The first Latin dictionary ever to be compiled on the basis of modern lexicographical principles.

THE NEW COLLEGE LATIN & ENGLISH DICTIONARY

COMPREHENSIVE: More than 63,000 words and phrases.

DEFINITIVE: Based on the foremost Classical authorities and organized to achieve the utmost clarity, precision, and convenience.

MODERN: Obsolete definitions have been replaced by fresh translations that correspond to current English usage.

A NEW LANDMARK
IN LATIN-ENGLISH DICTIONARIES
FOR THE MODERN STUDENT!

THE BANTAM NEW COLLEGE DICTIONARY SERIES

John C. Traupman, Author

JOHN C. TRAUPMAN received his B.A. in Latin and in German at Moravian College and his M.A. and Ph.D. in Classics at Princeton University. He is chairman of the Department of Classical Languages at St. Joseph's University (Philadelphia). He served as president of the Philadelphia Classical Society, of the Pennsylvania Classical Association, and of the Classical and Modern Language League. He has published widely in learned journals and is the author of *The Bantam New College German & English Dictionary* (Bantam Books, 1981) and an associate editor of *The Scribner-Bantam English Dictionary* (Scribner's, 1977; Bantam Books, 1979)

Edwin B. Williams, General Editor

EDWIN B. WILLIAMS (1891–1975), A.B., A.M., Ph.D., Doct. d'Univ., LL.D., L.H.D., was chairman of the Department of Romance Languages, dean of the Graduate School, and provost of the University of Pennsylvania. He was a member of the American Philosophical Society and the Hispanic Society of America. Among his many lexicographical works are *The Williams Spanish and English Dictionary* (Scribner's, formerly Holt and *The Bantam New College Spanish and English Dictionary*. He created and coordinated the Bantam series of original dictionaries—English, French, German, Italian, Latin, and Spanish. The University of Pennsylvania named "Williams Hall" in honor of Edwin B. Williams and his wife, Leonore, and is establishing the "Williams Chair in Lexicography," as the first chair in lexicography in an English-speaking country.

THE NEW COLLEGE
LATIN & ENGLISH DICTIONARY

JOHN C. TRAUPMAN, Ph.D.
St. Joseph's University, Philadelphia

BANTAM BOOKS
NEW YORK • TORONTO • LONDON • SYDNEY • AUCKLAND

THE NEW COLLEGE LATIN & ENGLISH DICTIONARY
Bantam Language Library edition / April 1966
23 printings through April 1988

Library of Congress Catalog Card Number: 66-12159

For information address: Bantam Books.

ISBN 0-553-27619-0

Published simultaneously in the United States and Canada

Bantam Books are published by Bantam Books, a division of Bantam Doubleday Dell Publishing Group, Inc. Its trademark, consisting of the words "Bantam Books" and the portrayal of a rooster, is Registered in U.S. Patent and Trademark Office and in other countries. Marca Registrada. Bantam Books, 666 Fifth Avenue, New York, New York 10103.

PRINTED IN THE UNITED STATES OF AMERICA

KR 32 31 30 29 28 27 26 25 24

INTRODUCTION

Both Latin and English entry words, as well as illustrative phrases under entry words, are treated in strictly alphabetical order.

Adverbs on the Latin-English side are inserted as separate entries and translated in that position without cross-reference to the corresponding adjective.

Adverbs on the English-Latin side ending in -ly are listed under their adjectives

Compound words are generally given in their assimilated forms, e.g., accurrō rather than adcurrō. Cross-references are provided as guides for those using texts which employ the unassimilated forms.

The letter j has been used in place of consonantal i because some recent texts have begun to use the former again and because students can thus more readily distinguish the consonant from the vowel.

If a feminine substantive, singular or plural, of the first declension, a neuter substantive, singular or plural, of the second declension, or a masculine substantive of the second declension falls alphabetically more than one word before or after the corresponding adjective, it is inserted as a separate entry and translated in that position, and a cross-reference to it is given under the adjective; for example, nāt•a -ae *f* occurs fifteen entries before nāt•us -a -um *adj* . . . ; *f* see nata.

If such a substantive does not fall alphabetically more than one word before or after the corresponding adjective, it is treated under the adjective.

Many of the variations in spelling of Latin words are indicated by means of cross-references, e.g., sēpiō see saepio.

Only those past participles are listed as separate entries whose difference in form from the first person singular present indicative warrants such listing, provided they fall alphabetically more than one word before or after the first person singular present indicative.

Only the first person singular present indicative and the present infinitive of regular active verbs of the first conjugation are given; in the case of deponent verbs, the perfect is added. For the other three conjugations and for irregular and defective verbs, all principal parts in use are given.

Discriminations between two or more meanings of the entry word are often shown by means of English words in parentheses.

Transitive and intransitive verbs, with their dependent

constructions, are clearly differentiated and are presented in a fixed order of transitive first and intransitive second.

Centered periods within entry words indicate division points at which inflectional elements are to be added.

All source words and phrases are printed in boldface type.

On the English-Latin side a boldface dash represents the vocabulary entry.

On the Latin-English side, the twofold purpose in marking the quantity of vowels is (1) to indicate accentuation of words and (2) to provide the basis for scansion of Classical Latin verse. Thus, all vowels that are long by nature and occur in open syllables are marked, whereas vowels in closed syllables, whether long or short by nature, are not marked, since the syllable in either case is long. However, since a vowel followed by a mute and a liquid can be open or closed, its quantity is marked when it is long. As a further aid to pronunciation, in words of three or more syllables, the short vowel of the penult is marked.

On the English-Latin side, Latin vowels have been marked to distinguish:

(a) words otherwise spelled alike: **lēvis, levis**

(b) the genitive singular and the nominative and accusative plural from the nominative singular of the fourth declension

(c) the ablative singular from the nominative singular of nouns of the first declension whenever the distinction is not clear from the context

(d) the nominative and genitive singular from the accusative plural of *i*-stem words of the third declension

(e) the infinitive of verbs of the second conjugation from the infinitive of verbs of the third conjugation.

On the English-Latin side, the genitive of the nouns of the fourth declension is provided in order to distinguish these nouns from nouns of the second declension ending in **-us**.

John C. Traupman

PRONUNCIATION

Vowels

	CLASSICAL METHOD	ECCLESIASTICAL METHOD
ă	Like *a* in *a*go: **compărō**	(Generally as in the Classical Method. However, in practice the different values of the vowels are frequently not rigidly adhered to.)
ā	Like *a* in f*a*ther: **imāgō**	
ĕ	Like *e* in p*e*t: **propĕrō**	
ē	Like *a* in l*a*te: **lēnis**	
ĭ	Like *i* in h*i*t: **ĭdem**	
ī	Like *ee* in k*ee*n; **amīcus**	
ŏ	Like *o* in *o*ften: **mŏdus**	
ō	Like *o* in h*o*pe: **nōmen**	
ŭ	Like *u* in p*u*t: **ŭt**	
ū	Like *u* in r*u*de: **ūtor**	
y̆	Like *ü* in German H*ü*tte: **my̆rīca**	
ȳ	Like *ü* in German *ü*ber: **Tȳdeus**	

Diphthongs

	CLASSICAL METHOD	ECCLESIASTICAL METHOD
ae	Like *y* in b*y*: **caecus**	Like *a* in l*a*te: **caecus**
au	Like *ow* in n*ow*: **nauta**	As in the Classical Method
ei	Like *ey* in gr*ey*: **deinde**	As in the Classical Method
eu	Like *eu* in f*eu*d: **Orpheus**	Like *eu* in Italian n*eu*tro: **euge**
oe	Like *oi* in *oi*l: **coepit**	Like *a* in l*a*te: **coepit**
ui	Like *uey* in gl*uey*: **cui** After **q**, like *wee* in *wee*k: **qui**	As in the Classical Method

Consonants

	CLASSICAL METHOD	ECCLESIASTICAL METHOD
b	As in English	As in English
c	Always like *c* in *c*an: **cīvis, cantō, actus**	Before **e, i, ae,** or **oe** like *ch* in *ch*erry; **excelsis, cīvis, caelum, coepit,** but before other letters like *c* in *c*an: **cantō, actus**
d	As in English	As in English
f	As in English	As in English
g	Always like *g* in *g*o: **genus, gula, gallīna, grātus**	Before **e** or **i** like *g* in *g*entle: **genus, regīna,** but before other letters except **g** and **n** (see under Consonant Groups) like *g* in *g*o: **gula, gallīna, fugō, grātus**
h	As in English	As in English
j	Like *y* in *y*es: **jungō, jam**	As in the Classical Method
k	As in English	As in English
l	As in English	As in English
m	As in English, but in verse final **m** before an initial vowel in the following word was presumably not pronounced	As in English
n	As in English	As in English
p	As in English	As in English
q	As in English and used only before consonantal **u**	As in English
r	Trilled as in the Romance languages	As in the Classical Method
s	Always like *s* in *s*ing: **miser, mors**	Like *s* in *s*ing: **salūs,** but when standing between two vowels or when final and preceded by a voiced consonant, like *z* in do*z*en: **miser, mors**
t	Like English *t*, but unaspirated	As in the Classical Method

	CLASSICAL METHOD	ECCLESIASTICAL METHOD
u	Like *w* in *w*ine, when unaccented, preceded by **q**, sometimes by **s**, and sometimes by **g**, and followed by a vowel: **qui·a, suā·vis** (but **su·ō·rum**), **dis·tin·guō** (but **ex·i·gŭ·us**)	As in the Classical Method
v	Like *w* in *w*ine: **vīvō**	As in English
x	Like *x* (= ks) in si*x*: **exactus**	Like *x* (=ks) in si*x*: **pax**; but in words beginning with **ex** and followed by a vowel, **h**, or **s**, like *x* (= gz) in e*x*haust: **exaudī, exhālō, exsolvō**
z	*Like dz* in a*dz*e: **zōna**	As in the Classical Method

Consonant Groups

	CLASSICAL METHOD	ECCLESIASTICAL METHOD
bs	Like *ps* in a*ps*e: **obsidĕō, urbs**	Like *bs* in o*bs*ession; **obsidĕō**, but in the final position, like *bs* in o*bs*erve: **urbs**
bt	Like *pt* in ca*pt*ain: **obtinēre**	Like *bt* in o*bt*ain: **obtinēre**
cc	Like *kk* in boo*kk*eeper: **ecce, occīdō, occāsum, occlūdō**	Before **e** or **i** like *tch* in ca*tch*: **ecce, occīdō**; but before other letters, like *kk* in boo*kk*eeper: **occāsum, occlūdō**
ch	Like *ch* in *ch*aotic: **pulcher**	As in the Classical Method
gg	Like *gg* in le*g* *g*uard: **agger**	Before **e** or **i** like *dj* in a*dj*ourn: **agger**; but before other letters, like *gg* in le*g* *g*uard: **aggrĕgō**
gn	As in English	Like *ny* in ca*ny*on: **dignus**
gu	See consonant **u**	As in the Classical Method
ph	Like *p-h* in to*p-h*eavy: **phōca**	Like *ph* in *ph*oenix: **phōca**
qu	See consonant *u*	As in the Classical Method
sc	Like *sc* in *sc*ope; **sciō, scūtum**	Before **e** or **i** like *sh* in *sh*in: **ascendō, sciō**; but before other letters, like *sc* in *sc*ope: **scandō, scūtum**
su	See consonant **u**	As in the Classical Method
th	Like *t* in *t*ake: **theātrum**	As in the Classical Method
ti	Like *ti* in English pa*ti*o: **nātiō**	When preceded by **s, t,** or **x** or when followed by a consonant, like *ti* in English pa*ti*o: **hostia, admixtiō, fortiter**; but when unaccented, followed by a vowel, and preceded by any letter except **s, t,** or **x**, like *tzy* in ri*tzy*: **nātiō, pretium**

SYLLABIFICATION

1. Every Latin word has as many syllables as it has vowels or diphthongs: **ae·ger, fī·li·us, Bai·ae**

2. When a word is divided into syllables:
   - **a)** a single consonant between two vowels goes with the following syllable (**h** is regarded as a consonant; **ch, ph, th, qu,** and somtimes **gu** and **su** are regarded as single consonants)*: **a·ger, ni·hil, a·qua, ci·cho·rē·um**
   - **b)** the first consonant of a combination of two or more consonants goes with the preceding vowel: **tor·men·tum, mit·tō, mon·strum**
   - **c)** a consonant group consisting of a mute (**b, d, g, p, t, c**) followed by **l** or **r** is generally left undivided and goes with the following vowel: **pa·trēs, a·cris, du·plex.** In Classical poetry this combination is often treated like any other pair of consonants: **pat·rēs, ac·ris, dup·lex**
   - **d)** prefixes form separate syllables even if the division is contrary to above rules: **ab·est, ob·lā·tus, abs·ti·nĕ·ō, ab·stō**

3. A syllable ending in a vowel or diphthong is called *open;* all others are called *closed*

4. The last syllable of a word is called the *ultima;* the next to last is called the *penult;* the one before the penult is called the *antepenult*

---

* The double consonant **x** goes with the preceding vowel: **dix·it**

QUANTITY OF VOWELS

1. A vowel is *long* (**lēvis**) or *short* (**lĕvis**) according to the length of time required for its pronunciation

2. A vowel is long:
   - **a)** before **ns, nf,** (and perhaps **gn**): **ingēns, īnfāns,** (**māgnus**)
   - **b)** when resulting from a contraction: **nīl** = **nihil, cōgō** = **cŏăgō, iniquus** = **inaequus**

3. A vowel is short:
   - **a)** before another vowel or **h: dĕa, trăhō**
   - **b)** generally before **nd** and **nt: amăndus, amănt**

4. Diphthongs are long: **causae**

QUANTITY OF SYLLABLES

1. Syllables are distinguished as *long* or *short* according to the length of time required for their pronunciation

2. A syllable is long:
   - **a)** if it contains a long vowel or a diphthong: **vē·nī, scrī·bō, cau·sae** (such a syllable is said to be *long by nature*)
   - **b)** if it contains a short vowel followed by **x, z,** or any two consonants except a mute (**b, d, g, p, t, c**) followed by **l** or **r: sax·um, gaz·a, mit·tō, cur·sor** (such a syllable is said to be *long by position,* but the vowel is pronounced *short*)

3. A syllable is short:
   - **a)** if it contains a short vowel followed by a vowel or by a single consonant (**h** is regarded as a consonant; **ch, ph, th, qu,** and sometimes **gu** and **su** are regarded as single consonants): **me·us, ni·hil, ge·rit, a·qua**
   - **b)** if it contains a short vowel followed by a mute (**b, d, g, p, t, c**) plus **l** or **r,** but it is sometimes long in verse: **flă·grans, ba·ră·thrum, ce·lĕ·brō** (such a syllable is said to be *common*)

NOTE: In this dictionary, long vowels are marked except before **x, z,** or two or more consonants unless the two consonants are a mute plus a liquid. Only the short penult of words of three or more syllables is marked.

ACCENT

1. Words of two syllables are accented on the first syllable: **om′nēs, tan′gō, ge′rit**

2. Words of more than two syllables are accented on the penult if it is long: **a·mī′cus, re·gun′tur** and on the antepenult if the penult is short: **fa·mi′li·a, ge′ri·tur**

3. These rules apply to words with enclitics appended (**-ce, -dum, -met, -ne, -que, -ve**): **vos′met, lau·dat′ne, de′ă·que** (nominative), **de·ā′que** (ablative)

4. In the second declension, the contracted genitive and the contracted vocative of nouns in **-ius** and the contracted genitive of those in **-ium** retain the accent of the nominative: **Vir·gi′lī, in·gĕ′nī**

5. Certain words which have lost a final **-e** retain the accent of the complete forms: **il·līc′** for **il·lī′ce, tan·tōn′** for **tan·tō′ne**

6. Certain compounds of **faciō**, in which a feeling for the individuality of the components was preserved, retain the accent of the simple verb: **be·ne·fă′cit**

ABBREVIATIONS

abbr	abbreviation
abl	ablative
acc	accusative
adj	adjective
adv	adverb
astr	astronomy
bot	botany
c.	circa, about
cent.	century
coll	colloquial
com	commercial
comp	comparative
conj	conjunction
d.	died
dat	dative
defect	defective
eccl	ecclesiastical
esp.	especially
f	feminine noun
fem	feminine
fig	figurative
fl	floruit
f pl	feminine plural noun
fut	future
genit	genitive
gram	grammar
impers	impersonal
impv	imperative
indecl	indeclinable
indef	indefinite
inf	infinitive
interj	interjection
interrog	interrogative
loc	locative
m	masculine noun
masc	masculine
math	mathematics
med	medicine
mil	military
m pl	masculine plural noun
mus	music
n	neuter noun
neut	neuter
nom	nominative
n pl	neuter plural noun
p	participle
phil	philosophy
pl	plural
pol	politics
pp	past participle
prep	preposition
pres	present
pron	pronoun
reflex	reflexive
rel	relative
rhet	rhetoric
s	substantive
singl	singular
subj	subjunctive
superl	superlative
v defect	defective verb
vi	intransitive verb
v impers	impersonal verb
vt	transitive verb

LATIN–ENGLISH

A

ā *interj* ah!
ā or **ab** *prep* (with *abl*) (of agency) by; (of time) since, after, from; (of space) from, away from; at, on, in; **a latere** on the side; **a tergo** in the rear
abactus *pp* of **abigo**
abăc·us -ī *m* cupboard; game board; abacus, counting board; panel; tray
abalienāti·ō -ōnis *f* transfer of property
abaliēn·ō -āre *vt* to alienate, estrange; to sell; to separate
Abantiăd·ēs -ae *m* descendant of Abas
Ab·ās -antis *m* king of Argos, father of Acrisius and grandfather of Perseus
abāv·us -ī *m* great-great-grandfather
abdicāti·ō -ōnis *f* abdication, renunciation, resignation
abdic·ō -āre *vt* to abdicate, renounce, resign; to disinherit; **se magistratu abdicare** to resign from office
ab·dicō -dicĕre -dixī -dictum *vt* (in augury) to disapprove of, forbid
abditē *adv* secretly, privately
abdit·us -a -um *adj* hidden, secret
ab·dō -dĕre -didī -ditum *vt* to hide; to remove, withdraw; to plunge (*e.g., a sword*)
abdōm·en -inis *n* abdomen, belly; (fig) gluttony, greed
ab·dūcō -dūcĕre -duxī -ductum *vt* to lead away, take away; to seduce; to alienate
ab·ĕō -īre -iī -itum *vi* to go away, depart; to vanish, disappear; to pass away, die; (of time) to pass, elapse; to change, be changed; to retire
abequit·ō -āre *vi* to ride off
aberrāti·ō -ōnis *f* wandering, escape, relief
aberr·ō -āre *vi* to wander, go astray; to deviate, differ
abesse *inf* of **absum**
abhinc *adv* ago
abhorr·ĕō -ēre -ŭī *vi* to shrink back; (with **ab** + *abl*) **a** to be averse to; **b** to be inconsistent with, differ from; **c** to be free from
abiegn·us -a -um *adj* fir
abi·ēs -ĕtis *f* fir; ship; spear; writing tablet
ab·igō -igĕre -ēgī -actum *vt* to drive away, get rid of; to banish, expel
abit·us -ūs *m* departure; outlet; end
abjectē *adv* abjectly, meanly
abject·us -a -um *adj* abject, mean; downhearted
ab·jiciō -jicĕre -jēcī -jectum *vt* to throw away, throw down; to slight; to give up; to humble, debase
abjūdic·ō -āre *vt* to take away (*by judicial decree*)
ab·jungō -jungĕre -junxī -junctum *vt* to unyoke; to detach
abjūr·ō -āre *vt* to deny on oath
ablātīv·us -a -um *adj & m* ablative
ablātus *pp* of **aufero**
ablēgāti·ō -ōnis *f* sending away, sending off; banishment
ablēg·ō -āre *vt* to send away; to remove, banish; to dismiss
abligurr·iō or **abligūr·iō -īre -īvī** or **-iī -ītum** *vt* to squander, waste
ablŏc·ō -āre *vt* to lease, rent out
ab·lūdō -lūdĕre -lūsī -lūsum *vi* to be unlike; (with **ab** + *abl*) to differ from
ab·lŭō -luĕre -lŭī -lūtum *vt* to wash away, cleanse, remove
ablūti·ō -ōnis *f* washing, cleansing
abnĕg·ō -āre *vt* to refuse, turn down
abnĕp·ōs -ōtis *m* great-great-grandson
abnept·is -is *f* great-great-granddaughter
abnoct·ō -āre *vi* to stay out all night, sleep out
abnorm·is -e *adj* irregular, unorthodox
ab·nŭō -nuĕre -nŭī -nūtum *vt* to refuse, deny
abol·ĕō -ēre -ēvī -itum *vt* to abolish, destroy, annihilate
abol·escō -escĕre -ēvī *vi* to decay, vanish, die out
aboliti·ō -ōnis *f* abolition
abōmin·or -ārī -ātus sum *vt* to detest
aborīgin·ēs -um *m pl* aborigines, original inhabitants
ab·orior -orīrī -ortus sum *vi* to miscarry; to fail; (of stars, etc.) to set
aborti·ō -ōnis *f* miscarriage
abortīv·us -a -um *adj* prematurely born
abort·us -ūs *m* miscarriage
ab·rādō -rādĕre -rāsī -rāsum *vt* to scrape off, shave; (fig) to squeeze out, rob
ab·ripiō -ripĕre -ripŭī -reptum *vt* to take away by force, carry off; to squander
ab·rōdō -rōdĕre -rōsī -rōsum *vt* to gnaw off

abrogātī·ō -ōnis *f* repeal
abrŏg·ō -āre *vt* to repeal, annul
abrotŏn·um -ī *n* southernwood (*aromatic, medicinal plant*)
ab·rumpō -rumpĕre -rūpī -ruptum *vt* to break off; to tear, sever
abruptē *adv* abruptly, rashly
abruptī·ō -ōnis *f* breaking off; divorce
abrupt·us -a -um *pp* of **abrumpo;** *adj* abrupt, steep; *n* precipice
abs *prep* (with *abl*, confined almost exclusively to the combination **abs te**) by, from
abs·cēdō -cēdĕre -cessī -cessum *vi* to go away, depart; to retire; to desist
abscessī·ō -ōnis *f* diminution
abscess·us -ūs *m* departure, absence, remoteness
abs·cīdō -cīdĕre -cīdī -cīsum *vt* to cut off, chop off; to cut short
ab·scindō -scindĕre -scĭdī -scissum *vt* to tear off, break off; to divide
abscīs·us -a -um *pp* of **abscido;** *adj* steep, precipitous; concise; abrupt
absconditē *adv* secretly; obscurely; profoundly
abscondit·us -a -um *adj* concealed, secret
abs·condō -condĕre -condī or **-condidī -conditum** *vt* to hide; to lose sight of, leave behind; to bury (*weapon*)
abs·ens -entis *pres p* of **absum;** *adj* absent
absentī·a -ae *f* absence
absil·iō -īre -iī or **-uī** *vi* to jump away
absimil·is -e *adj* unlike; (with *dat*) unlike
absinth·ium -iī or **-ī** *n* wormwood
abs·is -īdis *f* vault, arch; orbit (*of a star*)
ab·sistō -sistĕre -stitī *vi* to withdraw, depart; to cease, lay off
absolūtē *adv* perfectly
absolūtī·ō -ōnis *f* acquittal; perfection, completeness
absolūtōrī·us -a -um *adj* of acquittal, granting acquittal
absolūt·us -a -um *adj* perfect, complete, unqualified
ab·solvō -solvĕre -solvī -solūtum *vt* to release, set free, detach; to acquit; to finish off; to pay off, discharge
absŏn·us -a -um *adj* discordant, incongruous, incompatible
absorb·ĕō -ēre -ŭī *vt* to swallow, devour; to engross
absque *prep* (with *abl*) without, apart from, but for; **absque me foret** if it had not been for me
abstēmī·us -a -um *adj* abstemious, temperate, sober
abs·tergĕō -tergēre -tersī -tersum *vt* to wipe off, wipe dry; to expel, banish
absterr·ĕō -ēre -ŭī -ĭtum *vt* to scare away, deter
abstin·ens -entis *adj* temperate, forbearing; continent, chaste
abstinenter *adv* with restraint
abstinentī·a -ae *f* abstinence, self-control
abs·tinĕō -tinēre -tinŭī -tentum *vt* to withhold, keep away; *vi* to abstain, refrain; (with *genit*, *abl*, or with **ab** + *abl*, with *inf*, with **quin** or **quominus**) to refrain from
abst·ō -āre *vi* to stand at a distance, stand aloof
abs·trăhō -trahĕre -traxī -tractum *vt* to pull away, drag away, remove, detach
abs·trūdō -trūdĕre -trūsī -trūsum *vt* to push away; to conceal
abstrūs·us -a -um *adj* hidden, deep, abstruse; reserved
absum abesse afŭī *vi* to be away, be absent, be distant; (with *abl* or **ab** + *abl*) to be removed from, keep aloof from, be disinclined to; (with **ab** + *abl*) **a** to be different from, be inconsistent with; **b** to be free from; **c** to be unsuitable to, be unfit for; (with *dat*) to be of no help to
ab·sūmō -sūmĕre -sumpsī -sumptum *vt* to take away, diminish; to consume, use up, waste; to destroy, ruin
absurdē *adv* out of tune; absurdly
absurd·us -a -um *adj* out of tune; absurd, illogical, senseless, silly
Absyrt·us -ī *m* son of Aeëtes, king of Colchis, killed by his sister Medea when she eloped with Jason
abund·ans -antis *adj* overflowing, abundant; rich, affluent
abundanter *adv* copiously
abundantī·a -ae *f* abundance, wealth
abundē *adv* abundantly, amply
abund·ō -āre *vi* to overflow; to abound; to be rich
abūsī·ō -ōnis *f* incorrect use (*of figure of speech*)
abusque *prep* (with *abl*) all the way from
ab·ūtor -ūtī -ūsus sum *vi* (with *abl*) **a** to use up; **b** to misuse, abuse
Abȳd·os or **Abȳd·us -ī** *f* town on Hellespont, opposite Sestos
āc *conj* (usually used before consonants) and, and also, and moreover, and in particular; (in comparisons) than, as
Acadēmī·a -ae *f* Academy (*where Plato taught*); Platonic philosophy; Cicero's villa near Puteoli
Acadēmĭc·us -a -um *adj* Academic; *m* Academic philosopher; *n pl* Cicero's treatise on Academic philosophy
acalanth·is -ĭdis *f* thistlefinch
acanth·us -ī *m* acanthus
Acarnānī·a -ae *f* district of N.W. Greece
Acast·us -ī *m* son of Pelias

ac·cēdō -cēděre -cessī -cessum *vi* to come near, approach; (with *dat* or **ad** + *acc*) **a** to assent to, agree with, approve of; **b** to come near in resemblance, be like, resemble; **c** to be added to; (with **ad** or **in** + *acc*) to enter upon, undertake; **accedit ut** or **quod** there is the additional fact that
accelĕr·ō -āre *vt* to speed, quicken; *vi* to hurry
ac·cendō -cenděre -cendī -censum *vt* to light up, set on fire; (fig) to kindle, inflame, excite, awaken
accens·ĕō -ēre -ŭī -um *vt* to reckon, regard
accens·us -ī *m* attendant, orderly; *m pl* rear-echelon troops
accent·us -ūs *m* accent
accepti·ō -ōnis *f* accepting, receiving
accept·ō -āre *vt* to accept, receive
accept·or -ōris *m* recipient, approver
acceptr·ix -īcis *f* recipient (*female*)
accept·us -a -um *pp* of **accipio**; *adj* welcome, pleasing; *n* receipt; credit side (*in account books*)
accers·ō -ĕre -īvī -ītum *vt* to call, summon; to bring, procure
accessi·ō -ōnis *f* approach; passage, entrance; admittance
ac·cīdō -cīděre -cīdī -cīsum *vt* to cut down; to impair, weaken; to eat up
ac·cidō -ciděre -cidī *vi* to fall; to happen, occur; (with *dat*) to happen to, befall; (with **in** + *acc*) to fall on, fall upon; (with *dat* or **ad** + *acc*) to fall before, fall at (*e.g., someone's feet*); **aures** or **auribus** or **ad aures accidere** to reach or strike the ears
ac·cingō -cingěre -cinxī -cinctum *vt* to gird; to arm, equip, furnish; to make ready; **accingi** or **se accingere** (with *dat* or with **ad** or **in** + *acc*) to prepare oneself for, to enter upon, to undertake
ac·ciō -cīre -cīvī -cītum *vt* to call, send for, invite
ac·cipiō -cipěre -cēpī -ceptum *vt* to take, receive, accept; to admit, let in; to welcome, entertain; to hear, learn, understand; to interpret, explain; to undertake, assume, undergo; to approve of, assent to
accipit·er -ris *m* hawk, falcon
accīs·us -a -um *pp* of **accīdo**; *adj* impaired, ruined; troubled, disordered
accīt·us -ūs *m* summons, call
Acc·ius -iī or **ī** *m* Roman tragic poet (170-85? B.C.)
acclāmāti·ō -ōnis *f* shout, acclamation
acclām·ō -āre *vt* to hail, acclaim; *vi* to shout, cry out; (with *dat*) to shout at
acclār·ō -āre *vt* to make clear, make known
acclīnāt·us -a -um *adj* prostrate; sloping; (with *dat*) sloping toward
acclīn·is -e *adj* (with *dat*) **a** leaning on or against; **b** inclined toward, disposed to
acclīn·ō -āre *vt* (with *dat* or **in** + *acc*) to lean or rest (*something*) against; **se acclinare** (with **ad** + *acc*) (fig) to be inclined toward
acclīv·is -e *adj* sloping upwards, uphill, steep
acclīvit·ās -ātis *f* slope, ascent
accŏl·a -ae *m* neighbor
ac·cŏlō -colěre -colŭī -cultum *vt* to dwell near
accommodātē *adv* suitably, fittingly
accommodāti·ō -ōnis *f* adjustment, compliance, accommodation
accommŏdāt·us -a -um *adj* (with *dat* or **ad** + *acc*) fit for, adapted to, suitable to
accommŏd·ō -āre *vt* (with *dat* or **ad** + *acc*) to adjust or adapt or apply (*something*) to; **se accommodare** (with **ad** + *acc*) to apply or devote oneself to
accommŏd·us -a -um *adj* fit, suitable; (with *dat*) fit for, adapted to, suitable to
ac·crēdō -crēděre -crēdidī -crēditum *vi* (with *dat*) to believe, give credence to
ac·crescō -crescěre -crēvī -crētum *vi* to grow larger, increase, be added
accrēti·ō -ōnis *f* increase
accubiti·ō -ōnis *f* reclining at table
accŭb·ō -āre *vi* to lie nearby; to recline at table; (with *dat*) to lie near
accūd·ō -ĕre *vt* to coin
ac·cumbō -cumběre -cubŭī -cubitum *vi* to take one's place at table
accumulātē *adv* abundantly
accumulāt·or -ōris *m* hoarder
accumŭl·ō -āre *vt* to heap up, amass; to load, overwhelm
accūrātē *adv* carefully, accurately, exactly
accūrāti·ō -ōnis *f* carefulness, accuracy
accūrāt·us -a -um *adj* careful, accurate, exact, studied
accūr·ō -āre *vt* to take care of, attend to
ac·currō -currěre -currī -cursum *vi* to run up; (with **ad** or **in** + *acc*) to run to
accurs·us -ūs *m* running, concourse
accūsābil·is -e *adj* blameworthy
accūsāti·ō -ōnis *f* accusation; indictment, bill of indictment
accūsātīv·us -a -um *adj* & *m* accusative
accūsāt·or -ōris *m* accuser, prosecutor; informer
accūsātōriē *adv* like an accuser or prosecutor
accūsātōri·us -a -um *adj* accuser's, prosecutor's
accūsātr·ix -īcis *f* accuser (*female*)
accūsit·ō -āre *vt* to keep on accusing

accūs·ō -āre *vt* to accuse, prosecute; to reproach, blame
ac·er -ĕris *n* maple tree
ăc·er -ris -re *adj* sharp, pointed; pungent, stinging, penetrating, piercing, shrill; sagacious, keen, judicious; energetic, enthusiastic, ardent, brave; passionate, fierce, violent; severe, vigorous
acerbē *adv* bitterly, harshly
acerbĭt·ās -ātis *f* bitterness, harshness, sharpness, sourness; distress
acerb·ō -āre *vt* to embitter, aggravate
acerb·us -a -um *adj* bitter, harsh, sour; unripe; severe; morose, rough; untimely, premature; painful, troublesome; sad
acern·us -a -um *adj* maple
acerr·a -ae *f* incense box
acersecŏm·ēs -ae *m* young man, youth
acervātim *adv* in heaps; briefly
acerv·ō -āre *vt* to heap or pile up
acerv·us -ī *m* heap, pile; multitude; (in logic) sorites
acescō acescĕre acŭī *vi* to turn sour
Acest·ēs -ae *m* mythical king of Sicily
acētābŭl·um -ī *n* vinegar bottle
acēt·um -ī *n* sour wine, vinegar; (fig) pungent wit, shrewdness
Achaemĕn·ēs -is *m* first king of Persia, grandfather of Cyrus
Achaemenĭ·us -a -um *adj* Persian
Achae·us -a -um *adj & m* Achaean; Greek
Achai·a or **Achāĭ·a -ae** *f* province in northern part of the Peloponnesus on Gulf of Corinth; Greece
Achāĭc·us -a -um *adj & m* Achaean; Greek
Achāt·ēs -ae *m* companion of Aeneas; river in Sicily
Achelō·ūs -ī *m* river in N.W. Greece; river god
Achĕr·ōn -ontis or **Achĕr·os -ī** *m* river in Hades
Achill·ēs -is *m* Greek warrior, son of Peleus and Thetis
Achillē·us -a -um *adj* of Achilles
Achillīd·ēs -ae *m* descendant of Achilles
Achīv·us -a -um *adj* Achaean, Greek
Acīdalĭ·a -ae *f* Venus
acĭd·us -a -um *adj* sour, tart; (of sound) harsh, shrill; sharp, keen, pungent; unpleasant, disagreeable
acĭ·ēs -ēī *f* sharpness, sharp edge; keenness of vision, glance; eyesight, eye, pupil; mental power; battle line, battle array, battlefield, battle; debate
acīnăc·ēs -is *m* scimitar
acĭn·um -ī *n* or **acĭn·us -ī** *m* berry, grape; seed in berry
acipens·er -ĕris or **acipens·is -is** *m* sturgeon
Ăc·is -ĭdis *m* son of Faunus, loved by Galatea, changed into a river
acl·ys -ȳdis *f* small javelin
aconīt·um -ī *n* wolf's-bane; strong poison
ac·or -ōris *m* sour taste, sourness
acquī·escō -escĕre -ēvī -ētum *vi* to become quiet; to rest; to die; (with *abl, dat,* or with **in** + *abl*) to find rest in, acquiesce in, be content with, find pleasure in, rejoice in
ac·quīrō -quīrĕre -quīsīvī -quīsītum *vt* to acquire, obtain, gain, win
Acrăg·ās -antis *m* town on S.W. coast of Sicily
acrēdŭl·a -ae *f* bird (*perhaps owl or nightingale*)
ācricŭl·us -a -um *adj* irritable, peevish
ācrimōnĭ·a -ae *f* sharpness, pungency; irritation; energy
Acrisiōniăd·ēs -ae *m* descendant of Acrisius; Perseus
Acris·ius -iī or **-ī** *m* king of Argos, father of Danaë
ācrĭter *adv* sharply, keenly, vehemently, severely
acroām·a -ătis *n* entertainment; entertainer
Acroceraunĭ·a -ōrum *n pl* promontory on the Adriatic Sea in Epirus
Acrocorinth·us -ī *f* citadel of Corinth
act·a -ae *f* seashore, beach
act·a -ōrum *n pl* deeds, actions; public acts; proceedings of the senate; records, minutes; journal
Actae·ōn -ōnis *m* grandson of Cadmus, changed into a stag
Actae·us -a -um *adj* Attic, Athenian
actĭ·ō -ōnis *f* doing, performance, action, activity; proceedings; (law) suit, process, action, permission for a suit; delivery, gesticulation; plot, action (*of play*)
actĭt·ō -āre *vt* to plead (*cases*) often; to perform (*plays*) often
Act·ium -iī or **-ī** *n* promontory in Epirus (*where Octavian defeated Antony and Cleopatra in* 31 B.C.)
actīv·us -a -um *adj* (gram) active; practical (*opposite of contemplative*)
act·or -ōris *m* doer, performer; (law) plaintiff, pleader, advocate; agent, manager; player, actor; **actor summarum** cashier, accountant
Act·or -ōris *m* companion of Aeneas
actuāriŏl·um -ī *n* small barge
actuārĭ·us -a -um *adj* swift; *m* stenographer; *f* swift ship; *n* swift ship
actuōsē *adv* energetically
actuōs·us -a -um *adj* energetic, very active
actus *pp of* **ago**
act·us -ūs *m* act, performance; driving, motion, impulse; right of way; public business; presentation, delivery, gesture, recital; act (*of play*)
actūtum *adv* instantly, immediately
acŭl·a -ae *f* rivulet

aculeāt·us -a -um *adj* prickly; (fig) stinging, sharp, subtle
aculĕ·us -ī *m* barb, sting; point; sarcasm
acūm·en -inis *n* point, sharpness; sting (*of insect*); pungency; shrewdness, ingenuity, cunning
acŭō acuĕre acuī acūtum *vt* to make sharp or pointed, to whet; to exercise; to stimulate; to give an edge to, enhance; to tease
ac·us -ūs *f* needle, pin; **acu rem tangere** to hit the nail on the head
acūtē *adv* acutely, sharply, keenly
acūtŭl·us -a -um *adj* somewhat sharp, rather subtle
acūt·us -a -um *pp* of **acuo;** *adj* sharp, pointed; shrill; intelligent
ad *prep* (with *acc*) (of space) to, towards, near, at; (of time) toward, about, until, at, on, by; (with numbers) about, almost; for the purpose of, to; according to, in consequence of; with respect to; compared with
adacti·ō -ōnis *f* enforcing
adactus *pp* of **adigo**
adact·us -ūs *m* bringing together; snapping (*of jaws*)
adaequē *adv* equally
adaequ·ō -āre *vt* to make level; to equal, match; (fig) to put on the same level; *vi* to be on the same level, be equal; (with *dat*) to be level with
adamantē·us -a -um *adj* made of steel
adamantin·us -a -um *adj* hard as steel, adamantine
adăm·ās -antis *m* adamant; steel; diamond
adambŭl·ō -āre *vi* (with **ad** + *acc*) to walk about near
adăm·ō -āre *vt* to fall in love with
ad·aperiō -aperīre -aperŭī -apertum *vt* to uncover, throw open
adăqu·ō -āre *vt* to water; *vi* to fetch water
adauct·us -ūs *m* growth
ad·augĕō -augēre -auxī -auctum *vt* to increase, aggravate
adaugesc·ō -ĕre *vi* to begin to grow
ad·bĭbō -bibĕre -bibī -bibitum *vt* to drink in; to listen attentively to
adbīt·ō -ĕre *vi* to come near, approach
adc- = acc-
ad·dĕcet -decēre *v impers* it becomes
addens·ĕō -ēre or **addens·ō -āre** *vt* to close (*ranks*)
ad·dīcō -dīcĕre -dixī -dictum *vt* to assign; to doom; to dedicate, devote; *vi* (in augury) to be favorable
ad·discō -discĕre -didicī *vt* to learn in addition
additāment·um -ī *n* addition
ad·dō -dĕre -didī -ditum *vt* to add, increase; to impart, bestow
ad·docĕō -docēre -docŭī -doctum *vt* to teach in addition
addubit·ō -āre *vt* to call into doubt; *vi* to begin to feel doubt; to hesitate
ad·dūcō -dūcĕre -duxī -ductum *vt* to lead up, bring up; to draw together, wrinkle; to prompt, induce, persuade, move
adduct·us -a -um *adj* drawn tight, strained; narrow, tight (*place*); strict, serious, stern (*character*)
ad·ĕdō -esse -ēdī -ēsum *vt* to nibble at, to eat up, consume; to waste
ademptī·ō -ōnis *f* taking away
ad·ĕō -īre -iī or **-īvī -itum** *vt* to approach; to attack; to consult, apply to; to visit; to undertake, set about, undergo; *vi* to go up, come up; (with **ad** + *acc*) **a** to go to, approach; **b** to enter upon, undertake, set about, submit to
adĕō *adv* to such a degree, so; (following pronouns and numerals, to give emphasis) precisely, exactly, quite, just, chiefly; (at the beginning of sentence) thus far, to such an extent; even, indeed, truly
ad·eps -ipis *m* or *f* fat; corpulence
adepti·ō -ōnis *f* obtaining, attainment
adeptus *pp* of **adipiscor**
adequit·ō -āre *vi* to ride up; (with *dat* or **ad** + *acc*) to ride up to, ride towards
adesse *inf* of **adedo** or of **adsum**
adēsur·iō -īre -īvī *vi* to be very hungry
adēsus *pp* of **adedo**
ad·haerĕō -haerēre -haesī -haesum *vi* (with *dat* or *abl* or with **in** + *abl*) **a** to cling to, stick to; **b** to keep close to, hang on to
ad·haerescō -haerescĕre -haesī -haesum *vi* to stick; to falter; (with *dat* or *abl*, with **ad** + *acc*, or with **in** + *abl*) **a** to stick to, cling to; **b** to be devoted to; **c** to correspond to, accord with
adhaesi·ō -ōnis *f* clinging, adhesion
adhaes·us -ūs *m* adhering, adherence
adhib·ĕō -ēre -ŭī -itum *vt* to bring, put, add; to summon, invite; to apply; to use, employ; to consult; to handle, treat
adhinn·iō -īre -iī or **īvī -ītum** *vt* to whinny after, lust after; *vi* (with *dat* or with **ad** or **in** + *acc*) **a** to whinny after, lust after, crave; **b** to whinny in delight at
adhortāti·ō -ōnis *f* exhortation, encouragement
adhortāt·or -ōris *m* cheerer, supporter
adhort·or -ārī -ātus sum *vt* to cheer on, encourage
adhūc *adv* thus far, hitherto; till now; as yet, still; besides, in addition, moreover
ad·igō -igĕre -ēgī -actum *vt* to drive; to drive home, thrust; to compel; to inflict; to bind (*by oath*)
ad·imō -imĕre -ēmī -emptum *vt* to withdraw, take away; to carry off
adipāt·us -a -um *adj* fatty, greasy; gross, bombastic; *n* pastry (*made in fat*)

ad·ipiscor -ipiscī -eptus sum *vt* to reach, get, obtain, win
aditiāl·is -e *adj* inaugural
aditi·ō -ōnis *f* approach
adit·us -ūs *m* approach, access; entrance; admittance, audience, interview; beginning, commencement; chance, opportunity
adjac·eō -ēre -uī *vt* to adjoin; *vi* (with *dat* or **ad** + *acc*) **a** to lie near or at; **b** to border on, be contiguous with
adjecti·ō -ōnis *f* addition, annexation
adjectīv·us -a -um *adj* adjectival
ad·jiciō -jicĕre -jēcī -jectum *vt* to add, increase; (with *dat* or **ad** + *acc*) **a** to throw (*weapon*) at; **b** to add (*something*) to; **c** to turn or direct (*eyes, mind, etc.*) to; (with **in** + *acc*) to hurl (*weapon*) at
adjūdic·ō -āre *vt* to adjudge, award; to ascribe, assign
adjūment·um -ī *n* aid, help, support
adjunct·a -ōrum *n pl* accessory circumstances
adjuncti·ō -ōnis *f* joining, union; addition; (rhet) repetition
ad·jungō -jungĕre -junxī -junctum *vt* (with *dat*) to yoke or harness (*animal*) to; (with *dat* or **ad** + *acc*) **a** to add, attach, join (*something*) to; **b** to apply, direct (*mind, attention, etc.*) to
adjūr·ō -āre *vt* to swear to, confirm by oath; *vi* to swear
adjūtābil·is -e *adj* helpful
adjūt·ō -āre *vt* to help, assist; *vi* (with *dat*) to be of assistance to
adjūt·or -ōris *m* helper, assistant, promoter; aide, adjutant, deputy, secretary; supporting actor
adjūtōr·ium -iī or **-ī** *n* help, support
adjūtr·ix -īcis *f* helper, assistant (*female*)
ad·jŭvō -juvāre -jūvī -jūtum *vt* to help, encourage, sustain; *vi* to be of use, be profitable
adl- = all-
admātūr·ō -āre *vt* to bring to maturity; to hasten, expedite
ad·mētior -mētīrī -mensus sum *vt* to measure out
Admēt·us -ī *m* king of Pherae in Thessaly, husband of Alcestis
admigr·ō -āre *vi* (with **ad** + *acc*) **a** to go to; **b** to be added to
adminicŭl·ō -āre or **adminicŭl·or -ārī -ātus sum** *vt* to prop, support
adminicŭl·um -ī *n* prop, support, stake, pole; rudder; aid; assistant
administ·er -rī *m* assistant, attendant
administr·a -ae *f* assistant, attendant (*female*)
administrāti·ō -ōnis *f* help, aid; administration, management, government
administrāt·or -ōris *m* administrator, manager, director
administr·ō -āre *vt* to administer, manage, direct
admīrābil·is -e *adj* admirable, wonderful; strange, surprising, paradoxical
admīrābilit·ās -ātis *f* admiration, wonder, wonderfulness
admīrābiliter *adv* admirably; astonishingly, paradoxically
admīrāti·ō -ōnis *f* admiration, wonder, surprise
admīrāt·or -ōris *m* admirer
admīr·or -ārī -ātus sum *vt* to admire, wonder at, be surprised at
ad·miscĕō -miscēre -miscuī -mixtum *vt* to mix, add; to involve, implicate; to join, mingle; (with *dat*, with **ad** or **in** + *acc*, or with **cum** + *abl*) to add (*something*) to, to mix or mix up (*something*) with; **se admiscere** to get involved, to meddle
admissār·ius -iī or **-ī** *m* stallion, stud; lecherer
admissi·ō -ōnis *f* interview, audience
admiss·um -ī *n* crime
ad·mittō -mittĕre -mīsī -missum *vt* to let in, admit; to let go, let loose; to put at a gallop; to allow; to commit (*crime*)
admixti·ō -ōnis *f* admixture
admixtus *pp* of **admisceo**
admoderātē *adv* appropriately
admŏdum *adv* to the limit; very, quite, fully; (with numbers) just about; (with negatives) at all; (in answers) quite so, yes
admoen·iō -īre *vt* to besiege, blockade
admōl·ior -īrī -ītus sum *vt* to bring up, move up; **admoliri** (with *inf*) to strive to, struggle to
admon·ĕō -ēre -uī -itum *vt* to admonish, remind, suggest; to warn; to urge
admoniti·ō -ōnis *f* admonition, reminder, suggestion
admonit·or -ōris *m* admonisher, reminder
admonitr·ix -īcis *f* admonisher, reminder (*female*)
admonit·um -ī *n* admonition
admonit·us -ūs *m* suggestion; reproof
ad·mordĕō -mordēre -momordī -morsum *vt* to bite at, gnaw at; (fig) to fleece
admōti·ō -ōnis *f* moving, movement
ad·movĕō -movēre -mōvī -mōtum *vt* to move up, bring up, bring near; to lead on, conduct; (with *dat* or **ad** + *acc*) **a** to move or bring (*something*) to; **b** to apply (*something*) to; **c** to direct (*attention, etc.*) to; *vi* to draw near, approach
admūg·iō -īre *vi* (with *dat*) to low to, bellow to
admurmurāti·ō -ōnis *f* murmuring
admurmŭr·ō -āre *vi* to murmur (*in approval or disapproval*)
admutil·ō -āre *vt* to clip close; (fig) to clip, cheat

adn- = **ann-**
ad·olĕō -olēre -olŭī -ultum *vt* to magnify; to honor, worship; to sacrifice, burn; to pile up (*altars*); to sprinkle (*altars*)
adol·ĕō -ēre *vi* to smell
adolesc·ens -entis *m* young man; *f* young woman
adol·escō -escĕre -ēvī *vi* to grow, grow up; to be kindled, burn
Adōn·is -is or **-idis** *m* son of Cinyras, king of Cyprus, loved by Venus
adoper·iō -īre -ŭī -tum *vt* to cover up; to close
adopīn·or -ārī *vi* to suppose, conjecture
adoptāti·ō -ōnis *f* adopting (*of child*)
adopti·ō -ōnis *f* adoption (*of child*)
adoptīv·us -a -um *adj* adoptive, by adoption
adopt·ō -āre *vt* to adopt; to select; to graft (*plants*)
ad·or -ōris or **-ŏris** *n* spelt
adōrāti·ō -ōnis *f* adoration, worship
adōrĕ·a -ae *f* reward for valor; praise, glory
adōrĕ·us -a -um *adj* of spelt
ad·orior -orīrī -ortus sum *vt* to rise up against, attack, assault; to attempt; to undertake
adorn·ō -āre *vt* to equip, get ready; to adorn
adōr·ō -āre *vt* to implore, entreat; to ask for; to adore, worship
adp- = **app-**
ad·rādō -rādĕre -rāsī -rāsum *vt* to scrape, shave; to lop off
Adrast·us -ī *m* king of Argos, father-in-law of Tydeus and Polynices
adr- = **arr-**
adsc- = **asc-**
adse- = **ass-**
adsi- = **assi-**
adso- = **asso-**
adsp- = **asp-**
adst- = **ast-**
adsu- = **assu-**
ad·sum -esse -fŭī *vi* to be near, be present; to appear; to be at hand; to be of assistance; (with *dat*) to share in, participate in, stand by, assist; **animo** or **animis adesse** to pay attention; to cheer up
adt- = **att-**
adūlāti·ō -ōnis *f* fawning, cringing, servility, flattery
adūlāt·or -ōris *m* flatterer
adūlātōri·us -a -um *adj* flattering
adulesc·ens -entis *adj* young
adulesc·ens -entis *m* young man; *f* young woman
adulescenti·a -ae *f* youth, young people
adulescentŭl·a -ae *f* little girl
adulescentŭl·us -ī *m* young man
adūl·ō -āre *vi* to fawn
adūl·or -ārī -ātus sum *vt* to flatter (*in a servile manner*); *vi* (with *dat*) to kowtow to
adult·er -ĕra -ĕrum *adj* adulterous, unchaste; *m* adulterer; *f* adulteress
adulterīn·us -a -um *adj* adulterous; forged, counterfeit
adulter·ium -iī or **-ī** *n* adultery; adulteration
adultĕr·ō -āre *vt* to defile, corrupt; to falsify; *vi* to commit adultery
adult·us -a -um *adj* grown, mature, adult
adumbrātim *adv* in outline
adumbrāti·ō -ōnis *f* sketch, outline
adumbrāt·us -a -um *adj* shadowy, sketchy, unreal, fictitious, dim, imperfect
adumbr·ō -āre *vt* to shade, overshadow; to sketch; to represent
aduncit·ās -ātis *f* curvature
adunc·us -a -um *adj* curved, hooked
adurg·ĕō -ēre *vt* to pursue closely
ad·ūrō -ūrĕre -ussī -ustum *vt* to set on fire; to scorch; to nip, freeze; (fig) to inflame
adusque *adv* entirely, throughout
adusque *prep* (with *acc*) all the way to, as far as, right up to
adusti·ō -ōnis *f* burning
adust·us -a -um *pp* of **aduro**; *adj* scorched; sunburned
advectici·us -a -um *adj* imported, foreign
advecti·ō -ōnis *f* transportation
advect·ō -āre *vt* to keep on conveying
advect·us -ūs *m* conveyance
ad·vĕhō -vehĕre -vexī -vectum *vt* to carry, convey, transport; **(equo) advehi** (with **ad** or **in** + *acc*) to ride to; **(nave) advehi** (with **ad** + *acc*) to sail to
advēl·ō -āre *vt* to veil; to wreathe
advĕn·a -ae *m* or *f* stranger, foreigner
ad·veniō -venīre -vēnī -ventum *vi* to arrive; (with **ad** or **in** + *acc* or with *acc* of limit of motion) to arrive at, come to, reach
adventici·us -a -um *adj* foreign, strange, extraneous; unusual, extraordinary; unearned
advent·ō -āre *vi* to keep coming closer, approach
advent·or -ōris *m* visitor, guest; customer
advent·us -ūs *m* arrival, approach
adversārī·us -a -um *adj* (with *dat*) turned towards, opposed to, opposite; *m & f* adversary, enemy, rival; *n pl* journal, notebook, memoranda; assertions (*of opponent*)
adversātr·ix -īcis *f* opponent (*female*)
adversi·ō -ōnis *f* directing, direction
advers·ō -āre *vt* to direct (*attention*)
advers·or -ārī -ātus sum *vi* (with *dat*) to oppose, resist
adversum or **adversus** *adv* in the opposite direction; *prep* (with *acc*) facing, opposite, towards; compared with, contrary to
advers·us -a -um *adj* opposite, in front; facing; unfavorable, hostile;

adverso flumine upstream; *n* misfortune; opposite
ad·vertō or **ad·vortō -vertĕre -vertī -versum** *vt* (with *dat* or **in** + *acc*) **a** to turn or direct (*something*) to; **b** to steer (*ship*) to; **animum** or **animos advertere** to pay attention; **animum** or **animos advertere** (with *dat* or **ad** + *acc*) to give attention to, attend to, heed, observe; *vi* to land; (with **in** + *acc*) to punish
advesper·ascit -ascĕre -āvit *v impers* evening approaches
advigil·ō -āre *vi* to be vigilant, keep watch; (with *dat*) to keep watch over, bestow attention on; (with **pro** + *abl*) to watch out for
advocāti·ō -ōnis *f* legal assistance; legal counsel; the bar; period of time allowed to procure legal assistance; delay, adjournment
advocāt·us -ī *m* witness; advocate, counsel; helper, friend
advŏc·ō -āre *vt* to call, summon; to consult
advŏl·ō -āre *vi* (with *dat* or with **ad** or **in** + *acc*) **a** to fly to; **b** to dash to
ad·volvō -volvĕre -volvī -volūtum *vt* (with *dat* or **ad** + *acc*) to roll (*something*) to or toward; **advolvi** or **se advolvere genua** or **genibus** (*with genit*) to fall prostrate before
advor- = **adver-**
adȳt·um -ī *n* sanctuary; tomb
Aeacid·ēs -ae *m* descendant of Aeacus
Aeăc·us -ī *m* king of Aegina, father of Peleus, Telamon, and Phocus, and judge of the dead
aed·ēs or **aed·is -is** *f* shrine, temple; building; *f pl* rooms, apartments; house
aedicŭl·a -ae *f* chapel, shrine; small room, closet; small house; *f pl* small house
aedificāti·ō -ōnis *f* constructing, building; structure, building
aedificātiuncŭl·a -ae *f* tiny building
aedificāt·or -ōris *m* builder, architect
aedific·ium -iī or **-ī** *n* building
aedific·ō -āre *vt* to build, construct, establish
aedilici·us -a -um *adj* aedile's; *m* ex-aedile
aedīl·is -is *m* aedile
aedilit·ās -ātis *f* aedileship
aedis see **aedēs**
aeditŭ·us or **aeditim·us** or **aeditŭm·us -ī** *m* temple attendant, sacristan
Aeēt·ēs -ae *m* king of Colchis and father of Medea
Aegae·us -a -um *adj* Aegean; *n* Aegean Sea
Aegāt·ēs -um *f pl* three islands W. of Sicily
aeg·er -ra -rum *adj* sick, infirm, unsound; dejected; painful
Aeg·eus -ĕī *m* king of Athens, father of Theseus
Aegīd·ēs -ae *m* Theseus
Aegīn·a -ae *f* island off Attica; mother of Aeacus
aeg·is -idis *f* shield of Minerva and of Jupiter; aegis, protection
Aegisth·us -ī *m* son of Thyestes, seducer of Clytemnestra, and murderer of Agamemnon
aegrē *adv* painfully; with difficulty; reluctantly; hardly, scarcely
aegr·ĕō -ēre *vi* to be sick
aegr·escō -escĕre *vi* to become sick; to be aggravated, get worse; to be troubled
aegrimōnī·a -ae *f* sorrow, anxiety, trouble
aegritūd·ō -inis *f* sickness; sorrow
aegr·or -ōris *m* illness
aegrōtāti·ō -ōnis *f* sickness, disease
aegrōt·ō -āre *vi* to be sick; to languish
aegrōt·us -a -um *adj* sick
Aegypt·us -ī *f* Egypt; *m* mythical king of Egypt, whose 50 sons married the 50 daughters of his brother Danaüs
aelin·os -ī *m* dirge
aemŭl·a -ae *f* rival (*female*)
aemulāti·ō -ōnis *f* emulation, rivalry
aemulāt·or -ōris *m* rival, imitator
aemulāt·us -ūs *m* rivalry
aemŭl·or -ārī -ātus sum *vt* to emulate, rival; *vi* (with *dat*) to be envious of, be jealous of
aemŭl·us -a -um *adj* (with *genit* or *dat*) emulous of, envious of, jealous of, striving after; *m* rival
Aeneăd·ēs -ae *m* descendant of Aeneas; Trojan; Roman; Augustus
Aenē·ās -ae *m* son of Venus and Anchises, and hero of Virgil's epic
Aenē·is -idis or **-idos** *f* Aeneid (*Virgil's epic*)
aēnĕ·us or **ahēnĕ·us -a -um** *adj* bronze
aenigm·a -ătis *n* riddle, mystery
aēnip·ēs -ĕdis *adj* bronze-footed
aēn·us or **ahēn·us -a -um** *adj* bronze; (fig) firm, invincible; *n* cauldron
Aeoli·a -ae *f* realm of Aeolus, king of winds; group of islands near Sicily
Aeoli·ī -ōrum or **Aeŏl·ēs -um** *m pl* Aeolians (*inhabitants of N.W. Asia Minor*)
Aeŏl·is -idis *f* Aeolia, N.W. part of Asia Minor
Aeŏl·us -ī *m* god of winds
aequābil·is -e *adj* equal, alike; consistent, uniform; fair, impartial
aequābilit·ās -ātis *f* equality; uniformity; impartiality
aequābiliter *adv* equally; uniformly
aequaev·us -a -um *adj* of the same age
aequāl·is -e *adj* equal; even, level; of the same age, contemporary

aequāl·is -is *m* or *f* comrade; contemporary
aequālit·ās -ātis *f* equality; evenness; smoothness
aequāliter *adv* equally; evenly
aequanimit·ās -ātis *f* calmness, patience; kindness; impartiality
aequāti·ō -ōnis *f* equal distribution; **aequatio bonorum** communism
aequē *adv* equally; justly, fairly; **aeque . . . ac** or **atque** or **et** just as, as much as, as; **aeque . . . ac si** just as if; **aeque . . . quam** as . . . as, in the same way as
Aequ·ī -ōrum *m pl* people of central Italy
aequilibrit·ās -ātis *f* balance
aequilibr·ium -iī or **-ī** *n* horizontal position; equilibrium
aequinoctiāl·is -e *adj* equinoctial
aequinoct·ium -iī or **-ī** *n* equinox
aequiperābil·is -e *adj* (with *dat* or **cum** + *abl*) comparable to
aequipĕr·ō or **aequipăr·ō -āre** *vt* to compare; to equal, rival, come up to; (with *dat*, with **ad**+ *acc*, or **cum** + *abl*) to compare (*something*) to; *vi* (with *dat*) **a** to become equal to, be equal to; **b** to attain to
aequit·ās -ātis *f* evenness, conformity, symmetry, equity; calmness
aequ·or -ŏris *n* level surface; sea, ocean
aequorĕ·us -a -um *adj* of the sea, marine
aequ·us -a -um *adj* level, even, flat; favorable, friendly; fair, just; calm; *n* level, plain; justice, fairness
ā·ēr -ĕris *m* air, atmosphere, sky; weather; mist
aerāment·um -ī *n* bronze vessel or utensil
aerāri·us -a -um *adj* copper, bronze; of mines; financial, fiscal; *m* coppersmith; low-class Roman citizen; *f* mine; smelting furnace; *n* treasury
aerāt·us -a -um *adj* bronze; rich
āërĕ·us -a -um *adj* aerial, airy, lofty, high
aerĕ·us -a -um *adj* bronze
aerif·er -ĕra -ĕrum *adj* carrying cymbals
aerip·ēs -ĕdis *adj* bronze-footed
āëri·us -a -um *adj* aerial, airy, lofty, high
Aërŏp·ē -ēs or **Aërŏp·a -ae** *f* wife of Atreus, mother of Agamemnon and Menelaus
aerūginōs·us -a -um *adj* rusty
aerūg·ō -inis *f* copper rust, verdigris; corroding passion, envy, greed
aerumn·a -ae *f* need, want, trouble, hardship, calamity
aerumnābil·is -e *adj* full of troubles, calamitous
aerumnōs·us -a -um *adj* full of troubles, wretched, distressed
aes aeris *n* crude metal, copper, bronze; bronze object; armor, statue, utensil, trumpet; money; payment; reward; *n pl* wages, soldier's pay; **aes alienum** debt
Aeschyl·us -ī *m* Athenian tragic poet (525-456 B.C.)
Aesculāp·ius -iī or **-ī** *m* god of medicine, son of Apollo and Coronis
aesculēt·um -ī *n* oak forest
aesculĕ·us -a -um *adj* oak
aescŭl·us -ī *f* Italian oak
Aes·ōn -ŏnis *m* Thessalian prince, father of Jason, restored to youth by Medea
aest·ās -ātis *f* summer; summer heat
aestif·er -ĕra -ĕrum *adj* heat-bearing, sultry
aestimābil·is -e *adj* valuable
aestimāti·ō -ōnis *f* appraisal, assessment; esteem
aestimāt·or -ōris *m* appraiser
aestim·ō -āre *vt* to appraise, rate, value, estimate; to esteem, judge, hold
aestīv·a -ōrum *n pl* summer camp; campaign season, campaign; summer pastures
aestīv·ō -āre *vi* to pass the summer
aestīv·us -a -um *adj* summer
aestuār·ium -iī or **ī** *n* tidal waters, lagoon, estuary, marsh; air shaft
aestŭ·ō -āre *vi* to boil, seethe; to burn, glow; to undulate, swell, be tossed, heave; to waver, hesitate; to be excited
aestuōsē *adv* hotly, impetuously
aestuōs·us -a -um *adj* sultry; billowy
aest·us -ūs *m* agitation; glow, heat, sultriness; surge, billows, ebb and flow; tide; raging, seething, passion; uncertainty, irresolution
aet·ās -ātis *f* lifetime, age, generation
aetātŭl·a -ae *f* tender age
aeternit·ās -ātis *f* eternity, immortality
aetern·ō -āre *vt* to perpetuate, immortalize
aeternum *adv* forever; constantly, perpetually
aetern·us -a -um *adj* eternal, everlasting, immortal, imperishable
aeth·ēr -ĕris or **-ĕros** *m* upper air, sky, heaven
aetheri·us -a -um *adj* ethereal, heavenly, celestial; of the upper world
Aethi·ops -ŏpis *m* Ethiopian; Negro; blockhead
aethr·a -ae *f* ether, pure air, serene sky; air, sky, heavens
Aetn·a -ae or **Aetn·ē -ēs** *f* volcano in Sicily
Aetōli·a -ae *f* district in N. Greece
aevit·ās -ātis *f* age, lifetime
aev·um -ī *n* or **aev·us -ī** *m* age, lifetime, life; time, period; generation; eternity
Af·er -ra -rum *adj & m* African
affābil·is -e *adj* affable, courteous, kind
affābilit·ās -ātis *f* affability, courtesy

affābrē *adv* in a workmanlike manner, cunningly
affātim *adv* sufficiently, enough, satisfactorily
affāt·us -ūs *m* address, discourse
affectāti·ō -ōnis *f* eager desire; affectation, conceit
affectāt·or -ōris *m* affected person
affectāt·us -a -um *adj* choice, select; farfetched, studied
affecti·ō -ōnis *f* disposition, state of mind; inclination, partiality; affection, love
affect·ō -āre *vt* to grasp, seize; to pursue, strive after, aim at; to try to win over; to affect, feign
affect·us -a -um *adj* furnished, provided, gifted; weakened, impaired, sick; affected, moved, touched
affect·us -ūs *m* state, disposition, mood; feeling, passion, emotion; affection
affĕrō afferre attŭlī allātum *vt* to bring, carry, convey; to report, announce; to introduce, apply, employ, exert, exercise; to produce, cause, occasion, impart; to allege, assign; to contribute, help; **manus afferre** (with *dat*) to lay hands on, attack, do violence to, rob, plunder
af·ficiō -ficĕre -fēcī -fectum *vt* to treat, handle, manage; to affect, move, influence, impress; to attack, afflict; to impair, weaken; (*abl* and verb may be rendered by the verb corresponding to the *abl*): **cruce afficere** to crucify; **honoribus afficere** to honor; **supplicio afficere** to punish
af·fīgō -fīgĕre -fixī -fixum *vt* (with *dat* or **ad** + *acc*) to fasten, attach, affix, annex (*something*) to; (with *dat*) to impress (*something*) upon (*mind*)
af·fingō -fingĕre -finxī -fictum *vt* to form, fashion besides; to make up, invent; (with *dat*) to attach, affix, add, join, contribute (*something*) to
affīn·is -e *adj* adjoining, neighboring; related by marriage; (with *dat* or **ad** + *acc*) taking part in, privy to, associated with
affīn·is -is *m* or *f* in-law
affīnit·ās -ātis *f* relationship by marriage
affirmātē *adv* with solemn assurance, positively, certainly
affirmāti·ō -ōnis *f* affirmation, assertion, declaration
affirm·ō -āre *vt* to strengthen; to confirm, encourage; to aver, assert
afflāt·us -ūs *m* breeze, blast, breath; inspiration
affl·ĕō -ēre *vi* to weep
afflictāti·ō -ōnis *f* physical pain, torture
afflictō -āre *vt* to shatter, damage, harass, injure; to trouble, vex, distress, torment
afflict·or -ōris *m* destroyer, subverter
afflict·us -a -um *adj* damaged, shattered; cast down, downhearted; vile
af·flīgō -flīgĕre -flixī -flictum *vt* to knock, strike down; (*fig*) to crush
affl·ō -āre *vt* (with *dat*) **a** to breathe (*something*) upon; **b** to impart (*something*) to; *vi* (with *dat*) **a** to breathe upon; **b** to be favorable to
afflŭ·ens -entis *adj* flowing; rich, affluent; abounding, numerous
affluenter *adv* lavishly, abundantly
affluenti·a -ae *f* abundance
af·flŭō -fluĕre -fluxī -fluxum *vi* (with *dat* or **ad** + *acc*) **a** to flow to, flow towards, glide by; **b** to hasten to, flock to; (with *abl*) to abound in
af·for -fārī -fātus sum *vt* to address, accost, pray to
affŏre = adfuturus esse
affŏrem = adessem
affornīd·ō -āre *vi* to be afraid
af·fulgĕō -fulgēre -fulsī *vi* to shine, beam, dawn, appear; (with *dat*) to shine on
af·fundō -fundĕre -fūdī -fūsum *vt* (with *dat*) **a** to pour, sprinkle, scatter (*something*) on; **b** to send or despatch (*someone*) to; **affundi** or **se affundere** (with *dat*) to throw oneself at, prostrate oneself before
Afric·us -a -um *adj* African; *m* S.W. Wind; *f* originally the district of Carthage, made a Roman province in 146 B.C.; continent of Africa
Agamemn·ōn -ŏnis *m* king of Mycenae, son of Atreus and of Aërope, brother of Menelaus, and commander in chief of Greek forces at Troy
Aganipp·ē -ēs *f* fountain on Mount Helicon, sacred to the Muses
agās·ō -ōnis *m* driver, groom; lackey
agĕdum *interj* come on!; well!
agell·us -ī *m* little field, plot
agēm·a -ătis *n* corps or division (*of soldiers*)
Agēn·or -ŏris *m* son of Belus, king of Phoenicia, father of Cadmus and Europa, and ancestor of Dido
Agēnorīd·ēs -ae *m* descendant of Agenor; Cadmus; Perseus
ag·er -rī *m* field, ground, arable land, farm, estate; territory, district
agg·er -ĕris *m* fill dirt, rubbish, soil, mound; rampart, dike, dam, pier; fortification; causeway; funeral pile
aggĕr·ō -āre *vt* to pile up, fill up, amass, increase; stimulate
ag·gĕrō -gerĕre -gessī -gestum *vt* to bring forward, utter; (with *dat* or **ad** + *acc*) to bring, convey (*something*) to
aggest·us -ūs *m* accumulation
agglomĕr·ō -āre *vt* to wind up (*as on a ball*); to annex; **se agglomare** (with *dat*) to attach oneself to, join
agglūtin·ō -āre *vt* to glue, paste, solder, cement
aggravesc·ō -ĕre *vi* to grow heavy
aggrăv·ō -āre *vt* to make heavier; to make worse, aggravate
ag·gredior -grĕdī -gressus sum *vt* to approach; to address; to attack; to undertake, begin

aggrĕg·ō -āre *vt* to assemble, collect; to attach, join, include, implicate
aggressi·ō -ōnis *f* attack, assault; introduction
agil·is -e *adj* easily moved, agile, nimble, quick; busy, active
agilit·ās -ātis *f* mobility, agility, nimbleness, quickness, activity
agitābil·is -e *adj* easily moved, light
agitāti·ō -ōnis *f* motion, movement, agitation; activity, pursuit; prosecution
agitāt·or -ōris *m* driver, charioteer
agit·ō -āre *vt* to set in motion, drive on, impel; to hunt, chase, pursue; to drive, urge, support, insist on; to practice, exercise; to observe, keep, celebrate; to obey, carry out; to spend, pass (*time*); to shake, toss, disturb; to vex, distress; to stimulate, excite; to deride, insult; to criticize; to consider, deliberate on; to discuss, debate; *vi* to live, dwell, be
Aglaur·ōs -ī *f* daughter of Cecrops, changed by Mercury into a stone
agm·en -inis *n* herd, flock, troop, crowd; body, mass; army (*on march*), procession, train
agn·a -ae *f* ewe, lamb (*female*)
ag·nascor -nascī -nātus sum *vi* to be born (*after the father has made his will*)
agnāti·ō -ōnis *f* blood relationship (*on father's side*)
agnāt·us -ī *m* relative (*on father's side*)
agnell·us -ī *m* little lamb
agnīn·a -ae *f* mutton
agniti·ō -ōnis *f* recognition, acknowledgment, admission; knowledge
ag·noscō -noscĕre -nōvī -nitum *vt* to recognize, identify, acknowledge
agn·us -ī *m* lamb
agō agĕre ēgī actum *vt* to drive, lead, conduct; to chase, hunt; to drive away, steal; to spend (*time*); to do, act, perform; to manage, administer, carry on; to plead, transact, discuss, propose; to play, act the part of; to accuse, impeach; to exercise, practice, perform, deliver, pronounce; to treat; **agi** to be at stake; **se agere** to behave, deport oneself
ag·ōn -ōnis *m* contest, combat (*in public games*)
agrāri·us -a -um *adj* agrarian; *m pl* land-reform party
agrest·is -e *adj* rustic; boorish, wild, savage
agricŏl·a -ae *m* farmer, peasant
Agricŏl·a -ae *m* father-in-law of Tacitus
agricultūr·a -ae *f* agriculture
Agrigent·um -ī *n* city on south coast of Sicily (*sometimes called Acragas*)
agripĕt·a -ae *m* colonist, settler
Agripp·a -ae *m* son-in-law of Augustus, husband of Julia, and father of Agrippina
Agrippīn·a -ae *f* wife of Tiberius; daughter of Agrippa and Julia, and mother of Caligula
āh *interj* ah!, ha!, oh!
aha *interj* aha!
ai *interj* (denoting grief) alas!
āin = aisne (*see* **aio**)
aiō *vt & vi* (used mainly in present and imperfect indicative) I say; I say yes, I say so; I affirm, assert, tell, relate; **ain** (= **aisne**) **tandem?, ain tu?, ain tute?,** or **ain vero?** (colloquial phrase, expressing surprise) do you really mean it?, you don't say!, really?
Aj·ax -ācis *m* son of Telamon, king of Salamis; son of Oileus, king of the Locri
āl·a -ae *f* wing; armpit; squadron (*of cavalry*); flank (*of battle line*)
alăc·er -ris -re *adj* lively, brisk, quick, eager, active, cheerful
alacrit·ās -ātis *f* liveliness, briskness, eagerness, cheerfulness
alăp·a -ae *f* slap; emancipation (*of slave*)
ālārī·ī -ōrum *m pl* auxiliaries, allies
ālār·is -e *adj* (mil) on the flank, of the flank
ālāri·us -a -um *adj* (*mil*) on the flank, of the flank
ālāt·us -a -um *adj* winged
alaud·a -ae *f* lark
alāz·ōn -ŏnis *m* boaster
Alb·a -ae *f* town, also called Alba Longa, mother city of Rome, founded by Ascanius, son of Aeneas
albāt·us -a -um *adj* dressed in white
alb·ĕō -ēre -ŭī *vi* to be white
albesc·ō -ĕre *vi* to become white, whiten; to dawn
albic·ō -āre *vt* to make white, whiten *vi* to be white
albid·us -a -um *adj* white, whitish
Albi·ōn -ŏnis *f* Britain
albitūd·ō -inis *f* whiteness
Albŭl·a -ae *f* Tiber River
albŭl·us -a -um *adj* whitish
alb·um -ī *n* white; white tablet, record, list, register
Albunĕ·a or **Albūn·a -ae** *f* fountain at Tibur; nymph of the fountain
alb·us -a -um *adj* dead white, white, bright; favorable
Alcae·us -ī *m* Greek lyric poet of Lesbos, contemporary with Sappho (610 B.C.)
alcēd·ō -inis *f* kingfisher, halcyon
alcēdōni·a -ōrum *n pl* halcyon days; (fig) deep calm, tranquillity
alc·ēs -is *f* elk
Alcibiăd·ēs -is *m* Athenian politician, disciple of Socrates (450?-404 B.C.)
Alcīd·ēs -ae *m* Hercules
Alcimĕd·ē -ēs *f* wife of Aeson and mother of Jason
Alcinŏ·ūs -ī *m* king of the Phaea-

cians, by whom Ulysses was entertained

Alcmēn·a or **Alcumēn·a -ae** or **Alcmēn·ē -ēs** *f* wife of Amphitryon and mother of Hercules by Jupiter

ālě·a -ae *f* dice game; chance, risk, venture

āleāt·or -ōris *m* dice player, gambler

āleātōrĭ·us -a -um *adj* of dice, gambling

ālě·ō -ōnis *m* gambler

āl·es -ĭtis *adj* winged; swift

āl·es -ĭtis *m* or *f* winged creature, fowl, bird; *m* poet; *f* augury, omen, sign

al·escō -escěre *vi* to grow up, increase

Alexand·er -rī *m* Paris, son of Priam and Hecuba; Alexander the Great, king of Macedon

Alexandrē·a or **Alexandrī·a -ae** *f* city in Egypt, founded by Alexander the Great

alg·a -ae *f* seaweed

al·gěō -gēre -sī *vi* to be cold, feel cold

al·gescō -gescěre -sī *vi* to catch cold; to become cold

algĭd·us -a -um *adj* cold

alg·or -ōris *m* cold, chilliness

alg·us -ūs *m* cold

aliā *adv* by another way

aliās *adv* at another time; **alias . . . alias** at one time . . . at another, sometimes . . . sometimes

alibī *adv* elsewhere; otherwise, in other respects; **alibi . . . alibi** in one place . . . in another, here . . . there

alicŭbī *adv* at any place, somewhere, anywhere

alicunde *adv* from somewhere, from any place, from someone else

aliēnāti·ō -ōnis *f* transfer (*of property*); separation, alienation; aversion, dislike

aliēnigěn·a -ae *m* foreigner, alien, stranger

aliēn·ō -āre *vt* to make strange, transfer, sell; to alienate, set at variance; to remove, separate; to make insane, drive mad

aliēn·us -a -um *adj* another's; foreign; contrary, hostile; strange, unsuitable, incongruous, inconsistent, inconvenient; *m* stranger, foreigner

āli·ger -gěra -gěrum *adj* wearing wings, winged

alimentārĭ·us -a -um *adj* alimentary

aliment·um -ī *n* nourishment, food, provisions; fuel

alimōnĭ·a -ae *f* or **alimōn·ĭum -ĭī** or **-ī** *n* nourishment, food, support

aliō *adv* to another place, elsewhere

aliōquī or **aliōquīn** *adv* otherwise, in other respects, for the rest; besides; in general; in any case

aliorsum or **aliorsus** *adv* in another direction; in another manner, in a different sense

ālĭp·ēs -ědis *adj* wing-footed, swift-footed

alipt·ēs or **alipt·a -ae** *m* wrestling trainer

aliquā *adv* somehow, in any direction

aliquam *adv* in some degree

aliquamdĭū *adv* for some time

aliquandō *adv* sometime or other, once; at any time, ever; sometimes, now and then; for once, now; finally, now at last

aliquantisper *adv* for a while, for a time

aliquantō *adv* somewhat, a little, rather

aliquantŭlum *adv* somewhat

aliquantŭl·us -a -um *adj* little, small

aliquantum *adv* somewhat, a little, rather

aliquant·us -a -um *adj* considerable

aliquātěnus *adv* for some distance, to a certain extent, somewhat; in some respects, partly

alĭ·quī -qua -quod *adj* some, any

alĭquid *adv* to some extent, at all

alĭ·quid -cūjus *pron* something, anything; something important

alĭ·quis -cūjus *pron* someone, somebody, anyone; someone important

aliquō *adv* to some place, somewhere

aliquot (indecl) *adj* some, several, a few

aliquotiens *adv* several times

aliquōvorsum *adv* to some place, one way or another

alĭter *adv* otherwise, else, differently

aliŭbī *adv* elsewhere; **aliubi . . . aliubi** here . . . there

āl·ĭum -ĭī or **-ī** *n* garlic

aliunde *adv* from another source, from elsewhere

alĭ·us -a -ud *adj* another, other, different; *pron* another; **alii . . . alii** some . . . others; **alius . . . alius** one . . . another, the one . . . the other; **alius ex alio** one after another

al·lābor -lābī -lapsus sum *vi* to glide, slide, slip; to flow

allabōr·ō -āre *vi* to work hard

allacrĭmō -āre *vi* to weep, shed tears

allaps·us -ūs *m* stealthy approach

allātr·ō -āre *vt* to revile; (*of sea*) to break against, dash against

allātus *pp* of **affero**

allaud·ō -āre *vt* to praise highly

all·ēc -ēcis *n* fish sauce

Allectō (indecl) *f* one of the three Furies

allect·ō -āre *vt* to allure, entice

allēgāti·ō -ōnis *f* sending, despatching

allēg·ō -āre *vt* to commission, deputize, despatch; to allege; to instigate

al·lěgō -legěre -lēgī -lectum *vt* to select, elect

allevāment·um -ī *n* alleviation, relief

allevātī·ō -ōnis *f* raising, elevating; easing
allĕv·ō -āre *vt* to lift up, raise; to alleviate; to comfort; to lighten
all·ex -ĭcis *m* (the) big toe; midget
al·liciō -licĕre -lexī -lectum *vt* to attract
al·līdō -līdĕre -līsī -līsum *vt* (with *dat* or with **ad** or **in** + *acc*) to dash (*something*) against; **allidi** to be wrecked
allĭg·ō -āre *vt* to bind, fetter; to bandage; to hinder, detain; to impugn, accuse; (with **ad** + *acc*) to bind (*something*) to
al·linō -linĕre -lēvī -lĭtum *vt* to smudge; (with *dat*) to smear (*something*) on
all·ĭum -iī or **-ī** *n* garlic
Allobrŏg·ēs -um *m pl* Gallic tribe living between the Rhone and the Isère
allocūtī·ō -ōnis *f* address; consoling, comforting
alloqu·ĭum -iī or **-ī** *n* address, conversation; encouragement, consolation
al·lŏquor -lŏquī -locūtus sum *vt* to speak to, address; to exhort, rouse; to console, comfort
allūdī·ō -āre *vi* to play, jest
al·lūdō -lūdĕre -lūsī -lūsum *vi* to play, joke; (of waves) (with *dat*) to play against
al·lŭō -luĕre -lŭī *vt* to wash
alluvī·ēs -ēī *f* inundation, pool (*left by flood waters*); alluvial land
alluvī·ō -ōnis *f* inundation; alluvial land
alm·us -a -um *adj* nourishing; genial, kind, propitious, indulgent, bountiful
aln·us -ī *f* alder tree; ship
al·ō -ĕre -ŭī -tum or **-ĭtum** *vt* to feed, nourish, rear; to support, maintain; to promote; to increase, strengthen
alŏ·ē -ēs *f* aloe; bitterness
alogĭ·a -ae *f* folly
Alp·ēs -ĭum *f pl* Alps
alpha (indecl) *n* alpha (*first letter of Greek alphabet*)
Alphē·us or **Alphē·os -ī** *m* chief river of the Peloponnesus
Alpic·us -a -um *adj* Alpine
Alpīn·us -a -um *adj* Alpine
alsĭ·us or **als·us -a -um** *adj* chilly, cool, cold
altār·ĭa -ĭum *n pl* altar top, altar, high altar
altē *adv* high, on high, highly, deeply, far, remotely; loftily, profoundly
alt·er -ĕra -ĕrum *adj* one (*of two*); a second, the second, the next; *pron* one (*of two*), the one, the other; a second one, the second one, the next one; another (*one's fellow man*); **alter . . . alter** the one . . . the other, the former . . . the latter
altercātī·ō -ōnis *f* debate, dispute, discussion
alterc·ō -āre or **alterc·or -ārī -ātus sum** *vi* to quarrel, wrangle, bicker
alternīs *adv* by turns, alternately
altern·ō -āre *vt* to do by turns; to exchange; *vi* to alternate
altern·us -a -um *adj* one after another, alternate, mutual, every other
alterŭt·er -ra -rum (*f* also: **altĕra utra;** *n* also: **altĕrum utrum**) *adj* one (*of two*), either, one or the other; *pron* one, either one, one or the other
Althae·a -ae *f* daughter of Thestius, wife of Oeneus, king of Calydon, and mother of Meleager
alticinct·us -a -um *adj* active, busy, energetic
altĭl·is -e *adj* fattened, fat, full; rich
altisŏn·us -a -um *adj* high-sounding; sounding from on high
altitŏn·ans -antis *adj* thundering on high
altitūd·ō -ĭnis *f* height; depth; (fig) depth, reserve, secrecy
altivŏl·ans -antis *adj* high-flying
alt·or -ōris *m* foster father
altrinsĕcus *adv* on the other side
altr·ix -īcis *f* nourisher, foster mother
altrōvorsum *adv* on the other side
alt·us -a -um *adj* high; deep, profound; ancient, remote (*lineage*); *n* high seas, the deep; heaven; **ab alto** from on high, from heaven; **ex alto** farfetched
ālūcĭn·or -ārī *vi* to indulge in small talk, ramble
alumn·a -ae *f* foster daughter; pupil
alumn·us -ī *m* foster son; pupil
alūt·a -ae *f* soft leather; shoe; purse
alveār·ĭum -iī or **ī** *n* beehive
alveŏl·us -ī *m* tray, basin; bed of a stream; game board
alvĕ·us -ī *m* hollow, cavity; tub; bathtub; riverbed; hull of boat, boat; game board; beehive
alv·us -ī *m* belly, bowels, stomach; womb; boat; beehive
amābĭl·is -e *adj* lovable, lovely, attractive, pleasant
amābilĭt·ās -ātis *f* charm
amābilĭter *adv* lovingly, delightfully
Amalthē·a -ae *f* nymph who fed infant Jupiter with goat's milk; sibyl at Cumae
āmandātī·ō -ōnis *f* sending away
āmand·ō -āre *vt* to send away, remove
am·ans -antis *adj* loving, affectionate; **amans patriae** patriotic; *m* lover
amanter *adv* lovingly, affectionately
amārăc·us -ī *m* or *f* marjoram
amarant·us -ī *m* amaranth
amārē *adv* bitterly
amāritī·ēs -ēī *f* bitterness
amāritūd·ō -ĭnis *f* bitterness; sadness, sorrow, trouble
amār·or -ōris *m* bitterness
amār·us -a -um *adj* bitter; *n pl* disappointments
amās·ĭus -iī or **-ī** *m* lover

amāti·ō -ōnis *f* love affair
amāt·or -ōris *m* lover, friend; **amator patriae** patriot
amātorcŭl·us -ī *m* poor little lover
amātōri·us -a -um *adj* erotic, love; *n* love charm
amātr·ix -īcis *f* mistress, girl friend
Amāz·ōn -ōnis *or* **Amāzŏn·is -īdis** *f* Amazon (*member of mythical female warrior tribe dwelling in the Caucasus*)
ambact·us -ī *m* vassal
ambāg·ēs -is *f* winding, labyrinth; double-talk, evasion, digression; ambiguity, obscurity; **per ambages** enigmatically
amb·ĕdō -esse -ēdī -ēsum *vt* to eat up; (of fire) to char; to waste
ambĭg·ō -ĕre *vt* to go around, avoid; *vi* to waver, hesitate, be undecided; to argue, debate, wrangle; **ambigitur** it is uncertain
ambigŭē *adv* doubtfully, indecisively
ambiguit·ās -ātis *f* ambiguity, double meaning
ambigŭ·us -a -um *adj* wavering, changeable; uncertain, doubtful; disputed; unreliable, untrustworthy; ambiguous, dark, obscure; *n* doubt, uncertainty, paradox
amb·iō -īre *vt* to go around, encircle; (pol) ot canvass; to entreat, solicit, court
ambiti·ō -ōnis *f* (pol) campaigning (*by lawful means*); popularity, flattery; ambition (*in good or bad sense*); partiality, favortism; pomp, ostentation
ambitiōsē *adv* ostentatiously; from a desire to please
ambitiōs·us -a -um *adj* winding, entwining; publicity-conscious, eager for popularity, ambitious; ostentatious
ambit·us -ūs *m* winding, revolution; circuit, circumference, border, orbit; (pol) illegal campaigning, bribery; pomp, ostentation; circumlocution; (rhet) period
amb·ō -ae -ō *adj* both, two; *pron* both, the two
Ambraci·a -ae *f* district of Epirus in N.W. Greece
ambrosi·us -a -um *adj* ambrosial, divine, immortal; *f* food of the gods
ambūbāi·a -ae *f* Syrian flute player
ambulācr·um -ī *n* walk, avenue
ambulāti·ō -ōnis *f* (act) walk; (place) walk
ambulātiuncŭl·a -ae *f* short walk; (place) small promenade
ambulāt·or -ōris *m* peddler; idler
ambŭl·ō -āre *vt* to traverse, travel; *vi* to walk, take a walk; to march, travel; to strut
amb·ūrō -ūrĕre -ussī -ustum *vt* to burn up, scorch, singe; to consume; to numb, nip
amell·us -ī *m* wild aster
ām·ens -entis *adj* out of one's mind, mad; foolish, stupid
āmenti·a -ae *f* madness; folly
āment·ō -āre *vt* to fit (*a javelin*) with a strap
āment·um -ī *n* strap
am·es -ĭtis *m* pole for fowler's net
amethystin·us -a -um *adj* dressed in purple; *n pl* purple garments
amethyst·us -ī *f* amethyst
amic·a -ae *f* girl friend, lady friend
amicē *adv* in a friendly manner
amic·iō -īre -ŭī -tum *vt* to wrap around; to cover, clothe, wrap
amīcĭter *adv* in a friendly way
amīciti·a -ae *f* friendship
amict·us -ūs *m* wrap, cloak; style, fashion (*in dress*)
amicŭl·a -ae *f* girl friend
amicŭl·um -ī *n* wrap, mantle
amicŭl·us -ī *m* pal, buddy
amic·us -a -um *adj* friendly; *m* friend; patron
āmigr·ō -āre *vi* to move away, emigrate
āmissi·ō -ōnis *f* loss
amit·a -ae *f* aunt (*father's sister*)
ā·mittō -mittĕre -mīsī -missum *vt* to lose, let slip; **fidem amittere** to break one's word
amnicŏl·a -ae *m* or *f* riverside plant (*e.g., willow tree*)
amnicŭl·us -ī *m* brook
amn·is -is *m* river; **secundo amni** downstream
am·ō -āre *vt* to love, like, be fond of; to fall in love with; **amabo** or **amabo te** (coll) please
amoenē *adv* charmingly
amoenit·ās -ātis *f* charm
amoen·us -a -um *adj* charming, pleasant; *n pl* charming sights
amōl·ior -īrī *vt* to remove; to put aside, put away; **se amoliri** to remove oneself, clear out
amōm·um -ī *n* amomum plant (*aromatic shrub*)
am·or or **am·ōs -ōris** *m* love, affection; object of affection, love; Cupid; *m pl* love affair
āmōti·ō -ōnis *f* removal
ā·movĕō -movēre -mōvī -mōtum *vt* to remove, withdraw, put away, put aside; to steal; **se amovere** to retire, withdraw
Amphiarā·ūs -ī *m* famous Greek seer
amphiboli·a -ae *f* (rhet) ambiguity
Amphi·ōn -ŏnis *m* son of Antiope by Jupiter, twin brother of Zethus, king of Thebes, and husband of Niobe
amphitheātr·um -ī *n* amphitheater
Amphitrȳ·ō or **Amphitrȳ·ōn -ōnis** *m* husband of Alcmena
Amphitryōniăd·ēs -is *m* Hercules
amphŏr·a -ae *f* amphora; liquid measure (*about 7 gallons*)
amplē *adv* largely, abundantly, broadly, spaciously; splendidly
am·plector -plectī -plexus sum *vt* to embrace, entwine, enclose, encircle; to grab, get hold of; to understand, comprehend; to embrace, include, comprise; to sum up; to em-

brace affectionately, esteem, cling to; (mil) to occupy, cover
amplex·ō -āre or **amplex·or -ārī -ātus sum** *vt* to embrace; to honor, esteem
amplex·us -ūs *m* circuit; embrace, caress
amplificāti·ō -ōnis *f* extension, enlargement; (rhet) amplification, development
amplificāt·or -ōris *m* enlarger, amplifier
amplificē *adv* splendidly
amplific·ō -āre *vt* to enlarge, extend, widen; to increase; (rhet) to enlarge upon, develop
ampli·ō -āre *vt* to widen, enlarge; to enhance; to postpone (*judgment*), adjourn (*court, in order to gather further evidence*); to remand
ampliter *adv* splendidly
amplitūd·ō -inis *f* width, size, bulk, extent; greatness, dignity, importance, high rank; (rhet) development, amplification
amplius *adv* any further, any more, any longer, besides; further, more, longer; **amplius uno die** one day longer; longer than one day; **nec amplius** no longer
amplius *adj* (neuter comparative of **amplus**) more, further, else; (with numerals) more than; **hoc amplius** this further point; **nihil amplius** nothing further, no more; **quid amplius** what more, what else; *n* more, a larger amount; **amplius negoti** more trouble
ampl·us -a -um *adj* ample, large, wide, spacious; strong, great, powerful; grand, imposing, splendid; eminent, prominent, illustrious, distinguished
ampull·a -ae *f* bottle, jar, flask; bombast
ampullār·ius -iī or **-ī** *m* flask maker
ampull·or -ārī -ātus sum *vi* to be bombastic
amputāti·ō -ōnis *f* pruning
ampŭt·ō -āre *vt* to lop off, prune; to curtail, shorten; **amputata loqui** to speak disconnectedly
Amūl·ius -iī or **-ī** *m* king of Alba Longa, brother of Numitor, and granduncle of Romulus and Remus
amurc·a -ae *f* dregs of oil
amygdăl·a -ae *f* almond tree
amygdăl·um -ī *n* almond
amyst·is -idis *f* drinking bottoms up
an *conj* (introducing the latter clause of a disjunctive direct or indirect question) or
anabăthr·a -ōrum *n pl* bleachers
Anăcrĕ·ōn -ontis *m* famous lyric poet of Teos (*fl* 540 B.C.)
anadēm·a -ătis *n* fillet, headband
anagnost·ēs -ae *m* reader, reciter
analectr·is -idis *f* shoulder pad (*to improve the figure*)
anapaest·us -a -um *adj* anapestic; *m* anapest; *n* poem in anapestic meter
an·as -ătis *f* duck; **anas fluvialis** wild duck
anaticŭl·a -ae *f* duckling
anatīn·us -a -um *adj* duck's
anatocism·us -ī *m* compound interest
Anaxagŏr·ās -ae *m* Greek philosopher of Clazomenae, teacher of Pericles and Euripides (500?-428 B.C.)
Anaximand·er -rī *m* Greek philosopher of Miletus (610-547 B.C.)
Anaximĕn·ēs -is *m* Greek philosopher of Miletus (*fl* 544 B.C.)
an·ceps -cipitis *adj* two-headed; two-edged; twin-peaked; amphibious; double, twofold; doubtful, undecided, ambiguous; hazardous, critical; *n* danger, peril
Anchīs·ēs -ae *m* son of Capys and father of Aeneas
Anchīsiăd·ēs -ae *m* son of Anchises, Aeneas
ancīl·e -is *n* oval shield said to have fallen from heaven in reign of Numa, second king of Rome
ancill·a -ae *f* maidservant
ancillār·is -e *adj* maidservant's
ancillŭl·a -ae *f* young slave (*female*)
ancŏr·a -ae *f* anchor
ancorāl·e -is *n* cable
ancorār·ius -a -um *adj* of an anchor
Ancȳr·a -ae *f* Ankara, capital of Galatia
andabăt·a -ae *m* blindfold gladiator
And·ēs -ium *f pl* village near Mantua, birthplace of Virgil
androgȳn·us -ī *m* or **androgȳn·ē -ēs** *f* hermaphrodite
Andromăch·a -ae or **Andromăch·ē -ēs** *f* Hector's wife
Andromĕd·a -ae *f* daughter of Cepheus and Cassiope, rescued from a sea monster by Perseus
andr·ōn -ōnis *m* corridor
Andronīc·us -ī *m* Lucius Livius Andronicus (*fl* 241 B.C., *first epic and dramatic poet of the Romans*)
Andr·os -ī *f* Aegean island
ānell·us -ī *m* little ring
anēth·um -ī *n* anise, dill
anfract·us -ūs *m* curve, bend (*of road*); orbit; digression, prolixity
angell·us -ī *m* small corner
angīn·a -ae *f* tonsillitis, inflamation of the throat
angiport·us -ūs *m* or **angiport·um -ī** *n* alley
ang·ō -ĕre *vt* to choke, throttle; to distress, tease, trouble
ang·or -ōris *m* strangling, suffocation; anguish
anguicŏm·us -a -um *adj* snake-haired
anguicŭl·us -ī *m* small snake
anguif·er -ĕra -ĕrum *adj* snaky
anguigĕn·a -ae *m* offspring of a dragon; Theban
anguill·a -ae *f* eel
anguinĕ·us -a -um *adj* snaky; serpent-like
anguīn·us -a -um *adj* snaky

anguĭp•ēs -ĕdis *adj* serpent-footed
angu•is -is *m* or *f* snake, serpent
Angu•is -is *m* or *f* Dragon, Hydra (*constellation*)
Anguitĕn•ens -entis *m* Ophiuchus (*constellation*)
angulār•is -e *adj* angular
angulāt•us -a -um *adj* angular
angŭl•us -ī *m* angle, corner; nook, recess; **ad paris angulos** at right angles
angustē *adv* within narrow limits, closely, hardly, scarcely; briefly, concisely
angusti•ae -ārum *f pl* narrow place, defile; narrow passage, strait; (fig) shortness; scarcity, want, deficiency; difficulty, tight spot, perplexity, distress, straits; narrow-mindedness
angusticlāvi•us -a -um *adj* wearing a narrow purple stripe
angust•ō -āre *vt* to make narrow
angust•us -a -um *adj* narrow, close, short, brief (*time*); scanty (*means*); difficult, critical; narrow-minded; base, mean; *n* narrowness; critical condition, danger
anhēlĭt•us -ūs *m* panting, difficulty in breathing, puffing; breath, breathing; vapor
anhēl•ō -āre *vt* to breathe out; to pant after; *vi* to pant, puff; to exhale; (of fire) to roar
anhēl•us -a -um *adj* panting, puffing
anicŭl•a -ae *f* little old woman, silly old woman
Aniēns•is -e or **Aniēn•us -a -um** *adj* of the Anio (*tributary of the Tiber*)
anīl•is -e *adj* of an old woman
anīlĭt•ās -ātis *f* old age (*of women*)
anīlĭter *adv* like an old woman
anĭm•a -ae *f* air, wind, breeze; breath; breath of life, life; soul (*as the principle of life, opposed to* **animus** *as the principle of thought and feelings*); spirit, ghost
animadversi•ō -ōnis *f* attention, observation; reproach, criticism; punishment
animadvers•or -ōris *m* observer
animad•vertō or **animad•vortō -vertĕre -vertī -versum** *vt* to pay attention to, attend to; to notice, observe, realize; to reproach, criticize; to punish
anĭm•al -ālis *n* animal; living creature
animāl•is -e *adj* consisting of air; animate, living
anim•ans -antis *adj* living, animate; *m & f & n* living being; animal
animāti•ō -ōnis *f* living being
animāt•us -a -um *adj* courageous; inclined, disposed; (with **erga** or **in** + *acc*) disposed toward
anĭm•ō -āre *vt* to make alive, to animate; to encourage
animōsē *adv* courageously; eagerly
animōs•us -a -um *adj* full of air, airy; full of life, living, animate; blowing violently; full of courage, bold, spirited, undaunted; proud
animŭl•a -ae *f* little soul, life
animŭl•us -ī *m* darling
anim•us -ī *m* soul (*as principle of intellection and sensation, whereas* **anima** *is soul as principle of life*); intellect, understanding, mind, thought, reason; memory; knowledge; sense, consciousness; judgment, opinion; imagination; heart, feelings, passions; spirit, courage, morale; disposition, character; pride, haughtiness; will, purpose, desire, inclination; pleasure, delight; confident hope; **aequo animo** patiently, calmly; **animi causā** for amusement; **bono animo esse** to take heart; **ex animo** from the bottom of the heart, sincerely; **ex animo effluere** to slip one's mind; **in animo habere** (*with inf*) to intend to; **meo animo** in my opinion
Anī•ō -ēnis *m* tributary of the Tiber
An•ĭus -ĭī or **-ī** *m* king and priest on Delos who welcomed Aeneas
annāl•is -e *adj* lasting a year, annual; **lex annalis** law fixing minimum age for holding public offices; *m pl* annals, chronicle
annăt•ō -āre *vi* (with *dat* or **ad** + *acc*) to swim to
anne *conj* (pleonastic form of **an**) or
an•nectō -nectĕre -nexŭī -nexum *vt* (with *dat* or **ad** + *acc*) to tie, connect, annex (*something*) to; (with *dat*) to apply (*something*) to
annex•us -ūs *m* connection
annicŭl•us -a -um *adj* one year old, yearling
an•nītor -nītī -nīsus sum or **nixus sum** *vi* (with *dat* or **ad** + *acc*) to press against, lean on; (with **ut** or *inf*) to strive to
anniversārĭ•us -a -um *adj* annual, yearly
ann•ō -āre *vi* (with *dat*, with **ad** + *acc*, or with *acc* of limit of motion) to swim to or towards; (with *dat*) to swim with or along with
annōn *conj* or not
annōn•a -ae *f* year's crop; grain; price of grain; cost of living; high price
annōs•us -a -um *adj* aged, old
annotātĭ•ō -ōnis *f* notation, remark
annōtĭn•us -a -um *adj* last year's
annŏt•ō -āre *vt* to write down, note down; to comment on; to observe, perceive
annumĕr•ō -āre *vt* (with *dat*) to count out (*money*) to; (with *dat* or **in** + *acc*) to add (*something*) to, to include (*someone*) among
annuntĭ•ō -āre *vt* to announce, make known, proclaim
an•nŭō -nuĕre -nŭī -nūtum *vt* to designate by a nod; to indicate, declare; (with *dat*) to promise, grant (*something*) to; *vi* to nod, nod as-

sent; (with *dat*) to nod assent to, to be favorable to, smile on

ann·us -ī *m* year; season; age, time of life; year of office; **ad annum** for the coming year, a year hence; **annum** or **in annum** for a year; **per annos** year to year

annŭ·us -a -um *adj* lasting a year; annual, yearly; *n pl* yearly pay, pension

an·quīrō -quīrĕre -quīsīvī -quīsītum *vt* to search carefully; to examine, inquire into; (with *genit* or *abl* of the charge) to accuse (*someone*) of; *vi* to hold an inquest

ans·a -ae *f* handle; opportunity

ansāt·us -a -um *adj* having handles; **homo ansatus** man with arms akimbo

ans·er -ĕris *m* gander

ante *adv* before, previously; in front, forwards

ante *prep* (with *acc*) before; more than, above

antĕā *adv* before, previously, formerly

ante·capĭō -capĕre -cēpī -ceptum *vt* to receive beforehand; to take possession of beforehand, preoccupy; to anticipate

ante·cēdō -cēdĕre -cessī -cessum *vt* to precede; to excel, surpass; *vi* (with *dat*) **a** to have precedence over; **b** to excel, surpass

antecessĭ·ō -ōnis *f* antecedent cause

antecess·or -ōris *m* (mil) scout; *m pl* advance guard

antecurs·or -ōris *m* (mil) scout; *m pl* advance guard

ante·ĕō -īre -iī *vt* to precede; to excel, surpass; to anticipate, prevent; *vi* to precede; to take the lead; (with *dat*) **a** to go before; **b** to excel, surpass

ante·fĕrō -ferre -tŭlī -lātum *vt* to prefer; to anticipate

antefix·us -a -um *pp* of **antefigo**; *n pl* images, statues, etc., affixed to roofs and gutters of homes or temples

ante·gredĭor -grĕdī -gressus sum *vt* to precede

antehab·ĕō -ēre *vt* to prefer

antĕhāc *adv* before this time, before now, formerly

antelātus *pp* of **antefero**

antelūcān·us -a -um *adj* before dawn

antemerīdiān·us -a -um *adj* before noon

ante·mittō -mittĕre -mīsī -missum *vt* to send out ahead

antenn·a -ae *f* yardarm, sail yard

Antēn·or -ŏris *m* Trojan who after the fall of Troy went to Italy and founded Patavium

antepīlān·ī -ōrum *m pl* front ranks, front line

ante·pōnō -pōnĕre -posŭī -positum *vt* to prefer; to serve (*food*)

antepŏt·ens -entis *adj* very wealthy

antĕquam or **ante . . . quam** *conj* before

Antĕr·ōs -ōtis *m* avenger of unrequited love

ant·ēs -ium *m pl* rows (*e.g., of vines*)

antesignān·us -ī *m* soldier who fought in front of the standards to defend them; leader, commander

ante·stō or **anti·stō -stāre -stĕtī** *vi* to excel, be distinguished; (with *dat*) to be superior to

antest·or -ārī -ātus sum *vt* to call as witness

ante·venĭō -venīre -vēnī -ventum *vt* to anticipate, thwart; to surpass, excel; *vi* to become more distinguished; (with *dat*) **a** to anticipate; **b** to surpass, excel

ante·vertō -vertĕre -vertī -versum *vt* to go or come before, precede; to anticipate; to prefer

antevŏl·ō -āre *vi* to dash out ahead

anticipātĭ·ō -ōnis *f* preconception, foreknowledge

anticip·ō -āre *vt* to anticipate

antīc·us -a -um *adj* front, foremost

Antigŏn·ē -ēs *f* daughter of Theban king Oedipus; daughter of Trojan king Laomedon

Antilŏch·us -ī *m* son of Nestor, killed by Hector at Troy

Antiphăt·ēs -ae *m* king of the Laestrygones, who sank the fleet of Greeks returning from Troy with Ulysses

antīquārĭ·us -a -um *adj & m* antiquarian

antīquē *adv* in former times; in the good old style

antīquĭt·ās -ātis *f* antiquity; men of former times, the ancients; the good old days

antīquĭtus *adv* in former times, of old; from ancient times; in the old style

antīqu·ō -āre *vt* to reject (*law, bill*)

antīqu·us -a -um *adj* old, ancient; oldfashioned, venerable; *m pl* ancients, ancient authors; *n* antiquity; old custom

antist·es -ĭtis *m* priest presiding over temple, high priest

antist·es -ĭtis or **antistĭt·a -ae** *f* priestess presiding over temple, high priestess

Antisthĕn·ēs -is or **-ae** *m* pupil of Socrates and founder of Cynic philosophy

antithĕt·on -ī *n* (rhet) antithesis

antr·um -ī *n* cave, cavern

ānulār·ĭus -ĭī or **-ī** *m* ring maker

ānulāt·us -a -um *adj* wearing a ring

ānŭl·us -ī *m* ring, signet ring

ān·us -ī *m* anus, rectum; ring

an·us -ūs *f* old woman; hag

anxiē *adv* uneasily

anxiĕt·ās -ātis *f* anxiety, trouble

anxĭf·er -ĕra -ĕrum *adj* causing anxiety

anxĭ·us -a -um *adj* worried, troubled; disquieting

apăge *interj* go on!; scram!
apēliōt·ēs -ae *m* east wind
Apell·ēs -is *m* famous Greek painter (*fl 4th cent.* B.C.)
ap·er -rī *m* boar
aper·iō -īre -ŭī -tum *vt* to uncover, open, lay bare, disclose, reveal; to prove, demonstrate; to explain, recount
apertē *adv* openly, frankly, candidly
apert·ō -āre *vt* to keep on laying bare
apert·us -a -um *pp* of **aperio;** *adj* bare, uncovered, exposed; without decks; clear (*style*); frank, candid (*character*); manifest, plain, evident; accessible, unobstructed; *n* open space; **in aperto** in the open; **in aperto esse** to be clear, evident, well known, notorious
ap·ex -icis *m* point, top, summit; hat, cap, crown; crowning glory
aphract·us -ī *f* or **aphract·um -ī** *n* ship without deck
apiār·ius -iī or **-ī** *m* beekeeper
apicŭl·a -ae *f* little bee
ap·is -is *f* bee
ap·iscor -iscī -tus sum *vt* to pursue; to take, reach, gain, get
ap·ium -iī or **-ī** *n* celery
aplustr·e -is *n* stern
apoclēt·ī -ōrum *m pl* select committee (*of Aetolian League*)
apodytēr·ium -iī or **-ī** *n* dressing room (*at a bath*)
apolactiz·ō -āre *vt* to kick aside, scorn
Apoll·ō -inis *m* son of Jupiter and Latona, twin brother of Diana, god of the sun, divination, archery, healing, poetry, and music
Apollodōr·us -ī *m* famous rhetorician, teacher of Augustus; famous Athenian grammarian and author of an extant work on mythology (*fl* 140 B.C.)
apolŏg·us -ī *m* story, fable
apophorēt·a -ōrum *n pl* presents for house guests
aposphrāgism·a -ătis *n* device on signet ring, seal
apothēc·a -ae *f* warehouse, storehouse, magazine
apparātē *adv* with much preparation, sumptuously
apparātī·ō -ōnis *f* preparation
apparāt·us -a -um *adj* prepared, well prepared; sumptuous
apparāt·us -ūs *m* getting or making ready, preparing, providing; equipment, apparatus, paraphernalia; pomp, magnificence
appār·ĕō -ēre -ŭī -itum *vi* to appear, become visible; to be seen, show oneself; (with *dat*) to wait on, serve; **apparet** it is evident, clear, certain
appāritī·ō -ōnis *f* attendance, service; *f pl* household servants
appārit·or -ōris *m* servant; attendant of public official (*e.g., aide, lictor, secretary*)
appăr·ō -āre *vt* to prepare, make ready, provide
appellātī·ō -ōnis *f* addressing; appeal; naming, calling by name; name, title; pronunciation
ap·pellō -pellĕre -pŭlī -pulsum *vt* (with *dat* or **ad** + *acc*) to drive (*something*) to, steer (*ship*) to; *vi* (*of ship*) to land
appell·ō -āre *vt* to accost, address; to appeal to; (law) to sue; to name, call; to mention by name; to pronounce
appendicŭl·a -ae *f* small addition
append·ix -icis *f* addition, supplement
ap·pendō -pendĕre -pendī -pensum *vt* to weigh; to pay out; (fig) to weigh, consider
appĕt·ens -entis *adj* greedy, avaricious; (with *genit*) eager for, craving
appetenter *adv* eagerly, greedily
appetentī·a -ae *f* craving, desire; (with *genit*) craving for, desire for
appetītī·ō -ōnis *f* grasping, craving; (with *genit*) grasping at, craving for
appetīt·us -ūs *m* craving, desire; *m pl* appetites, passions
appĕt·ō -ĕre -īvī -ītum *vt* to try to reach; to lay hold of; to make for, head for; to attack, assail, assault; *vi* to approach, draw near
apping·ō -ĕre *vt* to paint; to write
ap·plaudō -plaudĕre -plausī -plausum *vt* (with *dat*) to strike (*something*) against; *vi* to applaud
applicātī·ō -ōnis *f* applying, application
applicāt·us -a -um *adj* (with **ad** + *acc*) inclined to; (with *dat*) lying close to, attached to
applicit·us -a -um *adj* (with *dat*) applied or joined to, attached to
applic·ō -āre -āvī or **-ŭī -ātum** or **itum** *vt* to bring in close contact; (with *dat* or **ad** + *acc*) **a** to apply, attach, add, join (*something*) to; **b** to steer (*ship*) toward; **c** to devote (*attention, mind*) to
applōr·ō -āre *vt* to deplore, lament
ap·pōnō -pōnĕre -posŭī -posĭtum *vt* to serve (*food*); (with *dat* or **ad** + *acc*) to put or lay (*something*) near, at, or beside; (with *dat*) **a** to set (*food*) before; **b** to appoint or designate (*someone*) to (*a duty, task*); **c** to reckon (*something*) as
apporrect·us -a -um *adj* stretched out
apport·ō -āre *vt* to carry or bring up; to cause; (with *dat*) to carry (*something*) to
apposc·ō -ĕre *vt* to demand in addition
appositē *adv* appropriately, pertinently
apposit·us -a -um *pp* of **appono;** *adj* fit, suitable, appropriate; (with *dat*) situated near, continguous with, bordering on; (with **ad** + *acc*) suited to, fit for
appōt·us -a -um *adj* drunk

apprĕc·or -ārī -ātus sum *vt* to pray to, worship
appre·hendō -hendĕre -hendī -hensum *vt* to seize, take hold of; (mil) to occupy
apprīmē *adv* chiefly, especially
ap·prīmō -primĕre -pressī -pressum *vt* (with *dat*) to press (*something*) close to
approbātĭ·ō -ōnis *f* approbation, approval; proof
approbāt·or -ōris *m* one who seconds or approves
apprŏbē *adv* very well
apprŏb·ō -āre *vt* to approve; to prove
appromitt·ō -ĕre *vt* to promise in addition
apropĕr·ō -āre *vt* to hasten, speed up; *vi* to hurry
appropinquātĭ·ō -ōnis *f* approach
appropinqu·ō -āre *vi* to approach; (with *dat* or **ad** + *acc*) to come near to, approach
appugn·ō -āre *vt* to fight, attack
appuls·us -ūs *m* landing, approach
aprīcātĭ·ō -ōnis *f* basking in the sun
aprīc·or -ārī *vi* to bask, sun oneself
aprīc·us -a -um *adj* sunny; *n* sunny spot
Aprīl·is *adj* of April; **mensis Aprīlis** April, month of April
aprugn·us -a -um *adj* of a wild boar
aps- = abs-
apsūmēd·ō -inis *f* devouring
aptē *adv* closely; suitably
apt·ō -āre *vt* to fasten, fit, adjust; to make ready, equip
apt·us -a -um *adj* suitable, adapted, appropriate, proper
apud *prep* (with *acc*) at, by, near, among; at the house of; before, in the presence of; in the writings of; over, (with influence) over
Āpūlĭ·a -ae *f* district in S.W. Italy
aqu·a -ae *f* water; *f pl* baths, spa; **aquā et ignī interdicere** to outlaw; **aquam praebere** (with *dat*) to entertain (*guests*)
aquaeduct·us -ūs *m* aqueduct
aquālicŭl·us -ī *m* belly, stomach
aquāl·is -e *adj* of water; *m & f* washbasin
aquārĭ·us -a -um *adj* of water; *m* water-conduit inspector
Aquār·ius -iī or **-ī** *m* Aquarius (*constellation; sign of the Zodiac*)
aquātic·us -a -um *adj* growing in water; watery, moist, humid
aquātĭl·is -e *adj* living or growing in water, aquatic
aquātĭ·ō -ōnis *f* fetching water; water hole
aquāt·or -ōris *m* water carrier
aquĭl·a -ae *f* eagle (*bird; Roman legionary standard*); (fig) legion; gable of house
aquĭl·ex -ĕgis *m* water finder, douser; water-conduit inspector
aquilĭf·er -ĕrī *m* standard-bearer
aquilīn·us -a -um *adj* eagle's
aquĭl·ō -ōnis *m* north wind; north
aquilōnĭ·us -a -um *adj* northerly
aquĭl·us -a -um *adj* swarthy
Aquīn·um -ī *n* town of the Volsci, birthplace of Juvenal
Aquitānĭ·a -ae *f* province in S.W. Gaul
aqu·or -ārī -ātus sum *vi* to fetch water
aquōs·us -a -um *adj* rainy, humid, full of water
aquŭl·a -ae *f* small stream, brook
ār·a -ae *f* altar
Ār·a -ae *f* Altar (*constellation*)
arabarch·ēs -ae *m* customs officer in Egypt
Arabĭ·a -ae *f* Arabia
Arabĭc·us or **Arabĭ·us** or **Arăb·us -a -um** *adj* Arabian
Arachn·ē -ēs *f* Lydian girl whom Minerva changed into a spider
arānĕ·a -ae *f* spider; cobweb
arāneŏl·a -ae *f* small spider
arāneŏl·us -ī *m* small spider
arāneōs·us -a -um *adj* full of cobwebs
arānĕ·us -a -um *adj* spider's; *m* spider; *n* spider web
Ar·ar -ăris *m* tributary of the Rhone
arātĭ·ō -ōnis *f* cultivation, tilling, agriculture; arable land
arātiuncŭl·a -ae *f* small plot, small farm
arāt·or -ōris *m* farmer; *m pl* farmers on state-owned land
arātr·um -ī *n* plow
Arāt·us -ī *m* Greek author of poem on astronomy (*fl* 270 B.C.)
arbĭt·er -rī *m* eyewitness; arbiter, judge, umpire; ruler, director, controller
arbĭtr·a -ae *f* eyewitness (*female*)
arbitrāriō *adv* uncertainly
arbitrārĭ·us -a -um *adj* uncertain
arbitrāt·us -ūs *m* decision; inclination, pleasure; direction, guidance
arbĭtr·ium -iī or **-ī** *n* decision, judgment; mastery, power, control, authority
arbĭtr·or -ārī -ātus sum *vt & vi* to decide or judge (*as an arbiter*); to testify; to think, suppose
arb·or or **arb·ōs -ŏris** *f* tree; mast, oar, ship; gallows
arborĕ·us -a -um *adj* of a tree; treelike
arbust·us -a -um *adj* wooded, planted with trees; *n* orchard; vineyard planted with trees; *n pl* trees
arbutĕ·us -a -um *adj* of arbutus
arbŭt·um -ī *n* fruit of arbutus
arbŭt·us -ī *f* arbutus, strawberry tree
arc·a -ae *f* chest, box, safe; coffin; prison cell
Arcadĭ·a -ae *f* district of central Peloponnesus
arcānō *adv* in secret, privately
arcān·us -a -um *adj* secret, concealed, private; *n* secret; sacred mystery
arc·ĕō -ēre -ŭī *vt* to shut up, en-

close; to keep at a distance, keep off; to hinder, prevent; (with *abl* or **ab** + *abl*) to keep (*someone*) off, away from

arcessīt·us -a -um *pp* of **arcesso;** *adj* farfetched

arcessīt·us -ūs *m* summons

arcess·ō -ĕre -īvī -ītum *vt* to send for, fetch, summon; (law) to arraign; to derive

archetȳp·us -a -um *adj & n* original

Archilŏch·us -ī Greek iambic poet of Paros (*c.* 714-676 B.C.)

archimagīr·us -ī *m* chief cook

Archimēd·ēs -is *m* scientist and mathematician of Syracuse (287-212 B.C.)

archipīrāt·a -ae *m* pirate captain

architect·ōn -ŏnis *m* architect, master builder; master in cunning

architect·or -ārī -ātus sum *vt* to build, construct

architectūr·a -ae *f* architecture

architect·us -ī *m* architect; deviser, author, inventor, contriver

arch·ōn -ŏntis *m* archon (*chief magistrate in Athens*)

arcitĕn·ens -entis *adj* holding a bow, wearing a bow

Arcitĕn·ens -entis *m* Archer (*constellation*)

Arctophȳl·ax -ăcis *m* Boötes (*constellation*)

Arct·os -ī *m* the Great and Little Bear (*double constellation*)

arct·os -ī *m* North Pole; North; north wind; night

Arctūr·us -ī *m* brightest star in Boötes

arcŭl·a -ae *f* small box, jewelry box; (rhet) ornament

arcŭ·ō -āre *vt* to curve

arc·us -ūs *m* bow; rainbow; curve; arch, triumphal arch

Ardĕ·a -ae *f* town in Latium

ardĕ·a -ae *f* heron

ardelĭ·ō -ōnis *m* busybody

ard·ens -entis *adj* blazing, burning, hot, fiery; gleaming, glittering; smarting, burning; (of emotions) glowing, hot, ardent

ardenter *adv* ardently, eagerly, passionately

ardĕō ardēre arsī *vi* to be on fire, burn, blaze; to flash, glow; to smart, burn

ardesc·ō -ĕre *vi* to catch fire; to gleam, glitter; (of passions) to become more intense, increase in violence

ard·or -ōris *m* heat, flame; flashing, brightness; heat (*of passions*); loved one, flame

ardŭ·us -a -um *adj* steep, high; difficult; *n* difficulty

ārĕ·a -ae *f* open space; park, playground; building site; threshing floor

arēna see **harena**

ār·ĕō -ēre *vi* to be dry; to be thirsty

āreŏl·a *f* small open space

Arēopăg·us -ī *m* criminal court in Athens; hill where criminal court met

Ar·ēs -is *m* Greek god of war

āresc·ō -ĕre *vi* to become dry; to wither

aretălŏg·us -ī *m* braggart

Arethūs·a -ae *f* nymph pursued by river god Alpheus in Peloponnesus and changed by Diana into a fountain; fountain near Syracuse

Argē·ī -ōrum *m pl* consecrated places in Rome ascribed to Numa; figures of men, made of rushes and thrown annually into the Tiber

argentārĭ·us -a -um *adj* silver; financial, pecuniary; *m* banker; *f* banking; bank; silver mine

argentāt·us -a -um *adj* plated or ornamented with silver

argenteŏl·us -a -um *adj* made of pretty silver

argentĕ·us -a -um *adj* silver, silvery

argent·um -ī *n* silver; silver plate; money

Argē·us or **Argīv·us** or **Argolic·us -a -um** *adj* Argive; Greek

Arg·ī -ōrum *m pl* Argos, town in N.E. Peloponnesus

Argīlēt·um -ī *n* district in Rome between the Quirinal and Capitoline

argill·a -ae *f* clay

Arg·ō -ūs *f* Jason's ship

Argŏl·is -ĭdis *f* district around Argos

Argonaut·ae -ārum *m pl* argonauts

Argos *n* (only *nom* and *acc*) Argos

argūmentātĭ·ō -ōnis *f* argumentation; proof

argūment·or -ārī -ātus sum *vt* to adduce as proof; (with **de** + *abl*) to conclude from; *vi* to bring evidence

argūment·um -ī *n* evidence, proof, argument; theme, plot; topic; subject, motif (*of artistic representation*)

arg·ŭō -uĕre -ŭī -ūtum *vt* to prove; to reveal, betray; to accuse, charge, impeach (*person*), find fault with (*thing*)

Arg·us -ī *n* many-eyed monster set over Io and killed by Mercury

argūtē *adv* subtly; craftily

argūtĭ·ae -ārum *f pl* subtlety; brightness, genius, cunning, shrewdness

argūtŭl·us -a -um *adj* somewhat subtle

argūt·us -a -um *adj* clearcut, clear, bright, distinct; penetrating, piercing; chatty; acute, subtle; bright, smart, witty; cunning, sly

argyrasp·is -ĭdis *adj* wearing a silver shield

Ariadn·a -ae *f* daughter of Minos, king of Crete, who extricated Theseus from the labyrinth

Arīcī·a -ae *f* town in Latium on the Via Appia

āridŭl·us -a -um *adj* somewhat dry

ārid·us -a -um *adj* dry, parched, withered; meager; (of style) dry, dull
ari·ēs -ĕtis *m* ram; battering ram; beam (*used as breakwater*)
Ari·ēs -ĕtis *m* Aries (*sign of the Zodiac*)
ariĕt·ō -āre *vt & vi* to butt, ram
Ariobarzān·ēs -is *m* king of Cappadocia
Ari·ōn -ŏnis *m* early Greek poet and musician, rescued from drowning by dolphin
arist·a -ae *f* ear of grain
Aristarch·us -ī *m* Alexandrine critic and scholar (*fl* 156 B.C.); stern critic
aristolochi·a -ae *f* birthwort
Aristophăn·ēs -is *m* the most famous Greek comic poet (*c.* 444-380 B.C.)
Aristotĕl·ēs -is *m* Aristotle (384-322 B.C.)
arithmētic·a -ōrum *n pl* arithmetic
āritūd·ō -inis *f* dryness
arm·a -ōrum *n pl* armor, defensive arms, arms; warfare; camp life; armed men; equipment, tools
armāment·a -ōrum *n pl* ship's gear
armāmentār·ium -iī or **-ī** *n* arsenal, armory
armāriŏl·um -ī *n* little chest, little closet
armār·ium -iī or **-ī** *n* cupboard, chest
armātūr·a -ae *f* outfit, equipment, armor; light-armed troops
armāt·us -a -um *adj* armed, equipped; *m* armed man
Armeni·a *f* country in N.E. Asia Minor
armeniăc·um -ī *n* apricot
armeniăc·us -ī *f* apricot tree
armentāl·is -e *adj* of a herd
armentār·ius -iī or **-ī** *m* herdsman
arment·um -ī *n* herd
armif·er -ĕra -ĕrum *adj* armed
armig·er -ĕra -ĕrum *adj* armed; producing warriors; *m* armed person; armor-bearer
armill·a -ae *f* armlet, bracelet
armillāt·us -a -um *adj* wearing a bracelet
armipŏt·ens -entis *adj* powerful in arms, warlike
armisŏn·us -a -um *adj* reverberating with arms
arm·ō -āre *vt* to furnish with arms, to arm; to rouse to arms
arm·us -ī *m* shoulder, shoulder blade, upper arm; flank (*of animal*)
ar·ō -āre *vt* to plow, till
Arpīn·um -ī *n* town in Latium, birthplace of Marius and Cicero
arquāt·us -a -um *adj* jaundiced
arrect·us -a -um *pp* of **arrigo**; *adj* upright; steep, precipitous
arrēp·ō -ĕre -sī *vi* (with *dat* or **ad** + *acc*) to creep towards, steal up on
arrhăb·ō -ōnis *m* deposit (*of money*)
ar·rīdĕō -rīdēre -rīsī -rīsum *vt* to smile at; *vi* (with *dat*) **a** to smile at or on, laugh with; **b** to be favorable to; **c** to be pleasing to, please
ar·rigō -rigĕre -rexī -rectum *vt* to erect, raise; to rouse, excite
ar·ripiō -ripĕre -ripŭī -reptum *vt* to snatch, seize; (fig) to grasp quickly; (law) to arrest, arraign; to satirize
ar·rōdō -rōdĕre -rōsī -rōsum *vt* to gnaw at
arrŏg·ans -antis *adj* arrogant
arroganter *adv* arrogantly
arroganti·a -ae *f* assumption, presumption; arrogance
arrŏg·ō -āre *vt* to question; to associate; to assume for oneself, claim
ars artis *f* skill; craft, trade; method, way, manner, means; artificial means; work of art; science, theory; manual, textbook; *f pl* cunning; moral qualities, character
artē *adv* closely, tightly; (to love) deeply, dearly; (to sleep) soundly
Artĕm·is -idis *f* Greek counterpart of Diana
artēri·a -ae *f* artery; windpipe
arthrītic·us -a -um *adj* arthritic
articulātim *adv* piecemeal; (to speak) articulately, distinctly
articŭl·ō -āre *vt* to utter distinctly, articulate
articŭl·us -ī *m* joint, knuckle; finger; limb; (gram) clause; turning point; **in ipso articulo temporis** in the nick of time
artĭf·ex -icis *adj* skillful, ingenious; artistic; broken, trained (*horse*); *m* craftsman, artist, master; originator, contriver, author
artificiōsē *adv* skillfully
artificiōs·us -a -um *adj* skillful, ingenious, accomplished; artificial
artific·ium -iī or **-ī** *n* skill, workmanship; artistic work, work of art; art, profession; cleverness, cunning; theory
art·ō -āre *vt* to pack closely; to compress, contract; to limit
artolagăn·us -ī *m* cake
artopt·a -ae *m* baker; bread pan (*to bake in*)
art·us -a -um *adj* close, tight; confined, restricted; dense, firm; scanty, small, needy; strict, severe; sound, deep (*sleep*); stingy; *n* narrow space; tight spot, difficulty
art·us -ūs *m* joint; *m pl* joints, limbs
ārŭl·a -ae *f* small altar
arund·ō -inis *f* reed; shaft, arrow; pipe, flute; pen; fishing rod; hobbyhorse; (in weaving) comb
arvīn·a -ae *f* grease
arv·us -a -um *adj* arable; *n* arable land, soil, land, plain, region; grain
arx arcis *f* fortress, stronghold, citadel, castle, protection, refuge, mainstay; height, summit; **arcem facere e cloaca** to make a mountain out of a molehill
ās assis *m* pound (*divisible into twelve ounces*); bronze coin; **heres ex asse** sole heir

Ascān·ius -iī or **-ī** *m* son of Aeneas and Creusa and founder of Alba Longa

ascendō ascendĕre ascendī ascensum *vt* to climb; to mount (*horse*); to board (*ship*); *vi* to climb up, ascend; (of voice) to rise; (with **ad** or **in** + *acc*) to climb, climb up to; (with **super** or **supra** + *acc*) to rise above, surpass

ascensi·ō -ōnis *f* climbing up, ascent

ascens·us -ūs *m* climbing up, ascent; means of ascending, approach; step, degree; (fig) climb, rise

asci·a -ae *f* ax; mason's trowel

asc·iō -īre *vt* to associate with oneself, admit

asc·iscō -iscĕre -īvī -ītum *vt* to adopt, approve (*bill*); to adopt (*custom*); to assume, claim, arrogate; to receive, admit (*e.g., as ally, citizen, etc.*); (with **in** + *acc*) to admit (*someone*) to

ascīt·us -a -um *adj* acquired (*as opposed to innate*)

Ascr·a -ae *f* birthplace of Hesiod in Boeotia

a·scrībō -scrībĕre -scripsī -scriptum *vt* to add (*by writing*); to impute, ascribe, attribute; to enroll, register; to reckon, number, class

ascripticī·us -a -um *adj* enrolled, registered

ascripti·ō -ōnis *f* addition (*in writing*)

ascriptīv·us -ī *m* (mil) reserve

ascript·or -ōris *m* supporter

asell·a -ae *f* little ass

asell·us -ī *m* little ass

Āsi·a -ae *f* Roman province; Asia Minor; Asia

asīl·us -ī *m* gadfly

asĭn·us -ī *m* ass; fool

Ās·is -ĭdis *f* Asia

asōt·us -ī *m* playboy

asparăg·us -ī *m* asparagus

aspargō see **aspergo**

aspectābil·is -e *adj* visible

aspect·ō -āre *vt* to look at, gaze at; to look with respect at; to face, lie in the direction of; to observe

aspect·us -ūs *m* look, sight, glance; sense of sight; manner of appearance, appearance, countenance

aspell·ō -ĕre *vt* to drive away

asp·er -ĕra -ĕrum *adj* rough, uneven; harsh, severe, stormy (*climate*); harsh, grating, hoarse (*sound*); pungent, strong (*smell*); rough, hard, unkind, rude (*character*); austere, rigid (*person*); wild fierce, savage (*animal*); rough, annoying, adverse (*circumstances*) rugged (*style*)

aspĕrē *adv* roughly; (fig) harshly, sternly, severely

a·spergō -spergĕre -spersī -spersum *vt* to sprinkle, scatter, taint; (with *dat*) to sprinkle (*something*) on

asperg·ō -ĭnis *f* sprinkling; spray

asperĭt·ās -ātis *f* uneveness, roughness; severity, fierceness; difficulty, trouble

aspernāti·ō -ōnis *f* disdain, contempt

aspern·or -ārī -ātus sum *vt* to disdain, despise, reject

aspĕr·ō -āre *vt* to make rough or uneven, roughen; to make fierce, exasperate; to excite

aspersi·ō -ōnis *f* sprinkling; laying on of colors

a·spiciō -spicĕre -spexī -spectum *vt* to catch sight of, spot; to look at; to examine closely, inspect; to observe, consider

aspīrāti·ō -ōnis *f* breathing, blowing; evaporation, exhalation; (gram) aspiration

aspīr·ō -āre *vi* to breathe, blow; (with *dat* or with **ad** or **in** + *acc*) to aspire to, desire to reach or obtain, come near to obtaining; (with *dat*) to favor

asp·is -ĭdis *f* asp

asportāti·ō -ōnis *f* removal

asport·ō -āre *vt* to carry away

asprēt·a -ōrum *n pl* rough terrain

assĕcl·a -ae *m* hanger-on

assectāti·ō -ōnis *f* (respectful) attendance

assectāt·or -ōris *m* attendant, escort; disciple

assect·or -ārī *vt* to follow, tail after

assecŭl·a -ae *m* hanger-on

assensi·ō -ōnis *f* assent, approval; *m pl* expressions of approval; (phil) realism

assens·or -ōris *m* backer, supporter

assens·us -ūs *m* assent, approval; *m pl* expressions of approval; (phil) realism; echo

assentāti·ō -ōnis *f* assent, agreement; flattery

assentātiuncŭl·a -ae *f* base flattery

assentāt·or -ōris *m* flatterer

assentātōriē *adv* flatteringly

assentātr·ix -īcis *f* flatterer (*female*)

as·sentiō -sentīre -sensī -sensum *vi* to agree; (with *dat*) to assent to, agree with, approve

as·sentior -sentīrī -sensus sum *vi* to agree; (with *dat*) to assent to, agree with, approve

assent·or -ārī -ātus sum *vi* to agree always; (with *dat*) to agree with always, to flatter

as·sĕquor -sĕquī -secūtus sum *vt* to pursue, catch up to, reach; to gain, obtain, procure; to come up to, equal, match; to comprehend, understand

ass·er -ĕris *m* pole, stake, post

as·sĕrō -serĕre -sēvī -situm *vt* (with *dat*) to plant (*something*) near

assĕr·ō -ĕre -uī -tum *vt* to set free, liberate (*slave*); to protect, defend; to claim, appropriate; **in servitutem asserere** to claim (*someone*) as one's slave

assertī·ō -ōnis *f* declaration of civil status
assert·or -ōris *m* defender, champion
asserv·iō -īre *vi* (with *dat*) to serve, assist
asserv·ō -āre *vt* to preserve, keep, watch over, guard
assessī·ō -ōnis *f* company, companionship
assess·or -ōris *m* companion, assistant; (law) assistant to a judge, counselor
assess·us -ūs *m* company, companionship
assevēranter *adv* emphatically
assevērātī·ō -ōnis *f* assertion, protestation; firmness, earnestness
assevēr·ō -āre *vt* to assert strongly, affirm, insist on
as·sidĕō -sidēre -sēdī -sessum *vi* to seat nearby; (with *dat*) **a** to sit near, stand by, attend upon, take care of, keep (*someone*) company; **b** to be busily engaged in; **c** to attend to, mind; **d** to be near (*in some respect*), be like, resemble
as·sīdō -sīdĕre -sēdī *vi* to sit down; (with *acc*) to sit down beside
assidŭē *adv* assiduously, continually, incessantly
assiduĭt·ās -ātis *f* constant presence or attendance; persistence; frequent recurrence
assidŭō *adv* continually
assidŭ·us -a -um *adj* continually present; persistent, tireless, incessant, busy; *m* taxpayer; rich man
assignātī·ō -ōnis *f* allotment (*of land*)
assign·ō -āre *vt* to mark out, allot, assign (*land*); to assign, confer; to ascribe, attribute; to consign; to seal
as·siliō -silīre -silŭī -sultum *vi* to jump; (with *dat*) to jump upon, leap at; (with **ad** + *acc*) **a** to jump to; **b** to have recourse to
assimiliter *adv* in like manner
assimĭl·is -e *adj* similar; (with *dat*) like
assimulātī·ō -ōnis *f* likeness, similarity
assimulāt·us -a -um *adj* similar; counterfeit
assimŭl·ō -āre *vt* to consider as similar, compare; to imitate, counterfeit
as·sistō -sistĕre -stitī *vi* to stand nearby; (with **ad** + *acc*) to stand at or by; (with *dat*) to assist, defend
assĭtus *pp* of **assero**
assol·ĕō -ēre *vi* to be usual
assŏn·ō -āre *vi* to echo; (with *dat*) to sound in response to, to echo (*a sound*)
assuē·faciō -facĕre -fēcī -factum *vt* to train; (with *dat*, with **ad** + *acc*, or with *inf*) to accustom (*someone*) to
assu·escō -escĕre -ēvī -ētum *vt* (with *dat*) to accustom (*someone*) to, make (*someone*) familiar with, familiarize (*someone*) with; *vi* (with *dat*, with **ad** + *acc*, or with *inf*) to become used to
assuētūd·ō -ĭnis *f* habit, custom
assuēt·us -a -um *pp* of **assuesco**; *adj* accustomed, customary, usual; (with *abl*) trained in; (with *dat*, with **ad** or **in** + *acc*, or with *inf*) accustomed to, used to
as·sūgō -ĕre — -suctum *vt* to suck in
assŭl·a -ae *f* splinter, chip, shaving
assulātim *adv* in splinters, in fragments, piecemeal
assult·ō -āre *vt* to assault, attack; *vi* to jump; (with *dat*) to jump to, jump at
assult·us -ūs *m* assault, attack
as·sūmō -ĕre -sumpsī -sumptum *vt* to take up, adopt, accept; to usurp, claim, assume; to receive, obtain, derive
assumptī·ō -ōnis *f* taking, receiving, assumption; adoption; (in logic) minor premise
assumptīv·us -a -um *adj* resting on external evidence, extrinsic
assŭ·ō -ĕre *vt* (with *dat*) to sew (*e.g., patch*) on (*e.g., clothes*)
as·surgō -surgĕre -surrexī -surrectum *vi* to rise up, rise, stand up; to mount up, increase, swell; (with *dat*) to yield to, stand up for (*out of respect*)
ass·us -a -um *adj* roasted; *n* roast; *n pl* steam bath, sweat bath
ast *conj* (older form of **at**) but
Astart·ē -ēs *f* Syro-Phoenician goddess, counterpart of Venus
a·釘sternō -sternĕre *vt* (with *dat*) to strew (*something*) on; **asterni** (with *dat*) to throw oneself down upon
astipulāt·or -ōris *m* legal assistant; supporter
astipŭl·or -ārī -ātus sum *vi* (with *dat*) to agree with
a·stō -stāre *vi* to stand erect, stand up, stand nearby; (with *dat*) to assist
Astrae·a -ae *f* goddess of justice
astrĕp·ō -ĕre -ŭī -ĭtum *vi* to roar; to make a noise; to applaud; (with *dat*) to assent loudly to, applaud
astrictē *adv* concisely; strictly
astrict·us -a -um *pp* of **astringo**; drawn together, tight; stingy, tight; concise
a·stringō -stringĕre -strinxī -strictum *vt* to tighten, bind fast; to put under obligation, obligate, oblige; (fig) to draw closer; to compress, abridge; to occupy (*attention*); to embarrass
astrologī·a -ae *f* astronomy
astrolŏg·us -ī *m* astronomer; astrologer
astr·um -ī *n* star; constellation; *n pl* stars, sky, heaven; immortality
astū (indecl) *n* city
astup·ĕō -ēre *vi* (with *dat*) to be amazed at
ast·us -ūs *m* cunning, cleverness

astutē *adv* slyly
astūti·a -ae *f* skill, dexterity; cunning, astuteness
astūt·us -a -um *adj* clever; sly, cunning
Astyăn·ax -actis *m* son of Hector and Andromache
asȳl·um -ī *n* refuge, sanctuary, asylum
at *conj* but; (in a transition) but, but on the other hand; (in anticipation of an opponent's objection) but, it may be objected; (in an ironical objection) but really, but after all; (after a negative clause, to introduce a qualification) but at least; **at contra** but on the contrary; **at tamen** and yet, but at least
Atābŭl·us -ī *m* sirocco, southeast wind
Atalant·a -ae *f* daughter of King Schoeneus, defeated by Hippomenes in a famous footrace; daughter of Iasius and participant in the Calydonian boar hunt
atat *interj* (expressing surprise, pain, warning) oh!
atăv·us -ī *m* great-great-great-grandfather; ancestor
Atell·a -ae *f* Oscan town in Campania
Atellān·us -a -um *adj* Atellan; **Atellana** or **fabula Atellana** comic farce which originated in Atella
āt·er -ra -rum *adj* (opposed to **niger** glossy black) dead black, black; dark, gloomy, eerie; black, unlucky; malicious; poisonous
Athăm·ās -antis *m* king of Thessaly, father of Helle and Phrixus by Nephele, and of Learchus and Melecerta by Ino
Athēn·ae -ārum *f pl* Athens
athě·os -ī *m* atheist
athlēt·a -ae *m* athlete, wrestler
athlēticē *adv* athletically
athlētic·us -a -um *adj* athletic
Atl·ās -antis *m* giant supporting the sky, son of Iapetus and Clymene
atŏm·os -ī *f* indivisible particle, atom
atque *conj* (denotes closer internal connection than is implied by **et** and gives prominence to what follows) and, as well as, together with, and even, and . . . too; (after words of comparison) as, than; **atque . . . atque** both . . . and; **atque adeo** and in fact
atquī *conj* but yet, but anyhow, however, rather, and yet
ātrāment·um -ī *n* ink
ātrāt·us -a -um *adj* clothed in black
Atr·eus -eī *m* son of Pelops, brother of Thyestes, father of Agamemnon and Menelaus
Atrīd·ēs -ae *m* descendant of Atreus
ātriens·is -is *m* butler
ātriŏl·um -ī *n* small hall, anteroom
ātrīt·ās -ātis *f* blackness
ātr·ium -iī or **-ī** *n* main room, entrance room (*of Roman house*); hall (*of temples or public buildings*)
atrōcit·ās -ātis *f* hideousness, repulsiveness (*of form, appearance*); fierceness, brutality, cruelty (*of character*); severity, rigidity (*of law*)
atrōciter *adv* horribly, fiercely, cruelly, grimly
Ătrŏp·os -ī *f* one of the three Fates
atr·ox -ōcis *adj* horrible, hideous, frightful; savage, cruel, fierce; harsh, stern, unyielding, grim
attactus *pp* of **attingo**
attact·us -ūs *m* touch, contact
attăg·ēn -ēnis *m* woodcock
attagēn·a -ae *f* woodcock
Attalic·us -a -um *adj* of Attalus; Pergamean; rich, splendid; *n pl* gold-brocaded garments
Attăl·us -ī *m* king of Pergamum in Asia Minor, who bequeathed his kingdom to Rome
attămen *conj* but still, but yet
attat or **attătae** *interj* (indicating surprise, joy, dismay) oh!
attegi·a -ae *f* hut, cottage
attemperātē *adv* on time, in the nick of time
attempt·ō -āre *vt* to try, attempt; to test; to tempt, try to corrupt; to attack
at·tendō -tendĕre -tendī -tentum *vt* to notice, mark; to pay attention to, mind, consider; (*with dat or* **ad** + *acc*) to direct (*mind, attention*) to; *vi* to pay attention, listen
attentē *adv* attentively
attenti·ō -ōnis *f* attention, attentiveness
attentō see **attempto**
attent·us -a -um *pp* of **attendo**; *adj* attentive; careful, frugal, industrious
attenuātē *adv* (rhet) without flowery language, simply
attenuāt·us -a -um *adj* weak, weakened; shortened, brief; over-refined, affected; plain, bald (*style*)
attenŭ·ō -āre *vt* to make weak, weaken; to thin, attenuate; to lessen, diminish; to humble
at·tĕrō -terĕre -trīvī -trītum *vt* to rub, wear away, wear out, weaken, exhaust; to waste, destroy
attest·or -ārī -ātus sum *vt* to attest, confirm, corroborate, prove
attex·ō -ĕre -ŭī -tum *vt* to weave; to add
Atth·is -idis *f* Attica
Attic·a -ae *f* district of Greece, of which Athens was the capital
atticē *adv* in the Attic or Athenian style
atticiss·ō -āre *vi* to speak in the Athenian manner
Attic·us -a -um *adj* Attic, Athenian; *m* T. Pomponius Atticus (*friend of Cicero,* 109-32 B.C.)
attigō see **attingo**
at·tinĕō -tinēre -tinŭī -tentum *vt* to hold tight, hold on to, hold, de-

tain, hold back; to reach for; *vi* (with **ad** + *acc*) to pertain to, relate to, refer to, concern; **quod ad me attinet** as far as I am concerned
at·tingō -tingĕre -tīgī -tactum *vt* to touch, come in contact with; to reach, arrive at; to touch (*food*), taste; to touch, lie near, border; to touch upon, mention lightly; to touch, strike, attack; to touch, affect; to undertake, engage in, take in hand, manage; to resemble; to concern, belong to
Att·is -idis *m* priest of Phrygian goddess Cybele
attoll·ō -ĕre *vt* to lift up, raise; to exalt, extol
at·tondĕō -tondēre -tondī -tonsum *vt* to clip, shave, shear; to prune; to crop; to clip, fleece, cheat
attonit·us -a -um *adj* thunderstruck, stunned, amazed, dazed, astonished; inspired; frantic
attorqu·ĕō -ēre *vt* to hurl up
at·trăhō -trahĕre -traxī -tractum *vt* to attract, draw, drag by force
attrect·ō -āre *vt* to touch, handle; to appropriate to oneself
attrepid·ō -āre *vi* to hobble along
attrib·ŭō -uĕre -ŭī -ūtum *vt* to allot, assign, bestow, give, annex; to impose (*taxes*)
attribūti·ō -ōnis *f* payment of a debt; (gram) predicate
attribūt·us -a -um *pp* of **attribuo;** *n* (gram) predicate
attrīt·us -a -um *pp* of **attero;** *adj* worn away, wasted; shameless
au *interj* ouch!
au·ceps -cŭpis *m* fowler, bird catcher; spy, eavesdropper
auctār·ium -iī or **-ī** *n* addition
auctific·us -a -um *adj* increasing
aucti·ō -ōnis *f* increase; auction
auctiōnāri·us -a -um *adj* auction
auctiōn·or -ārī -ātus sum *vi* to hold an auction
auctit·ō -āre *vt* to increase greatly
auct·ō -āre *vt* to increase, augment
auct·or -ōris *m* originator, author; writer, historian; reporter, informant (*of news*); authority (*for statement or theory*); proposer, backer, supporter; progenitor (*of race*); founder (*of city*); model, example; adviser, counselor; teacher; guarantor, security; leader, statesman
auctōrāment·um -ī *n* contract; pay, wages
auctōrit·ās -ātis *f* origination, source, cause; view, opinion, judgment; advice, counsel, encouragement; might, power, authority, weight, influence, leadership; importance, significance, worth, consequence; example, model, precedent; authority (*for establishing a fact*); document, record; decree (*of senate*); right of possession
auctōr·ō -āre *vt* to bind; **auctorari** or **se auctorare** to hire oneself out

auctus *pp* of **augeo**
auct·us -ūs *m* increase, growth, abundance
aucup·ium -iī or **-ī** *n* fowling; trap; eavesdropping; **aucupia verborum** quibbling
aucŭp·ō -āre or **aucŭp·or -ārī -ātus sum** *vt* to lie in wait for, watch for, chase, strive after, catch; *vi* to catch birds
audāci·a -ae *f* (in good sense) boldness, courage, daring; (in bad sense) recklessness, effrontery, audacity; bold deed; *f pl* adventures
audacter *adv* boldly, audaciously
aud·ax -ācis *adj* (in good sense) bold, daring; (in bad sense) reckless, rash, foolhardy
aud·ens -entis *adj* bold, daring, courageous
audenti·a -ae *f* daring, boldness
audĕō audēre ausus sum *vt* to dare, venture, risk; **vix ausim** (*old perf subj*) **credere** I could scarcely dare to believe; *vi* to dare, be bold
audi·ens -entis *m* hearer, listener; *m pl* audience
audienti·a -ae *f* hearing, attention; **audientiam facere** to command attention, to command silence
aud·iō -īre -īvī or **-iī ītum** *vt* to hear, listen to, give attention to; to hear, be taught by, learn from; to hear, listen to, grant; to accept, agree with, approve, yield to, grant, allow; to listen to, obey; to be called, be named, be reported, be regarded
audīti·ō -ōnis *f* hearsay, rumor, report, news
audītōr·ium -iī or **-ī** *n* lecture hall; the audience
audīt·us -ūs *m* sense of hearing; a hearing; report, rumor
aufĕrō auferre abstŭlī ablātum *vt* to bear or take away, bear off, remove, withdraw; to snatch away, steal, rob; to sweep away, kill, destroy; to gain, obtain, receive, get; to learn, understand; to mislead, lead into a digression; **auferri e conspectu** to disappear from sight
Aufid·us -ī *m* river in Apulia
au·fugiō -fugĕre -fūgī *vt* to escape, flee from; *vi* to escape, run away
Augē·ās -ae *m* king of Elis whose stables Hercules cleaned by diverting the River Alpheus through them
augĕō augēre auxī auctum *vt* to increase, enlarge, augment, spread; to magnify, extol, exalt; to exaggerate; to enrich; to honor, advance, promote; to feed (*flame*)
augesc·ō -ĕre *vi* to begin to grow; to become larger, increase
aug·ur -ŭris *m* or *f* augur (*priest who foretold the future by observing the flight of birds, lightning, etc.*), prophet, seer
augurāl·is -e *adj* of divination; au-

gur's; *n* area in Roman camp where the general took auspices
augurāti·ō -ōnis *f* prophesying
augurātō *adv* after taking the auguries
augurāt·us -ūs *m* office of augur
augur·ium -iī or **-ī** *n* observation of omens, interpretation of omen, augury; sign, omen; prophesy, prediction, forecast; foreboding
auguri·us -a -um *adj* of augurs; **jus augurium** the right to take auguries
augŭr·ō -āre or **augur·or -ārī -ātus sum** *vt* to consult by augury; to consecrate by augury; to conjecture, imagine; to foretell, predict, prophesy; *vi* to act as augur; to take auspices; to play augur
August·a -ae *f* (in imperial period) mother, wife, daughter, or sister of the emperor
Augustāl·is -e *adj* of Augustus; *n pl* games in honor of Augustus; **sodales Augustales** priests of deified Augustus
Augustān·us -a -um *adj* Augustan; imperial
augustē *adv* reverently
august·us -a -um *adj* august, sacred, venerable; majestic, magnificent
August·us -a -um *adj* Augustan, imperial; cognomen of Octavius Caesar and of subsequent emperors; **mensis Augustus** August
aul·a -ae *f* inner court, hall (*of house*); palace; royal court; people of the royal court, the court
aulae·um -ī *n* curtain, canopy; theater curtain; bed cover, sofa cover, tapestry
aulic·us -a -um *adj* courtly, princely; *n pl* courtiers
Aul·is -is or **-idis** *f* port in Boeotia from which the Greeks sailed for Troy
auloed·us -ī *m* singer (*accompanied by flute*)
aur·a -ae *f* breeze, breath of air, wind; air, atmosphere; heights, heaven; upper world; odor, exhalation; daylight, publicity; **ad auras ferre** to make known, publicize; **ad auras venire** to come to the upper world; **auram captare** to sniff the air; **aura popularis** popular favor; **auras fugere** to hide; **aura spei** breath of hope
aurāri·us -a -um *adj* of gold, golden, gold; *f* gold mine
aurāt·us -a -um *adj* decorated with gold, made of gold, gold-plated, golden; glittering
aureŏl·us -a -um *adj* gold; splendid
aurĕ·us -a -um *adj* of gold, golden; gilded; beautiful, magnificent, splendid; *m* gold coin
auricŏm·us -a -um *adj* golden-haired; with golden foliage
auricŭl·a *f* external ear, ear
aurif·er -ĕra -ĕrum *adj* producing or containing gold; (of tree) bearing golden apples
aurif·ex -icis *m* goldsmith
aurīg·a -ae *m* or *f* charioteer, driver; (fig) pilot
Aurīg·a -ae *m* Auriga, Wagoner (*constellation*)
aurigĕn·a -ae *m* offspring of gold (*i.e., Perseus*)
aurig·er -ĕra -ĕrum *adj* gold-bearing; gilded
aurīg·ō -āre *vi* to drive a chariot, compete in chariot race
aur·is -is *f* ear; *f pl* listeners; critical ears; **aurem admovere** to listen; **auribus servire** to flatter; **auris adhibere** to be attentive, pay attention; **in aurem dextram** or **in aurem utramvis dormire** to sleep soundly, i.e., to be unconcerned
aurītŭl·us -ī *m* ass
aurīt·us -a -um *adj* long-eared; attentive; nosey; **testis auritus** witness by hearsay only; *m* rabbit
aurōr·a -ae *f* morning, dawn, daybreak; the Orient, the East
Aurōr·a -ae *f* goddess of dawn
aur·um -ī *n* gold; color of gold, golden luster; gold cup; gold necklace; gold jewelry; gold plate; golden fleece; gold money; Golden Age
auscultāti·ō -ōnis *f* obedience
auscultāt·or -ōris *m* listener
auscult·ō -āre *vt* to hear (*with attention*), listen to; to overhear; *vi* (with *dat*) to obey, listen to
ausim see **audeo**
Ausŏn·ēs -um *m pl* Ausonians (*ancient inhabitants of central Italy*)
Ausonid·ae -ārum *m pl* Italians
Ausoni·us -a -um *adj* Ausonian, Italian; *m pl* Ausonians, Italians; *f* Ausonia, Italy
ausp·ex -icis *m* augur, soothsayer; author, founder, leader, director, protector; *m pl* witnesses (*at marriage ceremony*)
auspicātō *adv* after taking the auspices; under good omens, at a fortunate moment
auspicāt·us -a -um *adj* consecrated (*by auguries*); auspicious, favorable, lucky
auspic·ium -iī or **-ī** *n* divination (*through observation of flight of birds*), auspices; sign, omen, premonition; command, leadership, guidance, authority; right, power, will, inclination; **auspicium habere** to have the right to take auspices; **auspicium facere** (of birds) to give a sign, to yield an omen
auspic·or -ārī -ātus sum *vt* to begin, take up; *vi* to take auspices; to make a start
aust·er -rī *m* south wind; the South
austērē *adv* austerely, severely
austērit·ās -ātis *f* austerity
austēr·us -a -um *adj* austere, stern, harsh (*person*); pungent (*smell*); harsh (*taste*); drab, dark (*color*); se-

rious (*talk*); gloomy, sad, hard (*circumstances*)
austrāl·is -e *adj* southern; **cingulus, regio,** or **ora australis** torrid zone
austrīn·us -a -um *adj* from the south, southerly; southern
aus·us -a -um *pp* of **audeo;** *n* daring attempt, enterprise, adventure
aut *conj* or; (correcting what precedes) or, or rather, or else; (adding emphatic alternative) or at least; **aut . . . aut** either . . . or
autem *conj* (regularly follows an emphatic word) but, on the other hand, however; (in a transition) but, and now
autheps·a -ae *f* cooker, boiler (*utensil*)
autogrăph·us -a -um *adj* written with one's own hand, autograph
Autolўc·us -ī *m* father of Anticlea, maternal grandfather of Ulysses, and famous robber
automăt·on -ī *n* automaton
automăt·us -a -um *adj* automatic, spontaneous, voluntary
Automĕd·ōn -ontis *m* charioteer of Achilles
Autonŏ·ē -ēs *f* daughter of Cadmus, wife of Aristaeus, and mother of Actaeon
autumnāl·is -e *adj* autumn, autumnal
autumn·us -a -um *adj* autumn, autumnal; *m* autumn
autŭm·ō -āre *vt* to assert, affirm, say
auxiliār·ēs -ium *m pl* auxiliary troops
auxiliār·is -e *adj* auxiliary
auxiliāri·us -a -um *adj* auxiliary
auxiliāt·or -ōris *m* helper, assistant
auxiliāt·us -ūs *m* aid
auxili·or -ārī -ātus sum *vi* (with *dat*) **a** to help, aid, assist; **b** to relieve, heal, cure
auxil·ium -iī or **-ī** *n* help, aid, assistance; *n pl* auxiliary troops, auxiliaries; military force, military power; **auxilio esse** (with *dat*) to be of assistance to
avārē *adv* greedily
avārĭter *adv* greedily
avāriti·a -ae *f* greed, selfishness, avarice; gluttony
avāriti·ēs -ēī *f* avarice
avār·us -a -um *adj* greedy, covetous, avaricious; (with *genit*) desirous of, eager for
avē see **aveo**
ā·vĕhō -vehĕre -vexī -vectum *vt* to carry away; **avehi** to ride away, sail away
ā·vellō -vellĕre -vellī (or **-vulsī** or **-volsī**) **-vulsum** (or **-volsum**) *vt* to pull or pluck away; to tear off; to separate, remove; **avelli** or **se avellere** (with **ab** + *abl*) to tear oneself away from, withdraw from
avēn·a -ae *f* oats; reed, stalk, a straw; shepherd's pipe
Aventīn·us -a -um *adj* Aventine; *m* & *n* Aventine Hill (*one of the seven hills of Rome*)
av·ĕō -ēre *vt* to wish, desire, long for, crave; (with *inf*) to wish to, long to; *vi* to say good-bye; **ave!** or **avete!** hail!, hello!; good morning!; farewell!, good-bye!
Avernāl·is -e *adj* of Lake Avernus
Avern·us -a -um *adj* without birds; of Lake Avernus; *m* Lake Avernus (*near Cumae, said to be an entrance to the lower world*)
āverrunc·ō -āre *vt* to avert
āversābĭl·is -e *adj* abominable
āvers·or -ārī -ātus sum *vt* to repulse, reject, refuse, decline, shun, avoid, send away; *vi* to turn away (*in displeasure, contempt, shame, etc.*)
āvers·or -ōris *m* embezzler
āvers·us -a -um *adj* turned away (*in flight*); rear, in the rear; disinclined, alienated, unfavorable, hostile; (with *dat* or **ab** + *abl*) averse to, hostile to, opposed to, estranged from; *n* the back part, the back; *n pl* the back parts, the back; hinterland; **in adversum** backwards
ā-vertō (or **ā·vortō**) **-vertĕre -vertī -versum** *vt* to turn away, avert; to embezzle, misappropriate; to divert; to alienate; **se avertere** to retire; *vi* to withdraw, retire
avi·a -ae *f* grandmother; old wives' tale
āvi·a -ōrum *n pl* pathless, lonely places
aviāri·us -a -um *adj* of birds, bird; *n* aviary; haunt of wild birds
avidē *adv* eagerly, greedily
avidĭt·ās -ātis *f* eagerness, longing, great desire; avarice
avid·us -a -um *adj* eager, earnest, greedy; hungry, greedy, voracious, gluttonous, insatiable; (with *genit* or *dat* or with **in** + *acc*) desirous of, eager for
av·is -is *f* bird; sign, omen; **avis alba** rarity
avīt·us -a -um *adj* grandfather's, ancestral; old
āvi·us -a -um *adj* out-of-the-way, lonely; trackless, pathless, untrodden; wandering, straying; going astray
āvocāment·um -ī *n* diversion, recreation
āvocātī·ō -ōnis *f* distraction, diversion
āvŏc·ō -āre *vt* to call away; to divert, remove, withdraw; to divert, amuse
āvŏl·ō -āre *vi* to fly away; to hasten away, dash off
āvulsus *pp* of **avello**
avuncŭl·us -ī *m* mother's brother, maternal uncle; **avunculus magnus** great-uncle; **avunculus major** great-great-uncle

av·us -ī *m* grandfather; forefather, ancestor
Axĕn·us -ī *m* Black Sea
axicī·a -ae *f* scissors
axill·a -ae *f* armpit
ax·is -is *m* axle; chariot, wagon; axis, pole; North Pole; sky; the heavens; region, country; board, plank

B

babae *interj* wonderful!, strange!
Babȳl·ōn -ōnis *f* city on Euphrates
Babylōnī·a -ae *f* country between Tigris and Euphrates
bāc·a -ae *f* berry; olive; fruit; pearl
bācāt·us -a -um *adj* adorned with pearls
bacc·ar -āris *n* cyclamen (*plant whose root yields fragrant oil*)
Bacch·a -ae *f* bacchante, maenad
bacchābund·us -a -um *adj* raving, riotous
Bacchān·al -ālis *n* place sacred to Bacchus; *n pl* bacchanalian orgies
bacchātī·ō -ōnis *f* orgy; revelry
bacch·or -ārī -ātus sum *vi* to celebrate the festival of Bacchus; to revel, rave, rage
Bacch·us -ī *m* god of wine; (fig) vine; (fig) wine
bācīf·er -ĕra -ĕrum *adj* bearing berries or olives
bacill·um -ī *n* small staff, wand; lictor's staff
bacŭl·um -ī *n* or **bacŭl·us -ī** *m* stick; staff; scepter
badiss·ō -āre *vi* to go, walk
Baetic·us -a -um *adj* of the Baetis; *f* Baetica (*Roman province*)
Baet·is -is *m* river in Spain
Bāī·ae -ārum *f pl* resort town at northern extremity of Bay of Naples
bājŭl·ō -āre *vt* to carry, bear
bājŭl·us -ī *m* porter; day laborer
bālaen·a -ae *f* whale
balanāt·us -a -um *adj* anointed with balsam; embalmed
balăn·us -ī *m* or *f* acorn; date; balsam; shell-fish
balătr·ō -ōnis *m* jester, buffoon
bālāt·us -ūs *m* bleating
balb·us -a -um *adj* stammering
balbūt·iō -īre *vt & vi* to stammer, stutter
balinĕ·um -ī *n* bath
ballist·a -ae *f* large military device for hurling stones; heavy artillery
ballistār·ium -iī or **-ī** *n* artillery emplacement
balnĕ·ae -ārum *f pl* baths
balneārī·us -a -um *adj* of a bath; *n pl* baths
balneāt·or -ōris *m* bath superintendent
balneŏl·ae -ārum *f pl* baths
balneŏl·um -ī *n* small bath
balnĕ·um -ī *n* bath
bāl·ō -āre *vi* to bleat
balsăm·um -ī *n* balsam; balsam tree
baltĕ·us -ī *m* belt; baldric; girdle
baptister·ium -iī or **-ī** bath; swimming pool
barāthr·um -ī *n* abyss, chasm, pit; lower world
barb·a -ae *f* beard
barbărē *adv* in a foreign language; barbarously, cruelly
barbarī·a -ae or **barbarī·ēs -ēī** *f* foreign country, strange land; rudeness, want of culture
barbaric·us -a -um *adj* foreign, outlandish
barbariēs see **barbaria**
barbăr·us -a -um *adj* foreign; barbarous, savage, uncivilized, rude; *m* foreigner; barbarian
barbātŭl·us -a -um *adj* wearing a small beard
barbāt·us -a -um *adj* bearded; adult; old-time; *m* old-timer; philosopher, longhair; goat
barbig·er -ĕra -ĕrum *adj* wearing a beard, bearded
barbit·os -ī *m* lyre; lute
barbŭl·a -ae *f* small beard
bard·us -a -um *adj* stupid, dull
bard·us -ī *m* bard
bār·ō -ōnis *m* dunce, blockhead
barr·us -ī *m* elephant
bāsiātī·ō -ōnis *f* kissing; kiss
basilic·us -a -um *adj* royal; splendid; *f* public building, basilica (*used as law court and exchange*); portico
bāsī·ō -āre *vt* to kiss
bas·is -is *f* base, foundation, support; pedestal
bās·ium -iī or **-ī** kiss
Bassăr·eus -ĕī *m* Bacchus
batill·um -ī *n* brazier
battŭ·ō -ĕre -ī *vt* to beat, pound
beātē *adv* happily
beātit·ās -ātis *f* happiness
beātitūd·ō -inis *f* happiness
beāt·us -a -um *adj* happy; prosperous, rich; fertile; abundant; *n* happiness
Bēlid·ēs -um *f pl* descendants of Belus, the Danaids, who killed their husbands on their wedding night
bellārī·a -ōrum *m pl* dessert
bellāt·or -ōris *adj* warlike; valorous; spirited; *m* warrior
bellātr·ix -icis *adj* warlike, skilled in war; *f* warrior (*female*)
bellē *adv* prettily, neatly, nicely, well
Bellerŏph·ōn -ontis *m* slayer of Chimaera and rider of Pegasus
bellicōs·us -a -um *adj* warlike, martial, valorous

bellic·us -a -um *adj* war, military; warlike, fierce; *n* bugle; bugle call
bellig·er -ĕra -ĕrum *adj* belligerent, warlike, aggressive; martial; valiant
belligĕr·ō -āre or **belligĕr·or -ārī -ātus sum** *vi* to wage war, fight
bellipŏt·ens -entis *adj* mighty or valiant in war; *m* Mars
bell·ō -āre or **bell·or -ārī -ātus sum** *vi* to wage war, fight
Bellōn·a -ae *f* Roman goddess of war
bellŭl·us -a -um *adj* pretty, lovely, cute, fine
bell·um -ī *n* war; battle
bēlŭ·a -ae *f* beast, monster, brute
bēluōs·us -a -um *adj* full of monsters
Bēl·us -ī *m* Baal; king of Tyre and father of Dido; king of Egypt, father of Danaus and Aegyptus
bene *adv* well; thoroughly; very, quite
bene·dīcō -dīcĕre -dixī -dictum *vt* to speak well of, praise; (eccl) to bless
beneficenti·a -ae *f* beneficence, kindness
beneficiārī·ī -ōrum *m pl* soldiers exempt from menial tasks
benefic·ium -iī or **-ī** *n* kindness, favor, benefit, service; help, support; promotion; right, privilege
benefic·us -a -um *adj* generous, liberal, obliging
Benevent·um -ī *n* town in Samnium in S. Italy
benevŏlē *adv* kindly
benevŏl·ens -entis *adj* kind-hearted, obliging
benevolenti·a -ae *f* benevolence, kindness, goodwill; favor
benevŏl·us -a -um *adj* kind, friendly; devoted, faithful
benignē *adv* in a friendly manner, kindly, courteously; mildly, indulgently; liberally, generously
benignit·ās -ātis *f* kindness, friendliness, courtesy; liberality, bounty
benign·us -a -um *adj* kind-hearted; mild, affable; liberal; favorable; bounteous, fruitful
be·ō -āre *vt* to make happy; to bless; to enrich; to refresh
Berecynt·us -ī *m* mountain in Phrygia sacred to Cybele
bēryll·us -ī *m* precious stone, beryl
bēs bessis *m* two thirds
besti·a -ae *f* beast, wild beast
bestiārī·us -a -um *adj* of wild beasts; *m* wild-beast fighter
bestiŏl·a -ae *f* little beast
bēt·a -ae *f* beet
bēta (indecl) *n* second letter of Greek alphabet
bibliopōl·a -ae *m* bookseller
bibliothēc·a -ae *f* library
bibliothēcār·ius -iī or **-ī** *m* librarian
bib·ō -ĕre -ī *vt* to drink; to visit, reach, live near (*river*); (fig) to take in, absorb, listen eagerly to
bibŭl·us -a -um *adj* fond of drinking; absorbent; thirsty
bi·ceps -cipitis *adj* two-headed; twin-peaked
biclīn·ium -iī or **-ī** *n* table for two
bicŏl·or -ōris *adj* two-colored
bicorn·is -e *adj* two-horned; two-pronged
bid·ens -entis *adj* with two teeth; with two points; two-pronged; *m* hoe, mattock; sacrificial animal; sheep
bident·al -ālis *n* place struck by lightning
bīdŭ·um -ī *n* period of two days; two days
bienn·ium -iī or **-ī** *n* period of two years; two years
bifāriam *adv* on both sides, twofold, double, in two parts, in two directions
bifārī·us -a -um *adj* double, twofold
bif·er -ĕra -ĕrum *adj* bearing fruit twice a year; of twofold form
bifid·us -a -um *adj* split in two, forked, cloven
bifŏr·is -e *adj* having two doors; having two holes or openings; double
biformāt·us -a -um *adj* double, having two forms
biform·is -e *adj* double, having two forms
bifr·ons -ontis *adj* two-headed; two-faced
bifurc·us -a -um *adj* two-pronged, forked
bīg·a -ae *f* or **bīg·ae -ārum** *f pl* span of horses, team; two-horse chariot
bijŭg·ī -ōrum *m pl* team of horses; two-horse chariot
bijŭg·is -e *adj* yoked two together; drawn by a pair of horses
bijŭg·us -a -um *adj* yoked two together; two-horse
bilībr·is -e *adj* two-pound
bilingu·is -e *adj* two-tongued; bilingual; hypercritical, deceitful, false
bīl·is -is *f* gall, bile; wrath, anger; **bilis atra** melancholy; madness
bimăr·is -e *adj* situated between two seas
bimarīt·us -ī *m* bigamist
bimāt·er -ris *adj* having two mothers
bimembr·is -e *adj* half man, half beast
bimembr·is -is *m* centaur
bimestr·is -e *adj* two-month-old; lasting two months
bimŭl·us -a -um *adj* two-year-old
bīm·us -a -um *adj* two-year-old; for two years
bīn·ī -ae -a *adj* two by two; two to each, two each; two at a time; a pair of
binoct·ium -iī or **-ī** *n* two nights
binōmin·is -e *adj* having two names
bipalm·is -e *adj* two spans long
bipart·iō -īre — -ītum *vt* to divide into two parts; to bisect

bipartītō *adv* in two parts
bipăt·ens -entis *adj* open in two directions
bipedāl·is -e *adj* two feet long, broad, thick, or high
bipennif·er -ĕra -ĕrum *adj* wielding a two-edged ax
bipenn·is -e *adj* two-edged; *f* two-edged ax
bip·ēs -ĕdis *adj* two-footed, biped
birēm·is -e *adj* two-oared; with two banks of oars; *f* ship with two banks of oars
bis *adv* twice
Bistŏn·ēs -um *m pl* fierce tribesmen in Thessaly
bisulc·us -a -um *adj* split, cloven; forked
bīt·ō -ĕre *vi* to go
bitūm·en -ĭnis *n* bitumen, asphalt
bivi·us -a -um *adj* two-way; *n* crossroads, intersection
blaes·us -a -um *adj* lisping; indistinct
blandē *adv* flatteringly; courteously
blandiloquenti·a -ae *f* flattery
blandiloquentŭl·us -a -um *adj* smooth-tongued
blandīment·um -ī *n* flattery, compliment; charm
bland·ior -īrī -ītus sum *vt* to flatter; to coax; to allure; to please
blandĭter *adv* flatteringly
blandĭti·a -ae *f* caress, flattery, compliment; charm
blandītim *adv* flatteringly
bland·us -a -um *adj* smooth; flattering, fawning; alluring, charming, winsome, pleasant
blatĕr·ō -āre *vi* to talk foolishly, to babble
blatt·a -ae *f* cockroach; moth
blenn·us -ī *m* idiot, blockhead
blitĕ·us -a -um *adj* silly; tasteless
blit·um -ī *n* tasteless vegetable, kind of spinach
boārĭ·us -a -um *adj* cattle
Boeotĭ·a -ae *f* district north of Attica in central Greece, the capital of which was Thebes
bōlēt·us -ī *n* mushroom
bol·us -ī *m* throw (*of the dice*); cast (*of the net*); (fig) haul, piece of good luck, gain; choice morsel
bombax *interj* strange!; indeed!
bomb·us -ī *m* booming; buzzing, humming
bombȳcĭn·us -a -um *adj* silk, silken
bomb·ȳx -ȳcis *m* silkworm; silk; silk garment
Bon·a De·a (*genit:* **Bon·ae De·ae**) *f* goddess of chastity and fertility
bonĭt·ās -ātis *f* goodness, integrity; kindness, benevolence
bon·us -a -um *adj* good; honest, virtuous; faithful, patriotic; fit, suitable; able, clever; brave; noble; auspicious, favorable; useful, advantageous; *n* good; profit, advantage; *n pl* goods, property
bo·ō -āre *vi* to cry aloud; to roar
Boōt·ēs -ae *m* constellation containing the bright star Arcturus
borĕ·as -ae *m* north wind
borĕ·us -a -um *adj* north, northern
bōs bovis *m* or *f* ox, bull; cow
Bospŏr·us -ī *m* strait between Thrace and Asia Minor, connecting Propontis and Black Sea
botŭl·us -ī *m* sausage
bovīl·e -is *n* ox stall
bovill·us -a -um *adj* cattle
brāc·ae -ārum *f pl* pants, trousers
brācāt·us -a -um *adj* wearing trousers; foreign, barbarian; effeminate
bracchiāl·is -ē *adj* of the arm
bracchiŏl·um -ī *n* dainty arm
bracch·ium -iī or **-ī** *n* arm, lower arm; claw; bough; tendril; arm of the sea; sail yard
bractĕ·a -ae *f* gold leaf; gold foil
bracteŏl·a -ae *f* very thin gold leaf
brassĭc·a -ae *f* cabbage
breviār·ium -iī or **-ī** *n* summary, abridgement; statistics
brevicŭl·us -a -um *adj* rather short
brevilŏqu·ens -entis *adj* brief (*in speech*)
breviloquenti·a -ae *f* brevity
brevī *adv* briefly, in a few words; shortly, in a short time
brĕv·is -e *adj* short, little, brief; concise; small; shallow; narrow; *n pl* shoals, shallows
brevit·ās -ātis *f* brevity; smallness; shortness
breviter *adv* shortly, briefly
Britanni·a -ae *f* Britain; British Isles
Brom·ius -iī or **-ī** *m* Bacchus
brūm·a -ae *f* winter solstice; winter; winter's cold
brūmāl·is -e *adj* wintry
Brundis·ium -iī or **-ī** *n* port in S.E. Italy on Adriatic Sea
Brutti·ī -ōrum *m pl* inhabitants of toe of Italy
Brūt·us -ī *m* Lucius Junius Brutus (*credited with having driven out the last Roman king, Tarquinius Superbus*); Marcus Junius Brutus (*one of the murderers of Julius Caesar*)
brūt·us -a -um *adj* heavy, unwieldy; dull, stupid
būbīl·e -is *n* ox stall
būb·ō -ōnis *m* owl
būbŭl·a -ae *f* beef
bubulcĭt·or -ārī -ātus sum *vi* to be a herdsman; to ride herd
bubulc·us -ī *m* cowherd; plowman
būbŭl·us -a -um *adj* of cows or oxen
būcaed·a -ae *m* flogged slave
bucc·a -ae *f* cheek; loudmouthed person; trumpeter; parasite; mouthful
buccell·a -ae *f* small mouthful; morsel
buccŭl·a -ae *f*. little cheek; visor
buccŭlent·us -a -um *adj* loudmouthed
būcĕr(i)·us -a -um *adj* horned
būcĭn·a -ae *f* (curved) trumpet; war trumpet; shepherd's horn
būcĭnāt·or -ōris *m* trumpeter
būcolĭc·us -a -um *adj* pastoral, bucolic
būcŭl·a -ae *f* heifer

būf·ō -ōnis *m* toad
bulb·us -ī *m* onion
būl·ē -ēs *f* (Greek) council, senate
būleut·a -ae *m* councilor
būleuter·ium -iī *or* **-ī** *n* meeting place of Greek council
bull·a -ae *f* bubble; boss, stud, knob; amulet; badge (*symbol of boyhood*)
bullāt·us -a -um *adj* inflated, bombastic; studded; wearing a bulla, i.e., still a child
būmast·us -ī *f* species of grape with large clusters
būr·is -is *m* curved handle of plow
bustirăp·us -ī *m* ghoul, grave robber
bustuāri·us -a -um *adj* of a tomb or pyre
bust·um -ī *n* pyre; tomb, sepulcher
buxif·er -ĕra -ĕrum *adj* producing boxwood trees
bux·um -ī *n* boxwood; (spinning) top; comb; writing tablet (*made of boxwood*)
bux·us -ī *f* boxwood tree
Byzant·ium -iī or **-ī** *n* city on the Bosporus, later named Constantinople

C

caball·us -ī *m* pack horse, nag, hack
cachinnāti·ō -ōnis *f* loud or immoderate laughter
cachinn·ō -āre *vi* to laugh loud; to roar (*with laughter*)
cachinn·ō -ōnis *m* scoffer
cachinn·us -ī *m* loud laugh; jeering; rippling, roaring
cac·ō -āre *vt* to defile; *vi* to defecate
cacoēth·es -is *n* malignant disease; itch
cacūm·en -inis *n* point, tip, top, peak
cacūmin·ō -āre *vt* to make pointed; to sharpen
Căc·us -ī *m* son of Vulcan, a giant who lived on the Aventine Hill, killed by Hercules
cadāv·er -ĕris *n* corpse, carcass
cadāverōs·us -a -um *adj* cadaverous, ghastly
Cadmē·us -a -um *adj* Cadmean; Theban; *f* citadel of Thebes
Cadm·us -ī *m* son of Phoenician king Agenor, brother of Europa, and founder of Thebes
cadō cadĕre cecĭdī cāsum *vi* to fall, sink, drop; to be slain, die, be sacrificed; to happen; to belong, refer, be suitable, apply; to abate, subside, flag, decline, decay, vanish, fail, cease; to end, close
cadūceāt·or -ōris *m* herald
cadūcē·us -ī *m* herald's staff, caduceus
cadūcif·er -ĕra -ĕrum *adj* with herald's staff
cadūc·us -a -um *adj* falling, fallen; inclined to fall; frail, perishable, transitory; vain, futile, ineffectual; (law) lapsed, without heir
cad·us -ī *m* jar, flask, jug
caecigĕn·us -a -um *adj* born blind
caecit·ās -ātis *f* blindness
caec·ō -āre *vt* to make blind; to make obscure
Caecŭb·um -ī *n* famous wine from S. Latium
caec·us -a -um *adj* blind; invisible; vague, random, aimless, uncertain, unknown; making invisible, blinding; dark, gloomy, obscure
caed·ēs -is *f* murder, slaughter, massacre; bloodshed, gore; the slain
caed·ō caedĕre cecīdī caesum *vt* to hack at, chop; to strike, beat; to fell, cut down, cut off, cut to pieces; to kill, murder
caelām·en -inis *n* engraving, bas-relief
caelāt·or -ōris *m* engraver
caelātūr·a -ae *f* engraving
cael·ebs -ibis *adj* unmarried, single (*whether bachelor or widower*)
cael·es -itis *adj* heavenly, celestial
caelest·ia -ium *n pl* heavenly bodies
caelest·is -e *adj* heavenly, celestial; divine, supernatural
caelest·is -is *m* deity
caelibāt·us -ūs *m* celibacy
caelicŏl·a -ae *m* god
caelif·er -ĕra -ĕrum *adj* supporting the sky
caelipŏt·ens -entis *adj* powerful in heaven
caelit·ēs -um *m pl* inhabitants of heaven, gods
Cael·ius Mon·s (*genit:* **Cael·iī** or **-ī Mon·tis**) *m* Caelian Hill in Rome
cael·ō -āre *vt* to engrave in relief, to emboss, to carve; to cast; to fashion, compose; to adorn
cael·um -ī *n* sky, heaven, heavens; air, climate, weather; engraver's chisel, burin
caement·um -ī *n* quarry stone; rubble; cement
caenōs·us -a -um *adj* dirty, filthy, muddy
caen·um -ī *n* dirt, filth, mud, mire
caep·a -ae *f* or **caep·e -is** *n* onion
Caere (indecl) *n* city in Etruria
caerimōni·a -ae *f* rite; ritual, religious ceremony; sanctity, sacredness; awe, reverence, veneration
caerŭl·a -ōrum *n pl* sea
caerŭlē·us or **caerŭl·us -a -um** adj blue, azure, dark-blue, green, dark-green; dark, gloomy
Caes·ar -ăris *m* C. Julius Caesar (102?-44 B.C.)

caesariāt·us -a -um *adj* long-haired
caesari·ēs -ēī *f* hair
caesici·us -a -um *adj* bluish, dark blue
caesim *adv* by cutting; in short clauses, in a clipped style
caesi·us -a -um *adj* bluish-grey; blue-eyed; gray-eyed; cat-eyed
caesp·es -itis *m* sod, turf, grass; altar of sod
caest·us -ūs *m* boxing glove
caetr·a -ae *f* short Spanish shield
caetrāt·us -a -um *adj* armed with a shield
Caiēt·a -ae *f* nurse of Aeneas; town on coast of Latium
Caius see **Gaius**
Calăb·er -ra -rum *adj* Calabrian
Calabri·a -ae *f* S.W. peninsula of Italy
Cală·is -is *m* son of Boreas and Orithyia, and brother of Zetes
calamist·er -rī *m* hair curler, curling iron; (rhet) flowery language
calamistrāt·us -a -um *adj* curled (*with a hair curler*)
calamistr·um -ī *n* curling iron
calamit·ās -ātis *f* loss, injury, damage; misfortune, calamity, disaster; military defeat
calamitōsē *adv* unfortunately
calamitōs·us -a -um *adj* disastrous, ruinous, destructive; exposed to injury, suffering great damage, unfortunate
calăm·us -ī *m* reed, stalk; pen; arrow; fishing rod; pipe
calathisc·us -ī *m* small wicker basket
calăth·us -ī *m* wicker basket; milk pail; wine cup
calāt·or -ōris *m* servant, attendant
calc·ar -āris *n* spur; stimulus
calcānē·um -ī *n* heel
calceāment·um -ī *n* shoe
calceāt·us -ūs *m* sandal, shoe
calcĕ·ō -āre *vt* to furnish with shoes, to shoe
calceolār·ius -iī or **-ī** *m* shoemaker
calceŏl·us -ī *m* small shoe, half-boot
calcĕ·us -ī *m* shoe, half-boot
Calch·ās -antis *m* Greek prophet at Troy
calcitr·ō -āre *vi* to kick; to resist; to be stubborn; to kick up one's heels
calcitr·ō -ōnis *m* blusterer
calc·ō -āre *vt* to tread, tread under foot; to trample on, oppress; to scorn, abuse
calculāt·or -ōris *m* arithmetic teacher; accountant, bookkeeper
calcŭl·us -ī *m* pebble, stone; kidney stone; counter of an abacus; stone used in games; stone used in voting; vote, sentence, decision
caldāri·us -a -um *adj* warm-water; *n* hot bath
caldus see **calidus**
Calēdoni·a -ae *f* Highlands of Scotland
cale·faciō or **cal·faciō -facĕre -fēcī -factum** *vt* to warm, heat; to rouse up, excite, make angry
calefact·ō -āre *vt* to warm, heat
Calend·ae -ārum *f pl* first day of Roman month, calends
calendār·ium -iī or **-ī** *n* account book
cal·ĕō -ēre -ŭī *vi* to be warm, hot; to feel warm; to glow; to be hot with passion; to be troubled, be perplexed; to be zealously pursued; to be new or fresh
Cal·ēs -ium *f pl* Campanian town famous for its wine
cal·escō -escĕre -ŭī *vi* to get warm or hot; to become excited, be inflamed
calid·a or **cald·a -ae** *f* warm water
calidē *adv* quickly, promptly
calid·us or **cald·us -a -um** *adj* warm, hot; eager, rash, hasty, hotheaded, vehement; quick, ready, prompt; *n* warm drink; *f* see **calida**
caliendr·um -ī *n* wig (*for women*)
calig·a -ae *f* shoe, soldier's boot; soldier
caligāt·us -a -um *adj* wearing soldier's boots; (of a peasant) wearing clodhoppers
cālīg·ō -inis *f* mist, vapor, fog; gloom, darkness, obscurity; mental blindness; calamity, affliction
cālīg·ō -āre *vt* to veil in darkness, to obscure; to make dizzy; *vi* to steam, reek; to be wrapped in mist or darkness; to be blind, grope
caligŭl·a -ae *f* small military boot
Caligŭl·a -ae *m* pet name given by the soldiers to Gaius Caesar when he was a small boy
cal·ix -icis *m* cup; pot; (fig) wine
callaīn·us -a -um *adj* turquoise
call·ĕō -ēre -ŭī *vt* to know by experience or practice, to understand; (with *inf*) to know how to; *vi* to be callous, to be thick-skinned; to be insensible; to be experienced, clever, skillful
callidit·ās -ātis *f* skill; shrewdness; cunning, craft
callidē *adv* skillfully, expertly, shrewdly; well; cunningly
callid·us -a -um *adj* expert, adroit, skillful; ingenious, prudent, dexterous; clever, shrewd; sly, cunning, crafty, calculating
Callimăch·us -ī *m* famous Alexandrine poet and grammarian (*c.* 270 B.C.)
Calliŏp·ē -ēs or **Calliopē·a -ae** *f* Calliope (*muse of epic poetry*)
call·is -is *m* stony, uneven footpath; mountain path; cattle trail; mountain pasture; mountain pass, defile
Callist·ō -ūs *f* daughter of Lycaon, king of Arcadia, who was changed into the constellation Helice or Ursa Major
callōs·us -a -um *adj* hard-skinned; thick-skinned, callous; solid, hard, thick

call·um -ī *m* hard or thick skin; insensibility, stupidity
cal·ō -āre *vt* to call out, proclaim; to convoke
cāl·ō -ōnis *m* soldier's servant; menial servant, drudge
cal·or -ōris *m* warmth, heat, glow; passion, love; fire, zeal, impetuosity, vehemence
calth·a -ae *f* marigold
calthŭl·a -ae *f* yellow robe
calumnĭ·a -ae *f* trickery; pretense, evasion; false statement, misrepresentation, fallacy; false accusation, malicious charge; conviction for malicious prosecution
calumniāt·or -ōris *m* malicious prosecutor, perverter of the law, pettifogger
calumnĭ·or -ārī -ātus sum *vt* to accuse falsely; to misrepresent, calumniate; to blame unjustly; to put in a false light
calv·a -ae *f* scalp, bald head
calvit·ium -iī or **-ī** *n* baldness
calv·us -a -um *adj* bald
cal·x -cis *f* heel; (fig) foot, kick; **calcibus caedere** to kick
cal·x -cis *f* pebble; limestone, lime; finish line (*marked with lime*), goal; **ad calcem pervenire** to reach the goal; **ad carceres a calce revocari** to be recalled from the finish line to the starting gate; to have to start all over again
Calȳd·ōn -ōnis *f* town in Aetolia, scene of the famous boar hunt led by Meleager
Calyps·ō -ūs *f* nymph, daughter of Atlas, who entertained Ulysses on the island of Ogygia
camell·a -ae *f* drinking cup
camēl·us -ī *m* camel
Camēn·a -ae *f* Muse; poem; poetry
camĕr·a -ae *f* vault, arched roof, arch; houseboat
Camerin·um -ī *n* town in Umbria
Camill·a -ae *f* Volscian female warrior who assisted Turnus against Aeneas
Camill·us -ī *m* M. Furius Camillus, who freed Rome from the Gauls
camīn·us -ī *m* fireplace; furnace; forge; **oleum addere camino** to pour oil on the fire
cammăr·us -ī *m* lobster
Campānĭ·a -ae *f* district on E. coast of central Italy
campest·er -ris -re *adj* flat, level; overland (*march*); (of city) situated in a plain; (of army) fighting in a plain; (of sports, elections, etc.) held in the Campus Martius; *n* shorts (*worn in sports*); *n pl* flat lands
camp·us -ī *m* flat space, plain; sports field; level surface, surface (*of sea*); **Campus Martius** field near the Tiber used for sports, elections, military exercises, etc.
cam·ur -ŭra -ŭrum *adj* crooked, concave
canāl·is -is *m* pipe, conduit, gutter
cancell·ī -ōrum *m pl* railing, grating; barrier (*at sports, public events*); boundaries, limits
canc·er -rī *m* crab; the South; tropical heat; cancer (*disease*)
Canc·er -rī *m* Cancer (*northern zodiacal constellation; sign of the zodiac*)
cande·faciō -facĕre -fēcī -factum *vt* to make dazzling white; to make glow, make red-hot
candēl·a -ae *f* candle, torch, taper; waxed cord; **candelam apponere valvis** to set the house on fire
candelābr·um -ī *n* candlestick, candelabrum, chandelier; lamp stand
cand·ens -entis *adj* shining white, glittering, dazzling, glowing
cand·ĕō -ēre *vi* to be shining white, glitter, shine; to be white-hot
cand·escō -escĕre -ŭī *vi* to become white, begin to glisten; to get red-hot
candidātōrĭ·us -a -um *adj* of a candidate, candidate's
candidāt·us -a -um *adj* clothed in white; *m* candidate for office
candĭdē *adv* in dazzling white; clearly, simply, sincerely
candidŭl·us -a -um *adj* pretty white
candid·us -a -um *adj* (*cf* **albus**) shiny white, white, bright, dazzling, gleaming, sparkling; fair, radiant (*complexion*); candid, open, sincere, frank (*person*); bright, cheerful (*circumstances*); clear, bright (*day*); (of winds) bringing clear weather; white, silvery (*poplar, hair, etc.*); clear, unaffected (*style*); clothed in white; **candida sententia** vote of acquittal
cand·or -ōris *m* glossy whiteness, brightness, radiance; candor, sincerity; naturalness (*of style*); brilliance (*of discourse*)
cān·ens -entis *adj* grey, white
cān·ĕō -ēre -ŭī *vi* to be grey, be white
cānesc·ō -ĕre *vi* to grow white, become grey; to grow old; (of discourse) to lose force, grow dull
can·ī -ōrum *m pl* grey hair
canicŭl·a -ae *f* small dog, pup; (as term of abuse) little bitch
Canicŭl·a -ae *f* Canicula, Sirius, Dog Star (*brightest star in Canis Major*)
canīn·us -a -um *adj* canine; snarling, spiteful, caustic; **canina littera** letter R
can·is -is *m* or *f* dog, hound; (term of reproach to denote vile person, enraged person, hanger-on, etc.) dog; worst throw (*in dice*)
Can·is -is *m* Canis Major (*constellation, of which the brightest star is Canicula*)
canistr·um -ī *n* wicker basket (*for bread, fruit, flowers, etc.*)
cāniti·ēs (*genit* not in use) *f* greyness; grey hair; old age

cann·a -ae *f* reed; reed pipe, flute
cannăb·is -ae *f* or **cannăb·um -ī** *n* hemp
Cann·ae -ārum *f pl* village in Apulia where Hannibal won great victory over Romans in 216 B.C.
canō canĕre cecĭnī cantum *vt* to sing; to play; to speak in a singsong tone; to sing the praises of, celebrate; to prophesy, predict, foretell; (mil) to blow, sound; **signa canere** to sound the signal for battle; *vi* to sing; to play; (of birds) to sing; (of roosters) to crow; (of frogs) to croak; **receptui canere** to sound retreat; **tibiā canere** to play the flute
can·or -ōris *m* tune, sound, melody, song; tone (*of instruments*)
canōr·us -a -um *adj* melodious, musical; singsong, jingling; *n* melody, charm (*in speaking*)
Cantabri·a -ae *f* district in N.W. Spain
cantām·en -ĭnis *n* incantation, spell
cantāt·or -ōris *m* singer
canthăr·is -ĭdis *f* beetle; Spanish fly
canthăr·us -ī *m* wide-bellied drinking vessel with handles, tankard
canthēr·ĭus or **cantēr·ĭus -iī** or **-ī** *m* gelding; eunuch
canth·us -ī *m* iron tire; wheel
cantĭc·um -ī *n* song; aria in Roman comedy; (in delivery of speech) singsong
cantilēn·a -ae *f* old song, gossip; **cantilenam eandem canere** to sing the same old song, harp on the same theme
cantĭ·ō -ōnis *f* singing; incantation, charm, spell
cantĭt·ō -āre *vt* to keep on singing or playing, to sing or play repeatedly
cantiuncŭl·a -ae *f* catchy tune
cant·ō -āre *vt* to sing; to play; to sing of, celebrate, praise in song; to harp on, keep repeating; to predict; to drawl out; (of actor) to play the part of; *vi* to sing, to play; (of instruments) to sound; to drawl; (of rooster) to crow; **ad surdas aures cantare** to preach to deaf ears
cant·or -ōris *m* singer, poet; eulogist; actor, player; musician
cantr·ix -īcis *f* musician, singer (*female*)
cant·us -ūs *m* tune, melody, song, playing; incantation; prediction; magic spell
cān·us -a -um *adj* white, grey; aged, old venerable
capācit·ās -ātis *f* capacity
cap·ax -ācis *adj* capacious, spacious, wide, roomy; (of mind) able to grasp, receptive, capable
capēd·ō -ĭnis *f* cup or bowl used in sacrifices
capēduncŭl·a -ae *f* small cup or bowl used in sacrifices
capell·a -ae *f* she-goat, nanny goat
Capell·a -ae *f* Capella (*star of the first magnitude in Auriga*)
Capēn·a -ae *f* Porta Capena (*a gate in the Servian Wall which marked the start of the Via Appia*)
cap·er -rī *m* he-goat, billy goat
caperr·ō -āre *vt & vi* to wrinkle
capess·ō -ĕre -īvī or **-iī -ītum** *vt* to try to reach, make for, seize, get hold of, snatch at; to take up, undertake, engage in; **capessere rem publicam** to be engaged in politics
capillāt·us -a -um *adj* having hair, hairy; **bene capillatus** having a fine head of hair
capill·us -ī *m* hair
capiō capĕre cēpī captum *vt* (archaic *fut:* **capso**) to take hold of, grasp, seize; to occupy; to take up, assume (*office*); to catch, capture; to captivate, charm; to cheat, seduce, mislead, delude; to defeat, overcome (*in suite*); to convince (*in a dispute*); to reach, arrive at, land at; to exact, extort, accept as a bribe; to take, obtain, get, enjoy, reap (*profit, advantage*); to acquire, cherish, cultivate, adopt (*habits, etc.*); to form, conceive, come to, reach (*conclusions, plans, thoughts, resolutions, purposes*); to take, derive, draw, obtain (*examples, proofs, instances*); to entertain, conceive, receive, experience (*impressions, feelings*); (of feelings, experiences) to seize, overcome, occupy, take possession of; to suffer, be subjected to (*injury*); to hold, contain, be large enough for; to comprehend, grasp
cap·is -ĭdis *f* bowl (*with one handle, used in sacrifices*)
capistr·ō -āre *vt* to muzzle
capistr·um -ī *n* halter, muzzle
capĭt·al or **capit·āle -ālis** *n* capital offense
capitāl·is -e *adj* relating to the head or life; (law) affecting a man's life or civil status; (of crime) punishable by death, punishable by loss of civil rights, capital; dangerous, deadly, mortal; chief, preeminent, distinguished, of first rank
capĭt·ō -ōnis *m* big-head
Capitōlīn·us -a -um *adj* Capitoline; *m* Capitoline Hill; *m pl* persons in charge of the Capitoline games
Capitōl·ĭum -iī or **-ī** *n* the Capitol (*temple of Jupiter on the summit of Mons Tarpeius*); the Capitoline Hill (*including temple and citadel*); citadel (*of any city*)
capitulātim *adv* briefly, summarily
capitŭl·um -ī *n* small head; (as term of endearment) dear fellow
Cappadocĭ·a -ae *f* country in Asia Minor between the Taurus and Pontus
capr·a -ae *f* she-goat, nanny goat; body odor of armpits
caprĕ·a -ae *f* wild goat, roe
Caprĕ·ae -ārum *f pl* island at S. end of Bay of Naples off Sorrento

capreŏl·us -ī *m* roebuck, chamois; prop, support
Capricorn·us -ī *m* Capricorn (*sign of the zodiac*)
caprific·us -ī *f* wild fig tree
caprigĕn·us -a -um *adj* of goats; **caprigenum pecus** herd of goats
caprimulg·us -ī *m* rustic
caprīn·us -a -um *adj* of goats, goat; **de lana caprina rixari** to argue over nothing
caprĭp·ēs -ĕdis *adj* goat-footed
caps·a -ae *f* holder, container, box, case (*esp. for book rolls*)
capsō see **capio**
capsŭl·a -ae *f* small box
capt·a -ae *f* captive, prisoner (*female*)
captātī·ō -ōnis *f* hunt, quest; **captatio verborum** verbalism, sophistry
captāt·or -ōris *m* (fig) hound; **aurae popularis captator** publicity hound
captī·ō -ōnis *f* taking, catching; fraud; loss, disadvantage; sophism
captiōsē *adv* slyly, insidiously, deceptively
captiōs·us -a -um *adj* deceitful; captious, sophistical; dangerous, harmful
captiuncŭl·a -ae *f* quibble, sophism
captīvĭt·ās -ātis *f* captivity; conquest, capture
captīv·us -a -um *adj* caught, taken captive; prisoner's; captured, conquered; *mf* prisoner of war, captive
capt·ō -āre *vt* to catch at eagerly; to keep reaching for; to try to catch, chase after; to strive after, long for, desire earnestly; to try to hear; to try to trap, entice, allure; to adopt (*plan*); to try to cause (*laughter*); to watch for (*opportunity*); to begin (*conversation*)
captūr·a -ae *f* capture; quarry
capt·us -a -um *pp* of **capio**; *adj* **oculis et auribus captus** blind and deaf; **mente captus** mad, crazy; *m* captive, prisoner
capt·us -ūs *m* mental grasp, mental capacity; notion
Capŭ·a -ae *f* chief city of Campania
capulār·is -e *adj* with one foot in the grave
capŭl·us -ī *m* coffin; hilt, handle
cap·ut -ĭtis *n* head; top, summit, point, extremity; source (*of river*); root (*of plant*); top (*of tree*); head, leader; capital (*of country*); main point (*of discourse*); chapter, principal division, heading; substance, summary; (com) capital; main course; life, civil status; **capitis accusare** to accuse of a capital offense; **capitis damnare** to condemn to death; **capitis res** matter of life and death; **diminutio capitis** loss of civil rights; **diminutio capitis maxima** condemnation to death or slavery; **diminutio capitis media** loss of citizenship; **diminutio capitis minima** change of status (*as by adoption or, in the case of women, by marriage*)
Cap·ys -ўos *m* son of Assaracus and father of Anchises; companion of Aeneas; eighth king of Alba Longa
carbasĕ·us -a -um *adj* linen, canvas
carbăs·us -ī *f* (*pl:* **carbăs·a -ōrum** *n*) fine Spanish flax; linen garment; sail, canvas; awning
carb·ō -ōnis *m* charcoal
carbōnār·ius -iī or **-ī** *m* charcoal burner, collier
carbuncŭl·us -ī *m* small piece of coal; grief, sorrow; precious stone, garnet
carc·er -ĕris *m* prison, jail; prisoner; (term of reproach) jailbird; *m pl* starting gate (*at racetrack*); **ad carceres a calce revocari** to have to start all over again
carcerāri·us -a -um *adj* prison
carchēs·ium -iī or **-ī** *n* drinking cup (*slightly contracted in the middle*); upper part of mast (*similarly formed*)
cardiăc·us -ī *m* dyspeptic
card·ō -ĭnis *m* hinge; turning point, crisis; (astr) axis, pole; **cardo rerum** critical juncture, crisis
cardŭ·us -ī *m* thistle
cārē *adv* at a high price, dearly; highly
cārect·um -ī *m* sedge
căr·ĕō -ēre -ŭī *vi* (with *abl* or *genit*) **a** to be without; **b** to miss; **c** to be free from; **d** to keep away from, be absent from; **e** to abstain from
căr·ex -ĭcis *f* sedge
Cārĭ·a -ae *f* province in S.W. Asia Minor
cari·ēs (*genit* not in use) *f* decay, rot
carīn·a -ae *f* bottom of ship, keel; ship
Carīn·ae -ārum *f pl* the Keels (*district in Rome Between the Caelian and Esquiline Hills*)
carīnār·ius -iī or **-ī** *m* dyer of yellow
cariōs·us -a -um *adj* rotten, decayed, crumbled; wrinkled
cār·is -ĭdis *f* crab
cārĭt·ās -ātis *f* dearness, costliness, high price, high cost of living; affection, love
carm·en -ĭnis *n* song, tune; lyric poetry, poetry; incantation, charm; oracular utterance; ritual formula, legal formula; adage
Carment·a -ae or **Carment·is -is** *f* Roman goddess of prophecy, the mother of Evander, who came with him from Arcadia to Latium
Carmentāl·is -e *adj* of Carmenta; **Porta Carmentalis** gate at Rome near temple of Carmenta (*also called* **Porta Scelerata**, *i.e., ominous gate*)
carnār·ium -iī or **-ī** *n* meat hook; pantry
Carneăd·ēs -is *m* famous philoso-

pher, born at Cyrene, and founder of the New Academy (215-130 B.C.)

carnif·ex -ĭcis *m* hangman, executioner; murderer, butcher; scoundrel

carnificīn·a -ae *f* execution; torture, torment

carnific·ō -āre *vt* to mutilate, cut to pieces, behead

car·ō -nis or **carn·is -is** *f* flesh, meat; **caro ferina** venison; **caro putida** carrion; (fig) rotten egg

car·ō -ĕre *vt* to card (*wool*)

Carpăth·us -ī *f* island between Crete and Rhodes

carpatĭn·us -a -um *adj* of rough leather; *f* crude shoe

carpent·um -ī *n* two-wheeled covered carriage (*esp. used by women on holidays*)

carp·ō -ĕre -sī -tum *vt* to pluck, pick, cull; to carp at, criticize, take apart; to enjoy, make use of; to crop, browse on (*grass*); to pick, gather (*fruit*); to separate into parts, divide; (mil) to harass, weaken (*esp. by repeated attacks*); **auras vitales carpere** to breathe the breath of life; **diem carpere** to make the most of the present; **gyrum carpere** to go in a circle; **iter** or **viam carpere** to make one's way, pick one's way, travel; **vellera carpere** to spin

carptim *adv* piecemeal, separately, in parts; at different times; at different points; gradually

carpt·or -ōris *m* carver (*of food*)

Carrh·ae -ārum *f pl* town in Mesopotamia where Crassus was defeated and killed by the Parthians (53 B.C.)

carrūc·a -ae *f* four-wheeled carriage

carr·us -ī *m* four-wheeled wagon

Carthāginiens·is -e *adj & mf* Carthaginian

Carthāg·ō -ĭnis *f* Carthage (*city in N. Africa, founded as a Phoenician colony in 9th cent.* B.C.)

caruncŭl·a -ae *f* little piece of meat

cār·us -a -um *adj* dear, high-priced, expensive, costly; dear, beloved, esteemed; loving, affectionate

cas·a -ae *f* cottage, cabin, hut

casc·us -a -um *adj* old, primitive

cāseŏl·us -ī *m* small piece of cheese

cāsĕ·us -ī *m* cheese

casĭ·a -ae *f* mezereon (*fragrant plant with purple flowers*)

Cassandr·a -ae *f* daughter of Priam and Hecuba who had the gift of prophecy but was believed by no one

cass·ēs -ium *m pl* hunting net, snare; spider web

cassĭd·a -ae *f* metal helmet

Cassiŏp·ē -ēs or **Cassiopē·a -ae** *f* wife of Cepheus and mother of Andromeda, afterwards made a constellation

Cass·ius -iī or **-ī** *m* C. Cassius Longinus (*one of the murderers of Caesar*)

cass·is -ĭdis *f* metal helmet

cass·ō -āre *vi* to totter, trip

cass·us -a -um *adj* empty, hollow; (fig) empty, groundless, vain, pointless; (with *abl*) deprived of, devoid of, without; **cassus lumine** without life, dead; **in cassum** to no purpose, pointlessly

Castăl·is -ĭdis *adj* Castalian; **sorores Castalides** Muses; *f* Muse

Castalĭ·us -a -um *adj* Castalian; *f* fountain on Mt. Parnassus, sacred to Apollo and the Muses

castanĕ·a -ae *f* chestnut tree; chestnut

castē *adv* purely, chastely, spotlessly; virtuously; devoutly, piously

castellān·us -a -um *adj* of a fort, of a castle; *m* occupant of a castle or fortress; *m pl* garrison (*of a fortress*)

castellātim *adv* one fortress after another; **castellatim dissipati** (troops) stationed in various fortresses

castell·um -ī *n* fort, fortress, stronghold, castle; (fig) defense, shelter, refuge

castērĭ·a -ae *f* rowers' quarters

castīgābĭl·is -e *adj* punishable

castīgātĭ·ō -ōnis *f* correction, punishment; censure, reproof

castīgāt·or -ōris *m* corrector, critic

castīgātōrĭ·us -a -um *adj* reproving

castīgāt·us -a -um *adj* small, contracted, slender

castīg·ō -āre *vt* to correct, make right, blame, reprove, censure, chide, find fault with, punish; to correct, amend; to hold in check, restrain

castimōnĭ·a -ae *f* purity, morality; chastity, abstinence

castĭt·ās -ātis *f* purity, chastity

cast·or -ŏris *m* beaver

Cast·or -ŏris *m* son of Tyndareus, twin brother of Pollux, brother of Helen and Clytemnestra, and patron of sailors

castorĕ·um -ī *m* bitter, strong-smelling secretion of beavers

castrens·is -e *adj* camp, military

castr·ō -āre *vt* to castrate

castr·um -ī *n* fort, fortress, castle; *n pl* military camp; day's march; the service, army life; (pol) party; (phil) school; **bina castra** two camps; **castra facere** or **habere** to encamp; **castra movere** to break camp; **castra munire** to construct a camp; **castra ponere** to pitch camp; **castra una** one camp

cast·us -a -um *adj* (morally) pure, chaste, spotless, guiltless, virtuous; religious, pious, holy, sacred

casŭl·a -ae *f* little hut, little cottage

cās·us -ūs *m* falling; (fig) fall, downfall, overthrow, end; chance, event, happening, occurrence, emergency; occasion, opportunity; misfortune, mishap, accident, calamity; fall,

death; fate; (gram) case; **non consulto sed casu** not on purpose but by chance
catagelasĭm•us -a -um *adj* bantering, jeering; exposed to ridicule
catagrăph•us -a -um *adj* painted, colored
cataphract•ēs -ae *m* coat of mail
cataphract•us -a -um *adj* mail-clad
catăpl•us -ī *m* arrival of ship; arriving ship or fleet
catapult•a -ae *f* catapult; (fig) missile
catapultārĭ•us -a -um *adj* catapulted, shot (*from catapult*)
cataract•a or **catarract•a** or **catarract•ēs -ae** *f* waterfall, cataract (*esp. on the Nile*); floodgate; drawbridge
cataractrī•a -ae *f* spice
catast•a -ae *f* stage on which slaves were displayed for sale
catē *adv* skillfully, wisely
catēī•a -ae *f* javelin
catell•a -ae *f* puppy (*female*); small chain
catell•us -ī *m* puppy; small chain
catēn•a -ae *f* chain; series; barrier, restraint, bond
catēnāt•us -a -um *adj* chained
caterv•a -ae *f* crowd, throng, band, mob; troop (*of actors*); (mil) troop, horde
catervātim *adv* in companies, by troops; in crowds or flocks (*of plague-stricken people*)
cathĕdr•a -ae *f* armchair, cushioned seat; litter, sedan; professional chair
Catilīn•a -ae *m* L. Sergius Catiline (*Roman patrician whose conspiracy was exposed by Cicero in* 63 B.C.)
catill•ō -āre *vi* to lick the plate
catill•us -ī *m* plate
catīn•us -ī *m* plate, pot, bowl
Cat•ō -ōnis *m* M. Porcius Cato (*model of Roman aristocratic conservatism,* 239-149 B.C.); M. Porcius Cato Uticensis (*grandson of Porcius Cato, inveterate enemy of Caesar,* 95-45 B.C.)
catōn•ium -iī or **-ī** *n* lower world
Catull•us -ī *m* C. Valerius Catullus (*lyric and elegiac poet of Verona,* 86-54 B.C.)
catŭl•us -ī *m* puppy; whelp, cub
cat•us -a -um *adj* sharp, shrewd, keen; sly, cunning
Caucăs•us -ī *m* Caucasus mountains
caud•a -ae *f* tail (*of animal*); penis; **caudam jactare** (with *dat*) to flatter; **caudam trahere** to be mocked
caudĕ•us -a -um *adj* of wood, wooden
caud•ex or **cōd•ex -icis** *m* trunk (*of tree*); block (*of wood to which one was tied for punishment*); book, ledger; blockhead
caudicāl•is -e *adj* of wood cutting
Caud•ium -iī *or* **-ī** *n* town in Samnium
caul•ae -ārum *f pl* hole, opening passage; sheepfold, pen
caul•is -is *f* stalk, stem; cabbage stalk, cabbage
caup•ō -ōnis *m* innkeeper
caupōn•a -ae *f* inn, tavern; retail shop
caupōnĭ•us -a -um *adj* of a shop or tavern
caupōn•or -ārī -ātus sum *vt* to trade in or traffic in
caupōnŭl•a -ae *f* small inn or tavern
caus•a or **causs•a -ae** *f* (law) lawsuit, case; grounds, cause, motive, purpose, reason; good reason, just cause; pretext, pretense; inducement, occasion, opportunity; side, party, faction, cause; condition, situation, position; (rhet) matter of discussion, subject matter; matter, business, concern; commission, charge; personal relationship, connexion; **causā** (with *genit*) for the sake of, on account of; **causā cadere** to lose a case; **causam agere, causam dicere,** or **causam orare** to plead a case; **causam cognoscere** to examine a case (*as judge*); **vestrā causā** in your interests; **per causam** (with *genit*) under the pretext of; **sine causa** without good reason
causārĭ•us -a -um *adj* sick; *m* (mil) malingerer, goldbrick
causĭ•a -ae *f* Macedonian hat (*with wide brim*)
causidĭc•us -ī *m* pleader, lawyer; shyster
causifĭc•or -ārī -ātus sum *vi* to make excuses
caus•or -ārī -ātus sum *vt* to pretend, give as a reason
caussa see **causa**
causŭl•a -ae *f* petty lawsuit; minor cause
cautē *adv* cautiously, carefully; with security
cautēl•a -ae *f* precaution
caut•ēs -is *f* rock, crag
cautim *adv* warily, cautiously
cauti•ō -ōnis *f* caution, wariness; guarantee, provision; (law) bond, security, bail, warranty; **mea cautio est** I must see to it; **mihi cautio est** I must take care
caut•or -ōris *m* wary person; bondsman, surety
caut•us -a -um *adj* cautious, careful; safe, secure
cavaed•ium -iī or **-ī** *n* inner court of Roman house
cavĕ•a -ae *f* cavity; enclosure for animals: cage, den, stall, beehive, bird cage; auditorium, theater; **prima cavea** section of auditorium for nobility; **ultima cavea** section for lower classes
cavĕō cavēre cāvī cautum *vt* to guard against, beware of; to keep clear of; to stipulate, decree, order; to guarantee; *vi* to be careful, look out, be on one's guard; (with *abl* or

ab + *abl*) to be on one's guard against; (with **ab** + *abl*) to get a guarantee from; (with *dat*) **a** to guarantee, give a guarantee to; **b** to provide for, take care of; **cave tangere** (= **noli tangere**) do not touch
cavern·a -ae *f* hollow, cavity, cave, cavern; vault; hold (*of ship*)
cavill·a -ae *f* jeering, scoffing
cavillāti·ō -ōnis *f* banter, scoffing, raillery; sophistry, quibbling
cavillāt·or -ōris *m* scoffer; quibbler, sophist
cavill·or -ārī -ātus sum *vt* to scoff at, mock, criticize, satirize; *vi* to scoff, jeer; to quibble
cav·ō -āre *vt* to hollow out, excavate; to pierce, run through
cav·us -a -um *adj* hollow, hollowed; concave, vaulted; deep-channeled (*river*); *m & n* hole, cavity, hollow
-ce demonstrative enclitic appended to pronouns and adverbs (like colloquial English *here, there*, with *this* or *that*); **hice** (for **hicce**) this (*here*); **hujusce** of this (*here*); (when followed by the enclytic **-ne**, the form becomes **-ci: hicine, sicine**)
Cecropid·ae -ārum *m pl* descendants of Cecrops, Athenians
Cecrŏp·is -idis *f* female descendant of Cecrops (*esp. Aglauros*); Procne; Philomela; Athenian woman
Cecr·ops -ŏpis *m* first king of Athens
cēdō cēdĕre cessī cessum *vt* to grant, concede, yield, give up; *vi* to go, move, walk, walk along; to go away, depart, withdraw; (of time) to pass; (of events) to turn out; to pass away, die; (mil) to retreat; (with *dat*) **a** to befall, fall to the lot of, accrue to; **b** to yield to, submit to, give in to; **c** to yield (*in rank*) to, be inferior to; **d** to comply with, conform to, obey; (with **in** + *acc*) to be changed into, become; (with **pro** + *abl*) to pass for, be the equivalent of, be the price of; **bonis** or **possessionibus alicui cedere** to give up or cede one's property to someone; **foro cedere** to go bankrupt
cedo (*pl:* **cette**) (old *impv*) here with, bring here, give here; let's hear, tell, out with; look at; **cedo dum!** all right!; come now!; **cedo ut inspiciam** let me look
cedr·us -ī *f* cedar, juniper; cedar wood; cedar oil
Celaen·ō -ūs *f* daughter of Atlas and one of the Pleiades; one of the Harpies; greedy woman
cēlāt·um -ī *n* secret
celĕb·er -ris -re *adj* crowded, populous, frequented; well-attended; famous; well-known, common, usual; solemn, festive; numerous, repeated, frequent
celebrāti·ō -ōnis *f* large assembly; festival, celebration; *f pl* throngs
celebrāt·us -a -um *adj* much-frequented, much-visited, crowded, populous; celebrated, famous, renowned; customary, usual, frequent; solemn, festive; trite, familiar, often-repeated
celebrit·ās -ātis *f* throng, crowd, multitude, large assembly; publicity; repetition, frequency; fame, renown; celebration
celĕbr·ō -āre *vt* to frequent, crowd, fill, visit in crowds; to repeat, practice, exercise; to publicize, advertise, honor, glorify; to escort, attend; to cause to resound
cel·er -ĕris -ĕre *adj* swift, speedy, quick, rapid, hurried; rash, hasty
celĕrē *adv* quickly
Celĕr·ēs -um *m pl* mounted bodyguards of Roman kings
celerip·ēs -ĕdis *adj* swift-footed
celerit·ās -ātis *f* speed, quickness, rapidity
celeriter *adv* quickly, speedily
celĕr·ō -āre *vt* to quicken, speed up, accelerate; *vi* to be quick, rush, speed
cell·a -ae *f* storeroom, storehouse, grain elevator, silo; cheap apartment, garret; sanctuary (*of temple, where the cult image stood*); cell (*of beehive*)
cellāri·us -a -um *adj* of a storeroom; *m* storekeeper, butler
cellŭl·a -ae *f* small storeroom, small apartment
cēl·ō -āre *vt* to hide, conceal; to veil (*feelings*); to keep (*something*) secret, keep quiet about; (with *acc* of thing and *acc* of person from whom one conceals) to keep (*someone*) in the dark about, hide (*something*) from (*someone*); **celari** (with **de** + *abl*) to be kept in ignorance of
cel·ox -ōcis *adj* swift, quick; *f* swift-sailing ship, cutter, speedboat
cels·us -a -um *adj* high, lofty, towering, prominent, erect; lofty, elevated (*thoughts*); high (*rank*); proud, haughty
Celt·ae -ārum *m pl* Celts (*who occupied most of W. Europe*); (in more restricted sense) inhabitants of central Gaul
Celtibēr·ī -ōrum *m pl* Celtiberians (*early people of Central Spain*)
cēn·a -ae *f* principal meal, dinner; dish, course; company at dinner
cēnācŭl·um -ī *n* dining room (*usually on an upper floor*); attic
cēnātic·us -a -um *adj* dinner
cēnāti·ō -ōnis *f* dining room
cēnāt·us -a -um *adj* having dined; spent in feasting
cēnit·ō -āre *vi* to dine habitually, dine often
cēn·ō -āre *vt* to make a meal of, dine on, eat; *vi* to dine, eat dinner
cens·ĕō -ēre -ŭī -um *vt* to assess, rate, estimate, tax; to esteem, appreciate, value; (of senate) to decree, resolve; to propose, move, vote,

argue, suggest, advise; to think, believe, hold, suppose, imagine, expect

censi·ō -ōnis *f* rating, assessment, taxation; opinion

cens·or -ōris *m* censor (*one of two Roman magistrates who took the census and exercised general control over morals, etc.*); severe judge of morals, critic

censōri·us -a -um *adj* of the censors; subject to censure; rigid, stern, austere; **homo censorius** ex-censor; **lex censoria** contract (*drawn up by censors*) for leasing buildings

censūr·a -ae *f* office of censor, censorship; criticism

cens·us -ūs *m* census; register of the census; income bracket; wealth, property; rich presents, gifts; **censum agere** or **habere** to hold a census; **censu prohibere** to exclude from citizenship, disenfranchise

centaurē·um -ī *n* centaury (*medical herb*)

Centaur·us -ī *m* centaur (*creature fabled to be half man and half horse*); Centaurus (*southern constellation between the Southern Cross and Hydra*)

centēn·ī -ae -a *adj* one hundred each; **deciens centena milia passum** ten hundred thousand paces, one million paces

centēsim·us -a -um *adj* hundredth; *f* hundredth part, one percent; (com) 1% monthly (12% per annum)

centi·ceps -cipitis *adj* hundred-headed

centiēs or **centiens** *adv* a hundred times; (fig) a great many times

centimān·us -a -um *adj* hundred-handed

cent·ō -ōnis *m* patchwork, quilt

centum (indecl) *adj* hundred

centumgemin·us -a -um *adj* hundredfold

centumpl·ex -icis *adj* hundredfold

centumpond·ium -iī or **-ī** *n* hundred pounds, hundred-pound weight

centumvirāl·is -e *adj* of the centumviri

centumvir·ī -ōrum *m pl* panel of one hundred (*jurors chosen annually to try civil suits under a quaestor, esp. concerning inheritances*)

centuncŭl·us -ī *m* piece of patchwork, cloth of many colors, saddle cloth

centuri·a -ae *f* (mil) company, century (*theoretically composed of one hundred men*); (pol) century (*one of the* 193 *groups into which Servius Tullius divided the Roman people*)

centuriātim *adv* by companies, by centuries

centuriāt·us -a -um *adj* divided into companies or centuries; **comitia centuriata** centuriate assembly (*legislative body which met in the Campus Martius to elect high magistrates, decree war, etc.*)

centuri·ō -ōnis *m* centurion (*commander of an infantry company*)

centuri·ō -āre *vt* to divide into centuries

centuriōnāt·us -ūs *m* election of centurions

centuss·is -is *m* a hundred aces (*bronze coins*)

cēnŭl·a -ae *f* little dinner

Cephăl·us -ī *m* husband of Procris, whom he unintentionally shot

Ceph·eus -ĕī *m* king of Ethiopia, husband of Cassiope and father of Andromeda

Cephīs·us -ī *m* river in Attica; river in Phocis and Boeotia

cēr·a -ae *f* wax; writing tablet (*covered with wax*); wax seal; wax bust of an ancestor; cell (*of beehive*)

Ceramīc·us -ī *m* cemetery of Athens

cērār·ium -iī or **-ī** *n* fee for affixing a seal

cerast·ēs -ae *m* horned serpent

cerăs·us -ī *f* cherry tree; cherry

cērāt·us -a -um *adj* waxed

Cerbĕr·us -ī *m* three-headed dog which guarded the entrance to the lower world

cercopithēc·us -ī *m* long-tailed monkey

cercūr·us -ī *m* swift-sailing ship, cutter

cerd·ō -ōnis *m* workman, laborer

Cereāl·ia -ium *n pl* festival of Ceres (*April* 10*th*)

Cereāl·is -e *adj* of Ceres; of grain; **arma Cerealia** utensils for grinding and baking

cerebrōs·us -a -um *adj* hot-headed

cerĕbr·um -ī *n* brain; head, skull; understanding; hot temper

Cer·ēs -ĕris *f* goddess of agriculture and mother of Proserpine; grain bread, food

cērĕ·us -a -um *adj* of wax, waxen; wax-colored; soft, pliant; *m* candle

cērinth·a -ae *f* wax flower

cērin·us -a -um *adj* wax-colored; *n pl* wax-colored clothes

cernō cernĕre crēvī crētum *vt* (of sight) to discern, distinguish, make out, see; (of mind) to discern, see, understand; to decide, decree, determine; **hereditatem cernere** to formally declare oneself heir to an inheritance, accept an inheritance

cernŭ·us -a -um *adj* with face turned toward the earth, stooping forwards

cērōm·a -ătis *n* wrestler's oil

cērōmatĭc·us -a -um *adj* smeared with oil, oily, greasy

cerrīt·us -a -um *adj* crazy, frantic

certām·en -ĭnis *n* contest, match; rivalry; (mil) battle, combat

certātim *adv* with a struggle, in rivalry

certāti·ō -ōnis *f* contest; rivalry, discussion, debate

certē *adv* surely, certainly, unques-

tionably, undoubtedly, of course; (in answers) yes, certainly; (to restrict an assertion) at least, at any rate
certō *adv* for certain, for sure; surely, in fact, really
cert·ō -āre *vi* to fight, contend, struggle, do battle; to compete; (law) to debate; (with *inf*) to strive to
cert·us -a -um *adj* certain, determined, resolved, fixed, settled; specific, particular, certain, precise, definite; faithful, trusty, dependable; sure of aim, unerring; unwavering, inexorable; **certiorem facere** to inform; **certum est mihi** (with *inf*) I am determined to; **certum habere** to regard as certain; **pro certo** for sure; **pro certo habere** to be assured
cērŭl·a -ae *f* piece of wax; **cerula miniata** red pencil (*of a critic*)
cēruss·a -ae *f* ceruse, white paint
cērussāt·us -a -um *adj* painted white
cerv·a -ae *f* hind, deer
cervīc·al -ālis *n* pillow, cushion
cervīcŭl·a -ae *f* slender neck
cervīn·us -a -um *adj* of a stag or deer
cerv·ix -īcis *f* neck; nape of the neck; **in cervicibus nostris esse** to be on our necks., i.e., to have (*something or someone unpleasant*) on our hands; **a cervicibus nostris avertere** to get (*someone*) off our neck, get rid of (*someone*); **cervicibus sustinere** to shoulder (*responsibility*)
cerv·us -ī *m* stag, deer; (mil) palisade
cessātī·ō -ōnis *f* letup, delay; inactivity, idleness, cessation
cessāt·or -ōris *m* idler, loafer
cessī·ō -ōnis *f* surrendering, relinquishment
cess·ō -āre *vi* to let up, slack off, become remiss, stop; to be inactive, be idle, do nothing; to lie fallow
cestrosphendŏn·ē -ēs *f* artillery piece for hurling stones
cest·us or **cest·os -ī** *m* girdle (*esp. of Venus*)
cētār·ium -iī or **-ī** *n* fish pond
cētār·ius -iī or **-ī** *m* fish dealer
cētĕra *adv* otherwise, in all other respects, for the rest
cēterōquī or **cēterōquīn** *adv* otherwise, in all other respects, for the rest
cētĕrum *adv* otherwise, in all other respects, for the rest; but, yet, still, on the other hand
cētĕr·us -a -um *adj* the other, the remaining, the rest of; *pron m pl & f pl* the others, all the rest, everybody; *n* the rest
Cethēg·us -ī *m* C. Cernelius Cethegus (*fellow conspirator of Catiline*)
cette see **cedo**
cēt·us -ī (*pl:* **cēt·ē**) *m* sea monster: whale, shark, seal, dolphin
ceu *conj* (in comparisons) as, just as; (in comparative conditions) as if, just as if; **ceu cum** as when
cēv·ĕō -ēre *vi* (*cf* **criso**) (of a male) to move the haunches
Cē·yx -ȳcis *m* king of Trachis, who was changed into a kingfisher, as was his wife Alcyone
Chaldae·us -a -um *adj* Chaldaean; *m* astrologer, fortune-teller
chalybēi·us -a -um *adj* steel
Chalўb·es -um *m pl* people of Pontus in Asia Minor noted as steelworkers
chal·ybs -ȳbis *m* steel
Chāŏn·es -um *m pl* a tribe in Epirus
Chāoni·us -a -um *adj* Chaonian; of Epirus; *f* Chaonia (*district of Epirus*)
Cha·os -ī *n* chaos, the unformed world, empty space, shapeless mass from which the world was formed; **a Chao** from the beginning of the world
char·a -ae *f* wild cabbage
charisti·a -ōrum *n pl* Roman family festival
Charit·es -um *f pl* the Graces
Char·ōn -ontis *m* ferryman of the lower world
chart·a -ae *f* sheet of papyrus; sheet of paper; writing, letter, poem; book; record
chartŭl·a -ae *f* sheet of paper; letter, note
Charybd·is -is *f* whirlpool between Italy and Sicily, personified as a female monster
Chatt·ī -ōrum *m pl* people of central Germany
Chēl·ae -ārum *f pl* the Claws (*of Scorpio*); Libra (*constellation into which Scorpio extends*)
chelȳdr·us -ī *m* water snake
chely·s (*genit* not in use; *acc:* **chelyn**) *f* tortoise; lyre
cheragr·a -ae *f* arthritis in the hand
chīliarch·ēs -ae or **chīliarch·us -ī** *m* commander of 1000 men; Persian chancellor (*highest office next to the king*)
Chimaer·a -ae *f* fire-breathing monster, with lion's head, goat's body, and dragon's tail
Chi·os -ī *f* island off coast of Asia Minor, famous for its wine
chīrogrăph·um -ī *n* handwriting; autography; document; **falsa chirographa** forgeries
Chīr·ōn -ōnis *m* Chiron (*centaur, tutor of Aesculapius, Hercules, and Achilles, and famous for his knowledge of medicine and prophecy*)
chīronŏm·os -ī or **chīronŏm·ōn -ūntis** *m* pantomimist
chīrurgi·a -ae *f* surgery
Chi·us -a -um *adj & mf* Chian; *n* Chian wine; *n pl* Chian cloth
chlamydāt·us -a -um *adj* wearing a military uniform

chlam•ys -ȳdis *f* military cloak; gold-brocaded mantle
Choerĭl•us -ī *m* incompetent Greek panegyrist of Alexander the Great
chorāg•ĭum -iī or **-ī** *n* choreography
chorāg•us -ī *m* choragus (*man who finances the chorus*)
choraul•ēs -ae *m* flute player who accompanied the choral dance
chord•a -ae *f* gut string, string (*of musical instrument*); cord, rope
chorē•a -ae *f* dance
chorē•us -ī *m* trochee
chor•us -ī *m* chorus; choir
Chrem•ēs -ētis or **-is** or **-ī** *m* miserly old man (*in Roman comedy*)
Christiān•us -ī *m* Christian
Christ•us -ī *m* Christ
Chrȳsē•is -ĭdis *f* Agamemnon's slave girl, daughter of Chryses
Chrȳs•ēs -ae *m* priest of Apollo
Chrysipp•us -ī *m* famous Stoic philosopher (290-210 B.C.)
chrȳsolith•os -ī *m* chrysolite, topaz
chrȳs•os -ī *m* gold
cibārĭ•us -a -um *adj* of food; common, coarse (*food of slaves*); *n pl* rations, provisions, food allowance
cibāt•us -ūs *m* food
cib•ō -āre *vt* to feed
cibōr•ĭum -iī or **-ī** *n* drinking cup
cib•us -ī *m* food; feed; (fig) food, nourishment
cicād•a -ae *f* locust, harvest fly
cicātrīcōs•us -a -um *adj* scarred, covered with scars
cicātr•ix -īcis *f* scar
cicc•us -ī *m* core of pomegranate; something worthless, trifle
cic•er -ĕris *n* chick-pea
Cicĕr•ō -ōnis *m* M. Tullius Cicero (*orator and statesman,* 106-43 B.C.)
cīchorē•um -ī *n* endive
Cicŏn•es -um *m pl* Thracian tribe
cicōnĭ•a -ae *f* stork
cic•ur -ŭris *adj* tame
cicūt•a -ae *f* hemlock tree; hemlock poison; pipe, flute (*carved from hemlock tree*)
ciĕō ciēre cīvī citum *vt* to set in motion, move; to stir, agitate; to call for, send for; to summon for help; to invoke, appeal to; to call on by name, mention by name; to start, bring about; to renew (*combat*)
Cilicĭ•a -ae *f* country in S. Asia Minor
Cilicĭ•us -a -um *adj* Cilician; *n* garment of goat's hair
Cil•ix -ĭcis *adj & m* Cilician
Cimbr•ī -ōrum *m pl* Germanic tribe (*defeated by Marius in* 101 B.C.)
cīm•ex -ĭcis *m* bug
Cimmerĭ•ī -ōrum *m pl* people in the Crimea; mythical people living in perpetual darkness in caves at Cumae
cinaedĭc•us -a -um *adj* lewd
cinaed•us -ī *m* sodomite; lewd dancer
cincinnāt•us -a -um *adj* curly-haired
Cincinnāt•us -ī *m* L. Quinctius Cincinnatus (*famous Roman hero, dictator in* 458 B.C.)
cincinn•us -ī *m* curled hair, artificial curl (*of hair*); (rhet) highly artificial expression
cincticŭl•us -ī *m* small belt or sash
cinctūr•a -ae *f* belt, sash
cinct•us -ūs *m* tucking up; belt, sash; **cinctus Gabinius** Gabinian style of wearing toga (*usually employed at religious festivals*)
cinctūt•us -a -um *adj* wearing a belt or sash; old-fashioned
cinefact•us -a -um *adj* reduced to ashes
cinerār•ĭus -iī or **-ī** *m* curling iron, hair curler
cingō cingĕre cinxī cinctum *vt* to surround, encircle; to wreathe (*head*); to tuck up (*garment*); (mil) to beleaguer, invest; to cover, protect; **cingi in proelia** to prepare oneself for battle, get ready for battle; **ferrum cingi** to put on one's sword
cingŭl•a -ae *f* belt; sash (*worn by women*); girth (*worn by horses, etc.*); sword belt; chastity belt
cingŭl•um -ī *m* belt; sword belt; sash (*worn by women*); girdle, chastity belt
cingŭl•us -ī *m* zone (*of the earth*)
cinĭfl•ō -ōnis *m* hair curler
cin•is -ĕris *m* ashes; ruin, death
Cinn•a -ae *m* L. Cornelius Cinna (*consul* 87-84 B.C. *and supporter of Marius, d.* 84 B.C.)
cinnamōm•um or **cinnăm•um -ī** *n* cinnamon; *n pl* cinnamon sticks
Cinȳr•ās -ae *m* father of Myrrha and Adonis
cipp•us -ī *m* stake, post, pillar; gravestone; (mil) palisade
circā *adv* around, round about, all around, in the vicinity; *prep* (with *acc*) (of place) around, surrounding, about, among, through, in the neighborhood of, near; attending, escorting (*persons*); (of time) at about, around, towards; (with numerals) about, nearly, almost; concerning, in respect to
circamoer•ĭum -iī or **-ī** *n* area on both sides of a city wall
Circ•ē -ēs or **-ae** *f* daughter of Helios and Perse, famous for her witchcraft
circens•is -e *adj* of the racetrack; *m pl* races
circĭn•ō -āre *vt* to make round; to circle
circĭn•us -ī *m* (geometer's) compass, pair of compasses
circĭter *adv* (of time and number) nearly, about, approximately; *prep* (with *acc*) about, near
circlus see **circulus**
circuĕō see **circumeo**
circuitĭō see **circumitio**
circuĭt•us or **circumĭt•us -ūs** *m* circuit; going round, revolution; de-

tour; circumference; **circumlocution**; (rhet) period
circulāt·or -ōris *m* peddler, vendor
circŭl·or -ārī -ātus sum *vi* to gather around (*for conversation*); to stroll about
circŭl·us or **circl·us -ī** *m* circle, circuit; ring, hoop; social circle; (astr) orbit
circum *adv* about, all around; *prep* (with *acc*) around, about; in the neighborhood of
circum·ăgō -agĕre -ēgī -actum *vt* to turn around; to sway (*emotionally*); **circumagi** or **se circumagere** to go out of one's way, go in a round about way; (of time) to pass away, roll around
circumăr·ō -āre *vt* to plow around
circumcaesūr·ā -ae *f* contour, outline
circum·cīdo -cīdĕre -cīdī -cīsum *vt* to cut around, trim; to cut short, cut down on; to abridge, shorten; to circumcise
circumcircā *adv* all around
circumcīs·us -a -um *pp* of **circumcido**; *adj* steep; inaccessible; abridged, short
circum·clūdō -clūdĕre -clūsī -clūsum *vt* to shut in, hem in, enclose, surround
circumcŏl·ō -ĕre *vt* to live near
circumcurs·ō -āre *vt & vi* to run around
circum·dō -dare -dĕdī -dătum *vt* to surround, enclose, encircle; (with *dat*) to place or put (*something*) around
circum·dūcō -dūcĕre -duxī -ductum *vt* to lead around, draw around; (with double *acc*) to lead (*someone*) around to; **aliquem omnia praesidia circumducere** to take someone around to all the garrisons
circum·ĕō or **circu·ĕō -īre -īvī** or **-iī -ĭtum** *vt* to go around, go around to, visit, make the rounds of; to surround, encircle, enclose, encompass; to get around, circumvent, deceive, cheat; *vi* to go around, make a circuit
circumequit·ō -āre *vt* to ride around
circum·fĕrō -ferre -tŭlī -lātum *vt* to carry around, hand around; to publicize, spread abroad; to purify; **circumferri** to revolve; **oculos circumferre** to look around, glance about
circum·flectō -flectĕre -flexī -flexum *vt* to turn around, wheel about
circumfl·ō -āre *vt* to blow around; (fig) to buffet
circum·flŭō -fluĕre -fluxī *vt* to flow around; to surround; to overflow; *vi* to be overflowing, abound
circumflŭ·us -a -um *adj* flowing around; surrounded (*by water*)
circumforānĕ·us -a -um *adj* strolling about from market to market, itinerant; around the forum
circum·fundō -fundĕre -fūdī -fūsum *vt* to pour around; to surround, cover, envelop; **circumfundi** or **se circumfundere** to crowd around; **circumfundi** (with *dat*) to cling to
circumgĕm·ō -ĕre *vt* to growl around (*e.g., a sheepfold*)
circumgest·ō -āre *vt* to carry around
circum·gredior -grĕdī -gressus sum *vt* to surround
circumitĭ·ō or **circuitĭ·ō -ōnis** *f* going round; patrolling; circumlocution
circumitus see **circuitus**
circumjac·ĕō -ēre *vi* (with *dat*) to lie near, border on, be adjacent to
circum·jiciō -jicĕre -jēcī -jectum *vt* to throw or place around; to surround; (with *dat*) to throw (*something*) around (*someone or something*); **fossam circumjicere** to dig a trench all around
circumject·us -a -um *adj* surrounding, adjacent; (with *dat*) adjacent to; *n pl* neighborhood
circumject·us -ūs *m* surrounding; embrace
circumlātus *pp* of **circumfero**
circumlĭg·ō -āre *vt* to bind; (with *dat*) to bind or fasten (*something*) to
circum·linō -linĕre — -lĭtum *vt* to smear all over; to anoint
circumlŭ·ō -ĕre *vt* to flow around
circumluvĭ·ō -ōnis *f* island (*formed by a river flowing in a new channel*)
circum·mittō -mittĕre -mīsī -missum *vt* to send around
circummūn·iō or **circummoen·iō -īre** *vt* to fortify
circummūnītĭ·ō -ōnis *f* investment (*of town*); circumvallation
circumpadān·us -a -um *adj* situated along the Po River
circumpend·ĕō -ēre *vi* to hang around
circumplaud·ō -ĕre *vt* to applaud from every direction
circum·plector -plectī -plexus sum *vt* to clasp, embrace, surround
circumplic·ō -āre *vt* to wind; (with *dat*) to wind (*something*) around
circum·pōnō -pōnĕre -posŭī -positum *vt* (with *dat*) to place or set (*something*) around
circumpōtātĭ·ō -ōnis *f* round of drinks
circumrēt·iō -īre -īvī -ītum *vt* to snare
circum·rōdō -rōdĕre -rōsī *vt* to nibble all around; to hesitate to say; to slander, backbite
circumsaep·iō or **circumsēp·iō -īre -sī -tum** *vt* to fence in, enclose
circumscind·ō -ĕre *vt* to strip off
circum·scrībō -scrībĕre -scripsī -scriptum *vt* to draw a line around, mark the boundary of; to

limit, restrict; to set aside; to defeat the purpose of; to trap, defraud
circumscriptē *adv* comprehensively; (rhet) in periods
circumscripti·ō -ōnis *f* encircling; circle; circuit, limit, boundary; comprehensive statement; cheating, deceiving; (rhet) period
circumscript·or -ōris *m* cheat
circumscript·us -a -um *pp* of **circumscribo**; *adj* restricted, limited; (rhet) periodic
circumsĕc·ō -āre *vt* to cut around
circum·sedĕō -sedēre -sēdī -sessum *vt* to beset, besiege, invest, blockade
circumsēpĭō see **circumsaepio**
circumsessĭ·ō -ōnis *f* besieging, blockading
circumsīd·ō -ĕre *vt* to besiege
circumsil·ĭō -īre *vi* to hop around, dance around
circum·sistō -sistĕre -stĕtī *vt* to stand around, surround
circumsŏn·ō -āre *vt* to make resound, fill with sound; *vi* to resound everywhere; (with *dat*) to resound to
circumsŏn·us -a -um *adj* noisy
circumspectātr·ix -īcis *f* spy (*female*)
circumspectĭ·ō -ōnis *f* looking around; circumspection, caution
circumspect·ō -āre *vt* to search attentively, watch for; *vi* to keep looking around, look around anxiously
circumspect·us -a -um *pp* of **circumspicio**; *adj* well-considered; guarded (*words*); circumspect, cautious (*person*)
circumspect·us -ūs *m* consideration; view
circum·spicĭō -spicĕre -spexī -spectum *vt* to look around for, survey, see; to consider, examine; *vi* to be circumspect, be cautious, be on the watch; **se circumspicere** to think highly of oneself
circumstant·ēs -ĭum *m pl* bystanders
circum·stō -stāre -stĕtī *vt* to surround, envelop; (of terror, etc.) to grip, confront, overwhelm; *vi* to stand around
circumstrĕp·ō -ĕre *vt* to surround with noise or shouts
circumsurg·ō -ĕre *vi* (of mountains) to rise all around
circumtent·us -a -um *adj* tightly covered
circumtĕr·ō -ĕre *vt* to rub shoulders with, crowd around
circumtext·us -a -um *adj* with embroidered border
circumtŏn·ō -āre -ŭī *vt* to crash around (*someone*)
circumtons·us -a -um *adj* clipped
circum·vādō -vādĕre -vāsī *vt* to attack on every side; (of terror, etc.) to grip, confront
circumvăg·us -a -um *adj* flowing around, encircling
circumvall·ō -āre *vt* to blockade, invest
circumvectĭ·ō -ōnis *f* carting around (*of merchandise*); revolution (*of sun*)
circumvect·ō -āre *vt* to carry around
circumvect·or -ārī -ātus sum *vt* to ride or cruise around; to describe; *vi* to ride about, cruise about
circum·vĕhor -vĕhī -vectus sum *vt* to ride or cruise around; to describe, express by circumlocution; *vi* to ride about, cruise about
circumvēl·ō -āre *vt* to veil, envelop, cover
circum·venĭō -venīre -vēnī -ventum *vt* to encircle, surround; to go around to; to surround (*in a hostile manner*), invest; to distress, afflict, oppress; to circumvent, cheat, deceive
circumvert·ō -ĕre *vt* to turn (*something*) around; **circumverti** to turn oneself around, turn around; **circumverti axem** to turn around an axle
circumvest·ĭō -īre *vt* to clothe, wrap
circumvinc·ĭō -īre *vt* to bind, tie up
circumvīs·ō -ĕre *vt* to look around, glare around at
circumvolĭt·ō -āre *vt & vi* to fly around, dash about, rove around; to hover around
circumvŏl·ō -āre *vt* to fly around, hover about, flit about
circum·volvō -volvĕre — -volūtum *vt* to wind, roll around; **circumvolvi** or **se circumvolvere** (with *dat* or *acc*) to revolve around, wind oneself around
circ·us -ī *m* circle; racetrack; (astr) orbit
Circ·us Maxim·us (*genit:* **Circ·ī Maxim·ī**) *m* oldest racetrack in Rome, between the Palatine and Aventine, alleged to have been built by Tarquinius Priscus
cirrāt·us -a -um *adj* curly-haired
Cirrh·a -ae *f* town near Delphi, sacred to Apollo
cirr·us -ī *m* lock, curl; forelock; fringe
cis *prep* (with *acc*) on this side of; within
Cisalpīn·us -a -um *adj* Cisalpine, on the Roman side of the Alps
cis·ĭum -ĭī or **-ī** *n* light two-wheeled carriage
Cissē·is -ĭdis *f* Hecuba
Ciss·eus -ĕī *m* king of Thrace and father of Hecuba
cist·a -ae *f* box, chest
cistell·a -ae *f* small box
cistellātr·ix -īcis *f* female slave in charge of a money box
cistellŭl·a -ae *f* small box
cistern·a -ae *f* cistern, reservoir
cistophŏr·us -ī *m* Asiatic coin
cistŭl·a -ae *f* small box
citātim *adv* quickly, hastily

citāt·us -a -um *adj* quick, speedy, rapid; **citato equo** at full gallop
citeri·or -us *adj* on this side; nearer to earth, more down to earth, more mundane
Cithaer·ōn -ōnis *m* mountain range dividing Attica from Boeotia
cithăr·a -ae *f* zither, lyre, lute; art of playing the zither, lyre, or lute
citharist·a -ae *m* zither player, lute player
citharistri·a -ae *f* zither player, lutist (*female*)
cithariz·ō -āre *vt* to play the zither, lyre, or lute
citharoed·us -ī *m* singer accompanied by zither, lyre, or lute
citim·us -a -um *adj* nearest
citius *adv* sooner, rather; **dicto citius** no sooner said than done; **serius aut citius** sooner or later
cito *adv* quickly; soon
cit·ō -āre *vt* to excite, rouse; to call, summon, cite; to call to witness, appeal to
citrā *adv* on this side, on the near side; **citra cadere** to fall short; *prep* (with *acc*) on this side of, on the near side of; (of time) since, before; short of, less than
citrē·us -a -um *adj* of citrus wood
citrō *adv* to this side, this way; **ultro citro, ultro citroque,** or **ultro et citro** to and fro, up and down; mutually
citr·us -ī *f* citrous tree; citron tree
cit·us -a -um *pp* of **cieo**; *adj* quick, rapid, swift
cīvic·us -a -um *adj* civil; civic; **corona civica** oak-leaf crown awarded for saving a fellow soldier's life
cīvīl·is -e *adj* civil; civic; political; civilian; democratic; polite; **jus civile** rights as a citizen, civil rights; civil law; **ratio civilis** political science
cīvīlit·ās -ātis *f* politics; courtesy
cīvīliter *adv* like a citizen; as an ordinary citizen would; politely
cīv·is -is *m* or *f* citizen; fellow citizen; private citizen
cīvit·ās -ātis *f* citizenship; state, commonwealth, community
clād·ēs -is *f* disaster, ruin, damage, loss; (mil) defeat; (fig) scourge
clam *adv* secretly, privately, in secret; stealthily; *prep* (with *abl* or *acc*) without the knowledge of, unknown to; **clam habere aliquem** to keep someone in the dark; **neque clam me est** nor is it unknown to me
clāmāt·or -ōris *m* loudmouth
clāmitāti·ō -ōnis *f* bawling, noise, racket
clāmit·ō -āre *vt & vi* to cry out, yell
clām·ō -āre *vt* to call out, call upon; to proclaim, declare; to invoke; *vi* to cry out, yell, shout
clām·or -ōris *m* shout, cry, call; acclamation, applause; outcry, complaint; war cry; noise, sound, echo
clāmōs·us -a -um *adj* clamorous, noisy
clancŭlum *adv* secretly, privately; *prep* (with *acc*) unknown to
clandestīnō *adv* secretly
clandestīn·us -a -um *adj* clandestine, secret, hidden
clang·or -ōris *m* clang, din, shrill cry
clārē *adv* distinctly, clearly; brightly; with distinction
clār·ĕō -ēre *vi* to be clear, be bright, be distinct; to be evident; to be famous
clār·escō -escĕre -ŭī *vi* to become clear, become distinct, become bright; to become obvious; to become famous
clārigāti·ō -ōnis *f* demand for satisfaction, ultimatum; fine
clārig·ō -āre *vi* to give an ultimatum
clārisŏn·us -a -um *adj* clear-sounding, loud
clārit·ās -ātis *f* clarity, distinctness; clearness (*of style*); celebrity, distinction
clāritūd·ō -inis *f* brightness; distinction, fame
clār·ō -āre *vt* to make clear, explain, illustrate; to make famous; to illuminate
Clar·os -ī *f* town in Asia Minor near Colophon, famous for a temple and an oracle of Apollo
clār·us -a -um *adj* clear, distinct, bright; plain, manifest; famous, renowned; notorious
classiāri·us -a -um *adj* naval; *m pl* marines
classicŭl·a -ae *f* flotilla
classic·us -a -um *adj* first-class; naval; *m pl* marines; *n* battle signal; bugle
class·is -is *f* fleet; army; (pol) class
clāthr·ī or **clātr·ī -ōrum** *m pl* bars, cage, lattice
clātrāt·us -a -um *adj* barred
claud·ĕō -ēre or **claud·ō -ĕre** *vi* to limp; to falter, hesitate, waver
claudicāti·ō -ōnis *f* limping
claudic·ō -āre *vi* to be lame, limp; to waver; to be defective
Claud·ius -iī or **-ī** *m* Appius Claudius Caecus (*censor in* 312 B.C. *and builder of the Appian aqueduct and the Appian Way*); Roman emperor, 41-54 A.D.
claudō claudĕre clausī clausum *vt* to bolt, bar, shut, close; to bring to a close, conclude; to lock up, imprison; to blockade, hem in; to limit, restrict; to cut off, block; **agmen claudere** to bring up the rear; **numeris** or **pedibus claudere** to put into verse; **transitum claudere** to block traffic
claud·us -a -um *adj* lame, limping; crippled, imperfect, defective; wavering, untrustworthy
claustr·a -ōrum *n pl* lock, bar, bolt; gate, dam, dike; barrier, barricade; cage, den; fortress, defenses

clausŭl·a -ae *f* close, conclusion, end; (rhet) close of a period
claus·us -a -um *pp* of **claudo;** *n* enclosure
clāv·a -ae *f* cudgel, club, knotty branch
clāvār·ĭum -ĭī or **-ī** *n* allowance to soldiers for shoe nails
clāvicŭl·a -ae *f* tendril
clāvig·er -ĕra -ĕrum *adj* carrying a club; carrying keys; *m* club bearer (*Hercules*); key bearer (*Janus*)
clāv·is -is *f* key; **clavīs adimere uxori** to take the keys away from a wife, get a divorce
clāv·us -ī *m* nail; rudder, helm; purple stripe (*on a tunic, broad for senators, narrow for knights*); **clavus anni** beginning of the year; **clavus trabalis** spike; **trabali clavo figere** to nail down, clinch
Cleanth·ēs -is *m* Stoic philosopher, pupil of Zeno (300?-220 B.C.)
clēm·ens -entis *adj* gentle, mild, merciful, kind, compassionate; mitigated, qualified, toned down
clēmenter *adv* gently, mildly, mercifully, kindly, compassionately; by degrees, gradually
clēmentĭ·a -ae *f* mildness, mercy, clemency, compassion
Cle·ōn -ōnis *m* Athenian demagogue after death of Pericles in 429 B.C.
Cleopātr·a -ae *f* queen of Egypt (68-31 B.C.)
clep·ō -ĕre -sī -tum *vt* to steal
clepsȳdr·a -ae *f* water clock; (fig) time (*allotted to speakers*); **clepsydram dare** (with *dat*) to give (*someone*) the floor; **clepsydram petere** to ask for the floor
clept·a -ae *m* thief
cli·ens -entis *m* client, dependant (*freeman protected by a patron*); follower, retainer; companion, favorite; vassal
client·a -ae *f* client (*female*)
clientēl·a -ae *f* clientele; patronage, protection; *f pl* allies, dependants; clienteles
clientŭl·us -ī *m* poor client
clīnām·en -ĭnis *n* swerve
clīnāt·us -a -um *adj* bent, inclined
Clī·ō -ūs *f* Muse of history
clipeāt·us -a -um *adj* armed with a shield
clipĕ·um -ī *n* or **clipĕ·us -ī** *m* round bronze Roman shield; medallion; disc (*of sun*)
clītell·a -ae *f* saddlebag; *f pl* packsaddle
clitellārĭ·us -a -um *adj* carrying a packsaddle
clīvōs·us -a -um *adj* hilly, full of hills; steep
clīv·us -ī *m* slope, ascent, hill; slope, pitch; **adversus clivum** uphill; **primi clivi** foothills
Clīv·us Sac·er (*genit:* **Clīv·ī Sac·rī**) *m* part of the Via Sacra ascending the Capitoline Hill, also called Clivus Capitolinus
cloāc·a -ae *f* sewer, drain; **cloaca maxima** main sewer (*draining the valley between the Capitoline, Palatine, and Esquiline*)
Cloācīn·a -ae *f* Venus
Clōdĭ·a -ae *f* sister of Publius Clodius Pulcher and thought to be the person called Lesbia in Catullus' poems
Clōd·ĭus -ĭī or **-ī** *m* Publius Clodius Pulcher (*notorious enemy of Cicero who caused the latter to be exiled in* 58 B.C. *and was himself killed by Milo in* 52 B.C.)
Cloelĭ·a -ae *f* Roman girl who was given as hostage to Porsenna and escaped by swimming the Tiber
Clōth·ō (*genit* not in use; *acc:* **-ō**) *f* one of the three Fates
clu·ĕō -ēre or **clu·ĕor -ērī** *vi* to be named, be spoken of, be reputed, be famous
clūn·is -is *m* or *f* buttock
clūrīn·us -a -um *adj* of apes
Clūs·ĭum -ĭī or **-ī** *n* ancient Etruscan town
Clūs·ĭus -ĭī or **-ī** *m* Janus
Clymĕn·ē -ēs *f* wife of Merops and mother of Phaëthon
Clytaemnestr·a -ae *f* wife of Agamemnon, sister of Helen, Castor, and Pollux, and mother of Electra, Iphigenia, and Orestes, the latter of whom killed her
Cnid·us -ī *f* town in Caria, famous for worship of Venus
coacervātĭ·ō -ōnis *f* piling up, accumulation
coacerv·ō -āre *vt* to pile up, accumulate
coac·escō -escĕre -ŭī *vi* to become sour
coact·ō -āre *vt* to force
coact·or -ōris *m* collector (*of money*); **agminis coactores** rearguard elements
coactus *pp* of **cogo;** *adj* forced, unnatural, hypocritical; *n* felt
coact·us -ūs *m* coercion, compulsion
coaedific·ō -āre *vt* to build up (*an area*), fill with buildings; **loci coaedificati** built-up areas
coaequ·ō -āre *vt* to level off, make level, bring down to the same level
coagmentātĭ·ō -ōnis *f* combination, union
coagment·ō -āre *vt* to join, glue, cement
coagment·um -ī *n* joint
coāgŭl·um -ī *n* rennet
coal·escō -escĕre -ŭī -ĭtum *vi* to grow firm, take root; to increase, become strong, become established, thrive
coangust·ō -āre *vt* to contract, compress; to limit, restrict
coarct- = **coart-**
coargŭ·ō -ĕre -ī *vt* to prove conclusively, demonstrate; to refute, prove wrong or guilty; (with *genit* of the charge) to prove (*someone*) guilty of

coartāti·ō -ōnis *f* crowding together
coart·ō -āre *vt* to crowd together, confine; to shorten, abridge
coccināt·us -a -um *adj* clothed in scarlet
coccinĕ·us or **coccin·us -a -um** *adj* scarlet
cocc·um -ī *n* scarlet
coclĕ·a or **cochlĕ·a -ae** *f* snail
coclear·e -is *n* spoon
cocl·es -itis *m* person blind in one eye
Cocl·es -itis *m* Horatius Cocles (*famous for defending the Pons Sublicius against Porsenna's army*)
coctil·is -e *adj* baked; brick
coct·us -a -um *pp* of **coquo;** *adj* well-considered
Cōcȳt·us -ī *m* river of the lower world
cōdex see **caudex**
cōdicill·ī -ōrum *m pl* small trunks of trees, fire logs; note; petition; codicil
Codr·us -ī *m* last king of Athens, who sacrificed his life for an Athenian victory (1160-1132 B.C.)
coel- = **cael-**
co·ĕmō -emĕre -ēmī -emptum *vt* to buy up
coëmpti·ō -ōnis *f* marriage (*contracted by fictitious sale of contracting parties*); fictitious sale of an estate (*to relieve it of religious obligations*)
coëmptiōnāl·is -e *adj* of a fictitious marriage; used in a mock sale; worthless
coen- = **caen-**
co·ĕō -īre -īvī or **-iī -itum** *vt* **societatem coire** to enter an agreement, form an alliance; *vi* to come or go together; to meet, assemble; to be united, combine; to mate, copulate; to congeal, curdle; to agree; to conspire; to clash (*in combat*); (of wounds) to close, heal up
coep·iō -ĕre -ī -tum *vt & vi* to begin
coept·ō -āre *vt* to begin eagerly; to try; (with *inf*) to try to; *vi* to begin, make a beginning
coept·us -a -um *pp* of **coepio;** *n* beginning; undertaking
coept·us -ūs *m* beginning
coëpulōn·us -ī *m* dinner guest
coërc·ĕō -ēre -uī -itum *vt* to enclose, confine, hem in; to limit; to restrain, check, control
coërciti·ō -ōnis *f* coercion; right to punish
coët·us -ūs *m* coming together, meeting; crowd, company
Coe·us -ī *m* Titan, father of Latona
cōgitātē *adv* deliberately
cōgitāti·ō -ōnis *f* thinking, deliberating; reflection, meditation; thought, plan, design; reasoning power, imagination
cōgit·ō -āre *vt* to consider, ponder, reflect on; to imagine; (with *inf*) to intend to; *vi* to think, reflect, meditate
cōgitāt·us -a -um *adj* well-considered, deliberate; *n pl* thoughts, ideas
cognāti·ō -ōnis *f* relationship by birth; agreement, resemblance, affinity; relatives, family
cognāt·us -a -um *adj* related by birth; related, similar, connected; *mf* relative
cogniti·ō -ōnis *f* learning, acquiring knowledge; notion, idea, knowledge; recognition; (law) inquiry, investigation, trial; (with *genit*) knowledge of, acquaintance with
cognit·or -ōris *m* advocate, attorney; defender, protector; witness
cognitus *pp* of **cognosco;** *adj* acknowledged
cognōm·en -inis *n* surname, family name (*e.g., Caesar*); name
cognōment·um -ī *n* surname; name
cognōmināt·us -a -um *adj* synonymous
cognōmin·is -e *adj* like-named, of the same name
co·gnoscō -gnoscĕre -gnōvī -gnitum *vt* to become acquainted with, get to know, learn; to recognize, identify; to inquire into, investigate; to criticize, appreciate; to reconnoiter; **cognovisse** to know
cō·gō -gĕre -ēgī -actum *vt* to gather together, collect, convene; to thicken, condense, curdle; to pressure, bring pressure upon; to compel, force; to coax; to exact, extort; to infer, conclude; **agmen cogere** to bring up the rear
cohaer·ens -entis *adj* adjoining, continuous; consistent; harmonious
cohaerenti·a -ae *f* coherence, connection
co·haerĕō -haerēre -haesī -haesum *vi* to stick or cling together, cohere; to be consistent, be in agreement; (with *abl*) to consist of, be composed of; (with **cum** + *abl*) to be closely connected with, be in harmony with, be consistent with; **inter se cohaerere** to be consistent
co·haerescō -haerescĕre -haesī *vi* to cling together, cohere
cohēr·ēs -ēdis *m* or *f* coheir
cohib·ĕō -ēre -uī *vt* to hold together, hold close, confine; to hold back, repress, check, stop
cohonest·ō -āre *vt* to do honor to, celebrate
cohorr·escō -escĕre -uī *vi* to shiver all over
cohor·s -tis *f* yard (*esp. for cattle or chickens*); train, retinue, escort; (mil) cohort (*comprising 3 maniples or 6 centuries and forming one tenth of a legion*)
cohortāti·ō -ōnis *f* encouragement
cohorticŭl·a -ae *f* small cohort
cohort·or -ārī -ātus sum *vt* to encourage, cheer up, urge on
coïti·ō -ōnis *f* conspiracy, coalition; agreement
coït·us -ūs *m* meeting; sexual union
colăph·us -ī *m* slap, blow with a fist

Colch·is -idis *f* country on E. end of the Black Sea; Medea
cōlě·us -ī *m* sack, scrotum
cōl·is -is *m* stalk, cabbage
collabasc·ō -ĕre *vi* to waver, totter
collabefact·ō -āre *vt* to shake hard
collabe·fīō -fiĕrī -factus sum *vi* to collapse, be ruined, fall to pieces
col·lābor -lābī -lapsus sum *vi* to collapse, fall to pieces
collacerāt·us -a -um *adj* torn to pieces
collacrimāti·ō -ōnis *f* weeping
collacrim·ō -āre *vt* to cry bitterly over; *vi* to cry together
collactě·a -ae *f* foster sister
collār·e -is *n* collar
Collāti·a -ae *f* old town in Latium
Collātin·us -ī *m* husband of Lucretia
collāti·ō -ōnis *f* bringing together; contribution of money, collection; comparison, analogy; **signorum collatio** clash of troops
collāt·or -ōris *m* contributor
collātus *pp* of **confero**
collaudāti·ō -ōnis *f* warm praise
collaud·ō -āre *vt* to praise highly
collax·ō -āre *vt* to make loose
collect·a -ae *f* contribution of money
collectici·us -a -um *adj* hastily-gathered
collecti·ō -ōnis *f* gathering; summing up, recapitulation; inference
collectus *pp* of **colligo**
collect·us -ūs *m* collection
collēg·a -ae *m* colleague, partner (*in office*); associate, companion; fellow member (*of a club*)
collēg·ium -iī or **-ī** *n* association in office; official body, board, college, guild, company, corporation, society
collībert·us -ī *m* fellow freedman
collib·et or **collŭb·et -ēre -ŭit -itum** *v impers* it pleases
col·līdō -līdĕre -līsī -līsum *vt* to smash to pieces, shatter, crush; to cause to clash, set at variance
colligāti·ō -ōnis *f* binding together, connection
collig·ō -āre *vt* to tie together, connect; to unite, combine; to fasten, chain; to stop, hinder
col·ligō -ligĕre -lēgī -lectum *vt* to pick up, gather together, collect; to contract, compress, concentrate; to acquire gradually; to infer, conclude, gather; to assemble, bring together; to enumerate; to gather, repair; to check, control (*horse*); **animum colligere, mentem colligere,** or **se colligere** to collect or compose oneself, muster one's courage, rally, come to, come around; **vasa colligere** to pack up (*for the march*)
Collīn·a Port·a (*genit:* **Collīn·ae Port·ae**) *f* Colline Gate (*near the Quirinal Hill*)
collīně·ō -āre *vt* to aim straight; *vi* to hit the mark
col·linō -linĕre -lēvī -litum *vt* to smear; to defile
colliquefact·us -a -um *adj* dissolved, melted
coll·is -is *m* hill
collocāti·ō -ōnis *f* arrangement; giving in marriage
collŏc·ō -āre *vt* to place, put in order, arrange; to station, deploy; to give in marriage; to lodge, quarter; to occupy, employ; **se collocare** to settle, settle down (*in a place*)
collocuplēt·ō -āre *vt* to enrich, make quite rich
collocūti·ō -ōnis *f* conversation, conference
colloqu·ium -iī or **-ī** *n* conversation, conference
col·lŏquor -lŏquī -locūtus sum *vt* to talk to; *vi* to talk together, converse, hold a conference
collŭbet see **collibet**
collūc·ĕō -ēre *vi* to shine brightly, be entirely illuminated; (fig) to be resplendent
col·lūdō -lūdĕre -lūsī -lūsum *vi* to play together; to be in collusion; (with *dat*) to play with
coll·um -ī *n* neck
col·luō -luĕre -luī -lūtum *vt* to wash out, rinse, moisten; **ora colluere** to wet the mouth, quench the thirst
collūsi·ō -ōnis *f* collusion
collūs·or -ōris *m* playmate; fellow-gambler
collustr·ō -āre *vt* to light up; to survey, inspect; (in painting) to represent in bright colors
collutulent·ō -āre *vt* to soil, defile
colluvi·ō -ōnis or **colluvi·ēs** (*genit* not in use) *f* dregs, impurities, filth; rabble
collȳb·us -ī *m* conversion of currency; rate of exchange
collȳr·a -ae *f* noodles, macaroni
collȳr·ium -iī or **-ī** *n* eyewash
colō colĕre coluī cultum *vt* to till, cultivate, work; to live in (*a place*); to guard, protect; to honor, cherish, revere, worship; to adorn, dress; to practice, follow; to experience, live through, spend
colocāsi·a -ae *f* lotus, water lily
colōn·a -ae *f* peasant woman
colōni·a -ae *f* colony, settlement; colonists, settlers
colōnic·us -a -um *adj* colonial
colōn·us -ī *m* settler; farmer
col·or or **col·ōs -ōris** *m* color, hue, tint; external condition; complexion; tone, style; luster; grace; colorful pretext
colōrāt·us -a -um *adj* colored, tinted; healthily tanned
colōr·ō -āre *vt* to color, tan; (fig) to give a certain tone to
colossē·us -a -um *adj* colossal
coloss·us -ī *m* gigantic statue, colossus
colostr·a -ae *f* or **colostr·um -ī** *n* first milk after delivery, colostrum

colŭb·er -rī *m* snake, adder
colŭbr·a -ae *f* snake, adder (*female*)
colubrĭf·er -ĕra -ĕrum *adj* snaky
colubrīn·us -a -um *adj* snaky; wily, sly
cōl·um -ī *n* strainer
columb·a -ae *f* pigeon, dove (*female*)
columb·ar -āris *n* collar
columbār·ĭum -ĭī or **-ī** *n* pigeonhole; (fig) vault with niches for cinerary urns
columbīn·us -a -um *adj* of a dove or pigeon; *m* little dove
columb·us -ī *m* pigeon, dove
columell·a -ae *f* small column
colŭm·en -ĭnis *n* height, summit, peak; gable; pillar; head, leader; support, prop
column·a -ae *f* column, pillar, post; (fig) pillar, support; waterspout; **ad columnam** (i.e., **Maeniam**) **pervenire** or **ad columnam adhaerescere** to be brought to punishment (*because at the Columna Maenia in the Roman forum criminals and debtors were tried*); *f pl* display columns (*in bookshop*); bookshop
Column·a Maenĭ·a (*genit:* **Column·ae Maenĭ·ae**) *f* column in the Roman forum, possibly of the Basilica Porcia supporting a projecting balcony (**maenianum**), at which thieves and slaves were whipped and to which debtors were summoned for trial; whipping post
columnār·ĭum -ĭī or **-ī** *n* tax on house pillars
columnār·ĭus -ĭī or **-ī** *m* criminal debtor (*punished at the Columna Maenia*)
colurn·us -a -um *adj* made of hazel wood
col·us -ī *or* **-ūs** *m* or *f* distaff
cōlȳphĭ·a -ōrum *n pl* choice cuts of meat, loin cuts
com·a -ae *f* hair (*of the head*); mane (*of horse or lion*); fleece; foliage; grass; sunbeams
com·ans -antis *adj* hairy, long-haired; plumed (*helmet*); leafy; **comans stella** comet
cōmarch·us -ī *m* chief burgess
comāt·us -a -um *adj* long-haired; leafy
combĭb·ō -ĕre -ī *vt* to drink up; to absorb; to swallow, engulf; to repress, conceal (*tears*); to imbibe, acquire (*knowledge*)
combĭb·ō -ōnis *m* drinking partner
comb·ūrō -ūrĕre -ussī -ustum *vt* to burn up, consume; (fig) to ruin
com·ĕdō -edĕre (or **-esse**) **-ēdī -ēsum** (or **-estum**) *vt* to eat up, consume, devour; to waste, squander, dissipate, spend; **se comedere** to pine away
com·es -ĭtis *m* or *f* companion, fellow traveler; associate, comrade; attendant, retainer, dependant; concomitant, consequence
comēt·ēs -ae *m* comet
cōmĭcē *adv* like a comedy
cōmĭc·us -a -um *adj* of comedy, comic; **comicum aurum** stage money; *m* actor (*of comedy*); playwright (*of comedy*)
cōm·is -e *adj* courteous, polite; kind, friendly; (with *dat* or with **erga** or **in** + *acc*) friendly toward
cōmissābund·us -a -um *adj* parading in a riotous bacchanalian procession; carousing
cōmissātĭ·ō -ōnis *f* riotous bacchanalian procession; wild drinking party
cōmissāt·or -ōris *m* drinking partner, reveler, guzzler
cōmiss·or or **cōmīs·or -ārī -ātus sum** *vi* to join in a bacchanalian procession; to revel, guzzle
cōmĭt·ās -ātis *f* politeness, courteousness; kindness, friendliness
comitāt·us -ūs *m* escort, retinue; imperial retinue, court; company (*traveling together*), caravan
cōmĭter *adv* politely, courteously; kindly
comitĭ·a -ōrum *n pl* comitia, popular assembly; elections; **comitia consularia** or **comitia consulum** election of consuls; **comitia praetoria** election of praetors
comitiāl·is -e *adj* of the assembly; of the elections, election
comitiāt·us -ūs *m* assembly of the people in the comitia
comit·ĭum -ĭī or **-ī** *n* comitium, assembly place
comĭt·ō -āre or **comĭt·or -ārī -ātus sum** *vt* to accompany, attend, follow
commacŭl·ō -āre *vt* to spot, stain; to defile
commanipulār·is -is *m* comrade in the same brigade
commarīt·us -ī *m* fellow husband
commeāt·us -ūs *m* passage, thoroughfare; leave of absence, furlough; transport, passage, convoy; (mil) lines of communication; (mil) supplies; **in commeatu esse** to be on a furlough
commedĭt·or -ārī -ātus sum *vt* to practice; to imitate
commemĭn·ī -isse *vt & vi* to remember well
commemorābĭl·is -e *adj* memorable, worth mentioning
commemorātĭ·ō -ōnis *f* recollection, remembrance; mentioning, reminding
commemŏr·ō -āre *vt* to keep in mind, remember; to bring up (*in conversation*), to mention, recount, relate; *vi* (with **de** + *abl*) to be mindful of
commendābĭl·is -e *adj* commendable, praiseworthy
commendātĭcĭ·us -a -um *adj* of recommendation, of introduction; **litterae commendaticiae** letter of introduction or of recommendation

commendāti·ō -ōnis *f* recommendation, recommending; commendation, praise; excellence, worth
commendāt·or -ōris *m* backer, supporter
commendātr·ix -īcis *f* backer, supporter (*female*)
commendāt·us -a -um *adj* commended, recommended, acceptable, approved
commend·ō -āre *vt* to entrust, commit; to recommend; to render acceptable
commentāriŏl·um -ī *n* short treatise
commentār·ium -iī or **-ī** *n* or **commentār·ius -iī** or **-ī** *m* notebook, journal, diary, notes, memorandum; (law) brief; *pl* memoirs
commentāti·ō -ōnis *f* careful study, deep reflection; preparation; essay, treatise
commentīci·us -a -um *adj* thought out; invented, fictitious, imaginary; ideal; forged, false; legendary
comment·or -ārī -ātus sum *vt* to think over, consider well, study; to invent, contrive, make up; to prepare, produce (*writings*); to discuss, write about; to imitate, adopt the language of; *vi* to meditate, deliberate, reflect; to experiment in speaking, attempt to speak
comment·or -ōris *m* inventor
comment·us -a -um *pp* of **comminiscor;** *adj* fictitious, feigned, invented, pretended; *n* invention, fiction, fabrication; device, contrivance
commĕ·ō -āre *vi* to come and go; to go back and forth; to travel repeatedly; to make frequent visits
commerc·ium -iī or **-ī** *n* trade, commerce; right to trade; dealings, business; communication, correspondence; **belli commercia** ransom
commerc·or -ārī *vt* to deal in, purchase
commer·ĕo -ēre -uī -itum or **commer·ĕor -ērī -itus sum** *vt* to earn, merit, deserve fully; to be guilty of
com·mētior -mētīrī -mensus sum *vt* to measure; (with **cum** + *abl*) to measure (*something*) in terms of
commēt·ō -āre *vi* to go often
commigr·ō -āre *vi* to move, migrate
commīlit·ium -iī *or* **-ī** *n* comradeship, companionship, fellowship
commīlit·ō -ōnis *m* fellow soldier, army buddy
commināti·ō -ōnis *f* threatening, menacing; *f pl* violent threats
com·mingō -mingĕre -minxī -mictum *vt* to urinate on; to wet (*bed*); to defile, pollute; **commictum caenum** (term of reproach) dirty skunk
com·miniscor -miniscī -mentus sum *vt* to contrive, invent, devise
commīn·or -ārī -ātus sum *vt* to threaten violently
commin·ŭō -uĕre -uī -ūtum *vt* to lessen considerably, diminish; to break up, shatter; to weaken, impair; to humble, crush, humiliate
comminus *adv* hand to hand, at close quarters; near at hand, near; **comminus conferre signa** to engage in hand-to-hand fighting
com·miscĕō -miscēre -miscuī -mixtum *vt* to mix together, mix up, join together; to unite, bring together, mingle
commiserāti·ō -ōnis *f* pitying; (rhet) appeal to compassion
commideresc·ō -ĕre *vi* (with *genit*) to feel pity for; *v impers* (with *genit*) **me commiserescit ejus** I pity him
commisĕr·or -ārī -ātus sum *vt* to feel sympathy for; *vi* (rhet) to try to evoke sympathy
commissi·ō -ōnis *f* beginning (*of fight, game, etc.*)
commissūr·a -ae *f* connection; joint
commiss·us -a -um *pp* of **committo;** *n* offense, crime; secret; undertaking
commītig·ō -āre *vt* to soften up
com·mittō -mittĕre -mīsī -missum *vt* to connect, unite; to match (*for a fight, etc.*); to start, commence; to undertake; to commit, perpetrate; to entrust, commit; to engage in (*battle*); to incur (*penalty*); **se committere** (with *dat* or **in** + *acc*) to venture into
commodit·ās -ātis *f* proportion, symmetry; aptness of expression; convenience, comfort; right time; pleasantness (*of personality*); courtesy, kindness
commŏd·ō -āre *vt* to adjust, adapt; to bestow, supply, lend, give; *vi* to be obliging; (with *dat*) to adapt oneself to, be obliging to
commodŭlē or **commodŭlum** *adv* nicely, conveniently
commŏdum *adv* at a good time, in the nick of time; **commodum cum** just at the time when
commŏd·us -a -um *adj* adapted, suitable, fit, convenient; opportune (*time*); convenient, comfortable, advantageous; agreeable, obliging, pleasant (*person*); **quod commodum est** just as you please; *n* convenience, opportunity; profit, advantage; privilege, favor; loan; pay, reward; **commodo tuo** at your convenience
commōl·ior -īrī -ītus sum *vt* to set in motion
commone·faciō -facĕre -fēcī -factum *vt* to recall, call to mind; (with *acc* of person and *genit* of thing) to remind (*someone*) of
common·ĕō -ēre -uī -itum *vt* to remind, warn; (with *genit* or **de** + *abl*) to remind (*someone*) of
commonstr·ō -āre *vt* to point out clearly
commorāti·ō -ōnis *f* delaying, stay-

ing; residence, sojourn; (rhet) dwelling (*on some point*)
com·morior -mŏrī -mortŭus sum *vi* (with *dat* or with **cum** + *abl*) to die with, die at the same time as
commŏr·or -ārī -ātus sum *vt* to stop, detain; *vi* to linger, stay, stop off; (with **apud** + *acc*) to stay at the house of; **in sententia commorari** to stick to an opinion
commōtĭ·ō -ōnis *f* commotion; **animi commotio** excitement
commōtiuncŭl·a -ae *f* minor inconvenience
commōt·us -a -um *adj* excited, angry; deranged, insane; impassioned, lively (*style*)
com·movĕō -movēre -mōvī -mōtum *vt* to stir up, agitate, shake; to disturb, unsettle, disquiet, excite, shake up; to arouse, provoke; to stir up, generate, produce; to start, introduce (*novelties*); to displace, dislodge (*enemy*); to refute
commūn·e -is *n* community, state; **in commune** for general use, for all; in general
commūnicātĭ·ō -ōnis *f* imparting, communicating
commūnĭc·ō -āre or **commūnĭc·or -ārī** *vt* to make common; to communicate, impart, share; to share in, take part in; to unite, connect, join
commūnĭ·ō -ōnis *f* sharing in common
commūn·ĭō -īre -īvī or **-ĭī -ītum** *vt* to fortify, strengthen, barricade
commūn·is -e *adj* common, public, universal, general; familiar; courteous, affable; democratic; **loca communia** public places; **loci communes** commonplaces, general topics; **sensus communis** common sense; *n* see **commune**
commūnĭter *adv* in common, together
commūnītĭ·ō -ōnis *f* road building; (rhet) introduction
commurmŭr·ō -āre or **commurmŭr·or -ārī** *vi* to murmur, grumble
commūtābĭl·is -e *adj* changeable, subject to change; interchangeable
commūtātĭ·ō -ōnis *f* changing, change, alteration
commūtāt·us -ūs *m* change, alteration
commūt·ō -āre *vt* to change, alter; to interchange, exchange; (with *abl* or **cum** + *abl*) to exchange (*something*) for
cōm·ō -ĕre -psī -ptum *vt* to comb, arrange, braid; to adorn, deck out
cōmoedĭ·a -ae *f* comedy
cōmoedĭcē *adv* as in comedy
cōmoed·us -ī *m* comic actor
comōs·us -a -um *adj* with long hair, hairy; leafy
compact·us -a -um *pp* of **compingo**; *adj* compact, well built; *n* agreement
compāg·ēs -is *f* joining together, joint, structure, framework
compāg·ō -ĭnis *f* connection
comp·ar -ăris *adj* equal, on an equal level; (with *dat*) matching
comp·ar -ăris *m* or *f* comrade; playmate; perfect match; spouse
comparābĭl·is -e *adj* comparable
comparātĭ·ō -ōnis *f* comparison; arrangement; acquisition, preparation, provision; relative position (*of planets*)
comparātīv·us -a -um *adj* comparative
compār·ĕō -ēre -ŭī *vi* to be visible, be plain, be evident, appear; to be at hand, be present
compăr·ō -āre *vt* to put together, get together, provide; to prepare, arrange; to match; to compare; to procure, get, obtain, collect; to appoint, establish, constitute; **se comparare** (with **ad** or **in** + *acc*) to prepare oneself for, get ready for
comp·ascō -ascĕre — -astum *vt & vi* to feed together
compascŭ·us -a -um *adj* of public grazing
compec·iscor -iscī -tus sum *vi* to come to an agreement
compect·us -a -um *adj* in agreement, agreed; *n* agreement; **compecto** by agreement, according to the agreement
comped·ĭō -īre — -ītum *vt* to shackle
compellātĭ·ō -ōnis *f* rebuke, reprimand
compell·ō -āre *vt* to summon, call; to call to account, bring to book; to reproach; (law) to arraign
com·pellō -pellĕre -pŭlī -pulsum *vt* to drive together; to crowd, concentrate; to compel, force, urge, drive on
compendiārĭ·us -a -um *adj* short, abridged; **via compendiaria** shortcut
compend·ĭum -ĭī or **-ī** *n* careful weighing; saving (*of money*); profit; shortening, abridging; shortcut; **compendi facere** to save; **compendi fieri** to be brief; **suo privato compendio servire** to serve one's own private interests
compensātĭ·ō -ōnis *f* compensation, recompense
compens·ō -āre *vt* to compensate, make up for
com·percō -percĕre -persī *vt* to save, hoard up
comperendinātĭ·ō -ōnis *f* or **comperendināt·us -ūs** *m* (law) two-day adjournment
comperendĭn·ō -āre *vt* to adjourn (*court*) for two days; to put off (*defendant*) for two days
comper·ĭō -īre -ī -tum or **comper·ĭor -īrī -tus sum** *vt* to find out, ascertain, learn; **compertum habeo** or **compertum mihi est**

I have ascertained, I know for certain

compert·us -a -um *adj* discovered, well authenticated; (with *genit*) convicted of

comp·ēs -ĕdis *f* shackle (*for the feet*); (fig) bond

compesc·ō -ĕre -ŭī *vt* to confine, restrain, suppress, check, chain down

competīt·or -ōris *m* competitor, rival

competītr·ix -īcis *f* competitor, rival (*female*)

compĕt·ō -ĕre -īvī or **-iī -ītum** *vi* to coincide, come together, meet; to be adequate, be suitable; (with **ad** + *acc*) to be capable of

compīlāti·ō -ōnis *f* pillaging, plundering; (contemptuously said of a collection of documents) compilation

compīl·ō -āre *vt* to pillage, plunder

com·pingō -pingĕre -pēgī -pactum *vt* to put together, frame, compose; to confine, lock up, put (*in jail*)

compitāl·ia -ium or **-iōrum** *n pl* festival celebrated annually at the crossroads in honor of the Lares of the crossroads on a day appointed by the praetor

compitālici·us -a -um *adj* of the crossroads

compitāl·is -e *adj* of the crossroads

compit·um -ī *n* crossroads, intersection

complac·ĕō -ēre -ŭī or **-itus sum** *vi* (with *dat*) to be quite pleasing to, suit just fine

complān·ō -āre *vt* to make even or level; to raze to the ground, pull down

com·plector -plectī -plexus sum *vt* to embrace, clasp; to comprise; (of writings) to include; to grasp, understand; to display affection for, display esteem for; to enclose (*an area*); to seize, take possession of

complēment·um -ī *n* complement

compl·ĕō -ēre -ēvī -ētum *vt* to fill, fill up; (mil) to bring (*legion, etc.*) to full strength; (mil) to man; to complete; to impregnate; to fill with sound, make resound; to supply fully, furnish

complēt·us -a -um *adj* complete; perfect

complexi·ō -ōnis *f* combination, connection; conclusion in a syllogism; dilemma; (rhet) period

complex·us -ūs *m* embrace; (fig) love, affection; close combat; **in complexum alicujus venire** to come to close grips with someone

complicāt·us -a -um *adj* complicated, involved

complic·ō -āre *vt* to fold up

complōrāti·ō -ōnis *f* or **complōrāt·us -ūs** *m* groaning, lamentation, wailing

complōr·ō -āre *vt* to mourn for

complūr·ēs -ium *adj* several; a good many

complūriens or **complūriēs** *adv* several times, a good many times

compluscŭl·ī -ae -a *adj* a fair number of

compluv·ium -iī or **-ī** *n* rain trap (*quadrangular open space in middle of Roman house towards which the roof sloped so as to direct the rain into a basin, called impluvium, built into the floor*)

com·pōnō -pōnĕre -posŭī -positum *vt* to put together, join; to construct, build; to compose, write; to arrange, settle, agree upon, fix, set; to match, pair, couple; to compare, contrast; to put away; take down, lay aside; to lay out, bury (*the dead*); to compose, pacify, allay, calm, appease, quiet, reconcile; to feign, invent, concoct, contrive

comport·ō -āre *vt* to carry together, bring in, collect, gather, accumulate

comp·os -ŏtis *adj* (with *genit* or *abl*) in possession of, master of, having control over; having a share in, participating in; **compos animi** or **compos mentis** sane; **compos sui** self-controlled; **compos voti** having one's prayer answered

composĭtē *adv* in an orderly manner, orderly, regularly; **composite dicere** to speak logically

compositi·ō -ōnis *f* putting together, connecting, arranging, composition; matching (*of gladiators, etc.*); reconciliation (*of friends*); orderly arrangement (*of words*)

composit·or -ōris *m* composer, author

compositūr·a -ae *f* connection

composit·us -a -um *pp* of **compono**; *adj* compound (*words, etc.*); prepared, well arranged, orderly; made-up, feigned, false; adapted; composed, calm, settled; *n* agreement, compact; **composito** or **ex composito** by agreement, as agreed, as had been arranged

compotāti·ō -ōnis *f* drinking party

compot·iō -īre -īvī -ītum *vt* (with *acc* of person and *abl* of thing) to make (*someone*) master of, put (*someone*) in possession of

compōt·or -ōris *m* drinking partner

compōtr·ix -īcis *f* drinking partner (*female*)

comprans·or -ōris *m* dinner companion, fellow guest

comprecāti·ō -ōnis *f* public supplication

comprĕc·or -ārī -ātus sum *vt* to pray earnestly to, implore, supplicate

compre·hendō -hendĕre -hendī -hensum or **compren·dō -dĕre -dī -sum** *vt* to bind together, unite; to take hold of, grasp, seize, catch, apprehend; to attack, seize, arrest, capture, apprehend; to detect, discover; to occupy (*places*); to grasp, perceive, comprehend, take in; to

express, describe, narrate, recount; **ignem comprehendere** to catch fire; **memoriā comprehendere** to remember; **numero comprehendere** to enumerate, count
comprehensibil·is -e *adj* comprehensible, conceivable, intelligible
comprehensī·ō -ōnis *f* seizing, laying hold of; arrest; comprehension, perception; combining; (rhet) period
comprendō see **comprehendo**
compressi·ō -ōnis *f* pressing closely; embrace; (rhet) compression
compress·us -ūs *m* compression; embrace
com·prīmō -priměre -pressī -pressum *vt* to press together, bring together, compress, close; to embrace; to check, curb, restrain; to keep back, suppress, withhold, conceal; **animam comprimere** to hold the breath; **compressis manibus sedere** to sit on folded hands, to not lift a hand; **ordines comprimere** to close ranks
comprobāti·ō -ōnis *f* approbation, approval
comprobāt·or -ōris *m* enthusiastic backer
comprŏb·ō -āre *vt* to approve, sanction, acknowledge; to prove, establish, make good, confirm, verify
comprōmiss·um -ī *n* mutual agreement to abide by arbiter's decision
comprō-mittō -mittěre -mīsī -missum *vi* to agree to abide by an arbiter's decision
compt·us -a -um *pp* of **como**; *adj* neat, elegant
compt·us -ūs *m* hairdo
com·pungō -pungěre -punxī -punctum *vt* to puncture, prick; to tattoo; to prod
compŭt·ō -āre *vt* to compute, count
computresc·ō -ěre *vi* to become putrid, rot
Cōm·um -ī *n* Como (*town N. of the Po and birthplace of Pliny the Younger*)
cōnām·en -inis *n* effort, struggle; support, prop; **conamen mortis** attempt at suicide
cōnāt·um -ī *n* effort, exertion; attempt, undertaking, venture
cōnāt·us -ūs *m* effort; endeavor; impulse, inclination, tendency; undertaking
concăc·ō -āre *vt* to defile with excrement
concaed·ēs -ium *f pl* log barricade
concale·faciō -facěre -fēcī -factum *vt* to warm up
concall·escō -escěre -ŭī *vi* to grow hard; to become insensible; to become shrewd
concastīg·ō -āre *vt* to punish severely
concăv·ō -āre *vt* to curve, bend
concăv·us -a -um *adj* concave, hollow; curved, arched, bent, vaulted; deep (*valley*)
con·cēdō -cēděre -cessī -cessum *vt* to give up, relinquish, cede; to pardon, overlook; to allow, grant; *vi* to go away, give way, depart, withdraw, retire; (with *dat*) **a** to yield to, submit to, give way to, succumb to; **b** to submit to, comply with; **c** to make allowance for, pardon; **d** to be inferior to; (with **in** + *acc*) to pass over to, be merged in; **fato concedere, naturae concedere,** or **vitā concedere** to die
concelěbr·ō -āre *vt* to frequent, fill; to pursue (*studies*); to fill with life, enliven; to celebrate; to make widely known, proclaim, publish
concēnāti·ō -ōnis *f* dining together
concenti·ō -ōnis *f* singing together, harmony
concenturī·ō -āre *vt* to marshal by the hundreds; (with *dat*) to bring (*fear*) to
concent·us -ūs *m* concert, symphony; harmony; choir; concord, agreement, harmony
concepti·ō -ōnis *f* conception (*becoming pregnant*); (law) composing legal formulas
conceptīv·us -a -um *adj* movable (*holidays*)
concept·us -ūs *m* conception (*becoming pregnant*), pregnancy
concerp·ō -ěre -sī -tum *vt* to tear up, tear to shreds; (fig) to cut up, abuse, revile
concertāti·ō -ōnis *f* controversy, dispute
concertāt·or -ōris *m* rival
concertātōri·us -a -um *adj* controversial
concert·ō -āre *vi* to fight it out; to quarrel, debate
concessi·ō -ōnis *f* concession; admission (*of guilt with plea for mercy*)
concess·ō -āre *vt* (with *inf*) to stop (*doing something*)
concess·us -a -um *pp* of **concedo**; *n* concession (*thing allowed*)
concess·us -ūs *m* permission, leave
conch·a -ae *f* clam, oyster, mussel, murex; clam shell, oyster shell, mussel shell; pearl; purple dye; trumpet (*of Triton*); vessel (*containing ointments, etc.*); vulva
conch·is -is *f* bean
conchīt·a -ae *m* clam digger, conch digger
conchÿliāt·us -a -um *adj* purple
conchÿl·ium -iī or **-ī** *n* shellfish, clam, oyster; murex; purple dye, purple; purple garments
concĭd·ō -ěre -ī *vi* to collapse; to fall (*in battle*); (fig) to decline, fail, fall, decay, perish, go to ruin; (of winds) to subside
con·cīdō -cīděre -cīdī -cīsum *vt* to cut up, cut to pieces, kill; to beat severely; (fig) to crush (*with arguments*); (rhet) to chop up (*sentences*)
con·ciěō -ciēre -cīvī -cĭtum or **-cĭō**

-cīre -cīvī -cītum *vt* to assemble; to shake, stir up; (fig) to rouse, stir up, provoke
conciliābŭl·um -ī *n* public meeting place
conciliāti·ō -ōnis *f* union, bond; conciliating, winning over; inclination, bent, desire
conciliāt·or -ōris *m* mediator, promoter
conciliātrīcŭl·a -ae *f* procuress, madame
conciliātr·ix -īcis *f* mediator, promoter, match maker (*female*)
conciliāt·us -a -um *adj* (with **ad** + *acc*) endeared to, favorable to
conciliāt·us -ūs *m* union, connection, combination
concili·ō -āre *vt* to bring together, unite, connect; to unite (*in feeling*), make friendly, win over; to bring about (*by mediation*); to acquire, win
concil·ium -iī or **-ī** *n* gathering, meeting, assembly; council; combination, union
concinnē *adv* nicely, elegantly
concinnit·ās -ātis or **concinnitūd·ō -inis** *f* finish, elegance, symmetry (*of style*)
concinn·ō -āre *vt* to make symmetrical, get right, adjust; to bring about, produce, cause; to make (*e.g., insane*)
concinn·us -a -um *adj* symmetrical; neat, elegant; courteous, agreeable, nice; polished (*style*)
concin·ō -ĕre -ŭī *vt* to sing, celebrate; to prophesy; *vi* to sing or play together, harmonize; (fig) to agree, harmonize
conciō see **concieo**
conciō see **contio**
concipīl·ō -āre *vt* to carry off
con·cipiō -cipĕre -cēpī -ceptum *vt* to take hold of, take up, take, receive; to take in, absorb; to imagine, conceive, think; to understand, comprehend, perceive; to catch (*fire*); to entertain (*hope*); to draw up in formal language; to announce in formal language
concīsē *adv* concisely
concīsi·ō -ōnis *f* (rhet) dividing a sentence into short phrases
concīs·us -a -um *pp* of **concido**; *adj* cut up, short, concise
concitātē *adv* vigorously, vividly
concitāti·ō -ōnis *f* rapid movement; excitement; sedition, agitation
concitāt·or -ōris *m* instigator, ringleader; rabble-rouser
concitāt·us -a -um *adj* rapid, swift; excited
concit·ō -āre *vt* to stir up, rouse, urge; to cause, occasion
concit·or -ōris *m* instigator, ringleader; rabble-rouser
conclāmāti·ō -ōnis *f* loud shouting, yell; acclamation
conclāmit·ō -āre *vi* to keep on shouting, keep on yelling
conclām·ō -āre *vt* to shout, yell; to call to (*for help*); to call repeatedly by name, bewail (*the dead*); to exclaim; **jam conclamatum est** all's lost; **vasa conclamare** to give the signal to pack up (*for the march*); *vi* to shout, yell, cry out; **ad arma conclamare** to sound the alarm (*for an attack*)
conclāv·e -is *n* room; bedroom; dining room; cage, stall, coop
con·clūdō -clūdĕre -clūsī -clūsum *vt* to shut up, enclose; to include, comprise; to round off, conclude (*letter, speech*); to end rhythmically; to deduce, infer, conclude
conclūsē *adv* (rhet) in rhythmical cadence
conclūsi·ō -ōnis *f* blockade; end, conclusion; conclusion (*of a speech*), peroration; conclusion (*of syllogism*); (rhet) period
conclūsiuncŭl·a -ae *f* false conclusion
conclūs·us -a -um *pp* of **concludo**; *adj* confined; *n* logical conclusion
concŏl·or -ōris *adj* of the same color
concomitāt·us -a -um *adj* escorted
con·cŏquō -coquĕre -coxī -coctum *vt* to cook thoroughly; to boil down; to digest; to stomach, put up with; to cook up, concoct (*plans*); to weigh seriously, reflect upon, consider well; to prepare, ripen
concordi·a -ae *f* concord, harmony, good rapport; union
concorditer *adv* harmoniously
concord·ō -āre *vi* to be of one mind, be in harmony, agree
concor·s -dis *adj* of the same mind, concordant, agreeing, harmonious
concrēbr·escō -escĕre -ŭī *vi* to grow strong
concrēd·ō -ĕre -idī -itum *vt* to entrust, commit, consign
concrĕm·ō -āre *vt* to burn to ashes, burn up
concrĕp·ō -āre -ŭī -itum *vi* to rattle, creak, grate, clash, sound, make noise; **digitis concrepare** to snap the fingers
con·crescō -crescĕre -crēvī -crētum *vi* to grow together; to congeal, curdle, clot; to stiffen; to take shape, grow, increase
concrēti·ō -ōnis *f* condensing, congealing; matter, substance
concrēt·us -a -um *pp* of **concresco**; *adj* grown together, compounded; condensed, congealed, curdled, thick, stiff, hard; frozen; inveterate; dim (*light*); *n* hardness, solid matter
concrīmin·or -ārī *vi* to make bitter charges
concruci·ō -āre *vt* to torture
concubīn·a -ae *f* concubine
concubīnāt·us -ūs *m* concubinage, free love
concubīn·us -ī *m* adulterer
concubit·us -ūs *m* reclining together (*at table*); sexual intercourse
concubi·us -a -um *adj* used only in

the expression **concubiā nocte** early in the night, at bedtime; *n* bedtime
conculc·ō -āre *vt* to trample under foot, despise, treat with contempt
con·cumbō -cumbĕre -cubŭī -cubitum *vi* to lie together; (with **cum** + *abl*) to sleep with, have intercourse with
concup·iscō -iscĕre -īvī -ītum *vt* to long for, covet; to aspire to, strive after
concūr·ō -āre *vt* to take good care of
con·currō -currĕre -currī or **-cucurrī -cursum** *vi* to run together, flock together; to unite; to strike one another, crash; (mil) to clash, engage in combat; to happen at the same time, coincide; (with **ad** + *acc*) to have recourse to, run for help to; **concurritur** the armies meet, there is a clash
concursāti·ō -ōnis *f* running together; rushing about; (mil) skirmishing
concursāt·or -ōris *m* (mil) skirmisher
concursī·ō -ōnis *f* meeting, concurrence; (rhet) repetition for emphasis
concurs·ō -āre *vt* to run around to; **domos concursare** to run from house to house; *vi* to rush about excitedly, dash up and down; (mil) to skirmish
concurs·us -ūs *m* running together, concourse, assembly; union, combination; collision; (mil) rush, charge, clash
concuss·us -ūs *m* shaking, concussion
con·cutiō -cutĕre -cussī -cussum *vt* to strike together, bang together; to convulse; to strike, shake, shatter; to shock; to wave (*the hand*); to brandish (*weapon*); to shake out, ransack, examine; to shake, alarm, trouble, terrify
condal·ium -iī or **-ī** *n* slave's ring
condĕc·et -ēre *v impers* it befits, it becomes
condecŏr·ō -āre *vt* to grace, honor, adorn
condemnāt·or -ōris *m* accuser, prosecutor
condemn·ō -āre *vt* to condemn, convict, find guilty, sentence, doom; to blame, condemn; to prosecute successfully, bring a conviction against
condens·ō -āre *vt* to press close together, condense
condens·us -a -um *adj* close together, thick, crowded
condici·ō -ōnis *f* arrangement, settlement, agreement; stipulation, terms, condition; state, situation; circumstances, rank, place; marriage contract, marriage; **ea condicione ut** on condition that; **sub condicione** conditionally; **vitae condicio** way of life, living conditions
con·dīcō -dīcĕre -dixī -dictum *vt* to talk over, arrange together; to promise; **cenam condicere** (with *dat*) or **ad cenam condicere** (with *dat*) to make a dinner engagement with (*someone*)
condignē *adv* very worthily
condign·us -a -um *adj* fully deserving; (with *abl*) fully worthy of
condīment·um -ī *n* seasoning, spice
cond·iō -īre -īvī or **-iī -ītum** *vt* to preserve, pickle (*fruits, vegetables*); to season; to embalm (*the dead*); (fig) to spice, give spice to
condiscipulāt·us -ūs *m* companionship at school
condiscipŭl·us -ī *m* schoolmate, school companion, fellow student
con·discō -discĕre -didicī *vt* to learn by heart
conditiō see **condicio**
conditī·ō -ōnis *f* preserving (*of fruits, etc.*); seasoning, spicing
condit·or -ōris *m* founder, builder; author, composer
conditōr·ium -iī or **-ī** *n* coffin, cinerary urn; tomb
condit·us -a -um *pp* of **condio**; *adj* seasoned, spicy; polished (*style*)
con·dō -dĕre -didī -ditum *vt* to build, found; to write, compose (*poetry*); to establish (*an institution*); to store, treasure, hoard; to preserve, pickle; to bury; to conceal, hide, suppress; to shut (*eyes*); to sheathe (*sword*); to place (*soldiers*) in ambush; to plunge, bury (*sword*); to imprison; to memorize; to store up
condoce·faciō -facĕre -fēcī -factum *vt* to train well
condoc·ĕō -ēre -ŭī -tum *vt* to teach, instruct thoroughly
condol·escō -escĕre -ŭī *vi* to begin to ache, get very sore
condōnāti·ō -ōnis *f* donating, donation
condōn·ō -āre *vt* to give, present, deliver, abandon, surrender; to adjudge; (with double *acc*) to make (*someone*) a present of; (with *acc* of thing and *dat* of person) to forgive, pardon (*someone an offense*); **condonare alicui pecunias creditas** to remit someone's debt
condorm·iō -īre *vi* to sleep soundly
condorm·iscō -iscĕre -īvī *vi* to fall sound asleep
condūcibĭl·is -e *adj* advantageous, profitable; (with **ad** + *acc*) just right for
con·dūcō -dūcĕre -duxī -ductum *vt* to draw together, collect, assemble; to connect, unite; to hire, rent, borrow; to bribe; to employ; to induce; to contract for; *vi* to be of use; (with *dat*) to be useful to, profitable to; (with **ad** or **in** + *acc*) to be conducive to
conductīci·us -a -um *adj* hired, mercenary
conducti·ō -ōnis *f* bringing together; recapitulation; hiring, renting

conduct·or -ōris *m* contractor; lessee, tenant
conduct·us -a -um *pp* of **conduco;** *m pl* hired men; (mil) mercenaries; *n* rented apartment, rented house
conduplicātī·ō -ōnis *f* doubling; (humorously) embrace
conduplic·ō -āre *vt* to double; **corpora conduplicare** (humorously) to embrace
condūr·ō -āre *vt* to harden, make very hard
cond·us -ī *m* storeroom manager
cō·nectō -nectĕre -nexŭī -nexum *vt* to tie; to connect, join, link; to state as a conclusion; (with *dat*) to implicate (*someone or something*) in; (with *dat* or **cum** + *abl*) to join (*something*) to, connect (*something*) with
cōnexī·ō -ōnis *f* logical conclusion
cōnex·us -a -um *pp* of **conecto;** *adj* connected, joined; **per affinitatem conexus** (with *dat*) related by marriage to; *n* necessary inference, logical connection, necessary consequence
cōnex·us -ūs *m* combination
confābŭl·or -ārī -ātus sum *vt* to discuss; *vi* to converse, have a talk
confarreātī·ō -ōnis *f* solemn marriage ceremony in the presence of the Pontifex Maximus and ten witnesses
confarrĕ·ō -āre *vt* to marry with solemn rites
confātāl·is -e *adj* bound by the same fate
confectī·ō -ōnis *f* completion, successful completion; chewing, mastication
confect·or -ōris *m* finisher, executor; destroyer, consumer
con·fercĭō -fercīre — -fertum *vt* to stuff, cram, pack together; to stuff full
con·fĕrō -ferre -tŭlī -lātum *vt* to bring together; to contribute (*money, etc.*); to condense, compress; to bring together (*plans, ideas, etc.*), discuss, talk over; to bear, convey, direct; to devote, apply, confer, bestow, give, lend, grant; to ascribe, attribute, impute, assign; to put off, defer, postpone; (with **in** + *acc*) to change or transform (*someone or something*) into; to compare, contrast; **capita conferre** to put heads together, confer; **gradum conferre** (with **cum** + *abl*) to walk together with; **lites conferre** to quarrel; **pedem cum pede conferre** to fight toe to toe; **se conferre** (with **in** + *acc*) **a** to go to, head for; **b** to have recourse to; **c** to join (*a group, etc.*); **sermones conferre** (with **cum** + *abl*) to engage in conversation with, to engage (*someone*) in conversation; **signa conferre** to engage in combat, begin fighting
confertim *adv* (mil) shoulder to shoulder
confert·us -a -um *pp* of **confercio;** *adj* crowded, packed, thick, dense; (mil) shoulder to shoulder
confervēfac·iō -ĕre *vt* to make glow, make melt
con·fervescō -fervescĕre -ferbŭī *vi* to begin to boil, grow hot
confessī·ō -ōnis *f* confession, acknowledgment
confess·us -a -um *pp* of **confiteor;** *adj* acknowledged, incontrovertible, certain; *m* self-acknowledged criminal; *n* admission; **ex confesso** admittedly, beyond doubt; **in confessum venire** to be generally admitted
confestim *adv* immediately, without delay, suddenly
confici·ens -entis *adj* productive, efficient; (with *genit*) productive of; efficient in; *n pl* (with *genit*) sources of
con·ficiō -ficĕre -fēcī -fectum *vt* to make, manufacture, construct; to make ready, prepare, bring about, complete, accomplish, execute, fulfill; to bring about, cause; to bring together, collect; to get together, secure, obtain; to use up, wear out, exhaust; to finish off, weaken, sweep away, destroy, kill; to run through (*money, inheritance*); to chew (*food*); to complete, finish, spend, pass (*time*)
confictī·ō -ōnis *f* fabrication, invention (*of an accusation*)
confīd·ens -entis *adj* trustful; self-confident; presumptuous, smug
confīdenter *adv* confidently; smugly
confīdentī·a -ae *f* confidence; self-confidence, smugness
confīdentilŏqu·us -a -um *adj* speaking confidently
con·fīdō -fīdĕre -fīsus sum *vi* to have confidence, be confident, be sure; (with *dat*) to confide in, rely on, trust, believe; **sibi confidere** to rely on oneself, have self-confidence
con·fīgō -fīgĕre -fixī -fixum *vt* to fasten, join together; to pierce, transfix; (fig) to paralyze
con·fingō -fingĕre -finxī -fictum *vt* to make up, invent, fabricate
confīn·is -e *adj* having common boundaries, adjoining; (fig) closely related, akin
confīn·ium -iī or **-ī** *n* common boundary, frontier; (fig) borderline; *n pl* neighbors; confines
confirmātī·ō -ōnis *f* confirmation, encouragement; affirmation, verification, corroboration; (rhet) presentation of evidence
confirmāt·or -ōris *m* guarantor, surety
confirmāt·us -a -um *adj* resolute, confident, courageous; established, certain
confirmit·ās -ātis *f* firmness; stubbornness

confirm·ō -āre *vt* to strengthen, reinforce; to confirm, sanction, ratify; to encourage; to corroborate; to assert positively; **se confirmare** to recover, get back one's strength
confisc·ō -āre *vt* to deposit in a bank; to confiscate
confīsi·ō -ōnis *f* confidence, assurance
con·fitĕor -fitērī -fessus sum *vt* to confess, acknowledge, admit; to reveal; *vi* to confess
conflăgr·ō -āre *vi* to burn, be on fire; (fig) to burn
conflicti·ō -ōnis *f* conflict
conflict·ō -āre *vt* to beat down, strike down; to ruin; **conflictari** to be afflicted, be tormented; *vi* to contend, struggle, fight
conflict·or -ārī -ātus sum *vi* to struggle, wrestle
conflict·us -ūs *m* striking together; wrestling, struggle
con·flīgō -flīgĕre -flixī -flictum *vt* to throw or knock together; (with **cum** + *abl*) to contrast (*something*) with, compare (*something*) with; *vi* to come into conflict, clash, fight, battle; (with **cum** + *abl*) to come into conflict with, clash with; (with **adversus** + *acc* or **contra** + *acc*) to fight against; **inter se confligere** to collide, collide with one another
confl·ō -āre *vt* to kindle, ignite; to inflame (*passions*); to melt down (*metals*); to bring together, get up, raise (*army, money, etc.*); to forge, invent (*accusation*); to bring about, cause, occasion, produce
conflŭ·ens -entis *m* confluence, junction (*of rivers*); *m pl* confluence
con·flŭō -fluĕre -fluxī *vi* to flow or run together; (fig) to pour in together, come together in crowds
con·fodĭō -fodĕre -fōdī -fossum *vt* to dig up (*soil*); to stab; (fig) to stab
conformātĭ·ō -ōnis *f* shape, form, fashion; idea, notion; arrangement (*of words*); expression (*in the voice*); (rhet) figure of speech
conform·ō -āre *vt* to shape, fashion, put together; to modify, educate
confoss·us -a -um *pp* of **confodio**; *adj* full of holes
confractus *pp* of **confringo**
confragōs·us -a -um *adj* rough, rugged (*terrain*); *n pl* rough terrain
confrĕm·ō -ĕre -ŭī *vi* to grumble
confrĭc·ō -āre *vt* to rub vigorously, rub in; **genua confricare** to nag, pester
con·fringō -fringĕre -frēgī -fractum *vt* to smash, crush; to break down, destroy
con·fugĭō -fugĕre -fūgī *vi* to flee, take refuge, run for help; (with **ad** + *acc*) (fig) **a** to resort to, have recourse to; **b** to appeal to
confug·ĭum -ĭī or **-ī** *n* place of refuge, shelter
confulg·ĕō -ēre *vi* to glitter, sparkle
con·fundō -fundĕre -fūdī -fūsum *vt* to pour together, blend, mingle; to mix up, jumble together, confuse, bewilder, perplex; to spread, diffuse
confūsē *adv* in disorder, in confusion
confūsĭ·ō -ōnis *f* mixing, blending; confusion, mixup, trouble; **confusio oris** blush
confūs·us -a -um *pp* of **confundo**; *adj* confused, perplexed; troubled, confused (*look*)
confūt·ō -āre *vt* to prevent (*water, etc.*) from boiling over; to repress, stop; to silence, confute
congĕl·ō -āre *vt* to cause to freeze up, freeze, harden; **in lapidem congelare** to petrify; *vi* to freeze, freeze up
congeminātĭ·ō -ōnis *f* doubling
congemĭn·ō -āre *vt* to double
congĕm·ō -ĕre -ŭī *vt* to deplore deeply; *vi* to gasp, sigh, or groan deeply
cong·er -rī *m* eel
congerĭ·ēs -ēī *f* heap, pile, mass; funeral pile; accumulation
con·gĕrō -gerĕre -gessī -gestum *vt* to bring together; to heap up, build up; to keep up, multiply, repeat (*arguments*); (with **in** + *acc*) **a** to shower (*weapons*) upon, send a barrage of (*weapons*) upon; **b** to heap (*curses, favors, etc.*) upon
congĕr·ō -ōnis *m* thief
congerr·ō -ōnis *m* playmate
congestīcĭ·us -a -um *adj* piled up
congest·us -ūs *m* heap, mass, accumulation
congiāl·is -e *adj* holding a gallon
congiārĭ·us -a -um *adj* holding a gallon; *n* gift of one gallon (*e. g., of oil*) apiece to the people; bonus to the army; gift of money to the Roman people; gift of money among private friends
cong·ĭus -ĭī or **-ī** *m* Roman liquid measure equaling six sextarii, i.e., about six pints
conglacĭ·ō -āre *vi* to freeze up
conglisc·ō -ĕre *vi* to blaze up
conglobātĭ·ō -ōnis *f* massing together
conglŏb·ō -āre *vt* to make round, form into a ball, roll up
conglomĕr·ō -āre *vt* to roll up, group together, crowd together; **se in forum conglomerare** to crowd into the forum
conglūtinātĭ·ō -ōnis *f* gluing together; (fig) combining (*of words*)
conglūtĭn·ō -āre *vt* to glue, cement; (fig) to weld together, cement
congraec·ō -āre *vt* to squander like the Greeks
congrātŭl·or -ārī -ātus sum *vi* to offer congratulations
con·gredĭor -grĕdī -gressus sum *vt* to meet, accost, address, associate with; to fight; *vi* to come together, meet; to fight; (with **cum** + *abl*) **a**

to meet with; **b** to associate with; **c** to fight against
congregābĭl·is -e *adj* gregarious
congregātĭ·ō -ōnis *f* flocking together, congregation, union, association
congrĕg·ō -āre *vt* to herd together; to unite, associate
congressĭ·ō -ōnis *f* meeting, conference
congressus *pp* of **congredior**
congress·us -ūs *m* meeting, association, society, union; hostile encounter, contest, fight
congrŭ·ens -entis *adj* coinciding, corresponding; suitable, consistent; self-consistent, uniform, harmonious
congruenter *adv* consistently; (with *dat* or **ad** + *acc*) in conformity with; **congruenter naturae vivere** to live in conformity with nature
congruentĭ·a -ae *f* consistency, symmetry
congrŭ·ō -ĕre -ŭī *vi* to coincide; to correspond, agree, be consistent; (with **ad** + *acc* or with **cum** + *abl*) to coincide with; (with *dat* or **cum** + *abl*) to correspond to, agree with, be consistent with; (with *dat* or **in** + *acc*) to agree (*in feeling, opinion*) with
congrŭ·us -a -um *adj* agreeing, agreeable
cōnicĭō or **cōicĭō** see **conjicio**
cōnĭf·er -ĕra -ĕrum *adj* coniferous
cōnĭg·er -ĕra -ĕrum *adj* coniferous
cō·nītor -nītī -nixus sum or **-nīsus sum** *vi* to make a great effort, struggle, exert oneself; (with **in** + *acc*) to struggle toward, press on toward, try to reach
cōnīv·ĕō -ēre -ī *vi* to close the eyes (*in sleep, from light, from fear, etc.*), to blink; (of sun or moon) to be darkened, be eclipsed; (fig) to be drowsy; (with **in** + *abl*) to connive at, wink at, overlook
conjectĭ·ō -ōnis *f* throwing, barrage (*of missiles*); conjecture, interpretation
conject·ō -āre *vt* to conjecture, infer, conclude, guess
conject·or -ōris *m* interpreter of dreams, seer
conjectr·ix -īcis *f* interpreter of dreams, seer (*female*)
conjectūr·a -ae *f* conjecture, guess, inference; interpretation
conjectūrāl·is -e *adj* conjectural
conject·us -ūs *m* throwing together; crowding together; connecting; heap, crowd, pile; throwing, casting, hurling; turning, directing (*eyes*); casting (*a glance*); barrage (*of stones, weapons*); **ad** or **intra teli conjectum venire** to come within range of a weapon
con·jicĭō -jicĕre -jēcī -jectum *vt* to pile together (*e.g., baggage*); to conclude, infer, conjecture; to interpret (*omen*); to throw, fling, cast; to throw in (*e.g., words in a letter or speech*); **se in fugam** or **se in pedes conjicere** to take to one's heels
conjugāl·is -e *adj* conjugal
conjugātĭ·ō -ōnis *f* etymological relationship (*of words*)
conjugāt·or -ōris *m* uniter (*said of Hymen, god of marriage*)
conjugiāl·is -e *adj* marriage
conjug·ium -ĭī or **-ī** *n* union (*e.g., of body and soul*); marriage, wedlock; mating (*of animals*); (fig) husband, wife, spouse
conjŭg·ō -āre *vt* to form (*friendship*); **verba conjugata** cognates
conjunctē *adv* conjointly; at the same time; (in logic) conditionally, hypothetically; **conjuncte vivere** to live intimately together
conjunctim *adv* jointly
conjunctĭ·ō -ōnis *f* combination, union; association, connection; friendship; intimacy; marriage; relationship (*by blood or by marriage*); sympathy, affinity; (gram) conjunction
conjunct·us -a -um *adj* (with *dat* or *abl*) bordering upon, near; (with *dat* or *abl*, or with **cum** + *abl*) **a** connected with; **b** agreeing with, conforming with; *n* connection
con·jungō -jungĕre -junxī -junctum *vt* to join together, connect, unite; to unite in making (*war*); to unite or join in marriage; to unite (*by bonds of friendship*); (with *dat*) to add (*e.g., words*) to (*e.g., a letter*)
con·junx or **con·jux -jŭgis** *m* married person, spouse, husband; *m pl* married couple; *f* married person, spouse, wife; fiancee; bride; the female (*of animals*)
conjūrātĭ·ō -ōnis *f* conspiracy, plot; alliance
conjūrāt·us -a -um *adj* bound together by an oath, allied, associate; (mil) sworn in; *m pl* conspirators
conjūr·ō -āre *vi* to take an oath together; to plot, conspire
conjux see **conjunx**
conl- = **coll-**
conm- = **comm-**
Con·ōn -ōnis *m* famous Athenian admiral (*fl* 400 B.C.); famous mathematician and astronomer of Samos (283-222 B.C.)
cōnōpē·um or **cōnōpĕ·um -ī** *n* mosquito net
cōn·or -ārī -ātus sum *vt* to try, endeavor, venture, attempt
conquassātĭ·ō -ōnis *f* severe shaking; disturbance
conquass·ō -āre *vt* to shake hard; (fig) to shatter, upset, disturb
con·quĕror -quĕrī -questus sum *vt* to complain bitterly about, deplore; *vi* to complain, complain bitterly
conquestĭ·ō -ōnis *f* complaining, complaint; (rhet) appeal for sym-

pathy; (with *genit*, with **de** + *abl*, or with **adversus** + *acc*) complaint about

conquest·us -ūs *m* loud complaint

conqui·escō -escĕre -ēvī -ētum *vi* to rest, take a rest; to find rest, find recreation; to keep quiet, remain inactive; to slacken, flag; to lie dormant; to take a nap; to stop, pause

conquinisc·ō -ĕre *vi* to squat, stoop down

con·quīrō -quīrĕre -quīsīvī -quīsītum *vt* to search for, look for; to procure, bring together, collect; (fig) to search for, go after (*pleasures, etc.*)

conquīsīti·ō -ōnis *f* search; procuring, collection; (mil) conscription, draft, recruitment

conquīsīt·or -ōris *m* recruiting officer

conquīsīt·us -a -um *pp* of **conquiro**; *adj* chosen, select

conr- = corr-

consaep·iō or **consēp·iō -īre -sī -tum** *vt* to fence in, hedge in, enclose

consaept·um -ī *n* enclosure

consalūtāti·ō -ōnis *f* exchange of greetings

consalūt·ō -āre *vt* to greet (*as a group*), greet cordially; *vi* **inter se consalūtāre** to greet one another, exchange greetings

consān·escō -escĕre -ŭī *vi* to heal up; to recover

consanguinĕ·us -a -um *adj* related by blood; *m* brother; *m pl* relatives; *f* sister

consanguinit·ās -ātis *f* blood relationship; **consanguinitate propinquus** closely related

consauci·ō -āre *vt* to wound severely

consccelerāt·us -a -um *adj* wicked, depraved, criminal; (fig) rotten to the core

conscelĕr·ō -āre *vt* to stain with guilt, dishonor, disgrace

con·scendō -scendĕre -scendī -scensum *vt* to climb up, mount, ascend; to board (*ship*); **aequor navibus conscendere** to go to sea; *vi* to climb; to go aboard, board; (with **in** + *acc*) to go aboard (*ship*)

conscensi·ō -ōnis *f* embarkation; **in navīs conscensio** boarding the ships

conscienti·a -ae *f* joint knowledge; consciousness, knowledge; moral sense, conscience; good conscience; bad conscience; scruple; sense of guilt, remorse

con·scindō -scindĕre -scĭdī -scissum *vt* to tear up, tear to pieces; (fig) to tear to pieces, abuse

consc·iō -īre *vt* to become conscious of (*wrong*)

consc·iscō -iscĕre -īvī or **-iī -ītum** *vt* to approve or decide upon; **(sibi) mortem consciscere** to decide upon death for oneself, commit suicide

consci·us -a -um *adj* sharing knowledge with another; cognizant, conscious, aware; (with *genit* or *dat*) having knowledge of, aware of, privy to; *mf* partner, accomplice, confidant(e), confederate

conscrē·or -ārī -ātus sum *vi* to clear the throat

con·scrībō -scrībĕre -scripsī -scriptum *vt* to enlist, enroll; to write, write up, compose; to prescribe

conscripti·ō -ōnis *f* document, draft; record, report

conscript·us -a -um *pp* of **conscribo**; *m* senator; **patres conscripti** members of the senate

consĕc·ō -āre -ŭī -tum *vt* to cut up into small pieces, dismember

consecrāti·ō -ōnis *f* consecration; deification (*of emperors*)

consĕcr·ō -āre *vt* to make holy, consecrate, dedicate to a god; to dedicate to the gods below, doom to destruction, execrate; to immortalize, deify

consectāri·us -a -um *adj* logic; *n pl* conclusions, inferences

consectāti·ō -ōnis *f* eager pursuit

consectātr·ix -īcis *f* pursuer (*female*)

consecti·ō -ōnis *f* cutting up

consect·or -ārī -ātus sum *vt* to follow eagerly, go after; to follow up, pursue, chase, hunt; to overtake; to imitate, follow

consecūti·ō -ōnis *f* effect, consequences; (rhet) order, sequence

consen·escō -escĕre -ŭī *vi* to grow old, grow old together; to become gray; to become obsolete; to waste away, fade, decline; to degenerate, sink

consensi·ō -ōnis *f* agreement, unanimity; harmony; plot, conspiracy

consens·us -ūs *m* agreement, unanimity; agreement, harmony; plot, conspiracy; **consensū** with one accord; **in consensum vertere** to become a general custom; **omnium vestrum consensu** with the agreement of all of you, as you all agree

consentānĕ·us -a -um *adj* (with *dat* or **cum** + *abl*) agreeing with, according to, in accord with, proper for; **consentaneum est** it is reasonable; *n pl* concurrent circumstances

consenti·ens -entis *adj* unanimous

con·sentiō -sentīre -sensī -sensum *vt* **bellum consentire** to agree to war, vote for war; *vi* to agree; (with *inf*) to agree, plot, conspire to; (with **cum** + *abl*) to harmonize with, fit in with, be consistent with

consēp- = consaep-

consĕqu·ens -entis *adj* reasonable;

corresponding, logical, fit, suitable; *n* consequence, conclusion
consequenti·a -ae *f* consequence, natural sequence
con·sĕquor -sĕquī -secūtus sum *vt* to follow, follow up, pursue, go after; to catch up with, catch, reach, attain to, arrive at; (fig) to follow, copy, imitate; to obtain, get, acquire; to understand, perceive, learn; (of speech) to be equal to, do justice to; (of time) to come after, follow; to result from, be the consequence of, arise from
con·sĕrō -serĕre -serŭī -sertum *vt* to entwine, tie, join, string together; **manum** or **manūs conserere** to fight hand to hand, engage in close combat; **proelium conserere** to begin fighting
con·sĕrō -serĕre -sēvī -sītum *vt* to sow, plant
consertē *adv* in close connection, connectedly
conserv·a -ae *f* fellow slave (*female*)
conservāti·ō -ōnis *f* keeping, preserving
conservāt·or -ōris *m* preserver, defender
conservit·ĭum -ĭī or **-ī** *n* servitude
conserv·ō -āre *vt* to keep safe, preserve, maintain; (fig) to keep intact
conserv·us -ī *m* fellow slave
consess·or -ōris *m* table companion; fellow spectator; (law) assessor
consess·us -ūs *m* assembly, court
consīderātē *adv* with caution, deliberately
consīderāti·ō -ōnis *f* contemplation, consideration
consīderāt·us -a -um *adj* circumspect, cautious; well considered, deliberate
consīdĕr·ō -āre *vt* to look at closely, inspect, examine, survey; to consider, contemplate; reflect upon
con·sīdō -sīdĕre -sēdī -sessum *vi* to sit down, be seated, settle; (of assemblies) to hold sessions, be in session; (mil) to encamp, take up a position; to settle, stay (*in residence*); to settle, sink down, subside; (fig) to settle, sink, be buried; to diminish, subside, abate, die out
consign·ō -āre *vt* to seal, sign; to certify, attest, vouch for; to note, register, record
consil·escō -escĕre -ŭī *vi* to become still, calm down
consiliāri·us -a -um *adj* counseling; *m* counselor, adviser; interpreter, spokesman
consiliāt·or -ōris *m* counselor
consiliō *adv* intentionally, purposely
consili·or -ārī -ātus sum *vi* to take counsel, consult; (with *dat*) to give counsel to, advise
consil·ĭum -ĭī or **-ī** *n* consultation, deliberation; deliberative body, council; council of war; plan, measure, stratagem; decision; purpose, intention, design, policy; judgment, wisdom, prudence, discretion, sense; cabinet; advice, counsel; **consilium capere** or **consilium inire** or **consilium suscipere** to form a plan, come to a decision, decide, determine; **consilium est mihi** (with *inf*) I intend to; **non est consilium mihi** (with *inf*) I don't mean to; **privato consilio** for one's own purposes
consimil·is -e *adj* quite similar; (with *genit* or *dat*) completely similar to, just like
consip·iō -ĕre *vi* to be sane
con·sistō -sistĕre -stitī -stitum *vi* to come to a stop, come to rest, stop, pause, halt, take a stand, stand still; to grow hard, become solid, set; (mil) to take up a position, be posted, make a stand; (of ships) to come to anchorage, to ground; (of travelers) to halt on a journey; to be firm, be steadfast, continue, endure; to be, exist, occur, take place; (with *abl* or with **in** + *abl*) to consist of, depend on
consiti·ō -ōnis *f* sowing, planting
consit·or -ōris *m* sower, planter
consitūr·a -ae *f* sowing, planting
consōbrīn·a -ae *f* first cousin (*daughter of a mother's sister*)
consōbrīn·us -ī *m* first cousin (*son of mother's sister*)
consociāti·ō -ōnis *f* association, society
consociāt·us -a -um *adj* held in common, shared
consoci·ō -āre *vt* to associate, join, unite, connect, share
consōlābil·is -e *adj* consolable
consōlāti·ō -ōnis *f* consolation, comfort; encouragement; alleviation
consōlāt·or -ōris *m* comforter
consōlātōri·us -a -um *adj* comforting; **litterae consolatoriae** letter of condolence
consōl·or -ārī -ātus sum *vt* to console, comfort, reassure, soothe, encourage, cheer up; to relieve, alleviate, mitigate
consomni·ō -āre *vt* to dream about
consŏn·ō -āre -ŭī *vi* to sound together, ring, resound, reecho; (with *dat* or with **cum** + *abl*) to harmonize with, agree with; **inter se consonare** to agree, harmonize
consŏn·us -a -um *adj* harmonious; (fig) fit, suitable
consōp·iō -īre *vt* to put to sleep
consor·s -tis *adj* having a common lot, of the same fortune; common; shared in common; *mf* partner, associate; *m* brother; *f* wife; sister
consorti·ō -ōnis *f* partnership, association, fellowship
consort·ĭum -ĭī or **-ī** *n* partnership; participation; (with *genit*) partnership in
conspect·us -a -um *pp* of **conspicio**; *adj* visible; in full sight; conspicuous, striking
conspect·us -ūs *m* look, sight, view; sight (*power of seeing*); mental view;

being seen, appearance on the scene; **conspectu in medio** before all eyes

con·spergō -spergĕre -spersī -spersum *vt* to sprinkle, splatter

conspiciend·us -a -um *adj* worth seeing; distinguished

conspicill·um -ī *n* (with *genit*) keeping an eye on

con·spiciō -spicĕre -spexī -spectum *vt* to look at attentively, observe, fix the eyes upon; to catch sight of, spot; to look at with admiration; to face (*e.g., the forum*); to perceive, see, discern; **conspici** to be conspicuous, be noticed, be admired, attract attention

conspic·or -ārī -ātus sum *vt* to catch sight of, spot, see

conspicŭ·us -a -um *adj* visible, in sight; conspicuous, striking, remarkable, distinguished

conspīrātī·ō -ōnis *f* agreement, unanimity, harmony, concord; plot, conspiracy

conspīrāt·us -a -um *adj* conspiring, in conspiracy

conspīr·ō -āre *vi* to breathe together, blow together, sound together; to act in unison, to agree; to plot together, conspire

conspons·or -ōris *m* coguarantor

con·spŭō -spuĕre — -spūtum *vt* to spit on; **nive conspuere** to sprinkle with snow

conspurc·ō -āre *vt* to defile, mess up

conspūt·ō -āre *vt* to spit on in contempt

constabil·iō -īre -īvī -ītum *vt* to establish, confirm

const·ans -antis *adj* constant, uniform, steady, fixed, stable, regular, invariable, persistent; consistent, harmonious; (fig) faithful, constant, trustworthy

constanter *adv* constantly, steadily, uniformly, invariably; consistently; calmly

constanti·a -ae *f* steadiness, firmness, constancy, perseverance; harmony, symmetry, consistency; steadfastness; self-possession

consternātī·ō -ōnis *f* consternation, dismay, alarm; disorder, disturbance; mutiny; wild rush, stampede

con·sternō -sternĕre -strāvī -strātum *vt* to spread, cover; to pave; to thatch; **constrata navis** ship with deck

constīp·ō -āre *vt* to crowd together

constit·ŭō -uĕre -ŭī -ūtum *vt* to set up, erect, establish; to settle (*e.g., a people in a place*); to set up, establish (*authority*); to settle, determine, fix (*date, price, penalty*); to arrange, set in order, organize; to construct, erect; to designate, select, assign, appoint; to decide, arbitrate, decree, judge; (mil) to station, post, deploy

constitūtī·ō -ōnis *f* constitution, nature; disposition; regulation, ordinance, order; definition; (rhet) issue, point of discussion

constitūt·us -a -um *pp* of **constituo**; *adj* ordered, arranged; **bene constitutum corpus** good constitution; *n* agreement, arrangement

con·stō -stāre -stitī -stātum *vi* to stand together; to agree, correspond; to stand firm, remain unchanged, be constant; to stand still, stand firm; to be in existence; (of facts) to be established, be undisputed, be well known; (com) to tally, be correct; (with *abl* of price) to cost; **non mihi satis constat** I have not quite made up my mind; **ratio constat** the account tallies, is correct

constrāt·us -a -um *pp* of **consterno**; *n* flooring

con·stringō -stringĕre -strinxī -strictum *vt* to tie up; to shackle, chain; (fig) to bind, restrain; (rhet) to condense, compress

constructī·ō -ōnis *f* building, construction; arrangement (*of words*)

con·strŭō -struĕre -struxī -structum *vt* to heap up, pile up; to construct, build up; (gram) to construct

constuprāt·or -ōris *m* rapist

constŭpr·ō -āre *vt* to rape

consuād·ĕō -ēre *vi* (with *dat*) to advise strongly

Consuāl·ia -ium *n pl* feast of Consus, ancient Italian god of fertility, celebrated on August 21st

consuās·or -ōris *m* adviser

consūcid·us -a -um *adj* very juicy

consūd·ō -āre *vi* to sweat profusely

consuē·faciō -facĕre -fēcī -factum *vt* to accustom, inure

consu·escō -escĕre -ēvī -ētum *vt* to accustom, inure; *vi* to become accustomed; (with *inf*) to become accustomed to; (with **cum** + *abl*) to cohabit with

consuētī·ō -ōnis *f* sexual intercourse

consuētūd·ō -inis *f* custom, habit; usage, idiom; social intercourse, social ties; sexual intercourse; **ad consuetudinem** (with *genit*) according to the custom of; **consuetudine** or **ex consuetudine** according to custom, from habit; **pro consuetudine mea** according to my habit, as is my habit; **ut fert consuetudo** as is usual

consuēt·us -a -um *pp* of **consuesco**; *adj* usual, regular, customary

con·sul -sŭlis *m* consul (*one of the two highest magistrates of the Roman republic*); **consul designatus** consul-elect; **consulem creare, dicere,** or **facere** to elect a consul; **consul ordinarius** consul who entered office on the first of January; **consul suffectus** consul chosen in the course of the year to fill a vacancy in the consulship

consulār·is -e *adj* consular; **aetas**

consularis minimum legal age for election to consular office; **comitia consularia** consular elections; *m* ex-consul
consulāriter *adv* like a consul, in a manner worthy of a consul
consulāt·us -ūs *m* consulship; **consulatum petere** to run for the consulship; **se consulatu abdicare** to resign from the consulship
consŭl·ō -ĕre -ŭī -tum *vt* to consult, ask advice of; to consider; to advise (*something*), offer as advice; **boni consulere** to regard favorably; *vi* to deliberate, reflect; (with **ad** or **in** + *acc*) to reflect on, take into consideration; (with *dat*) to look after; (with **in** + *acc*) to take measures against; (with **de** + *abl*) to pass sentence on
consultāti·ō -ōnis *f* mature deliberation, consideration; consulting, inquiry; subject of consultation, case
consultē *adv* deliberately, after due consideration
consultō *adv* deliberately, on purpose
consult·ō -āre *vt* to reflect on, consider maturely; to ask (*someone*) for advice, consult; *vi* to deliberate, reflect; (with *dat*) to take into consideration, look after, care for; **in medium consultare** to look after the common good
consult·or -ōris *m* counselor, adviser; advisee, client
consultr·ix -īcis *f* protectress
consult·us -a -um *pp* of **consulo**; *adj* skilled, experienced; *m* expert; **juris consultus** legal expert, lawyer; *n* deliberation, consideration; decree, decision, resolution; response (*from an oracle*)
consummāt·us -a -um *adj* consummate, perfect
consumm·ō -āre *vt* to sum up; to finish, complete, accomplish, perfect
con·sūmō -sūmĕre -sumpsī -sumptum *vt* to use up, consume, exhaust; to devour; to squander; to wear out, destroy; to spend, waste (*money, time, effort*)
consumpti·ō -ōnis *f* consumption, wasting
consumpt·or -ōris *m* destroyer
con·sŭō -suĕre -sŭī -sūtum *vt* to stitch together, sew up
con·surgō -surgĕre -surrexī -surrectum *vi* to stand up; to rise in a body; (with **ad** or **in** + *acc*) to aspire to
consurrecti·ō -ōnis *f* rising up, standing up in a body
Cons·us -ī *m* ancient Italian deity of agriculture and fertility
consusurr·ō -āre *vi* to whisper together
contābēfac·iō -ĕre *vt* to wear out completely, consume, waste
contāb·escō -escĕre -ŭī *vi* to waste away
contabulāti·ō -ōnis *f* flooring; story
contabŭl·ō -āre *vt* to cover with boards; to build with (*several*) stories
contact·us -ūs *m* touch, contact; contagion; (fig) contagion, infection
contāg·ēs -is *f* touch, contact
contāgi·ō -ōnis *f* touching; touch; contact; contagion, infection; moral contagion, bad example
contāg·ium -iī or **-ī** *n* touch, contact; contagion; moral contamination
contāmināt·us -a -um *adj* polluted, contaminated, impure, vile, degraded; *m pl* perverted youths
contāmin·ō -āre *vt* to bring into contact, mingle, blend; to corrupt, defile; (fig) to corrupt, stain, taint, spoil
contechn·or -ārī -ātus sum *vi* to devise plots, think up tricks
con·tĕgō -tegĕre -texī -tectum *vt* to cover up; to hide; to protect
contemĕr·ō -āre *vt* to defile
con·temnō -temnĕre -tempsī -temptum *vt* to think little of, depreciate, slight, belittle, disregard; to despise, defy
contemplāti·ō -ōnis *f* viewing, surveying, contemplation
contemplāt·or -ōris *m* contemplator, observer
contemplāt·us -ūs *m* contemplation
contempl·ō -āre or **contempl·or -ārī -ātus sum** *vt* to observe, survey, gaze upon, contemplate
contemptim *adv* contemptuously
contempti·ō -ōnis *f* belittling, despising; **in contemptionem venire** (with *dat*) to become an object of contempt to
contempt·or -ōris *m* or **contemptr·ix -īcis** *f* scorner, despiser
contempt·us -a -um *pp* of **contemno**; *adj* contemptible, despicable
contempt·us -ūs *m* belittling, despising, scorn; **contemptui esse** to be an object of contempt
con·tendō -tendĕre -tendī -tentum *vt* to stretch, draw tight; to tune (*instrument*); to aim, shoot, hurl; (fig) to strain, stretch, exert; to hold, assert, maintain; to compare, contrast; to direct (*course*); *vi* to exert oneself; to compete, contend, fight; to travel, march; (with *inf*) to be in a hurry to; (with **in** + *acc*) to rush to, head for; (with **ad** + *acc*) to strive for, aspire to
contentē *adv* with great effort, earnestly; closely, scantily, sparingly
contenti·ō -ōnis *f* competition, struggle, dispute; straining, exertion, effort; contrast, comparison, antithesis
content·us -a -um *pp* of **contendo**; *adj* tense, tight, taut, strained; eager, intense
content·us -a -um *pp* of **contineo**; *adj* content, satisfied

contermin·us -a -um *adj* (with *dat*) bordering upon
con·tĕrō -terĕre -trīvī -trītum *vt* to grind to powder, pulverize, crumble; (fig) to wear away, wear out, use up; to consume, waste (*time*)
conterr·ĕō -ēre -ŭī -ĭtum *vt* to frighten, scare the life out of
contest·or -ārī -ātus sum *vt* to call to witness; (fig) to prove, attest; **litem contestari** to open a lawsuit by calling witnesses
contex·ō -ĕre -ŭī -tum *vt* to weave together; to brace together; to connect; to devise, build; to compose (*writings*); to dream up (*a charge*)
contextē *adv* in a coherent manner
context·us -a -um *pp* of **contexo;** *adj* connected
context·us -ūs *m* connection, coherence
contic·escō or **contic·iscō -escĕre -ŭī** *vi* to become quite still, fall completely silent, hush; to keep silence; (fig) to cease, abate
conticinnō *adv* in the evening
contignāti·ō -ōnis *f* floor, story
contign·ō -āre *vt* to lay a floor on
contigŭ·us -a -um *adj* touching, adjoining; within reach; (with *dat*) bordering on, near
contin·ens -entis *adj* contiguous, adjacent; unbroken, uninterrupted; self-controlled, continent; (with *dat*) bordering on, contiguous with, adjacent to
contin·ens -entis *f* continent, mainland
contin·ens -entis *n* chief point, main point (*of a speech*)
continenter *adv* in unbroken succession; without interruption; (sitting) close together; moderately, temperately
continenti·a -ae *f* self-control; continence
con·tinĕō -tinēre -tinŭī -tentum *vt* to hold or keep together; to keep within bounds, confine; to contain, comprise, include; to control, repress
con·tingō -tingĕre -tigī -tactum *vt* to come into contact with; (fig) to touch, affect; to touch, border on; to reach, reach to; to contaminate; *vi* to happen, turn out, come to pass; (with *dat*) **a** to touch, border on; **b** to happen to, befall
continuāti·ō -ōnis *f* unbroken series, succession; (rhet) period
continŭ·ō -āre *vt* to make continuous, join together, connect; to extend; to continue, carry on, draw out, prolong; to pass, occupy (*time*); **continuari** (with *dat*) **a** to be contiguous with, adjacent to; **b** to follow closely upon
continŭō *adv* immediately, without delay; as a necessary consequence, necessarily
continŭ·us -a -um *adj* continuous, unbroken; successive; **dies continuos quinque** for five successive days
conti·ō -ōnis *f* meeting, rally; public meeting (*of the people or of soldiers*); speech, pep talk, harangue
contiōnābund·us -a -um *adj* haranguing
contiōnāl·is -e *adj* typical of a public assembly; demagogic
contiōnāri·us -a -um *adj* mob-like
contiōnāt·or -ōris *m* demagogue, public agitator, rabble-rouser
contiōn·or -ārī -ātus sum *vi* to hold forth at a rally, to harangue; to come to a rally; to make a statement at a rally
contiuncŭl·a -ae *f* short harangue, trifling speech
contoll·ō -ĕre *vt* to bring together
contōn·at -āre *v impers* it is thundering hard
contor·quĕō -quēre -sī -tum *vt* to whirl, twist; to throw hard; to twist (*words*) around
contortē *adv* intricately
contortiōn·ēs -um *f pl* intricacies (*of language*)
contort·or -ōris *m* perverter; **contortor legum** pettifogger
contortŭl·us -a -um *adj* rather complicated
contortuplicāt·us -a -um *adj* all twisted up
contort·us -a -um *pp* of **contorqueo;** *adj* involved, intricate; vehement (*speech*)
contrā *adv* in opposition, opposite, in front, face to face; in turn, in return, on the other hand, on the other side; reversely, in the opposite way, the other way; on the contrary, conversely; **contra atque** or **ac** contrary to, otherwise than; **contra dicere** to reply, say in reply; to raise objections; **contra dicitur** the objection is raised; **contra ferire** to make a counterattack; **contra qua fas est** contrary to divine law; **contra quam senatus consuluisset** contrary to what the senate would have decided, contrary to the senate resolution; **quin contra** nay on the contrary, in fact it's just the opposite
contrā *prep* (with *acc*) opposite, opposite to, facing, towards, against; in answer to, in reply to; (in hostile sense) against, with, in opposition to, as the opponent of; against, injurious to, unfavorable to; contrary to, the reverse of; in violation of; against, in defiance of; **contra ea putare** to think otherwise; **quod contra** whereas, while; **valere contra** to counterbalance
contracti·ō -ōnis *f* drawing together, contraction; shortening (*of syllable*); despondency
contractiuncŭl·a -ae *f* slight mental depression
contract·us -a -um *pp* of **contraho;** *adj* contracted; narrow, lim-

ited (*place*); brief; pinching (*poverty*); in seclusion; **res contracta** contract
contract·us -ūs *m* shrinking
contrā·dīcō -dīcĕre -dixī -dictum *vi* (with *dat*) to contradict, speak against
contrādictĭ·ō -ōnis *f* objection, refutation
con·trăhō -trahĕre -traxī -tractum *vt* to draw together, collect, assemble; to contract, shorten, narrow, abridge, lessen, diminish; to wrinkle; (fig) to bring about, accomplish, cause, produce, incur; to conclude (*bargain*); to transact (*business*); to settle (*an account*); to complete (*business arrangements*)
contrāriē *adv* in opposite ways, in a different way
contrārĭ·us -a -um *adj* opposite; contrary, conflicting; hostile, antagonistic; from the opposite direction; (with *dat*) opposed to, contrary to; *n* the opposite, the contrary, the reverse; antithesis; **ex contrario** on the contrary, on the other hand; **in contraria** in opposite directions; **in contraria versus** changed into its opposite
contrectābilĭter *adv* appreciably, tangibly
contrectātĭ·ō -ōnis *f* handling, touching
contrect·ō -āre *vt* to touch, handle; (fig) to defile; (fig) to dwell upon, consider
contrem·iscō -iscĕre -ŭī *vt* to shudder at; *vi* to tremble all over; to waver
contrĕm·ō -ĕre -ŭī *vi* to tremble all over; to quake
contrib·ŭō -uĕre -ŭī -ūtum *vt* to bring together, enroll together, associate, unite, incorporate; to contribute, add
contrist·ō -āre *vt* to sadden, cover with gloom; (fig) to darken, cloud
contrīt·us -a -um *pp* of **contero;** *adj* worn out, common, trite
contrōversĭ·a -ae *f* controversy, quarrel, dispute, debate; civil lawsuit, litigation; subject of litigation; contradiction; question; **sine controversia** indisputably
contrōversiōs·us -a -um *adj* much disputed, controversial
contrōvers·us -a -um *adj* disputed, controversial, questionable, undecided
contrucīd·ō -āre *vt* to cut down, cut to pieces, massacre; (fig) to wreck, make a mess of
con·trūdō -trūdĕre -trūsī -trūsum *vt* to crowd together
contrunc·ō -āre *vt* to hack to pieces
contubernāl·is -is *m* army comrade, army buddy; junior staff officer; (coll) husband (*of slave*); personal attendant; comrade, companion, associate; colleague; *f* (coll) wife (*of slave*)
contubern·ĭum -ĭī or **-ī** *n* military companionship; common war tent; concubinage; marriage (*of slaves*); hovel (*of slaves*)
con·tuĕor -tuērī -tuĭtus sum *vt* to look at attentively, regard, survey
contuĭt·us or **contūt·us -ūs** *m* sight, observation
contumācĭ·a -ae *f* stubbornness, defiance, willfulness; constancy, firmness
contumācĭter *adv* stubbornly, defiantly
contŭm·ax -ācis *adj* stubborn, defiant
contumēlĭ·a -ae *f* mistreatment, rough treatment; outrage, insult, abuse, affront
contumēliōsē *adv* abusively
contumēliōs·us -a -um *adj* bringing dishonor; insulting, abusive; reproachful, insolent
contumŭl·ō -āre *vt* to bury
con·tundō -tundĕre -tŭdī -tūsum *vt* to crush, grind, pound, bruise; (fig) to crush, destroy, break, subdue; to baffle
conturbātĭ·ō -ōnis *f* confusion, consternation
conturbāt·us -a -um *adj* confused, distracted, disordered, in confusion
conturb·ō -āre *vt* to confuse, throw into confusion; to disquiet, disturb; to upset (*plans*); **rationes** or **rationem conturbare** to be bankrupt; *vi* to be bankrupt
cont·us -ī *m* pole
cōnūbiāl·is -e *adj* marriage, connubial
cōnūb·ĭum -ĭī or **-ī** *n* intermarriage; right to intermarry according to Roman law; marriage; sexual intercourse; **jus conubi** right to intermarry
cōn·us -ī *m* cone; apex (*of helmet*)
convăd·or -ārī -ātus sum *vt* to subpoena
conval·escō -escĕre -ŭī *vi* to grow strong; to regain strength, convalesce; (fig) to improve
convall·is -is *f* valley
convās·ō -āre *vt* to pack up, pack
convect·ō -āre *vt* to heap together; to bring home
convect·or -ōris *m* fellow passenger
con·vĕhō -vehĕre -vexī -vectum *vt* to collect, bring in (*esp. the harvest*)
con·vellō -vellĕre -vellī -vulsum *vt* to tear away, pull off, pluck, wrest; to tear to pieces, dismember; to break, shatter; (fig) to turn upside down, subvert, overthrow; **convellere signa** to break camp
convĕn·ae -ārum *m pl* or *f pl* strangers; refugees, vagabonds
convenĭ·ens -entis *adj* agreeing, harmonious, consistent; appropriate; (with *dat* or with **cum** + *abl*) consistent with, appropriate to; (with **ad** + *acc*) appropriate for, suitable for

convenienter *adv* consistently; suitably; (with **cum** + *abl* or with **ad** + *acc*) in conformity with
convenienti•a -ae *f* agreement, accord, harmony; conformity
con•veniō -venīre -vēnī -ventum *vt* to meet, go to meet; to interview; *vi* to come together, meet, gather, come in a body; to coincide; to unite, combine; to come to an agreement, agree; (with **ad** + *acc*) to fit (*as a shoe fits the foot*); (with *dat*, with **ad** or **in** + *acc*, or with **cum** + *abl*) to be applicable to, appropriate to, fit; **convenit** it is fitting, proper; **convenit inter se** (with *dat*) there is harmony among
conventīci•us -a -um *adj* coming together, gathering together; *n* fee for attending the assembly
conventicŭl•um -ī *n* small gathering; meeting place
conventi•ō -ōnis *f* agreement, contract
convent•us -a -um *pp* of **convenio**; *n* agreement, contract
convent•us -ūs *m* gathering, assembly; congress; district court; company, corporation; agreement; **ex conventu** by agreement; of one accord; **conventum agere** to hold court
con•verrō or **con•vorrō -verrĕre -verrī -versum** *vt* to sweep together, sweep up; to brush thoroughly; (fig) to scoop up (*e.g., an inheritance*)
conversāti•ō -ōnis *f* social intercourse; conversation
conversi•ō -ōnis *f* revolving, revolution; (fig) alteration, change; (rhet) repetition of word at end of clause; (rhet) balancing of phrases
convers•ō -āre *vt* to turn around; **se conversare** to revolve
con•vertō or **con•vortō -vertĕre -vertī -versum** *vt* to cause to turn, turn back, reverse; (fig) to turn, direct (*laughter, attention*); to convert, transform; to translate; to attract (*attention*); (mil) **sese convertere** to retreat; *vi* to return; to change, be changed, turn; (with **in** + *acc*) to be changed into, turn into
convest•iō -īre *vt* to clothe, cover
convex•us -a -um *pp* of **conveho**; *adj* rounded off; arched, convex; concave; sloping down; *n* vault, arch
convīciāt•or -ōris *m* reviler
convīci•or -ārī -ātus sum *vt* to revile
convīc•ium -iī or **-ī** *n* noise, chatter; wrangling; jeers, invective, abuse; cry of protest; reprimand; **conviciis consectari aliquem** to keep after someone with abuses
convicti•ō -ōnis *f* companionship; companions
convict•or -ōris *m* bosom friend
convict•us -ūs *m* association, socializing; close friends; feast, banquet
con•vincō -vincĕre -vīcī -victum *vt* to refute, prove wrong; to convict, prove guilty; to prove true, demonstrate clearly
convīs•ō -ĕre *vt* to examine, search; to shine on
convīv•a -ae *m* guest, table companion
convīvāl•is -e *adj* convivial, festive
convīvāt•or -ōris *m* master of ceremonies; host
convīv•ium -iī or **-ī** *n* banquet, dinner; dinner party; *n pl* dinner guests; **convivium agitare** to throw a party
con•vīvō -vīvĕre -vixī *vi* to live together; (with **cum** + *abl*) to feast with
convīv•or -ārī -ātus sum *vi* to feast together, have a party
convocāti•ō -ōnis *f* calling together
convŏc•ō -āre *vt* to call together, assemble
convŏl•ō -āre *vi* to flock together; (fig) to flock together, gather hastily
con•volvō -volvĕre -volvī -volūtum *vt* to roll together; to roll up (*a scroll*); to fasten together, interweave; to wrap; **se convolvere** to roll along; to go in a circle
convŏm•ō -ĕre *vt* to vomit on, vomit all over
convortō see **converto**
convulnĕr•ō -āre *vt* to wound seriously
convulsus *pp* of **convello**
coöper•iō -īre -ŭī -tum *vt* to cover; to overwhelm
coöptāti•ō -ōnis *f* cooption, election of a colleague by vote of incumbent members
coöpt•ō -āre *vt* to coopt
coör•ior -īrī -tus sum *vi* to rise, rise suddenly; (fig) (of war) to break out; (of wind) to arise
coört•us -ūs *m* rising, originating
cōp•a -ae *f* barmaid
cophĭn•us -ī *m* basket
cōpi•a -ae *f* abundance, supply, store, plenty; multitude, large number; wealth, prosperity; opportunity, means; command of language, fluency, richness of expression; (with *genit*) power over; (with *dat*) access to; **pro copia** according to opportunity, according to ability; *f pl* troops, armed forces; provisions, supplies
cōpiŏl•ae -ārum *f pl* small contingent of troops
cōpiōsē *adv* abundantly, plentifully; (rhet) fully, at length
cōpiōs•us -a -um *adj* plentiful; well supplied, rich, wealthy; eloquent, fluent (*speech*); (with *abl*) abounding in, rich in
cōp•is -e *adj* rich, well supplied
cōpŭl•a -ae *f* cord, string, rope, leash; (fig) tie, bond

cōpŭlāti·ō -ōnis *f* coupling, joining, union; combining (*of words*)
cōpŭl·ō -āre *vt* to couple, join; (fig) to unite; (with *dat* or with **cum** + *abl*) to couple with, join to, combine with
cōpŭl·or -ārī -ātus sum *vt* to join, clasp; **dexteras copulari** to shake hands
coqu·a -ae *f* cook (*female*)
coquīn·ō -āre *vi* to be a cook
co·quō -quĕre -xī -ctum *vt* to cook; to fry, roast, bake, boil; to prepare (*a meal*); to burn, parch; to ripen, mature; to digest; to disturb, worry, disquiet; to plan, concoct, dream up
coqu·us or **coc·us -ī** *m* cook
cor cordis *n* heart; mind, judgment; (as seat of feelings) heart, soul; dear friend; *n pl* persons, souls; **cordi esse** (with *dat*) to please, be dear to, be agreeable to
cōram *adv* in person, personally; publically, openly; in someone's presence, face to face; *prep* (coming before or after *abl*) before, in the presence of, face to face with
corb·is -is *m* or *f* wicker basket
corbīt·a -ae *f* slow-sailing merchant ship
corbŭl·a -ae *f* small basket
corcŭl·um -ī *n* little heart; sweetheart; poor fellow
Corcȳr·a -ae *f* island off the coast of Epirus, identified with Scheria, the island of Alcinous
cordātē *adv* wisely, prudently
cordol·ium -iī or **-ī** *n* heartache
Corfin·ium -iī or **-ī** *n* town in Central Italy which served as headquarters of Italian allies during the Social War against Rome in 90-89 B.C.
coriandr·um -ī *n* coriander
Corinthi·us -a -um *adj* Corinthian; **aes Corinthium** alloy of gold, silver, and copper, used in making expensive jewelry, etc.; *m pl* Corinthians; *n pl* costly Corinthian products
Corinth·us -ī *f* Corinth
Coriŏl·ī -ōrum *m pl* town in Latium, capital of the Volsci, from the capture of which, in 493 B.C., C. Marcius received the surname of Coriolanus
cor·ium -iī or **-ī** *n* or **cor·ius -iī** or **-ī** *m* skin, hide; bark; leather
Cornēli·us -a -um *adj* Cornelian; **gens Cornelia** Cornelian tribe (*famous Roman tribe, especially for the Scipios, the Gracchi, and Sulla*); *f* Cornelia (*daughter of Scipio Africanus Major and mother of the Gracchi*)
corneŏl·us -a -um *adj* horny
cornĕ·us -a -um *adj* horny; of the cornel tree; of cornel wood
cornĭc·en -inis *m* horn blower
cornīc·or -ārī -ātus sum *vi* to caw
cornīcŭl·a -ae *f* poor little crow
corniculār·ius -iī or **-ī** *m* soldier decorated with a horn-shaped medal for bravery; adjutant to a centurion
cornicŭl·um -ī *n* little horn; horn-shaped decoration, awarded for bravery
cornĭg·er -ĕra -ĕrum *adj* horn-bearing, horned
cornĭp·ēs -ĕdis *adj* hoofed
corn·ix -īcis *f* crow (*whose appearance on one's left side was considered a favorable omen and whose cries were regarded as a sign of rain*)
corn·ū -ūs or **corn·um -ī** *n* horn; horn, trumpet; lantern; funnel; oil cruet; hoof; bill (*of bird*); horn (*of moon*); branch (*of river*); arm (*of bay*); tongue (*of land*); crest socket (*of helmet*); roller end (*of book*); (mil) wing, flank; **cornua addere** (with *dat*) to give courage to, add strength to; **cornua sumere** to gain strength
corn·um -ī *n* cornel cherry
corn·us -ī *f* cornel cherry tree; dogwood tree; spear, shaft, javelin
coroll·a -ae *f* small garland
corollār·ium -iī or **-ī** *n* garland; gilt wreath given as reward to actors; gift, gratuity
corōn·a -ae *f* crown, garland; circle of bystanders; (mil) cordon of besiegers; ring of defense; **corona civica** decoration for saving a life; **corona muralis** decoration for being the first to scale an enemy wall; **corona navalis** decoration for naval victory; **sub corona vendere** to sell (*captives*) as slaves; **sub corona venire** (of captives) to be sold at public auction
Corōn·a -ae *f* Ariadne's crown, Corona Borealis (*constellation*)
corōnāri·us -a -um *adj* for a crown; **aurum coronarium** gold collected in the provinces for a victorious general
Corōnē·a -ae *f* town in Boeotia
Corōn·eus -ĕī *m* king of Phocis whose daughter was changed into a crow
Corōnīd·ēs -ae *m* Aesculapius, the son of Coronis
Corōn·is -īdis *f* daughter of Phylegyas and mother of Aesculapius
corōn·ō -āre *vt* to crown, wreathe; to enclose, encircle, shut in
corporĕ·us -a -um *adj* physical, of the body; corporeal, substantial; of flesh
corpulent·us -a -um *adj* corpulent
corp·us -ŏris *n* body; matter, substance; flesh; trunk; corpse; person, individual; body, frame, structure; framework; community; corporation; particle, grain
corpuscŭl·um -ī *n* puny body; particle, atom; (as term of endearment) little fellow
cor·rādō -rādĕre -rāsī -rāsum *vt* to scrape together, rake up; (fig) to scrape (*e.g., money*) together

correcti·ō -ōnis *f* correction, improvement, amendment; rhetorical restatement
correct·or -ōris *m* reformer; censor, critic
correctus *pp* of **corrigo**
cor·rēpō -rēpĕre -repsī *vi* to creep, slink; **in dumeta correpere** (fig) to beat around the bush, indulge in jargon
correptius *adv* more briefly; **correptius exire** to end in a short vowel, have a short vowel
correptus *pp* of **corripio**
corrīd·ĕō -ēre *vi* to laugh out loud
corrigi·a -ae *f* shoelace
cor·rigō -rigĕre -rexī -rectum *vt* to make straight, straighten out; to smooth out; to correct, improve, reform; to make up for (*delay*); to make the best of
cor·ripiō -ripĕre -ripŭī -reptum *vt* to seize, snatch up, carry off; to speed up, rush; to steal, carry off; to attack; to shorten, contract; to reprove, accuse, reproach; to cut (*a period of time*) short
corrōbŏr·ō -āre *vt* to strengthen, invigorate, corroborate; (fig) to fortify, encourage
cor·rōdo -rōdĕre -rōsī -rōsum *vt* to gnaw, chew up
corrŏg·ō -āre *vt* to go asking for, collect, drum up, solicit
corrōsus *pp* of **corrodo**
corrūg·ō -āre *vt* to wrinkle, corrugate; **nares corrugare** (with *dat*) to cause (*someone*) disgust
cor·rumpō -rumpĕre -rūpī -ruptum *vt* to burst; to break to pieces, smash; to destroy completely, ruin, waste; to mar, corrupt, adulterate; to falsify, tamper with (*documents*); to bribe; to seduce, corrupt
corrŭ·ō -ĕre -ī *vt* to shatter, wreck, ruin; *vi* to fall down, tumble, sink; (fig) to fall, fail, sink, go down
corruptē *adv* corruptly, perversely; in a lax manner
corruptēl·a -ae *f* corruption, seduction; bribery; seducer, misleader
corrupti·ō -ōnis *f* corrupting, ruining, breaking up; corrupt condition
corrupt·or -ōris *m* or **corruptr·ix -īcis** *f* corrupter, seducer, briber
corrupt·us -a -um *pp* of **corrumpo**; *adj* corrupt, spoiled, bad, ruined
cort·ex -icis *m* or *f* bark, shell, hull, rind; cork; **nare sine cortice** to swim without a cork life preserver; to be on one's own
cortīn·a -ae *f* kettle, caldron; tripod; (fig) vault of heaven
corŭlus see **corylus**
corusc·ō -āre *vt* to shake, brandish; *vi* to flit, flutter, to oscillate; to tremble; to flash, gleam
corusc·us -a -um *adj* oscillating, vibrating, tremulous; flashing, gleaming, glittering
corv·us -ī *m* raven; (mil) grapnel
Corybant·ēs -ium *m pl* Corybantes (*priests of Cybele*)
Corybanti·us -a -um *adj* of the Corybantes
cōrўc·us -ī *m* punching bag
corylēt·um -ī *n* cluster of hazel trees
corўl·us or **corŭl·us -ī** *f* hazel tree
corymbĭf·er -ĕra -ĕrum *adj* wearing or bearing clusters of ivy berries; *m* Bacchus
corymb·us -ī *m* cluster (*esp. of ivy berries*)
coryphae·us -ī *m* leader, head
cōrўt·os or **cōrўt·us -ī** *m* quiver (*for arrows*)
cōs cōtis *f* flint; grindstone, whetstone
Cō·s or **Co·ūs -ī** *f* small island in the Aegean Sea, famous for its wine and fine linen
cosmēt·a -ae *m* slave in charge of the wardrobe
cost·a -ae *f* rib; (fig) side, wall
cost·um -ī *n* perfume
cothurnāt·us -a -um *adj* wearing the tragic buskin; suitable to tragedy; tragic, of tragedy
cothurn·us -ī *m* high boot; hunting boot; buskin (*worn by tragic actors*); subject of tragedy; tragedy; lofty style of Greek tragedy
cōtid- = **cottid-**
cottăb·us -ī *m* game which consisted in flicking drops of wine on a bronze vessel
cottăn·a or **cottŏn·a -ōrum** *n pl* Syrian figs
cottīdiānō *adv* daily
cottīdiān·us or **cotīdiān·us -a -um** *adj* daily; everyday, ordinary
cottīdiē or **cōtīdiē** *adv* daily, every day
coturn·ix -īcis *f* quail
Cotytti·a -ōrum *n pl* festival of Cotytto
Cotytt·o -ūs *f* Thracian goddess of lewdness
Coūs see **Cos**
Cō·us -a -um *adj* Coan; *n* Coan wine; *n pl* Coan garments
covinnār·ius -iī or **-ī** *m* soldier who fought from a chariot
covinn·us -ī *m* war chariot of the Britons and the Belgae; coach
cox·a -ae *f* hipbone
coxend·ix -īcis *f* hip
crābr·ō -ōnis *m* hornet; **irritare crabrones** (fig) to stir up a hornet's nest
cramb·ē -ēs *f* cabbage; **crambe repetita** warmed-over cabbage; same old story
Crant·or -ōris *m* Greek Academic philosopher of Soli in Cilicia (*fl* 300 B.C.)
crāpŭl·a -ae *f* drunkenness; hangover
crāpulāri·us -a -um *adj* for (*i.e., to prevent*) a hangover
crās *adv* tomorrow; (fig) in the future

crassē *adv* thickly; rudely; confusedly; dimly
crassitūd·ō -inis *f* thickness, density; dregs
crass·us -a -um *adj* thick, dense; dense, dull, stupid
Crass·us -ī *m* L. Licinius Crassus (*famous orator, d* 90 B.C.); M. Licinius Crassus (*triumvir, together with Caesar and Pompey,* 112?-53 B.C.)
crastin·us -a -um *adj* tomorrow's; (old *abl* form) **die crastini** tomorrow; *n* tomorrow; **in crastinum differre** to put off till tomorrow
crāt·ēr -ēris *m* or **crātēr·a -ae** *f* mixing bowl; bowl; crater
Crāt·ēr -ēris *m* Bowl (*constellation*)
crāt·is -is *f* wickerwork; harrow; ribs of shield; (mil) faggots (*for filling trenches*); joint, rib (*of body*); honeycomb
creātī·ō -ōnis *f* election
creāt·or -ōris *m* creator; procreator, father; founder
creātr·ix -īcis *f* creatress; mother
crēb·er -ra -rum *adj* luxuriant, prolific (*growth*); numerous, crowded; repeated; frequent
crēbr·escō *or* **crēb·escō -escĕre -ŭī** *vi* to increase, become frequent; to gain strength
crēbrit·ās -ātis *f* frequency
crēbrō *adv* repeatedly, frequently, again and again
crēdibil·is -e *adj* credible, trustworthy
crēdibiliter *adv* credibly
crēdit·or -ōris *m* creditor, lender
crēd·ō -ĕre -idī -itum *vt* to lend, loan; to entrust, consign; to believe; to think, believe, suppose, imagine; *vi* (with *dat*) to believe, put faith in, have trust or confidence in; **credas** one would image; **satis creditum est** it is believed on good evidence
crēdulit·ās -ātis *f* credulity, trustfulness
crēdŭl·us -a -um *adj* credulous, trustful; gullible; (with *dat* or **in** with *acc*) trusting in
crem·ō -āre *vt* to burn to ashes; to cremate
Cremōn·a -ae *f* town in N. Italy, which became a Roman colony in 209 B.C.
crem·or -ōris *m* juice obtained from animal or vegetable substances; broth
cre·ō -āre *vt* to create, produce; to elect to office; to cause, occasion; to beget, bear
Cre·ō or **Cre·ōn -ontis** *m* brother of Jocaste and brother-in-law of Oedipus; king of Corinth who gave his daughter in marriage to Jason
crep·er -ĕra -ĕrum *adj* dark; (fig) uncertain, doubtful
crepid·a -ae *f* slipper, sandal
crepidāt·us -a -um *adj* sandal-wearing
crepīd·ō -inis *f* base, pedestal; quay, pier; dam, dike, causeway
crepidŭl·a -ae *f* small sandal
crepit·ō -āre *vi* to make noise, rattle, crackle, creak, chatter, rumble, rustle
crepit·us -ūs *m* noise, rattle, creak, chatter, rumble, rustle
crep·ō -āre -ŭī -itum *vt* to make rattle; to talk noisily about, chatter about; *vi* to make noise, rattle, crackle, creak, chatter, rumble, rustle
crepundi·a -ōrum *n pl* rattle; toys
crepuscŭl·um -ī *n* dusk, twilight; dimness, obscurity; *n pl* darkness
crescō crescĕre crēvī crētum *vi* to come into being, arise; to grow, grow up; to increase, swell; to prosper, thrive; to become great, attain honor
crēt·a -ae *f* chalk; white clay; cosmetic
Crēt·a -ae *f* Crete
crētāt·us -a -um *adj* chalked; dressed in white (*as candidate for office*)
crētě·us -a -um *adj* of chalk, of clay
crētī·ō -ōnis *f* (law) formal acceptance of an inheritance
crētōs·us -a -um *adj* abounding in chalk or clay
crētŭl·a -ae *f* white clay (*used for seals*)
crētus *pp* of **cerno**; *pp* of **cresco**
Creūs·a -ae *f* daughter of Priam and wife of Aeneas; daughter of Creon, king of Corinth and wife of Jason
crībr·um -ī *n* sieve; **imbrem in cribrum gerere** to carry coals to Newcastle
crīm·en -inis *n* charge, accusation; reproach; guilt, crime; **esse in crimine** to be accused
crīminātī·ō -ōnis *f* accusation; slander, false charge
crīmināt·or -ōris *m* accuser
crīmin·ō -āre or **crīmin·or -ārī -ātus sum** *vt* to accuse; to slander; to complain of, denounce
crīminōsē *adv* by way of accusation, accusingly, reproachfully
crīminōs·us -a -um *adj* accusing, reproachful, slanderous
crīnāl·is -e *adj* for the hair; *n* hairpin
crīn·is -is *m* hair; (fig) tail of a comet
crīnīt·us -a -um *adj* long-haired; **stella crinita** comet
crīs·ō -āre *vi* (of women) to wiggle the buttocks
crisp·ans -antis *adj* curled, wrinkled
crisp·ō -āre *vt* to curl, wave (*hair*); to swing, wave, brandish (*a weapon*)
crisp·us -a -um *adj* curled, waved (*hair*); curly-headed; curled, wrinkled; tremulous, quivering
crist·a -ae *f* cock's comb; crest, plume

cristāt·us -a -um *adj* crested, plumed
critic·us -ī *m* critic
crocē·us -a -um *adj* of saffron; saffron-colored, yellow, golden
crocĭn·um -ī *n* saffron
crōc·iō -īre *vi* to croak
crocodīl·us -ī *m* crocodile
crocōtārĭ·us -a -um *adj* of saffron-colored clothes
crocōtŭl·a -ae *f* saffron-colored dress
croc·us -ī *m* or **croc·um -ī** *n* crocus; saffron; saffron color
Croes·us -ī *m* king of Lydia, famous for his wealth (590?-546 B.C.)
crotalistrĭ·a -ae *f* castanet dancer
crotăl·um -ī *n* castanet
cruciābilitāt·ēs -um *f pl* torments
cruciābilĭter *adv* with torture
cruciāment·um -ī *n* torture
cruciāt·us -ūs *m* torture; mental torment; instrument of torture; (humorously) calamity
crucĭ·ō -āre *vt* to put to wrack, torture, torment; (fig) to grieve, torment
crūdēl·is -e *adj* cruel, hardhearted; (with **in** + *acc*) cruel toward
crūdēlĭt·ās -ātis *f* cruelty
crūdēlĭter *adv* cruelly
crūd·escō -escĕre -ŭī *vi* to grow violent, grow worse
crūdĭt·ās -ātis *f* indigestion
crūd·us -a -um *adj* bloody, bleeding; uncooked, raw; unripe, green; undressed (*hide*); undigested; suffering from indigestion; hoarse; fresh, vigorous (*old age*); cruel, merciless
cruent·ō -āre *vt* to bloody, stain with blood; (fig) to wound
cruent·us -a -um *adj* gory, bloodstained; bloodthirsty, cruel; blood-red
crumēn·a or **crumīn·a -ae** *f* purse, pouch; (fig) money
crumill·a -ae *f* purse
cru·or -ōris *m* gore, blood; *m pl* bloodshed, murder
cruppellārĭ·ī -ōrum *m pl* mail-clad combatants
crūrifrag·ĭus -ĭī or **-ī** *m* slave with broken shins
crūs crūris *n* leg, shin
crust·a -ae *f* crust, shell, rind, bark; inlaid work, mosaic; stucco
crustŭl·um -ī *n* cooky
crust·um -ī *n* pastry
crux crucis *f* cross, gallows; trouble, misery; gallows bird; tormentor; **i in malam crucem** (coll) go hang yourself
crypt·a -ae *f* underground passage, covered gallery
cryptoportĭc·us -ūs *f* covered walk
crystallĭn·us -a -um *adj* made of crystal; *n pl* crystal vases
crystall·us -ī *f* or **crystall·um -ī** *n* crystal
cubiculār·is -e *adj* bedroom
cubiculārĭ·us -a -um *adj* bedroom; *m* chamberlain
cubicŭl·um -ī *n* bedroom; emperor's box in the theater
cubīl·e -is *n* bed, couch; marriage bed; lair, nest, hole; kennel; **avaritiae cubilia** (fig) den of greediness
cubĭt·al -ālis *n* elbow cushion
cubitāl·is -e *adj* of the elbow; one cubit long
cubĭt·ō -āre *vi* to be in the habit of lying down; (with **cum** + *abl*) to go to bed with, have intercourse with
cubĭt·um -ī *n* elbow; cubit
cubĭt·us -ūs *m* lying down; intercourse
cub·ō -āre -ŭī or **-āvī -ĭtum** *vi* to lie, lie down; to recline at table; to lie in bed; to lie sick; (of roof) to slope; (of towns, etc.) to lie on a slope
cucull·us -ī *m* cowl, hood
cucūl·us -ī *m* cuckoo; lazy farmer
cucŭm·is -ĕris *m* cucumber
cucurbĭt·a -ae *f* gourd; (med) cupping glass
cūd·ō -ĕre *vt* to strike, beat, pound; thresh; to forge; to coin, stamp
cuicuimŏdī or **quoiquoimŏdī** *adj* any kind of
cuj·ās -ātis *pron* from what country
culcĭt·a -ae *f* mattress, feather tick; cushion, pillow
culcitell·a -ae *f* little cushion
cūlĕus see **culleus**
cul·ex -ĭcis *m* or *f* gnat
culīn·a -ae *f* kitchen; cuisine
cullĕ·us or **cūlĕ·us -ī** *m* leather bag (*for holding liquids*); scrotum
culm·en -ĭnis *n* stalk; top, summit; roof; (fig) height, pinnacle, zenith
culm·us -ī *m* stalk, stem; straw, thatch
culp·a -ae *f* fault, blame; immorality; **in culpa esse** or **in culpa versari** to be at fault
culpĭt·ō -āre *vt* to blame, find fault with
culp·ō -āre *vt* to blame, reproach, censure, find fault with, complain of
cult·a -ōrum *n pl* plantation; grain fields
cultē *adv* elegantly, sophisticatedly, with refinement
cultell·us -ī *m* small knife
cult·er -rī *m* knife; razor; plowshare
cultĭ·ō -ōnis *f* cultivation; tilling of the ground, agriculture
cult·or -ōris *m* tiller, planter, cultivator, farmer; inhabitant; supporter; worshiper
cultr·ix -īcis *f* cultivator (*female*); inhabitant (*female*); (fig) nurse
cultūr·a -ae *f* tilling, cultivating; agriculture; care, cultivation (*of the mind*); (with *genit*) playing up to (*e.g., influential friends*)
cult·us -a -um *pp* of **colo**; *adj* tilled, cultivated; neat, well dressed, prim; cultivated, refined, civilized (*person*); cultured, refined (*mind*)
cult·us -ūs *m* tilling, cultivation (*of land*); care, tending, keeping (*of flocks, etc.*); care (*of body*); training, education; culture, refinement, civilization; high style of living; luxury;

style of dress, fancy clothes; fancy outfit; worship, reverence, veneration
culull·us -ī *m* drinking cup
cūl·us -ī *m* buttock
cum *prep* (with *abl*) (accompaniment) with, together with, in company with; (time) at the same time with, at the time of, at, with; (circumstance, manner, etc.) with, under, in, in the midst of, among, in connection with; **cum eo quod** or **cum eo ut** on condition that; **cum pace** peacefully; **cum prima luce** at dawn; **cum primis** especially, particularly; **mecum** at my house
cum, quum, or **quom** *conj* when, at the time when; whenever; when, while, as; since, now that, because; although; **cum maxime** just when; especially when, just while; just then, just now; **cum primum** as soon as; **cum . . . tum** both . . . and, not only . . . but also, while . . . so too; **praesertim cum** or **cum praesertim** especially since, especially as; **quippe cum** since of course; **utpote cum** seeing that
Cūm·ae -ārum *f pl* town on coast of Campania and oldest Greek colony in Italy, famous as the residence of its Sibyl
Cūmān·us -a -um *adj* Cumaean; *n* Cicero's estate near Cumae
cumb·a or **cymb·a -ae** *f* boat, skiff
cumĕr·a -ae *f* bin
cumīn·um -ī *n* cumin (*medicinal plant, said to produce paleness*)
cumque, cunque, or **quomque** *adv* at any time
cumulātē *adv* fully, completely, abundantly, copiously
cumulāt·us -a -um *adj* increased, augmented; filled, full, perfect, complete
cumŭl·ō -āre *vt* to heap up, pile up; to amass, accumulate; to overload; to make complete, make perfect, crown
cumŭl·us -ī *m* heap, pile; increase, addition
cūnābŭl·a -ōrum *n pl* cradle
cūn·ae -ārum *f pl* cradle; nest
cunctābund·us -a -um *adj* hesitant, loitering, delaying
cunct·ans -antis *adj* hesitant, reluctant, dilatory
cunctanter *adv* hesitantly, slowly
cunctāti·ō -ōnis *f* hesitation, reluctance, delay
cunctāt·or -ōris *m* dawdler, slowpoke
cunct·or -ārī -ātus sum *vi* to hesitate, delay, linger, be in doubt; **cunctatus brevi** after a moment's hesitation
cunct·us -a -um *adj* all together, the whole, all, entire
cuneātim *adv* in the form of a wedge
cuneāt·us -a -um *adj* wedge-shaped
cunĕ·ō -āre *vt* to fasten with a wedge; (fig) to wedge in, squeeze in
cunĕ·us -ī *m* wedge; wedge-form sections of seats in the theater; (mil) troops formed up in the shape of a wedge
cunīcŭl·us -ī *m* rabbit; burrowing underground; (mil) mine
cunque see **cumque**
cūp·a -ae *f* vat
cuped- = cupped-
cupīdē *adv* eagerly
cupidĭt·ās -ātis *f* eagerness, enthusiasm, desire; passion, lust; ambition; greed, avarice; partisanship
cupīd·ō -ĭnis *m* eagerness, desire, longing; passion, lust; greed, avarice
Cupīd·ō -ĭnis *m* Cupid (*son of Venus*)
Cupīdinĕ·us -a -um *adj* Cupid's
cupĭd·us -a -um *adj* eager, enthusiastic, desirous, longing; ambitious; (with *genit*) desirous of, longing for, fond of, attached to
cupĭ·ens -entis *adj* eager, enthusiastic; (with *genit*) desirous of, longing for, fond of, enthusiastic about
cupienter *adv* eagerly, enthusiastically
cup·iō -ĕre -īvī or **iī -ītum** *vt* to wish, be eager for, long for, desire
cupīt·or -ōris *m* daydreamer
cuppēdi·a -ōrum *n pl* or **cupēdi·a -ae** *f* delicacies; sweet tooth
cuppēdinār·ĭus or **cupēdinār·ĭus -ĭī** or **-ī** *m* confectioner
cuppēd·ō -ĭnis *f* desire, longing
cupp·ēs -ĕdis *adj* fond of delicacies
cupressēt·um -ī *n* cypress grove
cupressĕ·us -a -um *adj* cypress
cupressĭf·er -ĕra -ĕrum *adj* cypress-bearing
cupress·us -ī or **-ūs** *f* cypress tree; box of cypress
cūr or **quor** *adv* why
cūr·a -ae *f* care, concern, worry; care, pains, attention; heartache; object of concern; sweetheart; administration, management, charge; trusteeship, guardianship; means of healing, cure, treatment; guardian, keeper; study, reflection; literary effort, literary work; **curae esse** (with *dat*) to be of concern to
cūrābĭl·is -e *adj* troublesome
cūral·ĭum -ĭī or **-ī** *n* coral
cūrātĭ·ō -ōnis *f* management, administration; office; treatment, cure
cūrātĭus *adv* more carefully
cūrāt·or -ōris *m* superintendent, manager; (law) guardian, keeper
cūrātūr·a -ae *f* care, attention; dieting
cūrāt·us -a -um *adj* cared-for, attended-to; anxious, earnest
curcŭlĭ·ō -ōnis *m* weevil
curculiuncŭl·us -ī *m* little weevil; (fig) trifle
Cur·ēs -ĭum *m pl* ancient Sabine town
Cūrēt·ēs -um *m pl* mythical people of Crete who attended Jupiter at his birth

cūrĭ·a -ae *f* curia, ward (*one of the thirty parts into which Romulus divided the Roman people*); meeting place of a curia; senate building
cūriāl·is -is *m* member of a curia or ward
cūriātim *adv* by curiae, by wards
cūriāt·us -a -um *adj* composed of curiae or wards; passed by the assembly of curiae; **comitia curiata** assembly of the curiae
cūrĭ·ō -ōnis *m* ward boss; **curio maximus** chief ward boss
cūrĭ·ō -ōnis *adj* lean, emaciated
cūriōsē *adv* carefully; curiously; (of style) affectedly
cūriōsĭt·ās -ātis *f* curiosity
cūriōs·us -a -um *adj* careful, diligent; curious, prying, inquisitive; careworn
cur·is or **quir·is -ītis** *f* spear
cūr·ō -āre *vt* to take care of, look after, attend to, trouble oneself about; to take charge of, see to; to provide for the payment of, settle up; to attend to (*the body with food, washing, etc.*); to cure; to worry about; **cura ut** see to it that; (at the end of a letter) **cura ut valeas** take care of yourself
curricŭlō *adv* at full speed, quickly
curricŭl·um -ī *n* race; lap (*of race*); racetrack; racing chariot; (fig) career
currō currĕre cucurrī cursum *vt* to run over, skim over, traverse; *vi* to run, dash, hurry; to sail; to move quickly, flow along; to fly; (of a speech) to move along; (of night, day) to pass away
curr·us -ūs *m* chariot, car; war chariot; triumphal car; triumph; racing chariot; plow wheel; ship
cursim *adv* on the double
cursĭt·ō -āre *vi* to keep running around, run up and down; to vibrate
curs·ō -āre *vi* to run around, run up and down
curs·or -ōris *m* runner, racer; courier; errand boy
cursūr·a -ae *f* running; haste, speed
curs·us -ūs *m* running, speeding, speed; trip; course, direction; suitable time or weather for travel; rapid movement, speed, flow; flow, progress; **magno cursu** at top speed; **cursus honorum** political career
curt·ō -āre *vt* to shorten; to circumcise
curt·us -a -um *adj* shortened; gelded, castrated; circumcised; broken; defective
curūl·is -e *adj* official, curule; **aedilis curulis** patrician aedile; **sella curulis** curule chair, official chair (*used by consuls, praetors, and patrician aediles*)
curvām·en -ĭnis *n* curve, bend
curvātūr·a -ae *f* curvature; **curvatura rotae** rim of a wheel
curv·ō -āre *vt* to curve, bend, arch; (fig) to affect, move, stir
curv·us -a -um *adj* curved, bent; crooked; concave, arched, hollow; winding (*stream, shore*); (fig) crooked; *n* wrong, crookedness
cusp·is -ĭdis *f* point, pointed end; bayonet; spearhead; spear, javelin; trident; scepter; sting (*of scorpion*)
custōdēl·a -ae *f* watch, guard, care
custōdĭ·a -ae *f* watch, guard, care; sentry, guard; sentry post; custody, prison; **custodiam agitare** to keep guard, be on guard; **in libera custodia** under surveillance, under house arrest
custōd·iō -īre -īvī or **-iī -ītum** *vt* to guard, watch over, protect, defend; to hold in custody; to keep an eye on; to keep carefully, preserve; **memoriā custodire** to keep in mind, remember well
cust·ōs -ōdis *m* guard, guardian, watchman; protector, bodyguard; jailer, warden; (mil) sentinel; spy; *m pl* garrison; *f* guardian; protectress; box, container
cuticŭl·a -ae *f* skin, cuticle
cut·is -is *f* skin; **cutem curare** (fig) to look after one's own skin
Cyān·ē -ēs *f* nymph who was changed into a fountain
cyathiss·ō -āre *vi* to serve wine
cyăth·us -ī *m* ladle; liquid measure (*one-twelfth of a sextarius, i.e., a half pint*)
cybae·a -ae *f* merchant ship
Cybĕl·ē or **Cybēl·ē -ēs** *f* originally a Phrygian goddess of fertility, later worshiped in Rome as Ops or Mater Magna
Cyclăd·es -um *f pl* Cyclades (*group of islands in Aegean Sea*)
cycl·as -ădis *f* woman's formal gown
cyclic·us -a -um *adj* cyclic; **poeta cyclicus** cyclic poet (*one of a group of poets treating the epic sagas revolving around the Trojan War*)
Cycl·ops -ōpis *m* mythical one-eyed giant of Sicily, esp. Polyphemus
cycnē·us -a -um *adj* swan's
cycn·us or **cygn·us -ī** *m* swan; (fig) poet
Cycn·us *or* **Cygn·us -ī** *m* king of the Ligurians, son of Sthenelus, changed into a swan, and placed among the stars; son of Neptune, changed into a swan
Cydōnĭ·us -a -um *adj* Cretan; *n* quince
cygnus see **cycnus**
cylindr·us -ī *m* cylinder; roller (*for rolling ground*)
Cyllēn·ē -ēs or **-ae** *f* mountain in Arcadia where Mercury was born
Cyllēnĭ·us -a -um *adj* of Mt. Cyllene; *m* Mercury
cymb·a -ae *f* boat, skiff
cymbăl·um -ī *n* cymbal
cymb·ium -iī or **-ī** *n* small cup

Cynicē *adv* like the Cynics
Cynic·us -a -um *adj* Cynic, relating to the Cynic philosophy; *m* Cynic philosopher, esp. Diogenes, its founder (412-323 B.C.)
cynocephăl·us -ī *m* dog-headed ape
Cynosūr·a -ae *f* Cynosure (*the northern constellation Ursa Minor*)
Cynthi·us -a -um *adj* of Mt. Cynthus; Cynthian; *m* Apollo; *f* Diana
Cynth·us -ī *m* mountain of Delos, famous as the birthplace of Apollo and Diana
cypariss·us -ī *f* cypress tree
Cypri·us -a -um *adj* Cypriote; *f* Venus
Cypr·us or **Cypr·os -ī** *f* Cyprus (*island off the coast of Asia Minor*)
Cypsĕl·us -ī *m* despot of Corinth (655-625 B.C.)
Cyrēn·ē -ēs *f* or **Cyrēn·ae -ārum** *f pl* chief city of Greek settlement in N.E. Africa
Cyr·us -ī *m* founder of the Persian monarchy in 559 B.C. (*d.* 529 B.C.); Cyrus the Younger (*under whom Xenophon served, d.* 401 B.C.)
Cyt·ae -ārum *f pl* town in Colchis, birthplace of Medea
Cytae·is -idis *f* Medea
Cythēr·a -ōrum *n pl* island off the S. coast of the Peloponnesus, famous for worship of Venus
Cytherē·is -idis *f* Venus
Cythereī·us -a -um *adj* Cytherean; **heros Cythereius** Aeneas; *f* Venus
Cytherē·us -a -um *adj* Cytherean; *f* Venus
cytis·us -ī *m* or *f* clover
Cytōriăc·us -a -um *adj* of Cytorus, Cytorian; **pecten Cytoriacus** comb made of boxwood
Cytōr·us or **Cytōr·os -ī** *m* mountain of Paphlagonia, famous for its boxwood
Cyzic·um -ī *n* or **Cyzic·us** or **Cyzic·os -ī** *f* town on Sea of Marmora

D

Dāc·ī -ōrum *m pl* Dacians (*people of the lower Danube*)
dactylic·us -a -um *adj* dactylic
dactўl·us -ī *m* dactyl
daedăl·us -a -um *adj* skillful, artistic, artfully constructed
Daedăl·us -ī *m* mythical builder of the labyrinth in Crete and the first to build wings and fly
Damascēn·us -a -um *adj* of Damascus
Damasc·us -ī *f* Damascus (*capital of Coele-Syria*)
damm·a or **dām·a -ae** *f* deer; venison
damnāti·ō -ōnis *f* condemnation
damnātōri·us -a -um *adj* guilty (*verdict*)
damnāt·us -a -um *adj* criminal; hateful
damnific·us -a -um *adj* harmful, injurious, pernicious
damnigerŭl·us -a -um *adj* harmful, injurious
damn·ō -āre *vt* to find guilty, sentence, condemn; to disapprove of, reject, blame; to consecrate, offer as a sacrifice, doom to the gods below; (with *genit* or *abl* of charge or punishment) to find (*someone*) guilty of; **capite** or **capitis damnare** to condemn to death; **de majestate damnare** to find guilty of treason; **voti damnare** to oblige (*someone*) to fulfill a vow
damnōsē *adv* destructively, so as to bring ruin
damnōs·us -a -um *adj* damaging, injurious, destructive, pernicious; prodigal; **canes damnosi** crap (*worst throw of the dice*); *m* spendthrift
damn·um -ī *n* loss, damage, harm, injury; misfortune; fine, penalty; fault; defect
Dană·ē -ēs *f* daughter of Acrisius and mother of Perseus
Danaïd·ēs -um *f pl* daughters of Danaus who killed their husbands on their wedding night, with the exception of Hypermnestra, and as punishment were made to carry water in the lower world
Dană·us -ī *m* king of Argos and father of fifty daughters; *m pl* Greeks
danist·a -ae *m* money lender, banker
danistic·us -a -um *adj* money-lending, banking, of bankers
danō see **dō**
Dānuv·ius -iī or **-ī** *m* Danube
Daphn·ē -ēs *f* nymph pursued by Apollo and changed into a laurel tree
Daphn·is -idis *m* handsome young Sicilian shepherd, the inventor of pastoral song
dapin·ō -āre *vt* to serve (*food*)
dap·s -is *f* ceremonial feast; sumptuous meal, banquet; simple food, poor meal
dapsil·is -e *adj* sumptuous, costly
Dardăn·us -a -um *adj* Dardanian, Trojan; Roman (*descendant of Aeneas*); *m* son of Jupiter and Electra and ancestor of the Trojan race; *m pl* people of Upper Moesia (*on Danube*)
Darē·us -ī *m* Darius (*king of Persia,* 521-485 B.C.); Darius Ochus or

Nothus (*king of Persia,* 424-405 B.C.); Darius Codomanus (*last king of Persia,* 336-331 B.C.)
datāri·us -a -um *adj* to be handed out, to give away
datātim *adv* giving in turn, passing from one to another
dati·ō -ōnis *f* giving, alloting; (law) right of alienation
datīv·us -a -um *adj* & *m* dative
dat·ō -āre *vt* to keep giving away, be in the habit of giving
dat·or -ōris *m* giver
dat·us -ūs *m* giving
Daul·is -idis *f* town in Phocis, famous for the fable of Procne and Philomela
Daun·us -ī *m* king of Apulia and ancestor of Turnus, the opponent of Aeneas
dē *prep* (with *abl*) (of space) down from, from, away from, out of; (of origin) from, of, descended from, derived from; (of separation) from among, out of; (of time) immediately after; about, concerning, of, in respect to; for, on account of, because of; according to, in imitation of; **de improviso** unexpectedly; **de industria** on purpose; **de integro** afresh, all over again; **de novo** anew
de·a -ae *f* goddess
dealb·ō -āre *vt* to whiten, whitewash, plaster
deambulāti·ō -ōnis *f* strolling, walking about, stroll, walk
deambŭl·ō -āre *vi* to go for a walk, take a stroll
deăm·ō -āre *vt* to be in love with; to be much obliged to
dearm·ō -āre *vt* to disarm
deartŭ·ō -āre *vt* to tear limb from limb, dismember; (fig) to waste, wreck
deasci·ō -āre *vt* to smooth with an ax; (coll) to cheat, con
dēbacch·or -ārī -ātus sum *vi* to rant and rave
dēbellāt·or -ōris *m* conqueror
dēbell·ō -āre *vt* to fight it out with, wear down, subdue; *vi* to fight it out to the end; to bring a war to an end
dēb·ĕō -ēre -ŭī -ĭtum *vt* to owe; to be responsible for; (with *inf*) **a** to have to, be bound to, be obliged to; **b** to be destined to, be fated to; (with *dat*) to owe (*e.g., a favor*) to, be indebted to (*someone*) for; **deberi** (with *dat*) to be due to
dēbil·is -e *adj* lame, crippled, frail, feeble, paralyzed
dēbilit·ās -ātis *f* lameness, debility, weakness, helplessness
dēbilitāti·ō -ōnis *f* disabling, paralyzing
dēbilit·ō -āre *vt* to lame; to disable, debilitate, weaken; to unnerve; to paralyze
dēbiti·ō -ōnis *f* debt
dēbit·or -ōris *m* debtor; person under obligation
dēbĭt·um -ī *n* debt; obligation
dēblatĕr·ō -āre *vt* to blurt out
dēcant·ō -āre *vt* to repeat monotonously; *vi* to sing on to the end; to stop singing
dē·cēdō -cēdĕre -cessī -cessum *vi* to withdraw, clear out, depart; to retire, retreat, fall back, abandon a position; to give place, make way, make room, yield; to depart, disappear, die; to abate, subside, cease; to go wrong, go awry; (with *dat*) to yield to, give in to; (with **de** + *abl*) to give up, relinquish, abandon
decem (indecl) *adj* ten; (fig) large number of
Decemb·er -ris *adj* & *m* December
decemjŭg·is -is *m* ten-horse chariot
decempĕd·a -ae *f* ten-foot measuring rod, ten-foot rule
decempedāt·or -ōris *m* surveyor
decempl·ex -icis *adj* tenfold
decemprīm·ī or **decem prīm·ī -ōrum** *m pl* board of ten (*governing Italian towns*)
decemscalm·us -a -um *adj* ten-oared
decemvirāl·is -e *adj* decemviral; **leges decemvirales** laws passed by the decemviri
decemvirāt·us -ūs *m* decemvirate
decemvĭr·ī -ōrum *m pl* decemviri, ten-man commission (*appointed in Rome at different times and for various purposes*); **decemviri legibus scribundis** commission to codify the laws (451 B.C.); **decemviri sacris faciundis** commission for attending to religious matters
decenn·is -e *adj* ten-year, lasting ten years
dec·ens -entis *adj* proper, becoming; handsome, pretty; decent, proper
decenter *adv* becomingly, decently, properly, with propriety
decenti·a -ae *f* propriety, decency
dē·cernō -cernĕre -crēvī -crētum *vt* to sift, separate; to decide, settle, determine, decree, resolve, vote; to decide by combat, fight out; to fight, combat; *vi* to contend, compete, struggle; to put forward a proposal; (with **de** or **pro** + *abl*) to fight over, fight for (*in court*)
dēcerp·ō -ĕre -sī -tum *vt* to pluck off, tear away, break off, gather, crop; to derive, enjoy (*e.g., benefits, satisfaction*); **aliquid de gravitate decerpere** to detract somewhat from the dignity
dēcertāti·ō -ōnis *f* decision, decisive struggle
dēcert·ō -āre *vi* to fight it out, decide the issue
dēcessi·ō -ōnis *f* withdrawing; retirement, departure (*from a province*); decrease; disappearance
dēcess·or -ōris *m* retiring official, predecessor in office
dēcess·us -ūs *m* withdrawal; retirement (*of official from a province*); decease, death

dec·et -ēre -ŭit (used only in 3d *sing* & *pl*) *vt* to befit, be becoming to; (with *inf*) it is fitting to (*someone*) to, it is proper for (*someone*) to; *vi* to be fitting, be proper; (with *dat* & *inf*) it is fitting to (*someone*) to, it is proper for (*someone*) to
dēcĭd·ō -ĕre -ī *vi* to fall down; to fall dead, die; to fall, drop, sink, fail, perish
dē·cīdō -cīdĕre -cīsī -cīsum *vt* to cut off, cut away; to cut short, terminate, put an end to, decide, settle; **pennas decidere** (fig) to clip (*someone's*) wings
deciens or **deciēs** *adv* ten times; **deciens centena milia** or **deciens** million
decimānus see **decumanus**
decĭm·us or **decŭm·us -a -um** *adj* the tenth; **cum decimo** tenfold; **cum decimo effecit ager** the field produced a tenfold return; **decimum** for the tenth time
dē·cipĭō -cipĕre -cēpī -ceptum *vt* to deceive, cheat; to snare, mislead, beguile; to escape the notice of; **aliquem laborum decipere** to make one forget his troubles; **laborum decipi** to be freed of troubles, forget one's troubles
dēcīsĭ·ō -ōnis *f* decision, settlement
decīsum *pp* of **decīdo**
Dec·ĭus -iī or **-ī** *m* P. Decius Mus (*Roman hero who voluntarily gave his life in battle during the Latin War in* 340 B.C. *to bring victory to the Roman army; his son who likewise gave his life in Samnite War in* 295 B.C.)
dēclāmātĭ·ō -ōnis *f* practice in public speaking; theme or subject matter in rhetorical exercise; loud talking, shouting, hubbub
dēclāmāt·or -ōris *m* elocutionist, declaimer; ranter
dēclāmātōrĭ·us -a -um *adj* rhetorical
dēclāmĭt·ō -āre *vt* to plead (*cases*); *vi* to practice public speaking; to bluster
dēclām·ō -āre *vt* to recite; *vi* to practice public speaking
dēclārātĭ·ō -ōnis *f* disclosure, declaration
dēclār·ō -āre *vt* to make clear, make evident, disclose; to proclaim, announce officially; to show, prove, demonstrate; to mean, express, signify; to declare (*as chosen for office*)
dēclīnātĭ·ō -ōnis *f* leaning away, bending aside, swerving; shunning, avoiding; digression; (gram) declension
dēclīn·ō -āre *vt* to deflect; to parry, avoid; to decline, conjugate; *vi* to deviate; to digress
dēclīv·e -is *n* declivity, slope
dēclīv·is -e *adj* sloping, steep, downhill
dēclīvĭt·ās -ātis *f* sloping terrain
dēcoct·a -ae *f* cold drink
dēcoct·or -ōris *m* bankrupt; (coll) old rake
dēcoct·us -a -um *pp* of **decoquo**; *adj* boiled down; mellow (*style*)
dēcoll·ō -āre *vt* to behead
dēcōl·ō -āre *vi* to trickle away, come to naught, fail
dēcŏl·or -ōris *adj* off-color, faded; dark, tanned; degenerate
dēcolōrātĭ·ō -ōnis *f* discoloring
dēcolōr·ō -āre *vt* to discolor, stain, deface
dē·cŏquō -coquĕre -coxī -coctum *vt* to boil down, boil thoroughly; to bring to ruin; *vi* to go bankrupt
dec·or -ōris *m* beauty, grace, elegance, charm; ornament
decōrē *adv* beautifully, gracefully; suitably, properly
decŏr·ō -āre *vt* to beautify, adorn, embellish; to decorate, honor
decōr·us -a -um *adj* beautiful, graceful, adorned; decorous, proper, suitable; fine, handsome; noble; *n* grace, propriety
dēcrepĭt·us -a -um *adj* decrepit, broken down, worn out
dē·crescō -crescĕre -crēvī -crētum *vi* to grow less, become fewer, diminish, subside, wane
dēcrēt·us -a -um *pp* of **decerno**; *n* decision, decree; principle, doctrine
decŭm·a or **decĭm·a -ae** *f* tenth part, tithe, land tax; largess to the people
decumān·us or **decimān·us -a -um** *adj* paying tithes; of the tenth cohort, of the tenth legion; *m* tax collector; *m pl* men of the tenth legion; *f* tax collector's wife; **porta decumana** main gate of a Roman camp on the side turned away from the enemy
decumāt·ēs -ium *adj* subject to tithes
dē·cumbō -cumbĕre -cubŭī *vi* to lie down; to recline at table; to fall (*in battle*)
decŭm·ō or **decĭmō -āre** *vt* to decimate
decurĭ·a -ae *f* decuria, group of ten; tenth part (*of a curia*); division, class (*without reference to number*); panel (*of judges*); social club
decuriātĭ·ō -ōnis *f* dividing into decuries
decuriāt·us -ūs *m* dividing into decuries
decurĭ·ō -āre *vt* (pol) to divide into groups of ten; (fig) to divide into groups
decurĭ·ō -ōnis *m* decurion (*head of a decuria*); (mil) cavalry officer (*in charge of ten men*); senator of a municipality or colony
dē·currō -currĕre -cucurrī or **-currī -cursum** *vt* to pass over, run over, traverse; to pass through (*life*); to get over (*troubles*); to discuss, treat; *vi* to run down; (mil) to parade, maneuver; (of river, ship) to run down to the sea; to run for

help; to sail; to land; **eo decursum est ut** it got to the point where
dēcursi·ō -ōnis *f* (mil) dress parade; maneuvers; raid, descent
dēcurs·us -ūs *m* running down; downward course; (mil) dress parade; (mil) maneuvers; (mil) raid; end of course, completion; **decursus honorum** completion of political career
dēcurtāt·us -a -um *adj* cut down, cut off short, mutilated; clipped (*style*)
dec·us -ŏris *n* beauty, glory, honor, dignity; virtue, worth; source of glory; *n pl* great deeds, distinctions
dēcuss·ō -āre *vt* to divide crosswise (*in the form of an* X)
dē·cutiō -cutĕre -cussī -cussum *vt* to shake off, beat off, strike down; to chop off (*head*); to break down (*wall with battering ram*)
dē·dĕcet -decēre -decŭit (used only in 3d *sing & pl*) *vt* it ill becomes, ill befits; (with *inf*) it is a disgrace to
dēdecŏr·ō -āre *vt* to disgrace, dishonor, bring shame to; to make a sham of
dēdecōr·us -a -um *adj* disgraceful, dishonorable, unbecoming
dēdĕc·us -ŏris *n* disgrace, dishonor, shame; vice, crime, outrage; (mil) disgraceful defeat; **dedecori esse** (with *dat*) to be a source of disgrace to; **dedecus admittere** to incur disgrace; **per dedecus** disgracefully
dēdicāti·ō -ōnis *f* dedication, consecration
dēdic·ō -āre *vt* to dedicate, consecrate, set aside; to declare (*property in a census return*)
dēdign·or -ārī -ātus sum *vt* to scorn, disdain, look down on; (with double *acc*) to scorn (*someone*) as; **aliquem maritum dedignari** to regard someone as an unworthy husband
dē·discō -discĕre -didĭcī *vt* to forget
dēditīc·ius -iī or **-ī** *m* captive; *m pl* prisoners of war
dēditi·ō -ōnis *f* surrender, capitulation
dēdit·us -a -um *pp* of **dedo**; *adj* (with *dat*) given to, devoted to, addicted to; (with **in** + *abl*) absorbed in; *m pl* prisoners of war, captives
dē·dō -dĕre -didī -ditum *vt* to give up, surrender; to devote; to apply; to abandon; **aliquem hostibus in cruciatum dedere** to hand someone over to the enemy to be tortured; **deditā operā** on purpose, intentionally; **neci** or **ad necem dedere** to put to death
dēdoc·ĕō -ēre -ŭī -tum *vt* to cause to forget; (with *inf*) to teach (*someone*) not to
dēdol·ĕō -ēre -ŭī *vi* to grieve no more
dēdŏl·ō -āre *vt* to chop away; to chop smooth
dē·dūcō -dūcĕre -duxī -ductum *vt* to lead or draw down; to launch (*ship*); to accompany, escort; to lead out (*colonists to new colony*); to conduct (*bride to her husband*), give away (*bride*); to evict; to subtract, deduct, diminish; to summon (*as witness*); to divert, mislead; to derive (*name*); to compose (*poetry*); to dissuade; to spin out (*thread*); to comb out (*hair*)
dēducti·ō -ōnis *f* leading or drawing off; settling (*of colonists*); (law) eviction; reduction; inference; **rationis deductio** train of reasoning
dēduct·us -a -um *pp* of **deduco**; *adj* drawn down; bent inwards, concave; lowered, modest; subtle, well wrought (*poem*)
deerr·ō -āre *vi* to go astray, wander away; **a vero deerrare** (fig) to stray from the truth
dēfaec·ō -āre *vt* to cleanse of dregs; to wash; (fig) to clear up, make clear
dēfatīgāti·ō -ōnis *f* exhaustion
dēfatīg·ō -āre *vt* to wear out, exhaust
dēfatiscor see **defetiscor**
dēfecti·ō -ōnis *f* failure; defection, desertion; weakening, exhaustion; eclipse; **defectio animi** mental breakdown; **in defectione esse** to be up in revolt
dēfect·or -ōris *m* defector, deserter; rebel
dēfect·us -a -um *pp* of **deficio**; *adj* weak, worn out
dēfect·us -ūs *m* failing, failure; desertion; revolt; eclipse
dē·fendō -fendĕre -fendī -fensum *vt* to repel, beat off, avert; to defend, protect, guard; to keep off (*the cold*); to answer (*a charge*); to champion (*a cause*); to support, uphold, maintain (*an argument*); to play the part of (*a character*); (law) to defend
dēfensi·ō -ōnis *f* defense
dēfensit·ō -āre *vt* to defend often; **causas defensitare** to be a lawyer
dēfens·ō -āre *vt* to defend, protect
dēfens·or -ōris *m* defender, protector; (law) defense lawyer; (law) guardian; champion (*of people*); *m pl* garrison
dēfensus *pp* of **defendo**
dē·fĕrō -ferre -tŭlī -lātum *vt* to bring or carry down; to bear off, carry away; to throw (*ship*) off course; to offer, confer, grant; to inform against, indict; to give an account of, announce, report; to recommend; to register; **ad aerarium deferre** to recommend (*someone*) for a monetary reward (*because of outstanding service to the State*); **ad consilium deferre** to take into consideration
dē·fervescō -fervescĕre -fervī or **-ferbŭī** *vt & vi* to cool off, calm down; (of a speech) to lose momentum; (of passions) to die out

dēfess·us -a -um *adj* weary, worn out, exhausted
dē·fetiscor or **dē·fatiscor -fetiscī -fessus sum** *vi* to become weary, tired
dē·ficiō -ficĕre -fēcī -fectum *vt* to fail, disappoint; to desert, abandon; *vi* to fail, be a failure; to defect, desert; to secede; (of arms, food, etc.) to run short, run out; (of strength, morale, etc.) to fail, grow weak, droop, sink; (of sun, moon) to be eclipsed; (of fire) to die out; (com) to be bankrupt
dē·fīgō -fīgĕre -fixī -fixum *vt* to fix, fasten down; to drive down; to fix, concentrate (*eyes, attention*); to root to the spot, astound, stupefy; to bewitch, enchant; **in terra defigere** to stick, plant, set up (*something*) in the ground
dē·fingō -fingĕre -finxī *vt* to form, mold; to portray; to disfigure, deface
dēfīn·iō -īre -īvī -ītum *vt* to set bounds to, limit; (fig) to limit, define, explain; to fix, determine, appoint; to delimit, bring to a finish, end; to assign, prescribe
dēfīnītē *adv* precisely
dēfīnīti·ō -ōnis *f* boundary; (fig) marking out, prescribing; definition
dēfīnītīv·us -a -um *adj* explanatory
dēfīnīt·us -a -um *adj* definite, precise
dē·fīō -fiĕrī *vi* to fail, be lacking
dēflagrāti·ō -ōnis *f* conflagration
dēflăgr·ō -āre *vt* to burn down; *vi* to burn down, go up in flames; to perish, be destroyed; (of passions) to cool off, be allayed, subside
dē·flectō -flectĕre -flexī -flexum *vt* to deflect, bend aside, turn away, divert; (fig) to turn away, lead astray; *vi* to turn away, digress, deviate
dēfl·ĕō -ēre -ēvī -ētum *vt* to cry bitterly for; to mourn as lost; *vi* to cry bitterly
dēfloccāt·us -a -um *adj* stripped of wool, shorn; bald (*head*)
dēflōr·escō -escĕre -ŭī *vi* to shed blossoms; (fig) to fade, droop
dēflŭ·ō -ĕre -xī *vi* to flow or float down; to glide down, slide, fall; to flow out, run dry; to vanish, pass away, disappear, cease; to go out of style, become obsolete
dē·fodiō -fodĕre -fōdī -fossum *vt* to dig down; to hollow out; to bury, hide, conceal
dēfŏre = dēfutūrum esse
dēformāti·ō -ōnis *f* disfiguring, defacing
dēform·is -e *adj* shapeless, amorphous; misshapen, disfigured, ugly; degrading; degraded; unbecoming, humiliating
dēformit·ās -ātis *f* deformity, ugliness, hideousness; vileness, turpitude
dēformiter *adv* without grace, without beauty
dēform·ō -āre *vt* to form from a pattern; to sketch, delineate; to deform, disfigure, mar
dēfossus *pp* of **defodio**
defraud·ō or **defrūd·ō -āre** *vt* to defraud, rob; to cheat; **genium suum defraudare** to deny oneself some pleasure
defrēnāt·us -a -um *adj* unbridled, uncontrolled
defric·ō -āre -ŭī -ātum *vt* to rub down; to brush (*teeth*); (fig) to satirize
de·fringō -fringĕre -frēgī -fractum *vt* to break off, break to pieces
defrūdo see **defraudo**
defrūt·um -ī *n* new wine
dē·fugiō -fugĕre -fūgī *vt* to run away from, avoid, shirk; to evade (*e.g., authority, law*); *vi* to run off, escape
dēfunct·us -a -um *pp* of **defungor;** *adj* finished; dead
dē·fundō -fundĕre -fūdī -fūsum *vt* to pour out; to empty (*e.g., bucket*)
dē·fungor -fungī -functus sum *vi* (with *abl*) **a** to perform, finish, be done with; **b** to have done with, get rid of; **defunctus jam sum** I'm safe now; **defungi vitā** or **defungi** to die; **parvo victu defungi** to do with or be content with little food
dēfūsus *pp* of **defundo**
dēgĕn·er -ĕris *adj* degenerate; unworthy; ignoble
dēgenĕr·ō -āre *vt* to disgrace, dishonor, fall short of; *vi* to be inferior to one's ancestors, be degenerate; (fig) to fall off, degenerate, decline
dēgĕr·ō -ĕre *vt* to carry off, carry away
dēg·ō -ĕre -ī *vt* to spend, pass (*time, life*); **aetatem degere** to live; *vi* to live
dēgrandinat *v impers* it is hailing hard
dēgrăv·ō -āre *vt* to weigh down; (fig) to burden, distress, inconvenience, overpower
dē·gredior -grĕdī -gressus sum *vi* to march down, go down, walk down, descend; **ad pedes degredi** to dismount
dēgrunn·iō -īre *vi* to grunt hard, grunt out loud
dēgust·ō -āre *vt* to taste; (fig) to taste, sample, try, experience; (of weapon) to graze
dehinc *adv* from here; from now on; then, next; hereafter
dehisc·ō -ĕre *vi* to part, divide, gape, yawn
dehonestāment·um -ī *n* blemish, disfigurement, dishonor, disgrace
dehonest·ō -āre *vt* to dishonor, disgrace
dehort·or -ārī -ātus sum *vt* to advise to the contrary, dissuade
Dēianīr·a -ae *f* daughter of Oeneus and wife of Hercules

dein see **deinde**
deinceps *adv* one after another, in succession, in order; in regular order, without interruption
deinde or **dein** *adv* (of place) from that place, from there; (of time) then, thereafter, thereupon, afterwards; (in enumerating facts, presenting arguments) secondly, next in order, in the next place
Dēiotăr·us -ī *m* king of Galatia (*defended by Cicero before Caesar in the latter's house*)
Dēiphŏb·us -ī *m* son of Priam and Hecuba, and husband of Helen after Paris' death
dējecti·ō -ōnis *f* (law) eviction
déject·us -a -um *pp* of **dejicio**; *adj* low, depressed, sunken (*place*); discouraged, downhearted, despondent
dēject·us -ūs *m* felling (*of trees*); steep slope
dējĕr·ō or **dējūrō -āre** *vi* to swear solemnly
dē·jiciō -jicĕre -jēcī -jectum *vt* to throw down, fling down; to fell, bring low, kill; to depose (*from office*); to lower (*eyes*); to drive off course; (law) to evict; (mil) to dislodge, drive out; to deprive; (with *abl* or **de** + *abl*) to deprive (*someone*) of, prevent (*someone*) from obtaining, rob (*someone*) of; **oculos dejicere** (with **ab** + *abl*) to divert the eyes from; to turn away from
dējung·ō -ĕre *vt* to unyoke; to sever
dējūrō see **dejero**
dējŭv·ō -āre *vt* to fail to help
dē·lābor -lābī -lapsus sum *vi* to slip down, fall down, sink down; to glide down, float down; (fig) to come down, sink; (fig) to stoop, condescend; (with **ad** + *acc*) to be inclined toward, be partial to, tend toward; (with **in** + *acc*) to sneak in among
dēlacĕr·ō -āre *vt* to tear to pieces
dēlāment·or -ārī -ātus sum *vt* to grieve deeply for
delass·ō -āre *vt* to tire out, weary
dēlāti·ō -ōnis *f* reporting; informing, denouncing; **nominis delatio** indicting of a person
dēlāt·or -ōris *m* reporter; informer, denouncer
dēlātus *pp* of **defero**
dēlectābĭl·is -e *adj* delightful, enjoyable
dēlectāment·um -ī *n* delight, amusement, pastime
dēlectāti·ō -ōnis *f* delight, pleasure, charm, amusement, satisfaction
dēlect·ō -āre *vt* to delight, amuse, charm; to attract, allure; **delectari** (with *abl*) to be delighted by, delight in; *v impers* **me ire delectat** I like to go, I enjoy going
dēlect·us -a -um *pp* of **deligo**; *adj* picked, choice, select
dēlect·us -ūs *m* choosing, choice
dēlēgāti·ō -ōnis *f* substitution, delegation (*of one person for another*); payment (*of debt*)
dēlēg·ō -āre *vt* to assign, transfer; to attribute, impute, ascribe
dēlēnific·us -a -um *adj* soothing, seductive
dēlēnīment·um -ī *n* palliative, solace, comfort; allurement, bait
dēlēn·iō or **dēlīn·iō -īre -īvī -ītum** *vt* to soothe, calm down, console, appease; to allure, seduce, win over
dēlēnīt·or -ōris *m* charmer, cajoler
dēl·ĕō -ēre -ēvī -ētum *vt* to destroy, annihilate, overthrow, extinguish, raze; to blot out, erase, obliterate (*writing*); to annul, put an end to, abolish, finish
dēlētr·ix -īcis *f* destroyer
Dēliăc·us -a -um *adj* Delian, of or from Delos
dēlīberābund·us -a -um *adj* deliberating maturely
dēlīberāti·ō -ōnis *f* considering, weighing; deliberation, consultation; **habet res deliberationem** the matter requires thought, needs consideration
dēlīberātīv·us -a -um *adj* deliberative; requiring deliberation
dēlīberāt·or -ōris *m* thoughtful person
dēlīberāt·us -a -um *adj* resolved upon, determined
dēlībĕr·ō -āre *vt* to weigh well, ponder; to resolve, determine; to consult (*oracle*); *vi* to reflect, deliberate; (with **de** + *abl*) to think seriously about, think over well
dēlīb·ō -āre *vt* to sip, take a sip of; to taste, take a taste of, nibble at; to take away, detract, subtract, remove
dēlibr·ō -āre *vt* to strip the bark off (*trees*); to peel
dēlibūt·us -a -um *adj* anointed; defiled, stained, smeared; steeped
dēlicātē *adv* delicately, softly, luxuriously
dēlicāt·us -a -um *adj* delicate, dainty, tender, soft; pampered, spoiled; dainty, fastidious
dēlici·ae -ārum *f pl* allurements, enticements, delights; whims, pet ideas, fanciful ideas; voluptuousness; favorite, sweetheart, darling; **delicias facere** to play tricks; **delicias facere** (with *dat*) to play around with (*a girl*); **esse in deliciis** (with *dat*) to be the pet or favorite of; **habere in deliciis** to have as a pet or favorite
dēliciŏl·ae -ārum *f pl* darling
delic·ĭum -iī or **-ī** *n* sweetheart; favorite
dēlic·ō -āre *vt* to make clear, explain
dēlict·um -ī *n* fault, offense, wrong, transgression, defect
dēlicŭ·us -a -um *adj* lacking, wanting
dēlig·ō -āre *vt* to tie up, bind together, bind fast
dē·ligō -ligĕre -lēgī -lectum *vt* to

choose, select, pick out, single out, elect; to gather, gather in
dē·lingō -lingĕre -linxī *vt* to lick off; to have a lick of
dēlīni- = **deleni-**
dē·linquō -linquĕre -līquī -lictum *vi* to fail, be wanting, fall short; to do wrong, commit a fault or crime
dē·liquescō -liquescĕre -licŭī *vi* to melt, melt away, dissolve; to pine away
dēliquī·ō -ōnis *f* failure; (with *genit*) failure to get
dēliqu·ĭum -ĭī or **-ī** *n* failure
dēlĭqu·ō or **dēlĭc·ō -āre** *vt* to clear up, explain
dēlīrāment·um -ī *n* nonsense, absurdity
dēlīrātī·ō -ōnis *f* silliness, folly, madness; infatuation; dotage
dēlīr·ō -āre *vi* to be off the beam, be crazy, be mad; to drivel
dēlīr·us -a -um *adj* crazy, demented, silly; in dotage
dēlit·escō -escĕre -ŭī *vi* to conceal oneself, lie hidden, lurk
dēlītig·ō -āre *vi* to rant
Dēli·us -a -um *adj* Delian, of Delos
Dēl·os -ī *f* sacred island in the Cyclades, where Apollo was born
Delph·ī -ōrum *m pl* town in Phocis, in Central Greece, famous for the shrine and oracle of Apollo; inhabitants of Delphi
delphīn·us -ī or **delph·īn -īnis** *m* dolphin
Delphīn·us -ī m Dolphin (*constellation*)
Deltōt·on -ī *n* Triangulum (*constellation*)
dēlūbr·um -ī *n* shrine, temple, sanctuary
dēluct·ō -āre or **dēluct·or -ārī -ātus sum** *vi* to wrestle
dēlūdific·ō -āre *vt* to make fun of
dē·lūdō -lūdĕre -lūsī -lūsum *vt* to dupe, mock, deceive, delude
dēlumb·is -e *adj* enervated, enfeebled, weakened
dēmad·escō -escĕre -ŭī *vi* to become drenched; to be moistened
dēmand·ō -āre *vt* to hand over, entrust
dēmarch·us -ī *m* demarch (*chief of a village in Attica*); (fig) tribune of the people
dēm·ens -entis *adj* out of one's mind, demented, distracted, mad; senseless, wild, reckless
dēmensus *pp* of **demetior;** *n* ration, allowance
dēmenter *adv* insanely
dēmentī·a -ae *f* insanity, madness; *f pl* follies
dement·iō -īre *vi* to be mad
dēmer·ĕō -ēre -ŭī -ĭtum or **dēmer·ĕor -ērī -ĭtus sum** *vt* to earn, merit, deserve; to serve well, do a service to
dē·mergō -mergĕre -mersī -mersum *vt* to sink, plunge, submerge; (fig) to plunge, cast down, overwhelm
dēmessus *pp* of **dēmeto**
dē·mētior -mētīrī -mensus sum *vt* to measure off, measure out
dē·mĕtō -metĕre -messŭī -messum *vt* to mow, reap, cut off, cut down, harvest
dēmigrātī·ō -ōnis *f* emigration
dēmigr·ō -āre *vi* to migrate, emigrate, move, depart; (fig) to depart, die
dēmin·ŭō -uĕre -ŭī -ūtum *vt* to make smaller, lessen, diminish; (fig) to remit, reduce, lessen; **capite deminuere** to deprive of citizenship
dēminūtī·ō -ōnis *f* lessening, diminution, abridging; (law) right of disposing of property; **capitis diminutio** loss of civil rights; **provinciae diminutio** shortening of term of office
dēmīr·or -ārī -ātus sum *vt* to be surprised at, be amazed at
dēmissē *adv* low; humbly, modestly; abjectly, meanly
dēmissīcī·us -a -um *adj* allowed to hang down, flowing
dēmissī·ō -ōnis *f* letting down, sinking, lowering; **demissio animi** low morale
demiss·us -a -um *pp* of **demitto;** *adj* low, low-lying (*place*); drooping (*lips, etc.*); bent (*head*); allowed to hang down, flowing, loose (*hair*); downhearted, dejected; shy, unassuming, retiring, humble; poor, humble
dēmītig·ō -āre *vt* to make mild; **demitigari** to grow more lenient
dē·mittō -mittĕre -mīsī -missum *vt* to drop, let drop, let sink, lower; to bring downstream; to land (*ship*); to grow (*beard*); to move down (*troops from higher place*); **se demittere** to descend; to stoop, bend down
dēmiurg·us or **dāmiurg·us -ī** *m* chief magistrate in a Greek state
dēm·ō -ĕre -psī -ptum *vt* to take away, remove, withdraw, subtract; (with *dat* or with **de** + *abl*) to take away from, subtract from, withhold from
Dēmocrĭt·us -ī *m* famous philosopher of Abdera, in Thrace, founder of the atomic theory (460-361 B.C.)
dēmōl·ĭor -īrī -ītus sum *vt* to demolish, pull down
dēmōlītī·ō -ōnis *f* pulling down (*of statues*)
dēmonstrātī·ō -ōnis *f* pointing out; explanation
dēmonstrātīv·us -a -um *adj* showy
dēmonstrāt·or -ōris *m* indicator
dēmonstr·ō -āre *vt* to point out clearly; to state precisely, explain, describe; to mention, speak of; to demonstrate, prove, establish
dē·morĭor -mŏrī -mortŭus sum *vi* to die, die off
dēmŏr·or -ārī -ātus sum *vt* to delay, detain; to hinder, block; *vi* to wait

Dēmosthĕn·ēs -is *m* greatest Greek orator (384-322 B.C.)
dē·movĕō -movēre -mōvī -mōtum *vt* to remove, move away, dispossess, expel; to remove, discharge (*from office*); (fig) to divert, turn away
demptus *pp* of **demo**
dēmūgīt·us -a -um *adj* bellowing, lowing
dē·mulcĕō -mulcēre -mulsī *vt* to stroke lovingly, to caress
dēmum *adv* at last, finally; not till then; (to give emphasis) precisely, exactly, just; (to give assurance) in fact, certainly, to be sure, as a matter of fact; **decimo demum anno** not till the tenth year; **modo demum** only now, not till now; **nunc demum** now at last, not till now; **post demum** not till after; **sic demum** thus finally; **tum demum** then at length, not till then
dēmurmŭr·ō -āre *vt* to grumble right through (*e.g., a performance*)
dēmūtāti·ō -ōnis *f* changing, perversion, degeneracy
dēmūt·ō -āre *vt* to change, alter; to make worse; *vi* to change one's mind
dēnār·ĭus -iī or **-ī** *m* Roman silver coin, originally containing ten aces, later eighteen, approximately equivalent to twenty-five cents; money
dēnarr·ō -āre *vt* to recount in detail
dēnās·ō -āre *vt* to bite the nose off (*the face*)
dēnăt·ō -āre *vi* to swim downstream
dēnĕg·ō -āre *vt* to deny, refuse, turn down; *vi* to say no, give a flat refusal
dēn·ī -ae -a *adj* in sets of ten, ten each, in tens; ten; tenth
dēnicāl·is -e *adj* purifying from death; **feriae denicales** purification service (*after death in the household*)
dēnique *adv* finally, at last; in short, in a word, briefly; (for emphasis) just, precisely; (ironical) of course; **octavo denique mense** not till after the eighth month; **tum denique** then at last, only then, not till then
dēnōmĭn·ō -āre *vt* to name, designate
dēnorm·ō -āre *vt* to make crooked or irregular; to disfigure, spoil
dēnŏt·ō -āre *vt* to mark down, specify; to take careful note of, observe closely
den·s -tis *m* tooth; ivory; point, prong, fluke; (fig) tooth (*of envy, hatred, time, etc.*); **albis dentibus deridere aliquem** to laugh heartily at someone; **dens Indus** elephant's tusk
densē *adv* closely, thickly; in quick succession, repeatedly
densĭt·ās -ātis *f* closeness, thickness
dens·ō -āre or **dens·ĕō -ēre — -ētum** *vt* to make thick, thicken; to press close together; to close (*ranks*); to condense (*a speech*)
dens·us -a -um *adj* dense, close, crowded, thick; frequent, continuous; intense (*love, cold*); concise (*style*)
dentāl·ia -ium *n pl* plow beam
dentāt·us -a -um *adj* toothed, having teeth; serrated; polished (*paper*)
dentifrangibŭl·us -a -um *adj* tooth-breaking; *m* thug; *n* fist
dentilĕg·us -ī *m* toothpicker (*one who picks up teeth after they have been knocked out*)
dent·iō -īre *vi* to teethe, cut one's teeth
dē·nūbō -nūbĕre -nupsī -nuptum *vi* (of a woman) to marry beneath one's rank
dēnūd·ō -āre *vt* to denude, strip naked, strip bare; (fig) to lay bare (*facts*)
dēnuntiāti·ō -ōnis *f* intimation, warning, threat; announcement, proclamation; **senatūs denuntiatio** senate ordinance; **testimoni denuntiatio** summons to testify
dēnunti·ō -āre *vt* to intimate; to give notice of; to announce officially; to give official warning to; (mil) to report to, give an official report to; to warn, threaten; **denuntiare testimonium** (with *dat*) to give (*someone*) a summons to testify
dēnŭō *adv* anew, afresh, once more, all over again
deonĕr·ō -āre *vt* to unload
deorsum or **deorsus** *adv* downwards, down; (of position) down, below
deoscŭl·or -ārī -ātus sum *vt* to kiss warmly, kiss up and down
dēpaciscor see **depeciscor**
dēpact·us -a -um *adj* lashed down; driven tight
dēparc·us -a -um *adj* very stingy
dē·pascō -pascĕre -pāvī -pastum or **dē·pascor -pascī -pastus sum** *vt* to feed off, graze on; to consume; to destroy, waste; (fig) to prune off (*excesses of style*)
dēpec·iscor or **dēpac·iscor -iscī -tus sum** *vt* to agree upon, bargain for, settle by bargaining
dē·pectō -pectĕre — -pexum *vt* to comb, curry; to curry (*one's hide*), flog
dēpeculāt·or -ōris *m* embezzler, plunderer
dēpecŭl·or -ārī -ātus sum *vt* to embezzle, plunder
dē·pellō -pellĕre -pŭlī -pulsum *vt* to drive off, drive away, drive out, expel; to avert; (mil) to dislodge; (with **quin** or with **de** or **ab** + *abl*) to avert, deter, dissuade, wean from; (with *abl*) to dislodge from; *vi* to deviate
dēpend·ĕō -ēre *vi* to hang down; (with *abl*) to be derived from; (with **de** + *abl*) to depend upon; (with **ex** + *abl*) to hang down from
dē·pendō -pendĕre -pendī -pen-

sum *vt* to pay up; **poenam dependere** (with *dat*) to pay the penalty to
dēper·dō -děre -didī -ditum *vt* to lose completely; to ruin, destroy
dēper·ěō -īre -iī *vt* to be hopelessly in love with; *vi* to go to ruin, perish; to be lost, finished
dē·pingō -pingěre -pinxī -pictum *vt* to paint, portray; to embroider; to portray, describe, represent (*in words or thoughts*)
dē·plangō -plangěre -planxī *vt* to grieve over, cry one's heart out over
deplex·us -a -um *adj* gripping firmly, grasping
deplōrābund·us -a -um *adj* weeping bitterly, sobbing
deplōr·ō -āre *vt* to cry over, mourn; to despair of; *vi* to take it hard, cry bitterly
deplŭ·it -ěre -it *v impers* it is raining hard, pouring down
dē·pōnō -pōněre -posŭī -positum *vt* to lay down; to put down, put aside, get rid of; to bet, wager; to deposit; (with **apud** + *acc*) to entrust to, commit to the care of; **bellum deponere** to give up war; **imperium deponere** to relinquish power, renounce power
dēpopulāti·ō -ōnis *f* ravaging, pillaging
dēpopulāt·or -ōris *m* pillager, marauder
dēpopŭl·ō -āre or **depopŭl·or -ārī -ātus sum** *vt* to ravage, pillage, lay waste; to depopulate; (fig) to waste, destroy, wreck
dēport·ō -āre *vt* to carry down; to carry away; to bring home (*victory*); to transport; to banish; (fig) to win
dē·poscō -poscěre -poposcī *vt* to demand, require; to request earnestly; to challenge; **sibi deposcere** to claim (*something*) for oneself
dēposit·us -a -um *pp* of **depono**; *adj* despaired of; *n* deposit (*of money as first payment*); deposit (*for safe keeping*)
dēprāvātē *adv* perversely
dēprāvāti·ō -ōnis *f* distorting; (fig) distortion
dēprāv·ō -āre *vt* to make crooked, distort; to pervert, corrupt, seduce; to misrepresent
dēprecābund·us -a -um *adj* imploring
dēprecāti·ō -ōnis *f* supplication; deprecation, averting by prayer; invocation, earnest entreaty; (with *genit*) intercession against (*danger, etc.*)
dēprecāt·or -ōris *m* intercessor (*generally against rather than for*)
dēprěc·or -ārī -ātus sum *vt* to pray against, avert by prayer; to pray for, beg for; to intercede in behalf of; to plead in excuse
dēpre·hendō -henděre -hendī -hensum or **dēpren·dō -děre -dī -sum** *vt* to get hold of; to arrest, intercept; to surprise, catch in the act; to detect, discover, find out; to perceive, understand; to embarrass
dēprehensi·ō -ōnis *f* detection
dēpress·us -a -um *pp* of **deprimo**; *adj* low, suppressed (*voice*); low (*land*)
dē·prīmō -priměre -pressī -pressum *vt* to depress, press down, weigh down; to plant deep; to dig (*e.g., a trench*) deep; to sink (*a ship*)
dēproeli·or -ārī -ātus sum *vi* to fight it out, battle fiercely
dē·prōmō -prōměre -prompsī -promptum *vt* to take down; to bring out, produce
dēproper·ō -āre *vt* to make in a hurry; *vi* to hurry
deps·ō -ěre -ŭī -tum *vt* to knead
dēpŭd·et -ēre -ŭit *v impers* **eum depudet** he has no sense of shame
dēpūg·is or **dēpȳg·is -is** *adj* without buttocks, with thin buttocks
dēpugn·ō -āre *vi* to fight hard; to fight it out; (with **cum** + *abl*) to be in a death struggle with
dēpulsi·ō -ōnis *f* averting; (rhet) defense
dēpuls·ō -āre *vt* to push aside; **de via depulsare** to push out of the way
dēpuls·or -ōris *m* averter
dēpulsus *pp* of **depello**
dēpung·ō -ěre *vt* to mark off, designate
dēpurg·ō -āre *vt* to clean
dēpŭt·ō -āre *vt* to prune; to reckon, consider
dēpȳgis see **depugis**
dēque *adv* down, downwards
dērect·us -a -um *pp* of **derigo**; *adj* straight, direct, level, upright, perpendicular; (fig) straightforward, direct, simple, right
dērelicti·ō -ōnis *f* dereliction, disregarding, neglecting
dēre·linquō -linquěre -līquī -lictum *vt* to leave behind, forsake, abandon
dērepente *adv* suddenly
dērēp·ō -ěre -sī *vi* to creep down
dēreptus *pp* of **deripio**
dē·rīděō -rīdēre -rīsī -rīsum *vt* to deride
dērīdicŭl·us -a -um *adj* quite ridiculous; *n* derision, mockery; absurdity; **deridiculo esse** to be the object of derision, be the butt of ridicule
dērig·escō -escěre -ŭī *vi* to grow stiff, grow rigid; to curdle
dē·rigō -rigěre -rexī -rectum *vt* to direct, aim; to steer (*ship*); to draw up in battle line; (fig) to direct, guide, regulate; (with *dat* or with **ad** or **in** + *acc*) to direct or aim at, guide to; (with **ad** + *acc*) to regulate (*e.g., life*) according to
dē·ripiō -ripěre -ripŭī -reptum *vt* to tear down, tear off, pull down
dērīs·or -ōris *m* scoffer, cynic

dērīs·us -ūs *m* derision
dērīvātī·ō -ōnis *f* diversion, diverting (*of river from its course*)
dērīv·ō -āre *vt* to draw off, divert; to derive
dērŏg·ō -āre *vt* to propose to repeal in part; to restrict, modify; to take away, diminish, impair
dērōs·us -a -um *adj* gnawed away, nibbled
dēruncĭn·ō -āre *vt* to plane off; to cheat
dērŭ·ō -ĕre -ŭī *vt* to throw down, overthrow, demolish; to detract
dērupt·us -a -um *adj* rough, steep, broken; *n pl* crevasses
dēsaev·iō -īre -iī *vi* to rage furiously; to run wild
dēsalt·ō -āre *vi* to dance
de·scendō -scendĕre -scendī -scensum *vi* to climb down, descend, come or go down; to dismount; to fall, sink, sink down, penetrate; (fig) to go down, sink, sink down, penetrate; (fig) to lower oneself, stoop, yield; (mil) to march down
descensī·ō -ōnis *f* going down; **descensio Tiberina** sailing down the Tiber
descens·us -ūs *m* climbing down, descent; slope, descent
desc·iscō -iscĕre -īvī or **-iī -ītum** *vi* to revolt, desert; (fig) to depart, deviate, fall off; (with **ab** + *abl*) **a** to revolt from, break allegiance with; **b** to deviate from, fall away from
de·scrībō -scrībĕre -scripsī -scriptum *vt* to write out, transcribe, copy; to describe, represent, portray, draw, design, sketch
descriptē see **discripte**
descriptī·ō -ōnis *f* copy; representation, diagram, sketch, map; description
descriptus *pp* of **describo**
dēsĕc·ō -āre -ŭī -tum *vt* to cut off
dēsĕr·ō -ĕre -ŭī -tum *vt* to desert, abandon, forsake; (law) to forfeit
dēsert·or -ōris *m* deserter
dēsert·us -a -um *pp* of **desero**; *adj* deserted; unpopulated, uninhabited; *n pl* wilderness, desert
dēserv·iō -īre *vi* (with *dat*) to be a slave to, serve devotedly
dēs·es -idis *adj* sitting down, sitting at ease; lazy; apathetic, lifeless, idle
dēsicc·ō -āre *vt* to dry up; to drain
dē·sidĕō -sidēre -sēdī *vi* to sit idle, remain inactive
dēsīderābĭl·is -e *adj* desirable
dēsīderātī·ō -ōnis *f* missing, feeling the absence; **desideratio voluptatum** the missing of pleasures, yearning for pleasures
dēsīder·ium -iī or **-ī** *n* longing, missing, feeling of loss; want, need, necessity; request, petition; **ex desiderio laborare** to be homesick; **me desiderium tenet** (with *genit*) I miss, am homesick for
dēsīdĕr·ō -āre *vt* to miss, long for, feel the want of; (mil) to lose (*men*) as casualties; **desiderari** (mil) to be missing, be lost, be a casualty
dēsidī·a -ae *f* idleness, inactivity; laziness; apathy
dēsidiābŭl·um -ī *n* place to lounge, hangout
dēsidiōsē *adv* idly
dēsidiōs·us -a -um *adj* idle, indolent, lazy; causing idleness or laziness; spent in idleness
dē·sīdō -sidĕre -sēdī *vi* to sink, settle down; (fig) to sink, deteriorate
dēsignātī·ō -ōnis *f* specification; designation, election to office
dēsignātor see **dissignator**
dēsign·ō -āre *vt* to mark out, point out, designate, define, trace; to denote, describe, represent; to appoint, choose, elect; **consul designatus** consul-elect
dē·siliō -silīre -silŭī -sultum *vi* to jump down, alight; **ab equo desilire** to dismount; **de nave desilire** to jump overboard; (fig) to venture forth
dē·sinō -sinĕre -siī -situm *vt* to give up, abandon; **furere desinere** to stop raging; *vi* to stop, come to a stop, end; (with **in** + *acc*) to end in; **similiter desinere** to have similar endings
dēsipī·ens -entis *adj* foolish, silly
dēsipientī·a -ae *f* folly, foolishness
dēsip·iō -ĕre *vi* to be silly, act foolishly
dē·sistō -sistĕre -stitī -stitum *vi* to stop, desist; to get stuck, stick; (with *abl* or with **ab** or **de** + *abl*) to desist from, abandon, give up (*an action begun*); **desistere a defensione** to give up the defense
dēsitus *pp* of **desino**
dēsōl·ō -āre *vt* to leave desolate, leave alone, forsake, abandon; **desolatus** (with *abl*) deprived of
despect·ō -āre *vt* to look down on, overlook, command a view of; to look down on, despise
despect·us -a -um *pp* of **despicio**; *adj* contemptible
despect·us -ūs *m* commanding view, view
despēranter *adv* hopelessly
despērātī·ō -ōnis *f* desperation, despair
despērāt·us -a -um *adj* despaired of; hopeless; desperate, hopeless
despēr·ō -āre *vt* to despair of; *vi* to despair, give up hope; (with **de** + *abl*) to despair of
despicātī·ō -ōnis *f* contempt; *f pl* feelings of contempt
despicāt·us -a -um *adj* despicable; **aliquem despicatum habere** to hold someone in contempt
despicī·ens -entis *adj* contemptuous; (with *genit*) contemptuous of
despicientī·a -ae *f* despising, contempt

de·spiciō -spicĕre -spexī -spectum *vt* to despise, look down on, express contempt for; *vi* to look down; (with **in** + *acc*) to look down on, have a view of
despic·or -ārī -ātus sum *vt* to despise, disdain
despoliāt·or -ōris *m* robber, plunderer, marauder
despoli·ō -āre *vt* to strip, rob, plunder
de·sponděō -spondēre -spondī -sponsum *vt* to pledge, promise solemnly; to promise in marriage; to give up, lose; **animum despondere** or **animos despondere** to lose heart
despūm·ō -āre *vt* to skim off, skim; *vi* to stop foaming
despŭ·ō -ĕre *vt* to spit upon, show contempt for; *vi* to spit (*on the ground*)
desquām·ō -āre *vt* to take the scales off, to scale (*fish*); (fig) to peel off
destill·ō -āre *vt* to drip, distil; *vi* to trickle down, drip
destimŭl·ō -āre *vt* to goad on, stimulate
destinātĭ·ō -ōnis *f* establishing; resolution, determination, purpose, design
destināt·us -a -um *adj* fixed, determined; **destinatum est mihi** (with *inf*) I have made up my mind to; *n pl* designs, intentions
destĭn·ō -āre *vt* to lash down, secure; (fig) to fix, determine, resolve; to design, destine; to appoint, designate; to take aim at
destit·ŭō -uĕre -ŭī -ūtum *vt* to set apart; to set down, place; to forsake, abandon; to leave in the lurch, leave high and dry, betray, desert; (with **ab** + *abl*) to rob of, leave destitute of
destitūtĭ·ō -ōnis *f* forsaking, abandonment; disappointment
destrict·us -a -um *adj* severe, rigid
de·stringō -stringĕre -strinxī -strictum *vt* to strip; to unsheathe; to give (*someone*) a rubdown; to brush gently against, skim; (of weapon) to graze; (fig) to criticize, satirize
destructĭ·ō -ōnis *f* pulling down (*e.g., of walls*); destruction, demolition; refutation
de·strŭō -struĕre -struxī -structum *vt* to pull down, demolish, destroy; (fig) to ruin
dēsubĭtō or **dē subĭtō** *adv* suddenly
dēsūdasc·ō -ĕre *vi* to begin to sweat all over
dēsūd·ō -āre *vi* to sweat; (with *dat*) (fig) to sweat over, work hard at
dēsuē·fīō -fĭerī -factus sum *vi* to become unused or unaccustomed
dēsu·escō -escĕre -ēvī -ētum *vi* to become unaccustomed
dēsuētūd·ō -ĭnis *f* disuse, lack of use
dēsuēt·us -a -um *pp* of **desuesco;** *adj* unused, out of use, obsolete; out of practice; (with *dat*) unused to, unfamiliar with
dēsult·or -ōris *m* circus rider who leaps from one horse to another; **amoris desultor** (fig) fickle lover
dēsultōrĭ·us -a -um *adj* of a circus rider; **equus desultorius** show horse
dēsultūr·a -ae *f* leaping down (*from horse*), dismounting
dē·sum -esse -fŭī -futūrus *vi* to fall short, fail; to fail in one's duty; to be absent, be missing; (with *dat*) to be absent from, be missing from, be lacking from; **sibi deesse** to cheat oneself, sell oneself short; **tempori deesse** or **occasioni temporis deesse** to pass up the opportunity, pass up the chance
dē·sūmō -sūmĕre -sumpsī -sumptum *vt* to pick out, choose; to assume, undertake; **sibi hostem desumere** to take on an enemy
dēsŭper *adv* from above, from overhead
dēsurg·ō -ĕre *vi* to rise; **cenā desurgere** to get up from the table
dē·tĕgō -tegĕre -texī -tectum *vt* to detect, uncover, expose, lay bare; to reveal, disclose, betray; **formidine detegi** to be betrayed by fear
dē·tendō -tendĕre — -tensum *vt* to unstretch; to take down (*tent*)
dētentus *pp* of **detineo**
dē·tergĕō -tergēre -tersī -tersum *vt* to wipe off, wipe away, wipe clean; (fig) to wipe clean; **mensam detergere** to eat up everything on the table
dēterĭ·or -us *adj* inferior, worse, poorer, meaner; less favorable, worse (*time*); degenerate (*person*); (mil) weaker (*e.g., in cavalry*)
dēterĭus *adv* worse
dēterminātĭ·ō -ōnis *f* boundary; conclusion, end; end (*of speech*)
dētermĭn·ō -āre *vt* to bound, limit, prescribe; to determine, settle
dē·tĕrō -terĕre -trīvī -trītum *vt* to rub away, wear away; to wear out; to lessen, weaken, detract from; **calces alicujus deterere** to tread on someone's heels
dēterr·ĕō -ēre -ŭī -ĭtum *vt* to deter, frighten away, discourage; (with *abl*, or with **ab** or **de** + *abl*, or with **ne, quin,** or **quominus**) to deter or discourage from; **deterruit quominus hostes persequerentur** he discouraged them from pursuing the enemy
dētersus *pp* of **detergeo**
dētestābĭl·is -e *adj* detestable, abominable
dētestātĭ·ō -ōnis *f* execration, curse; averting (*by sacrifices or prayers*)
dētest·or -ārī -ātus sum *vt* to curse, execrate; to invoke (*the gods*); to avert; to plead against; to detest, loathe, abhor; (with **in** + *acc*) to

call down (*e.g., vengeance*) upon; **invidiam detestari** to avert envy, avoid unpopularity

dētex·ō -ĕre -ŭī -tum *vt* to weave, finish weaving; (fig) to finish, finish off

dē·tinĕō -tinēre -tinŭī -tentum *vt* to hold back, keep back; to hold up, detain; to occupy, keep occupied; (with **ab** or **de** + *abl*) to keep back from; (with *abl* or with **in** + *abl*) to occupy (*e.g., day, mind*) with, keep (*someone*) busied with

dē·tondĕō -tondēre -totondī or **-tondī -tonsum** *vt* to cut off, clip off, shear off (*hair, wool*); (fig) to strip

dētŏn·ō -āre -ŭī *vi* to stop thundering; (of Jupiter) to thunder down

dētonsus *pp* of **detondeo**

dē·torquĕō -torquēre -torsī -tortum *vt* to twist or bend aside; to twist out of shape; to turn aside; to turn, direct; to avert (*eyes*); to divert, pervert; to distort, misrepresent (*words*)

dētractī·ō -ōnis *f* taking away, wresting; removal; (rhet) ellipsis

detractō see **detrecto**

detract·or -ōris *m* detractor

dē·trăhō -trahĕre -traxī -tractum *vt* to drag down, drag away, pull down, pull away; to remove, withdraw; to take away, deprive, rob, strip; to induce to come down, draw down (*e.g., an enemy from a strong position*); to disparage, detract, slander; (with *dat* or **de** + *abl*) to take away from (*someone*), rob (*someone*) of

dētrectātī·ō -ōnis *f* drawing back, avoidance; **militiae detrectatio** draft dodging

dētrectāt·or -ōris *m* detractor, disparager

dētrect·ō or **detract·ō -āre** *vt* to draw back from, shirk, decline, reject, refuse; to disparage, depreciate; to demean; **militiam detrectare** to dodge the draft

dētrīmentōs·us -a -um *adj* detrimental, harmful

dētrīment·um -ī *n* detriment, loss, damage; **detrimentum accipere** or **detrimentum capere** to incur or suffer harm; **detrimentum inferre** or **detrimentum afferre** to cause harm

dētrītus *pp* of **detero**

dē·trūdō -trūdĕre -trūsī -trūsum *vt* to push down, push away, push off; (mil) to dislodge; (law) to evict; to postpone, put off; **aliquem de sua sententia detrudere** to force someone to change his mind

detrunc·ō -āre *vt* to cut off, chop off; (fig) to mutilate, behead

dēturb·ō -āre *vt* to beat down, expel, tear down, strike down; (mil) to dislodge, force to come down; to eject, dispossess; **aliquem de sanitate deturbare** to drive a person mad

Deucalī·ōn -ōnis *m* son of Prometheus, who, together with his wife Pyrrha, was the sole survivor of the Deluge

de·unx -uncis *m* eleven twelfths; **heres ex deunce** heir to eleven twelfths

de·ūrō -ūrĕre -ussī -ustum *vt* to burn up, destroy; (of frost) to nip

de·us -ī (*nom pl:* **deī** or **dī**; *genit pl:* **deōrum** or **deum**) *m* god, deity; (of a person) god, divine being; *m pl* (of persons in high places) the powers that be; **di boni!** good heavens!; **di hominesque** all the world; **di meliora!** Heaven forbid!; **dis volentibus** with the help of the gods; **di te ament!** bless your little heart!

deustus *pp* of **deuro**

de·ūtor -ūtī -ūsus sum *vi* (with *abl*) to mistreat

dēvast·ō -āre *vt* to devastate, lay waste

dē·vĕhō -vehĕre -vexī -vectum *vt* to carry down, carry away, carry off; **devehi** to ride down, sail down

dē·vellō -vellĕre -vellī or **-volsī -vulsum** *vt* to pluck off

dēvēl·ō -āre *vt* to unveil

dēvenĕr·or -ārī -ātus sum *vt* to reverence, worship; to avert by prayer

dē·veniō -venīre -vēnī -ventum *vi* to come down, arrive; (with *acc* of extent of motion or with **ad** or **in** + *acc*) to arrive at, reach; (with **ad** + *acc*) to happen to, befall

dēverbĕr·ō -āre *vt* to thrash soundly

dēvers·or -ārī -ātus sum *vi* to stay as a guest; (with **apud** + *acc*) to stay at the house of

dēvers·or -ōris *m* guest

dēversōriŏl·um -ī *n* small inn, motel

dēversōrĭ·us or **dēvorsorĭ·us -a -um** *adj* of an inn; fit to stay at; **taberna deversoria** inn; *n* inn, hotel

dēverticŭl·um or **dēvorticŭl·um -ī** *n* side road, detour; digression; inn, hotel, tavern; low haunt, dive; refuge

dē·vertō (or **dē·vortō**) **-vertĕre -vertī -versum** or **dē·vertor -vertī -versus sum** *vi* to turn aside, turn away; to stay as guest, spend the night; (with **ad** or **apud** + *acc*) to stay with or at the house of; (with **ad** + *acc*) to have recourse to, resort to

dēvex·us -a -um *adj* inclining, sloping, steep; (with **ad** + *acc*) prone to, inclined to

dē·vinciō -vincīre -vinxī -vinctum *vt* to tie up, clamp; (fig) to bind fast, obligate, unite closely; **se vino devincire** (coll) to get tight

dē·vincō -vincĕre -vīcī -victum *vt* to conquer, subdue

dēvinct·us -a -um *pp* of **devincio;** *adj* (with *dat*) strongly attached to
dēvītāti·ō -ōnis *f* avoidance
dēvīt·ō -āre *vt* to avoid
dēvi·us -a -um *adj* out of the way, off the beaten track; devious; living apart, solitary, sequestered; inconsistent
dēvŏc·ō -āre *vt* to call down; to call off, recall, call away; to allure, seduce; **deos ad auxilium devocare** to invoke the gods for help
dēvŏl·ō -āre *vi* to fly down; to fly away; to hasten down, hasten away
dē·volvō -volvĕre -volvī -volūtum *vt* to roll down; **ad spem inanem pacis devolvi** to fall back on false hopes of peace; **devolvi** to roll down, go tumbling down, sink down
dēvŏr·ō -āre *vt* to devour, gulp down; to consume, waste, squander (*money, etc.*); (of the sea) to engulf, swallow up; to swallow, mumble (*words*); to repress (*tears*); to bear with patience
dēvor- = **dever-**
dēvorti·a -ōrum *n pl* side roads, detour
dēvōti·ō -ōnis *f* self-sacrifice; cursing, outlawing; incantation, spell; **capitis devotio** or **vitae devotio** sacrifice of one's life
dēvōt·ō -āre *vt* to lay a spell on, bewitch, jinx
dēvōt·us -a -um *pp* of **devoveo;** *adj* devoted, faithful; accursed; (with *dat*) **a** devoted to, faithful to; **b** addicted to, given to (*wine, drinking*)
dē·vovĕō -vovēre -vōvī -vōtum *vt* to devote, vow, sacrifice, dedicate; to mark out, doom, destine; to curse, execrate; to bewitch; **se devovere dis** to devote oneself to death
dēvulsus *pp* of **devello**
dext·ans -antis *m* five sixths
dextell·a -ae *f* little right hand; right-hand man
dext·er -ĕra -ĕrum or **-ra -rum** *adj* right, on the right side; handy, dexterous; lucky, propitious, favorable; opportune, right; *f* right hand; right side, the right; **a dextra laevaque** to the right and left, right and left, everywhere; **dextrā** with the right hand; (fig) with valor; **dextrā** (with *acc*) to the right of; **dextram dare** or **dextram tendere** to give a pledge of friendship; **dextram renovare** to renew a solemn pledge
dextĕrē or **dextrē** *adv* dexterously, skillfully; **dextre fortunā uti** (fig) to play the cards right
dexterĭt·ās -ātis *f* dexterity, adroitness; readiness
dextrorsum or **dextrorsus** or **dextrōvorsum** *adv* to the right, towards the right side
dī see **deus**

Dī·a -ae *f* ancient name of the island of Naxos; mother of Mercury
diabathrār·ius -iī or **-ī** *m* shoemaker
diadēm·a -ătis *n* diadem
diaet·a -ae *f* diet; living room
dialectĭcē *adv* logically
dialectĭc·us -a -um *adj* dialectical; *m* dialectician; *f* dialectics, logic; *n pl* dialectics, logical discussions
dialect·os -ī *f* dialect
Diāl·is -e *adj* of Jupiter; of Jupiter's high priest; **apex Dialis** high priest's miter; **conjux Dialis** high priest's wife; **flamen Dialis** high priest of Jupiter
dialŏg·us -ī *m* dialogue, conversation
Diān·a or **Dīān·a -ae** *f* Diana (*goddess of hunting, patroness of virginity, of the moon as Luna, of childbirth as Lucina, and of incantations and magic as Hecate*); (fig) Diana's temple; (fig) moon; **iracunda Diana** lunacy
diārĭ·a -ōrum *n pl* daily ration
dibăph·us -ī *f* crimson robe; official robe of magistrate
dic·a -ae *f* lawsuit, case, judicial process, judicial proceedings; **dicam scribere** (with *dat*) to sue (*someone*); **sortiri dicas** to select a jury
dicācĭt·ās -ātis *f* wittiness, sarcasm
dicācŭl·us -a -um *adj* quick-witted, sharp
dicāti·ō -ōnis *f* declaration of intent of becoming a citizen
dic·ax -ācis *adj* witty, sharp, sarcastic, caustic; pert
dichorē·us -ī *m* double trochee
dici·ō -ōnis *f* jurisdiction, sway, authority, control, rule, dominion, sovereignty; **in dicione esse** (with *genit*) or **sub dicione esse** (with *genit*) to be under the control of, be subject to, be under the jurisdiction of; **in dicionem redigere** (with *genit*) or **dicioni subjicere** (with *genit*) to bring (*someone*) under the control of
dicis causā or **grātiā** *adv* for show, for the sake of appearances
dic·ō -āre *vt* to dedicate, consecrate; to deify; to inaugurate; to set apart, devote; (with *dat*) to devote (*e.g., time, energy*) to; **se dicare** (with *dat* or **in** + *acc*) to dedicate oneself to
dīcō dīcĕre dixī dictum *vt* to say, tell; to indicate, mention, specify, point out; to nominate, appoint; to fix, set, appoint (*day or date*); to speak, deliver, recite; to pronounce, utter, articulate; to call, name; to assert, affirm; to describe, relate, celebrate; to tell, predict; (with double *acc*) to appoint (*someone*) as; **causam dicere** to plead or defend a case; **diem dicere** (with *dat*) to set a date for; **facete dictum!** well put!; **sententiam dicere** to

express an opinion; **testimonium dicere** to give evidence
dicrŏt·um -ī *n* bireme
dictamn·us -ī *f* dittany (*wild marjoram, growing in abundance on Mt. Dicte in Crete*)
dictāt·a -ōrum *n pl* lessons, rules; dictation
dictāt·or -ōris *m* dictator (*emergency magistrate in Rome with absolute authority, legally appointed for a maximum six-month term*); chief magistrate (*of Italic town*)
dictātōri·us -a -um *adj* dictatorial
dictātr·ix -īcis *f* mistress of ceremonies
dictātūr·a -ae *f* dictatorship
Dict·ē -ēs *f* mountain in Crete where Jupiter was hidden in a cave from his father Saturn
dicti·ō -ōnis *f* saying, speaking, uttering; diction, style; conversation; oracular response, prediction; **dictio causae** defense of a case; **dictio testimoni** right to give testimony; **juris dictio** administration of justice; jurisdiction
dictit·ō -āre *vt* to keep saying, to state emphatically; **causas dictitare** to practice law; **ut dictitabat** as he used to say, as he continually alleged
dict·ō -āre *vt* to say repeatedly, reiterate; to dictate; to compose; to suggest, remind
dict·us -a -um *pp* of **dīco;** *n* saying word, statement; witticism; maxim, proverb; prediction, prophecy; order, command, instruction; promise, assurance
Dictynn·a -ae *f* Diana
dī·dō or **dis·dō -dĕre -didī -ditum** *vt* to publicize, broadcast, disseminate; to distribute, hand out
Dīd·ō -ūs (*acc:* **Dīdō**) *f* daughter of Tyrian king Belus, sister of Pygmalion, foundress and queen of Carthage, also called Elissa
dī·dūcō -dūcĕre -duxī -ductum *vt* to draw apart, part, sever, separate, split; to undo, untie; to divide, distribute; to scatter, disperse; (in mathematics) to divide; **animus diductus** (with *abl*) the mind torn between (*alternatives*)
diēcŭl·a -ae *f* little while
diērect·us -a -um *adj* (coll) finished, done for; **i dierectus** or **abi dierectus!** go to the devil!
di·ēs -ēī *m* or *f* day; time, period, space of time, interval; daylight, light of day; anniversary; daybreak; season; **dicere diem** (with *dat*) to impeach, bring an accusation against; **diem ex die** from day to day, day after day; **diem noctemque** day and night, uninterruptedly; **dies meus** my birthday; **in diem** for the moment; for a future day; **in dies** (more and more) every day; **multo denique die** not till late in the day; **postridie ejus diei** the day after that; **post tertium ejus diei** two days after that
Diespĭt·er -ris *m* Jupiter
diffām·ō -āre *vt* to divulge (*something*); to defame (*someone*)
differenti·a -ae *f* difference, diversity; specific difference, species
differĭt·ās -ātis *f* difference
diffĕrō differre distŭlī dīlātum *vt* to carry in different directions; to scatter, disperse; to publicize, spread around, divulge; to defer, postpone, delay; to humor; to get rid of, put off; to distract, disquiet; *vi* to differ, be different, be distinguished; (with **ab** + *abl*) to differ from
differt·us -a -um *adj* stuffed, crowded, overcrowded
diffĭcĭl·is -e *adj* difficult, hard; surly, cantankerous; hard to manage, hard to please
difficilĭter *adv* with difficulty, barely
difficult·ās -ātis *f* difficulty, hardship, trouble, distress; surliness; poverty, financial embarrassment
difficulter *adv* with difficulty, barely
diffīd·ens -entis *adj* diffident, anxious, nervous
diffīdenter *adv* without confidence, distrustfully
diffīdenti·a -ae *f* diffidence, mistrust, distrust
dif·fīdō -fīdĕre -fīsus sum *vi* (with *dat*) to distrust, despair of
dif·findō -findĕre -fīdī -fissum *vt* to split, split apart, divide; (law) **diem diffindere** to cut short the business day; (fig) to detract
dif·fingō -ĕre *vt* to form differently, remodel; to alter
diffissus *pp* of **diffindo**
diffit·ĕor -ērī *vt* to disavow, disown
diffl·ō -āre *vi* to blow away; to disperse
difflŭ·ō -ĕre *vi* to flow in different directions, flow away; to dissolve, melt away, disappear; (with *abl*) to wallow in (*luxury, vice*)
dif·fringō -fringĕre — -fractum *vt* to shatter, break apart, smash
dif·fugĭō -fugĕre -fūgī *vi* to flee in different directions; to disperse; to disappear
diffug·ĭum -ĭī or **-ī** *n* dispersion
diffundĭt·ō -āre *vt* to pour out, scatter; to waste
dif·fundō -fundĕre -fūdī -fūsum *vt* to pour, pour out; to scatter, diffuse, spread, extend; to give vent to; to cheer up, gladden
diffūsē *adv* diffusely; fully, at length, in detail
diffūsĭl·is -e *adj* diffusive, expanding
diffūs·us -a -um *pp* of **diffundo;** *adj* spread out, spread abroad; wide; prolix; protracted
diffutūt·us -a -um *adj* exhausted by excessive sexual indulgence

Dīgenti·a -ae *f* small stream on Horace's Sabine farm
dī·gĕrō -gerĕre -gessī -gestum *vt* to spread about, distribute, divide; to arrange, assort, catalogue; to interpret; to digest
dīgestī·ō -ōnis *f* arrangement; (rhet) enumeration
dīgestus *pp* of **digero**
digitŭl·us -ī *m* little finger
digĭt·us -ī *m* finger; inch (*one sixteenth of a Roman foot*); toe; **caelum digito attingere** to reach the heights of happiness, be thrilled; **digitis concrepare** to snap the fingers; **digito uno attingere** to touch lightly, touch tenderly; **digitum intendere** (with **ad** + *acc*) to point the finger at; **digitus pollex** thumb; **in digitos arrectus** on tiptoe; **minimus digitus** little finger
digladĭ·or -ārī -ātus sum *vi* to fight hard
dignātĭ·ō -ōnis *f* esteem, respect; dignity, honor
dignē *adv* worthily, fitly
dignĭt·ās -ātis *f* worth, worthiness; dignity; authority, rank, reputation, distinction, majesty; self-respect; dignitary; political office; dignity (*of style*)
dign·ō -āre or **dign·or -ārī -ātus sum** *vt* to think worthy; (with *abl*) to think worthy of; (with double *acc*) to think (*someone*) worthy of being (*e.g., a son*)
dignosc·ō or **dīnosc·ō -ĕre** *vt* to distinguish; (with *abl*) to distinguish (*someone*) from; **dominum ac servum dignoscere** to know the difference between master and slave
dign·us -a -um *adj* worthy, deserving (*person*); fit, adequate, suitable, deserved, proper; (with *abl*) worthy of
dī·gredĭor -grĕdī -gressus sum *vi* to move apart, separate; to deviate; to digress
digressĭ·ō -ōnis *f* parting, separation; deviation; digression
digressus *pp* of **digredior**
digress·us -ūs *m* departure; digression
dījūdicātĭ·ō -ōnis *f* decision
dījūdĭc·ō -āre *vt* to decide, settle; **vera et falsa dijudicare** or **vera a falsis dijudicare** to distinguish between truth and falsehood
dījun = disjun
dī·lābor -lābī -lapsus sum *vi* to fall apart, break up; (of ice, etc.) to break up, dissolve; to disperse; to break up, decay; (of time) to slip away; (of water) to flow in different directions
dīlacĕr·ō -āre *vt* to tear to pieces
dīlāmĭn·ō -āre *vt* to split in two; **nuces dilaminare** to crack nuts
dīlanĭ·ō -āre *vt* to tear to pieces
dīlapĭd·ō -āre *vt* to demolish (*a structure of stone*); to squander
dīlapsus *pp* of **dilabor**
dīlarg·ĭor -īrī -ītus sum *vt* to hand out generously, lavish
dīlātĭ·ō -ōnis *f* postponement, delay
dīlāt·ō -āre *vt* to dilate, stretch, broaden, extend, enlarge; (fig) to amplify, spread, extend; to drawl out
dīlāt·or -ōris *m* procrastinator, slowpoke
dīlātus *pp* of **differo**
dīlaud·ō -āre *vt* to praise enthusiastically
dīlect·us -a -um *pp* of **diligo;** *adj* beloved
dīlect·us -ūs *m* selection; (mil) selective service, draft; draftees; recruitment; **dilectum habere** to conduct a draft; **legiones ex novo dilectu conficere** to bring the legions to full strength with new draftees
dīlĭg·ens -entis *adj* careful, conscientious, accurate; exacting, strict; thrifty, industrious; (with *genit*) observant of; (with **ad** + *acc* or with **in** + *abl*) careful in, careful to, conscientious about
dīligenter *adv* carefully, diligently, industriously
dīligentĭ·a -ae *f* diligence, care, industry, attentiveness, faithfulness; economy, frugality; (with *genit*) regard for
dī·lĭgō -ligĕre -lexī -lectum *vt* to single out; to esteem, love, value, prize; to approve, be content with, appreciate
dīlōrĭc·ō -āre *vt* to tear open
dīlūc·ĕō -ēre *vi* to be clear, be evident; (with *dat*) to be obvious to
dī·lūcescō -lūcescĕre -luxī *vi* to grow light, dawn
dīlūcĭdē *adv* clearly, distinctly, plainly
dīlūcĭd·us -a -um *adj* clear, distinct, plain, evident
dīlūcŭl·um -ī *n* daybreak, dawn
dīlūd·ĭum -ĭī or **-ī** *n* intermission
dīl·ŭō -uĕre -ŭī -ūtum *vt* to wash away, break up, separate; to dilute; to get rid of (*worries, annoyances*); to atone for; to explain, solve
dīluvĭ·ēs -ēī *f* inundation, flood, deluge
dīluvĭ·ō -āre *vt* to inundate, flood, deluge
dīluv·ĭum -ĭī or **-ī** *n* flood, deluge; (fig) destruction
dīmān·ō -āre *vi* to flow in different directions; (fig) to spread around
dīmensĭ·ō -ōnis *f* measurement
dī·mētĭor -mētīrī -mensus sum *vt* to measure out, measure off; to count off
dīmēt·ō -āre or **dīmēt·or -ārī -ātus sum** *vt* to measure out, mark out (*area*)
dīmicātĭ·ō -ōnis *f* fight, combat, struggle; contest, rivalry

dīmic•ō -āre *vi* to fight, struggle; to be in conflict, run a risk, be in peril; (with **cum** + *abl*) to fight against; **de capite dimicare** or **de vita dimicare** to fight for one's life

dīmidiāt•us -a -um *adj* half, in half

dīmidi•us -a -um *adj* half; broken in two, broken; **dimidius patrum, dimidius plebis** half patrician, half plebeian; *n* half; **dimidium militum quam** half as many soldiers as

dīmissi•ō -ōnis *f* dismissal, discharging, sending out

dī•mittō -mittĕre -mīsī -missum *vt* to send away, send around, send out, scatter, distribute; to break up, dismiss, disband; (mil) to discharge; to let loose; to divorce (*wife*); to leave, desert, abandon, give up, relinquish; to let go, let slip, forgo, forsake, renounce; to remit

dimminŭ•ō or **dīminŭ•ō -ĕre** *vt* to break to pieces, smash, shatter

dī•movĕō -movēre -mōvī -mōtum *vt* to move apart, part, separate; to disperse, dismiss, scatter; to lure away

Dindymēn•ē -ēs *f* Cybele (*also called Magna Mater by the Romans*)

Dindўm•us -ī *m* or **Dindўm•a -ōrum** *n pl* mountain in Asia Minor, sacred to Cybele

dīnoscō see **dignosco**

dīnumerātī•ō -ōnis *f* enumeration, counting up

dīnumĕr•ō -āre *vt* to enumerate, count up, compute; to count out, pay

diōbolār•is -e *adj* costing two obols

Diodŏt•us -ī *m* Stoic philosopher and tutor of Cicero (*d.* 59 B.C.)

dioecēs•is -is *f* district, governor's jurisdiction

dioecēt•ēs -ae *m* treasurer; secretary of revenue

Diogĕn•ēs -is *m* famous Ionic philosopher and pupil of Anaximenes (*5th cent.* B.C.); Cynic philosopher, born at Sinope, in Pontus (412?-323 B.C.)

Diomēd•ēs -is *m* son of Tydeus and king of Argos; hero at Troy

Diōn•ē -ēs or **Diōn•a -ae** *f* mother of Venus

Dionȳsī•a -ōrum *n pl* Greek festival of Bacchus

Dionȳsī•us -ī *m* tyrant of Syracuse (430-367 B.C.); Dionysus the Younger (397-330?)

Dionȳs•us or **Dionȳs•os -ī** *m* Bacchus

diōt•a -ae *f* two-handled wine jar

diplōm•a -ătis *n* official letter of recommendation

Dipȳl•on -ī *n* N.W. gate at Athens

Dīr•a -ae *f* a Fury; *f pl* the Furies (*goddesses of revenge and remorse*)

dīr•ae -ārum *f pl* curse, execration

Dircae•us -a -um *adj* Dircean, Boeotian; **cycnus Dircaeus** Dircean or Boeotian swan (*i.e., Pindar, famous lyric poet from Boeotia,* 522?-442 B.C.)

Dirc•ē -ēs *f* famous fountain in Boeotia

dīrect•us -a -um *pp* of **dirigo;** *adj* straight, direct; straightforward

diremptus *pp* of **dirimo**

dirempt•us -ūs *m* separation

dīreptī•ō -ōnis *f* plundering, pillaging; *f pl* acts of pillage

dīrept•or -ōris *m* plunderer

dīreptus *pp* of **diripio**

dirib•ĕō -ēre — -ĭtum *vt* to sort (*votes taken out of the ballot box*)

diribitī•ō -ōnis *f* sorting

diribĭt•or -ōris *m* sorter (*of ballots*)

diribitōr•ĭum -iī or **-ī** *n* sorting room

dī•rĭgō -rigĕre -rexī -rectum *vt* to put in order, arrange, line up, deploy

dir•ĭmō -imĕre -ēmī -emptum *vt* to take apart, part, separate, divide; to break off, disturb, interrupt; to separate, dissolve; to put off, delay; to break off, end, bring to an end; to nullify, bring to naught

dī•ripĭō -ripĕre -ripŭī -reptum *vt* to tear apart, tear to pieces; to lay waste, pillage, plunder, ravage; to snatch away, tear away; to whip out (*sword*); to steal

dīrĭt•ās -ātis *f* mischief; misfortune; cruelty

dī•rumpō or **dis•rumpō -rumpĕre -rūpī -ruptum** *vt* to break to pieces, smash, shatter; to break off (*friendship*); to sever (*ties*); **dirumpi** to burst (*with laughter, envy, indignation, etc.*)

dīrŭ•ō -ĕre -ī -tum *vt* to pull apart, demolish, destroy, overthrow; to scatter, disperse; (mil) to break up (*enemy formation*); to bankrupt

dīr•us -a -um *adj* fearful, awful; ominous, ill-omened; dreadful, awful, abominable; cruel, relentless, fierce; **temporibus diris** in the reign of terror; **venena dira** deadly poisons

dī•s -tis *adj* rich, wealthy; rich, fertile (*land*); rich, generous, expensive (*offerings*); (with *abl*) abounding in

Dī•s -tis *m* Pluto (*king of the lower world*)

dis•cēdō -cēdĕre -cessī -cessum *vi* to go away, depart; to separate, be severed; to disperse, scatter, be dissipated, disappear; (mil) to march off, break camp; to come off (*victorious, etc.*); to deviate; to swerve; to pass away, vanish, cease; (with **ab** + *abl*) **a** to forsake (*e.g., friends*); **b** to deviate from, swerve from; **c** to abandon, give up; (with **ex** or **de** + *abl*) to go away from, depart from; (with **ad** + *acc*) to depart for; (with **in** + *acc*) to vote for; **discedere in Catonis sen-**

tentiam to vote for Cato's proposal
disceptāti·ō -ōnis *f* dispute, difference of opinion; discussion, debate
disceptāt·or -ōris *m* or **disceptātr·ix -īcis** *f* arbitrator
discept·ō -āre *vt* to debate, dispute, discuss, treat; to decide, settle (*controversies, wars*); *vi* to act as umpire; to be at stake
dis·cernō -cernĕre -crēvī -crētum *vt* to separate, mark off, divide; to keep apart; to distinguish between; to discern, make out, distinguish
dis·cerpō -cerpĕre -cerpsī -cerptum *vt* to tear to pieces, mangle, mutilate; (fig) to tear apart (*with words, arguments*)
discessi·ō -ōnis *f* separation, division; separation, divorce; (in the senate) division, formal vote; **discessio sine ulla varietate** unanimous vote
discess·us -ūs *m* separation, parting; going away, departure; banishment; marching away, marching off
discid·ium -iī or **-ī** *n* parting, separation; discord, dissension, disagreement; divorce
discīd·ō -ĕre *vt* to cut to pieces, cut up
discinct·us -a -um *pp* of **discingo;** *adj* without a girdle; dissolute, loose; effeminate, voluptuous
di·scindō -scindĕre -scidī -scissum *vt* to tear apart, tear open, rend, tear; **amicitias discindere** to break off ties of friendship
dis·cingō -cingĕre -cinxī -cinctum *vt* to take off, ungird; to loose; (fig) to relax
disciplīn·a -ae *f* instruction, training, teaching, education; learning, knowledge, science; discipline; custom, habit; system; **militaris disciplina** basic training; **rei publicae disciplina** statesmanship
discipŭl·us -ī *m* or **discipŭl·a -ae** *f* pupil, student; disciple, follower
discissus *pp* of **discindo**
dis·clūdō -clūdĕre -clūsī -clūsum *vt* to keep apart, divide, shut off; **iram et cupiditatem locis discludere** to assign anger and passion to their proper places
discō discĕre didĭcī *vt* to learn, learn to know, become acquainted with; to be told (*e.g., the truth*); (with *inf*) to learn how to
discobŏl·us -ī *m* discus thrower
discŏl·or -ōris *adj* of a different color; different; (with *dat*) different from
discondūc·ō -ĕre *vi* to be unprofitable
disconven·iō -īre *vi* to disagree; to be inconsistent
discordābil·is -e *adj* discordant, disagreeing
discordi·a -ae *f* discord, dissension, disagreement; mutiny
discordiōs·us -a -um *adj* prone to discord, seditious
discord·ō -āre *vi* to quarrel, disagree; (with *dat* or **ab** + *abl*) to be out of harmony with, be opposed to
discor·s -dis *adj* discordant, inharmonious; disagreeing, at variance; contradictory, inconsistent; warring (*winds, etc.*); (with *abl*) inconsistent with, at variance with, different from
discrepanti·a -ae *f* discrepancy, dissimilarity, difference
discrepāti·ō -ōnis *f* disagreement, dispute
discrepit·ō -āre *vi* to be completely different
discrĕp·ō -āre -ŭī *vi* to be different in sound, sound different; to be out of tune; to disagree, be different, be inconsistent, vary, differ; to be disputed; (with *dat* or *abl* or with **ab** or **cum** + *abl*) to disagree with, be different from, be inconsistent with; *v impers* there is a difference of opinion, it is undecided, it is a matter of dispute; **discrepat inter scriptores rerum** there is a difference of opinion among historians
di·scrībō -scrībĕre -scripsī -scriptum *vt* to distribute, classify, divide; to assign, apportion; (with **in** + *acc*) to distribute among, divide among
discrīm·en -inis *n* dividing line; interval, intervening space, division, distance, separation; discrimination, difference, distinction; critical moment, turning point; decision, determination; crisis, jeopardy, peril, danger, risk; decisive battle
discrīmin·ō -āre *vt* to divide, separate; to apportion
discriptē *adv* orderly, lucidly, distinctly
discripti·ō -ōnis *f* distribution, classification
discript·us -a -um *pp* of **discribo;** *adj* well arranged; secluded
discruci·ō -āre *vt* to torture; to distress, torment
dis·cumbō -cumbĕre -cubŭī -cubitum *vi* to take their places at the table; (of several) to go to bed
discup·iō -ĕre *vt* (coll) to want badly; (with *inf*) (coll) to be dying to
dis·currō -currĕre -cucurrī or **-currī -cursum** *vi* to run in different directions, scamper about, run up and down, dash around
discurs·us -ūs *m* running up and down, running about; (mil) pincer movement
disc·us -ī *m* discus
dis·cutiō -cutĕre -cussī -cussum *vt* to knock apart; to smash to pieces, shatter; to break up, disperse, scatter, dispel; to frustrate, bring to naught; to suppress, destroy
disertē or **disertim** *adv* eloquently
disert·us -a -um *adj* fluent, well-spoken; clear, articulate

disject·ō -āre *vt* to toss about
disject·us -a -um *pp* of **disjicio;** *adj* scattered; dilapidated
disject·us -ūs *m* scattering
dis·jiciō -jicĕre -jēcī -jectum vt to drive apart, scatter, break up; to tear to pieces; to ruin, destroy; to thwart, frustrate, wreck; (mil) to break up (*enemy formation*)
disjuncti·ō or **dījuncti·ō -ōnis** *f* separation, alienation; diviation, variation; dilemma; asyndeton (*succession of clauses without conjunctions*)
disjunct·us -a -um *adj* separate, distinct; distant, remote; disjointed, disconnected, incoherent (*speech*); logically opposed; *n pl* opposites
dis·jungō or **dī·jungo -jungĕre -junxī -junctum** *vt* to unyoke; to sever, divide, part, remove; to separate, part, estrange, disunite, alienate
dispālesc·ō -ĕre *vi* to be divulged, spread
dispāl·or -ārī -ātus sum *vi* to wander about, straggle
dis·pandō (or **dis·pendō**) **-pandĕre — -pansum** (or **dis·pennō -pennĕre — -pessum**) *vt* to stretch out, extend; to spread out, expand
dis·pār -păris *adj* different, unlike; unequal, ill-matched; unequal, of different lengths
disparĭl·is -e *adj* different, dissimilar
disparĭliter *adv* differently
dispăr·ō -āre *vt* to separate, segregate
dispartĭō or **dispartĭor** see **dispertio**
dispectus *pp* of **dispicio**
dis·pellō -pellĕre -pŭlī -pulsum *vt* to disperse, scatter; to drive away, dispel
dispend·ĭum -ĭī or **-ī** *n* expense, cost; loss
dispendō see **dispando**
dispennō see **dispando**
dispensātĭ·ō -ōnis *f* weighing out, doling out; management, superintendence, direction, administration; position of superintendent or treasurer
dispensāt·or -ōris *m* household manager, chief butler; cashier, treasurer
dispens·ō -āre *vt* to weigh out, pay out; to distribute, manage (*household stores*); to regulate, manage, superintend
dispercut·iō -ĕre *vt* to knock out; **cerebrum dispercutere** (with *dat*) (coll) to knock out (*someone's*) brains
disper·dō -dĕre -dĭdī -dĭtum *vt* to spoil, ruin; to squander
disper·ĕō -īre -ĭī *vi* to go to ruin; to go to waste; to be undone, perish; **disperii!** (coll) I'm finished; **dispeream si** (coll) I'll be darned if
di·spergō -spergĕre -spersī -spersum *vt* to scatter about, disperse; to splatter; to distribute, scatter (*e.g., men*) without organization; to spread, extend (*war, rumor, etc.*)
dispersē *adv* here and there; occasionally
dispersus *pp* of **dispergo**
dispert·ĭō -īre -īvī or **-ĭī -ītum** or **dispert·ĭor** or **dispart·ĭor -īrī -ītus sum** *vt* to distribute, divide; to assign (*e.g., gates, areas*) as posts to be guarded
dispessus *pp* of **dispando**
di·spiciō -spicĕre -spexī -spectum *vt* to see clearly, make out, distinguish, detect; to consider carefully, perceive, detect, discern, discover, reflect on
displic·ĕō -ēre -ŭī -ĭtum *vi* to be unpleasant, be displeasing; (with *dat*) to displease; **sibi displicere** to be dissatisfied with oneself; to be in a bad humor
dis·plōdō -plōdĕre — -plōsum *vi* to explode
dis·pōnō -pōnĕre -posŭī -posĭtum *vt* to place here and there; to distribute, arrange, set in order; to station, post, assign; to adjust, order, dispose; **diem disponere** to arrange the day's schedule
disposĭtē *adv* orderly, methodically
disposĭtĭ·ō -ōnis *f* orderly arrangement, development (*of theme, essay*)
disposĭtūr·a -ae *f* orderly arrangement
disposĭt·us -a -um *pp* of **dispono;** *adj* well arranged; methodical, orderly
disposĭt·us -ūs *m* orderly arrangement
dispŭd·et -ēre -ŭit *v impers* (with *inf*) it is a great shame to
dispulsus *pp* of **dispello**
dis·pungō -pungĕre -punxī -punctum *vt* to check, balance, audit (*an account*)
disputātĭ·ō -ōnis *f* arguing; argument, debate
disputāt·or -ōris *m* disputant, debater
dispŭt·ō -āre *vt* to dispute, discuss; (com) to estimate, compute; to examine, treat, explain
disquīr·ō -ĕre *vt* to examine in detail
disquīsītĭ·ō -ōnis *f* inquiry, investigation
disrumpō see **dirumpo**
dissaep·ĭō -īre -sī -tum *vt* to separate, wall off, fence off
dissaept·um -ī *n* partition, barrier
dissāvĭ·or or **dissuāvĭ·or -ārī -ātus sum** *vt* to kiss passionately
dissĕc·ō -āre -ŭī -tum *vt* to cut apart, dissect
dissēmĭn·ō -āre *vt* to disseminate
dissensĭ·ō -ōnis *f* difference of opinion, disagreement; dissension; conflict, incompatibility
dissens·us -ūs *m* dissension, discord

dissentānĕ·us -a -um *adj* disagreeing, contrary
dis·sentiō -sentīre -sensī -sensum *vi* to differ in opinion, disagree, dissent; to differ, be in conflict, be inconsistent; (with *dat* or with **ab** or **cum** + *abl*) to differ with, disagree with; (with **ab** + *abl*) to differ from, be opposed to
dissserēn·at -āre *v impers* it is clearing up
dis·sĕrō -serĕre -sēvī -situm *vt* to scatter; to sow here and there; to stick in the ground at intervals
dissĕr·ō -ĕre -ŭī -tum *vt* to arrange; to examine; to discuss, argue, treat
disserp·ō -ĕre *vi* to creep about; to spread gradually
dissertī·ō -ōnis *f* gradual abolition, severance
dissert·ō -āre *vt* to discuss, treat
dissertus *pp* of **dissero** (to arrange)
dis·sidĕō -sidēre -sēdī -sessum *vi* to be located far apart, be distant, be remote; to disagree, be at variance; to differ, be unlike; (of a garment) to be on crooked; (with **ab** or **cum** + *abl*) to disagree with
dissignātī·ō -ōnis *f* arrangement
dissignāt·or -ōris *m* master of ceremonies; usher (*at the theater*); undertaker
dissign·ō -āre *vt* to regulate, arrange; to contrive
dissil·iō -īre -ŭī *vi* to fly apart, split, break up, burst; to be dissolved
dissimil·is -e *adj* dissimilar, unlike, different; (with *genit* or *dat* or with **atque** or **ac**) to be dissimilar to, different from
dissimiliter *adv* differently
dissimilitūd·ō -inis *f* difference
dissimulanter *adv* secretly, slyly
dissimulanti·a -ae *f* faking, hiding, dissembling
dissimulātī·ō -ōnis *f* concealing, disguising; Socratic irony
dissimulāt·or -ōris *m* dissembler, faker
dissimŭl·ō -āre *vt* to dissemble, conceal, disguise; to keep secret; to pretend not to see, ignore
dissipābil·is -e *adj* diffusible, dispersible
dissipātī·ō -ōnis *f* scattering, dispersal, dissipation; destruction
dissĭp·ō or **dissŭp·ō -āre** to scatter, disperse; to break up (*enemy formation*); to demolish, overthrow; to squander, dissipate; to circulate, spread; to drive away (*worries*)
dissit·us *pp* of **dissero** (to scatter)
dissociābil·is -e *adj* separating, estranging; incompatible
dissociātī·ō -ōnis *f* separation
dissoci·ō -āre *vt* to dissociate, separate; to ostracize; to set at variance, estrange; to divide into factions; to detach
dissolūbil·is -e *adj* dissoluble, separable
dissolūtē *adv* disconnectedly, loosely; carelessly
dissolūtī·ō -ōnis *f* dissolution, dissolving, breaking up; abolishing, destruction; refutation; looseness, dissoluteness; asyndeton (*succession of clauses without conjunctions*)
dissolūt·us -a -um *adj* disconnected, loose; careless, negligent, remiss; loose, licentious, dissolute; *n* asyndeton (*succession of clauses without conjunctions*)
dis·solvō -solvĕre -solvī -solūtum *vt* to dissolve, break up, loosen; to free, release; (fig) to break up; to pay; to refute; to unite; **animam dissolvere** to die; **legem dissolvere** to abrogate or annul a law; **poenam dissolvere** to pay the penalty
dissŏn·us -a -um *adj* dissonant, discordant, jarring, confused (*sounds, voices*); different; (with *abl*) differing from, different from
dissor·s -tis *adj* having a different fate; unshared
dis·suādĕō -suādēre -suāsī -suāsum *vt* to advise against, dissuade, object to, oppose
dissuāsī·ō -ōnis *f* dissuasion; (with *genit*) opposition to, objection to
dissuās·or -ōris *m* objector, opponent
dissuāvior see **dissavior**
dissult·ō -āre *vi* to fly apart, burst
dis·sŭō -suĕre — -sūtum *vt* to unstitch; to untie, undo, unfasten
dissŭpō see **dissipo**
distaed·et -ēre *v impers* it makes (*one*) tired; (with *genit*) it makes (*one*) tired of; **me distaedet loqui** I'm sick and tired of speaking
distanti·a -ae *f* distance, remoteness; difference, diversity
dis·tendō (or **dis·tennō**) **-tendĕre -tendī -tentum** *vt* to stretch apart, stretch out; to distend, swell; to distract, perplex
distent·us -a -um *pp* of **distendo;** *adj* distended; *pp* of **distineo;** *adj* busy, occupied, distracted
distermin·ō -āre *vt* to separate by a boundary, divide, limit
distich·on -ī *n* couplet
distinctē *adv* distinctly, clearly, with precision
distinctī·ō -ōnis *f* distinction, differentiation, discrimination; difference; (gram) punctuation
distinct·us -a -um *pp* of **distinguo;** *adj* distinct, separate; studded, adorned; varied, diversified; lucid (*speaker*); eminent
distinct·us -ūs *m* difference, distinction
dis·tinĕō -tinēre -tinŭī -tentum *vt* to keep apart, separate; to detain, hold back, hinder; to employ, engage, divert; to put off, delay; (mil) to keep (*troops*) from meet-

ing; to keep divided; to stand in the way of (*peace, victory, etc.*); to distract

di·stinguō -stinguĕre -stinxī -stinctum *vt* to mark off; to separate, part; to set off (*with colors, gold, etc.*); to distinguish, specify; to punctuate

dist·ō -āre *vi* to stand apart, be separate, be distant; to differ, be different; (with *dat* or **ab** + *abl*) to differ from; *v impers* there is a difference, it is important, makes a difference

dis·torquĕō -torquēre -torsī -tortum *vt* to twist, distort; to curl (*lips*); to roll (*eyes*)

distortī·ō -ōnis *f* twisting; contortion

distort·us -a -um *pp* of **distorqueo**; *adj* distorted, misshapen, deformed; perverse

distractī·ō -ōnis *f* pulling apart; dividing; discord, dissension

distract·us -a -um *adj* severed, separate

dis·trăhō -trahĕre -traxī -tractum *vt* to pull or drag apart, separate forcibly; to tear away, drag away, remove; to distract; to sever, break up; to estrange, alienate; to prevent, frustrate; to end, settle (*e.g., disputes*); to sell at retail, sell (*e.g., land*) in lots

distrib·ŭō -uĕre -ŭī -ūtum *vt* to distribute

distribūtē *adv* methodically

distribūtī·ō -ōnis *f* distribution, apportionment, division

district·us -a -um *adj* drawn in opposite directions; distracted, busied, engaged

di·stringō -stringĕre -strinxī -strictum *vt* to draw apart; to distract, draw the attention of

distrunc·ō -āre *vt* to cut in two, hack apart

disturbātī·ō -ōnis *f* destruction

disturb·ō -āre *vt* to throw into confusion; to smash up, demolish; to break up (*a marriage*); to frustrate

dītesc·ō -ĕre *vi* to grow rich

dīthyrambic·us -a -um *adj* dithyrambic; *m* dithyramb (*song in honor of Bacchus*)

dīthyramb·us -ī *m* dithyramb

dītī·ae -ārum *f pl* wealth

dīt·ō -āre *vt* to make rich, enrich; **ditari** to get rich

diū *adv* by day, in the daytime; long, for a long time; in a long time; **diu noctuque** by day and by night, continually; **iam diu** this long; **satis diu** long enough

diurn·us -a -um *adj* of the day, by day, day, daytime; daily, of each day; day's, of one day; **acta diurna** daily newspaper; **merum diurnum** daytime drinking; *n* account book; *n pl* record, journal, diary

dī·us -a -um *adj* godlike, divine, noble

diūtīnē *adv* for a long time

diūtīn·us -a -um *adj* long, lasting

diūtissimē *adv* for a very long time; longest; **iam diutissime** long, long ago

diūtius *adv* longer, still longer; **paulum diutius** a little too long

diūturnit·ās -ātis *f* length of time, long duration; durability

diūturn·us -a -um *adj* long, long-lasting

dīv·a -ae *f* goddess

dīvāric·ō -āre *vt* to stretch out, spread

dī·vellō -vellĕre -vellī -vulsum *vt* to tear apart, tear to pieces; to tear away; to untie; to wrest, remove, separate; to estrange

dī·vendō -vendĕre — -venditum *vt* to sell piecemeal, retail

dīverbĕr·ō -āre *vt* to zip through, fly through

dīverb·ium -iī *or* **-ī** *n* dialogue, verbal exchange

dīversē or **dīvorsē** *adv* in different directions; differently

dīversit·ās -ātis *f* diversity, difference; contradiction, direct opposite

dīvers·us or **dīvors·us -a -um** *pp* of **diverto**; *adj* in different directions; apart, separate; different; remote, opposite, diametrically opposed; hostile; unsettled, irresolute; dissimilar, distinct; *m pl* individuals; *n* opposite direction, different quarter, opposite side, opposite view

dī·vertō or **dī·vortō -vertĕre -vertī -versum** *vi* to go different ways; to turn off; to stop off, stay

dīv·es -itis *adj* rich, wealthy; costly, precious, sumptuous; plentiful, abundant; (with *genit* or *abl*) rich in, abounding in

dīvex·ō -āre *vt* to plunder; to violate

dīvidi·a -ae *f* worry, trouble, nuisance; dissension, antagonism

dī·vidō -vidĕre -vīsī -vīsum *vt* to divide, force apart; to divide, distribute, share; to break up, destroy; to arrange, apportion; to separate, distinguish; to separate, segregate, keep apart; to accompany (*songs with music*); **sententiam dividere** to break down a proposal (*so as to vote on each part separately*)

dīvidŭ·us -a -um *adj* divisible; divided, separated

dīvīnātī·ō -ōnis *f* clairvoyance; forecasting, predicting, divination; (law) selection of the most suitable prosecutor

dīvīnē *adv* through divine power; prophetically, by divine inspiration; divinely, gorgeously

dīvīnit·ās -ātis *f* divinity, godhead; prophetic power, clairvoyance; excellence

dīvīnitus *adv* from heaven, from god; providentially; prophetically; divinely, in a godlike manner; excellently

dīvīn·ō -āre *vt* to divine, predict, prophesy, foresee, dread
dīvīn·us -a -um *adj* divine, heavenly; divinely inspired, prophetic; godlike, superhuman, excellent, gorgeous; **divinum jus** natural law; **divinum jus et humanum** natural and positive law; **divinum scelus** sacrilege; **rerum divinarum et humanarum scientia** physics and ethics; **rem divinam facere** to worship; to sacrifice; **res divina** worship; sacrifice; **res divinae** religious affairs, religion; *m* prophet; *n* offering; *n pl* divine matters; religious duties; **agere divina humanaque** to perform religious and secular duties; **divina humanaque** things divine and human, the whole world
dīvīsi·ō -ōnis *f* division, distribution
dīvīs·or -ōris *m* distributer; person hired by a candidate to distribute bribes
dīvīs·us -a -um *pp* of **divido;** *adj* separate, distinct
dīvīs·us -ūs *m* distribution; **divisui facilis** easily divided, easy to divide
dīviti·ae -ārum *f pl* riches, wealth; richness (*of soil*); costly things
dīvolg- = divulg-
dīvor- = diver-
dīvort·ium -iī or **-ī** *n* separation; divorce; fork (*of road or river*); **divortium facere cum aliqua** to divorce some woman
dīvulgāt·us -a -um *adj* common, widespread
dīvulg·ō -āre *vt* to divulge, spread among the people; to publish (*a book*); to spread, publicize, advertise
dīvulsus *pp* of **divello**
dīv·us -a -um *adj* divine; deified; *m* god, deity; *n* sky; the open; **sub divo** out in the open, under the open sky; **sub divum rapere** to bring out in the open
dō dare dedī datum (danit = dat; danunt = dant; dane = dasne; duim = dem) *vt* to give; to offer; to offer, dedicate; to give out, pay (*money*); to bestow, confer; to permit, grant, concede, allow; to give up, hand over; to communicate, tell; to ascribe, impute, assign; to cause, produce, make; to furnish, afford, present; to grant, admit; to administer (*medicine*); to utter, give expression to, announce; **legem dare** to enact a law; **locum dare** (with *dat*) to make way for; **nomen dare** to enlist; **operam dare** to pay attention; **operam dare** (with *dat*) to pay attention to, give or devote attention to, look out for; **poenam** or **poenas dare** to pay the penalty; **sē dare** to present oneself; to plunge, rush; **velum dare** to set sail; **veniam dare** to grant pardon
doc·ĕō -ēre -uī -tum *vt* to teach, instruct; to instruct, give instructions to; (with double *acc*) to teach (*someone something*); **fabulam docere** to teach a play (*to the actors*), produce a play, put on a play
dochm·ius -iī or **-ī** *m* dochmaic foot (*consisting of a trochee and a cretic*)
docil·is -e *adj* docile, easily taught, teachable; docile, tractable
docilit·ās -ātis *f* docility, aptitude for learning
doctē *adv* learnedly, skillfully; shrewdly, cleverly
doct·or -ōris *m* teacher
doctrīn·a -ae *f* teaching, instruction, education, training; lesson; erudition, learning; science
doct·us -a -um *pp* of **doceo;** *adj* learned, skilled, experienced, clever, trained; cunning, shrewd; (with *abl*, with **ad** + *acc*, or **in** + *abl*) skilled in, experienced in, clever at
document·um -ī or **docūm·en -inis** *n* example, model, pattern; object lesson, warning; evidence, proof
Dōdōn·a -ae *f* town in Epirus, famous for the oracular oak tree sacred to Jupiter
Dōdōnae·us -a -um *adj* of Dodona
dodr·ans -antis *m* three fourths; **heres ex dodrante** heir entitled to three fourths of the estate
dogm·a -ătis *n* doctrine, tenet
dolābr·a -ae *f* pickax, mattock
dol·ens -entis *adj* painful, smarting; distressing
dolenter *adv* painfully; with sorrow
dol·ĕō -ēre -uī -itum *vt* to give pain to, hurt; *vi* to feel pain, be sore, ache, smart; to grieve, be sorry, be hurt; take offense; (with *dat*) to give pain to, afflict, hurt; **caput mihi dolet** I have a headache
dōliār·is -e *adj* fat, tubby
dōliōl·um -ī *n* small barrel
dōl·ium -iī or **-ī** *n* large wine jar
dol·ō -āre *vt* to chop; to beat, beat up, drub; (fig) to hack out (*e.g., a poem*)
dol·ō or **dol·ōn -ōnis** *m* pike; string; fore topsail
Dol·ō -ōnis *m* Dolon (*Trojan spy*)
Dolŏp·es -um *m pl* a people of Thessaly
dol·or -ōris *m* pain, ache, smart; pain, grief, distress, anguish; indignation, resentment, chagrin; pathos; object of grief; **capitis dolor** headache; **dentis dolor** toothache; **esse dolori** (with *dat*) to be a cause of grief or resentment to
dolōsē *adv* shrewdly, slyly
dolōs·us -a -um *adj* wily, cunning, deceitful
dol·us -ī *m* trick, device; deceit, cunning, trickery; **dolus malus** (law) intentional deceit, willful wrong, fraud, malice
domābil·is -e *adj* tameable
domesticātim *adv* at home
domestic·us -a -um *adj* of the house or home; domestic, household;

familiar, private, personal; domestic, native, of one's own country; **bellum domesticum** civil war; *m pl* members of the household or family

domī *adv* at home

domicil·ium -iī or **-ī** *n* residence, home

domin·a or **domn·a -ae** *f* lady of the house; mistress, owner; lady; sweetheart; wife

domin·ans -antis *adj* ruling, holding sway; **nomen dominans** word in its literal sense; *m* ruler

dominātī·ō -ōnis *f* mastery; tyranny, despotism, absolute power; *f pl* control, supremacy; rulers

dominātor -ōris *m* ruler, lord

dominātr·ix -īcis *f* ruler, mistress

dominat·us -ūs *m* absolute rule, sovereignty, tyranny; control, mastery

dominic·us -a -um *adj* of a lord, lord's, master's

Dominic·us -a -um *adj* (eccl) the Lord's

domin·ium -iī or **-ī** *n* absolute ownership; banquet, feast

domin·or -ārī -ātus sum *vi* to be master, be lord, have dominion; to play the master, domineer; (with **in** + *acc* or **in** + *abl*) to lord it over, tyrannize

domin·us -ī *m* owner, proprietor, possessor, master, ruler, lord; ruler, despot, tyrant; commander, chief; entertainer, host

Domin·us -ī *m* (eccl) Lord, Master

domiport·a -ae *f* snail

Domitiān·us -ī *m* T. Flavius Domitianus (*son of Vespasian, brother of Titus, and Roman emperor,* 81-96 A.D.)

domit·ō -āre *vt* to train, break in

domit·or -ōris *m* or **domitr·ix -īcis** *f* tamer

domit·us -ūs *m* taming

dom·ō -āre -uī -itum *vt* to tame, break in; to domesticate; to master, subdue, vanquish, conquer

dom·us -ūs or **-ī** (*dat:* **domuī** or **domō**; *abl:* **domō** or **domū**; *locat:* **domī** rarely **domō** or **domuī**; *genit pl:* **domuum** or **domōrum**) *f* house, building, mansion, palace; home, residence, family; native country; philosophical sect; **domi** at home; **domi militiaeque** at home and in the field, in peace and in war; **domum** homewards, home

dōnābil·is -e *adj* worthy of a gift

dōnār·ium -iī or **-ī** *n* gift repository of a temple; sanctuary; altar; votive offering

dōnātī·ō -ōnis *f* donation

dōnātīv·um -ī *n* (mil) bonus

dōnec *conj* while; as long as; until

dōn·ō -āre *vt* to present, bestow, grant, confer; to forgive, pardon; to give up, sacrifice; **aliquem civitate donare** to present someone with citizenship; **civitatem alicui donare** to bestow citizenship on someone

dōn·um -ī *n* gift, present; votive offering, sacrifice; **ultima dona** funeral rites, obsequies

dorc·as -ădis *f* gazelle

Dōr·ēs -um *m pl* Dorians (*one of the four Hellenic tribes*)

Dōric·us or **Dōrici·us -a -um** *adj* Dorian; Greek

Dōr·is -idis *f* daughter of Oceanus, wife of Nereus, and mother of fifty sea nymphs

dorm·iō -īre -īvī or **-iī -ītum** *vi* to sleep; to be inactive, be idle, be lazy

dormītāt·or -ōris *m* dreamer

dormīt·ō -āre *vi* to be sleepy, be drowsy; to nod, fall asleep

dormītōri·us -a -um *adj* for sleeping; **cubiculum dormitorium** bedroom

dors·um -ī *n* back; ridge; reef

dōs dōtis *f* dowry

Dossenn·us -ī *m* hunchback, clown (*well-known character in early Italic comedy*)

dōtāl·is -e *adj* of a dowry, given as a dowry, dotal

dōt·ō -āre *vt* to endow

drachm·a or **drachŭm·a -ae** *f* drachma (*Greek coin approximately the value of a denarius*)

drac·ō -ōnis *m* dragon; huge serpent

Drac·ō -ōnis *m* Dragon (*constellation*); Draco (*Athenian lawgiver, notorious for his severity, c.* 621 B.C.)

dracōnigĕn·us -a -um *adj* sprung from a dragon; **urbs draconigena** Thebes

drāpĕt·a -ae *m* runaway slave

drom·as -ădis *m* dromedary, camel

drom·os -ī *m* Spartan racetrack

Druid·ēs -um or **Druid·ae -ārum** *m pl* Druids (*priests and sages of the Gauls and Britons*)

Drūsill·a -ae *f* Livia Drusilla (*second wife of Augustus and mother of Tiberius,* 63 B.C.-29 A.D.)

Drūs·us -ī *m* Livius Drusus (*tribune of the people with C. Gracchus in* 122 B.C.); M. Livius Drusus (*former's son, famous orator and tribune of the people in* 91 B.C.); Nero Claudius Drusus (*son of Livia, brother of Tiberius,* 38-9 B.C.)

Dry·ad -ădis *f* dryad (*wood nymph*)

Dryŏp·es -um *m pl* people of Epirus

dubiē *adv* doubtfully; **haud dubie** undoubtedly, indubitably

dubitābil·is -e *adj* doubtful

dubitanter *adv* doubtingly, hesitantly

dubitātī·ō -ōnis *f* doubt, uncertainty; wavering, hesitancy, irresolution; hesitation, delay; (rhet) pretended embarrassment (*to win over the sympathy of the audience*)

dubit·ō -āre *vt* to doubt; to consider, ponder; *vi* to be doubtful, be in doubt, be uncertain, be perplexed;

to deliberate; to waver, hesitate, delay
dubi•us -a -um *adj* wavering, doubtful, dubious, uncertain, irresolute; dubious, undermined; precarious, critical, adverse, difficult; dim (*light*); overcast (*sky*); indecisive (*battle*); *n* doubt, question; **haud pro dubio habere** to regard as beyond doubt; **in dubium venire** to come in question; **in dubium vocare** to call in question; **procul dubio** beyond doubt, undoubtedly
ducēnāri•us -a -um *adj* receiving a salary of 200,000 sesterces
ducēn•ī -ae -a *adj* two hundred each
ducentēsim•a -ae *f* half percent
ducent•ī -ae -a *adj* two hundred
ducentiens or **ducentiēs** *adv* two hundred times
dūcō dūcere duxī ductum *vt* to lead, guide, direct, conduct; to lead, command; to lead, march; to draw, pull, haul; to draw out, protract, prolong; to put off, stall (*someone*); to pass, spend (*time*); to pull at (*oars*); to mislead, take in, fool, trick; to draw, attract; to draw (*lots*); to draw in, breathe in, inhale; to suck in, drink; to draw, trace; to construct, form, fashion, shape; to run (*a wall from one point to another*); to assume, get (*name*); to lead home, marry (*a woman*); to calculate, compute; to regard, consider, hold, account; to derive, trace (*lineage*); to spin (*wool*); (of a road) to lead, take (*someone*)
ductim *adv* in a continuous stream
ductit•ō -āre *vt* to take home, marry (*a woman*); to lead on, trick, deceive, cheat
duct•ō -āre *vt* to lead; to draw; to accompany, escort
duct•or -ōris *m* leader, commander, general; guide, pilot
duct•us -ūs *m* drawing, conducting; line, row; leadership, command; **oris ductus** facial expression
dūdum *adv* a short time ago, a little while ago; just now; once, formerly; **cum dudum** just as; **haud dudum** not long ago, just now; **jam dudum** for some time; **jam dudum eum exspecto** I have been expecting him; **quam dudum** how long; **ut dudum** just as
Duill•ius or **Duīl•ius -iī** or **-ī** *m* Roman consul who won Rome's first naval engagement against the Carthaginians off Sicily in 260 B.C.
duim see **do**
dulcēd•ō -inis *f* sweetness; pleasantness, charm, delightfulness
dulc•escō -escere -uī *vi* to become sweet
dulcicul•us -a -um *adj* rather sweet
dulcif•er -ĕra -ĕrum *adj* full of sweetness, sweet
dulc•is -e *adj* pleasant, charming, delightful; dear, friendly, kind; sweet
dulciter *adv* agreeably, pleasantly, sweetly
dulcitūd•ō -inis *f* sweetness
dūlicē *adv* like a slave
Dūlich•ium -iī or **-ī** *n* or **Dūlichi•a -ae** *f* island in the Ionian Sea, belonging to the realm of Ulysses
dum *adv* up to now, yet, as yet; now; **age dum!** or **agite dum!** come now!; all right!; **nemo dum** no one yet, no one as yet; **non dum** not yet, not as yet
dum *conj* while, during the time in which; as long as; until; provided that, if only; **dum modo** or **dummodo** provided that, if only; **exspectabam dum rediret** I was waiting for him to return
dūmēt•um -ī *n* thicket, underbrush
dummŏdo *conj* provided that, if only
dūmōs•us -a -um *adj* overgrown with bushes, bushy
dumtaxat *adv* strictly speaking, at least; only, simply, merely
dūm•us -ī *m* bush, bramble
du•o -ae -o *adj* two
duodeciens or **duodeciēs** *adv* twelve times
duodĕcim (indecl) *adj* twelve
duodecim•us -a -um *adj* twelfth
duodēn•ī -ae -a *adj* twelve each, twelve apiece, twelve; a dozen; **duodenis assibus** at twelve percent
duodēquadrāgēsim•us -a -um *adj* thirty-eighth
duodēquadrāgintā (indecl) *adj* thirty-eighth
duodēquinquāgēsim•us -a -um *adj* forty-eighth
duodētrīciens or **duodētrīciēs** *adv* twenty-eight times
duodētrīgintā (indecl) *adj* twenty-eight
duodēvīcēn•ī -ae -a *adj* eighteen each
duodēvīgintī (indecl) *adj* eighteen
duoetvīcēsimān•ī -ōrum *n pl* soldiers of the twenty-second legion
duoetvīcēsim•us -a -um *adj* twenty-second
duovirī see **duumviri**
dupl•a -ae *f* double the price
dupl•ex -icis *adj* twofold, double; divided into two; in double rows; double, twice as big, twice as long; complex, compound; two-faced, double-dealing, false
duplicār•ius -iī or **-ī** *m* soldier receiving double pay
dupliciter *adv* doubly, on two accounts
duplic•ō -āre *vt* to double; to bend double; to enlarge, lengthen, increase
dupl•us -a -um *adj* double, twice as much, twice as large; *n* double price; **in duplum** twice the amount, double; **in duplum ire** to pay twice as much, pay double

dupond·ius -iī or **-ī** *m* or **dupond·ium -iī** or **-ī** *n* two-ace coin, worth about five cents
dūrābil·is -e *adj* durable, lasting
dūrām·en -inis *n* hardness
dūratě·us -a -um *adj* wooden
dūrē or **dūriter** *adv* hard, sternly, rigorously, roughly; stiffly, awkwardly
dūr·escō -escěre -uī *vi* to grow hard, harden
dūrit·ās -ātis *f* hardness, toughness, harshness
dūriter see **dure**
dūriti·a -ae or **dūriti·ēs -ēī** *f* hardness; austerity; strictness, harshness, rigor; oppressiveness; insensibility, callousness
dūriuscŭl·us -a -um *adj* somewhat hard, rather harsh
dūr·ō -āre *vt* to make hard, harden, solidify; (fig) to harden, inure, toughen up; to make insensible, to dull, blunt; to bear, endure; *vi* to be inured, be tough; to endure, last, remain, continue, hold out; (of hills) to continue unbroken, extend
dūr·us -a -um *adj* hard; lasting; rough (*to the senses*); tough, hardy, hale; rough, rude, uncouth; shameless, brazen; harsh, cruel, callous, insensible; severe, oppressive; parsimonious, miserly
duum·vir -virī *m* member of a commission or board of two
duumvirāt·us -ūs *m* duumvirate, office of a duumvir
duumvir·ī -ōrum or **duovir·ī -ōrum** *m pl* two-man commission; **duumviri ad aedem faciendam** two-man commission for the construction of a temple; **duumviri juri dicundo** two-man board of colonial magistrates; pair of judges; **duumviri navales** two-man commission to equip the navy; **duumviri perduellionis** criminal court; **duumviri sacrorum** two-man commission in charge of the Sibylline books
dux ducis *m* or *f* conductor, guide; leader, head, author, ringleader; general
Dym·ās -antis *m* father of Hecuba, the queen of Troy
dynăm·is -is *f* store, plenty
dynast·ēs -ae *m* ruler, prince, petty monarch
Dyrrach·ium -iī or **-ī** *n* Adriatic port in Illyria which served as landing place for those who sailed from Italy

E

ē see **ex**
eā *adv* there, that way
ea ejus *f pron* she
eādem *adv* by the same way, the same way; at the same time; likewise, by the same token
eāpropter *adv* therefore
eapse see **ipse**
eātěnus *adv* to such a degree, so far
eběnus see **hebenus**
ēbĭb·ō -ěre -ī *vt* to drink up, drain; to absorb; to spend in drinks, squander
ēbland·ior -īrī -ītus sum *vt* to coax out, obtain by flattery
Eborāc·um or **Eburāc·um -ī** *n* town of the Brigantes in Britain, York
ēbriět·ās -ātis *f* drunkenness
ēbriŏl·us -a -um *adj* tipsy
ēbriōsĭt·ās -ātis *f* habitual drunkenness, heavy drinking
ēbriōs·us -a -um *adj & m* drunk
ēbri·us -a -um *adj* drunk; drunken (*acts, words*), of a drunk; (fig) intoxicated (*e.g., with love, power*)
ēbull·iō -īre *vt* to brag about; *vi* to bubble up, boil over
ebŭl·um -ī *n* or **ebŭl·us -ī** *m* danewort, dwarf elder
eb·ur -ŏris *n* ivory; ivory objects; statue, flute, scabbard; elephant
eburāt·us -a -um *adj* inlaid with ivory
eburneŏl·us -a -um *adj* ivory
eburně·us or **eburn·us -a -um** *adj* ivory; white as ivory; **ensis eburneus** sword with ivory hilt; **dentes eburnei** tusks (*of elephant*)
ēcastor *interj* by Castor!
ecca see **ecce**
eccam see **ecce**
ecce *interj* see!, look!, look here!, here!; **ecce me** here I am; (colloquially combined with the pronouns **is, ille,** and **iste**): **ecca** (i.e., **ecce + ea**) or **eccam** (i.e., **ecce + eam**) here she is; **eccilla** or **eccistam** there she is; **eccillum** or **eccum** here he is; **eccos** here they are
eccěrē *interj* there!
eccheum·a -ătis *n* pouring out
ecclēsi·a -ae *f* Greek assembly of people; (eccl) church, congregation
ecdic·us -ī *m* legal representative of a community
ecf- = **eff-**
echidn·a -ae *f* viper
Echidn·a -ae *f* hydra; **Echidna Lernaea** Lernaean hydra; monstrous mother of Cerberus, half woman and half serpent
Echīnăd·es -um *f pl* cluster of small islands off Acarnania
echīn·us -ī *m* sea urchin; dishpan
Echī·ōn -ŏnis *m* hero who sprang from the dragon's teeth sown by

Cadmus, married Agave, and became father of Pentheus

Ech·ō -ūs *f* nymph who was changed by Hera into an echo

eclog·a -ae *f* literary selection; eclogue

eclogāri·ī -ōrum *m pl* excerpted literary passages

ecquandō *adv* ever, at any time; (in indirect questions) whether ever

ecquī *conj* whether

ecqu·ī -ae or **-od** *adj* any

ec·quid -cūjus *pron* anything; (in indirect questions) whether, if at all

ec·quis -cūjus *pron* any, anyone; (in indirect questions) whether anyone

ecquō *adv* anywhere

eculĕ·us -ī *m* foal, colt; small equestrian statue; wooden torture rack

edācit·ās -ātis *f* gluttony

ed·ax -ācis *adj* gluttonous; (fig) devouring, destructive

ēdent·ō -āre *vt* to knock the teeth out of

ēdentŭl·us -a -um *adj* toothless, old

edĕpol *interj* by Pollux!, gad!

edĕra see **hedera**

ē·dīcō -dīcĕre -dīxī -dictum *vt* to proclaim, announce, decree, ordain, appoint

ēdicti·ō -ōnis *f* edict, order

ēdict·ō -āre *vt* to proclaim, publish

ēdict·um -ī *n* decree, edict, proclamation; edict of a praetor listing rules he would follow in his capacity as judge; order, command

ē·discō -discĕre -didicī *vt* to learn by heart, learn thoroughly

ēdissĕr·ō -ĕre -ŭī -tum *vt* to explain in detail, analyze fully

ēdissert·ō -āre *vt* to explain fully, explain in all details

ēditīci·us -a -um *adj* set forth, proposed; **judices editicii** panel of jurors (*subject to challenge by the defendant*)

ēditi·ō -ōnis *f* statement, account, published statement; publishing, publication; edition (*of a book*); (law) declaration (*of the form of judicial procedure to be followed*)

ēdit·us -a -um *adj* high; (with *abl*) descended from; *n* height; command, order

e·dō -dĕre -didī -ditum *vt* to give out, put forth, bring forth, emit; to give birth to, bear; to publish; to tell, announce, declare, disclose; to show, display, produce, perform; to bring about, cause; to promulgate

edō edĕre (or **esse**) **ēdī ēsum** *vt* to eat; (fig) to devour, consume, destroy; **pugnos edere** to eat fists, to get a good beating

ēdoc·ĕō -ēre -ŭī -tum *vt* to teach thoroughly; to instruct clearly; to inform; to show clearly; (with double *acc*) to teach (*someone something*) well

ēdŏl·ō -āre *vt* to chop out, hack out; to finish, prepare

ēdŏm·ō -āre -ŭī -itum *vt* to conquer, subdue

Ēdōn·ī -ōrum *m pl* Thracian tribe noted for its heavy drinking

Ēdōn·is -idis *adj* Edonian; *f* bacchante

ēdorm·iō -īre -īvī or **-iī** *vt* to sleep off; **crapulam edormire** to sleep off a hangover; *vi* to sleep soundly

ēdormisc·ō -ĕre *vt* to sleep off; **crapulam edormiscere** to sleep off a hangover

ēducāti·ō -ōnis *f* rearing; education

ēducāt·or -ōris *m* foster father; tutor, instructor

ēducātr·ix -īcis *f* nurse

ēdŭc·ō -āre *vt* to bring up; to train, educate, develop; to produce

ē·dūcō -dūcĕre -duxī -ductum *vt* to draw out; to take away; to draw (*sword*); to draw out, spend (*time*); to lead out, march out (*army*); to summon (*to court*); to hatch; to rear, bring up, educate, train; to raise, erect

edūl·is -e *adj* edible

ēdūr·ō -āre *vi* to last, continue

ēdūr·us -a -um *adj* hard, tough; (fig) tough

Ēëti·ōn -ōnis *m* father of Andromache and king of Thebe in Cilicia

effarciō see **effercio**

effāt·us -a -um *pp* of **effor;** *adj* solemnly pronounced; solemnly dedicated; *n* axiom; prediction

effecti·ō -ōnis *f* accomplishment, performing; efficient cause

effectīv·us -a -um *adj* producing, practical

effect·or -ōris *m* or **effectr·ix -īcis** *f* producer, author

effect·us -a -um *pp* of **efficio;** *adj* finished, complete; *n* effect

effect·us -ūs *m* effecting, completion; operation; effect, result, consequence

effēminātē *adv* effeminately, like a woman

effēmināt·us -a -um *adj* effeminate

effēmin·ō -āre *vt* to make a woman of; to represent as a woman; to effeminate, enervate

efferāt·us -a -um *adj* wild, brutal, savage

ef·ferciō or **ec·ferciō** or **ef·farciō -fercīre — -fertum** *vt* to stuff; to fill in (*e.g., a ditch*)

efferit·ās -ātis *f* wildness, barbarism

effĕr·ō -āre *vt* to make wild, brutalize; to exasperate

effĕrō or **ecfĕrō efferre extŭlī ēlātum** *vt* to carry out, bring out, bring forth; to utter, express; to publish, spread (*news*); to carry out for burial, bury; to produce, bear; to name, designate; to lift up, raise; to promote, advance; to bring out, expose; to praise, extol; to sweep off one's feet; **efferri** (fig) to be

carried away; **se efferre** to be haughty, be proud, be conceited
effert·us -a -um *pp* of **effercio;** *adj* full, crammed, bulging
effĕr·us -a -um *adj* wild, fierce, savage
ef·fervescō -fervescĕre -fervī *vi* to boil, boil over; to burst forth
efferv·ō -ĕre *vi* to boil over; (of bees) to swarm out; (of volcano) to erupt
effēt·us -a -um *adj* effete, spent; vain, delusive; (with *genit*) incapable of
efficācĭt·ās -ātis *f* efficiency
efficācĭter *adv* efficiently, effectively
effĭc·ax -ācis *adj* efficient, effective, efficacious
efficĭ·ens -entis *adj* efficient, effective; **res efficientes** causes
efficienter *adv* efficiently
efficientĭ·a -ae *f* efficiency, efficacy, influence
ef·ficĭō -ficĕre -fēcī -fectum *vt* to bring about, bring to pass, effect, cause, produce; to make, form; to finish, complete, accomplish; (of a field) to yield, produce; (of numbers) to amount to; to prove, show; **ita efficitur ut** thus it follows that
effictus *pp* of **effingo**
effigĭ·ēs -ēī or **effigĭ·a -ae** *f* effigy, likeness, semblance; opposite number; copy, imitation; image; statue, figure, portrait; ghost, phantom
ef·fingō -fingĕre -finxī -fictum *vt* to mold, form, fashion; to imitate; to wipe out, wipe clean; to represent, portray; to imagine
effīō passive of **efficio**
effĭāgitātĭ·ō -ōnis *f* urgent demand
effĭāgitāt·us -ūs *m* urgent request; **efflagitatu meo** at my insistence
effĭāgĭt·ō -āre *vt* to demand, insist upon
effictim *adv* (to love, desire) desperately
efflict·ō -āre *vt* to strike dead
ef·flīgō or **ecf·flīgō -flīgĕre -flixī -flictum** *vt* to strike dead, exterminate
effl·ō or **ecfl·ō -āre** *vt* to breathe out; **animam efflare** to expire
efflōr·esco -escĕre -ŭī *vi* to bloom, blossom, flourish
efflŭ·ō or **ecflŭ·ō -ĕre -xī** *vi* to flow out, flow forth, run out; to slip away, drop out, disappear; (of a rumor) to get out, circulate; **ex pectore effluere** to be forgotten
effluv·ĭum -ĭī or **-ī** *n* outlet; **effluvium lacūs** outlet of a lake
ef·fodĭō or **ecf·fodĭō -fodĕre -fōdī -fossum** *vt* to dig up; to gouge out (*eyes*); to root out, gut; to excavate
ef·for or **ec·for -fārī -fātus sum** *vt* to speak out, say out loud, tell; (in augury) to mark off, consecrate (*area*); *vi* to state a proposition
effossus *pp* of **effodio**
effrēnātē *adv* without restraint, out of control
effrēnātĭ·ō -ōnis *f* impetuosity
effrēnāt·us -a -um *adj* unbridled; (fig) unbridled, unrestrained
ef·fringō or **ec·fringō -fringĕre -frēgī -fractum** *vt* to break open, smash, break off; to break in (*door*)
ef·fugĭō -fugĕre -fūgī *vt* to escape; to escape the notice of; *vi* to escape; (with *abl* or with **ab** or **ex** + *abl*) to escape from
effug·ĭum -ĭī or **-ī** *n* escape, flight; means of escape; avoidance
ef·fulgĕō -fulgēre -fulsī *vi* to shine forth, gleam, glitter
effult·us -a -um *adj* propped up, supported
ef·fundō or **ec·fundō -fundĕre -fūdī -fūsum** *vt* to pour out, pour forth; to fling (*weapon*); to give up, let go, abandon, resign; to throw down; to produce in abundance; to lavish, waste, squander, run through; to empty out (*bags, etc.*); to given vent to, pour out; **effundi** or **se effundere** to pour out, rush out; to yield, indulge
effūsē *adv* far and wide; at random, in disorder; lavishly; immoderately
effūsĭ·ō -ōnis *f* outpouring, rushing out; shedding; effusion; profusion, lavishness, extravagance; *f pl* excesses
effūs·us -a -um *pp* of **effundo;** *adj* spread out, extensive, broad, wide; relaxed, loose; disheveled; lavish; straggly, disorderly; lavish; loose, dissolute
effūt·ĭō -īre — -ītum *vt & vi* to blab, babble, chatter
ef·futŭō or **ec·futŭō -futuĕre -futŭī -futūtum** *vt* to exhaust through excesses
ēgelĭd·us -a -um *adj* chilly, cool; lukewarm
eg·ens -entis *adj* needy, poor; (with *genit*) in need of
egēn·us -a -um *adj* needy, destitute; (with *genit* or *abl*) in need of
eg·ĕō -ēre -ŭī *vi* to be needy, suffer want; (with *genit* or *abl*) **a** to be in need of; **b** to lack, be without; **c** to want, desire, miss
Ēgerĭ·a -ae *f* nymph whom King Numa visited at night for advice
ē·gĕrō -gerĕre -gessī -gestum *vt* to carry out, take away, remove; to discharge, vomit, emit
egest·ās -ātis *f* need, want, poverty; (with *genit*) lack of
ēgestĭ·ō -ōnis *f* squandering
ēgestus *pp* of **egero**
ego *pron* I
egŏmet *pron* I personally, I and nobody else
ē·gredĭor -grĕdī -gressus sum *vt* to go beyond, pass; to quit; (fig) to go beyond, surpass; *vi* to go out, come out; to march out; to set sail, put out to sea; to disembark, land; to go up, climb; to digress
ēgregĭē *adv* exceptionally, singularly, uncommonly, splendidly

ēgregi·us -a -um *adj* exceptional, singular, uncommon; distinguished, illustrious; *n* honor, distinction
ēgressus *pp* of **egredior**
ēgress·us -ūs *m* departure; way out, exit; disembarking, landing; mouth (*of river*); digression; *m pl* comings and goings
ēgurgit·ō -āre *vt* to pour out, lavish
ehem *interj* (expressing pleasant surprise) ha!, aha!
eheu *interj* (expressing pain) oh!
eho *interj* (expressing rebuke) look here!, see here!; **eho dum!** look here now!
ei *interj* (expressing fear or dismay) golly!
ēia or **hēia** *interj* (expressing joy or surpise) ah!, ah ha!; good!; (expressing haste) quick!, come on!
ējacŭl·or -ārī -ātus sum *vt* to squirt (*e.g., water*); **se ejaculari** to squirt
ējectāment·a -ōrum *n pl* refuse; jetsam
ējecti·ō -ōnis *f* ejection; banishment, exile
ēject·ō -āre *vt* to spout forth; to keep throwing up (*e.g., blood*)
eject·us -ūs *m* emission
ējĕr·ō or **ējūr·ō -āre** *vt* to refuse upon oath, abjure, forswear; to deny on oath; to resign, abdicate; to disown, abandon
ē·jiciō -jicĕre -jēcī -jectum *vt* to throw out, drive out, put out, eject, expel; to banish, drive into exile; to utter; to run aground; to reject, disapprove; to boo (*someone*) off the stage; **ejici** to be stranded; **se ejicere** (of passions) to break out, come to the fore
ējulāti·ō -ōnis *f* wailing, lamenting
ējŭl·ō -āre *vi* to wail, lament
ējūrō see **ejero**
ē·lābor -lābī -lapsus sum *vi* to glide off; to slip away, escape; to pass away, disappear; (with *abl* or with **super** + *acc*) to glance off
ēlabōrāt·us -a -um *adj* studied, overdone; elaborate, finished
ēlabōr·ō -āre *vt* to work out, elaborate; to produce; *vi* to make a great effort, take great pains; (with *inf*) to strive to
ēlāmentābĭl·is -e *adj* pathetic
ēlangu·escō -escĕre -ī *vi* to slow down, slacken, let up
ēlapsus *pp* of **elabor**
ēlātē *adv* proudly
ēlāti·ō -ōnis *f* elation, ecstasy
ēlātr·ō -āre *vt* to bark out
ēlāt·us -a -um *pp* of **effero;** *adj* high, elevated; exalted; haughty, proud
ē·lāvō -lavāre -lāvī -lautum or **-lōtum** *vt* to wash out; (coll) to clean out, rob
Elĕ·a -ae *f* town in Lucania in S. Italy, birthplace of Eleatic philosophy
Eleātĭc·ī -ōrum *m pl* Eleatics, Eleatic philosophers
ēlecĕbr·a -ae *f* snare; seductress
ēlectē *adv* tastefully
ēlectĭl·is -e *adj* choice, dainty
ēlecti·ō -ōnis *f* choice; *f pl* selection
ēlect·ō -āre *vt* to select, choose; to wheedle out, coax out (*a secret*)
Ēlectr·a -ae *f* Pleiad, daughter of Atlas and Pleione and the mother of Dardanus by Jupiter; daughter of Agamemnon and Clytemnestra
ēlectr·um -ī *n* amber; electrum (*alloy of gold and silver*); *f pl* amber beads
ēlect·us -a -um *pp* of **eligo;** *adj* select, picked, choice; (mil) elite
ēlect·us -ūs *m* choice
ēlĕg·ans -antis *adj* fine, elegant, refined; choosy; fine, choice, select
ēleganter *adv* tastefully, neatly, elegantly
ēleganti·a -ae *f* elegance, refinement, taste, propriety
elĕg·ī -ōrum *m pl* elegiac verses
elegī·a or **elegē·a -ae** *f* elegy
Elĕl·ĕus -ĕī *m* (epithet of) Bacchus
elementārī·us -a -um *adj* elementary; **senex elementarius** old schoolteacher
element·um -ī *n* first principle, element; *n pl* elements, rudiments; beginnings; ABC's
elench·us -ī *m* pearl
elephantomăch·a -ae *m* fighter mounted on an elephant
elephant·us -ī or **elĕph·ās -antis** *m* elephant; (fig) ivory
Eleus·īn -īnis *f* Eleusis (*sacred city in Attica, famous for its cult of Demeter*)
Eleusīn·us -a -um *adj* Eleusinian; **Eleusina mater** Ceres
ēlĕv·ō -āre *vt* to lift up, raise; to alleviate; to lessen, diminish; to make light of, disparage
ē·liciō -licĕre -licŭī -licitum *vt* to elicit, draw out; to lure out, entice; to conjure up
Ēlic·ĭus -iī or **-ī** *m* (epithet of) Jupiter
ē·līdō -līdĕre -līsī -līsum *vt* to knock out, strike out, tear out, force out; to shatter, smash to pieces, crush; to force out, stamp out; (fig) to stamp out
ē·ligō -ligĕre -lēgī -lectum *vt* to pluck out; to pick out, choose
ēlīmĭn·ō -āre *vt* to carry outside; to spread abroad
ēlīm·ō -āre *vt* to file; to finish off, perfect
ēlingu·is -e *adj* without tongue, speechless; (fig) inarticulate
ēlingu·ō -āre *vt* (coll) to tear out the tongue of
Ēl·is or **Āl·is -ĭdis** *f* district and town on the W. coast of the Peloponnesus in which Olympia is located
Eliss·a or **Elīs·a -ae** *f* Dido
ēlīsus *pp* of **elido**

ēlix·us -a -um *adj* wet through and through, soaked
ellam = **ecce** + **illam**
elleborōs·us -a -um *adj* crazy
ellebŏr·us or **hellebŏr·us -ī** *m* or **ellebŏr·um -ī** *n* hellebore (*plant used for mental illness*)
ellips·is -is *f* ellipsis
ellum = **ecce** + **illum**
ēlŏc·ō -āre *vt* to lease out, rent out
ēlocūtī·ō -ōnis *f* style of speaking, delivery
ēlog·ium -iī or **-ī** *n* saying, maxim; inscription, epitaph; clause (*in a will*)
ēlŏqu·ens -entis *adj* eloquent
ēloquenter *adv* eloquently
ēloquentī·a -ae *f* eloquence
ēloqu·ium -iī or **-ī** *n* eloquence
ē·lŏquor -lŏquī -locūtus sum *vt* to speak out, declare; *vi* to give a speech
ēlōtus *pp* of **elavo**
ē·lūcĕō -lūcēre -luxī *vi* to shine forth; to glitter
ēluct·or -ārī -ātus sum *vt* to struggle out of, struggle through (*e.g., deep snow*); to surmount; *vi* to force a way out
ēlūcŭbr·ō -āre or **ēlūcŭbr·or -ārī -ātus sum** *vt* to compose by lamp light
ē·lūdō -lūdĕre -lūsī -lūsum *vt* to elude, parry, avoid; to escape, shun; to delude, deceive; to make fun of; to get the better of, outmaneuver; *vi* to end the game
ē·lūgĕō -lūgēre -luxī *vt* to mourn for; to cease to mourn
ēlumb·is -e *adj* loinless; bland (*style*)
ē·lŭō -luĕre -lŭī -lūtum *vt* to wash off, wash clean; to wash away; (fig) to wash away, remove, get rid of
ēlūsus *pp* of **eludo**
ēlūt·us -a -um *pp* of **eluo**; *adj* washed out, watery, insipid
ēluvī·ēs -ēī *f* inundation, overflow; sewage
ēluvī·ō -ōnis *f* deluge
Ēlys·ium -iī or **-ī** *n* realm of the blessed in the lower world
em *interj* (expressing wonder or emphasis) there!
emācit·ās -ātis *f* fondness for shopping
ēmancipātī·ō or **ēmancupātī·ō -ōnis** *f* emancipation; transfer of property
ēmancipāt·us -a -um *adj* made over, sold
ēmancip·ō or **ēmancŭp·ō -āre** *vt* to transfer; to declare (*a son*) free and independent, emancipate; to surrender, abandon
ēmān·ō -āre *vi* to flow out; to trickle out, leak out; to become known
Ēmathi·a -ae *f* Macedonia
Ēmăth·is -idis *adj* Macedonian; *f pl* the Pierides (*daughters of the Macedonian king Pierus*)
ēmātūr·escō -escĕre -ŭī *vi* to begin to ripen; to soften; (fig) to soften
em·ax -ācis *adj* fond of shopping
emblēm·a -ătis *n* mosaic, inlaid wood
embol·ium -iī or **-ī** *n* interlude
ēmendābil·is -e *adj* capable of correction
ēmendātē *adv* faultlessly
ēmendātī·ō -ōnis *f* emendation, correction
ēmendāt·or -ōris *m* or **ēmendātr·ix -īcis** *f* corrector
ēmendāt·us -a -um *adj* faultless
ēmendīc·ō -āre *vt* to obtain by begging
ēmend·ō -āre *vt* to emend, correct; to reform, improve, revise; to atone for
ēmensus *pp* of **emetior**
ēment·ior -īrī -ītus sum *vt* to falsify, fabricate, feign; *vi* to tell a lie
ēmerc·or -ārī -ātus sum *vt* to buy up; to bribe
ēmer·ĕō -ēre or **ēmer·ĕor -ērī -itus sum** *vt* to merit fully; to lay under obligation; (mil) to serve out (*term of service*); **aliquem emerere** to do someone a favor or favors
ē·mergō -mergĕre -mersī -mersum *vt* to raise (*from the water*); **emergi** or **se emergere** to raise oneself up, rise; *vi* to emerge; to rise (*in power*); to extricate oneself; (with **ex** + *abl*) to get clear of
ēmerit·us -a -um *pp* of **emereor**; *adj* worn out, unfit for service; *m* veteran
ēmersus *pp* of **emergo**
emetic·a -ae *f* emetic
ē·mētior -mētīrī -mensus sum *vt* to measure out; to traverse, travel over; to live through; to impart, bestow
ēmĕt·ō -ĕre *vt* to mow down
ēmic·ō -āre -ŭī -ātum *vi* to dart out, shoot out, dash out; to flash out; (fig) to shine, be prominent
ēmigr·ō -āre *vi* to move out, depart; **e vita migrare** to pass on, die
ēmin·ens -entis *adj* projecting out, prominent, high; eminent
ēminentī·a -ae *f* projection, prominence; (in painting) highlights
ēmin·ĕō -ēre -ŭī *vi* to stand out, project; to be conspicuous, stand out; (in painting) to be highlighted
ēmin·or -ārī -ātus sum *vt* to threaten
ēminus *adv* out of range, at a distance; from afar
ēmīr·or -ārī -ātus sum *vt* to be greatly surprised at, stand aghast at
ēmissār·ium -iī or **-ī** *n* drain, outlet
ēmissār·ius -iī or **-ī** *m* scout, spy
ēmissīci·us -a -um *adj* prying, spying
ēmissī·ō -ōnis *f* discharge, hurling, shooting; releasing, letting off
ēmissus *pp* of **emitto**
ēmiss·us -ūs *m* emission
ē·mittō -mittĕre -mīsī -missum *vt* to sound out; to hurl, discharge,

shoot; to let go, let slip, let loose, drop, release, let out; to send out, publish; to allow to escape; to emancipate, set at liberty; to utter; to pass up (*an opportunity*); **animam emittere** to give up the ghost; **emitti** or **se emittere** (with **ex** + *abl*) to break out of (*e.g., jail*)

emō emĕre ēmī emptum *vt* to buy; to pay for; to gain, obtain, acquire; to bribe; **bene emere** to buy cheap; **in diem emere** to buy on credit; **male emere** to pay dearly for

ēmodĕr·or -ārī -ātus sum *vt* to moderate

ēmodŭl·or -ārī -ātus sum *vt* to sing the praises of, celebrate in song

ēmōl·ior -īrī -ītus sum *vt* to accomplish

ēmoll·iō -īre -īvī or **-iī -ītum** *vt* to soften; to make mild; to enervate

ēmŏl·ō -ĕre — -ĭtum *vt* to grind up; to consume

ēmolument·um -ī *n* profit, gain, advantage

ēmon·ĕō -ēre *vt* to advise, admonish

ē·morior -mŏrī -mortŭus sum *vi* to die, die off; (fig) to die out

ēmortuāl·is -e *adj* of death; **dies emortualis** day of one's death

ēmortŭus *pp* of **emorior**

ē·movĕō -movēre -mōvī -mōtum *vt* to move out, remove, expel; to dislodge; to shake (*e.g., foundations of wall*)

Empedŏcl·ēs -is *m* philosopher of Sicily who is said to have jumped into the crater of Mt. Aetna (*fl* 444 B.C.)

emphăs·is -is *f* emphasis, stress

empīrĭc·us -ī *m* self-trained physician

empor·ium -iī or **-ī** *n* market town, market, mart

emptĭ·ō -ōnis *f* buying, purchase; thing purchased, purchase

emptĭt·ō -āre *vt* to be in the habit of buying

empt·or -ōris *m* buyer, purchaser

emptus *pp* of **emo**

ēmūg·iō -īre *vt* to bellow out

ē·mulgĕō -mulgēre — -mulsum *vt* to drain out; to exhaust

ēmunct·us -a -um *adj* discriminating; **naris emunctae esse** to have discriminating tastes

ē·mungō -mungĕre -munxī -munctum *vt* to blow the nose of; to swindle; (with *abl*) to cheat (*someone*) of; **emungi** to blow one's nose

ēmūn·iō -īre -īvī or **-iī -ītum** *vt* to build up; to fortify; to make a road through (*woods*)

ēn *interj* (in questions) really?; (in commands) come on!; (to call attention) look!, see!

ēnarrābĭl·is -e *adj* describable, intelligible

ēnarrātĭ·ō -ōnis *f* description; analysis

ēnarr·ō -āre *vt* to explain in detail, describe; to interpret

ē·nascor -nascī -nātus sum *vi* to grow out, sprout, arise

ēnăt·ō -āre *vi* to swim away, escape by swimming; (fig) to get away with it

ēnātus *pp* of **enascor**

ēnāvig·ō -āre *vt* to sail over, traverse; *vi* to sail away; (fig) to escape

Encelăd·us -ī *m* one of the giants whom Jupiter buried under Aetna

endrŏm·is -ĭdis *f* athlete's bathrobe

Endymĭ·ōn -ōnis *m* handsome young man with whom Luna fell in love and who was doomed to everlasting sleep on Mt. Patmos in Caria

ē·nĕcō (or **ē·nĭcō**) **-necāre -necŭī** (or **-nicāvī**) **-nectum** (or **-necātum**) *vt* to kill, kill off; to exhaust, wear out; (coll) to kill, pester to death

ēnervāt·us -a -um *adj* without sinews; without energy or force

ēnerv·is -e *adj* weak, feeble

ēnerv·ō -āre *vt* to weaken, enervate, render impotent

ēnīcō see **eneco**

enim *conj* namely, for instance; yes, indeed, certainly; in fact, to be sure; (in replies) of course, no doubt; for, because

enimvērō *adv* yes indeed, to be sure, certainly; (ironical) of course

Enīp·eus -ĕī *m* tributary of the Peneus in Thessaly

ēnīsus *pp* of **enitor**

ēnit·ĕō -ēre -ŭī *vi* to shine out, sparkle; to be distinguished or conspicuous

ēnitesc·ō -ĕre *vi* to begin to shine, begin to brighten, become conspicuous

ē·nītor -nītī -nīsus or **nixus sum** *vt* to work one's way up, climb; to give birth to; *vi* to exert oneself, make an effort; (with *inf*) to struggle to, strive to

ēnixē *adv* strenuously, earnestly

ēnix·us -a -um *pp* of **enitor**; *adj* strenuous, earnest

Ennĭ·us -ī *m* father of Latin literature, writer of tragedy, comedy, epic, and satire, born at Rudiae in Calabria (239-169 B.C.)

Ennosigae·us -ī *m* (epithet of Neptune) Earthshaker

ēn·ō -āre *vi* to swim out, swim away, escape by swimming

ēnōdātē *adv* without knots; plainly, clearly

ēnōdātĭ·ō -ōnis *f* solution, explanation

ēnōd·is -e *adj* without knots; plain, clear

ēnōd·ō -āre *vt* to explain, clarify

ēnorm·is -e *adj* irregular; enormous

ēnormĭt·ās -ātis *f* irregular shape

ēnōt·escō -escĕre -ŭī *vi* to become known

ēnŏt·ō -āre *vt* to take notes of, note down

ensicŭl·us -ī *m* small sword
ensĭf·er -ĕra -ĕrum *adj* with a sword, wearing a sword
ensĭg·er -ĕra -ĕrum *adj* with a sword, wearing a sword
ens·is -is *m* sword
enthȳmēm·a -ătis *n* thought, reflection; condensed syllogism
ē·nūbō -nūbĕre -nupsī *vi* (said of a woman) to marry out of one's rank
ēnucleātē *adv* plainly
ēnucleāt·us -a -um *adj* pure, clean; straightforward; simple, clear (*style*)
ēnuclĕ·ō -āre *vt* (fig) to give in a nutshell, explain to the point
ēnumerātĭ·ō -ōnis *f* enumeration
ēnumĕr·ō -āre *vt* to count up; to pay; to recount, relate, detail, describe
ēnuntiātĭ·ō -ōnis *f* (in logic) proposition
ēnuntĭ·ō -āre *vt* to disclose, reveal, betray; to say, assert, express
ēnuptĭ·ō -ōnis *f* right to marry outside the clan
ēnutr·ĭō -īre -īvī or **-ĭī -ītum** *vt* to nourish, raise, bring up (*children*)
eō īre īvī or **ĭī ītum** *vi* to go; to go, walk, sail, ride; (mil) to march; (of time) to pass; (of events) to go on, happen, turn out; **in sententiam ire** to vote for a bill
eō *adv* there, to that place; to that end, to that purpose; so far, to such an extent, to such a pitch; on that account, for that reason, with that in view; **eo ero brevior** I will be all the briefer; **eo magis** all the more; **eo maxime quod** especially because; **eo quo** to the place to which; **eo . . . quo** the . . . the . . .; **eo quod** because; **eo . . . ut** to such an extent . . . that
eōdem *adv* to the same place, purpose, or person
Ēōs (*nom* only) *f* Dawn
Ēō·us -ī *m* morning star; inhabitant of the East, Oriental; one of the horses of the sun
Epamīnond·ās -ae *m* famous Theban general who fought against the Spartans (*d.* 362 B.C.)
Epăph·us -ī *m* son of Jupiter and Io
ēpast·us -a -um *adj* eaten up
Epē·us or **Epī·us -ī** *m* builder of the Trojan horse
ephēb·us -ī *m* young man (18 *to* 20 *years of age*)
ephēmĕr·is -ĭdis *f* diary, journal
Ephĕs·us -ī *f* city in Asia Minor with famous temple of Diana
ephippiāt·us -a -um *adj* riding a saddled horse
ephipp·ĭum -ĭī or **-ī** *n* saddle
ephŏr·us -ī *m* ephor (*Spartan magistrate*)
Ephy̆r·a -ae or **Ephy̆r·ē -ēs** *f* ancient name of Corinth
Epicharm·us -ī *m* Greek philosopher and writer of early comedy (540-450 B.C.)
epichy̆s·is -is *f* jug
epicrŏc·us -a -um *adj* transparent, thin
Epicūr·us -ī *m* Greek philosopher, born on Samos (342-270 B.C.)
epic·us -a -um *adj* epic
epidictĭc·us -a -um *adj* for display
epidipn·is -ĭdis *f* dessert
epigramm·a -ătis *n* inscription; short poem, epigram
epilŏg·us -ī *m* epilogue, peroration
epimēnĭ·a -ōrum *n pl* month's rations
Epimēth·eus -ĕī *m* son of Iapetus and brother of Prometheus
epirēd·ĭum -ĭī or **-ī** *n* trace
epistol·ĭum -ĭī or **-ī** *n* note
epistŭl·a -ae *f* letter
epitaph·ĭum -ĭī or **-ī** *n* eulogy
epithalam·ĭum -ĭī or **-ī** *n* wedding song
epithēc·a -ae *f* addition, increase
epitŏm·a -ae or **epitŏm·ē -ēs** *f* epitome, abridgment
epity̆r·um -ī *n* olive salad
epŏd·es -um *m pl* seafish
ep·ops -ŏpis *m* hoopoe
epos (*nom & acc* only) *n* epic
ēpōt·us or **expōt·us -a -um** *adj* drained to the dregs; drunk dry
epŭl·ae -ārum *f pl* courses, dishes; sumptuous meal, banquet; **epulae regum** dinner fit for a king
epulār·is -e *adj* at dinner, of a dinner; **sermo epularis** talk at dinner
epŭl·ō -ōnis *m* dinner guest, guest at a banquet; **Tresviri** or **Septemviri Epulones** college of priests who superintended the state dinner to the gods
epŭl·or -ārī -ātus sum *vt* to feast on; *vi* to attend a dinner; (with *abl*) to feast on
epŭl·um -ī *n* banquet, feast
equ·a -ae *f* mare
equ·es -ĭtis *m* rider; (mil) trooper, cavalryman; cavalry; *m pl* cavalry
Equ·es -ĭtis *m* knight; capitalist (*member of Roman middle class*); equestrian order, bourgeoisie
equest·er -ris -re *adj* cavalry; equestrian; middle class, bourgeois, capitalist
equĭdem *adv* truly, indeed, in any event; (with first person) for my part, as far as I am concerned; of course, to be sure
equīn·us -a -um *adj* horse's
equirĭ·a -ōrum *n pl* horse race
equitāt·us -ūs *m* cavalry
equĭt·ō -āre *vi* to ride, ride a horse
equulĕ·us -ī *m* foal, colt; small equestrian statue; torture rack
equ·us -ī *m* horse; **equis virisque** or **equis viris** (fig) with might and main; **equo merere** to serve in the cavalry; **equo vehi** to ride, to ride a horse; **equus bipes** sea

horse; **in equo** mounted; *m pl* (fig) chariot
er·a -ae *f* mistress of the house
ērādīc·ō or **exrādīc·ō -āre** *vt* to root out, uproot, destroy
ē·rādō -rādĕre -rāsī -rāsum *vt* to scratch out, erase, obliterate
erăn·us -ī *m* mutual insurance society
Erătō (*nom* only) *f* Muse of erotic poetry; Muse
Eratosthĕn·ēs -is *m* famous Alexandrine geographer, poet, and philosopher (276-196 B.C.)
erc- see **herc-**
Erĕb·us -ī *m* god of darkness, son of Chaos and brother of Night; lower world
Erechth·eus -ĕī *m* mythical king of Athens, son of Hephaestus
ērect·us -a -um *pp* of **erigo;** *adj* erect, upright; noble, elevated, lofty; haughty; attentive, alert, tense; resolute, courageous
ē·rēpō -rēpĕre -repsī *vt* to crawl through (*field*); to crawl up (*mountain*); *vi* to crawl out
ēreptī·ō -ōnis *f* robbery
ērept·or -ōris *m* robber
ēreptus *pp* of **eripio**
ergā *prep* (with *acc*) to, towards; against
ergastŭl·um -ī n prison; *n pl* inmates
ergō *adv* therefore, consequently; (resumptive) well then, I say, as I was saying; (with imperatives) then, now; **quid ergo?** why then?; *prep* (with preceding *genit*) for the sake of; **illius ergo** for his sake
Erichthon·ĭus -ĭī or **-ī** *m* mythical king of Athens; son of Dardanus, father of Tros, and king of Troy
ēric·ĭus -ĭī or **-ī** *m* hedgehog; (mil) beam with iron spikes
Ēridăn·us -ī *m* Po river (*so called by the Greeks*)
erifŭg·a -ae *m* runaway slave
ē·rīgō -rigĕre -rexī -rectum *vt* to set up straight, straighten out (*e.g., tree*); to set up, erect; to cheer up, encourage; to arouse, excite; (mil) to deploy troops on a slope; **erigi** or **se erigere** to raise oneself, arise
Ērigŏn·ē -ēs *f* Virgo (*constellation*)
erīl·is -e *adj* master's, mistress's
Erīn·ys -ўos *f* Fury; (fig) frenzy
Eriphŷl·a -ae or **Eriphŷl·ē -ēs** *f* wife of the seer Amphiaraus and the mother of Alcmaeon, who killed her for betraying Amphiaraus
ē·ripĭō -ripĕre -ripŭī -reptum *vt* to snatch away, pull out, tear out; to deliver, rescue; to rob; (with *dat* or with **ab** or **ex** + *abl*) to take away from, wrest from, rescue from; **se eripere** to escape
ērogātī·ō -ōnis *f* paying out, payment
ērogīt·ō -āre *vt* to try to find out
ērŏg·ō -āre *vt* to allocate, expend; to bequeath; (with **in** + *acc*) **a** to allocate to, expend on; **b** to bequeath to
Er·ōs -ōtis *m* Cupid
errābund·us -a -um *adj* wandering, straggling
errātic·us -a -um *adj* erratic, roving, wandering
errātī·ō -ōnis *f* wandering
errāt·um -ī *n* error, mistake
errāt·us -ūs *m* roving, wandering about
err·ō -āre *vi* to wander, lose one's way, stray, roam; to waver; to err, make a mistake, be mistaken; (with **in** + *abl*) to be mistaken about
err·ō -ōnis *m* vagrant, vagabond
err·or -ōris *m* wandering, wavering, uncertainty; error; cause of error, deception; maze, winding, intricacy
ērub·escō -escĕre -ŭī *vt* to blush at; to be ashamed of; to respect; *vi* to grow red, redden; to blush
ērūc·a -ae *f* colewort
ēruct·ō -āre *vt* to belch, vomit, throw up; (fig) to belch
ērud·iō -īre -iī -ītum *vt* to educate, teach, instruct
ērudītē *adv* learnedly
ērudītī·ō -ōnis *f* instructing, instruction; erudition
ērudītŭl·us -a -um *adj* somewhat experienced, somewhat skilled
ērudīt·us -a -um *adj* educated, learned, accomplished
ē·rumpō -rumpĕre -rūpī -ruptum *vt* to cause to break out; to give vent to; **iram in hostes erumpere** to vent one's wrath on the enemy; *vi* to burst out, break out
ē·rŭō -ruĕre -rŭī -rŭtum *vt* to root up, uproot, dig out; to undermine, demolish, destroy; to draw out, elicit; to rescue; to plow up
ēruptī·ō -ōnis *f* eruption; (mil) sortie, sally
ēruptus *pp* of **erumpo**
er·us -ī *m* master of the house, head of the family; lord, owner, proprietor
ērŭtus *pp* of **eruo**
erv·um -ī *n* pulse, vetch
Erycīn·us -a -um *adj* of Mt. Eryx (*in Sicily*); of Venus; Sicilian; *f* Venus
Erymanth·is -ĭdis *f* Callisto (*changed into a bear and made a constellation*)
Erymanth·us -ī *m* mountain range in Arcadia, where Hercules killed a boar
Erysichth·ōn -ōnis *m* son of Thessalian king Triopas, punished with insatiable hunger for having cut down a grove sacred to Ceres
erythīn·us -ī *m* red mullet
Er·yx -ўcis or **Erўc·us -ī** *m* mountain on W. coast of Sicily, famous for its temple to Venus
esc·a -ae *f* dish; food; bait

escārī·us -a -um *adj* of food; of bait; *n pl* dishes, courses
e·scendō -scendĕre -scendī -scensum *vt & vi* to climb, climb up
escensī·ō or **exscensī·ō -ōnis** *f* climb, climbing
esculent·us -a -um *adj* edible; *n pl* edibles
esculētum see **aesculetum**
escŭlus see **aesculus**
ēsĭt·ō -āre *vt* to be accustomed to eating
Esquilī·ae -ārum *f pl* Esquiline Hill in Rome
Esquilīn·us -a -um *adj* Esquiline; *f* Esquiline gate
essedār·ĭus -ĭī or **-ī** *m* soldier fighting from a chariot
esse *inf* of **sum**; *inf* of **edo**
essĕd·um -ī *n* combat chariot (*used by Gauls and Britons*)
essentĭ·a -ae *f* essence
estr·ix -īcis *f* glutton (*female*)
essĭt·ō -āre *vt* to be accustomed to eating
ēsuriāl·is -e *adj* of hunger
ēsur·ĭō -īre — -ītum *vt* to be hungry for; *vi* to be hungry
ēsurītĭ·ō -ōnis *f* hunger
ēsus *pp* of **edo**
et *adv* besides, also; even, I mean
et *conj* and; (for emphasis) and even, yes and; (antithetical) however, but; **et . . . et** both . . . and, not only . . . but also
etĕnim *conj* for, and as a matter of fact
etēsĭ·ae -ārum *m pl* periodic winds (*on the Aegean Sea*)
ēthĭc·ē -ēs *f* ethics
ēthologĭ·a -ae *f* portrayal of character
ētholŏg·us -ī *m* impersonator
etĭam *conj* also, and also, besides, likewise; (of time) yet, as yet, still, even now; (in affirmation) yes, yes indeed, certainly, by all means; (emphatic) even, rather; (with emphatic imperatives) but just; **etiam atque etiam** again and again, repeatedly
etiamnunc or **etiamnum** *adv* even now, even at the present time, still
etiamsī *conj* even if, although
etiamtum or **etiamnunc** *adv* even then, till then, still
Etrūrĭ·a -ae *f* district N. of Rome
Etrusc·us -a -um *adj & mf* Etruscan
etsī *conj* even if, although
etymologĭ·a -ae *f* etymology
eu *interj* well done!, bravo!
Euan or **Euhan** *m* Bacchus
Euand·er or **Euandr·us -rī** *m* Evander (*Arcadian who founded Pallanteum at the foot of the Palatine hill*)
eu·ans or **euh·ans -antis** *adj* crying Euan or Euhan (*Bacchic cry*)
euax *interj* hurray!
Euboe·a -ae *f* island off the E. coast of Attica and Boeotia
Euēn·us -ī *m* river in Aetolia
euge or **eugĕpae** *interj* well done!, terrific!
euh·ans -antis *adj* shouting Euan (*Bacchic cry*)
Euhēmĕr·us -ī *m* Greek writer who attempted to prove that all the ancient myths were actually historical events (*fl* 316 B.C.)
Euh·ĭus -ĭī or **-ī** *m* Bacchus
Euhoe or **Euoe** *interj* ecstatic cry of revelers at festival of Bacchus
Eu·ĭus -ĭī or **-ī** *m* Bacchus
Eumenĭd·es -um *f pl* Erinyes or Furies (*goddesses of vengeance*)
eunūch·us -ī *m* eunuch
Euoe see **Euhoe**
Euphorb·us -ī *m* brave Trojan warrior whose soul Pythagoras asserted had transmigrated to himself
Euphrāt·ēs -is *m* Euphrates River
Eupŏl·is -ĭdis *m* famous Athenian comic poet (446?-411 B.C.)
Eurīpĭd·ēs -is *m* Athenian tragic poet (485-405 B.C.)
Eurīp·us -ī *m* strait between Boeotia and Euboea; channel, canal
Eurōp·a -ae or **Eurōp·ē -ēs** *f* daughter of Agenor and mother of Sarpedon and Minos by Jupiter; he, in the shape of a bull, carried her off to Crete
Eurōt·as -ae *m* chief river in Laconia
Eur·us -ī *m* S.E. wind; east wind; wind
Eurydĭc·ē -ēs *f* wife of Orpheus
Eurypȳl·us -ī *m* Greek warrior who fought at Troy
Eurysth·eus -ĕī *m* son of Sthenelus, grandson of Perseus, and king of Nycenae, who imposed the twelve labors of Hercules
Eurȳt·is -ĭdis *f* Iole (*with whom Hercules fell in love*)
Eurȳt·us -ī *m* king of Oechalia and father of Iole
euschēmē *adv* gracefully
Euterp·ē -ēs *f* Muse of lyric poetry
Euxīn·us Pont·us or **Euxīn·us -ī** *m* or **Pont·us -ī** *m* Black Sea
ē·vādō -vādĕre -vāsī -vāsum *vt* to pass, pass by; to pass through, escape; *vi* to go out; to turn out, become, prove to be, turn out to be; to get away, escape; to rise, climb
ēvăg·or -ārī -ātus sum *vt* to stray beyond, transgress; *vi* (mil) to maneuver; (fig) to spread
ēval·escō -escĕre -ŭī *vi* to grow strong; to increase; (of a word or expression) to gain currency; (with *inf*) to be able to; (with **in** + *acc*) to develop into
ēvān·escō -escĕre -ŭī *vi* to vanish, pass away, die away; (of wine) to become vapid; to be forgotten, perish
ēvānĭd·us -a -um *adj* vanishing
ēvast·ō -āre *vt* to devastate, wreck completely
evasus *pp* of **evado**

ē·věhō -vehěre -vexī -vectum *vt* to carry out, convey out; to carry abroad, spread abroad; to lift up, raise; **evehi** to ride, sail, drift
ē·vellō -vellěre -vellī or **-vulsī -vulsum** *vt* to tear or pluck out; to eradicate
ē·venĭō -venīre -vēnī -ventum *vi* to come out, come forth; to come to pass, happen; to follow, result, turn out, end; *v impers* it happens
ēvent·um -ī *n* event, occurrence; result, effect, consequence; fortune, experience
ēvent·us -ūs *m* event, accident, fortune, lot, fate; good fortune, success; issue, consequence, result
ēverběr·ō -āre *vt* to strike hard; to beat violently
ēverricŭl·um -ī *n* broom; dragnet
ē·verrō -verrěre -verrī -versum *vt* to sweep out; (fig) to clean out, strip
ēversĭ·ō -ōnis *f* overthrow, subversion, destruction
ēvers·or -ōris *m* subverter, destroyer
ēversus *pp* of **everro**; *pp* of **everto**
ē·vertō or **ē·vortō -vertěre -vertī -versum** *vt* to overturn, turn upside down; to overthrow, upset; to turn out, expel, eject; to subvert, destroy, ruin
ēvestīgāt·us -a -um *adj* tracked down
ēvictus *pp* of **evinco**
ēvĭd·ens -entis *adj* evident, visible, plain
ēvidenter *adv* evidently, plainly, clearly
ēvidentĭ·a -ae *f* distinctness, clearness (*in speech*)
ēvigĭl·ō -āre *vt* to watch through (*the night*); to work through the night writing (*e.g., books*); *vi* to be wide-awake; (fig) to be on one's toes
ēvīl·escō -escěre -ŭī *vi* to depreciate, become worthless
ē·vincĭō -vincīre -vinxī -vinctum *vt* to tie up; to crown, wreathe
e·vincō -vincěre -vīcī -victum *vt* to conquer completely, trounce; to prevail over
ēvinctus *pp* of **evincio**
ēvĭr·ō -āre *vt* to unman, castrate
ēviscěr·ō -āre *vt* to disembowel; to mangle
ēvitābĭl·is -e *adj* avoidable
ēvītātĭ·ō -ōnis *f* avoidance
ēvīt·ō -āre *vt* to avoid, escape
ēvocāt·ī -ōrum *m pl* veterans called up again; reenlisted veterans
ēvocāt·or -ōris *m* recruiter
ēvŏc·ō -āre *vt* to call out, summon; to challenge; (mil) to call up (*for service*); to evoke, excite, stir
ēvolgō see **evulgo**
ēvŏl·ō -āre *vi* to fly out, fly away; to rush out, dash out; (fig) to soar
ēvolūtĭ·ō -ōnis *f* unrolling a book; (fig) reading
ē·volvō -volvěre -volvī -volūtum *vt* to roll out, unroll, unfold; to spread; to unroll, read, study; to unfold, disclose; to free, extricate; to repel; to evolve, develop
ē·vŏmō -voměre -vomŭī -vomĭtum *vt* to vomit, spew out, disgorge
ēvulg·ō or **ēvolg·ō -āre** *vt* to divulge, make public
ēvulsĭ·ō -ōnis *f* pulling out, extraction (*of a tooth*)
ēvulsus *pp* of **evello**
ex or **ē** *prep* (with *abl*) (of space) out of, from; down from; up from, above; (of time) from, from . . . onward, immediately after, following, since; (cause or origin) from, through, by, on account of, by reason of; (transition) from, out of; from being; (conformity) after, according to, in conformity with; (means) with, by means of; (partitive) out of, from among, among; made of, out of
exacerb·ō -āre *vt* to exasperate, provoke
exactĭ·ō -ōnis *f* driving out, expulsion; supervision; exaction, collection; tax, tribute
exact·or -ōris *m* expeller; supervisor; tax collector
exact·us -a -um *pp* of **exigo**; *adj* exact, precise
exac·ŭō -uěre -ŭī -ūtum *vt* to sharpen; to sharpen, stimulate, excite, inflame
exadversum or **exadvorsum** or **exadversus** *adv* on the opposite side; *prep* (with *dat* or *acc*) across from, right opposite
exaedificātĭ·ō -ōnis *f* construction
exaedifĭc·ō -āre *vt* to finish building, build, construct; (fig) to complete
exaequātĭ·ō -ōnis *f* leveling; uniformity
exaequ·ō -āre *vt* to level, make level; (fig) to equal, regard as equal; **exaequari** (with *dat*) to be put on the same level with
exaestŭ·ō -āre *vi* to seethe, boil; to ferment
exaggerātĭ·ō -ōnis *f* (fig) elevation, enlargement; **animi exaggeratio** broadening of the mind
exaggěr·ō -āre *vt* to pile up; to enlarge; to enhance
exagitāt·or -ōris *m* critic
exagĭt·ō -āre *vt* to stir up, keep on the move; to scare away; to criticize, satirize; to irritate; to excite, stir up (*feelings*)
exagōg·a -ae *f* exportation
exalb·escō -escěre -ŭī *vi* to turn pale
exām·en -ĭnis *n* swarm; crowd; tongue of scale; weighing, consideration; examination
exāmĭn·ō -āre *vt* to weigh; to consider; to try, test, examine
examussim *adv* exactly

exancl·ō -āre *vt* to draw off, drain; to drain to the dregs
exanimāl·is -ē *adj* dead, lifeless; deadly
exanimāti·ō -ōnis *f* breathlessness; terror, panic
exanim·is -e or **exanim·us -a -um** *adj* breathless, terrified; dead, lifeless; fainting (*e.g., from fear*)
exanim·ō -āre *vt* to knock the breath out of; to wind, tire, weaken; to deprive of life, kill; to scare out of one's wits; to dishearten; to agitate
exanimus see **exanimis**
ex·ardescō -ardescĕre -arsī -arsum *vi* to catch fire; to flare up; (fig) to flare up, be provoked, be exasperated
exār·escō -escĕre -ŭī *vi* to become quite dry, dry up
exarm·ō -āre *vt* to disarm
exăr·ō -āre *vt* to plow up; to raise, produce; to write (*on wax with a stylus*), write down, note; to furrow, wrinkle; **frontem rugis exarare** to knit one's brow
exasciāt·us -a -um *adj* hewn out; properly planned, properly worked out
exaspĕr·ō -āre *vt* to make rough, roughen; to exasperate
exauctōr·ō -āre *vt* (mil) to discharge, cashier
exaud·iō -īre -īvī -ītum *vt* to hear clearly; to discern; to perceive, understand; to listen to; to grant
exaug·ĕō -ēre *vt* to increase; to confirm
exaugurāti·ō -ōnis *f* desecration, profaning
exaugŭr·ō -āre *vt* to desecrate, profane
exauspic·ō -āre *vi* to find the omens good
exballist·ō -āre *vt* to put an end to, finish off
exbĭbō see **ebibo**
excaec·ō -āre *vt* to blind; to stop up (*a river, pipe, etc.*); to darken
excandescenti·a -ae *f* mounting anger, outburst of anger
excand·escō -escĕre -ŭī *vi* to grow white hot; to reach a pitch (*of emotion*)
excant·ō -āre *vt* to charm away
excarnific·ō -āre *vt* to tear to pieces, torture to death
excăv·ō -āre *vt* to hollow out
ex·cēdō -cēdĕre -cessī -cessum *vt* to exceed, pass, surpass; *vi* to go out, go away, withdraw, depart, disappear; to die; **e medio excedere** or **e vita excedere** to depart from life, die
excell·ens -entis *adj* excellent, outstanding, distinguished, superior
excellenter *adv* excellently
excellenti·a -ae *f* excellence, superiority
ex·cellō -cellĕre *vi* to excel, be superior
excelsē *adv* high, loftily
excelsit·ās -ātis *f* loftiness
excels·us -a -um *adj* high, lofty; eminent; *n* height; high social status; **in excelso aetatem** or **vitam agere** to be in the limelight
excepti·ō -ōnis *f* exception, restriction, limitation; (law) objection raised by a defendant against an accuser's statement
except·ō -āre *vt* to catch, catch up to
exceptus *pp* of **excipio**
ex·cernō -cernĕre -crēvī -crētum *vt* to sift out, separate
ex·cerpō -cerpĕre -cerpsī -cerptum *vt* to pick out, extract; to pick out, choose, gather; to leave out, omit, except
excerpt·um -ī *n* excerpt
excess·us -ūs *m* departure; death; digression
excĕtr·a -ae *f* snake
excidi·ō -ōnis *f* destruction
excid·ium -iī or **-ī** *n* overthrow, destruction; cause of destruction
ex·cidō -cidĕre -cidī *vi* to fall out; (of an utterance) to slip out, escape; to pass away, perish; to degenerate; to disappear; to be forgotten; (with **in** + *acc*) to degenerate into; (with *abl* or **ex** + *abl*) **a** to be deprived of, lose; **b** to forget, miss; (with *dat* or **de** + *abl*) **a** to fall from; **b** to escape from (*lips*); **e memoria excidere** to slip the memory
ex·cīdō -cīdĕre -cīdī -cīsum *vt* to cut out, cut off, cut down; to raze, demolish; (fig) to banish, eliminate
exciĕō see **excio**
exc·iō -īre -īvī or **-iī -ītum** or **exci·ĕō -ēre** *vt* to call (*someone*) out, summon; to awaken (*from sleep*); to disturb; to frighten; to stir up, excite; to produce, occasion
ex·cipiō -cipĕre -cēpī -ceptum *vt* to take out, remove; to rescue; to exempt; to take, receive, catch, capture; to follow, succeed; to catch, intercept; to be exposed to; to incur; to receive, welcome; to take up eagerly; to listen to, overhear; to except, make an exception of; to reach (*a place*); to mention in particular; to take on, withstand
excīsi·ō -ōnis *f* destruction
excīsus *pp* of **excīdo**
excitāt·us -a -um *adj* excited, lively, vigorous; loud
excit·ō -āre *vt* to wake, rouse; to raise, stir up; to erect, construct, produce; to cause, occasion; (fig) to arouse, awaken, incite, inspire, stimulate, enliven, encourage; to startle
excītus *pp* of **excio**
exclāmāti·ō -ōnis *f* exclamation
exclām·ō -āre *vt* to exclaim; *vi* to shout, yell
ex·clūdō -clūdĕre -clūsī -clūsum *vt* to exclude, shut out, shut off; to

remove, separate; to hatch; (coll) to knock out (*an eye*); to prevent
exclūsi·ō -ōnis *f* exclusion
exclūsus *pp* of **excludo**
excoctus *pp* of **excoquo**
excōgitāti·ō -ōnis *f* thinking out, inventing, contriving
excōgitāt·us -a -um *adj* choice
excōgit·ō -āre *vt* to think out, devise, contrive
ex·cŏlō -colĕre -colŭī -cultum *vt* to tend, cultivate, work carefully; to refine, ennoble, perfect, improve; to worship
ex·cŏquō -coquĕre -coxī -coctum *vt* to cook out, boil away; to dry up, bake thoroughly; to harden, temper (*steel*)
excor·s -dis *adj* senseless, silly, stupid
excrēment·um -ī *n* excretion
excrĕō see **exscreo**
ex·crescō -crescĕre -crēvī -crētum *vi* to grow out; to grow up, rise up
excruciābĭl·is -e *adj* deserving torture
excrucĭ·ō -āre *vt* to torture, torment; to trouble, harass, distress
excubĭ·ae -ārum *f pl* standing guard; sentry; watchfire
excubĭt·or -ōris *m* sentry
excŭb·ō -āre -ŭī -ĭtum *vi* to sleep out of doors; to stand guard; to be attentive, be on the alert
ex·cūdō -cūdĕre -cūdī -cūsum *vt* to beat or strike out; to hammer out; to forge; (fig) to hatch (*eggs*); (fig) to hammer out, write up, hammer into shape
exculc·ō -āre *vt* to kick out; to tread down on; to stomp
excultus *pp* of **excolo**
excūrāt·us -a -um *adj* carefully attended to
ex·currō -currĕre -cucurrī or **-currī -cursum** *vi* to run or dash out; (mil) to sally forth, make an incursion; to project, extend; (fig) to fan out, expand
excursĭ·ō -ōnis *f* sally, sortie; inroad, invasion; outset, opening (*of a speech*)
excurs·or -ōris *m* skirmisher, scout
excurs·us -ūs *m* reconnoitering, running out ahead; raid, charge, attack, invasion; digression
excūsābĭl·is -e *adj* excusable
excūsātē *adv* excusably, without blame
excūsātĭ·ō -ōnis *f* excuse
excūsāt·us -a -um *adj* free from blame, exempt
excūs·ō -āre *vt* to free from blame, excuse; to exempt; to make excuses for, apologize for; to allege in excuse, plead as an excuse
excussus *pp* of **excutio**
excūsus *pp* of **excudo**
ex·cutĭō -cutĕre -cussī -cussum *vt* to shake out, shake off, shake loose; to knock out (*e.g., teeth*); (of horse) to throw, throw off; to shake out (*garment*); to jilt, give a cold shoulder to; to toss, throw; to shake out, search; to examine, investigate; (fig) to shake off, discard, banish
exdorsŭ·ō -āre *vt* to fillet
exec- see **exsec-**
ex·ĕdō -esse -ēdī -ēsum *vt* to eat up, consume; to destroy; to prey on; to hollow; to wear away, corrode
exĕdr·a -ae *f* sitting room; lecture room; hall
exedr·ĭum -ĭī or **-ī** *n* sitting room, parlor, living room
exempl·ar or **exempl·āre -āris** *n* copy; likeness; pattern, model, ideal
exemplār·is -e *adj* following a model
exempl·um -ī *n* sample, example, typical instance; precedent; pattern, make, character; model, pattern (*of conduct*); object lesson; warning; copy, transcript; portrait
exemptus *pp* of **eximo**
exentĕr·ō -āre *vt* to disembowel; to empty, exhaust; to torture, torment
ex·ĕō -īre -ĭī -ĭtum *vt* to pass beyond, cross; to parry, ward off, avoid; (fig) to exceed; *vi* to go out, go forth; to go away, withdraw, depart, retire; to march out; to disembark; to pour out, gush out, flow out; to escape, be freed; to pass away, perish; (of time) to run out, expire; to get out, become public; to burgeon forth; (of hills) to rise; **ex urna exire** to come out of, fall out of the urn (*said of lots*)
exeq- = **exseq-**
exerc·ĕō -ēre -ŭī -ĭtum *vt* to exercise, train; (mil) to drill, exercise, train; to keep (*someone*) busy, keep (*someone*) going; to supervise; to cultivate, work (*the soil*); to engage, occupy (*the mind*); to practice, follow (*a trade, occupation*); to carry into effect; to disturb, worry
exercitātĭ·ō -ōnis *f* exercise, practice, experience, training; (with *genit*) practice in
exercitāt·us -a -um *adj* experienced, trained, disciplined; troubled, worried, disturbed
exercit·ĭum -ĭī or **-ī** exercise, training
exercĭt·ō -āre *vt* to keep in training, exercise
exercĭt·or -ōris *m* trainer
exercĭt·us -a -um *pp* of **excerceo;** *adj* disciplined; experienced; trying, tough, harassing; harassed, vexed
exercĭt·us -ūs *m* army; infantry; (pol) assembly of the people; army of followers; swarm, flock, multitude
exĕrō see **exsero**
exēs·or -ōris *m* corrosive factor, underminer
exēsus *pp* of **exedo**
exhālātĭ·ō -ōnis *f* exhalation, vapor
exhāl·ō -āre *vt* to exhale, breathe out; *vi* to steam; to breathe one's last, expire

ex·hauriō -haurīre -hausī -haustum *vt* to draw out, empty, exhaust; to take away, remove; to drain dry; to bring to an end; to undergo, endure (*troubles*); to discuss fully
exhērēd·ō -āre *vt* to disinherit
exhēr·ēs -ēdis *adj* disinherited
exhib·ĕō -ēre -ŭī -ĭtum *vt* to hold out; to present, produce; to display, exhibit; to cause, occasion; to render, make
exhilăr·ō -āre *vt* to cheer up
exhorr·escō -escĕre -ŭī *vt* to shudder at; *vi* to be terrified
exhortātī·ō -ōnis *f* encouragement; *f pl* words of encouragement
exhort·or -ārī -ātus sum *vt* to encourage
ex·ĭgō -igĕre -ēgī -actum *vt* to drive out, push out, thrust out, expel; to demand, exact, collect, require; to pass, spend, complete, close (*life, time*); to finish, complete, conclude; to ascertain, determine; to weigh, consider, estimate, examine, try, test; to dispose of
exigŭē *adv* briefly, slightly, sparingly, barely
exiguĭt·ās -ātis *f* shortness, smallness, meagerness, scantiness, scarcity
exigŭ·us -a -um *adj* short, small, meager, scanty, poor, paltry, inadequate; a little, a bit of
exiliō see **exsilio**
exĭl·is -e *adj* thin, small, meager, feeble, poor; cheerless, dreary; depleted (*ranks*); worthless, insincere; dry, flat (*style*)
exīlĭt·ās -ātis *f* thinness; meagerness, dreariness
exīlĭter *adv* drily, drearily, jejunely
exilĭum see **exsilium**
exim see **exinde**
eximĭē *adv* exceptionally
eximĭ·us -a -um *adj* taken out, exempted; exempt; select, special, exceptional
ex·ĭmō -imĕre -ēmī -emptum *vt* to take out, take away, remove; to exempt; to free, release, let off; to make an exception of; to waste, lose (*time*); to banish (*e.g., worries*)
exin see **exinde**
exinān·ĭō -īre -īī -ītum *vt* to empty completely; to plunder; (fig) to clean out, fleece
exinde or **exim** or **exin** *adv* from that place, from that point; (in enumerating) after that, next, then; (of time) from that point, after that, then, furthermore, next; accordingly
existimātī·ō -ōnis *f* appraisal, judgment, estimate, opinion, decision, verdict; reputation, good name, character; (com) credit; **vulgi existimatio** public opinion
existimāt·or -ōris *m* critic, judge
existĭm·ō or **existŭm·ō -āre** *vt* to appraise, evaluate, value, estimate; to think, judge, consider, regard; **in hostium numero existimare** to regard as an enemy
existō see **exsisto**
exitiābĭl·is -e *adj* deadly, fatal, destructive; (with *dat*) fatal to
exitiāl·is -e *adj* deadly, fatal
exitĭ·ō -ōnis *f* going out, exit
exitiōs·us -a -um *adj* deadly, destructive
exit·ĭum -iī or **-ī** *n* destruction, ruin; cause of destruction
exĭt·us -ūs *m* going out, exit, departure; way out, outlet, exit; end, close, conclusion; **ad exitum adducere** to bring to a close
exlecĕbra see **elecebra**
ex·lex -lēgis *adj* without law, bound by no law; lawless, heedless of laws
exobsĕcr·ō or **exopsĕcr·ō -āre** *vi* to make an earnest entreaty
exocŭl·ō -āre *vt* to knock the eyes out of
exod·ĭum -iī or **-ī** *n* farce (*presented after the main feature*)
exol·escō -escĕre -ēvī -ētum *vi* to decay, fade; to become obsolete
exolēt·us -a -um *adj* full-grown; *m* (fig) old rake
exonĕr·ō -āre *vt* to unload; (fig) to relieve, free, exonerate
exoptābĭl·is -e *adj* highly desirable, long-awaited
exoptāt·us -a -um *adj* longed-for, welcome, desired
exopt·ō -āre *vt* to long for, wish earnestly, desire greatly
exōrābĭl·is -e *adj* accessible, sympathetic, placable
exōrābŭl·a -ōrum *n pl* enticements, bait, arguments
exōrāt·or -ōris *m* lucky petitioner
ex·ordĭor -ordīrī -orsus sum *vt & vi* to begin, start, commence
exord·ĭum -iī or **-ī** *n* beginning, start, commencement, origin; introduction
ex·orĭor -orīrī -ortus sum *vi* to come out, come forth, rise, appear; to begin, arise, be caused, be produced
exornātĭ·ō -ōnis *f* embellishment
exorn·ō -āre *vt* to fit out, furnish, equip, provide, supply; to adorn, embellish, decorate, set off, give luster to
exōr·ō -āre *vt* to prevail upon, win over; to gain or obtain by entreaty; to appease
exorsus *pp* of **exordior**; *n pl* beginning, commencement; introduction, preamble
exors·us -ūs *m* beginning, commencement; introduction
exortus *pp* of **exorior**
exort·us -ūs *m* rising; the East, the Orient
ex·os -ossis *adj* boneless
exoscŭl·or -ārī -ātus sum *vt* to kiss lovingly, kiss tenderly
exoss·ō -āre *vt* to bone, take the bones out of

exostr·a -ae *f* movable stage; **in exostra** in public
exōs·us -a -um *adj* hating, detesting; hated, detested
exōtic·us -a -um *adj* foreign, exotic
expall·escō -escĕre -ŭī *vt* to turn pale at, dread; *vi* to turn pale
expalliāt·us -a -um *adj* robbed of one's cloak
expalp·ō -āre *vt* to coax out
ex·pandō -pandĕre -pandī -pansum *vt* to spread out, unfold, expand
expătr·ō -āre *vt* to waste, squander
expav·escō -escĕre -ŭī *vt* to panic at; *vi* to panic
expect- = exspect-
expecūliāt·us -a -um *adj* stripped of property
exped·iō -īre -iī or **-īvī -ītum** *vt* to unfetter, extricate, disentangle; to get out, get ready; to clear for action; to clear (*roads of obstacles*); to free, extricate (*from troubles*); to put in order, arrange, settle, adjust, set right; to explain, unfold, clear up, disclose, recount, relate; **expedit** *v impers* it is expedient, useful, advantageous
expedītē *adv* without obstacles, without difficulty, quickly, promptly
expedīti·ō -ōnis *f* expedition, campaign, special mission
expedīt·us -a -um *adj* unencumbered, unhampered, unobstructed; (mil) lightly equipped; ready, prompt; ready at hand, convenient; **in expedito habere** to have at hand
ex·pellō -pellĕre -pŭlī -pulsum *vt* to drive out, eject, expel; to disown
ex·pendō -pendĕre -pendī -pensum *vt* to weigh out; to pay out, pay down, lay out, expend; to rate, estimate; to ponder, consider; to pay (*penalty*)
expens·us -a -um *adj* paid out, spent; *n* payment, expenditure
expergē·faciō -facĕre -fēcī -factum *vt* to awaken, wake up; to arouse, excite
exper·giscor -giscī -rectus sum *vi* to wake up; to be alert
experg·ō -ĕre -ī -itum *vt* to awaken, wake up
experi·ens -entis *adj* enterprising, active; (with *genit*) ready to undergo
experienti·a -ae *f* test, trial, experiment; experience, practice; effort
experīment·um -ī *n* test, experiment, proof; experience
exper·ior -īrī -tus sum *vt* to test, try, prove; to experience, endure, find out; to try to do, attempt; to measure strength with; *vi* to go to court
experrectus *pp* of **expergiscor**
exper·s -tis *adj* (with *genit*) having no share in, devoid of, free from, without
expert·us -a -um *pp* of **experior**; *adj* tried, proved, tested; (with *genit*) experienced in
expetess·ō -ĕre *vt* to desire, long for
expĕt·ō -ĕre -īvī or **-iī -ītum** *vt* to ask for, demand; to aim at, head for; to desire, long for, wish; *vi* (with **in** + *acc*) to befall; to fall upon, assail
expiāti·ō -ōnis *f* expiation, atonement; satisfaction
expictus *pp* of **expingo**
expīlāti·ō -ōnis *f* pillaging, plundering, ransacking
expīlāt·or -ōris *m* plunderer, robber
expīl·ō -āre *vt* to pillage, plunder, rob, ransack; to plagiarize
ex·pingō -pingĕre -pinxī -pictum *vt* to paint up; to depict; to paint true to life
expi·ō -āre *vt* to purify, cleanse ritually; to atone for, expiate; to avert (*curse, bad omen*)
expīrō see **exspiro**
expisc·or -ārī -ātus sum *vt* to fish for (*information*), ferret out, try to find out
explānātē *adv* plainly, clearly, distinctly
explānāti·ō -ōnis *f* explanation; clear pronunciation
explānāt·or -ōris *m* explainer; interpreter
explānāt·us -a -um *adj* plain, distinct
explān·ō -āre *vt* to explain, make clear; to pronounce clearly
ex·plaudō -plaudĕre -plausī -plausum *vt* to boo at, hiss at; to reject
explēment·um -ī *n* filling, stuffing
ex·plĕō -ēre -ēvī -ētum *vt* to fill out, fill up; to complete; to satisfy (*desires*); to make good, repair (*losses*); to fulfill, perform, accomplish, discharge
explēti·ō -ōnis *f* satisfying
explēt·us -a -um *adj* full, complete, perfect
explicātē *adv* clearly, plainly
explicāti·ō -ōnis *f* unfolding, uncoiling; analysis; interpretation
explicāt·or -ōris *m* or **explicātr·ix -īcis** *f* explainer
explicāt·us -a -um *adj* plain, clear-cut
explicāt·us -ūs *m* unfolding; explanation, interpretation
explicit·us -a -um *adj* disentangled; simple, easy
explic·ō -āre -āvī or **-ŭī -ātum** or **-itum** *vt* to unfold, unroll; to spread out; to loosen, undo; (mil) to exceed, deploy; to set free, release; to set in order, arrange, adjust, settle; to set forth, exhibit, explain
ex·plōdō or **ex·plaudō -plōdĕre -lōsī -plōsum** *vt* to drive off by clapping; to boo (*off the stage*); to disapprove, discredit
explōrātē *adv* after careful examination; for sure, for certain

explōrātĭ•ō -ōnis *f* exploration, examination
explōrāt•or -ōris *m* scout, spy
explōrāt•us -a -um *adj* sure, certain
explōr•ō -āre *vt* to explore, investigate; (mil) to reconnoiter; to probe, search; to test, try, try out
explōsĭ•ō -ōnis *f* booing (*of an actor*)
expol•iō -īre -īvī or -iī -ītum *vt* to polish; (fig) to polish, refine, adorn
expolītĭ•ō -ōnis *f* polishing, finishing off, embellishing
expolīt•us -a -um *adj* polished, lustrous; refined
ex•pōnō -pōnĕre -posŭī -positum or -postum *vt* to put out; to expose, abandon; to expose, lay open; to reveal, publish; to exhibit, relate, explain; to offer, tender; to set on shore, disembark, land
expor•rigō -rigĕre -rexī -rectum *vt* to stretch out, spread, spread out; **exporge frontem** (coll) smooth out your brow, quit frowning
exportātĭ•ō -ōnis *f* exportation
export•ō -āre *vt* to carry out; to export
ex•poscō -poscĕre -poposcī *vt* to demand, beg, insist upon; to demand the surrender of
expositīcĭ•us -a -um *adj* foundling
expositĭ•ō -ōnis *f* exposing; (rhet) narration, explanation (*of details of a case*)
exposit•us -a -um *pp* of **expono**; *adj* accessible; accessible, affable
expostulātĭ•ō -ōnis *f* insistent demand; complaint
expostŭl•ō -āre *vt* to demand, insist on; to complain of; (with **cum** + *abl* of person) to complain of (*something*) to (*someone*); *vi* to lodge a complaint; (with **cum** + *abl*) to lodge a complaint with
expostus *pp* of **expono**
expōtus see **epotus**
express•us -a -um *adj* distinct, clear, express; distinct, real
ex•prīmō -primĕre -pressī -pressum *vt* to press out, squeeze out; (fig) to squeeze out, wring, extort; to model, form, portray; to represent, imitate, copy, describe, express; to translate; to pronounce, articulate
exprobrātĭ•ō -ōnis *f* reproach
exprŏbr•ō -āre *vt* to reproach, find fault with; (with *dat*) to cast (*something*) up to, put the blame for (*something*) on; *vi* (with *dat*) to complain to
ex•prōmō -prōmĕre -prompsī -promptum *vt* to bring out, fetch out; to give vent to; to disclose, display, exhibit; to give utterance to, utter, express, state
expugnābĭl•is -e *adj* vulnerable to attack, pregnable
expugnācĭ•or -us *adj* more potent
expugnātĭ•ō -ōnis *f* assault; (with *genit*) assault on
expugnāt•or -ōris *m* attacker; **expugnator pudicitiae** assailant
expugn•ō -āre *vt* to assault, storm; to conquer (*persons*) in war; (fig) to conquer, overcome; (fig) to achieve, accomplish; (fig) to wrest, extort
expulsĭ•ō -ōnis *f* expulsion
expuls•ō -āre *vt* to drive out, expel
expuls•or -ōris *m* expeller
expulsus *pp* of **expello**
expultr•ix -īcis *f* expeller (*female*)
ex•pungō -pungĕre -punxī -punctum *vt* to expunge; to cancel; to remove
expurgātĭ•ō -ōnis *f* justification, excuse
expurg•ō -āre *vt* to cleanse, purify; to cure; to vindicate, excuse, justify
expŭtesc•ō -ĕre *vi* to rot away
expŭt•ō -āre *vt* to prune, lop off; to consider; to comprehend
ex•quīrō -quīrĕre -quīsīvī -quīsītum *vt* to investigate, scrutinize; to search for, look for; to ransack; to devise
exquīsītē *adv* carefully, accurately; exquisitely
exquīsīt•us -a -um *pp* of **exquiro**; *adj* carefully considered, choice, exquisite
exrādīcitus *adv* from the very roots
exsaev•iō -īre *vi* to cease raging, calm down
exsangu•is -e *adj* bloodless; pale; feeble; causing paleness
ex•sarciō or ex•serciō -sarcīre — -sartum *vt* to patch up; (fig) to repair
exsatĭ•ō -āre *vt* to satiate, satisfy fully, glut
exsaturābĭl•is -e *adj* appeasable
exsatŭr•ō -āre *vt* to satiate, satisfy completely
exsce- = esce
ex•scindō -scindĕre -scidī -scissum *vt* to annihilate, destroy
exscrĕ•ō -āre *vt* to cough up, spit out
ex•scrībō -scrībĕre -scripsī -scriptum *vt* to write down; to write out in full; to copy; (fig) to copy, take after, resemble
exsculp•ō -ĕre -sī -tum *vt* to carve out; to scratch out, erase; (fig) to extort
exsĕc•ō or exsic•ō -āre -ŭī -tum *vt* to cut out, cut away, cut off; to castrate; to deduct
exsecrābĭl•is -e *adj* accursed; bitter, merciless, deadly; execrating, cursing
exsecrātĭ•ō -ōnis *f* curse, execration; solemn oath
exsecrāt•us -a -um *adj* accursed, detestable
exsĕcr•or -ārī -ātus sum *vt* to curse, execrate; *vi* to take a solemn oath
exsectĭ•ō -ōnis *f* cutting out

exsecūti·ō -ōnis *f* execution, performance; discussion
exsecūtus *pp* of **exsequor**
exsequi·ae -ārum *f pl* funeral procession, funeral rites
exsequiāl·is -e *adj* funeral; **carmina exsequialia** dirges
ex·sĕquor -sĕquī -secūtus sum *vt* to follow out; to accompany to the grave; to perform, execute, accomplish, carry out; to follow up, investigate; to pursue, go after; to avenge, punish; to say, tell, describe, relate
exsĕr·ō -ĕre -ŭī -tum *vt* to untie, disconnect; to stretch out (*one's arms*); to stick out (*the tongue in disdain*); to bare, uncover
exsert·ō -āre *vt* to keep on stretching or sticking out
exsertus *pp* of **exsero;** *adj* uncovered, bare; protruding
exsībĭl·ō -āre *vt* to hiss off the stage
exsiccāt·us -a -um *adj* dry, uninteresting
exsicc·ō -āre *vt* to dry up; to drain dry
exsicō see **exseco**
exsign·ō -āre *vt* to mark down exactly, write down in detail
ex·siliō -silīre -silŭī *vi* to jump out, leap up; to start; **exsilire gaudio** to jump for joy
exsil·ĭum -ĭī or **-ī** *n* exile, banishment (*voluntary or involuntary*); place of exile
ex·sistō -sistĕre -stĭtī -stĭtum *vi* to come out, come forth; to appear, emerge; to exist, be; to arise, proceed; to turn into, become; to be visible
ex·solvō -solvĕre -solvī -solūtum *vt* to loosen, untie; to release, free, set free; to discharge, pay; to keep, fulfill; to satisfy (*hunger*); to break open, wound; to solve, explain; to throw off, get rid of; to repay, requite; to give out (*awards, punishment*)
exsomn·is -e *adj* sleepless
exsorb·ĕō -ēre -ŭī *vt* to suck up, drain; to drain, exhaust; to grasp at eagerly, welcome
exsor·s -tis *adj* without lots; chosen specially; (with *genit*) having no share in, free from
exspatĭ·or -ārī -ātus sum *vi* to go off course; to digress
exspectābĭl·is -e *adj* expected, anticipated
exspectātĭ·ō -ōnis *f* expectation, suspense; **exspectationem facere** to cause suspense
exspectāt·us -a -um *adj* expected, awaited, desired
exspect·ō -āre *vt* to await, wait for, look out for; to hope for, long for, anticipate
ex·spergō -spergĕre — -spersum *vt* to sprinkle, scatter
exspēs *adj* hopeless, forlorn; (with *genit*) without hope of
exspīrātĭ·ō -ōnis *f* breathing out, exhalation
exspīr·ō -āre or **expīr·ō -āre** *vt* to breathe out, exhale, emit; *vi* to expire, breathe one's last; (fig) to come to an end, cease
exsplend·escō -escĕre -ŭī *vi* to glitter, shine
exspolĭ·ō -āre *vt* to strip; to pillage
ex·spŭō -spuĕre -spŭī -spūtum *vt* to spit out; (fig) to banish (*e.g., worries*)
exstern·ō -āre *vt* to startle, scare; to terrify; to stampede (*horses*)
exstill·ō -āre *vi* to drop, trickle out; to melt
exstimulāt·or -ōris *m* instigator
exstimŭl·ō -āre *vt* to instigate, goad on
exstinctĭ·ō -ōnis *f* extinction
exstinct·or -ōris *m* extinguisher; suppressor; destroyer
ex·stinguō -stinguĕre -stinxī -stinctum *vt* to extinguish, put out; to destroy, kill; to abolish, annul; **extingui** to die, die out; to be forgotten
exstirp·ō -āre *vt* to extirpate, root out, eradicate
exst·ō -āre *vi* to stand out, protrude, project; to stand out, be prominent, be conspicuous; to be visible; to appear; to exist, be extant
exstructĭ·ō -ōnis *f* erection
ex·strŭō -struĕre -struxī -structum *vt* to pile up, heap up; to build, erect
exsuct·us -a -um *pp* of **exsugo;** *adj* dried up
exsūd·ō -āre *vt* to sweat; (fig) to sweat out, sweat over; *vi* to pour out
ex·sūgō -sūgĕre -suxī -suctum *vt* to suck out
exs·ul or **ex·ul -ŭlis** *m* or *f* exile, refugee
exsŭl·ō -āre *vi* to be an exile, be a refugee
exsultātĭ·ō -ōnis *f* exultation, jumping for joy
exsultim *adv* friskily
exsult·ō or **exult·ō -āre** *vi* to jump up; to frisk about; (of horses) to rear, prance; to exult, rejoice, jump for joy; to revel, run riot; to boast; (of speech) to range freely
exsuperābĭl·is -e *adj* climbable; superable
exsuperantĭ·a -ae *f* superiority
exsupĕr·ō -āre *vt* to surmount; to exceed, surpass; to overpower; *vi* to rise; (of flames) to shoot up; to be superior, excel, be conspicuous, prevail
exsurd·ō -āre *vt* to deafen; (fig) to dull
ex·surgō -surgĕre -surrexī *vi* to get up, rise, stand up; (fig) to rise, recover strength; **foras exsurgere** to get up and go out
exsuscĭt·ō -āre *vt* to rouse from sleep; to fan (*fire*); to excite, stir up

ext·a -ōrum *n pl* vital organs (*of sacrificial animals*)
extāb·escō -escĕre -ŭī *vi* to waste away, pine away; to disappear
extār·is -e *adj* used for cooking the sacrificial victim; sacrificial
extemplō or **extempŭlō** *adv* immediately, right away; on the spur of the moment
ex·tendō -tendĕre -tendī -tentum or **-tensum** *vt* to stretch out, spread out, extend; to enlarge, increase; to widen, broaden; to prolong, continue; to pass, spend; to exert, strain; **extendi** to stretch out, extend; **labellum extendere** to pout
extent·ō -āre *vt* to exert, strain
extent·us -a -um *pp* of **extendo;** *adj* extensive, wide; **extentis itineribus** by forced marches
extenuātī·ō -ōnis *f* extenuation; thinning out
extenuāt·us -a -um *adj* thinned, reduced; trifling; weak, faint
extenŭ·ō -āre *vt* to thin out; to lessen, diminish, extenuate, detract from
exter or **extĕr·us -a -um** *adj* external, outward; foreign, strange
exterĕbr·ō -āre *vt* to bore out; to extort
ex·tergĕō -tergēre -tersī -tersum *vt* to wipe out, wipe clean; (fig) to wipe out, plunder
exterī·or -us *adj* outer, exterior
exterius *adv* on the outside
extermĭn·ō -āre *vt* to drive out, banish; to put aside, put away, remove
extern·us -a -um *adj* external, outward; foreign, strange; *m* foreigner, stranger, foreign enemy; *n pl* foreign goods
ex·tĕrō -terĕre -trīvī -trītum *vt* to rub out, wear away; (fig) to crush
exterr·ĕō -ēre -ŭī -ĭtum *vt* to frighten, terrify
extersus *pp* of **extergeo**
extĕrus see **exter**
extex·ō -ĕre *vt* to unweave; (fig) to cheat
extim·escō -escĕre -ŭī *vt* to become terribly afraid of, dread; *vi* to become afraid
extĭm·us -a -um *adj* outermost, farthest, most remote
extisp·ex -ĭcis *m* soothsayer, diviner (*who makes predictions by inspecting the entrails of animals*)
extoll·ō -ĕre *vt* to lift up; to erect; to postpone; to extol, praise; to raise, exalt; to beautify; **animos extollere** to raise the morale
ex·torquĕō -torquēre -torsī -tortum *vt* to wrench, wrest; to dislocate; to extort
extorr·is -e *adj* driven out of one's country, banished, exiled
extort·or -ōris *m* extorter
extortus *pp* of **extorqueo;** *adj* deformed
extrā *adv* outside, on the outside; **extra quam** except in the case that; **extra quam si** unless; *prep* (with *acc*) outside, outside of, beyond; apart from, aside from; contrary to; except, besides; without; **extra jocum** all joking aside
ex·trăhō -trahĕre -traxī -tractum *vt* to pull out, drag out; to drag out, prolong; to waste (*time*); to extricate, release, rescue; to remove
extrānĕ·us -a -um *adj* extraneous, external, irrevelant, strange; *m* stranger
extrāordinārī·us -a -um *adj* extraordinary
extrārī·us -a -um *adj* outward, external; unrelated (*by family ties*)
extrēm·a -ōrum *n pl* end (*e.g., of a marching column, of strip of land, of life*)
extrēmĭt·ās -ātis *f* extremity, end
extrēmō *adv* finally, at last
extrēmum *adv* finally, at last; for the last time
extrēm·us -a -um *adj* extreme, outermost, on the end; latest, last; (of degree) utmost, extreme; lowest, meanest; **extrema aetas** advanced old age; **extrema cauda** tip of the tail; **extremā lineā amare** to love at a distance; **extrema manus** final touches; **extremis digitis attingere** to touch lightly; to touch lightly on; to hold tenderly; **extremus ignis** flickering flame; **in extremo libro secundo** at the end of the second book; *n* end; extremity; **ad extremum** at last; at the end; utterly; **in extremo** in mortal danger, in a crisis
extrīc·ō -āre or **extrīc·or -ārī -ātus sum** *vt* to extricate; to clear up; to obtain with difficulty
extrinsĕcus *adv* from outside, from abroad; on the outside, outside
extrītus *pp* of **extero**
ex·trūdō -trūdĕre -trūsī -trūsum *vt* to thrust out, drive out; to get rid of
extum·ĕō -ēre *vi* to swell up
ex·tundō -tundĕre -tūdī -tūsum *vt* to beat out, hammer out; to fashion; to devise; to extort
exturb·ō -āre *vt* to drive out, chase out, drive away; to divorce; to knock out
exūbĕr·ō -āre *vi* to grow luxuriantly; to abound
exulcĕr·ō -āre *vt* to make sore, aggravate; to exasperate
exulŭl·ō -āre *vt* to invoke with cries; *vi* to howl
exunctus *pp* of **exungo**
exund·ō -āre *vi* to overflow; **in litora exundare** to wash up on the shores
ex·ungō -ungĕre — -unctum *vt* to oil down, rub with oil

ex·ŭō -uĕre -ŭī -ūtum *vt* to take off, pull off; to shake off; to unclothe; to strip, deprive; to cast aside, cast off; to bare
exurg·ĕō -ēre *vt* to squeeze out
ex·ūrō -ūrĕre -ussī -ustum *vt* to burn out, burn up; to dry up; to consume, destroy; (fig) to inflame
exustī·ō -ōnis *f* conflagration
exustus *pp of* **exuro**
exūtus *pp of* **exuo**
exuvi·ae -ārum *f pl* clothing; equipment; arms; hide; slough; booty, spoils

F

fab·a -ae *f* bean
fabāl·is -e *adj* bean; **stipulae fabales** bean stalks
fābell·a -ae *f* short story; fable, tale; short play
fab·er -ra -rum *adj* skilled; *m* craftsman; smith; carpenter; (mil) engineer; **faber ferrarius** blacksmith; **faber tignarius** carpenter
Fab·ius -iī or **-ī** *m* Quintus Fabius Maximus Cunctator, elected consul five times and appointed dictator in 217 B.C. to conduct the war against Hannibal (*d.* 203 B.C.); Quintus Fabius Pictor, first Roman historian to use prose (*fl* 225 B.C.)
fabrē *adv* skillfully
fabrē·faciō -facĕre -fēcī -factum *vt* to build, make; to forge
fabrĭc·a -ae *f* trade, industry; workshop, factory; piece of work, structure, production; **fabricam fingere** (with **ad** + *acc*) (coll) to pull a trick on
fabricātī·ō -ōnis *f* structure, construction
fabricāt·or -ōris *m* builder, architect, producer, creator
fabrĭc·or -ārī -ātus sum or **fabrĭc·ō -āre** *vt* to build, construct, produce, forge; to prepare, form; to coin (*words*)
fabrīl·is -e *adj* craftman's, carpenter's, sculptor's; *n pl* tools
fābŭl·a -ae *f* story, tale; talk, conversation, conversation piece; small talk; affair, matter, concern; myth, legend; drama, play; dramatic poem; **fabulae!** (coll) baloney!; **lupus in fabula!** (coll) speak of the devil!
fābulār·is -e *adj* legendary
fābŭl·or -ārī -ātus sum *vt* to say, invent; *vi* to talk, chat, gossip
fābulōs·us -a -um *adj* legendary
fabŭl·us -ī *m* small bean
facess·ō -ĕre -īvī -ītum *vt* to do eagerly, perform, accomplish; to bring on, cause, create; **negotium alicui facessere** to cause someone trouble; *vi* to go away, depart
facētē *adv* facetiously, humorously, wittily, brilliantly
facētī·ae -ārum *f pl* clever thing, clever talk, witticism, humor
facēt·us -a -um *adj* witty, humorous; fine, polite; elegant; brilliant
facī·ēs -ēī *f* make, form, shape; face, look; look, appearance; nature, character; external appearance, pretense, pretext
facĭl·is -e *adj* easy; nimble; suitable, convenient; ready, quick; easy, easygoing, good-natured; favorable, prosperous; gentle (*breeze*); easily-borne, slight (*loss*); **ex** or **e facili** easily; **in facili esse** to be easy; **facilis victu** prosperous, well-off, well-to-do
facĭle *adv* easily, without trouble; unquestionably, by far, far; quite, fully; promptly, readily, willingly; pleasantly, well; **non facile** hardly
facilĭt·ās -ātis *f* facility, easiness, ease; readiness; fluency; suitability; good nature, affability, courteousness; levity
facinorōs·us or **facinerōs·us -a -um** *adj & m* criminal
facĭn·us -ŏris *n* deed, action; crime, villany
faciō facĕre fēcī factum (faxim = fēcĕrim; faxō = fēcĕrō) *vt* to make, fashion, frame, create, build, erect; to do, perform; to make, produce, compose; to bring about, cause, occasion; to acquire, gain, get, accumulate; to incur, suffer; to render, grant, give, confer; to grant, admit; to assume, suppose; to assert, say, represent, depict; to choose, appoint; to follow, practice; to regard, prize, value; **certiorem facere** to inform; **copiam facere** to afford the opportunity; **fac ita esse** suppose it were so, granted that it is so; **fidem facere** to give one's word; **pecuniam facere** or **stipendium facere** to make money, earn money; **promissum facere** to fulfill a promise; **sacra facere** to sacrifice; **verbum facere** to speak; **viam facere** (with *dat*) to make way for; *vi* to do, act; to take part, take sides; (with *dat* or with **ad** + *acc*) to be satisfactory for, be fit for, do for
factĕon = faciendum
factī·ō -ōnis *f* doing; making; party, faction; partisanship; company, social set, association, class; oligarchy; (with *genit*) right to make (*e.g., a will*)
factiōs·us -a -um *adj* busy; parti-

san; oligarchical; factious, revolutionary, seditious
factĭt·ō -āre *vt* to keep doing or making; to practice (*e.g., trade*); (with double *acc*) to declare (*someone*) to be (*e.g., heir*)
fact·or -ōris *m* (in playing ball) batter
fact·us -a -um *pp* of **facio;** *n* deed, act; accomplishment, exploit
facŭl·a -ae *f* little torch
facult·ās -ātis *f* opportunity, means; feasibility; ability, capacity, mental resources; material resources, means, supplies, abundance
fācundē *adv* eloquently
fācundĭ·a -ae *f* eloquence
fācundĭt·ās -ātis *f* eloquence
fācund·us -a -um *adj* eloquent, fluent
faecĕ·us -a -um *adj* morally impure, morally rotten
faecŭl·a -ae *f* wine lees
faenĕbr·is -e *adj* of interest, regarding interest; **res faenebris** indebtedness
faenerātĭ·ō -ōnis *f* lending at interest, investment
faenerātō *adv* with interest
faenerāt·or -ōris *m* money lender, investor, capitalist
faenĕr·or -ārī -ātus sum or **faenĕr·ō -āre** *vt* to lend at interest; to invest; to ruin through high interest rates; *vi* to bring interest, bring profit; **faeneratum beneficium** (fig) a favor richly repaid
faenĕ·us -a -um *adj* made of hay
faenīl·ĭa -ĭum *n pl* hayloft
faenisĕc·a -ae *m* peasant
faen·um or **fēn·um -ī** *n* hay; **faenum habet in cornu** (fig) he's crazy
faen·us or **fēn·us -ŏris** *n* interest; debt (*as result of heavy interest*); capital; (fig) profit, gain, advantage
faenuscŭl·um or **fēnuscŭl·um -ī** *n* a little interest
fae·x -cis *f* dregs, sediments, grounds, lees; (fig) dregs
fāginĕ·us or **fāgĭn·us** or **fāgĕ·us -a -um** *adj* beech
fāg·us -ī *f* beech tree
fal·a *or* **phal·a -ae** *f* movable wooden siege tower; scaffold
falārĭc·a or **phalārĭc·a -ae** *f* incendiary missile
falcār·ĭus -ĭī or **-ī** *m* sickle maker
falcāt·us -a -um *adj* fitted with scythes, scythed; sickle-shaped, curved
falcĭf·er -ĕra -ĕrum *adj* scythe-bearing
Falern·us -a -um *adj* Falernian; **ager Falernus** district in N. Campania, famous for its wine; *n* Falernian wine
Falisc·ī -ōrum *m pl* a people of S.E. Etruria
fallācĭ·a -ae *f* deception, deceit, trick
fallācĭter *adv* deceptively, deceitfully, fallaciously
fall·ax -ācis *adj* deceptive, deceitful, fallacious
fallō fallĕre fefellī falsum *vt* to cause to fall, trip; to lead into error; to deceive, trick, dupe, cheat; to fail to live up to, disappoint; to wile away; to escape the notice of, slip by; **fidem fallere** to break one's word; **me fallit** I do not know; **nisi** or **ni fallor** unless I'm mistaken; **opinionem fallere** (with *genit*) to fail to live up to the expectations of
falsē *adv* falsely
falsidĭc·us -a -um *adj* speaking falsely, lying
falsifĭc·us -a -um *adj* acting dishonestly
falsijūrĭ·us -a -um *adj* swearing falsely
falsilŏqu·us -a -um *adj* lying
falsimōnĭ·a -ae *f* trick
falsipăr·ens -entis *adj* bastard
falsō *adv* mistakenly, wrongly, erroneously; falsely, deceitfully, untruly
fals·us -a -um *pp* of **fallo;** *adj* mistaken, wrong, erroneous; false, untrue; lying, deceitful; vain, groundless, empty; spurious, sham, fictitious; *n* error; lying, perjury; lie, untruth, falsehood
fal·x -cis *f* sickle; pruning hook, pruning knife; (mil) hook for pulling down walls
fām·a -ae *f* talk, rumor, report; saying, tradition; reputation; fame, renown, glory, name; infamy, notoriety; public opinion
famēlĭc·us -a -um *adj* famished, starved
fam·ēs -is *f* hunger, starvation; poverty; famine; greed; (rhet) bald style, poverty of expression
fāmigerātĭ·ō -ōnis *f* rumor
fāmigerāt·or -ōris *m* gossip, rumormonger
famĭlĭ·a -ae or **-ās** *f* household slaves, domestics; household; house, family; family estate; fraternity; sect, school; **familiam ducere** to be the head of a sect; **pater familias** head of the household
familiār·is -e *adj* domestic, family, household; familiar, intimate; (in augury) one's own (*part of the sacrificial animal*); *m* servant, slave; acquaintance, friend, companion
familiārĭt·ās -ātis *f* familiarity, intimacy; association, friendship
familiārĭter *adv* on friendly terms
fāmōs·us -a -um *adj* much talked of; famous, renowned; infamous, notorious; slanderous, libelous; **carmen famosum** lampoon
famŭl·a -ae *f* slave, maid, maidservant
famulār·is -e *adj* of slaves, of servants
famulāt·us -ūs *m* servitude, slavery

famŭl·or -ārī -ātus sum *vi* to be a slave; (with *dat*) to serve
famŭl·us -a -um *adj* serviceable; *m* servant, attendant
fānātic·us -a -um *adj* fanatic, enthusiastic, inspired; wild, frantic
fān·um -ī *n* shrine, sanctuary, temple
fār farris *n* spelt; coarse meal, grits; sacrificial meal; bread; dog biscuit; *n pl* grain
far·ciō -cīre -sī -tum *vt* to stuff, cram
farfăr·us or **farfĕr·us -ī** *m* coltsfoot (*plant*)
farīn·a -ae *f* flour; powder; character, quality
farrāg·ō -inis *f* mash (*for cattle*); medley, hodgepodge
farrāt·us -a -um *adj* filled with grain; made with grain
fart·is -is *f* stuffing, filling, mincemeat; **fartim facere ex hostibus** to make mincemeat of the enemy
fart·or -ōris *m* fattener of fowls
fartus *pp* of **farcio**
fās (indecl) *n* divine law; sacred duty; divine will, fate; right; **fas est** it is right, it is lawful, it is permitted
fasci·a -ae *f* bandage, swathe; girth; fillet; wisp of cloud
fasciātim *adv* in bundles
fascicŭl·us -ī *m* small bundle
fascĭn·ō -āre *vt* to cast an evil eye on, bewitch, jinx; to envy
fascĭn·um -ī *n* or **fascĭn·us -ī** *m* evil eye; jinx; witchcraft; charm, amulet; penis
fasciŏl·a -ae *f* small bandage
fasc·is -is *m* bundle, pack, parcel, fagot; load, burden; baggage; *m pl* fasces (*bundle of rods and ax, carried before high magistrates by lictors as symbols of authority*); high office, supreme power, consulship
fassus *pp* of **fateor**
fast·ī -ōrum *m pl* calendar, almanac; annals; register of higher magistrates
fastīd·iō -īre -īvī or **-iī -ītum** *vt* to disdain, despise, snub, turn up the nose at; *vi* to feel disgust, feel squeamish; to be snobbish, be haughty
fastīdiōsē *adv* fastidiously, squeamishly; disdainfully, snobbishly
fastīdiōs·us -a -um *adj* fastidious, squeamish; disdainful, snobbish; refined, delicate
fastīd·ium -iī or **-ī** *n* fastidiousness, squeamishness, distaste, disgust, loathing; snobbishness, haughtiness, contempt
fastīgātē *adv* sloped (*like a gable*), sloping up, sloping down
fastīgāt·us -a -um *adj* rising to a point; sloping down
fastīg·ium -iī or **-ī** *n* gable; pediment; roof, ceiling; slope; height, elevation, top, edge; depth, depression; finish, completion; rank, dignity; main point, heading, highlight (*of story, etc.*)
fast·us -a -um *adj* legal (*day*); **dies fastus** court day
fast·us -ūs *m* disdain, contempt, arrogance; *m pl* brash deeds; calendar
fātāl·is -e *adj* fateful, destined, preordained; fatal, deadly; **deae fatales** the Fates
fātālĭter *adv* according to fate, by fate
fatĕor fatērī fassus sum *vt* to admit, acknowledge; to disclose, reveal
fātĭcăn·us or **fātĭcĭn·us -a -um** *adj* prophetic
fātidic·us -a -um *adj* prophetic
fātĭf·er -ĕra -ĕrum *adj* fatal, deadly
fatīgāti·ō -ōnis *f* fatigue, weariness
fatīg·ō -āre *vt* to fatigue, weary, tire; to worry, torment, harass, wear down; to importune, pray to constantly
fātilŏqu·a -ae *f* prophetess
fatisc·ō -ĕre or **fatisc·or -ī** *vi* to split, crack, give way; (fig) to crack, break down, collapse from exhaustion
fatuĭt·ās -ātis *f* silliness
fāt·um -ī *n* divine utterance, oracle; fate, destiny, doom; calamity, mishap, ruin; death; **ad fata novissima** to the last; **fato obire** to meet death, die; **fatum proferre** to prolong life
fātus *pp* of **for**
fatŭ·us -a -um *adj* silly, foolish; clumsy; *m* fool
fauc·ēs -ium *f pl* upper part of the throat, throat, gullet; strait, channel; pass, defile, gorge; (fig) jaws; **fauces premere** (with *genit*) to choke, throttle
Faun·us -ī *m* mythical king of Latium, father of Latinus, and worshiped as the Italian Pan; *m pl* Fauns, woodland spirits
faustē *adv* favorably, auspiciously
faustĭt·ās -ātis *f* fertility; good fortune, happiness
Faustŭl·us -ī *m* shepherd who raised Romulus and Remus
faust·us -a -um *adj* auspicious, favorable, fortunate, lucky
faut·or or **favĭt·or -ōris** *m* promoter, patron, supporter, fan
fautr·ix -īcis *f* patroness, protectress
favĕ·a -ae *f* favorite girl, pet slave girl
favĕō favēre fāvī fautum *vi* (with *dat*) to be favorable to, favor, support, side with; (with *inf*) to be eager to; **favere linguis** or **favere ore** to observe a reverent silence
favill·a -ae *f* ashes, embers; (fig) spark, beginning
favĭtor see **fautor**
Favōn·ius -iī or **-ī** *m* west wind (*also called Zephyrus*)

fav·or -ōris *m* favor, support; applause; appreciation (*shown by applause*)
favōrābĭl·is -e *adj* popular
fav·us -ī *m* honeycomb
fa·x -cis *f* torch; wedding torch; wedding; funeral torch; funeral; meteor, shooting star, comet; firebrand; fire, flame; guiding light; instigator; flame of love; stimulus, incitement; cause of ruin, destruction; **dicendi faces** fiery eloquence; **dolorum faces** pangs of grief
faxim see **facio**
febrīcŭl·a -ae *f* slight fever
febr·is -is *f* fever
Februŭ·a -ōrum *n pl* Roman festival of purification and expiation, celebrated on February 15th
Februārĭ·us -a -um *adj* & *m* February
februŭ·um -ī *n* purgation, purification
fēcundĭt·ās -ātis *f* fertility, fruitfulness; (rhet) overstatement
fēcund·ō -āre *vt* to fertilize
fēcund·us -a -um *adj* fertile, fruitful; abundant, rich; fertilizing; (with *genit* or *abl*) rich in, abounding in
fe·l -llis *n* gallbladder; gall, bile; bitterness, animosity; poison
fēl·ēs -is *f* cat
fēlīcĭt·ās -ātis *f* fertility; luck, good fortune, piece of luck; felicity, happiness
fēlīcĭter *adv* fruitfully, abundantly; favorably, auspiciously; luckily; happily; successfully
fēl·ix -īcis *adj* fruit-bearing; fruitful, fertile; favorable, auspicious; lucky; happy; successful
fēmell·a -ae *f* girl
fēmĭn·a -ae *f* female; woman
fēmĭnāt·us -a -um *adj* effeminate
fēmĭnĕ·us -a -um *adj* woman's; effeminate, unmanly
fēmĭnīn·us -a -um *adj* (gram) feminine
fem·ur -ŏris or **-ĭnis** *n* thigh
fēn- = faen-
fenestr·a -ae *f* window; hole (*for earrings*); (fig) opening, opportunity; (mil) breach (*in a wall*)
fer·a -ae *f* wild beast, wild animal
ferācius *adv* more fruitfully
Fērāl·ĭa -ĭum *n pl* festival of the dead, celebrated on February 17th or 21st
fērāl·is -e *adj* funeral; deadly, fatal; gloomy, dismal
fer·ax -ācis *adj* fertile, fruitful; (with *genit*) productive of
fercŭl·um -ī *n* food tray; dish, course; litter for carrying spoils in a victory parade or cult images in religious processions
fercŭl·us -ī *m* litter bearer
ferē or **fermē** *adv* approximately, nearly, almost, about, just about; generally, as a rule, usually; (with negatives) practically; **nemo fere** practically no one
ferentār·ĭus -ĭī or **-ī** *m* light-armed soldier; eager helper
Feretr·ĭus -ĭī or **-ī** *m* epithet of Jupiter
ferĕtr·um -ī *n* litter, bier
fērĭ·ae -ārum *f pl* holidays, vacation; (fig) leisure
fērĭāt·us -a -um *adj* vacationing, taking it easy, relaxing, taking time off
ferīn·us -a -um *adj* of wild animals; **caro ferina** venison; *f* game, venison
fer·ĭō -īre *vt* to strike, hit, shoot, knock; to kill; to slaughter, sacrifice (*an animal*); to coin; (fig) to strike, reach, affect; (fig) to cheat, trick; **cornu ferire** to butt; **foedus ferire** to make a treaty; **securi ferire** to behead; **verba ferire** to coin words
ferĭt·ās -ātis *f* wildness, fierceness
fermē see **fere**
ferment·um -ī *n* yeast; beer; (fig) ferment, provocation, vexation, anger, passion
ferō ferre tulī or **tetŭlī lātum** *vt* to bear, carry; to bear, produce, bring forth; to bear, endure; to lead, drive, conduct, direct; to bring, offer; to receive, acquire, obtain, win; to take by force, carry off, plunder, ravage; to manifest, display, make known, report, relate, say, tell; to propose, bring forward; to allow, permit; to cause, create; to set in motion; to call, name; (in accounting) to enter; **aegre ferre** to be annoyed at; **caelo supinas manus ferre** to raise the hands heavenward in prayer; **ferri** to move, rush; to sail; to fly; to flow along; (fig) to be carried away (*e.g., with ambition, greed*); **ferri** or **se ferre** to rush, flee; **iter ferre** to pursue a course; **laudibus ferre** to extol; **legem ferre** to propose a bill; **moleste ferre** to be annoyed at; **pedem ferre** to come, go, move, get going; **prae se ferre** to display, manifest; **se ferre obviam** (with *dat*) to rush to meet; **repulsam ferre** to experience defeat (*at the polls*); **sententiam ferre** to pass judgment; to cast a vote; **signa ferre** (mil) to begin marching; **ventrem ferre** to be pregnant; *vi* to say, e.g., **ut ferunt** as people say, as they say; to allow, permit, e.g., **si occasio tulerit** if occasion permit; to lead, e.g., **iter ad oppidum ferebat** the road led to the town
ferōcĭ·a -ae *f* courage, bravery, spirit; ferocity, barbarity; presumption
ferōcĭt·ās -ātis *f* courage, spirit, fierceness, aggressiveness; ferocity, barbarity; pride, presumption

ferōciter *adv* bravely, courageously, aggressively; defiantly; haughtily
Fērōni·a -ae *f* early Italic goddess of groves and fountains, and patroness of ex-slaves
fer·ox -ōcis *adj* brave, intrepid, warlike; defiant; overbearing, haughty, insolent
ferrāment·um -ī *n* tool, implement
ferrāri·us -a -um *adj* iron; **faber ferrarius** blacksmith; *m* blacksmith; *f pl* iron mines, iron works
ferrātil·is -e *adj* fit to be chained
ferrāt·us -a -um *adj* iron-plated; iron-tipped; in chains; in armor; **calx ferrata** spur; *m pl* soldiers in armor
ferrĕ·us -a -um *adj* iron, made of iron; hardhearted, cruel; firm, unyielding
ferricrepin·us -a -um *adj* (coll) clanking chains
ferriter·ium -iī or **-ī** *n* (coll) brig, jug
ferritĕr·us -ī *m* (coll) glutton for punishment
ferritrīb·ax -ācis *adj* (coll) chainsore (*sore from dragging chains*)
ferrūginĕ·us or **ferrūgin·us -a -um** *adj* rust-colored, dark, dusky
ferrūg·ō -inis *f* rust; verdigris; dark red; dark color; gloom
ferr·um -ī *n* iron; tool, implement; iron object: sword, dart, arrowhead, ax, plowshare, crowbar, spade, scissors, curling iron; **ferro atque igni** with fire and sword; **ferro decernere** to decide by force of arms
fertil·is -e *adj* fertile, fruitful, productive; fertilizing; (with *genit*) productive of
fertilit·ās -ātis *f* fertility, fruitfulness
ferŭl·a -ae *f* reed, stalk; rod, whip
fer·us -a -um *adj* wild; uncultivated, untamed; savage, uncivilized; rude, cruel, fierce; wild, desert (*place*); *m* wild beast, wild horse, lion, stag; *f* wild beast
fervē·faciō -facĕre -fēcī -factum *vt* to heat, boil
ferv·ens -entis *adj* seething, burning, hot; (fig) hot, heated, violent, impetuous
ferventer *adv* (fig) heatedly, impetuously
ferv·ĕō -ēre or **ferv·ō -ĕre -ī** *vi* to boil, seethe, steam; to foam; to swarm; to be busy, bustle about; (fig) to burn, glow, rage, rave
fervesc·ō -ĕre *vi* to become boiling hot, begin to boil, grow hot
fervid·us -a -um *adj* boiling, seething, hot; fermenting (*grapes*); hot, highly spiced; (fig) hot, fiery, violent, impetuous, hot-blooded
fervō see **ferveo**
ferv·or -ōris *m* heat, boiling heat; boiling; fermenting; fever; raging (*of the sea*); (fig) heat, vehemence, ardor, passion
Fescenni·a -ae *f* town in Etruria
Fescennīn·us -a -um *adj* Fescennine, of Fescennia; *m pl* Fescennine verses (*rude form of dramatic dialogue*)
fess·us -a -um *adj* tired, exhausted, worn out
festīnanter *adv* quickly
festīnāti·ō -ōnis *f* hurrying, haste, hurry
festīnātō *adv* hurriedly
festīn·ō -āre *vt & vi* to rush, hurry, accelerate; **jussa festinare** to carry out orders promptly
festīn·us -a -um *adj* hasty, quick, speedy
festīvē *adv* gaily; humorously
festīvit·ās -ātis *f* gaiety, fun; humor
festīv·us -a -um *adj* holiday, festal; gay, merry; agreeable, pleasing, pretty; humorous
festūc·a -ae *f* stalk; rod with which slaves were tapped when freed
fest·us -a -um *adj* joyous, festive, in holiday mood; *n* holiday; feast; **festum agere** to observe a holiday
fētiāl·is -is *m* member of a college of priests who performed the ritual in connection with declaring war and making peace
fetiāl·is -e *adj* negotiating, diplomatic; fetial, of the fetial priests
fetid·us -a -um *adj* fetid, stinking
fētūr·a -ae *f* breeding, bearing; offspring, young
fēt·us -a -um *adj* pregnant, breeding; fruitful, teeming, productive
fēt·us -ūs *m* breeding; (of plants) producing, bearing; offspring, young, brood; fruit, produce; (fig) growth, production
fi *interj* (expressing disgust at a bad smell) phew!
fib·er -rī *m* beaver
fibr·a -ae *f* fiber, filament; *f pl* entrails
fībŭl·a -ae *f* clasp, pin, brooch, buckle; brace, clamp
fīcedŭl·a or **fīcēdŭl·a -ae** *f* beccafico (*small bird*)
fictē *adv* falsely, fictitiously
fictīl·is -e *adj* clay, earthen; *n* jar; clay statue; *n pl* earthenware
ficti·ō -ōnis *f* forming, formation; disguising; supposition; fiction
fict·or -ōris *m* sculptor, molder, shaper
fictr·ix -īcis *f* maker, creator (*female*)
fict·um -ī *n* falsehood, fiction, pretense
fictūr·a -ae *f* shaping, fashioning
fict·us -a -um *pp* of **fingo;** *adj* false, fictitious; **vox ficta** falsehood
fīcŭl·us -ī *m* little fig
fīculn·us or **fīculnĕ·us -a -um** *adj* of a fig tree
fīc·us -ī or **-ūs** *f* fig; fig tree
fidēcommiss·um or **fideīcommiss·um -ī** *n* trust fund
fidēli·a -ae *f* earthen pot, pail,

bucket; **duo parietes de eadem fidelia dealbare** to whitewash two walls with one pail, to kill two birds with one stone
fidēl·is -e *adj* faithful, loyal; trusty, trustworthy, true, sure, safe (*ship, port, advice, etc.*); (with *dat* or **in** + *acc*) faithful to; *m* confidant
fidēlit·ās -ātis *f* faithfulness, loyalty, fidelity
fidēliter *adv* faithfully, loyally; securely, certainly
Fīdēn·ae -ārum *f pl* ancient town in Latium
fīd·ens -entis *adj* confident; resolute; bold
fīdenter *adv* confidently; resolutely; boldly
fīdenti·a -ae *f* self-confidence, boldness
fid·ēs -ēī *f* trust, faith, reliance, confidence; credence, belief; trustworthiness, conscientiousness, honesty; promise, assurance, word, word of honor; protection, guarantee; promise of protection, safe conduct; (com) credit; confirmation, proof, fulfilment; **de fide mala** in bad faith, dishonestly; **Di vostram fidem!** for heaven's sake!; **ex fide bona** in good faith, honestly; **fidem dare** to give one's word, offer a guarantee; **fidem facere** to inspire confidence; **fidem fallere** to break one's word; **fidem habere** (with *dat*) to have confidence in; to convince; **fidem servare** to keep one's word; **pro fidem deum!** for heaven's sake!; **res fidesque** capital and credit
fid·ēs -is *f* string (*of a musical instrument*); *f pl* stringed instrument: lyre, lute, zither
fidic·en -inis *m* lutist, lyre player; lyric poet
fidicin·us -a -um *adj* stringed-instrument; *f* lutist, lyre player (*female*)
fidicŭl·a -ae *f* or **fidicŭl·ae -ārum** *f pl* small lute
fīdissimē *adv* most faithfully
Fīd·ius -iī or **-ī** *m* epithet of Jupiter; **medius fidius!** honest to goodness!
fīdō fīdĕre fīsus sum *vi* (with *dat* or *abl*) to trust, put confidence in
fīdūci·a -ae *f* trust, confidence, reliance; self-confidence; trustworthiness; (law) deposit, pledge, security, mortgage
fīdūciāri·us -a -um *adj* held in trust
fīd·us -a -um *adj* trusty, dependable; certain, sure, safe
figlīn·us or **figulīn·us -a -um** *adj* potter's
fīgō fīgĕre fixī fixum *vt* to fix, fasten, affix, attach, nail; to drive in; to pierce; to erect, set up; to build; to post up, hang up
figulār·is -e *adj* potter's
figŭl·us -ī *m* potter; bricklayer
figūr·a -ae *f* figure, shape, form; phantom, ghost; nature, kind; figure of speech
figūrāt·us -a -um *adj* figurative
figūr·ō -āre *vt* to shape, form, mold, fashion; to train, educate
fīlātim *adv* thread by thread
fīli·a -ae *f* daughter
filicāt·us -a -um *adj* engraved with fern patterns
fīliŏl·a -ae *f* little daughter
fīliŏl·us -ī *m* little son
fīl·ius -iī or **-ī** *m* son; **terrae filius** a nobody
fil·ix -icis *f* fern
fīl·um -ī *n* thread; fillet; string, cord; wick; figure, shape (*of a woman*); texture, quality, style (*of speech*)
fimbri·ae -ārum *f pl* fringe, border, end
fim·us -ī *m* dung, manure; mire
findō findĕre fidī fissum *vt* to split, split in half
fingō fingĕre finxī fictum *vt* to shape, form; to mold, model (*in clay, stone, etc.*); to arrange, dress, trim; to imagine, suppose, think, conceive; to contrive, invent, pretend, feign; to compose (*poetry*); to disguise (*looks*); to trump up (*charges*); (with double *acc*) to represent as, depict as; **ars fingendi** sculpture; **linguā fingere** to lick; **se fingere** (with **ad** + *acc*) to adapt oneself to; to be subservient to
fīnient·ēs -ium *m pl* horizon
fīn·iō -īre -īvī or **-iī -ītum** *vt* to limit; (fig) to set bounds to, limit, restrain; to mark out, fix, determine; to put an end to, finish complete; **finiri** to come to an end, end; *vi* to come to an end; to die
fīn·is -is *m* or *f* boundary, border, limit; end; purpose, aim; extreme limit, summit, highest degree; starting point; goal; death; **fine** (with *genit*) up to, as far as; **finem facere** (with *genit* or *dat*) to put an end to; **quem ad finem** how long, to what extent; *m pl* boundaries, country, territory, land
fīnītē *adv* to a limited degree
fīnitĭm·us or **fīnitŭm·us -a -um** *adj* neighboring, bordering; (with *dat*) **a** bordering upon; **b** (fig) bordering upon, akin to; *m pl* neighbors
fīnīt·or -ōris *m* surveyor
fīnīt·us -a -um *adj* limited; (rhet) rhythmical
fīō fĭĕrī factus sum *vi* to come into being, arise; to be made, become, get; to happen; **fieri non potest quin** it is inevitable that; **fieri potest ut** it is possible that; **ita fit ut** or **quo fit ut** thus it happens that
firmām·en -inis *n* prop, support
firmāment·um -ī *n* prop, support; support, mainstay; main point
firmāt·or -ōris *m* establisher, promoter

firmē *adv* firmly, steadily
firmit·ās -ātis *f* firmness, strength; steadfastness, stamina, endurance
firmĭter *adv* firmly, steadily
firmitūd·ō -ĭnis *f* firmness, strength, durability; (fig) stability, constancy
firm·ō -āre *vt* to strengthen, fortify, support; to encourage, strengthen, fortify, assure, reinforce; to establish, prove, confirm; to declare, aver
firm·us -a -um *adj* firm, strong, hardy, stable; (fig) firm, steadfast, trusty, true, faithful, lasting; **firmus ad bellum** toughened for combat
fiscāl·is -e *adj* fiscal
fiscell·a -ae *f* small basket
fiscĭn·a -ae *f* small basket
fisc·us -ī *m* basket; money box; state treasury; imperial treasury, emperor's privy purse, imperial revenues
fissĭl·is -e *adj* easy to split; split
fissĭ·ō -ōnis *f* dividing, splitting
fiss·us -a -um *pp* of **findo**; *adj* cloven; *n* slit, fissure
fistūc·a -ae *f* mallet
fistŭl·a -ae *f* pipe, tube; water pipe; hollow stalk or reed; flute; fistula, ulcer
fīsus *pp* of **fido**
fix·us -a -um *pp* of **figo**; *adj* fixed, immovable; permanent
flābellifĕr·a -ae *f* female slave who waved a fan
flābell·um -ī *n* fan
flābĭl·is -e *adj* of air
flābr·a -ōrum *n pl* gusts of wind; breezes, winds
flacc·ĕō -ēre *vi* to be flabby; to lose heart; (of a speech) to get dull
flacc·escō -escĕre -ŭī *vi* to become flabby; to wither, droop
flaccĭd·us -a -um *adj* flabby; languid, feeble
flacc·us -a -um *adj* flabby
flagell·ō -āre *vt* to whip
flagell·um -ī *n* whip; scourge; riding crop; young shoot, sucker; arm (*of a polypus*); sting (*e.g., of conscience*)
flāgitātĭ·ō -ōnis *f* demand
flāgitāt·or -ōris *m* persistent demander
flāgitiōsē *adv* shamefully, disgracefully
flāgitiōs·us -a -um *adj* shameful, disgraceful, profligate
flāgit·ĭum -ĭī or **-ī** *n* shame, disgrace, scandalous conduct, scandal; rascal, good-for-nothing
flāgĭt·ō -āre *vt* to demand; (with double *acc* or with *acc* of thing or **ab** + *abl* of person) to demand (*something*) from (*someone*)
flagr·ans -antis *adj* blazing, flaming, hot; shining, glowing, glittering; ardent, hot, vehement, eager
flagranter *adv* vehemently, ardently
flagrantĭ·a -ae *f* blazing, glow; **flagiti flagrantia** utter disgrace
flagritrĭb·a -ae *m* (coll) (said of a slave) victim of constant whipping
flagr·ō -āre *vi* to blaze, be on fire; (with *abl*) **a** to glow with, flare up in; **b** to be the victim of (*e.g., envy*)
flagr·um -ī *n* whip
flām·en -ĭnis *m* flamen (*priest of a specific deity*); **flamen Dialis** priest of Jupiter
flām·en -ĭnis *n* gust, gale; breeze
flāminĭc·a -ae *f* wife of a flamen
Flāminīn·us -ī *m* T. Quintus Flamininus (*consul of* 198 B.C., *and conqueror of Philip of Macedon at Cynoscephalae, in Thessaly, in* 197 B.C.)
flāmin·ĭum -ĭī or **-ī** *n* office of flamen, priesthood
Flāminĭ·us -a -um *adj* Flaminian; **via Flaminia** road leading from Rome to Ariminum; *m* Gaius Flaminius (*conqueror of Insubrian Gauls in* 223 B.C., *builder of the Circus Flaminius and the Flaminian highway in* 220 B.C., *and casualty in the battle at Lake Trasimenus in* 217 B.C.)
flamm·a -ae *f* flame, fire, blaze; star; torch; flame of passion, fire of love, glow, passion; sweetheart; danger, destruction; **flamma fumo est proxima** where there's smoke there's fire; **flammam concipere** to catch fire
flammār·ĭus -ĭī or **-ī** *m* maker of bridal veils
flammeŏl·um -ī *n* bridal veil
flammesc·ō -ĕre *vi* to become inflamed, become fiery
flammĕ·us -a -um *adj* flaming, fiery; flashing (*eyes*); flame-covered; *n* bridal veil
flammĭf·er -ĕra -ĕrum *adj* fiery
flamm·ō -āre *vt* to set on fire; (fig) to inflame, incense; *vi* to burn, glow, blaze
flammŭl·a -ae *f* little flame
flāt·us -ūs *m* blowing, breathing, breath; breeze, wind; snorting; arrogance
flāv·ens -entis *adj* yellow, golden
flāvesc·ō -ĕre *vi* to become yellow, become golden-yellow
Flāvĭ·us -a -um *adj* Flavian; **gens Flavia** Flavian clan (*to which the emperors Vespasian, Titus, and Domitian belonged*)
flāv·us -a -um *adj* yellow, blond, reddish-yellow, golden
flēbĭl·is -e *adj* pitiful, pathetic, deplorable; crying, tearful
flēbilĭter *adv* tearfully, mournfully
flectō flectĕre flexī flexum *vt* to bend, curve; to turn, wheel about, turn around; to wind, twist, curl; to direct, avert, turn away (*eyes, mind, etc.*); to double, sail around (*a cape*); to modulate (*voice*); to change (*the mind*); to persuade, move, appease; **viam** or **iter flectere** (with **ad** + *acc*) to make one's way toward, head toward; *vi* to turn, go, march

flēmin•a -um *n pl* swollen, bloody ankles
fl•ĕō -ēre -ēvī -ētum *vt* to cry for, mourn for; *vi* to cry
flēt•us -ūs *m* crying; *m pl* tears
flexanim•us -a -um *adj* moving, touching
flexibil•is -e *adj* flexible; shifty, fickle
flexil•is -e *adj* flexible, pliant
flexilŏqu•us -a -um *adj* ambiguous
flexi•ō -ōnis *f* bending, turning; modulation (*of the voice*)
flexip•ēs -ĕdis *adj* creeping (*ivy*)
flexuōs•us -a -um *adj* winding (*road*)
flexūr•a -ae *f* bending, winding
flexus *pp* of **flecto**
flex•us -ūs *m* bending, turning, winding; shift, change, transition, crisis
flict•us -ūs *m* clashing, banging together
fl•ō -āre *vt* to blow, breathe; to coin (*money*); *vi* to blow
flocc•us -ī *m* lock (*of hair, wool*); down; **flocci facere** to think little of, disregard, not give a hoot about
Flōr•a -ae *f* goddess of flowers, whose festival was celebrated on April 28th
flōr•ens -entis *adj* blooming; prosperous; flourishing, in the prime; (with *abl*) in the prime of, at the height of
flōr•ĕō -ēre -ŭī *vi* to bloom, blossom; to be in one's prime; (of wine) to foam, ferment; to be prosperous, be eminent; (with *abl*) **a** to abound in; **b** to swarm with, be filled with
flōr•escō -escĕre -ŭī *vi* to begin to bloom, begin to blossom
flōrĕ•us -a -um *adj* flowery; made of flowers
flōrid•us -a -um *adj* flowery; fresh, pretty; florid (*style*)
flōrif•er -ĕra -ĕrum *adj* flowery
flōrilĕg•us -a -um *adj* (of bees) going from flower to flower
flōr•us -a -um *adj* luxuriant
fl•ōs -ōris *m* flower; bud, blossom; best (*of anything*); prime (*of life*); youthful beauty, innocence; crown, glory; nectar; literary ornament
floscŭl•us -ī *m* little flower, floweret; flower, pride, glory
fluctifrăg•us -a -um *adj* wave-breaking (*shore*), surging
fluctuātī•ō -ōnis *f* wavering, vacillating
fluctŭ•ō -āre or **fluctŭ•or -ārī -ātus sum** *vi* to fluctuate, undulate, wave; to be restless; to waver, vacillate, fluctuate
fluctuōs•us -a -um *adj* running (*sea*)
fluct•us -ūs *m* wave, billow; flowing, undulating; turbulence, commotion; disorder, unrest; **fluctus in simpulo** tempest in a tea cup
flu•ens -entis *adj* loose, flowing; (morally) loose; effeminate; fluent
fluent•a -ōrum *n pl* flow, stream, river
fluenter *adv* like a wave
fluid•us or **flūvid•us -a -um** *adj* flowing, fluid; soft; relaxing
fluit•ō or **flūt•ō -āre** *vi* to float, swim; to sail; to toss about; to hang loose, flap; to be uncertain, waver; to stagger
flūm•en -inis *n* flowing, stream, river, flood; fluency; (fig) flood (*e.g., of tears, words, etc.*); **flumine adverso** upstream; **secundo flumine** downstream
flūminĕ•us -a -um *adj* river
flu•ō -ĕre -xī -xum *vi* to flow; to run down, drip; to overflow; (of branches) to spread; to sink, drop, droop; to pass away, vanish, perish; to be fluent; to be monotonous; to spring, arise, proceed
flūtō see **fluito**
fluviāl•is -e *adj* river, of a river
fluviātil•is -e *adj* river, of a river
flūvidus see **fluidus**
fluv•ius -iī or **-ī** *m* river; running water, stream
flux•us -a -um *adj* flowing, loose; careless; loose, dissolute; frail, weak; transient, perishable
fōcāl•e -is *n* scarf
fōcill•ō -āre *vt* to warm, revive
focŭl•um -ī *n* stove
focŭl•us -ī *m* brazier; (fig) fire
foc•us -ī *m* hearth, fireplace; brazier; funeral pile; altar; home, family
fodic•ō -āre *vt* to poke, nudge
fodiō fodĕre fōdī fossum *vt* to dig, dig out; (fig) to prod, goad, prick
foecund- = **fecund-**
foedē *adv* foully, cruelly, shamefully
foederāt•us -a -um *adj* confederated, allied
foedifrăg•us -a -um *adj* treacherous, perfidious
foedit•ās -ātis *f* foulness, hideousness
foed•ō -āre *vt* to make hideous, disfigure; to pollute, defile, disgrace
foed•us -a -um *adj* foul, filthy, horrible, ugly, disgusting, repulsive; disgraceful, vile
foed•us -ĕris *n* treaty, charter, league; compact, agreement; law; **aequo foedere** on equal terms, mutually; **foedere certo** by fixed law; **foedere pacto** by fixed agreement
foen- = **faen-**
foet•ĕō -ēre *vi* to stink
foetid•us -a -um *adj* stinking
foet•or -ōris *m* stink, stench
foetu- = **fētu-**
foliāt•us -a -um *adj* leafy; *n* nard oil
fol•ium -iī or **-ī** *n* leaf; **folium recitare Sibyllae** to tell the gospel truth
follicŭl•us -ī *m* small bag, sack; shell, skin; eggshell
foll•is -is *m* bag; punching bag; bellows; money bag; puffed-out cheeks

fōment·um -ī *n* bandage; mitigation, alleviation
fōm·es -itis *m* tinder
fon·s -tis *m* spring, fountain; spring water, water; stream; lake; source, origin, fountainhead
fontān·us -a -um *adj* spring
fonticŭl·us -ī *m* little spring, little fountain
for fārī fātus sum *vt & vi* to say, speak, utter
forābĭl·is -e *adj* vulnerable
forām·en -ĭnis *n* hole, opening
forās *adv* out, outside; **foras dare** to publish (*writings*)
forc·eps -ĭpis *m* or *f* forceps, tongs
ford·a -ae *f* pregnant cow
fore = futur·us -a -um esse to be about to be
forem = essem
forens·is -e *adj* of the forum, in the forum; public, forensic
forf·ex -ĭcis *f* scissors
for·is -is *f* door, gate; *f pl* double doors; opening, entrance; (fig) door
forīs *adv* outside, out of doors; abroad, in foreign countries; from outside, from abroad
form·a -ae *f* form, shape, figure; beauty; shape, image; mold, stamp; shoemaker's last; vision, apparition, phantom; species, form, nature, sort, kind; outline, design, sketch, plan
formāment·um -ī *n* shape
formāt·or -ōris *m* fashioner
formātūr·a -ae *f* fashioning, shaping
Formĭ·ae -ārum *f pl* town in S. Latium
formīc·a -ae *f* ant
formīcīn·us -a -um *adj* ant-like
formīdābĭl·is -e *adj* terrifying
formīd·ō -āre *vt* to fear, dread; *vi* to be frightened
formīd·ō -ĭnis *f* fear, dread, awe, terror; scarecrow; threats
formīdolōsē *adv* dreadfully, terribly
formīdolōs·us -a -um *adj* dreadful, terrifying, terrible; afraid, terrified
form·ō -āre *vt* to form, shape, mold, build; to make, produce, invent; to imagine; to regulate, direct
formōsē *adv* beautifully, gracefully
formōsĭt·ās -ātis *f* beauty
formōs·us -a -um *adj* shapely, beautiful, handsome
formŭl·a -ae *f* nice shape, beauty; form, formula, draft; contract, agreement; rule, regulation; (law) regular method, formula, rule; (phil) principle
fornācāl·is -e *adj* of an oven
fornācŭl·a -ae *f* small oven
forn·ax -ācis *f* oven, furnace, kiln; forge
fornicāt·us -a -um *adj* arched
forn·ix -ĭcis *m* arch, vault; arcade; brothel
fornus see **furnus**
for·ō -āre *vt* to bore, pierce
fors *adv* perhaps, chances are, there is a chance, possibly
for·s -tis *f* chance, luck, fortune, accident; **forte** by chance, accidentally, by accident; as it happens, as it happened; perhaps
forsan, forsit, or **forsĭtan** *adv* perhaps
fortasse or **fortassis** *adv* perhaps
forte see **fors**
forticŭl·us -a -um *adj* quite bold, rather brave
fort·is -e *adj* strong, mighty, powerful; brave, courageous, valiant, resolute, steadfast, firm
fortĭter *adv* strongly, vigorously, firmly, bravely, boldly
fortitūd·ō -ĭnis *f* strength; bravery, courage, resolution
fortuītō *adv* by chance, accidentally, casually
fortuīt·us -a -um *adj* accidental, fortuitous, casual
fortūn·a -ae *f* chance, luck, fate, fortune; good luck, prosperity; bad luck, misfortune; lot, circumstances, state, rank, position; property, goods, fortune
fortūnātē *adv* fortunately, prosperously
fortūnāt·us -a -um *adj* fortunate, lucky, prosperous, happy; rich, well-off
fortūn·ō -āre *vt* to make happy, make prosperous, bless
forŭl·ī -ōrum *m pl* bookcase
for·um -ī *n* shopping center, market, marketplace; market town; trade, commerce; forum, civic center; court; public life, public affairs; jurisdiction; **cedere foro** to go bankrupt; **extra suum forum** beyond his jurisdiction; **forum agere** to hold court; **forum attingere** to enter public life; **in foro versari** to be engaged in commerce
For·um Appĭī (*genit*: **For·ī Appĭī**) *n* town in Latium on the Via Appia
For·um Aurēlĭī (*genit*: **For·ī Aurēlĭī**) *n* town N. of Rome on the Via Aurelia
For·um Julĭī (*genit*: **For·ī Julĭī**) *n* town in S. Gaul, colony of the eighth legion
for·us -ī *m* gangway; tier of seats; tier of a beehive
foss·a -ae *f* ditch, trench; **fossam deprimere** to dig a deep trench
fossĭ·ō -ōnis *f* digging
foss·or -ōris *m* digger; lout, clown
fossūr·a -ae *f* digging
fossus *pp* of **fodio**
fōtus *pp* of **foveo**
fovĕ·a -ae *f* small pit; (fig) pitfall
fovĕō fovēre fōvī fōtum *vt* to warm, keep warm; to fondle, caress; to love, cherish; to support, encourage; to pamper
fract·us -a -um *pp* of **frango;** *adj* interrupted, irregular; weak, feeble
frāg·a -ōrum *n pl* strawberries
fragĭl·is -e *adj* fragile, brittle;

crackling; weak, frail; unstable, fickle
fragilit•ās -ātis *f* weakness, frailty
fraglō see **fragro**
fragm•en -inis *n* fragment; *n pl* debris, ruins, wreckage
fragment•um -ī *n* fragment, remnant
frag•or -ōris *m* crash, noise, uproar, din; applause; clap of thunder
fragōs•us -a -um *adj* broken, uneven, rough; crashing, roaring
fragr•ō or **fragl•ō -āre** *vi* to smell sweet, be fragrant; to reek
framĕ•a -ae *f* German spear
frangō frangĕre frēgī fractum *vt* to break in pieces, smash to pieces, shatter; to grind, crush; (fig) to break down, overcome, crush, dishearten, humble, weaken, soften, move, touch; **diem mero frangere** to break up the day with wine
frāt•er -ris *m* brother; cousin; friend, comrade
frātercŭl•us -ī *m* little brother
frāternē *adv* like a brother
frāternit•ās -ātis *f* brotherhood
frātern•us -a -um *adj* brotherly; brother's; fraternal
frātricīd•a -ae *m* murderer of a brother, a fratricide
fraudātī•ō -ōnis *f* swindling
fraudāt•or -ōris *m* swindler
fraud•ō -āre *vt* to swindle, cheat, defraud; to embezzle; (with *abl*) to defraud (*someone*) of, cheat (*someone*) of
fraudulentī•a -ae *f* tendency to swindle, deceitfulness
fraudulent•us -a -um *adj* fraudulent; deceitful, treacherous
frau•s -dis *f* fraud, deception, trickery; error, delusion; crime, offense; harm, damage; deceiver, fraud, cheat; **sine fraude** without harm
fraxinĕ•us or **fraxin•us -a -um** *adj* of ash wood, ashen
fraxin•us -ī *f* ash tree; spear (*made of ash wood*)
Fregell•ae -ārum *f pl* ancient Volscan city on the Liris River, in Latium, made a Roman colony in 328 B.C.
fremebund•us -a -um *adj* roaring
fremit•us -ūs *m* roaring, growling, snorting; din, noise
frem•ō -ĕre -ŭī -ĭtum *vt* to grumble at, complain loudly of; to demand angrily; *vi* to roar, growl, snort, howl, grumble, murmur; to resound
frem•or -ōris *m* roaring, grumbling, murmuring
frend•ō -ĕre -ŭī *vi* to gnash the teeth; **dentibus frendere** to gnash the teeth
frēnī see **frenum**
frēn•ō -āre *vt* to bridle, curb; (fig) to curb, control
frēn•um -ī *n* or **frēn•a -ōrum** *n pl* or **frēn•ī -ōrum** *m pl* bridle, bit; (fig) curb, control, restraint
frequ•ens -entis *adj* crowded, in crowds, numerous, filled; frequent, repeated, usual, common; (may be rendered adverbially) often, repeatedly
frequentātī•ō -ōnis *f* piling up
frequenter *adv* frequently, often; in great numbers
frequentī•a -ae *f* crowd, throng; crowded assembly, large attendance
frequent•ō -āre *vt* to visit often, frequent, resort to; to do often, repeat; to crowd, people, stock; to attend (*e.g., games*) in large numbers
fretens•is -e *adj* **fretense mare** Strait of Messina
fret•um -ī *n* strait, channel; sea, waters; (fig) seething flood
frēt•us -a -um *adj* confident; (with *dat* or *abl*) supported by, relying on, depending on
fret•us -ūs *m* strait
fric•ō -āre -ŭī -tum *vt* to rub, rub down
frictus *pp* of **frigo**
frīgefact•ō -āre *vt* to make cold or cool
frīg•ĕō -ēre *vi* to be cold, be chilly; to freeze; (fig) to be numbed, be lifeless, be dull; (fig) to get a cool reception, be snubbed, get a cold shoulder; (fig) to fall flat
frīgesc•ō -ĕre *vi* to become cold, become chilled; to become lifeless
frīgidārī•us -a -um *adj* cooling
frīgidē *adv* feebly
frīgidŭl•us -a -um *adj* rather cold; rather faint
frīgid•us -a -um *adj* cold, cool; numbed, dull, lifeless, indifferent, unimpassioned, feeble; flat, insipid, trivial; *f* cold water
frīgō frīgĕre frixī frictum *vt* to fry, roast
frīg•us -ŏris *n* cold, coldness, chill, coolness; frost; cold of winter, winter; coldness of death, death; chill, fever; cold shudder, chill; cold region; cold reception; coolness, indifference; slowness, inactivity; *n pl* cold spell, cold season
frigutt•iō -īre *vi* to stutter
fri•ō -āre *vt* to crumble
fritill•us -ī *m* dice box
frīvŏl•us -a -um *adj* frivolous, trifling, worthless, sorry, pitiful; *n pl* trifles
frondāt•or -ōris *m* pruner
frond•ĕō -ēre *vi* to have leaves; to become green
frondesc•ō -ĕre *vi* to get leaves
frondĕ•us -a -um *adj* leafy, covered with leaves
frondĭf•er -ĕra -ĕrum *adj* leafy
frondōs•us -a -um *adj* full of leaves, leafy
fron•s -dis *f* foliage; leafy bough, green bough; chaplet, garland
fron•s -tis *f* forehead, brow; front end, front; countenance, face, look; face, façade; van, vanguard; exterior, appearance; outer end of a

scroll; sense of shame; **a fronte** in front; **frontem contrahere** to knit the brow, frown; **frontem ferire** to hit oneself on the head (*in self-annoyance*); **frontem remittere** to smooth the brow, to cheer up; **in fronte** (in measuring land) in breadth, frontage; **salvā fronte** without shame; **tenuis frons** low forehead
frontāl·ia -ium *n pl* frontlet (*ornament for forehead of a horse*)
front·ō -ōnis *m* one with a large forehead
fructuāri·us -a -um *adj* productive; subject to land tax
fructuōs·us -a -um *adj* fruitful, productive
fructus *pp* of **fruor**
fruct·us -ūs *m* produce, fruit; proceeds, profit, income, return, revenue; enjoyment, satisfaction; benefit, reward, results, consequence
frūgāl·is -e *adj* frugal; honest; worthy
frūgālit·ās -ātis *f* frugality, economy; temperance; honesty; worth
frūgāliter *adv* frugally, economically; temperately
frūgēs see **frux**
frūgī (indecl) *adj* frugal; temperate; honest, worthy; useful, proper
frūgif·er -ĕra -ĕrum *adj* fruitful, productive, fertile; profitable
frūgifĕr·ens -entis *adj* fruitful
frūgilĕg·us -a -um *adj* (of ants) food-gathering
frūgipăr·us -a -um *adj* fruitful
fruitus *pp* of **fruor**
frūmentāri·us -a -um *adj* of grain, grain; grain-producing; of provisions; **res frumentaria** (mil) supplies, quartermaster corps; *m* grain dealer
frūmentāti·ō -ōnis *f* (mil) foraging
frūmentāt·or -ōris *m* grain merchant; (mil) forager
frūment·or -ārī -ātus sum *vi* (mil) to forage
frūment·um -ī *n* grain; wheat; *n pl* grain fields, crops
frūn·iscor -iscī -ītus sum *vt* to enjoy
fruor fruī fructus sum or **fruitus sum** *vt* to enjoy; *vi* (with *abl*) **a** to enjoy, delight in; **b** to enjoy the company of; **c** (law) to have the use and enjoyment of
frustillātim *adv* in bits
frustrā *adv* in vain, uselessly, for nothing; without reason, groundlessly; **frustra discedere** to go away disappointed; **frustra esse** to be mistaken; **frustra habere** to have (*someone*) confused or baffled
frustrām·en -inis *n* deception
frustrāti·ō -ōnis *f* deception; frustration
frustrāt·us -ūs *m* deception; **frustratui habere** (coll) to take for a sucker
frustr·or -ārī -ātus sum or **frustr·ō -āre** *vt* to deceive, trick; to disappoint; to frustrate
frustulent·us -a -um *adj* crumby, full of crumbs
frust·um -ī *n* crumb, bit, scrap; **frustum pueri** (coll) whippersnapper
frut·ex -icis *m* shrub, bush; (coll) blockhead
fruticēt·um -ī *n* thicket, shrubbery
frutic·ō -āre or **frutic·or -ārī -ātus sum** *vi* to sprout; to become bushy; (fig) (of the hair) to become bushy
fruticōs·us -a -um *adj* bushy, overgrown with bushes
frux frūgis *f* or **frūg·ēs -um** *f pl* fruit, produce, grain, vegetables; barley meal (*for sacrifice*); fruits, benefit, result; **se ad frugem bonam recipere** to turn over a new leaf; **expers frugis** worthless
fūcāt·us -a -um *adj* dyed, colored, painted; artificial, spurious
fūc·ō -āre *vt* to dye red, redden, paint red; to disguise, falsify
fūcōs·us -a -um *adj* painted, colored; spurious, phoney
fūc·us -ī *m* red paint; rouge; drone; bee glue; disguise, pretense, deceit
fue or **fu** *interj* phui!
fug·a -ae *f* flight, escape; avoidance; exile; speed, swift passage; disappearance; (with *genit*) avoidance of, escape from; **fugae sese mandare, fugam capere, fugam capessere, fugam facere, se in fugam conferre, se in fugam conjicere,** or **sese in fugam dare** to flee, take flight; **in fugam conferre, in fugam conjicere, in fugam dare,** or **in fugam impellere** to put to flight
fugācius *adv* more cautiously, with one eye on flight
fug·ax -ācis *adj* apt to flee, fleeing; shy, timid; swift; passing, transitory; (with *genit*) shy of, shunning, avoiding, steering clear of, averse to
fugi·ens -entis *adj* fleeing, retreating; (with *genit*) avoiding, averse to
fugiō fugĕre fūgī fugitum *vt* to escape, escape from, run away from, shun, avoid; to leave (*esp. one's country*); to be averse to, dislike; to escape the notice of, escape, be unknown to; **fuge** (with *inf*) do not; **fugit me scribere** I forgot to write; *vi* to flee, escape, run away; to go into exile; to speed, hasten; to vanish, disappear; to pass away, perish
fugit·ans -antis *adj* fleeing; (with *genit*) averse to
fugitīv·us -a -um *adj & m* runaway, fugitive
fugit·ō -āre *vt* to run away from
fugit·or -ōris *m* deserter
fug·ō -āre *vt* to put to flight, drive away, chase away; to exile, banish; to avert
fulcīm·en -inis *n* support, prop, pillar

fulcĭō fulcīre fulsī fultum *vt* to prop up, support; to secure, sustain
fulcr·um -ī *n* bed post; couch, bed
fulgĕō fulgēre fulsī or **fulg·ō -ĕre** *vi* to gleam, flash, blaze, shine, glare; to shine, be conspicuous, be illustrious
fulgĭd·us -a -um *adj* flashing, shining
fulgō see **fulgeo**
fulg·or -ōris *m* flash of lightning, lightning; brightness; thing struck by lightning
fulgurāl·is -e *adj* of lightning; **libri fulgurales** books on lightning
fulgurāt·or -ōris *m* interpreter of lightning
fulgurīt·us -a -um *adj* struck by lightning
fulgŭr·ō -āre *vi* to lighten, send lightning; *v impers* it is lightning
fulic·a -ae or **ful·ix -icis** *f* coot (*waterfowl*)
fūlīg·ō -inis *f* soot; black paint
fulix see **fulica**
full·ō -ōnis *m* fuller
fullōnic·a -ae *f* fuller's craft, fulling
fullōni·us -a -um *adj* fuller's
fulm·en -inis *n* thunderbolt, lightning bolt; (fig) bolt, bolt out of the blue
fulment·a -ae *f* heel
fulminĕ·us -a -um *adj* of lightning, lightning; shine, sparkling, flashing
fulmĭn·ō -āre *vi* to lighten; (fig) to flash
fultūr·a -ae *f* support, prop
fultus *pp* of **fulcio**
fulv·us -a -um *adj* yellow, yellowish brown, reddish yellow, tawny; blond
fūmĕ·us -a -um *adj* smoky
fūmĭd·us -a -um *adj* smoking, smoky
fūmif·er -ĕra -ĕrum *adj* smoking
fūmific·ō -āre *vi* to smoke; to burn incense
fūmific·us -a -um *adj* smoking, steaming
fūm·ō -āre *vi* to smoke, fume, steam, reek
fūmōs·us -a -um *adj* smoked, smoky
fūm·us -ī *m* smoke, steam, fume
fūnāl·e -is *n* rope; torch; chandelier, candelabrum
fūnambŭl·us -ī *m* tightrope walker
functi·ō -ōnis *f* performance
functus *pp* of **fungor**
fund·a -ae *f* sling; sling stone; dragnet
fundām·en -inis *n* foundation
fundāment·um -ī *n* foundation; (fig) basis, ground, beginning; **a fundamentis** utterly, completely; **fundamenta agere, jacere,** or **locare** to lay the foundations
fundāt·or -ōris *m* founder
fundāt·us -a -um *adj* well-founded, established
fundĭt·ō -āre *vt* to sling, shoot with a sling; (fig) to sling (*e.g., words*) around
fundĭt·or -ōris *m* slinger
fundĭtus *adv* from the bottom, utterly, entirely
fund·ō -āre *vt* to found, build, establish; to secure to the ground, make fast
fundō fundĕre fūdī fūsum *vt* to pour, pour out; to melt (*metals*); to cast (*in metal*); to pour in streams, shower, hurl; (mil) to pour in (*troops*); (mil) to rout; to pour out, empty; to spread, extend, diffuse; to bring forth, bear, yield in abundance; to throw to the ground, bring down; to give up, lose, waste; to utter, pour out (*words*)
fund·us -ī *m* bottom; farm, estate; (law) sanctioner, authority
fūnĕbr·is -e *adj* funeral; deadly, murderous
fūnerāt·us -a -um *adj* done in, killed
fūnerĕ·us -a -um *adj* funeral; deadly, fatal
fūnĕr·ō -āre *vt* to bury; **prope funeratus** almost sent to my (*his, etc.*) grave
fūnest·ō -āre *vt* to defile with murder, desecrate
fūnest·us -a -um *adj* deadly, fatal, calamitous; sad, dismal, mournful; **annales funesti** obituary column
fungīn·us -a -um *adj* of a mushroom
fungor fungī functus sum *vi* (with *abl*) **a** to perform, execute, discharge, do; **b** to busy oneself with, be engaged in; **c** to finish, complete; **morte fungi** to suffer death, die
fung·us -ī *m* mushroom, fungus; candle snuff; (fig) clown
fūnicŭl·us -ī *m* cord
fūn·is -is *m* rope, cable, cord; rigging; **funem ducere** (fig) to command; **funem reducere** (fig) to change one's mind; **funem sequi** (fig) to serve, follow
fūn·us -ĕris *n* funeral rites, funeral, burial; corpse; death, murder; havoc; ruin, destruction; **sub funus** on the brink of the grave; *n pl* shades of the dead
fūr fūris *m* or *f* thief; (fig) rogue, rascal
fūrācissimē *adv* quite like a thief
fūr·ax -ācis *adj* thievish
furc·a -ae *f* fork; fork-shaped prop (*for supporting vines, bleachers, etc.*); wooden yoke (*put around slave's neck as punishment*)
furcif·er -ĕrī *m* rogue, rascal
furcill·a -ae *f* little fork
furcill·ō -āre *vt* to support, prop up
furcŭl·a -ae *f* fork-shaped prop; *f pl* narrow pass, defile
Furcŭl·ae Caudīn·ae (*genit*: **Furcŭl·ārum Caudīn·ārum**) *f pl* Caudine Forks (*mountain pass near Caudium, in Samnium, where the Roman army was trapped in* 321 B.C. *by the Samnites and made to pass under the yoke*)

furenter *adv* furiously
furf·ur -ŭris *m* chaff; bran
Furĭ·a -ae *f* Fury (*one of the three goddesses of frenzy and vengeance, who were named Megaera, Tisiphone, and Alecto*)
furĭ·a -ae *f* frenzy, madness, rage; remorse; madman
furiāl·is -e *adj* of the Furies; frenzied, frantic, furious; infuriated
furiālĭter *adv* frantically
furibund·us -a -um *adj* frenzied, frantic, mad; inspired
fūrīn·us -a -um *adj* of thieves
furĭ·ō -āre *vt* to drive mad, infuriate
furiōsē *adv* in a rage, in a frenzy
furiōs·us -a -um *adj* frenzied, frantic, mad, furious; maddening
furn·us or **forn·us -ī** *m* oven; bakery
fur·ō -ĕre *vi* to be crazy, be out of one's mind, rage, rave
fūr·or -ārī -ātus sum *vt* to steal, pilfer; to pillage; to plagiarize; to obtain by fraud; to withdraw in secret; to impersonate
fur·or -ōris *m* madness, rage, fury, passion; furor, excitement; prophetic frenzy, inspiration; passionate love
furtific·us -a -um *adj* thievish
furtim *adv* secretly, by stealth, clandestinely
furtīvē *adv* secretly, stealthily
furtīv·us -a -um *adj* stolen; secret, hidden, furtive
furt·um -ī *n* theft, robbery; trick, stratagem; secret action, intrigue; secret love; *n pl* intrigues; secret love affair; stolen goods
fūruncŭl·us -ī *m* petty thief
furv·us -a -um *adj* black, dark, gloomy, eerie
fuscĭn·a -ae *f* trident
fusc·ō -āre *vt* to blacken
fusc·us -a -um *adj* dark, swarthy; low, muffled, indistinct (*sound*)
fūsē *adv* widely; in great detail
fūsĭl·is -e *adj* molten, liquid
fūsĭ·ō -ōnis *f* outpouring, effusion
fust·is -is *m* club, stick, cudgel; beating to death (*as a military punishment*)
fustitudĭn·us -a -um *adj* (coll) whip-happy (*jail*)
fustuār·ĭum -ĭī or **-ī** *n* beating to death (*as a military punishment*)
fūs·us -a -um *pp* of **fundo;** *adj* spread out; broad, wide; diffuse (*style*)
fūs·us -ī *m* spindle
futtĭl·is or **fūtĭl·is -e** *adj* brittle; futile, worthless, untrustworthy
futtilĭt·ās or **fūtilĭt·ās -ātis** *f* futility, worthlessness
fut·ŭō -uĕre -ŭī -ūtum *vt* to have sexual intercourse with (*a woman*)
futūr·us -a -um *fut p* of **sum;** *adj* & *n* future

G

Gabĭ·ī -ōrum *m pl* ancient town in Latium
Gad·ēs -ĭum *f pl* Cadiz (*town in S. Spain*)
gaes·um -ī *n* Gallic spear
Gaetūl·ī -ōrum *m pl* a people in N.W. Africa along the Sahara Desert
Gā·ĭus -ī *m* Roman praenomen (*the names of Gaius and Gaia were formally given to the bridegroom and bride at the wedding ceremony*)
Galăt·ae -ārum *m pl* Galatians (*a people of central Asia Minor*)
Galatĭ·a -ae *f* Galatia (*country in central Asia Minor*)
Galb·a -ae *m* Servius Sulpicius Galba, the Roman emperor from June, 68 A.D., to January, 69 A.D. (5 B.C.-69 A.D.)
galbanĕ·us -a -um *adj* of galbanum
galban·um -ī *n* galbanum (*resinous sap of a Syrian plant*)
galbĭn·us -a -um *adj* chartreuse; (fig) effeminate; *n pl* pale green clothes
galĕ·a -ae *f* helmet
galeāt·us -a -um *adj* helmeted
galērīcŭl·um -ī *n* cap
galērīt·us -a -um *adj* wearing a farmer's cap, countryish
galēr·um -ī *n* or **galēr·us -ī** *m* cap; (fig) wig
gall·a -ae *f* gallnut
Gall·ī -ōrum *m pl* Gauls (*inhabitants of modern France and N. Italy*)
Gallĭ·a -ae *f* Gaul
Gallĭc·us -a -um *adj* Gallic
gallīn·a -ae *f* chicken, hen; (as term of endearment) chick
gallīnācĕ·us or **gallīnācĭ·us -a -um** *adj* poultry
gallīnār·ĭus -ĭī or **-ī** *m* poultry farmer
Gallograec·ī -ōrum *m pl* Galatians (*Celts who migrated from Gaul to Asia Minor in the 3rd cent. B.C.*)
Gall·us -a -um *adj* Gallic; *m* Gaul; priest of Cybele; C. Cornelius Gallus, lyric poet and friend of Virgil (69-27 B.C.)
gall·us -ī *m* rooster, cock
gānĕ·a -ae *f* or **gānĕ·um -ī** *n* brothel, dive; cheap restaurant
gānĕ·ō -ōnis *m* glutton
gānĕum see **ganea**
Gangarĭd·ae -ārum *m pl* an Indian people on the Ganges
Gang·es -is *m* Ganges River

gann·iō -īre *vi* to snarl, growl
gannīt·us -ūs *m* snarling, growling
Ganymēd·ēs -is *m* Ganymede (*handsome youth carried off to Olympus by the eagle of Jupiter to become the cupbearer of the gods*)
Garamant·es -um *m pl* tribe in N. Africa
Gargaphi·ē -ēs *f* valley in Boeotia sacred to Diana
Gargān·us -ī *m* mountain in S.E. Italy
garr·iō -īre *vt* to chatter, prattle, talk; **nugas garrire** to talk nonsense; *vi* to chatter, chat; (of frogs) to croak
garrulit·ās -ātis *f* talkativeness; chattering
garrŭl·us -a -um *adj* talkative, babbling, garrulous
gar·um -ī *n* fish sauce
gaud·ens -entis *adj* cheerful
gaudĕō gaudēre gāvīsus sum *vt* to rejoice at; **gaudium gaudere** to feel joy; *vi* to rejoice, be glad, feel pleased; (with *abl*) to delight in; **in se gaudere** or **in sinu gaudere** to be secretly glad
gaud·ium -iī or **-ī** *n* joy, gladness, delight; sensual pleasure, enjoyment; joy, cause of joy; **mala mentis gaudia** gloating
gaul·us -ī *m* bucket
gausăp·e -is or **gausăp·um -ī** *n* felt; (fig) shaggy beard
gāvīsus *pp* of **gaudeo**
gaz·a -ae *f* royal treasure; treasure, riches
gelidē *adv* coldly, indifferently
gelid·us -a -um *adj* cold, icy, frosty; icy cold, stiff, numbed; *f* cold water
gel·ō -āre *vt* & *vi* to freeze
Gelōn·ī -ōrum *m pl* Scythian tribe
gel·u -ūs *n* or **gel·um -ī** *n* or **gel·us -ūs** *m* coldness, cold, frost, ice; chill, coldness (*of death, old age, fear*)
gemebund·us -a -um *adj* sighing, groaning
gemellipăr·a -ae *f* mother of twins
gemell·us -a -um *adj* & *m* twin
gemināti·ō -ōnis *f* doubling; compounding
gemĭn·ō -āre *vt* to double; to join, unite, pair; to repeat, reproduce
gemĭn·us -a -um *adj* twin; double, twofold, two, both; similar; *m pl* twins
gemĭt·us -ūs *m* sigh, groan
gemm·a -ae *f* bud; gem, jewel; jeweled goblet; signet ring, signet; eye of a peacock's tail; literary gem
gemmāt·us -a -um *adj* set with jewels, jeweled
gemmĕ·us -a -um *adj* set with jewels, jeweled; brilliant, glittering, sparkling
gemmĭf·er -ĕra -ĕrum *adj* gem-producing
gemm·ō -āre *vi* to sprout, bud; to sparkle
gem·ō -ĕre -ŭī -ĭtum *vt* to sigh over, lament; *vi* to sigh, groan, moan; to creak
Gemōnĭ·ae -ārum *f pl* steps on the Capitoline slope from which criminals were thrown
gen·a -ae *f* or **gen·ae -ārum** *f pl* cheek; cheekbone; eye socket; eye
geneālŏg·us -ī *m* genealogist
gen·er -ĕrī *m* son-in-law; daughter's boyfriend or fiancé
generāl·is -e *adj* of a species, generic; general, universal
generālĭter *adv* in general, generally
generasc·ō -ĕre *vi* to be generated
generātim *adv* by species, by classes; in general, generally
generāt·or -ōris *m* producer, breeder
genĕr·ō -āre *vt* to beget, procreate, produce, engender
generōsĭus *adv* more nobly
generōs·us -a -um *adj* of good stock, highborn, noble; noble, noble-minded
genĕs·is -is *f* birth, creation; horoscope
genesta see **genista**
genetīv·us -a -um *adj* inborn, innate; (gram) genitive; *m* genitive case
genĕtr·ix -īcis *f* mother, ancestress
geniāl·is -e *adj* nuptial, bridal; genial; joyous, festive, merry
geniālĭter *adv* merrily
geniculāt·us -a -um *adj* knotted, having knots, jointed
genist·a or **genest·a -ae** *f* broom plant; broom
genitābĭl·is -e *adj* productive
genitāl·is -e *adj* generative, productive; of birth; **dies genitalis** birthday
genitālĭter *adv* fruitfully
genitīvus see **genetivus**
genĭt·or -ōris *m* father, creator
genĭtrix see **genetrix**
genĭtus *pp* of **gigno**
gen·ius -iī or **-ī** *m* guardian spirit; taste, appetite, natural inclination; talent, genius
gen·s -tis *f* clan; stock; tribe; folk, nation, people; species, breed; descendant, offspring; *f pl* foreign nations; **longe gentium abire** to be far, far away; **minime gentium** by no means; **ubi gentium** where in the world, where on earth
gentĭc·us -a -um *adj* tribal; national
gentīlicĭ·us -a -um *adj* family
gentīl·is -e *adj* family, hereditary; tribal; national; *m* clansman, kinsman
gentīlĭt·ās -ātis *f* clan relationship
gen·ū -ūs *n* knee; **genibus minor** kneeling; **genibus nixus** on one's knees; **genuum junctura** knee joint
genuāl·ia -ium *n pl* garters
genuīn·us -a -um *adj* innate, natural; of the cheek; jaw, of the jaw; *m pl* back teeth

gen·us -ĕris *n* race, descent, lineage, breed, stock, family; noble birth; tribe; nation, people; descendant, offspring, posterity; kind, sort, species, class; rank, order, division; fashion, way, style; matter, respect; genus; sex; gender; **aliquid id genus** (*acc* of description instead of *genit* of quality) something of that sort; **in omni genere** in every respect

geōgraphi·a -ae *f* geography

geōmĕtr·ēs -ae *m* geometer, mathematician

geōmetri·a -ae *f* geometry

geōmetric·us -a -um *adj* geometrical; *n pl* geometry

georgic·us -a -um *adj* agricultural; *n pl* Georgics (*poems on farming by Virgil*)

ger·ens -entis *adj* (with *genit*) managing (*e.g., a business*)

germān·a -ae *f* full sister, real sister

germānē *adv* sincerely

Germān·ī -ōrum *m pl* Germans

Germāni·a -ae *f* Germany

Germānic·us -a -um *adj* Germanic; *m* cognomen of Tiberius' nephew and adoptive son (15 B.C.-19 A.D.)

germānit·ās -ātis *f* brotherhood, sisterhood (*relationship between brothers and sisters of the same parents*); relationship between colonies of the same mother-city

germān·us -a -um *adj* having the same parents; brotherly; sisterly; genuine, real, true; *m* full brother, own brother; *f* see **germana**

germ·en -inis *n* sprout, bud, shoot, offspring; embryo

germin·ō -āre *vt* to put forth, grow (*hair, wings, etc.*); *vi* to sprout

gerō gerĕre gessī gestum *vt* to bear, carry, wear, have, hold; to bring; to display; exhibit, assume; to bear, produce; to carry on, manage, govern, regulate, administer; to carry out, transact, do, accomplish; **bellum gerere** to fight, carry on war; **dum ea geruntur** while that was going on; **gerere morem** (with *dat*) to gratify, please, humor; **personam gerere** (with *genit*) to play the part of; **rem gerere** to run a business, conduct an affair; **se gerere** to behave; **se gerere** (with **pro** + *abl*) to claim to be for; **se medium gerere** to remain neutral

ger·ō -ōnis *m* porter

gerr·ae -ārum *f pl* trifles, nonsense

gerr·ō -ōnis *m* (coll) loafer

gerulifigŭl·us -ī *m* accomplice; (with *genit*) accomplice in

gerŭl·us -ī *m* porter

Gēry̆·ōn -ōnis or **Gēryŏn·ēs -ae** *m* mythical three-headed king of Spain who was slain by Hercules

gestām·en -inis *n* that which is worn or carried, load; vehicle, litter; *n pl* ornaments; accouterments; arms

gestāti·ō -ōnis *f* drive (*place where one drives*)

gestāt·or -ōris *m* bearer, carrier

gesti·ō -ōnis *f* performance

gest·iō -īre -īvī or **-iī -ītum** *vi* to be delighted, be thrilled, be excited; to be eager; (with *inf*) to be itching to, long to

gestit·ō -āre *vt* to be in the habit of carrying or wearing

gest·ō -āre *vt* to bear, wear, carry; to carry about, blab, tell; to cherish; **gestari** to ride, drive, sail (*esp. for pleasure*)

gest·or -ōris *m* tattler

gestus *pp* of **gero;** *adj* **res gestae** accomplishments, exploits

gest·us -ūs *m* gesture; gesticulation; posture, bearing, attitude

Get·ae -ārum *m pl* Thracian tribe of the lower Danube

gibb·us -ī *m* hump

Gigant·es -um *m pl* Giants (*race of gigantic size, sprung from Earth as the blood of Uranus fell upon her. They tried to storm heaven but were repelled by the gods with the aid of Hercules and placed under various volcanoes*)

gignō gignĕre genŭī genitum *vt* to beget, bear, produce; to cause, occasion, create, begin

gilv·us -a -um *adj* pale-yellow; **equus gilvus** palomino

gingīv·a -ae *f* gum (*of the mouth*)

glab·er -ra -rum *adj* hairless, bald, smooth; *m* young slave, favorite slave

glaciāl·is -e *adj* icy, frozen

glaci·ēs -ēī *f* ice; *f pl* ice fields

glaci·ō -āre *vt* to turn into ice, freeze

gladiāt·or -ōris *m* gladiator; *m pl* gladiatorial combat, gladiatorial show; **gladiatores dare** or **gladiatores edere** to stage a gladiatorial show

gladiātōri·us -a -um *adj* gladiatorial; *n* gladiator's pay

gladiātūr·a -ae *f* gladiatorial profession

glad·ius -iī or **-ī** *m* sword; murder, death; **gladium educere** or **gladium stringere** to draw the sword; **gladium recondere** to sheathe the sword

glaeb·a -ae *f* lump of earth, clod; soil, land; lump, piece

glaebŭl·a -ae *f* small lump; bit of land, small farm

glaesum see **glesum**

glandĭf·er -ĕra -ĕrum *adj* acorn-producing

glandiōnid·a -ae *f* choice morsel

gland·ium -iī or **-ī** *n* choice cut (*of meat*)

glan·s -dis *f* mast; nut; acorn; chestnut; bullet

glārē·a -ae *f* gravel

glārеōs·us -a -um *adj* full of gravel, gravelly
glaucōm·a -ătis *n* cataract; **glaucomam ob oculos objicere** (*with dat*) to throw dust into the eyes of
glauc·us -a -um *adj* grey-green, greyish; bright, sparkling
Glauc·us -ī *m* leader of the Lycians in the Trojan War; fisherman of Anthedon, in Euboea, who was changed into a sea deity
glēba see **glaeba**
glēs·um or **glaes·um -ī** *n* amber
glī·s -ris *m* dormouse
glisc·ō -ĕre *vi* to grow, swell up, spread, blaze up; to grow, increase
globōs·us -a -um *adj* spherical
glob·us -ī *m* ball, sphere, globe; crowd, throng, gathering; clique
glomerām·en -ĭnis *n* ball, globe
glomĕr·ō -āre *vt* to form into a ball, gather up, roll up; to collect, gather together, assemble
glom·us -ĕris *n* ball of yarn
glōri·a -ae *f* glory, fame; glorious deed; thirst for glory, ambition; pride, boasting, bragging
glōriāti·ō -ōnis *f* boasting, bragging
glōriŏl·a -ae *f* bit of glory
glōri·or -ārī -ātus sum *vt* (*only with neut pron as object*) to boast about, e.g., **haec gloriari** to boast about this; **idem gloriari** to make the same boast; *vi* to boast, brag; (*with abl or with* **de** *or* **in** + *abl*) to take pride in, boast about; (*with* **adversus** + *acc*) to boast or brag to (*someone*)
glōriōsē *adv* gloriously; boastfully, pompously
glōriōs·us -a -um *adj* glorious, famous; boastful
glossēm·a -ătis *n* word to be glossed
glūt·en -ĭnis *n* glue
glūtināt·or -ōris *m* bookbinder
glūtin·ō -āre *vt* to glue together
glutt·iō or **glūt·iō -īre** *vt* to gulp down
glutt·ō -ōnis *m* glutton
Gnae·us or **Gnē·us -ī** *m* Roman praenomen
gnār·us -a -um or **gnārŭr·is -e** *adj* skillful, expert; known; (*with genit*) familiar with, versed in, expert in
gnātus see **natus**
gnāv- = nav-
gnōbĭlis see **nobilis**
Gnōsi·a -ae or **Gnōsi·as -ădis** or **Gnōs·is -ĭdis** *f* Ariadne (*daughter of King Minos*)
gnoscō see **nosco**
Gnoss·us or **Gnōs·us -ī** *f* Cnossos (*ancient capital of Crete and residence of Minos*)
gnōtus see **nosco**
gōb·ius or **cōb·ius -iī** or **-ī** or **gōbi·ō -ōnis** *m* goby (*small fish*)
Gorgi·as -ae *m* famous orator and sophist of Leontini, in Sicily (*c.* 480-390 B.C.)
Gorg·ō -ōnis *f* Gorgon (*a daughter of Phorcys and Ceto*); *f pl* Gorgons (*Stheno, Medusa, and Euryale*)
Gorgŏnĕ·us -a -um *adj* Gorgonian; **Gorgoneus equus** Pegasus; **Gorgoneus lacus** fountain Hippocrene on Mount Helicon
grabāt·us -ī *m* cot
Gracch·us -ī *m* Tiberius Sempronius Gracchus (*social reformer and tribune in* 133 B.C.); Gaius Sempronius Gracchus (*younger brother of Tiberius and tribune in* 123 B.C.)
gracĭl·is -e or **gracĭl·us -a -um** *adj* slim, slender; thin, skinny; poor; slight, insignificant; plain, simple (*style*)
gracilit·ās -ātis *f* slenderness; thinness, leanness, meagerness
grācŭl·us or **graccŭl·us -ī** *m* jackdaw
gradātim *adv* step by step, gradually, little by little
gradāti·ō -ōnis *f* climax
gradior gradī gressus sum *vi* to go, walk, step
Grādīv·us or **Grădīv·us -ī** *m* epithet of Mars
grad·us -ūs *m* step, pace, walk, gait; step, degree, grade, stage; approach, advance, progress; status, rank; station, position; step, rung, stair; footing; **concito gradu** on the double; **de gradu dejicere** (*fig*) to throw off balance; **gradum celerare** or **gradum corripere** to pick up the pace, speed up the pace; **gradum conferre** (*mil*) to come to close quarters; **gradūs ferre** (*mil*) to charge; **pleno gradu** on the double; **suspenso gradu** on tiptoe
Graecē *adv* Greek, in Greek; **Graece loqui** to speak Greek; **Graece scire** to know Greek
Graeci·a -ae *f* Greece; **Magna Graecia** southern Italy
graeciss·ō -āre *vi* to ape the Greeks
graec·or -ārī -ātus sum *vi* to go Greek, act like a Greek
Graecŭl·us -a -um *adj* (*in contemptuous sense*) Greek through and through, hundred-percent Greek; *mf* Greekling, dirty little Greek
Graec·us -a -um *adj & mf* Greek; *n* Greek, Greek language
Grā·iī or **Grā·ī -ōrum** *m pl* Greeks
Grāiugĕn·a -ae *m* Greek, Greek by birth
grall·ae -ārum *f pl* stilts
grallāt·or -ōris *m* stilt walker
grām·en -ĭnis *n* grass; meadow, pasture; plant, herb
grāminĕ·us -a -um *adj* grassy, of grass; of bamboo
grammatic·us -a -um *adj* grammatical, of grammar; *m* teacher of literature and language; philologist; *f & n pl* grammar; philology
grānāri·a -ōrum *n pl* granary
grandaev·us -a -um *adj* old, aged
grandesc·ō -ĕre *vi* to grow, grow big

grandicŭl·us -a -um *adj* rather large; pretty tall
grandĭf·er -ĕra -ĕrum *adj* productive
grandilŏqu·us -ī *m* braggart
grandĭn·at -āre *v impers* it is hailing
grand·iō -īre *vt* to enlarge, increase
grand·is -e *adj* full-grown, grown up, tall; large, great; aged; important, powerful, strong; grand, lofty, dignified (*style*); loud, strong (*voice*); heavy (*debt*); dignified (*speaker*)
grandĭt·ās -ātis *f* grandeur
grand·ō -ĭnis *f* hail
grānĭf·er -ĕra -ĕrum *adj* (of ants) grain-carrying
grān·um -ī *n* grain, seed
graphĭcē *adv* masterfully
graphĭc·us -a -um *adj* masterful
graph·ĭum -ĭī or **-ī** *n* stilus
grassāt·or -ōris *m* vagabond, tramp; bully; prowler
grass·or -ārī -ātus sum *vi* to walk about, prowl around; to hang around, loiter; to go, move, proceed; (with **adversus** or **in** + *acc*) to attack, waylay
grātē *adv* willingly, with pleasure; gratefully
grātēs (*genit* not in use) *f pl* thanks, gratitude; **grates agere** (with *dat*) to thank, give thanks to; **grates habere** (with *dat*) to feel grateful to
grātĭ·a -ae *f* grace, charm, pleasantness, loveliness; influence, prestige; love, friendship; service, favor, kindness; thanks, gratitude, acknowledgment; cause, reason, motive; **cum gratia** (with *genit*) to the satisfaction of; with the approval of; **eā gratiā ut** for the reason that; **exempli gratiā** for example; **gratiā** (with *genit*) for the sake of, on account of; **gratiam facere** (with *dat* of person and *genit* of thing) to pardon (*someone*) for (*a fault*); **gratias agere** (with *dat*) to thank, give thanks to; **gratias habere** (with *dat*) to feel grateful to; **in gratiam** (with *genit*) in order to win the favor of, in order to please; **in gratiam habere** to regard (*something*) as a favor; **meā gratiā** for my sake; **quā gratiā** why
Grātĭ·ae -ārum *f pl* Graces (*Aglaia, Euphrosyne, and Thalia, daughters of Jupiter by Eurynome*)
grātificātĭ·ō -ōnis *f* kindness
grātifĭc·or -ārī -ātus sum *vt* to give up, surrender, sacrifice; *vi* (with *dat*) **a** to do (*someone*) a favor; **b** to gratify, please
grātĭīs *adv* gratis, free, for nothing, gratuitously
grātiōs·us -a -um *adj* popular, influential; obliging
grātīs *adv* gratis, free, for nothing, gratuitously
grāt·or -ārī -ātus sum *vi* to rejoice; to express gratitude; (with *dat*) to congratulate; **invicem inter se gratari** to congratulate one another
grātuītō *adv* gratuitously, gratis, for nothing; for no particular reason
grātuīt·us -a -um *adj* gratuitous, free, spontaneous; voluntary; unprovoked
grātulābund·us -a -um *adj* congratulating
grātulātĭ·ō -ōnis *f* congratulation; rejoicing, joy; public thanksgiving
grātulāt·or -ōris *m* congratulator, well-wisher
grātŭl·or -ārī -ātus sum *vi* to be glad, rejoice, manifest joy; (with *dat*) **a** to congratulate; **b** to render thanks to
grāt·us -a -um *adj* pleasing, pleasant, agreeable, welcome; thankful, grateful; deserving thanks, earning gratitude; *n* favor; **gratum facere** (with *dat*) to do (*someone*) a favor
gravanter *adv* reluctantly
gravātē *adv* with difficulty; unwillingly, grudgingly
gravātim *adv* with difficulty; unwillingly
gravēdinōs·us -a -um *adj* prone to catch colds
gravēd·ō -ĭnis *f* cold, head cold
gravesc·ō -ĕre *vi* to grow heavy; (fig) to become worse
gravidĭt·ās -ātis *f* pregnancy
gravĭd·ō -āre *vt* to impregnate
gravĭd·us -a -um *adj* loaded, filled, full; pregnant; (with *abl*) teeming with
grav·is -e *adj* heavy, weighty; burdensome; troublesome, oppressive, painful, harsh, hard, severe, unpleasant; unwholesome, indigestible; important, influential, venerable, grave, serious; pregnant; hostile; low, deep, bass; flat (*note*); harsh, bitter, offensive (*smell or taste*); impressive (*speech*); stormy (*weather*); oppressive (*heat*)
gravĭt·ās -ātis *f* weight; severity, harshness, seriousness; importance; dignity, influence; pregnancy; violence, vehemence
gravĭter *adv* heavily, ponderously; hard, violently, vehemently; severely, harshly, unpleasantly, disagreeably; sadly, sorrowfully; with dignity, with propriety, with authority; (to feel) deeply; (to smell) offensive, strong; (to speak) impressively; **graviter ferre** to take (*something*) hard
grav·ō -āre *vt* to weigh down, load, load down; to burden, be oppressive to; to aggravate; to increase
grav·or -ārī -ātus sum *vt* to feel annoyed at, object to, refuse, decline; to bear with reluctance, regard as a burden; *vi* to feel annoyed, be vexed
gregāl·is -e *adj* of the herd or flock; common; **sagulum gregale** uni-

form of a private; *m pl* comrades, companions

gregāri·us -a -um *adj* common; (mil) of the same rank; **miles gregarius** private

gregātim *adv* in flocks, in herds, in crowds

grem·ium -iī or **-ī** *n* lap, bosom; womb

gressus *pp* of **gradior**

gress·us -ūs *m* step; course, way

gre·x -gis *m* flock, herd; swarm; company, group, crowd, troop, set, clique, gang; theatrical cast

gruis see **grus**

grunn·iō or **grund·iō -īre -īvī** or **-iī -ītum** *vi* to grunt

grunnīt·us -ūs *m* grunt, grunting

grū·s or **gru·is -is** *m* or *f* crane

grȳ (indecl) *n* scrap, crumb

gryps grȳpis *m* griffin

gubernācŭl·um or **gubernācl·um -ī** *n* rudder, tiller, helm; *n pl* (fig) helm

gubernāti·ō -ōnis *f* navigation

gubernāt·or -ōris *m* navigator, pilot; governor

gubernātr·ix -īcis *f* directress

gubern·ō -āre *vt* to navigate, pilot; to direct, govern

gul·a -ae *f* gullet, throat; palate, appetite, gluttony

gulōs·us -a -um *adj* appetizing, dainty

gurg·es -ĭtis *m* abyss, gulf, whirlpool; waters, flood, depths, sea; spendthrift

gurguli·ō -ōnis *m* gullet, windpipe

gurgust·ium -iī or **-ī** *n* dark hovel; (fig) hole in the wall

gustātōr·ium -iī or **-ī** *n* appetizer

gustāt·us -ūs *m* sense of taste; flavor, taste

gust·ō -āre *vt* to taste; (fig) to enjoy; to overhear; *vi* to have a snack

gust·us -ūs *m* tasting; appetizer

gutt·a -ae *f* drop; spot, speck

guttātim *adv* drop by drop

guttŭl·a -ae *f* tiny drop

gutt·ur -ŭris *n* gullet, throat, neck; *n pl* throat, neck

gūt·us or **gutt·us -ī** *m* cruet, flask

Gy·ās -ae *m* hundred-armed giant

Gȳg·ēs -is or **-ae** *m* king of Lydia (716-678 B.C.)

gymnasiarch·us -ī *m* manager of a gymnasium

gymnas·ium -iī or **-ī** *n* gymnasium

gymnastic·us -a -um *adj* gymnastic

gymnic·us -a -um *adj* gymnastic

gymnosophist·ae -ārum *m pl* Hindu Stoics

gynaecē·um or **gynaecī·um -ī** *n* women's apartments

gypsāt·us -a -um *adj* covered with plaster

gyps·um -ī *n* gypsum, plaster

gȳr·us -ī *m* circle, cycle, ring, orbit, course

H

ha, hahae, hahahae *interj* expression of joy, satisfaction, or laughter

habēn·a -ae *f* strap; *f pl* reins; (fig) reins, control; **habenae rerum** reins of the state; **habenas adducere, dare, effundere,** or **immittere** (with *dat*) to give free rein to

hab·ĕō -ēre -ŭī -ĭtum *vt* to have, hold, keep; to retain, detain; to contain; to possess, own; to wear; to treat, handle, use; to hold, conduct (*meeting*); to deliver (*speech*); to occupy, inhabit; to pronounce, utter (*words*); to hold, manage, govern, wield; to hold, think, consider, believe; to occupy, engage, busy; to occasion, produce, render; to know, be informed of, be acquainted with; to take, accept, endure, bear; **in animo habere** to have on one's mind; **in animo habere** (with *inf*) to intend to; **pro certo habere** to regard as certain; **secum** or **sibi habere** to keep (*something*) to oneself, keep secret; **se habere** (with *adv*) to be,feel (*well, etc.*); *vi* **bene habet** it is well, all is well; **sic habet** that's how it is

habĭl·is -e *adj* handy; suitable, convenient; active, nimble; skillful

habilĭt·ās -ātis *f* aptitude

habitābĭl·is -e *adj* habitable, fit to live in

habitāti·ō -ōnis *f* dwelling, house

habitāt·or -ōris *m* inhabitant, tenant

habĭt·ō -āre *vt* to inhabit; *vi* to dwell, live, stay, reside; (with **in** + *abl*) **a** to live in, reside at; **b** to be always in (*a certain place*); **c** (fig) to dwell upon

habitūd·ō -ĭnis *f* condition, appearance

habĭt·us -a -um *adj* well-kept, fat, stout

habĭt·us -ūs *m* condition (*of the body*); character, quality; style, style of dress, attire; disposition, state of feeling; habit

hāc *adv* this way, in this way

hactĕnus *adv* to this place, thus far; up till now, hitherto, so far; to this extent, so far, so much

Hadri·a -ae *f* city in Picenum, the birthplace of Hadrian; city in the country of the Veneti, on the coast of the sea named after it; *m* Adriatic Sea

Hadriān·us -ī *m* Hadrian (*Roman emperor,* 117-138 A.D.)
haec hōrum (*neut pl* of **hoc**) *adj & pron* these
haec hūjus (older form; **haece;** *genit:* **hujusce**) (*fem* of **hic**) *adj* this; the present, the actual; the latter; (occasionally) the former; **haec . . . haec** one . . . another; *pron* this one, she; the latter; (occasionally) the former; **haec . . . haec** one . . . another one; **haecine** (**haec** with *interrog* enclitic **-ne**) is this . . .?
haece see **haec**
haecĭne see **haec**
Haed·ī -ōrum *m pl* pair of stars in the constellation Auriga
haedilĭ·a -ae *f* little kid
haedill·us -ī *m* (term of endearment) little kid or goat
haedīn·us -a -um *adj* kid's, goat's
haedŭl·us -ī *m* little kid, little goat
haed·us -ī *m* young goat, kid
Haemonĭ·a -ae *f* Thessaly
Haem·us or **Haem·os -ī** *m* mountain range in Thrace
haerĕō haerēre haesī haesum *vi* to cling, stick; to hang around, linger, stay, remain fixed, remain in place; to be rooted to the spot, come to a standstill, stop; to be embarrassed, be at a loss, hesitate, be in doubt; (with *dat* or *abl* or with **in** + *abl*) **a** to cling to, stick to, adhere to, be attached to; **b** to loiter in, hang around in, waste time in (*a place*) or at (*an activity*); **c** to adhere to, stick by (*an opinion, purpose*); **d** to gaze upon; **e** to keep close to; **in terga, in tergis,** or **tergis hostium haerere** to pursue the enemy closely
haeresc·ō -ĕre *vi* to adhere
haerĕs·is -is *f* sect, school of thought
haesitābund·us -a -um *adj* hesitating, faltering
haesitantĭ·a -ae *f* stammering
haesitātĭ·ō -ōnis *f* hesitation, indecision; stammering
haesitāt·or -ōris *m* hesitator
haesĭt·ō -āre *vi* to get stuck; to stammer; to hesitate, be undecided, be at a loss
hahae hahahae *interj* expression of joy, satisfaction, or laughter
halagŏra -ae *f* salt market
hāl·ans -antis *adj* fragrant
hāl·ēc -ēcis *n* fish sauce
haliaeĕt·os -ī *m* sea eagle, osprey
hālĭt·us -ūs *m* breath; steam, vapor
hall·ex -ĭcis *m* big toe
hallūcĭn·or or **hālūcĭn·or -ārī -ātus sum** *vi* to daydream, have hallucinations, talk wildly
hāl·ō -āre *vt* to exhale; *vi* to exhale; to be fragrant
halophant·a -ae *m* scoundrel
hālūcinor see **hallucinor**
ham·a or **am·a -ae** *f* bucket, pail
Hamādrў·as -ădis *f* wood nymph
hāmātĭl·is -e *adj* with hooks
hāmāt·us -a -um *adj* hooked, hook-shaped
Hamĭlc·ar -ăris *m* famous Carthaginian general in the First Punic War, surnamed Barca, and father of Hannibal (*d.* 228 B.C.)
hāmiōt·a -ae *m* angler
hāmŭl·us -ī *m* small hook
hām·us -ī *m* hook, fishhook
Hannĭb·al -ălis *m* son of Hamilcar Barca and famous general in the Second Punic War (246-172 B.C.)
har·a -ae *f* pen, coop, stye
harēn·a -ae *f* sand; seashore, beach; arena; *f pl* desert
harēnōs·us -a -um *adj* sandy
hariŏl·or -ārī -ātus sum *vi* to foretell the future; to talk gibberish
hariŏl·us -ī *m* or **hariŏl·a -ae** *f* soothsayer
harmonĭ·a -ae *f* harmony
harpăg·ō -āre *vt* to steal
harpăg·ō -ōnis *m* hook, harpoon, grappling hook; greedy person
Harpalўc·ē -ēs *f* daughter of a Thracian king, brought up as a warrior
harp·ē -ēs *f* scimitar
Harpўĭ·ae -ārum *f pl* Harpies (*mythical monsters, half woman, half bird*)
harundĭf·er -ĕra -ĕrum *adj* reed-bearing
harundinĕ·us -a -um *adj* made of reed
harundinōs·us -a -um *adj* overgrown with reeds
harund·ō -ĭnis *f* reed, cane; fishing rod; pen; shepherd's pipe; arrow shaft, arrow; fowler's rod; weaver's comb; hobbyhorse (*toy*)
harusp·ex -ĭcis *m* soothsayer who foretold the future from the inspection of the vital organs of animals; prophet
haruspĭc·a -ae *f* soothsayer (*female*)
haruspicīn·us -a -um *adj* of divination; *f* art of divination
haruspic·ium -iī or **-ī** *n* divination
Hasdrŭb·al or **Asdrŭb·al -ălis** *m* brother of Hannibal (*d.* 207 B.C.); son-in-law of Hamilcar Barca (*d.* 221 B.C.)
hast·a -ae *f* spear; **sub hasta vendere** to sell at auction, auction off
hastāt·us -a -um *adj* armed with a spear; *m pl* soldiers in first line of a Roman battle formation
hastīl·e -is *n* shaft; spear, javelin
hau or **au** *interj* cry of pain or grief
haud or **haut** or **hau** *adv* not, hardly, not at all, by no means
hauddum *adv* not yet
haudquāquam *adv* not at all, by no means
haurĭō haurīre hausī haustum *vt* to draw, draw up, draw out; to drain, drink up; to spill, shed; to swallow, devour, consume, exhaust; to derive; (fig) to drink in, seize upon, imbibe
haustr·um -ī *n* scoop, bucket

haustus *pp* of **haurio**
haust·us -ūs *m* drawing (*of water*); drinking, swallowing; drink, draught; handful; stream (*of blood*)
haut see **haud**
havĕō see **aveo**
hebdŏm·as -ădis *f* week
Hēb·ē -ēs *f* goddess of youth, daughter of Juno, and cupbearer of the gods
hebĕn·us -ī *f* ebony
heb·ĕō -ēre *vi* to be blunt, be dull; (fig) to be inactive, be sluggish
heb·es -ĕtis *adj* blunt, dull; faint, dim; dull, obtuse, stupid
hebesc·ō -ĕre *vi* to grow blunt, grow dull; to become faint or dim; to lose vigor
hebĕt·ō -āre *vt* to blunt, dull, dim
Hebr·us -ī *m* principal river in Thrace
Hecăt·ē -ēs *f* goddess of magic and witchcraft and often identified with Diana
hecatomb·ē -ēs *f* hecatomb
Hect·or -ŏris *m* son of Priam and Hecuba, husband of Andromache, and bravest Trojan warrior in fighting the Greeks
Hecŭb·a -ae or **Hecŭb·ē -ēs** *f* wife of Priam who, after the destruction of Troy, became a captive of the Greeks and was eventually changed into a dog
hedĕr·a -ae *f* ivy
hederĭg·er -ĕra -ĕrum *adj* wearing ivy
hederōs·us -a -um *adj* overgrown with ivy
hēdȳchr·um -ī *n* perfume
hei hēia see **ei, ēia**
Helĕn·a -ae or **Helĕn·ē -ēs** *f* Helen (*wife of Menelaus, sister of Clytemnestra, Castor, and Pollux, who was abducted by Paris*)
Helĕn·us -ī *m* prophetic son of Priam and Hecuba
Hēliăd·es -um *f pl* daughters of Helios and sisters of Phaëthon, who were changed into poplars and whose tears were changed to amber
Helĭc·ē -ēs *f* Big Bear (*constellation*)
Helĭc·ōn -ōnis *m* mountain in Boeotia sacred to the Muses and to Apollo
Helicōniăd·es or **Helicōnĭd·es -um** *f pl* Muses
Hell·as -ădis *f* Greece
Hell·ē -ēs *f* daughter of Athamas and Nephele who, while riding the golden-fleeced ram, fell into the Hellespont and drowned
hellĕbor- = **ellebor-**
Hellespont·us -ī *m* Dardanelles
hellŭ·ō -ōnis *m* glutton, squanderer
hellŭ·or -ārī -ātus sum *vi* to be a glutton
hel·ops or **el·ops** or **ell·ops -ŏpis** *m* highly-prized fish (*perhaps the sturgeon*)
helvell·a -ae *f* delicious herb
Helvētĭ·ī -ōrum *m pl* people of Gallia Lugdunensis (*modern Switzerland*)
helv·us -a -um *adj* light-bay
hem *interj* (expression of surprise) well!
hēmerodrŏm·us -ī *m* courier
hēmicill·us -ī *m* mule
hēmicycl·ĭum -ĭī or **-ī** *n* semicircle of seats
hēmīn·a -ae *f* half of a sextarius (*half a pint*)
hendecasyllăb·ī -ōrum *m pl* hendecasyllabics (*verses with eleven syllables*)
hēpatārĭ·us -a -um *adj* of the liver
heptēr·is -is *f* galley with seven banks of oars
hera see **era**
Hēr·a -ae *f* Greek goddess identified with Juno
Hēraclīt·us -ī *m* early Greek philosopher of Ephesus who believed that fire was the primary element of all matter (*fl* 513 B.C.)
herb·a -ae *f* blade, stalk; herb, plant; grass, lawn; weed
herbesc·ō -ĕre *vi* to sprout
herbĕ·us -a -um *adj* grass-green
herbĭd·us -a -um *adj* grassy
herbĭf·er -ĕra -ĕrum *adj* grassy, grass-producing; made of herbs
herbōs·us -a -um *adj* grassy; made with herbs
herbŭl·a -ae *f* little herb
hercisc·ō -ĕre *vi* to divide an inheritance
herct·um or **erct·um -ī** *n* inheritance
Herculānĕ·um -ī *n* town on the seacoast of Campania which was destroyed with Pompeii in an eruption of Vesuvius in 79 A.D.
Hercŭl·ēs -is or **-ī** *m* son of Jupiter and Alcmena, husband of Deianira, and after his death and deification, husband of Hebe
hercŭlēs or **hercŭle** or **hercle** *interj* by Hercules!
here *adv* yesterday
hērēditārĭ·us -a -um *adj* of or about an inheritance; inherited, hereditary
hērēdĭt·ās -ātis *f* inheritance
hērēd·ĭum -ĭī or **-ī** *n* inherited estate
hēr·ēs -ēdis *m* heir; (fig) heir, successor; *f* heiress
herī or **here** *adv* yesterday
herif- herīl- = **erif- eril-**
Hermāphrodīt·us -ī *m* son of Hermes and Aphrodite who combined with the nymph Salmacis to become one person
Herm·ēs or **Herm·a -ae** *m* Greek god identified with Mercury
Hermiŏn·ē -ēs or **Hermiŏn·a -ae** *f* daughter of Helen and Menelaus and wife of Orestes
Hērodŏt·us -ī *m* father of Greek history, born at Halicarnassus on coast of Asia Minor (484-425 B.C.)

hērōic·us -a -um *adj* heroic, epic
hērōīn·a -ae *f* demigoddess
hērō·is -ĭdis *f* demigoddess
hēr·ōs -ōis *m* demigod, hero (*rarely used of men born of human parents*)
hērō·us -a -um *adj* heroic, epic
herus see **erus**
Hēsiŏd·us -ī *m* Hesiod (*early Greek poet, born in Boeotia, 8th cent.* B.C.)
Hēsiŏn·ē -ēs or **Hēsiŏn·a -ae** *f* daughter of Laomedon, king of Troy, whom Hercules rescued from a sea monster
Hespĕr·us or **Hespĕr·os -ī** *m* evening star
hestern·us -a -um *adj* yesterday's
hetairī·a -ae *f* secret society
hetairĭc·ē -ēs *f* Macedonian mounted guard
heu! *interj* (expression of pain or dismay) oh!, ah!
heus! *interj* (to draw attention) say there!, hey!
hexamĕt·er -rī *m* hexameter verse
hexēr·is -is *f* ship with six banks of oars
hiāt·us -ūs *m* opening; open or gaping mouth; mouthing, bluster; basin (*of fountain*); chasm; (gram) hiatus
Hibēr·es -um *m pl* Spaniards
hibern·a -ōrum *n pl* winter quarters
hībernācŭl·a -ōrum *n pl* winter bivouac; winter residence
hībern·ō -āre *vi* to spend the winter; to stay in winter quarters; (fig) to hibernate
hībern·us -a -um *adj* winter, in winter, wintry
hibisc·um -ī *n* hibiscus
hibrĭd·a or **hybrĭd·a -ae** *m* or *f* hybrid, mongrel, half-breed
hīc (or hĭc) hūjus (older form: **hīce hūjusce**) *adj* this; the present, the actual; the latter; (occasionally) the former; **hic . . . hic** one . . . another; *pron* this one, he; this man, myself, your's truly (*i.e., the speaker or writer*); the latter; (occasionally) the former; (in court) the defendant, my defendant; **hic . . . hic** one . . . another; **hicine** (**hic** with *interrog* enclitic **-ne**) is this . . . ?
hīc *adv* here, in this place; at this point; in this affair, in this particular, herein
hīce see **hic**
hīcine see **hic**
hiemāl·is -e *adj* winter, wintry; stormy
hiĕm·ō -āre *vi* to spend the winter, pass the winter; to be wintry, be cold, be stormy
hiem·s or **hiem·ps -is** *f* winter; cold; storm
Hiĕr·ō -ōnis *m* ruler of Syracuse and patron of philosophers and poets (?-466 B.C.); friend of the Romans in the First Punic War (306?-215 B.C.)
Hierosolȳm·a ōrum *m pl* Jerusalem
hiĕt·ō -āre *vi* to keep yawing
hilăre *adv* cheerfully, merrily, gaily
hilăr·is -e or **hilăr·us -a -um** adj cheerful, merry, gay
hilarĭt·ās -ātis *f* cheerfulness, gaiety
hilaritūd·ō -ĭnis *f* cheerfulness
hilăr·ō -āre *vt* to cheer up
hilarŭl·us -a -um *adj* merry little
hilărus see **hilaris**
hill·ae -ārum *f pl* smoked sausage
Hīlōt·ae or **Īlōt·ae -ārum** *m pl* Helots (*slaves of the Spartans*)
hīl·um -ī *n* something, trifle
hinc *adv* from here, from this place; on this side, here; for this reason; from this source; after this, henceforth, from now on
hinn·iō -īre *vi* to whinny, neigh
hinnīt·us -ūs *m* neighing
hinnulĕ·us -ī *m* fawn
hi·ō -āre *vt* to sing; *vi* to open, be open; to gape; to yawn; to make eyes (*in surprise or greedy longing*)
hippagōg·ī -ōrum *f pl* ships for transporting horses and cavalry
Hipparch·us -ī *m* son of Pisistratus, the tyrant of Athens, who was slain by Harmodius and Aristogiton in 514 B.C.
Hippi·ās -ae *m* son of Pisistratus, the tyrant of Athens, and tyrant of Athens himself, 527-510 B.C.
hippocentaur·us -ī *m* centaur
Hippocrăt·ēs -is *m* famous physician, founder of scientific medicine (*c.* 460-380 B.C.)
Hippocrēn·ē -ēs *f* spring on Mt. Helicon, sacred to the Muses and produced when the hoof of Pegasus hit the spot
Hippodăm·ē -ēs or **Hippodamē·a** or **Hippodamī·a -ae** *f* daughter of Oenamaus, the king of Elis, and wife of Pelops; daughter of Adrastus and wife of Pirithous
hippodrŏm·os -ī *m* racetrack
Hippolȳt·ē -ēs or **Hippolȳt·a -ae** *f* Amazonian wife of Theseus; wife of Acastus, king of Magnesia
Hippolȳt·us -ī *m* son of Theseus and Hippolyte
hippomăn·es -is *n* membrane of the head of a new-born foal; discharge of a mare in heat
Hippomĕn·ēs -ae *m* son of Megareus who competed with Atalanta in a race and won her as his bride
Hippōn·ax -actis *m* Greek satirist (*fl* 540 B.C.)
hippotoxŏt·ae -ārum *m pl* mounted archers
hippūr·us -ī *m* goldfish
hīr·a -ae *f* empty gut
hircīn·us or **hirquīn·us -a -um** *adj* goat, of a goat
hircōs·us -a -um *adj* smelling like a goat
hirc·us -ī *m* goat

hirnĕ·a -ae *f* jug
hirsūt·us -a -um *adj* hairy, shaggy, bristly; prickly; rude
Hirt·ius -iī or **-ī** *m* Aulus Hirtius (*consul in* 43 B.C. *and author of the eighth book of Caesar's Memoirs on the Gallic War*)
hirt·us -a -um *adj* hairy, shaggy; uncouth
hirūd·ō -inis *f* bloodsucker, leech
hirundinīn·us -a -um *adj* swallow's
hirund·ō -inis *f* swallow
hisc·ō -ĕre *vt* to murmur, utter; *vi* to open, gape, yawn; to open the mouth
Hispān·ī -ōrum *m pl* Spaniards
Hispāni·a -ae *f* Spain
Hispāniens·is -e *adj* Spanish
hispid·us -a -um *adj* hairy, shaggy, rough
Hist·er or **Ist·er -rī** *m* lower Danube
histori·a -ae *f* history; account, story; theme (*of a story*)
historic·us -a -um *adj* historical; *m* historian
histric·us -a -um *adj* theatrical
histri·ō -ōnis *m* actor
histriōnāl·is -e *adj* theatrical; histrionic
histriōni·a -ae *f* dramatics, art of acting
hiulcē *adv* with frequent hiatus
hiulc·ō -āre *vt* to split open
hiulc·us -a -um *adj* split, split open; open, gaping; with hiatus
hōc hūjus (older form: **hōce;** *genit:* **hūjusce)** (*neut* of **hic**); *adj* this; the present, the actual; the latter; (occasionally) the former; *pron* this one, it; the latter; (occasionally) the former; (with *genit*) this amount of, this degree of, so much; **hoc erat quod** this was the reason why; **hoc est** that is, I mean, namely; **hocine** (**hoc** with *interrog* enclitic **-ne**) is this . . . ?; **hoc facilius** all the more easily
hōce see **hoc**
hōcine see **hoc**
hodiē *adv* today; now, nowadays; still, to the present; at once, immediately; **hodie mane** this morning; **numquam hodie** (coll) never at all, never in the world
hodiern·us -a -um *adj* today's; **hodiernus dies** this day, today
holit·or -ōris *m* grocer
holitōri·us -a -um *adj* vegetable
hol·us -ĕris *n* vegetables
Homēr·us -ī *m* Homer
homicīd·a -ae *m* or *f* murderer, killer
homicīd·ium -iī or **-ī** *n* murder, manslaughter
hom·ō -inis *m* or *f* human being, man, person, mortal; mankind, human race; fellow; fellow creature; (coll) this one; *m pl* persons, people; infantry; bodies, corpses; members (*of the senate*); **inter homines esse** to be alive; to see the world
homull·us -ī or **homuci·ō -ōnis** or **homuncŭl·us -ī** *m* poor man, poor creature
honest·a -ae *f* lady
honestāment·um -ī *n* ornament
honest·ās -ātis *f* good reputation, respectability; sense of honor, respect; beauty, grace; honesty, integrity, uprightness; decency; *f pl* respectable persons, decent people
honestē *adv* honorably, respectably, decently, virtuously
honest·ō -āre *vt* to honor, dignify, embellish, grace
honest·us -a -um *adj* honored, respected; honorable, decent, respectable, virtuous; handsome; *m* gentleman; *n* virtue, good
hon·or or **hon·ōs -ōris** *m* honor, esteem; position, office, post; mark of honor, reward, acknowledgment; offering, rites (*to the gods or the dead*); beauty, grace, charm; glory, fame, reputation; **honoris causā** out of respect, with all respect
honōrābil·is -e *adj* honorable
honōrāri·us -a -um *adj* honored, respected, highly esteemed; honorary, conferring honor
honōrātē *adv* with honor, honorably
honōrāt·us -a -um *adj* honored, respected; in high office; honorable, respectable; **honoratum habere** to hold in honor
honōrificē *adv* honorably, respectfully
honōrific·us -a -um *adj* honorable, complimentary
honōr·ō -āre *vt* to honor, respect; to embellish, decorate
honōr·us -a -um *adj* honorable, complimentary
honōs see **honor**
hoplomăch·us -ī *m* gladiator
hōr·a -ae *f* hour; time; season; **in diem et horam** continually; **in horam vivere** to live from hand to mouth; **quota hora est?** what time is it?; *f pl* clock; **in horas** from hour to hour, every hour
Hor·a -ae *f* wife of Quirinus (*i.e., of deified Romulus*), called Hersilia before her death
Hōr·ae -ārum *f pl* Hours (*daughters of Jupiter and Themis and goddesses who kept watch at the gates of heaven*)
hōrae·us -a -um *adj* pickled
Horāt·ius -iī *or* **-ī** *m* Quintus Horatius Flaccus (65-8 B.C.); Horatius Cocles (*defender of the bridge across the Tiber in the war with Porsenna*)
hordĕ·um -ī *n* barley
hori·a -ae *f* fishing boat
horiŏl·a -ae *f* small fishing boat
hornō *adv* this year, during this year
hornōtin·us -a -um *adj* this year's
horn·us -a -um *adj* this year's

hōrolog·ium -iī or **-ī** *n* clock; water clock; sundial
horrend·us -a -um *adj* horrendous, horrible, terrible; awesome
horr·ens -entis *adj* bristling, bristly, shaggy
horr·ĕō -ēre -ŭī *vt* to dread; to shudder at, shrink from; to be amazed at; *vi* to stand on end, stand up straight; to get gooseflesh; to shiver, tremble, quake, shake; to look frightful, be rough
horr·escō -escĕre -ŭī *vt* to dread, become terrified at; *vi* to stand on end; (of the sea) to become rough; to begin to shake or shiver; to start (*in fear*)
horrĕ·um -ī *n* barn, shed; silo, granary; wine cellar; beehive
horribĭl·is -e *adj* horrible, terrifying; amazing
horrĭdē *adv* roughly, rudely, sternly
horridŭl·us -a -um *adj* rather shaggy; somewhat shabby; somewhat unsophisticated (*style*)
horrĭd·us -a -um *adj* bristling, bristly, shaggy, prickly; rude, uncouth, rough, rugged, wild; disheveled; blunt, unpolished, course (*manner*); frightful, frightened, awful
horrĭf·er -ĕra -ĕrum *adj* causing shudders; freezing, chilling; terrifying
horrificē *adv* awfully
horrific·ō -āre *vt* to make rough, ruffle; to terrify, appall
horrific·us -a -um *adj* frightful, terrifying
horrisŏn·us -a -um *adj* frightening (*sound*), frightening to hear
horr·or -ōris *m* bristling; shivering, shuddering, quaking; dread, horror; awe, reverence; chill; thrill
horsum *adv* this way, here
hortām·en -ĭnis *n* injunction; encouragement
hortāment·um -ī *n* encouragement
hortāti·ō -ōnis *f* exhortation, encouragement
hortāt·or -ōris *m* backer, supporter, rooter, instigator
hortāt·us -ūs *m* encouragement, cheering, cheer
Hortens·ius -iī or **-ī** *m* Quintus Hortensius (*famous orator and friendly competitor of Cicero,* 114-50 B.C.)
hort·or -ārī -ātus sum *vt* to encourage, cheer, incite, instigate; to give a pep talk to (*soldiers*)
hortŭl·us -ī *m* little garden, garden plot
hort·us -ī *m* garden; *m pl* park
hosp·es -ĭtis *m* host, entertainer; guest, visitor; friend; stranger, foreigner
hospit·a -ae *f* hostess; guest, visitor; friend; stranger, foreigner
hospitāl·is -e *adj* host's; guest's; hospitable
hospitālit·ās -ātis *f* hospitality
hospitāliter *adv* hospitably, as a guest
hospit·ium -iī or **-ī** *n* hospitality, friendship; welcome; guest room; lodging; inn
hosti·a -ae *f* victim, sacrifice
hostiāt·us -a -um *adj* bringing offerings
hostic·us -a -um *adj* hostile; foreign, strange; *n* enemy territory
hostīl·is -e *adj* enemy's, enemy, hostile
hostīliter *adv* hostilely, like an enemy
Hostīl·ius -iī or **-ī** *m* Tullus Hostilius (*third king of Rome*)
hostīment·um -ī *n* compensation, recompense
host·iō -īre *vi* to return like for like
host·is -is *m* or *f* enemy
hūc *adv* here, to this place; to this, to this point, so far; to such a pitch; for this purpose; **huc atque illuc** here and there, in different directions; **hucine?** (**huc** + *interrog* enclitic) so far?
hui! *interj* (expressing surprise or admiration) wow!
hūjusmŏdī or **hūjuscemŏdī** *adj* of this sort, such
humānē or **hūmāniter** *adv* like a man; politely, gently, with compassion
hūmānit·ās -ātis *f* human nature; mankind; kindness, compassion; courtesy; culture, refinement, civilization
hūmānitus *adv* humanly; humanely, kindly, compassionately
hūmān·us -a -um *adj* of man, human; humane, kind, compassionate; courteous; cultured, refined, civilized, well educated
humāti·ō -ōnis *f* burial
hūme- = ume-
humī *adv* on or in the ground
hūmid- = umid-
humĭl·is -e *adj* low, low-lying, low-growing; shallow; stunted; low, common, colloquial; lowly, humble, poor, obscure, insignificant; base, mean, small-minded, cheap
humilit·ās -ātis *f* lowness; lowliness, insignificance; smallness of mind, meanness, cheapness
humiliter *adv* low, deeply; meanly, abjectly
hum·ō -āre *vt* to bury
hum·us -ī *f* ground, earth; land, region, country
hyacinthin·us -a -um *adj* of the hyacinth; crimson
hyacinth·us or **hyacinth·os -ī** *m* hyacinth
Hyacinth·us or **Hyacinth·os -ī** *m* Spartan youth, who was accidently killed by his friend Apollo and from whose blood flowers of the same name sprang
Hyăd·es -um *f* Hyads (*group of sev-*

en stars in the head of the constellation Taurus whose rising with the sun was accompanied by rainy weather)
hyaen·a -ae *f* hyena
hyăl·us -ī *m* glass
Hybl·a -ae or **Hybl·ē -ēs** *f* Sicilian mountain, famous for its honey
hybrĭd·a -ae *m* or *f* hybrid, mongrel, half-breed
Hydasp·ēs -is *m* tributary of the Indus River
Hȳdr·a -ae *f* Hydra (*seven-headed dragon killed by Hercules*); Hydra or Anguis (*constellation*); fifty-headed monster at the gates of the lower world
hydraulĭc·us -a -um *adj* hydraulic
hydraul·us -ī water organ
hydrĭ·a -ae *f* jug, urn
Hydrochŏ·us -ī *m* Aquarius (*constellation*)
hydrōpĭc·us -a -um *adj* dropsical
hydr·ops -ōpis *m* dropsy
hydr·us or **hydr·os -ī** *m* serpent
Hyl·ās -ae *m* youthful companion of Hercules who was carried off by the nymphs as he was drawing water
Hyll·us or **Hūl·us -ī** *m* son of Hercules and husband of Iole
Hym·ēn -ĕnis or **Hymenae·us** or **Hymenae·os -ī** *m* Hymen (*god of marriage*); wedding ceremony; wedding; wedding song
Hymett·us or **Hymett·os -ī** *m* mountain in E. Attica, famous for its honey
Hypăn·is -is *m* river in Sarmatia (*modern Bug*)
hyperbăt·on -ī *n* (rhet) transposition of words
hyperbŏl·ē -ēs *f* hyperbole
Hyperborĕ·ī -ōrum *m pl* legendary people in the land of the midnight sun
Hyperī·ōn -ōnis *m* son of Titan and Earth, father of the Sun
Hypermestr·a -ae or **Hypermestr·ē -ēs** *f* the only one of the fifty daughters of Danaus who did not kill her husband on her wedding night
hypocaust·um or **hypocaust·on -ī** *n* sweat bath
hypodidascăl·us -ī *m* instructor
hypomnēm·a -ătis *n* memorandum, note
Hypsipȳl·ē -ēs *f* queen of Lemnos at the time of the Argonauts
Hyrcān·ī -ōrum *m pl* a people on the Caspian Sea

I

ia- = ja-
Iacch·us -ī *m* Bacchus; wine
iambē·us -a -um *adj* iambic
iamb·us -ī *m* iamb; iambic poem, iambic poetry
ianthĭn·a -ōrum *n pl* violet-colored garments
Īapĕt·us -ī *m* Titan, father of Prometheus, Epimetheus, and Atlas
Iāpȳd·es -um *m pl* Illyrian tribe
Iāp·yx -ȳgis *m* son of Daedalus who ruled in S. Italy; wind that blew from Apulia to Greece
Īas·ĭus -ĭī or **-ī** *m* son of Jupiter and Electra and brother of Dardanus
Iās·ōn -ŏnis *m* Jason (*son of Aeson, leader of the Argonauts, and husband of Medea and afterwards of Creusa*)
iasp·is -ĭdis *f* jasper
Ībēr- = Hiber-
ibi or **ibī** *adv* there, in that place; then, on that occasion; therein
ibīdem *adv* in the same place, just there; at that very moment; at the same time; in the same matter
Ib·is -is or **-ĭdis** *f* ibis (*bird sacred to the Egyptians*)
Icăr·us -ī *m* son of Daedalus, who, on his flight from Crete with his father, fell into the sea; father of Penelope
ichneum·ōn -ŏnis *m* ichneumon (*Egyptian rat that eats crocodile eggs*)
īcō īcĕre īcī ictum *vt* to hit, strike, shoot
īc·ōn -ŏnis *f* image
icterĭc·us -a -um *adj* jaundiced
ict·is -ĭdis *f* weasel
ictus *pp* of **īcō**
ict·us -ūs *m* stroke, blow, hit; cut, sting, bite, wound; range; stress, beat; **sub ictum** within range
id *adv* for that reason, therefore
id ejus (*neut* of **is**) *adj* this, that, the said, the aforesaid; *pron* it; a thing, the thing; **ad id** for that purpose; **aliquid id genus** something of that sort, something like that; **cum eo . . . ut** on condition that, with the stipulation that; **eo plus** the more; **ex eo** from that time on; as a result of that, consequently; **id consili** some sort of plan, some plan; **id quod** a thing which, the thing which; **id temporis** at that time; of that age; **in id** to that end; **in eo esse** to depend on it; **in eo esse . . . ut** to be so far gone that, to get to the point where
Īd·a -ae or **Īd·ē -ēs** *f* mountain near Troy; mountain in Crete where Jupiter was brought up
Īdal·ĭum -ĭī or **-ī** *n* city in Cyprus dear to Venus

idcircō *adv* on that account, for that reason, therefore
īdem eădem idem *adj* the same, the very same, exactly this; (often equivalent to a mere connective) also, likewise; *pron* the same one
identidem *adv* again and again, continually, habitually; now and then, at intervals
ideō *adv* therefore
idiōt·a -ae *m* uneducated person, ignorant person, layman
īdōl·on -ī *n* apparition, ghost
idōnĕē *adv* suitably
idōnĕ·us -a -um *adj* suitable, fit, proper; (with *dat* or with **ad** or **in** + *acc*) fit for, capable of, suited for, convenient for, sufficient for
Īd·ūs -ŭum *f pl* Ides (*fifteenth day of March, May, July, and October, and thirteenth of the other months; interest, debts, and tuition were often paid on the Ides*)
ie- = je-
iens euntis *pres p* of **eo**
igitur *adv* then, therefore, accordingly; (resumptive after parenthetical matter) as I was saying; (in summing up) so then, in short
ignār·us -a -um *adj* ignorant, unaware, inexperienced; unsuspecting; senseless; unknown, strange, unfamiliar; (with *genit*) unaware of, unfamiliar with
ignāvē *adv* listlessly, lazily
ignāvi·a -ae *f* listlessness, laziness; cowardice
ignāviter *adv* listlessly
ignāv·us -a -um *adj* listless, lazy, idle, inactive; relaxing; cowardly, bastardly; unproductive (*field, etc.*)
ignesc·ō -ĕre *vi* to catch fire, become inflamed, burn; (fig) to flare up
ignĕ·us -a -um *adj* of fire, on fire, fiery; red-hot, fiery
ignicŭl·us -ī *m* small fire, little flame, spark
ignĭf·er -ĕra -ĕrum *adj* fiery
ignigĕn·a -ae *m* son of fire (*epithet of Bacchus*)
ignip·ēs -ĕdis *adj* fiery-footed
ignipŏt·ens -entis *adj* lord of fire (*epithet of Vulcan*)
ign·is -is *m* fire; conflagration; watch fire, signal fire; torch; lightning, bolt of lightning; funeral pyre; star; brightness, glow, brilliancy, splendor; (fig) fire, rage, fury, love, passion; flame, sweetheart; agent of destruction, fanatic; *m pl* love poems
ignōbĭl·is -e *adj* insignificant, obscure, unknown, undistinguished; low-born, ignoble
ignōbilĭt·ās -ātis *f* obscurity; humble birth
ignōmini·a -ea *f* ignominy, dishonor, disgrace; **ignominiā afficere** to dishonor, disgrace; **ignominia senatūs** public censure imposed by the senate
ignōminiōs·us -a -um *adj* disgraced, degraded; disgraceful, shameful, ignominious; *m* infamous person
ignōrābĭl·is -e *adj* unknown
ignōranti·a -ae *f* ignorance
ignōrāti·ō -ōnis *f* ignorance
ignōr·ō -āre *vt* to not know, be ignorant of, be unfamiliar with; to mistake, misunderstand; to ignore, disregard, take no notice of
ignosc·ens -entis *adj* forgiving
ig·noscō -noscĕre -nōvī -nōtum *vt* (with *dat* of person and *acc* of the offense) to pardon, forgive, excuse (*someone a fault*); *vi* (with *dat*) to pardon, forgive, excuse
ignōt·us -a -um *adj* unknown, unfamiliar, strange; inglorious; unnoticed; low-born, ignoble; vulgar; ignorant
īl·ex -ĭcis *f* holm oak
Īli·a -ae *f* Rhea Silvia (*mother of Romulus and Remus*)
īl·ia -ium *n pl* guts, intestines; groin, belly
Īliăc·us -a -um *adj* Trojan
Īli·as -ădis *f* Iliad; Trojan woman
īlicet *adv* (ancient form for adjourning an assembly) let us go; all is lost, kaput; at once, immediately, instantly
īlicō *adv* on the spot, right then and there; immediately
īlign·us or **īlignĕ·us -a -um** *adj* of holm oak, oak
Īl·ios -iī or **-ī** *f* Troy
Īlīthȳi·a -ae *f* goddess who aided women in childbirth
Īl·ium -iī or **-ī** or **Īli·on -ī** *n* Troy
Īli·us -a -um *adj* Trojan
illa *adv* that way
ill·a -īus *adj fem* that; that famous; *pron* that one; she
illabefact·us -a -um *adj* unbroken, uninterrupted
il·lābor -lābī -lapsus sum *vi* to flow; to sink, fall; fall in, cave in; to slip; (with *dat* or with **ad** or **in** + *acc*) to flow into, enter into, penetrate
illabōr·ō -āre *vi* (with *dat*) to work at, work on
illāc *adv* that way
illacessīt·us -a -um *adj* unprovoked
illacrimābĭl·is -e *adj* unlamented, unwept; inexorable
illacrim·ō -āre or **illacrim·or -ārī -ātus sum** *vi* (with *dat*) to cry over
ill·aec (*acc:* **-anc**; *abl:* **-āc**) *adj fem* that; *pron* she
illaes·us -a -um *adj* unhurt, unharmed
illaetābĭl·is -e *adj* sad, melancholy
illapsus *pp* of **illabor**
illaquĕ·ō -āre *vt* to trap
illātus *pp* of **infero**
illaudāt·us -a -um *adj* without fame, obscure; detestable
ill·e -īus *adj masc* that; that famous; the former; **ille aut ille** this or

that, such and such; *pron* that one; he; the former one
illecĕbr·a -ae *f* attraction, allurement
illecebrōs·us -a -um *adj* alluring, seductive
illect·us -a -um *adj* unread
illect·us -ūs *m* allurement
illepĭdē *adv* inelegantly, rudely, impolitely
illepĭd·us -a -um *adj* inelegant, impolite, churlish
ill·ex -ĭcis *m* or *f* lure, decoy
ill·ex -ēgis *adj* lawless
illībāt·us -a -um *adj* undiminished, unimpaired
illīberāl·is -e *adj* ungenerous, stingy
illīberālĭt·ās -ātis *f* stinginess
ill·ic (*acc:* **-unc;** *abl:* **-ōc**) *adj masc* that; *pron* he
illic *adv* there, yonder, in that place; in that matter, therein
il·liciō -licĕre -lexī -lectum *vt* to allure, attract, seduce, mislead, lead astray
illicitāt·or -ōris *m* fake bidder (*one who bids at an auction to make others bid higher*)
illicĭt·us -a -um *adj* unlawful
il·līdō -līdĕre -līsī -līsum *vt* to smash to pieces, crush; (with *dat* or with **ad** or **in** + *acc*) to smash (*something*) against
illĭg·ō -āre *vt* to attach, connect; to tie, bind; to oblige; to impede, hamper
illim *adv* from there
illīm·is -e *adj* unmuddied, clear
illinc *adv* from there; on that side; **hinc illinc** from one side to another
il·lĭnō -linĕre -lēvī -lĭtum *vt* to cover; to smear; (with *dat*) to smear or spread (*something*) on
illiquefact·us -a -um *adj* melted
illīsus *pp* of **illido**
illiterāt·us -a -um *adj* uneducated, illiterate
illĭtus *pp* of **illino**
illō or **illōc** *adv* there, to that place; to that point
illōt·us -a -um *adj* unwashed, dirty
illūc *adv* to that place, in that direction; to that person, to him, to her; to that matter; to that point
ill·ūc (*acc:* **-ūc;** *abl:* **-ōc**) *adj neut* that; *pron* it
illuc·ĕō -ēre *vt* to shine on; *vi* to blaze
il·lucescō -lucescĕre -luxī *vi* to grow light, dawn, to begin to shine
ill·ud -īus *adj neut* that; the former; *pron* it
il·lūdō -lūdĕre -lūsī -lūsum *vt* to make fun of, ridicule; to waste, abuse; *vi* (with *dat*) to play around with, do mischief to
illūmĭnātē *adv* clearly
illūmĭn·ō -āre *vt* to light up, make bright, illuminate; to illustrate
illūsĭ·ō -ōnis *f* irony
illustr·is -e *adj* bright, clear, brilliant; plain, distinct, evident; distinguished, famous, illustrious, noble
illustr·ō -āre *vt* to light up, illuminate; to make clear, clear up, explain, illustrate; to adorn, embellish; to make famous
illūsus *pp* of **illudo**
illuvĭ·ēs -ēī *f* inundation; offscouring, filth, dirt
Illyrĭc·us -a -um *adj* Illyrian; *n* Illyria
Illyrĭ·us -a -um *adj* & *m* Illyrian; *f* Illyria (*country on the E. coast of the Adriatic Sea*)
Īl·us -ī *m* son of Tros, father of Laomedon, and founder of Ilium; Ascanius
imāginārĭ·us -a -um *adj* imaginary
imāginātĭōn·ēs -um *f pl* imaginings
imāgĭn·or -ārī -ātus sum *vt* to imagine
imāg·ō -ĭnis *f* image, likeness, picture, bust; bust of ancestor; ghost, vision; echo; appearance, semblance, shadow; mental picture, image, conception, thought, idea; figure of speech, simile, metaphor
imbēcillĭt·ās -ātis *f* weakness, feebleness; helplessness
imbēcillĭus *adv* more weakly, more faintly
imbēcill·us -a -um *adj* weak, feeble; helpless
imbell·is -e *adj* anti-war, pacifistic; peaceful; unfit for war, soft, cowardly; peaceful, quiet
imb·er -ris *m* rain, shower, rain storm; rain cloud; water; stream of tears; shower (*of gold, spears, etc.*)
imberb·is -e or **imberb·us -a -um** *adj* beardless
im·bĭbō -bibĕre -bĭbī *vt* to imbibe, drink in; to resolve on; **animo imbibere** to conceive, form (*e.g., an opinion*)
imbr·ex -ĭcis *f* tile
imbrĭc·us -a -um *adj* rainy
imbrĭf·er -ĕra -ĕrum *adj* rainy
im·bŭō -buĕre -bŭī -būtum *vt* to wet, soak, saturate; to stain, taint, infect, imbue, fill, steep; to instruct, train, educate
imitābĭl·is -e *adj* imitable
imitām·en -ĭnis *n* imitation; *n pl* likeness, image
imitāment·a -ōrum *n pl* pretense
imitātĭ·ō -ōnis *f* imitation; pretense
imitāt·or -ōris *m* or **imitātr·ix -īcis** *f* imitator
imitāt·us -a -um *adj* fictitious, copied
imĭt·or -ārī -ātus sum *vt* to imitate, copy, portray; to ape
immad·escō -escĕre -ŭī *vi* to become wet
immānē *adv* savagely
immān·is -e *adj* huge, enormous, monstrous; inhuman, savage, monstrous
immānĭt·ās -ātis *f* vastness, enor-

mity; savageness, cruelty, monstrousness, barbarity
immansuēt·us -a -um *adj* wild, savage
immātūrit·ās -ātis *f* overanxiousness
immātūr·us -a -um *adj* immature, unripe, premature
immedicābil·is -e *adj* incurable
immĕm·or -ŏris *adj* forgetful, forgetting; negligent
immemorābil·is -e *adj* not worth mentioning; untold
immemorāt·a -ōrum *n pl* novelties
immensit·ās -ātis *f* immensity; *f pl* immense stretches
immens·us -a -um *adj* immense, unending; *n* infinite space, infinity
immĕr·ens -entis *adj* undeserving, innocent
im·mergō -mergĕre -mersī -mersum *vt* to immerse, dip, plunge; (with **in** + *acc*) to dip (*something*) into; **se immergere** (with **in** + *acc*) **a** to plunge into; **b** to insinuate oneself into
immeritō *adv* undeservedly, innocently
immerit·us -a -um *adj* undeserving, innocent; undeserved, unmerited; **immerito meo** through no fault of mine
immersābil·is -e *adj* unsinkable
immersus *pp* of **immergo**
immētāt·us -a -um *adj* unmeasured
immigr·ō -āre *vi* to immigrate; (with **in** + *acc*) **a** to move into; **b** (fig) to invade
immin·ĕō -ēre *vi* to project, stick out; to be near, be imminent, be near at hand; to threaten, menace; (with *dat*) **a** to jut out over; **b** to look out over, overlook (*a view*); **c** to hover over, loom over, threaten; (with *dat* or **in** + *acc*) to be intent on, be eager for
immin·ŭō -uĕre -ŭī -ūtum *vt* to lessen, curtail; to weaken, impair; to infringe upon, encroach upon, violate, subvert, destroy
imminūtī·ō -ōnis *f* lessening; mutilation; understatement
im·miscĕō -miscēre -miscŭī -mixtum *vt* to mix in, intermix, blend; (fig) to mix up, confound; **immisceri** or **se immiscere** (with *dat*) **a** to join, join in with, mingle with, get lost in (*e.g., a crowd*); **b** to blend with, disappear in (*e.g., night, cloud, etc.*); **manūs manibus immiscere** (of boxers) to mix it up
immiserābil·is -e *adj* unpitied
immisericorditer *adv* unmercifully
immisericor·s -dis *adj* merciless, pitiless
immissī·ō -ōnis *f* letting grow, letting alone
immissus *pp* of **immitto**
immīt·is -e *adj* unripe, sour, green; rude, harsh, stern, severe; pitiless, inexorable
im·mittō -mittĕre -mīsī -missum *vt* to insert; to let in, let go in, admit; let go of, let drop; to let go, let fly, launch; to set on, incite, egg on; **immitti** or **se immittere** (with *dat* or **in** + *acc*) **a** to plunge or dive into; **b** to rush against, attack; **in terram immittere** to ground
immixtus *pp* of **immisceo**
immo or **immō** *adv* (in contradiction or correction of preceding words) no, on the contrary, or rather; (in confirmation of preceding words) quite so, yes indeed; **immo vero** yes and in fact
immōbil·is -e *adj* motionless, unshaken; immovable; clumsy
immoderātē *adv* without limit; immoderately, extravagantly
immoderātī·ō -ōnis *f* lack of moderation, excess
immoderāt·us -a -um *adj* unmeasured, limitless; immoderate, uncontrolled, excessive
immodestē *adv* immoderately, shamelessly
immodesti·a -ae *f* excesses; insubordination
immodest·us -a -um *adj* immoderate, uncontrolled
immodicē *adv* excessively
immodic·us -a -um *adj* huge, enormous; immoderate, excessive; (with *genit* or *abl*) given to, excessive in
immodulāt·us -a -um *adj* unrhythmical
immolātī·ō -ōnis *f* sacrifice
immolāt·or -ōris *m* sacrificer
immōlīt·us -a -um *adj* constructed, erected; *n pl* buildings
immŏl·ō or **inmŏl·ō -āre** *vt* to immolate, sacrifice, offer
im·morior -mŏrī -mortŭus sum *vi* (with *dat*) to die in, die upon; (fig) to get sick over
immŏr·or -ārī -ātus sum *vi* (with *dat*) to dwell upon
immors·us -a -um *adj* bitten into; excited
immortāl·is -e *adj* immortal
immortālit·ās -ātis *f* immortality
immortāliter *adv* infinitely
immortŭus *pp* of **immorior**
immōt·us -a -um *adj* unmoved, immovable; unshaken, undisturbed, steadfast
immūg·iō -īre -īvī or **-iī -ītum** *vi* to bellow, roar
immulg·ĕō -ēre *vt* to milk
immunditi·a -ae *f* dirtiness, filth
immund·us -a -um *adj* dirty, filthy, foul
immūn·iō -īre -īvī *vt* to reinforce, fortify
immūn·is -e *adj* without duty or office; tax-exempt, free, exempt; pure, innocent; (with *abl* or **ab** + *abl*) free from, exempt from; (with *genit*) free of, free from, devoid of, without

immūnit·ās -ātis *f* immunity, exemption, exemption from taxes
immūnīt·us -a -um *adj* unfortified, undefended; unpaved (*street*)
immurmŭr·ō -āre *vi* to grumble; (with *dat*) (of the wind) to whisper among
immūtābĭl·is -e *adj* immutable, unchangeable
immūtābilĭt·ās -ātis *f* immutability
immūtātĭ·ō -ōnis *f* exchange, substitution; metonymy
immūtāt·us -a -um *adj* unchanged
immūt·ō -āre *vt* to change, alter; to substitute
impācāt·us -a -um *adj* restless; aggressive
impactus *pp* of **impingo**
impall·escō -escĕre -ŭī *vi* (with *abl*) to turn pale at
im·pār -āris *adj* uneven, odd (*numbers*); uneven (*in size or length*); not matching, unlike (*in color or appearance*); unequal; unfair; ill-matched; uneven, crooked; (with *dat*) not a match for, inferior to, unable to cope with
imparāt·us -a -um *adj* unprepared
impărĭter *adv* unequally
impast·us -a -um *adj* unfed, hungry
impatĭ·ens -entis *adj* impatient; (with *genit*) unable to stand, endure, tolerate
impatienter *adv* impatiently; intolerably
impatientĭ·a -ae *f* impatience; (with *genit*) inability to stand or endure
impavĭdē *adv* fearlessly
impavĭd·us -a -um *adj* fearless, dauntless
impedīment·um -ī *n* impediment, hindrance; difficulty; *n pl* baggage, luggage; mule train
imped·iō -īre -īvī or **-iī -ītum** *vt* to entangle; to hamper, hinder; to entwine, encircle; to clasp, embrace; to block up (*road*); to hinder, prevent; to embarrass; **impedire** (with **ne, quin,** or **quominus**) to prevent (*someone*) from
impedītĭ·ō -ōnis *f* obstacle, obstruction
impedīt·us -a -um *adj* hampered; obstructed, blocked; difficult, intricate; impassable; busy, occupied
im·pellō -pellĕre -pŭlī -pulsum *vt* to strike against, strike, reach; to push, drive, drive forward, impel, propel; to urge, persuade, stimulate, induce; to force, compel; to put to rout; to swell (*sails*)
impend·ĕō -ēre *vi* to be near, be at hand, be imminent, threaten; (with *dat*) to hang over; (with *dat* or **in** + *acc*) to hover or loom over, threaten
impendiōs·us -a -um *adj* extravagant
impend·ium -iī or **-ī** *n* expense, cost, outlay; interest (*paid out*); loss
im·pendō -pendĕre -pendī -pensum *vt* to weigh out, pay out; to expend, devote, apply, employ; (with **in** + *acc*) **a** to spend (*money*) on; **b** to expend (*effort*) on, pay (*attention*) to
impenetrābĭl·is -e *adj* impenetrable
impens·a -ae *f* expense, cost, outlay; waste; contribution; **meis impensis** at my expense
impensē *adv* at a high cost, expensively; with great effort
impens·us -a -um *pp* of **impendo;** *adj* high, costly, expensive; strong, vehement, earnest; *n* high price
impĕr·ans -antis *m* master, ruler, conqueror
imperāt·or -ōris *m* commander, general; commander in chief; emperor; director, master, ruler, leader
imperātōrĭ·us -a -um *adj* of a general, general's; imperial
imperātr·ix -īcis *f* controller, mistress
imperāt·um -ī *n* command, order
impercept·us -a -um *adj* unperceived, unknown
impercuss·us -a -um *adj* noiseless
imperdĭt·us -a -um *adj* unscathed
imperfect·us -a -um *adj* unfinished, imperfect
imperfoss·us -a -um *adj* unpierced, not stabbed
imperiōs·us -a -um *adj* imperial; magisterial; tyrannical, overbearing, domineering, imperious
imperītē *adv* unskillfully, clumsily, ignorantly
imperītĭ·a -ae *f* inexperience, awkwardness, ignorance
imperĭt·ō -āre *vt & vi* to command, rule, govern
imperīt·us -a -um *adj* inexperienced, unfamiliar, ignorant, unskilled; (with *genit*) inexperienced in, unacquainted with, ignorant of
imper·ium -iī or **-ī** *n* command, order; right to command; exercise of authority; military commission, supreme command; mastery, sovereignty; realm, empire, dominion, supremacy, authority; public office, magistracy; term of office
imperjūrāt·us -a -um *adj* sacrosanct, inviolable
impermiss·us -a -um *adj* forbidden, unlawful
impĕr·ō -āre *vt* to requisition, give orders for, order, demand; (with *acc* of thing demanded and *dat* of source demanded from) to demand (*e.g., hostages*) from; *vi* to be in command, rule, be master; (with *dat*) to give orders to, order, command, govern, master
imperterrĭt·us -a -um *adj* undaunted, unterrified
impert·iō -īre *vt* (with *dat*) to impart, communicate, bestow, assign, direct (*something*) to, share (*something*) with; (with *acc* of person and *abl* of thing) to present (*someone*) with

imperturbāt•us -a -um *adj* unperturbed, unruffled
impervi•us -a -um *adj* impassable; (with *dat*) impervious to
impetibĭl•is -e *adj* intolerable
impĕt•ō -ĕre *vt* to make for; to attack
impetrābĭl•is -e *adj* obtainable; successful
impetrāti•ō -ōnis *f* obtaining, procurement
impetr•iō -īre *vt* to try to obtain through favorable omens
impĕtr•ō -āre *vt* to obtain, procure (*by asking*); to achieve, accomplish, bring to pass
impĕt•us -ūs *m* attack, assault; rush; impetus, impetuosity, vehemence, vigor, violence, fury, force; impulse, passion
impex•us -a -um *adj* uncombed; unpolished
impiē *adv* wickedly
impiĕt•ās -ātis *f* impiety, irreverence; disloyalty; treason
impĭg•er -ra -rum *adj* diligent, active, energetic
impĭgrē *adv* energetically, actively, quickly
impigrĭt•ās -ātis *f* energy, activity
im•pingō -pingĕre -pēgī -pactum *vt* (with *dat* or **in** + *acc*) **a** to fasten to; **b** to pin against, force against, dash against; **c** to press or force (*something*) on; **d** to fling at
impĭ•ō -āre *vt* to make irreverent
impĭ•us -a -um *adj* impious, irreverent; disobedient, undutiful; disloyal, unpatriotic; wicked, unscrupulous, shameless
implācābĭl•is -e *adj* implacable, unappeasable
implācāt•us -a -um *adj* unappeased, unsatisfied
implācĭd•us -a -um *adj* fierce, savage
impl•ĕō -ēre -ēvī -ētum *vt* to fill up; to satisfy; to fatten; to impregnate, make pregnant; to enrich; to cover with writing, fill up (*a book*); to discharge, fulfill, execute, implement; to complete, finish, end; to spend (*time*)
implex•us -a -um *adj* enfolded, entwined; involved
implicāti•ō -ōnis *f* entanglement; incorporation; embarrassment
implicāt•us -a -um *adj* entangled, involved, complicated, confused
impliciscor -ī *vi* to become confused
implicĭtē *adv* intricately
implicĭtus *pp* of **implico**; *adj* confused, confounded; **implicitus morbo** disabled by sickness, sick
implĭc•ō -āre -āvī -ātum or **-āre -ŭī -ĭtum** *vt* to entangle, involve, enfold, envelop; to embrace, clasp, grasp; to connect, unite, join; to involve, implicate, engage; to embarrass; **se dextrae implicare** to embrace, shake hands
implōrāti•ō -ōnis *f* begging, imploring
implōr•ō -āre *vt* to implore, appeal to, call upon for aid; (with double *acc*) to beg (*someone*) for; (with **ab** + *abl*) to ask for (*something*) from
implūm•is -e *adj* without feathers, unfledged
impl•ŭō -uĕre -ŭī -ūtum *vi* (with *dat*) to rain on
impluviāt•us -a -um *adj* shaped like an impluvium, square
impluv•ium -iī or **-ī** *n* skylight, impluvium (*opening in the roof of the atrium of the Roman house to get rid of smoke and let in light*); built-in basin in the atrium to catch the rain water; uncovered space in the atrium
impolītē *adv* simply, without fancy words
impolīt•us -a -um *adj* unpolished, rough; unrefined, inelegant; unfinished
impollūt•us -a -um *adj* unsullied
im•pōnō -pōnĕre -posŭī -posĭtum or **-postum** *vt* to impose; to establish, introduce; to place, set; to inflict, impose, dictate; to assign; to apply, give; to impose, assess, exact; to put (*someone*) in charge; (with *dat*, with **in** + *acc*, **in** + *abl*, or **supra** + *acc*) to place, put, set, lay (*someone or something*) on or in; (with *dat*) **a** to impose (*taxes, etc.*) upon; **b** to put (*someone*) in charge of; *vi* (with *dat*) to impose upon, trick, cheat
import•ō -āre *vt* to bring in, import; to introduce
importūnĭt•ās -ātis *f* importunity, rudeness, insolence; unfitness
importūn•us -a -um *adj* inconvenient, unsuitable; troublesome, annoying; lacking consideration for others, rude, ruthless, churlish; stormy; ill-omened
importuōs•us -a -um *adj* without a harbor
imp•os -ŏtis *adj* without control; (with *genit*) without control of
impositus *pp* of **impono**
impossibĭl•is -e *adj* impossible
impostus *pp* of **impono**
impŏt•ens -entis *adj* impotent, powerless; having no control of oneself, wild, uncontrollable, impetuous, violent
impotenter *adv* impotently, weakly
impotenti•a -ae *f* weakness, helplessness; lack of self-control, violence, fury, passion
impraesentiārum *adv* for the present, under present circumstances
imprans•us -a -um *adj* without breakfast, fasting
imprecāti•ō -ōnis *f* imprecation, curse
imprĕc•or -ārī -ātus sum *vt* to call down (*a curse*); to invoke
impressi•ō -ōnis *f* pressure; assault, attack, charge; rhythmical beat;

emphasis; impression (*on the mind*)
impressus *pp* of **imprimo**
imprīmīs or **in prīmīs** *adv* in the first place, chiefly, especially
im·prĭmō -primĕre -pressī -pressum *vt* to press down; to impress, imprint, stamp; (fig) to impress, engrave, mark
improbātĭ·ō -ōnis *f* disapprobation, blame
imprŏbē *adv* badly, wickedly, wrongfully; recklessly; persistently
improbĭt·ās -ātis *f* wickedness, depravity; roguishness
imprŏb·ō -āre *vt* disapprove, condemn, blame, reject
improbŭl·us -a -um *adj* naughty
imprŏb·us -a -um *adj* below standard, poor, inferior, bad, shameless; rebellious, unruly; restless, indomitable, self-willed; cruel, merciless; persistent
imprōcēr·us -a -um *adj* undersized
imprōdict·us -a -um *adj* not postponed
imprompt·us -a -um *adj* slow
improperāt·us -a -um *adj* slow, deliberate
impropri·us -a -um *adj* unsuitable
improsp·er -ĕra -ĕrum *adj* unfortunate
improspĕrē *adv* unfortunately
imprōvidē *adv* without foresight, thoughtlessly
imprōvĭd·us -a -um *adj* not foreseeing, not anticipating; (with *genit*) indifferent to
imprōvīs·us -a -um *adj* unexpected; **de improviso, ex improviso** or **improviso** unexpectedly; *n pl* emergencies
imprūd·ens -entis *adj* not foreseeing, not anticipating, unsuspecting, off one's guard; inconsiderate; (with *genit*) unaware of, ignorant of, heedless of, not experienced in
imprūdenter *adv* without foresight, thoughtlessly, inconsiderately, imprudently
imprūdentĭ·a -ae *f* thoughtlessness; ignorance, imprudence
impūb·ēs -ĕris or **-is** *adj* youthful, young; innocent, chaste, celibate, virgin
impŭd·ens -entis *adj* shameless
impudenter *adv* shamelessly
impudentĭ·a -ae *f* shamelessness
impudīcitĭ·a -ae *f* immodesty, lewdness, shamelessness
impudīc·us -a -um *adj* immodest, lewd, shameless
impugnātĭ·ō -ōnis *f* assault, attack
impugn·ō -āre *vt* to assault, attack; (fig) to impugn
impulsĭ·ō -ōnis *f* pressure; impulse
impuls·or -ōris *m* instigator
impulsus *pp* of **impello**
impuls·us -ūs *m* push, pressure, impulse, shock; instigation, incitement
impūne or **inpūne** *adv* with impunity, unpunished, scot-free; safely, unscathed
impūnĭt·ās -ātis *f* impunity
impūnītē *adv* with impunity
impūnīt·us -a -um *adj* unpunished; unrestrained
impūrē *adv* impurely
impūrĭt·ās -ātis *f* impurity
impūr·us -a -um *adj* impure, unclean, filthy; (morally) impure, filthy, vile
imputāt·us -a -um *adj* unpruned, untrimmed
impŭt·ō -āre *vt* to charge to someone's account, enter in an account; (with *dat*) to charge to, ascribe to, give credit for (*something*) to, put the blame for (*something*) on
īmŭl·us -a -um *adj* cute little
īm·us -a -um *adj* deepest, lowest; last; the bottom of, the foot of, the tip of; *n* bottom, depth; **ab imo** utterly; **ab imo ad summum** from top to bottom; **ex imo** utterly, completely; *n pl* lower world
in *prep* (with *abl*) in, on, upon, among, at; before; under; during, within, in, at, in the course of, on the point of, in case of, in relation to; subject to, affected by, engaged in, involved in; (with *acc*) into, up to, towards; till, to, for; in relation to, about, respecting, against; for, with a view to, according to, after
inaccess·us -a -um *adj* inaccessible
inac·escō -escĕre -ŭī *vi* to turn sour
Īnachĭd·ēs -ae *m* descendant of Inachus; Perseus; Epaphus
Īnăch·is -ĭdis *f* female descendant of Inachus (*esp. Io*)
Īnăch·us or **Īnăch·os -ī** *m* first king or Argos and father of Io
inadsc- = inasc-
inadt- = inatt-
inadust·us -a -um *adj* unburned
inaedifĭc·ō -āre *vt* to build on, build as an addition, erect, construct; to wall up, barricade; (with **in** + *abl*) to build (*something*) on top of
inaequābĭl·is -e *adj* uneven
inaequābilĭter *adv* unevenly, unequally
inaequāl·is -e *adj* uneven, unequal; unlike, changeable, inconstant
inaequālĭt·ās -ātis *f* unevenness
inaequālĭter *adv* unevenly
inaequāt·us -a -um *adj* unequal
inaequ·ō -āre *vt* to level off
inaestimābĭl·is -e *adj* inestimable; invaluable; valueless
inaestŭ·ō -āre *vi* **bilis inaestuat** anger flares up
inaffectāt·us -a -um *adj* unaffected, natural
inamābĭl·is -e *adj* hateful, revolting
inamāresc·ō -ĕre *vi* to become bitter
inambitiōs·us -um *adj* unambitious
inambulātĭ·ō -ōnis *f* walking about, strutting about

inambŭl·ō -āre *vi* to walk up and down
inamoen·us -a -um *adj* unpleasant
inānī·ae -ārum *f pl* emptiness
inānilogist·a -ae *m* chatterbox
inānīment·um -ī *n* empty space
inanim·us -a -um *adj* inanimate
inān·e -is *n* empty space, vacuum; emptiness; worthlessness
inān·is -e *adj* empty, void; deserted, abandoned, unoccupied; hollow; worthless, idle; lifeless, unsubstantial; penniless, poor; unprofitable; groundless, unfounded
inānit·ās -ātis *f* empty space, emptiness; uselessness, worthlessness
inānīter *adv* uselessly, vainly
inarāt·us -a -um *adj* untilled, fallow
in·ardescō -ardescĕre -arsī *vi* to catch fire, burn, glow
ināresc·ō -ĕre *vi* to become dry, dry up
inascens·us -a -um *adj* not climbed
inassuēt·us -a -um *adj* unaccustomed
inattenuāt·us -a -um *adj* undiminished; unappeased
inaud·ax -ācis *adj* timid, cowed
inaud·iō -īre -īvī or **-iī -ītum** *vt* to hear, learn
inaudīt·us -a -um *adj* unheard-of, unusual; without a hearing in court
inaugurātō *adv* after taking the auspices
inaugŭr·ō -āre *vt* to inaugurate, consecrate, install; *vi* to take the auspices
inaurāt·us -a -um *adj* gilded, gilt
inaur·ēs -ium *f pl* earrings
inaur·ō -āre *vt* to goldplate, gild; to line the pockets of (*someone*) with gold, to make rich
inauspicātō *adv* without consulting the auspices
inauspicāt·us -a -um *adj* undertaken without auspices; unlucky
inaus·us -a -um *adj* unattempted
inb- = imb-
inbīt·ō -ĕre *vt* enter
incaedŭ·us -a -um *adj* uncut
incal·escō -escĕre -ŭī *vi* to grow warm or hot; to get excited
incalfac·iō -ĕre *vt* to warm, heat
incallĭdē *adv* unskillfully
incallĭd·us -a -um *adj* unskillful; stupid, simple, clumsy
incand·escō -escĕre -ŭī *vi* to become white; to get white-hot
incān·escō -escĕre -ŭī *vi* to get grey
incantāt·us -a -um *adj* enchanted
incān·us -a -um *adj* grown grey
incassum *adv* in vain
incastīgāt·us -a -um *adj* unscolded, unpunished
incautē *adv* incautiously, recklessly
incaut·us -a -um *adj* incautious, inconsiderate, thoughtless, reckless; unforeseen, unexpected; unguarded
in·cēdō -cēdĕre -cessī -cessum *vi* to go, step, move, walk, stalk; to proceed, go forward; to come along, happen, occur, appear, arrive; to advance, go on
incelebrāt·us -a -um *adj* unheralded
incēnāt·us -a -um *adj* supperless
incendiār·ius -iī or **-ī** *m* agitator
incend·ium -iī or **-ī** fire; heat
in·cendō -cendĕre -cendī -censum *vt* to light, set on fire, burn; to light up, make bright; (fig) to inflame, fire, excite, enrage
incēn·is -e *adj* dinnerless, without dinner
incensi·ō -ōnis *f* burning
incensus *pp* of **incendo**
incens·us -a -um *adj* not registered (*with the censor*)
incepti·ō -ōnis *f* beginning; undertaking
incept·ō -āre *vt* to begin; to undertake
incept·or -ōris *m* beginner, originator
incept·us -a -um *pp* of **incipio**; *n* beginning; undertaking, attempt, enterprise; subject, theme
in·cernō -cernĕre -crēvī -crētum *vt* to sift
incēr·ō -āre *vt* to wax, cover with wax
incertō *adv* not for certain
incert·ō -āre *vt* to render doubtful, make uncertain
incert·us -a -um *adj* uncertain, vague, obscure; doubtful, dubious; unsure, hesitant; *n* uncertainty, insecurity; contingency; **in incertum** for an indefinite time
incess·ō -ĕre -īvī *vt* to fall upon, assault, reproach, accuse, attack; (fig) to attack
incess·us -ūs *m* walk, gait, pace; tread, trampling; invasion, attack
incestē *adv* impurely, sinfully; indecently
incest·ō -āre *vt* to pollute, defile; to violate (*a girl*)
incest·us -a -um *adj* polluted, defiled, unclean, impure, sinful; lewd, unchaste, incestuous
incest·us -ūs *m* indecency, incest
in·cĭdō -cidĕre -cidī -cāsum *vi* to happen, occur; (with **in** or **ad** + *acc*) to fall into, fall upon; (with **in** + *acc*) **a** to come upon unexpectedly, fall in with; **b** to attack; (with *dat* or **in** + *acc*) **a** to occur to (*mentally*); **b** to fall on (*a certain day*); **c** to befall; **d** to agree with
in·cīdō -cīdĕre -cīdī -cīsum *vt* to carve, engrave, inscribe; to cut, sever; (fig) to cut into, cut short, put an end to, break off, interrupt
incīl·e -is *n* ditch, trench
in·cingō -cingĕre -cinxī -cinctum *vt* to drape; to wreathe; to invest, surround
incĭn·ō -ĕre *vt* to sing; to play
incipessō see **incipisso**
in·cipiō -cipĕre -cēpī -ceptum *vt* & *vi* to begin, start

incipiss·ō -ĕre *vt* to begin
incīsē or **incīsim** *adv* in short phrases
incīsi·ō -ōnis *f* or **incīs·um -ī** *n* clause
incīsus *pp* of **incido**
incitāment·um -ī *n* incitement, incentive
incitāti·ō -ōnis *f* inciting, rousing; speed
incitātius *adv* rather impetuously
incitāt·us -a -um *adj* rapid, speedy; **equo incitato** at full gallop
incit·ō -āre *vt* to incite, urge on, spur on, drive on; to stimulate; to inspire; to stir up, arouse; to increase, augment; **currentem incitare** (fig) to spur a willing horse; **se incitare** to rush
incit·us -a -um *adj* rapid, swift; immovable; **ad incita redigere** to bring to a standstill
inclāmit·ō -āre *vt* to cry out against, abuse
inclām·ō -āre *vt* to shout at, scold, chide; *vi* to yell
inclār·escō -escĕre -ŭī *vi* to become famous
inclēm·ens -entis *adj* inclement, harsh, unmerciful
inclēmenter *adv* harshly, severely
inclēmenti·a -ae *f* harshness, severity, rigor
inclīnāti·ō -ōnis *f* leaning; inclination, tendency, bias; change; inflection
inclīnāt·us -a -um *adj* inclined, prone; sinking; low, deep
inclīn·ō -āre *vt* to bend, turn, to turn back, drive back, repulse; (fig) to divert, shift (*e.g., blame*); to change, alter; **inclinari** (mil) to fall back, give way; **inclinari** or **se inclinare** to lean, bend, turn; to change (*esp. for the worse*); *vi* to bend, turn, lean, dip, sink, (mil) to fall back, give way; (fig) to change, deteriorate; (fig) to change for the better
inclit·us -a -um *adj* famous
in·clūdō -clūdĕre -clūsī -clūsum *vt* to shut in, confine, lock up; to include, insert; to block, obstruct, shut off, stop up; (fig) to include, embrace, comprehend; to restrain, control; to close, end (*e.g., day*)
inclūsi·ō -ōnis *f* locking up, confinement
inclūt·us or **inclit·us -a -um** *adj* famous
incoct·us -a -um *pp* of **incoquo**; *adj* uncooked, raw
incōgitābil·is -e *adj* thoughtless, inconsiderate
incōgit·ans -antis *adj* unthinking, thoughtless
incōgitanti·a -ae *f* thoughtlessness
incōgitāt·us -a -um *adj* thoughtless, inconsiderate
incōgit·ō -āre *vt* to think up
incognit·us -a -um *adj* not investigated; unknown, unrecognized, unidentified; unparalleled
incohāt·us -a -um *adj* unfinished
incŏh·ō -āre *vt* to begin, start
incŏl·a -ae *m & f* inhabitant, resident
incŏl·ō -ĕre -ŭī *vt* to live in, inhabit, occupy; *vi* to live, reside
incolŭm·is -e *adj* unharmed, safe and sound, unscathed, alive; (with *abl*) safe from
incolumit·ās -ātis *f* safety
incomitāt·us -a -um *adj* unaccompanied
incommendāt·us -a -um *adj* unprotected
incommŏdē *adv* at the wrong time; inconveniently; unfortunately
incommodestic·us -a -um *adj* (coll) ill-timed, inconvenient
incommodit·ās -ātis *f* inconvenience; unsuitableness; disadvantage
incommŏd·ō -āre *vi* (with *dat*) to be inconvenient to, to be annoying to, to inconvenience
incommŏd·us -a -um *adj* inconvenient, annoying; *n* inconvenience; trouble, setback, disaster
incommūtābĭl·is -e *adj* unchangeable
incomparābĭl·is -e *adj* unequaled, incomparable
incompert·us -a -um *adj* unknown, forgotten
incompositē *adv* in disorder
incomposit·us -a -um *adj* disordered, confused, unstudied, uncouth; irregular
incomprehensibĭl·is -e *adj* incomprehensible
incompt·us -a -um *adj* unkempt, messy; primitive, rude (*discourse*)
inconcess·us -a -um *adj* forbidden, unlawful
inconcili·ō -āre *vt* to deceive, trick, to rob, fleece
inconcinn·us -a -um *adj* clumsy, awkward; absurd
inconcuss·us -a -um *adj* unshaken
inconditē *adv* confusedly
incondit·us -a -um *adj* unorganized, disorderly, confused, irregular; rough, undeveloped (*style*); raw (*jokes*)
inconsīderātē *adv* thoughtlessly
inconsīderāt·us -a -um *adj* thoughtless
inconsōlābĭl·is -e *adj* incurable
inconst·ans -antis *adj* inconsistent, fickle, shifty
inconstanter *adv* inconsistently
inconstanti·a -ae *f* inconsistency, fickleness
inconsultē *adv* indiscreetly
inconsult·us -a -um *adj* indiscreet, ill-advised, imprudent; not consulted
inconsult·us -ūs *m* **inconsultu meo** without consulting me
inconsumpt·us -a -um *adj* unconsumed
incontāmināt·us -a -um *adj* untainted

incontent·us -a -um *adj* loose, untuned (*string*)
incontin·ens -entis *adj* incontinent
incontinenter *adv* without self-control, incontinently
incontinenti·a -ae *f* lack of self-control
inconveni·ens -entis *adj* unsuitable, dissimilar
in·cōquō -coquĕre -coxī -coctum *vt* to boil, cook; to dye
incorrect·us -a -um *adj* uncorrected, unrevised
incorruptē *adv* justly, fairly
incorrupt·us -a -um *adj* untainted; uncorrupted, unspoiled; genuine, pure
incrēbr·escō or **incrēb·escō -escĕre -ŭī** *vi* to grow, rise, increase, spread
incrēdibĭl·is -e *adj* incredible
incrēdibiliter *adv* incredibly
incrēdŭl·us -a -um *adj* incredulous
incrēment·um -ī *n* growth, increase; increment, addition; addition to the family, offspring
increpĭt·ō -āre *vt* to scold, rebuke
incrĕp·ō -āre -ŭī (or **-āvī**) **-ĭtum** (or **-ātum**) *vt* to cause to make noise; to rattle; (*of Jupiter*) to thunder at; to scold, rebuke; *vi* to make a noise, to rustle, rattle, clatter, clash; to speak angrily
incr·escō -escĕre -ēvī *vi* to grow, increase; (with *dat* or *abl*) to grow in or upon
incrētus *pp* of **incerno**
incruentāt·us -a -um *adj* unbloodied
incruent·us -a -um *adj* bloodless, without bloodshed
incrust·ō -āre *vt* to cover with a coat, encrust
incŭb·ō -āre -ŭī -ĭtum *vi* (with *dat*) **a** to lie in or upon; **b** to lean on; **c** to brood over; **d** to watch jealously over
inculc·ō -āre *vt* to impress, inculcate; (with *dat*) to force (*something*) upon
inculpāt·us -a -um *adj* blameless
incultē *adv* uncouthly, roughly
incult·us -a -um *adj* untilled, uncultivated; neglected, slovenly; rough, uneducated, uncivilized; *n pl* desert, wilderness
incult·us -ūs *m* neglect; dirt, squalor
in·cumbō -cumbĕre -cubŭī -cubĭtum *vi* (with *dat* or **in** + *acc*) **a** to lean on or against; **b** to lie down on (*a couch, bed*); **c** to bend to (*the oars*); **d** to light on, fall on; **e** (fig) to press upon, burden, oppress, weigh down; **f** to apply onself to, take pains with, pay attention to; (with **ad** or **in** + *acc*) to be inclined towards, lean towards
incūnābŭl·a -ōrum *n pl* baby clothes, swaddling clothes; (fig) cradle, infancy, birthplace, source, origin
incūrāt·us -a -um *adj* neglected; uncured
incūrĭ·a -ae *f* carelessness, negligence
incūriōsē *adv* carelessly
incūriōs·us -a -um *adj* careless, unconcerned, indifferent; neglected
in·currō -currĕre -currī or **-cucurrī -cursum** *vt* to attack; *vi* (with *dat* or **in** + *acc*) **a** to run into, rush at, charge, attack, invade; **b** to extend to; **c** to meet, run into; **d** to fall on, coincide with
incursĭ·ō -ōnis *f* incursion, invasion, raid; assault, attack, collision
incurs·ō -āre *vt* to assault, attack; to invade; *vi* (with *dat* or **in** + *acc*) **a** to assault, attack; **b** to run into, bump against; **c** to strike, meet (*e.g., the eyes*); **d** to affect, touch, move
incurs·us -ūs *m* assault, attack; invasion; impulse
incurv·ō -āre *vt* to bend, curve
incurv·us -a -um *adj* bent, crooked
inc·ūs -ūdis *f* anvil
incūsātĭ·ō -ōnis *f* accusation
incūs·ō -āre *vt* to blame, find fault with, accuse
incuss·us -ūs *m* shock
incussus *pp* of **incutio**
incustōdīt·us -a -um *adj* unguarded; unconcealed; imprudent
incūs·us -a -um *adj* forged; **lapis incusus** indented millstone
in·cutĭō -cutĕre -cussī -cussum *vt* to throw; to produce; (with *dat* or **in** + *acc*) to strike (*something*) on or against; (with *dat*) **a** to strike into, instill in; **b** to throw at, to fling upon; **metum incutere** (with *dat*) to inspire fear in, strike fear in; **scipionem in caput alicujus incutere** to beat someone over the head with a stick
indāgātĭ·ō -ōnis *f* investigation, search
indāgāt·or -ōris *m* or **indāgātr·ix -īcis** *f* investigator
indāg·ō -āre *vt* to track down, hunt; (fig) to track down, investigate, explore
indāg·ō -ĭnis *f* dragnet; **indagine agere** to ferret out
indaudĭō see **inaudio**
inde *adv* from there; from that source, therefrom; from that time on, after that, thereafter; then; from that cause
indēbĭt·us -a -um *adj* not owed, not due
indĕc·ens -entis *adj* unbecoming, improper, indecent
indecenter *adv* improperly, indecently
indec·ĕō -ēre *vt* to be improper for
indeclīnāt·us -a -um *adj* unchanged, constant
indĕc·or -ŏris or **indecŏr·is -e** *adj* disgraceful, dishonorable, cowardly

indecōrē *adv* indecently, improperly
indecŏr·ō -āre *vt* to disgrace
indecōr·us -a -um *adj* unsightly, improper, disgraceful
indēfens·us -a -um *adj* undefended
indēfess·us -a -um *adj* tireless; not tired
indēflēt·us -a -um *adj* unwept
indēject·us -a -um *adj* undemolished
indēlēbil·is -e *adj* indestructible, indelible
indēlībāt·us -a -um *adj* undiminished
indemnāt·us -a -um *adj* unconvicted
indeplōrāt·us -a -um *adj* unwept
indeprens·us -a -um *adj* undetected
indeptus *pp* of **indipiscor**
indēsert·us -a -um *adj* unforsaken
indespect·us -a -um *adj* unfathomable
indestrict·us -a -um *adj* unscathed
indētons·us -a -um *adj* unshorn
indēvītāt·us -a -um *adj* unerring (*e.g., arrow*)
ind·ex -icis *m* index, sign, mark, indication, proof; title (*of book*); informer, spy; index finger
Indi·a -ae *f* India
indicāti·ō -ōnis *f* value; price
indīc·ens -entis *adj* not speaking; **me indicente** without a word from me
indic·ium -iī or **-ī** *n* information, disclosure, evidence; indication, proof, permission to give evidence; reward for giving evidence
indĭc·ō -āre *vt* to point out; to reveal, disclose, make known; to betray, inform against, accuse; to put a price on; *vi* to give evidence
in·dīcō -dīcĕre -dixī -dictum *vt* to proclaim, announce, publish; to summon, convoke; to impose (*a fine*); **bellum indicere** to declare war; **diem indicere** to set a date
indict·us -a -um *adj* unsaid; **causā indictā** without a hearing
Indĭc·us -a -um *adj* Indian; *m* Indian; *n* indigo
indĭdem *adv* from the same place; from the same source, from the same thing
indiffĕr·ens -entis *adj* (morally) indifferent; unconcerned, indifferent
indigĕn·a -ae *adj masc & fem* native
indĭg·ens -entis *adj* indigent; (with *genit*) in need of
indigenti·a -ae *f* indigence, want, need; craving
indig·ĕō -ēre -ŭī *vi* (with *genit* or *abl*) to need, be in need of, require; (with *genit*) to crave, desire
indĭg·es -ĕtis *adj* indigenous, native; *m* native god; national hero
indīgest·us -a -um *adj* unarranged, confused
indignābund·us -a -um *adj* indignant, highly indignant
indign·ans -antis *adj* indignant; impatient, reluctant
indignāti·ō -ōnis *f* indignation, displeasure; provocation, occasion for indignation; *f pl* expressions of indignation
indignē *adv* unworthily, undeservedly; indignantly
indignit·ās -ātis *f* unworthiness; indignation; indignity, shameful treatment; enormity, shamefulness
indign·or -ārī -ātus sum *vt* to be indignant at, displeased at, angry at, offended at
indign·us -a -um *adj* unworthy, undeserving; undeserved; (with *abl*) **a** unworthy of; **b** not deserving; **c** not worth; (with *genit*) unworthy of, undeserving of; **indignum!** shame!
indĭg·us -a -um *adj* (with *genit* or *abl*) in need of, needing
indīlig·ens -entis *adj* careless
indīligenter *adv* carelessly
indīligenti·a -ae *f* carelessness
ind·ipiscor -ipiscī -eptus sum or **indipisc·ō -ĕre** *vt* to obtain, get; to attain, reach
indīrept·us -a -um *adj* unplundered
indiscrēt·us -a -um *adj* closely connected; indiscriminate, undistinguishable; confused
indisertē *adv* without eloquence
indisert·us -a -um *adj* not eloquent; at a loss for words
indisposit·us -a -um *adj* confused, disorderly
indissolūbil·is -e *adj* imperishable, indestructible
indistinct·us -a -um *adj* indistinct, obscure; confused
indītus *pp* of **indo**
indīvidu·us -a -um *adj* indivisible; inseparable; *n* atom, indivisible particle
in·dō -dĕre -didī -ditum *vt* to put, place; to introduce; to impart, give; (with **in** + *acc*) to put or place (*something*) into or on, insert in
indocil·is -e *adj* difficult to teach, slow to learn; hard to learn; untaught
indoctē *adv* unskillfully
indoct·us -a -um *adj* untaught, untrained, unschooled; illiterate, ignorant
indolenti·a -ae *f* freedom from pain, insensibility
indŏl·ēs -is *f* inborn quality, natural quality; nature, character, disposition; natural ability, talent, genius
indol·escō -escĕre -ŭī *vi* to feel sorry; to feel resentment
indomābil·is -e *adj* untameable
indomit·us -a -um *adj* untamed, wild; (fig) wild, unmanageable
indorm·iō -īre -īvī or **-iī -ītum** *vi* to fall asleep; to grow careless; (with *dat* or *abl* or with **in** + *abl*) **a** to fall asleep at or on; **b** to fall asleep over; **c** to become careless about
indōtāt·us -a -um *adj* without dowry; poor; without funeral rites

or funeral honors; **ars indotata** unadorned style; **corpora indotata** bodies that have not been accorded the usual honors paid to the dead
indubitābil·is -e *adj* indubitable
indubitāt·us -a -um *adj* undoubted
indubit·ō -āre *vi* (with *dat*) to begin to distrust, begin to doubt
indubi·us -a -um *adj* undoubted, certain
indūci·ae -ārum *f pl* armistice, truce
in·dūcō -dūcĕre -duxī -ductum *vt* to lead or bring in; to bring in, introduce; to induce, persuade, seduce, move; to overlay, drape, wrap, cover, put on, clothe; to strike out, erase; to repeal, cancel; to present, exhibit; to mislead, delude; (with **in** + *acc*) **a** to lead to, lead into, lead against; **b** to bring into, introduce into; **c** (fig) to introduce (*e.g., a new custom*) into; **d** to enter into (*account books*), charge to (*someone's account*); (with *dat* or **super** + *acc*) to put (*item of apparel*) on, spread over, wrap around, draw over; **animum inducere** or **in animum inducere** to make up one's mind, convince oneself, be convinced, conclude, suppose, imagine
inducti·ō -ōnis *f* bringing in, introduction, admission; resolution, determination; intention; induction, generalization; **animi inductio** inclination; **erroris inductio** deception
induct·or -ōris *m* (referring to a whip) persuader
induct·us -ūs *m* persuasion, inducement
indūcŭl·a -ae *f* skirt, petticoat
indulg·ens -entis *adj* indulgent, lenient; (with *dat* or **in** + *acc*) lenient toward, kind toward
indulgenter *adv* indulgently, leniently, kindly
indulgenti·a -ae *f* indulgence, leniency, kindness
in·dulgĕō -dulgēre -dulsī *vt* (with *dat*) to grant, concede (*something*) to; **veniam indulgere** (with *dat*) to make allowances for; *vi* (with *dat*) **a** to be lenient toward, be kind to, be tender to; **b** to yield to, give way to; **c** to indulge in, be addicted to; **sibi indulgere** to be self-indulgent, take liberties
ind·ŭō -uĕre -ŭī -ūtum *vt* to put on (*e.g., a tunic*); to cover, wrap, clothe, array, envelop; to engage in; to assume, put on; to assume the part of; to involve, entangle; (with *dat*) to put (*e.g., a tunic*) on (*someone*)
indup- = **imp-**
indūr·escō -escĕre -ŭī *vi* to become hard, harden
indūr·ō -āre *vt* to harden
Ind·us -a -um *adj* Indian; *m* Indian; Ethiopian; mahout
industri·a -ae *f* industry, diligence; **industriā** or **de** or **ex industria** or **ob industriam** on purpose
industriē *adv* industriously, diligently
industri·us -a -um *adj* industrious, diligent, painstaking
indūti·ae or **indūci·ae -ārum** *f pl* armistice, truce
indūtus *pp* of **induo;** *adj* (with *acc* or *abl*) dressed in, wearing
indūt·us -ūs *m* wearing; clothing
induvi·ae -ārum *f pl* clothes
inebri·ō -āre *vt* to make drunk; (fig) to fill (*e.g., ear with gossip*)
inedi·a -ae *f* fasting; starvation
inēdit·us -a -um *adj* not made known, unknown, unpublished
inēlĕg·ans -antis *adj* inelegant, undistinguished
inēleganter *adv* without distinction
inēluctābil·is -e *adj* inescapable
inēmor·ior -ī *vi* (with *dat*) to die in or at
inempt·us -a -um *adj* unpurchased; without ransom
inēnarrābil·is -e *adj* indescribable
inēnarrābiliter *adv* indescribably
inēnōdābil·is -e *adj* inexplicable
in·ĕō -īre -iī -itum *vt* to enter; to enter upon, undertake, form; to begin, engage in; **consilium inire** to form a plan; **consilium inire ut, qua,** or **quemadmodum** to plan how to (*do something*); **inire numerum** (with *genit*) to go into an enumeration of, enumerate; **inire rationem** (with *genit*) to form an estimate of; **inire rationem ut, qua,** or **quemadmodum** to consider, find out, or figure out how to (*do something*); **viam inire** to begin a trip; to find a way, devise a means
ineptē *adv* foolishly, absurdly, inappropriately, pointlessly
inepti·a -ae *f* foolishness; *f pl* nonsense; trifles
inept·iō -īre *vi* to be absurd, make a fool of oneself
inept·us -a -um *adj* foolish, silly; inept, awkward, absurd; unsuitable, out of place; tactless, tasteless
inerm·is -e or **inerm·us -a -um** *adj* unarmed, defenseless; undefended; toothless (*gums*); harmless
inerr·ans -antis *adj* not wandering, fixed
inerr·ō -āre *vi* to wander about
iner·s -tis *adj* unskillful, incompetent; inactive, sluggish; weak, soft, helpless; stagnant, motionless; ineffective, dull, insipid; numbing (*cold*); expressionless (*eyes*); uneventful, leisurely (*time*)
inerti·a -ae *f* lack of skill, ignorance, rudeness; inactivity, laziness
inērudīt·us -a -um *adj* uneducated; crude, inconsiderate
inesc·ō -āre *vt* to bait; (fig) to bait, trap, deceive
inēvect·us -a -um *adj* mounted

inēvītābĭl·is -e *adj* inevitable, inescapable
inexcĭt·us -a -um *adj* unexcited, calm
inexcūsābĭl·is -e *adj* without excuse; admitting no excuse
inexercitāt·us -a -um *adj* untrained
inexhaust·us -a -um *adj* unexhausted, not wasted; inexhaustible
inexōrābĭl·is -e *adj* inexorable, relentless; unswerving, strict
inexperrect·us -a -um *adj* unawakened
inexpert·us -a -um *adj* untried, untested; novel; (with *abl*, or with **in** or **adversus** + *acc*) inexperienced in, unaccustomed to
inexpiābĭl·is -e *adj* inexpiable, not to be atoned for; irreconcilable, implacable
inexplēbĭl·is -e *adj* insatiable
inexplēt·us -a -um *adj* unsatisfied, unfilled
inexplicābĭl·is -e *adj* inextricable; inexplicable; impassable (*road*); involved, unending (*war*)
inexplōrātō *adv* without reconnoitering
inexplorāt·us -a -um *adj* unexplored; unfamiliar
inexpugnābĭl·is -e *adj* impregnable, unassailable; invincible
inexspectāt·us -a -um *adj* unexpected
inexstinct·us -a -um *adj* unextinguished; insatiable
inexsuperābĭl·is -e *adj* insuperable, insurmountable
inextrīcābĭl·is -e *adj* inextricable
infăbrē *adv* unskillfully
infabricāt·us -a -um *adj* unshaped, untrimmed
infacētē *adv* witlessly
infacētĭ·ae -ārum *f pl* coarse jokes
infacēt·us -a -um *adj* not witty, not funny, dull, stupid
infăcund·us -a -um *adj* ineloquent
infāmĭ·a -ae *f* bad reputation, bad name; disrepute, disgrace, scandal; embarrassment
infām·is -e *adj* infamous, notorious, disreputable, disgraceful
infām·ō -āre *vt* to defame, dishonor, disgrace
infand·us -a -um *adj* unspeakable, shocking
inf·ans -antis *adj* speechless, unable to speak; baby, infant, young; childish, silly; (fig) incapable of speaking, tongue-tied; *m* or *f* infant
infantĭ·a -ae *f* infancy; childishness; inability to speak; lack of eloquence
infar- = infer-
infatŭ·ō -āre *vt* to make a fool of
infaust·us -a -um *adj* ill-omened, unpropitious; unfortunate
infect·or -ōris *m* dyer
infect·us -a -um *pp* of **inficio**; *adj* not made, not done, undone, unfinished, unachieved; unfeasible; impossible
infēcundĭt·ās -ātis *f* unfruitfulness
infēcund·us -a -um *adj* unfruitful
infēlīcĭt·ās -ātis *f* bad luck, misfortune
infēlīcĭter *adv* unhappily; unluckily, unsuccessfully
infēlīc·ō -āre *vt* to make unhappy
infēl·ix -īcis *adj* unfruitful; unhappy, unfortunate; causing misfortune, ruinous; ill-omened; pessimistic
infensē *adv* hostilely, aggressively
infens·ō -āre *vt* to antagonize; to make dangerous; *vi* to be hostile
infens·us -a -um *adj* hostile, antagonistic; dangerous; (with *dat* or **in** + *acc*) **a** hostile to, antagonistic toward; **b** dangerous to
in·fercĭō or **infarcĭō -fercīre -fersī -fersum** or **-fertum** *vt* to stuff, cram
infĕr·a -ōrum *n pl* lower world
infĕr·ī -ōrum *m pl* the dead; the world below
inferĭ·ae -ārum *f pl* rites and offerings to the dead
inferĭ·or -us *adj* lower, farther down; (fig) inferior, lower; subsequent, later
inferĭus *adv* lower, too low
infernē *adv* below, beneath
infern·us -a -um *adj* lower; infernal, of the lower world
infĕrō inferre intŭlī illātum *vt* to bring in, introduce, carry in; to import; to bring forward, adduce, produce, make, occasion, incite, cause; to offer, render, sacrifice; to bury, inter; **arma, bellum, gradum, pedem,** or **signa inferre** to make an attack, make an advance, begin hostilities; **arma, bellum, pedem** or **signa inferre** (with *dat* or with **in** or **contra** + *acc*) to attack, advance against, invade; **conversa signa inferre** (with *dat*) to turn around and attack; **ignem inferre** (with *dat*) to set fire to; **se inferre** to go, march, rush, charge, plunge; **se in periculum inferre** to expose oneself to danger; *vi* to infer, conclude
infĕr·us -a -um *adj* lower; southern
in·fervescō -fervescĕre -ferbŭī *vi* to simmer, boil
infestē *adv* hostilely, violently, outrageously
infest·ō -āre *vt* to annoy; to infest; to attack
infest·us -a -um *adj* infested, molested, disturbed, unsafe; hostile, aggressive; dangerous; threatening
inficēt- = infacēt-
in·ficĭō -ficĕre -fēcī -fectum *vt* to dip, dye, tint; to infect; to stain; to corrupt, spoil; to imbue, instruct; (fig) to poison, infect
infidēl·is -e *adj* unfaithful, untrue, disloyal
infidēlĭt·ās -ātis *f* infidelity, unfaithfulness, disloyalty
infidēlĭter *adv* disloyally

infīd·us -a -um *adj* untrustworthy, treacherous
in·fīgō -fīgĕre -fixī -fixum *vt* to drive in, nail, thrust; to imprint, fix, impress; (with *dat*) **a** to drive into, thrust into; **b** to impale on; **c** to imprint on or in
infimātis see **infumatis**
infĭm·us or **infŭm·us -a -um** (*superl* of **inferus**) *adj* lowest, last; lowest, worst, humblest; **ab infimo colle** at the foot of the hill; **infimum mare** the botton of the sea; *n* bottom
in·findō -findĕre -fīdī -fissum *vt* (with *dat*) to cut (*e.g., furrows*) into
infīnīt·ās -ātis *f* endlessness, infinity
infīnītē *adv* without bounds, without end, infinitely; without exception
infīnītĭ·ō -ōnis *f* boundlessness, infinity
infīnīt·us -a -um *adj* unlimited, boundless; without end, endless, infinite; countless; indefinite
infirmātĭ·ō -ōnis *f* invalidation; refutation
infirmē *adv* weakly, faintly, feebly
infirmĭt·ās -ātis *f* weakness, feebleness; infirmity, sickness; inconstancy
infirm·ō -āre *vt* to weaken, enfeeble; to refute, disprove; to annul
infirm·us -a -um *adj* weak, faint, feeble; infirm, sick; trivial; inconstant
infissus *pp* of **infindo**
infit *v defect* he, she, it begins
infitĭ·ae -ārum *f pl* denial; **infitias ire** (with *acc*) to deny
infitiāl·is -e *adj* negative
infitiātĭ·ō -ōnis *f* denial
infitiāt·or -ōris *m* repudiator
infitĭ·or -ārī -ātus sum *vt* to deny, repudiate, contradict, disown
infixus *pp* of **infigo**
inflammātĭ·ō -ōnis *f* setting on fire; **inflammationem inferre** (with *dat*) to set on fire
inflamm·ō -āre *vt* to set on fire, kindle, light up; (fig) to inflame, excite
inflātĭ·ō -ōnis *f* swelling up; **habet inflationem faba** beans cause gas
inflātius *adv* too pompously
inflāt·us -a -um *adj* blown up, swollen, inflated; haughty; turgid (*style*)
inflāt·us -ūs *m* puff, blast; inspiration
in·flectō -flectĕre -flexī -flexum *vt* to bend, curve, bow, turn aside; to change; to influence; to inflect
inflēt·us -a -um *adj* unwept
inflexibĭl·is -e *adj* inflexible
inflexĭ·ō -ōnis *f* bending
inflexus *pp* of **inflecto**
inflex·us -ūs *m* curve
in·flīgō -flīgĕre -flixī -flictum *vt* to strike, smash, dash, swing; to inflict (*wound*); to bring (*e.g., disgrace*)
infl·ō -āre *vt* to blow (*horn*), play (*flute*); to inspire; to inflate, puff up, fill
in·flŭō -fluĕre -fluxī *vi* (with **in** + *acc*) **a** to flow into; **b** (fig) to spill over into, stream into, pour into
in·fodĭō -fodĕre -fōdī -fossum *vt* to dig; to bury
informātĭ·ō -ōnis *f* sketch; idea
inform·is -e *adj* unformed, shapeless; ugly, hideous
inform·ō -āre *vt* to form, shape
infŏr·ō -āre *vt* to bring into court
infortūnāt·us -a -um *adj* unfortunate
infortūn·ĭum -ĭī or **-ī** *n* misfortune, calamity; punishment
infossus *pp* of **infodio**
infrā *adv* below, underneath; down south, down the coast; *prep* (with *acc*) below, beneath, under; later than
infractĭ·ō -ōnis *f* weakening; **animi infractio** discouragement
infract·us -a -um *pp* of **infringo;** *adj* broken, weakened, exhausted; **infractos animos gerere** to feel down and out
infragĭl·is -e *adj* unbreakable, strong
infrĕm·ō -ĕre -ŭī *vi* to growl, bellow, roar; to rage
infrēnāt·us -a -um *adj* unbridled
infrend·ĕō -ēre or **infrend·ō -ĕre** *vi* **dentibus infrendere** to gnash the teeth
infrēn·is -e or **infrēn·us -a -um** *adj* unbridled
infrēn·ō -āre *vt* to put a bridle on; to harness; (fig) to curb
infrēnus see **infrenis**
infrĕqu·ens -entis *adj* uncrowded, not numerous; poorly attended; thinly populated; inconstant, irregular
infrequentĭ·a -ae *f* small number, scantiness; poor attendance; emptiness
in·fringō -fringĕre -frēgī -fractum *vt* to break, break in; to impair, affect, subdue, weaken, break down
infr·ons -ondis *adj* leafless
infructuōs·us -a -um *adj* unfruitful; pointless
infūcāt·us -a -um *adj* painted over, varnished; hidden
infŭl·a -ae *f* bandage; fillet; mark of distinction, badge of honor
infumāt·is or **infimāt·is -is** *m* one of the lowest (*in rank*)
infŭmus see **infimus**
in·fundō -fundĕre -fūdī -fūsum *vt* to pour in, pour on, pour out; (with *dat* or **in** + *acc*) **a** to pour into, pour upon; **b** to administer to; **infundi** or **se infundere** (with *dat*) to lay on, spread out on
infusc·ō -āre *vt* to darken, obscure; to stain, corrupt, sully
infūsus *pp* of **infundo;** *adj* diffused, permeating; fallen (*snow*); crowded

ingemin•ō -āre *vt* to redouble; to repeat, reiterate; *vi* to redouble
ingem•iscō or **ingem•escō -iscĕre -uī** *vi* to groan, heave a sigh; (with *dat* or **in** + *abl*) to groan over, sigh over
ingĕm•ō -ĕre -uī *vt* to groan over, sigh over; *vi* (with *dat*) to sigh over
ingenĕr•ō -āre *vt* to engender, generate, produce, create
ingeniāt•us -a -um *adj* naturally endowed, talented
ingeniōsē *adv* ingeniously
ingeniōs•us -a -um *adj* ingenious, clever, talented; (with *dat* or **ad** + *acc*) naturally suited to
ingenit•us -a -um *adj* inborn, natural
ingen•ium -iī or **-ī** *n* innate or natural quality; nature, temperament, character, bent, inclination; natural ability, talent, genius; clever person, genius
ing•ens -entis *adj* huge, vast; great, mighty, powerful
ingenuē *adv* liberally; frankly
ingenuit•ās -ātis *f* noble birth; noble character; frankness
ingenu•us -a -um *adj* native, indigenous; natural; free-born; like a freeman, noble; frank
in•gĕrō -gerĕre -gessī -gestum *vt* to carry in, throw in, heap; to hurl, shoot (*weapon*); to pour out (*angry words*), heap (*abuse*)
inglōri•us -a -um *adj* inglorious, without glory, inconspicuous
ingluvi•ēs -ēī *f* crop, maw; gluttony
ingrātē *adv* unpleasantly; unwillingly; ungratefully
ingrātific•us -a -um *adj* ungrateful
ingrātiīs or **ingrātīs** *adv* without thanks; unwillingly
ingrāt•us -a -um *adj* unpleasant, unwelcome; ungrateful; receiving no thanks, unappreciated; thankless
ingravesc•ō -ĕre *vi* to grow heavier; to become pregnant; to grow worse; to become more serious; to become weary; to become dearer (*in price*); to become more important
in•gredior -grĕdī -gressus sum *vt* to enter; to undertake; to begin; to walk in, follow (*footsteps*); *vi* to go in, enter; to go, walk, walk along; to begin, commence; to begin to speak; (with **in** + *acc*) **a** to go in, enter; **b** to enter upon, begin, take up, undertake; **in rem publicam ingredi** to enter politics, enter public life
ingressi•ō -ōnis *f* entering; walking; gait, pace; beginning
ingress•us -ūs *m* entering; (mil) inroad; walking; gait; beginning
ingru•ō -ĕre -ī *vi* to come, come on, rush on; (of war) to break out; (of rain) to pour down; (with *dat* or **in** + *acc*) to fall upon, attack
ingu•en -inis *n* groin; swelling, tumor; *n pl* private parts
ingurgit•ō -āre *vt* to gorge, stuff; **se ingurgitare** to stuff oneself; **se ingurgitare** (with **in** + *acc*) to steep oneself in, devote oneself to
ingustāt•us -a -um *adj* untasted
inhabil•is -e *adj* clumsy, unhandy; (with *dat* or **ad** + *acc*) unfit for
inhabitābil•is -e *adj* uninhabitable
inhabit•ō -āre *vt* inhabit
in•haerĕō -haerēre -haesī -haesum *vi* to stick, cling; (fig) to cling, adhere; to be inherent; (with *dat*, with **ad** + *acc*, or with **in** + *abl*) **a** to cling to; **b** to be closely connected with; **c** to gaze upon
in•haerescō -haerescĕre -haesī *vi* to stick fast, take hold
inhăl•ō -āre *vt* (with *dat*) to breathe (*e.g., bad breath*) on (*someone*)
inhib•ĕō -ēre -uī -itum *vt* to hold back, curb, check, control; to use, practice, perform; to apply, inflict; **retro navem inhibere** to back up the ship; *vi* to row backwards, backwater
inhibiti•ō -ōnis *f* backing up
inhi•ō -āre *vt* to gape at; to covet; *vi* to stand open-mouthed, be amazed
inhonestē *adv* dishonorably, disgracefully; dishonestly
inhonest•ō -āre *vt* to dishonor, disgrace
inhonest•us -a -um *adj* dishonorable, disgraceful, shameful, inglorious; indecent; ugly, degrading
inhonōrāt•us -a -um *adj* unhonored, disregarded, unrewarded
inhonōr•us -a -um *adj* defaced
inhorr•ĕō -ēre -uī *vi* to stand on end, bristle
inhorr•escō -escĕre -uī *vi* to stand on end, bristle; to vibrate; to shiver, tremble, shudder
inhospitāl•is -e *adj* inhospitable, unfriendly
inhospitālit•ās -ātis *f* inhospitality
inhospit•us -a -um *adj* inhospitable
inhūmānē *adv* inhumanly, savagely
inhūmānit•ās -ātis *f* inhumanity, barbarity; churlishness; extreme stinginess
inhūmāniter *adv* impolitely
inhūmān•us -a -um *adj* inhuman, savage; brutal; crude, impolite
inhumāt•us -a -um *adj* unburied
inibi or **inibī** *adv* there, in that place; near at hand
inimic•a -ae *f* (personal) enemy (*female*)
inimīcē *adv* hostilely, in an unfriendly way
inimīciti•a -ae *f* unfriendliness, enmity; *f pl* feuds
inimic•ō -āre *vt* to make into enemies, set at odds
inimic•us -a -um *adj* unfriendly, hostile; harmful; *m* (personal) enemy; **inimicissimus suus** his bitterest enemy
inīquē *adv* unequally, unevenly; unfairly
inīquit•ās -ātis *f* unevenness; in-

equality; disadvantage; unfairness
iniqu·us -a -um *adj* uneven, unequal; not level, sloping; unfair; adverse, harmful; dangerous, unfavorable; prejudiced; excessive; impatient, discontented; **iniquo animo** impatiently, unwillingly; *m* enemy, foe
initi·ō -āre *vt* to initiate, begin; to initiate (*into mysteries*)
init·ium -iī or **-ī** *n* entrance; beginning; *n pl* elements; first principles; sacred rites, sacred mysteries
inĭtus *pp* of **ineo**
inĭt·us -ūs *m* entrance; beginning
in·jiciō -jicĕre -jēcī -jectum *vt* to throw, inject; to impose, apply; to inspire, infuse; to cause, occasion; to furnish (*a cause*); to bring up, mention (*a name*); (with *dat* or **in** + *acc*) to throw or fling into, on or over; (with *dat* or **in** + *acc*) **a** to throw oneself into, rush into, expose oneself to; **b** to fling oneself down on; **c** (of the mind) to turn itself to, concentrate on, reflect on; **manum injicere** (with *dat*) to lay hands on, take possession of
injūcundĭt·ās -ātis *f* unpleasantness
injūcundĭus *adv* rather unpleasantly
injūcund·us -a -um *adj* unpleasant
injūdicāt·us -a -um *adj* undecided
in·jungō -jungĕre -junxī -junctum *vt* to join, attach, fasten; to inflict, impose; (with *dat*) **a** to join, attach, fasten to; **b** to inflict on, impose (*e.g., taxes, obligations*) on
injūrāt·us -a -um *adj* not under oath
injūrĭ·a -ae *f* injury, wrong, outrage, injustice; insult, affront; harshness, severity; revenge; damage, harm; ill-gotten goods; **injuriā** unjustly, undeservedly, innocently; **per injuriam** unjustly, outrageously
injūriōsē *adv* unjustly, wrongfully
injūriōs·us -a -um *adj* unjust, wrongful; harmful
injūrĭ·us -a -um *adj* unjust, wrong
injūr·us -a -um *adj* wrongful
injussū (*abl* only) *m* without orders; **injussu meo** without my orders
injuss·us -a -um *adj* unasked, unbidden, voluntary
injustē *adv* unjustly
injustitĭ·a -ae *f* injustice
injust·us -a -um *adj* unjust
inl- = ill-
inm- = imm-
innābĭl·is -e *adj* unswimmable
in·nascor -nascī -nātus sum *vi* (with *dat*) to be born in, grow in or on; (with **in** + *abl*) (fig) to originate in
innăt·ō -āre *vt* to swim; *vi* (with *dat*) to swim around in, float on; (with **in** + *acc*) to swim into
innāt·us -a -um *pp* of **innascor;** *adj* inborn, natural
innāvigābĭl·is -e *adj* unnavigable
in·nectō -nectĕre -nexŭī -nexum *vt* to entwine; to tie, fasten together; to join, attach, connect; (fig) to devise, invent, plan
in·nītor -nītī -nixus sum or **-nīsus sum** *vi* (with *abl*) to lean on, rest on, be supported by
inn·ō -āre *vt* to swim; to sail, sail over; *vi* (with *abl*) **a** to swim in, float on; **b** to sail on; **c** (of the sea) to wash against (*a shore*)
innŏc·ens -entis *adj* harmless; guiltless, innocent; upright; unselfish; (with *genit*) innocent of
innocenter *adv* blamelessly
innocentĭ·a -ae *f* innocence; integrity; unselfishness
innocŭē *adv* harmlessly; innocently
innocŭ·us -a -um *adj* harmless, innocuous; innocent; unharmed
innōt·escō -escĕre -ŭī *vi* to become known; to become notorious
innŏv·ō -āre *vt* to renew, restore; **se innovare** (with **ad** + *acc*) to return to
innoxĭ·us -a -um *adj* harmless; safe; innocent; unhurt; (with *genit*) innocent of
innūbĭl·us -a -um *adj* cloudless
innŭb·a -ae (*fem* only) *adj* unmarried
in·nūbō -nūbĕre -nupsī *vi* (with *dat*) to marry into
innumerābĭl·is -e *adj* innumerable
innumerābilĭt·ās -ātis *f* countless number
innumerābilĭter *adv* innumerably
innumerāl·is -e *adj* innumerable
innumĕr·us -a -um *adj* countless
in·nŭō -nuĕre -nŭī -nūtum *vi* to give a nod; (with *dat*) to nod to
innupt·a -ae (*fem* only) *adj* unmarried; *f* unmarried girl, maiden
innutr·iō -īre -īvī or **-iī -ītum** *vt* (with *dat*) to bring up in
Īn·ō -ūs *f* daughter of Cadmus and Harmonia, wife of Athamas, mother of Learchus and Melicerta, and stepmother of Phrixus and Helle; pursued by mad Athamas, she and Melicerta hurled themselves into the sea, whereupon they were changed into sea deities
inoblīt·us -a -um *adj* unforgetful
inobrŭt·us -a -um *adj* not overwhelmed
inobservābĭl·is -e *adj* unnoticed
inobservantĭ·a -ae *f* inattention
inobservāt·us -a -um *adj* unobserved
inoccidŭ·us -a -um *adj* never setting
inodōr·us -a -um *adj* odorless
inoffens·us -a -um *adj* unobstructed, uninterrupted, unhindered
inofficiōs·us -a -um *adj* irresponsible; not obliging
inŏl·ens -entis *adj* odorless
inol·escō -escĕre -ēvī *vi* to become inveterate; (with *dat*) to grow on or in

inōminät·us -a -um *adj* ill-omened, inauspicious
inopi·a -ae *f* lack, want, need, poverty; scarcity; barrenness (*of style*); helplessness
inopīn·ans -antis *adj* unsuspecting, taken by surprise
inopīnanter *adv* unexpectedly
inopīnātō *adv* unexpectedly, by surprise
inopīnāt·us -a -um *adj* not expected, unexpected, unsuspected, surprising; *n* surprise; **ex inopinato** by surprise
inopīn·us -a -um *adj* unexpected
inopiōs·us -a -um *adj* (with *genit*) in need of
in·ops -ŏpis *adj* without means or resources; poor, needy, destitute; helpless, weak, forlorn; bald (*style*); poor (*expression*); pitiful, wretched, contemptible; (with *genit*) destitute of, stripped of, without; (with *abl*) lacking in, deficient in, poor in
inōrāt·us -a -um *adj* not presented; **re inoratā** without presenting one's case
inordināt·us -a -um *adj* disordered
inornāt·us -a -um *adj* unadorned; plain (*style*); unheralded
inp- = imp-
inpendiōs·us -a -um *adj* extravagant
inperc·ō -ĕre *vi* (with *dat*) to spare
inpluviāt·us -a -um *adj* square, shaped like an impluvium
inpūrāt·us -a -um *adj* (morally) defiled
inpūritī·ae -ārum *f pl* (moral) impurity
inquam *v defect* say; after one or more words of direct quotation, e.g., **Desilite, inquit, milites et . . .** "Jump down, fellow soldiers", he says, "and . . ."; in emphatic repetition, e.g., **tuas, tuas inquam suspiciones . . .** your suspicions, yes I say yours . . . ; **inquit** it is said, one says
inquī·ēs -ētis *adj* restless
inquiēt·ō -āre *vt* to disquiet, disturb
inquiēt·us -a -um *adj* restless, unsettled
inquilīn·us -ī *m* tenant, inhabitant
inquinātē *adv* filthily
inquināt·us -a -um *adj* filthy, foul
inquīn·ō -āre *vt* to mess up, defile, contaminate
in·quīrō -quīrĕre quīsīvī -quīsītum *vt* to search for, inquire into, examine, pry into; *vi* to hold an investigation; to hold a preliminary hearing
inquīsītī·ō -ōnis *f* search, inquiry, investigation; preliminary hearing; (with *genit*) search for, inquiry into, investigation of
inquīsīt·or -ōris *m* inspector, examiner; spy; (law) investigator
inquīsīt·us -a -um *pp* of **inquiro;** *adj* not investigated

inquit see **inquam**
inr- = irr-
insalūbr·is -e *adj* unhealthy
insalūtāt·us -a -um *adj* ungreeted
insānābil·is -e *adj* incurable
insānē *adv* crazily, madly
insānī·a -ae *f* insanity, madness, frenzy; rapture; mania; excess; inspiration
insān·iō -īre -īvī or **-iī -ītum** *vi* to be crazy, be mad, be insane; to be absurd, be wild
insānīt·ās -ātis *f* unsoundness, disease
insān·us -a -um *adj* insane, mad, crazy; absurd, foolish; excessive, extravagant; monstrous, outrageous; inspired; maddening
insatiābil·is -e *adj* insatiable; that cannot cloy, uncloying
insatiābiliter *adv* insatiably
insatiĕt·ās -ātis *f* insatiety
insaturābil·is -e *adj* insatiable
insaturābiliter *adv* insatiably
in·scendō -scendĕre -scendī -scensum *vt & vi* to climb up, mount
inscensī·ō -ōnis *f* mounting; **in navem inscensio** boarding a ship
inscensus *pp* of **inscendo**
inscī·ens -entis *adj* unaware; silly, stupid
inscienter *adv* ignorantly, inadvertently
inscientī·a -ae *f* ignorance; inexperience; foolishness; awkwardness
inscīt·us -a -um *adj* ignorant, clumsy, stupid
inscī·us -a -um *adj* ignorant, unaware
in·scrībō -scrībĕre -scripsī -scriptum *vt* to inscribe; to ascribe; to title (*a book*); to assign, attribute, appropriate; to advertise; to address (*a letter*); (with *dat* or **in** + *abl*) to write (*something*) on or in
inscriptī·ō -ōnis *f* inscribing
inscript·us -a -um *pp* of **inscribo;** *adj* unwritten
in·sculpō -sculpĕre -sculpsī -sculptum *vt* to cut, carve, engrave; (with *abl* or **in** + *abl*) to cut, carve, or engrave upon
insectātī·ō -ōnis *f* hot pursuit
insectāt·or -ōris *m* persecutor
insect·or -ārī -ātus sum or **insect·ō -āre** *vt* to pursue, attack; to attack with words, criticize
insect·us -a -um *adj* indented, notched
insecūtus *pp* of **insequor**
insēdābiliter *adv* incessantly
insen·escō -escĕre -ŭī *vi* (with *dat*) to grow old amidst, grow old over
insensil·is -e *adj* imperceptible
insepult·us -a -um *adj* unburied
insĕqu·ens -entis *adj* next, following, succeeding
in·sĕquor -sĕquī -secūtus sum *vt* to follow, follow after; to succeed, to follow up; to attack; to prosecute; to pass, overtake; to reproach;

to strive after; *vi* to follow, come next
in·sĕrō -serĕre -sēvī -sĭtum *vt* to graft; (fig) to implant
in·sĕrō -serĕre -serŭī -sertum *vt* to insert; to introduce; to involve; to join, enroll, associate; to mingle, blend; to let in
insert·ō -āre *vt* to insert
inserv·iō -īre -īvī or **-iī -ītum** *vt* to serve, obey; *vi* to be a slave, be a subject; (with *dat*) to serve, be subservient to, be devoted to
insessus *pp* of **insido**
insībĭl·ō -āre *vi* (of the wind) to whistle, hiss
in·sidĕō -sidēre -sēdī -sessum *vt* to hold, occupy; *vi* to sit down; to settle down; to be deep-seated; (with *abl* or *in* + *abl*) **a** to sit on; **b** to settle down on or in; **c** (fig) to be fixed in, stamped in
insidĭ·ae -ārum *f pl* ambush; plot, trap; **insidias dare, comparare, collocare, parare,** or **struere** (with *dat*) to lay a trap for
insidiāt·or -ōris *m* soldier in ambush; (fig) plotter, subversive
insidĭ·or -ārī -ātus sum *vi* to lie in wait; (with *dat*) **a** to lie in wait for; **b** (fig) to plot against; **c** (fig) to watch for (*an opportunity*)
insidiōsē *adv* insidiously, by underhand means
insidiōs·us -a -um *adj* insidious, treacherous, tricky
in·sīdō -sīdĕre -sēdī -sessum *vt* to occupy, keep possession of, possess; *vi* (with *dat*) to settle in or on; (with **in** + *abl*) (fig) to become fixed in
insign·e -is *n* insignia, mark, token; (mil) decoration, medal; standard; coat of arms; signal; honor, distinction; brilliant passage, gem; *n pl* insignia, regalia, uniform, attire, accouterments
insign·iō -īre -īvī or **-iī -ītum** *vt* to make conspicuous, distinguish
insign·is -e *adj* conspicuous, distinguished; prominent, eminent, extraordinary, singular
insignītē *adv* extraordinarily, notably
insigniter *adv* remarkably
insignīt·us -a -um *adj* marked, conspicuous, clear, glaring; distinguished, striking, notable
insilĭ·a -ium *n pl* treadle (*of a loom*)
insil·iō -īre -ŭī or **-īvī** *vt* to jump up on, mount; *vi* (with *dat*) to jump on; (with **in** + *acc*) **a** to jump into or on; **b** to jump on, mount, climb aboard
insimulātĭ·ō -ōnis *f* charge, accusation
insimŭl·ō -āre *vt* to accuse, accuse falsely, allege
insincēr·us -a -um *adj* mixed, spoiled, not pure
insinuātĭ·ō -ōnis *f* winning sympathy
insinŭ·ō -āre *vt* to bring in secretly, sneak in; **se insinuare** (with **inter** + *acc*) to wriggle in between, work one's way between or among; **se insinuare in familiaritatem** (with *genit*) to ingratiate oneself with
insipĭ·ens -entis *adj* foolish
insipienter *adv* foolishly
insipientĭ·a -ae *f* foolishness
in·sistō -sistĕre -stitī *vt* to stand on, trample on; to set about, keep at (*a task, etc.*); to follow, chase after, pursue; **iter insistere** or **viam insistere** to enter upon a course, pursue a course; *vi* to stand, stop, come to a standstill; to pause; (with *dat*) **a** to tread on the heels of, pursue closely; **b** to press on with; **c** (fig) to dwell upon; (with *dat* or **in** + acc) to set foot on or in, step on, tread on, stand on; (with *dat* or **in** + *abl*) to persist in; (with **ad** or **in** + *acc*) to keep at, keep after, keep the pressure on, pursue vigorously
insitĭ·ō -ōnis *f* grafting; grafting time
insitīv·us -a -um *adj* grafted; (fig) spurious
insĭt·or -ōris *m* grafter
insĭt·us -a -um *pp* of **insero**; *adj* inborn, innate; incorporated
insociābĭl·is -e *adj* incompatible
insōlābiliter *adv* unconsolably
insŏl·ens -entis *adj* unaccustomed, unusual; immoderate, excessive; extravagant; insolent; (with *genit* or **in** + *abl*) unaccustomed to, inexperienced in; **in aliena re insolens** free with someone else's money
insolenter *adv* unusually; excessively; insolently
insolentĭ·a -ae *f* unusualness, strangeness, novelty; inexperience; affectation; insolence, arrogance
insolesc·ō -ĕre *vi* to become strange; to become insolent; to become elated
insolĭd·us -a -um *adj* soft
insolĭt·us -a -um *adj* unaccustomed, inexperienced; unusual, strange, uncommon; *n* the unusual
insomnĭ·a -ae *f* insomnia, sleeplessness
insomn·is -e *adj* sleepless
insomn·ium -iī or **-ī** *n* nightmare; dream
insŏn·ō -āre -ŭī *vi* to make noise; to sound, resound, roar; **calamis insonare** to make music with a reed pipe; **flagello insonare** to crack the whip; **pennis insonare** to flap the wings
ins·ons -ontis *adj* innocent; harmless
insōpīt·us -a -um *adj* sleepless
insŏp·or -ōris *adj* sleepless
inspect·ō -āre *vt* to look at, view, observe
inspectus *pp* of **inspicio**
inspēr·ans -antis *adj* not expecting

inspērāt·us -a -um *adj* unhoped for, unexpected, unforeseen; unwelcome; **ex insperato** unexpectedly
in·spergō -spergĕre -spersī -spersum *vt* to sprinkle
in·spiciō -spicĕre -spexī -spectum *vt* to inspect, look into, examine, consider; to inspect, review; to look at, consult (*books*)
inspīc·ō -āre *vt* to make pointed; to sharpen
inspīr·ō -āre *vt* to inspire, infuse, enkindle; *vi* (with *dat*) to blow on, breathe on
inspoliāt·us -a -um *adj* undespoiled
inspūt·ō -āre *vt* to spit on
instābīl·is -e *adj* unstable, unsteady; (fig) unsteady, changeable
inst·ans -antis *adj* present; immediate, threatening, urgent
instanter *adv* vehemently
instantī·a -ae *f* presence; vehemence
instar (indecl) *n* image, likeness, appearance, resemblance; (with *genit*) like, equal to, as large as, worth, as good as
instaurātī·ō -ōnis *f* renewal, repetition
instaurātīv·us -a -um *adj* begun anew, repeated
instaur·ō -āre *vt* to set up; to renew, repeat, start all over again (*esp. games and celebrations*); to repay, requite
in·sternō -sternĕre -strāvī -strātum *vt* to cover
instīgāt·or -ōris *m* or **instīgātr·ix -īcis** *f* instigator, ringleader
instīg·ō -āre *vt* to instigate, goad on, stimulate, incite
instill·ō -āre *vt* (with *dat*) to pour (*something*) on, instill (*something*) in
instimulāt·or -ōris *m* instigator
instimŭl·ō -āre *vt* to stimulate, urge on
instinct·or -ōris *m* instigator
instinct·us -a -um *adj* incited, inspired
instinct·us -ūs *m* inspiration, impulse
instipŭl·or -ārī -ātus sum *vi* to bargain
instĭt·a -ae *f* border, flounce; (fig) lady
institī·ō -ōnis *f* standing still
instĭt·or -ōris *m* salesman, huckster, hawker
instit·ŭō -uĕre -ŭī -ūtum *vt* to set, fix, plant; to set up, erect, establish; to arrange; to build, make, construct; to prepare, make ready; to provide, furnish; to institute, organize, set up; to appoint, designate; to undertake, begin; to decide, determine; to control, direct, govern; to teach, train, instruct, educate
institūtī·ō -ōnis *f* arrangement; custom; instruction, education; *f pl* principles of education
institūt·um -ī *n* practice, custom, usage; precedent; principle; decree, regulation, stipulation, terms; purpose, intention; **ex instituto** according to custom
in·stō -stāre -stitī *vt* to follow, pursue; to work hard at; to menace, threaten; *vi* to be at hand, approach, be impending; to insist; (with *dat* or **in** + *abl*) to stand on or in; (with *dat*) **a** to be close to; **b** to be on the heels of, pursue closely; **c** to harass
instrātus *pp* of **insterno**
instrēnŭ·us -a -um *adj* lethargic
instrēp·ō -āre -ŭī -ĭtum *vi* to creak, rattle
instructī·ō -ōnis *f* construction; array
instructĭus *adv* with better preparation
instruct·or -ōris *m* supervisor
instruct·us -a -um *pp* of **instruo**; *adj* provided, equipped, furnished; prepared, arranged; instructed, versed
instruct·us -ūs *m* equipment; stock-in-trade (*of an orator*)
instrūment·um -ī *n* instrument, tool, utensil; equipment; dress, outfit; repertory, stock-in-trade; means, supply, provisions; document
in·strŭō -struĕre -struxī -structum *vt* to build up, construct; to furnish, prepare, provide, fit out; to instruct; (mil) to deploy
insuās·um -ī *n* dark-orange color
insuāv·is -e *adj* unpleasant, disagreeable
insūd·ō -āre *vi* (with *dat*) to sweat on, drip sweat on
insuēfact·us -a -um *adj* accustomed
in·suescō -suescĕre -suēvī -suētum *vt* to accustom, familiarize; *vi* (with *dat*, with **ad** + *acc*, or with *inf*) to get used to
insuēt·us -a -um *adj* unusual; (with *genit* or *dat*, with **ad** + *acc*, or with *inf*) unused to
insŭl·a -ae *f* island; apartment building
insulān·us -ī *m* islander
insulsē *adv* in poor taste; insipidly, absurdly
insulsĭt·ās -ātis *f* lack of taste; silliness, absurdity
insuls·us -a -um *adj* unsalted, without taste; coarse, tasteless, insipid; silly, absurd; bungling; *f pl* silly creatures (*i.e., women*)
insult·ō -āre *vt* to insult, scoff at, taunt; (of votaries) to dance about in; *vi* to jump, gambol, prance; to gloat; (with *abl*) **a** to jump in, cavort in, gambol on, jump upon; **b** to gloat over; (with *dat* or **in** + *acc*) to scoff at, gloat over
insultūr·a -ae *f* jumping in
insum inesse infŭī *vi* to be there; (with *dat* or **in** + *abl*) **a** to be in, be on; **b** to be implied in, be contained in, be in, belong to

in·sūmō -sūměre -sumpsī -sumptum *vt* to spend, devote, waste; (with *dat* or **in** + *acc*) to devote to, apply to; (with *abl* or **in** + *abl*) to expend on; **operam insumere** (with *dat*) to devote effort to, waste effort on

in·suō -suěre -suī -sūtum *vt* to sew up; (wth *dat*) **a** to sew up in; **b** to embroider (*something*) on

insŭper *adv* above, overhead, on the top; from above; moreover, besides, in addition; *prep* (with *acc*) above, over, over and above; (with *abl*) in addition to, besides

insuperābil·is -e *adj* insurmountable; unconquerable

in·surgō -surgěre -surrexī -surrectum *vi* to rise, stand up; to rise, stand high, tower; to rise, increase, grow, grow intense; to rise to power; (with *dat*) **a** to rise up against; **b** to strain at (*e.g., oars*)

insusurr·ō -āre *vt* (with *dat*) to whisper (*something*) to; **insusurrare in aurem** (with *genit*) to whisper into the ear of; **sibi cantilenam insusurrare** to hum a tune to oneself; *vi* to whisper; (of wind) to blow gently

intāb·escō -escěre -ŭī *vi* to melt away gradually, dissolve gradually; (fig) to waste away, pine away

intactīl·is -e *adj* intangible

intact·us -a -um *adj* untouched; uninjured, intact; unpolluted; untried; unmarried; virgin, chaste

intact·us -ūs *m* intangibility

intāmināt·us -a -um *adj* unsullied

intect·us -a -um *pp* of **intego**; *adj* uncovered; naked; open, frank

integell·us -a -um *adj* fairly pure or chaste; in fair condition

intěg·er -ra -rum *adj* whole, complete, intact, unimpaired; unhurt, unwounded; healthy, sound, fresh; new, fresh; pure, chaste; untouched, unaffected; unbiased, unprejudiced; unattempted; unsubdued, unconquered; unbroken (*horse*); not worn, unused; inexperienced, ignorant; virtuous, honest, blameless, irreproachable; healthy, sane; **ab integro** or **de integro** anew, all over again; **in integrum restituere** to restore to a former condition; to pardon; **integrum alicui esse** (with *inf*) to be in someone's power to

in·tĕgō -tegěre -texī -tectum *vt* to cover up; to protect

integrasc·ō -ěre *vi* to break out fresh, start all over again

integrātī·ō -ōnis *f* renewal, new beginning

intěgrē *adv* wholly, entirely; honestly; correctly

integrit·ās -ātis *f* soundness; integrity; innocence; purity, chastity; correctness

intěgr·ō -āre *vt* to make whole; to heal, repair; to renew, begin again; to refresh

integument·um -ī *n* covering; lid; protection

intellectus *pp* of **intellego**

intellect·us -ūs *m* perception; comprehension, understanding; intellect

intellěg·ens -entis *adj* intelligent; (with *genit*) appreciative of; (with **in** + *abl*) versed in

intellegenter *adv* intelligently

intellegentī·a -ae *f* intelligence; understanding, knowledge; perception, judgment, discrimination, taste, skill; concept, notion; (with *genit*) knowledge or understanding of; (with **in** + *abl*) judgment in

intel·lĕgō -legěre -lexī -lectum *vt* to understand, perceive, discern, comprehend, gather; to realize, recognize; to have an accurate knowledge of, be an expert in; *vi* **intellego** (in answers) I understand, I get it

intemerāt·us -a -um *adj* undefiled, pure; pure, undiluted

intempěr·ans -antis *adj* intemperate, without restraint; profligate; excessive

intemperanter *adv* intemperately

intemperantī·a -ae *f* intemperance, lack of self-control; extravagance, excess

intemperātē *adv* intemperately

intemperāt·us -a -um *adj* excessive

intemperārī·ae -ārum *f pl* wild outbursts, wildness

intemperī·ēs -ēī *f* wildness, excess; outrageous conduct, excesses; **intemperies aquarum** heavy rain; **intemperies caeli** stormy weather

intempestīvē *adv* at a bad time, inopportunely

intempestīv·us -a -um *adj* untimely, unseasonable; poorly timed

intempest·us -a -um *adj* unseasonable; dark, dismal; unhealthy; **nox intempesta** dead of night

intemptāt·us or **intentāt·us -a -um** *adj* unattempted

in·tendō -tenděre -tendī -tentum or **-tensum** *vt* to stretch, stretch out, extend, spread out; to stretch, bend (*e.g., bow*); to aim, direct, shoot (*weapon*); to increase, magnify, intensify; to intend; to urge, incite; to aim at, intend; to assert, maintain; to aim, turn, direct; to raise (*voice*); to stretch (*truth*); to direct, turn, focus (*mind, attention*); to pitch (*tent*)

intentātus see **intemptatus**

intentē *adv* intently, attentively

intentī·ō -ōnis *f* stretching, straining, tension; attention; effort, exertion; accusation

intent·ō -āre *vt* to stretch out; to aim, direct; to threaten

intent·us -a -um *pp* of **intendo**; *adj* taut, tense; intent, attentive; eager, waiting, tense; strict (*discipline*); vigorous, tense, nervous (*speech*)

intent·us -ūs *m* stretching out, extending (*of the palms*)
intep·ĕō -ēre -ŭī *vi* to be lukewarm
intep·escō -pescĕre -ŭī *vi* to grow warm, be warmed
inter *prep* (with *acc*) between, among, amidst; during, within, in the course of; in spite of; (in classifying) among, in, with; **inter se** each other, one another, mutual, mutually
interaestŭ·ō -āre *vi* to retch
interāment·a -ōrum *n pl* framework of a ship
Interamn·a -ae *f* town in Latium, on the Liris; town in Umbria, birthplace of Tacitus
interapt·us -a -um *adj* joined together
interāresc·ō -ĕre *vi* to dry up
interātim *adv* meanwhile
interbīb·ō -ĕre *vt* to drink up
interbīt·ō -ĕre *vi* to come to nothing
intercalār·is -e *adj* intercalary, inserted
intercalārĭ·us -a -um *adj* intercalary, inserted
intercăl·ō -āre *vt* to intercalate, insert
intercapēd·ō -ĭnis *f* interruption, break, pause
inter·cēdō -cēdĕre -cessī -cessum *vi* to come or go in between; (of time) to intervene, pass, occur; to act as an intermediary; to intercede; (of tribunes) to exercise the veto; (with *dat*) **a** to veto, protest against; **b** to interfere with, obstruct, hinder
interceptĭ·ō -ōnis *f* interception
intercept·or -ōris *m* embezzler
interceptus *pp* of **intercipio**
intercessĭ·ō -ōnis *f* intercession, mediation; (tribune's) veto
intercess·or -ōris *m* intercessor, mediator; interferer, obstructor; tribune exercising the veto
inter·cĭdō -cidĕre -cĭdī *vi* to fall short, miss the mark; to happen in the meantime; to drop out, be lost
inter·cīdō -cīdĕre -cīdī -cīsum *vt* to cut through, sever, cut down
intercĭn·ō -ĕre *vt* to interrupt with song or music
inter·cipĭō -cipĕre -cēpī -ceptum *vt* to intercept; to cut off (*the enemy*); to interrupt, cut off, preclude; to appropriate; to misappropriate; to receive by mistake (*e.g., poison*)
intercīsē *adv* piecemeal
intercīsus *pp* of **intercido**
inter·clūdō -clūdĕre -clūsī -clūsum *vt* to shut off, shut out, cut off; to stop, block up; to hinder, prevent; to blockade, shut in; to cut off, intercept, separate, divide
interclūsĭ·ō -ōnis *f* stopping; parenthesis; **animae interclusio** shortwindedness
interclūsus *pp* of **intercludo**
intercolumn·ĭum -ĭī or **-ī** *n* space between columns, intercolumniation
inter·currō -currĕre -cucurrī -cursum *vi* to intervene, mediate; to mingle; to rush in
intercurs·ō -āre *vi* to crisscross; to infiltrate; **inter se intercursare** to crisscross each other
intercurs·us -ūs *m* intervention
interc·us -ŭtis *adj* between the skin and flesh; **aqua intercus** dropsy
inter·dīcō -dīcĕre -dixī -dictum *vt* to forbid, prohibit; *vi* to make a provisional decree; **aquā et igni interdicere** (with *dat*) to outlaw, banish
interdictĭ·ō -ōnis *f* prohibiting; **aquae et igni interdictio** banishment
interdict·um -ī *n* prohibition; contraband; provisional decree (*of a praetor*)
interdictus *pp* of **interdico**
interdĭū or **interdĭūs** *adv* by day, in the daytime
interd·ō -āre *vt* to give intermittently; to distribute
interduct·us -ūs *m* punctuation
interdum *adv* sometimes, now and then, occasionally; meanwhile
interdŭ·ō -āre *vt* **floccum interduo** or **nihil interduo** I don't give a hoot
interĕā *adv* meanwhile, in the interim; meanwhile, anyhow, nevertheless
interemptus *pp* of **interimo**
inter·ĕō -īre -ĭī -ĭtum *vi* to be done for, be finished, perish, be lost; to become extinct
ride in between
interequit·ō -āre *vt* to ride between (*e.g., the ranks or columns*); *vi* to
interfātĭ·ō -ōnis *f* interruption
interfectĭ·ō -ōnis *f* killing
interfect·or -ōris *m* or **interfectr·ix -īcis** *f* killer
inter·ficiō -ficĕre -fēcī -fectum *vt* to destroy; to kill
inter·fīō -fĭĕrī *vi* to pass away, be destroyed
inter·flŭō -fluĕre -fluxī *vt* to flow between; *vi* to flow in between
inter·fodĭō -fodĕre -fōdī -fossum *vi* to pierce
interf·or -ārī -ātus sum *vt & vi* to interrupt
interfug·ĭō -ĕre *vi* to scatter
interfulg·ĕō -ēre *vi* (with *abl*) to shine amidst or among
interfūs·us -a -um *adj* spread here and there; (with *acc*) flowing between
interĭbi *adv* in the meantime
intĕrim *adv* meanwhile; for the moment; sometimes; however, anyhow
inter·imō -imĕre -ēmī -emptum *vt* to do away with, abolish; to kill
inter·ior -ĭus *adj* inner, interior; inner side of; secret, private; deeper, more profound; more intimate, more personal, more confidential
interitĭ·ō -ōnis *f* ruin, destruction
interĭt·us -ūs *m* ruin; death

interius *adv* on the inside, in the middle; too short; (to listen) closely
interjac·ĕō -ēre *vi* (with *dat*) to lie between
interjaciō see **interjicio**
interjecti·ō -ōnis *f* interjection; parenthesis
interject·us -a -um *pp* of **interjicio;** *adj* (with *dat* or **inter** + *acc*) set or lying between
interject·us -ūs *m* interposition; interval
inter·jiciō -jicĕre -jēcī -jectum *vt* to interpose; (with *dat* or **inter** + *acc*) **a** to throw or set (*something*) between; **b** to intermingle (*something*) with, intermix (*something*) with
inter·jungō -jungĕre -junxī -junctum *vt* to join together; to clasp
inter·lābor -lābī -lapsus *vi* to glide or flow in between
inter·lĕgō -legĕre -lēgī -lectum *vt* to pick or pluck here and there
inter·linō -linĕre -lēvī -litum *vt* to smear; to alter by erasing
inter·lŏquor -lŏquī -locūtus sum *vi* to interrupt; (with *dat*) to interrupt (*someone*)
inter·lūcĕō -lūcēre -luxī *vi* to shine through; to lighten now and then; to be transparent; to be plainly visible
interlūnī·a -ōrum *n pl* new moon
interlŭ·ō -ĕre *vt* to flow between, wash
intermenstrŭ·us -a -um *adj* of the new moon; *n* new moon
intermināt·us -a -um *adj* endless
intermĭn·or -ārī -ātus sum *vt* (with *dat*) to threaten (*someone*) with (*something*); *vi* to threaten
inter·miscĕō -miscēre -miscŭī -mixtum *vt* to intermingle
intermissi·ō -ōnis *f* interruption
inter·mittō -mittĕre -mīsī -missum *vt* to interrupt, break off, suspend, omit, neglect; to leave gaps in, leave unoccupied, leave undefended; to allow (*time*) to pass; *vi* to pause, stop
intermixtus *pp* of **intermisceo**
inter·morĭor -mŏrī -mortŭus sum *vi* to die suddenly; to faint
intermortŭ·us -a -um *adj* dead; unconscious; (fig) half-dead, moribund
intermundĭ·a -ōrum *n pl* outer space
intermūrāl·is -e *adj* intermural, between two walls
internāt·us -a -um *adj* (with *dat*) growing among or between
internecīn·us -a -um *adj* internecine, exterminating, of extermination
interneci·ō -ōnis *f* massacre, extermination
internecīv·us -a -um *adj* exterminating; **bellum internecivum** war of extermination
internĕc·ō -āre *vt* to kill off, exterminate
internect·ō -ĕre *vt* to intertwine
internit·ĕō -ēre *vi* to shine out
internōd·ium -iī or **-ī** *n* space between two joints
inter·noscō -noscĕre -nōvī -nōtum *vt* to distinguish, recognize; (with **ab** + *abl*) to distinguish (*one thing*) from (*another*)
internunti·ō -āre *vi* to exchange messages
internunt·ius -iī or **-ī** *m* or **internunti·a -ae** *f* messenger, courier, mediator, go-between
intern·us -a -um *adj* internal; civil, domestic
in·tĕrō -terĕre -trīvī -trītum *vt* to rub in, mash together
interpellāti·ō -ōnis *f* interruption
interpellāt·or -ōris *m* interrupter, disturber
interpell·ō -āre *vt* to interrupt, break in on; to disturb, obstruct, hinder; to raise as an objection
interpŏl·is -e *adj* patched up
interpŏl·ō -āre *vt* to polish, dress up; to interpolate, falsify
inter·pōnō -pōnĕre -posŭī -positum *vt* to insert, interpose, intersperse; to introduce, insert; to introduce, admit (*a person*); to let (*time*) pass or elapse; to alter, falsify (*writings*); to allege, use as pretext; **operam** or **studium interponere** to apply effort; **se interponere** (with *dat* or **in** + *acc*) to interfere with, meddle with, get mixed up with
interpositi·ō -ōnis *f* insertion; introduction; parenthesis
interpositus *pp* of **interpono**
interposit·us -ūs *m* interposition
interpr·es -ĕtis *m & f* mediator, negotiator; middleman, broker; interpreter; expounder; translator
interpretāti·ō -ōnis *f* interpretation, explanation; meaning; translation
interprĕt·or -ārī -ātus sum *vt* to interpret, put a construction on, construe; to understand, infer, conclude; to decide, determine; to translate
inter·prĭmō -primĕre -pressī -pressum *vt* to squeeze
interpunct·a -ōrum *n pl* pauses, punctuation
interpuncti·ō -ōnis *f* punctuation
interpunct·us -a -um *adj* well-divided
inter·quiescō -quiescĕre -quiēvī *vi* to rest awhile; to pause awhile
interregn·um -ī *n* interregnum (*time between death of one king and election of another or similar interval between consuls*)
inter·rex -rēgis *m* interrex, regent
interrit·us -a -um *adj* undaunted
interrogāti·ō -ōnis *f* question; interrogation, cross-examination; syllogism

interrogāt·um -ī *n* question.
interrŏg·ō -āre *vt* to ask, question; to interrogate, cross-examine; to indict, sue
inter·rumpō -rumpĕre -rūpī -ruptum *vt* to break apart, break in half, break up, smash; to divide, scatter; to interrupt, break off
interruptē *adv* with interruptions
interruptus *pp* of **interrumpo**
inter·saepiō -saepīre -saepsī -saeptum *vt* to fence off, enclose; to stop up, close, cut off
inter·scindō -scindĕre -scidī -scissum *vt* to tear apart, tear down; to cut off, separate
inter·scrībō -scrībĕre -scripsī -scriptum *vt* to write (*something*) in between
inter·sĕrō -serĕre -serŭī *vt* to interpose; to allege as an excuse
interspīrāti·ō -ōnis *f* breathing pause, correct breathing (*in delivering a speech*)
interstinct·us -a -um *adj* blotchy
inter·stinguō -stinguĕre — -stinctum *vt* to spot, blotch; to extinguish
interstring·ō -ĕre *vt* to strangle
inter·sum -esse -fŭī *vi* to be present, assist, take part; to differ; to be of interest; (with *dat*) to be present at, attend, take part in; (with **in** + *abl*) to be present at; *v impers* there is a difference; it makes a difference; it is of importance; it is of interest; (with **inter** + *acc*) there is a difference between; (with **in** + *abl*) there is a difference among; (with *genit* or with *fem* of possessive pronouns **meā, tuā, nostrā,** *etc.*) it make a difference to, it is of importance to, it concerns (*me, you, us, etc.*); (with *genit* of value, e.g., **magni, permagni, tanti,** or with *adv* **multum, plurimum, maxime**) it makes a (*great, very great, such a great*) difference, it is of (*great, very great, such great*) importance, it is of (*great, very great, such great*) concern; **ne minimum quidem interest** there is not the slightest difference; **nihil omnino interest** there is no difference whatever
intertext·us -a -um *adj* interwoven
inter·trăhō -trahĕre -traxī *vt* (with *dat*) to take (*something*) away from
intertrīment·um -ī *n* wear and tear; loss, wastage
interturbāti·ō -ōnis *f* confusion, turmoil
interturb·ō -āre *vt* to confuse
intervall·um -ī *n* interval, space, distance; interval of time, spell, pause, intermission; contrast, difference
inter·vellō -vellĕre -vulsī -vulsum *vt* to pluck here and there
inter·veniō -venīre -vēnī -ventum *vt* to interfere with; *vi* to happen along; to intervene, intrude; to happen, occur; (with *dat*) to interfere with, interrupt, put a stop to, come in the way of, oppose, prevent
intervent·or -ōris *m* intruder, untimely visitor
intervent·us -ūs *m* intervention, intrusion; mediation
inter·vertō or **inter·vortō -vertĕre -vertī -versum** *vt* to divert, embezzle; (with *acc* of person and *abl* of thing) to rob or cheat (*someone*) of
inter·vīsō -vīsĕre -vīsī -vīsum *vt* to visit from time to time; to look after
intervolĭt·ō -āre *vi* to flit about
intervŏm·ō -ĕre -ŭī -ĭtum *vt* (with **inter** + *acc*) to throw up amongst
intervulsus *pp* of **intervello**
intestābĭl·is -e *adj* infamous, notorious; wicked
intestātō *adv* intestate
intestāt·us -a -um *adj* intestate; unconvicted by witnesses
intestāt·us -a -um *adj* castrated
intestīn·us -a -um *adj* internal; *n* & *n pl* intestines
in·texō -texĕre -texŭī -textum *vt* to interweave, interlace; to weave; to embroider; to surround, envelop
intĭb·um -ī *n* endive
intimē *adv* intimately, cordially
intĭm·us or **intŭm·us -a -um** *adj* innermost; deepest, most profound; most secret, most intimate; *m* intimate friend
in·tingō or **in·tinguō -tingĕre -tinxī -tinctum** *vt* to dip, soak
intolerābĭl·is -e *adj* intolerable; irresistible
intolerand·us -a -um *adj* intolerable
intolĕr·ans -antis *adj* intolerable, insufferable; (with *genit*) unable to stand, unable to put up with
intoleranter *adv* intolerably, immoderately, excessively
intoleranti·a -ae *f* unbearableness, insolence
intŏn·ō -āre -ŭī -ātus *vt* to thunder out; *vi* to thunder
intons·us -a -um *adj* unshorn, untrimmed; long-haired; rude
in·torquĕō -torquēre -torsī -tortum *vt* to twist, turn, roll; (with **circum** + *acc*) to wrap (*something*) around; (with *dat* or **in** + *acc*) to aim, cast, throw (*a weapon*) at
intort·us -a -um *adj* twisted; tangled; (fig) crooked
intrā *adv* on the inside, inside, within; inward; *prep* (with *acc*) inside, within; during, within, in the course of, in less than; less than, fewer than, within the limits of
intrābĭl·is -e *adj* inaccessible
intractābĭl·is -e *adj* intractable, unmanageable; formidable, dangerous
intractāt·us -a -um *adj* untamed, wild; unbroken (*horse*); unattempted

intrem·iscō -iscĕre -ŭī *vi* to begin to shake or tremble
intrĕm·ō -ĕre -ŭī *vi* to shake, tremble, shiver
intrepĭdē *adv* calmly, intrepidly
intrepĭd·us -a -um *adj* calm, intrepid, not nervous
intrīc·ō -āre *vt* to entangle, involve
intrinsĕcus *adv* on the inside
intrīt·us -a -um *adj* not worn away; (fig) not worn out
intrō *adv* inwards, inside, in
intr·ō -āre *vt & vi* to enter; to penetrate
intrō·dūcō -dūcĕre -duxī -ductum *vt* to introduce
intrōductī·ō -ōnis *f* introduction
intro·ĕō -īre -iī -ĭtum *vt & vi* to enter
intrō·fĕrō -ferre -tŭlī -lātum *vt* to carry in
intrō·gredĭor -grĕdī -gressus sum *vi* to step inside
introït·us -ūs *m* entrance; beginning, prelude
intrōlātus *pp* of **introfero**
intrō·mittō -mittĕre -mīsī -missum *vt* to let in, admit
introrsum or **introrsus** *adv* inwards, towards the inside; (fig) inwardly, inside
intrō·rumpō -rumpĕre -rūpī -ruptum *vi* to break in, enter by force
introspect·ō -āre *vt* to look in on
intrō·spicĭō -spicĕre -spexī -spectum *vt* to look into, look at; (fig) to inspect, examine, observe; *vi* (with **in** + *acc*) to look into; (fig) to look into, inspect, examine
intŭb·um -ī *n* endive
in·tuĕor -tuērī -tuĭtus sum *vt* to look at, gaze upon; to contemplate, consider; to look up to, have regard for, admire; to keep an eye on
intum·escō -escĕre -ŭī *vi* to swell up, rise; (of voice) to grow louder; (of river) to rise; to become angry; to get a big head, swell with pride
intumulāt·us -a -um *adj* unburied
in·tŭor -tŭī *vt* to look at, gaze at; to consider
inturbĭd·us -a -um *adj* undisturbed, quiet
intus *adv* inside, within; at home, in; to the inside; from within
intūt·us -a -um *adj* unguarded; unsafe
inŭl·a -ae *f* elecampane (*plant*)
inult·us -a -um *adj* unavenged; unpunished, without being punished
inumbr·ō -āre *vt* to shade; to cover
inundātĭ·ō -ōnis *f* inundation
inund·ō -āre *vt* to flood, inundate; *vi* to overflow; **sanguine inundare** to run red with blood
in·ungō -ungĕre -unxī -unctum *vt* to anoint
inurbānē *adv* impolitely, rudely; without wit
inurbān·us -a -um *adj* impolite, rude, rustic
in·urgĕō -urgēre -ursī *vi* to butt
in·ūrō -ūrĕre -ussī -ustum *vt* to burn in, brand, imprint; (with *dat*) **a** to brand upon, imprint upon, affix to; **b** to inflict upon
inūsĭtātē *adv* unusually, strangely
inūsĭtāt·us -a -um *adj* unusual, strange, uncommon, extraordinary
inustus *pp* of **inuro**
inūtĭl·is -e *adj* useless, unprofitable; impractical; injurious, harmful
inūtilĭt·ās -ātis *f* uselessness; harmfulness
inūtilĭter *adv* uselessly, unprofitably
in·vādō -vādĕre -vāsī -vāsum *vt* to come or go into, enter; to enter upon, undertake, attempt; to invade, attack, assault, rush upon; (fig) to seize, take possession of; *vi* to come or go in; to invade; (with **in** + *acc*) **a** to assail, attack, invade; **b** to seize, get possession of, usurp
inval·escō -escĕre -ŭī *vi* to grow stronger
invalĭd·us -a -um *adj* weak, feeble, impotent; inadequate, unsuitable
invāsus *pp* of **invado**
invectĭ·ō -ōnis *f* importing, importation; arrival by boat
in·vĕhō -vehĕre -vexī -vectum *vt* to carry in, bring in (*by cart, horse, boat, etc.*); (with *dat*) to bring (*e.g., evils*) upon; **invehi** (with *acc* or **in** + *acc*) **a** to ride into, sail into; **b** to attack; **c** to inveigh against, attack (*with words*); **invehi equo** to ride a horse; **invehi nave** to sail; **se invehere** (with *acc* or **in** + *acc*) to rush against, attack
invendibĭl·is -e *adj* unsalable
in·venĭō -venīre -vēnī -ventum *vt* to come upon, find, come across, discover; to find out, invent, devise; to learn, ascertain; to acquire, get, reach, earn
inventĭ·ō -ōnis *f* inventiveness; inventing, invention
invent·or -ōris *m* or **inventr·ix -īcis** *f* inventor, author, discoverer
invent·us -a -um *pp* of **invenio**; *n* invention, discovery
invenust·us -a -um *adj* having no sex appeal; homely, unattractive; unlucky in love
inverēcund·us -a -um *adj* disrespectful, immodest, shameless
inverg·ō -ĕre *vt* to pour upon
inversĭ·ō -ōnis *f* inversion (*of words*); irony; allegory
invers·us -a -um *adj* turned upside down; turned inside out
in·vertō -vertĕre -vertī -versum *vt* to invert, turn upside down, upset, reverse, turn inside out; to transpose, reverse; to pervert, abuse, misrepresent; to use ironically
invesperasc·it -ĕre *v impers* evening is approaching, twilight is falling
investīgātĭ·ō -ōnis *f* investigation

investīgāt·or -ōris *m* investigator, researcher
investīg·ō -āre *vt* to track, trace, search after; to investigate, search into, search after
inveter·ascō -ascĕre -āvī *vi* to begin to grow old, grow old; to become fixed, become established; to become rooted, grow inveterate; to become obsolete
inveterātī·ō -ōnis *f* chronic illness
inveterāt·us -a -um *adj* inveterate, long-standing
invicem or **in vicem** *adv* in turn, taking turns, one after another, alternately; mutually, each other
invict·us -a -um *adj* unconquered; invincible
invid·ens -entis *adj* envious, jealous
invidentī·a -ae *f* enviousness, jealousy
in·vidĕō -vidēre -vīdī -vīsum *vt* to cast an evil eye on; to envy, begrudge; *vi* (with *dat*) to envy, begrudge; (with *dat* of person and *abl* of cause or **in** + *abl*) to begrudge (*someone something*), envy (*someone because of something*)
invidī·a -ae *f* envy, jealousy; unpopularity; **invidiae esse** (with *dat*) to be a cause of envy to; **invidiam habere** to be unpopular, be hated
invidiōsē *adv* spitefully
invidiōs·us -a -um *adj* envious, spiteful; envied; causing envy
invid·us -a -um *adj* envious, jealous; (with *dat*) hostile to, unfavorable to
invigil·ō -āre *vi* to be alert, be on one's toes; (with *dat*) to be on the lookout for, keep an eye on, pay attention to, watch over; (with **pro** + *abl*) to watch over
inviolābil·is -e *adj* inviolable; invulnerable, indestructible
inviolātē *adv* inviolately
inviolāt·us -a -um *adj* inviolate, unhurt; inviolable
invīsitāt·us -a -um *adj* rarely seen; not seen before, unknown, strange
in·vīsō -vīsĕre -vīsī -vīsum *vt* to visit, get to see; to look into, inspect; to look after; to get sight of
invīs·us -a -um *pp* of **invideo**; *adj* unseen; hateful, detested; hostile
invītāment·um -ī *n* attraction, allurement, inducement
invītātī·ō -ōnis *f* invitation; challenge
invītāt·us -ūs *m* invitation
invītē *adv* unwillingly, against one's wish
invīt·ō -āre *vt* to invite; to entertain; to summon, challenge; to ask, request; to allure, attract; to encourage, court
invīt·us -a -um *adj* reluctant, unwilling, against one's will; **invitā Minervā** against one's better judgment, against the grain
invī·us -a -um *adj* without a road, trackless, impassable; *n pl* rough terrain
invocātī·ō -ōnis *f* invocation
invocāt·us -a -um *adj* unbidden
invŏc·ō -āre *vt* to invoke, call upon, appeal to
involāt·us -ūs *m* flight
involgō see **invulgo**
involit·ō -āre *vi* (with *dat*) (of long hair) to float over, trail over
invŏl·ō -āre *vt* to swoop down upon, pounce upon; *vi* to swoop down; (with **in** + *acc*) to swoop down upon, pounce upon
involūcr·e -is *n* smock
involūcr·um -ī *n* wrapper, cover, case, envelope; (fig) cover-up, front
involūt·us -a -um *adj* complicated
in·volvō -volvĕre -volvī -volūtum *vt* to wrap up, involve, envelop; to cover completely, overwhelm; (with *dat* or **in** + *acc*) to pile (*something*) on; **se involvere** (with *dat*) (fig) to get all wrapped up in
involvŏl·us -ī *m* caterpillar
invulg·ō -āre *vi* to give evidence
invulnerāt·us -a -um *adj* unwounded
iō *interj* ho!
io- = jo-
Ī·ō -ūs or **Ī·ōn -ōnis** *f* Io (*daughter of Argive King Inachus, changed by Jupiter into a heifer, and driven by Juno in this form over the world under the surveillance of hundred-eyed Argus*)
Iocast·a -ae or **Iocast·ē -ēs** *f* wife of Laius and mother as well as wife of Oedipus
Iolā·us -ī *m* son of Iphicles and companion of Hercules
Iŏl·ē -ēs *f* daughter of Eurytus, the king of Oechalia, who fell in love with Hercules
Iōn see **Io**
Iōn·es -um *m pl* Ionians (*Greek inhabitants of the W. coast of Asia Minor*)
Iōnĭ·cus -a -um *adj* Ionic; *m* Ionic dancer; *n pl* Ionic dance
Iōnĭ·us -a -um *adj* Ionian; *f* Ionia (*coastal district of Asia Minor*); *n* Ionian Sea (*off the W. Coast of Greece*)
iōta (*indecl*) *n* iota (*ninth letter of the Greek alphabet*)
Īphianass·a -ae *f* Iphigenia
Īphigenī·a -ae *f* daughter of Agamemnon and Clytemnestra, who was to have been sacrificed at Aulis but was saved by Diana and conveyed to the Tauric Chersonese, where she became priestess of Diana
Īphit·us -ī *m* Argonaut, son of Eurytus and Antiope
ips·a -īus or **-ĭus** *adj* self, very, just, mere, precisely; in person; by herself, alone; of herself, of her

own accord; *pron* she herself; mistress of the house
ips·e (or **ips·us**) **-īus** (or **-ĭus**) *adj* self, very, just, mere, precisely; in person; by himself, alone; of himself, of his own accord; *pron* he himself; master; host
ips·um -īus or **-ĭus** *adj* self, very, just, mere, precisely; by itself, alone; of itself, spontaneously; **nunc ipsum** just now; **tunc ipsum** just then; *pron* it itself, that itself; **ipsum quod . . .** the very fact that . . .
ipsus see **ipse**
īr·a -ae *f* ire, wrath, resentment
īrācundē *adv* angrily; passionately
īrācundĭ·a -ae *f* quick temper; anger, wrath, violence, passion; resentment
īrācund·us -a -um *adj* hot-tempered, quick-tempered, irritable; angry; resentful
īrasc·or -ī *vi* to get angry, fly into a rage; (with *dat*) to get angry at
īrātē *adv* angrily
īrāt·us -a -um *adj* angry, irate, enraged; (with *dat*) angry at
Īr·is -ĭdis *f* goddess of the rainbow and messenger of the gods
īrōnī·a -ae *f* irony
irrās·us -a -um *adj* unshaven
irratiōnāl·is -e *adj* irrational
ir·raucescō -raucescĕre -rausī *vi* to become hoarse
irredivīv·us -a -um *adj* irreparable
irrĕd·ux -ŭcis *adj* one-way (*road*)
irreligāt·us -a -um *adj* not tied
irreligiōsē *adv* impiously
irreligiōs·us -a -um *adj* impious, irreligious
irremeābĭl·is -e *adj* not to be traversed; one-way
irreparābĭl·is -e *adj* irretrievable
irrepert·us -a -um *adj* undiscovered, not found
ir·rēpō -rēpĕre -repsī -reptum *vi* to creep in; (fig) to sneak in; (with **ad** or **in** + *acc*) to creep toward or into; (fig) to sneak up on
irreprehens·us -a -um *adj* blameless
irrequiēt·us -a -um *adj* restless
irresect·us -a -um *adj* untrimmed
irresolūt·us -a -um *adj* not loosened, still tied
irrēt·iō -īre -īvī or **-iī -ītum** *vt* to trap
irretort·us -a -um *adj* not turned back
irrevĕr·ens -entis *adj* irreverent, disrespectful
irreverenter *adv* irreverently, disrespectfully
irreverentĭ·a -ae *f* irreverence, disrespect
irrevocābĭl·is -e *adj* irrevocable; implacable, relentless
irrevocāt·us -a -um *adj* not called back, not asked back
ir·rīdĕō -rīdēre -rīsī -rīsum *vt* to ridicule, laugh at, mock; *vi* to laugh, joke; (with *dat*) to laugh at
irrīdicŭlē *adv* with no sense of humor
irrigātĭ·ō -ōnis *f* irrigation
irrĭg·ō -āre *vt* to irrigate, water; to inundate; (fig) to diffuse; (fig) to flood, steep, soak
irrigŭ·us -a -um *adj* wet, soaked, well-watered; refreshing
irrīsĭ·ō -ōnis *f* ridicule, mockery
irrīs·or -ōris *m* reviler, mocker
irrīsus *pp* of **irrideo**
irrīs·us -ūs *m* mockery, derision; laughing stock, object of derision
irrītābĭl·is -e *adj* easily excited, easily enraged, irritable, sensitive
irrītām·en -ĭnis *n* incentive; provocation
irrītāment·um -ī *n* incentive; provocation
irrītātĭ·ō -ōnis *f* incitement; irritation, provocation; stimulant
irrīt·ō -āre *vt* to incite, excite, provoke, enrage
irrĭt·us -a -um *adj* invalid, null and void; futile, pointless, useless; unsuccessful (*person*)
irrogātĭ·ō -ōnis *f* imposing (*e.g., of a fine*)
irrŏg·ō -āre *vt* to impose, inflict; to object to (*proposals*)
irrōr·ō -āre *vt* to wet, moisten, sprinkle
irruct·ō -āre *vi* to belch
ir·rumpō -rumpĕre -rūpī -ruptum *vt* to rush into, break down; *vi* to rush in; (with *dat* or **in** + *acc*) **a** to rush into, rush through; **b** (fig) to intrude upon
ir·rŭō -ruĕre -rŭī *vi* to rush in, force one's way in; to make a slip (*in speaking*); (with **in** + *acc*) to rush into, rush on, invade, attack; **inruere in odium** (with *genit*) to incur the anger of
irruptĭ·ō -ōnis *f* invasion
irrupt·us -a -um *pp* of **irrumpo**; *adj* unbroken
Īr·us -ī *m* beggar in the palace of Ulysses in Ithaca
is ejus *adj* this, that, the said, the aforesaid; *pron* he; **is qui** he who, the person who, the one who
Īs·is -is or **-ĭdis** *f* Egyptian goddess
Ismarĭ·us -a -um *adj* of Mt. Ismarus in Thrace; Thracian
Īsocrăt·ēs -is *m* famous orator and teacher of rhetoric at Athens (436-338 B.C.)
ista see **iste**
istāc *adv* that way
istactĕnus *adv* thus far
istaec see **istic**
ist·e -a -ud *adj* that of yours; this, that, the very, that particular; such, of such a kind; that terrible, that despicable; *pron* that one; (in court) your client
Isthm·us or **Isthm·os -ī** *m* Isthmus of Corinth

ist·ic -aec -oc or **-uc** *adj* that, that of yours; *pron* the one, that one
istīc *adv* there, in that place; herein; on this occasion
istinc *adv* from there, from where you are
istīusmŏdī or **istīmŏdī** or **istīus modī** or **istī modī** *adj* that kind of, such
istō *adv* where you are; therefore; in that matter
istōc *adv* there, to where you are, yonder
istorsum *adv* in that direction
istūc *adv* there, to that place, to where you are, that way; **istuc veniam** I'll come to that matter
istūcine see **istic**
istud see **iste**
ita *adv* thus, so, in this manner, in this way; (of natural consequence) thus, accordingly, therefore, under these circumstances; (in affirmation) yes, true, exactly; (in questions) really?, truly?; **ita . . . ut** (in comparisons) just as, although . . . nevertheless; (as correlatives) both . . . and, both . . . as well as; (in restriction) on condition that, in sofar as, on the assumption that; (of degree) to such a degree . . . that, so much . . . that, so . . . that; **non ita** not very, not especially; **quid ita?** how so?, what do you mean?
Ītalĭ·a -ae *f* Italy
Ītalĭc·us -a -um *adj* Italian
Ītăl·is -ĭdis *adj* Italian; *f pl* Italian women
Ītalĭ·us -a -um *adj* Italian; *f* see **Italia**
Ītăl·us -a -um *adj* Italian
ităque *conj* and so, and thus, accordingly, therefore, consequently
item *adv* likewise, besides, moreover, also
it·er -inĕris *n* journey, trip, march, walk; day's march, day's journey; route; right of way; passage (*of voice, etc.*); method, course, way, road; **ex itinere** or **in itinere** en route; **iter flectere** to change course; **iter terrestre** overland route; **maximis itineribus** by marching at top speed
iterātĭ·ō -ōnis *f* repetition
itĕr·ō -āre *vt* to repeat, renew; to plow again
itĕrum *adv* again, a second time; **iterum atque iterum** repeatedly, again and again
Ithăc·a -ae or **Ithăc·ē -ēs** *f* island off the W. coast of Greece in the Ionian Sea and home of Odysseus
itĭdem *adv* in the same way
itĭ·ō -ōnis *f* going, walking
it·ō -āre *vi* to go
it·us -ūs *m* going; going away, departure
It·ys -ўos *m* son of Tereus and Procne, who was killed by Procne and served up as food to Tereus
iu- = ju-
Ixī·ōn -ōnis *m* son of Antion or of Jupiter, king of the Laipthae in Thessaly, and father of Pirithous; he was allowed into heaven by Jupiter after killing his father-in-law, but for trying to seduce Juno, was tied to a wheel and sent flying into Tartarus

J

jac·ĕō -ēre -ŭī *vi* to lie, lie down; to lie ill, be sick; to lie dead, to have fallen; to lie in ruins; to hang loose; to lie idle, rest; to lie, be situated; to lie flat, lie low; to feel low, be despondent; to lie prostrate, be powerless; to fall, fail, be refuted; to be low in someone's opinion; to linger, stay
jacĭō jacĕre jēcī jactum *vt* to lay, build, establish, set, found, construct; to throw, cast, fling; to emit, produce; to sow, scatter; to throw away; to mention, utter, declare, intimate
jact·ans -antis *adj* boasting, bragging, showing off
jactanter *adv* boastfully
jactantĭ·a -ae *f* boasting, showing off
jactātĭ·ō -ōnis *f* tossing to and fro; swaying; shaking; writhing; boasting, bragging, showing off; gesticulation; **jactatio animi** agitation; **jactatio maritima** seasickness
jactāt·us -ūs *m* tossing, waving
jactĭt·ō -āre *vt* to display, show off
jact·ō -āre *vt* to throw, hurl; to toss about, shake; to throw away, throw out, throw overboard; to disturb, disquiet, stir up; to consider, discuss; to throw out, mention; to brag about, show off; **jactari** to toss, rock; (of money) to fluctuate in value; **se jactare** to boast, show off, throw one's weight around
jactūr·a -ae *f* throwing away, throwing overboard; loss, sacrifice
jactus *pp* of **jacio**
jact·us -ūs *m* toss, throw, cast
jaculābĭl·is -e *adj* missile
jaculāt·or -ōris *m* thrower, shooter; light-armed soldier; spearman
jaculātr·ix -īcis *f* huntress
jacŭl·or -ārī -ātus sum *vt* to throw; to shoot at; (fig) to aim at, strive after
jacŭl·us -a -um *adj* throwing, casting; *n* dart, javelin; casting net
jājūn- = jejun-

jam *adv* (present) now, already; (past) already, by then; (future) very soon, right away; (in transition) now, next, moreover; (for emphasis) actually, precisely, quite; (in a conclusion) then surely; **jam dudum** long ago, long since; **jam inde** immediately; **jam jam** even now, at every moment; **jam . . . jam** at one time . . . at another; **jam nunc** even now; **jam pridem** long since; **jam tum** even then, even at that time
Jānicŭl·um -ī *n* Roman hill on the right bank of the Tiber
jānit·or -ōris *m* doorman
jānitr·ix -īcis *f* portress
jānŭ·a -ae *f* door, house door; entrance; (fig) entrance, approach
Jānuāri·us -a -um *adj & m* January
jān·us -ī *m* covered passage, arcade
Jān·us -ī *m* Janus (*old Italian deity, represented as having two faces*); temple of Janus (*at the bottom of the Argiletum in the Forum*)
jec·ur -ŏris *n* liver; (as the seat of emotions) anger, lust
jecuscŭl·um -ī *n* little liver
jējūnē *adv* (fig) drily
jējūniōs·ior or **jājūniōs·ior -ius** *adj* fasting, hungry
jējūnit·ās or **jājūnit·ās -ātis** *f* fasting; dryness (*of style*)
jējūn·ium -iī or **-ī** *n* fasting, fast; hunger; leanness
jējūn·us or **jājūn·us -a -um** *adj* fasting; hungry; poor (*land*); thin; insignificant, paltry, contemptible, low; dry (*style*)
jentācŭl·um -ī *n* breakfast
joc·or -ārī -ātus sum or **joc·ō -āre** *vt* to say in jest; *vi* to joke, crack a joke, be joking
jocōsē *adv* humorously, as a joke, jokingly
jocōs·us -a -um *adj* humorous, funny, clowning
joculār·is -e *adj* humorous, funny
joculāri·us -a -um *adj* ludicrous
joculāt·or -ōris *m* joker
jocul·or -ārī -ātus sum *vi* to joke
jocŭl·us -ī *m* joke
joc·us -ī (*pl:* **joc·ī -ōrum** *m* or **joc·a -ōrum** *n*) *m* joke; laughingstock; child's play; **joco remoto** all joking aside; **per jocum** as a joke, jokingly
jub·a -ae *f* mane; crest
jub·ar -ăris *n* radiance, brightness; sunshine
jubāt·us -a -um *adj* crested
jubĕō jubēre jussī jussum *vt* to order; (pol) to order, decree, enact, ratify; to designate, appoint, assign; (med) to prescribe; **jube fratrem tuum salvere** (in letters) best regards to your brother
jūcundē *adv* pleasantly, delightfully, agreeably
jūcundit·ās -ātis *f* pleasantness, delight, enjoyment, agreeableness; *f pl* favors
jūcund·us -a -um *adj* pleasant, delightful, agreeable
Jūdae·us -a -um *adj* Jewish; *m* Jew; *f* Jewess; Judaea, Palestine
jūd·ex -icis *m* judge; juror; arbitrator; umpire; critic, scholar; **judex morum** censor; **me judice** in my judgment
jūdicāti·ō -ōnis *f* judicial investigation; (fig) judgment, opinion
jūdicāt·us -a -um *adj* decided, determined; *m* condemned person; *n* decision, precedent; fine; **judicatum facere** to carry out a decision; **judicatum solvere** to pay a fine
jūdicāt·us -ūs *m* judgeship
jūdiciāl·is -e *adj* judicial, forensic
jūdiciāri·us -a -um *adj* judiciary
jūdic·ium -iī or **-ī** *n* trial, court, court of justice; sentence; jurisdiction; opinion, decision; faculty of judging, judgment, good judgment, taste, tact, discretion
jūdic·ō -āre *vt* to judge; to examine; to sentence, condemn; to form an opinion of; to conclude; to declare, proclaim; (with *dat* of person and *acc* of the offense) to convict (*someone*) of; (with *genit*) to find (*someone*) guilty of; (with *dat* of person and *genit* of the offense) to convict (*someone*) of
jugāl·is -e *adj* yoked together; nuptial
jugāti·ō -ōnis *f* tying up
jūgĕr·um -ī *n* jugerum (*land measure: about two thirds of an acre*)
jūg·is -e *adj* continual, perennial, inexhaustible
jugl·ans -andis *f* walnut tree
jugōs·us -a -um *adj* hilly
Jugŭl·ae -ārum *f pl* Orion's belt (*three stars in the constellation Orion*)
jugŭl·ō -āre *vt* to cut the throat of, kill, murder; to destroy; to silence
jugŭl·um -ī *n* or **jugŭl·us -ī** *m* throat
jug·um -ī *n* yoke, collar; pair, team; (mil) yoke (*consisting of a spear laid crosswise on two upright spears, under which the conquered had to pass*); crossbar (*of a loom*); thwart (*of a boat*); common bond, union; wedlock; pair, couple; mountain ridge; *n pl* heights
Jugurth·a -ae *m* king of Numidia (160-104 B.C.)
Jūli·a -ae *f* aunt of Julius Caesar and wife of Marius; daughter of Julius Caesar and wife of Pompey (*d.* 54 B.C.); daughter of Augustus by Scribonia (39 B.C.-14 A.D.)
Jūli·us -a -um *adj* Julian; of July; *m* Roman praenomen; July
jūment·um -ī *n* beast of burden, horse, mule
juncĕ·us -a -um *adj* of reeds; slim, slender
juncōs·us -a -um *adj* overgrown with reeds
juncti·ō -ōnis *f* joining

junctūr·a -ae *f* joining, uniting, joint, juncture; connection, relationship; combination
junct·us -a -um *pp of* **jungo;** *adj* connected, associated, united, attached
junc·us -ī *m* reed
jungō jungĕre junxī junctum *vt* to join, join together, unite, connect; to yoke, harness; to couple, pair, mate; to bridge (*a river*); to bring together, unite, associate, ally; to add; to compose (*poems*); to combine (*words*)
jūni·or -ōris *adj* younger
jūnipĕr·us -ī *f* juniper
Jūni·us -a -um *adj* June, of June; *m* Roman praenomen; June
jūn·ix -īcis *f* heifer
Jūn·ō -ōnis *f* daughter of Saturn and wife and sister of Jupiter
Juppĭter (or **Jupĭter** or **Diespĭter**) **Jovis** *m* son of Saturn, brother and husband of Juno, and chief god of the Romans
jūrāt·or -ōris *m* judge; assistant censor
jūreconsult·us -ī *m* legal expert, lawyer
jūrejūr·ō -āre *vi* to swear
jūreperītus see **jurisperitus**
jurg·ium -iī or **-ī** *n* quarrel; *n pl* reproaches
jurg·ō -āre *vi* to quarrel
jūridiciāl·is -e *adj* juridical
jūrisconsult·us or **jūreconsult·us -ī** *m* legal expert, lawyer
jūrisdictī·ō -ōnis *f* administration of justice; jurisdiction
jūrisperīt·us or **jūreperīt·us -ī** *m* legal expert, lawyer
jūr·ō -āre *vt* to swear; to swear by, attest, call to witness; to swear to, attest; *vi* to swear, take an oath; to conspire; (with **in** + *acc*) to swear allegiance to, swear to observe, vow obedience to; **in haec verba jurare** to swear according to the prescribed form; to conspire against; **jurare calumniam** to swear that the accusation is not false
jū·s -ris *n* juice, broth, gravy, soup; law (*as established by society and custom rather than statute law*); right, justice; law court, court of justice; legal right, authority, permission, prerogative; jurisdiction; **in jus ire** to go to court; **jure** by right, rightfully, in justice; **jus dicere** to sit as judge, hold court; **jus gentium** international law; **jus publicum** common right; **summum jus** strict letter of the law
jūs jūrand·um (*genit:* **jūr·is jūrand·ī**) *n* oath
jussū (*abl* only) *m* by order; **meo jussu** by my order
juss·us -a -um *pp of* **jubeo;** *n* order, command, bidding
justē *adv* justly, rightly
justific·us -a -um *adj* just-dealing
justitĭ·a -ae *f* justice, fairness
justit·ium -iī or **-ī** *n* suspension of legal business; (fig) standstill
just·us -a -um *adj* just, fair; justified, well-founded; formal; in due order, according to protocol, regular; *n* justice; due measure; **plus quam justo** more than due measure, too much; *n pl* rights; formalities; ceremonies, due ceremony; funeral rites, obsequies
Jūturn·a -ae *f* nymph, sister of Turnus, the king of the Rutuli
jūtus *pp of* **juvo**
juvenāl·is -e *adj* youthful; juvenile
Juvenāl·is -is *m* Juvenal (*D. Junius Juvenalis, Roman satirist in the time of Domitian and Trajan, c.* 62-142 A.D.)
juvenc·us -a -um *adj* young; *m* bullock; young man; *f* heifer; girl
juven·escō -escĕre -uī *vi* to grow up; to get young again
juvenīl·is -e *adj* youthful; juvenile; cheerful
juvenīliter *adv* youthfully, boyishly
juvĕn·is -e *adj* young; *m* young man (*between the ages of twenty and forty-five*); warrior; *f* young lady
juvĕn·or -ārī -ātus sum *vi* to act like a kid
juvent·a -ae *f* youth
juvent·ās -ātis *f* youth, prime of life, manhood; (collectively) young people, youth
juvent·ūs -ūtis *f* youth, prime of life, manhood; (collectively) young people, youth
juvō juvāre jūvī jūtum *vt* to help; to please, delight; **juvat** (with *inf*) it helps to; **juvat me** it delights me, I am glad
juxtā *adv* nearby, in close proximity; alike, in like manner, equally; (with **ac, atque, et, quam,** or **cum**) as well as, just the same as; *prep* (with *acc*) close to, near to, next to; next to, immediately after; near, bordering upon; next door to
juxtim *adv* near; equally

K

Kalend·ae or **Calend·ae -ārum** *f pl* Kalends (*first day of the Roman month*); **tristes Kalendae** gloomy Kalends (*because interest was due on the Kalends*)
Kalendār·ium -iī or **-ī** *n* account book
Karthāginiens·is -e *adj* Carthaginian
Karthāg·ō -inis *f* Carthage (*city of N. Africa*)

L

labasc·ō -ĕre *vi* to waver; to give in, yield
lābēcŭl·a -ae *f* blemish, spot, stain (*e.g., on someone's reputation*)
labe·faciō -facĕre -fēcī -factum *vt* to cause to totter, to shake, to weaken; (fig) to weaken, ruin, destroy
labefact·ō -āre *vt* to shake; (fig) to weaken, ruin, destroy
labell·um -ī *n* lip
lābell·um -ī *n* small basin
lāb·ēs -is *f* fall, falling down; stroke, blow, ruin, destruction; blemish, spot, defect; disgrace, discredit
labĭ·a -ae *f* lip
Labiēn·us -ī *m* Caesar's officer who defected to Pompey
labiōs·us -a -um *adj* thick-lipped
lab·ĭum -ĭī or **-ī** *n* lip
lab·ō -āre *vi* to totter, wobble; to waver, hesitate, be undecided; to fall to pieces, go to ruin
lābor lābī lapsus sum *vi* to glide, slide, slip; to slip, fall, sink; to slip away, disappear, escape; (of time) to slip by, pass, elapse; (fig) to fade
lab·or or **lab·ōs -ōris** *m* effort; trouble, distress, suffering; work, task
labōrĭf·er -ĕra -ĕrum *adj* struggling
labōriōs·us -a -um *adj* full of troubles, troublesome; energetic, industrious
labōr·ō -āre *vt* to work out, make, produce; *vi* to work; to suffer, be troubled; to be in danger; (with *inf*) to try to
labōs see **labor**
labr·um -ī *n* lip, edge
lābr·um -ī *n* basin, tub, bathtub
labrusc·a -ae *f* wild vine
labrusc·um -ī *n* wild grape
labyrinthē·us -a -um *adj* labyrinthine
labyrinth·us -ī *m* labyrinth
lac lactis *n* milk; milk of plants
Lacaen·a -ae *f* Spartan woman
Lacedaem·ōn -ōnis *f* Sparta
Lacedaemonĭ·us -a -um *adj* Spartan
lac·er -ĕra -ĕrum *adj* mangled, torn, lacerated, mutilated; lacerating, tearing
lacerātĭ·ō -ōnis *f* tearing, laceration, mangling
lacern·a -ae *f* coat, topcoat, overcoat
lacernāt·us -a -um *adj* wearing an overcoat
lacĕr·ō -āre *vt* to lacerate, tear, mangle; to slander, abuse; to waste, squander, destroy; to wreck (*ship*)
lacert·us -a -um *adj* muscular, brawny; *m* lizard; upper arm, muscle; *m pl* muscles, strength, brawn; *f* lizard
lacess·ō -ĕre -īvī or **-ĭī -ītum** *vt* to provoke, exasperate; to challenge; to move, arouse
Lachĕs·is -is *f* one of the three Fates
lacinĭ·a -ae *f* flap (*of a garment*)
Lacīn·ĭum -ĭī or **-ī** *n* promontory in Bruttium with a temple to Juno
Lac·ō or **Lac·ōn -ōnis** *m* Spartan; Spartan dog
Lacōnĭ·a -ae *f* district of the Peloponnesus of which Sparta was the chief city
Lacōnĭc·us -a -um *adj* Spartan; *n* sweat bath
lacrĭm·a or **lacrŭm·a -ae** *f* tear; gumdrop (*plant*)
lacrimābĭl·is -e *adj* worthy of tears, deplorable
lacrimābund·us -a -um *adj* tearful, about to break into tears
lacrĭm·ō or **lacrŭm·ō -āre** *vt* to cry for, shed tears over; (of trees) to drip; *vi* to cry, shed tears
lacrimōs·us -a -um *adj* crying, tearful; causing tears, bringing tears to the eyes
lacrimŭl·a -ae *f* teardrop, little tear; (fig) crocodile tear
lacrum- = lacrim-
lact·ans -antis *adj* milk-giving
lactārĭ·us -a -um *adj* milky
lactātĭ·ō -ōnis *f* allurement
lact·ens -entis *adj* suckling; milky, juicy, tender; full of milk; *m* suckling
lacteŏl·us -a -um *adj* milk-white
lact·ēs -ĭum *f pl* intestines; **laxae lactes** empty stomach
lactesc·ō -ĕre *vi* to turn to milk
lactĕ·us -a -um *adj* milky, full of milk, milk-colored, milk-white
lact·ō -āre *vt* to cajole, wheedle
lactūc·a -ae *f* lettuce
lacūn·a -ae *f* ditch, hole, pit; pond, pool; (fig) hole, gap
lacūn·ar -āris *n* paneled ceiling
lacūn·ō -āre *vt* to panel
lacūnōs·us -a -um *adj* sunken
lac·us -ūs *m* vat; tank, pool, reservoir, cistern; lake
laedō laedĕre laesī laesum *vt* to knock, strike; to hurt, rub open; to wound; to break (*promise, pledge*); to offend, outrage, violate; (with **ad** + *acc*) to smash (*something*) against
laen·a -ae *f* lined coat
Lāërt·ēs -ae *m* father of Ulysses
Lāërtiăd·ēs -ae *m* Ulysses
laesĭ·ō -ōnis *f* attack, provocation
Laestrȳg·ōn -ŏnis *m* Laestrygonian (*one of the mythical race of cannibals in Italy, founders of Formiae*)
laes·us *pp* of **laedo**
laetābĭl·is -e *adj* cheerful, glad
laet·ans -antis *adj* joyful, glad
laetātĭ·ō -ōnis *f* rejoicing, joy
laetē *adv* joyfully, gladly

laetific·ans -antis *adj* joyous
laetific·ō -āre *vt* to gladden, cheer up; **laetificari** to rejoice
laetific·us -a -um *adj* joyful, cheerful
laetiti·a -ae *f* joyfulness, gladness, exuberance
laet·or -ārī -ātus sum *vi* to rejoice, be glad
laet·us -a -um *adj* rejoicing, glad, cheerful; happy, fortunate, auspicious; fertile, rich, smiling (*grain*); sleek, fat (*cattle*); bright, cheerful (*appearance*); cheering, welcome (*news*)
laevē *adv* awkwardly
laev·us -a -um *adj* left, on the left side; awkward, stupid; ill-omened; lucky, propitious; *f* left hand, left side; *n* the left; *n pl* the area on the left
lagăn·um -ī *n* pancake
lagē·os -ī *f* Greek vine
lagoen·a or **lagōn·a -ae** *f* jug
lagō·is -ĭdis *f* grouse
laguncŭl·a -ae *f* flask
Lāïăd·ēs -ae *m* son of Laius (*Oedipus*)
Lāï·us -ī *m* Laius (*father of Oedipus*)
lall·ō -āre *vi* to sing a lullaby
lām·a -ae *f* swamp, bog
lambĕr·ō -āre *vt* to tear to pieces
lamb·ō -ĕre -ī *vt* to lick, lap; (of a river) to wash, flow by; (of ivy) to cling to
lāment·a -ōrum *n pl* wailing, moaning, lamentation
lāmentābĭl·is -e *adj* pitiable; doleful; mournful, sorrowful
lāmentārĭ·us -a -um *adj* sorrowful, pitiful
lāmentātĭ·ō -ōnis *f* lamentation
lāment·or -ārī -ātus sum *vt* to cry over, lament; *vi* to wail, cry
lamĭ·a -ae *f* witch, sorceress
lāmĭn·a or **lammĭn·a** or **lamn·a -ae** *f* plate, leaf (*of metal or wood*); blade; coin; peel, shell
lamp·as -ădis *f* torch; brightness; day; meteor; lamp
Lam·us -ī *m* mythical king of the Laestrygonians; son of Hercules and Omphale
lān·a -ae *f* wool; working in wool, spinning, **lana aurea** golden fleece; **lanam trahere** to card wool; **lanas ducere** to spin wool; **rixari de lana caprina** to argue over nothing
lānār·ĭus -ĭī or **-ī** *m* wool worker
lānāt·us -a -um *adj* woolly; *f pl* sheep
lancĕ·a -ae *f* lance, spear
lancĭn·ō -āre *vt* to squander, waste
lānĕ·us -a -um *adj* woolen; soft
langue·facĭō -facĕre -fēcī -factum *vt* to make tired
langu·ens -entis *adj* languid, drooping, listless
langu·ĕō -ēre *vi* to be tired, be weary; to be weak, feeble (*from disease*); (fig) to be dull, languid, listless; to be without energy
langu·escō -escĕre -ŭī *vi* to become weak, grow faint; (fig) to become listless; to decline, decrease; to relax
languĭdē *adj* weakly, faintly, without energy
languidŭl·us -a -um *adj* languid; withered, faded
languĭd·us -a -um *adj* weak, faint, languid, sluggish; listless; enervating
langu·or -ōris *m* weakness, faintness, languor; dullness, listlessness, sluggishness
laniāt·us -ūs *m* mangling; *f pl* mental anguish
laniēn·a -ae *f* butcher shop
lānific·ĭum -ĭī or **-ī** *n* weaving
lānific·us -a -um *adj* spinning, weaving, of spinning, of weaving
lānĭg·er -ĕra -ĕrum *adj* fleecy; *m* sheep (*ram*); *f* sheep (*ewe*)
lanĭ·ō -āre *vt* to tear to pieces, mangle
lanist·a -ae *m* gladiator trainer, fencing master; (*in derision*) ringleader
lānit·ĭum -ĭī or **-ī** *n* wool
lan·ĭus -ĭī or **-ī** *m* butcher; (*in derision*) executioner, butcher
lantern·a -ae *f* lantern
lanternār·ĭus -ĭī or **-ī** *m* guide
lānūg·ō -ĭnis *f* down (*of plants, cheeks, etc.*)
Lānuv·ĭum -ĭī or **-ī** *n* town in Latium on the Appian Way
lan·x -cis *f* dish, platter; scale
Lāocŏ·ōn -ontis *m* son of Priam and priest of Apollo, who, with his two sons, was killed by two serpents from the sea
Lāomĕd·ōn -ontis *m* king of Troy and father of Priam and Ganymede
Lāomedontē·us or **Lāomedontĭ·us -a -um** *adj* Trojan
Lāomedontiăd·ēs -ae *m* son of Laomedon; Priam; *m pl* Trojans
lapăth·um -ī *n* or **lapăth·us -ī** *f* sorrel (*plant*)
lapicīd·a -ae *m* stonecutter, quarry worker
lapicīdīn·ae -ārum *f pl* stone quarry
lapidārĭ·us -a -um *adj* stone; **latomiae lapidariae** stone quarries
lapidātĭ·ō -ōnis *f* throwing stones
lapidāt·or -ōris *m* stone thrower
lapidĕ·us -a -um *adj* of stones, stone, stony; **lapideus sum** (fig) I am petrified
lapĭd·ō -āre *vt* to throw stones at; *v impers* it is raining stones, it is hailing stones
lapidōs·us -a -um *adj* full of stones, stony; hard as stone; gritty (*bread*)
lapill·us -ī *m* pebble; precious stone, gem, jewel; *m pl* small stones (*esp. for mosaics*)
lap·is -ĭdis *m* stone; milestone; platform; boundary stone, landmark; tombstone; precious stone, gem, pearl, jewel, stone statue; marble

table; **lapides loqui** to speak harsh words
Lapith·ae -ārum *m pl* mountain tribe in Thessaly that fought the centaurs at the marriage of their king Pirithous
lapp·a -ae *f* burr
lapsi·ō -ōnis *f* sliding, slipping; (fig) tendency
laps·ō -āre *vi* to keep slipping, stumble
laps·us -a -um *pp* of **labor**; *adj* fallen
laps·us -ūs *m* falling, fall, sliding, slipping, gliding, flow, flight; blunder, error, fault, slip
laqueār·ia -ium *n pl* paneled ceiling
laqueāt·us -a -um *adj* paneled, having a paneled ceiling
laquĕ·us -ī *m* noose; snare; (fig) snare, trap; *m pl* (fig) subtleties
Lār Laris *m* tutelary deity, household god; hearth, home; *m pl* hearth, home, house, household, family
lard·um -ī *n* lard, fat
Larenti·a -ae *f* wife of Faustulus who reared Romulus and Remus
largē *adv* liberally, generously
largific·us -a -um *adj* bountiful
largiflŭ·us -a -um *adj* gushing
largilŏqu·us -a -um *adj* talkative
larg·ior -īrī -ītus sum *vt* to give generously, bestow freely; to lavish; to bestow, confer; to grant, concede; *vi* to give bribes, bribe
largīt·ās -ātis *f* generosity, bounty
largīti·ō -ōnis *f* generosity; bribery
largīt·or -ōris *m* generous donor; spendthrift; briber
larg·us -a -um *adj* abundant, plentiful, large, much; generous, liberal, bountiful, profuse
lārid·um -ī *n* lard, bacon fat
Lāriss·a -ae *f* town in Thessaly on the Peneus River
Lār·ius -iī or **-ī** *m* Lake Como
lar·ix -icis *f* larch tree
larv·a -ae *f* mask; ghost
larvāt·us -a -um *adj* bewitched
lasăn·um -ī *n* chamber pot
lasarpīcif·er -ĕra -ĕrum *adj* producing asafetida (*used as an antispasmodic*)
lascīvi·a -ae *f* playfulness; petulence; lewdness
lascīvībund·us -a -um *adj* petulant, roguish
lascīv·iō -īre -iī -ītum *vi* to frolic, be frisky; to run riot, run wild
lascīv·us -a -um *adj* playful, frisky; brash, impudent, petulant; licentious, lustful; luxuriant (*growth*)
lāserpīc·ium -iī or **-ī** *n* silphium (*plant which yielded asafetida*)
lassitūd·ō -inis *f* physical weariness, lassitude
lass·ō -āre *vt* to fatigue, exhaust
lassŭl·us -a -um *adj* somewhat tired
lass·us -a -um *adj* tired, weary, fatigued, exhausted
lātē *adv* widely, extensively; profusely; **late longeque** far and wide
latĕbr·a -ae *f* hiding place, hideaway, hideout; (fig) loophole
latebricŏl·a -ae *m* or *f* person who hangs around dives or brothels
latebrōsē *adv* secretly
latebrōs·us -a -um *adj* full of holes; hidden, secret; porous
lat·ens -entis *adj* hidden, secret
latenter *adv* in secret
lat·ĕō -ēre -uī *vi* to lie hidden, lie concealed, lurk; to keep out of sight, sulk; to live a retired life, remain in obscurity, remain unknown, escape notice; to be in safety; to avoid a summons, lie low; to be obscure
lat·er -ĕris *m* brick, tile; **laterem lavare** to waste effort
laterām·en -inis *n* earthenware
latercŭl·us -ī *m* small brick; tile; biscuit
latericī·us -a -um *adj* brick, made of brick; *n* brickwork
lātern·a -ae *f* lantern
latesc·ō -ĕre *vi* to hide
lat·ex -icis *m* liquid, fluid; water; spring; wine; oil
latibŭl·um -ī *n* hiding place, hideout, lair, den; (fig) refuge
lāticlāvi·us -a -um *adj* having a broad crimson stripe (*distinctive mark of senators, military tribunes of the equestrian order, and of sons of distinguished families*)
Latīnē *adv* Latin, in Latin; in proper Latin; in plain Latin; **Latine loqui** to speak Latin; to speak correct Latin; **Latine reddere** to translate into Latin; **Latine scire** to understand Latin
Latīnit·ās -ātis *f* pure Latin, Latinity; Latin rights and privileges
Latīn·us -a -um *adj* Latin; possessing Latin rights and privileges; *m* Latinus (*king of the Laurentians, who gave his daughter Lavinia in marriage to Aeneas*); *n* Latin language; **in Latinum convertere** to translate into Latin
lāti·ō -ōnis *f* bringing, rendering; proposing
latit·ō -āre *vi* to keep hiding oneself; to be concealed, hide, lurk; to lie low (*in order to avoid a summons*)
lātitūd·ō -inis *f* breadth, width; size, extent; broad pronunciation; richness of expression
lātius *adv* of late
Lati·us -a -um *adj* of Latium, Latin, Roman; *n* Latium (*district in W. central Italy, in which Rome was situated*); **jus Lati** or **Latium** Latin political rights and privileges
Lātō·is -idis *f* Diana
lātom- = lautom-
Lātōn·a -ae *f* daughter of the Titan Coeus and Phoebe, and mother of Apollo and Diana
Lātōnigĕn·a -ae *m* or *f* child of Latona; *m pl* children of Latona, i.e., Apollo and Diana

Lātōnĭ·us -a -um *adj* of Latona; *f* Diana
lāt·or -ōris *m* bringer, bearer; proposer (*of a law*)
Lātō·us -ī *m* Apollo
lātrāt·or -ōris *m* barker; dog
lātrāt·us -ūs *m* barking
lātrīn·a -ae *f* wash room, toilet
lātr·ō -āre *vt* to bark at, snarl at; to clamor for; *vi* to bark; (fig) to rant
latr·ō -ōnis *m* mercenary; freebooter; brigand, bandit; (in chess) pawn
latrōcin·ium -iī or **-ī** *n* military service (*as a mercenary*); freebooting; brigandage, banditry, vandalism, piracy, robbery, highway robbery; villany, outrage; band of robbers
latrōcĭn·or -ārī -ātus sum *vi* to serve as a mercenary, be a mercenary soldier; to be a bandit, be a highwayman, be a pirate
latruncŭl·us -ī *m* small-time bandit
lātumĭ·ae -ārum *f pl* stone quarry; prison
lātus *pp* of **fero**
lāt·us -a -um *adj* wide, broad; extensive; widespread; broad (*pronunciation*); diffuse (*style*)
lat·us -ĕris *n* side, flank; body, person; lungs; lateral surface; coast; (mil) flank, wing; **a latere** (mil) on the flank; **a latere** (with *genit*) **a** at the side of, in the company of; **b** from among the friends of; **aperto latere** (mil) on the exposed flank; **latere tecto** scot free; **latus dare** to expose oneself; **latus tegere** (with *genit*) to walk by the side of, to escort (*someone*)
latuscŭl·um -ī *n* small side
laudābĭl·is -e *adj* laudable, praiseworthy
laudābiliter *adv* laudably
laudātĭ·ō -ōnis *f* commendation; eulogy, panegyric, funeral oration; (in court) testimony by a character witness
laudāt·or -ōris *m* praiser; eulogist, panegyrist; (law) character witness
laudāt·us -a -um *adj* praiseworthy, commendable, excellent
laud·ō -āre *vt* to praise, commend; to name, quote, cite; to pronounce a funeral oration over
laurĕ·a -ae *f* laurel tree; laurel, laurel branch, laurel crown, bay wreath; triumph
laureāt·us -a -um *adj* laureate, laureled, crowned with laurel; **litterae laureatae** communiqué announcing victory
Laurent·ēs -um *m pl* Laurentians (*people of Lanuvium*)
Laurentīn·us or **Laurentĭ·us -a -um** *adj* Laurentian
laureŏl·a -ae *f* little laurel crown; triumph
laurĕ·us -a -um *adj* laurel, of laurel; *f* see **laurea**
lauricŏm·us -a -um *adj* laurel-covered (*mountain*)
laurĭf·er -ĕra -ĕrum *adj* crowned with laurel
laurĭg·er -ĕra -ĕrum *adj* wearing laurel
laur·us -ī *f* laurel tree, bay tree; triumph, victory
laus laudis *f* praise, commendation; fame, glory; approval, praiseworthy deed; merit, worth
Laus·us -ī *m* son of Numitor and brother of Rhea Silvia; son of Mezentius, killed by Aeneas
lautē *adv* sumptuously, splendidly; excellently
lautĭ·a -ōrum *n pl* state banquet (*given to foreign ambassadors and official guests*)
lautitĭ·a -ae *f* luxury, high living
lautumĭ·ae or **lātomĭ·ae** or **lātumĭ·ae -ārum** *f pl* stone quarry; prison
laut·us -a -um *adj* expensive, elegant, fine; well-heeled; refined, fashionable
lavābr·um -ī *n* bath
lavātĭ·o -ōnis *f* washing, bathing, bath; bathing kit
Lāvīnĭ·us -a -um *adj* Lavinian, of Lavinium; *n* town in Latium founded by Aeneas; *f* wife of Aeneas
lavō lavāre (or **lavĕre**) **lāvī lautum** (or **lavātum** or **lōtum**) *vt* to wash, bathe; to wet, drench; to wash away; **lavi** to wash, wash oneself, bathe; *vi* to wash, wash oneself, bathe
laxāment·um -ī *n* relaxation, respite, letup, mitigation
laxāt·us -a -um *adj* loose, extended (*e.g., ranks*)
laxē *adv* loosely, widely; freely
laxĭt·ās -ātis *f* roominess, extent
lax·ō -āre *vt* to extend, widen, expand, open; to open, undo, release; to relax, slacken; to mitigate; (fig) to release, relieve; *vi* (of price) to go down
lax·us -a -um *adj* roomy, wide; loose, slack; prolonged, extended (*time*); (fig) relaxed, easygoing, free; low (*price*)
le·a -ae *f* lioness
leaen·a -ae *f* lioness
Lēand·er -rī *m* youth of Abydos who swam across the Hellespont every night to his lover Hero of Sestos
Learch·us -ī *m* son of Athamas and Ino, killed by his mad father
leb·ēs -ētis *m* pan, cauldron, basin
lectīc·a -ae *f* litter; sofa, couch
lecticār·ius -iī or **-ī** *m* litter bearer
lectīcŭl·a -ae *f* small litter; small bier
lectĭ·ō -ōnis *f* selection; reading, reading aloud; perusal; **lectio senatūs** revision of the senate roll (*by the censor*)
lectisterniāt·or -ōris *m* slave who arranged the seating at table
lestistern·ium -iī or **-ī** *n* ritual feast (*at which images of the gods were placed on couches at the table*)

lectĭt·ō -āre *vt* to read and reread; to like to read
lectiuncŭl·a -ae *f* light reading
lect·or -ōris *m* reader (*esp. slave who read aloud to his master*)
lectŭl·us -ī *m* cot; small couch, settee; humble bier
lect·us -ī or **-ūs** *m* bed, couch; bier
lect·us -a -um *pp* of **lego;** *adj* select, choice, special, elite
Lēd·a -ae or **Lēd·ē -ēs** *f* Tyndarus's wife, whom Jupiter visited in the form of a swan and who bore Helen, Clytemnestra, Castor, and Pollux
lēgāti·ō -ōnis *f* embassy, mission, legation; members of an embassy; work or report of work of a mission; nominal staff appointment; command of a legion; **legatio libera** junket (*all-expenses-paid trip, a privilege granted to senators, nominally in an official capacity, to visit the provinces to transact private business*)
lēgāt·um -ī *n* bequest, legacy
lēgāt·us -ī *m* deputy, representative; ambassador, envoy; adjutant (*of a consul, proconsul, or praetor*); commander of a legion
lēgĭf·er -ĕra -ĕrum *adj* law-giving
legĭ·ō -ōnis *f* legion (*divided into* 10 *cohorts and numbering between* 4,200 *and* 6,000 *men*); army
legiōnārĭ·us -a -um *adj* legionary
lēgirŭp·a -ae or **lēgirup·iō -ōnis** *m* lawbreaker
lēgitĭmē *adv* legitimately, lawfully; properly
lēgitĭm·us -a -um *adj* legitimate, lawful; regular, right, just, proper; *n pl* legal formalities
legiuncŭl·a -ae *f* under-manned legion
lēg·ō -āre *vt* to commission; to send on a public mission, despatch; to delegate, deputize; to bequeath, will; (fig) to entrust
legō legĕre lēgī lectum *vt* to gather, collect, pick; to pick out, choose; to pick one's way through, cross; to sail by, coast along; to read, peruse; to recite, read out loud; to pick up, steal; to pick up (*news, rumor*); **fila legere** to wind up the thread of life; **senatum legere** to read off the senate roll
lēgulē·ius -iī or **-ī** pettifogger
legūm·en -ĭnis *n* leguminous plant; vegetable; pulse; bean
lemb·us -ī *m* cutter, yacht (*built for speed*), speedboat
lemm·a -ătis *n* theme, subject matter; epigram
Lemnicŏl·a -ae *m* inhabitant of Lemnos, i.e., Vulcan
lemniscāt·us -a -um *adj* heavily decorated (*with combat ribbons*)
lemnisc·us -ī *m* ribbon which hung down from a victor's wreath
Lemnĭ·us -a -um *adj* Lemnian; *m* Lemnian; Vulcan
Lemn·os or **Lemn·us -ī** *f* large island in the Aegean
Lemŭr·ēs -um *m pl* ghosts
Lemūrĭ·a -ōrum *n pl* night festival to drive ghosts from the house
lēn·a -ae *f* procuress, madame; seductress
Lēnae·us -a -um *adj* Lenaean, Bacchic; *m* Bacchus
lēnē *adv* gently
lēnĭm·en -ĭnis *n* consolation, comfort, compensation, reward
lēnīment·um -ī *n* alleviation
lēn·iō -īre -īvī *or* **-iī -ītum** *vt* to soften, alleviate, soothe, calm; *vi* to calm down
lēn·is -e *adj* soft, gentle, mild, smooth, calm; gradual (*slope*); (fig) gentle, mild, kind
lēnĭt·ās -ātis *f* softness, gentleness, mildness, smoothness; (fig) gentleness, mildness, tenderness, clemency
lēnĭter *adv* softly, gently, mildly; (fig) mildly, quietly, calmly; (of style) smoothly; halfheartedly
lēnitūd·ō -ĭnis *f* softness, mildness, gentleness, smoothness
lēn·ō -ōnis *m* pander, procurer, pimp; seducer
lēnōcin·ium -iī or **-ī** *n* pandering, pimping; allurement, attraction; bawdy or gaudy clothes; flattery
lēnōcĭn·or -ārī -ātus sum *vi* to be a pimp; (with *dat*) **a** to play up to, humor, pander to; **b** to stimulate, promote
lēnōnĭ·us -a -um *adj* pimp's
len·s -tis *f* lentil
lentē *adv* slowly; indifferently, halfheartedly; calmly, leisurely, deliberately
lent·esc·ō -ĕre *vi* to get sticky, soften; (fig) to soften, weaken; (with **ad** + *acc*) to stick to
lentiscĭf·er -ĕra -ĕrum *adj* (of a region) producing mastic trees
lentisc·us -ī *f* mastic tree; toothpick (*made of mastic wood*)
lentitūd·ō -ĭnis *f* slowness; insensibility, apathy, dullness
lent·ō -āre *vt* to bend
lentŭl·us -a -um *adj* somewhat slow
lent·us -a -um *adj* sticky, clinging; pliant, limber; slow, sluggish; lingering; irresponsive, reluctant, indifferent, backward; slow-moving; tedious; drawling; at rest, at leisure, lazy; calm, unconcerned
lēnŭl·us -ī *m* little pimp
lēnuncŭl·us -ī *m* little pimp; small sailboat, skiff
le·ō -ōnis *m* lion
Le·ō -ōnis *m* Lion (*constellation*)
Leōnĭd·ās -ae *m* king of Sparta (487-480 B.C.), who fell at Thermopylae in 480 B.C. after a gallant stand
leōnīn·us -a -um *adj* lion's, of a lion
Leontīn·ī -ōrum *m pl* town in E. Sicily
lep·as -ădis *f* limpet
lepĭdē *adv* pleasantly, charmingly,

neatly; (as affirmative answer) yes, indeed; (of approval) bravo!

lepĭd•us -a -um *adj* pleasant, charming, neat; effeminate

lep•ōs or **lep•or -ōris** *m* pleasantness, charm, attractiveness

lep•us -ŏris *m* hare

Lep•us -ŏris *m* Hare (*constellation*)

lepuscŭl•us -ī *m* little hare

Lern•a -ae or **Lern•ē -ēs** *f* marsh near Argos, where Hercules slew the Hydra

Lernae•us -a -um *adj* Lernaean

Lesbĭ•us -a -um *adj* Lesbian; *f* pseudonym for the girl friend of the poet Catullus; *n* Lesbian wine

Lesb•os or **Lesb•us -ī** *f* large island in the N. Aegean, the birthplace of the lyric poets Alcaeus and Sappho

less•us (only *acc*: **lessum** in use) *m* wailing

lētāl•is -e *adj* lethal, fatal, mortal

Lēthae•us -a -um *adj* of Lethe; infernal; causing drowsiness

lēthargĭc•us -ī *m* lazy fellow

lētharg•us -ī *m* lethargy

Lēth•ē -ēs *f* Lethe (*river of oblivion in the lower world*); forgetfulness

lētĭf•er -ĕra -ĕrum *adj* deadly, fatal; **locus letifer** mortal spot

lēt•ō -āre *vt* to kill

lēt•um -ī *n* death; ruin, destruction; **leto dare** to put to death

Leuc•as -ădis *f* island off W. Greece

leucasp•is -ĭdis *adj* armed with a white shield

Leucipp•us -ī *m* philosopher, teacher of Democritus, and one of the founders of Atomism (*5th cent.* B.C.)

Leucothĕ•a -ae or **Leucothĕ•ē -ēs** *f* name of Ino, daughter of Cadmus, after she was changed into a sea deity

Leuctr•a -ōrum *n pl* small town in Boeotia where Epaminondas defeated the Spartans in 371 B.C.

levām•en -ĭnis *n* alleviation, comfort, consolation

levāment•um -ī *n* alleviation, comfort, consolation

levātĭ•ō -ōnis *f* lightening; relief, comfort; lessening

levicŭl•us -a -um *adj* somewhat vain

levidens•is -e *adj* poor, inferior

levifĭd•us -a -um *adj* untrustworthy

lĕv•is -e *adj* light, not heavy; light-armed; lightly dressed; light, easily digested; thin, poor (*soil*); light, nimble; flitting; slight, small; unimportant, trivial; unfounded (*rumor*); easy, simple; mild; gentle, easygoing; capricious, unreliable, fickle

lēv•is -e *adj* smooth; slippery; smooth, hairless, beardless; delicate, tender; effeminate; smooth (*style*)

levisomn•us -a -um *adj* light-sleeping

levĭt•ās -ātis *f* lightness; mobility, nimbleness; levity, frivolity; (*fig*) shallowness

lēvĭt•as -ātis *f* smoothness; (*fig*) smoothness, fluency

levĭter *adv* lightly; slightly, a little, somewhat; easily, without difficulty; nimbly

lĕv•ō -āre *vt* to lift up, raise; to lighten, relieve, ease; to console, comfort; to lessen, weaken; to release, free; to take away; to avert

lēv•ō -āre *vt* to make smooth, polish; to soothe

lēv•or -ōris *m* smoothness

lex lēgis *f* motion, bill; law, statute; rule, regulation, principle, precept; condition, stipulation; **eā lege ut** with the stipulation that, on condition that; **lege** or **legibus** legally; **lege agere** to proceed legally; **legem abrogare** to repeal a law; **legem ferre** to propose a bill; **legem derogare** to amend a bill or law; **legem jubere** to sanction a law; **legem perferre** to pass a law; **sine legibus** without restraint, without control

lībām•en -ĭnis *n* libation; firstfruits

lībāment•um -ī *n* libation; firstfruits

lībātĭ•ō -ōnis *f* libation

lībell•a -ae *f* small silver coin, ace; small sum; level (*instrument*); **ad libellam** to a tee, exactly; **heres ex libella** sole heir

libell•us -ī *m* small book, pamphlet; notebook; journal, diary; program; handbill, advertisement; petition; answer to a petition; letter; written accusation, indictment, libel; satirical verse

lib•ens or **lub•ens -entis** *adj* willing, ready, glad; merry, cheerful

libenter or **lubenter** *adv* willingly, gladly, with pleasure

lib•er -rī *m* bark of a tree; book; work, treatise; catalog, list, register; letter, rescript

līb•er -ĕra -ĕrum *adj* free; open, unoccupied; unrestricted; unprejudiced; outspoken, frank; uncontrolled, unrestricted; (not slave) free; (of states or municipalities) independent, autonomous; exempt; free of charge; (with *abl* or **ab** + *abl*) free from, exempt from; (with *genit*) free of; *m pl* see **liberi**

Līb•er -ĕrī *m* Italian fertility god, later identified with Bacchus; wine

Lībĕr•a -ae *f* Proserpina; Ariadne, the wife of Bacchus

Līberāl•ĭa -ĭum *n pl* festival of Liber, held on March 17th, at which young men received the toga virilis

līberāl•is -e *adj* relating to freedom, relating to civil status, of free citizens; worthy of a freeman, honorable, gentleman's; courteous; liberal, generous; handsome

līberālĭt•ās -ātis *f* courtesy, politeness; liberality, generosity; grant, gift

līberālĭter *adv* like a freeman, nobly; liberally (*e.g., educated*); courteously; liberally, generously

līberāti·ō -ōnis *f* liberation, delivery, freeing, release; acquittal
līberāt·or -ōris *m* liberator
līberē *adv* freely; frankly, outspokenly; ungrudgingly; like a freeman, liberally
līber·ī -ōrum *m pl* children
līber·ō -āre *vt* to set free, free, release; to acquit, discharge; to cancel, get rid of (*e.g., debts*); to exempt; to manumit, set free; (with *abl* or with **ab** or **ex** + *abl*) to free or release from, acquit of; **fidem liberare** to keep one's promise; **nomina liberare** to cancel debts; **se aere alieno liberare** to pay up a debt
lībert·a -ae *f* freedwoman, ex-slave
lībert·ās -ātis *f* liberty, freedom; status of a freeman; political freedom; freedom of speech, freedom of thought; frankness
lībertīn·us -a -um *adj & mf* ex-slave; *m* freedman; *f* freedwoman
lībert·us -ī *m* freedman, ex-slave
lib·et (or **lub·et**) **-ēre -ŭit** (or **libĭtum est**) *v impers* (with *dat*) it pleases, is pleasant, is agreeable to, is nice for (*someone*); (with *inf*) it is nice, pleasant to (*do something*); **si lubet** if you please; **ut lubet** as you please
libīdin·or -ārī -ātus sum *vi* to gratify lust
libīdinōsē *adv* willfully; arbitrarily
libīdinōs·us -a -um *adj* willful; arbitrary; lustful, sensual
libīd·ō or **lubīd·ō -ĭnis** *f* desire, longing, inclination, pleasure; will, willfulness, arbitrariness, caprice, fancy; lust; rut, heat; **ex libidine** arbitrarily
libĭt·a -ōrum *n pl* will, pleasure, liking
Libitīn·a -ae *f* burial goddess; implements for burial; grave, death
līb·ō -āre *vt* to taste, sip; to pour as a libation, offer, consecrate; to touch lightly, barely touch, graze; to spill, waste; to extract, collect, compile
lībr·a -ae *f* balance, scales; plummet, level; pound (*of twelve ounces*)
lībrāment·um -ī *n* weight; balance, ballast; plane surface; gravity
lībrārĭ·a -ae *f* forelady (*who weighed out wool for slaves to spin*)
librāriŏl·us -ī *m* copyist, scribe
librārĭ·us -a -um *adj* book, of books; **taberna libraria** bookstore; *m* copyist, scribe; *n* bookcase
lībrāt·us -a -um *adj* poised; hurled; powerful
lībrīl·is -e *adj* one-pound, weighing a pound
lībrīt·or -ōris *m* artilleryman
lībr·ō -āre *vt* to balance; to poise, level, hurl, launch; to sway
līb·um -ī *n* cake; birthday cake
Liburnĭ·a -ae *f* district of Illyria between Istria and Dalmatia
Liburn·us -a -um *adj & mf* Liburnian; *f* Liburnian galley
Libȳ·a -ae or **Libȳ·ē -ēs** *f* Libya (*Africa*)
Libȳ·es -um *m pl* Libyans
Libȳc·us or **Libyss·us** or **Libystīn·us** or **Libȳ·us -a -um** or **Libyst·is -ĭdis** *adj* Libyan; (in general) African
lic·ens -entis *adj* free, bold
licenter *adv* freely, boldly, without restraint, licentiously
licentĭ·a -ae *f* license, liberty, freedom; lawlessness, licentiousness
lic·ĕō -ēre *vi* to cost; to be for sale
lic·ĕor -ērī -ĭtus sum *vt* to bid on, bid for, make an offer for; *vi* to bid, make a bid
lic·et -ēre -ŭit or **-ĭtum est** *v impers* it is permitted or lawful; (with *dat & inf*) it is all right for (*someone*) to; **licet** (to express assent) yes, all right
licet *conj* granted that, even if, although
Lich·ās -ae *m* companion of Hercules
līch·ēn -ēnis *m* ringworm
licitāti·ō -ōnis *f* bidding (*at auction*); haggling
licĭt·or -ārī -ātus sum *vt* to bid for
licĭt·us -a -um *adj* permissible, lawful
līc·ium -ĭī or **-ī** *n* thread
lict·or -ōris *m* lictor (*attendant and bodyguard of a magistrate, of whom twenty-four attended a dictator, twelve a consul, and six a praetor*)
li·ēn -ēnis *m* spleen
liēnōs·us -a -um *adj* splenetic
ligām·en -ĭnis *n* bandage
ligāment·um -ī *n* bandage
lignār·ius -ĭī or **-ī** *m* carpenter
lignāti·ō -ōnis *f* gathering of lumber
lignāt·or -ōris *m* woodcutter, lumberjack
ligneŏl·us -a -um *adj* wooden
lignĕ·us -a -um *adj* wooden
lign·or -ārī -ātus sum *vi* to gather wood
lign·um -ī *n* wood; timber, firewood, log, plank; writing tablet; tree; **in silvam ligna ferre** to carry coals to Newcastle
lig·ō -āre *vt* to tie, tie up, bandage; to close (*a deal*)
lig·ō -ōnis *m* mattock, hoe; farming
ligŭl·a -ae *f* shoe strap
Lig·ur or **Lig·us -ŭris** *m* or *f* Ligurian
Ligurĭ·a -ae *f* Liguria (*district along the N.W. coast of Italy*)
ligūr·iō or **ligurr·iō -īre -īvī** or **-ĭī -ītum** *vt* to lick, pick at; to eat daintily; (fig) to prey on; (fig) to be dying for
ligūrīti·ō -ōnis *f* daintiness
Ligus see **Ligur**
Ligusc·us or **Ligustic·us** or **Ligustīn·us -a -um** *adj* Ligurian
ligustr·um -ī *n* privet

līl·ium -iī or **-ī** *n* lily; (mil) trench lined with sharp stakes
līm·a -ae *f* file; (fig) pōlishing, revision
līmātius *adv* in a more polished manner
līmātŭl·us -a -um *adj* (fig) rather sharp (*judgment*)
līmāt·us -a -um *adj* (fig) polished, refined
līm·ax -ācis *m* or *f* snail
limbolārĭ·us -a -um *adj* **textores limbolarii** tassel makers, hemmers
limb·us -ī *m* fringe, hem, tassel
līm·en -ĭnis *n* lintel, threshold; doorway, entrance; threshold, outset, beginning; starting gate (*at racetrack*); house, home
līm·es -ĭtis *m* country trail; path; road along a boundary; boundary, frontier; channel, course, way; zodiac
līm·ō -āre *vt* to file; (fig) to polish, refine; to file down, take away from, lessen; to get down to (*the truth*)
līmōs·us -a -um *adj* muddy; mud, growing in mud
limpid·us -a -um *adj* limpid, clear
līmŭl·us -a -um *adj* squinting
līm·us -a -um *adj* squinting; sidelong, askance; *m* mud; dirt, grime; ceremonial apron (*worn by priests at sacrifice*)
līnĕ·a -ae *f* line, string, thread; fishing line; plumb line; outline; boundary line, limit; **ad lineam** or **rectā lineā** in a straight line, vertically; horizontally; **extremā lineā amare** to love at a distance; **lineas transire** to go out of bounds
līneāment·um -ī *n* line; characteristic, feature; outline
līnĕ·ō -āre *vt* to make straight, make perpendicular
līnĕ·us -a -um *adj* flaxen, linen
lingō lingĕre linxī linctum *vt* to lick up, lap up
lingu·a -ae *f* tongue; speech, language, dialect; (of animals) note, song, bark; tongue of land; eloquence; **linguā promptus** insolent; **utraque lingua** Greek and Latin
lingŭl·a -ae *f* tongue of land
lingulāc·a -ae *m* or *f* gossip, chatterbox
līnĭg·er -ĕra -ĕrum *adj* wearing linen
linō linĕre lēvī or **līvī litum** *vt* to smear; to erase; to cover, overlay; (fig) to mess up
linquō linquĕre līquī *vt* to leave, forsake, depart from; to leave or let alone; to leave in a pinch; **linqui animo** or **linqui** to faint; **linquitur** (with **ut**) it remains to (*do something*)
linteāt·us -a -um *adj* canvas
lintĕ·ō -ōnis *m* linen weaver
linteŏl·um -ī *n* small linen cloth
lint·er -ris *f* skiff; tub, vat
lintĕ·us -a -um *adj* linen; *n* linen, linen cloth; canvas, sail; kerchief
lintricŭl·us -ī *m* small boat
līn·um -ī *n* flax; linen; thread, rope, line; fishing line; net
Lin·us -ī *m* son of Apollo and instructor of Orpheus and Hercules
Lipăr·a -ae or **Lipăr·ē -ēs** *f* island off the N. coast of Sicily; *f pl* the Aeolian islands
Liparae·us -a -um or **Liparens·is -e** *adj* of Lipara
lipp·iō -īre -īvī *or* **-iī -ītum** *vi* to have sore eyes; (of eyes) to burn, ache
lippitūd·ō -ĭnis *f* running eyes, inflammation of the eyes
lipp·us -a -um *adj* with sore eyes, sore-eyed; burning (*eyes*); (fig) blind
lique·faciō -facĕre -fēcī -factum (*passive*: **lique·fīō -fĭerī -factus sum**) *vt* to melt, dissolve; to decompose; to waste, weaken
liqu·ens -entis *adj* clear, limpid; flowing, gliding; liquid, fluid
liquĕō liquēre licŭī *vi* to be liquid; *v impers* it is clear, is apparent, is evident; **liquet mihi** (with *inf*) I am free to; **non liquet** (law) it is not clear (*legal formula used by a hung jury*)
liquescō liquescĕre licŭī *vi* to melt; to decompose; to grow soft, grow effeminate; (fig) to melt away; to become clear
liquĭdē *adv* clearly; (fig) clearly, plainly
liquidiuscŭl·us -a -um *adj* somewhat softer
liquĭdō *adv* clearly, plainly, certainly
liquĭd·us -a -um *adj* liquid, fluid, flowing; clear, transparent; pure (*pleasure*); clear (*voice*); calm (*mind*); clear, evident, certain; *n* liquid, water; clearness, certainty
liqu·ō -āre *vt* to melt, dissolve; to strain, filter
līqu·or -ī *vi* to flow; to melt, dissolve; (fig) to melt away, waste away
liqu·or -ōris *m* fluidity; liquid, fluid; sea
Līr·is -is *m* river between Campania and Latium
līs lītis *f* lawsuit, litigation; matter of dispute; quarrel, wrangling; charge, accusation; **litem intendere** or **litem inferre** (with *dat*) to sue (*someone*); **litem aestimare** to assess damages; **lis capitis** criminal charge
litātĭ·ō -ōnis *f* success in sacrificing, efficacious sacrifice
litātō *adv* with favorable omens
lĭtĕra see **littera**
litĭc·en -ĭnis *m* clarion player
lītigāt·or -ōris *m* litigant
lītigiōs·us -a -um *adj* quarrelsome, litigious; contested, disputed
lītig·ium -iī or **-ī** *n* quarrel, dispute
lītĭg·ō -āre *vi* to quarrel, squabble; to go to court
lit·ō -āre *vt* to offer duly or accept-

ably; *vi* to offer acceptable sacrifice; to receive a good omen; (with *dat*) to propitiate, satisfy, appease
lītorāl·is -e *adj* shore, of the shore
lītorĕ·us -a -um *adj* seashore, at or along the seashore
littĕr·a or **lītĕr·a -ae** *f* letter (*of the alphabet*); handwriting; *f pl* epistle, letter, dispatch; edict, ordinance; literature, books, literary works; learning, liberal education, scholarship; records, accounts; **littera salutaris** (*i.e.*, **A** = **absolvo**) vote of acquittal; **littera tristis** (*i.e.*, **C** = **condemno**) vote of guilty; **litteras discere** to learn to read and write; **litteras scire** to know how to read and write
litterārĭ·us -a -um *adj* of reading and writing; **ludus litterarius** elementary school
litterātē *adv* legibly, in a clear handwriting; literally; learnedly
litterāt·or -ōris *m* elementary-school teacher; grammarian, philologist
litterātūr·a -ae *f* alphabet
litterāt·us -a -um *adj* marked with letters, engraved; learned, scholarly; liberally educated; devoted to literature
litterŭl·a -ae *f* small letter; *f pl* short letter, note; slight literary endeavors
litūr·a -ae *f* erasure; erased passage; correction, emendation; blot, smear; wrinkle
litus *pp* of **lino**
lit·us -ŏris *n* seashore, beach, coast; river bank; **in litus harenas fundere** to carry coals to Newcastle; **litus arare** to waste effort
litŭ·us -ī *m* cavalry trumpet, clarion; (fig) signal; augur's wand (*crooked staff carried by an augur*); **lituus meae profectionis** signal for my departure
līv·ens -entis *adj* black-and-blue, livid
līv·ĕō -ēre *vi* to be black and blue, be livid; to be envious; (with *dat*) to be jealous of
līvesc·ō -ĕre *vi* to turn black and blue
Līvĭ·a -ae *f* second wife of Augustus (58 B.C.-29 A.D.)
līvidŭl·us -a -um *adj* inclined to be jealous, somewhat envious
līvid·us -a -um *adj* leaden (*in color*); blue; black and blue; jealous, envious, spiteful
Līv·ĭus -ĭī or **-ī** *m* T. Livius Patavinus or Livy (*famous historian*, 59 B.C.-17 A.D.)
līv·or -ōris *m* leaden color; bluish color; black-and-blue mark; jealousy, envy, spite
lix·a -ae *m* camp follower
locātĭ·ō -ōnis *f* arrangement, placement; renting out, contract, lease
locāt·um -ī *n* lease, contract
locĭt·ō -āre *vt* to lease out
loc·ō -āre *vt* to place, put, set, lay; to establish, constitute, lay, set; to give in marriage, marry off; to let, rent out; to contract for; to invest
locŭl·us -ī *m* little place, spot; pocket
locŭpl·ēs -ētis *adj* rich; reliable, responsible
locuplēt·ō -āre *vt* to make rich, enrich
loc·us -ī (*pl*: **loc·ī -ōrum** *m*; **loc·a -ōrum** *n*) *m* place, site, spot, locality, district; place, seat; period, period of time; opportunity, room, occasion; situation, position, category; rank, degree, birth; passage in a book; topic, subject, point, division; (mil) position, post, station; **adhuc locorum** till now; **ad id locorum** till then; **ex aequo loco dicere** to speak in the senate; to hold a conversation; **ex** or **de loco superiore dicere** to speak from the rostrum; **ex loco inferiore dicere** to speak before a judge, speak in court; **inde loci** since then; **in eo loci** in such a condition; **interea loci** meanwhile; **loci communes** general topics; public places, parks; **loco** (with *genit*) instead of; **loco** or **in loco** at the right time; **loco cedere** to give way, yield; **postea loci** afterwards; **post id locorum** afterwards; **ubicumque loci** whenever
lōcust·a -ae *f* locust
Lōcust·a -ae *f* woman notorious as poisoner in the time of Claudius and Nero
locūtĭ·ō -ōnis *f* speech; way of speaking, pronunciation
locūtus *pp* of **loquor**
lōd·ix -īcis *f* blanket
logĭc·us -a -um *adj* logical; *n pl* logic
log·os or **log·us -ī** *m* word; witticism; *m pl* mere words, empty talk
lōlīgō see **lolligo**
lol·ĭum -ĭī or **-ī** *n* darnel
lollīg·ō or **lōlīg·ō -ĭnis** *f* cuttlefish
lollīguncŭl·a -ae *f* small cuttlefish
lōment·um -ī *n* face cream
Londīn·ĭum -ĭī or **-ī** *n* London
longaev·us -a -um *adj* aged
longē *adv* far, far off, long way off; away, distant; out of reach, of no avail; long, for a long period; (to speak) at greater length; (with comparatives) far, by far, much; **longe lateque** far and wide, everywhere
longinquĭt·ās -ātis *f* length, extent; remoteness, distance; length, duration
longinqu·us -a -um *adj* long, extensive; far off, distant, remote; from afar, foreign; long, prolonged, continued, tedious; **ex** or **e longinquo** from far away
longĭter *adv* far
longitūd·ō -ĭnis *f* length; **in longitudinem** lengthwise

longiuscŭl·us -a -um *adj* pretty long

longur·ĭus -iī or **-ī** *m* long pole

long·us -a -um *adj* long; spacious; long, protracted, drawn-out; tedious; **longa navis** battleship; **longum esse** (with *inf*) to be tedious to; *n* length; **in longum** for a long while; **ne longum faciam** in short

loquācĭt·ās -ātis *f* talkativeness

loquācĭter *adv* long-windedly; at length, in detail

loquācŭl·us -a -um *adj* rather talkative

loqu·ax -ācis *adj* talkative, loquacious

loquell·a -ae *f* speech, language

loquĭt·or -ārī -ātus *vi* to chatter away

loquor loquī locūtus sum *vt* to say; to talk of, speak about; to tell, tell of, mention; (fig) to declare, show, indicate; *vi* to speak; to rustle, murmur

lōrār·ĭus -iī or **-ī** *m* flogger, slave driver

lōrāt·us -a -um *adj* tied with thongs

lōrĕ·us -a -um *adj* striped

lōrīc·a -ae *f* breastplate; parapet; **libros mutare loricis** to exchange books for arms

lōrīcāt·us -a -um *adj* wearing a breastplate

lōrĭp·ēs -ĕdis *adj* bowlegged

lōr·um -ī *n* strip of leather, thong, strap; whip, scourge; leather badge; *n pl* reins

lōt·os or **lōt·us -ī** *f* lotus; flute (*of lotus wood*)

lōtus *pp* of **lavo**

lub- = lib-

lubentĭ·a -ae *f* pleasure

lūbrĭc·ō -āre *vt* to oil, grease, make smooth

lūbrĭc·us -a -um *adj* slippery; smooth; slimy; gliding; deceitful, tricky; precarious; *n* precarious situation, critical period

Lūc·a bōs (*genit:* **Lūc·ae bovis**) *f* elephant

Lūcānĭ·a -ae *f* district in S.W. Italy

Lūcānĭc·us -a -um *adj* Lucanian; *f* Lucanian sausage

Lūcān·us -a -um *adj* Lucanian; *m* Lucanian; Lucan (*M. Annaeus Lucanus, epic poet,* 39-65 A.D.)

lūc·ar -āris *n* forest tax

lucell·um -ī *n* slight profit

lūcĕō lūcēre luxī *vi* to shine, be light, glow, glitter, be clear; (fig) to be clear, be apparent, be conspicuous; *v impers* it is light, day is dawning

Lūcĕr·ēs -um *m pl* one of the three original Roman tribes

lucern·ae -ae *f* lamp; (fig) midnight oil

lūcescō or **lūciscō lūcescĕre luxī** *vi* to begin to shine; *v impers* it is getting light

lūcĭdē *adv* clearly, distinctly

lūcĭd·us -a -um *adj* shining, bright, clear; lucid, clear

lūcĭf·er -ĕra -ĕrum *adj* shiny

Lūcĭf·er -ĕrī *m* morning star; planet Venus; son of Aurora and Cephalus; day

lūcĭfŭg·us -a -um *adj* light-shunning

Lūcīl·ĭus -iī or **-ī** *m* C. Lucilius (*first Roman satiric poet, c.* 180-102 B.C.)

Lucīn·a -ae *f* goddess of childbirth; childbirth

lūciscō see **lucesco**

Lucrētĭ·a -ae *f* daughter of Spurius Lucretius and wife of Collatinus, who, having been raped by Sextus Tarquinius, committed suicide in 509 B.C.

Lucrēt·ĭus -iī or **-ī** *m* Spurius Lucretius (*father of Lucretia and consul in* 509 B.C.); Titus Lucretius Carus (*philosophical poet,* 94?-55? B.C.)

lucrificābĭl·is -e or **lucrifĭc·us -a -um** *adj* profitable

lucrifŭg·a -ae *m* or *f* person not out for gain, disinterested person

Lucrīn·us -a -um *adj* Lucrine; *m* Lake Lucrine (*small lake near Baiae, famous for its oysters*)

lucripĕt·a -ae *m* profiteer

lucr·or -ārī -ātus sum *vt* to gain, win, get

lucrōs·us -a -um *adj* profitable

lucr·um -ī *n* profit, gain; wealth; greed, love of gain; **lucri facere** to gain; **lucri fieri** to be gained; **lucro esse** (with *dat*) to be advantageous for (*someone*); **ponere in lucro** or **in lucris** to regard as gain

luctām·en -ĭnis *n* wrestling; struggle, effort

luct·ans -antis *adj* reluctant

luctātĭ·ō -ōnis *f* wrestling; struggle, contest

luctāt·or -ōris *m* wrestler

luctifĭc·us -a -um *adj* causing sorrow, doleful, woeful

luctisŏn·us -a -um *adj* sad-sounding

luct·or -ārī -ātus sum or **luct·ō -āre** *vi* to wrestle; (with *inf*) to struggle to

luctuōsĭus *adv* more pitifully

luctuōs·us -a -um *adj* causing sorrow, sorrowful; sad, feeling sad

luct·us -ūs *m* sorrow, mourning, grief, distress; signs of sorrow, mourning clothes; source of grief, affliction

lūcubrātĭ·ō -ōnis *f* moonlighting, working by lamp light; evening gossip; nighttime writing

lūcŭbr·ō -āre *vt* to compose at night; *vi* to moonlight, burn the midnight oil

lūculentē *adv* splendidly, well; (to beat) soundly

lūculenter *adv* brilliantly, smartly, very well

lūculent·us -a -um *adj* bright, brilliant; (fig) brilliant, smart, excellent; considerable (*wealth*); sound (*beating*); trustworthy (*sources*)
Lūcull·us -ī *m* Lucius Licinius Lucullus (*Roman general and politician*, 117-56 B.C.)
Lucŭm·ō or **Lucm·ō -ōnis** *m* Etruscan prince, Etruscan priest
lūc·us -ī *m* sacred grove; woods
lūdi·a -ae *f* actress; gladiator (*female*)
lūdibr·ium -iī or **-ī** *n* derision; subject of derision, butt of ridicule; (fig) plaything, sucker; **ludibrio esse** (with *dat*) to be made a fool of by (*someone*), be taken in by (*someone*); **ludibrio habere** to take for a sucker, make fun of
lūdibund·us -a -um *adj* playful, playing around; without effort, without danger
lūdic·er -ra -rum *adj* for sport, in sport; **ludicra exercitatio** sports; athletics; **ludicrum praemium** sports award; **ludicra res** drama; *n* sport, game; toy; show, public game; stage play
lūdificābil·is -e *adj* used in mockery
lūdificāti·ō -ōnis *f* ridiculing, mocking; fooling, tricking
lūdificāt·or -ōris *m* mocker
lūdificāt·us -ūs *m* mockery
lūdific·ō -āre or **lūdific·or -ārī -ātus sum** *vt* to make a fool of, fool, take for a sucker; to fool, trick, baffle
lūdi·ō -ōnis or **lūd·ius -iī** or **-ī** *m* actor
lūdō lūdĕre lūsī lūsum *vt* to play; to spend in play; to amuse oneself with, do for amusement, practice as a pastime; to imitate, mimic, mock, do a takeoff on, ridicule; to deceive, delude; *vi* to play; to frisk, frolic; to play around, make love; **aleā ludere** to shoot craps; **pilā ludere** to play ball, play tennis
lūd·us -ī *m* play, game, sport, pastime, diversion; school; mere child's play; joke, fun; playing around, fooling around, lovemaking; public show, public game; **amoto ludo** all joking aside; **in ludum ire** to go to school; **per ludum** as a joke, for fun; *m pl* public games, public exhibition; games, tricks; **ludos facere** or **ludos reddere** (with *dat*) to play tricks on, make fun of
luell·a -ae *f* expiation, atonement
lu·ēs -is *f* infection, contagion, plague, pestilence; calamity
Lugdūnens·is -e *adj* of Lyons
Lugdūn·um -ī *n* Lyons (*town in E. Gaul*)
lūgĕō lugēre luxī *vt* to mourn, lament, deplore; *vi* to mourn, be in mourning; to be in mourning clothes
lūgubr·ia -ium *n pl* mourning clothes
lūgŭbr·is -e *adj* mourning; doleful; disastrous
lumbifrag·ium -iī or **-ī** *n* physical wreck
lumbrīc·us -ī *m* worm; (as term of reproach) worm
lumb·us -ī *m* loin; *m pl* loins; genital organs
lūm·en -inis *n* light; lamp, torch; brightness, sheen, gleam; daylight; light of the eye, eye; light of life, life; window, window light; distinguished person, luminary, celebrity; glory, pride
lūminār·e -is *n* window
lūminōs·us -a -um *adj* luminous; (fig) bright, conspicuous
lūn·a -ae *f* moon; month; night; crescent (*worn as ornament by senators on their shoes*); **luna laborans** moon in eclipse, eclipse of the moon; **luna minor** waning moon
lūnār·is -e *adj* lunar, of the moon
lūnāt·us -a -um *adj* crescent-shaped
lūn·ō -āre *vt* to make crescent-shaped, to shape like a crescent
lūnŭl·a -ae *f* little crescent (*ornament worn by women*)
lu·ō -ĕre -ī *vt* to wash; to cleanse, purge; to set free, let go; to pay (*debt of penalty*); to suffer, undergo; to atone for, expiate; to satisfy, appease; to avert by expiation or punishment
lup·a -ae *f* she-wolf; flirt, prostitute
lupān·ar -āris *n* brothel
lupāt·us -a -um *adj* jagged (*like wolf's teeth*); *m pl* or *n pl* jagged bit
Luperc·al -ālis *n* shrine on the Palatine hill sacred to Pan
Lupercāl·ia -ium *n pl* festival of Lycaean Pan, celebrated in February
Luperc·us -ī *m* Pan
lupill·us -ī *m* small lupine (*plant*)
lupīn·us -a -um *adj* lupine, wolf's; *m & n* lupine, wolf's-bane (*plant*); stage money
lup·us -ī *m* wolf; (fish) pike; jagged bit; grapnel
lurc·ō -ōnis *m* glutton
lūrĭd·us -a -um *adj* pale-yellow, wan, ghastly, lurid; making pale
lūr·or -ōris *m* sallowness
luscini·a -ae *f* nightingale
lusciniŏl·a -ae *f* little nightingale
luscin·ius -iī or **-ī** *m* nightingale
lusciōs·us or **luscitiōs·us -a -um** *adj* purblind, partly blind
lusc·us -a -um *adj* one-eyed
lūsi·ō -ōnis *f* play, game
Lūsitān·ī -ōrum *m pl* Lusitanians
Lūsitāni·a -ae *f* Lusitania (*modern Portugal and W. part of Spain*)
lūsit·ō -āre *vi* to like to play
lūs·or -ōris *m* player, gambler; humorous writer; joker
lustrāl·is -e *adj* lustral, propitiatory; quinquennial
lustrāti·ō -ōnis *f* purification, lustration; wandering
lustr·ō -āre *vt* to purify; to travel

over, traverse; to check, examine; to go around, encircle; to survey; (mil) to review (*troops*); to light up, make bright, illuminate; to scan (*with the eyes*); to consider, review
lustr•or -ārī -ātus sum *vi* to frequent brothels
lustr•um -ī *n* haunt, den, lair; wilderness; brothel; sensuality; purificatory sacrifice, lustration; lustrum, period of five years; period of years; **ingens lustrum** one hundred years, century
lūsus *pp* of **ludo**
lūs•us -ūs *m* play, game, sport, amusement; playing around (*amorously*)
lūteŏl•us -a -um *adj* yellowish
lūtĕ•us -a -um *adj* of mud, of clay; muddy; dirty, grimy; (fig) dirty; mud-colored; golden-yellow, yellow, orange
lutit•ō -āre *vt* to splatter with mud; (fig) to throw mud at
lut•ō -āre *vt* to make dirty
lutulent•us -a -um *adj* muddy, filthy; (fig) filthy; turbid (*style*)
lut•um -ī *n* mud, mire; clay; yellow
lux lūcis *f* light; light of day, daylight; light of day, life; public view, publicity; the public, the world; light of hope, encouragement; glory; elucidation; **luce** or **luci** by daylight, in the daytime; **lux aestiva** summer; **lux brumalis** winter
lux•ō -āre *vt* to put out of joint, dislocate
lux•or -ārī -ātus sum *vi* to live riotously, have a ball
luxurĭ•a -ae or **luxurĭ•ēs -ēī** *f* luxurience; luxury, extravagance, excess
luxurĭ•ō -āre or **luxurĭ•or -ārī -ātus sum** *vi* to grow luxuriantly; to luxuriate; (of the body) to swell up; (of animals) to be frisky; to run riot, lead a wild life
luxuriōsē *adv* luxuriously, voluptuously
luxuriōs•us -a -um *adj* luxuriant; exuberant; extravagant, voluptuous
lux•us -ūs *m* extravagance, excess, luxury; splendor, pomp, magnificence
Lyae•us -a -um *adj* Bacchic; *m* Bacchus; wine
Lycae•us -a -um *adj* Lycaean (*esp. applied to Pan*); *m* mountain in Arcadia where Jupiter and Pan were worshiped
Lycā•ōn -ŏnis *m* king of Arcadia, the father of Callisto, who was changed into a wolf
Lycāŏn•is -ĭdis *f* Callisto, who was changed into the Great Bear
Lycē•um *or* **Lycī•um -ī** *n* Aristotle's school at Athens
Lycĭ•us -a -um *adj & m* Lycian; *f* country in S.W. Asia Minor
lychnūch•us -ī *m* lamp stand; chandelier
lychn•us -ī *m* lamp
Lyctĭ•us -a -um *adj* Cretan
Lycurg•us -ī *m* Thracian king who prohibited the worship of Bacchus and was punished with madness and death; Spartan lawgiver (*date unknown*); Athenian orator and friend of Demosthenes (390-324 B.C.)
Lyc•us or **Lyc•os -ī** *m* husband of Antiope, who divorced her to marry Dirce
Lȳdĭ•us -a -um *adj & m* Lydian; Etruscan; *f* country of Asia Minor, whose capital was Sardis
Lȳd•us -a -um *adj & m* Lydian; Etruscan
lymph•a -ae *f* water, spring water; water nymph
lymphātĭc•us -a -um *adj* crazy, frantic; *n* craziness
lymphāt•us -a -um *adj* crazy, mad
Lyncē•us -a -um *adj* sharp-eyed; *m* Argonaut, famous for keen vision; son of Egyptus and Hyperraestra
lyn•x -cis *m* or *f* lynx
lyr•a -ae *f* lyre; lyric poetry, lyric
Lyr•a -ae *f* Lyra (*constellation*)
lyrĭc•us -a -um *adj* lyric; of the lyre; *m pl* lyric poets; *n pl* lyric poems
lyrist•ēs -ae *m* lyrist
Lyrnēs•is or **Lyrness•is -ĭdis** *f* Briseis
Lyrnēs•us -ī *f* town in the Troad, the birthplace of Briseis
Lysĭ•ās -ae *m* Athenian orator in the time of Socrates (*c.* 450-370 B.C.)

M

Macăr•eus -ĕī or **-ĕos** *m* son of Aeolus, who lived in incest with his sister Canace
Macĕd•ō -ŏnis *m* Macedonian
Macedonĭc•us -a -um *adj* Macedonian
Macedonĭ•us -a -um *adj* Macedonian; *f* Macedonia (*country lying between Thessaly and Thrace*)
macell•um -ī *n* butcher shop, meat market
mac•ĕō -ēre *vi* to be lean, be skinny
mac•er -ĕra -ĕrum *adj* lean; skinny; thin, poor (*soil*)
Mac•er -rī *m* C. Licinius Macer (*Roman historian and orator who was impeached by Cicero and committed suicide in* 66 B.C.); C. Licinius Ma-

cer Calvus (*son of the former, and distinguished orator and poet, 82-46 B.C.*)
mācerī·a -ae *f* brick or stone wall; garden wall
mācĕr·ō -āre *vt* to knead, soften, make tender; to weaken, waste; to distress, vex, torment
macesc·ō -ĕre *vi* to grow thin
machaer·a -ae *f* sword
machaerophŏr·us -ī *m* soldier armed with sword
Machā·ōn -ŏnis *m* famous physician of the Greeks in the Trojan War and son of Aesculapius
Machāoni·us -a -um *adj* surgical
māchĭn·a -ae *f* machine, engine; crane; pulley, windlass, winch; (*fig*) scheme, stratagem
māchinàment·um -ī *n* machine, engine, contrivance
māchinātĭ·ō -ōnis *f* mechanism; machine; trick
māchināt·or -ōris *m* engineer, machinist; (*fig*) contriver
māchĭn·or -ārī -ātus sum *vt* to engineer, design, contrive; to scheme, plot
macĭ·ēs -ēī *f* leanness, thinness; barrenness; poverty (*of style*)
macilent·us -a -um *adj* skinny
macresc·ō -ĕre *vi* to grow thin, get skinny
macritūd·ō -inis *f* leanness, skinniness
macrocoll·um -ī *n* large-size sheet of paper
mactābĭl·is -e *adj* deadly
mactāt·us -ūs *m* sacrifice
mactē *interj* well done!; good luck!
mact·ō -āre *vt* to magnify, glorify, honor; to sacrifice; to slaughter, put to death; to destroy, ruin, overthrow; to trouble, afflict
mact·us -a -um *adj* glorified, honored, adored; **macte virtute (esto)** (congratulatory exclamation) good luck!; well done!
macŭl·a -ae *f* spot, stain, blemish; mesh (*of a net*); (*fig*) stigma, blemish, disgrace, defect
macŭl·ō -āre *vt* to spot; to stain; to defile, pollute; to dishonor
maculōs·us -a -um *adj* spotted; stained
made·faciō -facĕre -fēcī -factus (*passive*: **made·fīō -fĭerī -factus sum**) *vt* to wet, moisten, drench, soak, steep
mad·ens -entis *adj* wet, moist; flowing (*hair*); melting (*snow*); reeking (*with blood*)
mad·ĕō -ēre -ŭī *vi* to be wet, be moist, be soaked, be drenched; to drip; to flow; to be soused; to be full, overflow
mad·escō -escĕre -ŭī *vi* to become wet, become moist
madĭdē *adv* drunkenly
madĭd·us -a -um *adj* wet, moist, drenched; dyed, steeped; drunk
mad·or -ōris *m* moisture
maduls·a -ae *m* souse, drunkard
Maeand·er or **Maeandr·os** or **Maeandr·us -ī** *m* river in Asia Minor, famous for its winding course; winding; winding border; devious course
Maecēn·ās -ātis *m* C. Cilnius Maecenas (*adviser to Augustus and friend of Virgil and Horace, d. 8 B.C.*)
maen·a -ae *f* sprat (*fish*)
Maenăl·is -ĭdis *adj* **Maenalis ursa** Callisto (*who was changed into the Great Bear*)
Maenăl·us or **Maenăl·os -ī** *m* or **Maenăl·a -ōrum** *n pl* Mt. Maenalus (*mountain range in Arcadia, sacred to Pan*)
Maen·as -ădis *f* Bacchante
Maenĭ·us -a -um *adj* Maenian; **Maenia Columna** pillar in the forum at which thieves, slaves, and debtors were tried and flogged
Maeŏn·es -um *m pl* Maeonians (*ancient name of the Lydians*)
Maeonĭd·ēs -ae *m* native of Maeonia; Homer; Etrurian
Maeŏn·is -ĭdis *f* Maeonian woman (*esp. Arachne or Omphale*)
Maeonĭ·us -a -um *adj* Lydians; Homeric; Etruscan; *f* Maeonia, Lydia; Etruria
Maeōt·ae -ārum *m pl* Scythian tribe on Lake Maeotis on the N.E. coast of the Black Sea
Maeōt·is -ĭdis *adj* Maetoic; Scythian; **Maeotis lacus** Sea of Azov
maer·ĕō -ēre *vi* to mourn
maer·or -ōris *m* mourning, sadness
maestĭter *adv* like a mourner
maestitĭ·a -ae *f* sadness, gloom, melancholy
maestitūd·ō -inis *f* sadness
maest·us -a -um *adj* mourning, sad, gloomy
Maev·ius -iī or **-ī** *m* poetaster often ridiculed by Virgil and Horace
māgāl·ia -ium *n pl* huts
mage see **magis**
magĭc·us -a -um *adj* magic; **artes magicae** magic
magis or **mage** *adv* more, in a higher degree, rather; **eo magis** all the more, the more; **magis magisque** more and more; **magis . . . quam** or **magis . . . atque** rather . . . than; **non magis . . . quam** not so much . . . as
magist·er -rī *m* chief, master, director; teacher; adviser, guardian; ringleader, author; captain, pilot; (in apposition with another noun) expert; **magister morum** censor; **magister sacrorum** chief priest
magister·ium -iī or **-ī** *n* directorship, presidency; **magisterium morum** censorship
magistr·a -ae *f* directress, mistress, instructress
magistrāt·us -ūs *m* magisterial office, magistracy; magistrate, offi-

cial; body of magistrates; military command
magnanimit·ās -ātis *f* magnanimity; bravery
magnanim·us -a -um *adj* magnanimous; brave
Magn·ēs -ētis *adj & m* Magnesian; *f* city in Caria, near the Meander; city in Lydia near Mt. Sipylus; district in Thessaly on the Aegean Sea
magnidic·us -a -um *adj* talking big
magnificē *adv* magnificently, splendidly; pompously
magnificenti·a -ae *f* magnificence, grandeur, splendor; pompousness
magnific·ō -āre *vt* to think much of
magnific·us -a -um *adj* grand, great, splendid, august; rich, costly, magnificent; pompous
magniloquenti·a -ae *f* lofty style; pompous language
magnilŏqu·us -a -um *adj* sublime; bragging
magnitūd·ō -inis *f* greatness, magnitude, size; large quantity, large number; vastness, extent
magnopĕre or **magnō opĕre** *adv* greatly, very much, particularly; strongly, earnestly, heartily, urgently
magn·us -a -um (*comp*: **major;** *superl*: **maximus**) *adj* big, large, great; long (*time*); high (*price*); important, momentous; significant; impressive; high, powerful (*in rank*); loud (*voice*); heavy (*rain*); advanced (*age*); noble (*character*); proud, boastful; *n* great thing; great value; **magni (pretii) aestimare** or **magni habere** to value highly, have a high regard for; **magno emere** to buy at a high price; **magno vendere** to sell at a high price; **vir magno jam natu** aged man, man advanced in years
mag·us -a -um *adj* magic; **artes magae** magic; *m* learned man (*among the Persians*); magician
Māi·us -a -um *adj & m* May; *f* daughter of Atlas and Pleione, and mother of Mercury by Jupiter
mājāl·is -is *m* castrated hog; (as term of abuse) swine
mājest·ās -ātis *f* majesty, dignity, grandeur; high treason; sovereign power, sovereignty; authority
māj·or -us (*comp* of **magnus**) *adj* bigger, larger, greater; **annos natu major quadraginta** forty years older; **in majus ferre** to exaggerate; **majoris (pretii)** at a higher price; more highly; **major natu** elder, older
mājōr·ēs -um *m pl* ancestors, forefathers
mājuscŭl·us -a -um *adj* somewhat greater; a little older
māl·a -ae *f* cheekbone, upper jaw; *f pl* cheek; (fig) jaws (*e.g., of death*)
malaci·a -ae *f* calm at sea, dead calm
malaciss·ō -āre *vt* to soften, soften up
malăc·us -a -um *adj* soft; luxurious
male *adv* badly, wrongly; wickedly, cruelly, maliciously; unfortunately, unsuccessfully, awkwardly; excessively, extremely, very much; (with adjectives having a good sense) not, scarcely, not at all; (with adjectives having a bad sense) very much; terribly; **male audire** to be ill spoken of; **male dicere** (with *dat*) to say nasty things to, abuse; **male emere** to buy at a high price; **male facere** (with *dat*) to treat badly or cruelly; **male habere** to harass; **male metuere** to be terribly afraid of; **male vendere** to sell at a loss; **male vivere** to be a failure in life
maledic·ax -ācis *adj* abusive, foul-mouthed
maledicē *adv* abusively, slanderously
maledic·ens -entis *adj* abusive, foul-mouthed
male·dīcō -dīcĕre -dixī -dictum *vi* (with *dat*) **a** to speak ill of, abuse, slander; **b** to say nasty things to
maledicti·ō -ōnis *f* abusive language, abuse
maledictit·ō -āre *vi* (with *dat*) to keep saying nasty things to
maledict·um -ī *n* curse; abuse
maledic·us -a -um *adj* abusive, scurrilous, foul-mouthed
malefact·or -ōris *m* malefactor
malefact·um or **malfact·um -ī** *n* wrong, injury
maleficē *adv* mischievously
maleficenti·a -ae *f* harm, wrong, mischief
malefic·ium -iī or **-ī** *n* evil deed, crime, offense; harm, injury, wrong, mischief; **maleficium admittere** or **committere** to commit an offense or crime
malefic·us -a -um *adj* wicked, vicious, criminal; *m* mischief-maker
malesuād·us -a -um *adj* seductive, tempting
malevŏl·ens -entis *adj* spiteful
malevolenti·a -ae *f* spitefulness, malice, meanness
malevŏl·us -a -um *adj* spiteful, malicious, mean; *mf* enemy; jealous person
malif·er -ĕra -ĕrum *adj* apple-growing
malignē *adv* spitefully, jealously, meanly; stingily, grudgingly
malignit·ās -ātis *f* spite, malice, jealousy, meanness; stinginess
malign·us -a -um *adj* spiteful, malicious, jealous, mean; stingy; (fig) stingy, unproductive (*soil*); scanty (*light*)
maliti·a -ae *f* malice, ill-will, bad behavior; *f pl* devilish tricks
malitiōsē *adv* craftily, wickedly
malitiōs·us -a -um *adj* crafty, wicked, malicious, devilish
malleŏl·us -ī *m* small hammer, small mallet; fiery arrow

mallĕ·us -ī *m* hammer, mallet; pole-ax (*for slaughtering animals*)
mālō or **māvŏlō malle māluī** *vt* to prefer; *vi* (with *dat*) to incline toward, be more favorably disposed to
malobăthr·um -ī *n* malobathrum oil, betel juice
māl·um -ī *n* apple; **aureum malum** quince; **felix malum** lemon; **malum Punicum** or **malum granatum** pomegranate
mal·um -ī *n* evil, ill; harm; punishment; disaster; hardship
māl·us -ī *m* mast (*of ship*); pole; *f* apple tree
mal·us -a -um *adj* bad; ill, evil; ugly; unpatriotic; adverse, unsuccessful; unlucky; **i in malam rem** go to hell!; *n* see **malum**
malv·a -ae *f* mallow
Măm·ers -ertis *m* Mars
Māmertīn·ī -ōrum *m pl* (*mercenaries of Agathocles who after his death seized Messana, c.* 282 B.C., *and precipitated the First Punic War*)
mamill·a -ae *f* breast, teat
mamm·a -ae *f* breast (*of a woman*); dug
mammeāt·us -a -um *adj* large-breasted, full-bosomed
mānābĭl·is -e *adj* penetrating (*cold*)
manc·eps -ĭpis *m* purchaser; contractor
mancip·ĭum or **mancup·ĭum -iī** or **-ī** *n* formal purchase; possession, right of ownership; slave; **mancipio accipere** to take possession of; **mancipio dare** to turn over possession of; **res mancipi** possessions basic to running a farm (*e.g., land, slaves, livestock, farm implements*); **res nec mancipi** possessions other than those needed to run a farm
mancĭp·ō or **mancŭp·ō -āre** *vt* to sell, transfer
manc·us -a -um *adj* crippled, maimed; (fig) defective, imperfect
mandāt·um -ī *n* command, order, commission; *n pl* instructions
mandāt·us -ūs *m* command, order
mand·ō -āre *vt* to commit, entrust; to command, order, enjoin, commission
mandō mandĕre mandī mansum *vt* to chew; to champ; to eat, devour; **humum mandere** to bite the dust (*said of those who fall in battle*)
mandr·a -ae *f* stable, stall; drove of cattle; checkerboard
mandūc·us -ī *m* mask representing a glutton
māne (indecl) *n* morning; *adv* early in the morning; **bene mane** very early; **cras mane** tomorrow morning; **heri mane** yesterday morning; **hodie mane** this morning; **postridie ejus diei mane** the following morning
manĕō manēre mansī mansum *vt* to wait for, await; *vi* to stay, remain; to stop off, pass the night; to last, endure, continue, persist; **in condicione manere** to stick by an agreement; **in sententia manere** to stick to an opinion
mān·ēs -ĭum *m pl* souls of the dead; ghosts; lower world; last remains (*of the body*), ashes
mang·ō -ōnis *m* pushy salesman; slave dealer
manĭc·ae -ārum *f pl* handcuffs; grappling hook; long sleeves; gloves
manicāt·us -a -um *adj* long-sleeved
manicŭl·a -ae *f* little hand
manifestē *adv* plainly, distinctly
manifestō *adv* manifestly, evidently, plainly
manifest·ō -āre *vt* to reveal, betray
manifest·us -a -um *adj* manifest, plain, clear, distinct; exposed, brought to light, detected, caught; (with *genit*) convicted of, caught in; (with *inf*) known to
manipl- = manipul-
manipulār·is -e *adj* of a maniple or company; **miles manipularis** private
manipulār·is -is *m* private; soldier of the same company; comrade
manipulātim *adv* by companies
manipŭl·us or **manipl·us -ī** *m* handful (*esp. of hay*); (coll) gang; (mil) maniple, company (*three of which constituted a cohort*)
Manl·ĭus -iī or **-ī** *m* M. Manlius Capitolinus (*consul in* 392 B.C., *who, in* 389 B.C., *saved the Capitoline from the invading Gauls*); T. Manlius Torquatus (*consul in* 340 B.C., *famous for his military discipline*)
mannŭl·us -ī *m* pony
mann·us -ī *m* small Gallic horse
mān·ō -āre *vi* to drip, trickle, flow; to stream; (fig) to spread, emanate
mansĭ·ō -ōnis *f* stopover
mansĭt·ō -āre *vi* to stay on
mansuē·faciō -facĕre -fēcī -factum (*passive*: **mansuē·fīō -fiĕrī -factus sum**) *vt* to tame; (fig) to tame, pacify, civilize
mansu·ēs -is or **-ētis** *adj* tame, mild
mansu·escō -escĕre -ēvī -ētum *vt* to tame; *vi* to grow tame, become tame; (fig) to grow gentle, grow mild
mansuētē *adv* gently, mildly
mansuētūd·ō -ĭnis *f* mildness, gentleness
mansuēt·us -a -um *adj* tame; mild, gentle
mansus *pp* of **mando** and **maneo**
mantēl·e -is *n* napkin, towel
mantell·um or **mantēl·um -ī** *n* mantle
mantĭc·a -ae *f* knapsack
manticĭn·or -ārī -ātus sum *vi* to predict, prophesy
mant·ō -āre *vt* to wait for; *vi* to stay, remain, wait
Mant·ō -ūs *f* prophetic daughter of Tiresias

Mantŭ·a -ae *f* birthplace of Virgil, in N. Italy
manuāl·is -e *adj* that can be held in hand, hand-sized (*e.g., rocks*)
manubi·ae -ārum *f pl* money derived from the sale of booty
manubiāri·us -a -um *adj* (coll) bringing in the loot
manūbr·ium -iī or **-ī** *n* handle; hilt
manufestāri·us -a -um *adj* plain, obvious
manulě·a -ae *f* long sleeve
manuleār·ius -iī or **-ī** *m* sleeve maker
manuleāt·us -a -um *adj* long-sleeved
manūmissi·ō -ōnis *f* manumission, freeing of a slave
manū·mittō or **manū·mittō -mittěre -mīsī -missum** *vt* to manumit, emancipate, set free (*a slave*)
manupret·ium -iī or **-ī** *n* workman's pay, wages; (fig) pay, reward
man·us -ūs *f* hand; band, company; gang; force, violence, close combat; finishing touch; handwriting; work; workmanship; elephant's trunk; grappling irons; power; (law) power of the husband over his wife; **ad manum habere** to have at hand, have in readiness; **ad manum venire** to come within reach; **e manu** at a distance, from a distance; **in manibus esse** to be in everyone's hands, be well known; to be near, be at hand; to be present; **in manu esse** (with *genit*) to be in the power of, be under the jurisdiction of; **in manu esse** (with *dat*) to be obvious to; **inter manus** under one's hands, with one's care; in one's hands, in one's arms; **manibus pedibusque** (fig) with might and main; **manu** by hand, artificially; (mil) by force of arms; **manu tenere** to know for sure; **manum committere, conserere,** or **conferre** to begin to fight; **manum dare** to lend a hand; **manum injicere** (with *dat*) to lay hands on, arrest; **manus dare** or **manus dedere** to give oneself up, surrender; **per manus** by hand; by force, by main force; from hand to hand, from mouth to mouth, from father to son; **plenā manu** generously; **prae manibus** or **prae manu** at hand, in readiness; **sub manu** or **sub manum** at hand, near; immediately
mapāl·ia -ium *n pl* African huts; African village, kraal
mapp·a -ae *f* napkin; flag (*used in starting races at the racetrack*)
Marăth·ōn -ōnis *f* site, in E. Attica, of victory by Miltiades over the Persians (490 B.C.)
Marcell·us -ī *m* Roman cognomen in the gens Claudia; M. Claudius Marcellus (*nephew of Augustus, whose premature death is referred to in the Aeneid,* 43-23 B.C.)
marc·ěō -ēre *vi* to wither, droop, shrivel; to be weak, be feeble, be decrepit, be run-down; to slack off
marcesc·ō -ěre *vi* to begin to wither, begin to droop; to become weak, become run-down; to become lazy
marcid·us -a -um *adj* withered, drooping; groggy
Marc·ius -iī or **-ī** *m* Ancus Marcius (*fourth king of Rome*)
marcŭl·us -ī *m* small hammer
mar·e -is *n* sea; seawater, saltwater; **mare inferum** Tyrrhenian Sea; **mare nostrum** Mediterranean Sea; **mare superum** Adriatic Sea
Mareōt·a -ae *f* town and lake near Alexandria in Egypt
Mareōtic·us -a -um *adj* Mareotic; Egyptian
margarīt·a -ae *f* or **margarīt·um -ī** *n* pearl
margin·ō -āre *vt* to furnish with a border; to curb (*a street*)
marg·ō -inis *f* margin, edge, border; frontier
Mariān·ī -ōrum *m pl* partisans of Marius
Marīc·a -ae *f* nymph of Minturnae, mother of Latinus
marīn·us -a -um *adj* sea, of the sea, marine
marisc·a -ae *f* fig; **tumidae mariscae** the piles
marīt·a -ae *f* wife, married woman
marītāl·is -e *adj* marital, nuptial, matrimonial
maritimus or **maritŭm·us -a -um** *adj* sea, of the sea; seafaring, maritime; (fig) changeable (*like the sea*); **ora maritima** seacoast; *n pl* seacoast
marīt·ō -āre *vt* to marry; to train (*a vine to a tree*)
marīt·us -a -um *adj* matrimonial nuptial; *m* husband, married man; lover; *f* see **marita**
Mar·ius -iī or **-ī** *m* C. Marius (*conqueror of Jugurtha and of the Cimbri and Teutons, and seven times consul,* 157-86 B.C.)
marm·or -ŏris *n* marble; marble statue, marble monument; smooth surface of the sea
marmorě·us -a -um *adj* marble, made of marble; marble-like
Mar·ō -ōnis *m* cognomen of Virgil
marr·a -ae *f* hoe, weeding hook
Mar·s -tis *m* god of war and father of Romulus and Remus; battle, war; engagement; planet; **aequo Marte** on an equal footing; **suo Marte** by one's own exertions, independently
Mars·ī -ōrum *m pl* Marsians (*a people of S. central Italy, regarded as tough warriors*)
marsupp·ium -iī or **-ī** *n* pouch, purse
Marsȳ·ās or **Marsȳ·a -ae** *m* satyr who challenged Apollo with the flute and was flayed alive upon his defeat; statue in the Roman forum of Marsyas

Martiāl·is -is *m* M. Valerius Martialis (*commonly called Martial and famous for his epigrams, c.* 40-120 A.D.)
Marticŏl·a -ae *m* worshiper of Mars
Martī·us -a -um *adj* Martian, of Mars; sacred to Mars; descended from Mars; March; *m* March, month of March
mās maris *adj* male, masculine; manly, masculine, brave; *m* male
masculīn·us -a -um *adj* male, masculine
mascŭl·us -a -um *adj* male, masculine; manly, vigorous; *m* male
mass·a -ae *f* mass, lump; (coll) chunk of money
Massic·us -a -um *adj* Massic; *m* Mt. Massicus (*between Latium and Campania, famous for its wine*); *n* Massic (*wine*)
Massilī·a -ae *f* Greek colony on S. coast of Gaul (*modern Marseilles*)
Massȳl·ī -ōrum *m pl* tribe of E. Numidia
mastīgī·a ae *m* rascal
mastrūc·a -ae *f* sheepskin; (as term of abuse) ninny
mastrūcāt·us -a -um *adj* clothed in sheepskin
matăr·a -ae or **matăr·is -is** *f* Celtic javelin
matell·a -ae *f* chamber pot
matellī·ō -ōnis *m* pot
māt·er -ris *f* mother; matron; **mater familias** lady of the house; (of animals) dam; cause, origin, source
mātercŭl·a -ae *f* a little mother, poor mother
māt·erfamiliās -risfamiliās *f* lady of the house, mistress of the household
māterī·a -ae or **māterī·ēs -ēī** f matter, stuff, material; lumber, wood, timber; fuel; subject, subject matter, theme, topic; cause, source, occasion, opportunity; capacity, natural ability, disposition
māteriār·ius -iī or **-ī** *m* timber merchant
māteriāt·us -a -um *adj* built with lumber; **male materiatus** built with poor lumber
māteriēs see **materia**
māterī·or -ārī -ātus sum *vi* to fetch or gather wood
mātern·us -a -um *adj* maternal, mother's, of a mother
mātertĕr·a -ae *f* aunt, mother's sister
mathēmatic·us -ī *m* mathematician; astrologer
Matīn·us -ī *m* mountain in Apulia, near Horace's birthplace
mātricīd·a -ae *m* matricide, mother's murderer
mātricīd·ium -iī or **-ī** *n* matricide, murder of one's mother
mātrimōn·ium -iī or **-ī** *n* matrimony, marriage; **in matrimonium ire** to enter matrimony, get married; **in matrimonium aliquam ducere** to marry some girl
mātrīm·us -a -um *adj* having a mother still living
mātrōn·a -ae *f* married woman, matron, wife; woman of quality, lady
Mātrōnāl·ia -ium *n pl* festival celebrated by matrons on March 1 in honor of Mars
mātrōnāl·is -e *adj* matronly, womanly, wifely
matt·a -ae *f* straw mat
matŭl·a -ae *f* pot; chamber pot
mātūrātē *adv* in good time
mātūrē *adv* at the right time; in time; betimes, in good time, promptly, quickly; prematurely
mātūr·escō -escĕre -ŭī *vi* to get ripe, ripen, mature
mātūrit·ās -ātis *f* ripeness, maturity; (fig) maturity, height, perfection
mātūr·ō -āre *vt* to ripen, bring to maturity; to accelerate, speed up; (with *inf*) to be too quick in doing; *vi* to hasten
mātūr·us -a -um *adj* ripe, mature, full-grown; opportune, at the right time; early, coming early (*e.g., winter*); advanced in years; marriageable; mellow (*with age*)
Mātūt·a -ae *f* goddess of the dawn
mātūtīn·us -a -um *adj* morning, early; **tempora matutina** morning hours
Mauritānī·a -ae *f* country of N.W. Africa
Maur·us -a -um *adj* Moorish; African
Maurūsī·us -a -um *adj* Moorish, Mauretanian
Māvor·s -tis *m* Mars
Māvortī·us -a -um *adj* Martian, of Mars
maxill·a -ae *f* jaw
maximē or **maxŭmē** *adv* very, most, especially, particularly; just, precisely, exactly; (in sequences) in the first place, first of all; (in affirmations) by all means, certainly, yes; **immo maxime** certainly not; **nuper maxime** just recently; **quam maxime** as much as possible; **tum cum maxime** at the precise moment when; **tum maxime** just then, precisely at that time; **ut maxime . . . ita maxime** the more . . . so much the more
maximĭt·ās -ātis *f* magnitude
maxĭmus or **maxŭmus** (*superl* of **magnus**) see **magnus**
mazonŏm·us -ī *m* large dish
meāmet = **meā,** *abl fem sing* of **meus,** strengthened by **-met**
meapte = **mea,** *nom fem sing* of **meus,** strengthened by **-pte**
meāt·us -ūs *m* motion, movement; course, channel
mecastor *interj* by Castor!
mēd = **me**
mēcum = **cum me**
medd·ix or **med·ix -icis** *m* magis-

trate (*among the Oscans*); **meddix tuticus** senior magistrate (*among the Oscans*)
Mēdē·a -ae *f* daughter of Aeetes, the king of Colchis, and wife of Jason, famous for her magic
Mēdē·is -ĭdis *adj* magic
med·ens -entis *m* physician
med·ĕor -ērī *vt* to heal; *vi* (with *dat*) to heal, cure, be good for, remedy
Mēd·ī -ōrum *m pl* Medes; Persians; Parthians
Mēdi·a -ae *f* Asian country between Armenia, Parthia, Hyrcania, and Assyria
mediastīn·us -ī *m* servant, drudge
mēdic·a -ae *f* alfalfa
medicābĭl·is -e *adj* curable
medicām·en -ĭnis *n* medicine, remedy, drug, antidote; tincture; cosmetic; (fig) cure, remedy
medicāment·um -ī *n* medication, medicine; potion; (fig) relief, antidote; (rhet) embellishment
medicāt·us -ūs *m* magic charm
medicīn·a -ae *f* medicine, medical science; medicine, remedy; doctor's office; (with *genit*) (fig) cure for, remedy for
medĭc·ō -āre *vt* to medicate, cure; to dye
medĭc·or -ārī -ātus sum *vt* to cure; *vi* (with *dat*) to heal, cure
medĭc·us -a -um *adj* medical; healing; *m* doctor, surgeon
Mēdĭc·us -a -um *adj* Median, of the Medes
mediē *adv* moderately
mediĕt·ās -ātis *f* mean
medimn·um -ī *n* or **medimn·us -ī** *m* bushel, medimnus (*containing six modii*)
mediŏcr·is -e *adj* medium, average, ordinary; mediocre; narrow, small
mediocrĭt·ās -ātis *f* mean; moderation; mediocrity; *f pl* moderate passions
mediocrĭter *adv* moderately, fairly; not particularly, not very, not much; calmly
Mediolān·um -ī *n* Milan
medioxŭm·us -a -um *adj* (coll) in the middle
meditāment·um -ī *n* practice, drill
meditātē *adv* purposely
meditāti·ō -ōnis *f* reflection, contemplation; practice; rehearsal; (with *genit*) reflection on, contemplation of
meditāt·us -a -um *adj* premeditated
mediterrānĕ·us -a -um *adj* inland
medĭt·or -ārī -ātus sum *vt* to think over, reflect on; to practice; to plan, design
medi·us -a -um *adj* middle, central, the middle of, in the middle; intervening (*time*); middling, ordinary, common; undecided, neutral, ambiguous; meddling; **in mediā insulā** in the middle of the island; **media pars** half, one half; *m* mediator; *n* middle, center; community, common good; public, publicity; **e medio abire** to disappear; **in medio relinquere** to leave undecided, leave hanging in the air; **in medium** into the center; on behalf of the public; for the common good; **in medium proferre** to publish
medius fidius *interj* by Heaven!
med·ix -icis *m* magistrate (*among the Oscans*); **medix tuticus** senior magistrate
medull·a -ae *f* marrow; middle, center
medullĭtus *adv* (fig) with all one's heart
Medūs·a -ae *f* one of the three Gorgons, the daughter of Phorcys, whose eyes turned everything they looked upon into stone
Medūsae·us -a -um *adj* Medusan; **equus Medusaeus** Pegasus
Megaer·a -ae *f* one of the three Furies
Megalens·ia or **Megalēs·ia -ium** *n pl* festival of Cybele, celebrated on the 4th of April
Megăr·a -ae *f* or **Megăr·a -ōrum** *n pl* town near Athens
Megarē·us or **Megarĭc·us -a -um** *adj* Megarean
megistān·es -um *m pl* grandees
mehercle or **mehercŭle** or **mehercŭles** *interj* by Hercules!
mēi·ō -ĕre *vi* to urinate
mel mellis *n* honey; **meum mel** (as term of endearment) my honey!; *n pl* drops of honey
melancholĭc·us -a -um *adj* melancholy
melandrȳ·um -ī *n* piece of salted tuna
Melanth·ius -iī or **-ī** *m* goatherd of Ulysses
melcŭl·um -ī *n* (*term of endearment*) little honey
Meleăg·er or **Meleăg·ros -rī** *m* son of King Oeneus of Calydon and participant in the famous Calydonian boar hunt
Meleagrĭd·es -um *f pl* sisters of Meleager, who were changed into birds
Melicert·a or **Melicert·ēs -ae** *m* son of Ino and Athamas, who was changed into a sea god, called by the Greeks Palaemon and by the Romans Portunus
melĭc·us -a -um *adj* musical; lyric
melilōt·os -ī *m* clover
melimēl·a -ōrum *n pl* honey apples
melīn·a -ae *f* mead
mēlīn·a -ae *f* leather wallet
Mēlīn·um -ī *n* pigment; Melian white
meli·or -us (*comp* of **bonus**) *adj* better
melisphyll·um -ī *n* balm
Melĭt·a or **Melĭt·ē -ēs** *f* Malta
Melitens·is -e *adj* Maltese
melius (*comp* of **bene**) *adv* better
meliuscŭlē *adv* pretty well

meliuscŭl·us -a -um *adj* a little better
mell·a -ae *f* mead
mellicŭl·us -a -um *adj* sweet as honey
mellĭf·er -ĕra -ĕrum *adj* honey-producing
mellifĭc·ō -āre *vi* to make honey
mellill·a -ae *f* (term of endearment) little honey
mellīn·a -ae *f* sweetness, delight
mellīn·a -ae *f* leather wallet
mellīt·us -a -um *adj* honeyed, sweetened with honey; sweet as honey
mel·os -ī (Greek *pl*: **mel·e**) *n* tune, melody, song
Melpomĕn·ē -ēs *f* Muse of tragic poetry
membrān·a -ae *f* membrane, skin; slough; parchment; film
membrānŭl·a -ae *f* small piece of parchment
membrātim *adv* limb by limb; piecemeal, singly; in short sentences
membr·um -ī *n* limb, member; part, division; clause
mēmet *pron* (emphatic form of **me**) me
memĭn·ī -isse *vt* to remember; *vi* (with *genit*) to be mindful of, remember
Memn·ōn -ŏnis *m* son of Tithonus and Aurora, king of the Ethiopians, and ally of the Trojans, who was killed by Achilles
Memnŏnĭd·es -um *f pl* birds that rose from the pyre of Memnon
Memnŏni·us -a -um *adj* Memnonian; Oriental, Moorish, black
mem·or -ŏris *adj* mindful, remembering; having a good memory; reminding; (with *genit*) mindful of, remembering
memorābĭl·is -e *adj* memorable, remarkable
memorand·us -a -um *adj* worth mentioning, notable
memorāt·us -ūs *m* mention
memorĭ·a -ae *f* memory; remembrance; period of recollection, recollection, time, lifetime; a memory, past event, history; historical account; **memoriae prodere** to hand down to posterity; **paulo supra hanc memoriam** not long ago; **post hominum memoriam** within the memory of man; **superiore memoriā** in earlier times
memoriŏl·a -ae *f* weak memory
memorĭter *adv* from memory, by heart; accurately, correctly
memŏr·ō -āre *vt* to mention, bring up, relate; to name, call; *vi* (with **de** + *abl*) to speak of
Memph·is or **-ĭdos** *f* city in central Egypt
Memphitĭc·us -a -um *adj* Egyptian
Menand·er or **Menand·ros -rī** *m* Greek comic playwright, the most important representative of the Attic New Comedy (342-291 B.C.)
Menandrē·us -a -um *adj* of Menander
mend·a -ae *f* fault, blemish
mendāciloquĭ·or -us *adj* more false, more mendacious
mendāc·ium -iī or **-ī** *n* lie
mendāciuncŭl·um *n* white lie, fib
mend·ax -ācis *adj* mendacious, given to lying, false; *m* liar
mendicābŭl·um -ī *n* beggar
mendicĭt·ās -ātis *f* beggary
mendĭc·ō -āre or **mendĭc·or -ārī -ātus sum** *vt* to beg, beg for; *vi* to beg, go begging
mendicŭl·us -a -um *adj* beggarly
mendĭc·us -a -um *adj* needy, poor, poverty-stricken; (fig) poor, sorry, paltry; *m* beggar
mendōsē *adv* faultily, carelessly
mendōs·us -a -um *adj* full of physical defects; full of faults, faulty, incorrect, erroneous; blundering
mend·um -ī *n* defect, fault; blunder
Menelā·us -ī *m* son of Atreus, brother of Agamemnon, and husband of Helen
Menen·ius -iī or **ī** *m* Menenius Agrippa (*patriotic Roman who told the plebs the fable of the belly and the limbs during the secession of the plebs in* 494 B.C.)
Menoec·eus -ĕī or **-ĕos** *m* son of Theban king Creon, who hurled himself off the city walls to save the city
Menoetiăd·ēs -ae *m* Patroclus
Menoet·ius -iī or **-ī** *m* father of Patroclus
men·s -tis *f* mind, intellect; understanding, reason; thought, opinion, idea; feeling, heart, soul; purpose, intention, plan; courage, boldness; passion, impulse; **addere mentem** to give courage; **captus mente** crazy; **demittere mentem** to lose heart; **in mentem venire** to come to mind; **mentis suae esse** to be in one's right mind
mens·a -ae *f* table; meal, course, dinner; guests at table; counter; bank; sacrificial table, altar; **mensa secunda** dessert
mensār·ius -iī or **-ī** *m* banker; treasurer, treasury-board member
mensĭ·ō -ōnis *f* measure, measuring; quantity (*of a syllable*)
mens·is -is *m* month; **primo mense** at the beginning of the month
mens·or -ōris *m* surveyor
menstruāl·is -e *adj* for a month
menstrŭ·us -a -um *adj* monthly; lasting for a month; *n* rations for a month; month's term of office
mensŭl·a -ae *f* little table
mensūr·a -ae *f* measuring, measurement; standard of measure; amount, size, proportion, capacity, extent, limit, degree
mensus *pp* of **metior**
ment·a or **menth·a -ae** *f* mint
mentĭ·ens -entis *m* sophism, fallacy
mentĭ·ō -ōnis *f* mention; **mentio-**

nem facere (with *genit* or **de** + *abl*) to make mention of; **mentiones serere** (with **ad** + *acc*) to throw hints to
ment·ior -īrī -ītus sum *vt* to invent, fabricate; to feign, imitate, fake; *vi* to lie; to act deceitfully
Ment·or -ŏris *m* friend of Ulysses; famous artist in metalwork; ornamental cup
ment·um -ī *n* chin
mĕ·ō -āre *vi* to go, pass
mephīt·is -is *f* malaria
mepte *pron* (emphatic form of **mē**) me, me myself
merăcŭl·us or **merācl·us -a -um** *adj* pretty pure, rather pure
merāc·us -a -um *adj* pure, unmixed, undiluted, straight
mercābĭl·is -e *adj* buyable
mercāt·or -ōris *m* merchant, trader, dealer, wholesale dealer
mercātōrĭ·us -a -um *adj* merchant, trading; **navis mercatoria** merchant ship
mercātūr·a -ae *f* trading, trade, commerce; purchase; *f pl* goods
mercāt·us -ūs *m* trade, traffic; market, marketplace; fair
mercēdŭl·a -ae *f* poor pay; low rent, low income
mercēnārĭ·us -a -um *adj* hired, paid, mercenary; *m* common laborer, servant
merc·ēs -ēdis *f* pay, wages, salary; bribe; reward, recompense; cost; injury, detriment; stipulation, condition, retribution, punishment; rent, income, interest
mercimōn·ium -iī or **-ī** *n* merchandise
mer·cor -ārī -ātus sum *vt* to deal in, trade in, purchase
Mercuriāl·is -e *adj* of Mercury; *m pl* corporation of merchants in Rome
Mercur·ius -iī or **-ī** *m* Mercury (*son of Jupiter and Maia, messenger of the gods, patron of commerce, diplomacy, lying, gambling, and conductor of departed souls to the world below*); Mercury (*planet*)
merd·a -ae *f* droppings, excrement
merend·a -ae *f* lunch, snack
mer·ĕo -ēre -ŭī -ĭtum or **mer·ĕor -ērī -ĭtus sum** *vt* to deserve, merit, be entitled to; to win, earn, acquire, merit; *vi* to serve; to serve in the army; (with **de** + *abl*) to serve, render service to, do a favor for; **bene de re publica merere** or **mereri** to serve one's country well; **de te merui** I have done you a favor, I have treated you well; **equo merere** to serve in the cavalry
meretrīcĭ·us -a -um *adj* prostitute's
meretrīcŭl·a -ae *f* cute little wench
merĕtr·ix -īcis *f* prostitute, harlot, wench, strumpet
merg·ae -ārum *f pl* pitchfork
merg·es -ĭtis *f* sheaf
mergō mergĕre mersī mersum *vt* to dip, plunge, sink; to engulf, swallow up; to swamp, overwhelm, bury, drown; **mergi** to sink, drown; to go bankrupt
merg·us -ī *m* diver (*bird*)
merīdiān·us -a -um *adj* midday, noon; southern, southerly
merīdiātĭ·ō -ōnis *f* siesta
merīdĭ·ēs -ēī *m* midday, noon; south; **spectare ad meridiem** to face south
merīdĭ·ō -āre *vi* to take a siesta
Mērĭŏn·ēs -ae *m* charioteer of Idomeneus
merĭtō *adv* deservedly, rightly
merĭt·ō -āre *vt* to earn regularly
meritōr·ius -a -um *adj* rented, hired; *n pl* rented apartment
merĭt·us -a -um *adj* deserved, just, right, proper, deserving; guilty; *n* service, favor, kindness; blame, fault, offense; merit, worth
merobĭb·us -a -um *adj* drinking unmixed wine
Merŏp·ē -ēs *f* one of the Pleiades, the daughter of Atlas and Pleione
Mer·ops -ŏpis *m* king of Ethiopia, husband of Clymene, and reputed father of Phaethon
mer·ops -ŏpis *f* bee eater (*bird*)
mers·ō -āre *vt* to keep dipping or plunging, to immerse; (fig) to engulf; **mersari** (with *dat*) to plunge into
mersus *pp* of **mergo**
merŭl·a -ae *f* blackbird
mer·us -a -um *adj* pure, unmixed, undiluted, unadulterated; (fig) undiluted; (fig) nothing but, mere; *n* wine
mer·x -cis *f* merchandise, wares; **mala merx** (fig) bad lot
Messallīn·a -ae *f* wife of the Emperor Claudius; wife of Nero
Messān·a -ae *f* town in N.E. Sicily
Messāpĭ·us -a -um *adj* Apulian; *f* town and district in S.E. Italy, named after the mythical founder Messapus
mess·is -is *f* harvest; harvest time; **adhuc tua messis in herba est** (fig) don't count your chickens before they are hatched
mess·or -ōris *m* reaper, mower
messōr·ius -a -um *adj* reaper's
messus *pp* of **meto**
mēt·a -ae *f* marker for measuring the distance at a racetrack; (fig) goal, end; (fig) turning point, critical moment
metall·um -ī *n* metal; *n pl* mine
metamorphōs·is -is *f* transformation
metaphŏr·a -ae *f* metaphor
mētāt·or -ōris *m* planner; **metator urbis** city planner
Metaur·us -ī *m* small river in Umbria, at the banks of which Hasdrubal was defeated in 207 B.C.

Metell·us -ī *m* Roman surname; Q. Caecilius Metellus Numidicus (*commander of the Roman forces against Jugurtha from* 109 B.C. *until replaced by Marius in* 107 B.C.)
Methymn·a -ae *f* town on the island of Lesbos
mētior mētīrī mensus sum *vt* to measure; to traverse, travel; to judge, estimate; (with *dat*) to measure (*something*) out to, distribute (*something*) among; (with *abl*) to judge (*someone*) by the standard of
metō metĕre messŭī messum *vt* to reap, mow, gather, collect, harvest; (fig) to mow down (*e.g., with the sword*)
mēt·or -ārī -ātus sum *vt* to measure off; to lay out (*e.g., a camp*)
metrēt·a -ae *f* liquid measure (*about nine gallons*)
metuculōs·us -a -um *adj* fearful; scary
metŭ·ens -entis *adj* afraid, apprehensive, anxious
metŭ·ō -ĕre -ī *vt* to fear, be afraid of; *vi* to be afraid, be apprehensive
met·us -ūs *m* fear, anxiety, apprehension
me·us -a -um *adj* my; *pron* mine; **meā interest** it is of importance to me; **meum est** (with *inf*) it is my duty to; **meus est** (coll) I've got him
Mezent·ius -iī or **-ī** *m* Etruscan tyrant of Caere, slain by Aeneas
mī = mihi
mīc·a -ae *f* crumb, morsel
Micips·a -ae *m* son of Masinissa and king of Numidia (148-118 B.C.); *m pl* (fig) Numidians, Africans
mic·ō -āre *vi* to vibrate, quiver, twinkle, sparkle, flash
mictur·iō -īre *vi* to have to urinate
Mid·ās -ae *m* king of Phrygia, at whose touch everything turned to gold (8*th cent.* B.C.)
migrātī·ō -ōnis *f* moving, changing residence; metaphorical use
migrāt·us -ūs *m* transporting
migr·ō -āre *vt* to transport; (fig) to transgress, violate; *vi* to move, change residence, depart, migrate; (fig) to go away, change, turn
mīl·es -itis *m* soldier; infantryman; private; army
Mīlēsi·us -a -um *adj* Milesian, of Miletus
Mīlēt·us -ī *f* Miletus (*town on the W. coast of Asia Minor*)
mīl·ia -ium *n pl* thousands; see **mille**
mīliār·ium -iī or **-ī** *n* milestone
mīlitār·is -e *adj* military
mīlitāriter *adv* in a military manner, like a soldier
mīlitāri·us -a -um *adj* soldierly, military
mīliti·a -ae *f* army; war; the military; military discipline; **militiae** in war, on the battlefield, in the army; **militiae domique** abroad and at home, on the war front and on the home front
mīlit·ō -āre *vt* to carry on (*war*); *vi* to serve as a soldier, be in the service
mil·ium -iī or **-ī** *n* millet
mille (indecl) *adj* thousand; *n* thousand; **mille homines** a thousand men; **milia** *n pl* thousands; **duo milia passuum** two miles
millēsim·us or **millensim·us -a -um** *adj* thousandth
milliār·ium -iī or **-ī** *n* milestone
milliens or **milliēs** *adv* a thousand times; innumerable times
Mil·ō -ōnis *m* T. Annius Milo (*friend of Cicero and enemy of Clodius, defended by Cicero on a charge of having murdered Clodius in* 52 B.C.)
Miltiăd·ēs -is *m* Athenian general victorious at Marathon (490 B.C.)
mīluīn·us -a -um *adj* rapacious
mīlŭ·us or **mīlŭ·os -ī** *m* kite (*bird of prey*); gurnard (*fish*)
Mīlŭ·us -ī *m* Kite (*constellation*)
mīm·a -ae *f* actress
Mimallŏn·is -idis *f* Bacchante
Mim·ās -antis *m* one of the giants
mīmicē *adv* like a mime actor
mīmic·us -a -um *adj* suitable for the mime, farcical
Mimnerm·us -ī *m* Greek elegiac poet of Colophon (*fl.* 560 B.C.)
mīmŭl·a -ae *f* miserable little actress
mīm·us -ī *m* mime, farce; actor of a mime; (fig) farce
min·a -ae *f* Greek coin (*about* 100 *denarii*)
mināci·ae -ārum *f pl* menaces, threats
mināciter *adv* threateningly
min·ae -ārum *f pl* menaces, threats; projecting points of a wall
minanter *adv* threateningly
minātī·ō -ōnis *f* threatening
min·ax -ācis *adj* threatening, menacing; projecting, jutting out
min·ĕō -ēre *vi* to project, jut out
Minerv·a -ae *f* goddess of wisdom and of the arts and sciences, identified with Pallas Athene; (fig) skill, genius; spinning and weaving; **invitā Minervā** against one's better judgment
mingō mingĕre minxī mictum *vi* to urinate
miniān·us -a -um *adj* vermilion
miniātŭl·us -a -um *adj* reddish
minimē or **minŭmē** *adv* least of all, least, very little; by no means, certainly not, not in the least; **minume gentium** (coll) by no means
minim·us or **minŭm·us -a -um** (*superl* of **parvus**) *adj* smallest, least, very small; slightest, very insignificant; youngest; shortest (*time*); **minimus natu** youngest; *n* the least, minimum; lowest price; **minimo emere** to buy at a very low price; **minimo provocare** to

provoke for the least thing or on the flimsiest pretext
minĭ·ō -āre *vt* to color red, paint red
minist·er -rī *m* servant, attendant, helper; agent, tool, instrument
minister·ĭum -ĭī or **-ī** *n* office, ministry, service, occupation, work, employment; retinue
ministr·a -ae *f* servant, attendant, helper; waitress; handmaid
ministrāt·or -ōris *m or* **ministrātr·ix -īcis** *f* assistant, helper
ministr·ō -āre *vt* to serve, wait on; to tend; to execute, carry out (*orders*); (with *dat*) to hand out (*something*) to; (with *abl*) to supply (*someone or something*) with
minitābund·us -a -um *adj* threatening
minĭt·ō -āre or **minĭt·or -ārī -ātus sum** *vt* to make threats of (*e.g., war*); (with *acc* of thing and *dat* of person) to threaten to bring (*e.g., evil, death*) upon, hold (*something*) threateningly over (*someone*); *vi* to make threats; (with *dat* of person threatened and *abl* of means) to threaten (*somone*) with
min·ĭum -ĭī or **-ī** *n* vermilion; red lead
Mīnō·is -ĭdis *f* Ariadne
Mīnōĭ·us or **Mīnō·us -a -um** *adj* of Minos, Cretan
min·or -ārī -ātus sum *vt* to threaten; to promise boastfully; (with *dat* of person and *acc* of thing) to threaten (*someone*) with (*something*), to hold (*something*) over (*someone*) as a threat; *vi* to jut out, project; to be menacing, make threats; (with *dat*) to threaten, make threats to
min·or -us (*comp* of **parvus**) *adj* smaller, less; less, shorter (*time*); younger; inferior, less important; (with *abl*) **a** (of time) too short for; **b** inferior to; **c** unworthy of; (with *inf*) unfit to, incapable of; **dimidio minor quam** half as small as; **minores facere filios quam** to think less of the sons than of; **minor natu** younger; *m pl* descendants, posterity; *n* less, smaller amount; **minoris emere** to buy at a lower price; **minus praedae** less booty
Mīn·ōs -ōis or **-ōnis** *m* son of Zeus and Europa, king of Crete, and, after his death, judge in the lower world; grandson of the former, likewise king of Crete, husband of Pasiphaë, and father of Ariadne and Phaedra
Mīnōtaur·us -ī *m* monstrous offspring of Pasiphaë, half man and half bull, and kept in the labyrinth
minŭmē see **minime**
minŭmus see **minimus**
min·ŭō -uĕre -ŭī -ūtum *vt* to diminish, lessen, reduce; to weaken, lower; to modify (*plans*); to settle (*controversies*); to limit, restrict (*authority*); to offend against, try to cheapen (*e.g., the majesty of the Roman people*); *vi* to diminish, abate, ebb; **minuente aestu** at ebbtide
minus *adv* less; not; by no means, not at all
minuscŭl·us -a -um *adj* rather small, smallish
minūt·al -ālis *n* hamburger, hash
minūtātim *adv* piecemeal; bit by bit
minūtē *adv* in a small-minded way
minūtŭl·us -a -um *adj* tiny
minūt·us -a -um *adj* small, minute; petty, narrow-minded
Minȳ·ae -ārum *m pl* Argonauts, the companions of Jason
Minȳ·ās -ae *m* mythical king of Thessaly
mīrābĭl·is -e *adj* wonderful, marvelous, amazing, extraordinary
mīrābilĭter *adv* wonderfully, amazingly
mīrābund·us -a -um *adj* full of amazement, astonished
mīrācŭl·um -ī *n* wonder, marvel; surprise, amazement
mīrand·us -a -um *adj* fantastic
mīrātĭ·ō -ōnis *f* admiration, wonder
mīrāt·or -ōris *m* admirer
mīrātr·ix -īcis *adj fem* admiring
mīrē *adv* wonderfully, uncommonly, strangely; **mire quam** it is strange how, strangely
mīrificē *adv* wonderfully
mīrific·us -a -um *adj* causing wonder, wonderful
mīrimŏdīs *adv* in a strange way
mirmill·ō -ōnis *m* gladiator (*who fought with Gallic arms*)
mīr·or -ārī -ātus sum *vt* to be amazed at, be surprised at; to look at with wonder, admire
mīr·us -a -um *adj* amazing, surprising, astonishing; wonderful; **mirum est** (with *acc & inf*) it is surprising that; **mirum quam** or **mirum quantum** it is amazing how, it is amazing to what extent
miscellānĕ·a -ōrum *n pl* hash
miscĕō miscēre miscŭī mixtum *vt* to mix, blend, mingle; to combine, associate, share; to mix up, confuse, turn upside down; to mix, prepare, brew
misell·us -a -um *adj* poor little
Mīsēn·um -ī *n* promontory and town near the bay of Naples
mis·er -ĕra -ĕrum *adj* poor; wretched, miserable, unhappy; sorry, worthless
miserābĭl·is -e *adj* miserable, pitiable; piteous
miserābilĭter *adv* pitiably; piteously
miserand·us -a -um *adj* pitiful, deplorable
miserātĭ·ō -ōnis *f* pity, compassion, sympathy; appeal for sympathy
misĕrē *adv* wretchedly, miserably, unhappily; pitifully; desperately
miser·ĕō -ēre -ŭī -ĭtum or **miser·ĕor -ērī -ĭtus sum** *vi* (with *genit*) to pity, feel sorry for, sympathize with; *v impers* (with *acc* of

person who feels pity and *genit* of object of pity), e.g., **miseret** or **miseretur me aliorum** I feel sorry for the others
miseresc·ō -ĕre *vi* to feel pity, feel sympathetic; (with *genit*) to pity, feel sorry for; *v impers* (with *acc* of person who feels pity and *genit* of object of pity), e.g., **me miserescit tui** I feel sorry for you, I pity you
miserĭ·a -ae *f* poverty; misery, unhappiness, distress, trouble
misericordĭ·a -ae *f* pity, sympathy, compassion; mercy
misericor·s -dis *adj* sympathetic, merciful
miserĭter *adv* sadly
misĕr·or -ārī -ātus sum *vt* to deplore; to pity; *vi* to feel pity
missicŭl·ō -āre *vt* to keep sending
missĭl·is -e *adj* missile, flying; *n pl* missiles
missĭ·ō -ōnis *f* release, liberation; sending off, despatching; military discharge; dismissal from office; cessation, end; **sine missione** without letup, to the death
missĭt·ō -āre *vt* to keep sending
missus *pp* of **mitto**
miss·us -ūs *m* letting go, throwing, hurling; sending
mītesc·ō -ĕre *vi* to grow mild, grow mellow, become ripe; (fig) to get soft; (fig) to become gentle, become tame
Mithr·ās -ae *m* Mithra (*sun-god of the Persians*)
Mithridāt·ēs -is *m* Mithridates the Great (*king of Pontus from* 120 B.C. *to* 63 B.C.)
Mithridātē·us or **Mithridātĭc·us -a -um** *adj* Mithridatic
mītigātĭ·ō -ōnis *f* mitigation, soothing
mītĭg·ō -āre *vt* to mellow, ripen; to soften; to calm down, appease, pacify
mīt·is -e *adj* mellow, ripe, soft; calm, placid; mild, gentle
mitr·a -ae *f* miter, turban
mittō mittĕre mīsī missum *vt* to send; let fly, throw, fling, launch; to emit, shed; to let out, utter; to let go of, drop; to free, release, discharge, dismiss; to pass over in silence, omit; to send for, invite; to pass up, forego; to dedicate (*a book*); to yield, produce, export; to dismiss, forget; **sanguinem mittere** to bleed; **sanguinem provinciae mittere** (fig) to bleed a province dry
mītŭl·us -ī *m* limpet
mixtim *adv* promiscuously
mixtūr·a -ae *f* mixing, blending
Mnēmosȳn·ē -ēs *f* mother of the Muses
mnēmosȳn·on -ī *n* souvenir
mōbĭl·is -e *adj* mobile, moveable, portable; nimble, active; shifty, changing; impressionable, excitable
mōbilĭt·ās -ātis *f* mobility; agility, quickness; shiftiness
mōbilĭter *adv* quickly, rapidly
mōbilĭt·ō -āre *vt* to impart motion to, endow with motion
moderābĭl·is -e *adj* moderate
moderām·en -ĭnis *n* control
moderanter *adv* under control
moderātē *adv* with moderation
moderātim *adv* gradually
moderātĭ·ō -ōnis *f* controlling, control, regulation, guidance; moderation, self-control; rules, regulation
moderāt·or -ōris *m* or **moderātr·ix -īcis** *f* controller, director, guide
moderāt·us -a -um *adj* controlled, well regulated, orderly, restrained
modĕr·ō -āre or **modĕr·or -ārī -ātus sum** *vt* to control, direct, guide; *vi* (with *dat*) **a** to moderate, restrain, put restraint upon; **b** to allay, mitigate
modestē *adv* with moderation, discreetly; modestly
modestĭ·a -ae *f* moderation, restraint; discretion; modesty, sense of shame, sense of honor, dignity; propriety; mildness (*of weather*)
modest·us -a -um *adj* moderate, restrained; modest, discreet; orderly, obedient
modiāl·is -e *adj* containing a modius or peck
modĭcē *adv* moderately, with restraint; in an orderly manner; only slightly
modĭc·us -a -um *adj* moderate; small; modest, unassuming; ordinary, puny, trifling
modificāt·us -a -um *adj* regulated (*in length*)
mod·ius -iī or **-ī** *m* modius, peck (*one sixth of a medimnus*); measure; **pleno modio** in full measure
modo *adv* only, merely, simply, solely; (of time) just now, just recently, lately; presently, in a moment; **modo . . . deinde** (or **tum** or **postea** or **interdum**) first . . . then, at one time . . . next time; **modo . . . modo** now . . . now, sometimes . . . sometimes, at one moment . . . at another; **non modo . . . sed etiam** or **verum etiam** not only . . . but also; *conj* if only, provided that
modulātē *adv* according to measure, in time; melodiously
modulāt·or -ōris *m* director, musician
modŭl·or -ārī -ātus sum *vt* to regulate the time of, measure rhythmically; to modulate; to sing; to play
modŭl·us -ī *m* small measure, small stature
mod·us -ī *m* standard of measurement, measure; time, rhythm; size; limit, boundary; rule, regulation; way, manner, mode; **ad modum** (with *genit*) or **in modum** (with *genit*) or **modo** (with *genit*) in the

manner of, according to the style of, like; **ejus modi homo** that kind of man; **hujus modi homo** this kind of man

moech·a -ae *f* adultress

moechiss·ō -āre *vt* to ravish, rape

moech·or -ārī -ātus sum *vi* to have an affair, commit adultery

moech·us -ī *m* adulterer

moen·ĭa -ĭum *n pl* town walls, ramparts, fortifications; fortified town; castle, stronghold; defenses

moeniō see **munio**

moerus see **murus**

Moes·ī -ōrum *m pl* a people on the lower Danube

mol·a -ae *f* millstone; mill; flour; *f pl* mill

molār·is -is *m* millstone; molar (*tooth*)

mōl·ēs -is *f* mass, bulk, pile; massive structure, dam, mole, pier; mass (*of people, etc.*); burden, effort, trouble; calamity; might, greatness

molestē *adv* with annoyance; with difficulty, with trouble; **moleste ferre** to be annoyed at, be disgruntled at, just about stand

molestĭ·a -ae *f* annoyance, trouble; worry; affectation (*in style*)

molest·us -a -um *adj* annoying, troublesome, distressing; labored, affected (*style*)

mōlīm·en -ĭnis *n* great exertion, great effort; attempt, undertaking

mōlīment·um -ī *n* great exertion, great effort

mōl·ior -īrī -ītus sum *vt* to do with great effort, strain at, exert oneself over; to wield, heave, hurl; to work hard at; to build, erect; to rouse; to displace; to undertake, attempt; to perform; to cause, occasion; *vi* to exert oneself, struggle, take great pains

mōlītĭ·ō -ōnis *f* building, erection; demolition

mōlīt·or -ōris *m* builder

molĭtus *pp* of **molo**

molītus *pp* of **molior**

mollesc·ō -ĕre *vi* to become soft; to become gentle; to become effeminate

mollicŭl·us -a -um *adj* tender, dainty

moll·ĭō -īre -īvī or **-ĭī -ītum** *vt* to make soft, soften; (fig) to soften, mitigate; to demoralize

mollĭp·ēs -ĕdis *adj* soft-footed

moll·is -e *adj* soft; springy; flexible; flabby; mild, calm; easy; gentle (*slope*); sensitive, impressionable; tender, touching; weak, effeminate; amatory (*verses*); complaint; changeable, untrustworthy

mollĭter *adv* softly; gently, smoothly; effeminately; voluptuously; patiently, with fortitude

mollitĭ·a -ae or **mollitĭ·ēs -ēī** *f* softness; flexi[illegible] tenderness; sensitivity; wea[illegible] irresolution; effeminacy, vol[illegible]ess

mollitūd·ō -ĭnis *f* softness; flexibility; susceptibility

mol·ō -ĕre -ŭī -ĭtum *vt* to grind

Moloss·us -a -um *adj* Molossian; *m* Molossian hound; *m pl* Molassians (*a people of Epirus*)

mōl·y -ўos *n* magic herb

mōm·en -ĭnis *n* movement, motion; momentum

mōment·um -ī *n* movement, motion; alteration; turn, critical time; moment; impulse; momentum; influence, importance; motive

Mon·a -ae *f* Isle of Man

monēdŭl·a -ae *f* jackdaw

mon·ĕō -ēre -ŭī -ĭtum *vt* to call to mind, remind, advise, point out; to warn; to foretell; to teach, instruct, inform

monēr·is -is *f* galley

Monēt·a -ae *f* Juno Moneta, in whose temple on the Capitoline Hill money was kept; coin, money; stamp or die (*for money*)

monētāl·is -e *adj* of the mint; *m* (coll) money man

monīl·e -is *n* necklace

monim- = monum-

monĭt·a -ōrum *n pl* warnings; prophecies

monitĭ·ō -ōnis *f* reminder

monĭt·or -ōris *m* reminder, counselor; teacher

monĭt·us -ūs *m* reminder, warning

monogramm·us -a -um *adj* sketchy, shadowy

monopod·ĭum -ĭī or **-ī** *n* table with a single central leg

monotrŏp·us -a -um *adj* single, alone

mon·s -tis *m* mountain, mountain range; mass, heap; hill; **montis auri polliceri** to make wild promises; **summus mons** mountain top

monstrātĭ·ō -ōnis *f* pointing out

monstrāt·or -ōris *m* displayer; inventor

monstr·ō -āre *vt* to show, to point out, exhibit, make known, advise, teach; to appoint, institute, ordain; to advise, urge

monstr·um -ī *n* sign, portent, wonder; warning; monster, monstrosity; miracle, marvel

monstruōsē *adv* unnaturally

monstruōs·us -a -um *adj* unnatural, strange, monstrous

montān·us -a -um *adj* mountain, of a mountain; mountainous; *m pl* mountaineers; *n pl* mountainous regions

monticŏl·a -ae *m* mountaineer, highlander

montivăg·us -a -um *adj* wandering over the mountains

montōs·us or **montuōs·us -a -um** *adj* mountainous

monument·um -ī *n* reminder; monument, memorial; record (*written or oral*); token of identification

Mopsopĭ·us -a -um *adj* Athenian; *f* Attica, Athens

mor·a -ae *f* delay; pause; spell, period of time; stop-off; division of the Spartan army consisting of from three to seven hundred men
mōrāl·is -e *adj* moral
morāt·or -ōris *m* obstructionist; (in court) lawyer who spoke only to gain time
mōrāt·us -a -um *adj* -mannered; -natured; in character; **bene moratus** well-mannered; **male moratus** ill-mannered, rude
morbid·us -a -um *adj* sickly; causing sickness, unwholesome
morbōs·us -a -um *adj* debauched
morb·us -ī *m* sickness, disease; fault, vice; distress; **in morbum cadere** or **in morbum incidere** to fall sick
mordācius *adv* more bitingly; (fig) more radically
mord·ax -ācis *adj* biting, snapping; (fig) sharp, stinging, caustic, snarling; pungent (*taste*)
mordĕō mordēre momordī morsum *vt* to bite; to eat, devour; to bite, grip, (of cold) to nip; (of words) to cut, hurt; (of a river) to bite its way through
mordic·ēs -um *m pl* bites
mordicus *adv* by biting, with the teeth; (fig) tightly, doggedly
mōrē *adv* foolishly
morēt·um -ī *n* salad
moribund·us -a -um *adj* dying, at the point of death; mortal; deadly
mōrigĕr·ō -āre or **mōrigĕr·or -ārī -ātus sum** *vi* (with *dat*) to humor, pamper, yield to, comply with
mōrigĕr·us -a -um *adj* obedient, obsequious
morior morī mortŭus sum *vi* to die; (fig) to die out, wither, decay, pass away
morm·yr -ўris *f* Pontic fish
mōrolŏg·us -a -um *adj* speaking nonsense, foolish
mor·or -ārī -ātus sum *vt* to delay, detain; to entertain, hold the attention of; to hinder, prevent; **nihil morari** (with *acc*) **a** to disregard, care nothing for, not value; **b** to have nothing against, have nothing to say against; *vi* to delay, linger, tarry, loiter; to stay, remain, wait; **quid moror?** or **quid multis morer?** why should I drag out the point?, to make a long story short
mōrōsē *adv* morosely, crabbily
mōrōsit·ās -ātis *f* moroseness, peevishness, crabbiness
mōrōs·us -a -um *adj* morose, peevish, crabby; fastidious, particular; (fig) stubborn (*disease*)
Morph·eus -ĕos *m* god of dreams
mors mortis *f* death; destruction; corpse; **mortem obire** to meet death; **mortis poena** death penalty; **sibi mortem consciscere** to commit suicide
mors·a -ōrum *n pl* bits, little pieces
morsiuncŭl·a -ae *f* peck, kiss
morsus *pp* of **mordeo**
mors·us -ūs *m* bite; pungency; grip; corrosion; gnawing pain; sting, vicious attack
mortāl·is -e *adj* mortal, subject to death; human, mortal; transient; man-made; *m* mortal, human being
mortālit·ās -ātis *f* mortality; mortals, mankind
morticīn·us -a -um *adj* dead; corpse-like, rotting
mortif·er or **mortif·ĕrus -ĕra -ĕrum** *adj* lethal, deadly
mortifĕrē *adv* mortally
mortuāl·ia -ium *n pl* dirges
mortŭ·us -a -um *pp* of **morior;** *adj* dead, deceased; withered, decayed; scared to death; *m* corpse
mōrŭl·us -a -um *adj* dark, black
mōr·um -ī *n* blackberry, mulberry
mōr·us -ī *f* mulberry tree
mōr·us -a -um *adj* foolish; *mf* fool
mōs mōris *m* caprice, mood; nature, manner; custom, usage, practice; fashion, style; rule, regulation, law; **de more** or **ex more** according to custom; **morem gerere** (with *dat*) to humor (*someone*); *m pl* morals, character, behavior; customs; laws
Mōs·ēs or **Moys·ēs -is** *m* Moses
mōti·ō -ōnis *f* motion
mōt·ō -āre *vt* to keep moving, keep shifting
mōtus *pp* of **moveo**
mōt·us -ūs *m* motion, movement; gesture; dancing; change (*e.g., of fortune*); impulse, inspiration; emotion, passion; rebellion, riot; **motus animi** emotion; **motus terrae** earthquake
mov·ens -entis *adj* movable; **res moventes** personal property; *n pl* motives
movĕō movēre mōvī mōtum *vt* to move; to stir, shake, disturb; to dislodge (*the enemy*); to eject, expel; to degrade; to remove, take away; to plow; to cause, occasion, promote; to begin; to undertake; to trouble, torment; to move, influence, affect; to dissuade; to exert, exercise; to turn over in the mind, ponder; **se ex loco movere** to budge from the spot; **se movere** to dance; *vi* to move
mox *adv* soon, presently; hereafter; next, then, later on
Moys·ēs -is *m* Moses
mūcid·us -a -um *adj* sniveling, driveling; moldy, musty
Mūc·ius -iī or **-ī** *m* Roman family name
mūcr·ō -ōnis *m* sharp point, sharp edge; sword; edge, boundary; keenness
mūc·us -ī *m* nasal mucus
mūgient·ēs -ium *m pl* oxen
mūgil or **mūgil·is -is** *m* mullet
mugin·or -ārī -ātus sum *vi* to dillydally

mūg·iō -īre -īvī or **-iī -ītum** *vi* to bellow, low; to rumble, roar
mūgīt·us -ūs *m* bellowing, lowing; rumbling, roaring
mūl·a -ae *f* mule
mulcĕō mulcēre mulsī mulsum *vt* to stroke, pet; to stir gently; to soothe, alleviate; to appease; to flatter, delight
Mulcīb·er -ĕrī or **-ĕris** *m* Vulcan; fire
mulc·ō -āre *vt* to beat, cudgel; to mistreat, injure
mulctr·a -ae *f* milk pail
muctrār·ium -iī or **-ī** or **muctr·um -ī** *n* milk pail
mulgĕō mulgēre mulsī mulsum or **mulctum** *vt* to milk
mulĭĕbr·is -e *adj* woman's, womanly, feminine; womanish, effeminate
muliebrĭter *adv* like a woman; effeminately
mulĭ·er -ĕris *f* woman; wife
mulierārĭ·us -a -um *adj* woman's; *m* woman chaser, wolf
muliercŭl·a -ae *f* little woman; little hussy
mulierōsĭt·ās -ātis *f* weakness for women
mulierōs·us -a -um *adj* woman-crazy
mūlīn·us -a -um *adj* mulish
mūlĭ·ō -ōnis *m* mule driver
mūliōnĭ·us -a -um *adj* mule driver's
mullŭl·us -ī *m* little mullet
mull·us -ī *m* mullet
muls·us -a -um *pp* of **mulceo;** *adj* honeyed, sweet as honey; *f* (term of endearment) honey; *n* mead (*wine mixed with honey*)
mult·a -ae *f* fine; penalty; loss of money; **multam certare** to contest a fine; **multam committere** to incur a fine; **multam dicere** (with *dat* of person and *acc* of the fine) to fine (*someone a certain amount*); **multam subire** to incur a fine, be fined
multa *adv* much, very, greatly, earnestly
mult·a -ōrum *n pl* many things; much; **ne multa** in short, to be brief
multangŭl·us -a -um *adj* many-angled
multātīcĭ·us -a -um *adj* fine, of a fine; **multaticia pecunia** fine
multātĭ·ō -ōnis *f* fine, penalty
multēsĭm·us -a -um *adj* trifling, negligible
mult·ī -ōrum *m pl* many men, many; multitude, mass, common people
multibĭb·us -a -um *adj* heavy-drinking
multicăv·us -a -um *adj* porous
multīcĭ·a -ōrum *n pl* diaphanous garments
multifārĭam *adv* in many places
multifĭd·us -a -um *adj* divided into many parts; (of a river) having many tributaries; **dens multifida** comb
multiform·is -e *adj* multiform, manifold
multifŏr·us -a -um *adj* many-holed; (flute) having many stops
multigenĕr·is -e or **multigĕn·us -a -um** *adj* of many kinds, various, complex
multijŭg·is -e or **multijŭg·us -a -um** *adj* yoked together; (fig) various, complex
multilŏqu·ax -ācis *adj* talkative
multiloqu·ium -iī or **-ī** *n* talkativeness
multilŏqu·us -a -um *adj* talkative
multimŏdīs *adv* in many ways
multĭpl·ex -icis *adj* with many folds; winding, labyrinthine, serpentine; manifold; many; (in implied comparisons) many times as great, far greater; varied, complicated; changeable, versatile, many-sided; sly, cunning; *n* manifold return
multiplicābĭl·is -e *adj* manifold, many
multiplicĭter *adv* in various ways
multiplĭc·ō -āre *vt* to multiply, increase, enlarge
multipŏt·ens -entis *adj* mighty, powerful
multitūd·ō -inis *f* great number, multitude, crowd, throng; rabble, common people
multivŏl·us -a -um *adj* passionate
multō *adv* (with comparatives) much, far, by far, a great deal; **multo aliter ac** far otherwise than, much different from; **multo ante** long before; **multo post** long after; **non multo secus fieri** to turn out just about the same
mult·ō -āre *vt* to punish, fine
mult·us -a -um (*comp:* **plures;** *superl:* **plurimus**) *adj* many a, much, great; abundant, considerable, extensive; tedious, long-winded; full, numerous, thick, loud, heavy, constant; **ad multum diem** till late in the day; **multā nocte** late at night; **multo die** late in the day; (with plural nouns) many; *m pl* see **multi;** *n* much; **multi** of great value, highly; **multi facere** to think highly of, make much of, think much of; **multum est** it is of great importance; **multum temporis** a great deal of time, much time; *n pl* see **multa**
multum *adv* much, greatly, very, often, frequently, far; (with comparatives) much, far; **multum valere** to have considerable influence
mūl·us -ī *m* mule
Mulvĭ·us -a -um *adj* Mulvian; **Mulvius pons** Mulvian bridge (*across the Tiber, above Rome, on the Via Flaminia*)
Mumm·ius -iī or **-ī** *m* L. Mummius Achaicus (*conqueror of Corinth,* 146 B.C.)
mundān·us -ī *m* world citizen

mundē or **munditer** *adv* neatly, cleanly
munditi·a -ae or **munditi·ēs -ēī** *f* neatness, cleanness; elegance; politeness
mundŭl·us -a -um *adj* trim, neat, sharp
mund·us -a -um *adj* neat, clean, nice; fine, smart, sharp, elegant; choice (*words*); *m* neat person; world, universe, heavens; earth, mankind; beauty aids
mūnerigerŭl·us -ī *m* bearer of presents
mūnĕr·ō -āre or **munĕr·or -ārī -ātus sum** *vt* to reward, honor, present; (with *acc* of thing and *dat* of person) to present to
mūni·a -ōrum *n pl* official duties or functions
mūnic·eps -ipis *m* or *f* citizen of a municipality; fellow citizen, fellow countryman
mūnicipāl·is -e *adj* municipal; (as term of contempt) provincial, country
mūnicip·ium -iī or **-ī** *n* municipality, town (*whose people were Roman citizens, but otherwise autonomous*)
mūnificē *adv* generously
mūnificenti·a -ae *f* generosity
mūnific·ō -āre *vt* to treat generously
mūnific·us -a -um *adj* generous; splendid
mūnim·en -inis *f* defense
mūniment·um -ī *n* defense, protection, fortification, rampart; (fig) shelter, defense
mūn·iō or **moen·iō -īre -īvī** or **-iī -ītum** *vt* to wall, defend with a wall, fortify, strengthen, defend, protect, guard, secure; to build (*road*); (fig) to guard, shelter, protect, support
mūn·is -e *adj* obliging
mūniti·ō -ōnis *f* building, fortifying, defending; fortification, rampart, trenches, lines; **munitio fluminum** bridging of rivers; **munitio viae** road construction
mūnit·ō -āre *vt* to open up (*a road*)
mūnit·or -ōris *m* builder, engineer
mūnit·us -a -um *adj* fortified; (fig) protected, safe
mūn·us or **moen·us -ĕris** *n* service, function, duty; gift; service, favor, kindness; duty, tribute; public entertainment, gladiatorial show, extravaganza; tribute (*to the dead*), rite, sacrifice; public office
mūnuscŭl·um -ī *n* small present
mūraen·a -ae *f* moray (*eel-like fish*)
mūrāl·is -e *adj* wall; wall-destroying; wall-defending; **corona muralis** mural crown (*award for being the first to scale the enemy walls*)
mūr·ex -icis *m* murex, mollusk (*yielding purple dye*); purple dye, purple; jagged rock; spiked trap (*as defense against cavalry attack*)
muri·a -ae *f* brine
muriātic·um -ī *n* pickled fish
mūricīd·us -ī *m* mouse killer; (fig) coward
murmill·ō -ōnis *m* gladiator with Gallic arms, who fought against a retarius
murm·ur -ŭris *n* murmur, murmuring; buzz, hum; roar, crash; growling, grumbling; rumbling; hubbub
murmurill·um -ī *n* low murmur
murmŭr·ō -āre *vi* to murmur; to mutter, grumble; to rumble, roar
murr·a or **murrh·a** or **myrrh·a -ae** *f* myrrh tree; myrrh
murrĕ·us or **myrrhĕ·us -a -um** *adj* made of myrrh; perfumed with myrrh; myrrh-colored, yellowish
murrin·us or **myrrhin·us -a -um** *adj* of myrrh; *f* drink flavored with myrrh; *n pl* vases
murt- = **myrt-**
mūr·us -ī *m* wall, city wall; dam, dike; rim (*of dish or pot*); (fig) wall, protection
mūs mūris *m* or *f* mouse, rat
Mūs·a -ae *f* Muse (*patron goddess of poetry, song, dance, literature, astronomy, etc.*); poem, song; talent, genius, taste; *f pl* studies
Mūsae·us -ī *m* mythical pre-Homeric bard and musician in the time of Orpheus
musc·a -ae *f* fly
muscār·ium -iī or **-ī** *n* fly swatter
muscipŭl·a -ae *f* or **muscipŭl·um -ī** *n* mousetrap
muscōs·us -a -um *adj* mossy
muscŭl·us -ī *m* little mouse; muscle; (mil) mantelet
musc·us -ī *m* moss
Mūsē·us or **Mūsae·us -a -um** *adj* of the Muses, musical, poetic
mūsic·a -ae or **mūsic·ē -ēs** *f* or **mūsic·ā -ōrum** *n pl* music, art of music (*including poetry*)
mūsicē *adv* pleasantly
mūsic·us -a -um *adj* musical; poetic; cultural; *m* musician
mussit·ō -āre *vt* to bear in silence; *vi* to be silent; to mutter, grumble
muss·ō -āre *vt* to bear in silence, bear silently; to brood over; *vi* to mutter, murmur; (of bees) to hum; to hesitate
mustācĕ·us -ī *m* or **mustācĕ·um -ī** *n* cake, wedding cake
mustell·a or **mustēl·a -ae** *f* weasel
mustellīn·us or **mustēlīn·us -a -um** *adj* of a weasel
must·um -ī *n* fresh grape juice, unfermented wine, must; vintage
mūtābil·is -e *adj* changeable; fickle
mūtābilit·ās -ātis *f* mutability; fickleness
mūtāti·ō -ōnis *f* mutation, change, alteration; exchange, interchange
mutil·ō -āre *vt* to cut off, lop off, crop; to mutilate; to reduce, shorten, lessen; to rob
mutil·us -a -um *adj* maimed, mutilated; defective

Mutīn·a -ae *f* town of N. central Italy, S. of the Po, which played a role in the civil war after the death of Julius Caesar
mūtiō see **muttio**
mūtītiō see **muttitio**
mūt·ō -āre *vt* to move, shift, change, alter; to exchange, interchange, barter, sell; to modify, transform, vary; to change for the better; to change for the worse; (with *abl* or **pro** + *abl*) to exchange or substitute (*something or someone*) for; *vi* to change
mūt·ō -ōnis *m* penis
mutt·iō or **mūt·iō -īre -īvī -ītum** *vi* to mutter, mumble
muttīti·ō or **mūtīti·ō -ōnis** *f* muttering, mumbling
mūtuāti·ō -ōnis *f* borrowing
mūtŭē *adv* mutually; in return
mūtuit·ō -āre *vt* to wish to borrow
mūtŭō *adv* mutually, in return
mūtŭ·or -ārī -ātus sum *vt* to borrow; to derive, obtain, get
mūt·us -a -um *adj* mute, speechless; silent, still; *n pl* brutes
mūtŭ·us -a -um *adj* mutual, reciprocal, interchangeable; borrowed, lent; *n* reciprocity; loan; **mutuum dare** (with **cum** + *abl*) to lend to (*someone*); **mutuas pecunias sumere** (with **ab** + *abl*) to borrow money from (*someone*); **mutuum argentum rogare** to ask for a loan of cash
Mycēn·ae -ārum *f pl* or **Mycēn·ē -ēs** *f* Mycene (*city of Agamemnon in Argolis*)
Mycēnae·us -a -um or **Mycēnens·is -e** *adj* Mycenean
Mycēn·is -idis *f* Mycenaean girl (*Iphigenia*)
Mygdŏn·es -um *m pl* a people of Thrace, some of whom later migrated to Phrygia
Mygdoni·us -a -um *adj* Phrygian
myopăr·ō -ōnis *m* pirate ship
myrīc·a -ae or **myrīc·ē -ēs** *f* tamarisk
Myrmidŏn·es -um *m pl* Myrmidons (*people of Thessaly whom Achilles led in battle*)
Myr·ōn -ōnis *m* famous Greek sculptor, whose most famous work is the Discus Thrower, 5th cent. B.C.
myropōl·a -ae *m* perfumer
myropōl·ium -iī or **-ī** *n* perfume shop
myrrh- = **murr-**
myrtēt·um or **murtēt·um -ī** *n* myrtle grove
myrtě·us or **murtě·us -a -um** *adj* myrtle; crowned with myrtle
Myrtō·um mar·e (*genit:* **Myrtō·ī mar·is**) *n* sea between the Peloponnesus and the Cyclades
myrt·um -ī *n* myrtle berry
myrt·us -ūs or **-ī** *f* myrtle
Mȳsi·us -a -um *adj* Mysian; *f* Mysia (*country in N.W. Asia Minor*)
myst·a or **myst·ēs -ae** *m* priest of the mysteries of Ceres; an initiate
mystagōg·us -ī *m* initiator
mystēr·ium -iī or **-ī** *n* secret religion, secret service, secret rite or worship, divine mystery; secret; **mysteria facere** to hold service; **mysteria Romana** festival of Bona Dea
myst·ēs -ae *m* priest of the mysteries of Ceres
mystic·us -a -um *adj* mystic
Mytilēn·ae -ārum *f pl* or **Mytilēn·ē -ēs** *f* capital of the island of Lesbos

N

Nabatae·us -a -um *adj* Nabataean; Arabian, Eastern, Oriental; *m pl* Nabataeans; *f* Nabataea (*ancient Arab kingdom S.E. of Palestine*)
nabl·ium -iī or **-ī** *n* Phoenician harp (*an instrument of ten or twelve strings, played with both hands*)
nactus *pp* of **nanciscor**
Naeviān·us -a -um *adj* of Naevius
Naev·ius -iī or **-ī** *m* Cn. Naevius (*early Roman dramatic and epic poet*, c. 270-200 B.C.)
naev·us -ī *m* body mole
Nāi·as -ădis or **Nā·is -idis** or **-idos** *f* Naiad, water nymph
nam *conj* for; for instance; (transitional) now, but now, on the other hand
namque *conj* for, for in fact, for no doubt, for surely
nanciscor nancisci nanctus sum or **nactus sum** *vt* to get by accident (*esp. by good luck*), obtain, chance upon, find
nān·us -ī *m* dwarf, midget
Napae·ae -ārum *f pl* dell nymphs
nāp·us -ī *m* turnip
Narb·ō -ōnis *m* town in S. Gaul, from which the province of Narbonese Gaul took its name
Narbōnens·is -e *adj* Narbonese
narciss·us -ī *m* narcissus
Narciss·us -ī *m* son of Cephisus and the nymph Liriope, who was changed into a flower of the same name; powerful freedman of Claudius
nard·um -ī *n* or **nard·us -ī** *f* nard, spikenard (*fragrant ointment*)
nār·is -is *f* nostril; *f pl* nostrils, nose; **acutae nares** keen perception; **homo naris obesae** dimwit;

naribus ducere to smell; **naribus uti** (with **ad** + *acc*) to turn up the nose at
narrābĭl·is -e *adj* to be told
narrātĭ·ō -ōnis *f* narration, narrative
narrātiuncŭl·a -ae *f* short story
narrāt·or -ōris *m* narrator, historian
narrāt·um -ī *n* account, statement, narrative
narrāt·us -ūs *m* narration, narrative
narr·ō -āre *vt* to tell, relate, narrate, recount; to describe; *vi* to speak, tell; **bene narrare** (with **de** + *abl*) to tell good news about (*someone*); **male narrare** (with **de** + *abl*) to tell bad news about (*someone*); **tibi narro** I'm telling you, I assure you
narthēc·ĭum -ĭī or **-ī** *n* medicine chest
narus see **gnarus**
Nārycĭ·us -a -um *adj* of Naryx (*city of the Opuntian Locrians and birthplace of Ajax Oileus*)
nascor nascī nātus sum or **gnātus sum** *vi* to be born; to rise, begin, originate, be produced, spring forth, proceed, grow, be found; **post homines natos** since the beginning of the world
Nās·ō -ōnis *m* Publius Ovidius Naso (*Roman poet, born in Sulmo, in central Italy,* 43 B.C.-*c.* 17 A.D.)
nass·a -ae *f* wicker trap (*for catching fish*); (fig) trap
nassitern·a -ae *f* large water jug
nasturc·ĭum -ĭī or **-ī** *n* garden cress
nās·us -ī *m* or **nās·um -ī** *n* nose; sense of smell; sagacity; anger; scorn; nozzle, spout
nāsūtē *adv* sarcastically
nāsūt·us -a -um *adj* big-nosed; satirical, sarcastic
nāt·a or **gnāt·a -ae** *f* daughter
nātālicĭ·us -a -um *adj* birthday, natal; *n pl* birthday party
nātāl·is -e *adj* of birth, natal; *m* birthday; *m pl* birth, origin, lineage
nat·ans -antis *m* or *f* fish
natātĭ·ō -ōnis *f* swimming
natāt·or -ōris *m* swimmer
nat·ēs -ĭum *f pl* buttocks, rear, rear end
nātĭ·ō -ōnis *f* race, stock; tribe, nation, people; (in contemptuous sense) breed, set
nat·is -is *f* buttock, rump; *f pl* see **nates**
nātīv·us -a -um *adj* born; inborn, innate, original; produced by nature, natural; primitive (*words*)
nat·ō -āre *vi* to swim, float; to flow; to swim, overflow, be flooded; (of the eyes) to be glassy; (of birds) to fly, glide; to waver, fluctuate, be uncertain; to hover, move to and fro
nātr·ix -īcis *f* water snake
nātūr·a -ae *f* blood relationship, natural affinity, birth; nature, natural constitution, quality, property; nature, natural disposition, character; physical nature, world, universe; order of the world, course of things; element, substance; reproductive organs
nātūrāl·is -e *adj* natural; by birth, one's own (*e.g., father, son*); produced by nature; according to nature
nātūrālĭter *adv* naturally, by nature
nāt·us or **gnāt·us -a -um** *pp* of **nascor;** *adj* born, made, destined, fit; (with *dat* or with **ad** or **in** or **propter** + *acc*) born for, made for, naturally suited to; (with **annos**) at the age of . . . , . . . years old, e.g., **annos viginti natus** at the age of twenty, twenty years old; **non amplius novem annos natus** no more than nine years old; **pro** or **e re nata** under the existing circumstances, as matters stand; *m* son; *m pl* children; *f* see **nata**
nauarch·us -ī *m* captain of a ship, skipper
nauclērĭc·us -a -um *adj* ship owner's, skipper's
nauclēr·us -ī *m* ship owner, skipper
nauc·um -ī *n* trifle; (mostly in genitive of value with a negative) **non nauci esse** to be of no value, be good for nothing; **non nauci facere** or **non nauci habere** to regard as worthless, regard as good for nothing
naufrag·ĭum -ĭī or **-ī** *n* shipwreck; wreck, ruin, destruction; wreckage; **naufragium facere** to be shipwrecked
naufrăg·us -a -um *adj* shipwrecked, wrecked, of the shipwrecked; causing shipwreck, dangerous to shipping; (fig) ruined; *m* shipwrecked person
naul·um -ī *n* fare
naumachĭ·a -ae *f* simulated sea engagement (*staged as an exercise or for amusement*)
nausĕ·a -ae *f* seasickness; vomiting, nausea
nausĕ·ō -āre *vt* to make (*someone*) throw up; (fig) to belch forth, throw up, utter; *vi* to be seasick; to vomit; to feel squeamish, feel disgust; to cause disgust
nauseŏl·a -ae *f* slight squeamishness
Nausică·a -ae *f* daughter of Alcinous, king of the Phaeacians
naut·a or **nāvĭt·a -ae** *m* sailor, seaman, mariner; captain
nautĕ·a -ae *f* nausea; stinking liquid
nautĭc·us -a -um *adj* nautical, sailors'; *m pl* sailors, seamen
nāvāl·is -e *adj* naval, of ships, of a ship; **castra navalia** camp for the protection of ships; **forma navalis** shape of a ship; *n* tackle, rigging; *n pl* dock, dockyard, shipyard; rigging

nāviculā·a -ae *f* small ship
nāviculāri·us -a -um *adj* of a small ship; *m* skipper; ship owner; *f* shipping business
nāvifrăg·us -a -um *adj* dangerous, treacherous, causing shipwreck
nāvigābil·is -e *adj* navigable
nāvigāti·ō -ōnis *f* sailing, navigation, voyage
nāvig·er -ĕra -ĕrum *adj* navigable
nāvig·ium -iī or **-ī** *n* ship
nāvig·ō -āre *vt* to sail across, navigate; *vi* to sail, put to sea; (fig) to swim
nāv·is -is *f* ship; **navem appellere** or **navem terrae applicare** to land a ship; **navem deducere** to launch a ship; **navem solvere** to set sail; **navem subducere** to beach a ship; **navis aperta** ship without a deck; **navis longa** battleship; **navis mercatoria** merchant vessel; **navis oneraria** transport, cargo ship; **navis praetoria** flagship; **navis tecta** ship with a deck
nāvit·a -ae *m* sailor, seaman; captain
nāvit·ās -ātis *f* energy, zeal
nāviter *adv* energetically, zealously, actively, busily; utterly, completely
nāv·ō -āre *vt* to do or perform energetically, conduct or prosecute with vigor; **operam navare** to act energetically; **operam navare** (with *dat*) to render assistance to
nāv·us or **gnāv·us -a -um** *adj* energetic, busy
Nax·os -ī *f* largest island of the Cyclades, famous for its wine and as the place where Theseus abandoned Ariadne
nē *interj* (always with a personal or demonstrative pronoun) indeed, certainly, surely; *adv* not; **ne . . . quidem** (to negate emphatically the words placed between) not even; (in negative commands) not; **ne timete** do not fear; *conj* that not, lest; (after verbs and nouns denoting fear) lest, that
-ne enclitic (introducing a question and added to the first important word of a clause)
nebŭl·a -ae *f* mist, fog, vapor; cloud; smoke; darkness, obscurity
nebŭl·ō -ōnis *m* loafer, good-for-nothing
nebulōs·us -a -um *adj* foggy
nec or **neque** *adv* not; *conj* nor, and not; **nec . . . et** not only not . . . but also; **nec . . . nec** or **neque . . . neque** neither . . . nor; **nec non** (introducing an emphatic affirmative) and certainly, and besides
necdum or **neque dum** *conj* and not yet, nor yet
necessāriē or **necessāriō** *adv* necessarily, of necessity
necessāri·us -a -um *adj* necessary, indispensable, needful, requisite; necessary, inevitable; pressing, urgent; connected by blood or friendship, related, closely connected; *mf* relative, kinsman; friend; *n pl* necessities
necesse (indecl) *adj* necessary; unavoidable, inevitable; requisite; **necesse esse** to be necessary; **necesse habere** to regard as necessary, regard as inevitable
necessit·ās -ātis *f* necessity, inevitableness, compulsion, urgency; requirement; privation, want; relationship, friendship, connection
necessitūd·ō -ĭnis *f* necessity, need, want, distress; relationship, bond, connection, relationship, friendship; *f pl* ties of friendship; relatives, friends, personal connections
necessum (indecl) *adj* necessary, requisite; inevitable
necne *adv* or not
necnōn *adv* also, besides, moreover
nec·ō -āre *vt* to kill, murder, slay, destroy
necopīn·ans -antis *adj* unaware
necopīnātō *adv* unexpectedly, by surprise
necopīnāt·us -a -um *adj* unexpected
necopīn·us -a -um *adj* unexpected; unsuspecting, careless, off guard
nect·ar -ăris *n* nectar (*drink of the gods*); nectar (*as term for honey, milk, wine, poetry, sweetness, etc.*)
nectarĕ·us -a -um *adj* of nectar, sweet or delicious as nectar
nectō nectĕre nexŭī or **nexī nexum** *vt* to tie, connect, fasten together, join; to weave; to clasp; to imprison, fetter; to devise, contrive; (fig) to attach, affix
nēcŭbi *conj* lest anywhere, so that nowhere
nēcunde *conj* lest from anywhere
nēdum *adv* (after an expressed or implied negative) much less, still less; (after an affirmative) not to say, much more
nefand·us -a -um *adj* unspeakable, impious, abominable
nefāriē *adv* impiously, abominably
nefāri·us -a -um *adj* impious, abominable, criminal; *n* crime, criminal act
nefās (indecl) *n* crime, wrong, wickedness, act contrary to divine law, sin; criminal, monster; **per omne fas ac nefas** by hook or by crook
nefast·us -a -um *adj* forbidden, unlawful; impious, irreligious; criminal; unlucky, inauspicious; *n* crime, outrage
negāti·ō -ōnis *f* denial
negĭt·ō -āre *vt* to deny, refuse, turn down
neglecti·ō -ōnis *f* neglect
neglectus *pp* of **neglego**
neglect·us -ūs *m* neglect
neglĕg·ens -entis *adj* negligent, careless, indifferent
neglegenter *adv* carelessly
neglegenti·a -ae *f* negligence, carelessness, neglect
neg·lĕgō -legĕre -lexī -lectum *vt*

to be unconcerned about; to neglect, disregard, overlook; to slight, despise
neg·ō -āre *vt* to deny, refuse, decline; *vi* to say no; to refuse
negōtiāl·is -e *adj* business
negōti·ans -antis *m* business man
negōtiāti·ō -ōnis *f* banking, banking business
negōtiāt·or -ōris *m* business man; banker; salesman, dealer
negōtiŏl·um -ī *n* minor matter
negōti·or -ārī -ātus sum *vi* to do business, do banking; to trade
negōtiōs·us -a -um *adj* business; busy
negōt·ĭum -ĭī or **-ī** *n* business, occupation, employment; matter, thing, affair; situation; trouble; banking, money lending; trade, commerce; **negotium suum** private affairs; **quid negoti est?** what's the matter?; **quid negoti tibi est?** what business is it of yours?
Nēl·eus -ĕī or **-ĕos** *m* son of Neptune and the nymph Tyro, king of Pylos, and father of Nestor
Nemae·us -a -um *adj* Nemean
Nemĕ·a -ae or **Nemĕ·ē -ēs** *f* town in Argolis, where Hercules slew the Nemean lion and founded the Nemean games
Nemĕ·a -ōrum *n pl* Nemean games (*held every two years at Nemea*)
Nemĕs·is -is or **-ios** *f* goddess of vengeance
nēm·ō -ĭnis *m* or *f* no one, nobody; **nemo quisquam** nobody at all; **nemo unus** no single person, no one by himself; **non nemo** someone, many a one
nemorāl·is -e *adj* sylvan
nemorens·is -e *adj* of a grove; of Diana's grove
nemoricultr·ix -īcis *f* denizen of the forest
nemorivăg·us -a -um *adj* roaming the woods
nemorōs·us -a -um *adj* wooded; covered with foliage
nempe *adv* (in confirmation or in sarcasm) certainly, to be sure, of course, naturally; (in questions) do you mean?
nem·us -ŏris *n* grove; sacred grove; plantation
nēnĭ·a or **naenĭ·a -ae** *f* funeral dirge; doleful song; incantation; ditty
neō nēre nēvī nētum *vt* to spin; to weave
Neoptolĕm·us -ī *m* Pyrrhus, the son of Achilles
nep·a -ae *f* scorpion; crab
Nephelē·is -ĭdos *f* Helle (*daughter of Nephele and Athamas*)
nep·ōs -ōtis *m* grandson; nephew; descendant; spendthrift
Nep·ōs -ōtis *m* Cornelius Nepos (*Roman biographer and friend of Cicero*, c. 100- c. 25 B.C.)
nepōtŭl·us -ī *m* little grandson
nept·is -is *f* granddaughter
Neptūnĭ·us -a -um *adj* of Neptune
Neptūn·us -ī *m* Neptune (*god of the sea and brother of Jupiter*)
nēquam (indecl) *adj* worthless, bad, good for nothing
nēquāquam *adv* by no means, not at all
neque see **nec**
nequĕdum see **necdum**
nequ·ĕō -īre -īvī or **-ĭī -ĭtum** *vi* to be unable; (with *inf*) to be unable to, not to be able to, be incapable of; **nequit** (with **quin**) it is impossible to
nēquĭ·or -us *adj* (*comp* of **nequam**) worse, more worthless
nēquīquam or **nēquicquam** *adv* pointlessly, for nothing, to no purpose; without good reason; with impunity
nēquissĭm·us -a -um *adj* (*superl* of **nequam**) worst, most worthless
nēquĭter *adv* worthlessly, wretchedly, miserably, vilely, wrongly
nēquitĭ·a -ae or **nēquitĭ·ēs -ēī** *f* worthlessness, vileness, wickedness
Nērē·is -ĭdis *f* sea nymph, Nereid (*daughter of Nereus, of whom there were* 50)
Nēr·eus -ĕī or **-ĕos** *m* son of Oceanus and Tethys, husband of Doris and father of the Nereids; sea
Nērīn·ē -ēs *f* daughter of Nereus
Nērītĭ·us -a -um *adj* of Neritos; **Neritius dux** Ulysses
Nērĭt·os or **Nērĭt·us -ī** *m* island near Ithaca
Nēr·ō -ōnis *m* Nero Claudius Caesar (*Roman emperor* 38-68 A.D.; *reigned* 54-68 A.D.)
Nērōniān·us -a -um *adj* Nero's, Neronian
Nerv·a -ae *m* M. Cocceius Nerva (*Roman emperor* 30-98 A.D., *reigned* 96-98 A.D.)
nervōsē *adv* strongly, vigorously
nervōs·us -a -um *adj* sinewy, brawny, strong
nervŭl·us -ī *m* a little vigor
nerv·us -ī *m* sinew, tendon, muscle; string, wire; bowstring; thong, strap; penis; leather covering of a shield; prison; power, vigor, strength, nerve, force, energy
nesc·ĭō -īre -īvī or **-ĭī -ītum** *vt* not to know, be ignorant of, be unacquainted with; (with *inf*) **a** not to know how to; **b** to be unable to; **nescio modo** somehow or other; **nescio quando** sometime or other; **nescio quid** something or other; **nescio quis** someone or other
nescĭ·us -a -um *adj* unaware, not knowing, ignorant; unknown; (with *genit* or **de** + *abl*) ignorant of, unaware of; (with *inf*) not knowing how to, unable to, incapable of; (with *acc & inf*) unaware that, not knowing that
Ness·us -ī *m* centaur who was slain by Hercules with a poisoned arrow for trying to molest his wife
Nest·or -ŏris *m* son of Neleus, king

of Pylos, and wise counselor of the Greeks at Troy
neu see **neve**
neut·er -ra -rum *adj* neither (*of two*); neuter; of neither sex; *pron* neither one (*of two*)
neutiquam or **ne utiquam** *adv* on no account, in no way
neutrō *adv* to neither side
neutrŭbi *adv* in neither the one place nor the other
nēve or **neu** *conj* or not, and not; **neve . . . neve** or **neu . . . neu** neither . . . nor
nex necis *f* death, murder, slaughter
nexĭl·is -e *adj* tied up, bound together
nex·um -ī *n* slavery for debt; voluntary servitude for debt
nex·us -a -um *pp* of **necto;** *m* free person who has pledged his person as security for a debt
nex·us -ūs *m* grip; bond; enslavement for debt
nī *adv* not; **quid ni?** why not?; *conj* (in prohibition or negative purpose) that not; (in negative condition) if not, unless
nīcētēr·ium -ĭī or **-ī** *n* prize
nic·ō -ĕre -ī *vi* to beckon
nict·ō -āre *vi* to wink; (with *dat*) to wink at
nīdāment·um -ī *n* material for a nest
nīd·or -ōris *m* steam, vapor, smell
nīdŭl·us -ī *m* little nest
nīd·us -ī *m* nest; (fig) home; *m pl* nestlings, brood
nig·er -ra -rum *adj* black; swarthy, dark; dismal; unlucky, ill-omened; black, bad (*character*); malicious
nigr·ans -antis *adj* black, dusky
nigr·escō -escĕre -ŭī *vi* to grow black, grow dark
nigr·ō -āre *vi* to be black
nigr·or -ōris *m* blackness, darkness
nihil or **nīl** (indecl) *n* nothing; (with *genit*) no, not a bit of; **nihil boni** no good, not a bit of good; **nil est** it is pointless, it's no good
nihil or **nīl** *adv* not, not at all, in no respect
nihilōmĭnus *adv* nonetheless, nevertheless, just the same; no less
nihĭl·um or **nīl·um -ī** *n* nothing; **de nihilo** for nothing, for no reason; **nihil est quod, cur,** or **quam ob rem** there is no reason why; **nihili esse** to be worthless, be of no value; **nihili facere** or **nihili pandere** to consider as worthless; **nihilo minus** nonetheless, nevertheless; **nihil quicquam** nothing whatever, nothing at all; **pro nihilo putare** to regard as worthless
nīl see **nihil**
Nīliăc·us -a -um *adj* Nile, of the Nile, Egyptian
Nīligĕn·a -ae *masc & fem adj* born on the Nile, Egyptian
nīlum see **nihilum**
Nīl·us -ī *m* Nile River; god of the Nile
nimbāt·us -a -um *adj* light, frivolous
nimbĭf·er -ĕra -ĕrum *adj* stormy
nimbōs·us -a -um *adj* stormy, rainy
nimb·us -ī *m* cloud; storm cloud, black rain cloud; rainstorm, heavy shower, pouring rain; (fig) storm
nimiō *adv* far, much; **nimio plus** far more, much more
nīmīrum *adv* no doubt, certainly, surely; (ironically) doubtless, of course
nimis *adv* very, very much, too much; **non nimis** not particularly
nimĭum *adv* too, too much; very, very much; **nimium quam** or **nimium quantum** very much indeed, ever so much, very; **nimium quam es barbarus** you are as barbarous as can be; **non nimium** not particularly, not very much
nimĭ·us -a -um *adj* very much, very great; too great, excessive; *n* excess, abundance
ningit (or **ninguit**) **ningĕre ninguit** (or **ninxit**) *v impers* it is snowing
ningu·ēs -ĭum *f pl* snowflakes, snow
Nin·us -ī *m* son of Belus, the first king of Assyria, husband of Semiramis, and builder of Nineveh; Nineveh
Niŏb·a -ae or **Niŏb·ē -ēs** *f* daughter of Tantalus and wife of Amphion, who was turned into a weeping mountain after Apollo and Diana had slain her seven sons and seven daughters
Nīr·eus -ĕī or **-ĕos** *m* handsomest Greek at Troy
Nīsē·is -ĭdis *f* Scylla (*daughter of Nisus*)
nisi *conj* unless, if not; except, but
nīsus *pp* of **nitor**
nīs·us or **nix·us -ūs** *m* pressure, effort; labor pain (*of childbirth*); soaring, flight; posture; **nisu immotus eodem** immobile in the same posture
Nīs·us -ī *m* king of Megara, father of Scylla, who betrayed her country by cutting off his purple lock of hair; friend of Euryalus in the Aeneid
nītēdŭl·a -ae *f* dormouse
nit·ens -entis *adj* shining, bright; brilliant; beautiful, glowing with beauty, glamorous; sleek (*cattle*); greasy
nit·ĕō -ēre -ŭī *vi* to shine, gleam, glisten; to be glamorous; to glow with health; (of animals) to be sleek; to be greasy; to be flashy
nit·escō -escĕre -ŭī *vi* to become shiny, become bright; to begin to glow (*with health or beauty*); to grow sleek
nitĭdē *adv* brightly
nitidiuscŭlē *adv* somewhat more sprucely
nitidiuscŭl·us -a -um *adj* a little more shiny

nitĭd·us -a -um *adj* shining, bright; glowing (*with health or beauty*); shiny, greasy; glamorous, flashy; smart, spruce, handsome; cultivated, refined; sleek (*cattle*)

nit·or -ōris *m* brightness, sheen; luster; glamour, beauty, healthy glow; elegance (*of style*); dignity (*of character*)

nītor nītī nixus sum (usually in the literal sense) or **nīsus sum** (usually in the figurative sense) *vi* to make an effort, struggle, strain, strive; to be in labor; to push forward, advance, climb, fly; to contend, insist; (with *abl* or **in** + *acc*) to lean on, support oneself on; (with *abl* or **in** + *abl*) (fig) to depend on, rely on, trust to; (with **ad** + *acc*) to aspire to; (with *inf*) to try to, endeavor to, struggle to

nitr·um -ī *n* soda; soap, cleanser

nivāl·is -e *adj* snowy; covered with snow; cold, wintry; (fig) cold, chilly

nivĕ·us -a -um *adj* of snow, snowy, snow; covered with snow; snow-white

nivōs·us -a -um *adj* snowy

nix nivis *f* snow; *f pl* (fig) grey hair

nix·or -ārī -ātus sum *vi* to struggle hard; (with *abl*) to lean upon, rest on

nixus *pp* of **nitor**

nix·us -ūs see **nisus**

nō nāre *vi* to swim, float; to sail; to fly; (of eyes) to be glazed

nōbĭl·is -e *adj* known; noted; notable, famous; notorious; noble; thorough-bred (*horse*); fine, excellent; *m pl* notables, nobles

nōbilĭt·ās -ātis *f* fame, renown; noble birth; the nobility; excellence

nōbilĭt·ō -āre *vt* to make famous; to make notorious

noc·ens -entis *adj* harmful; guilty criminal

noc·ĕō -ēre -ŭī -ĭtum *vi* (with *dat*) to harm, injure

nocīv·us -a -um *adj* harmful, injurious

noctĭf·er -ĕrī *m* evening star

noctilūc·a -ae *f* moon

noctivăg·us -a -um *adj* night-wandering

noctū *adv* by night, at night

noctŭ·a -ae *f* owl

noctuābund·us -a -um *adj* traveling by night

noctuīn·us -a -um *adj* of owls

nocturn·us -a -um *adj* nocturnal, of night, at night, by night, night

noctuvigĭl·us -a -um *adj* awake at night

nocŭ·us -a -um *adj* harmful, injurious

nōd·ō -āre *vt* to tie in a knot, knot, tie

nōdōs·us -a -um *adj* knotty

nōd·us -ī *m* knot; knob, knot (*in wood*); girdle; bond, tie; obligation; knotty point, difficulty, crisis

nōlō nolle nōlŭī *vt* (with *inf*) to be unwilling to, wish not to, refuse to; *vi* to be unwilling

nom·as -ădis *m* or *f* nomad; Numidian

nōm·en -ĭnis *n* name; gentile name (*e.g., Julius, as distinct from the praenomen*); race, stock; title; noun; bond, claim, debt; debtor; name, fame, reputation; title, pretext, pretense, excuse, account, reason, responsibility, authority, sake, behalf; mere name (*as opposed to reality*); **aetatis nomine** on the pretext of age, on account of age; **eo nomine** on that account; **nomen dare** or **nomen profiteri** to enlist (*in the army*); **nomen deferre** (with *genit*) to bring an accusation against, accuse (*someone*); **nomen dissolvere** or **nomen expedire** or **nomen solvere** to liquidate an account, pay a debt; **nomina sua exigere** to collect one's debt

nōmenclāt·or -ōris *m* name caller (*slave who accompanied his master and identified those whom they met, esp. during a political campaign*)

nōminātim *adv* by name, expressly

nōminātĭ·ō -ōnis *f* nomination for office

nōminātīv·us -a -um *adj & m* nominative

nōmināt·us -a -um *adj* renowned

nōminĭt·ō -āre *vt* to usually call

nōmĭn·ō -āre *vt* to name, call by name; to mention by name; to make famous; to nominate for an office; to denounce, arraign

nomism·a -ătis *n* coin

nōn *adv* not; no; by no means

Nōn·ae -ārum *f pl* Nones (*fifth day in all months, except March, May, July, and October, in which they occurred on the seventh*)

nōnāgensĭm·us or **nōnāgēsĭm·us -a -um** *adj* ninetieth

nōnāgiens or **nōnāgiēs** *adv* ninety times

nōnāgintā (indecl) *adj* ninety

nōnān·us -a -um *adj* of the ninth legion; *m* soldier of the ninth legion

nōnārĭ·a -ae *f* prostitute

nondum *adv* not yet

nongent·ī -ae -a *adj* nine hundred

nonne *adv* is it not?; (in indirect questions) whether not; **nonne vides?** don't you see?, you see, don't you?; **quaeritur nonne ire statim velis** the question is whether you do not wish to go at once

nonnull·us -a -um *adj* some, many a; **nonnulli** some, some people

nonnunquam *adv* sometimes

nonnusquam *adv* in some places

nōn·us -a -um *adj* ninth; *f* ninth hour

nōn·us decĭm·us -a -um *adj* nineteenth

Nōrĭc·us -a -um *adj* of Noricum; *n* region between the Danube and the Alps

norm·a -ae *f* square (*carpenter's tool*); (fig) rule, standard

nōs *pron* we; us

noscit·ō -āre *vt* to examine closely, observe; to recognize, know
noscō noscĕre nōvī nōtum or **gnoscō — gnōvī gnōtum** *vt* to get to know, become acquainted with, recognize, learn; to examine, inquire into; to approve of; **novisse** to have become acquainted with, (*and therefore*) to know
nosmet *pron* (emphatic form of **nōs**) we ourselves; us
nost·er -ra -rum *adj* our, our own; *pron* ours; **noster** our friend; **nostri** our men, our soldiers, our side
nostr·ās -ātis *adj* native, of our country
not·a -ae *f* note, mark, sign; letter, character; note, short letter; punctuation mark; brand (*of wine*); marginal note, critical mark; tattoo marks, brand; distinctive mark, distinctive quality; stamp (*on coin*); brand, stigma; nickname; black mark (*against one's name*); reproach, disgrace; nod, sign, beck; *f pl* letters of the alphabet; shorthand notes; memoranda
notābĭl·is -e *adj* notable, noteworthy, memorable; notorious
notābilĭter *adv* notably, remarkably; perceptibly
notār·ĭus -ĭī or **-ī** *m* stenographer; secretary
notātĭ·ō -ōnis *f* notation, mark; black mark (*of a censor*); choice; observation; etymology
notāt·us -a -um *adj* noted, distinguished
nōt·escō -escĕre -ŭī *vi* to become known
noth·us -a -um *adj* bastard, illegitimate; mongrel; not genuine, phoney
nōtĭ·ō -ōnis *f* acquaintance; (law) investigation; (fig) notion, idea
nōtitĭ·a -ae or **nōtitĭ·ēs -ēī** *f* acquaintance; fame; notion, conception
not·ō -āre *vt* to mark; to mark out; to note, mark, observe; to write down; to record; to take down in shorthand; to mark critically; to brand; to indicate, denote; to brand, reproach
not·us or **not·os -ī** *m* south wind; wind
nōt·us -a -um *pp* of **nosco;** *adj* known, well known; notorious; familiar, customary; *m pl* acquaintances
novācŭl·a -ae *f* razor
novāl·is -is *f* or **novāl·e -is** *n* field plowed for the first time, reclaimed land; cultivated field; fallow land; crops
novātr·ix -īcis *f* renovator, renewer (*female*)
novē *adv* newly, in an unusual manner
novell·us -a -um *adj* new, fresh, young, newly acquired
novem (indecl) *adj* nine
Novemb·er or **Novemb·ris -re** *adj & m* November
novendĕcim or **novemdĕcim** (indecl) *adj* nineteen
novendiāl·is or **novemdiāl·is -e** *adj* nine-day; occurring on the ninth day
novensĭl·ēs -ĭum *m pl* new gods (*introduced from abroad*)
novēn·ī -ae -a *adj* in groups of nine, nine each, nine
noverc·a -ae *f* stepmother
novercāl·is -e *adj* stepmother's, of a stepmother, like a stepmother
novīcĭ·us -a -um *adj* new, brand new
novīens or **noviēs** *adv* nine times
novissĭmē *adv* very recently, of late
novissĭm·us -a -um *adj* latest, last, most recent; **novissimum agmen** (mil) the rear; **novissima verba** parting words; *m pl* (mil) rear guard
novĭt·ās -ātis *f* newness, novelty; rareness, strangeness, unusualness; novelty of high rank, recently acquired rank
nov·ō -āre *vt* to make new, renovate, renew; to repair, fix; to refresh; to change, alter; to invent, coin (*words*); **res novare** to bring about a revolution
nov·us -a -um *adj* new, young, fresh, novel; strange, unusual, unheard-of; recent, modern; new, unused; inexperienced; renewed, revived; **homo novus** self-made man (*first man of a family to reach a curule office*); **res novae** political innovations, revolution; *n* news
nox noctis *f* night; night activity; sleep; death; darkness, blindness; mental darkness, ignorance; gloom; **ad multam noctem** till late at night; **nocte** or **de nocte** at night, by night; **noctem et dies** night and day; **sub noctem** at nightfall
nox·a -ae *f* harm, injury; offense, fault, guilt, responsibility; punishment
noxĭ·us -a -um *adj* harmful, noxious; guilty; (with *genit* or *abl*) guilty of; *f* harm, damage, injury; blame, guilt; fault, offense; **in noxia esse** to be at fault
nūbĕcŭl·a -ae *f* little cloud; gloomy expression
nūb·ēs -is *f* or **nūb·is -is** *m* cloud; gloom; veil
nūbĭf·er -ĕra -ĕrum *adj* cloudy; cloud-capped (*mountain*); cloud-bringing (*wind*)
nūbigĕn·a -ae *adj masc* or *fem* born of clouds
nūbĭl·is -e *adj* marriageable
nūbĭl·us -a -um *adj* cloudy; cloud-bringing (*wind*); troubled; dark, gloomy, melancholy
nūbō nūbĕre nupsi nuptum *vi* (of women) to marry; (with *dat*) to marry (*a man*), be married to (*a man*)

nucifrangibŭl·um -ī *n* (colloquially of teeth) nutcracker
nuclĕ·us -ī *m* nut; kernel, stone (*of fruit*)
nudius *adv* it is now the . . . day since, e.g., **nudius tertius dedi ad te epistolam** it is now the third day since I mailed you a letter; ago, e.g., **nudius tertius decimus** twelve days ago
nūd·ō -āre *vt* to strip, bare; to lay bare, uncover; (mil) to leave undefended; (with *abl*) to divest of
nūd·us -a -um *adj* nude, naked; lightly clothed; bare, empty; defenseless; poor, needy; bare, mere, simple, sole, only; (with *genit* or *abl* or with **ab** + *abl*) bare of, without, stripped of, destitute of, deprived of
nūg·ae -ārum *f pl* trifles, nonsense; good-for-nothing, a nobody
nūgāt·or -ōris *m* joker; fibber, babbler, braggart
nūgātōrĭ·us -a -um *adj* worthless, useless, nonsensical
nūg·ax -ācis *adj* nonsensical
nūgivend·us -ī *m* dealer in women's apparel
nūg·or -ārī -ātus sum *vi* to talk nonsense; (with *dat*) to trick, cheat
null·us -a -um *adj* no; (coll) not, not at all; non-existent, of no account; *pron* none
num *adv* (of time, used only with **etiam**) now, e.g., **etiam num** now, even now, still; *interrog particle* (expecting negative answer) surely not, really, actually, e.g., **num ista est nostra culpa?** is that really our fault?, that isn't our fault, is it?; *conj* (in indirect questions) whether
Num·a -ae *m* Numa Pompilius (*second king of Rome*)
numcŭbi *adv* ever?, at any time?
numell·a -ae *f* shackle
nūm·en -ĭnis *n* nod; will, consent; divine will; divine power, divinity; deity, godhead
numerābĭl·is -e *adj* easily counted, few in number
numerāt·um -ī *n* ready cash
numĕrō *adv* at the right time, just now; too soon
numĕr·ō -āre *vt* to number, count; to pay out (*money*); to consider; to enumerate, mention; to relate, recount; to reckon as one's own, possess, own
numerōsē *adv* rhythmically
numerōs·us -a -um *adj* numerous; rhythmical
numĕr·us -ī *m* member; (mil) division, troop; mere cipher; class, category; rank, position; estimation, regard; rhythm, meter, verse; quantity, measure; portion (*of work*), part, function; **aliquo numero esse** to be of some account; **in numero haberi** (with *genit*) to be regarded as, be ranked among; **nullo numero esse** to be of no account; *m pl* mathematics, astronomy
Numĭd·a -ae *m* Numidian
Numidĭ·a -ae *f* Numidia (*a country of N. Africa*)
Numidic·us -a -um *adj* Numidian
Numĭt·or -ōris *m* king of Alba, brother of Amulius, father of Ilia, and grandfather of Romulus and Remus
nummārĭ·us -a -um *adj* financial; mercenary
nummāt·us -a -um *adj* rich; **bene nummatus** well-off, well-to-do
nummulār·ius -iī or **-ī** *m* banker
nummŭl·ī -ōrum *m pl* petty cash
numm·us -ī *m* coin, cash, money; sesterce (*small silver coin, worth about a nickel*); small sum, trifle, mere nothing; **in nummis habere** to have in ready cash
numquam or **nunquam** *adv* never; **non numquam** sometimes
numquid *adv* (to introduce direct question): **numquid meministi?** do you remember?; (to introduce indirect question): whether
nunc *adv* now; nowadays, today; now, in view of this, but as matters now stand; **nunc . . . nunc** at one time . . . at another, once . . . once
nuncupātĭ·ō -ōnis *f* name, appellation; public pronouncing (*of vows*)
nuncŭp·ō -āre *vt* to name, call; to take or make (*a vow*) publicly; to proclaim publicly
nundĭn·ae -ārum *f pl* market day; marketplace, market town; trade, sale
nundināl·is -e *adj* market
nundinātĭ·ō -ōnis *f* trading, bargaining, buying and selling
nundĭn·or -ārī -ātus sum *vt* to buy; *vi* to hold a market, attend a market; to trade; to gather in large numbers
nundĭn·um -ī *n* market time; **trinum nundinum** period of three market times, i.e., seventeen days
nunq- = numq-
nuntiātĭ·ō -ōnis *f* announcement (*by an augur*)
nuntĭ·ō -āre *vt* to announce, declare, report, relate
nuntĭ·us -a -um *adj* bringing news; *m* messenger, courier; news, message; order, injunction; **nuntium remittere** (with *dat*) to send a letter of divorce to, to divorce (*a wife*); *n pl* message, news
nūper *adv* recently
nūpĕr·us -a -um *adj* recent
nupt·a -ae *f* bride, wife
nuptĭ·ae -ārum *f pl* marriage, wedding
nuptiāl·is -e *adj* nuptial, wedding
nur·us -ūs *f* daughter-in-law; young lady, young married woman
nusquam *adv* nowhere; on no occasion; for nothing, to nothing; **nus-**

quam alibi nowhere else; **nusquam esse** to not exist; **nusquam gentium** nowhere in the world
nūt·ō -āre *vi* to keep nodding; to sway to and fro, totter; to hesitate, waver
nūtrīcāt·us -ūs *m* nursing (*of babies*)
nūtrīc·ius -iī or **-ī** *m* tutor
nūtrīc·ō -āre or **nūtrīc·or -ārī -ātus sum** *vt* to nurse, suckle; to rear, bring up
nūtrīcŭl·a -ae *f* nurse
nūtrīm·en -inis *n* nourishment
nūtrīment·um -ī *n* nutriment, nourishment, support; fuel (*for fire*)
nūtr·iō -īre -īvī or **-iī -ītum** *vt* to nurse, suckle, nourish, feed; to rear, bring up, support, maintain, foster; to take care of, attend to; to cherish, cultivate
nūtr·ix -īcis *f* nurse; *f pl* breasts
nūt·us -ūs *m* nod; hint, intimation; will, pleasure, command; gravity
nux nucis *f* nut; nut tree, almond tree; **nuces relinquere** (fig) to put away childish things
Nyctē·is -idis *f* Antiope (*wife of Lycus, the king of Thebes, and mother of Amphion and Zethus*)
Nyct·eus -ĕī or **-ĕos** *m* father of Antiope
nymph·a -ae or **nymph·ē -ēs** *f* bride; nymph (*demi-goddesses who inhabit fountains, rivers, sea, woods, and mountains*); water
Nȳs·a -ae *f* mythical birthplace of Bacchus
Nȳsae·us or **Nȳsi·us -a -um** *adj* of Nysa, Nysaean
Nȳs·eus -ĕī or **-ĕos** *m* Bacchus
Nȳsigĕn·a -ae *m* native of Nysa

O

ō *interj* oh!
Oax·ēs or **Oax·is -is** *m* river in Crete
ob *prep* (with *acc*) before, in front of; on account of, because of; for the sake of, in the interest of; in return for, instead of; in proportion to, balanced against; **ob rem** to the purpose, usefully, profitably; **quam ob rem** wherefore, accordingly
obaerāt·us -a -um *adj* deeply in debt; *m* debtor
obambŭl·ō -āre *vt* to prowl all over, prowl about (*e.g., the city*); *vi* to walk about, wander, prowl about; (with *dat*) to prowl about near; (with **ante** + *acc*) to wander around in front of
obarm·ō -āre *vt* to arm
obăr·ō -āre *vt* to plow up, plow over
obbrūtesc·ō -ĕre *vi* to grow dull
obc- = occ-
ob·dō -dĕre -didī -ditum *vt* to close, lock; to expose
obdorm·iō -īre -īvī or **-iī -ītum** *vi* to fall asleep
obdorm·iscō -iscĕre -īvī — *vi* to fall asleep
ob·dūcō -dūcĕre -duxī -ductum *vt* to put on (*clothes*); to cover, veil, surround, envelop; to hide; to swallow; to pass (*time*); to bring forward as a candidate; to run or dig (*ditch*); (with *dat* of thing protected) to draw or place (*something*) over; (with *dat* or **ad** + *acc*) to pit (*someone or something*) against
obducti·ō -ōnis *f* veiling
obduct·ō -āre *vt* to introduce as a rival
obdūr·escō -escĕre -uī *vi* to grow hard, harden; to become insensitive
obdūr·ō -āre *vi* to persist, stick it out
ob·ĕō -īre -īvī or **-iī -ītum** *vt* to go to meet; to travel, travel to, travel over, wander through, traverse, encircle, visit; to run over, review, enumerate (*in a speech*); to undertake, engage in; **diem edicti obire** to meet one's death; *vi* to go; to pass away, die; to fade, disappear; (of heavenly bodies) to go down, set
obequit·ō -āre *vi* to ride up; (with *dat*) to ride up to
oberr·ō -āre *vi* to ramble about, wander around; (with *abl*) **a** to wander about, wander among; **b** to make a mistake on or at
obēs·us -a -um *adj* fat, plump; swollen; crude, coarse
ōb·ex -icis *m* or *f* bar, bolt; barrier; obstacle, hindrance
obf- = off-
obg- = ogg-
ob·haerescō -haerescĕre -haesī *vi* to get stuck
obīr·ascor -ascī -ātus sum *vi* (with *dat*) to get angry at
obiter *adv* on the way, as one goes along; (fig) in passing, incidentally
obitus *pp* of **obeo**
obit·us -ūs *m* approach, visit; death, passing, ruin, downfall; setting (*of heavenly bodies*)
objac·ĕō -ēre -uī *vi* (with *dat*) to lie before, lie at
objectāti·ō -ōnis *f* reproach
object·ō -āre *vt* to oppose; to expose, endanger; to throw in the way; to cause (*delay*); (with *dat*) **a** to expose to, abandon to; **b** to impute to, throw up (*faults*) to, bring a charge of (*e.g., madness*) against, fling (*charges, abuse*) at; (with *dat & acc & inf*) to throw a hint to (*someone*) that
object·us -a -um *adj* lying in the

way, lying in front; (with *dat*) **a** opposite; **b** exposed to; *n pl* charges, accusations

object·us -ūs *m* interposition; obstacle, hindrance; protection; (with *genit*) protection afforded by

ob·jiciō -jicĕre -jēcī -jectum *vt* to cast, hurl; to present, offer, expose; to hold up as an example; to set up as a defense, use as a defense; (with *dat*) **a** to cast before, throw to, offer to, expose to, set up as a defense against; **b** to throw up (*faults, weaknesses, etc.*) to; **c** to bring upon, inflict on, inspire in; **objici** (with *dat*) to happen to, befall, occur to; **se objicere** (with *dat*) to expose oneself to

objurgāti·ō -ōnis *f* scolding, rebuke

objurgāt·or -ōris *m* critic

objurgātōri·us -a -um *adj* scolding, reproachful

objurgit·ō -āre *vt* to keep on scolding

objurg·ō -āre *vt* to scold, rebuke, blame, reprimand; to chastise, correct; to deter

oblangu·escō -escĕre -ŭī *vi* to taper off

oblātrātr·ix -īcis *f* nagging woman, nag

oblātus *pp* of **offero**

oblectām·en -ĭnis *n* delight

oblectāment·um -ī *n* delight, amusement, pastime

oblectāti·ō -ōnis *f* delight, amusement; attraction; (with *genit*) diversion from

oblect·ō -āre *vt* to attract, delight, amuse, divert; to spend (*time*) pleasantly; **se oblectare** to amuse oneself, enjoy oneself

ob·līdō -lidĕre -līsī -līsum *vt* to crush; to squeeze together, strangle

obligāti·ō -ōnis *f* binding, pledging, obligation

obligāt·us -a -um *adj* obliged, under obligation; (with *dat*) (vow) made to

oblĭg·ō -āre *vt* to tie up, bandage; to bind, oblige, put under obligation, make liable; to hamper, tie down; to embarrass; to mortgage; **fidem obligare** to pledge one's word; **obligari** (with *abl*) **a** to be guilty of; **b** to be obliged to, compelled to

oblīm·ō -āre *vt* to cover with mud; to dissipate, squander

ob·linō -linĕre -lēvī -lĭtum *vt* to smear; (fig) to smear, defile; (fig) to overload

oblīquē *adv* sideways; (fig) indirectly

oblīqu·ō -āre *vt* to turn aside, twist, shift, slant

oblīqu·us -a -um *adj* slanting, crosswise; from the side; indirect; sly; envious; downhill (*road*); **obliquus oculus** disapproving look, envious look; *n* side; **ab obliquo** from the side; **per obliquum** across

oblīsus *pp* of **oblido**

oblit·escō -escĕre -ŭī *vi* to hide

oblittĕr·ō -āre *vt* to erase; to cancel; (fig) to blot out; **nomina oblitterare** to cancel debts

oblĭtus *pp* of **oblino**

oblītus *pp* of **obliviscor**

oblīvi·ō -ōnis *f* oblivion; forgetting; forgetfulness

oblīviōs·us -a -um *adj* forgetful, oblivious; (wine) causing forgetfulness

ob·līviscor -līviscī -lītus sum *vt* to forget; *vi* to forget; (with *genit*) to forget, neglect, disregard, be indifferent to

oblīv·ium -iī or **-ī** *n* forgetfulness, oblivion

oblocūt·or -ōris *m* contradictor

oblong·us -a -um *adj* oblong

ob·lŏquor -lŏquī -locūtus sum *vt* (with *dat*) **a** to interrupt; **b** to answer (*in argument*), contradict; **c** to speak against, abuse, rail at; **d** to accompany (*in music*), sing to

obluct·or -ārī -ātus sum *vi* (with *dat*) to struggle with, fight against, struggle against

oblūd·ō -ĕre *vt* to play jokes on

obmōl·ior -īrī -ītus sum *vt* to make a barricade of

obmurmŭr·ō -āre *vi* (with *dat*) to roar in answer to

obmūt·escō -escĕre -ŭī *vi* to become silent, hush up; to cease

obnāt·us -a -um *adj* growing on (*e.g., the bank of a river*)

ob·nītor -nītī -nixus sum *vi* to strain, struggle, put on the pressure; (with *dat*) **a** to press against, lean against; **b** to resist, oppose

obnīxē *adv* with all one's might, obstinately

obnix·us -a -um *pp* of **obnitor;** *adj* steadfast, firm, resolute

obnoxiē *adv* guiltily; timidly

obnoxiōsius *adv* more slavishly

obnoxiōs·us -a -um *adj* submissive

obnoxi·us -a -um *adj* liable, addicted, guilty; submissive, servile, obedient; weak, timid; obliged, under obligation, indebted; answerable, responsible; liable, subject, exposed; **obnoxium est** (with *inf*) it is dangerous to

ob·nūbō -nūbĕre -nupsī -nuptum *vt* to veil, cover

obnuntiāti·ō -ōnis *f* announcement (of omens)

obnunti·ō -āre *vi* to make an announcement; to make an announcement that the omens are adverse; to announce bad news

oboedi·ens -entis *adj* obedient; (with *dat* or **ad** + *acc*) obedient to

oboedienter *adv* obediently

oboedienti·a -ae *f* obedience

oboed·iō -īre -īvī or **-iī -ītum** *vi* (with *dat*) to give ear to, listen to, obey

obol·ĕō -ēre -ŭī *vt* to smell of; *vi* to smell

ob·orior -orīrī -ortus sum *vi* to rise, appear
obp- = opp-
ob·rēpō -rēpĕre -repsī -reptum *vt* to creep up on, sneak up on; *vi* to creep up; (with *dat*) **a** to creep up on, sneak up on, take by surprise; **b** to trick, cheat; (with **in** + *acc*) to steal over; **obrepere ad honores** to worm one's way into high positions
obrept·ō -āre *vi* to sneak up
obrēt·iō -īre -īvī or **-iī -ītum** *vt* to entangle
obrig·escō -escĕre -ŭī *vi* to stiffen; to freeze
obrōd·ō -ĕre *vt* to gnaw at
obrŏg·ō -āre *vi* (with *dat*) to supersede (*a law*)
ob·rŭō -ruĕre -rŭī -rŭtum *vt* to cover up, cover, hide, bury; to overwhelm, overthrow; to sink, cover with water, swamp, overflow; to overpower, surpass, obscure, eclipse; *vi* to fall to ruin
obruss·a -ae *f* test, proof
obsaep·iō -īre -sī -tum *vt* to fence in; to block (*road*); (fig) to close, block
obsatŭr·ō -āre *vt* to sate, cloy; **istius obsaturari** to have enough of him
obscaen- = obscen-
obscaev·ō -āre *vi* to give a bad omen
obscēnē *adv* obscenely
obscēnĭt·ās -ātis *f* obscenity
obscēn·us -a -um *adj* dirty, filthy; indecent, obscene; ominous
obscūrātĭ·ō -ōnis *f* obscuring, darkening; disappearance
obscūrē *adv* indistinctly; secretly, imperceptibly
obscūrit·ās -ātis *f* obscurity
obscūr·ō -āre *vt* to obscure, darken; to cover, hide; to veil (*words*); (of love) to blind; to hide, suppress
obscūr·us -a -um *adj* obscure, dark, shady; obscure, lowly, mean; dim, indistinct, unintelligible; secret; reserved; vague, uncertain; gloomy; *n* the dark, darkness; obscurity
obsecrātĭ·ō -ōnis *f* entreaty; public appeal to the gods
obsĕcr·ō -āre *vt* to entreat, appeal to, implore
obsecund·ō -āre *vi* (with *dat*) to comply with, humor
obsecūtus *pp* of **obsequor**
obsēp- = obsaep-
obsĕqu·ens -entis *adj* compliant, obedient; indulgent, gracious (*gods*); (with *dat*) obedient to
obsequenter *adv* compliantly, obsequiously
obsequentĭ·a -ae *f* obsequiousness
obsequiōs·us -a -um *adj* obsequious
obsequ·ium -iī or **-ī** *n* compliance, indulgence; obedience, allegiance
ob·sĕquor -sĕquī -secūtus sum *vi* (with *dat*) to comply with, yield to, give into, gratify, humor
obsĕr·ō -āre *vt* to bolt, bar, lock up
ob·sĕrō -serĕre -sēvī -situm *vt* to sow or plant thickly; to fill, cover
observ·ans -antis *adj* attentive, respectful; (with *genit*) respectful of, attentive to, careful about
observantĭ·a -ae *f* regard, respect; (with *genit* or **in** + *acc*) regard for, respect for
observātĭ·ō -ōnis *f* observation; caution, care
observāt·or -ōris *m* observer
observĭt·ō -āre *vt* to watch carefully, note carefully
observ·ō -āre *vt* to watch, watch out for, take careful note of; to guard; to observe, keep, obey, comply with; to pay attention to, pay respect to
obs·es -idis *m* or *f* hostage; guarantee
obsessĭ·ō -ōnis *f* blockade
obsess·or -ōris *m* frequenter, regular visitor; blockader
ob·sidĕō -sidēre -sēdī -sessum *vt* to sit near or at, remain by or near; to frequent; (mil) to besiege, invest, blockade; to block, choke; to occupy, fill; to look out for, watch closely; to keep guard over
obsidiāl·is -e *adj* for breaking a blockade; **corona obsidialis** decoration for breaking a blockade
obsidĭ·ō -ōnis *f* blockade, siege; imminent danger
obsid·ium -iī or **-ī** *n* blockade, siege; imminent danger, great peril; status of hostage
ob·sīdō -sīdĕre -sēdī -sessum *vt* to besiege, invest, beset, blockade; to take possession of, occupy
obsignāt·or -ōris *m* sealer; witness; **obsignator testamenti** witness to a will
obsign·ō -āre *vt* to seal, seal up; to sign and seal; (fig) to stamp, impress
ob·sistō -sistĕre -stitī -stitum *vi* (with *dat*) to stand in the way of, block, resist, oppose, disapprove of, forbid
obsĭtus *pp* of **obsero** (to sow)
obsole·fīō -fiĕrī -factus sum *vi* to wear out, become spoiled; to become worthless
obsol·escō -escĕre -ēvī -ētum *vi* to wear out, go out of style, become obsolete, get shabby, lose value
obsolētĭus *adv* rather shabbily
obsolēt·us -a -um *adj* out of date, old, obsolete, worn out; shabby, threadbare; low, mean, poor
obsōnāt·or -ōris *m* shopper
obsōnāt·us -ūs *m* shopping
obsōn·ium -iī or **-ī** *n* shopping items, food
obsōn·ō -āre or **obsōn·or -ārī -ātus sum** *vt* to shop for; **famem obsonare** to work up an appetite; *vi* to go shopping; to provide food; (with **de** + *abl*) to provide a feast for
obsŏn·ō -āre *vi* (with *dat*) to drown out
obsorb·ĕō -ēre -ŭī *vt* to gulp down

obstant·ia -ium *n pl* obstacles, obstructions
obstētr·ix -īcis *f* midwife
obstinātē *adv* resolutely, with determination; obstinately, stubbornly
obstinātī·ō -ōnis *f* resolution, determination; obstinacy, stubbornness
obstināt·us -a -um *adj* resolute, determined, fixed; obstinate, stubborn
obstin·ō -āre *vt* to be resolved on, resolve, determine; (with *inf*) to resolve to, determine to; *vi* to be determined, be resolved; (with **ad** + *acc*) to be set on
obstipescō see **obstupesco**
obstīp·us -a -um *adj* bent, bent to one side; bent forwards, bowed; **capite obstipo stare** to stand with head bowed
ob·stō -stāre -stĕtī *vi* to stand in the way, be in the way, raise opposition; (with *dat*) to stand in the way of, oppose, object to, resist, hinder, obstruct; (with **ne, quin, quominus,** or **cur non**) to prevent (*someone*) from
obstrĕp·ō -ĕre -ŭī -ĭtum *vt* to fill with noise, drown out; *vi* to make a racket, make noise; **a** (with *dat*) to shout at, drown out with shouts, interrupt with shouts; **b** (*of the sea*) to resound against
ob·stringō -stringĕre -strinxī -strictum *vt* to shut in, confine, tie up; (fig) to tie up, involve, put under obligation, oblige; **fidem obstringere** (with *dat*) to pledge one's word to; **obstringi** or **se obstringere** (with *abl*) to get involved in, be guilty of
obstructī·ō -ōnis *f* obstruction
obstructus *pp* of **obstruo**
obs·trūdō or **ob·trūdō -trūdĕre -trūsī -trūsum** *vt* to gulp down; (with *dat*) to force (*something*) upon, thrust (*something*) upon
ob·strŭō -struĕre -struxī -structum *vt* to pile up, block up, stop up; (with *dat*) to block or close (*e.g., the road*) against
obstrūsus *pp* of **obstrudo**
obstupe·faciō -facĕre -fēcī -factum *vt* to astound, astonish, paralyze, stupefy
obstup·escō or **obstip·escō -escĕre -ŭī** *vi* to be astounded, be struck dumb, be paralyzed
obstupĭd·us -a -um *adj* stupefied
ob·sum -esse -fŭī *vi* (with *dat*) to be opposed to, be against; to be prejudicial to, harm; **nihil obest dicere** there is no harm in saying
ob·sŭō -suĕre -sŭī -sūtum *vt* to sew on; to sew up
obsurd·escō -escĕre -ŭī *vi* to become deaf; (fig) to turn a deaf ear
ob·tĕgō -tegĕre -texī -tectum *vt* to cover up; to protect; (fig) to conceal, keep secret; **animus sui obtegens** secretive mind
obtemperātī·ō -ōnis *f* compliance, obedience
obtempĕr·ō -āre *vi* (with *dat*) to comply with, submit to, obey
ob·tendō -tendĕre -tendī -tentum *vt* to spread, stretch out; to offer as an excuse; to envelop, conceal; **obtendi** (with *dat*) to lie opposite; **obtentā nocte** under cover of darkness
obtentus *pp* of **obtineo**
obtent·us -ūs *m* screen, cover; pretext, pretense
ob·tĕrō -terĕre -trīvī -trītum *vt* to trample on, trample down, crush; (fig) to trample on, crush, degrade, destroy
obtestātī·ō -ōnis *f* adjuring, adjuration; solemn entreaty, supplication
obtest·or -ārī -ātum sum *vt* to call as witness; to make an appeal to, implore, entreat
obtex·ō -ĕre -ŭī *vt* to cover, veil
obtic·ĕō -ēre *vi* to be silent
obtic·escō -escĕre -ŭī *vi* to fall silent, be dumbstruck
ob·tinĕō -tinēre -tinŭī -tentum *vt* to get hold of; to hold on to, keep, maintain, preserve, uphold; to assert, maintain; to obtain, gain, acquire; *vi* to continue
ob·tingō -tingĕre -tĭgī *vi* to happen, occur; (with *dat*) to happen to, befall, occur to
obtorp·escō -escĕre -ŭī *vi* to become numb, become stiff, become insensible
ob·torquĕō -torquēre -torsī -tortum *vt* to twist
obtrectātī·ō -ōnis *f* detraction, disparagement
obtrectāt·or -ōris *m* detractor, disparager
obtrect·ō -āre *vt* to treat spitefully, mistreat, disparage; to carp at; *vi* (with *dat*) to detract from, disparage, belittle
obtrītus *pp* of **obtero**
obtrūdō see **obstrudo**
obtrunc·ō -āre *vt* to cut off, cut down; (in battle) to cut down, kill
ob·tuĕor -tuērī -tuĭtus sum *vt* to gaze at, gaze upon; to see clearly
ob·tundo -tundĕre -tŭdī -tūsum or **-tunsum** *vt* to beat, beat on, thump on; to blunt; (fig) to pound away at, stun, deafen, annoy, molest, importune
obturb·ō -āre *vt* to throw into disorder; (fig) to disturb, confuse, distract
obturgesc·ō -ĕre *vi* to begin to swell up
obtūr·ō -āre *vt* to block up, stop up, plug up; **aures obturare** to refuse to listen
obtūsus or **obtunsus** *pp* of **obtundo**; *adj* blunt, dull; (fig) dulled, blurred
obtūt·us -ūs *m* stare, gaze
obumbr·ō -āre *vt* to overshadow, shade; to darken, obscure; to cover, screen
obunc·us -a -um *adj* hooked

obust·us -a -um *adj* singed; hardened in the fire; nipped (*by cold*)
obvāg·iō -īre *vi* to whimper
obvall·ō -āre *vt* to fortify
ob·veniō -venīre -vēnī -ventum *vi* to come up, happen, occur; (with *dat*) to fall to the lot of, be alloted to
obvers·or -ārī -ātus sum *vi* to make an appearance, show oneself; (fig) hover
obvers·us -a -um *adj* (with **ad** + *acc*) **a** turned toward, facing; **b** inclined to; (with *dat*) engaged in; *m pl* opponents
ob·vertō or **ob·vortō -vertĕre -vertī -versum** *vt* (with *dat* or **ad** + *acc*) to turn (*something*) towards or in the direction of; (with **in** + *acc*) to turn (*e.g., the soldiers*) to face (*e.g., the enemy*); **obverti** (with **ad** + *acc*) to turn toward
obviam or **ob viam** *adv* (with *dat*) **a** to meet, in order to meet, in the way of; **b** (fig) opposed to; **effundi obviam** (with *dat*) to pour out to meet, go out in great numbers to meet; **obviam esse** (with *dat*) **a** to meet; **b** to oppose, resist; **obviam ire** (with *dat*) or **obviam procedere** (with *dat*) to go to meet; **obviam obsistere** (with *dat*) to stand in the way of (*someone*); **obviam prodire** or **obviam proficisci** or **obviam progredi** (with *dat*) to go out to meet; **obviam venire** (with *dat*) to go to meet, come to meet
obvigilāt·um -ī *n* vigilance
obvi·us -a -um *adj* in the way; exposed, open; accessible (*person*); ready, at hand; (with *dat*) **a** to meet, so as to meet; **b** opposed to; **c** exposed or open to; **obvius esse** (with *dat*) to meet, encounter; **obvius venire** (with *dat*) to come to meet
ob·volvō -volvĕre -volvī -volūtum *vt* to wrap up, cover up
occaec·ō -āre *vt* to blind, make blind; to darken, obscure; to hide; to numb
occall·escō -escĕre -ŭī *vi* to become thick-skinned; (fig) to become callous
occăn·ō -ĕre -ŭī *vi* to sound the charge
occāsĭ·ō -ōnis *f* occasion, opportunity, good time, chance; pretext; (mil) surprise, raid; **occasionem amittere** to lose the opportunity; **occasionem arripere** to seize the opportunity; **per occasionem** at the right time
occāsiuncŭl·a -ae *f* nice little opportunity
occās·us -ūs *m* setting; sunset, west; (fig) downfall, ruin, death
occātĭ·ō -ōnis *f* harrowing
occāt·or -ōris *m* harrower
oc·cēdō -cēdĕre -cessī -cessum *vi* to go up; **obviam occedere** (with *dat*) to go to meet
occent·ō -āre *vt* to serenade; to satirize in verse
occept·ō -āre *vt* to begin
occĭd·ens -entis *m* the setting sun; west
occīdĭ·ō -ōnis *f* massacre, annihilation; **occidione occidere** to massacre, annihilate, wipe out
oc·cīdō -cīdĕre -cīdī -cīsum *vt* to knock down; to cut down, slay, kill; to murder; to ruin; to pester to death; **se occidere** to commit suicide
oc·cĭdō -cidĕre -cĭdī -cāsum *vi* to fall, fall down; (of the sun) to go down, set; to fall, be slain, perish; (of hope, etc.) to fade, die; (fig) to be ruined, be lost; **occidi!** I'm finished!
occidŭ·us -a -um *adj* setting; western; (fig) sinking, fading, dying
occill·ō -āre *vt* to smash
oc·cĭnō -cinĕre -cecĭnī or **-cinŭī** *vi* to sound ominous
oc·cipĭō -cipĕre -cēpī -ceptum *vt* & *vi* to begin
occipit·ĭum -iī or **-ī** or **occĭp·ut -ĭtis** *n* back of the head
occīsĭ·ō -ōnis *f* massacre; **occisionem facere** to cause a massacre
occīs·or -ōris *m* killer, murderer
occīsus *pp* of **occīdo**
occlāmĭt·ō -āre *vt* to shout at; *vi* to cry out, bawl
oc·clūdō -clūdĕre -clūsī -clūsum *vt* to close up, shut up, lock up; to check, control
occ·ō -āre *vt* to harrow
occŭb·ō -āre *vi* to lie; to rest
occulc·ō -āre *vt* to trample down
occŭl·ō -ĕre -ŭī -tum *vt* to cover; to cover up, hide
occultātĭ·ō -ōnis *f* concealment, hiding
occultāt·or -ōris *m* hideout
occultē *adv* secretly, in concealment
occult·ō -āre *vt* to hide
occult·us -a -um *adj* hidden, secret; reserved (*person*); *n* concealment; secret; **ex occulto** from a place of concealment; secretly
oc·cumbō -cumbĕre -cubŭī -cubĭtum *vt* to fall to, meet; **mortem occumbere** to meet death; *vi* to sink down in death, fall dying; **certae morti occumbere** to meet certain death; **morti occumbere** to fall prey to death; **occumbere** (with **per** + *acc*) to die at the hands of
occupātĭ·ō -ōnis *f* occupation (*e.g., of a town*); occupation, employment, business; business engagement, task; job; involvement, concern
occupāt·us -a -um *adj* occupied, busied, engaged, involved
occŭp·ō -āre *vt* to occupy, seize; to win, gain; to attack, strike down; to outstrip, overtake; to fill, take up; to invest, loan, lend; (with *inf*) to be the first to
oc·currō -currĕre -currī or **-cu-**

currī -cursum *vi* to run up; (with *dat*) a to run up to, run to meet, meet; b to rush against, attack; c to resist, oppose, counteract; d to meet, answer, reply to, object to; e to relieve, remedy; f to occur to, suggest itself to, present itself to; g (fig) to run into, run up against, get involved in

occursāti·ō -ōnis *f* hustle and bustle; excited welcome; officiousness

occurs·ō -āre *vt* to run to meet; *vi* (with *dat*) a to run to meet, go or come to meet, meet; b to go to meet (*the enemy*), attack, charge, oppose; c (of thoughts) to occur to

occurs·us -ūs *m* meeting; (with *genit*) running into (*someone or something*)

Ōceanīt·is -idis *f* ocean nymph

Ōceăn·us -ī *m* ocean; Oceanus (*son of Caelus and Terra, husband of Tethys, and father of rivers and of ocean nymphs*)

ocell·us -ī *m* eye; gem; darling

ōcim·um -ī *n* basil

ōci·or -us *adj* swifter, quicker

ōcius *adv* more swiftly, more quickly; sooner; more easily; immediately, on the spot; (with *abl*) rather than; **ocius serius** sooner or later; **quam ocissime** as quickly as possible

ocrě·a -ae *f* greave, shin guard

ocreāt·us -a -um *adj* wearing shin guards

Octāvi·a -ae *f* sister of Augustus, wife of C. Marcellus, and later of M. Antony (64-11 B.C.); daughter of Claudius and wife of Nero (*murdered in* 62 A.D.)

Octāv·ius -iī or **-ī** *m* C. Octavius (*Emperor Augustus, who, upon adoption by Julius Caesar, became C. Julius Caesar Octavianus,* 63 B.C.-14 A.D.)

octāvum *adv* for the eighth time

octāv·us -a -um *adj* eighth; **octava pars** one eighth; *f* eighth hour of the day (*i.e.,* 2 *p.m.*); *n* **cum octavo efficere** to produce eightfold

octāv·us decim·us -a -um *adj* eighteenth

octiens or **octiēs** *adv* eight times

octingentēsim·us or **octingentensim·us -a -um** *adj* eight hundredth

octingent·ī -ae -a *adj* eight hundred

octip·ēs -ědis *adj* eight-footed

octō (indecl) *adj* eight

Octōb·er -ris *adj & m* October

octōděcim (indecl) *adj* eighteen

octōgēnāri·us -a -um *adj & m* octogenarian

octōgēn·ī -ae -a *adj* eighty each

octōgēsim·us or **octōgensim·us -a -um** *adj* eightieth

octōgiēs or **octōgiens** *adv* eighty times

octōgintā (indecl) *adj* eighty

octōjūg·is -e *adj* eight-team

octōn·ī -ae -a *adj* eight at a time, eight each

octōphŏr·os -on *adj* carried by eight carriers; *n* eight-man litter

octuplicāt·us -a -um *adj* eightfold

octŭpl·us -a -um *adj* eightfold; *n* eightfold fine

octuss·is *m* sum of eight aces

oculāt·us -a -um *adj* having eyes; exposed to view, conspicuous; **oculatus testis** eyewitness

oculě·us -a -um *adj* many-eyed

oculissim·us -a -um *adj* dearest

oculitus *adv* like one's own eyes, dearly

ocŭl·us -ī *m* eye; eye, bud (*in plants*); sight, vision; mind's eye; apple of the eye; **aequis oculis** contentedly; **altero oculo captus** blind in one eye; **ante oculos** in full view; (fig) obvious; **ante oculos ponere** to imagine; **ex oculis abire** to go out of sight, disappear; **in oculis** in view, in public, in the limelight; **in oculis ferre** or **gestare** to hold dear, value; **oculos adjicere** (with **ad** + *acc*) to eye; to covet; **oculos dejicere** (with **ab** + *abl*) to take one's eyes off; (fig) to lose sight of; **oculos pascere** (with *abl*) to feast one's eyes on; **sub oculis** (with *genit*) in the presence of, under the very nose of

ōd·ī -isse *vt* to have taken a dislike to, dislike, hate, be disgusted at

ōdiōsē *adv* hatefully; unpleasantly

ōdiōsic·us -a -um *adj* odious, unpleasant, annoying

ōdiōs·us -a -um *adj* odious, unpleasant, annoying

ōd·ium -iī or **-ī** *n* dislike, hatred, aversion; object of hatred, nuisance; dissatisfaction, disgust; offensive conduct, insolence; **odio esse** (with *dat*) to be hateful to, be disliked by, be hated by; *n pl* feelings of hatred

od·or or **od·ōs -ōris** *m* odor, smell, scent; stench, stink; pleasant smell, fragrance, perfume; inkling, suggestion, hint; *m pl* perfume

odōrāti·ō -ōnis *f* smell, smelling

odōrāt·us -a -um *adj* fragrant, scented

odōrāt·us -ūs *m* smell, smelling; sense of smell

odōrif·er -ěra -ěrum *adj* fragrant

odōr·ō -āre *vt* to make fragrant

odōr·or -ārī -ātus sum *vt* to sniff at, scent; to aspire to, aim at; to be sniffing after, search for, investigate; to get a smattering of

odōr·us -a -um *adj* smelly, fragrant; keen-scented

odōs see **odor**

Odrysi·us -a -um *adj & m* Thracian

Odyssē·a or **Odyssī·a -ae** *f* the Odyssey

Oeăg·er -rī *m* king of Thrace and father of Orpheus

Oeagri·us -a -um *adj* Thracian

Oebalid·ēs -ae *m* male descendant of Oebalus; *m pl* Castor and Pollux

Oebalĭ·us -a -um *adj* Spartan; Tarentine; Sabine; *f* Tarentum (*Spartan colony in S. Italy*)
Oebăl·us -ī *m* king of Sparta, father of Tyndareus, and grandfather of Helen and Clytemnestra
Oedĭp·ūs -ŏdis or **-ī** *m* Oedipus
Oen·eus -ĕī or **-ĕos** *m* king of Calydon, husband of Althaea, and father of Meleager and Deianira
Oenīd·ēs -ae *m* descendant of Oeneus; Meleager; Diomedes (*son of Tydeus*)
Oenomă·us -ī *m* king of Pisa in the Peloponnesus and father of Hippodamia
oenophŏr·um -ī *n* wine-bottle basket
Oenopĭ·a -ae *f* ancient name of Aegina (*island between Attica and Argolis*)
oenopōl·ium -iī or **-ī** *n* wine shop, tavern
Oenōtrĭ·us -a -um *adj* Oenotrian, Italian; *f* ancient name of S.E. Italy; Italy
oestr·us -ī *m* horsefly, gadfly; fancy, inspiration
oesȳp·um -ī *n* lanolin
Oet·a -ae or **Oet·ē -ēs** *f* Mt. Oete (*mountain in S. Thessaly, on which Hercules died*)
Oetae·us -a -um *adj* Oetean; *m* Hercules
ofell·a -ae *f* bit, morsel
off·a -ae *f* pellet, lump, dumpling; swelling; shapeless mass
offātim *adv* in bits, in little lumps
offectus *pp* of **officio**
of·fendō -fendĕre -fendī -fensum *vt* to bump, bump against, stub, strike, hit; to hit upon, come upon, meet with, bump into, stumble upon, find; to offend, shock, vex, disgust; to hurt (*feelings*); to injure (*reputation*); **nihil offendere** to suffer no damage, receive no injury; *vi* to make a blunder, make a mistake, blunder; to give offense, be offensive; to fail, take a loss, be defeated, come to grief; to run aground; (with *dat* or **in** + *abl*) to hit against, bump against; (with *dat*) to give offense to; (with **in** + *acc*) to take offense at; **terrae offendere** to run aground
offens·a -ae *f* offense, affront, injury; displeasure, resentment, hatred; crime; **offensā** (with *genit*) out of hatred for
offensĭ·ō -ōnis *f* stubbing; tripping, stumbling; dislike, displeasure, hatred, digust, aversion; discredit, bad reputation, mishap, failure, disaster, accident, defeat; *f pl* offensive acts; feelings of displeasure
offensiuncŭl·a -ae *f* slight displeasure; minor setback; disappointment
offens·ō -āre *vt & vi* to bump
offens·us -a -um *pp* of **offendo;** *adj* offensive, odious; offended, displeased, annoyed
offens·us -ūs *m* bump; shock; offense
offĕrō offerre obtŭlī oblātum *vt* to offer, bring forward, present, show; to cause, occasion; to confer, bestow, inflict; **se offerre** (with *dat*) **a** to meet, encounter; **b** to expose oneself to
offerūment·a -ae *f* (*said humorously of a blow or welt*) present
officīn·a or **opificīn·a -ae** *f* shop, workshop, factory, office
of·ficiō -ficĕre -fēcī -fectum *vi* (with *dat*) to get in the way of, interfere with, oppose, obstruct, be detrimental to, hinder
officiōsē *adv* obligingly, courteously
officiōs·us -a -um *adj* ready to serve, obliging; dutiful, obligatory
offic·ium -iī or **-ī** *n* service, favor, kindness, courtesy; obligation, duty, function, office, part; social obligation, social call, social visit; ceremony, ceremonial observance, attendance; official duty; employment, business, job; sense of duty, conscience; allegiance
of·fīgō -fīgĕre -fixī -fixum *vt* to fasten down, nail down, drive in
offirmāt·us -a -um *adj* determined, resolute
offirm·ō -āre *vt* **se offirmare** to steel oneself, be determined; *vi* to be determined
offlect·ō -ĕre *vt* to turn (*something*) around
offrēnāt·us -a -um *adj* curbed
offūcĭ·a -ae *f* cosmetic; (fig) trick
of·fulgĕō -fulgēre -fulsī -fulsum *vi* (with *dat*) to shine on
of·fundō -fundĕre -fūdī -fūsum *vt* to pour out; to cover, fill; to eclipse; **offundi** (with *dat*) to pour out over, spread over
oggan·iō -īre -īvī or **-iī -ītum** *vt & vi* to growl
og·gĕrō -gerĕre *vt* to bring, offer, give
Ōgȳg·ēs -is or **Ōgȳg·us -ī** *m* mythical king of Thebes, in whose reign the Deluge occurred
Ōgygĭ·us -a -um *adj* Theban
oh *interj* oh!
ōhē or **ōhĕ** *interj* whoa!
oi *interj* (*express complaint*) oh no!
Oīl·eus -ĕī or **-ĕos** *m* king of Locris and father of Ajax the archer
olĕ·a -ae *f* olive; olive tree
oleāgĭn·us -a -um *adj* olive, of an olive tree
oleārĭ·us -a -um *adj* oil, of oil; *m* oil merchant
oleast·er -rī *m* oleaster, wild olive tree
Ōlenĭ·us -a -um *adj* of Olenus (*town in Achaia and Aetolia*); Achaian, Aetolian
ol·ens -entis *adj* smelling; fragrant; smelly, stinking; musty
ol·ĕō -ēre -ŭī *vt* to smell of, smell like; (fig) to betray; *vi* to smell; (with *abl*) to smell of
olĕ·um -ī *n* olive oil, oil; (fig) palaestra; **oleum addere camino** (fig) to pour oil on the fire; **oleum**

et operam perdere to waste time and effort
ol·faciō -facĕre -fēcī -factum *vt* to smell
olfact·ō -āre *vt* to sniff at
olid·us -a -um *adj* smelly
ōlim *adv* once, once upon a time; at the time; for a good while; someday, in the future, hereafter; now and then, at times; ever, at any time
olit- = **holit-**
olīv·a -ae *f* olive; olive tree; olive wreath; olive branch; olive staff
olīvēt·um -ī *n* olive grove
olīvif·er -ĕra -ĕrum *adj* olive-producing, olive-growing
olīv·um -ī *n* oil; ointment; (fig) palaestra
oll·a -ae *f* pot, jar
olle or **ollus** = **ille**
ol·or -ōris *m* swan
olōrīn·us -a -um *adj* swan, of a swan
olus see **holus**
Olympī·a -ae *f* Olympia (*region in Elis, in the Peloponnesus, where the Olympian games were held*)
Olympī·a -ōrum *n pl* Olympian games
Olympiăc·us -a -um *adj* Olympian
Olympī·as -ădis *f* Olympiad (*period of four years between Olympian games, starting in the year* 776 B.C., *according to which the Greeks reckoned time*); wife of Philip V of Macedon and mother of Alexander the Great
Olympĭc·us or **Olympī·us -a -um** *adj* Olympian
Olympionīc·ēs -ae *m* Olympic victor
Olymp·us -ī *m* Mt. Olympus (*mountain on the boundary of Macedonia and Thessaly, regarded as the home of the gods or heaven*)
omās·um -ī *n* tripe; (fig) paunch, belly
ōm·en -ĭnis *n* omen, sign, token, foreboding; solemn assurance
ōment·um -ī *n* fat; bowels
ōminăt·or -ōris *m* diviner
ōmĭn·or -ārī -ātus sum *vt* to forebode, predict, prophesy
ōminōs·us -a -um *adj* ominous
omiss·us -a -um *adj* remiss, negligent
omitto omittĕre omīsī omissum *vt* to let go, let fall, let go of; to give up, abandon; to omit, pass over, say nothing of; to overlook, disregard
omnĭf·er -ĕra -ĕrum *adj* all-sustaining
omnigĕn·us -a -um *adj* of every kind
omnimŏdīs or **omnimŏdo** *adv* by all means, wholly
omnīnō *adv* altogether, entirely, wholly; (with numerals) in all; (in generalizations) in general; (in concessions) no doubt, to be sure, yes, by all means, certainly; **haud omnino** or **non omnino** not quite, not entirely; absolutely not, not at all; not expressly; **omnino nemo** no one at all
omnipăr·ens -entis *adj* all-producing (*earth*)
omnipŏt·ens -entis *adj* almighty
omn·is -e *adj* all, every; every kind of, every sort of; the whole; *m pl* all, all men, everybody; *n* the universe; *n pl* all things, everything, all nature, all the world
omnitŭ·ens -entis *adj* all-seeing
omnivăg·us -a -um *adj* roving everywhere
omnivŏl·us -a -um *adj* all-craving
Omphăl·ē -ēs *f* Lydian queen whom Hercules had to serve
onăg·er or **onagr·us -ī** *m* wild ass
onăg·os -ī *m* ass driver
Onchesmīt·ēs -ae *m* wind blowing from Onchesmus (*harbor in Epirus*)
onerārī·us -a -um *adj* carrying freight; **jumenta oneraria** beasts of burden; **oneraria** or **navis oneraria** freighter, transport
onĕr·ō -āre *vt* to load, load down, burden; (fig) to overload, oppress; (fig) to pile on, aggravate
onerōs·us -a -um *adj* onerous, burdensome, oppressive, heavy
on·us -ĕris *n* load, burden; freight, cargo; burden, difficulty; trouble; tax expense; foetus, embryo; **oneri esse** (with *dat*) to be a burden to
onust·us -a -um *adj* loaded, burdened; filled, full
on·yx -ȳchis *m* or *f* onyx; onyx box
opācĭt·ās -ātis *f* shade, darkness
opāc·ō -āre *vt* to shade
opāc·us -a -um *adj* shady; dark, obscure; *n pl* **per opaca locorum** through shady places
opell·a -ae *f* light work
opĕr·a -ae *f* effort, pains, exertion, work, labor; care, attention; service, assistance; leisure, spare time; laborer, workman, artisan; **operae esse** or **operae pretium esse** to be worthwhile; **operam dare** to take pains, exert oneself, be busied, pay attention, give attention; **operam funeri dare** to attend a funeral; **operam sermoni dare** to listen to a conversation; **operam tonsori dare** to see a barber, get a haircut; **operā meā (tuā,** etc.) through my (*your, etc.*) agency, thanks to me (*you, etc.*)
operārī·us -a -um *adj* working; *m* working man, workman, laborer; *f* working woman
opercŭl·um -ī *n* lid, cover
operīment·um -ī *n* lid, cover
oper·iō -īre -ŭī -tum *vt* to cover, cover up; to shut, close; to hide; to overwhelm
opĕr·or -ārī -ātus sum *vi* to work, work hard, take pains; (with *dat*) **a** to work hard at, be busied with, be engaged in; **b** to perform (*religious services*); **c** to attend; **d** to worship

operōsē *adv* with great effort, at great pains
operōs·us -a -um *adj* active, busy, painstaking; troublesome, difficult, elaborate; efficacious, powerful (*drugs*)
opert·us -a -um *pp* of **operio**; *adj* closed; hidden; secret; *n* secret; secret place; **in operto** inside, in secret; *n pl* depths; veiled oracles
opēs see **ops**
ophīt·ēs -ae *m* serpentine (*type of marble*)
Ophiūsi·us -a -um *adj* Cyprian; *f* old name of Cyprus
ophthalmi·ās -ae *m* a fish
opic·us -a -um *adj* boorish
opif·er -ĕra -ĕrum *adj* helpful
opif·ex -icis *m* maker, framer, creator; craftsman, mechanic
opificīn·a -ae *f* workshop
ōpili·ō -ōnis *m* shepherd
opīmē *adv* richly, splendidly
opīmit·ās -ātis *f* abundance
opīm·us -a -um *adj* fat, plump; fertile, fruitful; rich, enriched; abundant, copious, plentiful; sumptuous, splendid; lucrative; noble; **spolia opima** armor stripped from one general by another on the field of battle
opīnābil·is -e *adj* conjectural, imaginary
opīnāti·ō -ōnis *f* mere opinion, conjecture, supposition, hunch
opīnāt·or -ōris *m* guesser
opīnāt·us -a -um *adj* supposed, imagined
opīnāt·us -ūs *m* supposition
opīni·ō -ōnis *f* opinion, conjecture, supposition, guess, belief, expectation; general impression, estimation; rumor; reputation, bad reputation; **amplius opinione** beyond expectation, beyond all hopes; **celerius opinione** sooner than expected; **hac opinione ut** under the impression that; **in opinione esse** (with *acc & inf*) to be of the opinion that; **praebere opinionem timoris** to convey the impression of fear; **praeter opinionem** contrary to expectation, sooner than expected; **ut opinio mea est** as I suppose
opīniōs·us -a -um *adj* opinionated
opīn·ō -āre or **opīn·or -ārī -ātus sum** *vt* to suppose, imagine, conjecture; *vi* (parenthetical) to suppose, imagine
opipărē *adv* splendidly, sumptuously
opipăr·us -a -um *adj* splendid, sumptuous, ritzy
opisthogrăph·us -a -um *adj* written on the back
opitŭl·or -ārī -ātus sum *vi* (with *dat*) to bring help to, assist
oport·et -ēre -ŭit *v impers* it is right, it is proper; **me ire oportet** I ought to go, should go
op·pangō -pangĕre -pēgī -pactum *vt* to affix, imprint
oppect·ō -ĕre *vt* to comb off; (coll) to pluck, pick, eat
oppēd·ō -ĕre *vi* (with *dat*) **a** to break wind at; **b** (fig) to deride, mock
opper·ior -īrī -tus sum *vt* to wait for, await; (with **num**) to wait and see whether; *vi* to wait
oppĕt·ō -ĕre -īvī or **-iī -ītum** *vt* to go to meet; **mortem oppetere** to go to meet death, perish, die; *vi* to perish, die
oppidān·us -a -um *adj* of a town, in a town; (disparagingly) provincial; *m pl* townsfolk, townspeople
oppidō *adv* absolutely, quite, completely; (as affirmative answer) exactly
oppidŭl·um -ī *n* small town
oppid·um -ī *n* town
oppignĕr·ō -āre *vt* to pledge
oppīl·ō -āre *vt* to shut up, shut off
op·plĕō -plēre -plēvī -plētum *vt* to fill up, choke up
op·pōnō -pōnĕre -posŭī -positum *vt* to put, place, station; to oppose; to expose, lay bare, open; to wager, mortgage; to bring forward, present, adduce, allege; to reply, respond, object; to compare
opportūnē *adv* opportunely, at the right time
opportūnit·ās -ātis *f* suitableness, fitness, convenience; opportunity, right time; advantage
opportūn·us -a -um *adj* suitable, fit, convenient; advantageous, useful; exposed; **tempore opportunissimo** in the nick of time; *n pl* exposed parts
oppositi·ō -ōnis *f* opposition
opposit·us -a -um *pp* of **oppono**; *adj* opposite; (with *dat*) opposite, across from
opposit·us -ūs *m* opposing, opposition
oppressi·ō -ōnis *f* force, violence; violent seizure; suppression, overthrow
oppressiuncŭl·a -ae *f* slight pressure
oppressus *pp* of **opprimo**
oppress·us -ūs *m* pressure
op·primō -primĕre -pressī -pressum *vt* to press down, weigh down; to pressure, put pressure on; to close, shut; to overwhelm; to put down, suppress, quell; to sink (*a ship*); to subvert, overthrow, crush, subdue, overpower; to conceal, suppress; to seize, catch, surprise
opprobrāment·um -ī *n* disgrace, scandal
opprobr·ium -iī or **-ī** *n* disgrace, scandal, reproach; cause of disgrace; taunt, abuse, abusive word
opprŏbr·ō -āre *vt* to taunt
oppugnāti·ō -ōnis *f* assault; (fig) attack, assault, accusation
oppugnāt·or -ōris *m* assailant, attacker
oppugn·ō -āre *vt* to assault, assail, attack, storm; (fig) to attack, assail

ops opis *f* power, might; help, aid; influence, weight; **opem ferre** (with *dat*) to bring help to, help; *f pl* wealth, resources, means; military or political resources
Ops Opis *f* goddess of abundance, sister and wife of Saturn, and identified with Earth
ops- = **obs-**
optābil·is -e *adj* desirable
optāti·ō -ōnis *f* wishing, wish
optātō *adv* according to one's wish
optāt·us -a -um *adj* longed-for, desired, welcome; *n* wish, desire
optigō see **obtego**
optim·ās -ātis *m* aristocrat; *m pl* aristocracy, aristocratic party
optimē or **optumē** (*superl* of **bene**) *adv* very well, thoroughly, best; most opportunely, just in time
optim·us or **optum·us -a -um** (*superl* of **bonus**) *adj* very good, best; excellent
opti·ō -ōnis *m* helper, assistant; (mil) adjutant
optīv·us -a -um *adj* chosen
opt·ō -āre *vt* to choose, select; to wish for, desire
optum- = **optim-**
opŭl·ens -entis *adj* opulent, rich
opulentē or **opulenter** *adv* richly, splendidly
opulenti·a -ae *f* opulence, wealth; resources; power
opulentit·ās -ātis *f* opulence; power
opulent·ō -āre *vt* to make rich, enrich
opulent·us -a -um *adj* opulent, rich, wealthy; powerful; sumptuous
op·us -ĕris *n* work; product of work, structure, building; literary work, composition, book; work of art, workmanship; deed, achievement; (mil) offensive works, siege works; (mil) defensive works, fortifications; **magno opere** greatly; **quanto opere** how much, how greatly; **tanto opere** so much, so greatly; **opus est** (with *inf*) it is useful or beneficial to; **opus est** (with *dat* of person in need and *abl* of person or thing needed) to need, e.g., **vobis duce opus est** you need a leader
opuscŭl·um -ī *n* little work, minor work
ōr·a -ae *f* boundary, border, edge; coastline, coast; region, district; cable, hawser; (fig) people of the coast, people of the region; **ora maritima** seacoast
ōrācŭl·um or **ōrācl·um -ī** *n* oracle; prophesy
ōrāri·us -a -um *adj* coasting; **navis oraria** coaster, coasting vessel
ōrāt·a -ōrum *n pl* prayers, requests
ōrāti·ō -ōnis *f* faculty of speech; speech, language; style of speech, manner of speaking, style, expression; oration, speech; theme, subject; prose; eloquence; imperial rescript; **orationem habere** to give a speech
ōrātiuncŭl·a -ae *f* short speech, insignificant speech
ōrāt·or -ōris *m* orator, speaker; spokesman; suppliant
ōrātōriē *adv* oratorically
ōrātōri·us -a -um *adj* orator's, oratorical
ōrātr·ix -īcis *f* suppliant (*female*)
ōrāt·us -ūs *m* request
orb·a -ae *f* orphan; widow
orbāt·or -ōris *m* murderer (*of someone's children or parents*)
Orbil·ius -iī or **-ī** *m* Horace's teacher in Venusia
orb·is -is *m* circle; disk, ring, orbit; quoit; hoop; wheel; round shield; eye socket, eye; globe, earth, world, universe; region, territory, country; circuit, round; rotation; cycle, period; (rhet) balance; zodiac; **orbis lacteus** Milky Way; **orbis terrae** or **terrarum** earth, world, universe
orbīt·a -ae *f* rut, wheel track; (fig) rut, routine
orbīt·ās -ātis *f* childlessness, widowhood, orphanhood
orbitōs·us -a -um *adj* full of ruts
orb·ō -āre *vt* to bereave of parents, father, mother, children, husband, or wife; to strip, rob, deprive, make destitute
orb·us -a -um *adj* bereaved, bereft; destitute; orphaned, fatherless; childless; widowed; (with *genit* or *abl* or with **ab** + *abl*) bereft of, deprived of, without; *m* orphan; *f* see **orba**
orc·a -ae *f* vat, barrel
Orcăd·es -um *f pl* islands N. of Scotland (*modern Orkneys*)
orch·as -ădis *f* olive
orchestr·a -ae *f* senatorial seats (*in the theater*); (fig) senate
Orc·us -ī *m* lower world; Pluto (*king of the lower world*); death
orde- = **horde-**
ordināri·us -a -um *adj* ordinary, usual, regular
ordinātim *adv* in order, in good order, in succession; regularly, properly
ordināti·ō -ōnis *f* orderly arrangement; orderly government
ordināt·us -a -um *adj* regular; appointed
ordĭn·ō -āre *vt* to set in order, arrange, regulate; to govern, rule; to record chronologically
ordior ordīrī orsus sum *vt* to begin, undertake; to describe; *vi* to begin, begin to speak
ord·ō -ĭnis *m* line, row, series; row of seats (*in a theater*); order, methodical arrangement; (pol) rank, order, class; (mil) line, file (*of soldiers*), company, century, command of a company or century; *m pl* officers of a company; promotions; **amplissimus ordo** senatorial order; **ex ordine** in succession, with-

out a break; **extra ordinem** extraordinarily, especially, uncommonly; **ordine, in ordine,** or **per ordinem** in order, in sequence, in detail, with regularity, regularly
Orē·as -ădis *f* Oread, mountain nymph
Orest·ēs -is or **-ae** *m* son of Agamemnon and Clytemnestra who avenged his father's death by killing his mother
orex·is -is *f* longing, appetite
organĭc·us -ī *m* organist
orgăn·um -ī *n* instrument, implement; musical instrument, organ
orgĭ·a -ōrum *n pl* Bacchic revels; orgies
orichalc·um -ī *n* copper ore; brass
ōricill·a -ae *f* lobe
orĭ·ens -entis *m* rising sun, morning sun; morning; day; land of the rising sun, Orient, the East
orĭg·ō -ĭnis *f* origin, source, beginning, start; birth, lineage, descent; race, stock, family; founder, progenitor
Ŏrī·ōn or **Orī·ōn -ŏnis** or **-ōnis** *m* mythical hunter, turned into a constellation
orĭor orīrī ortus sum *vi* to rise, get up; to become visible, appear; to be born, originate, be descended; to proceed, begin, start
Ŏrīthўī·a -ae *f* daughter of Erechtheus and mother of Calais and Zetes by Boreas
oriund·us -a -um *adj* descended, sprung, born
ornāment·um -ī *n* equipment, trappings, apparatus; ornament, adornment, decoration; trinket, jewel; (fig) distinction; rhetorical ornament; pride and joy
ornātē *adv* ornately, elegantly
ornātr·ix -īcis *f* hairdresser (*female*)
ornātŭl·us -a -um *adj* fancy
ornāt·us -a -um *adj* equipped, fitted out, furnished, dressed, harnessed; adorned, decorated, embellished; handsome; illustrious, excellent
ornāt·us -ūs *m* equipment; attire, apparel, outfit; furniture; decoration, ornament; world, universe
orn·ō -āre *vt* to equip, fit out, furnish, dress; to set off, decorate, adorn; to honor, praise, commend
orn·us -ī *f* mountain ash
ōr·ō -āre *vt* to beg, entreat, implore, plead with; to ask for; to plead (*a case*); (with double *acc*) to ask (*someone*) for; *vi* to plead, beg, pray; (with **cum** + *abl*) to plead or argue with
Oront·ēs -is or **-ae** *m* chief river of Syria; companion of Aeneas
Orontē·us -a -um *adj* Syrian
Orph·eus -ĕī or **-ĕos** *m* son of Oeagrus and Calliope, husband of Eurydice, and famous musician and poet
Orphē·us or **Orphĭc·us -a -um** *adj* Orphic
ors·us -a -um *pp* of **ordior;** *n pl* beginnings; utterance, words; attempt
ors·us -ūs *m* beginning; attempt, undertaking
ortus *pp* of **orior**
ort·us -ūs *m* rising; the East; birth, origin; source
Ortygĭ·a -ae or **Ortygĭ·ē -ēs** *f* Delos; island in the port of Syracuse
or·yx -ўgis *m* gazelle
oryz·a -ae *f* rice
os ossis *n* bone; marrow, innermost parts; *n pl* skeleton
ōs ōris *n* mouth; beak; voice, speech, expression; lip, face, countenance, look; sight, presence (*of a person*); impudence; mask, mouth, opening, orifice, front; **habere aliquid in ore** to be talking about something continually; **in ore omnium esse** to be on the lips of everyone, be talked about
osc·en -ĭnis *m* bird of augury (*e.g., crow, raven, owl*)
oscill·um -ī *n* small mask
oscĭt·ans -antis *adj* yawning; (fig) indifferent, bored
oscĭt·ō -āre or **oscĭt·or -ārī -ātus sum** *vi* to gape; to yawn
osculātĭ·ō -ōnis *f* kissing
oscŭl·or -ārī -ātus sum *vt* to kiss; (fig) to make a fuss over
oscŭl·um -ī *n* little mouth; kiss; **breve osculum** peck
Osc·us -a -um *adj* Oscan; *m pl* Oscans (*ancient people of Campania and Samnium*)
Osīr·is -is or **-idis** *m* Egyptian god, the husband of Isis
ōs·or -ōris *m* hater
Oss·a -ae *f* mountain in N.E. Thessaly
ossĕ·us -a -um *adj* bony
ossifrăg·a -ae *f* osprey
ostendō ostendĕre ostendī ostentum *vt* to stretch out, stretch forth; to expose; to show, exhibit, display, present; to reveal, disclose; to declare, make known
ostentātĭ·ō -ōnis *f* display; ostentation, showing off; mere show, pretense
ostentāt·or -ōris *m* show-off
ostent·ō -āre *vt* to show, exhibit; to show off, display, parade, boast of; to declare, point out, set forth
ostent·um -ī *n* portent, prodigy
ostent·us -ūs *m* display, show; **ostentui** for appearances, in pretense
Ostĭ·a -ae *f* or **Ostĭ·a -ōrum** *n pl* Ostia (*port and town at the mouth of the Tiber*)
ostiār·ium -iī or **-ī** *n* tax on doors
ostiātim *adv* from door to door
ost·ium -iī or **-ī** *n* door; entrance, mouth
ostrĕ·a -ae *f* or **ostrĕ·um -ī** *n* oyster
ostreāt·us -a -um *adj* covered with oyster shells; (fig) black and blue

ostreōs·us -a -um *adj* abounding in oysters
ostrif·er -ĕra -ĕrum *adj* oyster-growing
ostrīn·us -a -um *adj* purple
ostr·um -ī *n* purple; purple dress, purple covering
ōsus *pp* of **odi**
Oth·ō -ōnis *m* L. Roscius Otho (*author of the law in* 67 B.C. *reserving fourteen rows in the theaters for the equestrian order*); M. Salvius Otho (*Roman emperor in* 69 A.D.)
Othr·ys -ўos *m* mountain in S. Thessaly
ōtiŏl·um -ī *n* bit of leisure
ōti·or -ārī -ātus sum *vi* to take it easy
ōtiōsē *adv* at leisure; leisurely, without haste; calmly, fearlessly
ōtiōs·us -a -um *adj* at leisure, relaxing; free from official obligations; quiet, calm; unconcerned, indifferent, neutral; passionless; *m* private person (*not holding public office*); *m pl* civilians, non-combatants
ōt·ium -iī or **-ī** *n* leisure, free time, relaxation; freedom from public affairs, retirement; peace, quiet; ease, idleness, inactivity
Ovid·ius -iī or **-ī** *m* P. Ovidius Naso or Ovid (*Latin poet, born at Sulmo,* 43 B.C.-17 A.D.)
ovīl·e -is *n* sheepfold; voting enclosures in the Campus Martius
ovīl·is -e *adj* sheep, of sheep
ovill·us -a -um *adj* sheep, of sheep
ov·is -is *f* sheep; wool; simpleton
ov·ō -āre *vi* to rejoice; to hold a celebration; to celebrate a minor triumph
ōv·um -ī *n* egg; *n pl* wooden balls used to mark the laps at the racetrack

P

pābulāti·ō -ōnis *f* foraging
pābulāt·or -ōris *m* forager
pābŭl·or -ārī -ātus sum *vi* to forage; (coll) to make a living
pābŭl·um -ī *n* food, fodder; pasturage, grass; (fig) nourishment
pācāl·is -e *adj* of peace
pācāt·us -a -um *adj* peaceful, quiet, calm; *n* friendly country
Pachўn·um -ī *n* S.E. point of Sicily
pācif·er -ĕra -ĕrum *adj* peace-bringing, peaceful
pācificāti·ō -ōnis *f* pacification
pācificāt·or -ōris *m* peacemaker
pācificātōri·us -a -um *adj* peace-making
pācific·ō -āre *vt* to pacify, appease; *vi* to make peace, conclude peace
pācific·us -a -um *adj* peace-making; peaceable
paciscor pasciscī pactus sum *vt* to bargain for, agree upon; to stipulate; to barter; to betroth; *vi* to come to an agreement, agree, make a bargain, make a contract; (with *inf*) to agree to, pledge oneself to
pac·ō -āre *vt* to pacify, soothe, subdue
pact·a -ae *f* fiancee; bride
pacti·ō -ōnis *f* pact, contract, agreement, treaty; condition, stipulation; collusion
Pactōl·us -ī *m* river in Lydia famous for its gold
pact·or -ōris *m* contractor, negotiator, party (*in a contract*)
pact·us -a -um *pp* of **paciscor** and of **pango**; *n* pact, contract, agreement; way, manner; **aliquo pacto** somehow; **hoc pacto** in this way; **in pacto manere** to stick to the agreement; **quo pacto** how, in what way
Pācuv·ius -iī or **-ī** *m* Roman tragic poet, native of Brundisium, and nephew of Ennius (*c.* 220-130 B.C.)
Pad·us -ī *m* Po River (*in N. Italy*)
pae·ān -ānis *m* epithet of Apollo as the god of healing; paean, hymn of praise, victory song
paedagōg·ium -iī or **-ī** *n* training school for pages
paedagōg·us -ī *m* slave in charge of school children; (fig) guide, leader
paedic·ō -āre *vt* to have abnormal relations with (*young boys*)
paed·or -ōris *m* filth
pael·ex -icis *f* concubine, mistress
paelicāt·us -ūs *m* concubinage
Paelign·ī -ōrum *m pl* a people of central Italy
paenē *adv* almost, nearly
paeninsŭl·a -ae *f* peninsula
paenitend·us -a -um *adj* regrettable
paenitenti·a -ae *f* repentance, regret
paenit·ĕō -ēre -ŭī *vt* to cause to regret; to displease; *vi* (with *genit*) to regret; *v impers* (with *acc* of person), e.g., **me paenitet** I am sorry; (with *acc* of person and *genit* of thing), e.g., **me paenitet consili** I regret the plan, I am dissatisfied with the plan; (with *acc* of person and *inf* or **quod**), e.g., **eos paenitet animum tuum offendisse** or **eos paenitet quod animum tuum offenderint** they regret having offended your feelings
paenŭl·a -ae *f* traveling coat; raincoat
paenulāt·us -a -um *adj* wearing a traveling coat
pae·ōn -ōnis *m* metrical foot con-

taining one long and three short syllables
paeōni·us -a -um *adj* healing, medicinal
Paest·um -ī *n* town in Lucania in S. Italy
paetŭl·us -a -um *adj* slightly squint-eyed
paet·us -a -um *adj* squinting, squint-eyed; leering
pāgān·us -a -um *adj* of a village, rustic; ignorant, untaught; *m* villager, peasant; (as term of contempt) yokel
Pagăs·a -ae *f* or **Pagăs·ae -ārum** *f pl* town on the coast of Thessaly, from which the Argonauts sailed
Pagasae·us -a -um *adj* Pagasaean; *m* Jason
pāgātim *adv* by villages, in every village
pāgell·a -ae *f* small page
pāgĭn·a -ae *f* page (*of book*)
pāginŭl·a -ae *f* small page
pāg·us -ī *m* village; canton, province; country people, villagers
pāl·a -ae *f* spade
palaestr·a -ae *f* palaestra, wrestling school, gymnasium; school of rhetoric; rhetorical training; school; wrestling; exercise; brothel
palaestrĭcē *adv* as at the palaestra
palaestrĭc·us -a -um *adj* of the palaestra, gymnastic; *f* gymnastics
palaestrīt·a -ae *m* professional wrestler; director of a palaestra
palam *adv* openly, publicly, plainly; **palam esse** to be public, be well known; **palam facere** to make public, disclose; *prep* (with *abl*) before, in the presence of, face to face with
Palātīn·us -a -um *adj* Palatine; imperial
Palāt·ium -iī or **-ī** *n* Palatine Hill (*residential area of distinguished Romans and several Roman emperors*); palace
palāt·um -ī *n* or **palāt·us -ī** *m* palate; taste; literary taste
palĕ·a -ae *f* chaff
paleār·ia -ium *n pl* dewlap
Pal·ēs -is *f* Italic goddess of shepherds and flocks
Palīc·ī -ōrum *m pl* twin sons of Jupiter and the nymph Thalia
Palīl·is -e *adj* of Pales; *n pl* festival of Pales celebrated on April 21st
palimpsest·us -ī *m* palimpsest
Palinūr·us -ī *m* pilot of Aeneas who fell overboard and drowned; promontory named after him
paliūr·us -ī *m* Christ's thorn (*plant*)
pall·a -ae *f* ladies' long robe; outer garment, mantle; tragic actor's costume
Palladi·us -a -um *adj* of Pallas; *n* statue of Pallas, Palladium
Pall·as -ădis or **-ădos** *f* Athene; olive oil, oil; olive tree; Palladium (*Trojan statue of Pallas*)
pall·ens -entis *adj* pale, sallow; grey-green, yellow-green, chartreuse, yellowish, sickly-looking
pall·ĕō -ēre -ŭī *vi* to be pale, look pale; to be yellow, look yellow; to change color, fade; (with *dat*) to grow pale over, worry about
pall·escō -escĕre -ŭī *vt* to turn pale at; *vi* to turn pale; to turn yellow; to fade
palliāt·us -a -um *adj* wearing a Greek cloak; **fabula palliata** Latin play with Greek setting and characters
pallidŭl·us -a -um *adj* somewhat pale
pallĭd·us -a -um *adj* pale, sallow; grey-green, yellow-green, chartreuse
palliolātim *adv* in a mantle
palliolāt·us -a -um *adj* wearing a short mantle, wearing a hood
palliŏl·um -ī *n* short cloak; cape, hood
pall·ium -iī or **-ī** *n* coverlet, cover; Greek cloak
pall·or -ōris *m* paleness, pallor; **pallorem ducere** to turn pale
pallŭl·a -ae *f* short cloak
palm·a -ae *f* palm of the hand, hand; palm tree, date; palm branch, palm wreath; palm of victory, prize, victory, honor, distinction; blade of an oar
palmār·is -e *adj* excellent, deserving the palm or prize
palmāri·us -a -um *adj* prize-winning, excellent; *n* masterpiece
palmāt·us -a -um *adj* embroidered with palm branches; **tunica palmata** palm-embroidered tunic (*worn by a general*)
palm·es -ĭtis *m* vine sprout, vine branch; branch, bough
palmēt·um -ī *n* palm grove
palmĭf·er -ĕra -ĕrum *adj* palm-growing, full of palm trees
palmōs·us -a -um *adj* full of palm trees
palmŭl·a -ae *f* oar blade
pāl·or -ārī -ātus sum *vi* to roam about, wander aimlessly
palpāti·ō -ōnis *f* stroking; *f pl* flattering
palpāt·or -ōris *m* flatterer
palpĕbr·a -ae *f* eyelid
palpĭt·ō -āre *vi* to throb, palpitate, quiver
palp·ō -āre or **palp·or -ārī -ātus sum** *vt* to stroke, pat; to wheedle, coax; to flatter; *vi* (with *dat*) **a** to coax; **b** to flatter
palp·us -ī *m* palm of the hand; coaxing
palūdāment·um -ī *n* military coat; general's coat
palūdāt·us -a -um *adj* wearing a general's coat
palūdōs·us -a -um *adj* swampy, marshy
palumb·ēs -is *m* or *f* pigeon, dove
pāl·us -ī *m* stake, post; wooden post used in sword practice

pal·ūs -ūdis *f* swamp, marsh; sedge
palust·er -ris -re *adj* swampy, marshy, in the swamps
pampinĕ·us -a -um *adj* of vine tendrils, made of vine leaves; **odor pampineus** bouquet of wines
pampin·us -ī *m* vine shoot, tendril; vine leaf; tendril (*of any plant*)
Pān Pānos *m* Pan (*Greek god of flocks, shepherds, and woods, often identified with Faunus*)
panacē·a -ae *f* or **panăc·es -is** *n* panacea
Panaetōlic·us -a -um *adj* Pan-Aetolian
pānār·ium -iī or **-ī** *n* bread basket
Panchāi·a -ae *f* region in Arabia famous for its frankincense
panchrest·us or **panchrist·us -a -um** *adj* good for everything, universally useful
pancraticē *adv* (coll) fine, splendidly; **pancratice valere** to get along splendidly
pancrat·ium or **pancrat·ion -iī** or **-ī** *n* contest which included both boxing and wrestling
Pandăr·us -ī *m* famous Lycian archer in the Trojan army; companion of Aeneas, killed by Turnus
pandicŭl·or -ārī -ātus sum *vi* to stretch oneself
Pandī·ōn -ōnis *m* king of Athens and father of Procne and Philomela
Pandīoni·us -a -um *adj* of Pandion
pandō pandĕre pandī pansum or **passum** *vt* to spread out, extend, expand, unfold; to open, lay open, throw open; to reveal, make known, publish
pand·us -a -um *adj* crooked, bent, curved
pangō pangĕre panxī or **pepĕgī -pactum** *vt* to fasten, fix, drive in; to fix, settle, agree upon, determine; to write, compose, celebrate, record; to promise in marriage; **indutias pangere** (with **cum** + *abl*) to conclude an armistice with
pānicē·us -a -um *adj* made of bread; **milites panicei** (coll) Breadville brigade
pānicŭl·a -ae *f* tuft
pānic·um -ī *n* millet
pān·is -is *m* bread, loaf; **panis cibarius** coarse bread; **panis secundus** stale bread
Pānisc·us -ī *m* little Pan
pannicŭl·us -ī *m* rag
Pannoni·us -a -um *adj* Pannonian; *f* Pannonia (*country on the Danube*)
pannōs·us -a -um *adj* tattered, ragged; shriveled, wrinkled, sad-looking
pannūcē·us or **pannūci·us -a -um** *adj* ragged; shriveled, wrinkled
pann·us -ī *m* patch; rag
Panŏp·ē -ēs or **Panopē·a -ae** *f* a sea nymph
pans·a -ae *masc & fem adj* flat-footed, splayfooted
pansus *pp of* **pando**
panthēr·a -ae *f* panther
Panthoid·ēs -ae *m* Euphorbus (*Trojan warrior*)
Panth·us -ī *m* priest of Apollo at Troy and father of Euphorbus
pantic·ēs -um *m pl* bowels; sausages
papae *interj* great!, wonderful!
pāp·as -ae or **-ătis** *m* tutor
papāv·er -ĕris *n* poppy
papāverĕ·us -a -um *adj* of poppies
Paphi·ē -ēs *f* Venus
Paphi·us -a -um *adj* Paphian, of Paphos
Paph·os -ī *f* town in Cyprus sacred to Venus
pāpili·ō -ōnis *m* butterfly
papill·a -ae *f* nipple, teat; breast
papp·ō -āre *vi* to eat baby food, eat pap
papp·us -ī *m* hairy seed (*of certain plants*)
papŭl·a -ae *f* pimple
papȳrĭf·er -ĕra -ĕrum *adj* papyrus-producing
papȳr·us -ī *m & f* or **papȳr·um -ī** *n* papyrus; paper; garment (*made of papyrus*)
pār paris *adj* equal, like, on a par, equally matched, well matched; suitable, adequate; of equal size; (with *dat* or **cum** + *abl*) equal to, comparable to, similar to, as large as; (with limiting *abl*, **ad** + *acc*, or **in** + *abl*) equal, similar, alike in; **par est** it is right, it is proper; **par proelium** indecisive battle; **ut par est** (used parenthetically) as is only right; *m* companion, comrade; equal; mate, spouse; **pares cum paribus facillime congregantur** birds of a feather flock together; *n* pair, couple; the like; **par pari** like for like, tit for tat
parābil·is -e *adj* available
parasīt·a -ae *f* parasite (*female*)
parasītast·er -rī *m* poor parasite
parasītāti·ō -ōnis *f* sponging
parasītic·us -a -um *adj* parasitical
parasīt·or -ārī -ātus sum *vi* to sponge, freeload, be a parasite
parasīt·us -ī *m* parasite, sponger, freeloader
parātē *adv* with preparation; carefully; readily, promptly
parāti·ō -ōnis *f* preparing, procuring, acquisition
paratragoed·ō -āre *vi* to talk in a tragic style, be melodramatic
parāt·us -a -um *adj* prepared, ready; well prepared, furnished, equipped; learned, well versed, skilled; (with *dat* or **ad** + *acc*) **a** ready for; **b** equipped to; (with *inf*) prepared to, ready to; (with *abl* or **in** + *abl*) versed in, experienced in
parāt·us -ūs *m* preparation, provision, equipment, outfit; clothing, apparel
Parc·a -ae *f* goddess of Fate, Fate
parcē *adv* sparingly, thriftily; moderately, with restraint; stingily; rarely, seldom

parceprōm·us -ī *m* stingy person
parcō parcĕre pepercī parsum *vt* to spare, use sparingly; *vi* to be sparing, economize; (with *dat*) **a** to spare, use carefully; **b** to show mercy to; **c** to abstain from, refrain from; **d** to refuse (*help*); (with *inf*) to cease, stop (*e.g., doing, talking*)
parc·us -a -um *adj* thrifty, economical, frugal; niggardly, stingy; moderate, conservative; slight, little, scanty, paltry (*thing given*)
pard·us -ī *m* panther
par·ens -entis *adj* obedient; *m* parent, father; ancestor, grandparent; founder, inventor; *m pl* subjects; ancestors; *f* parent, mother
parentāl·is -e *adj* parental; **dies parentalis** memorial day; *n pl* festival in honor of dead ancestors and relatives
parent·ō -āre *vi* to hold memorial service in honor of dead parents or relatives; (with *dat*) **a** to offer sacrifice to (*the dead*); **b** to avenge (*a dead person*) with the death of another person; **c** to appease, satisfy
pār·ĕō -ēre -ŭī *vi* to appear, be visible, be evident, be at hand; (with *dat*) **a** to obey, be obedient to, comply with, be subject to, be subservient to; **b** to yield to, gratify, satisfy (*pleasures, etc.*); **c** to fulfill (*promises*)
pari·ēs -ĕtis *m* wall (*esp. partition in a house or building*)
parietīn·ae -ārum *f pl* tumbled-down walls; ruins; (fig) ruins
Parīl·ia -ium *n pl* festival of Pales (*celebrated on April 21st*)
parĭl·is -e *adj* equal, like; **aetas parilis** same age, like age
pariō parĕre pepĕrī partum *vt* to bear, bring forth, give birth to; (of animals) to lay, spawn, produce; (fig) to produce, create, devise, cause, effect, accomplish, acquire, obtain
Par·is -ĭdis *m* son of Priam and Hecuba, also called Alexandros; famous pantomime actor in the reign of Nero; famous pantomime actor in the reign of Domitian, the freedman of Domitia
parĭter *adv* equally, in like manner, as well, alike; at the same time, simultaneously, together, at once; **pariter ac** (or **atque**), **pariter ut** as well as; **pariter ac si** just as if; **pariter** (with **cum** + *abl*) together with, at the same time as
parĭt·ō -āre *vt* (with *inf*) to get ready to
Pari·us -a -um *adj & mf* Parian
parm·a -ae *f* small round shield; shield
parmāt·us -a -um *adj* armed with a shield, light-armed
parmŭl·a -ae *f* small shield
Parnās·is -ĭdis or **Parnāsĭ·us -a -um** *adj* of Parnassus, Parnassian
Parnās·us or **Parnās·os -ī** *m* mountain in Phocis, in central Greece, sacred to Apollo and the Muses, on whose slopes Delphi was located
par·ō -āre *vt* to prepare, make ready, provide, furnish; to get, procure, acquire, gather, purchase; **se parare** to prepare oneself, get ready; *vi* to get ready, make preparations, make arrangements; (with *dat* or **ad** + *acc*) to get ready for
parŏch·a -ae *f* room and board (*required of provincials for traveling Roman officials*)
parŏch·us -ī *m* official host (*local official who provided accommodations for traveling Roman dignitaries*); host
parops·is -ĭdis *f* dish, dessert dish
Par·os or **Par·us -ī** *f* island of the Cyclades, famous for its white marble
parr·a -ae *f* owl
Parrhăs·is -ĭdis *f* Arcadian woman; Callisto
Parrhasĭ·us -a -um *adj* Arcadian; **Parrhasia virgo** Callisto; *f* district in Arcadia
parricīd·a -ae *m* or *f* parricide (*murder of a parent or close relative*); assassin of a high magistrate; murderer, assassin; traitor, outlaw, criminal
parricīd·ium -iī or **-ī** *n* parricide (*murderer of a parent or close relative*); murder, assassination; treason, high treason
par·s -tis *f* part, portion, share, section, fraction; side, direction, region; part, function, duty; part of body, member (*esp. genital organs*); *f pl* part, role, character; political party; **ab omni parte** in all respects; **ex altera parte** on the other hand; **ex magna parte** to a great extent; **ex parte** partly; **in eam partem** in that direction; in that sense; in such a manner; **in perjorem partem rapere** to put a worse construction on; **in utramque partem** in both directions; **major pars populi** the majority; **maximam partem** for the most part; **minor pars populi** the minority; **omnibus partibus** in all respects; **pars . . . pars, pars . . . alii** some . . . others; **parte** in part, partly; **pro mea parte** to the best of my abilities; **tres partes** three fourths
parsimōnĭ·a -ae *f* parsimony
parsus *pp* of **parco**
parthenĭc·ē -ēs *f* parthenium (*plant*)
Parthenopae·us -ī *m* son of Meleager and Atalanta and one of the Seven who fought against Thebes
Parthenŏp·ē -ēs *f* one of the Sirens, after whom Naples was originally named
Parthĭ·a -ae *f* Parthia (*country located S.E. of the Caspian*)
Parthĭc·us -a -um *adj* Parthian
Parth·us -a -um *adj & m* Parthian

partic·eps -ipis *adj* (with *genit*) sharing in, taking part in; *m* partner, confederate
particip·ō -āre *vt* to make (*someone*) a partner; to share (*something*)
particŭl·a -ae *f* bit, particle, grain
partim *adv* partly, in part, to some extent; for the most part, mostly; (with *genit* or **ex** + *abl*) some of; **partim . . . partim** some . . . others
parti·ō -ōnis *f* bringing forth, producing
part·iō -īre -īvī or **-iī -ītum** or **part·ior -īrī -ītus sum** *vt* to share, distribute, apportion, divide
partītē *adv* with proper divisions, methodically
partīti·ō -ōnis *f* division, distribution, sharing; division of a speech
partitūd·ō -inis *f* bearing (*of young*)
partur·iō -īre -īvī or **-iī** *vt* to teem with; to be ready to produce; to bring forth, yield; (fig) to brood over; *vi* to be in labor
partus *pp* of **pario;** *adj* acquired; *n* acquisition, gain, store
part·us -ūs *m* birth; young, offspring; (fig) beginnings
parum *adv* a little, too little, insufficiently; **parum est** it is not enough, it does not suffice; **parum habere** to regard as unsatisfactory; **satis eloquentiae sapientiae parum** enough eloquence but too little wisdom
parumper *adv* for a little while, a moment; **operire parumper** wait a moment
parvit·ās -ātis *f* smallness
parvŭl·us or **parvŏl·us -a -um** *adj* tiny; slight, petty; young; *n* childhood, infancy; **ab parvulis** from childhood, from infancy
parv·us -a -um (*comp* **minor;** *superl* **minimus**) *adj* small, little, puny; short; young; brief, short (*time*); small, insignificant, unimportant; low, cheap (*price*); *n* a little, trifle; childhood, infancy; **a parvis** or **a parvo** from childhood, from infancy; **parvi esse** to be of little importance; **parvi facere, aestimare, habere,** or **ducere** to think little of, care little for; **parvi refert** it makes little difference, it matters little
pasceŏl·us -ī *m* money bag
pascō pascĕre pāvī pastum *vt* to feed, pasture, keep, raise (*animals*); to cultivate, cherish; to feed (*flames, passions*); to pile up (*debts*); to grow (*beard*); to lay waste, ravage (*fields*); to feast, gratify (*the eyes*); to cherish (*hope*)
pascor pascī pastus sum *vi* to graze, browse, be fed; (with *abl*) **a** to graze on; **b** (fig) to feed on, feast on, thrive on
pascŭ·us -a -um *adj* grazing, pasture; *n* pasture
Pāsiphă·ē -ēs or **Pāsiphă·a -ae** *f* daughter of Helios, sister of Circe, husband of Minos, and mother of Androgeos, Ariadne, Phaedra, and the Minotaur
pass·er -ĕris *m* sparrow; plaice, flounder; **passer marinus** ostrich
passercŭl·us -ī *m* little sparrow
passim *adv* here and there, all over, at random; without order, indiscriminately, promiscuously
passus *pp* of **pando** and of **patior;** *adj* spread out, extended, open; disheveled; dried, dry; *n* wine made from dried grapes, raisin wine
pass·us -ūs *m* step, pace; footstep, track; **mille passūs** mile; **tria milia passuum** three miles
pastill·us -ī *m* lozenge
pasti·ō -ōnis *f* pasture, grazing
past·or -ōris *m* shepherd
pastorāl·is -e *adj* shepherd's, pastoral
pastōrici·us or **pastōri·us -a -um** *adj* shepherd's, pastoral
pastus *pp* of **pasco**
past·us -ūs *m* pasture, fodder, food; (fig) food
patagiār·ius -iī or **-ī** *m* fringe maker
patagiāt·us -a -um *adj* (tunic) with fringes
Patăr·a -ae *f* town in Lycia with an oracle of Apollo
Patăr·eus -ĕī or **-ĕos** *m* Apollo
Patavīn·us -a -um *adj* of Patavium
Patav·ium -iī or **-ī** *n* city in N. Italy, the birthplace of Livy (*modern Padua*)
pate-faciō -facĕre -fēcī -factus (passive; **pate·fīō -fiĕrī**) *vt* to throw open; to open up, make accessible; to bring to light
patefacti·ō -ōnis *f* disclosure
patell·a -ae *f* pan, dish, plate
pat·ens -entis *adj* open, accessible; extensive; exposed; evident
patentius *adv* more openly, more clearly
pat·ĕō -ēre -ŭī *vi* to stand open, be open; to be accessible; to be exposed; to open, stretch out, extend; to be clear, be plain, be well known; to be accessible, be attainable, be free; (of the mind) to be open, be receptive
pat·er -ris *m* father; **pater cenae** host; **pater familias** head of the household, head of the family; *m pl* forefathers; senators
patĕr·a -ae *f* flat dish (*used esp. in making libations*)
pat·erfamiliās -risfamiliās *m* head of the household, head of the family
patern·us -a -um *adj* father's, paternal; ancestral; of a native country, native
pat·escō -escĕre -ŭī *vi* to be opened, be open; to stretch out, extend; to be disclosed, be divulged, become evident
pathic·us -a -um *adj* lustful
patibĭl·is -e *adj* tolerable, endurable; sensitive

patibulāt·us -a -um *adj* gibbeted; wearing a yoke
patibŭl·um -ī *m* fork-shaped yoke (*tied around the neck of a criminal*); fork-shaped gibbet
pati·ens -entis *adj* hardy, tough; hard; stubborn, unyielding, patient, tolerant; (with *genit* or **ad** + *acc*) able to endure, inured to, able to take; **amnis patiens navium** navigable river
patienter *adv* patiently
patientĭ·a -ae *f* patience, endurance; resignation, forbearance; submissiveness; sexual submission
patĭn·a -ae *f* dish, pan
patinārĭ·us -a -um *adj* of pans; in a pan; **strues patinaria** pile of dishes
patĭor pātī passus sum *vt* to experience, undergo, suffer; to put up with, allow; to submit to sexually; **aequo animo pati** to suffer patiently; **aegre pati** to resent, be displeased with
patrāt·or -ōris *m* perpetrator
patrāt·us *adj masc* **pater patratus** plenipotentiary
patrĭ·a -ae *f* native land, native city, home
patrĭcē *adv* paternally
patricĭ·us -a -um *adj* of patrician status, patrician; *m pl* patricians, patrician class
patrīmōn·ĭum -ĭī or **-ī** *n* patrimony, inheritance
patrĭm·us -a -um *adj* having a father living
patriss·ō -āre *vi* to take after one's father
patrīt·us -a -um *adj* father's, inherited from one's father
patrĭ·us -a -um *adj* father's, of a father, fatherly, paternal; ancestral, traditional, heriditary; native; *f* see **patria**
patr·ō -āre *vt* to bring about, effect, achieve, accomplish, perform, finish, conclude; **bellum patrare** to bring the war to an end; **jus jurandum patrare** to take an oath (*confirming a treaty*); **pacem patrare** to conclude a peace
patrōcin·ĭum -ĭī or **-ī** *n* patronage, protection, legal defense, legal representation
patrōcĭn·or -ārī -ātus sum *vi* to be a patron, afford protection; (with *dat*) to serve (*someone*) as patron, protect, defend
Patrŏcl·us -ī *m* son of Menoetius and friend of Achilles, who wearing the armor of Achilles, was killed by Hector
patrōn·a -ae *f* legal protectress, patroness; advocate; defender, safeguard
patrōn·us -ī *m* legal protector, patron; advocate (*in court*); defender
patruēl·is -e *adj* of or descended from a father's brother, cousin's; *m* cousin
patrŭ·us -a -um *adj* uncle's; *m* (paternal) uncle
patŭl·us -a -um *adj* open, standing open; spreading, spread out, broad
pauciloqu·ĭum -ĭī or **-ī** *n* reticence
paucĭt·ās -ātis *f* paucity, scarcity, small number
paucŭl·ī -ae -a *adj* just a few, very few; *n pl* few words
pauc·us -a -um *adj* few, little; *pron masc pl* few, a few; the select few, elite; **inter paucos (paucas)** or **in paucis** especially; *pron neut pl* a few things, a few words; **paucis** in a few words, briefly
paulātim *adv* little by little, gradually, by degrees; a few at a time
paulisper *adv* for a little while
paulō *adv* (as *abl* of degree of difference in expressions of comparison) by a little, a little, somewhat; **paulo antea** a little before; **paulo post** a little later
paulŭlō *adv* somewhat, a little; cheaply, at a low price
paulŭlum *adv* somewhat, a little
paulŭl·us -a -um *adj* very little; *n* a bit; **paululum pecuniae** a bit of money
paulum *adv* a little, to some extent, to some degree
paul·us -a -um *adj* small, little; *n* bit, trifle; **post paulum** after a bit, after a while
Paul·us -ī *m* L. Aemilius Paulus (*conqueror of Macedonia through the victory at Pydna in* 168 B.C.)
paup·er -ĕris *adj* poor; scanty, meager; (with *genit*) poor in; *m* poor man, pauper
paupercŭl·us -a -um *adj* poor
pauperĭ·ēs -ēī *f* poverty
paupĕr·ō -āre *vt* to impoverish; (with *abl*) to rob (*someone*) of
paupert·ās -ātis *f* poverty
paus·a -ae *f* pause, stop, end
pausĭ·a -ae *f* plump olive
pauxillātim *adv* bit by bit, little by little
pauxillisper *adv* by degrees
pauxillŭlum *adv* a little, a bit
pauxillŭl·us -a -um *adj* very little, tiny; *n* bit
pauxillum *adv* a little, a bit
pauxill·us -a -um *adj* very little, tiny; *n* small amount
pavefact·us -a -um *adj* frightened, scared
pavĕō pavēre pāvī *vt* to be scared of; *vi* to be terrified, tremble, or shiver with fear
pavesc·ō -ĕre *vt* to get scared of; *vi* to begin to be alarmed
pavĭdē *adv* in panic
pavĭd·us -a -um *adj* panicky, alarmed, shivering or trembling with fear, startled; with beating heart, nervous; causing alarm
pavīment·ō -āre *vt* to pave
pavīment·um -ī *n* pavement; floor
pav·ĭō -īre -īvī or **-ĭī -ītum** *vt* to strike, beat

pavit·ō -āre *vt* to be panicky over; *vi* to quake with fear, be scared to death; to shiver (*with fever*)
pāv·ō -ōnis *m* peacock
pav·or -ōris *m* panic, terror, dismay, quaking, shivering; **pavorem injicere** (with *dat*) to throw the fear of the Lord into, to terrify
pax pācis *f* peace; peace treaty, reconciliation, compact, agreement; harmony, tranquility; favor, pardon (*from the gods*); **pace tua** with your permission, with your leave
pecc·ans -antis *m* offender, sinner
peccāt·um -ī *n* fault, mistake, slip, transgression, sin
pecc·ō -āre *vi* to make a mistake, commit a fault, sin
pecorōs·us -a -um *adj* rich in cattle
pect·en -inis *m* comb; plectrum (*for strumming a lyre*); scallop (*sea food*)
pectō pectĕre pexī pexum *vt* to comb; to card (*wool*); (coll) to clobber (*with stick or fist*)
pect·us -ŏris *n* breast; heart, feeling; soul, conscience, mind, understanding; character, person
pecū (*genit* not in use) *n* flock; *n pl* cattle; pastures
pecuārĭ·us -a -um *adj* of sheep, of cattle; **res pecuaria** livestock; *m* cattle man, cattle breeder, rancher; *f* livestock; *n pl* herds of cattle, herds of sheep
pecūlāt·or -ōris *m* embezzler
pecūlāt·us -ūs *m* embezzlement
pecūliār·is -e *adj* one's own, as one's own private property; special
pecūliāt·us -a -um *adj* rich, well off
pecūlĭ·ō -āre *vt* to give away for good
pecūliōs·us -a -um *adj* owning private property
pecūl·ium -iī or **-ī** *n* small savings (*esp. accumulated by slaves*); private property
pecūnĭ·a -ae *f* money; **pecunia praesens** ready cash
pecūniārĭ·us -a -um *adj* pecuniary, financial, money
pecūniōs·us -a -um *adj* rich, wealthy, loaded with money; profitable, bringing in money
pec·us -ŏris *n* cattle, herd, flock; sheep; head of cattle; **pecus equinum** stud; (as term of scorn) cattle
pec·us -ŭdis *f* head of cattle; beast; sheep; domestic animal; land animal (*as opposed to birds*); (as term of abuse) brute, beast, swine
pedāl·is -e *adj* one-foot-long
pedār·ius -iī or **-ī** *m* inferior senator (*who let others step all over him*)
ped·es -itis *m* infantryman; pedestrian; infantry
pedest·er -ris -re *adj* infantry; pedestrian; on land, by land; written in prose; prosaic, plain
pedetemptim *adv* by feeling one's way, step by step, slowly, cautiously
pedĭc·a -ae *f* foot chain; trap, snare
pedīculōs·us -a -um *adj* lousy
ped·is -is *m* or *f* louse
pedisĕqu·a -ae *f* attendant, handmaid
pedisĕqu·us -ī *m* footman, page, lackey
peditastell·us -ī *m* poor infantryman
peditāt·us -ūs *m* infantry
pēdĭt·um -ī *n* wind, gas
pēdō pēdĕre pepēdī *vi* to break wind
ped·um -ī *n* shepherd's hook
Pēgasē·us or **Pēgasei·us -a -um** *adj* of Pegasus, Pegasean
Pēgasĭd·es -um *f pl* Muses
Pēgăs·us -ī *m* winged horse which sprang from the blood of Medusa and whose hoof, as it hit Mt. Helicon, caused Hippocrene, a fountain dear to the Muses, to flow
pegm·a -ătis *n* bookcase; scaffolding
pējerātiuncŭl·a -ae *f* petty oath
pējerāt·us or **pējurāt·us -a -um** *adj* offended by false oaths; **jus pejeratum** false oath
pējĕr·ō or **perjūr·ō -āre** *vt* to swear falsely by; *vi* to swear a false oath; (coll) to lie
pējerōs·us -a -um *adj* perjured
pēj·or -us (*comp* of **malus**) *adj* worse
pējus (*comp* of **male**) *adv* worse
pelagĭ·us -a -um *adj* of the sea
pelăg·us -ī *n* sea, open sea
pēlăm·is -idis or **pēlăm·ys -ydis** *f* young tuna fish
Pelasg·ī -ōrum *m pl* aborigines of Greece
Pēl·eus -ĕī or **-ĕos** *m* king of Thessaly, son of Aeacus, husband of Thetis, and father of Achilles
Pelĭ·ās -ae *m* king of Iolcos in Thessaly and uncle of Jason
Pēlīd·ēs -ae *m* descendant of Peleus; Achilles; Neoptolemus
Pēlĭ·on -ī *n* mountain in E. Thessaly
Pēlĭ·us or **Pēliăc·us -a -um** *adj* of Mt. Pelion
Pell·a -ae or **Pell·ē -ēs** *f* city of Macedonia and birthplace of Alexander the Great
pellācĭ·a -ae *f* charm, allurement
Pellae·us -a -um *adj* of or from Apella; **Pellaeus juvenis** Alexander
pell·ax -ācis *adj* seductive, alluring
pellectĭ·ō -ōnis *f* perusal
pel·liciō -licĕre -lexī -lectum *vt* to allure, entice, coax, wheedle
pellicŭl·a -ae *f* small hide, skin, fleece
pellĭ·ō -ōnis *m* furrier
pell·is -is *f* skin, hide; leather; felt; tent; shield cover; **detrahere pellem** to expose one's true character
pellīt·us -a -um *adj* clothed in skins, wearing leather coat
pellō pellĕre pepŭlī pulsum *vt* to push, beat, strike, knock, hurl; to

drive out or away, expel, banish; to repel, drive back, rout; to play or strum (*lyre, etc.*); to affect, impress, move, strike; to stamp (*the earth*)
pelluc- = **perl-**
Pelopei·as -ădis or **Pelopē·is -ĭdis** *adj* Peloponnesian
Pelopei·us or **Pelopē·us -a -um** *adj* Pelopian; Mycenaean; Phrygian
Pelopĭd·ae -ārum *m pl* descendants of Pelops
Peloponnens·is -e *adj* Peloponnesian
Peloponnēsiăc·us or **Peloponnēsĭ·us -a -um** *adj* Peloponnesian
Peloponnēs·us -ī *f* the Peloponnesus (*modern Morea*)
Pel·ops -ŏpis *m* son of Tantalus, father of Atreus and Thyestes, and grandfather of Agamemnon and Menelaus
pelōr·is -ĭdis *f* large shellfish
Pelōr·us or **Pelōr·os -ī** *m* N.E. promontory of Sicily
pelt·a -ae *f* small leather shield
peltast·ēs or **peltast·a -ae** *m* soldier armed with a small leather shield
peltāt·us -a -um *adj* armed with a small leather shield
Pēlūs·ium -ĭī or **-ī** *n* city on the E. mouth of the Nile
pelv·is -is *f* bucket, basin
penārĭ·us -a -um *adj* food, supply, storage
Penāt·ēs -ium *m pl* Penates, household gods; hearth, home, house; cells (*of bees*)
penātĭg·er -ĕra -ĕrum *adj* carrying the household gods
pendĕō pendēre pependī *vi* to hang, hang down, be suspended; to hang loose; to hang down, be flabby, be weak; to depend, be dependent; to be in suspense, be uncertain, hesitate; to hang around, loiter; to hang in the air, be suspended, hover, float, overhang; (with *abl* or with **ab, de** or **ex** + *abl*) **a** to hang down from, hang by; **b** to depend on, be dependent upon; **c** to hang on to, be devoted to; (with **in** + *abl*) to be poised on, hover in, hover over
pendō pendĕre pependī pensum *vt* to weigh, weigh out; to pay, pay out; to weigh, ponder, consider, value, esteem; to pay (*penalty*); **flocci pendere** to think little of; **magni pendere** to think much of, value highly; *vi* to weigh, have weight
pendŭl·us -a -um *adj* hanging, hanging down; doubtful, uncertain
Pēnē·is -ĭdis or **Pēnēĭ·us -a -um** *adj* of Peneus
Pēnelŏp·a -ae or **Pēnelŏp·ē -ēs** *f* daughter of Icarius and Periboea and wife of Ulysses
penes *prep* (with *acc* of person only) in the possession of, in the power of, belonging to, resting with; at the house of, with; **penes se esse** to be in one's senses
penetrābĭl·is -e *adj* penetrating, piercing; penetrable
penetrāl·is -e *adj* penetrating, piercing; inner, internal, interior; *n pl* the interior, center; inner chambers; sanctuary; the interior, hinterlands
penĕtr·ō -āre *vt & vi* to penetrate, enter
Pēnē·us -a -um *adj* of Peneus, of the Peneus River; *m* Peneus River (*largest river in Thessaly*); river god, the father of Cyrene and Daphne
pēnicill·us -ī *m* paint brush, pencil
pēnicŭl·us -ī *m* brush; sponge
pēn·is -is *m* tail; penis; lechery
penĭtē *adv* inwardly
penĭtus *adv* internally, inside, deep within, deeply; from within; thoroughly, completely, through and through; heartily
penĭt·us -a -um *adj* inner, inward
penn·a -ae *f* feather; wing; flight
pennāt·us -a -um *adj* feathered
pennĭg·er -ĕra -ĕrum *adj* winged, feathered
pennipŏt·ens -entis *adj* winged, able to fly
pennŭl·a -ae *f* little wing
pensĭl·is -e *adj* hanging; **uva pensilis** grape hung out to dry
pensĭ·ō -ōnis *f* payment, instalment
pensĭt·ō -āre *vt* to pay; to weigh, ponder, consider; *vi* to be taxable
pens·ō -āre *vt* to weigh out; to weigh, ponder, consider, examine; to compare, contrast; to pay, atone for; to repay, compensate, requite
pens·um -ī *n* work quota; duty, task; consideration, scruple; **pensi esse** to be of value, be of importance; **pensi habere** to value, consider of importance
pensus *pp* of **pendo**
pentēr·is -is *f* galley, quinquereme
Penthesilē·a -ae *f* Amazon, warrior queen who was killed by Achilles at Troy
Penth·eus -ĕī or **-ĕos** *m* king of Thebes, son of Echion and Agave, grandson of Cadmus, and opponent of the Bacchic cult
pen·um -ī *n* supplies, provisions, food
pēnūrĭ·a -ae *f* want, need, dearth
pen·us -ūs or **-ī** *m* or **pen·us -ŏris** *n* supplies, provisions, food
pepl·um -ī *n* or **pepl·us -ī** *m* robe for the statue of Athena
per *prep* (with *acc*) (of space) through, throughout, all over, along; (of time) through, during, for, in the course of, at, at the time of; (of agency) through, by, by means of, at the hands of; (of means or manner) through, by, under pretense of; for the sake of, with a view to; (in oath) by
pēr·a -ae *f* wallet
perabsurd·us -a -um *adj* completely absurd

peraccommodāt·us -a -um *adj* very convenient
perāc·er -ris -re *adj* very sharp
peracerb·us -a -um *adj* very harsh, very sour
perac·escō -escĕre -ŭī *vi* to become completely sour
peractī·ō -ōnis *f* conclusion, last act (*of a play*)
peractus *pp* of **perago**
peracūtē *adv* very acutely
peracūt·us -a -um *adj* very sharp; very clear (*voice, intellect*)
peradulesc·ens -entis *adj* very young
peradulescentŭl·us -ī *m* very young man
peraequē *adv* quite evenly, uniformly
peragĭt·ō -āre *vt* to harass
per·ăgō -agĕre -ēgī -actum *vt* to carry through to the end, complete, accomplish; to pierce; to travel through; to harass, disturb, trouble; to describe, relate, go over; to work over, till, cultivate; to deliver (*speech*); (law) to prosecute to a conviction
peragrātī·ō -ōnis *f* traveling
perăgr·ō -āre *vt* to travel through, travel, traverse; *vi* (fig) to spread, penetrate
peralt·us -a -um *adj* very high
perăm·ans -antis *adj* (with *genit*) very fond of
peramanter *adv* very lovingly
perambŭl·ō -āre *vt* to travel, traverse, walk through
peramoen·us -a -um *adj* very pleasant, very charming
perampl·us -a -um *adj* very large, very spacious
perangustē *adv* very narrowly
perangust·us -a -um *adj* very narrow
perantīqu·us -a -um *adj* very ancient, very old
perapposĭt·us -a -um *adj* very suitable
perardŭ·us -a -um *adj* very difficult
perargūt·us -a -um *adj* very clear; very sharp, very witty
perarmāt·us -a -um *adj* heavily armed
per·ărō -āre *vt* to plow through; to furrow; to write on (*a wax tablet*); to write
pērātim *adv* bag by bag
perattentē *adv* very attentively
perattent·us -a -um *adj* very attentive
peraudiend·us -a -um *adj* that must be heard to the end
perbacch·or -ārī -ātus sum *vt* to carouse through (*e.g., many days*)
perbeāt·us -a -um *adj* very happy
perbellē *adv* very prettily
perbĕne *adv* very well
perbenevŏl·us -a -um *adj* very friendly
perbenignē *adv* very kindly
perbĭb·ō -ĕre -ī *vt* to drink up, drink in, imbibe
perbīt·ō -ĕre *vi* to go to ruin
perbland·us -a -um *adj* very attractive, very charming
perbŏn·us -a -um *adj* very good, excellent
perbrĕv·is -e *adj* very short, very brief; **perbrevi** or **perbrevi tempore** in a very short time
perbreviter *adv* very briefly
perc·a -ae *f* perch
percalefact·us -a -um *adj* warmed through and through
percal·escō -escĕre -ŭī *vi* to become quite hot
percall·escō -escĕre -ŭī *vt* to become thoroughly versed in; *vi* to become very hardened
percār·us -a -um *adj* very dear, very costly; very dear, much loved
percaut·us -a -um *adj* very cautious
percelĕbr·or -ārī -ātus sum *vi* to be quite famous
percĕl·er -ĕris *adj* very quick
perceleriter *adv* very quickly
per·cellō -cellĕre -cŭlī -culsum *vt* to knock down, beat down, overthrow; to scare to death; to overthrow, ruin; to send scurrying; to hit hard
percens·ĕō -ēre -ŭī *vt* to count up; to review, survey; to travel through, traverse
perceptī·ō -ōnis *f* harvesting; comprehension; *f pl* concepts
percept·us -a -um *pp* of **percipio;** *n* precept, rule, doctrine
per·cīdō -cīdĕre -cīdī -cīsum *vt* to smash to pieces
percī·ĕō -ēre or **perc·īō -īre -īvī** or **-iī -ītum** *vt* to stir up, excite
per·cipĭō -cipĕre -cēpī -ceptum *vt* to get a good hold of; to catch; to occupy, seize; to gather in, harvest, reap; (of the senses) to take in, perceive, feel; (of feelings) to get hold of, get the better of; to learn, know, comprehend, understand, perceive
percĭt·us -a -um *pp* of **percieo;** *adj* aroused, provoked; impetuous, excitable
percoctus *pp* of **percoquo**
percŏl·ō -āre *vt* to strain, filter
per·cŏlō -colĕre -colŭī -cultum *vt* to reverence, revere, worship; to beautify; to crown, complete
percōm·is -e *adj* very courteous
percommŏdē *adv* very conveniently, very well, very suitably
percommŏd·us -a -um *adj* very convenient, very suitable
percontātī·ō -ōnis *f* thorough investigation
percontāt·or -ōris *m* inquisitive fellow
percont·or -ārī -ātus sum *vt* to question, investigate, interrogate; (with double *acc*) to ask (*someone something*)
percontŭm·ax -ācis *adj* very stubborn

per·cŏquō -coquĕre -coxī -coctum *vt* to cook through and through, cook thoroughly; to heat thoroughly; to ripen; to scorch, blacken
percrēb·escō or **percrēbr·escō -escĕre -ŭī** *vi* to become prevalent, be spread abroad
percrĕp·ō -āre -ŭī -ĭtum *vi* to resound, ring
percruci·or -ārī -ātus sum *vi* to torment oneself
perculsus *pp* of **percello**
percult·us -a -um *pp* of **percolo;** *adj* decked out; (coll) dolled up (*woman*)
percupĭd·us -a -um *adj* (with *genit*) very fond of
percup·ĭō -ĕre *vt* (with *inf*) to be eager to, desire very much to, be dying to
percūriōs·us -a -um *adj* very curious
percūr·ō -āre *vt* to heal completely
per·currō -currĕre -cucurrī or **currī -cursum** *vt* to run through, run along, run over, pass over, speed over; (fig) to scan briefly, look over; (in a speech) to treat in succession, go over, run over; (of feelings) to run through, penetrate, pierce; *vi* to run fast, hurry along; (with **ad** + *acc*) to dash to (*e.g., the Forum*); (with **per** + *acc*) **a** to run through or across, travel through; **b** (fig) to run through, mention quickly, treat in succession
percursātĭ·ō -ōnis *f* traveling; **percursatio Italiae** traveling through Italy
percursĭ·ō -ōnis *f* quick survey
percurs·ō -āre *vi* to roam about, range about
percussĭ·ō -ōnis *f* hitting, striking; snapping (*of fingers*); (mus) beat, time
percuss·or -ōris *m* assailant; assassin
percussus *pp* of **percutio**
percuss·us -ūs *m* beating, striking
per·cutĭō -cutĕre -cussī -cussum *vt* to beat or hit hard; to pierce, transfix, run through; to shoot, kill; to shock, impress, move, astound; to cut through; to dig (*ditch*); to coin, stamp (*money*); to cheat, trick
perdecōr·us -a -um *adj* very pretty
perdēlīr·us -a -um *adj* very silly, quite mad
perdeps·ō -ĕre -ŭī *vt* to knead thoroughly; (fig) to seduce
perdifficĭl·is -e *adj* very difficult
perdifficiliter *adv* with great difficulty
perdign·us -a -um *adj* (with *abl*) quite worthy of
perdīlĭg·ens -entis *adj* very diligent, very conscientious
perdīligenter *adv* very diligently, very conscientiously
per·discō -discĕre -didĭcī *vt* to learn thoroughly, learn by heart
perdisertē *adv* very eloquently
perdĭtē *adv* recklessly, desperately
perdĭt·or -ōris *m* destroyer
perdĭt·us -a -um *adj* ruined, lost; profligate, degenerate, infamous, reckless, incorrigible, hopeless
perdĭū *adv* for a very long time
perdĭūturn·us -a -um *adj* longlasting, protracted
perdīv·es -ĭtis *adj* very rich
perd·ix -īcis *m* partridge
per·dō -dĕre -dĭdī -dĭtum *vt* to wreck, ruin, destroy; to waste, squander; to lose
perdoc·ĕō -ēre -ŭī -tum *vt* to teach thoroughly
perdoctē *adv* very skillfully
perdoct·us -a -um *pp* of **perdoceo;** *adj* very learned, very skillful
perdol·escō -escĕre -ŭī *vi* to become resentful
perdŏm·ō -āre -ŭī -ĭtum *vt* to tame completely, subdue, subjugate
perdormisc·ō -ĕre *vi* to sleep on, keep on sleeping
per·dūcō -dūcĕre -duxī -ductum *vt* to lead, guide; to cover, spread; to prolong, drag out; to induce; to seduce; (with **ad** + *acc*) **a** to lead, bring, guide, escort to; **b** to build, run (*wall, ditch, road, etc.*) to; **c** to prolong, protract, drag out, continue (*something*) to or till; **d** to win over to, convince of
perduct·ō -āre *vt* to lead, conduct
perduct·or -ōris *m* guide; pimp
perdūdum *adv* long long ago
perduellĭ·ō -ōnis *f* treason, high treason
perduell·is -is *m* enemy
perdūr·ō -āre *vi* to hold out, last, endure
per·ĕdō -esse -ēdī -ēsum *vt* to eat up, devour
perĕgrē *adv* abroad, away from home; from abroad; **peregre abire** or **peregre exire** to go abroad
peregrīnābund·us -a -um *adj* traveling around
peregrīnātĭ·ō -ōnis *f* living abroad, travel, touring; roaming, ranging (*said of animals*)
peregrīnāt·or -ōris *m* traveler, wanderer
peregrīnĭt·ās -ātis *f* foreign manners, strange ways
peregrīn·or -ārī -ātus sum *vi* to live abroad, travel abroad, travel around; (fig) to be a stranger
peregrīn·us -a -um *adj* foreign, strange, alien, exotic; (fig) strange, inexperienced; **amores peregrini** love affairs with foreign women; **praetor peregrinus** praetor who tried cases involving foreigners and Roman citizens; **terror peregrinus** fear of a foreign enemy; *mf* foreigner, alien
perēlĕg·ans -antis *adj* very elegant
perēleganter *adv* very elegantly
perēlŏqu·ens -entis *adv* very eloquent

peremn·ia -ium *n pl* auspices taken before crossing a river
peremptus *pp* of **perimo**
perendiē *adv* the day after tomorrow
perendin·us -a -um *adj* **dies perendinus** the day after tomorrow; *m* the day after tomorrow
perenn·is -e *adj* perennial, continual, everlasting
perenniserv·os -ī *m* slave for life
perennit·ās -ātis *f* continuance, perpetuity
perenn·ō -āre *vi* to last
pērenticīd·a -ae *m* (coll) crook
per·ĕō -īre -iī -itum *vi* to pass away, pass on, die; to go to waste, perish, be destroyed; to be lost, be ruined, be undone; to be desperately in love, pine away; (of snow) to melt away; (of iron) to rust away; **perii!** I'm ruined!, I'm finished!, I'm washed up!
perequit·ō -āre *vt* to ride up through; *vi* to ride around
pererr·ō -āre *vt* to roam around, wander through; to survey, look (*someone*) over
perērudīt·us -a -um *adj* very learned
perēsus *pp* of **peredo**
perexcels·us -a -um *adj* very high, exalted
perexiguē *adv* very sparingly
perexigu·us -a -um *adj* tiny; insignificant; very short (*day*)
perfacētē *adv* very wittily
perfacēt·us -a -um *adj* very witty, very sharp
perfacile *adv* very easily, very readily
perfacil·is -ē *adj* very easy; very courteous
perfamiliār·is -e *adj* very close, intimate; *m* very close friend
perfectē *adv* completely, perfectly
perfecti·ō -ōnis *f* completion; perfection
perfect·or -ōris *m* perfecter; **dicendi perfector** stylist
perfect·us -a -um *pp* of **perficio**; *adj* complete, finished, perfect, excellent
per·fĕrō -ferre -tŭlī -lātum *vt* to carry through; to endure to the end, bear with patience, put up with; to pass (*a law*); to bring, announce, report (*news*)
per·ficiō -ficĕre -fēcī -fectum *vt* to complete, finish, accomplish, carry out, perform, execute, bring to an end; to bring to completion, finish, perfect; to bring about, cause
perfic·us -a -um *adj* perfecting; **natura perfica** nature which perfects
perfidēl·is -e *adj* very faithful, very trusty
perfidi·a -ae *f* perfidy, treachery
perfidiōsē *adv* treacherously
perfidiōs·us -a -um *adj* treacherous, faithless
perfid·us -a -um *adj* treacherous, untrustworthy, dishonest, sneaky; *m* sneak
per·fīgō -fīgĕre -fixī -fixum *vt* to pierce
perflābil·is -e *adj* airy; invisible (*gods*)
perflāgitiōs·us -a -um *adj* utterly disgraceful
perfl·ō -āre *vt* to blow through, blow across
perfluctŭ·ō -āre *vt* to surge through
per·fodiō -fodĕre -fōdī -fossum *vt* to dig through; to pierce
perfŏr·ō -āre *vt* to bore through, pierce; to make by boring
perfortiter *adv* very bravely
perfoss·or -ōris *m* **perfossor parietum** burglar
perfossus *pp* of **perfodio**
perfractus *pp* of **perfringo**
perfrĕm·ō -ĕre -ŭī *vi* to snort loud
perfrĕqu·ens -entis *adj* very crowded, over-crowded
perfric·ō -āre -ŭī -ātum or **-tum** *vt* to rub well, rub all over; **os perfricare** to rub away blushes, put on a bold front
perfrīgefac·iō -ĕre *vt* (fig) to send a chill over, make shudder
per·frīgescō -frīgescĕre -frixī *vi* to catch a bad cold
perfrīgid·us -a -um *adj* very cold, ice-cold
per·fringō -fringĕre -frēgī -fractum *vt* to break through; to break to pieces, batter in, smash; (fig) to break (*laws, etc.*), break up (*conspiracy*)
per·frŭor -frŭī -fructus sum *vi* (with *abl*) to experience to the full, fully enjoy, be delighted by, perform gladly
perfŭg·a -ae *m* military deserter; political turncoat
per·fugiō -fugĕre -fūgī *vi* (with **ad** or **in** + *acc*) **a** to flee to for refuge; **b** to desert to; **c** (fig) to have recourse to, find comfort in
perfuncti·ō -ōnis *f* performance, performing, discharge
perfunctus *pp* of **perfungor**
per·fundō -fundĕre -fūdī -fūsum *vt* to drench, bathe; to sprinkle; to dye; (fig) to fill, flood, steep, inspire
per·fungor -fungī -functus sum *vt* to enjoy; *vi* (with *abl*) **a** to perform, discharge, fulfill; **b** to go through, endure, undergo; **c** to get rid of; **d** to be finished with, be done with; **e** to enjoy
perfŭr·ō -ĕre *vi* to rage wildly, rage on
perfūsus *pp* of **perfundo**
Pergăm·a -ōrum *n pl* or **Pergăm·us -ī** *f* citadel of Troy, Troy
Pergamĕ·us -a -um *adj* Trojan; *m pl* Trojans
Pergăm·um -ī *n* Troy; Pergamum (*city in Mysia, the capital of the Attalid kingdom, famous for its library*)

pergaud·ĕō -ēre *vi* to be very glad
per·gō -gĕre -rexī -rectum *vt* to go on uninterruptedly with, continue; (with *inf*) to continue to; *vi* to go straight on, continue, proceed; (with **ad** + *acc*) to pass on to, proceed to (*esp. in speaking*)
pergraec·or -ārī -ātus sum *vi* to go completely Greek, have a ball
pergrand·is -e *adj* very large, huge; **pergrandis natu** very old
pergraphic·us -a -um *adj* very cunning
pergrāt·us -a -um *adj* very pleasant; *n* distinct pleasure
pergrăv·is -e *adj* very heavy; very important; very impressive
pergraviter *adv* very seriously
pergŭl·a -ae *f* veranda, balcony; school; brothel
Perg·us -ī *m* lake in Sicily, near Henna, where Pluto carried off Proserpina
perhib·ĕō -ēre -ŭī -ĭtum *vt* to hold, assert, maintain; to call, name; to adduce, cite
perhīlum *adv* very little
perhonōrificē *adv* very respectfully, with all due respect
perhonōrific·us -a -um *adj* very honorable, very complimentary; very respectful
perhorr·escō -escĕre -ŭī *vt* to begin to shudder at; to develop a terror of; *vi* to begin to quake, begin to tremble violently
perhorrĭd·us -a -um *adj* horrible, dreadful
perhūmanĭter *adv* very kindly
perhūmān·us -a -um *adj* very courteous
Pericl·ēs -is or **-ī** *m* Athenian statesman, son of Xanthippus and political leader of Athens during the city's most flourishing period (c. 495-429 B.C.)
perīclitāti·ō -ōnis *f* test, experiment
perīclit·or -ārī -ātus sum *vt* to test, put to the test, try; to jeopardize; to risk; *vi* to be in danger, be in jeopardy; to run a risk; (with *abl*) to be in danger of losing (*e.g., life, reputation*); **capite periclitari** to be in danger of losing one's life, risk one's life
perīculōsē *adv* dangerously
perīculōs·us -a -um *adj* dangerous, perilous, risky
perīcŭl·um or **perīcl·um -ī** *n* danger, peril, risk; trial, attempt, experiment, test; literary venture; (law) trial, case, lawsuit, legal record, writ, sentence
peridōnĕ·us -a -um *adj* very suitable; (with *dat* or **ad** + *acc*) well adapted to, well suited to
perillustr·is -e *adj* very clear; very illustrious, very distinguished
perimbēcill·us -a -um *adj* very weak, very feeble
per·ĭmō -imĕre -ēmī -emptum *vt* to take away completely; to destroy; to slay, kill
perimpedīt·us -a -um *adj* rough (*terrain*), full of obstacles
perincommŏdē *adv* very inconveniently
perincommŏd·us -a -um *adj* very inconvenient
perinde *adv* in the same manner, equally, just as, quite as; (with **atque, ac, ut,** or **quam**) just as, exactly as; (with **ac si, quasi, tamquam,** or **quam si**) just as if
perindulg·ens -entis *adj* very tender; (with **ad** + *acc*) very tender toward
perinfirm·us -a -um *adj* very weak
peringeniōs·us -a -um *adj* very clever
perinīqu·us -a -um *adj* very unfair; very upset, very annoyed, very impatient, very reluctant; **periniquo animo pati** or **ferre** to be quite upset at, be quite annoyed at, be very reluctant about
perinsign·is -e *adj* very remarkable
perinvīt·us -a -um *adj* very unwilling
periŏd·us -ī *f* sentence, rhetorical period
peripatētic·us -a -um *adj* peripatetic, Aristotelian; *m pl* peripatetics, Aristotelians
peripetasmăt·a -um *n pl* curtains, drapes
perīrāt·us -a -um *adv* very angry; (with *dat*) very angry with
periscĕl·is -īdis *f* anklet
peristrōm·a -ătis *n* carpet
peristyl·ium -iī or **-ī** *n* peristyle (*open court surrounded by a colonnade*)
peristȳl·um -ī *n* colonnade around a building, peristyle
perītē *adv* skillfully, expertly
perīti·a -ae *f* experience, practical knowledge, skill; (with *genit*) experience in, familiarity with, knowledge of
perīt·us -a -um *adj* experienced, skillful, expert, familiar; (with *genit* or *abl*, with **in** + *abl*, or with **ad** + *acc*) experienced in, skillful in, expert in or at, familiar with; (with *inf*) skilled in, expert at, e.g., **peritus cantare** skilled in singing, expert at singing
perjūcundē *adv* very pleasantly
perjūcund·us -a -um *adj* very pleasant
perjūr·ium -iī or **-ī** *n* perjury, false oath
perjūrō see **pejero**
perjūr·us or **pejĕr·us -a -um** *adj* perjured, oath-breaking; lying, dishonest
per·lābor -lābī -lapsus sum *vi* to glide along, skim across or over; (with **per** + *acc*) to slip through; (with **ad** + *acc*) to come, move, glide, or slip toward; (with **in** + *acc*) to glide into, slip into

perlaet·us -a -um *adv* very glad, most joyful
perlapsus *pp* of **perlabor**
perlātē *adv* very extensively
perlat·ĕō -ēre -ŭī *vi* to be completely hidden
perlātus *pp* of **perfero**
perlectī·ō -ōnis *f* thorough perusal
per·lĕgō -legĕre -lēgī -lectum *vt* to scan, survey thoroughly; to read through
perlepidē *adv* very nicely
perlĕv·is -e *adj* very light, very slight
perlevĭter *adv* very lightly, very slightly
perlīb·ens or **perlŭb·ens -entis** *adj* very willing
perlibenter or **perlubenter** *adv* very gladly
perlīberāl·is -e *adj* very genteel
perlīb·et or **perlŭb·et -ēre** *v impers* (with *inf*) I should very much like to
perliciō see **pellicio**
perlĭt·ō -āre *vi* to sacrifice with favorable omens
perlongē *adv* a long way off, very far
perlonginqu·us -a -um *adj* very long; very tedious
perlub- = **perlib-**
per·lūcĕō or **pel·lūcĕō -lūcēre -luxī** *vi* to shine clearly, be bright; to be clearly visible; to be transparent; to be clear, be intelligible
perlūcidŭl·us -a -um *adj* somewhat transparent
perlūcĭd·us or **pellūcĭd·us -a -um** *adj* very bright; transparent
perluctuōs·us -a -um *adj* very sad
per·lŭō -luĕre -lŭī -lūtum *vt* to wash thoroughly, wash off, bathe
perlustr·ō -āre *vt* to traverse; to scan, survey, review
permadefac·iō -ĕre *vt* to soak through and through, drench
permagn·us -a -um *adj* very great; very important; *n* great thing; **permagno** at a very high price, very dearly; **permagnum aestimare** (with *inf*) to think it quite something to
permānanter *adv* by flowing through
permānasc·ō -ĕre *vi* (*of a report*) to begin to spread
per·manĕō -manēre -mansī -mansum *vi* to last, continue, hold out, remain, persist, endure
permān·ō -āre *vt* to seep through, penetrate; *vi* to penetrate; (with **ad** or **in** + *acc*) **a** to seep through to, seep into, penetrate; **b** (fig) to reach, extend to, penetrate
permansī·ō -ōnis *f* persistence, continuance
permarīn·us -a -um *adj* sea-going
permātūr·escō -escĕre -ŭī *vi* to become fully ripe
permediŏcr·is -e *adj* completely normal
permeditāt·us -a -um *adj* well rehearsed, well trained
permensus *pp* of **permetior**
permĕ·ō -āre *vt* to go through, cross over, cross; *vi* (with **in** + *acc*) to penetrate; (with **per** + *acc*) to penetrate, permeate
Permess·us -ī *m* river in Boeotia sacred to Apollo and the Muses
per·mētĭor -mētīrī -mensus sum *vt* to measure out, measure; to traverse, travel, travel over
per·mingō -mingĕre -minxī *vt* to soak with urine; to pollute
permīr·us -a -um *adj* very surprising, truly amazing
per·miscĕō -miscēre -miscŭī -mixtum *vt* to mix together, intermingle; (fig) to mix together, mix up, confuse
permissī·ō -ōnis *f* unconditional surrender; permission
permiss·us -a -um *pp* of **permitto**; *n* permission
permiss·us -ūs *m* permission, leave
permitiāl·is -e *adj* destructive, deadly
permitĭ·ēs -ēī *f* wasting away; ruin, decay
per·mittō -mittĕre -mīsī -missum *vt* to let through, let go through; to throw, hurl; to give up, surrender; to concede, relinquish; to let loose, let go; to let, permit, allow, grant; (with *dat*) to give up to, surrender (*something*) to, entrust (*something*) to, grant (*something*) to; (with **in** + *acc*) to send flying at, hurl or throw at
permixtē or **permixtim** *adv* confusedly, promiscuously
permixtī·ō -ōnis *f* mixture; confusion, bedlam
permixt·us -a -um *pp* of **permisceo**; *adj* confused, promiscuous
permodest·us -a -um *adj* very modest, very moderate
permolestē *adv* with much trouble; **permoleste ferre** to be quite annoyed at
permolest·us -a -um *adj* very troublesome, very annoying
permŏl·ō -ĕre *vt* to grind up; **alienas uxores permolere** (fig) to seduce other men's wives
permōtĭ·ō -ōnis *f* excitement; **animi permotio** or **mentis permotio** excitement, deep emotion
per·movĕō -movēre -mōvī -mōtum *vt* to stir up, churn up (*the sea*); to move deeply, make a deep impression upon; to excite, agitate, rouse; to influence, induce, prevail on
per·mulcĕō -mulcēre -mulsī -mulsum *vt* to stroke, pet, caress; to soothe, charm; to delight, flatter; to appease, tame, mitigate, allay
permultō *adv* (with comparatives) by far, far, much
permultum *adv* very much; **permultum ante** very often before; **permultum interest** it makes a world of difference

permult·us -a -um *adj* very much, very many; *n* a lot, much
permūn·iō -īre -īvī or **-iī -ītum** *vt* to fortify thoroughly; to finish fortifying
permūtāti·ō -ōnis *f* permutation, complete change; change, alteration; crisis, revolution; exchange, barter; substitution
permūt·ō -āre *vt* to change completely, alter completely; to exchange, interchange
pern·a -ae *f* ham
pernecessāri·us -a -um *adj* very necessary; very closely related; *m* close friend; close relative
pernecesse (indecl) *adj* very necessary, indispensable
pernĕg·ō -āre *vt* to deny flatly; to turn down flat
per·nĕō -nēre -nēvī -nētum *vt* (of the Fates) to spin out
perniciābil·is -e *adj* ruinous
pernici·ēs -ēī *f* ruin, destruction, disaster, calamity; pest, curse
perniciōsē *adj* perniciously, ruinously
perniciōs·us -a -um *adj* pernicious, ruinous
pernīcit·ās -ātis *f* agility, nimbleness, swiftness
perniciter *adv* nimbly, swiftly
pernig·er -ra -rum *adj* jet black
pernimi·us -a -um *adj* much too much
pern·ix -īcis *adj* agile, nimble, active, swift
pernōbil·is -e *adj* famous, illustrious
pernoct·ō -āre *vi* to spend the night
per·noscō -noscĕre -nōvī -nōtum *vt* to examine thoroughly; to become fully acquainted with, get an accurate knowledge of
pernōt·escō -escĕre -ŭī *vi* to become generally known
pern·ox -octis *adj* all-night; **luna pernox** full moon
pernumĕr·ō -āre *vt* to count up
pēr·ō -ōnis *m* clodhopper, brogue (*worn by peasants and soldiers*)
perobscūr·us -a -um *adj* very obscure
perodiōs·us -a -um *adj* very annoying
perofficiōsē *adv* with devotion, with attention
perol·ĕō -ēre *vi* to have a strong odor
pērōnāt·us -a -um *adj* wearing clodhoppers
peropportūnē *adv* very opportunely, very conveniently
peropportūn·us -a -um *adj* very opportune, very convenient, well timed
peroptātō *adv* very much to one's wish
perŏpus (indecl) *n* great need; **perŏpus est** it is absolutely essential
perōrāti·ō -ōnis *f* peroration, conclusion of a speech
perōrnāt·us -a -um *adj* very flowery (*style*)
perorn·ō -āre *vt* to enhance the prestige of (*e.g., the senate*)
perōr·ō -āre *vt* to plead (*a case*) all by oneself; to wind up, conclude (*a speech, case*), rest (*a case*); *vi* to give the summation
perōs·us -a -um *adj* hating, detesting
perpāc·ō -āre *vt* to silence completely; to pacify thoroughly
perparcē *adv* very stingily
perparvŭl·us -a -um *adj* tiny
perparv·us -a -um *adj* very small
perpast·us -a -um *adj* well fed
perpauc·ī -ae -a *adj* very few; *n pl* very few words; **perpauca dicere** to speak very briefly
perpaucŭl·ī -ae -a *adj* very few
perpaulum *adv* somewhat, slightly
perpaul·um -ī *n* small bit
perpaup·er -ĕris *adj* very poor
perpauxill·um -ī *n* little bit
perpavefac·iō -ĕre *vt* to frighten the daylight out of
per·pellō -pellĕre -pulsī -pulsum *vt* to push hard; to urge strongly, force
perpendicŭl·um -ī *n* plumb line, plummet; **ad perpendiculum** perpendicularly
per·pendō -pendĕre -pendī -pensum *vt* to weigh carefully, consider; to value, judge
perpĕram *adv* incorrectly, falsely
perp·es -ĕtis *adj* continuous, uninterrupted
perpessi·ō -ōnis *f* suffering, endurance
per·petior -pĕtī -pessus sum *vt* to endure, put up with, stand; to allow, permit
perpĕtr·ō -āre *vt* to accomplish, go through with, carry out, achieve, perform; to perpetrate, commit
perpetuit·ās -ātis *f* perpetuity
perpetŭō *adv* constantly, without interruption, forever
perpetŭ·ō -āre *vt* to perpetuate
perpetŭ·us -a -um *adj* perpetual, continuous, uninterrupted; general, universal; whole, entire; **quaestiones perpetuae** standing courts; permanent committee; *n* **in perpetuum** without a break, continuously; for all time, forever
perplac·ĕō -ēre -ŭī *vi* (with *dat*) to please immensely
perplexābil·is -e *adj* obscure, perplexing
perplexābiliter *adv* perplexingly
perplexē or **perplexim** *adv* confusedly, unintelligibly
perplex·or -ārī -ātus sum *vi* to cause confusion
perplex·us -a -um *adj* intricate, confused; ambiguous, obscure; *n* ambiguity, confusion
perplicāt·us -a -um *adj* entangled
perplŭ·ō -ĕre *vt* (fig) to rain, pour; *vi* (of roof, etc.) to leak, let the rain in

perpol·iō -īre -īvī or **-iī -ītum** *vt* to polish well, bring to a high polish; (fig) to polish up, perfect
perpolīt·us -a -um *adj* polished, refined
perpopŭl·or -ārī -ātus sum *vt* to ravage, devastate
perpōtāti·ō -ōnis *f* heavy drinking; drinking party
perpōt·ō -āre *vt* to drink off; *vi* to drink heavily, drink constantly
per·prĭmō -primĕre -pressī *vt* to press hard, squeeze hard; to lie on
perpropinqu·us -a -um *adj* very near
perprūrisc·ō -ĕre *vi* to begin to itch all over
perpugn·ax -ācis *adj* very belligerent
perpulch·er -ra -rum *adj* very beautiful, very handsome
perpulsus *pp* of **perpello**
perpurg·ō -āre *vt* to cleanse thoroughly, clean up; (fig) to clear up, explain
perpusill·us -a -um *adj* puny
perpŭt·ō -āre *vt* to prune back hard; to clear up, explain in detail
perquam *adv* very, extremely
per·quīrō -quīrĕre -quīsīvī -quīsītum *vt* to search carefully for; to examine carefully
perquīsītius *adv* more accurately, more critically
perquīsīt·or -ōris *m* enthusiast; **auctionum perquisitor** auction enthusiast
perrārō *adv* very rarely, very seldom
perrār·us -a -um *adj* very rare, quite uncommon
perrecondĭt·us -a -um *adj* recondite, abstruse
perrectus *pp* of **pergo**
per·rēpō -rēpĕre -repsī -reptum *vt* to crawl over, crawl along
perrept·ō -āre *vt* to creep through, sneak through; *vi* to creep around
perrīdicŭlē *adv* most absurdly
perrīdicŭl·us -a -um *adj* utterly absurd
perrogāti·ō -ōnis *f* passage (*of a law*)
perrŏg·ō -āre *vt* to ask in succession; to poll (*opinions*); **sententias perrogare** to have roll call (*in the senate*)
per·rumpō -rumpĕre -rūpī -ruptum *vt* to break through, force one's way through; to break in two, shatter, smash; to offend against, violate; *vi* to break through, make a breakthrough
Pers·a or **Pers·ēs -ae** *m* Persian
persaepe *adv* very often
persalsē *adv* very wittily
persals·us -a -um *adj* very witty
persalūtāti·ō -ōnis *f* round of greetings, greeting all in turn
persalūt·ō -āre *vt* to salute one after another
persanctē *adv* very solemnly
persapi·ens -entis *adj* very wise
persapienter *adv* very wisely
perscienter *adv* very wisely, very discreetly
per·scindō -scindĕre -scĭdī -scissum *vt* to tear to pieces; to scatter (*e.g., clouds*)
perscīt·us -a -um *adj* very clever, very smart
per·scrībō -scrībĕre -scripsī -scriptum *vt* to write out; to describe fully, give in detail; to record, register; to enter (*into an account book*); to make over by writing; to pay by check
perscripti·ō -ōnis *f* entry, official record; check, payment by check
perscript·or -ōris *m* bookkeeper, accountant
perscriptus *pp* of **perscribo**
perscrūt·ō -āre or **perscrūt·or -ārī -ātus sum** *vt* to search or examine thoroughly, scrutinize
per·sĕcō -secāre -secŭī -sectum *vt* to dissect, cut into pieces; (fig) to cut through, cut out, eliminate
persect·or -ārī -ātus sum *vt* to follow eagerly, investigate
persecūti·ō -ōnis *f* prosecution, suing, lawsuit
persecūtus *pp* of **persequor**
per·sedĕō or **per·sidĕō -sedēre -sēdī -sessum** *vi* to remain seated
persegn·is -e *adj* very slow-moving, dull, tedious
per·sentiō -sentīre -sensī -sensum *vt* to perceive clearly; to feel deeply
persentisc·ō -ĕre *vt* to detect; to feel deeply
Persephŏn·ē -ēs *f* daughter of Demeter and queen of the lower world, called Proserpina by the Romans
persĕqu·ens -entis *adj* pursuing; (with *genit*) given to the practice of
per·sĕquor -sĕquī -secūtus sum *vt* to follow persistently, follow up; to be in hot pursuit of, be on the heels of; to chase after, catch up to; to follow verbatim; to imitate, copy; to prosecute; to take vengeance on; to follow out, execute, perform; to describe, explain
Pers·ēs -ae or **Pers·eus -ĕī** *m* last king of Macedonia, conquered by Aemilius Paulus at Pydna (169 B.C.)
Pers·eus -ĕī or **-ĕos** *m* son of Jupiter and Danae, who killed Medusa and slew the sea monster who was about to devour Andromeda
Persē·us or **Persēi·us -a -um** *adj* of Perseus
persevēr·ans -antis *adj* persevering, persistent, relentless
persevēranter *adv* persistently, relentlessly
persevēranti·a -ae *f* perseverance, persistence
persevēr·ō -āre *vt* to persist in; *vi* to persist
persevēr·us -a -um *adj* very strict

Persĭ·a -ae or **Pers·is -ĭdis** *f* Persia
Persĭc·us -a -um *adj* Persian; (fig) luxurious, soft; of Perses (*king of Macedonia*); *m pl* Persians; *f* peach tree; *n* peach; *n pl* Persian history
per·sīdō -sīdĕre -sēdī -sessum *vi* to sink down, penetrate
persign·ō -āre *vt* to record in detail
persimĭl·is -e *adj* very similar; (with *genit* or *dat*) very similar to, very much like
persimpl·ex -ĭcis *adj* very plain, very simple
Pers·is -ĭdis *adj* Persian; *f* Persia; Persian woman
Pers·ius -iī or **-ī** *m* A. Persius Flaccus (*famous satirist in the reign of Nero*, 34-62 A.D.)
persoll·a -ae *f* little mask; (as term of abuse) you ugly little thing!
persōl·us -a -um *adj* completely alone
per·solvō -solvĕre -solvī -solūtum *vt* to solve, explain; to pay up; to pay (*a penalty*); to fulfill (*a vow*); to render (*thanks*); to offer (*sacrifice*); **poenas persolvere** (with *dat*) to suffer at the hands of
persōn·a -ae *f* mask; part, character; mask, pretense; personality, person, character
personāt·us -a -um *adj* wearing a mask, masked; under false pretenses; **pater personatus** father on the stage
persŏn·ō -āre *vt* to make resound, make ring; to shout; **aurem personare** to make the ear ring; *vi* to resound, reecho; **citharā personare** to play the zither loudly
perspectē *adv* intelligently
perspect·ō -āre *vt* to look all around
perspect·us -a -um *pp* of **perspicio**; *adj* well known, clear, evident
perspecŭl·or -ārī -ātus sum *vt* to examine thoroughly, explore thoroughly
persperg·ō -ĕre *vt* to sprinkle
perspĭc·ax -ācis *adj* sharp-sighted; keen, penetrating, perspicacious
perspicienti·a -ae *f* clear perception
per·spiciō -spicĕre -spexī -spectum *vt* to see through; to look closely at, examine, inspect, observe
perspicŭē *adv* clearly
perspicuit·ās -ātis *f* clarity
perspicŭ·us -a -um *adj* clear, transparent; clear, evident, perspicuous
per·sternō -sternĕre -strāvī -strātum *vt* to pave
perstimŭl·ō -āre *vt* to stimulate violently
per·stō -stāre -stitī -stātum *vi* to stand firm, hold one's ground; to keep standing; to remain unchanged, last; to be firm, persevere, persist, hold out
perstrātus *pp* of **persterno**
perstrĕp·ō -ĕre -ŭī -ĭtum *vi* to make a loud noise, make a lot of noise
per·stringō -stringĕre -strinxī -strictum *vt* to tie, tie up; to blunt, deaden (*the senses*), dazzle (*the eyes*), deafen (*the ears*); to touch lightly, graze, graze against; to glance over, touch lightly on; to belittle, slight
perstudiōsē *adv* enthusiastically
perstudiōs·us -a -um *adj* very eager, enthusiastic; (with *genit*) very fond of, enthusiastic about
per·suādĕō -suādēre -suāsī -suāsum *vi* (with *dat*) to persuade, convince; **sibi persuasum habere** to convince oneself, be convinced
persuāsĭ·ō -ōnis *f* convincing
persuastr·ix -īcis *f* seductress
persuāsus *pp* of **persuadeo**
persuās·us -ūs *m* persuasion
persubtīl·is -e *adj* very subtle, very ingenious
persult·ō -āre *vt* to gambol about, prance about; to scour (*woods*); *vi* to gambol, prance, run around
per·taedet -taedēre -taesum est *v impers* (with *acc* of person = subject in English and *genit* of thing = object in English) to be weary of, be sick and tired of, be bored with, e.g., **me negotii pertaedet** I am sick and tired of this business
per·tĕgō -tegĕre -texī -tectum *vt* to cover, cover up
pertempt·ō -āre *vt* to test thoroughly; to sound (*someone*) out; to consider well; (fig) to pervade, fill, overwhelm; **gaudia pertemptant pectus** joy fills (*their*) hearts
per·tendō -tendĕre -tendī -tensum or **-tentum** *vt* to press on with, continue, carry out; *vi* to press on, continue, persevere, persist, keep going
pertenŭ·is -e *adj* very thin, very slight, very small, very fine
pertereĕbr·ō -āre *vt* to bore through
per·tergĕō -tergēre -tersī -tersum *vt* to wipe off; (of air) to brush lightly against
perterre·faciō -facĕre -fēcī -factum *vt* to scare the life out of
perterr·ĕō -ēre -ŭī -ĭtum *vt* to frighten, terrify; (with **ab** + abl) to frighten (*someone*) away from
perterricrĕp·us -a -um *adj* terrible-sounding, rattling frightfully
per·texō -texĕre -texŭī -textum *vt* to bring to an end, go through with, accomplish
pertĭc·a -ae *f* pole, rod, staff; measuring pole; (fig) measure
pertim·escō -escĕre -ŭī *vt* to be alarmed at, become afraid of; *vi* to become very frightened, become alarmed
pertināci·ā -ae *f* stubbornness; perseverance, determination
pertinācĭter *adv* stubbornly, tenaciously; perseveringly, constantly
pertĭn·ax -ācis *adj* very tenacious; persevering, steadfast; unyielding, stubborn, obstinate

pertin·ĕō -ēre -ŭī *vi* to reach, extend; (with **per** + acc) to pervade, reach; (with **ad** + *acc*) **a** to extend to, reach; **b** to pertain to, relate to, concern; **c** to apply to, be applicable to, suit, be suitable to; **d** to tend toward, be conducive to; **e** to belong to; **quod pertinet** (with **ad** + *acc*) as regards, as far as concerns

perting·ō -ĕre *vi* to extend

pertolĕr·ō -āre *vt* to put up with, endure to the end

pertorqu·ĕō -ēre *vt* to twist, distort

pertractātē *adv* systematically

pertractāti·ō -ōnis *f* handling, treatment

pertract·ō -āre *vt* to handle, fondle; (fig) to handle carefully, treat systematically; to influence

per·trăhō -trahĕre -traxī -tractum *vt* to drag; to allure, lead on, decoy

pertrect- = pertract-

pertrist·is -e *adj* very sad, very gloomy

pertumultuōsē *adv* very excitedly, hysterically

per·tundō -tundĕre -tŭdī -tūsum *vt* to punch a hole through, perforate

perturbātē *adv* confusedly, in confusion

perturbāti·ō -ōnis *f* confusion, disorder; political disturbance, revolution; mental disturbance; disturbing emotion

perturbātr·ix -īcis *f* disturbing element

perturbāt·us -a -um *adj* disturbed, troubled; excited, alarmed; embarrassed

perturb·is -e *adj* downright shameful

perturb·ō -āre *vt* to throw into confusion, confuse, disturb; to embarrass; to upset, alarm

pertūs·us -a -um *pp* of **pertundo;** *adj* perforated; tattered (*clothes*)

per·ungō -ungĕre -unxī -unctum *vt* to oil well, anoint thoroughly

perurbān·us -a -um *adj* very urbane, very sophisticated; *m* sophisticate

per·ūrō -ūrĕre -ussī -ustum *vt* to burn up; to consume; to inflame, rub sore; to scorch; (of cold) to nip, bite; (fig) to fire, inflame

Perusi·a -ae *f* town in Etruria

perustus *pp* of **peruro**

perūtil·is -e *adj* very useful, very practical

per·vādō -vādĕre -vāsī -vāsum *vt* to pass through, go through; to spread throughout, pervade; to penetrate, reach; *vi* to spread, penetrate; (with **ad** or **in** + *acc*) to go as far as, spread to, reach, arrive at, penetrate; (with **per** + *acc*) to spread through or over

pervagāt·us -a -um *adj* widespread, prevalent, well known; general, common

pervăg·or -ārī -ātus sum *vt* to spread through or over, pervade; *vi* to wander all over, range about; (with **ad** + *acc*) to spread to, extend to, be known as far as

pervăg·us -a -um *adj* wandering about

pervariē *adv* in various versions

pervast·ō -āre *vt* to devastate

pervāsus *pp* of **pervado**

per·vĕhō -vehĕre -vexī -vectum *vt* to bring, carry, convey; to bring (*e.g., supplies*) through; **pervehi** to ride, drive, sail; to reach; **in portum pervehi** to sail into port, reach port

per·vellō -vellĕre -vellī *vt* to pull hard; to pinch hard; to excite, arouse; (fig) to tear apart (*with words*), disparage

per·veniō -venīre -vēnī -ventum *vt* to come to, reach; *vi* to come up, arrive; (with **ad** or **in** + *acc*) **a** to arrive at, reach; **b** (fig) to attain to

pervēn·or -ārī -ātus sum *vt* to search through (*e.g., all the city*)

perversē or **pervorsē** *adv* wrongly, perversely

perversĭt·ās -ātis *f* perversity, distortion

pervers·us or **pervors·us -a -um** *adj* turned the wrong way, awry, crooked; cross-eyed; (fig) crooked, wrong, perverse; spiteful, malicious

per·vertō or **per·vortō -vertĕre -vertī -versum** *vt* to overturn, upset, knock down; (fig) to abuse, misuse, undo, destroy, pervert

pervespĕrī *adv* late in the evening

pervestīgāti·ō -ōnis *f* thorough search, examining, investigation

pervestīg·ō -āre *vt* to track down, hunt down; (fig) to trace, detect

pervĕt·us -ĕris *adj* very old, ancient

pervetust·us -a -um *adj* outdated, antiquated

perviam *adv* **perviam facere** to make accessible

pervicāci·a -ae *f* persistence; stubbornness

pervicācius *adv* more obstinately, more stubbornly

pervĭc·ax -ācis *adj* persistent, determined; headstrong, stubborn, obstinate

pervictus *pp* of **pervinco**

per·vidĕō -vidēre -vīdī -vīsum *vt* to look over, overlook, survey; to see through; to examine, investigate; to realize

pervig·ĕō -ēre -ŭī *vi* to continue to thrive

pervĭg·il (*genit:* **-ĭlis**) *adj* wide awake, ever watchful

pervigilāti·ō -ōnis *f* religious vigil

pervigil·ium -iī or **-ī** *n* all-night vigil

pervigĭl·ō -āre *vt* to spend or pass (*nights, days*) without sleep; *vi* to

stay awake all night, keep an all-night vigil
pervīl·is -e *adj* very cheap
per·vincō -vincĕre -vīcī -victum *vt* to defeat completely, completely overcome, completely get the better of; to outdo, surpass, exceed; to outbid; to convince; to prove; *vi* to win, succeed; to carry a point; (with **ut**) to succeed in, bring it about that; **non pervicit ut referrent consules** he did not succeed in having the consuls make a formal proposal
pervīsus *pp* of **pervideo**
perví·us -a -um *adj* crossable, passable, accessible; *n* passage, thoroughfare
per·vīvō -vīvĕre -vixī *vi* to live on; **pervivere usque ad summam aetatem** to live on to a ripe old age
pervolgō see **pervulgo**
pervolit·ō -āre *vt & vi* to fly about, flit about
pervŏl·ō -āre *vt* to fly through or about, flit about; to dart through, pass quickly over; *vi* to fly about, flit about; (with **in** + *acc*) to fly through to, arrive at, reach
per·vŏlō -velle -volŭī *vt* to want badly, wish very much; (with *inf*) to wish very much to; (with *acc & inf*) to eagerly wish (*someone*) to
pervolūt·ō -āre *vt* to turn over often, read through (*books*)
per·volvō -volvĕre -volvī -volūtum *vt* to roll (*someone*) over; to keep reading, read through (*books*); **pervolvi** to be busy, be engaged
pervor- see **perver-**
pervulgāt·us or **pervolgāt·us -a -um** *adj* widely known, very common
pervulg·ō or **pervolg·ō -āre** *vt* to make known, make public, publicize; to frequent; **se pervulgare** to prostitute oneself, become a prostitute
pēs pedis *m* foot; foot (*measure*); foot, meter (*in verse*); leg (*of table, couch, etc.*); sail rope, sheet; **ad pedes descendere** to dismount (*in order to fight on foot*); **aequis pedibus labi** to sail on an even keel; **ante pedes** in plain view; **pede dextro, felice,** or **secundo** auspiciously; **pedem conferre** to come to close quarters; **pedem ferre** to come; to go; **pedem ponere** (with **in** + *abl*) to set foot on; **pedem referre** to go back, retreat; **pedibus** on foot; **pedibus claudere** to set to verse, put in meter; **pedibus ire in sententiam** (with *genit*) to vote in favor of the proposal of; **pedibus itur in sententiam** the proposal is put to a vote, a vote is taken on the proposal; **pedibus merere** or **pedibus mereri** to serve in the infantry; **pedibus vincere** to win a footrace; **pugna ad pedes** infantry battle; **se in pedes conjicere** to take to one's heels; **servus a pedibus** footman; **sub pedibus** under one's sway
pessimē (*superl* of **male**) *adv* very badly, most wretchedly
pessim·us -a -um (*superl* of **malus**) *adj* worst; *m* scoundrel
pessŭl·us -ī *m* bolt (*of a door*)
pessum *adv* down, to the ground, to the bottom; **pessum dare** to send to the bottom, sink, drown, ruin, destroy; **pessum ire** to go down, sink, go to ruin
pestĭf·er -ĕra -ĕrum *adj* pestilential; destructive, pernicious; *m* trouble maker
pestifĕrē *adv* balefully
pestĭl·ens -entis *adj* pestilential, unhealthful; (fig) destructive, pernicious
pestilentĭ·a -ae *f* unhealthful atmosphere, unhealthful climate; pestilence, plague; destruction, death
pestilĭt·ās -ātis *f* pestilence, plague
pest·is -is *f* contagious disease, plague; destruction, death; trouble maker, anarchist, subversive
petasāt·us -a -um *adj* wearing a hat; (fig) ready to travel
petasĭ·ō or **petăs·ō -ōnis** *m* ham
petasuncŭl·us -ī *m* little ham
petăs·us -ī *m* hat
petaur·um -ī *n* springboard
petess·ō or **petiss·ō -ĕre** *vt* to be eager for, pursue; **pugnam petessere** to be spoiling for a fight
petītĭ·ō -ōnis *f* attack, blow, thrust, aim; petition, request, application; candidacy, political campaign; claim, suit, suing; right to sue; **petitioni se dare** to become a candidate
petīt·or -ōris *m* applicant; political candidate; plaintiff
petītur·ĭō -īre *vi* to be eager for office
petīt·us -a -um *pp* of **peto;** *n* request, desire
petīt·us -ūs *m* (with *genit*) heading for
pet·ō -ĕre -īvī *or* **-ĭī -ītum** *vt* to make for, head for; to attack; to strive for, aim at; to demand, require, exact; to claim, sue for; to beg, desire, entreat; to look for, go in search of, search for; to run after, chase, court (*girls*); to fetch, bring, obtain, draw; to run for (*office*); to refer to, relate to
petorrĭt·um -ī *n* open four-wheeled carriage
petr·a -ae *f* rock, crag
petr·ō -ōnis *m* yokel
Petrōn·ĭus -ĭī or **-ī** *m* Petronius Arbiter (*author and master of ceremonies at the court of Nero*)
petŭl·ans -antis *adj* pert, impudent, smart-alecky, petulant, forward
petulanter *adv* pertly, impudently, petulantly

petulanti·a -ae *f* pertness, impudence, forwardness; carelessness
petulc·us -a -um *adj* butting, apt to butt
pex·us -a -um *pp of* **pecto;** *adj* combed; new, still having the nap on
Phaeāc·es -um *m pl* Phaeacians (*people described in the Odyssey as living on a utopian island*)
Phaeāci·us -a -um *adj* Phaeacian; *f* Phaeacia
Phaeāc·us -a -um *adj* Phaeacian
Phaedr·a -ae *f* daughter of Minos and Pasiphae and wife of Theseus
Phaedr·us -ī *m* pupil of Socrates; freedman of Augustus and famous writer of Latin fables
Phaest·um -ī *n* town in Crete
Phaëth·ōn -ontis *m* son of Helios and Clymene who was killed trying to drive his father's chariot
Phaëthontē·us -a -um *adj* of Phaethon
Phaëthontiăd·es -um *f pl* sisters of Phaethon
phalang·ae -ārum *f pl* wooden rollers
phalangīt·ae -ārum *m pl* soldiers belonging to a Macedonian phalanx
phal·anx -angis *f* phalanx, battalion (*compact body of heavy-armed men in battle array first developed by the Macedonians*)
phalărīc·a or **falărīc·a -ae** *f* firebrand, fiery missile (*shot by a catapult or thrown by hand*)
phalĕr·ae -ārum *f pl* military medals; medallions (*worn by horses on forehead and chest*)
phalerāt·us -a -um *adj* wearing medals, decorated; ornamental
Phalērĭc·us -a -um *adj* of Phaleron
Phalēr·um -ī *n* Athenian harbor
pharĕtr·a -ae *f* quiver
pharetrāt·us -a -um *adj* wearing a quiver
pharmaceutrĭ·a -ae *f* witch, sorceress
pharmacopōl·a -ae *m* druggist; quack
Pharsālic·us -a -um *adj* of Pharsalus
Pharsāli·us -a -um *adj* Pharsalian; *f* district of Pharsalia
Pharsāl·os or **Pharsāl·us -ī** *f* town in Thessaly near which Caesar defeated Pompey (48 B.C.)
Phar·os or **Phar·us -ī** *m* or *f* island in the harbor at Alexandria famous for its lighthouse; lighthouse
phasēl·us -ī *m* or *f* kidney bean; pinnace (*light boat*); yacht
Phāsiăc·us -a -um *adj* Colchian
Phāsiān·a -ae *f* pheasant (*female*)
Phāsiān·us -ī *m* pheasant
Phāsi·as -ădis *adj* Colchian
Phās·is -ĭdis or **-ĭdos** *m* river in Colchis
phasm·a -ătis *n* ghost
Pher·ae -ārum *f pl* city in Thessaly, the home of Admetus
Pherae·us -a -um *adj* of Pherae
phiăl·a -ae *f* saucer
Phīdĭ·ās -ae *m* famous Greek sculptor and friend of Pericles (*fl* 440 B.C.)
philēm·a -ătis *n* kiss
Philēm·ōn -ŏnis *m* pious rustic who was changed into an oak tree while his wife Baucis was changed into a linden tree
Philipp·ī -ōrum *m pl* city in Macedonia where Octavian and Antony defeated Brutus and Cassius (42 B.C.)
Philippic·ae -ārum *f pl* series of vitriolic speeches directed at Antony by Cicero
Philipp·us -ī *m* name of several kings of Macedon (*esp. Philip II, son of Amyntas, and father of Alexander the Great, c.* 382-336 B.C.)
philitī·a or **phiditī·a -ōrum** *n pl* communal meals at Sparta
Phil·ō or **Phil·ōn -ōnis** *m* Academic philosopher and teacher of Cicero
Philoctēt·ēs -ae *m* Greek warrior and famous archer who was abandoned by the Greek army on the island of Lemnos
philologī·a -ae *f* love of study, study of literature
philolŏg·us -a -um *adj* learned, scholarly
Philomēl·a -ae *f* daughter of Pandion and sister of Procne, who was changed into a nightingale
philosŏphē *adv* philosophically
philosophī·a -ae *f* philosophy
philosŏph·or -ārī *vi* to pursue philosophy
philosŏph·us -a -um *adj* philosophical; *mf* philosopher
phitr·um -ī *n* love potion
phily̆r·a -ae *f* inner bark of the lime tree; linden tree
phīm·us -ī *m* dice box
Phīn·eus -ĕī or **-ĕos** *m* king of Salmydessus in Thrace, whom the Argonauts rescued from the torments which the Harpies visited upon him
Phlegĕth·ōn -ontis *m* river of fire in the lower world
Phlegethont·is -ĭdis *adj* of Phlegethon
Phlegy̆·ās -ae *m* king of the Lapiths and father of Ixion
Phlī·ūs -untis *f* city in N.E. Peloponnesus
phōc·a -ae or **phōc·ē -ēs** *f* seal
Phōcaic·us or **Phōcē·us** or **Phōcī·us -a -um** *adj & mf* Phocian
Phōc·is -ĭdis *f* a country of Greece W. of Boeotia
Phoeb·as -ădis *f* prophetess, priestess of Apollo
Phoeb·ē -ēs *f* moon goddess, the sister of Phoebus; night
Phoebigĕn·a -ae *m* son of Phoebus (*i.e., Asculapius*)
Phoeb·us -ī *m* Apollo as sun god; sun
Phoenīc·ē -ēs *f* Phoenicia

Phoenīc·es -um *m pl* Phoenicians
phoenīcoptĕr·us -ī *m* flamingo
Phoeniss·a -ae *f* Phoenician woman (*esp. Dido*)
phoen·ix -īcis *m* phoenix (*famous Arabian bird which was said to live 500 years and from whose ashes a young phoenix would be born*)
Phoen·ix -īcis *m* son of Amyntor and companion of Achilles
Phorc·is -ĭdos *f* female descendant of Phorcus; Medusa
Phorc·us -ī *m* son of Neptune and father of Medusa and the other Gorgons
Phorcȳn·is -ĭdis or **-ĭdos** *f* Medusa
Phraāt·ēs or **Phrahāt·ēs -ae** *m* king of Parthia
phrenēs·is -is *f* frenzy, delirium
phrenētic·us -a -um *adj* frenetic, frantic, delirious
Phrix·us -ī *m* son of Athamas and Nephele and brother of Helle, with whom he fled to Colchis mounted on the ram with the golden fleece
Phryg·es -um *m pl* Phrygians (*a people of Asia Minor*)
phrygĭ·ō -ōnis *m* embroiderer
Phrygĭ·us -a -um *adj & mf* Phrygian; Trojan; *f* Phrygia (*a country of Asia Minor*)
Phthī·a -ae *f* home of Achilles in Thessaly
Phthīōt·a or **Phthīōt·ēs -ae** *m* native of Phthia
phthis·is -is *f* consumption, tuberculosis
phy *interj* bah!
phylăc·a -ae *f* jail
phylacist·a -ae *m* jailer; overanxious creditor
phylarch·us -ī *m* tribal chief
physĭc·a -ae or **physĭc·ē -ēs** *f* physics
physĭc·us -a -um *adj* natural, physical, belonging to natural philosophy or physics; *m* natural philosopher, physicist, scientist; *n pl* physics
physiognōm·ōn -ōnis *m* physiognomist
physiologĭ·a -ae *f* natural philosophy, natural science
piābĭl·is -e *adj* expiable
piāculār·is -e *adj* expiatory, atoning; *n pl* expiatory sacrifices
piācŭl·um -ī *n* propitiatory sacrifice; victim; atonement, expiation; remedy; crime, sacrilege; punishment
piām·en -ĭnis *n* atonement
pīc·a -ae *f* magpie
picārĭ·a -ae *f* place where pitch is made
picĕ·a -ae *f* pine tree
Pīc·ens -entis *adj* Picene, of Picenum
Pīcēn·us -a -um *adj & m* Picene; *n* district of Central Italy on the Adriatic coast
picĕ·us -a -um *adj* made of pitch; pitch-black
pict·or -ōris *m* painter
Pict·or -ōris *m* Q. Fabius Pictor (*earliest Roman historian, who wrote a history of Rome in Greek, fl 225 B.C.*)
pictūr·a -ae *f* painting, art of painting; a painting, picture; embroidery
pictūrāt·us -a -um *adj* painted; embroidered
pict·us -a -um *pp of* **pingo;** *adj* decorated, colored; tattooed; ornate (*style*); false, unreal
pīc·us -ī *m* woodpecker; griffin (*fabulous bird*)
Pīc·us -ī *m* son of Saturn and grandfather of Latinus, who was changed by Circe into a woodpecker
piē *adv* dutifully, affectionately
Pīerĭ·a -ae *f* district in Macedonia
Pīĕr·is -ĭdis or **-ĭdos** *f* daughter of Pieros; Muse; *f pl* the nine Muses
Pīerĭ·us -a -um *adj* Pierian; poetic; musical; *f* see **Pieria;** *f pl* Muses
Pīĕr·os or **Pīĕr·us -ī** *m* father of the nine Muses
piĕt·ās -ātis *f* responsibility, sense of responsibility, sense of duty; devotion, piety; kindness, tenderness; loyalty, patriotism
pig·er -ra -rum *adj* reluctant, unwilling; apathetic, slow, lazy; numbing (*cold*); slow-moving, tedious, dull (*war, etc.*); backward, slow, dull (*person*)
pig·et -ēre -ŭit or **-ĭtum est** *v impers* it irks, pains, annoys, makes regretful; (with *genit* of cause of feeling), e.g., **piget stultitiae meae** I am irked by my foolishness; (with *inf*), e.g., **illa me composuisse piget** I repent having written those verses
pigmentār·ius -iī *or* **-ī** *m* paint dealer
pigment·um -ī *n* pigment, paint, color; coloring, color (*of style*)
pignerāt·or -ōris *m* mortgagee
pignĕr·ō -āre *vt* to pledge, mortgage, pawn; (fig) to pledge
pignĕr·or -ārī -ātus sum *vt* to take as pledge, accept in good faith; to claim to
pign·us -ĕris or **-ŏris** *n* pledge, security, guarantee; hostage; mortgage; income from mortgages; wager, stake; (fig) pledge, assurance, proof; *n pl* children
pigrē *adv* slowly, sluggishly
pigritĭ·a -ae or **pigritĭ·ēs -ēī** *f* sluggishness, laziness
pigr·ō -āre or **pigr·or -ārī -ātus sum** *vi* to be slow, be sluggish, be lazy
pīl·a -ae *f* a mortar; pillar; pier
pĭl·a -ae *f* ball; ball game; ballot (*used by jury*); **mea pila est** the ball is mine, I've won; **pilā ludere** to play ball
pīlān·us -ī *m* soldier in the third rank in battle
pīlāt·us -a -um *adj* armed with javelin
pīlent·um -ī *n* ladies' carriage

pilleāt·us -a -um *adj* wearing a felt skullcap (*as a symbol of free status*)
pilleŏl·us -ī *m* skullcap
pillĕ·um -ī *n* or **pillĕ·us -ī** *m* felt cap or hat (*worn by Romans at festivals, esp. at the Saturnalia, and given to a slave when freed as a symbol of his freedom*); freedom, liberty
pilōs·us -a -um *adj* hairy
pīl·um -ī *n* javelin
pīl·us -ī *m* maniple or company of the triarii, company of veteran reserves; **primi pili centurio** chief centurion of a legion (*centurion of the first century of the triarii*); **primus pilus** chief centurion of the triarii and therefore of the legion
pĭl·us -ī *m* hair; (fig) whit; **non pili facere** to care not a whit for
Pimpl·a -ae *f* town in Pieria sacred to the Muses
Pimplē·a -ae or **Pimplē·is -ĭdis** *f* Muse
Pindaric·us -a -um *adj* Pindaric
Pindăr·us -ī *m* Pindar (*famous lyric poet from Thebes in Boeotia*, 518-438 B.C.)
Pind·us -ī *m* mountain range separating Thessaly from Epirus
pīnēt·um -ī *n* pine forest
pīnĕ·us -a -um *adj* pine, of pine
pingō pingĕre pinxī pictum *vt* to draw, paint; to embroider; to depict, represent, portray; to stain, color; to decorate; to color, embellish (*style*)
pingu·e -is *n* fat, grease
pinguesc·ō -ĕre *vi* to get fat; to become fertile
pingu·is -e *adj* fat; oily, greasy; juicy; rich, fertile; thick, dense; stupid, dull; quiet, comfortable
pīnĭf·er -ĕra -ĕrum *adj* pine-producing, pine-covered
pīnĭg·er -ĕra -ĕrum *adj* pine-producing, pine-covered
pinn·a -ae *f* feather; wing; flight; fin; feathered arrow; pinnacle, battlement
pinnāt·us -a -um *adj* feathered, winged
pinnĭg·er -ĕra -ĕrum *adj* winged; having fins, finny
pinnĭp·ēs -ĕdis *adj* wing-footed
pinnirăp·us -ī *m* crest-snatcher (*gladiator who tried to get his opponent's helmet crest*)
pinnŭl·a -ae *f* little wing
pīnotēr·ēs -ae *m* hermit crab
pins·ō -ĕre -ī (or **-ŭī**) **-um** (or **-ĭtum**) *vt* to pound
pīn·us -ūs or **-ī** *f* pine tree, fir tree; pine forest; ship; torch; wreath of pine
pi·ō -āre *vt* to appease by sacrifice, propitiate; to honor with religious rites, worship; to purify with religious rites; to atone for, expiate; to avert
pip·er -ĕris *n* pepper
pīpĭl·ō -āre *vi* to chirp
pīpŭl·um -ī *n* or **pīpĭl·us -ī** *m* shrieking, yelling
Pīrae·eus or **Pīrae·us -ī** *m* or **Pīrae·a -ōrum** *n pl* principal harbor of Athens
pīrāt·a -ae *m* pirate
pīrātĭc·us -a -um *adj* pirate; *f* piracy; **piraticam facere** to practice piracy
Pīrēn·ē -ēs *f* fountain on the citadel of Corinth near which Bellerophon caught Pegasus
Pīrithŏ·us -ī *m* son of Ixion and king of the Lapiths
pir·um -ī *n* pear
pir·us -ī *f* pear tree
Pīs·a -ae *f* of **Pīs·ae -ārum** *f pl* Pisa (*city in Elis on the Alpheus River near which the Olympic games were held*)
Pīs·ae -ārum *f pl* Pisa (*ancient city of N. Etruria*)
Pīsae·us -a -um *adj* of Pisa; *f* Hippodamia
piscārĭ·us -a -um *adj* fish, of fishing or fish; **forum piscarium** fish market
piscāt·or -ōris *m* fisherman; fishmonger
piscātōrĭ·us -a -um *adj* fishing; fish
piscāt·us -ūs *m* fishing; fish; (fig) good haul
piscicŭl·us -ī *m* little fish
piscīn·a -ae *f* fish pond; swimming pool
piscīnār·ĭus -ĭī or **-ī** *m* person fond of swimming pools or fish ponds
pisc·is -is *m* fish
Pisc·is -is *m* Piscis (*constellation*)
pisc·or -ārī -ātus sum *vi* to fish
piscōs·us -a -um *adj* full of fish
pisculent·us -a -um *adj* well stocked with fish
Pīsistratĭd·ae -ārum *m pl* sons of Pisistratus (*i.e., Hippias and Hipparchus*)
Pīsistrăt·us -ī *m* enlightened tyrant of Athens (560-527 B.C.)
pistill·um -ī *n* pestle
pist·or -ōris *m* miller; baker
pistrill·a -ae *f* little mill
pistrīn·um -ī *n* flour mill; bakery; drudgery
pistr·is -is or **pistr·ix -īcis** *f* sea monster (*of any kind*); whale, shark; swift ship
pithēc·ĭum -ĭī or **-ī** *n* little ape
Pitth·eus -ĕī or **-ĕos** *m* king of Troezen and father of Aethra, the mother of Theseus
pītuīt·a -ae *f* phlegm; rheum; head cold
pītuītōs·us -a -um *adj* full of phlegm, phlegmatic
pi·us -a -um *adj* conscientious; god-fearing, godly, holy; fatherly, motherly, brotherly, sisterly; affectionate; patriotic; good; sacred, holy (*objects connected with religion*)
pix picis *f* pitch; *f pl* chunks of pitch
plācābĭl·is -e *adj* easily appeased; pacifying, appeasing
plācābilĭt·ās -ātis *f* readiness to forgive, conciliatory disposition

plācām·en -ĭnis *n* means of appeasing, peace offering
plācāment·um -ī *n* means of appeasing, peace offering
plācātē *adv* calmly, quietly
plācātĭ·ō -ōnis *f* pacifying, propitiating
plācāt·us -a -um *adj* calm, quiet; appeased, reconciled
plac·ens -entis *adj* pleasing
placent·a -ae *f* cake
plac·ĕō -ēre -ŭī -ĭtum *vi* (with *dat*) to please, satisfy, give pleasure to, be acceptable to; **sibi placere** to be satisfied with oneself, pride oneself; *v impers* it seems right, seems proper; it is settled, is agreed; it is resolved, is decided; **eis placitum est ut considerent** they decided to consider; **senatui placuit** the senate decreed
placĭdē *adv* calmly, placidly, gently, quietly
placĭd·us -a -um *adj* calm, placid, gentle, quiet
placĭt·ō -āre *vi* to be very pleasing
placĭt·us -a -um *adj* pleasing, acceptable; agreed upon; *n* principle, belief, tenet; **ultra placitum laudare** to praise excessively
plāc·ō -āre *vt* to calm, quiet; to appease; to reconcile
plāg·a -ae *f* blow; wound; (fig) blow
plăg·a -ae *f* region, tract, zone; hunting net; mesh of a net; curtain; (fig) trap
plagiār·ĭus -ĭī or **-ī** *n* plunderer; kidnapper; plagiarist
plāgĭg·er -ĕra -ĕrum *adj* covered with welts
plāgigerŭl·us -a -um *adj* covered with welts
plāgipatĭd·a -ae *m* whipping boy
plāgōs·us -a -um *adj* quick to use the rod
plagŭl·a -ae *f* curtain
plagūsĭ·a -ae *f* a fish
planctus *pp* of **plango**
planct·us -ūs *m* beating
plānē *adv* clearly, distinctly; legibly; completely, entirely, quite; certainly, to be sure
plangō plangĕre planxī planctum *vt* to strike, beat; to beat (*breast, head as sigh of grief*); to lament, bewail; *vi* to wail, lament; (fig) to wring the hands
plang·or -ōris *m* striking, beating; beating of the breast; wailing
plānilŏqu·os -a -om *adj* speaking clearly
plānip·ēs -ĕdis *m* ballet dancer
plānĭt·ās -ātis *f* distinctness
plānitĭ·ēs -ēī or **plānitĭ·a -ae** *f* flat surface, level ground, plain
plant·a -ae *f* sprout, shoot; young plant, slip; sole (*of the foot*)
plantār·ĭa -ĭum *n pl* slips; young trees; hair
plān·us -a -um *adj* flat, level, even; plain, clear; *n* level ground, plain
plan·us -ī *m* tramp; imposter, cheat
plasm·a -ătis *n* phoney accent
Platae·ae -ārum *f pl* Plataea (*town in Boeotia near which the Greeks defeated the Persians in 479 B.C.*)
plataleĕ·a -ae *f* waterfowl, spoonbill
platăn·us -ī or **-ūs** *f* plane tree
platē·a or **platĕ·a -ae** *f* street
Plat·ō or **Plat·ōn -ōnis** *m* Plato (*famous Greek philosopher, 429-348 B.C.*)
Platōnĭc·us -a -um *adj* Platonic; *m pl* Platonists
plaudō plaudĕre plausī plausum *vt* to slap, clap, beat; *vi* to flap, beat, clap; (with *dat*) to applaud, approve of; **alis plaudere** to flap the wings; **manibus plaudere** to clap the hands
plausibĭl·is -e *adj* deserving applause
plaus·or -ōris *m* applauder
plaustr·um -ī *n* wagon, cart
Plaustr·um -ī *n* the Great Bear (*constellation*)
plausus *pp* of **plaudo**
plaus·us -ūs *m* clapping, flapping; clapping of the hands; applause
Plaut·us -ī *m* T. Maccius Plautus (*famous Roman writer of comedies, born at Sarsina in Umbria, c. 254-184 B.C.*)
plēbēcŭl·a -ae *f* rabble
plēbēĭ·us or **plēbēj·us -a -um** *adj* plebeian, of the common people; common, low, vulgar
plēbicŏl·a -ae *m* democrat; demagogue
plēbiscīt·um -ī *n* decree of the commons
pleb·s -is or **plēb·ēs -ēī** or **-ī** *f* plebeians, common people; the masses, proletariat
plectĭl·is -e *adj* plaited
plectō plectĕre plexī or **plexŭī plexum** *vt* to plait, braid
plect·ō -ĕre *vt* to punish
Plēĭ·as -ădis *f* Pleiad; *f pl* Pleiades (*seven daughters of Atlas and Pleione, who were placed among the stars*)
Plēĭŏn·ē -ēs *f* daughter of Oceanus and Tethys, wife of Atlas, and mother of the Pleiades
plēnē *adv* fully, completely
plēn·us -a -um *adj* full; stout, plump; pregnant; filled, satisfied; full, packed; full, strong, loud (*voice*); full-length, unabridged, uncontracted; abundant, plentiful; advanced, mature (*years*); complete, finished
plērumque *adv* generally, mostly; often, frequently
plēr·usque -ăque -umque *adj* a very great part of, the greater part of, most; very many, a good many; *n* the greatest part
plex·us -a -um *pp* of **plecto**; *adj* plaited
plicātr·ix -īcis *f* woman who folds clothes, folder

plic·ō -āre -āvī or **-ŭī -ātum** or **-ĭtum** *vt* to fold, wind, coil up
Plīn·ius -iī or **-ī** *m* C. Plinius Secundus (*author of a work on natural history, who perished in the eruption of Vesuvius in* 79 A.D.); C. Plinius Caecilius (*his nephew, author of Letters and a Panegyric to Trajan,* 62 A.D.-*c.* 114 A.D.)
plōrābil·is -e *adj* deplorable
plōrāt·or -ōris *m* mourner
plōrāt·us -ūs *m* wailing, wail
plōr·ō -āre *vt* to cry over; *vi* to cry aloud, wail
plostell·um -ī *n* cart
ploxĕm·um -ī *n* wagon frame
pluit pluĕre pluit *vt* it is raining (*stones, blood, etc.*); *vi* it is raining; (with *abl*) it is raining (*stones, etc.*)
plūm·a -ae *f* down, soft feather; (collectively) feathers, down
plūmātil·e -is *n* dress embroidered with feathers
plūmāt·us -a -um *adj* covered with feathers
plumbĕ·us -a -um *adj* lead, of lead; leaden, oppressive (*weather*); dull, stupid
plumb·um -ī *n* lead; bullet; pipe; ruler (*for drawing lines*); **plumbum album** tin
plūmĕ·us -a -um *adj* downy, filled with down; like feathers
plūmip·ēs -ĕdis *adj* with feathered feet
plūmōs·us -a -um *adj* downy, feathered
plūrimum *adv* very much, especially, commonly, generally, most
plūrim·us -a -um (*superl* of **multus**) *adj* many a; most; very much; very many; very great, very intense; **plurimam salutem dare** to send warmest greetings; *n* a great deal; **plurimi facere** to think very highly of, think a great deal of; **quam plurimum** as much as possible
plūs *adv* more; **multo plus** much more; **paulo plus** a little more
plūs plūris (*comp* of **multus**) *adj* more; *n* more; too much; **et, quod plus est, Romani estis** and what is more, you are Romans; **plus animi** more courage; **plus nimio** much too much; **plus plusque** more and more; **uno viro plus habere** to have one man too much; **pluris esse** (*genit* of value) to be of more value, of a higher price, worth more, be higher, be dearer; *n pl* more words; **quid plura?** why should I say more?, in short
plūscŭl·us -a -um *adj* a little more, somewhat more; *n* a little more; **plusculum negoti** a little more business
plutĕ·us -ī *m* or **plutĕ·um -ī** *n* (mil) movable mantlet or shed used to protect soldiers in siege work; parapet; couch, dining couch; book shelf; book case; board, slab
Plūt·ō or **Plūt·ōn -ōnis** *m* king of the lower world, husband of Proserpina, and brother of Jupiter and Neptune
pluvī·a -ae *f* rain
pluviāl·is -e *adj* rain, of rain, rainy; **fungi pluviales** mushrooms brought out by the rain
pluvī·us -a -um *adj* rain, of rain, rainy; **pluvia aqua** rain water; **pluvius arcus** rainbow; *f* see **pluvia**
pōcill·um -ī *n* small drinking cup
pōcŭl·um -ī *n* drinking cup; drink, draught; **poculum ducere** or **exhaurire** to drain a cup
podăgr·a -ae *f* arthritis
podagrōs·us -a -um *adj* arthritic
pōd·ex -ĭcis *m* anus, rectum
pod·ium -iī or **-ī** balcony; box seat (*for the emperor*)
Poeantiăd·ēs -ae *m* Philoctetes
Poe·ās -antis *m* father of Philoctetes
poēm·a -ătis *n* poem
poēmat·ium -iī or **-ī** *n* short poem
poen·a -ae *f* compensation, recompense, retribution, satisfaction, penalty, fine, punishment; hardship, loss, pain; (in games) penalty; **poenam** or **poenas dare, dependere, pendere, persolvere, reddere, solvere, suscipere,** or **sufferre** to pay the penalty, make restitution, give satisfaction; **poenam** or **poenas capere, persequi, petere, repetere,** or **reposcere** to exact a penalty, demand satisfaction; **poena mortis** capital punishment, death penalty
poeniō see **punio**
Poen·us -a -um *adj & m* Carthaginian
poēs·is -is *f* art of poetry; poetry, poems
poēt·a -ae *m* maker, contriver; poet
poētic·a -ae or **poētic·ē -ēs** *f* art of poetry; poetics
poēticē *adv* poetically
poētic·us -a -um *adj* poetic, poetical; *f* see **poetica**
poētrī·a -ae *f* poetess
poētr·is -ĭdis or **-ĭdos** *f* poetess
pol *interj* by Pollux!; Lord!
polent·a -ae *f* pearl barley
polentāri·us -a -um *adj* caused by eating barley
pol·iō -īre -īvī or **-iī -ītum** *vt* to polish, smooth; (fig) to polish, improve, perfect
polītē *adv* in a polished manner, with taste, smoothly, elegantly
politic·us -a -um *adj* political
polīt·us -a -um *adj* polished, smooth; (fig) polished, smooth, smooth-spoken, smooth-mannered, refined, cultivated
poll·en -ĭnis *n* or **poll·is -ĭnis** *m* or *f* flour
poll·ens -entis *adj* strong, powerful, thriving, able
pollentī·a -ae *f* might, power

poll·ĕō -ēre *vi* to be strong, be powerful; to be capable, be able; (*of medicines*) to be powerful, be efficacious; to have influence; **in re publica plurimum pollere** to have tremendous influence in politics
poll·ex -icis *m* thumb; big toe
pollic·ĕor -ērī -itus sum *vt* to promise
pollicitāti·ō -ōnis *f* promise
pollicit·or -ārī -ātus sum *vt* to keep promising
pollicit·us -a -um *pp* of **polliceor;** *n* promise
pollinārĭ·us -a -um *adj* flour, for flour
pollinct·or -ōris *m* embalmer
pol·lingō -lingĕre -linxī -linctum *vt* to lay out, embalm
Pollĭ·ō -ōnis *m* C. Asinius Pollio (*distinguished orator, poet, historian, patron of literature, and statesman*, 76 B.C.-4 A.D.)
poll·is -inis *m* or *f* flour
pol·lūcĕō -lūcēre -luxī -luctum *vt* to offer, offer up as sacrifice; to serve (*meal*); to entertain
pollūcibiliter *adv* sumptuously, in grand style
polluctūr·a -ae *f* sumptuous dinner
polluct·us -a -um *pp* of **polluceo;** *n* offering, sacrificial meal
pol·lŭō -luĕre -lŭī -lūtum *vt* to pollute, defile, soil, mess up; to defile, violate
Poll·ux or **Poll·ūcēs -ūcis** *m* son of Tyndareus and Leda, twin brother of Castor, and famous boxer
pol·us -ī *m* end of an axis, pole; North Pole; **polus australis** South Pole
Polyb·ius -iī or **-ī** *m* Greek historian and friend of Scipio Aemilianus (*c.* 203-120 B.C.)
Polydăm·ās -antis *m* son of Panthus and friend of Hector
Polydōr·us -ī *m* son of Priam and Hecuba, murdered by Polymestor the king of Thrace
Polyhymnĭ·a -ae *f* one of the nine Muses
Polymest·ōr -ŏris *m* king of the Thracian Chersonese, husband of Ilione the daughter of Priam
Polynīc·ēs -is *m* son of Oedipus and Jocasta and brother of Eteocles
Polyphēm·us -ī *m* son of Neptune and one of the Cyclops of Sicily
pōlўp·us -ī *m* polyp (*sea animal; tumor*)
Polyxĕn·a -ae *f* daughter of Priam whom Pyrrhus, the son of Achilles, sacrificed at his father's tomb
pōmārĭ·us -a -um *adj* fruit, of fruit trees; *m* fruit vendor; *n* orchard
pōmerīdiān·us -a -um *adj* afternoon
pōmēr·ium or **pōmoer·ium -iī** or **-ī** *n* space kept free of buildings inside and outside a city wall
pōmif·er -ĕra -ĕrum *adj* fruit-bearing
pōmōs·us -a -um *adj* loaded with fruit
pomp·a -ae *f* solemn or religious procession; retinue; pomp, ostentation
Pompēi·us or **Pompēj·us -ī** *m* Pompey the Great (*Roman general and statesman*, 106-48 B.C.)
Pompējān·us -a -um *adj* Pompeian; *m pl* inhabitants of Pompeii; soldiers or followers of Pompey
Pompēj·ī -ōrum *m pl* city south of Naples, destroyed by the eruption of Vesuvius in 79 A.D.
Pompil·ius -iī or **-ī** *m* Numa Pompilius (*second king of Rome and traditional founder of Roman state religion*)
Pomptīn·us -a -um *adj* Pomptine; **Pomptinae paludes** Pomptine Marshes in Latium
pōm·um -ī *n* fruit; fruit tree
pōm·us -ī *f* fruit tree
pondĕr·ō -āre *vt* to weigh; to consider, ponder
ponderōs·us -a -um *adj* weighty, heavy; full of meaning
pondō *adv* in weight
pondō (*indecl*) *n* pound, pounds; **auri quinque pondo** five pounds of gold
pond·us -ĕris *n* weight; mass; burden; importance; stability of character; *n pl* balance, equilibrium
pōne *adv* behind, after, back; *prep* (*with acc*) behind
pōnō pōnĕre posŭī positum or **postum** *vt* to put, place, put down, set down, set, fix, deposit; to lay aside, lay down; to lay out, spend; to stake; to place, station, post; to set up, erect, build, found; to regard, consider; to cite, assert; to suppose, assume; to lay out for burial; to smooth, calm; to arrange, smooth (*hair*); *vi* to abate, calm down
pons pontis *m* bridge; gangway; drawbridge; deck
pontĭcŭl·us -ī *m* small bridge
pontĭf·ex -icis *m* pontiff, pontifex, priest (*one of a board of fifteen*); **pontifex maximus** chief pontiff
pontificāl·is -e *adj* pontifical
pontificāt·us -ūs *m* pontificate
pontific·us -a -um *adj* pontifical
pont·ō -ōnis *m* ferry
pont·us -ī *m* sea; sea water
Pont·us -ī *m* Euxine or Black Sea; region around the Black Sea; kingdom of Mithridates between Bithynia and Armenia, subsequently a Roman province
pop·a -ae *m* priest's assistant (*attendant who slew the victim*)
popăn·um -ī *n* sacrificial cake
popell·us -ī *m* rabble, mob
popīn·a -ae *f* restaurant; food sold at a restaurant
popīn·ō -ōnis *m* diner at a restaurant
popl·es -itis *m* hollow of the knee;

knee; **duplicato poplite** on bended knee; **contento poplite** with a stiff knee
Pōplicŏla see **Publicola**
poppysm·a -ătis *n* clicking with the tongue (*as sign of approval*)
populābĭl·is -e *adj* destructible
populābund·us -a -um *adj* ravaging, laying waste
populār·ēs -ĭum *m pl* people's party, democrats
populār·ia -ĭum *n pl* general-admission seats
populār·is -e *adj* of the people, by the people, for the people, people's, popular; approved by the people, popular; favoring the people, democratic; demagogic; of the same country, native; common, coarse
populār·is -is *m* or *f* fellow countryman; party member; fellow member, associate; (with *genit*) partner or associate in
populārĭt·ās -ātis *f* fellow citizenship; popularity
populārĭter *adv* like the people; like a demagogue; **populariter loqui** to use slang
populātĭ·ō -ōnis *f* ravaging, devastation
populāt·or -ōris *m* ravager, destroyer
populāt·us -ūs *m* devastation
pōpulĕ·us -a -um *adj* of poplars, poplar
pōpulĭf·er -ĕra -ĕrum *adj* filled with poplar trees
pōpuln·us -a -um *adj* of poplars, poplar
popŭl·ō -āre or **popŭl·or -ārī -ātus sum** *vt* to ravage, devastate, lay waste; (fig) to pillage, ruin, destroy, spoil
popŭl·us -ī *m* people (*as a political community*), nation; people, crowd, public; citizens (*as opposed to soldiers*), civilians; region, district
pōpŭl·us -ī *f* poplar tree
porc·a -ae *f* sow
porcell·a -ae *f* little sow
porcell·us -ī *m* little hog
porcīnār·ĭus -ĭī or **-ī** *m* pork seller
porcīn·us -a -um *adj* hog's, pig's; *f* pork
Porc·ĭus -ĭī or **-ī** *m* M. Porcius Cato the Censor (235-149 B.C.); M. Porcius Cato Uticensis (95-46 B.C.)
porcŭl·a or **porculēn·a -ae** *f* little sow
porcŭl·us -ī *m* little pig
porc·us -ī *m* pig, hog
porgō see **porrigo**
Porphyrĭ·ōn -ōnis *m* a Giant
porrect·a -ōrum *n pl* offering; **inter caesa et porrecta** (fig) at the eleventh hour
porrectĭ·ō -ōnis *f* extending, stretching out
porrect·us -a -um *pp* of **porrigo**; *adj* stretched out, extended, extensive, long; protracted (*delay*); laid out, dead; (fig) wide-spread
porric·ĭō -ĕre *vt* to offer up, make an offering of
por·rĭgō or **porg·ō -rigĕre -rexī -rectum** *vt* to reach out, stretch out, extend; to offer, present, hand; to lengthen (*a syllable*); **se porrigere** to extend
porrīg·ō -ĭnis *f* dandruff
porrō *adv* forwards, farther on, on; far off, at a distance; long ago; in the future, hereafter; again, in turn; next, furthermore, moreover, on the other hand
porr·um -ī *n* leek; chive
Porsenn·a or **Porsēn·a** or **Porsinn·a -ae** *m* king of Clusium in Etruria who sided with Tarquin in a war against Rome
port·a -ae *f* city gate; gate; entrance; outlet; camp gate (*of which there were always four*)
portātĭ·ō -ōnis *f* carrying, conveyance
por·tendō -tendĕre -tendī -tentum *vt* to indicate, foretell, portend, predict
portentifĭc·us -a -um *adj* monstrous, abnormal
portentōs·us -a -um *adj* monstrous, abnormal, unnatural, portentous
portent·um -ī *n* portent, omen, sign; monstrosity, monster; fantasy, farfetched fiction; (as term of contempt) monster, demon
portentus *pp* of **portendo**
porthm·eus -ĕī or **-ĕos** *m* ferryman (*i.e., Charon, who piloted the ferry across the Styx*)
porticŭl·a -ae *f* small portico
portĭc·us -ūs *f* colonnade, portico; (mil) gallery (*formed by placing vineae end to end*); Stoicism
portĭ·ō -ōnis *f* portion, share; ratio, portion; instalment, payment; **pro portione** proportionally, relatively
portiscŭl·us -ī *m* gavel
portĭt·or -ōris *m* customs officer; ferryman, boatman
port·ō -āre *vt* to carry; to bring
portōr·ĭum -ĭī or **-ī** *n* port duty, customs duty; tax (*on peddlers*)
portŭl·a -ae *f* small gate
Portūn·us -ī *m* tutelary deity of harbors
portuōs·us -a -um *adj* having good harbors
port·us -ūs *m* port, harbor; haven, refuge; mouth of a river
posc·a -ae *f* sour drink
poscō poscĕre poposcī *vt* to ask, request, beg, demand; (of things) to require, demand, need, call for, make necessary; (with **ab** + *abl*) to ask for (*something*) from, demand (*something*) of; (with double *acc*) to demand (*something*) of, ask (*someone*) for
Posīdōn·ĭus -ĭī or **-ī** *m* Stoic philosopher at Rhodes, teacher of Cicero
positĭ·ō -ōnis *f* putting, placing, setting; position, posture; situation

posĭt·or -ōris *m* builder
positūr·a -ae *f* posture; formation
posĭt·us -a -um *pp* of **pono;** *adj* situated, located
posĭt·us -ūs *m* position; arrangement
possessĭ·ō -ōnis *f* possession; getting possession, occupation; possession, estate
possessiuncŭl·a -ae *f* small estate
possess·or -ōris *m* possessor, occupant; (law) defendant
possibĭl·is -e *adj* possible
pos·sidĕō -sidēre -sēdī -sessum *vt* to possess, occupy; to have, own; to dwell in, live in; (fig) to take hold of
pos·sīdo -sīdĕre -sēdī -sessum *vt* to take possession of, occupy, seize
possum posse potŭī *vi* to be able; **multum (plus, plurimum) posse** to have much (*more, very great*) influence; **non possum quin exclamem** I can't help exclaiming; **quantum** or **ut fieri potest** as far as is possible
post *adv* (of place) behind, back, backwards; (of time) later, afterwards; (of order) next; **aliquanto post** somewhat later; **multis post annis** many years later; *prep* (with *acc*) (of place) behind; (of time) after, since
postĕā *adv* afterwards, after this, after that, hereafter, thereafter
posteāquam *conj* after
posterĭ·or -us *adj* later, next, following; latter, posterior; inferior, worse; hind
posterĭt·ās -ātis *f* the future, afterages, posterity, later generations; offspring (*of animals*); **in posteritatem** in the future
posterius *adv* later, at a later date
postĕr·us -a -um *adj* following, ensuing, next, subsequent, future; *m pl* future generations, posterity, descendants; *n* future time; next day; consequence; **in posterum** till the next day; for the future
post·fĕrō -ferre *vt* to put after; to esteem less; to sacrifice
postgenĭt·us -a -um *adj* born later; *m pl* later generations
posthab·ĕō -ēre -ŭī -ĭtum *vt* to consider of secondary importance; to slight, neglect; (with *dat*) to think (*something*) less important than
posthāc *adv* hereafter, in the future
posthinc or **post hinc** *adv* from here, from this place, next
posthōc or **post hōc** *adv* after this, afterwards
postĭbī *adv* afterwards, then
postīcŭl·um -ī *n* small building in the rear
postīc·us -a -um *adj* hind, back, rear; *n* back door
postidĕā *adv* afterwards, after that
postilēn·a -ae *f* crupper; buttocks
postillā *adv* afterwards

post·is -is *m* door post; door; *m pl* double doors
postlīmin·ĭum -ĭī or **-ī** *n* right to return home and resume one's former rank and privileges, right of recovery; **postliminio** by the right of recovery
postmerīdiān·us -a -um *adj* afternoon
postmŏdo or **postmŏdum** *adv* after a bit, a little later, afterwards
postpart·or -ōris *m* successor, heir
post·pōnō -pōnĕre -posŭī -posĭtum or **-postum** *vt* to consider of secondary importance; to neglect, disregard; (with *dat*) to consider (*something*) of less importance than, set (*something*) aside in favor of
postprincipĭ·a -ōrum *n pl* sequel
postpŭt·ō -āre *vt* to consider of secondary importance; (with **prae** + *abl*) to consider (*something*) less important than
postquam *conj* after, when
postrēmō *adv* at last, finally; **primo . . . deinde . . . postremo** first . . . then . . . finally
postrēmum *adv* for the last time, last of all
postrēm·us -a -um (*superl* of **posterus**) *adj* last, last in line, rear; lowest, worst
postrīdiē *adv* on the day after, on the following day; **postridie mane** the next morning; *prep* (with *genit*), e.g., **postridie ejus diei** on the day after that; (with *acc*), e.g., **postridie ludos** on the day after the games
postrīdŭō *adv* on the day after
postscaen·ĭum -ĭī or **-ī** *n* backstage
post·scrībō -scrībĕre -scripsī scriptum *vt* (with *dat*) to add (*e.g., a name*) to; **Tiberi nomen suo postscribere** to add the name of Tiberius to his own name
postulāt·a -ōrum *n pl* demands, claims, requests
postulātĭ·ō -ōnis *f* demand, request, desire; complaint; (law) application for permission to present a claim
postulāt·us -ūs *m* claim, suit
postŭl·ō -āre *vt* to demand, claim; to arraign, prosecute; to apply for (*a writ from the praetor to prosecute*)
postŭm·us -a -um *adj* last, lateborn
postus *pp* of **pono**
pōtātĭ·ō -ōnis *f* drinking, drinking party
pōtāt·or -ōris *m* drinker
pot·ens -entis *adj* capable; mighty, powerful, strong; efficacious, potent; fit, capable, equal; influential; (with *genit*) **a** capable of, equal to, fit for; **b** having power over; **c** presiding over; **d** having obtained (*one's wish*); **e** having carried out (*an order*)

potentāt·us -ūs *m* political power, rule, dominion
potenter *adv* powerfully, mightily, effectually, vigorously; according to one's ability
potenti·a -ae *f* force, power; political power (*esp. unconstitutional power*)
potēr·ium -ii or **-ī** *n* goblet
potest·ās -ātis *f* power, ability, capacity; efficacy, force; public authority, rule, power, sway, dominion, sovereignty, empire, rule; magisterial power, magistracy, office; possibility, opportunity, permission; person in office, magistrate, ruler; property, quality
potin or **potin'** = **potisne** can you?, are you able?
pōti·ō -ōnis *f* drinking; drink, draught; magic potion
pot·ior -īrī -ītus sum *vt* to acquire, get possession of; *vi* (with *genit* or *abl*) to acquire, get possession of, become master of, get hold of, get
poti·or -us (*comp* of **potis**) *adj* better, preferable, superior; more important
potis or **pote** (indecl) *adj* able, capable; possible
potissimum *adv* chiefly, especially, eminently
potissim·us -a -um *adj* chief, principal, most important
potius *adv* rather, more, by preference; **potius quam** more than, rather than
pōt·ō -āre *vt* to drink; to absorb
pōt·or -ōris *m* drinker
pōtr·ix -īcis *f* drinker (*female*)
pōtulent·us -a -um *adj* drinkable; *n pl* drinks
pōt·us -a -um *adj* drunk
pōt·us -ūs *m* drink
prae *adv* before, in front; in preference; *prep* (with *abl*) before, in front of; compared with, in comparison with; in view of; because of; by reason of, on account of, through; **prae manu** at hand; **prae se** publicly, openly, plainly; **prae se ferre** to display, manifest, exhibit, profess
praeacū·ō -ĕre *vt* to sharpen to a point
praeacūt·us -a -um *adj* pointed
praealt·us -a -um *adj* very high; very deep
praeb·ĕō -ēre -ŭī -ĭtum *vt* to hold out, offer, present; to supply, give; to exhibit, represent, show; to give up, yield, surrender; to cause, occasion; to permit, allow; **se praebere** to show oneself, behave
praebĭb·ō -ĕre -ī *vt* (with *dat*) to drink (*e.g., a toast*) to
praebĭt·or -ōris *m* supplier
praecalid·us -a -um *adj* very warm, hot
praecantr·ix -īcis *f* witch, enchantress
praecān·us -a -um *adj* prematurely grey
prae·cavĕō -cavēre -cāvī -cautum *vt* to guard against, try to avoid; *vi* to take precautions, be on one's guard; (with *dat*) to look out for, look after; (with *abl*) to guard against, be on one's guard against
prae·cēdō -cēdĕre -cessī -cessum *vt* to precede, go out before, lead; to surpass, excel; *vi* to excel, be superior; (with *dat*) to excel, be superior to
praecell·ens -entis *adj* superior, excellent, preeminent
praecell·ō -ĕre *vt* to surpass, outdo; *vi* to distinguish oneself, excel; (with *dat*) to rule over
praecels·us -a -um *adj* towering
praecenti·ō -ōnis *f* musical prelude (*before a sacrifice*)
praecent·ō -āre *vi* (with *dat*) to sing to
praecentus *pp* of **praecino**
praec·eps -ipitis *adj* headfirst; downhill, steep, precipitous; sinking (*sun*); swift, rushing, violent; hasty, rash, inconsiderate; dangerous; *n* edge of a cliff, cliff, precipice; danger, critical situation
praeceps *adv* headfirst
praecepti·ō -ōnis *f* preconception; precept, rule; priority
praecept·or -ōris *m* or **praeceptr·ix -īcis** *f* teacher, preceptor
praecept·um -ī *n* rule, maxim; order, command, direction
prae·cerpō -cerpĕre -cerpsī -cerptum *vt* to pick or gather before time; (with *dat*) (fig) to snatch away from
prae·cīdō -cīdĕre -cīdī -cīsum *vt* to lop off, cut short; to cut, cut through; to damage, mutilate; to break off, finish abruptly, end suddenly (*a speech, etc.*); to end, destroy (*hopes, etc.*); to refuse, decline
prae·cingō -cingĕre -cinxī -cinctum *vt* to gird; to surround, ring; to dress; **ense cingi** to wear a sword; **male cinctus** improperly dressed; **recte cinctus** properly dressed
prae·cīnō -cinĕre -cinŭī -centum *vt* to predict; (with *dat*) to predict (*something*) to; *vi* to make predictions; (with *dat*) to sing or play before or at (*e.g., dinner, sacrifice*)
prae·cipĭō -cipĕre -cēpī -ceptum *vt* to take or receive in advance; to grasp beforehand, anticipate; to teach, instruct, direct, warn; to prescribe; **animo praecipere** or **cogitatione praecipere** to imagine beforehand, reckon on, anticipate, expect; **oculis praecipere** to see beforehand, get a preview of; **opinione praecipere** to suspect in advance; **pecuniam mutuam praecipere** to get an advance loan
praecipitanter *adv* at a high speed
praecipĭt·ō -āre *vt* to throw down

head first; to hasten, hurry, precipitate; **se praecipitare** to throw oneself down, throw oneself down headfirst, jump down, dive; to sink; *vi* to rush headfirst, rush at top speed, rush thoughtlessly; to fall, sink; to be ruined
praecipŭē *adv* especially, chiefly
praecipŭ·us -a -um *adj* special, peculiar, particular; chief, principal; distinguished, excellent, extraordinary; *n* excellence, superiority; *n pl* outstanding or important elements; **praecipua rerum** highlights
praecīsē *adv* briefly, concisely; absolutely
praecīs·us -a -um *pp of* **praecido;** *adj* abrupt, precipitous; rugged, rough; brief, abrupt (*speech*)
praeclārē *adv* very clearly; excellently; (to express agreement) very good, splendid
praeclār·us -a -um *adj* very clear; very nice; splendid, noble, distinguished, excellent; famous, distinguished; notorious
prae·clūdō -clūdĕre -clūsī -clūsum *vt* to shut, shut off, obstruct; to hinder, stop, impede; **portas consuli praecludere** to shut the gates on the consul, shut the gates in the consul's face; **vocem praecludere alicui** to shut someone up, to hush someone up
praec·ō -ōnis *m* crier, herald; auctioneer; (fig) pangyrist
precōgit·ō -āre *vt* to premeditate
praecognīt·us -a -um *adj* known beforehand, foreseen
prae-cōlō -colĕre — -cultum *vt* to cultivate prematurely; (fig) to embrace prematurely
praecomposit·us -a -um *adj* arranged beforehand; studied, self-conscious
praecōnī·us -a -um *adj* of a public crier, of an auctioneer; *n* crier's office; proclamation, announcement; praising, praise
praecon·sūmō -sumĕre -sumpsī -sumptum *vt* to spend or use up beforehand
praecontrect·ō -āre *vt* to consider in advance
praecordi·a -ōrum *n pl* diaphragm, midriff; insides, stomach; breast, heart
praecor·rumpō -rumpĕre -rūpī -ruptum *vt* to bribe in advance
praec·ox -ŏcis *adj* premature, hasty, rash
praecurrent·ia -ium *n pl* antecedents
prae·currō -currĕre -cucurrī or **-currī -cursum** *vt* to precede, anticipate; to outdo, surpass; *vi* to run out ahead, take the lead; (with **ante** + *acc*) to run out ahead of; (with *dat*) to outdo
praecursi·ō -ōnis *f* previous occurrence; (mil) skirmish; (rhet) warm-up (*of the audience*)
praecurs·or -ōris *m* forerunner; spy; (mil) scout; advance guard
praecursōri·us -a -um *adj* sent in advance
prae·cutiō -cutĕre -cussī -cussum *vt* to wave, brandish in front
praed·a -ae *f* booty, spoils, plunder; prey; **praedae esse** (with *dat*) to fall prey to
praedābund·us -a -um *adj* pillaging, plundering
praedamn·ō -āre *vt* to condemn beforehand; **spem praedamnare** to give up hope too soon
praedāti·ō -ōnis *f* pillaging, plunder
praedāt·or -ōris *m* marauder, looter, vandal; hunter; greedy man
praedātōri·us -a -um *adj* marauding, looting; graspy, greedy
praedēlass·ō -āre *vt* to tire out, weaken beforehand
praedestin·ō -āre *vt* to predetermine
praediāt·or -ōris *m* real-estate agent
praediātōri·us -a -um *adj* real-estate; **jus praediatorium** mortgage law
praedicābil·is -e *adj* praiseworthy, laudable
praedicāti·ō -ōnis *f* announcement, publication; praising
praedicāt·or -ōris *m* appreciator; eulogist
praedic·ō -āre *vt* to announce, proclaim; to report; to assert; to praise
prae·dīcō -dīcĕre -dixī -dictum *vt* to mention beforehand or earlier; to prearrange; to predict; to order, command beforehand
praedicti·ō -ōnis *f* prediction
praedict·um -ī *n* prediction, prophecy; command, order; **velut ex praedicto** as if by prearrangement
praediŏl·um -ī *n* small estate, small farm
praedisc·ō -ĕre *vt* to learn beforehand, find out in advance
praedisposit·us -a -um *adj* previously arranged
praedit·us -a -um *adj* endowed, gifted, provided, furnished; (with *abl*) endowed with, provided with, furnished with
praed·ium -iī or **-ī** *n* estate, farm; **praedia urbana** city lots
praedīv·es -itis *adj* very rich
praedīvin·ō -āre *vt* to know in advance, have a presentiment of
praed·ō -ōnis *m* marauder, looter, robber, pirate
praedoct·us -a -um *adj* instructed beforehand
praed·or -ārī -ātus sum *vt* to raid, plunder, loot, rob; (fig) to rob, ravish; **amores alicujus praedari** to steal away someone's sweetheart; *vi* to plunder, loot, make a raid; (with **ex** + *abl*) to prey on, profit by, take advantage of, e.g., **ex al-**

terius inscientiā praedari to prey on someone else's ignorance
prae-dūcō -dūcĕre -duxī -ductum *vt* to run or construct (*trench, wall*) out in front (*for defensive purposes*)
praedulc·is -e *adj* very sweet; (fig) very satisfying (*honor, reward*)
praedūr·us -a -um *adj* very tough (*skin*); tough, brawny
praeēmin·ĕō -ēre *vt* to surpass, excel; *vi* to project forward, stick out
prae·ĕō -īre -īvī or **-iī -itum** *vt* to lead, precede; to read out, dictate, lead (*prayers*); *vi* to go out ahead, take the lead; (with *dat*) to walk in front of
praefāti·ō -ōnis *f* preface, introduction; formula
praefātus *pp* of **praefor**
praefectūr·a -ae *f* supervision, superintendence; prefectship, office of prefect, superintendency; government of a district; prefecture (*Italian city governed by a Roman prefect*); territory of a prefecture, district
praefect·us -ī *m* prefect, supervisor, superintendent; commander; governor; (with *genit* or *dat*) supervisor of, commander of, prefect or governor of
prae-fĕrō -ferre -tŭlī -lātum *vt* to hold out, carry in front; to prefer; to anticipate; to display, reveal, betray; to offer, present; to offer as a model; **praeferri** to ride past, ride by, march past, outflank; **praeferri** or **se praeferri** (with *dat*) to surpass
praefĕr·ox -ōcis *adj* very belligerent, very defiant
praeferrāt·us -a -um *adj* iron-tipped; (coll) chained (*slave*)
praefervĭd·us -a -um *adj* boiling; (fig) boiling; **ira praefervida** boiling anger
praefestīn·ō -āre *vt* to hurry past; (with *inf*) to be in a hurry to
praefĭc·a -ae *f* hired mourner (*female*)
prae·ficiō -ficĕre -fēcī -fectum *vt* to put (*someone*) in charge; (with double *acc*) to appoint (*someone*) as; (with *dat*) to put (*someone*) in charge of, set (*someone*) over, appoint (*someone*) to command
praefīd·ens -entis *adj* too trustful, overconfident; (with *dat*) too trustful of; **homines sibi praefidentes** overconfident men
prae·fīgō -fīgĕre -fixī -fixum *vt* to fix, fasten, set up in front, fasten on the end; to tip, point; to transfix; **capistris praefigere** to muzzle; **cuspidibus praefixus** pointed; **ferro praefixus** iron-tipped
praefīn·iō -īre -īvī or **-iī -ītum** *vt* to determine in advance; to prescribe, appoint; to limit
praefīnītō *adv* in the prescribed manner
praefiscĭnē or **praefiscĭnī** *adv* meaning no offense
praeflōr·ō -āre *vt* to deflower, deprive of its bloom; (fig) to tarnish, spoil
praeflŭ·ō -ĕre *vt & vi* to flow by
praefōc·ō -āre *vt* to choke, choke up, strangle
prae·fodiō -fodĕre -fōdī *vt* to bury beforehand; to dig in front of; **portas praefodire** to dig trenches in front of the gates
prae·for -fārī -fātus sum *vt* to say beforehand, utter in advance, preface; to address in prayer beforehand; to foretell; to invoke; *vi* to pray beforehand; (with *dat*) to pray before
praefractē *adv* obstinately
praefract·us -a -um *pp* of **praefringo;** resolute, determined; abrupt
praefrīgĭd·us -a -um *adj* very cold, freezing
prae·fringō -fringĕre -frēgī -fractum *vt* to break off at the tip or end, break to pieces, smash
prae·fulciō -fulcīre -fulsī -fultum *vt* to prop up, support in front; (with *dat*) to use (*someone*) as a prop or support for; **illud praefulci ut** make sure that
prae·fulgĕō -fulgēre -fulsī *vi* to shine forth, glitter, sparkle
praegelĭd·us -a -um *adj* very cold
praegest·iō -īre *vi* to be very eager
praegn·ans -antis or **praegn·ās -ātis** *adj* pregnant; (with *abl*) full of, swollen with
praegracĭl·is -e *adj* very lean or slender
praegrand·is -e *adj* huge, very great; very powerful
praegrăv·is -e *adj* very heavy; very fat; oppressive; very tiresome
praegrăv·ō -āre *vt* to weigh down; to outweigh; (fig) to burden
prae·gredior -grĕdī -gressus sum *vt* to go in advance of, go ahead of; to go by, go past; *vi* to walk out in front; (with *dat*) to precede, lead
praegressi·ō -ōnis *f* procession; (fig) precedence
praegustāt·or -ōris *m* taster, sampler
praegust·ō -āre *vt* to taste beforehand, get a sample of
praehib·ĕō -ēre *vt* to offer, furnish, supply; to utter, speak (*words*); **praehibere operam** (with *dat*) to offer to help
praejac·ĕō -ēre *vt* to lie before, be located in front of; *vi* (with *dat*) to lie before
praejūdicāt·us -a -um *adj* decided beforehand; prejudiced; *n* prejudged matter; prejudice; **id pro praejudicato ferre** to take it as a foregone conclusion
praejūdic·ium -iī or **-ī** *n* preliminary hearing; prejudgment; precedent, example

praejūdic·ō -āre *vt* to decide beforehand, prejudge
prae·jūvō -juvāre -jūvī *vt* to help in advance
prae·lābor -lābī -lapsus sum *vt & vi* to glide along, glide by, float by
praelamb·ō -ĕre *vt* to pretaste
praelarg·us -a -um *adj* very ample
praelātus *pp* of **praefero**
prae·lĕgō -legĕre -lēgī -lectum *vt* to sail past
praelig·ō -āre *vt* to tie up; (with *dat*) to tie (*something*) to
praelong·us -a -um *adj* very long
prae·lŏquor -lŏquī -locūtus sum *vt* to make (*a speech*) before someone else; to present (*a case*) first; to say by way of preface; *vi* to speak first
prae·lūcĕō -lūcēre -luxī *vi* (with *dat*) **a** to throw light on; **b** to outshine, outdo, surpass
praelūsi·ō -ōnis *f* prelude
praelustr·is -e *adj* magnificent
praemandāt·a -ōrum *n pl* warrant for arrest
praemand·ō -āre *vt* to order in advance
praemātūrē *adv* too soon, prematurely
praemātūr·us -a -um *adj* premature
praemedicāt·us -a -um *adj* protected by charms
praemeditāti·ō -ōnis *f* premeditation, prior consideration
praemedit·or -ārī -ātus sum *vt* to think over beforehand; to practice, practice on (*a musical instrument*)
praemerc·or -ārī -ātus sum *vt* to buy in advance
praemetŭ·ens -entis *adj* apprehensive
praemetuenter *adv* anxiously
praemetŭ·ō -ĕre *vt* to fear beforehand; *vi* (with *dat*) to be apprehensive about
prae·mittō -mittĕre -mīsī -missum *vt* to send out ahead, send in advance; *vi* to send word
praem·ium -iī or **-ī** *n* prize, reward, recompense; exploit (*worthy of reward*); gift, bribe
praemolesti·a -ae *f* apprehension, presentiment of trouble
praemōl·ior -īrī *vt* to prepare beforehand
praemon·ĕō -ēre -ŭī -itum *vt* to forewarn; to warn of; to foreshadow, presage, predict
praemonit·us -ūs *m* forewarning, premonition
praemonstrāt·or -ōris *m* director, guide
praemonstr·ō -āre *vt* to point out the way to, guide, direct; to predict
prae·mordĕō -mordēre -mordī or **morsī -morsum** *vt* to bite the tip off of; (fig) to crib, pilfer
prae·morior -mŏrī -mortŭus sum *vi* to die too soon, die prematurely
praemūn·iō -īre -īvī -ītum *vt* to fortify, protect, secure
praemūnīti·ō -ōnis *f* (rhet) preparation, conditioning (*of the minds of the hearers*)
praenarr·ō -āre *vt* to relate beforehand
praenăt·ō -āre *vt* to float past, flow by
Praenest·e -is *n* or *f* ancient town in Latium (*modern Palestrina*)
Praenestīn·us -a -um *adj & m* Praenestine
praenit·ĕō -ēre -ŭī *vi* (with *dat*) **a** to outshine; **b** to appear more attractive to
praenōm·en -inis *n* first name
praenosc·ō -ĕre *vt* to find out beforehand, foreknow
praenōti·ō -ōnis *f* innate idea, preconception
praenūbil·us -a -um *adj* heavily clouded; dark, gloomy
praenunti·a -ae *f* harbinger, foreteller, omen
praenunti·ō -āre *vt* to foretell
praenunti·us -a -um *adj* foreboding; *m* forecaster, harbinger, omen
praeoccupāti·ō -ōnis *f* seizing beforehand, advance occupation
praeoccŭp·ō -āre *vt* to occupy before another; to preoccupy; to anticipate, prevent
praeŏl·it -ĕre *v impers* a smell is emitted, there is a strong smell; **praeolit mihi quod tu velis** I scent your wishes before you express them
praeopt·ō -āre *vt* to prefer
praepand·ō -ĕre *vt* to spread, extend
praeparāti·ō -ōnis *f* preparation
praeparāt·us -a -um *adj* prepared, supplied, furnished, ready; *n* stores; **ex ante preparato** from the stores; (fig) by previous arrangement
praepăr·ō -āre *vt* to get ready, prepare, prepare for; to gather together
praepedīment·um -ī *n* impediment, hindrance
praeped·iō -īre -īvī or **-iī -ītum** *vt* to shackle, chain; to hinder, obstruct, hamper; to embarrass
praepend·ĕō -ēre *vi* to hang down in front
praep·es -ĕtis *adj* nimble, fast; winged; of good omen, favorable; *m* or *f* bird of good omen; bird, large bird
praepilāt·us -a -um *adj* tipped with a ball; **missile prapilatum** blunted missile
praepingu·is -e *adj* very fat; very fertile
praepoll·ĕō -ēre *vi* to be powerful; to be superior; (with *dat*) to surpass in power
praeponděr·ō -āre *vt* to outweigh; to regard as superior
prae·pōnō -pōnĕre -posŭī -posi-

tum *vt* (with *dat*) **a** to place, set, put (*something*) in front of or before; **b** to entrust (*someone*) with, put (*someone*) in command of, in charge of; **c** to prefer (*someone or something*) to
praeport·ō -āre *vt* to carry before oneself
praepositi·ō -ōnis *f* preference; prefixing
praeposit·us -a -um *pp* of **praepono;** *adj* preferred, preferable; *m* prefect, commander; *n* that which is desirable, a desirable good
prae·possum -posse -potŭī *vi* to get the upper hand, have the better of it
praepostĕrē *adv* in reversed order, out of order
praepostĕr·us -a -um *adj* inverted, in reverse order; absurd, preposterous
praepŏt·ens -entis *adj* very powerful; (with *genit*) in full control of, fully controlling
praeproperanter or **praeproperē** *adv* very quickly
praeproper·us -a -um *adj* very quick; overhasty, sudden
praepūt·ĭum -ĭī or **-ī** *n* foreskin
praequam *conj* in comparison to; **nihil hoc est, praequam alios sumptus facit** this is nothing in comparison to the other expenses that he runs up
praequest·us -a -um *adj* complaining beforehand; **multa praequestus** having first raised many complaints
praeradĭ·ō -āre *vt* to outshine
praerapĭd·us -a -um *adj* very swift
praereptus *pp* of **praeripio**
praerig·escō -escĕre -ŭī *vi* to become very stiff
prae·ripĭō -ripĕre -ripŭī -reptum *vt* to snatch away, carry off; to anticipate, forestall; to count on too soon, presume upon; (with *dat*) to snatch from, steal from
prae·rōdō -rōdĕre -rōsī -rōsum *vt* to bite the ends of, nibble at; **digitos praerodere** to bite the fingernails
praerogātīv·us -a -um *adj* asked before others; voting first, privileged; *f* first tribe or century to vote; vote of the first tribe or century; previous election; sure sign, omen
praerōsus *pp* of **praerodo**
prae·rumpō -rumpĕre -rūpī -ruptum *vt* to break off, tear away (*something*) in front
praerupt·us -a -um *adj* broken off, broken up; broken up, rough (*terrain*); steep; hasty, impetuous
praes praedis *m* bondsman, surety; collateral
praesaep- = praesep-
praesāg·iō -īre -īvī or **praesāg·ior -īrī** *vt* to have forebodings of, feel beforehand; to cause
praesāgītĭ·ō -ōnis *f* presentiment, strange feeling, foreboding, prophetic power
praesāg·ĭum -ĭī or **-ī** *n* presentiment, presage, prediction
praesāg·us -a -um *adj* divining, prophetic
praesc·iō -īre -īvī *vt* to know beforehand
praescisc·ō -ĕre *vt* to find out or learn beforehand
praescĭ·us -a -um *adj* prescient; (with *genit*) foreseeing; **praescius venturi** foreseeing the future
prae·scrībō -scrībĕre -scripsī -scriptum *vt* to prefix in writing; to describe beforehand; to determine in advance, prescribe, ordain; to dictate; to outline, map out; to put forward as an excuse
praescriptĭ·ō -ōnis *f* heading, title; preface; pretext; rule, law; limit, restriction
praescript·um -ī *n* regulation, rule, proviso
praesĕc·ō -āre -ŭī -tum *vt* to cut off, cut out, cut short
praesegmĭn·a -um *n pl* clippings
praes·ens -entis *adj* present, in person, at hand; existing, contemporary; prompt, immediate, impending; efficacious, powerful, effective; influential; resolute; propitious; **sermo praesens** a face-to-face talk; *n* present time; **ad praesens** or **in praesens** for the present
praesensĭ·ō -ōnis *f* presentiment; preconception
praesensus *pp* of **praesentio**
praesentārĭ·us -a -um *adj* ready, at hand
praesentĭ·a -ae *f* presence; efficacy, effect; **animi praesentia** presence of mind; **in praesentia** at the present time, just now, for the present
praesent·ĭa -ĭum *n pl* present circumstances, present state of affairs
prae·sentĭō -sentīre -sensī -sensum *vt* to feel beforehand, to realize in advance, have strange feelings about, divine
praesēp·e or **praesaep·e -is** *n* or **praesēp·is** or **praesēp·es -is** *f* stall, stable; crib, manger; room, lodgings; tavern; hovel; beehive
praesēp·iō or **praesaep·iō -īre -sī -tum** *vt* to fence in, barricade
praesertim *adv* especially, particularly, principally; **praesertim cum** especially because
praeserv·iō -īre *vi* (with *dat*) to serve as a slave to
praes·es -ĭdis *m* guard, guardian, protector, defender; president, superintendent; captain, pilot; *f* guardian, protectress
praesĭd·ens -entis *m* president, ruler
prae·sidĕō -sidēre -sēdī *vt* to guard, protect, defend; to command, be in comand of; *vi* to be in charge,

be in command; (with *dat*) **a** to watch over, guard, protect; **b** to preside over, direct, manage, command

praesidiāri·us -a -um *adj* on garrison duty

praesid·ium -iī or **-ī** *n* protection, defense; help, assistance; guard, garrison; convoy, escort; garrison post, defensive position

praesignific·ō -āre *vt* to indicate in advance, foretoken

praesign·is -e *adj* outstanding

praesŏn·ō -āre -ŭī *vi* to sound beforehand

praesparg·ō -ĕre *vt* to strew, scatter

praestābil·is -e *adj* excellent, outstanding

praest·ans -antis *adj* outstanding, eminent, exceptional

praestanti·a -ae *f* excellence, superiority, preeminence

praestern·ō -ĕre *vt* to strew

praest·es -itis *adj* guardian, protecting, presiding

praestigi·ae -ārum *f pl* sleight of hand, juggling, tricks, illusion, deception

praestigiāt·or -ōris *m* or **praestigiātr·ix -īcis** *f* juggler, magician; imposter

praestin·ō -āre *vt* to buy, shop for

prae·stitŭō -stituĕre -stitŭī -stitūtum *vt* to fix or set up beforehand, prescribe

praestitus *pp* of **praesto**

praestō *adv* at hand, ready, present; **praesto esse** (with *dat*) **a** to be on hand for, attend, serve, be helpful to, aid; **b** to be in the way of, resist, oppose

prae·stō -stāre -stitī -stitum *vt* to excel, be superior to; to show, exhibit, give evidence of, display; to answer for, be responsible for, take upon oneself; to perform, discharge, fulfill; to keep, maintain, retain; **fidem praestare** to keep one's word; **impetūs populi praestare** to be responsible for popular outbreaks; **nihil praestare** to be answerable for nothing; **officia praestare** to perform duties; **se praestare** to show oneself, behave; **socios salvos praestare** to keep the allies safe; **terga hosti praestare** to show one's back to the enemy, retreat; **virtutem praestare** to display courage; *vi* to stand out, be outstanding, be preeminent, be superior; *v impers* it is preferable, it is better

praestōl·or -ārī -ātus sum *vt* to wait for, expect; *vi* (with *dat*) to wait for

prae·stringō -stringĕre -strinxī -strictum *vt* to draw together, squeeze; to blunt (*an edge*); to blind, dazzle (*the eyes*); to dazzle, baffle, confuse

prae·strŭō -struĕre -struxī -structum *vt* to build up, block up, block, stop up; to build up (*e.g., confidence*) beforehand

praes·ul -ŭlis *m* or *f* public dancer

praesult·ō -āre *vi* (with *dat*) to jump around in front of

prae·sum -esse -fŭī *vi* to preside, be in charge, be in command; (with *dat*) **a** to preside over, be in charge of, be in command of; **b** to protect; (with **in** + *abl*) to be governor in

prae·sūmō -sūmĕre -sumpsī -sumptum *vt* to take in advance; to anticipate, take for granted, presume

praesumpti·ō -ōnis *f* anticipation

praesūt·us -a -um *adj* sewed up; covered

praetĕg·ō -ĕre *vt* to protect

praetempt·ō -āre *vt* to try out in advance, test in advance; to grope for

prae·tendō -tendĕre -tendī -tentum *vt* to hold or stretch in front of oneself; to present; to offer as an excuse, give as pretext, allege, pretend; (with *dat*) to hold or draw (*e.g., a toga*) in front of (*e.g., the eyes*); **praetendi** (of places) to lie to the front or opposite; **praetendi** (with *dat*) to lie or be situated opposite or over against

praetentō see **praetempto**

praetentus *pp* of **praetendo**

praetep·escō -escĕre -ŭī *vi* (of love) to glow

praeter *conj* besides, other than; *prep* (with *acc*) (of place) past, by, along, before, in front of; (in comparison) above, beyond, more than; against, contrary to, aside from; besides, apart from, except; besides, in addition to

praeterăg·ō -ĕre *vt* (with double *acc*) to drive (*e.g., a horse*) past (*a place*)

praeterbīt·ō -ĕre *vt & vi* to go by or past

praeterĕā *adv* besides, moreover; hereafter, thereafter

praeter·ĕō -īre -īvī or **-iī -itum** *vt* to go past, pass by; to skip, pass over in silence, neglect; to escape the notice of; to go beyond; to surpass

praeterequit·ans -antis *adj* riding by

praeter·fĕrō -ferre -tŭlī -lātum *vt* (with double *acc*) to carry or take (*someone*) past (*something*); **praeterferri** to move or sweep by (*a place*)

praeterflŭ·ō -ĕre *vt & vi* to flow by

praeter·gredior -grĕdī -gressus sum *vt* to march by, go past; to surpass

praeterhāc *adv* in addition

praeterit·us -a -um *pp* of **praetereo**; *adj* past, past and gone, bygone; *n pl* bygone events, the past

praeter·lābor -lābī -lapsus sum *vt* to glide by; *vi* to glide by, slip away

praeterlātus *pp* of **praeterfero**

praetermĕ·ō -āre *vt & vi* to go past or by

praetermissi·ō -ōnis *f* leaving out, omission; passing over, neglecting; (with *genit*) omission of, neglecting of

praeter·mittō -mittĕre -mīsī -missum *vt* to let pass, let go by; to leave undone; to pass over, omit, disregard, overlook, neglect

praetĕr·ō -ĕre *vt* to wear down in front

praeterquam *adv* besides, other than; **praeterquam quod** apart from the fact that

praetervecti·ō -ōnis *f* passing by

praeter·vĕhor -vĕhī -vectus sum *vt & vi* to ride by; to sail by; to march or go by

praetervŏl·ō -āre *vt & vi* to fly by; (of opportunity) to slip by; to escape

praetex·ō -ĕre -ŭī -tum *vt* to border, edge, fringe; to adorn in front; (fig) to cloak, conceal, disguise; to allege as a pretext

praetextāt·us -a -um *adj* wearing the toga praetexta (*crimson-bordered toga*); underage, juvenile, **mores praetextati** loose morals

praetext·us -a -um *pp* of **praetexo;** *adj* bordered; wearing the crimson-bordered toga; **fabula praetexta** Roman tragic drama; *f* toga praetexta (*crimson-bordered toga which was worn by higher magistrates and by freeborn boys*); tragedy; **praetextas docere** to put on tragedies; *n* pretext, pretense, excuse

praetext·us -ūs *m* outward show, splendor; pretense, pretext

praetim·ĕō -ēre *vi* to be apprehensive

praetinct·us -a -um *adj* previously dipped

praet·or -ōris *m* praetor (*judicial magistrate, accompanied by six lictors*); commander; (during the early years of the republic) chief magistrate, chief executive; (in Italian municipalities) chief magistrate; **praetor peregrinus** praetor who had jurisdiction over cases involving foreigners; **praetor urbanus** or **praetor urbis** praetor who had jurisdiction over cases involving Roman citizens

praetōriān·us -a -um *adj* praetorian, belonging to the emperor's bodyguard; *m pl* praetorian guard, soldiers of the praetorian guard

praetōrici·us -a -um *adj* received from the praetor (*at public games*)

praetōri·us -a -um *adj* of the commander in chief, of the commander or general; praetor's, of the praetor; propraetor's; **cohors praetoria** general's bodyguard; **comitia praetoria** praetorian elections; **navis praetoria** flagship; **porta praetoria** camp gate nearest the general's tent; **turba praetoria** crowd around the praetor; *n* general's quarters, headquarters; official residence of the governor in a province; council of war; emperor's bodyguard; palace, mansion

praetorqu·ĕō -ēre *vt* to twist beforehand; to strangle first

praetrepĭd·ans -antis *adj* very nervous

praetrepĭd·us -a -um *adj* very nervous, trembling

praetrunc·ō -āre *vt* to cut off, cut short

praetūr·a -ae *f* praetorship; **praeturā se abdicare** to resign the praetorship

praeumbr·ans -antis *adj* casting a shadow; (fig) overshadowing

praeust·us -a -um *adj* burnt at the tip; hardened by fire at the point; frost-bitten

praeut *conj* as compared with, when compared with

praeval·ĕō -ēre -ŭī *vi* to be stronger, have more power; to have greater influence; to have the upper hand

praevalĭd·us -a -um *adj* of superior strength, unusually strong, unusually powerful, imposing; too strong

praevāricāti·ō -ōnis *f* collusion

praevāricāt·or -ōris *m* phoney accuser, prosecutor in collusion, prevaricator

praevāric·or -ārī -ātus sum *vi* to make a sham defense or prosecution; (with *dat*) to favor because of collusion

prae·vĕhor -vĕhī -vectus sum *vt* (of a river) to flow past; *vi* to ride in front, ride by; to sail by

prae·venĭo -venīre -vēnī -ventum *vt* to come before, precede, get the jump on, anticipate; to prevent; *vi* to come before, precede

praeverr·ō -ĕre *vt* to sweep before

praevert·ō -ĕre -ī or **prae·vertor -vertī** *vt* to go before, precede, outrun, outstrip; to turn to first, attend to first; to prefer; to come before, anticipate, prevent; to preoccupy; (with *dat* or **prae** + *abl*) to prefer (*someone or something*) to; *vi* (with *dat* or **ad** + *acc*) to go to first, turn to first, attend to first

prae·vidĕō -vidēre -vīdī -vīsum *vt* to foresee

praeviti·ō -āre *vt* to taint or pollute beforehand

praevĭ·us -a -um *adj* going before, leading the way

praevŏl·ō -āre *vi* to fly out in front

pragmatĭc·us -a -um *adj* experienced; *m* lawyer, attorney

prandĕō prandēre prandī pransum *vt* to eat for breakfast, eat for lunch; *vi* to have breakfast, have lunch

prand·ium -iī or **-ī** *n* breakfast, lunch

pransĭt·ō -āre *vt* to usually eat for lunch

prans·or -ōris *m* guest at lunch

prans·us -a -um *pp* of **prandeo;** *adj* having had breakfast, after eating; well fed; **pransus potus** having been wined and dined

prasin·us -a -um *adj* green; **factio prasina** the Greens (*one of the stables of horses at the racetrack in Rome*)

prātens·is -e *adj* meadow, growing in the meadow

prātŭl·um -ī *n* small meadow

prāt·um -ī *n* meadow; (fig) plain (*of the sea*); *n pl* meadow grass

prāvē *adv* crookedly; improperly, wrongly, badly, poorly; **prave facti versūs** poorly written verses

prāvit·ās -ātis *f* crookedness, distortion; impropriety, irregularity; perverseness, depravity

prāv·us -a -um *adj* crooked, distorted, deformed; irregular, improper, wrong, bad; perverse, vicious

Praxitĕl·ēs -is *m* famous Greek Athenian sculptor (*4th cent.* B.C.)

precāriō *adv* upon request

precāri·us -a -um *adj* obtained by prayer; dependent on another's will, uncertain, precarious

precāti·ō -ōnis *f* prayer; **precationes facere** to say prayers

precāt·or -ōris *m* intercessor, suppliant

precēs = *pl* of **prex**

preci·ae -ārum *f pl* grapevine

prec·or -ārī -ātus sum *vt* to entreat, supplicate, pray to; to pray for; to wish for; (with double *acc*) to pray to (*someone*) for; (with *acc* of thing and *abl* of person) to request (*something*) from; (with **pro** + *abl*) to entreat (*e.g., the gods*) on behalf of; (with **ut** or **ne**) to pray that, pray that not; **longum Augusto diem precari** to wish Augustus long life; *vi* to pray; (with **ad** + *acc*) to pray to, e.g., **di ad quos precantur** the gods to whom they pray; **male precari** to curse, utter curses

pre·hendō -hendĕre -hendī -hensum or **prendō prendĕre prendī prensum** *vt* to take hold of, grasp, seize; to detain; to arrest; to occupy; to catch, surprise; to reach, arrive at; to grasp, understand

prēl·um -ī *n* wine press, oil press; clothes press

premō premĕre pressī pressum *vt* to press, squeeze; to lie down on; to hug (*shore*); to suppress, hide; to cover, crown; to press hard, bear down on; to chase, attack; to weigh down, load; to press together, close; to curb, stop; to depress, lower; to mark, impress; to prune; to pressure, urge, importune; to degrade, humble, disparage; to abridge; to subjugate

prensāti·ō -ōnis *f* campaigning (*for office*)

prens·ō or **prehens·ō -āre** *vt* to take hold of, clutch at, grab; to stop, detain; *vi* to campaign, be a candidate

prensus *pp* of **prendo**

pressē *adv* distinctly, with articulation; concisely; accurately; simply

pressi·ō -ōnis *f* fulcrum; leverage

press·ō -āre *vt* to press

press·us -a -um *pp* of **premo;** *adj* closed, shut tight; suppressed; slow; lowered, low, subdued; concise, precise, accurate; articulate

press·us -ūs *m* pressing, pressure; expression (*of the face*)

prest·ēr -ēris *m* waterspout

pretiōsē *adv* at great cost, expensively

pretiōs·us -a -um *adj* previous, valuable; expensive; extravagant

pret·ium -iī or **-ī** *n* price; value, worth; reward, return, recompense; bribe; pay, wages; **in pretio esse** to be prized; to be held in high esteem; **in pretio habere** to prize, hold in high esteem; **pretium curae esse** to be worth the trouble; **pretium habere** to have value, be worth something; **pretium facere** to set a price; **pretium operae esse** to be worth the effort, be worthwhile

prex precis *f* prayer, request; curse, imprecation; intercession

Priamē·is -idis *f* daughter of Priam

Priamēi·us -a -um *adj* Priam's, of Priam

Priamid·ēs -ae *m* son of Priam

Priăm·us -ī *m* Priam (*son of Laomedon, husband of Hecuba, father of Hector, Paris, etc., king of Troy at the time of its fall*)

prīdem *adv* long ago, long, since; **haud ita pridem** not so long ago; not long before; **quam pridem** how long ago

prīdiē *adv* the day before, the previous day

prīm·a -ōrum *n pl* first part, beginning; first principles or elements; **cum primus** among the first, especially; **in primis** above all, chiefly, particularly, especially, principally

prīm·ae -ārum *f pl* lead, first rank, highest place, highest importance; **primas dare** (with *dat*) to attach supreme importance to

prīmaev·us -a -um *adj* young, youthful

prīmān·ī -ōrum *m pl* soldiers of the first legion

prīmāri·us -a -um *adj* first in rank; first-rate

prīmigĕn·us -a -um *adj* original

prīmipīl·us -ī *m* first-ranking centurion of a legion

prīmiti·ae -ārum *f pl* firstfruits

prīmitus *adv* originally, at first; for the first time

prīmō *adv* first, in the first place; at first, at the beginning

prīmord·ium -iī or **-ī** *n* origin, beginning; commencement; beginning of a new reign

prīmōr·ēs -um *m pl* chiefs, nobles, leaders; (mil) front line
prīmōr·is -e *adj* first, foremost, extreme, tip of; first, principal; **digituli primores** fingertips; **primori in acie** all the way up front
prīmŭlum *adv* first of all, at first
prīmŭl·us -a -um *adj* very first
prīmum *adv* first, in the first place, before all else; at first; for the first time; **cum primum, ubi primum, ut primum** as soon as; **primum dum** in the first place; **quam primum** as soon as possible
prīm·us -a -um *adj* first, foremost; principal; eminent, distinguished; earliest; **primas partes agere** to play the lead role; **primis digitis** with or at the fingertips; **primo anno** at the beginning of the year or season; **primus in provinciam introiit** he was the first to enter the province; **primus quisque** the very first, the first possible; *f pl* see **primae;** *n* beginning, front; **a primo** from the first, from the beginning; **in primo** in the beginning; (mil) at the head of the column; *n pl* see **prima**
princ·eps -ĭpis *adj* first, in front; foremost, chief; *m* leader, chief; emperor; (mil) maniple, company; captain, company commander, centurion; captaincy, centurionship; *m pl* soldiers of the second line (*between the hastati and triarii*), second line
principāl·is -e *adj* first, foremost; original, primitive; chief, principal; of the emperor; **via principalis** (mil) main street of a camp; **porta principalis** (mil) main gate of a camp
principāt·us -ūs *m* first place; post of commander in chief; principate, rule, sovereignty; origin, beginning
principi·a -ōrum *n pl* first principles; foundations; front line, front-line troops; headquarters
principiāl·is -e *adj* initial
princip·ium -iī or **-ī** *n* start, commencement, origin; beginner, originator; first to vote; right to vote first; **a principio** or **principio** at the beginning, at first
pri·or -us *adj* previous, preceding, prior, former; first; better, superior, preferable
priōr·ēs -um *m pl* forefathers, ancestors, ancients; *f pl* (only *acc*) lead, preference
priscē *adv* in the old-fashioned style
prisc·us -a -um *adj* old, ancient; old-time, old-fashioned; former, previous
pristĭn·us -a -um *adj* former, earlier; pristine, primitive, original; preceding, previous, yesterday's; *n* former condition; **in pristinum restituere** to restore to its former condition
pristis see **pistrix**
prius *adv* earlier, before, previously, sooner, first; sooner, rather
priusquam *conj* before
prīvātim *adv* privately, in private, in a private capacity, as a private citizen; at home
prīvāti·ō -ōnis *f* removal
prīvātō *adv* at home
prīvāt·us -a -um *adj* private; personal, individual, peculiar; isolated, withdrawn; ordinary (*language*); *m* private citizen, civilian; *n* privacy, retirement; private property, private land; **ex privato** out of one's own pocket; **in privato** in private; **in privatum** for private use
prīvign·a -ae *f* stepdaughter
prīvign·us -ī *m* stepson; *m pl* stepchildren
prīvilēg·ium -iī or **-ī** *n* special bill directed against an individual; special bill in favor of an individual
prīv·ō -āre *vt* to deprive, rob, strip; to free, release
prīv·us -a -um *adj* every, each single; own, private; (with *genit*) deprived of
prō *adv* (with **quam** or **ut**) just as, according as; *prep* (with *abl*) before, in front of, in, on, in the presence of; for, in behalf of, in favor of, in the service of, on the side of; instead of, in place of, for; in return for, in exchange for, for; just as, as, the same as, for; in proportion to, according to, in comparison with, by virtue of; **pro eo** just the same; **pro eo atque** or **ac** just as, the same as; **pro eo quod** in view of the fact that; **pro se quisque** each one for himself, individually; **pro ut** or **pro eo quantum** as, in proportion as; *interj* oh!; **pro di immortales!** Oh, heavens above!
proāgŏr·us -ī *m* chief magistrate in some provincial towns
proavi·a -ae *f* great-grandmother
proavīt·us -a -um *adj* great-grandfather's, ancestral
proăv·us -ī *m* great-grandfather; ancestor, forefather
probābil·is -e *adj* worthy of approval, commendable, acceptable, pleasing, agreeable; probable, plausible, credible, likely
probābilit·ās -ātis *f* probability, plausibility
probābilĭter *adv* probably
probāti·ō -ōnis *f* approval, approbation, assent; test, trial; proof
probāt·or -ōris *m* approver, supporter, backer
probāt·us -a -um *adj* approved, acceptable; tried, tested, good; esteemed
probē *adv* well, properly, correctly; well, thoroughly, very, very much
probĭt·ās -ātis *f* probity, honesty, worth, goodness
prob·ō -āre *vt* to approve, commend, esteem; to make good, represent as good, make acceptable; to pronounce judgment on; to pro-

nounce approval of; to make credible, prove, show, demonstrate; to test, try, inspect; **probare pro** (with *abl*) to pass (*someone*) off for; **probari pro** (with *abl*) to pass for, be taken for

probriperlecĕbr·ae -ārum *f pl* temptations

probrōs·us -a -um *adj* scandalous, shameful, abusive

probr·um -ī *n* abuse, invective, reproach; shameful act, vile deed; lewdness, indecency; shame, disgrace; charge of disgraceful conduct

prob·us -a -um *adj* good, honest, upright, virtuous, decent; (coll) real, proper, downright

Proc·a or **Proc·ās -ae** *m* king of Alba and father of Numitor and Amulius

procācit·ās -ātis *f* brashness

procāciter *adv* brashly

proc·ax -ācis *adj* brash

prō·cēdō -cēdĕre -cessī -cessum *vi* to proceed, go forward, advance; to make progress, advance; to come out (*in public*), show oneself, appear; to come forth, arise; (of time) to pass, elapse; to turn out, result, succeed; to continue

procell·a -ae *f* violent wind, squall, hurricane, storm; (fig) violence, commotion, storm; (mil) charge, sudden attack

prōcell·ō -ĕre *vt* to throw down; **se procellere in mensam** to lie down at the table

procellōs·us -a -um *adj* gusty

proc·er -ĕris *m* chief, noble, prince, leader

prōcērit·ās -ātis *f* height, tallness; length; *f pl* the different heights

prōcērius *adv* farther, to a greater extent, more

prōcēr·us -a -um *adj* tall; long; **palmae procerae** upraised palms

prōcessi·ō -ōnis *f* advance

prōcessus *pp* of **procedo**

prōcess·us -ūs *m* advance, progress

Prochȳt·a -ae or **Prochȳt·ē -ēs** *f* small island off the Campanian coast

prō·cīdō -cidĕre -cīdī *vi* to fall forwards, fall over, fall down, fall prostrate

prōcinctū (*abl* only) *m* **in procinctu** under arms, ready for combat

prōclāmāt·or -ōris *m* loudmouth

prōclām·ō -āre *vi* to yell

prōclīn·ō -āre *vt* to bend forward, bend; **res proclinata** critical situation, crisis

prōclīv·e -is *n* slope, descent; **in proclivi esse** to be easy

prōclīve *adv* downward, downhill; rapidly

prōclīv·is -e or **prōclīv·us -a -um** *adj* sloping forward; downhill; easy; inclined, disposed, subject, ready, willing

prōclīvit·ās -ātis *f* proclivity, tendency, predisposition

prōclīvus see **proclivis**

Procn·ē or **Progn·ē -ēs** *f* daughter of Pandion, sister of Philomela, wife of Tereus, and mother of Itys, who was changed into a swallow; swallow

proc·ō -āre *vt* to require, demand

prōcons·ul -ŭlis *m* vice-consul, proconsul; governor of a province; military commander

prōconsulār·is -e *adj* proconsular

prōconsulāt·us -ūs *m* proconsulship, proconsulate

prōcrastinātī·ō -onis *f* procrastination

prōcrastin·ō -āre *vt* to postpone, put off from day to day

prōcreātī·ō -ōnis *f* procreation, breeding

prōcreāt·or -ōris *m* procreator, sire, parent, father

prōcreātr·ix -īcis *f* mother

prōcrĕ·ō -āre *vt* to procreate, beget, produce

prōcresc·ō -ĕre *vi* to spring forth, be produced; to continue to grow, grow up

Procr·is -is or **-idis** *f* wife of Cephalus who mistook her for a wild beast and shot her

Procrust·ēs -ae *m* notorious robber in Attica who stretched his victims to the length of his bed or mutilated them if they were too tall

prōcŭb·ō -āre *vi* to lie stretched out

prō·cūdō -cūdĕre -cūdī -cūsum *vt* to forge, fashion; to bring forth, produce

procul *adv* at a distance, in the distance, far; from a distance, from far; **haud procul afuit quin legatos violarent** they came close to outraging the ambassadors

prōculc·ō -āre *vt* to trample upon, trample down

prō·cumbō -cumbĕre -cubŭī -cubitum *vi* to fall down, sink down; to lean forward, bend over, be broken down; to extend, spread; (fig) to go to ruin

prōcūrātī·ō -ōnis *f* management, administration, superintendence; expiation, expiatory sacrifice

prōcūrāt·or -ōris *m* procurator, manager, administrator, superintendent, agent, deputy; governor of a province

prōcūrātr·ix -īcis *f* governess, protectress

prōcūr·ō -āre *vt* to manage, administer; to take care of, attend to; to avert by sacrifice; to expiate; *vi* to serve as procurator

prō·currō -currĕre -cucurrī or **-currī -cursum** *vi* to run out ahead, dash forward; to jut out, project

prōcursātī·ō -ōnis *f* sally, charge

prōcursātōr·ēs -um *m pl* skirmishers

prōcurs·ō -āre *vi* to keep charging out, continue to skirmish
prōcurs·us -ūs *m* sally, charge, onset
prōcurv·us -a -um *adj* curving forwards; curving, winding (*shore*)
proc·us -ī *m* noble; gigolo; **impudentes proci** shameless candidates
Procȳ·ōn -ōnis *m* Lesser Dog Star, Sirius
prōdactus *pp* of **prodigo**
prōdeambŭl·ō -āre *vi* to go out for a walk
prōd·ĕō -īre -iī -ĭtum *vi* to go out, come out, go forth, come forth; (of a cliff) to project; (of plants) to come out, appear; to appear in public; to go ahead, advance, proceed
prō·dīcō -dīcĕre -dixī -dictum *vt* to put off, defer, postpone; **diem prodicere** to adjourn a case to a later date
prōdictāt·or -ōris *m* vice-dictator
prōdĭgē *adv* lavishly
prōdigenti·a -ae *f* profusion, extravagance; openhandedness
prōdigiālĭter *adv* to a fantastic degree
prōdigiōs·us -a -um *adj* prodigious; freakish
prōdig·ium -iī or **-ī** *n* portent; unnatural crime, monstrous crime; monster, freak
prōd·ĭgō -igĕre -ēgī -actum *vt* to squander, waste
prōdĭg·us -a -um *adj* wasteful; lavish, openhanded; (with *genit*) free with; **animae prodigus** free with or careless with one's life; **herbae prodigus locus** spot with luxuriant growth of grass
prōditi·ō -ōnis *f* betrayal, treason; **proditionem agere** (with *dat*) to commit treason against, betray
prōdĭt·or -ōris *m* betrayer, traitor
prō·dō -dĕre -dĭdī -dĭtum *vt* to bring out, bring forth, produce; to reveal, disclose; to record, relate, report, hand down, transmit; to proclaim, appoint, elect; to give up, surrender; to forsake, betray; to prolong, protract; (fig) to display, exhibit
prōdoc·ĕō -ēre *vt* to preach publicly
prodrŏm·us -ī *m* forerunner, advance messenger
prō·dūcō -dūcĕre -duxī -ductum *vt* to bring out, bring forth; to produce; to promote, advance; to bring to light, reveal; to bring into the world, produce, raise, bring up; to educate; to drag out, protract, stretch out, lengthen; to lead on, induce; to put off, adjourn; to put (*a slave*) up for sale; to produce (*on the stage*), perform; to bring to court
prōductē *adv* long; **producte litteram dicere** to lengthen the letter or vowel
prōducti·ō -ōnis *f* lengthening
prōduct·ō -āre *vt* to drag out, delay
prōduct·us -a -um *pp* of **produco**; *adj* lengthened, prolonged, long
proēgmĕn·on -ī *n* preference
proeliār·is -e *adj* battle, of battle
proeliāt·or -ōris *m* combatant
proeli·or -ārī -ātus sum *vi* to battle, fight
proel·ium -iī or **-ī** *n* battle, combat, fight; *n pl* fighting men, warriors
Proet·us -ī *m* king of Tiryns
prōfān·ō -āre *vt* to profane, desecrate
profān·us -a -um *adj* unconsecrated, ordinary, common; impious, wicked; ill-omened
profātus *pp* of **profor**
profecti·ō -ōnis *f* setting out, departure; source (*of money*)
profectō *adv* really, actually
profectus *pp* of **proficiscor**
prōfectus *pp* of **proficio**
prōfect·us -ūs *m* progress, advance, success; increase, profit
prō·fĕrō -ferre -tŭlī -lātum *vt* to bring forward, advance, bring out; to extend, enlarge; to put off, postpone, defer; to produce, discover, invent; to make known, reveal, publish; to mention, cite, quote; **pedem proferre** to advance; **signa proferre** to march forward
profess·ae -ārum *f pl* professional prostitutes, professionals
professi·ō -ōnis *f* public acknowledgment, profession, declaration; registration (*at which property, etc., was declared*); profession, business
profess·or -ōris *m* professor, teacher
professōri·us -a -um *adj* professorial; professional, expert
professus *pp* of **profiteor**
profest·us -a -um *adj* non-holiday, ordinary; **dies profestus** working day
prō·ficiō -ficĕre -fēcī -fectum *vi* to make progress, make headway, advance, have success, succeed; to be useful, do good, help, be conducive; **nihil proficere** to do no good
pro·ficiscor -ficiscī -fectus sum *vi* to set out, start, go, depart; to originate, proceed, arise
pro·fitĕor -fitērī -fessus sum *vt* to declare publicly, acknowledge, confess, profess; to offer freely, promise, volunteer; to follow as a profession, practice (*e.g., law*); to make a declaration of, register (*property, etc.*) before a public official; **indicium profiteri** to volunteer evidence, testify freely; **nomen profiteri** to put one's name in as a candidate, announce oneself a candidate; **se adjutorem profiteri** (with **ad** + *acc*) to volunteer to help (*someone*); **se amicum profiteri** to avow oneself a friend, profess to be a friend; *vi* to make a confession, make an admission; to be a professor, be a teacher

prōflīgāt·or -ōris *m* big spender
prōflīgāt·us -a -um *adj* profligate, dissolute
prōflīg·ō -āre *vt* to knock to the ground, knock down; to defeat, conquer; to bring to an end, do away with, finish off; to ruin, crush; to debase, degrade
prōfl·ō -āre *vt* to breathe out
prōflŭ·ens -entis *adj* flowing along; fluent (*speech*); *f* running water
prōfluenter *adv* easily, effortlessly
prōfluentĭ·a -ae *f* fluency
prō·flŭō -fluĕre -fluxī *vi* to flow out; to flow along; (fig) to proceed
prōfluv·ĭum -ĭī or **-ī** *n* flow
prof·or -ārī -ātus sum *vt* to say, declare; *vi* to speak out
pro·fugĭō -fugĕre -fūgī *vt* to run away from, escape from; *vi* to run away, escape; (with **ad** + *acc*) to take refuge with, take refuge at the house of
profŭg·us -a -um *adj* fugitive; banished, exile; nomadic; *m* fugitive, refugee
pro·fundō -fundĕre -fūdī -fūsum *vt* to pour, pour out; to shed; to utter; to give vent to; to spend freely, waste, squander; **se profundere** (of things) to come pouring out; (of persons) to come pouring out, come charging out, break out
profund·us -a -um *adj* deep; boundless, vast; dense (*forest, cloud*); high (*heaven*); infernal; (fig) bottomless, boundless; *n* depth; the deep, deep sea; (fig) abyss
profūsē *adv* in disorder, helter-skelter, haphazardly; extravagantly
profūsĭ·ō -ōnis *f* profusion
profūs·us -a -um *pp* of **profundo**; *adj* extravagant, lavish, profuse; excessive, expensive
prōgĕn·er -ĕrī *m* granddaughter's husband
prōgenĕr·ō -āre *vt* to beget, produce
prōgenĭ·ēs -ēī *f* line, lineage; progeny, descendants, offspring, posterity
prōgenĭt·or -ōris *m* progenitor, founder, ancestor
prō·gignō -gignĕre -genŭī -genĭtum *vt* to beget, produce
prognārĭter *adv* precisely, exactly
prognāt·us -a -um *adj* born, descended; (with *abl* or with **ab** or **ex** + *abl*) born of, descended from; *m* child; grandson
Prognē see **Procne**
prognostĭc·on or **prognostĭc·um -ī** *n* sign of the future, prognostic
prō·gredĭor -grĕdī -gressus sum *vi* to go forward, march forward, proceed, advance; to go on, make headway, make progress; to go forth, go out
prōgressĭ·ō -ōnis *f* progress, advancement; increase, growth; (rhet) climax
prōgressus *pp* of **progredior**
prōgress·us -ūs *m* progress, advance; march (*of time or events*)
prōh *interj* oh!, O!
prohĭb·ĕō -ēre -ŭī -ĭtum *vt* to hold back, check, hinder, prevent, avert, keep off; to prohibit, forbid; to keep away; to defend, protect
prohibitĭ·ō -ōnis *f* prohibition
proïnde or **proïn** *adv* consequently, accordingly; **proinde atque** (or **ac**), **proinde ut**, or **proinde quam** just as, exactly as; **proinde atque si** (or **ac si**), **proinde quasi** just as if
prōjectĭcĭ·us -a -um *adj* exposed (*child*)
prōjectĭ·ō -ōnis *f* stretching out; **projectio bracchii** stretching out of the arm
prōject·ō -āre *vt* to accuse, blame
prōject·us -a -um *pp* of **projicio**; *adj* jutting out, projecting; prostrate, stretched out; inclined; prone; abject, contemptible; downcast
prōject·us -ūs *m* projection, extension
prō·jiciō -jicĕre -jēcī -jectum *vt* to throw down, throw out, throw; to throw away, abandon, forsake; to hold out, extend; to throw out, banish, exile; to neglect, desert; to blurt out; to throw away, give up, sacrifice; to put off, delay; to throw overboard; **se projicere ad pedes** (with *genit*) to throw oneself at the feet of, fall prostrate before; **se projicere ex nave** to jump overboard; **se projicere in forum** to rush into the forum
prō·lābor -lābī -lapsus sum *vi* to glide forward, slip or move forward; to fall forwards, fall on one's face; to slip out; (of words) to slip out, escape; to be led on, led astray (*by greed, fear, etc.*); (fig) to fail, go to ruin, collapse
prōlapsĭ·ō -ōnis *f* falling, collapse
prōlapsus *pp* of **prolabor**
prōlātĭ·ō -ōnis *f* expansion, extension (*of territory*); adducing, mentioning (*of precedents*); delay, postponement
prōlāt·ō -āre *vt* to extend; to put off, delay
prōlātus *pp* of **profero**
prōl·ēs -is *f* offspring, progeny, children, descendants; race, stock; child; young man
prōlētār·ĭus -ĭī or **-ī** *m* proletarian; *m pl* proletariat
prō·licĭō -licĕre -lixī *vt* to entice, bring out, incite
prōlixē *adv* freely, wildly; readily, cheerfully, freely
prōlix·us -a -um *adj* long, freely growing, wild (*beard, hair, etc.*); obliging, ready and unwilling; favorable (*circumstances*)
prōlocūtus *pp* of **proloquor**
prōlŏg·us -ī *m* prologue (*of a play*); actor who gives the prologue

prō·lŏquor -lŏquī -locūtus sum *vt & vi* to speak out

prōlub·ium -iī or **-ī** *n* desire, inclination, yen

prō·lūdō -lūdĕre -lūsī -lūsum *vi* to practice; (of boxers) to spar, shadowbox

prō·lŭō -luĕre -lŭī -lūtum *vt* to wash out, flush, wash off, wash away; to wet, drench

prōlūsi·ō -ōnis *f* sparring, shadowboxing

prōlūtus *pp* of **proluo**

prōluvi·ēs -ēī *f* flood; refuse, sewage

prōmer·ĕō -ēre -ŭī -itum or **prōmer·ĕor -ērī -itus sum** *vt* to deserve, merit, earn; *vi* to be deserving; (with **de** + *abl*) to deserve the gratitude of; **bene de multis promerere** or **promereri** to deserve the full gratitude of many people

prōmerit·um -ī *n* reward, due; merit; guilt

Promēth·eus -ĕī or **-ĕos** *m* son of Iapetus and Clymene, brother of Epimetheus, and father of Deucalion, who by teaching men the use of fire, incurred the wrath of Jupiter

Promēthē·us -a -um *adj* Promethean, of Prometheus

Promēthīd·ēs -ae *m* son of Prometheus, Deucalion (*who, with his wife Pyrrha, was the sole survivor of the Deluge*)

prōmin·ens -entis *adj* projecting, prominent; *n* headland

prōmin·ĕō -ēre -ŭī *vi* to jut out, hang forward, bend forward, extend; (with **in** + *acc*) to reach down to

prōmiscam or **prōmiscē** *adv* in common, without distinction, indiscriminately

prōmiscŭē *adv* indiscriminately, promiscuously

prōmiscŭ·us or **prōmisc·us -a -um** *adj* promiscuous, haphazard, indiscriminate, in common, open to all; common, ordinary

prōmissi·ō -ōnis *f* promise

prōmiss·or -ōris *m* promiser, fourflusher

prōmiss·us -a -um *adj* allowed to grow, long, hanging down; *n* promise

prō·mittō -mittĕre -mīsī -missum *vt* to let (*e.g., the hair*) grow; to promise; to give promise of, give hope of; *vi* to promise to go; **ad cenam promittere** to promise to go to dinner, make a dinner engagement

prōmō prōmĕre prompsī promptum *vt* to bring out, draw out; to produce (*arguments*); to bring to light, reveal; to bring out, express (*feelings, ideas, emotions*)

prōmontōr·ium -iī or **-ī** *n* promontory

prōmōt·a -ōrum *n pl* second choice (*things preferred next after absolute good*)

prō·movĕō -movēre -mōvī -mōtum *vt* to move (*something*) forward, cause to advance; to enlarge, extend; to effect, accomplish; to promote (*to higher office*); to bring to light, reveal; to put off, postpone; **nihil promovere** to accomplish nothing, do no good, make no progress

promptē *adv* readily, quickly; easily; frankly

prompt·ō -āre *vt* to give out, distribute

promptū (only *abl*) *m* **in promptu** in readiness, ready, at hand; public, visible, manifest; **in promptu gerere, habere,** or **ponere** to display

promptuāri·us -a -um *adj* of a storehouse, storage; **cella promptuaria** (coll) jail

prompt·us -a -um *pp* of **promo;** *adj* prompt, ready; easy; brought to light, evident; bold, enterprising; (with *dat* or with **ad** or **in** + *acc*) **a** ready or prepared for, set for; **b** inclined to, disposed to; (with **in** + *abl*) quick at, prompt at; (with **adversus** + *acc*) ready for, prepared against; (with *inf*) ready to, quick to

prōmulgāti·ō -ōnis *f* promulgation, publication

prōmulg·ō -āre *vt* to promulgate, publish

prōmuls·is -idis *f* hors d'oeuvres

prōmuntūr·ium -iī or **-ī** *n* promontory

prōm·us -ī *m* butler

prōmūtŭ·us -a -um *adj* on credit, advanced, given in advance

prōnē *adv* downwards

pronĕp·ōs -ōtis *m* great-grandson

pronept·is -is *f* great-granddaughter

pronoe·a -ae *f* providence

prōnŭb·a -ae *f* patroness of marriage

prōnuntiāti·ō -ōnis *f* proclamation, declaration; announcement (*of the jury's verdict*); delivery (*of a speech*); proposition (*in logic*)

prōnuntiāt·or -ōris *m* narrator

prōnuntiāt·um -ī *n* proposition (*in logic*)

prōnunti·ō -āre *vt* to proclaim, announce; to utter, pronounce, express (*opinion, judgment*); to hold out, promise, offer; to recite, deliver, narrate, relate; (in the senate) to formulate, announce, put to a vote

prōnŭr·us -ūs *f* grandson's wife

prōn·us -a -um *adj* leaning, inclined, bending, stooping, bent over, bent forwards; swift, rushing, dashing, moving swiftly along; sloping, steep (*hill, road*); sinking, setting (*sun, etc.*); downhill; easy; inclined, disposed, prone; *n* downward tendency, gravity; *n pl* slopes

prooemi·or -ārī *vi* to make an introduction or preface
prooem·ium -iī or **-ī** *n* preface; prelude; (fig) prelude (*e.g., to a fight*)
propāgāti·ō -ōnis *f* propagation; extension, prolongation; **nominis propagatio** perpetuation of the name
propāg·ō -āre *vt* to propagate (*race*); to extend (*territory*); to prolong (*life*)
prōpălam *adv* openly, publicly
prōpatŭl·us -a -um *adj* open; *n* open space; **in propatulo habere** to display
prope *adv* near, nearby; (of time) near, at hand; (of degree) nearly, almost, practically, just about; (with **ab** + *abl*) close by, near to; **prope est cum** the time has come when; *prep* (with *acc*) near, near to; **prope diem** very soon, presently
prō·pellō -pellĕre -pŭlī -pulsum *vt* to drive forward, push forward; to drive away, drive out
propemŏdo or **propemŏdum** *adv* nearly, practically, almost
prō·pendĕō -pendēre -pendī -pensum *vi* to hang down; to preponderate; (with **in** + *acc*) to be inclined to, be favorably disposed to
prōpensē *adv* readily, willingly
prōpensi·ō -ōnis *f* propensity, inclination, tendency
prōpens·us -a -um *pp* of **propendeo**; *adj* important; coming near, approaching; inclined, disposed, ready, willing; **propenso animo** with a ready mind, willingly; **propensus in alteram partem** inclined toward the other point of view
properanter *adv* quickly, hastily
properanti·a -ae *f* haste
properāti·ō -ōnis *f* haste
properātō *adv* quickly, speedily
properāt·us -a -um *adj* hurried, quick, speedy; *n* haste, speed; **properato opus est** speed is required
propĕrē *adv* quickly, in haste, hastily
properĭp·ēs -ĕdis *adj* quick-moving
propĕr·ō -āre *vt* to speed up, accelerate; to prepare hastily, do in haste; *vi* to be quick; to go or move quickly
Propert·ius -iī or **-ī** *m* Sextus Propertius (*Latin elegiac poet, c.* 50-15 B.C.)
propĕr·us -a -um *adj* quick, speedy
prōpex·us -a -um *adj* combed forward
prōpīnāti·ō -ōnis *f* toast
propīn·ō or **prōpīn·ō -āre** *vt* to drink (*e.g., a cup of wine*) as a toast; to drink a toast to, toast; (with *dat*) **a** to drink (*e.g., a cup of wine*) as a toast to; **b** to pass on (*a cup*) to
propinqu·a -ae *f* relative (*female*)
propinquē *adv* near at hand
propinquit·ās -ātis *f* proximity, nearness, vicinity; (fig) relationship, affinity; friendship
propinqu·ō -āre *vt* to bring on; to accelerate, hasten; *vi* to draw near, approach; (with *dat*) to draw near to, approach
propinqu·us -a -um *adj* near, neighboring; (of time) near, at hand; related; *m* relative; *f* see **propinqua**; *n* neighborhood, vicinity
propi·or -us *adj* nearer, closer; later, more recent; more closely related, more like, more nearly resembling; more intimate, closer; of more concern, of greater import; (with *dat*) **a** nearer to, closer to; **b** closer to in resemblance, more like; (with *acc* or with **ab** + *abl*) closer to
propiōr·a -um *n pl* closer side (*e.g., of a river*); more recent events
propiti·ō -āre *vt* to propitiate, appease
propiti·us -a -um *adj* propitious, well-disposed, favorable
propnigē·um -ī *n* room where the bath was heated
propōl·a -ae *m* retailer
prōpollŭ·ō -ĕre *vt* to pollute further
prō·pōnō -pōnĕre -posŭī -posĭtum *vt* to put or place forward, expose to view, display; to propose; to imagine; to offer, propose; to say, report, relate, publish; to threaten; to denounce; to design, determine, intend
Propont·is -ĭdis or **-ĭdos** *f* Sea of Marmora
prōporrō *adv* furthermore; wholly, completely
prōporti·ō -ōnis *f* proportion, symmetry; analogy
prōpositi·ō -ōnis *f* proposition; intention, purpose; theme; basic assumption (*in logic*)
prōposĭt·us -a -um *pp* of **propono**; *adj* exposed, open; accessible; impending, at hand; *n* intention, design, purpose, resolution; main point, theme; first premise (*in logic*)
prōpraet·or -ōris *m* propraetor (*expraetor who was made governor of a province*)
propriē *adv* in the strict sense; strictly for oneself, personally; peculiarly, especially
propriĕt·ās -ātis *f* property, peculiarity, quality
proprītim *adv* specifically, properly
propri·us -a -um *adj* own; very own; special, peculiar, individual, particular, personal; lasting, permanent
propter *adv* near, near at hand
propter *prep* (with *acc*) near, close to, next to; on account of, because of, for the sake of; through, by means of
propterĕā *adv* for that reason, therefore, on that account; **propterea quod** for the very reason that
prōpudiōs·us -a -um *adj* shameful, disgraceful

prōpud·ium -iī or **-ī** *n* shameful act; (said of a person) disgrace
prōpugnācŭl·um -ī *n* rampart, battlement; defense; (fig) safeguard
prōpugnāti·ō -ōnis *f* defense, vindication
prōpugnāt·or -ōris *m* defender, champion
prōpugn·ō -āre *vt* to defend; *vi* to come out and fight; to fight a defensive action, repel an assault; (fig) to put up a defense
prōpulsāti·ō -ōnis *f* repulse
prōpuls·ō -āre *vt* to drive back, repel, repulse; (fig) to ward off, repel
prōpulsus *pp* of **propello**
Propylae·a -ōrum *n pl* entrance to the Athenian Acropolis
prōquam *conj* according as
prōr·a -ae *f* prow; (fig) ship; **mihi prora et puppis est** my intention from first to last is
prō·rēpō -rēpěre -repsī *vi* to creep ahead, crawl out
prōrēt·a -ae *m* look-out at the prow
prōrě·us -ī *m* look-out at the prow
prō·ripiō -ripěre -ripŭī -reptum *vt* to drag forth, drag out; to rush; **se proripere** to rush, dash
prōrogāti·ō -ōnis *f* extension, prolongation (*of a term of office*); postponement
prōrŏg·ō -āre *vt* to prolong, extend; to put off, postpone
prorsum *adv* forwards; (with a negative) absolutely, at all, e.g., **prorsum nihil** absolutely nothing, nothing at all
prorsus *adv* forward; by all means, certainly; in short, in a word; (with a negative) absolutely, at all, e.g., **nullo prorsus modo assentior** I don't agree in any way at all
prō·rumpō -rumpěre -rūpī -ruptum *vt* to make (*something*) break forth, fling forth; **prorumpi** to burst forth; *vi* to break out, rush out, make an attack
prō·rŭō -ruěre -rŭī -rŭtum *vt* to overthrow, demolish; *vi* to rush forth; to tumble
prōrupt·us -a -um *pp* of **prorumpo**; *adj* unrestrained
prōsāpi·a -ae *f* stock, race, line
proscaen·ium -iī or **-ī** *n* front part of a stage; *n pl* stage; theater
pro·scindō -scinděre -scidī -scissum *vt* to plow up, break up; (fig) to criticize harshly, satirize, cut to pieces
pro·scrībō -scrīběre -scripsī -scriptum *vt* to publish in writing; to proclaim, announce; to advertise (*for sale, etc.*); to confiscate (*property*); to punish with confiscation of property, deprive of property; to proscribe, outlaw
proscripti·ō -ōnis *f* advertisement; proscription, notice of confiscation, notice of outlawry
proscriptur·iō -īre *vi* to be anxious to hold a proscription
proscript·us -a -um *pp* of **proscribo**; *m* proscribed person, outlaw
prōsěc·ō -āre -ŭī -tum *vt* to cut off (*esp. parts of a sacrificial victim*)
prōsecūtus *pp* of **prosequor**
prōsěd·a -ae *f* prostitute
prōsēmin·ō -āre *vt* to sow, scatter about, plant; to propagate, raise (*family*)
prō·sentiō -sentīre -sensī *vt* to sense or realize beforehand
prō·sěquor -sěquī -secūtus sum *vt* to escort, attend; to pursue (*enemy*); to chase, follow; to pursue, go on with, continue (*a topic*); to describe in detail; to follow, imitate; to attend, honor
Proserpin·a -ae *f* daughter of Ceres and wife of Pluto
prōserp·ō -ěre *vi* to creep or crawl forwards, creep along
proseuch·a -ae *f* synagogue
prōsil·iō -īre -ŭī *vi* to jump forward, jump up; to jump to one's feet; (of blood) to spurt; (of sparks) to shoot out; to rush, dash
prōsŏc·er -ěrī *m* wife's grandfather
prospect·ō -āre *vt* to view, look out at, gaze upon; (of places) to look towards, command a view of; to look for, hope for, expect, await
prospectus *pp* of **prospicio**
prospect·us -ūs *m* distant view; sight, view; faculty of sight; sight (*thing seen*)
prospecŭl·or -ārī -ātus sum *vt* to look out for, watch for; *vi* to look around, reconnoiter
prosp·er see **prosperus**
prospěrē *adv* favorably, luckily, as desired, successfully
prosperit·ās -ātis *f* success, good fortune, prosperity; **prosperitas valetudinis** good health
prospěr·ō -āre *vt* to cause to succeed, make happy, make fortunate
prosp·ěrus or **prosp·er -ěra -ěrum** *adj* successful, fortunate, lucky, favorable, prosperous
prospicienti·a -ae *f* foresight, precaution
pro·spiciō -spicěre -spexī -spectum *vt* to see far off, see in the distance; to spot; to command a view of; to watch for; to look out for, provide for; to foresee; *vi* to look forward; to look into the distance, have a distant view, have a view; to be on the lookout, exercise foresight; (with **in** + *acc*) to command a view of, overlook; **ex superioribus in urbem prospicere** to have a view of the city from a vantage point; **parum prospiciunt oculi** the eyes are nearsighted
pro·sternō -sterněre -strāvī -strātum *vt* to throw to the ground, throw down, knock down; to wreck, ruin, overthrow, subvert; to debase; **se prosternere** to debase oneself; **se prosternere ad**

pedes (with *genit*) to throw oneself at the feet of, fall down before
prostibĭl·is -is *f* prostitute
prostibŭl·um -ī *n* prostitute
prostit·ŭō -uĕre -ŭī -ūtum *vt* to expose for sale; to prostitute
pro·stō -stāre -stĭtī *vi* to project; (of wares) to be set out for sale; to prostitute oneself, be a prostitute
prostrātus *pp* of **prosterno**
prōsubĭg·ō -ĕre *vt* to dig up, root up
prō·sum -desse -fŭī *vi* to be useful, be of use, do good, be profitable; **multum prodesse** to do a lot of good
Prōtagŏr·ās -ae *m* Greek sophist, contemporary of Socrates, born at Abdera (*c.* 485-415 B.C.)
prō·tĕgō -tegĕre -texī -tectum *vt* to cover in front, cover, cover up; to cover with a roof; to shelter, protect; (fig) to cover, defend, protect
prōtēl·ō -āre *vt* to chase away, drive off
prōtēl·um -ī *n* team of oxen; (fig) row, series
prō·tendō -tendĕre -tendī -tentum *vt* to stretch forth, stretch out, extend
prōtent·us -a -um *adj* extended
prōtĕnus see **protinus**
prō·tĕrō -terĕre -trīvī -trītum *vt* to wear down, rub out; to trample down, trample under foot; (fig) to trample upon, rub out, crush
prōterr·ĕō -ēre -ŭī -ĭtum *vt* to scare away
protervē *adv* boldly, brashly, impudently, brazenly
protervĭt·ās -ātis *f* brashness, brazenness
proterv·us -a -um *adj* bold, brash, brazen, impudent
Prōtesilā·us -ī *m* first Greek casualty in the Trojan War
Prōt·eus -ĕī or **-ĕos** *m* god of the sea with power to assume various forms
prothȳmē *adv* willingly, readily
prothymĭ·a -ae *f* willingness, readiness
prōtĭnam *adv* immediately
prōtĭnus or **prōtĕnus** *adv* straight on, forward, farther on; continuously, right on, without pause; immediately, at once, on the spot
prōtoll·ō -ĕre *vt* to stretch out (*hand*); to put off, postpone
prōtopraxĭ·a -ae *f* priority (*among creditors in receiving payment*)
prō·trăhō -trahĕre -traxī -tractum *vt* to drag forward, drag out; to produce; to reveal, expose, disclose, bring to light
prōtrītus *pp* of **protero**
prō·trūdō -trūdĕre -trūsī -trūsum *vt* to push forwards, push out; to push off, postpone
prōturb·ō -āre *vt* to drive ahead, drive on, drive away, repel; to knock down
proŭt *conj* as, just as
prōvect·us -a -um *adj* advanced; **aetate provectus** advanced in years; **nox provecta erat** the night had been far advanced
prō·vĕhō -vehĕre -vexī -vectum *vt* to carry forwards; to transport, convey; to lead, lead on; to promote, advance, raise; **provehi** to ride, drive, move, or sail ahead
prō·veniō -venīre -vēnī -ventum *vi* to go on, proceed; to succeed; to come out, appear; to come out, grow, be produced; to come about, happen
prōvent·us -ūs *m* result, outcome; success; yield, produce; harvest
prōverb·ĭum -iī or **-ī** *n* proverb
prōvĭd·ens -entis *adj* prudent
prōvidenter *adv* prudently, with foresight
prōvidentĭ·a -ae *f* foresight, foreknowledge; precaution; **providentia deorum** providence
prō·vidĕō -vidēre -vīdī -vīsum *vt* to see in the distance; to see coming; to foresee; to provide for; to provide against, guard against, avert, avoid; to look after, look out for, care for; to prepare, make ready
prōvĭd·us -a -um *adj* foreseeing; prudent, cautious; provident; (with *genit*) providing
prōvincĭ·a -ae *f* sphere of administration; sphere of jurisdiction; office, duty, charge; public office, commission, command, administration; sphere of action; province
prōvinciāl·is -e *adj* provincial, of a province, in a province; **bellum provinciale** war in a province; **molestia provincialis** annoyance of administering a province; *m* provincial
prōvīsĭ·ō -ōnis *f* foresight; precaution; (with *genit*) precaution against
prōvīsō *adv* with forethought
prōvīs·ō -ĕre *vt* to go out to see; to be on the lookout for
prōvīs·or -ōris *m* lookout (*person*); provider
prōvīsū (only *abl*) *m* by looking forward; (with objective *genit*) **a** by foreseeing (*e.g., danger*); **b** by providing, providing for
prōvīsus *pp* of **provideo**
prō·vīvō -vivĕre -vixī *vi* to live on
prōvocātĭ·ō -ōnis *f* appeal (*to a higher court*); challenge
prōvocāt·or -ōris *m* challenger; type of gladiator
prōvŏc·ō -āre *vt* to challenge; to provoke; to exasperate; to stir, stimulate; **bellum provocare** to provoke a war; **beneficio provocatus** touched or stirred by an act of kindness; **in aleam provocare** to challenge to a game of dice; **provocare maledictis** to provoke or exasperate with nasty remarks
prōvŏl·ō -āre *vi* to fly out, rush out, dash out

prō·volvō -volvĕre -volvī -volūtum *vt* to roll forward, roll along; to roll over, overturn; to humble, ruin; **se provolvere** to prostrate oneself, fall down, grovel, humble oneself
prōvŏm·ō -ĕre *vt* to vomit, throw up
proximē or **proxŭmē** *adv* (of place) nearest, next; (of time) most recently, just recently; (with *acc*) close to, next to, at the side of, very much like, closely resembling; (with *dat*) (of place) next to; **proxime atque** almost as much as, nearly the same as; **proxime Pompeium sedebam** I was sitting next to Pompey; **quam proxime** (with *dat* or *acc*) as close as possible to
proximĭt·ās -ātis *f* proximity, vicinity; resemblance, similarity; close relationship
proximō *adv* very recently, just recently
proxĭm·us or **proxŭm·us -a -um** *adj* nearest, next; next, following, ensuing; previous, most recent, latest, last; closely related; adjoining; most direct (*route*); *m* close relative, next of kin; *n* neighborhood; next door, next-door neighbor
prūd·ens -entis *adj* foreseeing, foreknowing; conscious, aware; skilled, skillful, experienced, versed; prudent, discreet, sensible, intelligent; (with *genit* or *abl* or with **in** + *abl*) aware of, conscious of, familiar with, skilled in, experienced in
prūdenter *adv* prudently, cautiously; skillfully
prūdenti·a -ae *f* foreseeing; prudence, discretion, good sense; **prudentia juris publici** knowledge of or experience in public law
pruīn·a -ae *f* frost; winter
pruīnōs·us -a -um *adj* frosty
prūn·a -ae *f* live coal
prūnitĭ·us -a -um *adj* of plum-tree wood
prūn·um -ī *n* plum
prūn·us -ī *f* plum tree
prūrīg·ō -ĭnis *f* itching, itch; yen
prūr·iō -īre *vi* to itch; to have an itch; (with **in** + *acc*) to be itching for
prytanē·um -ī *n* state dining hall (*where the Prytanes dined*)
prytăn·is -is *m* prytane (*member of the executive body in some Greek states*)
psall·ō -ĕre -ī *vi* to play the lyre or lute
psaltēr·ĭum -ĭī or **-ī** *n* stringed instrument, lute
psaltri·a -ae *f* lutist, musician (*female*)
psec·as -ădis *f* female slave who perfumed her lady's hair
psēphism·a -ătis *n* plebiscite of the Greek assembly
pseudocăt·ō -ōnis *m* a make-believe Cato
pseudomĕn·os or **pseudomĕn·us -ī** *m* fallacious syllogism
pseudothỹr·um -ī *n* back door
psittăc·us -ī *m* parrot
Psych·ē -ēs *f* maiden loved by Cupid and made immortal by Jupiter
psychomantī·um or **psychomantē·um -ī** *n* place where people attempted to communicate with the dead
-pte *enclitic* (added to pronouns) self, own
ptisanār·ĭum -ĭī or **-ī** *n* gruel
Ptolemae·us -ī *m* Ptolemy (*name of a series of Egyptian kings descended from Lagus, a general of Alexander the Great*)
pūb·ens -entis *adj* mature; juicy (*plant*)
pūber see **pubes**
pūbert·ās -ātis *f* puberty; manhood, virility; sign of maturity, beard
pūb·ēs or **pūb·er -ĕris** *adj* grown up, adult; downy, covered with down; *m pl* grown-ups, adults, men;
pūb·ēs -is *f* pubic hair; groin; youth, young men, grown-up males; throng, people; bullocks
pūb·escō -escĕre -ŭī *vi* to reach the age of puberty, arrive at maturity; (of plants) to grow up, ripen; (of meadows, etc.) to be clothed, covered (*e.g., with flowers*)
pūblicān·us -a -um *adj* of public revenues; *m* revenue agent
pūblicātĭ·ō -ōnis *f* confiscation
pūblĭcē *adv* publicly, officially, in behalf of the state, for the state; at public expense; generally, universally; **publice dicere** to speak officially
pūblicĭtus *adv* at public expense, at the expense of the state; publicly
pūblĭc·ō -āre *vt* to confiscate; to throw open to the general public; to prostitute
Pūblicŏl·a or **Pōplicŏl·a -ae** *m* Publius Valerius Publicola (*fl* 509 B.C.)
pūblĭc·us -a -um *adj* of the people, public, common; of the state, state, federal, national; common, ordinary, vulgar; common, general, public; **causa publica** affair of national importance; (law) federal case (*i.e., criminal case*); **res publica** state, government, politics, public life, country; *m* public official; *n* public, publicity; public property, national treasury, federal revenue; **de publico** at public expense; **in publico** in public, publicly; **in publicum prodire** to go out in public; **in publicum redigere** to hand over to the national treasury
pudend·us -a -um *adj* shameful, scandalous
pud·ens -entis *adj* modest, bashful
pudenter *adv* modestly, bashfully
pud·ĕō -ēre -ŭī or **pudĭtum est** *vt* to make ashamed; *v impers* (with *acc* of person and *genit* or *abl* of

cause of feeling), e.g., **me tui pudet** I am ashamed of you
pudibund·us -a -um *adj* modest, bashful
pudīcē *adv* chastely, modestly, virtuously
pudīciti·a -ae *f* chastity, modesty, purity
pudīc·us -a -um *adj* chaste, modest, virtuous, pure
pud·or -ōris *m* shame, decency, modesty, sense of shame; sense of honor, propriety; cause for shame, shame, disgrace; blush
puell·a -ae *f* girl; girl friend, sweetheart; young wife
puellār·is -e *adj* young girl's, girlish, youthful
puellāriter *adv* girlishly
puellŭl·a -ae *f* little girl; little sweetheart
puell·us -ī *m* little boy, lad
pu·er -ĕrī *m* boy, lad, young man; servant, slave, page; bachelor; **a pueris** or **a puero** from boyhood, from childhood; **ex pueris excedere** to outgrow childhood
puerīl·is -e *adj* boyish, childish, youthful, puerile
puerīliter *adv* like a child, childishly
pueriti·a or **puerti·a -ae** *f* childhood, boyhood
puerper·ium -iī or **-ī** *n* childbirth, lying-in, giving birth
puerpĕr·us -a -um *adj* helping childbirth, easing labor pains; *f* woman in labor
puertia see **pueritia**
puerŭl·us -ī *m* little boy, little slave
pūg·a or **pȳg·a -ae** *f* rump, rear, buttocks
pug·il -ilis *m* boxer
pugilāti·ō -ōnis *f* boxing
pugilāt·us -ūs *m* boxing
pugilicē *adv* like a boxer
pugillār·is -e *adj* hand-size; *m pl & n pl* notebook
pugillātōri·us -a -um *adj* boxing, punching; **follis pugillatorius** punching bag
pugi·ō -ōnis *m* dagger
pugiuncŭl·us -ī *m* small dagger
pugn·a -ae *f* fist fight, brawl; fight, combat, battle
pugnācit·ās -ātis *f* pugnacity, aggressiveness
pugnāciter *adv* pugnaciously, doggedly
pugnācŭl·um -ī *n* fortress
pugnant·ēs -ium *m pl* fighters, warriors
pugnant·ia -ium *n pl* contradictions, inconsistencies
pugnāt·or -ōris *m* fighter, combatant
pugn·ax -ācis *adj* pugnacious, scrappy, aggressive; quarrelsome; dogged, obstinate
pugnĕ·us -a -um *adj* of the fist; **mergae pugneae** punches
pugn·ō -āre *vt* to fight; *vi* to fight; to contend, dispute; (with *dat* or **cum** + *abl*) **a** to fight, fight against, struggle with, oppose; **b** to contradict
pugn·us -ī *m* fist
pulchell·us -a -um *adj* cute little
pulch·er -ra -rum *adj* beautiful, fair, handsome
pulchrē *adv* beautifully; (as exclamation of applause) fine!; **pulchre mihi est** I am fine
pulchritūd·ō -inis *f* beauty; excellence, attractiveness
pūlē·ium or **pūleg·ium -iī** or **-ī** *n* pennyroyal, mint; (fig) fragrance, pleasantness
pūl·ex -icis *m* flea
pullār·ius -iī or **-ī** *m* keeper of the sacred chickens
pullāt·us -a -um *adj* wearing black, in black, in mourning
pullŭl·ō -āre *vi* to sprout; (of animals) to produce young
pull·us -a -um *adj* dark-grey, dark, blackish; mourning; **toga pulla** mourning toga; *n* dark-grey garment
pull·us -ī *m* young (*of animals*), foal, offspring, chick, chicken
pulmentār·ium -iī or **-ī** *n* relish, appetizer
pulment·um -ī *n* relish; food, rations
pulm·ō -ōnis *f* lung
pulmōnĕ·us -a -um *adj* of the lungs, pulmonary
pulp·a -ae *f* meat, flesh
pulpāment·um -ī *n* meat; game
pulpĭt·um -ī *n* platform; stage
puls pultis *f* pulse, porridge, mush
pulsāti·ō -ōnis *f* knock
puls·ō -āre *vt* to batter, keep hitting; to knock at; to strum (*lyre*); to beat on, strike against; (fig) to jolt, disquiet; *vi* to throb
pulsus *pp* of **pello**
puls·us -ūs *m* push, pushing; beat, beating, striking, stamping, blow, stroke; trample; (fig) impression, influence
pultāti·ō -ōnis *f* knocking (*at the door*)
pultiphagōnid·ēs -ae *m* porridge eater
pultiphăg·us -ī *m* porridge eater
pult·ō -āre *vt* to knock at
pulverĕ·us -a -um *adj* dust, of dust; dusty; fine as dust; raising dust
pulverulent·us -a -um *adj* dusty; raising dust; covered with dust
pulvill·us -ī *m* small cushion
pulvīn·ar -āris *n* cushioned couch, couch; sacred couch for the images of the gods; seat of honor; shrine, temple
pulvīnār·ium -iī or **-ī** *n* cushioned seat of a god; dry dock
pulvīn·us -ī *m* pillow, cushion; seat of honor
pulv·is -ĕris *m* dust, powder; scene of action, arena, field; effort, work
pulviscŭl·us -ī *m* fine dust, fine powder

pūm·ex -icis *m* pumice stone; porous stone, lava
pūmicĕ·us -a -um *adj* pumice, lava
pūmic·ō -āre *vt* to smooth or polish with pumice stone
pūmili·ō -ōnis *m* or *f* midget, dwarf, pygmy
punctim *adv* with the point, with the pointed end
punct·um -ī *n* prick, puncture; point, mathematical point; point, spot; vote, ballot; clause, phrase; moment; **puncto temporis eodem** at the same instant; **punctum temporis** moment, instant, point of time
pungō pungĕre pupŭgī punctum *vt* to prick, puncture, dent; to sting, bite; to cause (*a wound*); to stab; (fig) to sting, annoy, trouble, disturb
Pūnicān·us -a -um *adj* Punic, Carthaginian, in the Carthaginian style
Pūnicē *adv* Punic, in the Punic language
pūnicĕ·us -a -um *adj* reddish, red, crimson, pink
Pūnic·us -a -um *adj* Punic, Carthagianian; red, crimson, reddish, pink; *n* pomegranate
pūn·iō -īre -īvī or **-iī -ītum** or **pūn·ior -īrī -ītus sum** *vt* to punish, chastise; to avenge, revenge
pūnīt·or -ōris *m* avenger
pūp·a -ae *f* doll, puppet; girl, lass
pūpill·a -ae *f* orphan girl, ward; minor; pupil (*of the eye*)
pūpillār·is -e *adj* of an orphan, belonging to an orphan
pūpill·us -ī *m* orphan boy, orphan, ward
pupp·is -is *f* stern; ship; (coll) back; **a puppi** astern
pūpŭl·a -ae *f* pupil; eye
pūpŭl·us -ī *m* little boy
pūrē *adv* clearly, brightly; plainly, simply; purely, chastely
purgām·en -inis *n* dirt, filth; means of expiation, purification
purgāment·a -ōrum *n pl* offscourings, refuse, dirt, filth, garbage; (term of abuse) trash, dregs, garbage
purgāti·ō -ōnis *f* cleansing, cleaning, cleanup; apology, justification
purgāt·us -a -um *adj* cleansed, clean, pure
purg·ō -āre *vt* to clean, cleanse, clear, clear away, remove; to clear of a charge, exculpate, excuse, justify; to refute; to cleanse, purify ritually; to purge (*the body*)
pūrific·ō -āre *vt* to purify
pūriter *adv* purely, cleanly; **vitam puriter agere** to lead a clean life
purpŭr·a -ae *f* purple, deep-red, dark-red; purple or deep-red cloth or garment; royal-purple robe; royalty; consular dignity, imperial dignity
purpurāt·us -a -um *adj* wearing royal purple; *m* courtier
purpurĕ·us -a -um *adj* deep-red, crimson, pink, violet, royal-purple (*and various shades, as applied to roses, poppies, lips, flesh, blood, wine, dawn, hair*)
purpurissāt·us -a -um *adj* rouged
purpuriss·um -ī *m* rouge; red dye
pūr·us -a -um *adj* pure, clear, clean; cleared, cleansed; cleansing, purifying; pure, chaste; plain, naked, unadorned, natural; plain (*toga*), without crimson border; pure, accurate, faultless (*style*); (law) unconditional, absolute; subject to no religious claims; *n* clear sky
pūs pūris *n* pus; (fig) venom, malice
pusill·us -a -um *adj* petty, puny; *n* bit, trifle
pūsi·ō -ōnis *m* little boy
pustŭl·a -ae *f* pimple; blister
pustulāt·us or **pusulāt·us -a -um** *adj* refined, purified
putām·en -inis *n* clipping, peeling, shell, husk
putāti·ō -ōnis *f* pruning
putāt·or -ōris *m* pruner
putĕ·al -ālis *n* low wall (*around a well or sacred spot*), stone enclosure; **puteal Libonis** stone enclosure in the Roman Forum near which much business was transacted
puteāl·is -e *adj* well, of a well
pūt·ĕō -ēre *vi* to stink; to be rotten, be putrid
Puteolān·us -a -um *adj* of Puteoli
Puteŏl·ī -ōrum *m pl* commercial city on the coast of Campania (*modern Pozzuolo*)
put·er or **put·ris -e** *adj* putrid, rotting; crumbling; flabby
pūt·escō -escĕre -ŭī *vi* to become rotten
putĕ·us -ī *m* well; pit; dungeon
pūtidē *adv* disgustingly, disagreeably
pūtidiuscŭl·us -a -um *adj* rather tedious
pūtid·us -a -um *adj* stinking, rotten; affected, unnatural (*style*)
putill·us -a -um *adj* tiny
put·ō -āre *vt* to trim, prune; to think, ponder, consider, judge, suppose, imagine; to reckon, estimate, value; to believe in, recognize (*gods*); to clear up, settle (*accounts*); **magni putare** to think highly of; **pro certo putare** to regard as certain; *vi* to think, imagine, suppose
pūt·or -ōris *m* stench
putre·faciō -facĕre -fēcī -factum *vt* to make rotten, rot; to cause to crumble, soften
putresc·ō -ĕre *vi* to become rotten, get moldy
putrid·us -a -um *adj* rotten; flabby
putris see **puter**
put·us -a -um *adj* pure, bright, perfectly pure; splendid; unmixed; unmitigated; *m* boy
pyct·a or **pyct·ēs -ae** *m* boxer
Pydn·a -ae *f* city in Macedonia near which Aemilius Paulus defeated

Perseus, the Macedonian king (169 B.C.)
pȳg·a -ae *f* rump, rear, buttocks
Pygmali·ōn -ōnis *m* son of Belus the king of Cyprus and brother of Dido; king of Cyprus who fell in love with a statue
Pylăd·ēs -ae *m* son of Strophius and friend of Orestes
Pyl·ae -ārum *f pl* Thermopylae (*narrow pass in E. Thessaly*)
Pyli·us -a -um *adj* of Pylos
Pyl·os -ī *f* Pylos (*home of Nestor in S.E. Peloponnesus*)
pyr·a -ae *f* pyre
pȳrăm·is -ĭdis *f* pyramid; cone
Pȳrăm·us -ī *m* neighbor and boy friend of Thisbe
Pȳrēnae·us -a -um *adj* of the Pyrenees
Pȳrēn·ē -ēs *f* the Pyrenees Mountains
pyrēthr·on or **pyrēthr·um -ī** *n* Spanish camomile (*plant*)
pyrōp·us -ī *m* bronze
Pyrrh·a -ae or **Pyrrh·ē -ēs** *f* daughter of Epimetheus, wife of Deucalion, and survivor of the Deluge
Pyrrh·ō -ōnis *m* philosopher of Elis, contemporary of Aristotle, and founder of the philosophical school of Skepticism (*c.* 360-270 B.C.)
Pyrrh·us -ī *m* son of Achilles and founder of Epirus (*also called Neoptolemus*); king of Epirus who invaded Italy to assist the Tarentines against the Romans in 280 B.C. (319-272 B.C.)
Pȳthagŏr·ās -ae *m* Greek philosopher and mathematician (*6th cent.* B.C.)
Pȳthagorē·us or **Pythagoric·us -a -um** *adj* Pythagorean
Pȳthi·us -a -um *adj* Pythian, Delphic; *m* Apollo; *f* Pythia (*priestess of Apollo at Delphi*); *n pl* Pythian games (*held in honor of Apollo every four years*)
Pȳth·ō -ūs *f* Delphi
Pȳth·ōn -ōnis *m* dragon slain by Apollo near Delphi
pȳtism·a -ătis *n* spit, squirt of wine
pȳtiss·ō -āre *vt* to spit, spit out (*wine*)
pyx·is -ĭdis *f* powder box, cosmetic box

Q

quā *adv* where, in what direction, by what way; to what extent, as far as; whereby, how, by what means; in any way, to any degree; **qua . . . qua** partly . . . partly, both . . . and
quācumque *adv* wherever, by whatever way, in whatever way; by whatever means, howsoever
quādam tenus *adv* to a certain point, only so far and no farther
quadr·a -ae *f* square table, dining table; square crust; square morsel, square bit (*of cheese, etc.*)
quadrāgēn·ī -ae -a *adj* forty each
quadrāgēsim·us or **quadrāgensim·us -a -um** *adj* fortieth; *f* one fortieth; 2½ percent tax
quadrāgiēs or **quadrāgiens** *adv* forty times
quadrāgintā (indecl) *adj* forty
quadr·ans -antis *m* fourth part, a fourth, a quarter; cent (*smallest coin, worth one sixth of an ace*); quarter of a pound; quarter pint (*quarter of a sextarius*); **quadrante lavatum ire** take a bath for one cent (*usual price of a bath*)
quadrant·al -ālis *n* five-gallon jar
quadrantāri·us -a -um *adj* quarter; **mulier quadrantaria** two-bit wench (*woman who sold herself for a pittance*); **tabulae quadrantariae** record of debts reduced to a fourth
quadrāt·us -a -um *adj* squared, square; *n* square
quadrīdu·um -ī *n* four-day period, four days
quadrienn·ium -iī or **-ī** *n* four-year period, four years
quadrifāriam *adv* in four parts
quadrifid·us -a -um *adj* split into four parts
quadrig·ae -ārum *f pl* four-horse team; four-horse chariot
quadrīgār·ius -iī or **-ī** *m* chariot racer
quadrīgāt·us -a -um *adj* stamped with a four-horse chariot
quadrīgŭl·ae -ārum *f pl* little four-horse team
quadrijŭg·is -e *adj* four-horse-team
quadrijŭg·us -a -um *adj* four-horse-team; *m pl* four-horse team
quadrilībr·is -e *adj* four-pound
quadrīmŭl·us -a -um *adj* only four years old
quadrīm·us -a -um *adj* four-year-old
quadringēnāri·us -a -um *adj* consisting of four hundred men each
quadringēn·ī -ae -a *adj* four hundred each
quadringentēsim·us -a -um *adj* four-hundredth
quadringentiēs *adv* four hundred times
quadripertīt·us -a -um *adj* fourfold
quadrirēm·is -e *adj* having four banks of oars; *f* quadrireme
quadriv·ium -iī or **-ī** *n* crossroads

quadr·ō -āre *vt* to make square; to complete; to round out, give rhythmic finish to (*a speech*); *vi* to make a square; to be exact; (of accounts) to agree, come out right, tally; (with *dat* or **in** + *acc*) to suit, fit, seem proper to

quadr·um -ī *n* square; **in quadrum redigere sententias** to balance sentences

quadrupĕd·ans -antis *adj* galloping; *m pl* horses

quadrŭp·ēs -ĕdis *adj* four-footed; on all fours; *mf* quadruped

quadruplāt·or -ōris *m* informer (*who received one fourth of the forfeiture*); corrupt judge

quadrŭpl·ex -ĭcis *adj* quadruple, fourfold

quadruplĭc·ō -āre *vt* to quadruple, increase fourfold

quadrŭpl·or -ārī -ātus sum *vi* to be an informer

quadrŭpl·us -a -um *adj* quadruple, fourfold; *n* four times the amount

quaerĭt·ō -āre *vt* to keep looking for; to keep asking

quaerō quaerĕre quaesīvī quaesītum *vt* to look for, search for; to try to get; to get, obtain; to try to gain, earn, acquire; to miss, lack; to require, demand, call for; to ask, interrogate; to examine, investigate; to plan, devise, aim at; (with *inf*) to try to, wish to; (with **ab** or **de** or **ex** + *abl*) to ask (*something*) of or from (*someone*); *vi* to hold an examination; (with **de** + *abl*) to ask about, inquire about; **si quaeris** or **si quaerimus** (coll) to tell the truth

quaesītĭ·ō -ōnis *f* questioning under torture

quaesīt·or -ōris *m* judge (*praetor or other official who presided over a criminal trial*)

quaesīt·us -a -um *pp* of **quaero;** *adj* select, special; far-fetched, artificial, affected; *n* question; *n pl* gains, earnings, acquisitions, store

quaes·ō -ĕre *vt* to beg, ask; **quaeso** (usually parenthetical) please

quaesticŭl·us -ī *m* slight profit

quaesti·ō -ōnis *f* inquiry, investigation, questioning, examination; judicial investigation, criminal trial; court of inquiry, court; questioning under torture, third degree; question, subject of investigation, case; court record; (with **de** + *abl* of the nature of the charge) court investigating a charge of (*e.g., forgery, etc.*); **in quaestione versare** to be under investigation; **quaestio extraordinaria** investigation by a special board; **quaestio inter sicarios** murder trial, court investigating a murder; **quaestio perpetua** standing court; **quaestioni praeesse** to preside over a case, be judge at a trial; **servos in quaestionem dare** or **ferre** to hand over slaves for questioning under torture

quaestiuncŭl·a -ae *f* minor or trifling question

quaest·or -ōris *m* quaestor; financial officer; treasury official; public prosecutor of criminal offenses

quaestōrī·us -a -um *adj* quaestor's, of a quaestor; *m* ex-quaestor; *n* quaestor's tent in a camp; quaestor's residence in a province

quaestuōs·us -a -um *adj* profitable, lucrative, productive; acquiring wealth; eager to make a profit, acquisitive; enriched, wealthy

quaestūr·a -ae *f* quaestorship; quaestor's safe, public funds

quaest·us -ūs *m* gain, profit; acquisition; way of making money, job, occupation, business, trade; (fig) profit, gain, benefit, advantage; **ad quaestum** for profit, to make a profit; **quaestui rem publicam habere** to use public office for personal profit; **quaestum facere** to make money

quālĭbet or **quālŭbet** *adv* anywhere, everywhere; in any way, as you please

quāl·is -e *adj* what sort of, what kind of; of such a kind, such as, as; (with quotations and citations) as, as for example; **in hoc bello, quale** in this war, the likes of which; **qualis erat!** what a man he was!

quāl·iscumque -ecumque *adj* of whatever kind; of any kind whatever, any at all; **homines, qualescumque sunt** men, no matter what kind they are

quāl·islĭbet -elĭbet *adj* of whatever kind, of whatever sort

quālĭt·ās -ātis *f* quality, nature, property

quālĭter *adv* as, just as

quāl·us -ī *m* wicker basket, straw basket

quam *adv* (in questions and exclamations) to what extent, how, how much; (in comparisons) as, than; (with superlatives) as . . . as possible, e.g., **quam celerrime** as fast as possible; **quam plurimo vendere** to sell at the highest price possible; **quam primum** as soon as possible; (*after verbs implying preference*) rather than

quamdĭū or **quam diū** *adv* how long; *conj* as long as, until

quamlĭbet or **quamlŭbet** *adv* as much as you please

quamŏbrem or **quam ob rem** *adv* for what reason, why; for which reason, wherefore, why

quamquam *conj* though, although

quamvīs *adv* (with *adj* or *adv*) however; ever so; *conj* although

quānam *adv* by what route, by what way

quandō *adv* (in questions) when, at what time; (indefinite, after **si, ne,**

num) ever, at any time; *conj* when; because, since

quandōcumque or **quandōcunque** *adv* at some time or other, some day; *conj* whenever; as often as, no matter when

quandōque *adv* at some time, at one time or other, some day; *conj* whenever; as often as; since

quandōquĭdem *conj* in as much as, whereas, seeing that

quantill·us -a -um *adj* how much, how little

quantĭt·ās -ātis *f* quantity

quantō *adv* by how much, how much; **quanto ante** how much earlier; **quanto . . . tanto** the . . . the

quantopĕre *adv* how much, how greatly; with how great effort, how carefully

quantŭlum *adv* how little; **quantulum interest utrum** how little difference it makes whether

quantŭl·us -a -um *adj* how great, how much, how little, how small, how insignificant

quantul·uscumque -acumque -umcumque *adj* however small, however unimportant

quantum *adv* as much as, so much as, as great an extent; how much, how far, to what extent; (with comparatives) the more, the greater; **quantum in me fuit** as much as I could, to the best of my ability; **quantum maximā voce potuit** at the the top of his voice; **quantum potest** as much (*or fast, quickly, soon, long, etc.*) as possible

quantumcumque *adv* as much as

quantumlĭbet *adv* however much

quantumvīs *adv* however; **quantumvis rusticus** however unsophisticated, although unsophisticated

quant·us -a -um *adj* how great, how much; **quantus quantus** however great, however much; *pron neut* what amount; (with *genit*) how much; **in quantum** to whatever extent, as far as; **quanti** (*genit* of price) at what price, how much, how dearly, how high; **quanto** (*abl* of price) at what price, for how much; **quantum frumenti** how much grain

quant·uscumque -acumque -umcumque *adj* however great; of whatever size; however small, however trifling, however unimportant

quant·uslĭbet -alĭbet -umlĭbet *adj* however great; ever so great

quant·usvīs -ăvīs -umvīs *adj* however great

quāpropter *adv* wherefore, why

quāquā *adv* by whatever route, whatever way

quāquam *adv* by any way

quārē or **quā rē** *adv* by what means, how; from what cause, why; whereby; wherefore

quartadecumān·ī -ōrum *m pl* soldiers of the fourteenth legion

quartān·us -a -um *adj* occurring every fourth day; *f* quartan fever; *m pl* soldiers of the fourteenth legion

quartār·ĭus -ĭī or **-ī** *m* quarter pint

quartō *adv* for the fourth time

quartum *adv* for the fourth time

quart·us -a -um *adj* fourth

quart·us decĭm·us -a -um *adj* fourteenth

quasi *conj* as if, just as if, as though

quasi *adv* as it were, so to speak; about, nearly, almost

quasill·um -ī *n* or **quasill·us -ī** *m* small basket

quassātĭ·ō -ōnis *f* shaking

quass·ō -āre *vt* to keep shaking, keep tossing, keep waving; to batter, shatter, smash to pieces; (fig) to shake, weaken

quass·us -a -um *pp* of **quatio**; *adj* shattered, broken; **vox quassa** weak voice

quate·facĭō -facĕre -fēcī -factum *vt* to shake; (fig) to weaken

quātĕnus *adv* how far, to what point; as far as; till when, how long; to what extent; **est quatenus** there is an extent to which; *conj* as far as; insofar as, inasmuch as, seeing that, since, as

quater *adv* four times

quater decĭens or **quater deciēs** *adv* fourteen times

quatern·ī -ae -a *adj* four together, four in a group, four each

quatĭō quatĕre — -quassum *vt* to shake, cause to tremble, cause to vibrate; to brandish, wave about; to beat, strike, drive; to batter, crush; (fig) to touch, move, affect; (fig) to plague, harass

quattŭor (indecl) *adj* four

quattuordĕcim (indecl) *adj* fourteen

quattuorvirāt·us -ūs *m* membership on the board of four

quattuorvĭr·ī -ōrum *m pl* board of four officials (*executive board of municipalities and colonies*)

-que *conj* and

quemadmŏdum or **quem ad modum** *adv* in what way, how; *conj* just as, as

qu·ĕō -īre -īvī or **-ĭī -ĭtum** *vi* to be able; (with *inf*) to be able to

quercēt·um -ī *n* oak forest

quercĕ·us -a -um *adj* oak, of oak

querc·us -ūs *f* oak tree; oak-leaf crown (*awarded to a soldier who saved citizen in battle*); acorns

querell·a or **querēl·a -ae** *f* complaint

queribund·us -a -um *adj* complaining; **vox queribunda** whining voice

querimōnĭ·a -ae *f* complaint, grievance; elegy

querĭt·or -ārī -ātus sum *vi* to keep complaining

quern·us -a -um *adj* oak, of oak

queror querī questus sum *vt* to

complain of, complain about; to lament; *vi* to complain; (of birds) to sing, warble, sing sadly, coo mournfully

querquētulān·us -a -um *adj* oak, covered with oak trees

querŭl·us -a -um *adj* complaining, full of complaints, querulous; plaintive; warbling, cooing

questus *pp* of **queror**

quest·us -ūs *m* complaint; plaintive note (*of the nightingale*)

quī quae quod *adj* (interrog) which, what, what kind of; (indefinite) any; *pron* (rel) who, that; (indef, after **si, nisi, num, ne**) anyone

quī *adv* how; why; at what price; whereby; in some way, somehow

quia *conj* because

quiănam *adv* why

quicquam cūjusquam *pron* anything

quicque cūjusque *pron* each, each one

quidquid (*genit* not in use) *pron* whatever

quīcum (old *abl* + **cum**) *pron* with whom, with which

quīcumque quaecumque quodcumque or **quīcunque quaecunque quodcunque** *pron* (rel) whoever, whosoever, everyone who, whatever, whatsoever, everything that, all that; (indef) any whatsoever, any possible, every possible

quid *adv* why

quid cūjus *pron* (interrog) what; (indef, after **si, nisi, num,** or **ne**) anything

quīdam quaedam quiddam *pron* a certain one, a certain person, a certain thing

quīdam quaedam quoddam *adj* a certain; (to soften an expression) a kind of, what one might call

quidem *adv* (emphasizing the word that is placed before it) indeed, in fact; (qualifying or limiting) at least, at any rate; (concessive) it is true; of course; all right; (exemplifying) for example; **ne . . . quidem** (emphasizing the intervening word) not even, e.g., **ne tu quidem** not even you

quidnam cūjusnam *pron* (interrog) what

quidnam *adv* why, why in the world

quidnī *adv* why not

quidpĭam cūjuspĭam *pron* anything, something

quidquid (*genit* not in use; *abl:* **quoquo**) *pron* whatever, whatsoever, everything which; **per quiquid deorum** by all the gods

quidquid *adv* to whatever extent, the further

qui·ēs -ētis *f* quiet, peace, rest; calm, lull; neutrality; sleep; dream; sleep of death, death

qui·escō -escĕre -ēvī -ētum *vt* to stand by and watch, quietly allow; *vi* to rest, keep quiet, be inactive; to rest, sleep, be asleep; to lie still, be still, be undisturbed; to pause, make a pause; to be calm, be unruffled; to be neutral, keep neutral; (with *inf*) to cease to, stop; (with **ab** + *abl*) to be free from

quiētē *adv* quietly, calmly

quiēt·us -a -um *adj* at rest, resting, free from exertion, inactive; quiet, peaceful, undisturbed; neutral; calm, quiet; still, silent; idle; *n pl* period of peace

quilĭbet quaelĭbet quidlĭbet *pron* anyone, any you wish, no matter who, anything, anything you wish, not matter what, everything

quilĭbet quaelĭbet quodlĭbet *adj* any, any at all, any you wish

quīn *adv* (interrog) why not; (corroborative) in fact, as a matter of fact; *conj* so that not, without; **facere non possum, quin ad te mittam librum** I can't help sending you the book; **nullo modo introire possem, quin viderent me** I just couldn't walk in without their seeing me; (after verbs of preventing, opposing) from: **milites aegre sunt retenti quin oppidum oppugnarent** the soldiers could barely be kept from assaulting the town; (after verbs of hesitation, doubt, suspicion): **non dubito quin** I do not doubt that; (esp. representing a nominative of a relative pronoun with a negative) that . . . not, without: **nemo aspicere potest quin dicat** no one can look on without saying; **nemo est quin velit** there is no one who does not prefer

quīnam quaenam quodnam *adj* which, what, just which, just what

Quinct- = **Quint-**

quinc·unx -uncis *m* five twelfths; five percent (*interest*); the figure five (*as arranged on dice or cards*)

quindecĭens or **quindecĭēs** *adv* fifteen times

quindĕcim (indecl) *adj* fifteen

quindecimprīm·ī -ōrum *m pl* executive board of fifteen (*magistrates of a municipality*)

quindecimvirāl·is -e *adj* of the board of fifteen

quindecimvĭr·ī -ōrum *m pl* board of fifteen; **quindecimviri Sibyllini** board of fifteen in charge of the Sibylline Books

quingēnārĭ·us -a -um *adj* of five hundred each, consisting of five hundred men

quingēn·ī -ae -a *adj* five hundred each

quingentēsĭm·us -a -um *adj* five-hundredth

quingent·ī -ae -a *adj* five hundred

quingentĭens or **quingentĭēs** *adv* five hundred times

quīn·ī -ae -a *adj* five each; **quini deni** fifteen each; **quini viceni** twenty-five each

quinquāgēn·ī -ae -a *adj* fifty each

quinquāgēsim·us -a -um *adj* fiftieth; *f* two-percent tax
quinquāginta (indecl) *adj* fifty
Quinquātr·ūs -ŭum *f pl* or **Quinquātr·ia -ium** *n pl* festival in honor of Minerva (*celebrated from March 19th to 23rd*)
quinque (indecl) *adj* five
quinquennāl·is -e *adj* quinquennial, occurring every five years; five-year, lasting five years
quinquenn·is -e *adj* five years old, of five years
quinquenn·ium -iī or **-ī** *n* five-year period, five years
quinquepartīt·us -a -um *adj* fivefold, divided into five parts
quinqueprīm·ī -ōrum *m pl* five-man board of magistrates
quinquerēm·is -e *adj* having five banks of oars; *f* quinquereme
quinquĕ·vir -virī *m* member of a five-man board
quinquevirāt·us -ūs *m* membership on a board of five
quinquevir·ī -ōrum *m pl* five-man board (*created at various times to serve various purposes*)
quinquiens or **quinquiēs** *adv* five times
quinquiplic·ō -āre *vt* to multiply by five
quintadecimān·ī -ōrum *m pl* soldiers of the fifteenth legion
quintān·us -a -um *adj* of the fifth; *m pl* members of the fifth legion; *f* camp street running between the fifth and sixth maniple (*used as the market street of the camp*)
Quintiliān·us or **Quinctiliān·us -ī** *m* M. Fabius Quintilianus (*Quintilian, famous orator and rhetoric teacher, c.* 35-*c.* 95 A.D.)
Quintīl·is or **Quinctīl·is -e** *adj & m* July
quintō or **quintum** *adv* for the fifth time
quint·us -a -um *adj* fifth
Quint·us -ī *m* Roman first name
quint·us decim·us -a -um *adj* fifteenth
quippe *adv* of course, naturally, obviously, by all means; *conj* since, for; **quippe qui** since he (*is, was, will be one who*), inasmuch as he; **multa Caesar questus est quippe qui vidisset** Caesar complained a lot since he had seen
quippiam = quidpiam
quippinī *adv* why not?; of course, to be sure
Quirīnāl·ia -ium *n pl* festival in honor of Romulus (*celebrated on the 17th of February*)
Quirīnāl·is -e *adj* of Quirinus; **collis Quirinalis** Quirinal Hill (*one of the seven hills of Rome*)
Quirīn·us -a -um *adj* of Quirinus; *m* Quirinus (*epithet applied to Romulus after his deification, to Janus, to Augustus, and to Antony*)
Quir·īs -ītis *m* Roman citizen; inhabitant of Cures (*Sabine town*)
quirītāti·ō -ōnis *f* shrieking, shriek
quirītāt·us -ūs *m* scream, shriek
Quirītēs = *pl* of **Quiris**
quirīt·ō -āre *vi* to scream, shriek
quis cūjus *pron* (interrog) who, which one; (indef) anyone
quīs = quibus
quisnam quaenam (see **quidnam**) *pron* (interrog) who
quispiam cūjuspiam *pron* someone
quispiam quaepiam quodpiam *adj* any
quisquam cūjusquam *pron* anyone, anybody, any person
quisque cūjusque *pron* each, each one, everybody, every one; **doctissimus quisque** every one of great learning, all the most learned; **optimus quisque** all the best ones
quisque quaeque quodque *adj* each
quisquili·ae -ārum *f pl* refuse, trash, junk, rubbish, odds and ends
quisquis (*genit* not in use; *abl:* **quoquo**) *pron* whoever, whosoever, every one who; every one, each
quīvīs quaevīs quidvīs *pron* anyone, anyone you please, anyone at all; **quivis unus** any one person
quīvīs quaevīs quodvīs *adj* any, any you please, any at all
quō *adv* (interrog) where, to what place; what for, to what purpose; (after **si, nisi,** or **ne**) to any place, anywhere; **quo . . . eo** the . . . the; **quo magis . . . eo magis** the more . . . the more; *conj* where, to which place; whereby, wherefore; (replacing **ut** when the clause contains a comparative) in order that, so that
quoad *adv* how far; how long; *conj* as long as; as far as; until
quōcircā *adv* for which reason, wherefore, therefore, that's the reason why
quōcumque *adv* to whatever place, wherever
quod *conj* because; as for the fact that; for the fact that; insofar as; as far as; **quod si** or **quodsi** but if
quōdammŏdo or **quōdam modo** *adv* in a way
quoi = cui
quōjus = cujus
quōlĭbet *adv* anywhere you please
quom see **cum**
quōminus *conj* that not; (after verbs of hindering) from, e.g., **deterrere aliquem quominus habeat** to keep someone from having
quōmŏdo *adv* (interrog) in what way, how; (rel) just as, as
quōmodocumque *adv* in whatever way, however
quōmodŏnam *adv* in just what way, how then
quōnam *adv* where, where to; to what purpose, to what end
quondam *adv* once, at one time, formerly; at times, sometimes, once in a while; some day, one day (*in the future*)

quōniam *conj* because, seeing that, now that
quōpiam *adv* to any place, anywhere
quoque *adv* too, also
quōquō *adv* to whatever place, wherever
quōquōmŏdo *adv* in whatever way, however
quōquōversum or **quōquōversus** *adv* in every direction, every way
quorsum or **quorsus** *adv* in what direction, where to; to what end, why
quot (indecl) *adj* (interrog) how many; (correlative) as many; **quot Kalendis** every first of the month; **quot mensibus** every month
quotannīs *adv* every year
quotcumque (indecl) *adj* however many
quotēn·ī -ae -a *adj* how many each
quotīdiē *adv* daily
quotiens or **quotiēs** *adv* (interrog) how many times; (correlative) as often as
quotienscumque or **quotienscunque** *adv* however often, as often as
quotquot (indecl) *adj* however many, no matter how many
quotŭm·us -a -um *adj* which in number, which in order
quot·us -a -um *adj* which, what; what a small, what a trifling; **quota hora est?** what time is it?; **quota pars** what part; **quot erit iste liber qui . . .** which will be the book which . . .; **quotus quisque philosophorum invenitur** how rarely is one of the philosophers found, how few philosophers are found
quot·uscumque -acumque -umcumque *adj* just what, just which; **quotacumque pars** just what part
quōusque *adv* how far, how long
quōvīs *adv* to any place whatsoever, anywhere; **quovis gentium** anywhere in the world
quum see **cum** *conj*

R

rabĭdē *adv* rabidly, madly, furiously
rabĭd·us -a -um *adj* rabid, mad, furious, raving, uncontrolled
rabĭ·ēs (*genit* not in use) *f* rage, madness; (fig) rage, anger, fury, wild passion, eagerness
rabĭōsē *adv* furiously, ravingly
rabiōsŭl·us -a -um *adj* half-crazy
rabiōs·us -a -um *adj* rabid, mad, raving, crazy
rabŭl·a -ae *m* ranting lawyer
racēmĭf·er -ĕra -ĕrum *adj* clustered; covered with grape clusters
racēm·us -ī *m* cluster, bunch (*esp. of grapes*); (fig) wine
radĭ·ans -antis *adj* shining, beaming, radiant
radiāt·us -a -um *adj* spoked; having rays, radiant
rādīcitus *adv* by the roots, root and all; completely
rādīcŭl·a -ae *f* small root
radĭ·ō -āre or **radĭ·or -ārī -ātus sum** *vt* to radiate; *vi* to radiate, shine, gleam
radiōs·us -a -um *adj* radiant
rad·ĭus -iī or **-ī** *m* stake, stick; spoke; ray, beam; shuttle; radius; measuring rod; elongated olive
rād·ix -īcis *f* root; radish; foot (*of hill or mountain*); base, foundation; basis, origin
rādō rādĕre rāsī rāsum *vt* to scrape, scratch; to shave; to scratch out, erase; to graze, touch in passing; to strip off; (of the wind) to lash
raed·a -ae *f* four-wheeled carriage, coach
raedār·ĭus -iī or **-ī** *m* coach driver
Raetĭ·us -a -um *adj* Raetian; *f* Raetia (*Alpine country between Germany and Italy*)
Raet·us -a -um *adj & m* Raetian
rall·us -a -um *adj* thin, threadbare
rāmāl·ĭa -ĭum *n pl* brushwood, undergrowth
rāment·um -ī *n* or **rament·a -ae** *f* chip, shaving
rāmĕ·us -a -um *adj* of branches, of boughs
rām·ex -ĭcis *m* hernia, rupture; blood vessel of the lung
Ramn·ēs or **Ramnens·ēs -ĭum** *m pl* one of the three original Roman tribes; (fig) blue bloods
rāmōs·us -a -um *adj* branchy, branching; branch-like
rāmŭl·us -ī *m* twig
rām·us -ī *m* branch, bough; branch (*of an antler*); stick, club
rān·a -ae *f* frog; **rana marina** frog fish
ranc·ens -entis *adj* putrid, stinking
rancidŭl·us -a -um *adj* rank, stinking; disgusting
rancĭd·us -a -um *adj* rancid, rank, stinking; disgusting
rānuncŭl·us -ī *m* little frog, tadpole
rapācĭd·a -ae *m* son of a thief
rapācĭt·ās -ātis *f* rapacity, greediness
rap·ax -ācis *adj* rapacious, grasping, grabby, greedy for plunder; insatiable
raphăn·us -ī *m* radish
rapĭdē *adv* rapidly; (to burn) fiercely
rapidĭt·ās -ātis *f* rapidity, velocity, swiftness, rush
rapĭd·us -a -um *adj* tearing away,

seizing; fierce, consuming, white-hot (*fire*); rapid, swift, rushing, hurrying, impetuous
rapīn·a -ae *f* rapine, pillage; prey, booty
rapiō rapĕre rapŭī raptum *vt* to seize and carry off, to snatch, tear, pluck; to drag off; to hurry, drive, cause to rush; to carry off by force, rob, ravish, ravage, lay waste; to lead on hurriedly; **flammam rapere** to catch fire; **in jus rapere** to drag off to court, hale before a court; **se rapere** to hurry, dash, take off
raptim *adv* hurriedly, speedily, suddenly
raptĭ·ō -ōnis *f* abduction, ravishing, rape
rapt·ō -āre *vt* to seize and carry off, drag away; to drag along; to plunder; to hale, arraign
rapt·or -ōris *m* plunderer, robber; rapist
rapt·us -a -um *pp* of **rapio;** *n* plunder, loot
rapt·us -ūs *m* snatching away; looting, robbery; rape, abduction
rāpŭl·um -ī *n* little turnip
rāp·um -ī *n* turnip
rārē *adv* rarely, seldom
rārē·faciō -facĕre -fēcī -factum *vt* to rarefy, thin out
rāresc·ō -ĕre *vi* to grow thin, lose density, become rarefied; to grow wider, widen out, open up; to become fewer; to disappear, die away
rārĭt·ās -ātis *f* looseness of texture; thinness; small number
rārō *adv* rarely, seldom
rār·us -a -um *adj* wide apart, of loose texture, thin; far apart, scattered far apart; scarce, sparse; few; (mil) in open rank; uncommon, rare, unusual
rāsĭl·is -e *adj* shaved smooth, scraped, polished
rastr·um -ī *n* rake; mattock
rāsus *pp* of **rado**
ratĭ·ō -ōnis *f* calculation, computation, reckoning, account; matter, affair, business, transaction; consideration, respect, regard; grounds; scheme, system, method, procedure; theory, doctrine; science; relation, connection, reference; fashion, way, style; reasoning, reason, judgment, understanding; reasonableness, order, law, rule; view, opinion; **propter rationem** (with *genit*) out of regard for; **ratio aeraria** rate of exchange; **ratio atque usus** theory and practice; **ratio constat** the accounts tally; **rationem conferre, referre,** or **deferre** (with *genit*) to render or give an account of, account for; **rationem ducere** to make a calculation, reckon; **rationem habere** (with **cum** + *abl*) to have to do with; **rationem inire** to calculate, make a calculation
ratiōcinātĭ·ō -ōnis *f* (rhet) exercise of the reasoning powers, reasoning; syllogism
ratiōcinātīv·us -a -um *adj* syllogistic
ratiōcināt·or -ōris *m* accountant
ratiōcĭn·or -ārī -ātus sum *vt & vi* to calculate, reckon; to reason, argue, conclude, infer
rat·is -is *f* raft; boat; *f pl* pontoons
ratiuncŭl·a -ae *f* small account; trifling reason; petty syllogism
rat·us -a -um *pp* of **reor;** *adj* reckoned, calculated; fixed, established, settled, certain, sure, approved; **pro rata parte** or **pro rata** in proportion, proportionately; **ratum facere** or **ratum efficere** to confirm, ratify, approve; **ratum habere** or **ducere** to consider valid, regard as certain or sure
raucisŏn·us -a -um *adj* hoarse
rauc·us -a -um *adj* raucous, hoarse; screaming, strident; scraping; deep, deep-voiced
raud·us or **rūd·us -ĕris** *n* copper coin
rauduscŭl·um or **rūduscŭl·um -ī** *n* bit of money
rāv·ĭō -īre *vi* to talk oneself hoarse
rāv·is -is *f* hoarseness
rāv·us -a -um *adj* greyish
re·a -ae *f* defendant, guilty woman
reapse *adv* in fact, actually, really
Reāt·e -is *n* Sabine town
Reātīn·us -a -um *adj & m* Reatine
rebellātĭ·ō -ōnis *f* rebellion
rebellātr·ix -īcis *f* rebel; **Germania rebellatrix** rebel Germany
rebellĭ·ō -ōnis *f* rebellion
rebell·is -e *adj* rebellious; *m pl* rebels
rebell·ĭum -ĭī or **-ī** *n* rebellion
rebell·ō -āre *vi* to rebel
rebīt·ō -ĕre *vi* to go back
rebŏ·ō -āre *vt* to make reecho; *vi* to reecho, bellow back
recalcĭtr·ō -āre *vi* to kick back
recal·ĕō -ēre *vi* to be warmed; (of a river) to run warm (*e.g., with blood*)
recal·escō -escĕre -ŭī *vi* to grow warm again
recal·faciō -facĕre -fēcī *vt* to make warm again, warm up again
recalv·us -a -um *adj* bald in front, with receding hairline
recand·escō -escĕre -ŭī *vi* to grow white; to grow hot, glow; (with *dat*) to grow white, grow hot, glow in response to
recant·ō -āre *vt* to recant; to charm back, charm away; *vi* to reecho
re·cēdō -cēdĕre -cessī -cessum *vi* to go back, go away, withdraw, recede, give ground, fall back; to depart; to vanish, disappear; to stand back, be distant
recell·ō -ĕre *vi* to spring back, recoil
rec·ens -entis *adj* recent, fresh, young; newly arrived, just arrived; modern; fresh, rested; *n pl* recent events

recens *adv* just, recently, lately, newly

recens·ĕō -ēre -ŭī -um *vt* to count, enumerate, number, survey; to review, hold a review of (*the army*); (of a censor) to revise the roll of, review, enroll; to recount, go over again, retell

recensī·ō -ōnis *f* revision

recensus *pp* of **recenseo**

recens·us -ūs *m* review

receptācŭl·um -ī *n* receptacle, container; reservoir; place of refuge, shelter; hiding place

receptī·ō -ōnis *f* reception

recept·ō -āre *vt* to take back; to welcome frequently into the home, entertain; to tug at; **se receptare** to beat a hasty retreat

recept·or -ōris *m* or **receptr·ix -īcis** *f* shelterer; concealer

recept·us -a -um *pp* of **recipio**; *n* obligation

recept·us -ūs *m* taking back, recantation; (mil) retreat; way of escape; refuge, place of retreat; return; **(signum) receptui canere** to sound retreat

recessim *adv* backwards

recess·us -ūs *m* retreat, withdrawal; departure; secluded spot, retreat; inner room, central chamber; recess; background

recharmĭd·ō -āre *vi* to stop being a Charmides (*character in Roman comedy*)

recidīv·us -a -um *adj* recurring, returning; rebuilt

re·cīdo -cīdĕre -cīdī -cīsum *vt* to cut back, cut away, cut off, cut down; to abridge, cut short

re·cĭdō -cidĕre -cĭdī -cāsum or **rec·cĭdō -cidĕre** *vi* to fall back; to jump back, recoil; to suffer a relapse; (fig) to fall back, fall, sink, relapse; to turn out, result; (with **ad** or **in** + *acc*) to pass to, be handed over to

re·cingō -cingĕre — -cinctum *vt* to loosen, undo, take off

recĭn·ō -ĕre *vt* to repeat, reecho; *vi* to sound a warning

reciper- = **recuper-**

re·cipiō -cipĕre -cēpī -ceptum *vt* to keep back, keep in reserve; to take back, withdraw, bring back, carry back, retake, recover, regain; to take in, accept, receive, welcome; to gain, collect, take in, make (*money*); to take up, assume, undertake; to guarantee, pledge; (mil) to retake, reoccupy, recapture, seize, take, occupy; **ad se** or **in se recipere** to take upon oneself, take responsibility for, promise, guarantee; **se recipere** to get hold of oneself again, regain self-composure, recover, come to again; to retreat, escape; **se recipere** (with **ad** or **in** + *acc*) to retreat to, escape to, find refuge in

reciprŏc·ō -āre *vt* to move back and forth; to turn back; to back (*e.g., a ship*) about, reverse the direction of; to reverse, convert (*a proposition*); *vi* (of the tide) to ebb and flow, rise and fall

reciprŏc·us -a -um *adj* ebbing and flowing, going backwards and forwards

recīsus *pp* of **recīdo**

recitātī·ō -ōnis *f* reading aloud, recitation

recitāt·or -ōris *m* reader, reciter

recĭt·ō -āre *vt* to read out, read aloud, recite; to name in writing, appoint, constitute; **senatum recitare** to have roll call in the senate

reclāmātī·ō -ōnis *f* cry of disapproval

reclāmĭt·ō -āre *vi* to voice disapproval

reclām·ō -āre *vt* to protest; *vi* to raise a protest, voice disapproval, shout objections; to reverberate; (with *dat*) to express disapproval to, contradict

reclīn·is -e *adj* reclining, leaning back

reclīn·ō -āre *vt* to bend back, lean back, rest; (with **ab** + *abl*) to distract (*someone*) from; **se reclinare** to lean

re·clūdō -clūdĕre -clūsī -clūsum *vt* to open; to lay open, disclose; to draw (*sword*); to break up (*the soil*)

recoctus *pp* of **recoquo**

recōgĭt·ō -āre *vi* (with **de** + *abl*) to think again about, reconsider, reflect on

recognitī·ō -ōnis *f* reinvestigation

reco·gnoscō -gnoscĕre -gnōvī -gnĭtum *vt* to call to mind again, review; to recognize; to look over, examine, inspect, investigate; to certify, authorize

recol·ligō -ligĕre -lēgī -lectum *vt* to gather again, gather up, collect; **te recollige** get hold of yourself, pluck up your courage

re·cŏlō -colĕre -colŭī -cultum *vt* to till again; to honor again; to recall to mind, think over, consider; to cultivate once more, practice again, resume

recomminisc·or -ī *vt* to call to mind again, recall

recomposĭt·us -a -um *adj* rearranged

reconciliātī·ō -ōnis *f* winning back again, reestablishment, restoration; reconciling, reconciliation

reconcilī·ō -āre *vt* to bring back, regain, recover; to restore, reestablish; to win over again, conciliate; to bring together again, reconcile

reconcinn·ō -āre *vt* to set right again, repair

recondĭt·us -a -um *adj* hidden, concealed; recondite, abstruse, profound; reserved (*person*)

recon·dō -dĕre -dĭdī -dĭtum *vt* to put back again, put away, hoard; to hide, conceal; to plunge (*sword*); to close (*eyes*) again; to store up (*in the mind*)

reconfl·ō -āre *vt* to blow up again, rekindle

re·cŏquō -coquĕre -coxī -coctum *vt* to cook, boil, or bake again; to recast, remold

recordātī·ō -ōnis *f* recollection, remembrance

record·or -ārī -ātus sum *vt* to recall, recollect, remember

recrĕ·ō -āre *vt* to recreate, restore, renew; (fig) to revive, refresh

recrĕp·ō -ĕre *vt & vi* to reecho

re·crescō -crescĕre -crēvī *vi* to grow again; to be renewed

recrūd·escō -escĕre -ŭī *vi* to become raw again; (of a wound) to open up again; (of a revolt) to break out again

rectā *adv* by a direct route, right on, directly

rectē *adv* in a straight line; rightly, correctly, suitably, properly, well; quite; (in answers) well, right, quite well, fine

rectī·ō -ōnis *f* direction, controlling

rect·or -ōris *m* guide, controller, leader, ruler, master, pilot

rect·us -a -um *pp* of **rego;** *adj* in a straight line, straight, direct; correct, right, proper, appropriate; just, upright, conscientious, virtuous; *n* right; uprightness, rectitude, virtue

recŭb·ō -āre *vi* to lie on one's back, lie down, rest

rēcŭl·a -ae *f* little thing

recultus *pp* of **recolo**

re·cumbō -cumbĕre -cubŭī *vi* to lie down again, lie down; to recline (*esp. at table*); to sink down (*e.g., in a swamp*); to fall; (of fog) to settle down

recuperātī·ō -ōnis *f* recovery

recuperāt·or or **reciperāt·or -ōris** *m* recoverer, regainer; (law) arbiter (*member of a bench of from three to five men who expedited cases needing speedy decisions*)

recuperātōrī·us or **reciperātōrī·us -a -um** *adj* of the special court for summary civil suits

recupĕr·ō or **recipĕr·ō -āre** *vt* to regain, recover, get back; to win over again

recūr·ō -āre *vt* to restore, refresh, restore to health

re·currō -currĕre -currī *vi* to run back, hurry back; to return, recur, come back

recurs·ō -āre *vi* to keep running back; to keep recurring

recurs·us -ūs *m* return; retreat

recurv·ō -āre *vt* to curve, bend back

recurv·us -a -um *adj* curving, curved, bent, crooked

recusātī·ō -ōnis *f* refusal; (law) objection, protest; counterplea

recūs·ō -āre *vt* to raise objections to, reject, refuse; (with *inf*) to be reluctant to, refuse to; *vi* to raise an objection, object; to make a rebuttal

recuss·us -a -um *adj* reverberating

recutīt·us -a -um *adj* with the foreskin cut back, circumcised; Jewish

redactus *pp* of **redigo**

redambŭl·ō -āre *vi* to walk back

redăm·ō -āre *vt* to love in return

redargu·ō -ĕre -ī *vt* to disprove, contradict, refute

redauspĭc·ō -āre *vi* to take the return auspices; (coll) to return

red·dō -dĕre -dĭdī -dĭtum *vt* to give back, return, restore, replace; to repay; to repeat, recite (*words*); to translate; to render, make; to give as due, pay, deliver; to reflect, reproduce, imitate; **se reddere** to return, come back

redemptī·ō -ōnis *f* ransoming; bribing; revenue collection

redempt·ō -āre *vt* to ransom, repeatedly

redempt·or -ōris *m* contractor; revenue agent

redemptūr·a -ae *f* revenue collection

redemptus *pp* of **redimo**

red·ĕō -īre -ĭī -ĭtum *vi* to go or come back, return; (of a speaker) to return (*to the main theme*); (with **ad** + *acc*) **a** to return to, revert to; **b** to fall back on, have recourse to, be reduced to; **c** (of power, inheritances, etc.) to revert to, devolve upon; **ad se redire** to come to again, regain consciousness; to control oneself

redhāl·ō -āre *vt* to exhale

redhib·ĕō -ēre — -ĭtum *vt* to take back

red·ĭgō -igĕre -ēgī -actum *vt* to drive back, lead back, bring back; to call in, collect, raise (*money, revenues*); to reduce, diminish (*numbers*); to force, compel, subdue, reduce; (with double *acc*) to render, make; (with **in** or **sub** + *acc*) to bring under the power of; **ad vanum et irritum redigere** to make meaningless; **in memoriam redigere** to remember, recall; **in provinciam redigere** to reduce to the rank of a province

redimĭcŭl·um -ī *n* band, chaplet, fillet; chain, fetter

redim·ĭō -īre -ĭī -ītum *vt* to crown, wreathe

red·ĭmō -imĕre -ēmī -emptum *vt* to buy back; to ransom, redeem; to buy off, rescue by payment, rescue, release, set free; to buy up; to buy off, ward off, avert; to pay for, compensate for, atone for; to get by contract, collect under contract

redintĕgr·ō -āre *vt* to make whole again, restore, refresh; (mil) to bring to full strength

redipisc·or -ī *vt* to get back

reditī·ō -ōnis *f* return

redĭt·us -ūs *m* return; revenue, proceeds, returns; (of heavenly bodies) revolution, orbit; (fig) restoration
redivĭa see **reduvia**
redivīv·us -a -um *adj* second-hand (*building materials*)
redol·ĕō -ēre -ŭī *vt* to smell of; *vi* to smell, be redolent
redomĭt·us -a -um *adj* retamed, broken in again
redōn·ō -āre *vt* to restore, give back again; to give up, abandon
redorm·ĭō -īre *vi* to go to sleep again
re·dūcō -dūcĕre -duxī -ductum *vt* to draw back; to lead back, bring back; to escort (*official as mark of honor to his home*); to remarry (*after a separation*); to restore to normal; to withdraw (*troops*); **in gratiam reducere** to restore to favor
reductĭ·ō -ōnis *f* restoration
reduct·or -ōris *m* restorer
reduct·us -a -um *pp* of **reduco**; remote, secluded, aloof, removed
redunc·us -a -um *adj* bent backwards, curved backwards
redundantĭ·a -ae *f* excess; redundancy
redund·ō -āre *vi* to overflow; to be too numerous, be too large; to be soaked (*e.g., with blood*); (with *abl*) to abound in; (with **de** or **ex** + *abl*) to stream from, overflow with
reduvĭ·a or **redivĭ·a -ae** *f* hangnail, loose fingernail
red·ux -ūcis *adj* guiding back, rescuing; brought back, restored
refectus *pp* of **reficio**
refell·ō -ĕre -ī *vt* to refute, disprove
re·fercĭō -fercīre -fersī -fertum *vt* to stuff, cram, choke, crowd
refer·ĭō -īre *vt* to strike back, hit back
refĕrō referre rettŭlī relātum *vt* to bring back, carry back; to give back, return, restore, pay back, repay; to bring back, return, echo (*a sound*); to renew, revive, repeat; to bring back, direct, focus, turn (*mind, attention*); to present again, represent; to say in turn, answer, reply; to announce, report, relate, tell; to note down, enter, register, record; to reckon, consider, regard; to refer, attribute, ascribe; to bring up, spit out, vomit; **gradum referre** to go back, retreat; **gratiam** or **gratias referre** to return thanks, show gratitude; **in rationibus referendis** in accounting; **pedem referre** to go back, retreat, withdraw, retire; **pedes fertque refertque** he walks up and down; **rationes referre ad aerarium** to make an accounting to the treasury; **se referre** to go back, return; **vestigia referre** to retrace footsteps, return; *vi* to make a motion, make a proposal; **ad senatum referre** (with **de** + *abl*) to bring before the senate the matter of, make a proposal to the senate about; *v impers* it is of importance, it is of consequence; **meā (tuā, nostrā) refert** it is of importance, of consequence, of advantage to me (*you, us*); **non refert utrum** it makes no difference whether; **parvi refert** (with *inf*) it is of little importance, of little advantage to; **quid refert?** what's the difference?
refert·us -a -um *pp* of **refercio**; *adj* stuffed, packed, crammed; crowded
referv·ĕō -ēre *vi* to boil over, bubble over
refervesc·ō -ĕre *vi* to begin to boil or bubble
re·ficĭō -ficĕre -fēcī -fectum *vt* to rebuild, repair, restore; to revive (*hope, etc.*); to refresh, invigorate; to get (*e.g., money*) back again; to reappoint, reelect
re·fīgō -fīgĕre -fixī -fixum *vt* to unfasten, undo; to take down (*pictures, posters, etc.*); to annul (*laws*)
refing·ō -ĕre *vt* to refashion
refixus *pp* of **refigo**
reflāgĭt·ō -āre *vt* to demand again, ask back
reflāt·us -ūs *m* head wind
re·flectō -flectĕre -flexī -flexum *vt* to bend back or backwards, turn around, turn away; (fig) to turn back, bring back, change
refl·ō -āre *vt* to breathe out again; *vi* to blow in the wrong direction
reflŭ·ō -ĕre *vi* to flow back, run back; to overflow
reflŭ·us -a -um *adj* ebbing, receding
refocill·ō -āre *vt* to rewarm; to revive
reformāt·or -ōris *m* reformer
reformīdātĭ·ō -ōnis *f* dread
reformīd·ō -āre *vt* to dread, stand in awe of; to shrink from, shun
reform·ō -āre *vt* to reshape, remold, transform
re·fovĕō -fovēre -fōvī -fōtum *vt* to warm again; to restore, revive, refresh
refractārĭŏl·us -a -um *adj* a bit refractory, somewhat stubborn
refractus *pp* of **refringo**
refrāg·or -ārī -ātus sum *vi* (with *dat*) to oppose, resist, thwart
refrēn·ō -āre *vt* to curb, restrain, keep down, control
refrĭc·ō -āre -ŭī -ātum *vt* to rub open, scratch open; to irritate, reopen, inflame (*a wound*); (fig) to irritate, exasperate; (fig) to renew; *vi* to break out again
refrīgerātĭ·ō -ōnis *f* coolness
refrīgĕr·ō -āre *vt* to cool off, cool, chill; to refresh; to weary, exhaust; **refrigerari** to grow cool, grow weary
re·frīgescō -frīgescĕre -frixī *vi* to grow cool, become cool; (fig) to lose

force, flag, abate, fail, grow dull, grow stale, fall flat

re·fringō -fringĕre -frēgī -fractum *vt* to break open, break down; to tear off (*clothes*); (fig) to break, check, destroy, put an end to

re·fugiō -fugĕre -fūgī *vt* to run away from; to avoid; *vi* to run away, escape; to disappear

refug·ium -iī or **-ī** *n* place of refuge; recourse

refŭg·us -a -um *adj* receding, vanishing; *m* fugitive

re·fulgĕō -fulgēre -fulsī *vi* to gleam, reflect, reflect light, glitter

re·fundō -fundĕre -fūdī -fūsum *vt* to pour back, pour out; **refundi** to flow back, overflow

refūtāti·ō -ōnis *f* refutation

refūtāt·us -ūs *m* refutation

refūt·ō -āre *vt* to repress, suppress; to refute, disprove

rēgāl·is -e *adj* kingly, regal; king's, of a king, royal

rēgāliter *adv* royally, in royal style, splendidly; despotically

regĕl·ō -āre *vt* to cool off; to thaw

re·gĕrō -gerĕre -gessī -gestum *vt* to carry back, throw back; (fig) to throw back (*remarks*)

rēgi·a -ae *f* palace, castle, court; fortress, residence; (in camp) king's tent; royal family, king and courtiers, court; regia (*originally the palace of King Numa on the Sacred Way in the Roman Forum and later the residence of the Pontifex Maximus*)

rēgiē *adv* royally; despotically

Rēgiens·is -e or **Rēgīn·us -a -um** *adj* of Regium; *m pl* inhabitants of Regium

rēgific·us -a -um *adj* royal, kingly, magnificent

regign·ō -ĕre *vt* to reproduce

Rēgillān·us -a -um or **Rēgillens·is -e** *adj* of or at Lake Regillus

rēgill·us -a -um *adj* royal, magnificent

Rēgill·us -ī *m* lake in Latium famous for the victory over the Latins won by the Romans under the dictator Postumius (496 B.C.)

regim·en -inis *n* steering, controlling; rudder; government, rule, command, guidance; director, ruler, governor

rēgīn·a -ae *f* queen; princess; noble woman, lady

regi·ō -ōnis *f* straight line, line, direction; boundary, boundary line; region, area, quarter, neighborhood; ward (*of Rome*); district, province (*of a country*); department, sphere; **ab recta regione** in a straight line; **de recta regione deflectere** to veer off from a straight path; **e regione** in a straight line, directly; **e regione** (with *genit*) in the opposite direction to, exactly opposite; **rectā regione** by a direct route

regiōnātim *adv* by wards, by districts

Rēg·ium or **Rhēg·ium -iī** or **-ī** *n* city on the toe of Italy; town in Cisalpine Gaul

rēgi·us -a -um *adj* king's, kingly, royal, regal; like a king, worthy of a king, magnificent; *m pl* the king's troops; *f* see **regia**

reglūtin·ō -āre *vt* to unglue

regnāt·or -ōris *m* ruler, sovereign

regnātr·ix -īcis *adj fem* imperial

regn·ō -āre *vi* to be king, reign; to be supreme, hold sway; to domineer; (with *genit*) to be king of; (with **in** + *acc*) to rule over; **regnari** to be ruled by a king, be under a king

regn·um -ī *n* monarchy, royal power, kingship; absolute power, despotism, power; supremacy, control, direction, sovereignty; realm, kingdom; domain, estate

regō regĕre rexī rectum *vt* to keep in a straight line; keep in a proper course; to guide, conduct; to govern, rule, command; to manage, direct; **regere finīs** (law) to mark out the limits

re·gredior -grĕdī -gressus sum *vi* to step or go back; to come back, return; to march back, retreat

regress·us -ūs *m* return; retreat

rēgŭl·a -ae *f* ruler (*for measuring*); straight stick; straight board; rule, standard, example, model, principle

rēgŭl·us -ī *m* petty king, prince, chieftain; prince

Rēgŭl·us -ī *m* M. Atilius Regulus (*Roman general who was taken prisoner by the Carthaginians in the First Punic War, refused to let himself be ransomed, and was killed in* 250 B.C.)

regust·ō -āre *vt* to taste again; (fig) to delve again into (*e.g., literature*)

rē·iciō -icĕre -jēcī -jectum *vt* to throw back, fling back; to throw over one's shoulders or behind one; to beat back, repel, repulse; to reject, refuse, disdain, scorn; (of judges) to challenge, overrule; to refer, direct, assign; to postpone; **rem reicere** (with **ad** + *acc*) to turn over or refer the matter to (*someone for consideration or decision*); **potestas reiciendi** (law) right to challenge

rējectānĕ·us -a -um *adj* to be rejected

rējecti·ō -ōnis *f* rejection; (law) challenging; **rejectio judicum** challenging of the members of the jury

rēject·ō -āre *vt* to throw back

rējectus *pp* of **reicio**

re·lābor -lābī -lapsus sum *vi* to slide or glide back; to sink down (*upon a couch*); (of rivers) to flow back; to sail back; (fig) to return

relangu·escō -escĕre -ī *vi* to faint; to be relaxed, relax; to weaken

relāti·ō -ōnis *f* report (*made by a*

magistrate to the senate or emperor); repetition, reiteration; **relatio criminis** (law) answering to a charge

relāt·or -ōris *m* proposer of a motion

relātus *pp* of **refero**

relāt·us -ūs *m* official report; narration, recital, listing; **relatus carminum** recital of poems

relaxāti·ō -ōnis *f* relaxation, easing; mitigation

relax·ō -āre *vt* to stretch out, widen, open; to loosen, open; to release, set free; to ease, ease the tensions of, relieve, cheer up; to alleviate, mitigate

relectus *pp* of **relego**

relēgāti·ō -ōnis *f* banishment, sending into retirement

relēg·ō -āre *vt* to send away, remove, send into retirement, retire; to banish; to put aside, reject; to refer

re·lĕgō -legĕre -lēgī -lectum *vt* to collect again, gather up, gather together, to travel over, sail over again; to go over, review (*in thought, in a speech*); to reread

relentesc·ō -ĕre *vi* to slack off, cool off

relĕv·ō -āre *vt* to lighten; to lift up or raise again; (fig) to relieve, free, lighten, soothe, alleviate

relicti·ō -ōnis *f* abandonment

relictus *pp* of **relinquo**

relicŭus see **reliquus**

religāti·ō -ōnis *f* tying back, tying up

religi·ō -ōnis *f* religious scruple, conscientiousness, sense of right; misgivings; reverence, awe; religion; superstition; sanctity, holiness; religion, sect, cult, mode of worship; object of veneration, sacred object, sacred place; divine service, worship, religious observation

religiōsē *adv* scrupulously, conscientiously, carefully, exactly; reverently, piously, religiously

religiōs·us -a -um *adj* scrupulous, conscientious, exact, precise, accurate; religious, reverent, pious, devout; superstitious; sacred, holy, consecrated; subject to religious claims, under religious liability

relig·ō -āre *vt* to bind back, tie up; to moor (*a ship*); to unbind, untie, loosen; (fig) to bind

re·lĭnō -linĕre -lēvī — *vt* to unseal, open

re·linquō -linquĕre -līquī -lictum *vt* to leave behind, not take along; to leave behind, bequeath; to permit to remain, let remain; to leave alive; to forsake, abandon, desert, leave in a lurch; to give up, abandon, relinquish, resign; to leave unmentioned; **locum integrum relinquere** to leave the place untouched

reliquī·ae -ārum *f pl* remains, remnants

reliqu·us or **relicŭ·us -a -um** *adj* remaining, left over, left; remaining, subsequent, future (*time*); outstanding (*debt*); *m pl* the others; *n* remainder, rest, residue; **in reliquum** in the future, for the future; **nihil reliqui facere** to leave nothing undone, omit nothing, leave no stone unturned; **reliqui omnes** all the rest; **reliquum est** (with *inf* or **ut**) it only remains to; **reliquum aliquem facere** to leave someone behind; to spare someone; **reliquum aliquid facere** or **aliquid reliqui facere** to leave something remaining, leave something behind, neglect something

rellig- = relig-

relliq- = reliq-

re·lūcĕō -lūcēre -luxī *vi* to reflect light, gleam, shine out, blaze

re·lūcescō -lūcescĕre -luxī *vi* to grow bright again, clear

reluct·or -ārī -ātus sum *vi* to fight back, put up a struggle, resist; to be reluctant

re·manĕō -manēre -mansī *vi* to stay behind; to remain, continue (*in a certain state*)

remān·ō -āre *vi* to flow back

remansi·ō -ōnis *f* staying behind, stay

remed·ium -iī or **-ī** *n* remedy, cure, antidote, medicine

remensus *pp* of **remetior**

remĕ·ō -āre *vt* to retrace, relive; *vi* to go or come back, return

re·mētior -mētīrī -mensus sum *vt* to remeasure; to retrace, go back over

rēm·ex -igis *m* rower, crew member, oarsman

Rēm·ī -ōrum *m pl* a people of Gaul (*near modern Rheims*)

rēmigāti·ō -ōnis *f* rowing

rēmig·ium -iī or **-ī** *n* rowing; oars; oarsmen, rowers

rēmig·ō -āre *vi* to row

remigr·ō -āre *vi* to move back, go back, return

reminisc·or -ī *vt* to call to mind, remember; *vi* to remember; (with *genit*) to be mindful of, conscious of, remember

re·miscĕō -miscēre — -mixtum *vt* to mix up, intermingle; **veris falsa remiscere** to intermingle lies with truth

remissē *adv* mildly, gently

remissi·ō -ōnis *f* release; easing, letting down, lowering; relaxing (*of muscles*); relaxation, recreation; mildness, gentleness; submissiveness; abatement, diminishing; remission (*of debts*)

remiss·us -a -um *adj* relaxed, loose, slack; mild, gentle; negligent, remiss; easy-going, indulgent, yielding; gay, merry, light; low, cheap (*price*)

re·mittō -mittĕre -mīsī -missum *vt* to send back; to release; to slacken, loosen; to emit, produce, let out,

yield, send forth, give off; to send back, return, restore; to give up, reject, resign, concede; to relax, relieve (*the mind*); to pardon; to remit, remove (*penalty*); (with *inf*) to stop (*doing something*); *vi* (of wind, rain, etc.) to slack off, abate
remixtus *pp* of **remisceo**
remŏl·ĭor -īrī -ītus sum *vt* to push or move back or away, heave back
remollesc·ō -ĕre *vi* to get soft again, soften; to weaken
remŏr·a -ae *f* hindrance, delay
remorāmin·a -um *n pl* hindrances, delays
re·mordĕō -mordēre — -morsum *vt* to bite back; to attack in return; to disturb, annoy, worry, torture
remŏr·or -ārī -ātus sum *vt* to delay, hinder, hold back, detain; *vi* to loiter, delay, linger, stay behind
remōtē *adv* at a distance, far away
remōtĭ·ō -ōnis *f* removal
remōt·us -a -um *adj* removed, out of the way, far off, remote, distant; (fig) remote, apart, separate, clear, free; dead; (with **ab** + *abl*) removed from, separate from, apart from, clear of, free from
re·movĕō -movēre -mōvī -mōtum *vt* to move back, withdraw, put away, remove; to shroud, veil; (fig) put out of sight, set aside, abolish; to subtract
remūg·ĭō -īre *vi* to bellow back; to resound, reecho
re·mulcĕō -mulcēre -mulsī *vt* to stroke, smooth back; **caudam remulcere** to put the tail between the legs (*in fear*)
remulc·um -ī *n* tow rope, tow line
remūnerātĭ·ō -ōnis *f* remuneration, reward, recompense, repayment
remūnĕr·or -ārī -ātus sum *vt* to repay, reward
remurmŭr·ō -āre *vi* to murmur back in reply
rēm·us -ī *m* oar; (fig) wing; **remi corporis** hands and feet (*of a swimmer*)
Rem·us -ī *m* brother of Romulus
renarr·ō -āre *vt* to tell over again, recount
re·nascor -nascī -nātus sum *vi* to be born again; to rise again, spring up again, be restored; to reappear; to recur
renāvĭg·ō -āre *vi* to sail back
ren·ĕō -ēre *vt* to unravel, undo
rēn·ēs -um *m pl* kidneys
renīd·ens -entis *adj* beaming, glad
renīd·ĕō -ēre *vi* to reflect, reflect light, glitter, shine; to smile, grin all over; to beam with joy
renīdesc·ō -ĕre *vi* to begin to reflect light, begin to glitter
renīt·or -ī *vi* to put up a struggle, fight back, resist
ren·ō -āre *vi* to swim back, float back
rēn·ō or **rhēn·ō -ōnis** *m* fur
renōd·ō -āre *vt* to tie back in a knot; to untie
renovām·en -ĭnis *n* renewal, new condition
renovātĭ·ō -ōnis *f* renovation, renewal; revision; compound interest
renŏv·ō -āre *vt* to make new again; to renovate, repair, restore; to plow up (*a fallow field*); to reopen (*wounds*); to revive (*old customs, etc.*); to start (*battles*) all over again; to refresh (*the memory*); to repeat, keep repeating, reaffirm; **faenus renovare in singulos annos** to compound the interest on a yearly basis
renumĕr·ō -āre *vt* to count over again, recount; to pay back, repay
renuntiātĭ·ō -ōnis *f* formal or official report, announcement
renuntĭ·ō -āre *vt* to report; to announce; to retract (*promise, etc.*); to renounce, call off, reject; (with double *acc*) to announce or declare elected as; (with *acc & inf*) to bring back word that
renunt·ius -iī or **-ī** *m* bringer of news, reporter
re·nŭō -nuĕre -nŭī *vt* to nod refusal to, deny, refuse, turn down, decline, say not to, reject; *vi* to shake the head in refusal, refuse, say no; (with *dat*) to say no to, deny (*a charge*)
renūt·ō -āre *vt* to refuse emphatically
reor rērī ratus sum *vt* to think, deem; (with *acc & inf*) to think that; (with *acc & adj* as objective complement) to regard (*something*) as; *vi* to think, suppose
repāgŭl·a -ōrum *n pl* bolts, bars; (fig) restraints, regulations, rules, limits
repand·us´-a -um *adj* curved backwards, concave; (*shoes*) with turned-up toes
reparābĭl·is -e *adj* capable of being repaired, reparable, retrievable
reparc·ō -ĕre *vi* (with *dat*) to be sparing with, take it easy with
repăr·ō -āre *vt* to get again, acquire again; to recover, retrieve, make good; to restore, renew, repair; to recruit (*a new army*); **vina merce reparare** to get wine in exchange for wares, barter for wine
repastinātĭ·ō -ōnis *f* digging up again
re·pectō -pectĕre — -pexum *vt* to comb back; to comb again, recomb
repellō repellĕre reppŭlī repulsum *vt* to drive back, push back, repel, repulse; to reject; to remove; to refute
re·pendō -pendĕre -pendī -pensum *vt* to repay, pay back; to ransom, redeem; (fig) to repay in kind, requite, recompense, reward; to compensate for; to balance, balance out; **magna rependere** to pay back in full
rep·ens -entis *adj* sudden, unexpected, unlooked-for, hasty
repensus *pp* of **rependo**

repentē *adv* suddenly, unexpectedly, all of a sudden
repentīnō *adv* suddenly, unexpectedly
repentīn·us -a -um *adj* sudden, unpected, unlooked-for; hasty, impetuous
reperc·ō -ĕre *vi* (with *dat*) **a** to be sparing with; **b** to refrain from
repercussus *pp* of **repercutio;** *adj* rebounding; reflected, reflecting; echoed, echoing
repercuss·us -ūs *m* rebounding, reverberation, echo, repercussion
reper·cutiō -cutĕre -cussī -cussum *vt* to make (*something*) rebound, reverberate, or reflect
reperiō reperīre reppĕrī repertum *vt* to find, find again, discover; to get, procure, obtain, win; to find out, ascertain, learn, realize; to invent, devise
repert·or -ōris *m* discoverer, inventor, author
repert·us -a -um *pp* of **reperio;** *n pl* discoveries, inventions
repetītī·ō -ōnis *f* repetition; (rhet) anaphora, repetition
repetīt·or -ōris *m* claimant
repĕt·ō -ĕre -īvī or **-iī -ītum** *vt* to head back to, try to reach again, return to; to aim at again; to fetch back; to attack again; to prosecute again; to demand anew; to demand back, claim, demand in compensation, retake; to trace back, retrace; to trace in thought, think over, recall, recollect; to trace back (*in speech*); to repeat, undertake again, resume, renew; **lex de pecuniis** (or **rebus**) **repetundis** law on extortion, extortion law; **pecuniam repetere** to sue for the recovery of money; **res repetere** to sue for the recovery of property; **reus pecuniarum repetundarum** guilty of extortion
repetund·ae -ārum *f pl* extortion; money extorted; **repetundarum argui** to be charged with extortion; **repetundarum teneri** to be held on an extortion charge
repexus *pp* of **repecto**
replĕō -plēre -plēvī -plētum *vt* to refill, fill up, replenish; to fill to overflowing; to make up for, replace, compensate for; to recruit, bring (*an army*) to full strength
replēt·us -a -um *adj* filled, full; well provided
replicātī·ō -ōnis *f* folding back, rolling back, rolling up; reflex action
replic·ō -āre *vt* to fold back, unfold, turn back
rēp·ō -ĕre -sī *vi* to creep, crawl
re·pōnō -pōnĕre -posŭī -posĭtum or **repostum** *vt* to put back, set back, lay (*e.g., the head*) back; to replace; to restore; to substitute; to lay out, stretch out (*the body*); to lay aside, store, keep, preserve; to lay aside, put away; to renew, repeat; to place, class; to replay, requite; **in sceptra reponere** to reinstate in power; **membra reponere** (with *abl* or **in** + *abl*) to stretch out on (*e.g., a bed*); **se in cubitum reponere** to rest on one's elbow, prop oneself up on one's elbow; **spem reponere** (with **in** + *abl*) to put one's hope in or on, count on
report·ō -āre *vt* to bring back; to report; to carry off, gain, obtain; **victoriam reportare** to win a victory
reposc·ō -ĕre *vt* to demand back; to ask for, claim, require, demand
reposĭt·us -a -um *pp* of **repono;** *adj* distant, remote
repost·or -ōris *m* restorer
repostus *pp* of **repono**
repōtĭ·a -ōrum *n pl* second round of drinks
repraesentātĭ·ō -ōnis *f* vivid presentation; cash payment
repraesent·ō -āre *vt* to present again, show, exhibit, display, depict; to pay in cash; to do immediately, accomplish instantly, do on the spot; to rush, speed up (*e.g., plans*); to anticipate; to apply (*medicines*) immediately
repreh·endō or **repr·endō -endĕre -endī -ensum** *vt* to hold back; to restrain, check; to blame, find fault with, rebuke, criticize; (law) to prosecute, convict, condemn; to refute
reprehensĭ·ō -ōnis *f* checking, check; interruption (*of a speech*); blame, rebuke, criticism; refutation
reprehens·ō -āre *vt* to hold back continually; to detain from time to time
reprehens·or -ōris *m* critic
repress·or -ōris *m* restrainer
re·prĭmō -primĕre -pressī -pressum *vt* to hold back, keep back; to restrain, limit, confine, curb, repress, suppress; **se reprimere** to control oneself; **se reprimere** (with **ab** + *abl*) to refrain from
reprōmissĭ·ō -ōnis *f* return promise
reprō·mittō -mittĕre -mīsī -missum *vt* to promise in return
rept·ō -āre *vi* to creep or crawl around
repudiātĭ·ō -ōnis *f* repudiation; refusal, rejection
repudĭ·ō -āre *vt* to repudiate, scorn; to refuse, reject; to jilt; to divorce
repudiōs·us -a -um *adj* objectionable, offensive
repud·ium -iī or **-ī** *n* repudiation, separation, divorce; **repudium renuntiare** or **repudium remittere** (with *dat*) to send a letter of divorce to, divorce
repuerasc·ō -ĕre *vi* to become a child again; to behave childishly
repugn·ans -antis *n* contradiction
repugnanter *adv* reluctantly
repugnantĭ·a -ae *f* incompatibility
repugn·ō -āre *vi* to fight back; (with *dat*) **a** to oppose, offer opposition to, fight against, be against; **b** to

disagree with, be inconsistent with, be incompatible with; (with **contra** + *acc*) to fight against
repuls·a -ae *f* defeat at the polls; rebuff, cold shoulder; **repulsa consulatūs** defeat in running for the consulship; **repulsam ferre** to lose an election
repuls·ans -antis *adj* throbbing; re-echoing
repulsus *pp* of **repello**
repuls·us -ūs *m* reverberation, echo
repung·ō -ĕre *vt* to goad again
repurg·ō -āre *vt* to clean or clear again; to purge away, remove
reputātī·ō -ōnis *f* reconsideration, review
repŭt·ō -āre *vt* to count back, calculate; to think over, reflect upon, reconsider
requī·ēs -ētis *f* rest, relief; relaxation, recreation
requi·escō -escĕre -ēvī -ētum *vt* to put to rest, quiet down, calm down; *vi* to rest, take a rest, come to rest, stop, end; to rest, relax; to find rest, be consoled, find relief; to rest, lie quietly, sleep; (of the dead) to rest, sleep
requiēt·us -a -um *adj* rested up, refreshed
requīrĭt·ō -āre *vt* to keep asking for, be on a constant lookout for
re·quīrō -quīrĕre -quīsīvī or **-quīsiī -quīsītum** *vt* to look for, search for, hunt for; to look around for, miss; to ask; to ask for, demand, require; (with **ab** or **de** + *abl*) to ask or demand (*something*) from or of
rēs reī or **rēī** *f* thing, matter, affair, object, business, circumstance, event, occurrence, deed, condition, case; reality, truth, fact; property, possessions, estate, effects; benefit, advantage, interest, profit; business affair, transaction; cause, reason, motive, ground; (law) case, suit; (mil) operation, campaign, battle; state, government, politics; historical event; theme, topic, subject matter; **ab re** contrary to interests, disadvantageous, useless; **contra rem publicam** unconstitutional(ly), contrary to public interests; **eā re** therefore, for that reason; **ex re** according to the circumstances, according to the situation; **ex re istius** for his good; **ex re publicā** constitutionally, for the common good, in the public interest; **ex tuā re** to your advantage; **in re** in fact, in reality; **in rem** for the good; useful, advantageous; **ob eam rem** for that reason; **ob rem** to the purpose; **pro re** according to circumstances; **re** in fact, in practice, in reality, in truth, actually, really; **rem gerere** to conduct a military operation; **rerum potiri** to get control of the government; **rerum scriptor** historian, annalist; **res est mihi tecum** I have some business with you; **res sit mihi cum his** let me handle them; **res frumentaria** foraging; grain situation, grain supply; **res gestae** exploits, achievements, military achievements; **res judiciaria** administration of justice, department of justice; **res novae** revolution; **res pecuaria et rustica** livestock; **res Persicae** Persian history, Parthian history; **res rustica** agriculture; **res publica** state, government, politics, public life, commonwealth, country; **res secundae** prosperous times, prosperity; **res uxoria** marriage; dowry; **summa rerum** world, universe
resăcr·ō -āre *vt* to ask again for; to free from a curse
resaev·iō -īre *vi* to go wild again
resalūt·ō -āre *vt* to greet in return
resān·escō -escĕre -ŭī *vi* to heal up again
re·sarciō -sarcīre — -sartum *vt* to patch up, repair; to make good (*a loss*)
re·scindō -scindĕre -scĭdī -scissum *vt* to tear off; to cut down; to tear open; to rescind, repeal, abrogate; (fig) to tear open, expose
re·sciscō -sciscĕre -scīvī or **-sciī -scītum** *vt* to find out, learn, ascertain
re·scrībō -scrībĕre -scripsī -scriptum *vt* to write back in reply; to rewrite, revise; to enlist, enroll; to repay, pay back; *vi* to write a reply
rescript·um -ī *n* imperial rescript
resĕc·ō -āre -ŭī -tum *vt* to cut back, cut short; to reap; (fig) to trim, curtail; **ad vivum resecare** to cut to the quick
resĕcr·ō or **resăcr·ō -āre** *vt* to ask again for; to free from a curse
resectus *pp* of **reseco**
resecūtus *pp* of **resequor**
resēmĭn·ō -āre *vt* to reproduce
re·sĕquor -sĕquī -secūtus sum *vt* to reply to, answer
resĕr·ō -āre *vt* to unlock, unbar, open; to disclose; to open, begin (*a year*)
reserv·ō - āre *vt* to reserve, hold back; to spare; to hold on to
res·es -ĭdis *adj* remaining, left; lazy, idle, inactive; slow, sluggish; calm
re·sidĕō -sidēre -sēdī *vi* to remain seated; to stay behind, be left, remain; to tarry, linger; to stay, reside
re·sīdō -sīdĕre -sēdī *vi* to sit down, settle back; to sink down, sink, settle, subside; to calm down
residŭ·us -a -um *adj* remaining, left; in arrears, outstanding (*money*); *n* the remainder, rest
resign·ō -āre *vt* to unseal, open; to disclose, reveal; to give up, resign; to annul, cancel; to destroy (*confidence*)
resil·iō -īre -ŭī *vi* to spring back,

jump back; to recoil; to contract; to shrink back
resīm·us -a -um *adj* turned up, snub
rēsīn·a -ae *f* resin
resīnāt·us -a -um *adj* resined, rubbed with resin
resip·iō -ĕre *vt* to taste of, have the flavor of
resip·iscō -iscĕre -īvī or **-iī** or **-ŭī** *vi* to come to one's senses
resist·ens -entis *adj* firm, tough
re·sistō -sistĕre -stitī *vi* to stand still, stop, pause; to stay, stay behind, remain, continue; to resist, put up resistance; to rise again; (with *dat*) **a** to be opposed to, resist; **b** to reply to
re·solvō -solvĕre -solvī -solūtum *vt* to untie, unfasten, undo; to open; to dissolve, melt, thaw; to relax (*the body*); stretch out (*the limbs*); to unravel; to cancel; to dispel; to unnerve, enervate; to release, set free
resonābĭl·is -e *adj* resounding, answering (*echo*)
resŏn·ō -āre *vt* to repeat, reecho, resound with, make ring; *vi* to resound, ring, reecho; (with *dat* or **ad** + *acc*) to resound in answer to
resŏn·us -a -um *adj* resounding, reechoing
resorb·ĕō -ēre *vt* to suck in, swallow again
respect·ō -āre *vt* to look back on; to keep an eye on, care for; to have regard for; to gaze at, look at; *vi* to look back; to look around
respectus *pp* of **respicio**
respect·us -ūs *m* backward glance, looking back; looking around; refuge, asylum; regard, respect, consideration; **respectum habere** (with *dat* or **ad** + *acc*) to have respect for
re·spergō -spergĕre -spersī spersum *vt* to sprinkle, splash, spray; to defile
respersĭ·ō -ōnis *f* sprinkling, splashing
respersus *pp* of **respergo**
re·spiciō -spicĕre -spexī -spectum *vt* to look back at, see behind oneself; to look back for, look around for; to look back upon (*the past, etc.*); to look at, gaze at, look upon, regard, contemplate, consider; to notice; to look after, take care of, see to; to respect; *vi* to look back; to look around; (with **ad** + *acc*) to look at, gaze at
respīrām·en -ĭnis *n* windpipe
respīrātĭ·ō -ōnis *f* respiration, breathing; exhalation; letup, rest, pause (*to catch one's breath*), breathing space
respīrāt·us -ūs *m* respiration
respīr·ō -āre *vt* to breathe, breathe out, exhale; *vi* to breathe, take a breath; to catch one's breath, breathe again, recover (*from fright, etc.*); (of combat, passions, etc.) to slack off, die down, subside; **a continuis cladibus respirare** to catch one's breathe again after continuous fighting; **ab metu respirare** to breathe again after a shock
resplend·ĕō -ēre *vi* to glitter
re·spondĕō -spondēre -spondī -sponsum *vt* to answer; to say in reply; **ficta respondere** to make up answers; **multa respondere** to give a lengthly reply; **par pari respondere** to answer tit for tat; **verbum verbo respondere** to answer word for word; *vi* to answer, respond, reply; to echo; (law) to answer (*to bail*), appeal (*in court*); (of lawyers) to give an opinion, give legal advice; (of priests, oracles) to give a response; (with *dat*) **a** to answer, reply to; **b** to match, balance, correspond to, be equal to, resemble, measure up to; **amori amore respondere** to return love for love
responsĭ·ō -ōnis *f* response, answer, reply; refutation; **sibi ipsi responsio** a reply to one's own arguments
responsĭt·ō -āre *vi* to give professional advice
respons·ō -āre *vi* to answer, reply; to reecho; (with *dat*) **a** to answer to, agree with; **b** to resist, defy; **c** to answer back to (*in disobedience or defiance*)
respons·or -ōris *m* answerer
respons·us -a -um *pp* of **respondeo**; *n* answer, response, reply; professional advice, oracular response; **responsum auferre** or **ferre** (with **ab** + *abl*) to receive an answer from; **responsum referre** to deliver an answer
rēspūblica reīpūblicae *f* state, government, politics, public life, commonwealth, country
respŭ·ō -ĕre -ī *vt* to spit out, cast out, eject, expel; to reject, refuse, dislike, spurn
restagn·ō -āre *vi* to form pools; to run over, overflow; to be inundated
restaur·ō -āre *vt* to restore, rebuild
restĭcŭl·a -ae *f* thin rope, cord
restinctĭ·ō -ōnis *f* quenching
re·stinguō -stinguĕre -stinxī -stinctum *vt* to quench, extinguish, put out; to snuff out, extinguish, exterminate, destroy
restĭ·ō -ōnis *m* rope maker; (coll) roper (*person who whipped with ropes*)
restipulātĭ·ō -ōnis *f* counterclaim
restipŭl·or -ārī -ātus sum *vt* to stipulate in return
rest·is -is *f* rope
restĭt·ō -āre *vi* to stay behind, lag behind, hold back, hang back
restĭtr·ix -īcis *f* stay-behind (*female*)
re·stitŭō -stituĕre -stitŭī -stitūtum *vt* to set up again; to restore, rebuild, reconstruct; to renew, reestablish, revive; to bring back, re-

store, reinstate; to give back, return, replace; to restore, repair, remedy; to reenact (*a law*); to reverse, revoke, make void, undo, cancel; to make good, compensate for, repair
restitūti·ō -ōnis *f* restoration; reinstatement, pardon; recall (*from exile*)
restitūt·or -ōris *m* restorer, rebuilder
restitūtus *pp* of **restituo**
re·stō -stāre -stitī *vi* to stand firm, stand one's ground, resist; to stay behind, stay in reserve; to be left, be left over; *v impers* (with *inf* or **ut**) it remains to (*do something*)
restrictē *adv* sparingly; exactly, precisely
restrict·us -a -um *adj* tied back, tight; stingy; moderate; strict, stern
re·stringō -stringĕre -strinxī -strictum *vt* to draw back tightly, tie back, tighten; (of dogs) to show (*the teeth*); (fig) to restrain
resūd·ō -āre *vt & vi* to sweat
result·ō -āre *vi* to rebound; to reverberate, resound
re·sūmō -sūmĕre -sumpsī -sumptum *vt* to take up again, resume; to recover (*strength*)
resupīn·ō -āre *vt* to throw (*someone*) on his back, throw over, throw down; (coll) to knock for a loop; to break down (*doors*)
resupīn·us -a -um *adj* bent back, thrown back; supine, lying on the back; leaning backward; proud, haughty (*gait*)
re·surgō -surgĕre -surrexī -surrectum *vi* to rise again, appear again
resuscīt·ō -āre *vt* to resuscitate, revive, renew
retardāti·ō -ōnis *f* retarding, delaying
retard·ō -āre *vt* to slow down, retard, hold back, delay, keep back, check, hinder
rēt·e -is *n* net; (fig) trap
re·tĕgō -tegĕre -texī -tectum *vt* to uncover; to open
retempt·ō -are *vt* to attempt again, try again, test again
re·tendō -tendĕre -tendī -tentum or **-tensum** *vt* to release from tension, unbend, relax
retenti·ō -ōnis *f* holding back, slowing down; withholding (*of assent*)
retent·ō -āre *vt* to hold back, hold tight; to attempt again, try again, test again
retentus *pp of* **retendo** and **retineo**
re·texō -texĕre -texŭī -textum *vt* to unravel; to cancel, annul, reverse, undo; to weave anew; to renew, repeat; to correct, revise; to take back, retract (*words*)
rētiār·ius -iī or **-ī** *m* gladiator who tried to entangle his opponent in a net
reticenti·a -ae *f* reticence, silence; (rhet) abrupt pause; **poena reticentiae** punishment for suppressing the truth
retic·ĕō -ēre *vt* to be silent about, suppress, keep secret; *vi* to be silent, keep silence; (with *dat*) to make no answer to
rētĭcŭl·um -ī *n* small net; hair net; network bag, reticule (*for protecting bottles*); racket (*for playing ball*)
retinācŭl·a -ōrum *n pl* cable, rope, hawser, tether
retin·ens -entis *adj* (with *genit*) clinging to
retinenti·a -ae *f* recollection, retention
re·tinĕō -tinēre -tinŭī -tentum *vt* to hold back, keep back; to restrain; to keep, retain; to hold in reserve; to keep, preserve, maintain, uphold; to hold, engross (*attention*); to detain, delay
retinn·iō -īre *vi* to ring again, ring out
retōn·ō -āre *vi* to resound
re·torquĕō -torquēre -torsī -tortum *vt* to twist or bend back; to hurl back (*weapons*); **mentem retorquere** to change the mind; **oculos retorquere** (with **ad** + *acc*) to look back wistfully at
retorrĭd·us -a -um *adj* parched, dried out, withered; wily, old, shrewd
retortus *pp* of **retorqueo**
retractāti·ō -ōnis *f* rehandling, retreatment; hesitation
retract·ō or **retrect·ō -āre** *vt* to rehandle, take in hand again, undertake once more, take up once more; to reexamine, review; to revise; *vi* to refuse, decline; to be reluctant
retract·us -a -um *adj* withdrawn, distant, remote
re·trăhō -trahĕre -traxī -tractum *vt* to draw back, withdraw, drag back; to bring to light again, make known again; (fig) to drag away, divert, remove, turn
retrectō see **retracto**
retrib·ŭō -uĕre -ŭī -ūtum *vt* to give back, restore, repay
retrō *adv* backwards, back, to the rear; behind, on the rear; in the past, formerly, back, past; in return, on the contrary, on the other hand
retrorsum or **retrorsus** *adv* back, backwards, behind; in reversed order
re·trūdō -trūdĕre — -trūsum *vt* to push back; to hide, conceal
retundō retundĕre retŭdī (or **rettŭdī**) **retunsum** (or **retūsum**) *vt* to pound back; to dull, blunt; (fig) to deaden, weaken, repress, restrain
retuns·us or **retūs·us -a -um** *adj* blunt, dull; (fig) dull
re·us -ī *m* defendant, plaintiff, the accused; convict, criminal, culprit

reval·escō -escĕre -ŭī *vi* to regain one's strength, recover; to become valid again
re·vĕhō -vehĕre -vexī -vectum *vt* to carry back, bring back; **revehi** to ride or drive back, sail back; (fig) to go back (*e.g., to an earlier period*)
re·vellō -vellĕre -vellī -vulsum *vt* to pull out, pull back, tear off, tear out; to tear up (*the ground*), dig up; (fig) to abolish, remove
revēl·ō -āre *vt* to unveil, uncover
re·venĭō -venīre -vēnī -ventum *vi* to come again, come back, return
rēvērā *adv* in fact, actually
rēverbĕr·ō -āre *vt* to beat back, repel
reverend·us -a -um *adj* venerable, awe-inspiring
revĕr·ens -entis *adj* reverent, respectful
reverenter *adv* respectfully
reverentĭ·a -ae *f* awe, respect, reverence
rever·ĕor -ērī -ĭtus sum *vt* to revere, respect, stand in awe of
reversĭ·ō or **revorsĭ·ō -ōnis** *f* turning back (*before reaching one's destination*); recurrence (*of fever, etc.*)
revert·ō -ĕre -ī or **re·vertor** (or **re·vortor**) **-vertī -versus sum** *vi* to turn back, turn around, come back, return; (in speaking) to return, revert, recur
revictus *pp* of **revinco**
revid·ĕō -ēre *vt* to go back to see, revisit
re·vincĭō -vincīre -vinxī -vinctum *vt* to tie back, tie behind, tie up
re·vincō -vincĕre -vīcī -victum *vt* to conquer, crush, repress; to refute, disprove, convict
revinctus *pp* of **revincio**
revir·escō -escĕre -ŭī *vi* to grow green again, become green again; to grow young again; to grow again, grow strong again, revive
revīs·ō -ĕre *vt* to go to see again, revisit; to look back to see; *vi* to come or go back; (with **ad** + *acc*) **a** to look at again, look back at; **b** to return to, revisit
re·vīviscō or **re·vīvescō -vīvescĕre -vixī** *vi* to come back to life, be restored to life, revive; (fig) to revive, recover, gain strength
revocābĭl·is -e *adj* revocable, capable of being recalled
revocām·en -ĭnis *n* recall
revocātĭ·ō -ōnis *f* calling back, calling away, recall; revoking, retracting (*of a word*)
revŏc·ō -āre *vt* to call back, recall; to recall, call off, withdraw (*troops*); to call back (*an actor, singer*) for an encore; to bring back to life, revive; (law) to arraign again; to recover, regain (*strength, etc.*); to resume (*career, studies*); to revoke, retract; to check, control; to cancel; (with **ad** + *acc*) to refer, apply, subject, submit (*someone or something*) to
revŏl·ō -āre *vi* to fly back
revolsus see **revulsus**
revolūbĭl·is -e *adj* able to be rolled back; **non revolubilis** irrevocable (*fate*)
re·volvō -volvĕre -volvī -volūtum *vt* to roll back, unroll, unwind; to retravel (*a road*); to unroll, read over, read again (*a book*); to reexperience; to go over, think over; **revolvi** to revolve, come around again, recur, return
revŏm·ō -ĕre -ŭī *vt* to vomit forth again, disgorge
revor- = rever-
revorr·ō -ĕre *vt* to sweep back, scatter again
revulsus *pp* of **revello**
rex rēgis *m* king; (with bad connotations during the republican period) tyrant, dictator; patron; rich man; leader, king (*in children's game*); queen bee
Rhadamanth·us -ī *m* son of Jupiter, brother of Minos, and one of the three judges in the lower world
Rhaet·ī -ōrum *m pl* people of Raetia
Rhaetĭ·a -ae *f* Alpine country between Germany and Italy
rhapsōdĭ·a -ae *f* Homeric lay, selection from Homer
Rhe·a -ae *f* Cybele
Rhe·a Silvĭ·a -ae *f* daughter of Numitor and mother of Romulus and Remus
rhēd- = raed-
Rhēg·ium -ĭī or **-ī** *n* town on the toe of Italy
rhēn·ō -ōnis *m* fur
Rhēnān·us -a -um *adj* Rhenish
Rhēn·us -ī *m* Rhine
Rhēs·us -ī *m* Thracian king who fought as an ally of Troy
rhēt·or -ŏris *m* rhetorician, teacher of rhetoric; orator
rhētorĭc·a -ae or **rhētorĭc·ē -ēs** *f* rhetoric
rhētorĭc·a -ōrum *n pl* treatise on rhetoric
rhētorĭcē *adv* rhetorically, in an oratorical manner
rhētorĭc·us -a -um *adj* rhetorician's, rhetorical; **doctores rhetorici** rhetoric professors; **libri rhetorici** rhetoric textbooks
rhīnocĕr·ōs -ōtis *m* rhinoceros; vessel made of a rhinoceros's tusk
rhō (indecl) *n* seventeenth letter of the Greek alphabet
Rhodăn·us -ī *m* Rhone
Rhodiens·is -e or **Rhodĭ·us -a -um** *adj* Rhodian, of Rhodes; *m pl* Rhodians
Rhodŏp·ē -ēs *f* mountain range in Thrace
Rhodopēĭ·us -a -um *adj* Thracian
Rhod·os or **Rhod·us -ī** *f* Rhodes (*island off the coast of Asia Minor*)
Rhoetē·us -a -um *adj* Trojan;

Rhoeteus ductor Aeneas; *m* promontory on the Dardanelles near Troy; sea near the promontory of Rhoeteum
rhomb·us -ī *m* magic wheel; turbot (*fish*)
rhomphae·a -ae *f* long javelin
rhythmĭc·us -a -um *adj* rhythmical; *m* teacher of prose rhythm
rhythm·os or **rhythm·us -ī** *m* rhythm, symmetry
rīc·a -ae *f* veil (*worn by Roman women at sacrifices*)
rīcīn·ium -iī or **-ī** *n* short mantle with a cowl
rict·um -ī *n* snout; wide-open mouth
rict·us -ūs *m* snout; wide-open mouth; **risū rictum diducere** to break into a grin; *m pl* jaws, gaping jaws
rīdĕō rīdēre rīsī rīsum *vt* to laugh at, ridicule; to smile upon; *vi* to smile, laugh; (with *dat* or **ad** + *acc*) to smile to
rīdibund·us -a -um *adj* laughing
rīdiculāri·us -a -um *adj* laughable, funny; *n pl* jokes
rīdicŭlē *adv* jokingly, humorously; ridiculously, absurdly
rīdiculōs·us -a -um *adj* funny, amusing; ridiculous
rīdicŭl·us -a -um *adj* funny, amusing, laughable; ridiculous, silly; *m* joker, clown; *n* joke
rig·ens -entis *adj* stiff, rigid, unbending
rig·ĕō -ēre *vi* to be still, be numb, stiffen; to be rigid, stand on end, stand erect; to stand stiff, rise
rig·escō -escĕre -ŭī *vi* to grow stiff, become numbed, stiffen, harden; to stand on end
rigĭdē *adv* rigorously, severely
rigĭd·us -a -um *adj* rigid, stiff, hard, inflexible; stern, rigid, severe; rough, rude
rig·ō -āre *vt* to wet, moisten, water; to conduct, convey (*water*)
rig·or -ōris *m* stiffness; numbness, cold; hardness; sternness, severity
rigŭ·us -a -um *adj* irrigating, watering; irrigated, watered
rīm·a -ae *f* crack; **rimas agere** to be cracked
rīm·or -ārī -ātus sum *vt* to lay open, tear open; to pry into, search, tear at, examine; to ransack; **naribus rimari** to sniff at
rīmōs·us -a -um *adj* full of cracks, leaky
ringor ringī rictus sum *vi* to open the mouth wide, to show the teeth; to snarl; (fig) to be snappy, snarl
rīp·a -ae *f* bank, shore
rīpŭl·a -ae *f* river bank
risc·us -ī *m* chest, trunk
rīsiōn·ēs -um *f pl* laughs
rīs·or -ōris *m* scoffer, teaser
rīs·us -ūs *m* laugh, smile, laughter; laughingstock; **risum continere** to keep back a laugh, keep from laughing; **risum movere** (with *dat* of person) to make (*someone*) laugh; **risūs captare** to try to make people laugh, try to get laughs
rīte *adv* according to religious usage; duly, justly, rightly, fitly; in the usual way, customarily
rīt·us -ūs *m* ceremony, rite; custom, habit, way, manner, style; **ritū** (with *genit*) in the manner of, like; **pecudum ritū** like cattle
rīvāl·is -is *m* one who uses the same stream, neighbor; one who uses the same mistress, rival
rīvālĭt·ās -ātis *f* rivalry in love
rīvŭl·us or **rīvŏl·us -ī** *m* brook, rivulet
rīv·us -ī *m* brook, stream
rix·a -ae *f* brawl, fight; quarrel, squabble
rix·or -ārī -ātus sum *vi* to brawl, come to blows, fight; to quarrel, squabble
rōbīginōs·us or **rūbīginōs·us -a -um** *adj* rusty; envious
rōbīg·ō -ĭnis *f* rust; blight, mildew; film (*on teeth*), tartar
rōborĕ·us -a -um *adj* oak, of oak
rōbŏr·ō -āre *vt* to make strong, strengthen
rōb·ur or **rōb·us -ŏris** *n* hard wood; oak; prison (*at Rome, also called Tullianum*); objects made of hard wood: lance, club, bench; physical strength, power, vigor, toughness; vigor, strength, power, quality (*of mind*); best part, flower, choice, cream, élite; stronghold
rōbust·us -a -um *adj* hardwood; oak; robust, strong, firm, tough (*body*); firm, vigorous, solid (*character*)
rōdō rōdĕre rōsī rōsum *vt* to gnaw, gnaw at; to rust, corrode; to say nasty things about, slander, run down
rogāl·is -e *adj* of a pyre
rogātĭ·ō -ōnis *f* proposal, referendum, bill, resolution; request; (rhet) question; **rogationem ferre** to introduce a bill; **rogationem perferre** to pass a bill; **rogationem suadere** to back, push, speak in favor of a bill; **rogationi intercedere** to veto a bill
rogātiuncŭl·a -ae *f* inconsequential bill; little question
rogāt·or -ōris *m* proposer (*of a bill to the people*); poll clerk (*who collected and counted votes*); beggar
rogāt·us -ūs *m* request
rogitātĭ·ō -ōnis *f* proposal
rogĭt·ō -āre *vt* to keep asking, keep asking for
rog·ō -āre *vt* to ask, ask for, beg, request, solicit, question; to invite; to nominate for election; to bring forward for approval, introduce, propose (*bill or resolution*); (with double *acc*) to ask (*someone for something*), ask (*someone something*); **legem rogare** to introduce a bill; **milites sacramento rogare** to

swear in soldiers; **senatorem sententiam rogare** to ask a senator for his opinion, ask a senator how he votes; **sententias rogare** to call the roll (*in the senate*); **populum rogare** to ask the people about a bill, to propose or introduce a bill; **primus sententiam rogari** to have the honor of being the first (*senator*) to be asked his view, be the first to vote

rog·us -ī *m* funeral pile, pyre; (fig) grave, destruction

Rōm·a -ae *f* Rome

Rōmān·us -a -um *adj* Roman; *m pl* Romans

Rōmulě·us -a -um *adj* of Romulus

Rōmulĭd·ae -ārum *m pl* descendants of Romulus, Romans

Rōmŭl·us -a -um *adj* of Romulus; *m* Romulus (*son of Rhea Silvia and Mars, twin brother of Remus, and founder as well as first king of Rome*)

rōrārĭ·ī -ōrum *m pl* skirmishers (*light-armed Roman troops who usually initiated an attack and then withdrew*)

rōrĭd·us -a -um *adj* dewy

rōrĭf·er -ĕra -ĕrum *adj* dew-bringing, dewy

rōr·ō -āre *vt* to drip, trickle, pour drop by drop; to moisten; *vi* to drop dew, scatter dew

rōs rōris *m* dew; moisture; water; teardrop; **ros Arabus** perfume; **ros marinus** or **ros maris** rosemary; **rores pluvii** rain drops; **rores sanguinei** drops of blood

ros·a -ae *f* rose; rose bush; rose bed; wreath of roses

rosār·ĭum -ĭī or **-ī** *n* rose garden

roscĭd·us -a -um *adj* dewy; moistened, sprayed

Rosc·ĭus -ĭī or **-ī** *m* L. Roscius Otho (*friend of Cicero, whose law in* 67 B.C. *reserved fourteen rows of seats in the theater for members of equestrian order*); Q. Roscius (*famous Roman actor and friend of Cicero, d.* 62 B.C.); Sextus Roscius (*of Ameria, defended by Cicero in a patricide trial in* 80 B.C.)

rosēt·um -ī *n* rose bed, rose garden

rosě·us -a -um *adj* rosy, rose-colored; of roses

rosmarīn·um -ī *n* rosemary (*spice*)

rostrāt·us -a -um *adj* beaked; (ship) having a pointed bow; **columna rostrata** column adorned with the beaks of conquered vessels to commemorate a naval victory; **corona rostrata** navy medal (*awarded to the first man to board the enemy's ship*)

rostr·um -ī *n* bill, beak; snout, muzzle; curved bow (*of a ship*); *n pl* speaker's stand in the Roman Forum (*so called because it was adorned with the beaks of ships taken from the battle of Antium,* 338 B.C.)

rōsus *pp of* **rodo**

rot·a -ae *f* wheel; potter's wheel; torture wheel; disk; chariot, car

rot·ō -āre *vt* to turn, whirl about; **rotari** to roll around; to revolve

rotŭl·a -ae *f* little wheel

rotundē *adv* smoothly, elegantly

rotund·ō -āre *vt* to make round, round off; to round out, complete

rotund·us -a -um *adj* rolling, revolving; round, circular, spherical; rounded, perfect; well-turned, smooth, polished, balanced (*style*)

rube·facĭō -facĕre -fēcī -factum *vt* to make red, redden

rubell·us -a -um *adj* reddish

rub·ens -entis *adj* red; blushing

rub·ĕō -ēre *vi* to be red, be ruddy; to be bloody; to blush

rub·er -ra -rum *adj* red; ruddy

rub·escō -escĕre -ŭī *vi* to grow red, redden; to blush

rubēt·a -ae *f* toad

rubēt·a -ōrum *n pl* bramble bush

rubě·us -a -um *adj* bramble, of brambles

Rubĭc·ō -ōnis *m* small stream marking the boundary between Italy and Cisalpine Gaul

rubicundŭl·us -a -um *adj* reddish

rubicund·us -a -um *adj* red; ruddy

rubĭd·us -a -um *adj* reddish, red

rūbīg- = robig-

rub·or -ōris *m* redness; blush; bashfulness, sense of shame; shame, disgrace

rubrīc·a -ae *f* red clay; red ochre; red chalk; rubric, law

rub·us -ī *m* bramble bush; blackberry bush; blackberry

ruct·ō -āre or **ruct·or -ārī -ātus sum** *vt & vi* to belch

ruct·us -ūs *m* belch, belching

rud·ens -entis *m* rope; *m pl* rigging

Rudĭ·ae -ārum *f pl* town in Calabria in S. Italy (*birthplace of Ennius*)

rudiār·ĭus -ĭī or **-ī** *m* retired gladiator

rudīment·um -ī *n* first attempt, beginning, commencement; **rudimentum adulescentiae ponere** to pass the novitiate; **rudimentum militare** basic training

Rudīn·us -a -um *adj* of Rudiae

rud·is -e *adj* in the natural state; raw, undeveloped, rough, wild, unformed; inexperienced, unskilled, ignorant, awkward, uncultured, uncivilized; (with *genit* or *abl*, with **ad** + *acc*, or with **in** + *abl*) inexperienced in, ignorant of, awkward at

rud·is -is *f* stick, rod; practice sword

rud·ō -ĕre -īvī -ītum *vi* to roar, bellow, bray; to creak

rūd·us -ĕris *n* crushed stone; rubble; rubbish; piece of brass or copper

rūfŭl·us -a -um *adj* reddish

Rūfŭl·ī -ōrum *m pl* military tribunes appointed by a general (*as opposed to military tribunes elected by the people*)

rūf·us -a -um *adj* red, reddish
rūg·a -ae *f* wrinkle
rūg·ō -āre *vi* to become wrinkled, become creased
rūgōs·us -a -um *adj* wrinkled, shriveled; corrugated
ruīn·a -ae *f* tumbling down, falling down, fall; collapse; debris, ruins; crash; catastrophe, disaster, destruction, defeat; wrecker, destroyer; **ruinam dare** or **trahere** to fall with a crash
ruīnōs·us -a -um *adj* going to ruin, ruinous, ruined, tumbling, fallen
rum·ex -icis *f* sorrel
rūmific·ō -āre *vt* to report
Rūmīn·a -ae *f* Roman goddess who was worshiped near the fig tree under which the she-wolf had suckled Romulus and Remus
Rūmīnāl·is -e *adj* **ficus Ruminalis** fig tree of Romulus and Remus
rūminātī·ō -ōnis *f* chewing of the cud; (fig) rumination
rūmin·ō -āre *vt* to chew again; *vi* to chew the cud
rūm·or -ōris *m* shouting, cheering, noise; rumor, hearsay; popular opinion, current opinion; reputation, fame; notoriety; calumny; **adverso rumore esse** to be in bad repute, be unpopular
rumpī·a -ae *f* long javelin
rumpō rumpěre rūpī ruptum *vt* to break, break down, break open; to burst, burst through; to tear, split; to force, make (*e.g., a path*) by force; to break in on, interrupt, cut short; to break (*a law, treaty*); to break out in, utter (*complaints, etc.*)
rūmuscŭl·ī -ōrum *m pl* gossip
rūn·a -ae *f* dart
runc·ō -āre *vt* to weed, weed out
ru·ō -ěre -ī -tum *vt* to throw down, hurl to the ground; to level (*e.g., sand dunes*); to destroy, overthrow, lay waste; to throw up, upturn, churn up; *vi* to fall hard, fall in ruins, totter; to run, dash, rush on, hurry; (of rain) to come pouring down; (of the sun) to set rapidly
rūp·ēs -is *f* cliff
rupt·or -ōris *m* breaker, violator
ruptus *pp* of **rumpo**
rūricŏl·a -ae *m* or *f* rustic, peasant, farmer; *m* ox
rūrigěn·a -ae *m* rustic, peasant, farmer
rūr·ō -āre *vi* to live in the country
rursus or **rursum** or **rūsum** *adv* back, backwards; on the contrary, on the other hand, in turn; again, back again, once more; **rursus rursusque** again and again
rūs rūris *n* the country, countryside, lands, fields; farm, estate; **rure redire** to return from the country; **ruri** or **rure vitam agere** to live in the country; **rus ire** to go into the country; *n pl* countryside
rusc·um -ī *n* or **rusc·us -ī** *f* broom (*of twigs*)
russ·us -a -um *adj* red, russet
rusticān·us -a -um *adj* rustic, country, rural
rusticātī·ō -ōnis *f* country life
rusticē *adv* like a farmer; plainly, simply; unsophisticatedly, boorishly
rusticit·ās -ātis *f* simple country ways, rusticity; boorishness, coarseness
rustic·or -ārī -ātus sum *vi* to live in the country
rusticŭl·us -a -um *adj* somewhat coarse; *m* peasant
rustic·us -a -um *adj* of or in the country, country, rural; plain, simple, unspoiled, unsophisticated; coarse, boorish, rude; *m* farmer, peasant; *f* country girl
rūsum see **rursus**
rūt·a -ae *f* rue (*bitter herb*); bitterness, unpleasantness
rūt·a -ōrum *n pl* minerals; **ruta caesa** or **ruta et caesa** (law) everything mined or cut down on an estate, timber and minerals
rutil·ō -āre *vt* to make red, color red, dye red; *vi* to glow red
rutil·us -a -um *adj* red, reddish yellow; strawberry-blond
rutr·um -ī *n* spade
rūtŭl·a -ae *f* a bit of rue
Rutŭl·ī -ōrum *m pl* ancient people of Latium whose capital was Ardea
rutus *pp* of **ruo**

S

Sab·a -ae *f* town in Arabia Felix, famous for its incense
Sabae·us -a -um *adj* Sabaean
Sabāz·ius -iī or **-ī** *m* Bacchus; *n pl* festival in honor of Bacchus
sabbăt·a -ōrum *n pl* Sabbath
sabbatāri·ī -ōrum *m pl* Sabbath-keepers, Jews
Sabell·us -a -um *adj* Sabellian, Sabine; *m* Sabine (*i.e., Horace*)
Sabīn·us -a -um *adj & mf* Sabine; *n* Sabine wine; Horace's Sabine estate
Sabrīn·a -ae *f* Severn River
saburr·a -ae *f* sand, ballast
saburr·ō -āre *vt* to ballast; (coll) to gorge with food
Sac·ae -ārum *m pl* Scythian tribe
saccipēr·ium -iī or **-ī** *n* purse pocket
sacc·ō -āre *vt* to filter, strain

saccŭl·us -ī *m* little bag; purse
sacc·us -ī *m* sack, bag; wallet; filter, strainer
sacell·um -ī *n* chapel
sac·er -ra -rum *adj* sacred, holy, consecrated; devoted to a deity for destruction, accursed; detestable; criminal, infamous; *n* see **sacrum**
sacerd·ōs -ōtis *m* priest; *f* priestess
sacerdōtāl·is -e *adj* sacerdotal
sacerdōt·ĭum -ĭī or **-ī** *n* priesthood
sacrāment·um -ī *n* guarantee, deposit (*sum of money which each of the parties to a law suit deposited and which was forfeited by the loser*); civil law suit; dispute; oath; voluntary oath of recruits; military oath; **eum obligare militiae sacramento** to swear him in; **justis sacramentis contendere** to argue on equal terms; **omnes sacramento adigere** or **rogare** to swear in everyone; **sacramentum dicere** to sign up, swear in; **sacramentum dicere** (with *dat*) to swear allegiance to (*a general or emperor*)
sacrār·ĭum -ĭī or **-ī** *n* sacristy; shrine, chapel
sacrāt·us -a -um *adj* hallowed, consecrated, holy, sacred
sacrĭf·er -ĕra -ĕrum *adj* carrying sacred objects
sacrificāl·is -e *adj* sacrificial
sacrificātĭ·ō -ōnis *f* sacrifice, sacrificing
sacrific·ĭum -ĭī or **-ī** *n* sacrifice
sacrifĭc·ō or **sacrufĭc·ō -āre** *vt & vi* to sacrifice
sacrificŭl·us -ī *m* sacrificing priest
sacrifĭc·us -a -um *adj* sacrificial
sacrileg·ĭum -ĭī or **-ī** *n* sacrilege; temple robbing
sacrilĕg·us -a -um *adj* sacrilegious; profane, impious, wicked; *m* temple robber; wicked person; *f* impious woman
sacr·ō -āre *vt* to consecrate; to dedicate; to set apart, devote, give; to doom, curse; to hallow, declare inviolable; to hold sacred, worship; to immortalize
sacrōsanct·us -a -um *adj* sacred, inviolable, sacrosanct
sacrufĭcō see **sacrifico**
sacr·um -ī *n* holy object, sacred vessel; holy place, temple, sanctuary; religious rite, act of worship, religious service, sacrifice; victim; *n pl* worship, religion; secret, mystery; **sacra facere** to sacrifice
saeclum see **saeculum**
saeculār·is or **sēculār·is -e** *adj* centennial
saecŭl·um or **sēcŭl·um** or **saecl·um -ī** *n* generation, lifetime; century; spirit of the age, fashion
saepe *adv* often
saepenumĕrō or **saepe numĕrō** *adv* very often, again and again, oftentimes
saep·ēs or **sēp·ēs -is** *f* hedge, fence, enclosure
saepīment·um or **sēpīment·um -ī** *n* hedge, fence, enclosure
saep·ĭō or **sēp·ĭō -īre -sī -tum** *vt* to fence in, hedge in, enclose; to surround, encircle; to guard, fortify, protect, strengthen
saept·um or **sept·um -ī** *n* fence, wall, enclosure; stake; sheepfold; voting booth; *n pl* enclosure; voting booths, polls
saet·a -ae or **sēt·a -ae** *f* stiff hair, bristle
saetĭg·er -ĕra -ĕrum *adj* bristly; *m* boar
saetōs·us -a -um *adj* bristly, hairy
saevē *adv* fiercely, savagely
saevidĭc·us -a -um *adj* spoken in anger, savage
saev·ĭō -īre -ĭī -ītum *vi* to be fierce, be savage, be furious; (of persons) to be brutal, be violent
saevĭter *adv* savagely, ferociously, cruelly
saevitĭ·a -ae *f* rage, fierceness; brutality, savageness, barbarity (*of persons*)
saev·us -a -um *adj* raging, fierce, furious, cruel; brutal, savage, barbarous (*persons*)
sāg·a -ae *f* fortune-teller (*female*)
sagācĭt·ās -ātis *f* keenness; sagacity, keenness of perception, shrewdness
sagācĭter *adv* keenly; shrewdly, accurately, acutely, sagaciously
sagāt·us -a -um *adj* wearing a military coat
sag·ax -ācis *adj* keen, sharp, acute; intellectually quick, sharp, shrewd; prophetic
sagīn·a -ae *f* stuffing, cramming, fattening up; food, rations; rich food; fattened animal; fatness (*from overeating*)
sagīn·ō -āre *vt* to fatten
sāg·ĭō -īre *vi* to perceive quickly, catch on quickly
sagitt·a -ae *f* arrow
Sagitt·a -ae *f* Sagitta (*constellation*)
sagittārĭ·us -a -um *adj* of or for an arrow; *m* archer, bowman
Sagittār·ĭus -ĭī or **-ī** *m* Sagittarius (*constellation*)
sagittĭf·er -ĕra -ĕrum *adj* arrow-bearing
Sagittipŏt·ens -entis *m* Sagittarius (*constellation*)
sagitt·ō -āre *vt* to shoot (*arrows*); *vi* to shoot arrows
sagm·en -ĭnis *n* tuft of sacred herbs (*plucked in the Capitol by the consul or praetor and worn by the fetiales as a sign of inviolability*)
sagŭl·um -ī *n* short military coat (*esp. that of general officers*)
sag·um -ī *n* coarse mantle; military uniform; **ad sagum ire** or **sagum sumere** to get into uniform; **in sagis esse** to be in uniform, be in the armed forces

Saguntīn·us -a -um *adj & m* Saguntine
Sagunt·um -ī *m* Saguntum (*city on the E. coast of Spain which Hannibal attacked and which thereby brought on the First Punic War*)
sāl salis *m* salt; salt water, sea water, sea; seasoning, flavor; good taste, elegance; pungency (*of words*), wit, humor; sarcasm; *m pl* witticisms, jokes, sarcastic remarks
salăc·ō -ōnis *m* braggart, show-off
salamandr·a -ae *f* salamander
Salamīnĭ·us -a -um *adj* of Salamis; *m pl* people of Salamis
Salăm·īs -īnis *f* island in the Saronic gulf near Athens; city in Cyprus founded by Teucer
salapūt·ium -iī or **-ī** *n* midget
Salārĭ·a -ae *f* Via Salaria (*from the Porta Collina to the Sabine district*)
salārĭ·us -a -um *adj* salt, of salt; **annona salaria** revenue from salt mines; *m* salt-fish dealer; *n* salary; allowance; a meal
sal·ax -ācis *adj* lustful; salacious, provocative
salĕbr·a -ae *f* jolting; rut; harshness, roughness (*of speech*)
Saliār·is -e *adj* Salian, of the Salii; sumptuous
Saliāt·us -ūs *m* office of Salius, Salian priesthood
salict·um -ī *n* willow grove
salient·ēs -ium *f pl* springs, fountains
salign·us -a -um *adj* willow, of willow
Salĭ·ī -ōrum *m pl* college of twelve priests dedicated to Mars who went in solemn procession through Rome on the Kalends of March
salill·um -ī *n* small salt cellar
salīn·ae -ārum *f pl* salt pits, salt works; **salinae Romanae** salt works at Ostia (*a state monopoly*)
salīn·um -ī *n* salt cellar
sal·ĭō -īre -ŭī or **-iī -tum** *vi* to jump, leap, bound, hop
Salisubsŭl·ī -ōrum *m pl* dancing priests of Mars
saliunc·a -ae *f* wild nard (*aromatic plant*)
salīv·a -ae *f* saliva; taste, flavor
sal·ix -icis *f* willow tree
Sallust·ius -iī or **-ī** *m* Sallust (*C. Sallustius Crispus, a Roman historian*, 86-35 B.C.)
Salmăc·is -idis *f* fountain in Caria which made all who drank from it soft and effeminate
Salmōn·eus -ĕos *m* son of Aeolus and brother of Sisyphus who imitated lightning and was thrown by Jupiter into Tartarus
Salmōn·is -idis *f* Tyro (*daughter of Salmoneus*)
salsāment·um -ī *n* salted or pickled fish; brine
salsē *adv* facetiously, humorously
Salsipŏt·ens -entis *adj* ruling the sea
sals·us -a -um *adj* salted; briny, salty; facetious, humorous, sharp, witty; *n pl* salty food; witty remarks, satirical writings
saltātĭ·ō -ōnis *f* dancing, dance
saltāt·or -ōris *m* dancer
saltātōrĭ·us -a -um *adj* dance, for dancing
saltātr·ix -icis *f* dancing girl, dancer
saltāt·us -ūs *m* dance, religious dance
saltem *adv* at least, in any event, anyhow; **non saltem** not even
salt·ō -āre *vt & vi* to dance
saltuōs·us -a -um *adj* wooded, covered with forest
salt·us -ūs *m* wooded pasture, forest; upland; jungle; ravine; valley, glen; (coll) female organ; leap, leaping; **saltum dare** to leap
salūb·er (or **salūb·ris**) **-re** *adj* healthful, healthy, wholesome; (with *dat* or with **ad** + *acc*) healthful for, good for, beneficial to
salūbrit·ās -ātis *f* healthiness, wholesomeness; health, soundness
salūbriter *adv* healthfully; healthily; beneficially
sal·um -ī *n* seas, high seas
sal·ūs -ūtis *f* health; welfare; prosperity, safety; greeting, good wish, best regards; **salutem dicere** (abbreviated **s. d.**) to say hello, send greetings; (at the end of a letter) to say good-bye; **salutem magnam dicere** to send warm greetings; (at the end of a letter) to say good-bye; **salutem plurimam dicere** (abbreviated **s.p.d.**) to send warmest greetings; (at the end of a letter) to give best regards
salūtār·is -e *adj* salutary, healthful, wholesome; beneficial, advantageous, useful; **ars salutaris** art of healing; **salutaris littera** vote of acquittal
salūtāriter *adv* beneficially, profitably, advantageously
salūtātĭ·ō -ōnis *f* greeting, salutation; formal morning reception or morning call at the house of an important person; callers; **ubi salutatio defluxit** when the morning callers have dispersed
salūtāt·or -ōris *m* or **salūtātr·ix -icis** *f* morning caller
salūtĭf·er -ĕra -ĕrum *adj* health-giving
salūtigerŭl·us -a -um *adj* bringing greetings
salūt·ō -āre *vt* to greet, wish well, salute; to send greetings to; to visit, pay respects to, pay a morning call on; to pay reverence to (*gods*); to greet, welcome; (with double *acc*) to salute as, hail as, e.g., **aliquem imperatorem salutare** to hail someone as a victorious general
salvē *adv* well; in good health; **satine salve?** (coll) everything O.K.?
salv·ĕō -ēre *vi* to be well, be in good

health; to be getting along well; **salve, salvete,** or **salveto!** hello!, good morning!, good day!; goodbye!; **te salvere jubeo** I bid you good day

salv·us or **salv·os -a -um** or **-om** *adj* well, sound, safe, unharmed, unscathed; living, alive; (with substantive in an *abl* absolute) without violation of, without breaking, e.g., **salvā lege** without breaking the law; **salvos sum** (coll) I'm all right, I'm O.K.

sambūc·a -ae *f* triangular stringed instrument, harp

sambūcin·a -ae *f* harpist (*female*)

sambūcistrĭ·a -ae *f* harpist (*female*)

Sam·ē -ēs *f* ancient name of the island of Cephallenia

Samĭ·us -a -um *adj* of Samos; **Juno Samia** Juno worshiped at Samos; **vir Samius** Pythagoras

Samn·īs -ītis *adj* Samnite; *m* Samnite gladiator; *m pl* Samnites

Samn·ium -ĭī or **-ī** *n* district of central Italy

Sam·os or **Sam·us -ī** *f* island off the W. coast of Asia Minor, famous for temple to Juno and as the birthplace of Pythagoras

Samothrāc·ēs -um *m pl* Samothracians

Samothrācĭ·us -a -um *adj* Samothracian; *f* Samothrace (*island in the N. Aegean*)

sānābĭl·is -e *adj* curable

sānātĭ·ō -ōnis *f* healing, curing

sanciō sancīre sanxī sanctum *vt* to consecrate, hallow, make inviolable; to ratify; to condemn; (with *abl*) to forbid under penalty of

sanctē *adv* solemnly, reverently, religiously, conscientiously, purely

sanctimōnĭ·a -ae *f* sanctity, sacredness; chastity

sanctĭ·ō -ōnis *f* consecration, confirmation, sanctioning; penalty clause (*that part of the law that provided for penalties against those breaking that law*), sanction

sanctĭt·ās -ātis *f* sanctity, sacredness, inviolability; integrity, purity, chastity, holiness

sanctitūd·ō -ĭnis *f* sanctity, sacredness

sanct·or -ōris *m* enactor (*of laws*)

sanct·us -a -um *adj* consecrated, hallowed, sacred, inviolable; venerable, august, divine; pure, holy, chaste, virtuous

sandaligerŭl·ae -ārum *f pl* maids who brought their mistress's slippers

sandal·ium -ĭī or **-ī** *n* slipper, sandal

sandapĭl·a -ae *f* cheap coffin (*for people of the lower classes*)

sand·yx -ȳcis *f* vermilion

sānē *adv* reasonably, sanely, sensibly; certainly, doubtless, truly, very; (ironically) of course, naturally; (with negatives) really, at all; (in concessions) to be sure, however; (in answers) yes, of course, to be sure; (with imperatives) then; (with **quam**) how very

sanguen see **sanguis**

sanguĭn·ans -antis *adj* bleeding; (fig) bloodthirsty, savage

sanguinārĭ·us -a -um *adj* bloodthirsty, savage

sanguinĕ·us -a -um *adj* bloody, bloodstained; bloodred

sanguinolent·us -a -um *adj* bloody, bloodstained; bloodred; sanguinary

sangu·is or **sangu·īs -ĭnis** *m* or **sangu·en -ĭnis** *n* blood; blood, consanguinity, descent, family; descendant, offspring; slaughter, murder, bloodshed; forcefulness, life, vigor (*of a speech*); life, strength; **pugnatum plurimo sanguine** fought out in a real massacre; **sanguinem dare** to bleed; **sanguinem effundere** or **profundere** to bleed heavily; **sanguinem haurire** to shed (*someone else's*) blood; **sanguinem mittere** (of a physician) to let blood, bleed

sanĭēs (*genit* not found) *f* blood (*from a wound*); gore; foam, froth, slaver; venom

sānĭt·ās -ātis *f* health; sanity; common sense, discretion; solidity, healthy foundation (*for victory, etc.*); soundness, propriety (*of style*)

sann·a -ae *f* mocking grimace, face

sannĭ·ō -ōnis *m* one who makes faces, clown

sān·ō -āre *vt* to cure, heal; to correct, repair; to allay, quiet, relieve

Sanquāl·is -e *adj* of Sangus (*Sabine deity*); **Sanqualis avis** osprey (*bird*)

sān·us -a -um *adj* sound, hale, healthy; sane, rational, sensible; sober; (with **ab** + *abl*) free from (*faults, vices*)

sap·a -ae *f* new wine

sāperd·a -ae *m* a fish (*from the Black Sea*)

sapĭ·ens -entis *adj* wise, sensible, judicious, discreet; *m* sensible person; sage, philosopher; man of discriminating taste, connoisseur

sapienter *adv* wisely, sensibly, prudently

sapientĭ·a -ae *f* good taste, common sense, prudence, wisdom; science; philosophy

sap·iō -ĕre -īvī or **-ĭī** *vt* to have the flavor of, taste of; to have the smell of, smell like; to have knowledge of, understand; *vi* to have a sense of taste; to have sense, be sensible, be discreet, be wise; **sero sapiunt** they are wise too late

sāp·ō -ōnis *m* soap

sap·or -ōris *m* taste, flavor; delicacy, dainty; elegance, refinement, sense of taste

Sapph·ō -ūs *f* celebrated Greek lyric poetess of Lesbos

sarcin·a -ae *f* package, bundle, pack; burden (*of the womb*); sorrow, trouble; *f pl* luggage, gear
sarcinārĭ·us -a -um *adj* pack, of luggage; **jumenta sarcinaria** pack animals
sarcināt·or -ōris *m* patcher, botcher
sarcināt·us -a -um *adj* loaded down, burdened
sarcinŭl·ae -ārum *f pl* small bundles, little trousseau
sarciō sarcīre sarsī sartum *vt* to patch, fix, repair
sarcophăg·us -ī *m* sarcophagus, tomb
sarcŭl·um -ī *n* light hoe, garden hoe
Sard·ēs or **Sard·īs -ium** *f pl* Sardis (*capital of Lydia*)
Sardiān·us -a -um *adj* Sardian
Sardinĭ·a -ae *f* Sardinia
Sardiniens·is -e *adj* Sardinian
Sardīs see **Sardes**
sardŏn·yx -ўchis *m* sardonyx (*precious stone*)
Sardō·us or **Sard·us -a -um** *adj* & *m* Sardianian
sarg·us -ī *m* bream (*fish*)
sar·iō or **sarr·io -īre -īvī** or **-ŭī** *vt* to hoe, weed
sarīs·a -ae *f* long Macedonian lance
sarīsophŏr·os -ī *m* Macedonian lancer
sarīt·or or **sart·or -ōris** *m* hoer, weeder
Sarmăt·ae -ārum *m pl* Sarmatians (*barbarous people of S.E. Russia*)
Sarmatĭ·a -ae *f* Sarmatia
Sarmatĭc·us -a -um *adj* Sarmatian
sarm·en -inis or **sarment·um -ī** *n* brushwood; *n pl* twigs, fagots
Sarpēd·ōn -ŏnis *m* king of Lycia who was killed by Patroclus at Troy
Sarr·a -ae *f* Tyre
sarrāc·um or **serrāc·um -ī** *n* cart
Sarrān·us -a -um *adj* Tyrian
sarrĭō see **sario**
sartāg·ō -inis *f* frying pan
sartor see **saritor**
sart·us -a -um *pp* of **sarcio;** *adj* (occurring only with **tectus**) in good repair; **aedem Castoris sartam tectam tradere** to hand over the temple of Castor in good repair; *n pl* repairs; **sarta tecta exigere** to complete the repairs
sat (indecl) *adj* enough, sufficient, adequate; *n* enough; **sat agere** (with *genit*) to have enough of, have the hands full with
sat *adv* sufficiently, quite; **sat scio** I am quite sure
sat·a -ae *f* daughter
sat·a -ōrum *n pl* crops
satăg·ō -ĕre *vi* to have trouble enough, have one's hands full
satell·es -itis *m* or *f* attendant, follower; partisan; accomplice
satĭ·ās -ātis *f* sufficiency; overabundance, satiety, satisfied desire
satiĕt·ās -atis *f* sufficiency, adequacy; satiety, weariness, disgust
satin' or **satine** *adv* quite, really
satĭ·ō -āre *vt* to satisfy, appease; to fill, glut; to saturate; to cloy
satĭ·ō -ōnis *f* sowing, planting; *f pl* sown fields
satis (indecl) *adj* enough, sufficient, adequate; *n* enough; (law) satisfaction, security, guarantee; **satis accipere** to accept a guarantee; **satis dare** (with *dat*) to give a guarantee to; **satis facere** (with *dat*) to satisfy; to pay (*a creditor*); to make amends to (*by word or deed*), apologize to; **satis facere** (with *dat* of person and *acc* & *inf*) to satisfy (*someone*) with proof that, demonstrate sufficiently to (*someone*) that; **satis superque dictum est** more than enough has been said
satis *adv* enough, sufficiently, adequately, fully; **satis bene** pretty well
satisdatĭ·ō -ōnis *f* putting up bail, giving a guarantee
satisfactĭ·ō -ōnis *f* amends, satisfaction, apology
satĭus (*comp* of **satis**) *adj* **satius est** (with *inf*) it is better or preferable to
sat·or -ōris *m* sower, planter; father; promoter, author
satrapē·a or **satrapī·a -ae** *f* satrapy (*office or province of a satrap*)
satrăp·ēs -is *m* satrap (*governor of a province of the Persian empire*)
sat·ur -ŭra -ŭrum *adj* full, well fed, stuffed; plump; rich, fertile; rich, deep (*colors*); *f* mixture, hotchpotch; medley; satire, satirical poem; **per saturam** at random, pell-mell
saturei·a -ōrum *n pl* savory (*aromatic herb used as seasoning*)
saturĭt·ās -ātis *f* satiety; plenty, overabundance
Sāturnālĭ·a -ōrum *n pl* festival in honor of Saturn, beginning on the 17th of December and lasting several days
Sāturnĭ·a -ae *f* Juno (*daughter of Saturn*)
Sāturnīn·us -ī *m* L. Appuleius Saturninus (*demagogic tribune in* 103 B.C. *and* 100 B.C.)
Sāturnĭ·us -a -um *adj* Saturnian; **Saturnius numerus** Saturnian meter (*archaic Latin meter based on stress accent*); *m* Jupiter; Pluto
Sāturn·us -ī *m* Saturn (*Italic god of agriculture, equated with the Greek god Cronos, ruler of the Golden Age, and father of Jupiter, Neptune, Juno, and Pluto*)
satŭr·ō -āre *vt* to fill, satisfy, glut, cloy, saturate; to satisfy, content
sat·us -a -um *pp* of **sero;** *m* son; *f* see **sata;** *n pl* see **sata**
sat·us -ūs *m* sowing, planting; begetting; race, stock; seed (*of knowledge*)
satyrisc·us -ī *m* little satyr

satўr·us -ī *m* satyr; satyr play (*Greek drama in which satyrs often formed the chorus*)
sauciāti·ō -ōnis *f* wounding
sauci·ō -āre *vt* to wound
sauci·us -a -um *adj* wounded; (fig) smitten, offended, hurt; melted (*snow*)
Sauromăt·ae -ārum *m pl* Sarmatians (*barbaric tribe of S. Russia*)
sāviāti·ō or **suāviāti·ō -ōnis** *f* kissing
sāviŏl·um or **suāviŏl·um -ī** *n* little kiss
sāvi·or -ārī -ātus sum *vt* to kiss
sāv·ium or **suāv·ium -iī** or **-ī** *n* puckered lips; kiss
saxātil·is -e *adj* rock, living among rocks; *m* saxatile (*fish*)
saxēt·um -ī *n* rocky place
saxĕ·us -a -um *adj* rocky, stony; **umbra saxea** shade of the rocks
saxific·us -a -um *adj* petrifying, changing objects into stone
saxōs·us -a -um *adj* rocky, stony
saxŭl·um -ī *n* small rock, little crag
sax·um -ī *n* bolder, rock; Tarpeian Cliff (*W. side of the Capitoline Hill*)
scabellum see **scabillum**
scab·er -ra -rum *adj* itchy; rough, scurfy
scab·iēs (*genit* not found) *f* itch; roughness, scurf; (fig) itch
scabill·um or **scabell·um -ī** *n* stool, footstool; castanet tied to the foot
scabiōs·us -a -um *adj* itchy, mangy; moldy
scab·ō -ĕre -ī *vt* to scratch
Scae·a port·a -ae *f* Scaean gate (*W. gate of Troy*)
scaen·a or **scēn·a -ae** *f* stage setting, stage; scene; (fig) public view, publicity; pretense, pretext; **tibi scenae serviendum est** you must keep yourself in the limelight
scaenāl·is or **scēnāl·is -e** *adj* theatrical, scenic
scaenic·us or **scēnic·us -a -um** *adj* of the stage, theatrical, scenic; *m* actor
Scaevŏl·a -ae *m* C. Mucius Scaevola (*Roman hero who infiltrated into Porsenna's camp to kill Porsenna, and, on being discovered, burned off his own right hand*)
scaev·us -a -um *adj* left, on the left; perverse; *f* sign or omen appearing on the left
scāl·ae -ārum *f pl* ladder, flight of steps, stairs
scalm·us -ī *m* oarlock; oar; boat
scalpell·um -ī *n* scalpel
scalp·ō -ĕre -sī -tum *vt* to carve; to scratch; to tickle
scalpr·um -ī *n* chisel; knife; penknife
scalpurr·iō -īre *vi* to scratch
Scamand·er -rī *m* river at Troy, also called Xanthus
scammōnĕ·a -ae *f* scammony (*plant*)
scamn·um -ī *n* bench, stool; throne
scandō scandĕre scandī scansum *vt & vi* to climb, mount, ascend
scandŭl·a -ae *f* shingle (*for roof*)
scaph·a -ae *f* light boat, skiff
scaph·ium -iī or **-ī** *n* boat-shaped drinking cup; chamber pot
scapŭl·ae -ārum *f pl* shoulder blades; shoulders, back
scāp·us -ī *m* shaft; yarn beam (*of a loom*)
scarīf·ō -āre *vt* to scratch open
scar·us -ī *m* scar (*fish*)
scatĕbr·a -ae *f* bubbling, gushing, jet
scat·ĕō -ēre or **scat·ō -ĕre** *vi* to bubble up, gush out, jet; to teem
scatūrīgin·ēs or **scaturrīgin·ēs -um** *f pl* springs
scaturr·iō -īre *vi* to bubble, gush; to bubble over with enthusiasm
scaur·us -a -um *adj* clubfooted
scaz·ōn -ontis *m* scazon (*iambic trimeter with a spondee or trochee in the last foot*)
scelerātē *adv* criminally, wickedly
scelerāt·us -a -um *adj* profaned, desecrated; outlawed; criminal, wicked, infamous; *m* villain, criminal
scelĕr·ō -āre *vt* to pollute, desecrate
scelerōs·us -a -um *adj* full of wickedness, vicious
scel·us -ĕris *n* wicked deed, crime, wickedness; calamity; scoundrel, criminal
scēn- = scaen-
sceptrif·er -ĕra -ĕrum *adj* sceptered
sceptr·um -ī *n* scepter; kingship, dominion, authority; kingdom
sceptūch·us -ī *m* scepter-bearer (*high officer of state in the East*)
sched·a or **scid·a -ae** *f* sheet, page
schēm·a -ae *f* figure, form, style; figure of speech
Schoenē·is -idis *f* Atalanta
Schoenei·us -a -um *adj* of Schoeneus; *f* Atalanta
Schoen·eus -ĕī *m* king of Boeotia and father of Atalanta
schoenobăt·ēs -ae *m* ropewalker
schol·a -ae *f* learned debate, dissertation, lecture; school; sect, followers
scholastic·us -a -um *adj* school, scholastic; *m* rhetoric teacher, rhetorician
scida see **scheda**
sci·ens -entis *adj* having knowledge; having full knowledge, with one's eyes open; (with *genit*) having knowledge of, familiar or acquainted with, expert in; (with *inf*) knowing how to
scienter *adv* wisely, expertly
scienti·a -ae *f* knowledge, skill
scilicet *adv* of course, evidently, certainly; (ironically) naturally, of course, to be sure; (as an explanatory particle) namely, that is to say, in other words

scill·a or **squill·a -ae** *f* shrimp
scin = **scisne,** i.e., **scis** + **ne**
scindō scindĕre scidī scissum *vt* to cut, split, tear apart or open; to divide, separate; to interrupt
scindŭla see **scandula**
scintill·a -ae *f* spark
scintill·ō -āre *vi* to sparkle, flash
scintillŭl·a -ae *f* little spark
sciō scīre scīvī or **sciī scītum** *vt* to know; to realize, understand; to have skill in; (with *inf*) to know how to
Scīpiăd·ēs -ae *m* a Scipio, one of the Scipio family
Scīpi·ō -ōnis *m* famous family in the gens Cornelia; P. Cornelius Scipio Africanus Major (*conqueror of the Carthaginians in the Second Punic War,* 236-184 B.C.); P. Cornelius Scipio Aemilianus Africanus Minor (*conqueror of the Carthaginians in the Third Punic War, c.* 185-132 B.C.)
scirpĕ·us or **sirpĕ·us -a -um** *adj* wicker, of wicker; *f* wickerwork
scirpicŭl·a -ae *f* wicker basket
scirpicŭl·us -ī *m* wicker basket
scirp·us or **sirp·us -ī** *m* bulrush
sciscĭt·ō -āre or **sciscĭt·or -ārī -ātus sum** *vt* to ask, question, interrogate; to consult; (with *acc* of thing asked about and **ex** or **ab** + *abl* of person) to ask (*something*) of (*someone*), check on (*something*) with (*someone*); *vi* (with **de** + *abl*) to ask about
sciscō sciscĕre scīvī scītum *vt* (pol) to approve, adopt, enact, decree; to learn, ascertain
sciss·us -a -um *pp* of **scindo;** *adj* split, rent; furrowed (*cheeks*); shrill, harsh (*voice*)
scītāment·a -ōrum *n pl* dainties, delicacies
scītē *adv* expertly
scīt·or -ārī -ātus sum *vt* to ask; to consult (*oracle*); (with *acc* of thing and **ab** or **ex** + *abl*) to ask (*something*) of (*someone*); *vi* (with **de** + *abl*) to ask or inquire about
scītŭl·us -a -um *adj* neat, trim, smart
scīt·um -ī *n* statute, decree
scīt·us -a -um *adj* experienced, skillful; suitable, proper; judicious, sensible, witty (*words*); smart, sharp (*appearance*); (with *genit*) skilled in, expert at
scīt·us -ūs *m* decree, enactment
sciūr·us -ī *m* squirrel
scob·is -is *f* sawdust, scrapings, filings
scomb·er -rī *m* mackerel
scōp·ae -ārum *f pl* twigs, shoots; broom
Scop·ās -ae *m* famous Greek sculptor of Paros (*4th cent.* B.C.)
scopulōs·us -a -um *adj* rocky, craggy
scopŭl·us -ī *m* rock, cliff, crag; promontory
scorpī·ō -ōnis or **scorp·ius** or **scorp·ios -iī** or **-ī** *m* scorpion; (mil) artillery piece, catapult
Scorpī·ō -ōnis *m* Scorpion (*sign of the zodiac*)
scortāt·or -ōris *m* fornicator, lecher
scortĕ·us -a -um *adj* leather, of leather
scort·or -ārī -ātus sum *vi* to associate with prostitutes
scort·um -ī *n* prostitute; sex fiend
screāt·or -ōris *m* one who clears his throat noisily, hawker
screāt·us -ūs *m* clearing the throat, hawking
scre·ō -āre *vi* to clear the throat, hawk, hem
scrīb·a -ae *m* clerk, secretary
scriblīt·a -ae *f* tart
scrībō scrībĕre scripsī scriptum *vt* to write, draw; to write down; to write out, compose, produce; to enlist (*soldiers*); (with double *acc*) to appoint (*someone*) as
scrīn·ium -iī or **-ī** *n* bookcase, letter case, portfolio
scripti·ō -ōnis *f* writing, composition, authorship; wording, text
scriptĭt·ō -āre *vt* to keep writing, write regularly
script·or -ōris *m* writer; scribe, secretary; composer, author; **rerum scriptor** historian
scriptŭl·a -ōrum *n pl* lines on a game board
scriptūr·a -ae *f* writing; composing; a writing, written work; tax paid on public pastures; testamentary provision
script·us -a -um *pp* of **scribo;** *n* written composition, treatise, work, book; literal meaning, letter; **orationem de scripto dicere** to read off a speech; **scriptum legis** or **scriptum** written ordinance, law
scrīpŭl·um or **scrūpŭl·um -ī** *n* small weight, smallest measure of weight, scruple (*one twenty fourth of an uncia*)
scrob·is -is *m* ditch, trench; grave
scrōf·a -ae *f* breeding sow
scrōfipasc·us -ī *m* swine keeper, pig breeder
scrūpĕ·us -a -um *adj* stony, rugged, jagged, rough
scrūpōs·us -a -um *adj* full of sharp stones, rugged, jagged, rough
scrūpŭlōsē *adv* precisely, carefully
scrūpulōs·us -a -um *adj* rough, rugged, jagged; precise, careful
scrūpŭlum see **scripulum**
scrūpŭl·us -ī *m* small sharp pebble; uneasy feeling, scruple
scrūp·us -ī *m* rough or sharp stone; uneasiness
scrūt·a -ōrum *n pl* trash, junk
scrūtāt·or -ōris *m* examiner
scrūt·or -ārī -ātus sum *vt* to scrutinize, examine
sculp·ō -ĕre -sī -tum *vt* to carve, chisel, engrave

sculpōnĕ·ae -ārum *f pl* clogs
sculptĭl·is -e *adj* carved, engraved
sculpt·or -ōris *m* sculptor
sculptūr·a -ae *f* carving; sculpture
sculptus *pp* of **sculpo**
scurr·a -ae *m* jester, comedian; man-about-town
scurrīl·is -e *adj* scurrilous
scurrīlĭt·ās -ātis *f* scurrility
scurrīliter *adv* jeeringly
scurr·or -ārī -ātus sum *vi* to clown around
scūtāl·e -is *n* thong of a sling
scūtār·ĭus -ĭī or **-ī** *m* shield maker
scūtāt·us -a -um *adj* carrying a shield; *m pl* troops armed with shields
scutell·a -ae *f* saucer, shallow bowl
scutĭc·a -ae *f* whip
scūtigerŭl·us -ī *m* shield bearer
scutr·a -ae *f* pan, flat dish
scutŭl·a or **scytăl·a** or **scytăl·ē -ae** *f* platter; eye patch; wooden cylinder; secret letter
scutulāt·us -a -um *adj* diamond-shaped; *n pl* checkered clothing
scūtŭl·um -ī *n* small shield
scūt·um -ī *n* oblong shield; (fig) shield, defense, protection
Scyll·a -ae *f* dangerous rock on the Italian side of Straits of Messina, said to have been the daughter of Phorcus and transformed by Circe into a sea monster with howling dogs about her midriff; daughter of Nisus who betrayed her father by cutting off his purple lock of hair
Scyllae·us -a -um *adj* Scyllan
scymn·us -ī *m* cub, whelp
scyph·us -ī *m* goblet, cup
Scyr·os or **Scyr·us -ī** *f* island off Euboea
scytăla see **scutula**
scytălē see **scutula**
Scyth·a or **Scyth·ēs -ae** *m* Scythian; *m pl* Scythians (*general name for the nomadic tribes of the section of Europe and Asia beyond the Black Sea*)
Scythĭ·a -ae *f* Scythia
Scythĭc·us -a -um *adj* Scythian
Scyth·is -ĭdis *f* Scythian woman
sē or **sēsē** (*genit:* **suī**; *dat:* **sibī** or **sibi**; *abl* **sē** or **sēsē**) *pron acc* (reflex) himself, herself, itself, themselves; one another; **ad se** or **apud se** at home; **apud se** in one's senses; **inter se** one another, mutually
sēb·um -ī *n* tallow, grease
sē·cēdō -cēdĕre -cessī -cessum *vi* to go apart, go aside, withdraw; to rebel
sē·cernō -cernĕre -crēvī -crētum *vt* to separate; to dissociate; to distinguish; to reject, set aside
sēcessĭ·ō -ōnis *f* withdrawal; secession
sēcess·us -ūs *m* retirement, retreat; isolated spot
sē·clūdō -clūdĕre -clūsī -clūsum *vt* to shut off, shut up; to seclude, bar; to hide
sec·ō -āre -ŭī -tum *vt* to cut, cut off, reap, carve; (in surgery) to cut out, excise, cut off, amputate; to scratch, tear, wound, injure; to cut through, traverse; to cut short, settle, decide; to follow, chase
sēcordĭa see **socordia**
sēcrētĭ·ō -ōnis *f* dividing, separating
sēcrētō *adv* separately, apart; secretly; in private
sēcrēt·us -a -um *pp* of **secerno;** separate; isolated, solitary; secret; (with *genit* or *abl*) deprived of, in need of; *n* secret, mystery; private conversation or interview; isolated place, solitude
sect·a -ae *f* path; way, method, course; school of thought; political party
sectārĭ·us -a -um *adj* gelded; leading
sectāt·or -ōris *m* follower, adherent
sectĭl·is -e *adj* cut, divided
sectĭ·ō -ōnis *f* cutting; auctioning off of confiscated property; right to confiscated property; confiscated property
sect·or -ōris *m* cutter; buyer at a sale of confiscated property, speculator in confiscated estates
sect·or -ārī -ātus sum *vt* to keep following, follow eagerly, run after, keep trailing after; to chase, hunt
sectūr·a -ae *f* digging, excavation; *f pl* diggings, mines
sectus *pp* of **seco**
sēcubĭt·us -ūs *m* sleeping alone
sēcŭb·ō -āre -ŭī *vi* to lie alone, sleep by oneself; to live alone
sēcul- = saecul-
secund·a -ōrum *n pl* success, good fortune
secund·ae -ārum *f pl* secondary role (*in a play*); second fiddle
secundān·ī -ōrum *m pl* soldiers of the second legion
secundārĭ·us -a -um *adj* secondary, second-rate, inferior
secundō *adv* secondly
secund·ō -āre *vt* to favor, further, back, support
secundum *adv* after, behind; *prep* (with *acc*) (of space) beside, by, along; (of time) immediately after, after; (in rank) next to, after; (of agreement) according to, in compliance with; in favor of, to the advantage of
secund·us -a -um *adj* following; next, second (*in time*); backing, favorable, supporting; next, second (*in rank*); secondary, subordinate, inferior, second-string; **anno secundo** the next year; **a mensis fine secunda dies** the second-last day of the month; **in secundam aquam** with the current; **secunda mensa** dessert; **secundo flumine** downstream, with the current; **se-**

cundo lumine on the following day; **secundo mari** with the tide; **secundo populo** with the backing of the people; **secundus panis** inferior bread, stale bread; **secundus ventus** tail wind, fair wind; *f pl* see **secundae**; *n pl* see **secunda**
sēcūrē *adv* securely, safely
secūricŭl·a -ae *f* hatchet
secūrif·er -ĕra -ĕrum *adj* carrying an ax, ax-carrying
secūrig·er -ĕra -ĕrum *adj* ax-carrying
secūr·is -is *f* ax, hatchet; blow, mortal blow; power of life and death; supreme authority, sovereignty
sēcūrit·ās -ātis *f* freedom from care, unconcern, composure; freedom from danger, security, safety; false sense of security; carelessness
sēcūr·us -a -um *adj* carefree; secure, safe; cheerful; careless; offhand
secus (indecl) *n* sex; **secus muliebre** females; **secus viriles** males
secus *adv* otherwise, differently; **non secus ac** or **non secus quam** not otherwise than, just as, exactly as; **si secus accidet** if it turns out otherwise (*than expected*), if it turns out badly
secūt·or -ōris *m* gladiator (*who fought against an opponent who had a net*)
secūtus *pp* of **sequor**
sed or **set** *conj* but; but also; but in fact
sēdātē *adv* sedately, calmly
sēdāti·ō -ōnis *f* calming
sēdāt·us -a -um *adj* calm, composed
sēdĕcim (indecl) *adj* sixteen
sēdĕcŭl·a -ae *f* little seat, low stool
sedentāri·us -a -um *adj* sedentary
sedĕō sedēre sēdī sessum *vi* to sit, remain sitting; (of magistrates, esp. judges) to sit, preside, hold court, be a judge; (of an army) to remain encamped; to keep the field; to settle down in blockade; to be idle, be inactive; (of clothes) to fit; (of places) to be low-lying; to sink, settle; to be firm, be fixed, be established; to stick fast, be stuck; to be determined, be firmly resolved
sēd·ēs -is *f* seat, chair, throne; residence, home; last home, burial place; base, foundation, bottom
sedīl·e -is *n* seat, chair, bench, stool; *n pl* seats in the theater; rowers' benches
sēditi·ō -ōnis *f* sedition, insurrection, mutiny; dissension, quarrel, disagreement; warring (*of elements, etc.*)
sēditiōsē *adv* seditiously
sēditiōs·us -a -um *adj* seditious, mutinous; quarrelsome; troubled, disturbed
sēd·ō -āre *vt* to calm, settle, still, allay
sē·dūcō -dūcĕre -duxī -ductum *vt* to lead aside, draw aside, lead away, carry off; to put aside; to separate, divide
sēducti·ō -ōnis *f* taking sides, siding
sēduct·us -a -um *pp* of **seduco;** distant, remote
sēdulit·ās -ātis *f* application, earnestness; officiousness
sēdŭlō *adv* diligently; intentionally, on purpose
sēdŭl·us -a -um *adj* diligent, busy; officious
seg·es -ĕtis *f* grain field; crop
Segest·a -ae *f* town in N.W. Sicily
Segestān·us -a -um *adj* of Segesta; *m pl* people of Segesta; *n* territory of Segesta
segmentāt·us -a -um *adj* trimmed with a flounce
segment·um -ī *n* trimming, flounce; brocade
segnip·ēs -ĕdis *adj* slow-footed
segn·is -e *adj* slow, inactive; sluggish, lazy
segniter *adv* slowly, lazily
segniti·a -ae or **segniti·ēs** (*genit* not found) *f* slowness, inactivity, laziness
sēgrĕg·ō -āre *vt* to segregate, separate
sējugāt·us -a -um *adj* separated
sējŭg·is -is *m* six-horse chariot
sējunctim *adv* separately
sējuncti·ō -ōnis *f* separation, division
sē·jungō -jungĕre -junxī -junctum *vt* to separate, disunite, part, sever; (fig) to sever, part, disconnect; to distinguish
sēlecti·ō -ōnis *f* selection
sēlectus *pp* of **seligo**
Seleuc·us -ī *m* name of a line of kings of Syria
sēlībr·a -ae *f* half pound
sē·ligō -ligĕre -lēgī -lectum *vt* to pick out, select, choose
sell·a -ae *f* chair, stool; sedan; magistrate's chair
sellāriŏl·us -a -um *adj* (place) for sitting or lounging
sellār·ius -iī or **-ī** *m* lecherer
sellisterni·a -ōrum *n pl* sacred banquets in honor of goddesses
sellŭl·a -ae *f* stool; sedan
sellulār·ius -iī or **-ī** *m* mechanic
sēmanĭmis see **semianimis**
semel *adv* once, one time; but once, once for all; first, the first time; once, ever, at some time, at any time
Semĕl·ē -ēs or **Semĕl·a -ae** *f* daughter of Cadmus and mother of Bacchus by Jupiter
Semelei·us -a -um *adj* of Semele
sēm·en -ĭnis *n* seed, germ; seedling, young plant, shoot; offspring; race, stock; (in physics) particle; instigator, cause
sēmenstris see **semestris**
sēmentĭf·er -ĕra -ĕrum *adj* seed-bearing, fruitful
sēmentīn·us -a -um *adj* of the sowing season

sēment·is -is *f* sowing, planting; young crops
sēmentīv·us -a -um *adj* at seed time, of the sowing season
sēmerm·is -e *adj* half-armed
sēmestr·is or **sēmenstr·is -e** *adj* for six months, half-yearly, semiannual
sēmēs·us -a -um *adj* half-eaten
sēmet = emphatic form of **se**
sēmiadapert·us -a -um *adj* half-open
sēmianĭm·is -e or **sēmianĭm·us** or **sēmanĭm·us -a -um** *adj* half-dead
sēmiapert·us -a -um *adj* half-open
sēmĭb·ōs -ōvis *adj masc* half-ox; **semibos vir** Minotaur
sēmicăp·er -rī *adj masc* half-goat
sēmicremāt·us or **sēmicrĕm·us -a -um** *adj* half-burned
sēmicubitāl·is -e *adj* half-cubit long
sēmidĕ·us -a -um *adj* semidivine; *m* demigod
sēmidoct·us -a -um *adj* half-educated
sēmierm·is -e or **sēmierm·us -a -um** *adj* half-armed
sēmiēs·us -a -um *adj* half-eaten
sēmifact·us -a -um *adj* half-finished
sēmĭf·er -ĕra -ĕrum *adj* half-beast; half-savage; *m* centaur
sēmifult·us -a -um *adj* half-propped
sēmigermān·us -a -um *adj* half-German
sēmigrăv·is -e *adj* half-drunk
sēmĭgr·ō -āre *vi* to go away, depart
sēmihĭ·ans -antis *adj* half-open
sēmihŏm·ō -ĭnis *m* half man, half beast; subhuman
sēmihōr·a -ae *f* half hour
sēmilăc·er -ĕra -ĕrum *adj* half-mangled
sēmilaut·us -a -um *adj* half-washed
sēmilīb·er -ĕra -ĕrum *adj* half-free
sēmilix·a -ae *m* (term of reproach) sad sack
sēmimarīn·us -a -um *adj* semisubmerged (*in the sea*)
sēmĭm·ās -ăris *adj* gelded, castrated; *m* hermaphrodite
sēmimortŭ·us -a -um *adj* half-dead
sēminār·ĭum -ĭī or **-ī** *n* nursery garden; (fig) breeding ground
sēmināt·or -ōris *m* originator, cause, source
sēminĕcis (*genit; nom does not occur*) *adj* half-killed, half-dead
sēmin·ĭum -ĭī or **-ī** *n* breeding; stock
sēmĭn·ō -āre *vt* to sow; to beget, procreate; to produce
sēminūd·us -a -um *adj* half-stripped; half-unarmed
sēmipāgān·us -ī *m* little clown
sēmiplēn·us -a -um *adj* (garrison) at half strength
sēmiputāt·us -a -um *adj* half-pruned
Semīrăm·is -is or **-ĭdis** *f* famous queen of Assyria, the consort and successor of Ninus
Semīramĭ·us -a -um *adj* of Semiramis
sēmirās·us -a -um *adj* half-shaven
sēmireduct·us -a -um *adj* bent back halfway
sēmirefect·us -a -um *adj* half-repaired
sēmirŭt·us -a -um *adj* half-ruined, half-demolished
sēm·is -issis *m* half; half an ace (*coin*); one half percent a month or six-percent per annum; **non semissis homo** man not worth a penny, worthless fellow
sēmisĕn·ex -is *m* elderly gent
sēmisepult·us -a -um *adj* half-buried
sēmisomn·is -e or **sēmisomn·us -a -um** *adj* half-asleep
sēmisupīn·us -a -um *adj* half-prone
sēmĭt·a -ae *f* path, lane
sēmitāl·is -a -um *adj* of byways
sēmitārĭ·us -a -um *adj* back-alley
sēmiustilāt·us or **sēmiustulāt·us -a -um** *adj* half-burned
sēmĭv·ir -īrī *adj* half-man, half-beast; unmanned; unmanly, effeminate; *m* half-man; eunuch
sēmivīv·us -a -um *adj* half-alive, half-dead
sēmod·ĭus -ĭī or **-ī** *m* half a peck
sēmōt·us -a -um *adj* remote, distant; *n pl* faraway places
sē·movĕō -movēre -mōvī -mōtum *vt* to move apart, separate, remove, put aside
semper *adv* always, ever; regularly, on each occasion
sempitern·us -a -um *adj* everlasting
Semprōnĭus see **Gracchus**
sēmuncĭ·a -ae *f* half ounce (*one twenty-fourth of a Roman pound*); trifle
sēmunciārĭ·us -a -um *adj* half-ounce; **faenus semunciarium** interest at the rate of one twenty-fourth of the capital (*i.e., about five percent per annum*)
sēmust·us -a -um *adj* half-burned
senācŭl·um -ī *n* open-air meeting place of the senate in the Forum
sēnāriŏl·us -ī *m* trifling trimeter
sēnārĭ·us -a -um *adj* six-foot (*verse*); *m* iambic trimeter
senāt·or -ōris *m* senator
senātōrĭ·us -a -um *adj* senatorial; in the senate; of a senator
sĕnāt·us -ūs *m* senate; senate session; **senatūs consultum** decree of the senate
Senĕc·a -ae *m* L. Annaeus Seneca (*Stoic philosopher and instructor of Nero, 4 B.C.-65 A.D.*)
senect·us -a -um *adj* aged, old; *f* old age, senility
senect·ūs -ūtis *f* old age; old people

sen·ĕō -ēre *vi* to be old
sen·escō -escĕre -ŭī *vi* to grow old; to decline, become feeble, lose strength; to wane, draw to a close
sen·ex -is *adj* aged, old; *m* old man; *f* old woman
sēn·ī -ae -a *adj* six each, six in a group, six at a time; **seni deni** sixteen each
senīl·is -e *adj* of old people, of an old man; aged; senile
sēnī·ō -ōnis *m* a six (*on dice*)
seni·or -us (*comp* of **senex**) *adj* older, elder; more mature (*years*); *m* elderly person, an elder (*over forty-five years of age*)
sen·ium -iī or **-ī** *n* feebleness of age, decline, senility; decay; grief, trouble; gloom; crabbiness; old man
sens·a -ōrum *n pl* thoughts, sentiments, ideas
sensicŭl·us -ī *m* short sentence
sensif·er -ĕra -ĕrum *adj* producing sensation
sensīl·is -e *adj* capable of sensation, sentient
sensim *adv* gropingly; tentatively; carefully, gradually, gently
sens·us -a -um *pp* of **sentio**; *n pl* see **sensa**
sens·us -ūs *m* sense faculty, capacity for feeling, sensation; feeling, emotion, sentiment; attitude, frame of mind, view; understanding, judgment, intelligence; meaning, intent, sense; sentence; **communes sensūs** commonplaces; universal human feelings
sententi·a -ae *f* opinion, view, judgment; purpose, intention; (law) sentence, verdict; (in the senate) motion, proposal, view; meaning, sense; sentence; maxim; **de sententia** (with *genit*) in accordance with the wishes of; **ex animi (mei) sententia** (in an oath) to the best of (*my*) knowledge and belief; **ex mea sententia** in my opinion, to my liking; **in sententiam alicujus pedibus ire** to vote in favor of someone's proposal; **sententia est** (with *inf*) I intend to; **sententiam dicere** (in the senate) to express a view; **sententiam pronuntiare** or **dicere** to pronounce or give the verdict
sententiŏl·a -ae *f* phrase; maxim
sententiōsē *adv* sententiously
sententiōs·us -a -um sententious, full of meaning
senticēt·um -ī *n* thorny bush
sentīn·a -ae *f* bilge water; cesspool; bilge; (fig) dregs, scum, rabble
sentiō sentīre sensī sensum *vt* to perceive with the senses, feel, hear, see, smell; to realize; to feel, observe, notice; to experience; to think, judge; *vi* (law) to vote, decide
sent·is -is *m* thorny bush, bramble, brier
sentisc·ō -ĕre *vt* to begin to realize; to begin to observe, perceive
sent·us -a -um *adj* thorny; untidy (*person*)
seorsum or **seorsus** *adv* apart, separately; (with *abl* or **ab** + *abl*) apart from
sēparābil·is -e *adj* separable
sēparātim *adv* apart, separately
sēparāti·ō -ōnis *f* severing, separation
sēparātius *adv* less closely, more widely
sēparāt·us -a -um *adj* separate, distinct, different
sēpăr·ō -āre *vt* to separate, divide, part; to distinguish
sepelībil·is -e *adj* that may be buried
sepeliō sepelīre sepelīvī or **sepeliī sepultum** *vt* to bury; (fig) to bury, overwhelm, ruin, destroy, suppress
sēpēs see **saepes**
sēpi·a -ae *f* cuttlefish
sēpīmentum see **saepīmentum**
sēpiō see **saepio**
sēpiŏl·a -ae *f* little cuttlefish
sē·pōnō -pōnĕre -posŭī -positum *vt* to put aside; to separate, pick out, select; to assign, reserve; to remove, take away, exclude; to distinguish
sēposit·us -a -um *adj* remote, distant; select; distinct, private
seps sēpis *m* or *f* snake
sepse = emphatic **sē**
septem (indecl) *adj* seven
Septemb·er -ris *adj* & *m* September
septemdĕcim (indecl) *adj* seventeen
septemflŭ·us -a -um *adj* seven-mouthed (*Nile*)
septemgemin·us -a -um *adj* sevenfold
septempedāl·is -e *adj* seven-foot, seven-feet-high
septempl·ex -icis *adj* sevenfold
septemtriōnāl·ia -ium *n pl* northern regions, northern part
septemtriōnāl·is -e *adj* northern
septemtriōn·ēs or **septentriōn·ēs -um** *m pl* seven stars near the North Pole belonging to the Great Bear; the seven stars of the Little Bear; northern regions, the North; north wind
septemvirāl·is -e *adj* of the septemvirs, septemviral; *m pl* septemvirs
septemvirāt·us -ūs *m* septemvirate, office of the septemvirs
septemvĭr·ī -ōrum *m pl* septemvirs (*board of seven officials*)
septēnār·ius -iī or **-ī** *m* heptameter (*verse of seven feet*)
septendĕcim or **septemdĕcim** (indecl) *adj* seventeen
septēn·ī -ae -a *adj* seven each, seven in a group; **septeni deni** seventeen each, seventeen in a group
septentr- = **septemtr-**
septiens or **septiēs** *adv* seven times

septimān·us -a -um *adj* of or on the seventh; *n pl* soldiers of the seventh legion
septimum *adv* for the seventh time
septim·us or **septŭm·us -a -um** *adj* seventh
septim·us decim·us -a -um *adj* seventeenth
septingentēsim·us -a -um *adj* seven hundredth
septingent·ī -ae -a *adj* seven hundred
septuāgēsim·us -a -um *adj* seventieth
septuāgintā (indecl) *adj* seventy
septuenn·is -e *adj* seven-year-old
septum see **saeptum**
septun·x -cis *m* seven ounces; seven twelfths
septus *pp* of **saepio**
sepulcrāl·is -e *adj* of a tomb, sepulchral, funeral
sepulcrēt·um -ī *n* grave, tomb
sepulcr·um -ī *n* grave, tomb
sepultūr·a -ae *f* burial
sepultus *pp* of **sepelio**
Sēquăn·a -ae *m* Seine
sequ·ax -ācis *adj* following, pursuing; penetrating (*fumes*); eager
sequ·ens -entis *adj* next, following
sequest·er -ris (or **-ra**) **-re** *adj* intermediate; negotiating, mediating; **pace sequestrā** under the protection of a truce; *m* trustee; agent, mediator, go-between
sequius or **sētius** (*comp* of **secus**) *adv* less; worse, more unfavorably; **nihilo setius** or **nilo setius** nevertheless
sequor sequī secūtus sum *vt* to follow, escort, accompany, go with; to chase, pursue; to come after (*in time*); to go after, aim at; to head for (*a place*); *vi* to go after, follow, come next; (of words) to come naturally
ser·a -ae *f* bolt, bar (*of door*)
Serāp·is -is or **-idis** *m* Egyptian god of healing
serēnit·ās -ātis *f* fair weather; serenity; favorableness
serēn·ō -āre *vt* to make fair, clear up, brighten
serēn·us -a -um *adj* clear, bright, fair, cloudless; cheerful, serene; *n* clear sky, fair weather
Sēr·es -um *m pl* Chinese
seresc·ō -ĕre *vi* to dry off
sēri·a -ae *f* large jar
sēri·a -ōrum *n pl* serious matters, serious business
Sēric·us -a -um *adj* Chinese; *n pl* silks
seri·ēs (*genit* not found) series, row, succession; train, sequence, order, connection; lineage
sēriō *adv* seriously, in all sincerity
sēri·us -a -um *adj* serious, earnest; *n* serious matter; seriousness, earnestness; *n pl* see **seria**
serm·ō -ōnis *m* conversation, talk; discussion, discourse; common talk, rumor, gossip; language, diction; prose, everyday language
sermōcin·or -ārī -ātus sum *vi* to talk, converse
sermuncŭl·us -ī *m* small talk, chitchat
serō serĕre serŭī sertum *vt* to join, connect; to entwine, wreathe; to compose, combine, contrive
serō serĕre sēvī satum *vt* to sow, plant; (fig) to sow the seeds of
sērō *adv* late
serp·ens -entis *m* or *f* creeping thing, snake, serpent, dragon
Serp·ens -entis *m* Serpent, Draco (*constellation*)
serpentigĕn·a -ae *m* dragon offspring
serpentip·ēs -ĕdis *adj* dragon-footed
serperastr·a -ōrum *n pl* splints (*for straightening the crooked legs of children*); officer who keeps his soldiers in check
serpillum see **serpyllum**
serpō serpĕre serpsī serptum *vi* to creep, crawl; to move along slowly, spread slowly
serpyll·um or **serpill·um** or **serpull·um -ī** *n* wild thyme
serr·a -ae *f* saw
serrāt·us -a -um *adj* serrated, notched
serrŭl·a -ae *f* small saw
sert·a -ae *f* wreath
sert·a -ōrum *n pl* wreaths, festoons
Sertōr·ius -iī or **-ī** *m* general of Marius who held out in Spain against the partisans of Sulla until he was assassinated by Perperna (*c.* 122-72 B.C.)
sert·us -a -um *pp* of **sero** (to join); *f* see **serta;** *n pl* see **serta**
ser·um -ī *n* whey; serum
sēr·us -a -um *adj* late; too late; **anni seri** ripe years; **ulmus sera** slow-growing elm; *n* late hour; **in serum rem trahere** to drag out the matter until late
serv·a -ae *f* slave (*female*)
servābil·is -e *adj* retrievable
serv·ans -antis *adj* keeping; (with *genit*) observant of
servāt·or -ōris *m* or **servātr·ix -īcis** *f* savior, preserver, deliverer
servīl·is -e *adj* slave, servile
servīliter *adv* slavishly
serv·iō -īre -īvī or **-iī -ītum** *vi* to be a servant or slave; to be obedient; (of buildings, land) to be mortgaged; (with *dat*) **a** to be a slave to, be subservient to; **b** to serve; **c** to comply with, conform to, humor; **d** to be devoted to, work at; **e** to serve, be of use to
servit·ium -iī or **-ī** *n* slavery, servitude; slaves
servitūd·ō -inis *f* servitude, slavery
servit·ūs -ūtis *f* slavery; serfdom; slaves; property liability, easement
Serv·ius Tull·ius -iī or **-ī** *m* sixth king of Rome

serv·ō -āre *vt* to watch over, preserve, protect; to store, reserve; to keep, retain; to observe; to keep to, continue to dwell in
servŏl·a -ae *f* young slave girl
servolicŏl·a -ae *f* slave of a slave (*female*)
servŏl·us -ī *m* young slave
serv·us or **serv·os -a -um** *adj* slave, servant; *mf* slave, servant
sescēnār·is -e *adj* a year and a half old
sescēnārĭ·us -a -um *adj* six-hundred-man (*cohort*)
sescēn·ī -ae -a *adj* six hundred each, six hundred in a group
sescentēsĭm·us -a -um *adj* six hundredth
sescent·ī -ae -a *adj* six hundred
sescentĭens or **sescentĭēs** *adv* six hundred times
sēsē see **se**
sescuncĭ·us -a -um *adj* inch and a half thick
sesĕl·is -is *f* seseli (*plant*)
sesqui *adv* more by a half, one and a half times
sesquialt·er -ĕra -ĕrum *adj* one and a half
sesquihōr·a -ae *f* an hour and a half
sesquimod·ĭus -ĭī or **-ī** *m* peck and a half
sesquioctāv·us -a -um *adj* having a ratio of nine to eight
sesquiŏp·us -ĕris *n* day and a half's work
sesquipedāl·is -e *adj* foot and a half long or wide
sesquiplāg·a -ae *f* blow and a half
sesquipl·ex -ĭcis *adj* one and a half times as much
sesquitertĭ·us -a -um *adj* containing one and a third; having a ratio of four to three
sessibŭl·um -ī *n* chair, seat, easy chair
sessĭl·is -e *adj* for sitting on; (plants) growing close to the ground, low-growing
sessĭ·ō -ōnis *f* sitting; session; loafing
sessĭt·ō -āre *vi* to sit much, keep sitting, rest
sessiuncŭl·a -ae *f* small group, small circle
sess·or -ōris *m* spectator; resident
sestert·ĭum -ĭī or **-ī** *n* sesterce
sestert·ĭus -ĭī or **-ī** (*genit pl:* **sestertĭum**) (abbreviated HS) *m* sesterce (*small silver coin, equal to one fourth of a denarius, i.e., about 8¢, and used as the ordinary Roman unit in accounting*); **centena milia sestertium** 100,000 sesterces; **deciens** (i.e., **deciens centena milia**) **sestertium** 1,000,000 sesterces
Sest·os or **Sest·us -ī** *f* city on the Hellespont
sēt- = saet-
Sētĭ·a -ae *f* town in Latium famous for its wine
Sētīn·us -a -um *adj* Setine; *n* Setine wine
sētius see **sequius**
seu *conj* or if; or; **seu . . . seu** whether . . . or
sevērē *adv* seriously; severely, austerely
sevērĭt·ās -ātis *f* severity, sternness, strictness
sevērĭtūd·ō -ĭnis *f* austerity
sevēr·us -a -um *adj* serious, grave; severe, strict, austere; ruthless, grim
sēvŏc·ō -āre *vt* to call aside, call away; to remove, withdraw, separate
sēv·um -ī *n* tallow, grease
sex (indecl) *adj* six
sexāgēnārĭ·us -a -um *adj* sixty-year-old
sexāgēn·ī -ae -a *adj* sixty each, sixty in a group
sexāgēsĭm·us -a -um *adj* sixtieth
sexāgĭens or **sexāgĭēs** *adv* sixty times
sexāgintā (indecl) *adj* sixty
sexangŭl·us -a -um *adj* hexagonal
sexcen- = sescen-
sexcēnārĭ·us -a -um *adj* six-hundred-man (*cohort*)
sexenn·is -e *adj* six-year-old, of six years; **sexenni die** in a six-year period
sexenn·ĭum -ĭī or **-ī** *n* six-year period, six years
sexĭens or **sexĭēs** *adv* six times
sexprīm·ī or **sex prīm·ī -ōrum** *m pl* six-member council (*in provincial towns*)
sextadecimān·ī -ōrum *m pl* soldiers of the sixteenth legion
sext·ans -antis *m* one sixth; small coin (*one sixth of an ace*); one sixth of a pint
sextār·ĭus -ĭī or **-ī** *m* pint
Sextīl·is -e *adj* of or belonging to the sixth month of the old Roman year which was afterwards called August in honor of Augustus
sextŭl·a -ae *f* sixth of an ounce
sextum *adv* for the sixth time
sext·us -a -um *adj* sixth
sext·us decĭm·us -a -um *adj* sixteenth
sexungŭl·a -ae *f* six-clawed woman, rapacious woman
sex·us -ūs *m* sex
sī *conj* if, if only; **quod si** but if; **si forte** if perchance, in the hope that; **si minus** if not
sibī see **se**
sībĭl·a -ōrum *n pl* hisses, hissing
sībĭl·ō -āre *vt* to hiss at; *vi* to hiss
sībĭl·us -a -um *adj & m* hissing
Sibyll·a or **Sibull·a -ae** *f* sibyl, prophetess
Sibyllīn·us -a -um *adj* sibylline
sīc *adv* thus, so, in this way; thus, as follows; in these circumstances; in such a way, to such a degree; (in assent) yes

Sicān·ī -ōrum *m pl* ancient people of Italy who migrated to Sicily
Sicānī·a -ae *f* Sicily
Sicān·is -ĭdis *adj* Sicilian
Sicānī·us -a -um *adj* Sicilian; *f* see **Sicania**
Sicān·us -a -um *adj* Sicilian; *m pl* see **Sicani**
sīcār·ĭus -ĭī or **-ī** *m* murderer, assassin; **inter sicarios accusare (defendere)** to prosecute (defend) on a murder charge
siccē *adv* firmly, solidly
siccĭt·ās -ātis *f* dryness; drought; firmness, solidity; dullness (*of style*)
sicc·ō -āre *vt* to dry, dry up, drain; to stanch, heal
siccocŭl·us -a -um *adj* dry-eyed
sicc·us -a -um *adj* dry; thirsty; sober; firm, solid (*body*); solid (*argument*); dry, insipid (*style*)
Sicilĭ·a -ae *f* Sicily
sicilicissĭt·ō -āre *vi* to act like a Sicilian
sīcīlicŭl·a -ae *f* sickle
Siciliens·is -e *adj* Sicilian
sīcine *adv* is this how . . . ?
sīcŭbi *adv* if anywhere, wheresoever
sīcŭl·a -ae *f* little dagger
Sicŭl·ī -ōrum *m pl* ancient Italian people who migrated to Sicily
sīcunde *conj* if from some place, if from anywhere
sīcut or **sīcŭtī** *conj* as, just as; (in elliptical clauses) just as, like; (introducing a comparison) as it were, so to speak; (introducing an example) as, as for instance; (of condition) as, in the same condition as; as if, just as if; **sicut . . . ita** although . . . yet
Sicy̆·ōn -ōnis *f* town in the N. Peloponnesus
Sicyōnĭ·us -a -um *adj* of Sicyon; *m pl* inhabitants of Sicyon
sīdereˇ·us -a -um *adj* starry; star-spangled; heavenly, divine
sīdō sīdĕre sīdī or **sēdī sessum** *vi* to sit down; to settle; (of birds) to alight, land; to sink; to settle down, subside; (of ships) to be grounded
Sīd·ōn -ōnis *f* city of Phoenicia
Sīdōn·is -ĭdis *adj* Phoenician; *f* Dido; Europa
Sīdōnĭ·us -a -um *adj* Sidonian, Phoenician; Theban; *m pl* Sidonians
sīd·us -ĕris *n* constellation; star, heavenly body; sky, heaven; light, glory, beauty, pride; season; climate, weather; (in astrology) star, destiny
Sigambr·ī -ōrum *m pl* powerful German tribe
Sīgē·um -ī *n* promontory near Troy where Achilles was said to have been buried
Sīgē·us -a -um *adj* Sigean
sigill·a -ōrum *n pl* figurines; seal (*on a seal ring*)
sigillāt·us -a -um *adj* adorned with little figures
signāt·or -ōris *m* sealer, signer; witness
signāt·us -a -um *adj* sealed, secured
signĭf·er -ĕra -ĕrum *adj* bearing the constellations, starry; *m* standard-bearer; chief, leader
signĭfĭc·ans -antis *adj* clear, distinct, expressive
significanter *adv* clearly, graphically
significātĭ·ō -ōnis *f* signal, indication, sign, mark; expression of approval, applause; meaning, sense, signification; emphasis
signĭfĭc·ō -āre *vt* to show, indicate, point out, express; to intimate; to notify, publish, make known; to portend; to mean, signify
sign·ō -āre *vt* to mark, stamp, impress, imprint; to seal, seal up; to coin; to point out, signify, indicate, express; to adorn, decorate; to distinguish, mark, note
sign·um -ī *n* sign, indication, proof; military standard, banner; password; cohort, maniple; omen, symptom; statue, picture; device on a seal, seal, signet; heavenly sign, constellation; **ab signis discedere** to break ranks, disband; **signa conferre** to engage in close combat; to concentrate troops; **signa constituere** to halt; **signa conversa ferre** to wheel around and attack; **signa ferre** to break camp; **signa movere** to advance; **signa movere in hostem** to advance against the enemy, attack the enemy; **signa proferre** to march forward, advance; **signa servare** to keep the order of battle; **signa sequi** to march in rank; **signa subsequi** to keep the order of battle; **signa transferre** to desert, join the other side; **signis collatis** in regular battle
sīlān·us -ī *m* jet of water
Silăr·us -ī *m* river forming the boundary between Lucania and Campania
sil·ens -entis *adj* silent, calm, quiet; *mf pl* the dead
silent·ĭum -ĭī or **-ī** *n* silence; inactivity; **silentium facere** to obtain silence; to keep silence; **silentium significare** to call for silence
Sīlēn·us -ī *m* teacher and constant companion of Bacchus, usually drunk
sil·ĕō -ēre -ŭī *vt* to leave unmentioned, say nothing about; *vi* to be silent, be still; to keep silence; to be hushed; to rest, cease
sil·er -ĕris *n* willow
silesc·ō -ĕre *vi* to become silent, fall silent, become hushed
sil·ex -ĭcis *m* flint, flint stone; cliff, crag; hardheartedness
silicern·ĭum -ĭī or **-ī** *n* funeral feast; (coll) old fossil
silīg·ō -ĭnis *f* winter wheat; wheat flour

silĭqu·a -ae *f* pod, husk; *f pl* pulse
sillўb·us -ī *m* label giving book's title
sīl·ō -ōnis *m* (man) button nose, snub nose
silūr·us -ī *m* sheatfish
sīl·us -a -um *adj* having a turned-up nose, snub-nosed
silv·a or **silŭ·a -ae** *f* woods, forest; shrubbery, bush, foliage, crop, growth; mass, abundance, quantity, material, supply
Silvān·us -ī *m* god of woods; *m pl* woodland gods
silvesc·ō -ĕre *vi* (of a vine) to run wild
silvestr·is -e *adj* wooded, overgrown with woods; woodland, living in woods; wild, growing wild; rural, pastoral; *n pl* woodlands
silvicŏl·a -ae *m* or *f* denizen of the forest
silvicultr·ix -īcis *adj fem* living in the woods
silvifrăg·us -a -um *adj* forest-smashing (*wind*)
silvōs·us -a -um *adj* wooded, woody
sīmĭ·a -ae *f* ape
simĭl·is -e *adj* similar; (with *genit* or *dat*) resembling, like, similar to; **homines inter se similes** men resembling one another; **veri similis** probable; realistic; *n* comparison, parallel
similiter *adv* similarly; **similiter atque** or **ac** just as; **similiter ut si** just as if
similitūd·ō -ĭnis *f* likeness, resemblance; imitation; analogy; comparison, simile; monotony; (with *genit*) similarity to; **est homini cum deo similitudo** there is a resemblance between a god and man
sīmiŏl·us -ī *m* monkey
simĭtū *adv* at the same time; (with **cum** + *abl*) together with
sīm·ĭus -ĭī or **-ī** *m* ape
Simŏ·īs -entis *m* river at Troy
Simōnĭd·ēs -is *m* famous lyric poet of Ceos (*fl* 500 B.C.); celebrated iambic poet of Amorgos (*7th cent.* B.C.)
simpl·ex -ĭcis *adj* single, simple, unmixed; plain, natural; frank; naive; in single file
simplicĭt·ās -ātis *f* simplicity; candor, frankness
simplicĭter *adv* simply, plainly; candidly, frankly
simpl·us -a -um *adj* simple; *n* simple sum
simpŭl·um -ī *n* small ladle
simpuv·ĭum -ĭī or **-ī** *n* libation bowl
simul *adv* together, at the same time; likewise, also; (with *abl* or **cum** + *abl*) with, together with; **simul atque** or **ac** or **et** as soon as; **simul . . . simul** both . . . and; *conj* as soon as
simulăcr·um -ī *n* image, likeness, representation; form, shape, phantom, ghost; conception; sign, emblem; mere shadow; portraiture, characterization
simulām·en -ĭnis *n* imitation, copy
simŭl·ans -antis *adj* imitating; (with *genit*) imitative of
simulātē *adv* insincerely, deceitfully
simulātĭ·ō -ōnis *f* faking, bluffing, bluff, pretense; **simulatione** (with *genit*) under the pretense of, under the guise of
simulāt·or -ōris *m* imitator; pretender, phoney
simŭl·ō -āre *vt* to imitate, copy, represent; to put on the appearance of, simulate
simult·ās -ātis *f* enmity, rivalry, feud, jealousy, grudge
sīmŭl·us -a -um *adj* rather snub-nosed
sīm·us -a -um *adj* snub-nosed, pug-nosed
sīn *conj* if however, if on the other hand, but if
sināp·i -is *n* or **sināp·is -is** *f* mustard
sincērē *adv* sincerely, honestly, frankly
sincērĭt·ās -ātis *f* soundness, integrity
sincēr·us -a -um *adj* sound, whole, clean, untainted; real, genuine
sincĭp·ut -ĭtis or **sincipitāment·um -ī** *n* half a head; cheek, jowl (*of a hog*); brain
sind·ōn -ŏnis *f* fine cotton or linen fabric, muslin
sine *prep* (with *abl*) without; **flammā sine** flameless
singillātim *adv* one by one, singly
singlārĭter see **singulariter**
singulār·is -e *adj* single, alone, one at a time; unique, unparalleled; *m pl* crack troops
singulārĭter or **singlārĭter** *adv* singly; particularly
singulārĭ·us -a -um *adj* single, separate
singulātim *adv* singly, individually
singŭl·ī -ae -a *adj* single, one at a time, individual; one each, one apiece; **in singulos dies** on each successive day; every day, daily; *m pl* individuals
singultim *adv* sobbingly, gaspingly; falteringly
singult·ĭō -īre *vi* to hiccup; to throb
singult·ō -āre *vt* to gasp out, spurt out; *vi* to sob, gasp; to gurgle
singult·us -ūs *m* sob, gasp; squirt (*of water, etc.*); death rattle
singŭl·us -a -um *adj* one by one, single; each one, one apiece
sinist·er -ra -rum *adj* left, on the left; (because in Roman augury the augur faced south, having the East on the left) favorable, auspicious, lucky; (because in Greek augury the augur faced north, having the East on his right) unfavorable, inauspicious, unlucky; wrong, perverse, improper; *m pl* soldiers on the left

flank; *f* left, left hand; left side; *n* left side; **a sinistra** on the left
sinisterit·ās -ātis *f* awkwardness
sinistrē *adv* badly, wrongly, perversely
sinistrorsum or **sinistrorsus** *adv* to the left
sinō sinĕre sīvī or **siī situm** *vt* to allow; **sine modo** only let, if only
Sin·ōn -ōnis *m* Greek soldier through whose treachery the Greeks were able to get the horse into Troy
Sinōp·a -ae or **Sinīp·ē -ēs** *f* Greek colony on the S. coast of the Euxine Sea
Sinuess·a -ae *f* city on the border between Latium and Campania
sīn·um -ī *n* large drinking cup
sinŭ·ō -āre *vt* to wind, curve, arch
sinuōs·us -a -um *adj* winding, sinuous, serpentine
sin·us -ūs *m* curved or bent surface, indentation, curve, fold, hollow; fold of the toga about the breast; pocket, purse; breast, bosom, lap; bay, gulf, lagoon; winding coast; valley, hollow; heart (*e.g., of a city*), interior; intimacy; **in sinu meo est** he is dear to me
sīn·us -ī *m* large drinking cup
sīpar·ium -iī or **-ī** *n* theater curtain; **post siparium** behind the scenes
sīph·ō -ōnis *m* siphon; fire engine
sīphuncŭl·us -ī *m* small pipe
Sipȳl·us -ī *m* mountain in Lydia
sīquandō or **sī quandō** *conj* if ever
sīquidem *conj* if in fact
sirempse or **sirempse** = **si rem ipsam** *adj* the same, e.g., **sirempse legem** the same law
Sīr·ēn -ēnis *f* Siren (*sea nymph who had the power of charming with her song*)
Sīri·us -a -um *adj* of Sirius, of the Dog Star; *m* Sirius, Dog Star
sirp·e -is *n* silphium (*plant*)
sīr·us -ī *m* underground granary
sīs = **sī vīs** please, if you please
sistō sistĕre stitī statum *vt* to cause to stand, make stand, put, place, set; to set up (*monument*); to establish; to stop, check, arrest; to put an end to; to produce in court; **pedem sistere** or **gradum sistere** to halt, stop; **se sistere** to present oneself, appear, come; **sisti non potest** the crisis cannot be met, the case is hopeless; **vadimonium sistere** to answer bail, show up in court; *vi* to stand, rest; to stop, stay; to stand firm, last, endure; to show up in court; (with *dat* or **contra** + *acc*) to stand firm against
sistrāt·us -a -um *adj* with a tambourine
sistr·um -ī *n* rattle, tambourine
Sīsyphīd·ēs -ae *m* descendant of Sisyphus, i.e., Ulysses
Sīsȳph·us -ī *m* son of Aeolus, king of Corinth, whose punishment in Hades was to roll a rock repeatedly up a hill
sitell·a -ae *f* lottery urn
Sīth·ōn -ōnis *adj* Thracian
Sīthŏn·is -idis or **Sīthoni·us -a -um** *adj* Thracian; *m pl* Thracians
sitīculōs·us -a -um *adj* thirsty, dry
sitī·ens -entis *adj* thirsting, thirsty; arid, parched; parching; (with *genit*) eager for
sitienter *adv* thirstily, eagerly
sit·iō -īre -īvī -iī *vt* to thirst for; *vi* to be thirsty
sit·is -is *f* thirst; (with *genit*) thirst for
sitīt·or -ōris *m* thirsty person; **sititor aquae** thirster for water
sittȳbus see **sillybus**
sitŭl·a -ae *f* bucket
sit·us -a -um *pp* of **sino**; *adj* lying, situated; founded; (with **in** + *abl*) resting on, dependent on
sit·us -ūs *m* position, situation, site; structure; neglect; mustiness; dust, dirt; idleness, inactivity, lack of use
sīve *conj* or if; or; **sive . . . sive** whether . . . or
smaragd·us -ī *m* or *f* emerald
smar·is -idis *f* a small sea fish
smīl·ax -ăcis *f* smilax, bindweed (*plant*)
Sminth·eus -ĕī *m* epithet of Apollo
Smyrn·a -ae *f* town in Asia Minor
sobol- = **subol-**
sōbriē *adv* soberly, moderately; sensibly
sōbriĕt·ās -ātis *f* temperance (*in drinking*)
sōbrīn·a -ae *f* cousin (*female, on the mother's side*)
sōbrīn·us -ī *m* cousin (*on the mother's side*)
sōbri·us -a -um *adj* sober; temperate, continent; sensible, reasonable
soccŭl·us -ī *m* small or short sock
socc·us -ī *m* sock; slipper; low shoe worn by actors in comedies; comedy
soc·er or **soc·ĕrus -ĕrī** *m* father-in-law
soci·a -ae *f* associate, companion, ally, partner (*female*)
sociābil·is -e *adj* compatible, intimate
sociāl·is -e *adj* allied, confederate; nuptial, conjugal; companionable, sociable
sociāliter *adv* sociably, in comradeship
sociènn·us -ī *m* comrade
sociĕt·ās -ātis *f* companionship, fellowship; association, society, partnership, alliance, confederacy
soci·ō -āre *vt* to unite, associate; to share
sociofraud·us -ī *m* heel, double crosser
soci·us -a -um *adj* joint, allied, confederate; held in common, common; *m* associate, companion, ally, partner; *f* see **socia**
sōcordi·a or **sēcordi·a -ae** *f* silliness, stupidity; apathy, laziness

sōcordius *adv* too apathetically
sōc·ors -ordis *adj* silly, stupid; apathetic, lazy, inactive
Sōcrăt·ēs -is *m* famous Athenian philosopher (469-399 B.C.)
Sōcratic·ī -ōrum *m pl* Socratics, disciples of Socrates
socr·us -ūs *f* mother-in-law
sodālici·us -a -um *adj* of companionship; *n* companionship, intimacy; society, secret society
sodāl·is -is *m* or *f* comrade, companion, fellow; member (*of a society, priestly college, etc.*); accomplice, conspirator; gallant
sodālit·ās -ātis *f* companionship, fellowship; society, club, association; secret society
sodālit- = sodalic-
sōdēs = si audes if you will, please
sōl sōlis *m* sun; sunlight, sunshine; day
sōlāciŏl·um -ī *n* bit of comfort
sōlāc·ĭum -ĭī or **-ī** *n* comfort, relief
sōlām·en -ĭnis *n* comfort
sōlār·is -e *adj* sun; **lumen solare** sunlight, sunshine
sōlār·ĭum -ĭī or **-ī** *n* sundial; clock; sunny spot, balcony
sōlāt- = solac-
sōlāt·or -ōris *m* comforter
soldūrĭ·ī -ōrum *m pl* retainers (*of a chieftain*)
soldus see **solidus**
solĕ·a -ae *f* sole; sandal; fetter; sole (*flat fish*)
soleār·ĭus -ĭī or **-ī** *m* sandal maker
soleāt·us -a -um *adj* wearing sandals
solĕō solēre solĭtus sum *vi* (with *inf*) to be in the habit of, usually, e.g., **solet cenare sero** he usually eats late; (with **cum** + *abl*) to have intercourse with
solĭdē *adv* for certain; fully, wholly
solidĭt·ās -ātis *f* solidity
solĭd·ō -āre *vt* to make firm, make dense; to strengthen
solĭd·us or **sold·us -a -um** *adj* solid, firm, dense; whole, entire; genuine, real; trustworthy; firm, resolute; *n* entire sum, total; solid, solid body, mass, substance; solid earth
sōliferrĕ·um -ī *n* all-iron spear
sōlistĭm·us -a -um *adj* perfect; **tripudium solistimum** perfectly auspicious omen
sōlitārĭ·us -a -um *adj* solitary, lonely
sōlitūd·ō -ĭnis *f* loneliness; deprivation; wilderness
solĭt·us -a -um *adj* usual, customary, characteristic; *n* the usual, the customary; **formosior solito** more handsome than usual, unusually handsome; **magis solito** or **plus solito** more than usual
sol·ĭum -ĭī or **-ī** *n* seat, chair; throne; dominion, sway; bathtub; stone coffin, sarcophagus
sōlivăg·us -a -um *adj* roaming alone; single, solitary
sollemn·is -e *adj* annual, periodic; religious, solemn; usual; *n* usage, practice; solemn rite, solemnity, ceremony, feast, sacrifice; festival, games (*in observance of Roman holy days*)
sollemnĭter *adv* solemnly, religiously
soll·ers -ertis *adj* skilled, skillful, expert, clever
sollerter *adv* skillfully, expertly, cleverly
sollertĭ·a -ae *f* skill, ingenuity, shrewdness; clever plan; (with *genit*) skill in
sollicitātĭ·ō -ōnis *f* vexation, anxiety; incitement, instigation
sollicĭtē *adv* anxiously, with solicitude; diligently
sollicĭt·ō -āre *vt* to shake, disturb; to disquiet, annoy, molest; to worry, make anxious; to provoke, tempt; to stir up, incite, incite to revolt
sollicitūd·ō -ĭnis *f* anxiety, uneasiness
sollicĭt·us -a -um *adj* stirred up, stormy (*sea*); tossed (*by the waves*); troubled, disturbed, disquieted, restless; anxious, solicitous, apprehensive, worried
sollif- = solif-
sollist- = solist-
soloecism·us -ī *m* grammatical mistake, solecism
Sol·ōn -ōnis *m* famous Athenian legislator (*c.* 640-*c.* 560 B.C.)
sōl·or -ārī -ātus sum *vt* to console, comfort; to relieve, mitigate (*fear, worry*)
sōlstitiāl·is -e *adj* of the summer solstice; midsummer's; solar
sōlstit·ĭum -ĭī or **-ī** *n* summer solstice; midsummer, summer heat
sol·um -ī *n* bottom, ground, floor; soil, land, country; sole (*of foot or shoe*)
sōlum *adv* only, merely, barely; **non solum . . . sed etiam** not only . . . but also
sōl·us -a -um *adj* only, single, sole, alone; lonely, solitary
solūtē *adv* loosely, freely, without hindrance; negligently; without vigor
solūt·us -a -um *adj* loose, untied, unbandaged; negligent; free; fluent; unrhythmical; uncontrolled; exempt, free; unbiased; unbridled, loose
solūtĭ·ō -ōnis *f* loosening; payment
solvō solvĕre solvī or **solŭī solūtum** *vt* to loosen, untie; to free, release; to dissolve, break up; detach, disengage; to unlock, open; to melt, turn, change; to relax, smooth, soothe; to impair, weaken, destroy; to acquit, absolve; to accomplish, fulfill; to pay, pay off; to solve, explain; to suffer, undergo (*punishment*); to remove, get rid of (*feelings*); *vi* to weigh anchor, set sail
Solўm·a -ōrum *n pl* Jerusalem

somniculōsē *adv* sleepily, drowsily
somniculōs·us -a -um *adj* sleepy, drowsy
somnif·er -ĕra -ĕrum *adj* sleep-inducing, soporific; deadly (*poison*)
somni·ō -āre *vt* to dream of; to day-dream about, imagine; **somnium somniare** to have a dream
somn·ium -iī or **-ī** *n* dream; day-dreaming; nightmare
somn·us -ī *m* sleep; night; sleep of death; indolence
sonābil·is -e *adj* noisy
sonip·ēs -ĕdis *adj* loud-hoofed; *m* steed
sonit·us -ūs *m* sound, noise
sonivi·us -a -um *adj* noisy
son·ō -āre -ŭī -itum *vt* to speak, sound, express; to mean; to sound like; *vi* to sound, ring, resound, make a noise
son·or -ōris *m* sound, noise, clang
sonōr·us -a -um *adj* sonorous, loud, noisy, clanging
sons sontis *adj* guilty, criminal
sontic·us -a -um *adj* important
son·us -ī *m* sound, noise; tone (*of style*)
sophi·a -ae *f* wisdom
sophist·ēs -ae *m* sophist
Sophŏcl·ēs -is *m* famous Greek writer of tragedies (*c.* 495-406 B.C.)
Sophoclē·us -a -um *adj* Sophoclean, of Sophocles
soph·us -a -um *adj* wise; *m* wise man, sage
sōp·iō -īre -īvī or **-iī -ītum** *vt* to put to sleep; to stun, knock unconscious; (fig) to calm, still, settle, lull
sop·or -ōris *m* deep sleep; stupor; apathy, indifference; sleeping potion
sopōrāt·us -a -um *adj* stupefied; unconscious; buried in sleep; allayed (*grief*); soporific
sopōrif·er -ĕra -ĕrum *adj* sleep-inducing
sopōr·us -a -um *adj* drowsy
Sōract·e -is *n* mountain in Etruria about twenty-six miles from Rome
sōrăc·um -ī *n* hamper
sorb·ĕō -ēre -ŭī *vt* to suck in, gulp down; to absorb; (fig) to swallow (*e.g., hatred*)
sorbill·ō -āre *vt* to sip
sorbilō *adv* drop by drop, bit by bit
sorbiti·ō -ōnis *f* drink, pleasant drink
sorb·um -ī *n* Juneberry, serviceberry
sorb·us -ī *f* Juneberry tree, serviceberry tree
sord·ĕō -ēre *vi* to be dirty, be shabby; to appear worthless
sord·ēs -is *f* dirt, filth; shabbiness, squalor; *f pl* shabby clothes, rags (*often worn as a sign of mourning*); mourning; meanness (*of behavior*); low rank, low condition, vileness; dregs, rabble; vulgarity
sord·escō -escĕre -ŭī *vi* to become dirty, become soiled
sordidāt·us -a -um *adj* in dirty or shabby clothes (*esp. as a sign of mourning*)
sordidē *adv* vilely, meanly, vulgarly
sordidŭl·us -a -um *adj* rather soiled, rather shabby; (fig) low, mean
sordid·us -a -um *adj* dirty, filthy, shabby; soiled, stained; dressed in mourning clothes; low (*rank*); vile, vulgar (*behavior*)
sorditūd·ō -inis *f* dirt, filth
sōr·ex -icis *m* shrewmouse
sōricīn·us -a -um *adj* squealing like mice
sōrīt·ēs -ae *m* sorites (*logical conclusion drawn from cumulative arguments*)
sor·or -ōris *f* sister; cousin; companion, playmate; **sorores doctae** Muses; **sorores tres** three Fates; **sorores tristes** gloomy Fates
sorōricīd·a -ae *f* murderer of a sister
sorōri·us -a -um *adj* sister's, of a sister; sisterly; **stuprum sororium** incest with a sister
sors sortis *f* lot; casting of lots, decision by lot; prophecy; fate, destiny, lot in life; portion, share; sort, kind, class
sorsum see **seorsum**
sortilĕg·us -a -um *adj* prophetic; *m* soothsayer, fortune-teller
sorti·ō -īre or **sort·ior -īrī -ītus sum** *vt* to cast or draw lots for; to allot, assign by lot, appoint by lot; to obtain by lot; to choose, select; to share, divide; to receive, get by chance; *vi* to cast or draw lots
sortīti·ō -ōnis *f* drawing lots, determining by lots
sortītō *adv* by lot; by fate
sortīt·us -ūs *m* lottery
Sosi·ī -ōrum *m pl* the Sosii (*two brothers famous as booksellers in Rome at the time of Horace*)
sosp·es -itis *adj* safe and sound; auspicious, lucky
sospit·a -ae *f* preserver (*epithet of Juno*)
sospitāl·is -e *adj* beneficial
sospit·ō -āre *vt* to preserve, protect
sōt·ēr -ēris *m* savior, deliverer, protector
sōtēri·a -ōrum *n pl* party thrown for a person recovering from an illness
spād·ix -īcis *adj* chestnut-brown
spad·ō -ōnis *m* eunuch
spargō spargĕre sparsī sparsum *vt* to scatter, sprinkle, strew; to scatter, disperse; to disseminate, broadcast; to spot, dapple
sparsi·ō -ōnis *f* sprinkling
spars·us -a -um *pp* of **spargo**; *adj* freckled, spotty
Spart·a -ae or **Spart·ē -ēs** *f* Sparta (*capital of Laconia, also called Lacedaemon*)
Spartăc·us -ī *m* Thracian gladiator who led a revolt of gladiators against Rome in 73-71 B.C.

Spartān·us -a -um *adj* Spartan
Spartiāt·ēs -ae *m* Spartan
Spartiātic·us or **Spartic·us -a -um** *adj* Spartan
spart·um -ī *n* Spanish broom (*plant, used in making ropes, nets, etc.*)
sparŭl·us -ī *m* bream (*fish*)
spar·us -ī *m* hunting spear
spath·a -ae *f* broad two-edged sword
spatĭ·or -ārī -ātus sum *vi* to walk, stroll, take a walk; to walk solemnly; to spread out
spatiōsē *adv* extensively; long, for a long time
spatiōs·us -a -um *adj* spacious; broad, large; prolonged
spat·ium -iī or **-ī** *n* room, space, extent; open space, public square; distance (*between two points*); walk, promenade (*place*); interval, period; time, opportunity; measure, quantity (*in metrics*); lap; race track
specĭ·ēs -ēī *f* sight, view; outward appearance, outline, shape; fine appearance, beauty; deceptive appearance, show, semblance, pretense, pretext; resemblance, likeness; display, splendor; vision, apparition; image, statue; idea, notion; reputation; species, sort; **in speciem** or **per speciem** as a pretext, for the sake of appearances
specill·um -ī *n* probe (*surgical instrument*)
specĭm·en -ĭnis *n* mark, sign, proof, example; model, ideal
speciō specĕre spexī *vt* to look at, behold
speciōsē *adv* splendidly
speciōs·us -a -um *adj* handsome, good-looking, beautiful; plausible; specious
spectābĭl·is -e *adj* visible; remarkable
spectācŭl·um or **spectācl·um -ī** *n* sight, spectacle; public performance; stage play; theater
spectām·en -ĭnis *n* sign, proof
spectātĭ·ō -ōnis *f* observation, view; examining, testing
spectāt·or -ōris *m* observer; spectator; critic, judge
spectātr·ix -īcis *f* on-looker, observer; spectator
spectāt·us -a -um *adj* tried, tested, proved; esteemed
spectĭ·ō -ōnis *f* observing the auspices; right to take the auspices
spect·ō -āre *vt* to observe, watch; to face in the direction of; to consider; to bear in mind; to aim at, tend towards; to examine, test
spectr·um -ī *n* specter, apparition
specŭl·a -ae *f* look-out, watch tower; summit
spēcŭl·a -ae *f* bit of hope
speculābund·us -a -um *adj* on the look-out
speculār·is -e *adj* transparent; *n pl* windowpane, window
speculāt·or -ōris *m* spy; explorer
speculātōrĭ·us -a -um *adj* for spying, for reconnaissance; *f* reconnaissance ship
speculātr·ix -īcis *f* spy (*female*)
specŭl·or -ārī -ātus sum *vt* to reconnoiter, observe, watch for
specŭl·um -ī *n* mirror (*made of polished metal*)
spec·us -ūs *m* or *n* cave, cavern; artificial excavation, ditch, canal, channel, pit; hole, cavity (*of a wound, etc.*)
spēlae·um -ī *n* den, cave
spēlunc·a -ae *f* cave
spērābĭl·is -e *adj* possible (*able to be hoped for*)
spērāt·us -a -um *adj* hoped for, longed for, desired; *f* fiancee, bride-to-be
Sperchē·is -ĭdis *adj* of the Spercheos
Sperchē·os or **Sperchī·us -ī** *m* large river in S. Thessaly
spernō spernĕre sprēvī sprētum *vt* to remove; to scorn, reject
spēr·ō -āre *vt* to hope for, expect, look forward to; to trust, trust in; to anticipate, await with fear
spēs speī *f* hope, expectation; anticipation, apprehension (*of evil*); **praeter spem** beyond all expectation; unexpectedly
Speusipp·us -ī *m* nephew of Plato and his successor as head of the Academy (347-339 B.C.)
sphaer·a -ae *f* sphere, globe, ball
sphaeristēr·ium -iī or **-ī** *n* tennis court
Sphin·x -gis *f* sphinx
spīc·a -ae *f* point; ear (*of grain*); tuft, top, head (*of plants*)
spīcĕ·us -a -um *adj* made of ears of grain
spīcŭl·um -ī *n* point; sting; dart, arrow
spīc·um -ī *n* ear (*of grain*)
spīn·a -ae *f* thorn; thorn bush; prickle (*of animals*); backbone, spine; back; *f pl* subtleties
spīnēt·um -ī *n* thorn hedge, thorny thicket
spīnĕ·us -a -um *adj* made of thorns, thorn
spīnĭf·er -ĕra -ĕrum *adj* prickly
spīnōs·us -a -um *adj* thorny, prickly; (fig) stinging, irritating (*worries*); confused, obscure (*style*)
spint·ēr -ēris *m* elastic bracelet
spintrĭ·a -ae *m* male prostitute
spinturnīc·ium -iī or **-ī** *n* bird of ill omen
spīn·us -ī *f* blackthorn, sloe tree
spīr·a -ae *f* coil (*of a serpent*); chin strap
spīrābĭl·is -e *adj* good to breathe, life-giving (*air*)
spīrācŭl·um -ī *n* pore, vent; breathing space
spīrāment·um -ī *n* pore, vent; breathing space, pause, instant
spīrit·us -ūs *m* breathing, breath; breeze; air; breath of life, life; in-

spiration; spirit, character, courage; pride, arrogance; morale; **spiritum ducere** to take a breath, breathe
spīr·ō -āre *vt* to exhale, breathe out; to aspire to, aim at; *vi* to breathe; to be alive; to be favorable; to have poetic inspiration
spissāt·us -a -um *adj* condensed, concentrated
spissē *adv* thickly, closely, tightly; slowly
spissesc·ō -ĕre *vi* to condense, become thick
spissigrăd·us -a -um *adj* slow-paced
spiss·ō -āre *vt* to condense, concentrate
spiss·us -a -um *adj* thick, tight, dense; slow, late; difficult
splēn splēnis *m* spleen
splend·ĕō -ēre *vi* to be clear and bright, shine, gleam; to be illustrious, be glorious
splendesc·ō -ĕre *vi* to become clear and bright
splendĭd·us -a -um *adj* clear and bright, gleaming, glistening, sparkling; spotless, noble (*character*); splendid, magnificent; sumptuous; showy; illustrious
splend·or -ōris *m* brightness, brilliance; clearness; splendor, magnificence; noble
splēniāt·us -a -um *adj* wearing a patch
splēn·ium -iī or **-ī** *n* patch (*for the face*)
spoliāti·ō -ōnis *f* stripping, plundering; unjust deprivation (*of honor or dignity*); ousting (*from public office*)
spoliāt·or -ōris *m* or **spoliātr·ix -īcis** *f* despoiler, robber
spoliāt·us -a -um *adj* stripped, robbed
spoli·ō -āre *vt* to strip of clothes; to pillage, plunder, rob
spol·ium -iī or **-ī** *n* hide, skin; spoils, booty, loot
spond·a -ae *f* bed frame, sofa frame; bed, sofa
spondāl·ium or **spondaul·ium -iī** or **-ī** *n* ritual hymn accompanied by a flute
spondĕō spondēre spopondī sponsum *vt* to promise solemnly, pledge, vow; to promise in marriage; *vi* (law) to give a guarantee, put up bail; (with **pro** + *abl*) to vouch for
spondē·us -ī *m* spondee
spondÿl·us -ī *m* mussel
spongi·a -ae *f* sponge; coat of mail
spons·a -ae *f* fiancée
sponsāl·ia -ium *n pl* engagement; engagement party
sponsi·ō -ōnis *f* solemn promise, guarantee; bet; (law) agreement between two parties that the loser pay a certain sum to the other
spons·or -ōris *m* guarantor, surety
spons·us -a -um *pp* of **spondeo;** *m* fiancé, bridegroom; *f* see **sponsa;** *n* agreement, engagement
spons·us -ūs *m* contract
sponte (only *abl*) *f* (of persons, mostly with possessive *adj*) of one's own accord, voluntarily; by oneself, unaided; (of things) of itself, spontaneously; on its own account, for its own sake
sport·a -ae *f* plaited basket; sieve
sportell·a -ae *f* little basket, lunch basket
sportŭl·a -ae *f* little basket (*in which gifts of food were given by the patron to his clients*); dole, present (*of food or money*); gift
sprēti·ō -ōnis *f* scorn, contempt
sprēt·or -ōris *m* despiser
sprētus *pp* of **sperno**
spūm·a -ae *f* foam, froth; lather; scum
spūmāt·us -a -um *adj* covered with foam
spūmesc·ō -ĕre *vi* to grow foamy
spūmĕ·us -a -um *adj* foaming, frothing
spūmĭf·er -ĕra -ĕrum *adj* foaming
spūmĭg·er -ĕra -ĕrum *adj* foaming
spūm·ō -āre *vi* to foam, froth
spūmōs·us -a -um *adj* full of foam, foaming; bombastic (*poem*)
spuō spuĕre spuī spūtum *vt* to spit, spit out; *vi* to spit
spurcāt·us -a -um *adj* foul, filthy
spurcē *adv* filthily; in filthy language
spurcidĭc·us -a -um *adj* foul-mouthed, filthy, smutty, obscene
spurcĭfĭc·us -a -um *adj* smutty, obscene
spurciti·a -ae or **spurciti·ēs -ēī** *f* filth, smut
spurc·ō -āre *vt* to make filthy, foul up; to defile
spurc·us -a -um *adj* (morally) filthy, dirty
spūtātilĭc·us -a -um *adj* deserving to be spit at, contemptible, disgusting
spūtāt·or -ōris *m* spitter
spūt·ō -āre *vt* to spit, spit out; to avert by spitting
spūt·um -ī *n* spit
squāl·ĕō -ēre -uī *vi* to be rough, be scaly, be parched, be wrankled; to be coated, be clotted, be stiff; to be covered with filth; to be covered with weeds, be overgrown; to wear mourning clothes, go in mourning
squālĭdē *adv* coarsely
squālĭd·us -a -um *adj* rough, scaly; stiff, coated with dirt, squalid; in mourning; rough, coarse (*speech*); cracked, parched (*land*)
squāl·or -ōris *m* squalor, dirtiness; desolation; filthy garments (*neglected as a sign of mourning*)
squal·us -ī *m* shark
squām·a -ae *f* scale; scale armor; fish
squāmĕ·us -a -um *adj* scaly
squāmĭf·er -ĕra -ĕrum *adj* scaly

squāmĭg·er -ĕra -ĕrum *adj* scaly; *m pl* fish
squāmōs·us -a -um *adj* covered with scales, scaly
squill·a or **scill·a -ae** *f* shrimp
st *interj* sh!
stabilīment·um -ī *n* support
stabil·iō -īre -īvī -ītum *vt* to stabilize; to establish
stabĭl·is -ē *adj* stable, firm, steady; steadfast, unwavering, immutable
stabilĭt·ās -ātis *f* stability, firmness, steadiness, durability
stabiliter *adv* firmly
stabŭl·ō -āre *vt* to stable or house (*animals*); *vi* to have a stall
stabŭl·um -ī *n* stable, stall; lair; hut; brothel
stact·a -ae or **stact·ē -ēs** *f* myrrh oil
stad·ium -iī or **-ī** *n* furlong; race track
Stagīr·a -ōrum *n pl* town in Macedonia, the birthplace of Aristotle
Stagīrīt·es -ae *m* Aristotle
stagn·ō -āre *vt* to overflow, inundate; *vi* to form a pool; to be inundated
stagn·um -ī *n* pool, swamp, lake, lagoon; straits; waters
stalagm·ium -iī or **-ī** *n* eardrop, earring (*with pendant*)
stām·en -ĭnis *n* warp (*of a loom*); thread; string (*of an instrument*); fillet (*worn by priests*)
stāminĕ·us -a -um *adj* full of threads, consisting of threads, wrapped in threads
Stat·a -ae *f* surname of Vesta
statārĭ·us -a -um *adj* standing, stationary; steady, calm; *m pl* actors in a type of comedy; *f* quiet or refined comedy
statēr·a -ae *f* scales; **statera aurificis** goldsmith's scales
staticŭl·us -ī *m* a dance
statim *adv* at once, immediately, on the spot
statĭ·ō -ōnis *f* standing still; station, post; position; residence; anchorage; *f pl* sentries
Stāt·ius -iī or **-ī** *m* P. Papinius Statius (*poet of the Silver Age of Latin literature, c.* 40-96 A.D.)
statīv·us -a -um *adj* stationary; *n pl* bivouac
stat·or -ōris *m* magistrate's attendant
Stat·or -ōris *m* Stayer (*epithet of Jupiter, who kept the Roman soldiers from retreating*)
statŭ·a -ae *f* statue
statūm·en -ĭnis *n* rib (*of a hull*)
stat·ŭō -uĕre -ŭī -ūtum *vt* to cause to stand, bring to a stop; to set up, erect; to establish (*precedent, etc.*); to set, fix, determine; to decide, settle; to decree; to strengthen, support; to appoint, create; to inflict, pass (*sentence, punishment*); to hold, think, consider; to fix (*a price*); to draw up, arrange (*a battle line*)
stat·us -a -um *pp* of **sisto;** *adj* fixed, set, appointed
stat·us -ūs *m* position, posture; position, situation, condition; social status, rank; form of government; (mil) position; **status rei publicae** type of government
statūt·us -a -um *adj* tall
steg·a -ae *f* deck
stell·a -ae *f* star; constellation; **stella comans** comet; **stella diurna** Lucifer; **stella errans** planet
stell·ans -antis *adj* starry
stellāt·us -a -um *adj* set with stars, starry; made into a star
stellĭf·er -ĕra -ĕrum *adj* star-bearing, starry
stellĭg·er -ĕra -ĕrum *adj* star-bearing, starry
stellĭ·ō -ōnis *m* newt, lizard with spotted back
stemm·a -ătis *n* genealogical tree, pedigree; *n pl* antiquity, history
stercorĕ·us -a -um *adj* full of dung
stercŏr·ō -āre *vt* to manure, fertilize
sterc·us -ŏris *n* manure, dung
sterĭl·is -e *adj* sterile, barren; causing barrenness, blighting; empty, bare; unprofitable; unrequited (*love*); wild (*trees*)
sterilĭt·ās -ātis *f* sterility, barrenness
stern·ax -ācis *adj* bucking (*horse*)
sternō sternĕre strāvī strātum *vt* to strew, spread; to pave (*roads, etc.*); to knock down, bring low, slay; to raze, level; to flatten, smooth; to calm, calm down; **sterni** to stretch out (*on the ground*)
sternūment·um -ī *n* sneezing, sneeze
sternŭ·ō -ĕre -ī *vt* to give (*e.g., an omen*) by sneezing; *vi* to sneeze; to sputter
Sterŏp·ē -ēs *f* one of the Pleiades
sterquilīnĭ·um -iī or **-ī** or **sterquilīn·um -ī** *n* dung heap; (term of abuse) heap of dung
stert·ō -ĕre *vi* to snore
Stēsichŏr·us -ī *m* Greek lyric poet of Himera in Sicily (*c.* 640-*c.* 555 B.C.)
Sthenĕl·us -ī *m* king of Mycenae, son of Perseus, and father of Eurystheus; king of the Ligurians and father of Cycnus who was changed into a swan
stibad·ium -iī or **-ī** *n* semicircular seat
stigm·a -ătis *n* mark, brand; stigma (*of disgrace*)
stigmatĭ·ās -ae *m* branded slave
stigmōs·us -a -um *adj* branded
still·a -ae *f* drop; mere drop
still·ō -āre *vt & vi* to drip
stil·us -ī *m* stylus (*pointed instrument for writing*); writing, composition; style (*of writing or speaking*)
stimulātĭ·ō -ōnis *f* stimulation, incitement

stimulātr·ix -īcis *f* inciter (*female*)
stimulĕ·us -a -um *adj* of goads
stimŭlō -āre *vt* to goad, torment; to spur on, incite, excite
stimŭl·us -ī *m* or **stimŭl·um -ī** *n* goad, prick; (mil) pointed stake concealed below the ground; (fig) stimulus, incentive, spur
stingu·ō -ĕre *vt* to quench, extinguish
stīpātī·ō -ōnis *f* crowd, throng
stīpāt·or -ōris *m* attendant; *m pl* retinue
stīpendārī·us -a -um *adj* liable to tax, tributary; *m pl* tributary peoples; mercenary troops
stīpend·ĭum -ĭī or **-ī** *n* tax, tribute, tariff; (mil) pay; military service; year's service, campaign; **emereri stipendia** to have served out one's term; **emeritis stipendiis** at the end of one's military service, at discharge; **merere stipendia** or **mereri stipendia** to serve, serve in the army
stīp·es -ĭtis *m* log, trunk; branch, tree; blockhead
stīp·ō -āre *vt* to crowd, cram, pack; to crowd around, accompany in a group
stips stipis *f* gift, donation, alms
stipŭl·a -ae *f* stalk, blade; stubble; reed pipe
stipulātī·ō -ōnis *f* agreement, bargain; (law) formal promise
stipulātiuncŭl·a -ae *f* insignificant promise, slight stipulation
stipulāt·us -a -um *adj* promised
stipŭl·or -ārī -ātus sum *vt* to stipulate; *vi* to bargain; (law) to make a formal promise
stīrī·a -ae *f* icicle
stirpĭtus *adv* by the roots
stirp·s or **stirp·ēs** or **stirp·is -is** *f* stock, stem, stalk, root; plant, shrub; race, lineage; offspring, descendant; character, nature; root, source, foundation, beginning, origin
stīv·a -ae *f* plow handle
stlattārī·us or **stlātārī·us -a -um** *adj* imported, costly
stlopp·us -ī *m* slap (*sound produced by slapping an inflated cheek*)
stō stāre stetī statum *vi* to stand, stand still, remain standing; to stand firm, hold one's ground; to stand upright; (of hair) to stand up straight, stand on end; (of eyes) to remain fixed; (of battle) to continue; (of a ship) to be moored, ride at anchor; to be motionless; to be stuck; to depend, rest; to take sides, take part; (with *abl* of price) to come to, cost; (with *abl* or **in** + *abl*) to depend on, rest with; (with **per** + *acc* of person) to depend on, be due to, be the fault of, thanks to
Stōĭc·a -ōrum *n pl* Stoic philosophy
Stōĭcē *adv* like a Stoic
Stōĭc·us -a -um *adj* Stoic; *m* Stoic, Stoic philosopher; *n pl* see **Stoica**
stol·a -ae *f* dress (*long outer garment worn by Roman women and reaching from the neck to the ankles*); ceremonial gown (*worn by musicians*)
stolāt·us -a -um *adj* wearing a stola; (fig) proper for a lady, lady-like
stolĭdē *adv* stupidly
stolĭd·us -a -um *adj* dull, stupid, stolid, slow
stomăch·or -ārī -ātus sum *vi* to be annoyed, fret, fume, glower
stomachōsĭus *adv* rather angrily
stomachōs·us -a -um *adj* irritable, resentful
stomăch·us -ī *m* stomach; taste, appetite; irritation, anger, resentment; **stomachus bonus** good appetite; good humor, patience
storĕ·a or **storĭ·a -ae** *f* straw mat, rope mat
strab·ō -ōnis *m* squinter
străg·ēs -is *f* heap, confused mass, pile of debris; havoc, massacre
strāgŭl·us -a -um *adj* covering, serving as a covering; *n* rug, carpet; bedspread; horse blanket
strām·en -ĭnis *n* straw
strāment·um -ī *n* straw; covering, saddle cloth; **stramentum agreste** straw bed
strāmĭnĕ·us -a -um *adj* straw, made of straw
strangŭl·ō -āre *vt* to choke, stifle
strangūrĭ·a -ae *f* strangury
stratēgēm·a -ătis *n* stratagem; trick
stratēg·us -ī *m* commander, general; master of ceremonies
stratiōtĭc·us -a -um *adj* soldier-like, soldierly, military
strāt·us -a -um *pp* of **sterno**; *n* quilt, blanket; bed, couch; horse blanket, pack saddle; pavement
strēn·a -ae *f* good-luck omen
strēnŭē *adv* briskly, quickly, actively, strenuously
strēnuĭt·ās -ātis *f* briskness, vigor, liveliness
strēnŭ·ō -āre *vi* to be brisk
strēnŭ·us -a -um *adj* brisk, vigorous, active; fast (*ship*); restless
strepĭt·ō -āre *vi* to be noisy, clatter, rustle
strepĭt·us -ūs *m* noise, din, racket; crash, bang, clank, rumble, rustle, creak, squeak; sound (*of musical instruments*)
strep·ō -ĕre -ŭī -ĭtum *vt* to shout; *vi* to make a noise (*of any kind*); to rattle, clatter, clang, rumble, rustle, creak, squeak; to roar; to hum, murmur; (of musical instruments) to sound, blare; (of places) to ring, resound, be filled
strĭāt·a -ae *f* scallop
strictim *adv* superficially, cursorily
strictūr·a -ae *f* mass of molten iron
strict·us -a -um *pp* of **stringo**; *adj* close, tight, narrow
strīd·ĕō -ēre -ī or **strīd·ō -ĕre -ī** *vi* to make a high-pitched noise; to hiss, whistle, whizz, shriek, scream; to grate, buzz, rattle

strīd·or -ōris *m* shrill sound, hiss, shriek, scream, whine; harsh noise, grating, rattle, buzz
strīdŭl·us -a -um *adj* shrill, strident, hissing, whistling, creaking
strigĭl·is -is *f* scraper
strig·ō -āre *vi* to stop, halt; to lose strength, give out
strigōs·us -a -um *adj* lean, thin; bald (*style*)
stringō stringĕre strinxī strictum *vt* to strip, clip; to draw (*sword*); to draw tight, tie tight; to press together, compress; to touch lightly, graze; to border on, touch (*places*); to affect, touch, move, pain, wound (*mind, good name, etc.*); to waste, consume
string·or -ōris *m* twinge, shock
strix strigis *f* owl, screech owl
stroph·a -ae *f* trick
Strophăd·es -um *f pl* island home of the Harpies
strophiār·ius -iī or **-ī** *m* brassiere maker
stroph·ium -iī or **-ī** *n* brassiere; head band, chaplet
Stroph·ius -iī or **-ī** *m* king of Phocis and father of Pylades
structĭl·is -e *adj* building, for building
struct·or -ōris *m* builder, mason, carpenter; carver (*at table*)
structūr·a -ae *f* construction; structure
structus *pp of* **struo**
stru·ēs -is *f* pile, heap
stru·ix -īcis *f* pile, heap
strūm·a -ae *f* tumor, swollen gland
strūmōs·us -a -um *adj* scrofulous
struō struĕre struxī structum *vt* to build, build up, erect; to arrange, deploy (*troops*); to arrange, regulate; to occasion, contrive, plot
strūthĕ·us -a -um *adj* sparrow's
strūthiocamēl·us -ī *m* ostrich
Strȳm·ōn -ŏnis *m* river forming the border between Macedonia and Thrace
Strȳmonĭ·us -a -um *adj* Strymonian, Thracian
stud·eō -ēre -uī *vt* to desire, be eager for; *vi* to be eager; (*with dat*) **a** to be eager for, be keen on, be enthusiastic about, take pains with, busy oneself with, apply oneself to; **b** to study; **c** to be a partisan of
studiōsē *adv* eagerly, enthusiastically, diligently
studiōs·us -a -um *adj* eager, keen, enthusiastic; studious; (*with genit*) partial to (*a person or cause*); (*with genit or dat*) eager for, keen on, enthusiastic about, devoted to, fond of, desirous of; **litterarum studiosus** studious
stud·ium -iī or **-ī** *n* eagerness, keenness, enthusiasm; devotion (*to a person*); party spirit; study; (*with genit*) eagerness for, enthusiasm for
stultē *adv* foolishly
stultiloquentĭ·a -ae *f* or **stultiloqu·ium -iī** or **-ī** *n* silly talk
stultilŏqu·us -a -um *adj* talking foolishly
stultitĭ·a -ae *f* foolishness, silliness
stultivĭd·us -a -um *adj* foolish-looking
stult·us -a -um *adj* foolish, silly, stupid
stūp·a -ae *f* tow, coarse flax, hemp
stupe·faciō -facĕre -fēcī -factum (*passive:* **stupe·fīō -fĭerī -factus sum**) *vt* to stupefy, stun, astonish, knock senseless
stup·ĕō -ēre -uī *vt* to be amazed at; *vi* to be knocked senseless, be stunned, be stupefied, be astounded, be amazed; to be stopped in one's tracks
stup·escō -escĕre -uī *vi* to become amazed, become bewildered
stūpĕ·us -a -um *adj* of tow, hempen
stupidĭt·ās -ātis *f* stupidity
stupĭd·us -a -um *adj* amazed, astounded; dull, stupid
stup·or -ōris *m* numbness, bewilderment, confusion; dullness, stupidity
stupp·a -ae *f* tow, coarse flax, hemp
stuppĕ·us -a -um *adj* of tow, hempen
stupr·ō -āre *vt* to ravish, rape; to defile
stupr·um -ī *n* immorality; rape; disgrace (*esp. from a sex crime*)
sturn·us -ī *m* starling
Stygiāl·is -e *adj* Stygian
Stygĭ·us -a -um *adj* Stygian, infernal; deadly
Stymphalĭc·us or **Stymphalĭ·us -a -um** *adj* Stymphalian
Stymphăl·um -ī *n* or **Stymphăl·us -ī** *m* district in Arcadia famous for its vicious birds of prey which were killed by Hercules as one of his twelve labors
Sty·x -gis or **-gos** *f* chief river in the lower world; river in Arcadia
suādēl·a -ae *f* persuasion
suādĕō suādēre suāsī suāsum *vt* to recommend, propose, suggest; to urge, impel, induce; *vi* (*with dat*) to advise, urge, suggest to, propose to; **sibi suadere** (*with acc & inf*) to satisfy oneself that
suās·iō -ōnis *f* recommendation; support, backing (*a proposal*); persuasive eloquence
suās·or -ōris *m* adviser; advocate, supporter
suās·um -ī *n* dye
suāsus *pp of* **suadeo**
suās·us -ūs *m* advice
suāveŏl·ens -entis *adj* fragrant
suāviātiō see **saviatio**
suāvidĭc·us -a -um *adj* charming
suāvilŏqu·ens -entis *adj* charming
suāviloquentĭ·a -ae *f* charming manner of speech
suāviŏlum see **saviolum**
suāvĭor see **savior**
suāv·is -e *adj* charming, pleasant, agreeable, attractive

suāvit·ās -ātis *f* charm, pleasantness, sweetness, attractiveness
suāvĭter *adv* pleasantly, sweetly, charmingly, attractively
suāvitūd·ō -ĭnis *f* (term of endearment) honey
suāvium see **savium**
sub *prep* (with *abl*) under, beneath, underneath, behind; at the foot of, close to, near (*mountain, wall*); during, in, within, at, by, in the time of, just before; during the reign of; (with *acc*) under, along under; up to (*walls*); approaching, about, just before, just after
subabsurdē *adv* a bit absurdly
subabsurd·us -a -um *adj* rather absurd
subaccūs·ō -āre *vt* to blame, find fault with
subactĭ·ō -ōnis *f* working (*of the soil*); development (*of the mind*)
subactus *pp* of **subigo**
subaerāt·us -a -um *adj* (gold) having an inner layer of bronze
subagrest·is -e *adj* rather uncouth
subālār·is -e *adj* carried under the arms
subalb·us -a -um *adj* whitish
subamār·us -a -um *adj* somewhat bitter
subaquĭl·us -a -um *adj* somewhat dark, brownish
subarroganter *adv* rather arrogantly
subauscult·ō -āre *vt* to eavesdrop on; *vi* to eavesdrop
subbasilicān·us -ī *m* loafer (*person who hangs around the basilicas*)
subbĭb·ō -ĕre -ī *vt* to drink a little
subbland·ior -īrī -ītus sum *vi* (with *dat*) to flirt with
subc- = succ-
subdifficĭl·is -e *adj* rather difficult
subdiffĭd·ō -ĕre *vi* to be a little distrustful
subditīci·us -a -um *adj* substituted, phoney
subditīv·us -a -um *adj* substituted, phoney
subdĭtus *pp* of **subdo**
subdiū *adv* by day
sub·dō -dĕre -dĭdī -dĭtum *vt* to put under; to subdue; to substitute; to forge, make up; to spread (*a rumor*) falsely; (with *dat*) **a** to put or apply (*something*) to, add (*something*) to; **b** to subject (*someone*) to; **se aquis subdere** to plunge into the water
subdoc·ĕō -ēre *vt* to instruct (*as an assistant teacher*)
subdŏlē *adv* rather cunningly
subdŏl·us -a -um *adj* underhand, sly, cunning
subdŏm·ō -āre *vt* to tame somewhat
subdubĭt·ō -āre *vi* to be rather undecided
sub·dūcō -dūcĕre -duxī -ductum *vt* to draw up from below; to pull up, raise, to remove, take away, steal; to haul up, beach (*a ship*); to withdraw (*troops*); to balance (*accounts*)
subductĭ·ō -ōnis *f* drydocking, beaching; calculation, computation
sub·ĕdō -esse -ēdī *vt* to eat away or wear away at the bottom; **scopulum unda subedit** water wears away the bottom of the cliff
sub·ĕō -īre -īvī or **-iī -ĭtum** *vt* to enter (*a place*), enter (*the mind*); to approach, attack; to undergo (*dangers, punishment, etc.*); to help, support; to climb; to slip under; to dodge (*a blow*); *vi* to come or go up, climb; to follow; to advance, press forward; (with **ad** or **in** + *acc*) **a** to come up against, attack; **b** to climb (*a mountain*); **c** to approach, enter
sūb·er -ĕris *n* cork tree; cork
subf- = suff-
subg- = sugg-
subhorrĭd·us -a -um *adj* rather coarse, rather uncouth
sub·iciō -icĕre -jēcī -jectum *vt* to throw up, fling up; to bring up; to bring up close, expose; to suggest; to add, append; to suborn; to substitute; to forge; (with *dat* or **sub** + *acc*) **a** to put, place (*something*) under; **b** to subject (*someone*) to (*authority, danger, risk*); **c** to classify (*something*) under; **d** to submit (*something*) to (*one's judgment*)
subigitātĭ·ō -ōnis *f* lewdness; intercourse
subigitātr·ix -īcis *f* loose woman
subigĭt·ō -āre *vt* to lie with
sub·igō -igĕre -ēgī -actum *vt* to turn up, till, plow; to knead; to whet, sharpen; to rub down; to tame; to train, discipline (*the mind*); to conquer, subdue, subjugate, reduce; to force, impel, constrain; to incite; to row, propel (*a boat*)
subimpŭd·ens -entis *adj* rather shameless
subinān·is -e *adj* rather empty, rather pointless
subinde *adv* immediately afterwards; from time to time
subinsuls·us -a -um *adj* rather insipid
subinvid·ĕō -ēre *vi* (with *dat*) to envy (*someone*) a little
subinvīs·us -a -um *adj* rather disliked, rather unpopular
subinvīt·ō -āre *vt* to invite unenthusiastically
subīr·ascor -ascī -ātus sum *vi* to be annoyed; (with *dat*) to be peeved at
subitārĭ·us -a -um *adj* (mil) suddenly called up (*to meet an emergency*); built in a hurry
subĭtō *adv* suddenly, unexpectedly, at once; **subito dicere** to speak ex-tempore
subĭt·us -a -um *adj* coming on suddenly, sudden, unexpected; rash

(*man*); emergency (*troops*); *n* emergency
subjac·ĕō -ēre -ŭī *vi* to lie nearby; (with *dat*) to lie under or close to; **monti subjacere** to lie at the foot of the mountain
subjectĭ·ō -ōnis *f* subjection; substitution; forgery
subjectissimē *adv* most humbly
subject·ō -āre *vt* to toss up
subject·or -ōris *m* forger
subject·us -a -um *pp* of **subicio;** *adj* (with *dat*) **a** located near, bordering on; **b** subject to; *m* subject (*conquered person*)
sub·jungō -jungĕre -junxī -junctum *vt* (with *dat*) **a** to yoke or harness to; **b** to join to, connect with, add to; **c** to make subject to
sub·lābor -lābī -lapsus sum *vi* to sink, fall down, collapse; to glide imperceptibly; to fall back, fail
sublātē *adv* loftily, in lofty tones
sublātĭ·ō -ōnis *f* elevation, raising
sublāt·us -a -um *pp* of **suffero** and of **tollo;** *adj* elated
sublect·ō -āre *vt* to coax, cajole
sub·lĕgō -legĕre -lēgī -lectum *vt* to gather up, pick up; to pick up stealthily, steal, kidnap; to substitute; to overhear, pick up
sublest·us -a -um *adj* weak, trifling
sublevātĭ·ō -ōnis *f* alleviation, lightening
sublĕv·ō -āre *vt* to lift up, raise, support
sublĭc·a -ae *f* stake, pile (*esp. for a bridge*)
sublicĭ·us -a -um *adj* resting upon piles; **pons sublicious** wooden bridge across the Tiber, built by Ancus Marcius
subligācŭl·um -ī *n* short apron
sublĭg·ar -āris *n* apron
sublĭg·ō -āre *vt* (with *dat*) to tie or fasten (*e.g., a sword*) to or below
sublīmē *adv* aloft, on high
sublīmen *adv* upwards, on high
sublīm·is -e *adj* high, raised up, lifted high; lofty, elevated, exalted; raised high, borne aloft, through the sky; aspiring; eminent, distinguished
sublīm·us -a -um *adj* high, lofty
sublīmit·ās -ātis *f* loftiness, sublimity
sublingĭ·ō -ōnis *m* scullion
sub·linō -linĕre -lēvī -lĭtum *vt* to smear secretly; **os sublinere** (with *dat*) to cheat (*someone*)
sublūc·ĕō -ēre *vi* to shine faintly, glimmer
sub·lŭō -luĕre — -lūtum *vt* to wash underneath; to flow at the foot of (*a mountain*)
sublustr·is -e *adj* dimly lighted, throwing some light, glimmering, flickering
subm- = summ-
sub·nascor -nascī -nātus sum *vi* (with *dat*) to grow up underneath
sub·nectō -nectĕre -nexŭī -nexum *vt* to fasten, tie (*something*) underneath; to confine; (with *dat*) to fasten or tie (*something*) below (*something else*)
subnĕg·ō -āre *vt* to halfway refuse; (with *dat*) to halfway refuse (*something*) to (*someone*)
subnĭg·er -ra -rum *adj* blackish
subnimĭ·a -ae *f* robe
subnīs·us or **subnix·us -a -um** *adj* propped up, resting, leaning; (with *dat*) **a** propped up on, resting on, leaning on; **b** relying on, depending on, confiding in
subnŏt·ō -āre *vt* to note down, record, register; to observe secretly
subnŭb·a -ae *f* rival (*female*)
subnūbĭl·us -a -um *adj* somewhat cloudy, overcast
sub·ō -āre *vi* to be in heat
subobscēn·us -a -um *adj* somewhat obscene, shady
subobscūr·us -a -um *adj* rather obscure
subodiōs·us -a -um *adj* annoying
suboffend·ō -ĕre *vi* to give some offense
subŏl·et -ēre *v impers* there is a faint smell; **mihi subolet** I have an inkling, I have a sneaking suspicion, I have a faint idea
subŏl·ēs -is *f* offspring
subolesc·ō -ĕre *vi* to grow up instead
subor·ior -īrī *vi* to rise up in succession, arise, proceed
suborn·ō -āre *vt* to equip, supply, provide; to employ as a secret agent, incite secretly, suborn
subp- = supp-
subr- = surr-
sub·scrībō -scrībĕre -scripsī -scriptum *vt* to write underneath; to sign; to write down, record, register; *vi* to sign an accusation, act as prosecutor; (with *dat*) **a** to add (*something*) to, attach (*something*) in writing to; **b** to assent to, agree to; (with **in** + *acc*) to sign an accusation against, indict, accuse, prosecute
subscriptĭ·ō -ōnis *f* inscription underneath; signature; (law) subscription; recording (*of an offense by the censor*); record, register
subscript·or -ōris *m* signer or joint-signer (*of an accusation*)
subscriptus *pp* of **subscribo**
subsc·ūs -ūdis *f* tenon of a dovetail
subsecīvus see **subsicivus**
subsĕc·ō -āre -ŭī -tum *vt* to clip, trim, cut off
subsecūtus *pp* of **subsĕquor**
subsell·ium -ĭī or **-ī** *n* low seat or bench; seat or bench on a lower level; judge's seat, the bench; tribunal, court; seat in the senate, senator's seat; bleachers (*where the poor people sat*); **versatus in utrisque subsellis** experienced as judge and lawyer

sub·sentĭō -sentīre -sensī *vt* to have some inkling of
sub·sĕquor -sĕquī -secūtus sum *vt* to follow close after, chase, pursue; to back up, support; to imitate; to adhere to, conform to; to come after, succeed (*in time or order*); *vi* to ensue
subserv·iō -īre *vi* (with *dat*) **a** to be subject to; **b** to accommodate oneself to, humor; **c** to support, aid
subsicīv·us -a -um *adj* left over; extra, spare (*time*); extra, overtime (*work*)
subsidiārĭ·us -a -um *adj* (mil) reserve; *m pl* reserves
subsid·ium -iī or **-ī** *n* aid, support; place of refuge, asylum; protection; (mil) reserves, triarii; military support, relief, aid; **subsidio esse** (with *dat*) to act as support to; **subsidio mittere** to send in support
sub·sīdō -sīdĕre -sēdī -sessum *vt* to lie in wait for; *vi* to sit down, crouch down, settle down; to sink, subside, settle; to establish oneself, settle down, establish residence, stay
subsignān·us -a -um *adj* special reserve (*troops*)
subsign·ō -āre *vt* to endorse, subscribe to (*an opinion*); to register, enter, record; to guarantee
subsil·iō -īre -iī *vi* to jump up
sub·sistō -sistĕre -stitī *vt* to hold out against; *vi* to stand up; to make a stand, take a firm stand; to come to a standstill, stop; to stay behind; (with *dat*) **a** to take a stand against, oppose, fight; **b** to meet (*an expense*)
subsort·ior -īrī -ītus sum *vt* to choose as a substitute by lot; *vi* to choose a substitute by lot; (in a passive sense) to be chosen as a substitute
subsortītĭ·ō -ōnis *f* substitution by lot
substantĭ·a -ae *f* substance, essence; means, wealth, property
sub·sternō -sternĕre -strāvī -strātum *vt* to spread underneath; to cover; (with *dat*) to put at the disposal of, make subservient to; **rem publicam libidini suae substernere** to misuse high office to serve one's lust
substit·ŭō -uĕre -ŭī -ūtum *vt* to submit, present; to substitute; (with *dat* or **in locum** with *genit*) to substitute for or in place of; **animo** or **oculis substituere** to imagine
subst·ō -āre *vi* to stand firm, hold out; (with *dat*) to stand up to
substrātus *pp* of **substerno**
substrict·us -a -um *adj* tight, narrow, small
sub·stringō -stringĕre -strinxī -strictum *vt* to tie up, draw up; to restrain, control; (with *dat*) to press (*something*) close to
substructĭ·ō -ōnis *f* substructure, foundation
sub·strŭō -struĕre -struxī -structum *vt* to lay (*foundation*); **vias glareā substruere** to lay a foundation of gravel on the roads
subsult·ō -āre *vi* to jump up, jump up and down
sub·sum -esse *vi* to be near, be at hand; (with *dat*) **a** to be below or beneath, be under; **b** to be concealed in; **c** to be subject to, subservient to
subsūt·us -a -um *adj* trimmed at the bottom
subtēm·en -ĭnis *n* woof; thread, yarn
subter *adv* below, underneath; *prep* (with *abl*) beneath, below, underneath, under; (with *acc*) underneath, beneath; up to, close to, close beneath
subter·dūcō -dūcĕre -duxī -ductum *vt* to withdraw secretly, lead away secretly
subter·fugĭō -fugĕre -fūgī *vt* to evade, avoid; *vi* to run away secretly, get off
subter·lābor -lābī *vt* to glide or flow under; *vi* to slip away, escape
sub·tĕrō -terĕre -trīvī -trītum *vt* to wear away underneath
subterrānĕ·us -ā -um *adj* subterranean, underground
subtex·ō -ĕre -ŭī -tum *vt* to sew on; to veil, cover; (fig) to work up, compose; (with *dat*) **a** to sew onto; **b** to throw (*a covering*) over; **c** to work (*something*) into (*a story or plot*)
subtīl·is -e *adj* woven fine, of fine texture; delicate; subtle; discriminating, precise; plain, direct (*style*)
subtīlĭt·ās -ātis *f* fineness, minuteness; slenderness; exactness, precision; simplicity (*of style*)
subtīlĭter *adv* finely, delicately; accurately; plainly, simply
subtim·ĕō -ēre *vt* to be a bit afraid of
sub·trăhō -trahĕre -traxī -tractum *vt* to drag up from beneath, drag out, draw off, withdraw, remove; to avert (*the eyes*); (with *dat*) to drag or draw (*something*) away from
subtrist·is -e *adj* rather sad
subtrītus *pp* of **subtero**
subturpicŭl·us -a -um *adj* somewhat disgraceful
subturp·is -e *adj* rather disgraceful
subtus *adv* below, underneath
subtūs·us -a -um *adj* somewhat bruised
subūcŭl·a -ae *f* man's undershirt
sūbŭl·a -ae *f* awl
subulc·us -ī *m* swineherd
Subūr·a -ae *f* rough, noisy district in Rome, N.E. of the Forum between the Esquiline and Quirinal
Subūrān·us -a -um *adj* of the Subura
suburbānĭt·ās -ātis *f* nearness to Rome

suburbān·us -a -um *adj* suburban, near Rome; *m* suburbanite; *n* suburban home
suburb·ium -iī or **-ī** *n* suburb
suburg·ĕō -ēre *vt* (with **ad** + *acc*) to keep or turn (*a ship*) close to
subvectī·ō -ōnis *f* transportation
subvect·ō -āre *vt* to bring up regularly
subvectus *pp* of **suveho**
subvect·us -ūs *m* bringing up, transportation
sub·vĕhō -vehĕre -vexī -vectum *vt* to carry or bring up, transport
sub·veniō -venīre -vēnī -ventum *vi* (with *dat*) to come up to aid, reinforce, relieve
subvent·ō -āre *vi* (with *dat*) to rush to the aid of
subver·ĕor -ērī *vi* to be a bit apprehensive
subvers·ō or **subvors·ō -āre** *vt* to ruin completely
subvers·or -ōris *m* subverter, repealer
sub·vertō or **sub·vortō -vertĕre -vertī -versum** *vt* to turn upside down, upset, overthrow, throw over, subvert
subvex·us -a -um *adj* sloping upward
subvŏl·ō -āre *vi* to fly up
subvolv·ō -ĕre *vt* to roll up
subvor- = **subver-**
subvulturī·us -a -um *adj* vulturelike
succăv·us -a -um *adj* hollow underneath
succēdānĕ·us or **succīdānĕ·us -a -um** *adj* substitute
suc·cēdō -cēdĕre -cessī -cessum *vt* to climb; to march on or against, advance to or as far as; *vi* to come up, climb; to come next, follow in succession; to turn out (*successfully*); (with **ad, in,** or **sub** + *acc*) to climb, climb up; (with *dat*) **a** to come next to, follow; **b** to succeed in (*an undertaking*); **c** to yield to, submit to; **d** to relieve, take the place of (*e.g., tired troops*); **e** to enter, go below to (*e.g., a shelter; grave*); (with **in** or **ad** + *acc*) (fig) to reach, attain (*e.g., high honors*), receive by succession, enter upon (*an inheritance*)
suc·cendō -cendĕre -cendī -censum *vt* to set on fire, set fire to; to light (*a fire*); (fig) to inflame
succens·ĕō or **suscens·ĕō -ēre -ī** *vi* to be angry, be enraged; (*with dat*) to be enraged at
succensus *pp* of **succendo**
succenturiāt·us -a -um *adj* in reserve
succenturī·ō -āre *vt* to receive (*someone*) as a substitute into a century or company
succenturī·ō -ōnis *m* assistant centurion, substitute for a centurion
successī·ō -ōnis *f* succession
success·or -ōris *m* successor
success·us -ūs *m* approach, advance uphill; outcome, success
succīdānĕus see **succedaneus**
succīdī·a -ae *f* leg or side of meat; (fig) extra income
suc·cīdō -cīdĕre -cīdī -cīsum *vt* to cut down, cut off, mow down
suc·cĭdō -cidĕre -cĭdī *vi* to sink, give way; to collapse, fail
succĭd·us or **sūcĭd·us -a -um** *adj* juicy; (coll) fresh, plump (*girl*)
succidŭ·us -a -um *adj* sinking, falling
suc·cingō -cingĕre -cinxī -cinctum *vt* to tuck up; to put on (*e.g., a sword*); to equip, arm, fit out
succingŭl·um -ī *n* belt
succĭn·ō -ĕre *vi* to chime in (*in conversation*)
succīsus *pp* of **succīdo**
succlāmātī·ō -ōnis *f* shouting in reply
succlām·ō -āre *vt* to shout out after, interrupt with shouts; (with *dat*) to shout out (*words*) at
succontumēliōsē *adv* rather insolently
suc·crescō -crescĕre -crēvī *vi* to grow up; to be replenished; (with *dat*) to attain to
succrisp·us -a -um *adj* rather curled
suc·cumbō -cumbĕre -cubŭī -cubĭtum *vi* to fall or sink back; to yield, succumb, submit
suc·currō -currĕre -currī -cursum *vi* (with *dat*) **a** to run up to; **b** to run to help; **c** to occur to, enter the mind of
succ·us or **sūc·us -ī** *m* sap, juice; taste, flavor
succuss·us -ūs *m* shaking, jolt
succust·ōs -ōdis *m* assistant guard
suc·cutiō -cutĕre -cussī -cussum *vt* to toss up
sūcĭdus see **succidus**
sūcĭn·us -a -um *adj* & *n* amber
suctus *pp* of **sūgō**
sucŭl·a -ae *f* little pig; winch, windlass
sūcus see **succus**
sūdār·ium -iī or **-ī** *n* handkerchief, towel
sūdātōrī·us -a -um *adj* sweat, for sweating; *n* sweat room
sūdātr·ix -īcis *adj* causing sweat
sud·is -is *f* stake, pile; pike (*weapon*); dorsal fin
sūd·ō -āre *vt* to sweat, exude; to soak with sweat; (fig) to sweat over; *vi* to sweat; to drip
sūd·or -ōris *m* sweat; moisture; hard work
sūducŭl·um -ī *n* sweat-maker (*i.e., whip*)
sūd·us -a -um *adj* dry; clear, cloudless (*weather*); *n* clear weather, bright sky
su·ĕō -ēre *vi* to be accustomed; (with *inf*) be accustomed or used to
su·escō -escĕre -ēvī -ētum *vt* to

accustom, familiarize; *vi* to become used; (with *dat*) to get used to
Suess·a -ae *f* town in Latium
suēt·us *pp* of **suesco;** *adj* usual, familiar
Suēv·ī -ōrum *m pl* a people of N.E. Germany
sūf·es -ĕtis *m* chief magistrate at Carthage
suffarcināt·us -a -um *adj* stuffed full
suffarcĭn·ō -āre *vt* to stuff full, cram
suffectus *pp* of **sufficio**
suffĕrō sufferre sustŭlī sublātum *vt* to suffer, bear, endure
suf·ficĭō -ficĕre -fēcī -fectum *vt* to lay the foundation for; to dip, tinge, dye; to appoint to a vacancy; to yield, supply, afford; **consul suffectus** substitute cousul (*consul appointed to complete an unexpired term of another consul*); *vi* to suffice, be sufficient; (with *dat* or with **ad** or **in** + *acc*) to suffice for, be adequate to
suf·fīgō -fīgĕre -fixī -fixum *vt* to nail up, fasten
suffīm·en -ĭnis *n* incense
suffīment·um -ī *n* incense
suffixus *pp* of **suffigo**
sufflām·en -ĭnis *n* brake (*on a vehicle*)
sufflāt·us -a -um *adj* puffed up, bloated; (fig) fuming (*with anger*)
suffl·ō -āre *vt* to blow up, inflate; *vi* to blow, puff
suffōc·ō -āre *vt* to choke, strangle
suf·fodĭō -fodĕre -fōdī -fossum *vt* to stab, pierce; to dig under (*walls*)
suffrāgātĭ·ō -ōnis *f* voting (*in someone's favor*), support
suffrāgāt·or -ōris *m* supporter (*at the polls*), partisan
suffrāgātōrĭ·us -a -um *adj* partisan
suffrāg·ĭum -ĭī or **-ī** *n* ballot, vote; right to vote, franchise; decision, judgment; applause, approbation; **suffragium ferre** to cast a ballot; **suffragium ferre** (with **de** or **in** + *abl*) to vote on
suffrāg·or -ārī -ātus sum *vi* to cast a favorable vote; (with *dat*) to vote in favor of, support, vote for; **fortunā suffragante** with luck on our side
suffring·ō -ĕre *vt* to break, smash
suf·fugĭō -fugĕre -fūgī *vt* to escape, avoid; *vi* (with **in** + *acc*) to run to for cover
suffug·ĭum -ĭī or **-ī** *n* shelter, cover
suf·fulcĭō -fulcīre -fulsī -fultum *vt* to prop up, underpin, support
suf·fundō -fundĕre -fūdī -fūsum *vt* to pour in, fill; to suffuse, spread; to tinge, color; to infuse; **virgineum ore ruborem suffundere** (with *dat*) to cause (*someone*) to blush
suffūr·or -ārī *vt* to filch
suffusc·us -a -um *adj* darkish, brownish
suffūsus *pp* of **suffundo**
sug·gĕrō -gerĕre -gessī -gestum *vt* to supply, add; to prompt, suggest
suggest·um -ī *m* platform; stage
suggestus *pp* of **suggero**
suggest·us -ūs *m* platform; stage
suggrand·is -e *adj* rather huge
sug·gredĭor -grĕdī -gressus sum *vt & vi* to approach
sūgillātĭ·ō -ōnis *f* bruise; affront
sūgill·ō -āre *vt* to beat black and blue; to affront, insult
sūgō sūgĕre suxī suctum *vt* to suck
suī see **se**
suill·us -a -um *adj* of swine; **grex suillus** herd of swine
sulc·ō -āre *vt* to furrow, plow; to make a line in (*sand*)
sulc·us -ī *m* furrow; ditch, trench (*for plants*); track (*of a wheel or meteor*); wrinkle; plowing; wake (*of ship*)
sulf·ur -ŭris *m* sulfur
Sull·a -ae *m* Sulla (*Cornelius Sulla Felix, Roman general, dictator, champion of the aristocratic party, and political reformer,* 138-78 B.C.)
Sullān·ī -ōrum *m pl* partisans of Sulla
sullātur·ĭō -īre *vi* to wish to be a Sulla
Sulm·ō -ōnis *m* town about ninety miles east of Rome and birthplace of Ovid
Sulmōnens·is -e *adj* of Sulmo
sulp·ur or **sulf·ur -ŭris** *m* sulfur
sulpurāt·us -a -um *adj* saturated with sulfur; *n pl* matches
sulpurĕ·us -a -um *adj* sulfurous
sultis = **si vultis** if you please, please
sum esse fuī *vi* to be, exist; (with *genit* of possession) to belong to, pertain to, be characteristic of, be the duty of; (with *genit* or *abl* of quality) to be of, be possessed of, have; (with *genit* or *abl* of value) to be valued at, cost; (with *dat*) to belong to; (with **ab** + *abl*) to belong to; (with **ad** + *acc*) to be designed for; (with **ex** + *abl*) to consist of; **est** (with *inf*) it is possible to, it is permissible to; **est** (with **ut**) it is possible that; **sunt qui** there are those who, there are people who, they are of the type that
sūm·en -ĭnis *n* breast, teat, udder; breeding sow
summ·a -ae *f* main thing; chief point, gist, summary; sum, amount, contents, substance; sum of money; **ad summam** generally, on the whole; in short; **summa rerum** the world; supreme power; **summa summarum** the whole universe
summān·ō -āre *vi* to drip a bit
Summān·us -ī *m* Roman god of night lightning

summ·ās -ātis *adj* high-born, aristocratic, noble
summātim *adv* on the surface; generally, summarily
summāt·us -ūs *m* supremacy, supreme power
summē *adv* very, extremely
sum·mergō -mergĕre -mersī -mersum *vt* to sink, submerge, drown
summĕr·us -a -um *adj* pure, straight (*wine*)
sumministr·ō -āre *vt* to supply, furnish
summissē or **summissim** *adv* in a low voice, softly; modestly, humbly
summissī·ō -ōnis *f* lowering, dropping
summiss·us -a -um *adj* lowered, stooping; lowered, soft (*voice*); humble, unassuming; submissive; too submissive, abject
sum·mittō -mittĕre -mīsī -missum *vt* to let down, lower; sink, drop; to let (*hair*) grow long; to lower, reduce, moderate, relax, lessen; to bring down, humble; to rear, put forth, produce; to send secretly; to send as a reinforcement; to send as a substitute; **animum summittere** (with *dat*) to yield to; **se summittere** to bend down, stoop over; to condescend; **se summittere** (with *dat*) to yield to, give in to
summolestē *adv* with some annoyance
summolest·us -a -um *adj* rather annoying
summon·ĕō -ēre -ŭī *vt* to give (*someone*) a gentle reminder, remind privately
summopĕre *adv* with the greatest diligence, completely
summōrōs·us -a -um *adj* rather crabby
sum·movĕō -movēre -mōvī -mōtum *vt* to move up, advance; to clear (*e.g., the court*); to remove; to expel, banish; (mil) to dislodge; (fig) to drive away, forget about (*e.g., worries*)
summ·us -a -um *adj* uppermost, highest; the top of, the surface of; last, latest, the end of; greatest, best, top, consummate; most distinguished; most important; *m* head of the table; *f* see **summa;** *n* top, surface, highest place, head of the table
summum *adv* at most; at latest; **uno aut summum altero proelio** in one or at most in two battles
sūmō sūmĕre sumpsī sumptum *vt* to take up; to put on, dress oneself in, wear; to exact, inflect (*penalty*); to take up, begin, enter upon; to eat, consume; to assume, suppose, take for granted; to cite, adduce, mention; to assume, appropriate; to select; to purchase, buy
sumptĭ·ō -ōnis *f* assumption
sumptuārĭ·us -a -um *adj* expense, relating to expenses, sumptuary, against extravagance
sumptuōsē *adv* sumptuously, expensively
sumptuōs·us -a -um *adj* costly, expensive; lavish, wasteful
sumptus *pp* of **sumo**
sumpt·us -ūs *m* cost, expense, charge; **sumptui esse** (with *dat*) to be costly to, be expensive to; **sumptum suum exercere** to earn one's keep; **sumptu tuo** at your expense, out of your pocket
Sūn·ĭum -ĭī or **-ī** *n* S.E. promontory of Attica
suō suĕre suī sūtum *vt* to sew, stitch, tack together
suōmet = emphatic form of **suo**
suopte = emphatic form of **suo**
suovetaurīl·ĭa -ĭum *n pl* sacrifice of a pig, sheep, and bull
supell·ex -ectĭlis *f* furniture, household utensils; (fig) outfit, qualification
super *adv* on the top, above; besides, moreover; **super esse** to be left over; *prep* (with *abl*) above, over, upon, on; concerning, about; besides, in addition to; at, on (*time*); (with *acc*) over, above, upon; (with numbers) over, more than; besides, over and above
supĕr·a -ōrum *n pl* upper world, sky, Heaven; heavenly bodies
supĕrā *adv* above
superābĭl·is -e *adj* surmountable, climbable; conquerable
super·addō -addĕre — -addĭtum *vt* to add besides, add to boot
supĕr·ans -antis *adj* predominant
superast·ō -āre *vi* (with *dat*) to stand on
superāt·or -ōris *m* conqueror
superbē *adv* arrogantly, haughtily, snobbishly
superbĭ·a -ae *f* arrogance, haughtiness, snobbishness; (justifiable) pride
superbiloquentĭ·a -ae *f* haughty tone, arrogant speech
superb·ĭō -īre *vi* to be haughty; to be superb, be magnificent; (with *abl*) to take pride in
superb·us -a -um *adj* arrogant, haughty, snobbish; overbearing, tyrannical, despotic; fastidious, disdainful; superb, magnificent
supercil·ĭum -ĭī or **-ī** *n* eyebrow; frown, will (*of Jupiter*); summit, brow (*of a hill, etc.*); arrogance, superciliousness
superēmin·ĕō -ēre -ŭī *vt* to tower over, top
superficĭ·ēs -ēī *f* top, surface; (law) fixtures, improvements, buildings (*i.e., anything upon the property, but not the land itself*)
super·fīō -fĭĕrī *vi* to be over and above; to be left over

superfix·us -a -um *adj* attached above
superflu·ens -entis *adj* superabundant, running over; (with *abl*) abounding in
superflŭ·ō -ĕre *vi* to overflow
super·fundō -fundĕre -fūdī -fūsum *vt* (with *abl*) to shower (*something*) with; (with *dat*) to pour (*something*) upon; **superfundi** or **se superfundere** to spread, spread out, extend; **fama superfudit se in Asiam** the report spread to Asia
super·gredior -grĕdī -gressus sum *vt* to walk or step over; to surpass
supĕr·ī -ōrum *m pl* the gods above; men on earth; mortals; upper world
superimmin·ĕō -ēre *vt* to tower above
superimpend·ens -entis *adj* overhanging, towering overhead
superim·pōnō -pōnĕre -posŭī -positum *vt* to place on top, place overhead
superimposit·us -a -um *adj* superimposed
superincĭd·ens -entis *adj* falling from above
superincŭb·ans -antis *adj* lying above or on top
superin·cumbō -cumbĕre -cubŭī *vi* (with *dat*) to lay oneself down upon
superingĕr·ō -ĕre *vt* to pour down
superin·iciō -icĕre — -jectum *vt* to throw on top
superin·sternō -sternĕre -strāvī *vt* to cover
superi·or -us (*comp* of **supĕrus**) *adj* higher, upper; the upper part of; past, previous, preceding; older, elder, more advanced; victorious, conquering; superior, stronger; superior, greater; **de loco superiore dicere** to speak from the tribunal, handle a case in court; to speak from the rostra, deliver a formal address; **ex loco superiore pugnare** to fight from a vantage point
superin·jaciō -jacĕre -jēcī -jectum or **-jactum** *vt* to overspread, overwhelm; to overdo, exaggerate
superinjectus *pp* of **superinicio**
superlātĭ·ō -ōnis *f* exaggeration
superlāt·us -a -um *adj* exaggerated
supernē *adv* above, from above
supern·us -a -um *adj* upper; situated high up; supernal, celestial
supĕr·ō -āre *vt* to go over, pass over, rise above; to pass or go past, go beyond; to sail past, double; to outdo, surpass; to overcome, vanquish; *vi* to mount, ascend; to be superior, have the advantage; to be left over, survive; to be superfluous; to be abundant; (with *dat*) to pass over, pass above
superobrŭ·ō -ĕre *vt* to cover completely, smother
superpend·ens -entis *adj* towering overhead
super·pōnō -pōnĕre -posŭī -positum *vt* (with *dat*) to put or place (*something*) upon; (with **in** + *acc*) to put (*someone*) in charge of
superscand·ō -ĕre *vt* to step over, climb over
super·sedĕō -sedēre -sēdī -sessum *vi* (with *abl*) to refrain from, give up
superstagn·ō -āre *vi* (of a river) to overflow and form swamps
superst·es -ĭtis *adj* standing by as a witness; surviving; posthumous; (with *genit* or *dat*) outliving, surviving; **superstes esse** to live on; **superstes esse** (with *genit* or *dat*) to outlive (*someone or something*)
superstitĭ·ō -ōnis *f* excessive fear; superstition
superstitiōsē *adv* superstitiously
superstitiōs·us -a -um *adj* superstitious; having magical powers
superstĭt·ō -āre *vi* to be remaining, be left
superst·ō -āre *vt* to stand over; *vi* (with *dat*) to stand on, stand over
superstrāt·us -a -um *adj* spread over (*as a covering*)
super·strŭō -struĕre -struxī -structum *vt* to build on top
super·sum -esse -fŭī *vi* to be left over, still exist, survive; to abound; to be in excess, be superfluous; to be adequate, suffice; (with *dat*) to outlive, survive (*someone*)
supertĕg·ō -ĕre *vt* to cover, cover over
superurg·ens -entis *adj* putting on pressure, adding pressure
supĕr·us -a -um *adj* upper; of this world, of this life; northern; **ad auras superas redire** to return to the upper air, come back to life; **mare superum** Adriatic Sea; *m pl* see **superi**; *n pl* see **supera**
supervacānĕ·us -a -um *adj* superfluous
supervacŭ·us -a -um *adj* superfluous, needless
supervād·ō -ĕre *vt* to go over, climb over
super·vĕhor -vĕhī -vectus sum *vt* to sail, ride, or drive by or past
super·veniō -venīre -vēnī -ventum *vt* to come upon, come on top of; to overtake; to come over, close over, cover; to surprise; *vi* to arrive suddenly; (with *dat*) to come upon by surprise
supervent·us -ūs *m* sudden arrival, unexpected arrival
supervolĭt·ō -āre *vt* to hover over
supervŏl·ō -āre *vt* to fly over; *vi* to fly across
supīn·ō -āre *vt* to turn up, lay on its back; to turn over (*by plowing*)
supīn·us -a -um *adj* face-up; lying

upwards, turned upwards; sloping, sloping upwards; (streams) flowing upwards (*to their source*); on one's back; lazy, careless, indifferent
suppactus *pp* of **suppingo**
suppaenit·et -ēre *v impers* (with *acc* of person and *genit* of thing regretted), e.g., **illum furoris suppaenitet** he somewhat regrets the outburst
suppalp·or -ārī *vi* (with *dat*) to coax (*someone*) a little
supp·ār -ăris *adj* nearly equal
supparasīt·or -ārī -ātus sum *vi* (with *dat*) to flatter (*someone*) a little like a parasite
suppăr·um -ī *n* or **suppăr·us -ī** *m* linen dress; small sail
suppeditāti·ō -ōnis *f* good supply, abundance
suppedit·ō -āre *vt* to supply, furnish; *vi* to stand by; to be at hand, be in stock, be available; (with *dat*) to be at hand for; (with **ad** or **in** + *acc*) to be adequate for, suffice for
suppēd·ō -ĕre *vi* to break wind quietly
suppeti·ae -ārum *f pl* help, assistance
suppeti·or -ārī -ātus sum *vi* (with *dat*) to help, assist
suppĕt·ō -ĕre -īvī or **-iī -ītum** *vi* to be at hand, be in stock, be available; (with *dat*) **a** to be at hand for, be available to; **b** to be equal to, suffice for, be sufficient for; **c** to correspond to
suppīl·ō -āre *vt* to filch
sup·pingō -pingĕre — -pactum *vt* to fasten underneath
supplant·ō -āre *vt* to trip up
supplēment·um -ī *n* full complement; reinforcements
suppl·ĕō -ēre -ēvī -ētum *vt* to fill up; to make good (*losses, damage, etc.*); (mil) to bring to full strength
suppl·ex -icis *adj* kneeling, on one's knees, in entreaty; humble, submissive; *m* suppliant
supplicāti·ō -ōnis *f* public thanksgiving, day of prayer; thanksgiving for victory; day of humiliation
suppliciter *adv* suppliantly, humbly, submissively
supplic·ium -iī or **-ī** *n* kneeling down, bowing down, humble entreaty; public prayer, supplication; (because criminals were beheaded kneeling) execution, death penalty; punishment, torture; suffering, distress, pain
supplic·ō -āre *vi* (with *dat*) to go on one's knees to, entreat, beg
sup·plōdō -plōdĕre -plōsī *vt* to stamp (*the foot*)
supplōsi·ō -ōnis *f* stamping; **supplosio pedis** stamping of the foot
sup·pōnō -pōnĕre -posŭī -positum *vt* (with *dat*) **a** to put, place, set (*something*) under; **b** to put (*something*) next to, add (*something*) to; **c** to substitute (*something*) for; **potentiam in gratiae locum supponere** to put power in place of influence, substitute power for influence
support·ō -āre *vt* to bring or carry up, transport
supposītīci·us -a -um *adj* spurious
suppositi·ō -ōnis *f* substitution
suppositus *pp* of **suppono**
suppostr·ix -īcis *f* unfair substituter (*female*)
suppressi·ō -ōnis *f* holding back (*of money*), embezzlement
sup·primō -primĕre -pressī -ressum *vt* to press down or under; to sink; to repress, stop; to suppress, keep secret
supprōm·us -ī *m* assistant butler
suppŭd·et -ēre *v impers* to cause (*someone*) a slight feeling of shame; (with *acc* of person and *genit* of cause), e.g., **eorum me suppudet** I am a bit ashamed of them
suppūr·ō -āre *vi* to fester
supp·us -a -um *adj* (animals) facing the ground
suppŭt·ō -āre *vt* to trim up; to count, compute
suprā *adv* on top, above; up above; earlier; beyond, more; **supra quam** more than; *prep* (with *acc*) over, above; beyond; (of time) before; (of amount) over, beyond; in charge of
suprascand·ō -ĕre *vt* to climb over
suprēmum *adv* for the last time
suprēm·us -a -um (*superl* of **superus**) *adj* highest, topmost; the top of; last, latest, final; greatest, supreme, extreme; closing, dying, final; **suprema manus** the finishing touches; **supremus mons** summit of the mountain, mountain top; *n* last moment; *n pl* moment of death; funeral rites, obsequies; testament
sūr·a -ae *f* calf of the leg
surcŭl·us -ī *m* shoot, sprout, twig; slip, graft
surdast·er -ra -rum *adj* somewhat deaf
surdit·ās -ātis *f* deafness
surd·us -a -um *adj* deaf; silent, noiseless; unheeding; dull, faint, indistinct
surēn·a -ae *f* grand vizier (*in the Parthian empire*)
surgō surgĕre surrexī surrectum *vi* to get up, rise, stand up; to get up (*from sleep*); to grow up, spring up
surp·ō -ĕre -ŭī *vt* to snatch, wrest; to pilfer
surrancid·us or **subrancid·us -a -um** *adj* somewhat rancid
surrauc·us or **subrauc·us -a -um** *adj* somewhat hoarse
surrectus *pp* of **surgo**
surrēmig·ō or **subrēmig·ō -āre** *vi* to row along
sur·rēpō or **sub·rēpō -rēpĕre -repsī -reptum** *vt* to creep under, crawl under; *vi* to creep up; (with *dat*) to creep up on, steal upon

surrepticī·us or **subrepticī·us -a -um** *adj* surreptitious; stolen
surreptus *pp* of **surrepo** and of **surripio**
sur·rīdĕō or **sub·rīdĕō -rīdēre -rīsī** *vi* to smile
surrīdicŭlē or **subrīdicŭlē** *adv* rather humorously
sur·rigō or **sub·rigō -rigĕre -rexī -rectum** *vt* to raise, lift up, erect
surring·or or **subring·or -ī** *vi* to grimace, make a face; to be somewhat annoyed
sur·ripiō or **sub·ripiō -ripĕre -ripŭī -reptum** *vt* to snatch secretly, pilfer; (with *dat*) to pilfer (*something*) from
surrŏg·ō -āre *vt* to propose as a substitute
surrostrān·ī or **subrostrān·ī -ōrum** *m pl* loafers around the rostra
surrub·ĕō or **subrub·ĕō -ēre** *vi* to blush slightly
surrūf·us or **subrūf·us -a -um** *adj* reddish
sur·rŭō or **sub·rŭō -ruĕre -rŭī -rŭtum** *vt* to undermine, dig under; to tear down, demolish; (fig) to wreck, stamp out, destroy
surrustic·us or **subrustic·us -a -um** *adj* rather unsophisticated
surrŭtus *pp* of **surruo**
sursum or **sursus** *adv* upwards, high up; **sursum deorsum** up and down, to and fro
sūs suis *m* pig, hog, boar; *f* sow
Sūs·a -ōrum *n pl* capital of Persia
suscensĕō see **succenseo**
suscepti·ō -ōnis *f* undertaking
sus·cipiō -cipĕre -cēpī -ceptum *vt* to catch (*something before it falls*); to support; to pick up, resume (*conversation*); to bear (*children*); to accept, receive (*under one's protection*); to take up, undertake; to acknowledge, recognize (*a child*) as one's own
suscit·ō -āre *vt* to stir up; to erect, build; to awaken; to encourage; (fig) to stir up (*rebellion, love, etc.*)
suspect·ō -āre *vt* to gaze up at; to distrust, suspect
suspect·us -a -um *pp* of **suspicio**; *adj* suspected, mistrusted
suspect·us -ūs *m* respect, esteem
suspend·ium -iī or **-ī** *n* hanging; hanging oneself
sus·pendō -pendĕre -pendī -pensum *vt* to hang up, hang; to prop up, support; to keep in suspense; to check (*temporarily*); to interrupt; **suspendi** (with **ex** + *abl*) to depend on
suspens·us -a -um *adj* hanging, balanced; raised, poised; in suspense, uncertain, hesitant; (with **ex** + *abl*) dependent upon
suspic·ax -ācis *adj* suspicious; mistrusted, causing mistrust, suspicious
su·spiciō -spicĕre -spexī -spectum *vt* to look up at; to look up to, admire; to mistrust, suspect; *vi* to look up; (with **in** + *acc*) to look up at or into
suspīciōsē *adv* suspiciously
suspīciōs·us -a -um *adj* mistrustful, suspicious; suspicious-looking, suspicious; (with **in** + *acc*) suspicious of
suspic·ō -āre or **suspic·or -ārī -ātus sum** *vt* to mistrust, suspect; to suppose, believe, surmise
suspīrāt·us -ūs *m* deep breath, sigh
suspīr·ium -iī or **-ī** *n* deep breath, sigh; **suspirium ducere, repetere,** or **trahere** to draw a deep breath, sigh
suspīr·ō -āre *vt* to sigh for; *vi* to sigh, heave a sigh
susque deque *adv* up and down; **de Octavio susque deque est** it's all one (*i.e., of no consequence*) as far as Octavian is concerned
sustentācŭl·um -ī *n* prop, support
sustentāti·ō -ōnis *f* forbearance, patience
sustent·ō -āre *vt* to hold up, hold upright, support; to sustain (*with food*); to hold (*enemy*); to uphold (*law*); to delay; to postpone
sus·tinĕō -tinēre -tinŭī -tentum *vt* to hold up, support; to hold back, hold in, check; to uphold (*law*); to sustain, support (*with food*); to bear (*trouble*); to hold up, delay, put off
sustoll·ō -ĕre *vt* to lift up, raise; to destroy
susurrāt·or -ōris *m* mutterer, whisperer
susurr·ō -āre *vt & vi* to mutter, murmur, whisper
susurr·us -ī *m* low, gentle noise; murmur, whisper, buzz, hum
sūtēl·ae -ārum *f pl* patches; tricks
sūtil·is -e *adj* sewn together, fastened together
sūt·or -ōris *m* shoemaker
sūtōri·us -a -um *adj* shoemaker's; *m* ex-shoemaker
sūtrīn·us -a -um *adj* shoemaker's; *f* shoemaker's shop; shoemaker's trade
sūtūr·a -ae *f* seam; suture
sūt·us -a -um *pp* of **suo**; *n pl* joints
su·us -a -um *adj* his, her, its, their, one's own; due, proper, peculiar; *pron masc pl* one's own people, one's own friends, one's own family; *pron neut pl* one's own property
Sybăr·is -is *f* town in S. Italy noted for its luxurious living
Sybarīt·a -ae *m* Sybarite
Sȳchae·us -ī *m* husband of Dido
sȳcophant·a -ae *m* sycophant; blackmailer; cheat; slanderer
sȳcophanti·a -ae *f* cunning, deceit
sȳcophantiōsē *adv* deceitfully
sȳcophant·or -ārī -ātus sum *vi* to cheat; (with *dat*) to play a trick on
Syēn·ē -ēs *f* town in S. Egypt
syllăb·a -ae *f* syllable
syllabātim *adv* syllable by syllable

symbŏl·a -ae *f* contribution (*of money to a feast*); (coll) blows
symbŏl·us -ī *m* symbol, mark, token
symphōnī·a -ae *f* agreement of sound, symphony, harmony
symphōniăc·us -a -um *adj* concert, musical; **puerī symphoniacī** choristers; *m pl* musicians
Symplēgăd·es -um *f pl* two islands in the Euxine which floated about and dashed against each other until they were fixed in place as the Argo sailed by them
symplegm·a -ătis *m* group (*of persons embracing or wrestling*)
synĕdr·us -ī *m* senator (*in Macedonia*)
syngrăph·a -ae *f* promissory note
syngrăph·us -ī *m* written contract; pass, passport
synŏd·ūs -ontis *m* bream (*fish*)
synthĕs·is -is *f* dinner service; suit of clothes; dinner clothes
Syph·ax -ācis *m* king of Numidia at the time of the Second Punic War, siding with Carthage (*d.* 203 B.C.)
Syrācosī·us -a -um *adj* Syracusan; *m pl* Syracusans
Syrācūs·ae -ārum *f pl* Syracuse (*chief city in Sicily*)
Syrācūsān·us or **Syrācūsī·us -a -um** *adj* Syracusan
Syrī·us -a -um *adj* Syrian; *m pl* Syrians; *f* Syria
Syr·us -a -um *adj* Syrian; *m pl* Syrians
Sȳr·inx -ingis *f* nymph who was pursued by Pan and changed into a reed
syrm·a -ae *f* robe with a train (*worn esp. by actors in tragedies*); tragedy
syrt·is -is *f* sand dune; quicksand
Syrt·is -is *f* Gulf of Sidra in N. Africa; Gulf of Cabes; *f pl* the Syrtes (*lakes and sand dunes of that area as representative of a wild, forbidding place*)

T

tabell·a -ae *f* small board; door sill; game board; writing tablet; ballot; picture, painting; votive tablet
tabellārī·us -a -um *adj* (law) regulating voting; *m* mailman, courier
tāb·ĕō -ēre *vi* to waste away; to melt away; to stream, run
tabern·a -ae *f* hut, hovel, cottage; booth, stall, shop; inn
tabernācŭl·um -ī *n* tent; **tabernaculum capere** to choose a place for a tent outside the city in which to take the auspices
tabernārī·ī -ōrum *m pl* shopkeepers
tāb·ēs -is *f* melting, wasting, decay, dwindling, shrinking; decaying matter, rot; disease, pestilence
tāb·escō -escĕre -ŭī to begin to decay, begin to melt, melt gradually
tābidŭl·us -a -um *adj* wasting, consuming
tābĭd·us -a -um *adj* wasting, decaying, melting; corrupting, infectious
tābific·us -a -um *adj* melting, wasting; (fig) gnawing
tabŭl·a -ae *f* plank, board; writing tablet; advertisement; auction; picture, painting; map; votive tablet; *f pl* account books, records, registers, lists
tabulār·ium -iī or **-ī** *n* archives, archives building
tabulātĭ·ō -ōnis *f* flooring, floor, story
tabulāt·us -a -um *adj* boarded; *n* floor, story; layer; row (*of trees*)
tāb·um -ī *n* putrid matter, decay, rot; disease, plague, pestilence
tac·ĕō -ēre -ŭī -ĭtum *vt* to be silent about, pass over in silence; *vi* to be silent, hold one's tongue; to be still, be noiseless
tacitē *adv* silently, secretly
taciturnit·ās -ātis *f* silence, taciturnity
taciturn·us -a -um *adj* silent, taciturn; noiseless, hushed, quiet
tacĭt·us -a -um *adj* silent, mute; unmentioned, secret; (law) assumed, implied, tacit; **per tacitum** in silence
Tacĭt·us -ī *m* C. Cornelius Tacitus (*Roman historian, c.* 55-*c.* 115 A.D.)
tactĭl·is -e *adj* tangible
tactĭ·ō -ōnis *f* touch, touching; feeling, sense of touch
tactus *pp* of **tango**
tact·us -ūs *m* touch; handling; influence, effect
taed·a -ae *f* pine wood, pitch pine; torch; wedding torch; wedding; pine board
taedet taedēre taeduit or **taesum est** *v impers* it irks; (with *acc* of person and *genit* of the cause), e.g., **me taedet stultitiae meae** my foolishness irks me, I am annoyed at my foolishness
taedĭf·er -ĕra -ĕrum *adj* torch-bearing
taed·ium -iī or **-ī** *n* irksomeness, tediousness, weariness, boredom
taenī·a -ae *f* band, ribbon
Taenarĭd·ēs -ae *m* Spartan (*esp. Hyacinthus*)
Taenăr·is -ĭdis *adj* Spartan
Taenăr·um or **Taenăr·on -ī** *n* or **Taenăr·us** or **Taenăr·os -ī** *m* or *f* most southerly point of the Pelo-

ponnesus (*thought to be the entrance to the lower world*); lower world, Hades

taet·er -ra -rum *adj* foul, revolting, offensive, shocking, loathsome; ugly, hideous; disgraceful; *n* offensiveness, repulsiveness

taetrē *adv* foully, hideously, shockingly

taetricus see **tetricus**

tag·ax -ācis *adj* light-fingered

tālār·is -e *adj* ankle-length; *n pl* angle-length clothes; sandals

tālār·ius -a -um *adj* of dice; **ludus talarius** game of dice

talāsiō or **talassiō** *interj* wedding cry

tālĕ·a -ae *f* rod, bar, stake

talent·um -ī *n* talent (*Greek weight, varying from state to state, but equal to about fifty pounds*); sum of money (*consisting of sixty minae*)

tāli·ō -ōnis *f* (law) punishment in kind

tāl·is -e *adj* such, of such kind, of that kind; so great, so excellent, so distinguished

talp·a -ae *m* or *f* mole (*animal*)

Talthyb·ius -iī or **-ī** *m* herald of Agamemnon

tāl·us -ī *m* ankle, anklebone; heel, foot; die (*used in playing dice*)

tam *adv* to such an extent, to such a degree, so, so much; **tam . . . quam** the . . . the; **tam magis . . . quam magis** the more . . . the more

tamăr·ix -īcis *f* tamarisk

tamdiū *adv* so long, how long; **tuamdiu quam** or **tuamdiu dum** as long as

tamen *adv* yet, nevertheless, still, all the same; in the same way

Tāmĕs·is -is or **Tāmĕs·a -ae** *m* Thames

tametsī *conj* even if, although

tamquam or **tanquam** *conj* as, just as, as much as; just as if; **tamquam si** just as if

Tanăgr·a -ae *f* town in Boeotia

Tană·is -is *m* river of Sarmatia (*modern Don*)

Tanăqu·il -īlis *f* wife of the elder Tarquin

tandem *adv* at last, in the end, finally; (expressing urgency or impatience) now, tell me, please

tangō tangĕre tetigī tactum *vt* to touch; to handle, meddle with; to taste; to come to, reach; to border on; to hit, beat; to wash, anoint; to affect, gall, move to pity; to dupe; to touch upon, mention; to touch, be related to; to undertake

Tantalĕ·us -a -um *adj* of Tantalus

Tantalid·ēs -ae *m* descendant of Tantalus

Tantăl·is -idis *f* descendant of Tantalus (*female*)

Tantăl·us -ī *m* son of Jupiter and father of Pelops who was punished in the lower world with constant hunger and thirst

tantill·us -a -um *adj* so small, so little; *n* a bit

tantisper *adv* just so long (*and no longer*); just for the moment

tantopĕre or **tantō opĕre** *adv* so much, so greatly, to such a degree, so earnestly, so hard

tantŭlum *adv* so little, in the least

tantŭl·us -a -um *adj* so little, so small; *n* so little, such a trifle; **tantulo vendere** to sell for such a trifling amount

tantum *adv* so much, so greatly, to such a degree, so far, so long, so; only, just, but just, hardly, scarcely; **tantum modo** only

tantummŏdo *adv* only

tantundem *adv* just so much, just as far, to the same extent

tant·us -a -um *adj* of such size, so great; so much; so little; so important; *pron neut* so much; so little; so small an amount, so small a number; **tanti** of such value, worth so much, at so high a price; of little account, of such small importance; **tanto** (with comparatives) by so much, so much the; **tanto melior!** so much the better!, bravo!, excellent!; **tanto nequior!** so much the worse!

tant·usdem -ădem -undem *adj* so great, just as great, just as large

tapēt·a -ae *m* or **tapēt·a -ōrum** or **tapēt·ia -ium** *n pl* carpet; tapestry; coverlet

tardē *adv* slowly

tardesc·ō -ĕre *vi* to become slow; to falter

tardĭp·ēs -ĕdis *adj* limping

tardĭt·ās -ātis *f* tardiness, slowness; dullness, stupidity

tarditūd·ō -inis *f* tardiness, slowness

tardiuscŭl·us -a -um *adj* rather slow, slowish, dragging

tard·ō -āre *vt* to slow down, delay, hinder; *vi* to go slow, take it easy

tard·us -a -um *adj* tardy, slow; lingering; mentally slow, mentally retarded; deliberate; crippling

Tarentīn·us -a -um *adj* Tarentine; *m pl* Tarentines

Tarent·um -ī *n* town on S. coast of Italy, founded by the Spartans around 700 B.C.

tarm·es -ĭtis *m* wood worm, borer

Tarpēĭ·us -a -um *adj* Tarpeian; **mons Tarpeius** Tarpeian cliff on the Capitoline Hill from which criminals were thrown; *f* Roman girl who treacherously opened the citadel to the Sabine attackers

tarpezīt·a or **trapezīt·a -ae** *m* banker

Tarquiniens·is -e *adj* of the town of Tarquinii

Tarquinĭ·us -a -um *adj* Tarquinian; *m* Tarquinius Priscus (*fifth king of Rome and husband of Tanaquil*); Tarquinius Superbus (*seventh

and last king of Rome); *m pl* important Etrurian town
Tarracīn·a -ae *f* or **Terracīn·ae -ārum** *f pl* town in Latium
Tartăr·a -ōrum *n pl* or **Tartăr·us** or **Tartăr·os -ī** *m* Tartarus (*lower level of Hades reserved for criminals*)
Tartarĕ·us -a -um *adj* of Tartarus, infernal
tat or **tatae** *interj* exclamation of surprise
tat·a -ae *m* (coll) daddy
Tat·ius -iī or **-ī** *m* Titus Tatius (*king of the Sabines who later ruled jointly with Romulus until the latter had him killed*)
taurĕ·us -a -um *adj* bull's, of a bull; **terga taurea** bulls' hides; drums; *f* rawhide, whip
Taur·ī -ōrum *m pl* barbarous people living in the peninsula now called the Crimea
Tauric·us -a -um *adj* Tauric
taurif·er -ĕra -ĕrum *adj* bull-producing (*regions*)
tauriform·is -e *adj* bull-shaped
taurīn·us -a -um *adj* bull's; made of bull's hide; bull-like
taur·us -ī *m* bull
Taur·us -ī *m* Taurus (*constellation*)
taxāti·ō -ōnis *f* rating, appraisal
taxill·us -ī *m* small die (*for playing dice*)
tax·ō -āre *vt* to appraise
tax·us -ī *f* yew, yew tree
Tāўgĕt·ē -ēs *f* one of the Pleiades, the daughter of Atlas and Pleione
Tāўgĕt·us -ī *m* mountain range in Laconia
tē *acc & abl* of **tu**
-te = suffix for **tu** and **te**
Teān·um -ī *n* town in Campania; town in Apulia
techn·a or **techĭn·a -ae** *f* trick
Tecmess·a -ae *f* wife of Ajax the son of Telamon
tectē *adv* cautiously, guardedly
tect·or -ōris *m* plasterer
tectōriŏl·um -ī *n* bit of plaster work
tectōri·us -a -um *adj* roofing; plasterer's; painter's; *n* plaster, stucco; fresco painting; beauty preparation
tect·us -a -um *pp* of **tego;** *adj* concealed; secret; guarded (*words*); reserved, secretive (*person*); *n* roof; ceiling; canopy; cover, shelter; house
tēcum = **cum te**
Tegĕ·a -ae *f* town in Arcadia
Tegeae·us -a -um *adj* Tegean, Arcadian; *m* Pan; *f* Arcadian maiden (*i.e., Atalanta*)
Tegeāt·ae -ārum *m pl* Tegeans
teg·es -ĕtis *f* mat
tegill·um -ī *n* hood, cowl
tegĭm·en or **tegm·en** or **tegŭm·en -ĭnis** *n* cover, covering; vault (*of heaven*)
tegiment·um or **tegment·um** or **tegument·um -ī** *n* cover, covering
tegō tegĕre texī tectum *vt* to cover; to protect, shelter, defend; to hide; to bury; **tegere latus** (with *genit*) to escort (*someone*)
tēgŭl·a -ae *f* tile; *f pl* roof tiles, tiled roof
tegŭmen see **tegimen**
tegumentum see **tegimentum**
tēl·a -ae *f* web; warp (*threads that run lengthwise in the loom*); yarn beam; loom; design, plan
Telăm·ōn -ōnis *m* son of Aeacus, brother of Peleus, king of Salamis, and father of Ajax and Teucer
Telamōniăd·ēs -ae *m* son of Telamon (*i.e., Ajax*)
Telamōn·ius -iī or **-ī** *m* Ajax
Tēlegŏn·us -ī *m* son of Ulysses and Circe
Tēlemăch·us -ī *m* son of Ulysses and Penelope
Tēlĕph·us -ī *m* king of Mysia, wounded by the spear of Achilles and later cured by its rust
tell·ūs -ūris *f* the earth; ground, earth; land, country
tēl·um -ī *n* missile, weapon; spear, javelin, dart; sword, dagger, ax; shaft
temerārĭ·us -a -um *adj* casual, accidental; rash, thoughtless
temĕre *adv* by chance, without cause; at random; rashly, thoughtlessly; **non temere** not lightly; not easily; hardly ever; **nullus dies temere intercessit quo non scriberet** hardly a day ever passed without his writing
temerĭt·ās -ātis *f* chance, accident; rashness, thoughtlessness; *f pl* foolhardy acts
temĕr·ō -āre *vt* to darken, blacken; to violate, disgrace, defile
tēmēt·um -ī *n* alcohol, wine
temnō temnĕre tempsī temptum *vt* to slight, offend
tēm·ō -ōnis *m* pole, tongue (*of a carriage or plow*); wagon
Tempē (indecl) *n pl* scenic valley between Olympus and Ossa in Thessaly
temperāment·um -ī *n* moderation
tempĕr·ans -antis *adj* moderate, temperate
temperanter *adv* moderately
temperantĭ·a -ae *f* self-control, moderation
temperātē *adv* moderately, with due moderation
temperātĭ·ō -ōnis *f* blending, proportion, symmetry; temperament; organization, constitution; control
temperāt·or -ōris *m* controller
temperāt·us -a -um *adj* tempered; self-controlled, temperate
tempĕrī *adv* in time, on time; in due time, at the right time
temperi·ēs -ēī *f* blending, tempering; temperature, mild temperature
tempĕr·ō -āre *vt* to compound, combine, blend, temper; to regulate, moderate; to tune; to govern, con-

trol, rule; *vi* to be moderate, exercise restraint; (with *abl* or **ab** + *abl*) to abstain from
tempest·ās -ātis *f* time, period, season; stormy weather, storm, tempest
tempestīvē *adv* at the right time, seasonably
tempestīvit·ās -ātis *f* right time, timeliness
tempestīv·us -a -um *adv* timely, seasonable, fit; ripe, mature; in good time, early
templ·um -ī *n* space marked off in the sky or on the earth for observation of omens; open space, quarter; temple, shrine, sanctuary
temporāl·is -e *adj* temporary, transitory
temporārĭ·us -a -um *adj* temporary; changeable (*character*)
tempŏre or **tempŏrī** *adv* in time, on time; in due time, at the right time
temptābund·us -a -um *adj* making constant attempts, trying
temptāment·um -ī *n* attempt, effort; temptation, trial
temptāmĭn·a -um *n pl* attempts, trials
temptātĭ·ō -ōnis *f* trial; attack (*of sickness*)
temptāt·or -ōris *m* assailant
tempt·ō or **tent·ō -āre** *vt* to test, feel, probe; to try, attempt; to attack; to try to influence, tamper with, tempt, try to induce; to urge, incite, sound out; to worry, distress, disquiet
temptus *pp* of **temno**
temp·us -ŏris *n* temple (*of the head*); time, period, season; occasion, opportunity; right time, good time, proper period; times, condition, state, position; need, emergency; measure, quantity, cadence (*in metrics*); **ad tempus** punctually; at the right time, at the appointed time; for the time being, for the moment; for the occasion; **ante tempus** before time, too soon, prematurely; **ex tempore** on the spur of the moment; **id temporis** at that time; **in ipso tempore** in the nick of time; **in tempore** at the right moment, just in time; **in tempus** temporarily, for a time; **per tempus** just in time; **pro tempore** as time permits, according to circumstances; **tempori cedere** to yield to circumstances; **tempus in ultimum** to the last extremity
tēmulent·us -a -um *adj* intoxicated
tenācit·ās -ātis *f* tenacity; miserliness
tenācĭter *adv* tightly, firmly
ten·ax -ācis *adj* holding tight, gripping, clinging; sticky; firm; obstinate; stingy; (with *genit*) clinging to, holding on to
tendicŭl·ae -ārum *f pl* little snare, little noose, little trap
tendō tendĕre tetendī tentum or **tensum** *vt* to stretch, stretch out, hold out, spread, strain; to head for (*a place*); to aim, shoot (*an arrow*); to bend (*a bow*); to tune (*an instrument*); to pitch (*a tent*); *vi* to pitch tents, be encamped; to travel, sail, move, march; to endeavor; to contend, fight; to exert oneself; (with *inf*) to try to, endeavor to; (with **ad** + *acc*) **a** to tend toward, be inclined toward; **b** to move toward, travel to, aim for; (with **contra** + *acc*) to fight against
tenĕbr·ae -ārum *f pl* darkness; night; blindness; dark place, haunts; lower world; unconsciousness; death; obscurity, low station; ignorance
tenebricōs·us -a -um *adj* gloomy; darkened (*senses*); blind (*lust*)
tenebrĭc·us -a -um *adj* dark, gloomy
tenebrōs·us -a -um *adj* dark, gloomy
Tenĕd·os or **Tenĕd·us -ī** *f* island off the coast of Troy
tenellŭl·us -a -um *adj* tender little, dainty little
tenell·us -a -um *adj* dainty
ten·ĕō -ēre -ŭī -tum *vt* to hold, hold tight, keep; to grasp, comprehend; to comprise; to possess, occupy, be master of; to hold back, restrain, repress; to hold, charm, amuse; to have control of, get the better of; to keep, detain; *vi* to hold out, last, keep on
ten·er -ĕra -ĕrum *adj* tender, soft, delicate; young, youthful; impressionable; weak; effeminate; voluptuous
tenerasc·ō -ĕre *vi* to grow weak
tenĕrē *adv* softly
tenerĭt·ās -ātis *f* weakness
tēnesm·os -ī *m* straining at stool
ten·or -ōris *m* uninterrupted course; **uno tenore** uninterruptedly
tens·a -ae *f* car carrying images of the gods in procession
tens·us -a -um *pp* of **tendo**; *adj* stretched, drawn tight, stretched out
tentīg·ō -ĭnis *f* lust
tentō see **tempto**
tentōr·ĭum -ĭī or **-ī** *n* tent
tent·us -a -um *pp* of **tendo** and of **teneo**; *adj* stretched, drawn tight, stretched out
tenuicŭl·us -a -um *adj* poor, paltry
tenŭ·is -e *adj* thin, fine; delicate; precise; shallow (*groove, etc.*); slight, puny, poor, insignificant; plain, simple; small, narrow
tenuĭt·ās -ātis *f* thinness, fineness; leanness; simplicity; precision; poverty
tenuĭter *adv* thinly; slightly; poorly, indifferently; exactly, minutely; superficially
tenŭ·ō -āre *vt* to make thin; to con-

tract; to dissolve; to lessen, diminish, weaken
ten·us -ŏris *n* trap, snare
tenus *prep* (with *abl*, always placed after the noun) as far as, up to, down to; **nomine tenus** or **verbo tenus** as far as the name goes, nominally, in name
Te·os or **Te·us -ī** *f* town on the coast of Asia Minor, the birthplace of Anacreon
tepe·faciō -facĕre -fēcī -factum *vt* to make warm, warm up
tep·ĕō -ēre -ŭī *vi* to be warm, be lukewarm; to glow with love; to be lukewarm, indifferent
tep·escō -escĕre -ŭī *vi* to grow warm; to grow lukewarm, grow indifferent
tepidius *adv* rather tepidly
tepid·us -a -um *adj* warm, lukewarm, tepid
tep·or -ōris *m* warmth; coolness, lack of heat (*in the bath*); lack of fire (*in a speech*)
ter *adv* three times, thrice
terdeciens or **terdeciēs** *adv* thirteen times
terebinth·us -ī *f* terebinth, turpentine tree
terĕbr·a -ae *f* borer, drill
terĕbr·ō -āre *vt* to bore, drill, bore out
terēd·ō -inis *f* grub worm
Tēreïd·ēs -ae *m* Itys (*son of Tereus*)
Terent·ius -iī or **-ī** *m* Terence (*M. Terentius Afer, Roman comic poet, c.* 190-159 B.C.)
ter·es -ĕtis *adj* smooth, well-rounded; smooth and round, polished, shapely; round, cylindrical; (fig) smooth, elegant, fine
Tēr·eus -ĕī or **-ĕos** *m* king of Thrace, husband of Procne, and father of Itys
tergemin·us -a -um *adj* triple, threefold
tergĕō tergēre tersī tersum or **terg·ō -ĕre** *vt* to scour, wipe off, wipe dry, clean, cleanse
tergin·um -ī *n* rawhide; scourge
tergiversāti·ō -ōnis *f* refusal; evasion, subterfuge
tergivers·or -ārī -ātus sum *vi* to keep turning one's back; to be shifty, be evasive
tergō see **tergeo**
terg·um -ī or **terg·us -ŏris** *n* back; ridge; hide, leather; leather objects: bag, shield, drum; (mil) rear; **a tergo** in the rear, from behind; **in tergum** backward
term·es -itis *m* branch
Terminā̆l·ia -ium or **-iōrum** *n pl* festival of Terminus (*the god of boundaries, celebrated on the* 23*rd of February*)
terminăt·iō -ōnis *f* decision, determining; arrangement, ending (*of a sentence*)
termin·ō -āre *vt* to mark off with boundaries, bound, limit; to fix, determine, define; (rhet) to end, round out (*a sentence*)
termin·us -ī *m* boundary, limit
Termin·us -ī *m* god of boundaries
tern·ī -ae -a *adj* three in a group, three apiece, three each
terō terĕre trīvī trītum *vt* to wear, rub, wear out, crush; to spend, waste; to smooth, grind, sharpen
Terpsichŏr·ē -ēs *f* Muse of dancing; poetry
terr·a -ae *f* the earth; land; earth, ground, soil; country, region, territory
terrāneŏl·a -ae *f* crested lark
terrēn·us -a -um *adj* earthly, terrestrial; earthen, made of earth; *n* land, ground
terr·ĕō -ēre -ŭī -itum *vt* to frighten, scare, terrify; to deter
terrestr·is -e *adj* of the earth, on the earth; land, earth; **proelium terrestre** land battle
terrĕ·us -a -um *adj* sprung from the earth, earth-born
terribĭl·is -e *adj* terrible, frightful
terricŭl·a -ōrum *n pl* scarecrow
terrific·ō -āre *vt* to terrify
terrific·us -a -um *adj* terrifying, awe-inspiring, alarming
terrigĕn·a -ae *m* or *f* earth-born creature
terrilŏqu·us -a -um *adj* ominous, alarming
territ·ō -āre *vt* to keep frightening; to intimidate
territōr·ium -iī or **-ī** *n* land around a town, territory, suburbs
terr·or -ōris *m* terror, alarm, dread, fright
ters·us -a -um *pp* of **tergeo**; *adj* clean, neat; neat, terse
tertiadecimān·ī -ōrum *m pl* soldiers of the thirteenth legion
tertiān·us -a -um *adj* recurring every second day, tertian; *m pl* soldiers of the third legion; *f* tertian fever
tertiō *adv* in the third place, thirdly; the third time
tertium *adv* for the third time
terti·us -a -um *adj* third
terti·us decim·us -a -um *adj* thirteenth
terunc·ius -iī or **-ī** *m* three twelfths of an ace, quarter ace; **heres ex teruncio** heir to one fourth of the estate
tervenēfic·us -ī *m* (term of abuse) three-time killer
tesqu·a -ōrum *n pl* wilderness, wilds
tessell·a -ae *f* cubed mosaic stone
tessellāt·us -a -um *adj* tesselated
tessĕr·a -ae *f* cube; die; watchword, countersign; tally, token; ticket
tesserār·ius -iī or **-ī** *m* officer of the day
tesserŭl·a -ae *f* small cube; ticket
test·a -ae *f* brick, tile; jug, crock; potsherd; shell fish; shell
testāmentāri·us -a -um *adj* per-

taining to a will or testament; *m* forger of a will
testāment·um -ī *n* will, testament
testātī·ō -ōnis *f* invoking as witness
testāt·us -a -um *adj* attested, public
testicŭl·us -ī *m* testicle
testificāti·ō -ōnis *f* giving evidence, testifying; proof, evidence
testific·or -ārī -ātus sum *vt* to give as evidence, attest; to vouch for; to bring to light; to call to witness
testimōn·ium -iī or **-ī** *n* testimony, deposition
test·is -is *m* or *f* witness; *m* testicle
test·or -ārī -ātus sum *vt* to give as evidence; to show, prove, vouch for; to call to witness, appeal to; *vi* to be a witness, testify; to make a will
testūdinĕ·us -a -um *adj* of a tortoise; made of tortoise shell
testūd·ō -ĭnis *f* tortoise; tortoise shell; lyre, lute; arch, vault; (mil) protective shed (*for besiegers*)
test·um -ī *n* earthenware lid; pot with a lid
tēte = emphatic form of **te**
Tēth·ys -ȳos *f* wife of Oceanus and mother of the sea nymphs; sea
tetradrachm·um or **tetrachm·um -ī** *n* Greek silver coin (*worth four drachmas*)
tetrarch·ēs -ae *m* tetrarch (*ruler of one fourth of a country*); petty prince
tetrarchī·a -ae *f* tetrarchy
tetric·us -a -um *adj* gloomy, sour, crabby
Teuc·er or **Teuc·rus -rī** *m* son of Telamon and brother of Ajax; son of Scamander of Crete, son-in-law of Dardanus, and later king of Troy
Teucrī·a -ae *f* Troy
Teucr·us -a -um *adj* Teucrian, Trojan; *m pl* Trojans
Teutŏn·ēs -um or **Teutŏn·ī -ōrum** *m pl* Teutons
texō texĕre texŭī textum *vt* to weave; to plait; to build; to compose
textĭl·is -e *adj* woven; brocaded; *n* fabric
text·or -ōris *m* weaver
textrīn·um -ī *n* weaving
textr·ix -īcis *f* weaver (*female*)
textūr·a -ae *f* texture; web; fabric
text·us -a -um *pp* of **texo**; *n* woven cloth, fabric; web
text·us -ūs *m* texture
Thā·is -ĭdis *f* Athenian courtesan
thalăm·us -ī *m* woman's room; bedroom; marriage bed; marriage
thalassĭc·us -a -um *adj* sea-green
thalassĭn·us -a -um *adj* sea-green
Thal·ēs -is or **-ētis** *m* early Ionian philosopher of Miletus, regarded as one of the Seven Sages (*fl* 575 B.C.)
Thalī·a -ae *f* Muse of comedy; sea nymph
thall·us -ī *m* green bough, green stalk
Thaps·os or **Thaps·us -ī** *f* city in Africa where Caesar defeated the Pompeians (46 B.C.)
Thas·os or **Thas·us -ī** *f* island in the Aegean Sea, off the coast of Thrace
Thaumantī·as -ădis or **Thaumant·is -ĭdis** *f* Iris (*daughter of Thaumas*)
theātrāl·is -e *adj* theatrical
theātr·um -ī *n* theater
Thēb·ae -ārum *f pl* Thebes (*capital of Boeotia, founded by Cadmus*); Thebes (*city of Upper Egypt*)
Thēbae·us -a -um *adj & mf* Theban (*of Egypt*)
Thēbān·us -a -um *adj & mf* Theban (*of Boeotia*)
thēc·a -ae *f* case; envelope
Them·is -ĭdis *f* goddess of justice and of prophecy
Themistŏcl·ēs -is or **-ī** *m* Themistocles (*Athenian general and statesman, c.* 528-459 B.C.)
thensaurārĭ·us -a -um *adj* treasure, of treasure
thensaurus see **thesaurus**
Theocrĭt·us -ī *m* founder of Greek pastoral poetry, born at Syracuse (*3rd cent.* B.C.)
theolŏg·us -ī *m* theologian
therm·ae -ārum *f pl* hot springs, hot baths
thermopōl·ium -iī or **-ī** *n* hot-drink shop
thermopŏt·ō -āre *vt* to warm with a drink
Thermopȳl·ae -ārum *f pl* famous pass in Thessaly between Mt. Oeta and the sea, defended by Leonidas and his four hundred Spartans (490 B.C.)
thermŭl·ae -ārum *f pl* little hot bath
Thersīt·ēs -ae *m* Greek soldier at Troy notorious for his ugliness
thēsaur·us or **thensaur·us -ī** *m* storehouse; store, treasure, hoard
Thēs·eus -ĕī or **-ĕos** *m* king of Athens, son of Aegeus and Aethra, and husband first of Ariadne and later of Phaedra
Thēsē·us -a -um *adj* of Theseus
Thēsīd·ae -ārum *m pl* Athenians
Thēsīd·ēs -ae *m* Hippolytus (*son of Theseus*)
Thespiăd·es -um *f pl* Muses
Thesp·is -is *m* traditional founder of Greek tragedy
Thespī·us -a -um *adj* Thespian; *f pl* town in Boeotia near Mt. Helicon
Thessalī·a -ae *f* Thessaly (*most northerly district of Greece*)
Thessalĭc·us -a -um *adj* Thessalian
Thessăl·us -a -um *adj* Thessalian; *m pl* people of Thessaly, Thessalians
Thestorĭd·ēs -ae *m* Calchas (*famous Greek seer who joined the expedition to Troy*)
Thet·is -ĭdis or **-ĭdos** *f* sea nymph, daughter of Nereus and Doris, wife of Peleus, and mother of Achilles

thiăs·us -ī *m* Bacchic dance; Bacchic troop of dancers
Thisb·ē -ēs *f* girl in Babylon, loved by Pyramus
Tho·ās -antis *m* king of Tauris, slain by Orestes; king of Lemnos and father of Hypsipyle
thol·us -ī *m* rotunda
thōr·ax -ācis *m* breastplate
Thrāc·a -ae or **Thrāc·ē -ēs** *f* Thrace (*wild country to the N. of the Aegean*)
Thrācĭ·us -a -um *adj* Thracian; *f* Thrace
Thress·a or **Threiss·a -ae** *f* Thracian woman
Thr·ex -ēcis or **Thr·ax -ācis** *m* Thracian gladiator
thron·us -ī *m* throne
Thūcydĭd·ēs -is *m* Thucydides (*famous Greek historian of the Peloponnesian War, c.* 456-*c.* 400 B.C.)
thunn·us -ī *m* tuna fish
thūr- = tur-
Thūrĭ·ī -ōrum *m pl* city on the Tarentine Gulf in S. Italy
Thūrīn·us -a -um *adj & m* Thurian
thūs thūris *n* incense, frankincense
Thybris see **Tiberis**
Thyēn·ē -ēs *f* nymph who nursed Bacchus
Thyest·ēs -ae *m* son of Pelops, brother of Atreus, and father of Aegisthus
thymbr·a -ae *f* savory (*plant*)
thym·um -ī *n* thyme
Thȳnĭ·a -ae *f* Bithynia (*country in Asia Minor*)
Thȳniăc·us -a -um *adj* Bithynian
Thȳn·us -a -um *adj & m* Bithynian
thynn·us -ī *m* tuna fish
Thyōn·eus -ĕī *m* Bacchus
thyrs·us -ī *m* Bacchic wand twined with vine tendrils and ivy, and crowned with a fir cone
tiār·a -ae *f* or **tiār·ās -ae** *m* tiara
Tiberīn·is -ĭdis *adj* of the Tiber
Tiberīn·us -a -um *adj* of the Tiber; *m* river god of the Tiber
Tibĕr·is or **Tibr·is** or **Thybr·is -is** *m* Tiber River
Tiber·ĭus -ĭī or **-ī** *m* Tiberius (*Tiberius Claudius Nero Caesar, successor of Augustus,* 42 B.C.-37 A.D., *ruling from* 14 A.D. *to* 37 A.D.)
tībĭ·a -ae *f* shinbone, tibia; flute
tībīc·en -ĭnis *m* flutist; prop; pillar
tībīcĭn·a -ae *f* flutist (*female*)
Tibull·us -ī *m* Albius Tibullus (*Roman elegiac poet, c.* 54-*c.* 19 B.C.)
Tīb·ur -ŭris *n* town of Latium on the Anio (*modern Tivoli*)
Tīburt·ēs -um *m pl* Tiburtines
Tīburtīn·us or **Tīburn·us -a -um** *adj* Tiburtine
Tīcīn·us -ī *m* tributary of the Po
Tigellīn·us -ī *m* notorious favorite of the emperor Nero
tigill·um -ī *n* beam, log
tignārĭ·us -a -um *adj* **faber tignarius** carpenter
tign·um -ī *n* trunk, log, beam, board

tigr·is -is or **-ĭdis** *f* tigress
Tigr·is -is or **-ĭdis** *m* large river of W. Asia which joins with the Euphrates
tīlĭ·a -ae *f* lime tree
Tīmae·us -ī *m* Greek historian of Sicily (*c.* 346-*c.* 250 B.C.); Pythagorean philosopher of Locri in S. Italy after whom Plato named one of his dialogues (*5th cent.* B.C.)
Timāgĕn·ēs -is *m* brilliant rhetorician in the time of Augustus
timefact·us -a -um *adj* alarmed, frightened
tim·ĕō -ēre -ŭī *vt* to fear, be afraid of; *vi* to fear, be afraid
timĭdē *adv* timidly, fearfully
timidĭt·ās -ātis *f* timidity, fearfulness, cowardice
timĭd·us -a -um *adj* timid, fearful, cowardly; (with *genit*) fearful of, afraid of
tim·or -ōris *m* fear, alarm; dread; a terror
tinctĭl·is -e *adj* used for dipping
tinct·us -a -um *pp* of **tingo**
tinĕ·a -ae *f* moth; bookworm
tingō tingĕre tinxī tinctum *vt* to dip, soak; to dye, color; to tinge, imbue
tinnīment·um -ī *n* ringing
tinn·ĭō -īre -īvī -ĭī -ītum *vt & vi* to ring
tinnīt·us -ūs *m* ring, ringing, tinkling, jingling
tinnŭl·us -a -um *adj* ringing, tinkling; shrill
tintinnābŭl·um -ī *n* bell, door bell, cattle bell
tintinnācŭl·us -a -um *adj* jingling; *m pl* chain gang
tintĭn·ō -āre *vi* to ring
tīn·us -ī *m* laurustinus (*shrub*)
Tīph·ys -ȳos *m* pilot of the Argo
tippŭl·a -ae *f* water spider
Tīresĭ·ās -ae *m* famous seer at Thebes at the time of Oedipus
Tīridāt·ēs -ae *m* king of Armenia
tīr·ō -ōnis *m* recruit; beginner
tīrōcin·ĭum -ĭī or **-ī** *n* first campaign; inexperience in military life; body of raw recruits; beginning, first try
tīruncŭl·us -ī *m* young beginner
Tīryn·s -this or **-thos** *f* town in Argolis where Hercules was raised
Tīrynthĭ·us -a -um *adj* Tirynthian
Tīsamĕn·us -ī *m* son of Orestes and king of Argos
Tīsiphŏn·ē -ēs *f* one of the three Furies who haunted murderers
Tīsiphonē·us -a -um *adj* guilty
Tīt·ān -ānis or **Tītān·us -ī** *m* Titan; sun; *m pl* giant sons of Uranus and Ge who rebelled against Uranus and put Cronus on the throne
Tītānĭ·us -a -um *adj* of the Titans, Titanic; *f* Latona (*the mother of Apollo and Diana*); Pyrrha (*as descendant of Prometheus*); Circe (*as daughter of Sol*)

Tīthōnī·us -a -um *adj* Tithonian; *f* Aurora
Tīthōn·us -ī *m* son of Laomedon and husband of Aurora from whom he received the gift of immortality without eternal youth
Tit·iēs -ium *m pl* one of the three original tribes of Rome
tītillātī·ō -ōnis *f* tickling
tītill·ō -āre *vt* to tickle
titivillīt·ium -iī or **-ī** *n* trifle
titubanter *adv* falteringly
titubātī·ō -ōnis *f* staggering
titŭb·ō -āre *vi* to stagger, reel, totter; to falter, waver (*in speech*)
titŭl·us -ī *m* inscription; label; notice, advertisement; title of honor; renown; pretext
Tity̆·os -ī *m* giant slain by Apollo for insulting Latona and thrown into Tartarus
Tīty̆r·us -ī *m* shepherd in Vergil's pastorals, sometimes identified with Virgil himself
Tlēpolĕm·us -ī *m* son of Hercules
Tmōl·us or **Timōl·us -ī** *m* mountain in Lydia famous for its wines
toculli·ō -ōnis *m* banker
tōf·us or **tōph·us -ī** *m* tufa (*volcanic rock*)
tog·a -ae *f* outer garment of a Roman citizen; **toga candida** white toga (*worn by candidates for office*); **toga picta** brocaded toga (*worn by triumphant generals*); **toga praetexta** crimson-bordered toga (*worn by magistrates and freeborn children*); **toga pulla** dark-grey toga (*worn by mourners*); **toga pura** or **virilis** or **libera** toga of manhood (*worn by young men from about the age of sixteen*)
togāt·us -a -um *adj* wearing a toga; *m* Roman citizen; civilian; humble client; *f* Roman drama (*treating of Roman themes*); prostitute
togŭl·a -ae *f* little toga
tolerābĭl·is -e *adj* tolerable; patient
tolerābilius *adv* more patiently, fairly patiently
tolĕr·ans -antis *adj* tolerant; (*with genit*) tolerant of, enduring
toleranter *adv* patiently
toleranti·a -ae *f* toleration, endurance
tolerāti·ō -ōnis *f* toleration, endurance
tolerāt·us -a -um *adj* tolerable, endurable
tolĕr·ō -āre *vt* to tolerate, bear, endure; to support, maintain, sustain
tollēn·ō -ōnis *m* crane, lift, derrick
tollō tollĕre sustŭlī sublātum *vt* to lift, raise; to have (*a child*); to acknowledge (*a child*); to raise, educate; to weigh (*anchor*); to take on, take on board; to remove; to do away with, destroy; to cancel, abolish, abrogate; to lift, steal; to uplift, cheer up, excite; to erect, build up; to waste (*time*); **amicum tollere** to cheer up a friend; **animos tollere** to boost the morale; **deos tollere** to deny the existence of the gods; **hominem de medio tollere** to make away with or kill a man; **pecunias ex fano tollere** to steal money from a shrine; **signa tollere** to break camp
tolūtim *adv* at a trot
tomācŭl·um or **tomācl·um -ī** *n* sausage
tōment·um -ī *n* stuffing (*for pillows*)
Tom·ī -ōrum *m pl* or **Tom·is -is** *f* town in Moesia on the Black Sea to which Ovid was exiled
Tomīt·ae -ārum *m pl* people of Tomi
Tomītān·us -a -um *adj* of Tomi
Ton·ans -antis *m* Thunderer (*epithet of several gods, esp. Jupiter*)
tondĕō tondēre totondī tonsum *vt* to clip, shear, shave; to prune; to reap, mow; to crop, browse on; (fig) to fleece, rob; **usque ad cutem tondere** to swindle, fleece
tonitrāl·is -e *adj* thunderous
tonitr·us -ūs *m* or **tonitrŭ·um -ī** *n* thunder; *m pl* or *n pl* claps of thunder
ton·ō -āre -ŭī -ĭtum *vt* to thunder out (*words*); *vi* to thunder
tons·a -ae *f* oar blade
tonsĭl·is -e *adj* clipped
tonsill·ae -ārum *f pl* tonsils
tonsĭt·ō -āre *vt* to shear regularly
tons·or -ōris *m* shearer, barber
tonsōri·us -a -um *adj* shaving; barber's
tonstrīcŭl·a -ae *f* little hairdresser, little barber (*female*)
tonstrīn·a -ae *f* barber shop
tonstr·ix -īcis *f* hairdresser, barber (*female*)
tonsūr·a -ae *f* clipping, shearing; **capillorum tonsura** haircut
tons·us -a -um *pp* of **tondeo**; *f* see **tonsa**
tons·us -ūs *m* haircut; hairdo
tōph·us -ī *m* tufa (*volcanic rock*)
topiāri·us -a -um *adj* garden, landscape; *m* gardener, landscaper; *f* landscaping
topĭc·e -ēs *f* resourcefulness in finding topics for speeches
tor·al -ālis *n* valance
torcŭl·ar -āris or **torcŭl·um -ī** *n* wine press, oil press
toreum·a -ătis *n* embossing, relief
torment·um -ī *n* windlass; catapult, artillery piece; shot; torture rack, torture; (fig) torture; *n pl* artillery
tormĭn·a -um *n pl* colic
torminōs·us -a -um *adj* prone to colic
torn·ō -āre *vt* to form with a lathe, turn on a lathe
torn·us -ī *m* lathe; burin
torōs·us -a -um *adj* brawny, muscular
torpēd·ō -inis *f* numbness, lethargy, listnessness; crampfish, torpedo (*fish*)

torp·ĕō -ēre -ŭī *vi* to be numb; to be stiff; to be stupefied; to be groggy
torp·escō -escĕre -ŭī *vi* to grow numb, grow listless
torpĭd·us -a -um *adj* groggy
torp·or -ōris *m* torpor, numbness; grogginess
torquāt·us -a -um *adj* wearing a necklace
Torquāt·us -ī *m* T. Manlius Torquatus (*legendary Roman hero who is said to have slain a gigantic Gaul in single combat and to have worn the Gaul's necklace*)
torquĕō torquēre torsī tortum *vt* to twist, turn, wind, wrench; to whirl, hurl, wind up and hurl; to rack; (fig) to torment
torqu·ēs or **torqu·is -is** *m* or *f* necklace; collar; festoon
torr·ens -entis *adj* burning, seething; rushing, roaring (*stream*); fiery (*speech*); *m* roaring stream, torrent
torrĕō torrēre torrŭī tostum *vt* to roast, bake, burn, scorch; to parch, dry up
torr·escō -escĕre -ŭī *vi* to become burned or parched
torrĭd·us -a -um *adj* baked, parched, dried up; frostbitten
torr·is -is *m* firebrand
tortē *adv* crookedly
tortĭl·is -e *adj* twisted, winding, spiral
tort·ō -āre *vt* to twist; **tortari** to writhe
tort·or -ōris *m* torturer, executioner
tortuōs·us -a -um *adj* full of turns, winding; (fig) tortuous, complicated
tort·us -a -um *pp* of **torqueo;** *adj* twisted, crooked; gnarled (*oak*); complicated
tort·us -ūs *m* twisting, twist, spiral; **tortūs dare** (of a serpent) to form loops
torŭl·us -ī *m* tuft (*of hair*)
tor·us -ī *m* knot; bulge; muscle, brawn; bed, couch; mattress; mound; boss; flowery expression
torvĭt·ās -ātis *f* grimness, wildness
torv·us -a -um *adj* grim, fierce, stern, savage
tostus *pp* of **torreo**
tot (indecl) *adj* so many, as many
totĭdem (indecl) *adj* just so many, just as many
totĭens or **totĭēs** *adv* so often, so many times
tōt·us -a -um *adj* the whole, all, entire; **totus in illis** wholly absorbed in those matters; *n* the whole matter, all; **ex toto** wholly, totally; **in toto** on the whole, in general; **in totum** wholly, totally
toxĭc·um -ī *n* poison
trabāl·is -e *adj* of or for beams; **clavus trabalis** spike; **telum trabale** beam-like shaft
trabĕ·a -ae *f* ceremonial robe (*woven in stripes and worn by magistrates, augurs, etc.*)
trabeāt·us -a -um *adj* wearing a ceremonial robe
trab·s -is *f* beam, plank; timber; tree; object made of beams: roof, shaft, table, battering ram
tractābĭl·is -e *adj* manageable; (weather) fit for navigation
tractātĭ·ō -ōnis *f* handling, management, treatment; discussion, treatment (*of a subject*)
tractāt·us -ūs *m* touching, handling, management
tractim *adv* little by little, slowly; at length, in a drawn-out manner
tract·ō -āre *vt* to drag around, haul, pull; to touch, handle; to manage, control, wield; to conduct, carry on, transact, practice; to discuss; **se tractare** to behave oneself, conduct oneself
tract·us -a -um *pp* of **traho;** *adj* flowing, fluent, continuous (*discourse*)
tract·us -ūs *m* dragging; drawing out, dragging out, extension (*e.g., of a war*); track, trail; tract, extent, distance; region, district
trādĭtĭ·ō -ōnis *f* handing over, surrender; transmission
trādĭt·or -ōris *m* betrayer, traitor
trādō trādĕre trādĭdī trādĭtum *vt* to hand over, surrender, deliver; to betray; to hand down, bequeath, transmit, pass on; to relate, recount; to teach; **se tradere** (with *dat*) **a** to surrender to; **b** to devote oneself to
trā·dūcō -dūcĕre -duxī -ductum *vt* to lead across, bring over, transfer, to lead in parade, make a show of; to disgrace, degrade; to broadcast, proclaim; to pass, spend
trāductĭ·ō -ōnis *f* transfer, transference; course, passage (*of time*); metonymy
trāduct·or -ōris *m* conveyor
trāductus *pp* of **traduco**
trād·ux -ŭcis *m* vine branch
tragĭcē *adv* as in tragedy
tragicocōmoedĭ·a -ae *f* melodrama
tragĭc·us -a -um *adj* of tragedy, tragic; in the tragic style, grand, solemn; of a tragic nature, tragic, moving, terrible; **actor tragicus** tragedian; *m* tragic playwright
tragoedĭ·a -ae *f* tragedy
tragoed·us -ī *m* tragic actor, tragedian
trāgŭl·a -ae *f* javelin
trag·us -ī *m* body odor of the armpits; a fish (*of unknown type*)
trah·ax -ācis *adj* greedy
trahĕ·a -ae *f* sledge, drag
trahō trahĕre traxī tractum *vt* to draw, drag, trail; to draw out, pull out, extract; to lead, take along, be followed by; to contract, wrinkle; to inhale; to quaff; to take on, assume, acquire, get; to squander, dissipate; to spin, manufacture; to attract, allure, influence; to win over (*to the other side*); to refer,

ascribe; to distract; to consider, ponder; to spin out, prolong, protract
Trājān·us -ī *m* Trajan (*M. Ulpius Trajanus, Roman emperor,* 97-117 A.D.)
trājectī·ō -ōnis *f* crossing, passage; transposition (*of words*); shift of meaning; exaggeration
trājectus *pp* of **trajicio**
trāject·us -ūs *m* crossing over, passage
trā·jiciō or **trans·iciō** or **trans·jiciō -jicĕre -jēcī -jectum** *vt* to have go across, cause to go across, transfer; to ship across, transport; to pass through, break through; to stab through, pierce; (with double *acc*) to bring (*e.g., troops*) across (*river, mountain*); (with **trans** + *acc*) to lead across; (with **in** + *acc*) to lead over into
trālāt- = **translat-**
Trall·ēs -ium *f pl* town in Lydia
trālŏqu·or -ī *vt* to talk over, enumerate, recount
trālūcĕō see **transluceo**
trām·a -ae *f* woof, web
trāmĕō = **transmeo**
trām·es -ĭtis *m* path, track, trail
trāmi- = **transmi-**
trānătō = **transnato**
trān·ō or **transn·ō -āre** *vt* to swim across; to pass through, permeate; *vi* to swim across; to pass through
tranquillē *adv* quietly, calmly
tranquillĭt·ās -ātis *f* tranquillity, stillness, calmness
tranquill·ō -āre *vt* to calm, quiet, tranquillize
tranquill·us -a -um *adj* calm, quiet, tranquil; *n* calm, calmness, peace, quiet, tranquillity; quiet sea
trans *prep* (with *acc*) across, over, beyond
transab·ĕō -īre -iī *vt* to go through, pierce
transact·or -ōris *m* manager
transactus *pp* of **transigo**
transad·ĭgō -igĕre -ēgī -actum *vt* to pierce; to run (*someone*) through; (with double *acc*) to run (*e.g., a sword*) through (*someone*)
Transalpīn·us -a -um *adj* Transalpine, lying beyond the Alps
tran·scendō or **trans·scendō -scendĕre -scendī -scensum** *vt* to climb or step over, surmount; to overstep, transgress; *vi* to climb or step across
trans·cīdō -cīdĕre -cīdī *vt* to flog soundly
tran·scrībō or **trans·scrībō -scrībĕre -scripsī -scriptum** *vt* to transcribe, copy off; (law) to transfer, convey; to transfer, remove
trans·currō -currĕre -currī or **-cucurrī -cursum** *vt & vi* to run or dash over; to run or dash through; to run or dash by or past
transcurs·us -ūs *m* running through, passage; cursory mention
transd- = **trad-**
transenn·a -ae *f* grating; lattice work, trellis work; lattice window; fowler's net
trans·ĕō -īre -iī -ĭtum *vt* to pass over, cross; to desert; to pass (*in a race*); to pass over, make no mention of; to treat cursorily; to overstep, pass beyond; to surpass; *vi* to go over, go across, pass over; to pass by, go by; to shift (*to another opinion, topic, etc.*); (of time) to pass, go by; to pass away; (with **ad** + *acc*) **a** to cross over to (*a place*); **b** to cross over to, desert to; (with **in** + *acc*) to change into, be transformed into; (with **per** + *acc*) to penetrate, permeate, pervade
trans·fĕrō -ferre -tŭlī -lātum (or **trālātum**) *vt* to carry or bring across; to transfer by writing, to copy; to shift, transfer; to transform; to postpone; to translate; to use (*words*) figuratively
trans·fīgō -fīgĕre -fixī -fixum *vt* to pierce, transfix; to run (*someone*) through
transfigūr·ō -āre *vt* to transform
transfixus *pp* of **transfigo**
trans·fodĭō -fodĕre -fōdī -fossum *vt* to run through, stab, pierce
transform·is -e *adj* transformed, changed in shape
transform·ō -āre *vt* to change in shape, transform
transfossus *pp* of **transfodio**
transfŭg·a -ae *m* or *f* deserter, turncoat
trans·fugĭō -fugĕre -fūgī *vi* to desert
transfug·ĭum -iī or **-ī** *n* desertion
trans·fundō -fundĕre -fūdī -fūsum *vt* to transfuse; to pour; (with **in** + *acc*) to pour (*a liquid*) into; (with **ad** + *acc*) (fig) to shift (*affection, allegiance*) to (*another person*)
transfūsī·ō -ōnis *f* transmigration
transfūsus *pp* of **transfundo**
trans·gredĭor -grĕdī -gressus sum *vt* to cross, pass over; to exceed; *vi* to go across; to cross over (*to another party*)
transgressī·ō -ōnis *f* crossing, passage; transposition (*of words*)
transgressus *pp* of **transgredior**
transgress·us -ūs *m* crossing
transiciō see **trajicio**
transiect- = **traject-**
trans·ĭgō -igĕre -ēgī -actum *vt* to pierce, run through; to finish, settle, transact, accomplish, perform, conclude; to pass, spend (*time*); *vi* to come to an agreement, reach an understanding
transil·ĭō or **transsil·ĭō -īre -ŭī** *vt* to jump over, jump across; to overstep, exceed; to skip, omit; *vi* to jump across
transĭt·ans -antis *adj* passing through
transitĭ·ō -ōnis *f* crossing, passage;

switching (*to another party*); contagion, infection; passageway
transitus *pp* of **transeo**
transit·us -ūs *m* crossing, passage; passing; traffic; crossing over, desertion; change, period of change, transition; fading (*of colors*); **in transitu** in passing
translātīci·us or **trālātīci·us -a -um** *adj* transmitted, traditional, customary; usual, common
translāti·ō or **trālāti·ō -ōnis** *f* transfer, shift; transporting; translation; metaphor, figure
translātīv·us -a -um *adj* transferable
translāt·or -ōris *m* middleman (*in a transfer*)
translātus *pp* of **transfero**
translĕg·ō -ĕre *vt* to read through
translūc·ĕō or **trālūc·ĕō -ēre** *vi* to be reflected; to shine through
transmarīn·us -a -um *adj* from beyond the seas, foreign, overseas
transmĕ·ō or **trāmĕ·ō -āre** *vi* to cross, pass
transmigr·ō -āre *vi* to move, migrate, emigrate
transmissi·ō -ōnis *f* crossing, passage
transmissus *pp* of **transmitto**
transmiss·us -ūs *m* passing over, crossing, passage
trans·mittō or **trā·mittō -mittĕre mīsī -missum** *vt* to send across; to transmit; to let pass; to hand over, entrust, commit; to pass over, leave unmentioned; to pass through, endure; (with **in** + *acc*) to send (*someone*) across to or into; (with **per** + *acc*) to let (*someone*) pass through; *vi* to cross over, cross, pass (*from one place to another*)
transmontān·ī -ōrum *m pl* people across the mountains
trans·movĕō -movēre -mōvī -mōtum *vt* to move, transfer
transmūt·ō -āre *vt* to change, shift
transnăt·ō or **trānăt·ō -āre** *vt* to swim; *vi* to swim across
transnō see **trano**
Transpadān·us -a -um *adj* Transpadane, beyond or N. of the Po River
transpect·us -ūs *m* view, prospect
transpic·iō or **transspic·iō -ĕre** *vt* to look through
trans·pōnō -pōnĕre -posŭī -posĭtum *vt* to transfer
transport·ō -āre *vt* to transport
transposĭtus *pp* of **transpono**
Transrhēnān·us -a -um *adj* beyond the Rhine, E. of the Rhine
transs- = **trans-**
Transtiberīn·us -a -um *adj* across the Tiber
transtin·ĕō -ēre *vi* to pass through
transtr·um -ī *n* thwart
transult·ō -āre *vi* to jump across
transūt·us -a -um *adj* pierced through
transvecti·ō or **trāvecti·ō -ōnis** *f* transportation, crossing
trans·vĕhō or **trā·vĕhō -vehĕre vexī -vectum** *vt* to transport; to carry, lead (*in a parade*); **transvehi** to ride by (*in a parade*); (of time) to elapse
transverbĕr·ō -āre *vt* to pierce through and through, transfix
transversa *adv* sideways; across one's course
transversārĭ·us -a -um *adj* transverse, lying crosswise
transvers·us or **trāvers·us** or **transvors·us -a -um** *adj* lying across, lying crosswise; inopportune; astray; in the wrong direction; *n* wrong direction, opposite direction; **de transverso** unexpectedly; **ex transverso** unexpectedly; sideways
transvolĭt·ō -āre *vt* to flit through, fly through
transvŏl·ō or **trāvŏl·ō -āre** *vt & vi* to fly over, fly across, fly by, zip by
transvorsus see **transversus**
trapēt·us -ī *m* oil press
trapezīt·a -ae *m* banker
Trapĕz·ūs -untis *f* city in Pontus on the Black Sea
Trasimenn·us or **Trasumenn·us -ī** *m* lake in Etruria where Hannibal defeated the Romans (217 B.C.)
trāv- = **transv-**
trecēn·ī -ae -a *adj* three hundred each
trecentēsĭm·us -a -um *adj* three hundredth
trecentiēs *adv* three hundred times
trechedipn·um -ī *n* light garment worn to dinner
tredĕcim (indecl) *adj* thirteen
tremebund·us -a -um *adj* trembling, shivering
treme·faciō -facĕre -fēcī -factum *vt* to shake, cause to shake
tremend·us -a -um *adj* terrible, frightful
trem·escō or **trem·iscō -escĕre -ŭī** *vt* to tremble at; *vi* to tremble
trem·ō -ĕre -ŭī *vt* to tremble at; *vi* to tremble, shiver, quake
trem·or -ōris *adj* trembling, shaking, shivering; dread
tremŭl·us -a -um *adj* trembling, quivering, tremulous, shivering
trepidanter *adv* tremblingly, nervously
trepidāti·ō -ōnis *f* nervousness, alarm
trepidē *adv* nervously, in alarm
trepĭd·ō -āre *vt* to start at, be jumpy or nervous at; *vi* to be nervous, be jumpy, be alarmed; (of a flame) to flicker; (of streams) to rush along
trepĭd·us -a -um *adj* nervous, jumpy, agitated, hurried, restless; bubbling; perilous, critical, alarming; **in re trepida** in a ticklish situation
trēs (or **trīs**) **tria** *adj* three; (denoting a small number) a couple of

tress·is -is *m* small coin: mere trifle
tresvīrī (*genit:* **triumvirōrum**) *m pl* three-man board, triumvirs
Trēvĕr·ī -ōrum *m pl* people of E. Gaul
triangŭl·us -a -um *adj* triangular; *n* triangle
triārī·ī -ōrum *m pl* soldiers of the third rank in a battle line, reserves
tribuārī·us -a -um *adj* tribal
tribūl·is -is *m* fellow tribesman
trībŭl·um -ī *n* threshing sledge (*wooden platform with iron teeth underneath*)
tribŭl·us -ī *m* caltrop (*thistle*)
tribūn·al -ālis *n* raised platform; tribunal, judgment seat; (in camp) general's platform; cenotaph
tribūnāt·us -ūs *m* tribuneship, rank of tribune
tribūnicī·us -a -um *adj* tribunician, tribune's; *m* ex-tribune
tribūn·us -ī *m* tribune; **tribunus aerarius** paymaster; **tribunus militaris** or **tribunus militum** military tribune (*six in each legion, serving under the legatus, and elected by the people or at times appointed by a commander*); **tribunus plebis** tribune of the people (*ten in number, serving the interests of the plebeians*)
trib·ŭō -uĕre -ŭī -ūtum *vt* to divide; to distribute, bestow, confer, assign; to give, present; to concede, grant, allow; to ascribe, impute; to devote, spend
trib·us -ūs *m* tribe (*originally three in number and eventually increased to thirty-five*)
tribūtārī·us -a -um *adj* subject to tribute; **tributariae tabellae** letters of credit
tribūtim *adv* by tribes
tribūtī·ō -ōnis *f* distribution
tribūt·us -a -um *pp* of **tribuo;** *adj* arranged by tribes; *n* tribute, tax, contribution
trīc·ae -ārum *f pl* tricks; nonsense
trīcēn·ī -ae -a *adj* thirty each
tric·eps -ipĭtis *adj* three-headed
trīcēsim·us -a -um *adj* thirtieth
trichīl·a -ae *f* bower, arbor; summer home
trīciens or **trīciēs** *adv* thirty times
trīclīn·ium -iī or **-ī** *n* dining couch (*running around three sides of a table*); dining room
trīc·ō -ōnis *m* practical joker, trickster
trīc·or -ārī -ātus sum *vi* to cause trouble; to pull tricks
tricorp·or -ŏris *adj* three-bodied
tricusp·is -ĭdis *adj* three-pronged
trid·ens -entis *adj* three-pronged; *m* trident
Tridentĭf·er or **Tridentĭg·er -ĕrī** *m* Trident Bearer (*epithet of Neptune*)
tridŭ·um -ī *n* three-day period, three days
trienn·ia -ĭum *n pl* triennial festival, festival celebrated every three years
trienn·ium -iī or **-ī** *n* three-year period, three years
tri·ens -entis *m* one third; coin (*one third of an ace*); third of a pint
trientābŭl·um -ī *n* land given by the state as an equivalent for one third of the sum which the state owed
trientī·us -a -um *adj* sold for a third
triērarch·us -ī *m* captain of a trireme
triēr·is -is *f* trireme
trietērĭc·us -a -um *adj* triennial, recurring every three years; *n pl* festival of Bacchus
trietēr·is -ĭdis *f* three-year period; triennial festival
trifārĭam *adv* in three places, on three sides
trifau·x -cis *adj* triple-throated
trifĭd·us -a -um *adj* three-forked; split into three parts
triform·is -e *adj* triple
trifīl·is -e *adj* having three threads or hairs
tri·fūr -fūris *m* archthief
trifurcĭf·er -ĕrī *m* archvillain, hardened criminal
trigemĭn·us or **tergemĭn·us -a -um** *adj* threefold, triple; *m pl* triplets
trīgintā (indecl) *adj* thirty
trig·ōn -ōnis *m* ball game
trilībr·is -e *adj* three-pound
trilingu·is -e *adj* triple-tongued
tril·ix -īcis *adj* three-ply, triple-stranded
trimestr·is -e *adj* of three months
trimĕtr·us -ī *m* trimeter
trīm·us -a -um *adj* three-year-old
Trīnăcr·is -ĭdis *adj* Sicilian
Trīnacrī·us -a -um *adj* Sicilian; *f* Sicily
trīn·ī -ae -a *adj* threefold, triple; three each
trinōd·is -e *adj* having three knots, triple-knotted
triōbŏl·us -ī *m* three-obol coin, half-drachma piece
Triōn·ēs -um *m pl* Great Bear and Little Bear (*constellation*)
tripartītō *adv* in three parts, into three parts
tripartīt·us or **tripertīt·us -a -um** *adj* divided into three parts, threefold
tripectŏr·us -a -um *adj* triple-bodied, triple-breasted
tripedāl·is -e *adj* three-foot
tripertītus see **tripartitus**
trip·ēs -ĕdis *adj* three-legged
tripl·ex -ĭcis *adj* threefold, triple; *n* three times as much, threefold portion
tripl·us -a -um *adj* triple, threefold
Triptolĕm·us -a -um *m* son of Celeus the king of Eleusis, favorite of Ceres, inventor of agriculture, and one of the judges in the lower world

tripudi·ō -āre *vi* to dance (*as a religious act*); to do a war dance; to leap, dance, hop about
tripudium -iī or **-ī** *n* solemn religious dance; war dance; dance (*in general*); favorable omen (*when the sacred chickens ate hungrily*)
trip·us -ŏdis *f* tripod (*three-footed vessel*); oracle, Delphic oracle
triquĕtr·us -a -um *adj* triangular; Sicilian
trirēm·is -e *adj* having three banks of oars; *f* trireme
trīs see **tres**
triscurrī·a -ōrum *n pl* broad humor, fantastic nonsense
tristicŭl·us -a -um *adj* somewhat sad
tristific·us -a -um *adj* ominous; saddening
tristimōnī·a -ae *f* sadness
trist·is -e *adj* sad, sorrowful, melancholy, glum, dispirited; bringing sorrow, saddening, dismal; gloomy, sullen; stern, harsh; disagreeable, offensive (*odor*); bitter (*taste*)
tristiti·a -ae *f* sadness, gloom, gloominess, melancholy; severity, sternness
tristitī·ēs -ēī *f* sadness, sorrow, melancholy
trisulc·us -a -um *adj* three-forked
trităv·us -ī *m* great-great-great-grandfather
trīticĕ·us -a -um *adj* wheat, of wheat
trītic·um -ī *n* wheat
Trīt·ōn -ōnis *m* son of Neptune who blows through a shell to calm the seas; lake in Africa where Minerva was said to be born
Trītōniăc·us -a -um *adj* Tritonian
Trītōn·is -ĭdis or **-ĭdos** *f* Minerva
Trītōnĭ·us -a -um *adj* Tritonian; *f* Minerva
trīt·or -ōris *m* grinder
trītūr·a -ae *f* threshing
trīt·us -a -um *pp* of **tero**; *adj* worn, well-worn; beaten (*path*); experienced, expert; common, trite (*language*)
trīt·us -ūs *m* rubbing, friction
triumphāl·is -e *adj* triumphal; having had a triumph; *n pl* triumphal insignia (*without the actual triumph*)
triumph·ō -āre *vt* to triumph over, conquer completely, vanquish; *vi* to make a triumphal procession, celebrate a triumph, triumph
triumph·us or **triump·us -ī** *m* victory parade, triumph; victory, triumph; **triumphum agere** (with **de** or **ex** + *abl*) to celebrate a triumph over
triumv·ir -īrī *m* triumvir, commissioner; mayor (*of a provincial town*)
triumvirāl·is -e *adj* triumviral, of the triumvirs
triumvirāt·us -ūs *m* triumvirate, office of triumvir
triumvĭr·ī -ōrum *m pl* triumvirs, three commissioners, three-man commission (*appointed at various times to serve various purposes*); **triumviri capitales** police commissioners, superintendents of prisons and executions
trivenēfĭc·a -ae *f* nasty old witch
Trivĭ·a -ae *f* Diana
triviāl·is *adj* of the crossroads; found everywhere, common, ordinary
triv·ium -iī or **-ī** *n* crossroads, intersection; public street, highway
trivĭ·us -a -um *adj* of or at the crossroads
Trō·as -ădis *adj* Trojan; *f* Troad, district of Troy; Trojan woman
trochae·us -ī *m* trochee; tribrach (*metrical foot of three short syllables*)
trochlĕ·a -ae *f* block and tackle
troch·us -ī *m* hoop
Trōĭ·a or **Trōj·a -ae** *f* Troy
Trōiăd·es -um *f pl* Trojan women
Trōĭc·us -a -um *adj* Trojan
Trōīl·us -ī *m* son of Priam, killed by Achilles
Trōĭ·us -a -um *adj* Trojan; *f* see **Troia**
Trōjān·us -a -um *adj* Trojan; *m pl* Trojans
Trōjugĕn·a *masc & fem adj* Trojan-born, born at Troy, of Trojan descent, Trojan; *m* Trojan
tropae·um -ī *n* trophy, victory memorial; victory; mark, token, memorial, monument
Trōs Trōis *m* Tros (*king of Phrygia after whom Troy was named*)
trucīdātī·ō -ōnis *f* slaughter, massacre, butchery
trucīd·ō -āre *vt* to slaughter, massacre, cut down
truculentē or **truculenter** *adv* grimly, fiercely
truculenti·a -ae *f* savagery, ferocity; harshness; inclemency
truculent·us -a -um *adj* savage, grim, fierce, cruel
trud·is -is *f* pointed pole, pike
trūdō trūdĕre trūsī trūsum *vt* to push, thrust, drive, shove; to put forth (*buds*)
trull·a -ae *f* dipper, ladle, scoop; brazier; wash basin
trunc·ō -āre *vt* to lop off, mutilate, maim
trunc·us -a -um *adj* lopped; stripped (*of branches and leaves*), trimmed; maimed, mutilated; imperfect, undeveloped; *m* trunk, tree trunk; trunk, body (*of human being*); chunk of meat; blockhead
trūsĭt·ō -āre *vt* to keep pushing, keep shoving
trūsus *pp* of **trudo**
trutĭn·a -ae *f* balance, pair of scales; criterion
trutĭn·or -ārī -ātus sum *vt* to weigh, balance

trux trucis *adj* savage, grim, fierce, wild
trȳgōn·us -ī *m* stingray
tu *pron* you (*singular*)
tuātim *adv* in your manner, as is typical of you
tub·a -ae *f* bugle, war trumpet
tūb·er -ĕris *n* lump, bump, swelling; truffle (*food*)
tub·er -ĕris *f* apple tree; *m* apple
tubĭc·en -ĭnis *m* bugler, trumpeter
tubilustr·ium -iī or **-ī** *n* festival of bugles or trumpets (*celebrated on March 23rd and May 23rd and including a ritual cleaning of the bugles or trumpets*)
tuburcin·or -ārī -ātus sum *vt* to devour, gobble up
tub·us -ī *m* tube, pipe
tuccēt·um or **tūcēt·um -ī** *n* sausage
tudĭt·ō -āre *vt* to keep hitting, keep beating
tuĕor *or* **tu·or tuērī tuĭtus sum** or **tūtus sum** *vt* to see, look at, gaze at, watch, observe; to look after, take care of, guard, defend, protect
tugur·ium -iī or **-ī** *n* hut, hovel, cottage
tuiti·ō -ōnis *f* guarding, defense; **tuitio sui** self-defense
Tulliān·um -ī *n* state prison in Rome, reputedly built by Servius Tullius
Tulliŏl·a -ae *f* little Tullia (*Cicero's daughter*)
Tull·ius -iī or **-ī** *m* Servius Tullius (*sixth king of Rome*)
tum *adv* then, at that time; next; moreover, besides; **cum . . . tum** both . . . and especially, not only . . . but also, if . . . then surely; **tum cum** at the point when, at the time when, just then when; **tum . . . tum** first . . . then, at one time . . . at another, now . . . now, both . . . and, partly . . . partly
tume·faciō -facĕre -fēcī -factum *vt* to make swell; (fig) to inflate
tum·ĕō -ēre -ŭī *vi* to be swollen, swell up, be inflated; (of business) to be in ferment, be cooking; (of language) to be bombastic; (of a person) to be excited, be in a dither, be in a rage; to be proud
tum·escō -escĕre -ŭī *vi* to begin to swell, begin to swell up; (of wars) to brew; to grow excited, become enraged, become inflated
tumid·us -a -um *adj* swollen, swelling; bloated; rising high; proud, inflated, puffed up; arrogant; incensed, enraged, exasperated; bombastic
tum·or -ōris *m* tumor, swelling; protuberance, bulging; elevation (*of the ground*); commotion, excitement, anger, rage; vanity, pride, arrogance
tumŭl·ō -āre *vt* to bury
tumulōs·us -a -um *adj* full of hills, hilly, rolling
tumultuāri·us -a -um *adj* hurried, confused, disorderly; (mil) emergency, drafted hurriedly to meet an emergency; **exercitus tumultuarius** emergency army; **pugna tumultuaria** irregular fight or battle (*i.e., not fought in regular battle formation*)
tumultuāti·ō -ōnis *f* confusion, hustle and bustle, panic
tumultŭ·ō -āre or **tumultŭ·or -ārī -ātus sum** *vi* to make a disturbance; to be in uproar, be topsyturvy
tumultuōsē *adv* disorderly, in confusion
tumultuōs·us -a -um *adj* boisterous, uproarious, turbulent, panicky
tumult·us -ūs *m* commotion, uproar; insurrection, rebellion, civil war; confusion, agitation (*of the mind*); outbreak (*of crime*)
tumŭl·us -ī *m* mound; rising; ground swell; burial mound; **tumulus inanis** cenotaph
tūn = **tūne (tū & ne)**
tunc *adv* (of time past) then, at that time, on that occasion, just then; (of future time) then, at that time, in that event; (of succession in time) thereupon; (in conclusion) accordingly, consequently, in that case; **tunc . . . cum** then . . . when, just when, just at the time when; only when, whenever; **tunc demum** not until, then only, not till then; **tunc primum** then for the first time; **tunc quando** whenever; **tunc quoque** then too; **tunc vero** then to be sure, exactly then
tundō tundĕre tutŭdī tunsum or **tūsum** *vt* to beat, pound, hammer, thump; to buffet; to thresh; (fig) to harp on, keep at, importune
tunĭc·a -ae *f* tunic (*ordinary sleeved garment worn by both sexes*); skin, peel, husk, coating
tunicāt·us -a -um *adj* wearing a tunic; in shirt sleeves; coated, covered with skin
tunicŭl·a -ae *f* short tunic; thin skin or coating
tunsus *pp of* **tundo**
tuor see **tueor**
turb·a -ae *f* turmoil, disorder, uproar, commotion; brawl; crowd, disorderly crowd, mob, gang; multitude; common crowd, the masses; a large number
turbāment·a -ōrum *n pl* means of disturbance
turbātē *adv* in confusion, confusedly
turbāti·ō -ōnis *f* confusion, disorder
turbāt·or -ōris *m* ringleader, troublemaker, disturber
turbāt·us -a -um *adj* confused, disorderly; disturbed, annoyed
turbell·ae -ārum *f pl* stir, row; **turbellas facere** to cause a row
turben see **turbo** *m*
turbĭdē *adv* confusedly, in disorder
turbid·us -a -um *adj* wild, confused, boisterous; muddy, turbid;

troubled, perplexed; vehement; disheveled (*hair*); stormy (*sky, weather*)

turbinĕ·us -a -um *adj* cone-shaped

turb·ō -ĭnis *m* or **turb·en -ĭnis** *n* whirl, twirl, eddy; spinning, revolution; coil; spinning top; reel; spindle; wheel; tornado, whirlwind; wheel of fortune; (fig) whirlwind, storm

turb·ō -āre *vt* to throw into confusion, disturb, agitate; to break, disorganize (*in battle*), cause to break ranks; to confuse, confound; to muddy

turbulentē or **turbulenter** *adv* boisterously, tumultuously, confusedly

turbulent·us -a -um *adj* turbulent, wild, stormy; disturbed, confused; seditious, trouble-making

turd·a -ae *f* or **turd·us -ī** *m* thrush

tūrĕ·us -a -um *adj* of frankincense

turgĕō turgēre tursī *vi* to be swollen, be puffed up; to be bombastic

turgesc·ō -ĕre *vi* to begin to swell, begin to swell up; to begin to blow up (*in anger*)

turgidŭl·us -a -um *adj* poor swollen, swollen little (*eyes*)

turgĭd·us -a -um *adj* swollen, puffed up, inflated; turgid, bombastic

tūribŭl·um -ī *n* censer

tūricrĕm·us -a -um *adj* incense-burning

tūrĭf·er -ĕra -ĕrum *adj* incense-producing

tūrilĕg·us -a -um *adj* incense-gathering

turm·a -ae *f* troop, squadron (*of cavalry*); crowd, group

turmāl·is -e *adj* of a squadron; equestrian; *m pl* troopers

turmātim *adv* by troops, by squadrons, squadron by squadron

Turn·us -ī *m* king of the Rutuli, killed by Aeneas

turpicŭl·us -a -um *adj* ugly little; somewhat indecent

turpificāt·us -a -um *adj* corrupted, debased, degenerate

turpilucricupĭd·us -a -um *adj* (coll) eager to make a fast buck

turp·is -e *adj* ugly, deformed; foul, filthy, nasty; disgraceful, shameless; dirty, obscene, indecent

turpĭter *adv* repulsively; disgracefully, scandalously, shamelessly

turpitūd·ō -ĭnis *f* ugliness, deformity; foulness; disgrace; moral turpitude

turp·ō -āre *vt* to make ugly, disfigure; to soil, dirty, defile, pollute

turrĭg·er -ĕra -ĕrum *adj* turreted; (Cybele) wearing a turreted crown (*representing the earth with its cities*)

turr·is -is *f* turret, tower; howdah (*on an elephant*); (fig) castle, mansion

turrīt·us -a -um *adj* turreted; fortified with turrets; crowned with turrets, adorned with a turret crown

turt·ur -ŭris *m* turtledove

tūs tūris *m* incense, frankincense

Tusculān·us -a -um or **Tusculens·is -e** *adj* Tusculan, of Tusculum; *m pl* Tusculans

Tuscŭl·us -a -um *adj* Tusculan; *n* Tusculum (*town in Latium near Alba Longa, about twelve miles from Rome*)

Tusc·us -a -um *adj* Etruscan

tussicŭl·a -ae *f* slight cough

tuss·iō -īre *vi* to cough, have a cough

tuss·is -is *f* cough

tūsus *pp* of **tundo**

tūtām·en -ĭnis or **tūtāment·um -ī** *n* means of defense, defense, protection

tūte = tū & te emphatic form of **tū**

tūtē *adv* safely

tūtēl·a or **tūtell·a -ae** *f* care, charge, patronage, protection, defense; guardianship; charge, thing protected; guardian, keeper, watcher

tūtĕmet = tū & te & met emphatic form of **tū**

tūt·ō -āre or **tūt·or -ārī -ātus sum** *vt* to guard, protect, defend; to keep safe, watch, preserve; to ward off, avert; (with **ab** + *abl* or with **ad** or **adversus** + *acc*) to protect (*someone*) from, guard (*someone*) against

tūt·or -ōris *m* protector; guardian (*of minors, women, etc.*)

tūt·us -a -um *pp* of **tueor**; *adj* safe, secure; cautious, prudent; *n* safe place, safety, shelter, security; **ex tuto** from a safe place, in safety, safely

tūtō *adv* safely, in safety

tu·us -a -um *adj* your; right for you, proper for you; *pron* yours; **tuā interest** it is of importance to you; **tui** your friends, your people, your family; **tuum est** (with *inf*) it is your duty to, it is up to you to

tuxtax *adv* (word meant to imitate the sound of blows) whack, wham; **tuxtax meo tergo erit** (coll) it's going to go whack, wham, bang over my back

Tȳd·eus -ĕī or **-ĕos** *m* Tydeus (*son of Oeneus, one of the Seven against Thebes, and father of Diomedes*)

Tȳdīd·ēs -ae *m* Diomedes (*son of Tydeus*)

tympanotrīb·a -ae *m* timbrel player, drummer

tympăn·um or **typăn·um -ī** *n* timbrel, drum

Tyndar·ĕus -ĕī or **Tyndăr·us -ī** *m* king of Sparta, husband of Leda, father of Castor and Clytemnestra, and reputed father of Pollux and Helen

Tyndarid•ēs -ae *m* descendant of Tyndareus
Tyndăr•is -ĭdis *f* descendant of Tyndareus (*female*)
Typhō•ĕus -ĕī or **ĕos** or **Typh•ōn -ōnis** *m* giant who was struck with lightning by Jupiter and buried under Mount Etna
typ•us -ī *m* figure, image (*on the wall*)
tyrannactŏn•us -ī *m* tyrannicide, assassin of a tyrant
tyrannicē *adv* tyrannically; arbitrarily, cruelly
tyrannicīd•a -ae *m* tyrannicide, assassin of a tyrant
tyrannic•us -a -um *adj* tyrannical; arbitrary, cruel
tyrann•is -ĭdis *f* tyranny, despotism
tyrianthĭn•a -ōrum *n pl* violet-colored clothes
Tyrĭ•us -a -um *adj* Tyrian, Phoenician; Carthaginian; Theban; crimson (*because of the famous dye produced at Tyre*); *m pl* Tyrians, Carthaginians
Tyr•ō -ūs *f* daughter of Salmoneus and mother of Pelias and Neleus by Poseidon
Tyr•os or **Tyr•us -ī** *f* Tyre (*famous commercial city of Phoenicia*)
tȳrotarīch•os -ī *m* dish of salted fish and cheese
Tyrrhēnĭ•a -ae *f* Etruria
Tyrrhēnic•us -a -um *adj* Etrurian, Etruscan
Tyrrhēn•us -a -um *adj* Etrurian, Etruscan; *m pl* Etruscans (*Pelasgian people who migrated to Italy perhaps from Lydia in Asia Minor and settled to the N. of the Tiber*)
Tyrtae•us -ī *m* Spartan poet (*7th cent.* B.C.)

U

ūb•er -ĕris *adj* rich, fruitful, fertile, plentiful, productive; rich, imaginative (*style*); (fig) fruitful, productive; *n* richness, fruitfulness, fertility; fertile soil, fruitful field; breast, teat; udder, dug
ūberĭus *adv* more fully, more copiously, more fruitfully
ūbert•ās -ātis *f* richness, fertility, productiveness
ūbertim *adv* abundantly, copiously
ubī *adv* (interrog) where; **ubi gentium** (coll) where in the world; *conj* where, in which, whereby, with whom, by whom; when, whenever
ubīcumque *adv* wherever, wheresoever; anywhere, everywhere
Ubĭ•ī -ōrum *m pl* German tribe on the lower Rhine
ubīnam *adv* where; **ubinam gentium** (coll) where in the world
ubīquāque *adv* everywhere
ubīque *adv* anywhere, everywhere
ubiŭbī *adv* wherever
ubīvīs *adv* anywhere, everywhere, wherever you please; **ubivis gentium** (coll) anywhere in the world
ūd•us -a -um *adj* wet, moist, damp, humid
ulcĕr•ō -āre *vt* to make sore; (fig) to wound
ulcerōs•us -a -um *adj* full of sores, ulcerous
ulciscor ulciscī ultus sum *vt* to avenge oneself on, take vengeance on, punish; to avenge, requite, repay
ulc•us -ĕris *n* sore, ulcer
ūlīg•ō -ĭnis *f* moisture, dampness
Ulix•ēs -is or **-ēī** or **-ei** *m* Ulysses (*king of Ithaca, son of Laertes, husband of Penelope, and father of Telemachus and Telegonus*)
ull•us -a -um *adj* any
ulmĕ•us -a -um *adj* elm, made of elm
ulmitrĭb•a -ae *m* (coll) slaphappy (*from being flogged with elm whips*)
ulm•us -ī *f* elm tree; *f pl* elm rods
uln•a -ae *f* elbow; arm; (as measure of length) ell
ulpĭc•um -ī *n* leek
ulterĭ•or -ūs *adj* farther, on the farther side, more remote; further, more, longer, in a higher degree; worse; *m pl* more remote people, those beyond; *n pl* things beyond
ultĭmum *adv* finally, for the last time
ultĭm•us -a -um *adj* farthest, most distant, extreme; earliest; latest, final, last; greatest; lowest; meanest; *n* last thing; end; **ad ultimum** to the end, to the extreme, in the highest degree, to the last degree, utterly; *n pl* extremes; the worst
ultĭ•ō -ōnis *f* vengeance, revenge
ult•or -ōris *m* avenger, punisher, revenger
ultrā *adv* beyond, farther, besides; *prep* (with *acc*) beyond, past; (of number, measure, degree) over, beyond, more than, over and above
ultr•ix īcis *adj* avenging
ultrō *adv* to the farther side, beyond; on the other side; besides, moreover, too; of one's own accord, without being asked; without being spoken to; **ultro tributa** expenditure incurred by the government for public works
ultus *pp* of **ulciscor**

ulŭl·a -ae *f* screech owl
ululāt·us -ūs *m* crying, wailing (*esp. of mourners*); war cry
ulŭl·ō -āre *vt* to cry out to; *vi* to shriek, yell; (of places) to ring, resound
ulv·a -ae *f* sedge
umbell·a -ae *f* umbrella, parasol
umbilīc·us -ī *m* navel, belly button; midriff; middle, center; projecting end of dowels on which books were rolled; cockle, sea snail
umb·ō -ōnis *m* boss (*of a shield*); shield; elbow
umbr·a -ae *f* shade, shadow; phantom, shade, ghost; mere shadow (*of one's former self, etc.*); shelter, cover; constant companion; grayling, umber (*fish*); **rhetorica umbra** rhetorician's school
umbrācŭl·um -ī *n* bower, arbor; school; umbrella, parasol
umbrāticŏl·a -ae *m* lounger, loafer (*in the shade*)
umbrātic·us -a -um *adj* too fond of the shade, lazy
umbrātĭl·is -e *adj* remaining in the shade, private, retired; academic
Umbri·a -ae *f* Umbria (*district in central Italy*)
umbrĭf·er -ĕra -ĕrum *adj* shady
umbr·ō -āre *vt* to shade, cover
umbrōs·us -a -um *adj* shady
ūmect·ō -āre *vt* to wet, moisten
ūmect·us -a -um *adj* moist, damp
ūm·ĕō -ēre *vi* to be moist, be damp, be wet
umĕr·us -ī *m* shoulder
ūmesc·ō -ĕre *vi* to become moist or wet
ūmidŭl·us -a -um *adj* dampish
ūmid·us -a -um *adj* moist, damp, wet; green (*lumber*); *n* wet place
ūm·or -ōris *m* moisture; liquid, fluid
umquam or **unquam** *adv* ever, at any time
ūnā *adv* together; **ūnā venire** to come along
ūnanim·ans -antis *adj* of one mind, of one accord
ūnanimĭt·ās -ātis *f* unanimity
ūnanimus -a -um *adj* unanimous; of one mind, of one heart, harmonious
ūnci·a -ae *f* a twelfth; ounce (*one twelfth of a pound or libra*)
ūnciāri·us -a -um *adj* containing a twelfth; **faenus unciarium** eight and one third percent interest per annum
ūnciātim *adv* little by little
uncīnāt·us -a -um *adj* hooked, barbed
ūnciŏl·a -ae *f* a mere twelfth
uncti·ō -ōnis *f* rubdown; (fig) wrestling
unctĭt·ō -āre *vt* to keep rubbing with oil, keep oiling
unctiuscŭl·us -a -um *adj* somewhat too unctuous
unct·or -ōris *m* anointer, rubdown man
unct·um -ī *n* sumptuous dinner; ointment
unctūr·a -ae *f* anointing
unct·us -a -um *pp* of **ungo;** *adj* greasy; resinous; sumptuous; *n* sumptuous dinner; ointment
unc·us -a -um *adj* hooked, crooked, barbed; *m* hook, clamp; grappling iron
und·a -ae *f* water; liquid; wave, billow; (fig) stream, tide, agitated mass
unde *adv* from where, whence; from whom; **unde unde** or **undeunde** from some place or other, somehow or other, by hook or by crook
undeciens or **undeciēs** *adv* eleven times
undĕcim (indecl) *adj* eleven
undecim·us -a -um *adj* eleventh
undecumque or **undecunque** *adv* from whatever place, from whatever source
undēn·ō -ae -a *adj* eleven in a group, eleven each, eleven
undēnōnāgintā (indecl) *adj* eighty-nine
undeoctōgintā (indecl) *adj* seventy-nine
undēquadrāgintā (indecl) *adj* thirty-nine
undēquinquāgensĭm·us or **undēquinquāgēsĭm·us -a -um** *adj* forty-ninth
undēquinquāgintā (indecl) *adj* forty-nine
undēsexāgintā (indecl) *adj* fifty-nine
undētrīcensĭm·us or **undētrīcēsĭm·us -a -um** *adj* twenty-ninth
undēvīcēsimān·ī -ōrum *m pl* soldiers of the nineteenth legion
undēvīcēsĭm·us -a -um *adj* nineteenth
undēvīgintī (indecl) *adj* nineteen
undĭque *adv* from all directions, on all sides, everywhere; in all respects, completely
undisŏn·us -a -um *adj* sea-roaring; **undisoni dei** gods of the roaring waves
und·ō -āre *vi* to move in waves, undulate; to billow; to overflow
undōs·us -a -um *adj* full of waves, billowy
ūnetvīcensĭm·us or **ūnetvīcēsĭm·us -a -um** *adj* twenty-first
ūnetvīcēsimān·ī -ōrum *m pl* soldiers of the twenty-first legion
ungō or **unguō ungĕre unxī unctum** *vt* to oil, grease, anoint
ungu·en -ĭnis *n* fat, grease, ointment
unguentār·ius -iī or **-ī** *m* perfumer
unguentāt·us -a -um *adj* anointed; perfumed, wearing perfume
unguent·um -ī *n* ointment; perfume
unguicŭl·us -ī *m* fingernail; toenail; **a teneris unguiculis** from earliest childhood
ungu·is -is *m* fingernail; toenail; claw, talon, hoof; **ad unguen** to a

tee, complete, perfect; **de tenero ungui** from earliest childhood; **transversum unguem** a hair's breadth
ungŭl·a -ae *f* hoof, claw, talon; (fig) horse
unguō see **ungo**
ūnicē *adv* singularly, solely
ūnicŏl·or -ōris *adj* of one and the same color
ūnicorn·is -e *adj* one-horned
ūnĭ·cus -a -um *adj* sole, only, single, singular, unique; uncommon, unparalleled, outstanding, unique
ūniform·is -e *adj* uniform
ūnigĕn·a -ae *masc & fem adj* only-begotten, only; of the same parentage
ūnimăn·us -a -um *adj* with one hand, one-handed
ūnĭ·ō -ōnis *m* single large pearl
ūniter *adv* jointly, conjointly
ūniversāl·is -e *adj* universal
ūniversē *adv* generally, in general
ūniversĭt·ās -ātis *f* aggregate, entirety, whole; whole world, universe
ūnivers·us -a -um *adj* all together, all taken collectively, whole, entire; *n* the whole; whole world, universe; **in universum** on the whole, in general
ūnocŭl·us -ī *m* one-eyed person
ūnomammĭ·a -ae *f* (coll) single-breasted land (*country of the Amazons*)
unquam or **umquam** *adv* ever, at any time
ūn·us -a -um *adj* one; single, only, sole; one and the same; (indef) a, an, one, some; *pron* some one, a mere individual; **ad unum** to a man; **unus et alter** one or two; **unus quisque** every one individually, every single one
ūpilĭ·ō or **ōpilĭ·ō -ōnis** *m* shepherd
upŭp·a -ae *f* hoopoe; hoe, mattock
Ūranĭ·a -ae or **Ūranĭ·ē -ēs** *f* Muse of astronomy
urbānē *adv* politely, courteously; with sophistication; wittily, elegantly
urbānĭt·ās -ātis *f* living in the city, city life; refinement, politeness; sophistication; wit; raillery
urbān·us -a -um *adj* of the city, of the town, city, town; courteous; sophisticated; witty, facetious, humorous; forward, brash; *m* city man; city slicker
urbicăp·us -ī *m* conqueror of cities
urbs urbis *f* city; the city of Rome, the capital
urceŏl·us -ī *m* little pitcher, little pot
urcĕ·us -ī *m* pitcher, water pot
ūrēd·ō -ĭnis *f* blight (*of plants*)
urgĕō urgēre ursī *vt* to prod on, urge, urge forward; to pressure, put pressure on (*someone*); to crowd, hem in; to follow up, keep at, stick by; *vi* to be pressing, be urgent; to be insistent
ūrīn·a -ae *f* urine
ūrīnāt·or -ōris *m* diver
ūrīn·ō -āre or **ūrīn·or -ārī -ātus sum** *vi* to dive
urn·a -ae *f* pot, jar; water pot; voting urn; urn of fate; cinerary urn; money jar
ūrō ūrĕre ussī ustum *vt* to burn; to burn up, reduce to ashes, consume; to scorch, parch, dry up; to sting, pain; to nip, frostbite; to rub sore; to corrode; to annoy, gall, burn up, make angry; to inflame (*with love*), kindle, set on fire
urnŭl·a -ae *f* small urn
urs·a -ae *f* she-bear
Urs·a Major (*genit:* **Urs·ae Major·is**) *f* Great Bear (*constellation*)
Urs·a Minor (*genit:* **Urs·ae Minor·is**) *f* Little Bear (*constellation*)
ursīn·us -a -um *adj* bear, bear's
urs·us -ī *m* bear
urtīc·a -ae *f* nettle; desire, itch
ūr·us -ī *m* wild ox
Usipĕt·ēs -um *m pl* German tribe on the Rhine
ūsitātē *adv* in the usual way, as usual
ūsitāt·us -a -um *adj* usual, customary, familiar; **usitatum est** (with *inf*) it is customary to
uspiam *adv* anywhere, somewhere; in any matter
usquam *adv* anywhere, in any place; anywhere, to any place
usque *adv* all the way, right on, straight on; all the time, continuously; even, as much as; **usque** (with **ab** + *abl*) all the way from; **usque** (with **ad** + *acc*) all the way to; **usque quaque** every moment, continually; on all occasions, in everything
ust·or -ōris *m* cremator
ustŭl·ō -āre *vt* to burn a little, scorch, singe; to burn up
ustus *pp* of **uro**
ūsū·capiō -capĕre -cēpī -captum *vt* (law) to acquire possession of, acquire ownership of (*by long use, by prescription*)
ūsūcapĭ·ō -ōnis *f* (law) acquisition of ownership through long use or long possession
ūsūr·a -ae *f* use, enjoyment; interest (*on capital*)
ūsūrārĭ·us -a -um *adj* for use and enjoyment; paying interest
ūsurpātĭ·ō -ōnis *f* use; (with *genit*) making use of, use of
ūsurp·ō -āre *vt* to make use of, use, employ, adopt, practice, exercise; (law) to take possession of, acquire; to seize wrongfully, usurp; to name, call, speak of; to adopt, assume; to perceive (*with the senses*), observe, experience
ūsus *pp* of **utor**
ūs·us -ūs *m* use, enjoyment; practice, employment; experience, skill; usage, custom; familiarity; usefulness, advantage, benefit; occasion,

need, necessity; **ex usu esse** or **usui esse** (with *dat*) to be useful to, be beneficial to, be a good thing for; **si usus veniat** if the need should arise, if the opportunity should present itself; **usus adest** a good opportunity comes along; **usus est** (with *abl*) there is need of; **usus et fructus** use and enjoyment; **usu venit** it happens, it occurs

ūsusfructus (*genit:* **ūsūsfructūs**) *m* use and enjoyment

ut or **utī** *adv* how, in what way; *conj* (comparative) as; (adversative) although; (temporal) when, while; (purpose) in order that; (result) that; (concessive) granted that; (introducing examples) as, as for example; (after verbs of fearing) lest, that not; (introducing an explanation or reason) as, as being, inasmuch as; (introducing indirect commands) that

utcumque or **utcunque** *adv* however; whenever; one way or another

ūtensil·is -e *adj* useful; *n pl* utensils, materials

ūt·er -ris *m* bag, skin, bottle

ut·er -ra -rum *adj* which (*of the two*); *pron* which one (*of the two*); one or the other

ut·ercumque -racumque -rumcumque *adj* whichever (*of the two*); *pron* whichever one (*of the two*)

ut·erlibet -ralibet -rumlibet *adj* whichever (*of the two*) you please; *pron* whichever one (*of the two*) you please, either one (*of the two*)

ut·erque -răque -rumque *adj* each (*of the two*), both; **sermones utriusque linguae** conversations in both languages; *pron* each one (*of the two*), both; **uterque insaniunt** both are insane

utĕr·us -ī *m* or **utĕr·um -ī** *n* womb; belly, paunch (*of a man*)

ut·ĕrvīs -răvīs -rumvīs *adj* whichever (*of the two*) you please, either; *pron* whichever one (*of the two*) you please, either one

utī see **ut**

ūtibil·is -e *adj* useful, practical

Utic·a -ae *f* city in Africa, N.W. of Carthage, where the younger Cato committed suicide

Uticens·is -is *adj* of Utica, Utican

ūtil·is -e *adj* useful, profitable, expedient, practical; (with *dat* or **ad** + *acc*) fit for, useful for, practical in

ūtilit·ās -ātis *f* usefulness, advantage

ūtiliter *adv* usefully, profitably

utinam *conj* (introducing a wish) if only, would that

utique *adv* anyhow, at least, at any rate

ūtor ūtī ūsus sum *vi* (with *abl*) **a** to use, make use of; **b** to enjoy; **c** to practice, experience; **d** to enjoy the friendship or companionship of

utpŏte *conj* as, inasmuch as; **utpote qui** inasmuch as (*he is one*) who, inasmuch as he, because he

ūtrār·ius -iī or **-ī** *m* water carrier, water boy

utrimque or **utrinque** *adv* from or on both sides, on either side; **utrimque constitit fides** on both sides the word of honor held good, both parties kept their word

utrō *adv* to which of the two sides, in which direction

utrobīque *adv* on both sides, on either hand

utrōlibet *adv* to either side

utrōque *adv* to both places, in both directions

utrŭbi or **utrŭbī** *adv* at or on which of two sides

utrubīque *adv* on both sides, on either hand

utrum *conj* either; whether

utut or **ut ut** *adv* however, in whatever way

ūv·a -ae *f* grape; bunch or cluster of grapes; vine; cluster of bees

ūvesc·ō -ĕre *vi* to become moist; (fig) to get drunk

ūvidŭl·us -a -um *adj* moist

ūvid·us -a -um *adj* wet, moist, damp, humid; drunken

ux·or -ōris *f* wife; mate (*of animals*)

uxorcŭl·a -ae *f* dear little wife

uxōri·us -a -um *adj* of a wife, wifely; very fond of a wife; henpecked

V

vac·ans -antis *adj* vacant, unoccupied; at leisure, unemployed; unengaged, single; (with *abl*) lacking, without; *n pl* unoccupied estates

vacāti·ō -ōnis *f* freedom, exemption (*from duty, service, etc.*); exemption from military service; payment for exemption from military service

vacc·a -ae *f* cow

vaccīn·ium -iī or **-ī** *n* hyacinth

vaccŭl·a -ae *f* heifer

vacē·fīō -fĭerī -factus sum *vi* to become empty, be emptied

vacill·ō -āre *vi* to stagger, reel; to vacillate, waver; to be untrustworthy

vacīvē *adv* at leisure

vacīvit·ās -ātis *f* want, lack

vacīv·us or **vocīv·us -a -um** *adj* empty; free; (with *genit*) free of, void of, free from

vac·ō -āre *vi* to be empty, be vacant,

be unoccupied; to be free, be carefree; to be at leisure, have free time; (with *abl* or **ab** + *abl*) to be free from; (with *dat* or with **ad** or **in** + *acc*) to be free for, have time for; *v impers* there is time, room, leisure; (with *inf*) there is time to or for
vacuāt·us -a -um *adj* empty
vacuē·faciō -facĕre -fēcī -factum *vt* to empty, clear, free
vacuĭt·ās -ātis *f* freedom, exemption; vacancy (*in an office*)
vacŭ·ō -āre *vt* to empty, clear, free
vacŭ·us -a -um *adj* empty, clear, free; vacant; worthless, useless; single, unmarried; widowed; at leisure; carefree; (with *genit* or *abl* or with **ab** + *abl*) free from, devoid of, without; (with *dat*) free for
vadimōn·ĭum -ĭī or **-ī** *n* (law) promise (*to appear in court*), bail (*given as a guarantee of one's appearance in court*); **vadimonium deserere** to default, fail to show up in court; **vadimonium differre** to postpone appearance in court, grant a continuance; **vadimonium facere** to put up bail; **vadimonium sistere** to appear in court
vād·ō -ĕre *vi* to go, make one's way, advance
vad·or -ārī -ātus sum *vt* to put (*someone*) under bail
vadōs·us -a -um *adj* shallow
vad·um -ī *n* shallow place, shallow, shoal, ford; body of water, stream, sea; bottom, depths
vae *interj* woe! (with *acc* or *dat*) woe to
vaf·er -ra -rum *adj* sly, cunning; subtle
vafrē *adv* slyly, cunningly
vagē *adv* far and wide
vāgīn·a -ae *f* sheath, scabbard; sheath (*of ear of grain*), hull, husk; vagina
vāg·iō -īre -īvī -iī *vi* (esp. of an infant) to cry; (of swine) to squeal
vāgīt·us -ūs *m* cry; bleating
vāg·or -ōris *m* cry, wail (*of an infant*)
vag·or -ārī -ātus sum or **vag·ō -āre** *vi* to wander, range, roam
vag·us -a -um *adj* wandering, ranging, roaming; unsteady, inconstant; vague, uncertain
vah *interj* ah!, oh!
valdē *adv* greatly, intensely; (with *adj* or *adv*) very; (as affirmative reply) yes, certainly; to be sure
valē *interj* good-bye
val·ens -entis *adj* strong, powerful; healthy, hale, well
valenter *adv* strongly; energetically
valentŭl·us -a -um *adj* a strong little
val·ĕō -ēre -ŭī *vi* to be strong, be vigorous; to be powerful, be effective; to avail, prevail, succeed; to be influential; to be valid; to be strong enough, be adequate, be capable, be able; to be of value, be of worth; to mean, signify; **te valere jubeo** I bid you farewell, good-by to you; **vale!** or **valete!** good-bye!; **vale dicere** to say good-bye, take leave
valesc·ō -ĕre *vi* to grow strong, acquire strength, thrive
valētūdinār·ĭum -ĭī or **-ī** *n* hospital
valētūd·ō -ĭnis *f* state of health; good health; ill health, illness
valg·us -a -um *adj* bowlegged
validē *adv* strongly, vehemently; (in replies) of course, certainly, definitely
valid·us -a -um *adj* strong, powerful, able; healthy, robust; fortified; influential; efficacious
vallār·is -e *adj* (decoration) awarded for scaling a rampart
vall·ēs or **vall·is -is** *f* valley
vall·ō -āre *vt* to fortify with a rampart, wall in; to protect, defend
vall·um -ī *n* rampart, palisade, entrenchment; protection
vall·us -ī *m* stake, pale; rampart with palisades, stockade; tooth (*of a comb*)
valv·ae -ārum *f pl* folding doors, double doors
vanesc·ō -ĕre *vi* to vanish, fade, disappear
vānidic·us -a -um *adj* lying, boasting; *m* liar, boaster
vāniloquentĭ·a -ae *f* empty talk
vāniloquidōr·us -ī *m* liar
vānilŏqu·us -a -um *adj* talking nonsense; lying, boasting, bragging
vānĭt·ās -ātis *f* falsity, unreality, deception, untruth; boasting, lying; vanity, conceit; worthlessness, frivolity, fickleness
vānitūd·ō -ĭnis *f* falsehood
vann·us -ī *f* fan, winnowing fan
vān·us -a -um *adj* empty, vacant; groundless, pointless; hollow, unreal; lying, false; boastful, conceited, vain; *n* emptiness, uselessness, deceptive appearance
vapĭdē *adv* poorly, badly
vapĭd·us -a -um *adj* flat, vapid, spoiled, bad; morally corrupt
vap·or -ōris *m* vapor, steam, smoke; exhalation, warmth, heat
vapōrār·ĭum -ĭī or **-ī** *n* steam pipe
vapōr·ō -āre *vt* to steam, steam up; to warm, heat; *vi* to steam, smoke
vapp·a -ae *f* sour wine; spoiled lad, good-for-nothing
vāpulār·is -e *adj* in for a flogging
vāpŭl·ō -āre *vi* to get a beating; (of savings, etc.) (fig) to take a beating
variantĭ·a -ae *f* diversity, variations
variātĭ·ō -ōnis *f* variation, difference
vārĭc·ō -āre *vt* to straddle
varicōs·us -a -um *adj* varicose
vārĭc·us -a -um *adj* with legs wide apart
varĭē *adv* variously, in various ways, differently

variĕt·ās -ātis *f* variety, difference, diversity; vicissitudes; inconstancy
vari·ō -āre *vt* to diversify, vary, change, make different; to variegate; *vi* to change color; to vary, differ, change; to differ in opinion; to waver
vari·us -a -um *adj* colored, variegated, spotted, striped; different, varying, various, changeable; versatile; inconstant, unsteady, untrustworthy
Var·ius -iī or **-ī** *m* epic and tragic poet and friend of Virgil and Horace (*d. c.* 12 B.C.)
var·ix -icis *f* varicose vein
Varr·ō -ōnis *m* M. Terentius Varro (*Roman antiquarian and philologist whose wide erudition earned him the title of the most learned of the Romans,* 116-27 B.C.)
vār·us -a -um *adj* knock-kneed; bent, crooked; opposed, contrary
vas vadis *m* bail, surety
vās vāsis or **vās·um -ī** (*pl:* **vās·a -ōrum**) *n* vessel, dish; utensil, implement; *n pl* equipment, gear; **vasa conclamare** (mil) to give the signal to pack the gear
vāsār·ium -iī or **-ī** *n* allowance for furnishings (*given to a provincial governor*)
vasculār·ius -iī or **-ī** *m* metal worker; goldsmith
vascŭl·um -ī *n* small vessel
vastāti·ō -ōnis *f* devastation, ravaging
vastāt·or -ōris *m* devastator, ravager
vastē *adv* vastly, widely; coarsely, harshly; violently
vastific·us -a -um *adj* devastating
vastit·ās -ātis *f* wasteland, desert; state of desolation, emptiness; devastation, destruction; vastness, immensity; (fig) destroyer
vastiti·ēs -ēī *f* ruin, destruction
vast·ō -āre *vt* to make empty, make desolate, vacate, empty; (mil) to lay waste, ravage, devastate, destroy
vast·us -a -um *adj* empty, deserted, desolate; ravaged, devastated; vast, enormous; uncouth, rude, uncultivated, clumsy
vāt·ēs -is *m* soothsayer, prophet; bard, poet; *f* prophetess; poetess
Vāticān·us -a -um *adj* Vatican; **mons** or **collis Vaticanus** hill in Rome on the right bank of the Tiber
vāticināti·ō -ōnis *f* prophesying, prediction, soothsaying
vāticināt·or -ōris *m* prophet, soothsayer
vāticin·ium -iī or **-ī** *n* prediction, prophecy
vāticini·us -a -um *adj* prophetic
vāticin·or -ārī -ātus sum *vt* to foretell, prophesy; to keep harping on; *vi* to prophesy; to rant and rave, talk wildly
vatill·um -ī *n* brazier
-ve *conj* (enclitic) or; **-ve . . . -ve** either . . . or
vēcordi·a -ae *f* senselessness; insanity, madness
vēc·ors -ordis *adj* senseless; foolish; mad
vectīg·al -ālis *n* tax, toll, tariff; revenue, income (*of an individual*); honorarium (*given to a magistrate*)
vectīgāl·is -e *adj* tax, toll, tariff; paying tribute, subject to taxes, taxable, taxed; **pecunia vectigalis** tax money, tribute
vecti·ō -ōnis *f* conveyance, transporting
vect·is -is *m* crowbar, lever; bar, bolt (*on a door or gate*)
vect·ō -āre *vt* to carry around; **vectari** to keep riding around
vect·or -ōris *m* bearer, carrier; rider, passenger
vectōri·us -a -um *adj* transportation, of transportation; **navigia vectoria** transport ships, transports
vectūr·a -ae *f* transport, transportation, conveyance; freight costs; fare
vectus *pp* of **veho**
Vēdiŏv·is or **Vējŏv·is -is** *m* Anti-Jove (*Etruscan divinity of the lower world, identified with Apollo and with the Jupiter of the lower world*); Little Jove (*identified with the infant Jupiter*)
vegĕt·us -a -um *adj* lively, vigorous, vivacious
vēgrand·is -e *adj* not huge, small
vehĕm·ens -entis *adj* vehement, violent, impetuous, ardent; great, tremendous; vigorous, active
vehementer or **vēmenter** *adv* vehemently, impetuously, violently, eagerly
vehementi·a -ae *f* vehemence
vehicŭl·um -ī *n* vehicle, carriage, cart; vessel, ship
vehō vehĕre vexī vectum *vt* to carry, convey, transport; **vehi** to ride, sail, be borne along
Vei·ens -entis or **Veientān·us -a -um** *adj* of Veii
Vei·ī -ōrum *m pl* old Etrurian city about twelve miles from Rome, captured by Camillus (396 B.C.)
vel *adv* even, actually; perhaps; for instance; *conj* or, or perhaps; or rather; **vel . . . vel** either . . . or
Vēlābr·um -ī *n* low ground between the Capitoline and Palatine
vēlām·en -inis *n* drape, covering, veil; clothing, robe
vēlāment·um -ī *n* curtain, veil; *n pl* olive branches draped with woolen fillets
vēlār·ium -iī or **-ī** *n* awning (*over the open-air theater*)
vēlāt·ī -ōrum *m pl* (mil) reserves
vēl·es -itis *m* light-armed soldier, skirmisher
vēlif·er -ĕra -ĕrum *adj* sail, sailing;

carina velifera sail boat, sailing ship
vēlificāti·ō -ōnis *f* sailing
vēlific·ō -āre or **vēlific·or -ārī -ātus sum** *vt* to sail through; *vi* to sail; (with *dat*) (fig) to be under full sail toward, be hell-bent for (*e.g., high office*)
Velīn·us -ī *m* river and lake in the Sabine territory
vēlitār·is -e *adj* of the light-armed troops
vēlitāti·ō -ōnis *f* skirmishing
vēlitēs = *pl* of **veles**
vēlit·or -ōris *m* skirmisher
vēlivŏl·us -a -um *adj* sail-flying (*ship*); sail-covered (*sea*)
vellic·ō -āre *vt* to pluck, pinch, nip; to carp at, rail at
vellō vellĕre vellī (or **vulsī**) **vulsum** (or **volsum**) *vt* to pluck, pull, tear at, tear away, tear out; to tear up, tear down, destroy
vell·us -ĕris *n* fleece; skin, pelt; wool; *n pl* fleecy clouds
vēl·ō -āre *vt* to veil, wrap, envelop, cover, cover up; to encircle, crown; to cover up, hide, conceal
vēlōcit·ās -ātis *f* speed, velocity
vēlōciter *adv* speedily, swiftly
vēl·ox -ōcis *adj* speedy, swift
vēl·um -ī *n* sail; veil, curtain, awning, covering; **vela dare** or **vela facere** to set sail; **remis velisque** with might and main
velut or **velŭtī** *conj* as, just as, even as; as for example; (to introduce a simile) as, as it were; (in elliptical clauses) like; **velut** or **velut si** just as if, just as though, as if, as though
vēmens see **vehemens**
vēn·a -ae *f* vein, artery; vein of metal; water course; vein (*in wood, stone, etc.*); natural bent or disposition, genius; penis; strength; *f pl* (fig) heart, core
vēnābŭl·um -ī *n* hunting spear
Venāfrān·us -a -um *adj* of Venafrum
Venāfr·um -ī *n* town in S. central Italy
vēnālici·us -a -um *adj* for sale; *m* slave dealer; *n pl* merchandise, imports and exports
vēnāl·is -e *adj* for sale; open to bribes; *mf* slave offered for sale
vēnātic·us -a -um *adj* hunting
vēnāti·ō -ōnis *f* hunt, hunting; wild-beast show; game
vēnāt·or -ōris *m* hunter
vēnātōri·us -a -um *adj* hunter's
vēnātr·ix -īcis *f* huntress
vēnātūr·a -ae *f* hunting
vēnāt·us -ūs *m* hunting
vendibil·is -e *adj* salable; attractive, popular, acceptable, on sale
venditāti·ō -ōnis *f* boasting, showing off
venditi·ō -ōnis *f* sale
vendit·ō -āre *vt* to try to sell; to advertise; to give as a bribe; **se venditare** (with *dat*) to ingratiate oneself with
vendit·or -ōris *m* vendor, seller; recipient of a bribe
vend·ō -ĕre -idī -itum *vt* to put up for sale; to sell, vend; to sell (*someone*) out, betray; to advertise; to praise, recommend
venēfic·a -ae *f* poisoner; sorceress, witch; (term of abuse) hag, witch
venēfici·um -iī or **-ī** *n* poisoning witchcraft, magic
venēfic·us -a -um *adj* poisoning, poisonous; magic; *m* poisoner; sorcerer, magician
venēnāt·us -a -um *adj* poisonous, venomous; filled with poison; magic; bewitched, enchanted; (fig) venomous, bitter
venēnif·er -ĕra -ĕrum *adj* poisonous, venemous
venēn·ō -āre *vt* to poison; (fig) to poison, injure by slander
venēn·um -ī *n* poison; drug, potion; magic charm; sorcery; ruin, destruction
vēn·eō -īre -iī -itum *vi* to go up for sale, be sold
venerābil·is -e *adj* venerable
venerābund·us -a -um *adj* reverent, reverential
venerand·us -a -um *adj* venerable
venerāti·ō -ōnis *f* veneration, reverence, great respect
venerāt·or -ōris *m* respecter, adorer; admirer
Venerĕ·us or **Veneri·us -a -um** *adj* of Venus; of sexual love, venereal; *m* Venus-throw (*best throw in playing dice*); *m pl* attendants in Venus's temple
venĕr·or -ārī -ātus sum *vt* to venerate, revere, worship, pray to; to implore, beg; to pray for
Venĕt·ī -ōrum *m pl* a people in N.E. Italy in the region around modern Venice
Veneti·a -ae *f* district of the Veneti
Venetic·us -a -um *adj* Venetian
Venĕt·us -a -um *adj* Venetian; bluish; *m* Venetian; a Blue (*i.e., a member of one of the racing factions in Rome which were called Blues, Greens, etc.*)
veni·a -ae *f* kindness, favor, goodwill; permission; pardon, forgiveness; **veniam dare** (with *dat*) to grant forgiveness to, do a favor to, grant permission to; **veniam petere** to ask for permission; **veniā vestrā** with your leave
veniō venīre vēnī ventum *vi* to come; (with **in** + *acc*) **a** to come into, enter into (*e.g., agreement, friendship*); **b** to fall into (*e.g., trouble, disgrace*)
vēn·or -ārī -ātus sum *vt & vi* to hunt
vent·er -ris *m* stomach, belly; womb; embryo, unborn child; belly, protuberance; appetite, gluttony

ventīl·ō -āre *vt* to fan, wave; to display, show off
ventī·ō -ōnis *f* coming
ventĭt·ō -āre *vi* to keep coming, come regularly
ventōs·us -a -um *adj* windy, full of wind; of the wind; wind-like, swift as the wind; conceited; fickle
ventricŭl·us -ī *m* belly; ventricle (*of the heart*)
ventriōs·us -a -um *adj* pot-bellied
ventŭl·us -ī *m* breeze
vent·us -ī *m* wind
vēnūcŭl·a -ae *f* grape (*of the type well suited for preserving*)
vēnum (*genit* not in use; *dat:* **vēnō**) *n* sale, that which is for sale; **venum** or **veno dare** to sell, sell as a slave; **venum** or **veno dari** to be sold; **venum** or **veno ire** to go up for sale, be sold
vēnum·dō or **vēnun·dō -dare -dědī -dătum** *vt* to put up for sale, sell
ven·us -ĕris *f* beauty, charm; pleasure of love, sexual indulgence, mating; beloved, love
Ven·us -ĕris *f* Venus (*goddess of love and beauty; planet*); Venus-throw (*highest throw of the dice*)
Venusĭ·a -ae *f* town in Apulia, the birthplace of Horace
Venusīn·us -a -um *adj* of Venusia
venust·ās -ātis *f* beauty, charm, attraction
venustē *adv* prettily, charmingly
venustŭl·us -a -um *adj* cute, pretty, charming little
venust·us -a -um *adj* beautiful, charming, attractive
vēpallĭd·us -a -um *adj* very pale
veprēcŭl·a -ae *f* little brier bush
vepr·ēs -is *m* thorn bush, bramble bush
vēr vēris *n* spring, springtime; youth
vērātr·um -ī *n* hellebore
vēr·ax -ācis *adj* truthful
verbēn·a -ae *f* vervain; *f pl* sacred branches worn by heralds and priests
verb·er -ĕris *n* scourge, rod, whip; flogging, scourging; thong (*of a sling and similar weapons*); *n pl* strokes, flogging
verberābilissŭm·us -a -um *adj* altogether deserving of a flogging
verberātĭ·ō -ōnis *f* flogging
verberĕ·us -a -um *adj* deserving of a flogging
verbĕr·ō -āre *vt* to scourge, flog, whip; to batter, beat
verbĕr·ō -ōnis *m* rascal
verbōsē *adv* verbosely
verbōs·us -a -um *adj* verbose, wordy
verb·um -ī *n* word; saying, expression; verb; proverb; mere talk, mere words; formula; **ad verbum** word for word, verbatim; **verba dare** (with *dat*) to cheat (*someone*); **verba facere** to speak, make a speech; **verbi causā** or **verbi gratiā** for instance; **verbo** orally; in a word, briefly; nominally, in name only; in theory; **verbum de verbo, verbum pro verbo, verbum verbo** word for word
Vercingetŏr·ix -īgis *m* famous leader of the Arverni in the Gallic War
vercŭl·um -ī *n* (term of endearment) sweet springtime
vērē *adv* really, truly
verēcundē *adv* bashfully, shyly, modestly
verēcundĭ·a -ae *f* bashfulness, shyness, modesty; respect, awe, reverence; sense of shame, feeling of disgrace, disgrace, shame
verēcund·or -ārī *vi* to be bashful, be shy, feel ashamed
verēcund·us -a -um *adj* bashful, shy, modest, reserved
verēd·us -ī *m* fast hunting horse
verend·us -a -um *adj* venerable; *n pl* the private parts
ver·ĕor -ērī -ĭtus sum *vt* to revere, have respect for, respect; to fear; *vi* to feel uneasy, be apprehensive, be afraid, be anxious; (with *genit*) to stand in awe of, be afraid of; (with *dat*) to be afraid for; (with **de** + *abl*) to be apprehensive about; (with **ut**) to be afraid that not; (with **ne**) to be afraid that
verētr·um -ī *n* the private parts
Vergilĭ·ae -ārum *f pl* Pleiads
Vergil·ĭus or **Virgil·ĭus -ĭī** or **-ī** *m* Virgil (*P. Vergilius Maro, famous epic poet of the Augustan Age,* 70-19 B.C.)
verg·ō -ĕre *vt* to turn, incline; *vi* to turn, incline; to decline; to lie, be situated; (with **ad** + *acc*) **a** to verge toward; **b** to face, face toward
vēridĭc·us -a -um *adj* truthful, speaking the truth; truly spoken
vērīsimĭl·is -e *adj* probable, likely; realistic
vērīsimilitūd·ō -ĭnis *f* probability, likelihood
vērĭt·ās -ātis *f* truth, truthfulness; the truth, the real facts; real life, reality; honesty, integrity; correctness (*in etymology or grammar*); **ex veritate** in accordance with the truth
vēriverb·ĭum -ĭī or **-ī** *n* truthfulness
vermiculāt·us -a -um *adj* inlaid with wavy lines, vermiculated
vermicŭl·us -ī *m* grub worm
vermĭn·a -um *n pl* stomach pains
verm·is -is *m* worm
vern·a -ae *m* or *f* slave (*born in the master's house*), home-born slave; native
vernācŭl·us -a -um *adj* of home-born slaves; native, domestic; *m pl* jesters
vernīl·is -e *adj* slavish, servile; pert, smart
vernīlĭt·ās -ātis *f* slavishness, subservience; pertness

vernīliter *adv* slavishly
vern·ō -āre *vi* to show signs of spring; to burgeon, break into bloom; to be young
vernŭl·a -ae *m or f* little home-born slave, young home-born slave; native
vern·us -a -um *adj* spring; **tempus vernum** springtime
vērō *adv* in truth, in fact; certainly, to be sure; even; however
Verōn·a -ae *f* city in N. Italy, the birthplace of Catullus and of Pliny the Elder
Vērōnens·is -e *adj* Veronese
verp·a -ae *f* penis
verp·us -ī *m* circumcised man
verr·ēs -is *m* boar, pig
Verr·ēs -is *m* C. Cornelius Verres (*notorious for outrageous conduct in governing Sicily in* 73-70 B.C.)
verrīn·us -a -um *adj* of a boar, boar, hog, pork
verrō verrĕre verrī versum *vt* to pull, drag, drag away, carry off; to sweep, scour, brush; (of the wind) to whip across, sweep (*the land*)
verrūc·a -ae *f* wart (*on the body*); small failing, minor blemish
verrūcōs·us -a -um *adj* full of warts; (fig) faulty, full of blemishes
verrunc·ō -āre *vi* to turn out well
versābĭl·is -e *adj* shifting, movable
versābund·us -a -um *adj* revolving
versātĭl·is -e *adj* capable of turning, revolving, movable; versatile
versicŏl·or -ōris *adj* changing color, of various colors
versicŭl·us -ī *m* short line, single line (*of verse or prose*), versicle; *m pl* poor little verses
versificāt·or -ōris *m* versifier
versipell·is -e *adj* changing appearance, of changed appearance; sly; *m* werwolf
vers·ō or **vors·ō -āre** *vt* to keep turning, twist, wind; to roll; to bend, shift; to move about, agitate; to disturb, harass; to handle; to consider
vers·or or **vors·or -ārī -ātus sum** *vi* to live, stay; (with **in** + *abl*) to be involved in, be engaged in, be busy with
versum or **vorsum** *adv* (usually after another *adv* of direction) back; **rusum vorsum** backward; **sursum versum** up and down
versūr·a or **vorsūr·a -ae** *f* rotation; loan (*of money to pay another debt*); **versuram facere** (with **ab** + *abl*) to get a loan from (*someone to pay another*); **versurā solvere** to pay off (*another debt*) with borrowed money
versus *pp* of **verro** and of **verto**
vers·us or **vors·us -ūs** *m* turning; furrow; line, row; line, verse; line (*in writing*); turn, step (*in a dance*)
versus or **vorsus** *adv* (with **ad** + *acc*) towards, in the direction of; (with **in** + *acc*) into, in towards; **si in urbem versus venturi erunt** if they intend to come into the city; **sursum versus** upwards
versūtē *adv* cunningly
versūtī·ae -ārum *f pl* cunning
versūtilŏqu·us -a -um *adj* smooth-speaking, sly
versūt·us or **vorsūt·us -a -um** *adj* clever, shrewd, ingenious; sly, crafty, cunning, deceitful
vert·ex or **vort·ex -icis** *m* whirlpool, eddy, strong current; whirlwind, tornado; crown or top of the head; head; top, summit (*of mountain*); pole (*of the heavens*); **ex vertice** from above
verticōs·us or **vorticōs·us -a -um** *adj* swirling, full of whirlpools
vertīg·ō -inis *f* turning, whirling; dizziness
vert·ō or **vort·ō vertĕre vertī versum** *vt* to turn, turn around; to invert, tilt; to change, alter, transform; to overturn, overthrow, destroy; to ascribe, impute; to translate; **se vertere** or **verti** (with **in** + *acc*) to change into, change oneself into; **verti** (with **in** + *abl*) **a** to be in (*a place or condition*); **b** to be engaged in, be involved in; *vi* to turn; to change; to turn out; (with **in** + abl) to center upon, depend upon
Vertumn·us -ī *m* god of the changing seasons
ver·ū -ūs *n* spit (*for roasting*); javelin, dart
veruīn·a -ae *f* small javelin
vērum *adv* truly, yes; true but; but in fact; but yet, but even; yet, still; **verum tamen** or **verumtamen** nevertheless, but yet
vēr·us -a -um *adj* true, actual, genuine, real; fair, reasonable; *n* truth, the truth, reality; honor, duty, right; **veri similis** probable; realistic; **veri similitudo** probability
verūt·um -ī *n* dart, javelin
verūt·us -a -um *adj* armed with a dart or a javelin
verv·ex -ēcis *m* wether, castrated hog; (term of abuse) muttonhead
vēsānī·a -ae *f* insanity, madness
vēsānī·ens -entis *adj* furious
vēsān·us -a -um *adj* insane, mad; furious, savage, raging
vesc·or -ī *vi* (with *abl*) to feed on, eat, feast on, enjoy
vesc·us -a -um *adj* nibbled off; little, feeble; corroding, consuming
vēsīc·a or **vensīc·a -ae** *f* bladder; bombast; objects made of bladder: purse, cap, football, lantern
vēsīcŭl·a -ae *f* little bladder; little bag
vesp·a -ae *f* wasp
Vespasiān·us -ī *m* Vespasian (*T. Flavius Vespasianus Sabinus, Roman emperor,* 70-79 A.D., *and father of Domitian and Titus*)
vesp·er -ĕris or **-ĕrī** *m* evening; supper; the West; **ad vesperum**

towards evening; **primo vespere** early in the evening; **sub vesperum** towards evening; **tam vesperi** so late in the evening; **vespere** or **vesperi** in the evening
vespĕr·a -ae *f* evening
vesperasc·ō -āre *vi* to become evening, grow towards evening; to get late
vespertīlĭ·ō -ōnis *m* bat
vespertīn·us -a -um *adj* evening, in the evening; eastern
vesperūg·ō -ĭnis *f* evening star
vespill·ō -ōnis *m* undertaker
Vest·a -ae *f* Roman goddess of the hearth
Vestāl·is -e *adj* Vestal, of Vesta, Vesta's; *f* Vestal, Vestal virgin
vest·er or **vost·er -ra -rum** *adj* (in addressing more than one person) your; *pron* yours; **voster** your master; your own stock or lineage
vestibŭl·um -ī *n* entrance, forecourt; beginning
vestīg·ium -iī or **-ī** *n* footstep, step; footprint, track; trace, vestige; moment, instant
vestīg·ō -āre *vt* to track, trace; to check, find out
vestīment·um -ī *n* garment, clothes
vest·iō -īre -īvī or **-iī -ītum** *vt* to dress, clothe; to adorn, deck, array, attire; (fig) to dress, clothe
vestiplic·a -ae *f* laundress
vest·is -is *f* garment, clothing; coverlet, tapestry; blanket; slough, skin (*of a snake*); **mutare vestem** to change one's clothes; to put on mourning clothes
vestispic·a -ae *f* wardrobe woman
vestīt·us -ūs *m* clothes, clothing, dress, apparel, attire; ornament (*of speech*); **mutare vestitum** to put on mourning clothes; **redire ad suum vestitum** to end the mourning period
vetĕr·a -um *n pl* tradition, antiquity
veterān·us -a -um *adj & m* veteran
veter·ascō -ascĕre -āvī *vi* to grow old
veterāt·or -ōris *m* old hand, expert; sly old fox
veterātōriē *adv* cunningly, slyly
veterātōri·us -a -um *adj* cunning, sly
vetĕr·ēs -um *m pl* the ancients; ancient authors
veterīn·us -a -um *adj* of burden; *f pl & n pl* beasts of burden
veternōs·us -a -um *adj* lethargic; sleepy, drowsy
vetern·us -ī *m* lethargy; old age; drowsiness; listlessness
vetĭt·um -ī *n* prohibition
vet·ō or **vot·ō -āre -ŭī** or **-āvī -ĭtum** *vt* to forbid, prohibit, oppose
vetŭl·us -a -um *adj* poor old
vet·us -ĕris *adj* old, aged; long-standing; *m pl* see **veteres**; *n pl* see **vetera**
vetust·ās -ātis *f* age; ancient times, antiquity; long duration, great age
vetust·us -a -um *adj* old, ancient; old-time, old-fashioned, good old (*days, etc.*); antiquated
vexām·en -ĭnis *n* shaking, quaking
vexātĭ·ō -ōnis *f* shaking, jolting, tossing; distress
vexāt·or -ōris *m* jostler; harasser; troublemaker
vexillār·ius -iī or **-ī** *m* standard-bearer, ensign; *m pl* special reserves
vexill·um -ī *n* standard, ensign, flag (*esp. the red flag hoisted above the general's tent as a signal for battle*); troops; **vexillum praeponere** to hoist the red flag (*as a signal for battle*)
vex·ō -āre *vt* to shake, toss; to vex, annoy; to harass (*troops*), attack
vi·a -ae *f* way, road, street, highway; march, journey; method; right way, right method; **inter vias** on the road
viāl·is -e *adj* highway
viārĭ·us -a -um *adj* for highway maintenance
viāticāt·us -a -um *adj* provided with traveling money
viātic·us -a -um *adj* for a trip, for traveling, travel; *n* travel allowance, provisions for the journey; (mil) soldiers' saving fund
viāt·or -ōris *m* traveler; passenger; (law) summoner
vīb·ix -īcis *f* weal, welt (*from a blow*)
vibr·ō -āre *vt* to brandish, shake, wave around; to hurl, fling; *vi* to vibrate, quiver; (of the tongue) to flick
vīburn·um -ī *n* wayfaring tree, guelder rose
vīcān·us -a -um *adj* village; *m pl* villagers
Vic·a Pot·a (*genit:* **Vic·ae Pot·ae**) *f* goddess of victory
vicārĭ·us -a -um *adj* substituted; *m* substitute, deputy, proxy; underslave (*kept by another slave*)
vīcātim *adv* from street to street; from village to village; in hamlets
vice *prep* (with *genit*) on account of; like, after the manner of
vicem *adv* in turn; *prep* (with *genit*) instead of, in place of; on account of; like, after the manner of
vīcēnārĭ·us -a -um *adj* of the number twenty
vīcēn·ī -ae -a *adj* twenty each, twenty in a group
vīcēsimān·ī -ōrum *m pl* soldiers of the twentieth legion
vīcēsimārĭ·us -a -um *adj* derived from the five-percent tax
vīcēsim·us -a -um *adj* twentieth; *f* five-percent tax
vicĭ·a -ae *f* vetch
vīciens or **vīciēs** *adv* twenty times
vīcīnāl·is -e *adj* neighboring, nearby
vīcīnĭ·a -ae *f* neighborhood, nearness, proximity
vīcīnit·ās -ātis *f* neighborhood, proximity; the neighborhood (*i.e., the neighbors*)

vīcīn·us -a -um *adj* neighboring, nearby, near; *mf* neighbor; *n* neighborhood

vicis (*genit;* the *nom* does not occur; *acc:* **vicem;** *abl:* **vice**) *f* change, interchange, alteration, succession; return, recompense, retaliation; fortune, misfortune, condition, fate, changes of fate; duty, office, position; function, office; **in vicem** or **invicem** by turns, alternately, mutually; **in vicem** or **invicem** (with *genit*) instead of, in place of; **in vicīs** by turns, alternately, mutually

vicissim or **vicissātim** *adv* in turn, again

vicissitūd·ō -inis *f* change, interchange, alternation

victim·a -ae *f* victim; sacrifice

victimār·ius -iī or **-ī** *m* assistant at sacrifices

victit·ō -āre *vi* to live, subsist; (with *abl*) to live on, subsist on

vict·or -ōris *m* conqueror; (in apposition) **victor exercitus** victorious army

victōriāt·us -ī *m* silver coin stamped with the image of victory

Victōriŏl·a -ae *f* small statue of Victory

victr·ix -īcis *f* or *n* conqueror, victor

victus *pp* of **vinco**

vict·us -ūs *m* living, means of livelihood; way of life

vīcŭl·us -ī *m* hamlet

vīc·us -ī *m* village, hamlet; ward, quarter (*in a town or city*); street, alley (*running through the quarter*)

vidēlicet *adv* clearly, evidently; (in irony) of course, naturally; (in explanations) namely

viden = videsne? do you see?, do you get it?

vidĕō vidēre vīdī vīsum *vt* to see, look at; to know; to consider; to understand, realize; (with **ut**) to see to it that, take care that; **vidēri** to seem, appear, seem right, seem good

vidŭ·a -ae *f* widow; spinster

viduit·ās -ātis *f* bereavement; want, lack; widowhood

vīdŭl·us -ī *m* leather travel bag, suitcase, knapsack

vidŭ·ō -āre *vt* to deprive, bereave; (with *genit* or *abl*) to deprive of, bereave of; **viduata** left a widow

vidŭ·us -a -um *adj* bereft, destitute; unmarried; (with *abl* or **ab** + *abl*) bereft of, destitute of, without; *f* see **vidua**

viēt·or -ōris *m* cooper

viēt·us -a -um *adj* shriveled

vig·ĕō -ēre -ŭī *vi* to thrive, be vigorous, flourish

vig·escō -escĕre -ŭī *vi* to become vigorous, gain strength, become lively

vīgēsim·us -a -um *adj* twentieth

vig·il -ĭlis *adj* awake, wakeful; alert, on one's toes; *m* watchman, guard, sentinel

vigil·ans -antis *adj* watchful, alert; disquieting (*worries*)

vigilanter *adv* vigilantly, alertly

vigilanti·a -ae *f* wakefulness; alertness

vigil·ax -ācis *adj* alert; sleep-disturbing, disquieting (*worries*)

vigili·a -ae *f* wakefulness, sleeplessness, insomnia; standing guard; guards, sentinels; vigil; vigilance, alertness

vigil·ō -āre *vt* to spend (*the night*) awake; to make, do, perform, write (*something*) while awake at night; *vi* to remain awake, stay awake; to be alert; (with *dat*) to be attentive to

vīgintī (indecl) *adj* twenty

vīgintīvirāt·us -ūs *m* membership on a board of twenty

vīgintīvir·ī -ōrum *m pl* twenty-man board or commission

vig·or -ōris *m* vigor, liveliness, energy

vīlic·a -ae *f* foreman's wife, manager's wife

vīlic·ō -āre *vi* to be a foreman, be a manager

vīlic·us -ī *m* foreman, manager (*of an estate*)

vīl·is -e *adj* cheap, inexpensive; cheap, mean, common, worthless

vīlit·ās -ātis *f* lowness of price, cheapness, low price; worthlessness

vīliter *adv* cheaply

vill·a -ae *f* villa, country home, farm

villic- = vilic-

villōs·us -a -um *adj* hairy, shaggy

villŭl·a -ae *f* small villa

vill·um -ī *n* drop of wine

vill·us -ī *m* hair, fleece; nap (*of cloth*)

vīm·en -ĭnis *n* osier; basket

vīment·um -ī *n* osier

Vīmināl·is coll·is (*genit:* **Vīmināl·is coll·is**) *m* one of the seven hills of Rome

vīminĕ·us -a -um *adj* made of osiers

vīn or **vīn' = visne?** do you wish

vīnācĕ·us -a -um *adj* grape, of a grape; *m* a grape seed

Vīnāl·ia -ium *n pl* wine festival (*celebrated on the 23rd of April and on the 19th of August*)

vīnāri·us -a -um *adj* wine; *m* wine dealer, vintner; *n pl* wine flasks

vincibil·is -e *adj* easily won

vinciō vincīre vinxī vinctum *vt* to bind; to encircle, surround; to restrain; (rhet) to bind together, link together, arrange rhythmically

vincō vincĕre vīcī victum *vt* to conquer, vanquish; to get the better of, beat, defeat, outdo; to surpass, excel; to convince, refute, persuade; to prove, demonstrate; to outlast, outlive; *vi* to be victorious; to prevail, succeed

vinctus *pp* of **vincio**

vincŭl·um or **vincl·um -ī** *n* chain, fetter, cord, band; *n pl* prison

vindēmi·a -ae *f* vintage

vindēmiāt·or -ōris *m* vintager, grape gatherer
vindēmiŏl·a -ae *f* small vintage; minor sources of income
vind·ex -icis *adj* avenging; *m* (law) claimant; defender, protector, champion; deliverer, liberator; avenger, punisher
vindicāti·ō -ōnis *f* (law) claim; avenging, punishment
vindici·ae -ārum *f pl* legal claim; things or persons claimed; championship, protection; **vindicias dare, dicere,** or **decernere** to hand over the things or persons claimed
vindic·ō -āre *vt* to lay a legal claim to; to protect, defend; to appropriate; to demand; to demand unfairly; to claim as one's own; to avenge, punish; **in libertatem vindicare** to claim for freedom, set free, free, liberate, emancipate
vindict·a -ae *f* rod used in the ceremony of setting slaves free; defense, protection; vengeance, revenge, satisfaction
vīnĕ·a -ae *f* vineyard; vine; (mil) shed (*used to defend besiegers against the missiles of the enemy*)
vīnēt·um -ī *n* vineyard
vīnit·or -ōris *m* vinedresser
vinnŭl·us -a -um *adj* charming, pleasant
vīnolenti·a -ae *f* wine drinking, intoxication
vīnolent·us -a -um *adj* intoxicated, drunk
vīnōs·us -a -um *adj* fond of wine
vīn·um -ī *n* wine
viŏl·a -ae *f* violet; violet color
violābil·is -e *adj* vulnerable
violār·ium -iī or **-ī** *n* bed of violets
violār·ius -iī or **-ī** *m* dyer of violet color
violāti·ō -ōnis *f* violation, profanation
violāt·or -ōris *m* violator, profaner, desecrator
viŏl·ens -entis *adj* violent, raging, impetuous
violenter *adv* violently, vehemently, impetuously
violenti·a -ae *f* violence, vehemence, impetuosity
violent·us -a -um *adj* violent, vehement, impetuous, boisterous
viŏl·ō -āre *vt* to do violence to, outrage, harm or injure by violence; to violate, break
vīpĕr·a -ae *f* viper; adder, snake
vīperĕ·us -a -um *adj* viper's, adder's, snake's
vīperīn·us -a -um *adj* of a viper or snake
vir virī *m* male person, man; real man; hero; husband; manhood, virility; (mil) infantryman
virāg·ō -inis *f* female warrior; heroine
virect·a -ōrum *n pl* green places; lawn
vir·ĕō -ēre -ŭī *vi* to be green; to be fresh, be vigorous, flourish
vīrēs = *pl of* **vis**
vir·escō -escĕre -ŭī *vt* to grow green
virg·a -ae *f* twig, sprout; graft; rod, switch (*for flogging*); walking stick, cane, staff; magic wand; wand; colored stripe in a garment; branch of a family tree
virgāt·or -ōris *m* flogger
virgāt·us -a -um *adj* made of twigs or osiers; striped
virgēt·um -ī *n* osier thicket
virgĕ·us -a -um *adj* of twigs, of kindling wood
virgidēmi·a -ae *f* (coll) harvest of birch rods (*i.e., sound flogging*)
virgināl·is -e *adj* maiden's, girl's, girlish; *n* female organ
virgināri·us -a -um *adj* maiden's, girl's
virginĕ·us -a -um *adj* maidenly, virgin, of virgins
virginit·ās -ātis *f* virginity, girlhood
virg·ō -inis *f* virgin, maiden, girl, young woman; young married woman
Virg·ō -inis *f* Virgo (*constellation; aqueduct constructed by M. Vipsanius Agrippa*)
virgŭl·a -ae *f* little twig; wand; **virgula divina** divining rod
virgult·a -ōrum *n pl* thickets, brushwood; slips (*of trees*)
virguncŭl·a -ae *f* lass, young girl
virid·ans -antis *adj* growing green, green
viridār·ium -iī or **-ī** *n* garden; plantation
virid·is -e *adj* green; fresh, young; *n pl* greenery
viridit·ās -ātis *f* greenness; freshness
virid·or -ārī *vi* to become green
virīl·is -e *adj* male, masculine; adult; manly; **pro virili parte** or **partione** to the best of one's ability; *n pl* manly or heroic deeds
virīlit·ās -ātis *f* manhood, virility
virīliter *adv* manfully
vīripŏt·ens -entis *adj* almighty
virītim *adv* individually, separately
vīrōs·us -a -um *adj* slimy; strong-smelling, fetid, stinking
virt·ūs -ūtis *f* manliness, manhood, virility; strength; valor, bravery, gallantry; gallant deeds; excellence, worth; virtue, moral perfection, good quality; *f pl* achievements
vīr·us -ī *n* slime; poison; pungency; saltiness
vīs (*genit* not in use) *f* power, strength, force; energy; hostile force, violence, attack, assault; amount, quantity; meaning (*of words*); **vires** *f pl* strength, resources; (mil) troops; **per vim** forcibly, violently; **pro viribus** with all one's might
viscāt·us -a -um *adj* limed

viscĕr·a -um *n pl* viscera, internal organs; womb; heart, vitals, bowels; (fig) innermost part, bowels, heart, center; bosom friend, favorite

viscerātī·ō -ōnis *f* public distribution of meat

visc·ō -āre *vt* to make sticky

visc·um -ī *n* mistletoe; birdlime

visc·us -ĕris *n* organ (*of the body*); entrails

vīsī·ō -ōnis *f* appearance, apparition; notion, idea

vīsĭt·ō -āre *vt* to keep seeing; to visit, go to visit

vīs·ō -ĕre -ī -um *vt* to look at with attention, view; to come or go to look at; to find out; to visit

vīs·um -ī *n* sight, appearance

vīs·us -ūs *m* faculty of sight, sight; thing seen, sight, vision

vīt·a -ae *f* life, way of life; livelihood; course of life, career; biography

vītābĭl·is -e *adj* undesirable, deserving to be shunned

vītābund·us -a -um *adj* avoiding, evading

vītāl·is -e *adj* of life, vital; likely to live, staying alive; *n* means of life; *n pl* vital parts

vītālĭter *adv* vitally

vītātī·ō -ōnis *f* avoidance

Vitell·ius -iī or **-ī** *m* A. Vitellius (*Roman emperor,* 69 A.D.)

vitell·us -ī *m* little calf; yolk (*of egg*)

vītĕ·us -a -um *adj* of the vine

vītĭcŭl·a -ae *f* little vine

vītĭf·er -ĕra -ĕrum *adj* vine-producing

vītigĕn·us -a -um *adj* produced from the vine

vitilēn·a -ae *f* procuress

vitī·ō -āre *vt* to corrupt, spoil, violate, mar; to falsify

vitiōsē *adv* faultily, badly, corruptly

vitiōsĭt·ās -ātis *f* corrupt or bad condition

vitiōs·us -a -um *adj* faulty, defective, corrupt, bad; vicious

vīt·is -is *f* vine; vine branch; centurion's staff; centurionship

vītisāt·or -ōris *m* vine planter

vit·ium -iī or **-ī** *n* fault, defect, flaw; sin, offense, vice; flaw in the auspices

vīt·ō -āre *vt* to avoid, evade

vīt·or -ōris *m* basket maker

vitrĕ·us -a -um *adj* glass, of glass; glassy; *n pl* glassware

vītrĭc·us -ī *m* stepfather

vitr·um -ī *n* glass

vitt·a -ae *f* headband, fillet

vittāt·us -a -um *adj* wearing a fillet

vitŭl·a -ae *f* heifer

vitulīn·us -a -um *adj & f* veal

vītŭl·or -ārī *vi* to celebrate, hold a celebration

vitŭl·us -ī *m* calf, young bull; foal; seal

vituperābĭl·is -e *adj* blameworthy

vituperātī·ō -ōnis *f* blaming, censuring; blame; scandalous conduct, blameworthiness

vituperāt·or -ōris *m* censurer

vitupĕr·ō -āre *vt* to spoil (*omen*), render void; to blame

vīvācĭt·ās -ātis *f* will to live

vivār·ium -iī or **-ī** *n* game preserve; fish pond

vīvāt·us -a -um *adj* animated, lively

vīv·ax -ācis *adj* long-lived; long-lasting, enduring; quick to learn

vīvescō or **vīviscō vīvescĕre vixī** *vi* to become alive, come to life; to grow lively, get full of life

vīvĭd·us -a -um *adj* teeming with life, full of life; true to life, vivid, realistic; quick, lively (*mind*)

vīvirād·ix -īcis *f* development of roots

vīviscō see **vivesco**

vīvō vīvĕre vixī victum *vi* to be alive, live; to be still alive, survive; to reside; (with *abl* or **dē** + *abl*) to live on, subsist on

vīv·us -a -um *adj* alive, living; lively; fresh; natural (*rock*); speaking (*voice*); *n* (com) capital; **ad vivum resecare** to cut to the quick

vix *adv* with difficulty, hardly; scarcely

vixdum *adv* hardly then, scarcely yet

vocābŭl·um -ī *n* designation, name; noun

vōcāl·is -ē *adj* having a voice, gifted with speech or song, singing, speaking; tuneful; *f* vowel

vocām·en -inis *f* designation, name

vocātī·ō -ōnis *f* summons (*to court*); invitation (*to dinner*)

vocāt·or -ōris *m* inviter, host

vocāt·us -ūs *m* summons, call

vōciferātī·ō -ōnis *f* loud cry, yell

vōcifĕr·ō -āre or **vōcifĕr·or -ārī -ātus sum** *vt & vi* to shout, yell

vocĭt·ō -āre *vt* to usually call, name; to shout out again and again

voc·ō -āre *vt* to summon; to call, name; to call upon (*the gods*); to invite; (mil) to challenge; **in dubium vocare** to call in question; **in odium vocare** to bring into disfavor; **in periculum vocare** to lead into danger

vōcŭl·a -ae *f* small or weak voice; soft note, soft tone; whisper, gossip

volaem·um -ī *n* large pear

Volaterr·ae -ārum *f pl* old Etruscan town

Volaterrān·us -a -um *adj* of Volaterrae

volātĭc·us -a -um *adj* flying, winged; transitory, passing; inconstant

volātĭl·is -e *adj* flying, winged; rapid, swift; fleeting, transitory

volāt·us -ūs *m* flight

Volcānāl·ia -ium *n pl* festival of Vulcan (*celebrated on the 23rd of August*)

Volcān·us or **Vulcān·us -ī** *m* Vulcan (*god of fire and son of Juno and Jupiter*)

vol•ens -entis *adj* willing, permitting; willing, ready; favorable; *m* well-wisher

volg- = vulg-

volit•ans -antis *m* winged insect

volit•ō -āre *vi* to flit about, fly about, flutter; to move quickly; to hover, soar

volō velle voluī *vt* to wish, want; to propose, determine; to hold, maintain; to mean; to prefer; *vi* to be willing

volōn•ēs -um *m pl* volunteers (*slaves who enlisted after the battle of Cannae,* 216 B.C.)

volpēs see **vulpes**

Volsc•us -a -um *adj* Vulscan; *m pl* an ancient people in S. Latium

volsell•a -ae *f* tweezers

volsus *pp* of **vello**

volt = older form of **vult** he, she, it wishes

voltis = older form of **vultis** you wish

Voltumn•a -ae *f* Etruscan goddess in whose temple the Etruscan states met

voltus see **vultus**

volūbil•is -e *adj* turning, spinning, revolving, swirling; voluble, rapid, fluent; changeable

volūbilit•ās -ātis *f* whirling motion; roundness; volubility, fluency; mutability

volūbiliter *adv* volubly, rapidly, fluently

volŭc•er -ris -re *adj* flying, winged; rapid, speedy; *mf* bird; *f* insect

volūm•en -inis *n* roll, book; chapter, book; whirl, eddy; coil; fold

voluntāri•us -a -um *adj* voluntary; *m pl* volunteers

volunt•ās -ātis *f* will, wish, desire, purpose, aim; goodwill; last will, testament; attitude (*good or bad*); **ad voluntatem** (with *genit*) according to the wishes of; **de** or **ex voluntate** (with *genit*) at the desire of

volup *adv* to one's satisfaction, agreeably

voluptābil•is -e *adj* agreeable, pleasant

voluptāri•us -a -um *adj* pleasant, agreeable; voluptuous; *m* voluptary

volupt•ās -atis *f* pleasure, enjoyment, delight; *f pl* sensual pleasures; games, sports, public performances

voluptuōs•us -a -um *adj* pleasant, agreeable

volūtābr•um -ī *n* wallow (*for swine*)

volūtābund•us -a -um *adj* wallowing about

volūtāti•ō -ōnis *f* rolling about, tossing about; wallowing; restlessness

volūt•ō -āre *vt* to roll about, turn over; to engross; to think over; **volutari** to wallow, luxuriate

volūtus *pp* of **volvo**

volv•a or **vulv•a -ae** *f* wrapper, cover; womb; sow's womb (*as a favorite dish*)

volvō volvěre volvī volūtum *vt* to roll, turn about, wind; (e.g., of a river) to roll (*rocks, etc.*) along; to breathe; to unroll, read (*books*); to pour out, utter fluently; to consider, weigh; (of time) to bring on, bring around; to form (*a circle*); to undergo (*troubles*); **volvi** to roll, tumble, revolve; *vi* to revolve; to roll on, elapse

vōm•er or **vōm•is -ěris** *m* plowshare; penis

vomic•a -ae *f* sore, boil, abscess, ulcer; annoyance

vōmis see **vomer**

vomiti•ō -ōnis *f* vomiting

vom•ō -ěre -uī -itum *vt & vi* to vomit, throw up

vorāg•ō -inis *f* deep hole, abyss, chasm, depth

vor•ax -ācis *adj* swallowing, devouring; greedy, ravenous

vor•ō -āre *vt* to swallow, devour; (fig) to devour (*by reading*)

vors- = vers-

vort- = vert-

vōs *pron* you; (reflex) yourselves

vosmet *pron* (emphatic form of **vōs**) you yourselves

voster see **vester**

vōtīv•us -a -um *adj* votive, promised in a vow

votō see **veto**

vōt•um -ī *n* solemn vow (*made to a deity*), vow; votive offering; wish, prayer

vověō vovēre vōvī vōtum *vt* to vow, promise solemnly, pledge, devote (*to a deity*); to wish, wish for, desire

vox vōcis *f* voice; sound, tone, cry, call; word, utterance, saying, expression; proverb; language; accent

Vulcānus see **Volcanus**

vulgār•is or **volgār•is -e** *adj* common, general, usual

vulgāriter or **volgariter** *adv* in the common or usual way

vulgāt•or or **volgāt•or -ōris** *m* divulger

vulgāt•us or **volgāt•us -a -um** *adj* common, general; well known; notorious

vulgivăg•us or **volgivăg•us -a -um** *adj* roving; inconstant

vulg•ō or **volg•ō -āre** *vt* to spread, publish, broadcast; to divulge; to prostitute; to level, make common

vulgō or **volgō** *adv* generally, publicly, everywhere

vulg•us or **volg•us -ī** *n* masses, people, public; crowd, herd; rabble, populace

vulnerāti•ō or **volnerāti•ō -ōnis** *f* wounding, wound

vulněr•ō or **volněr•ō -āre** *vt* to wound; to damage

vulnific·us -a -um *adj* inflicting wounds
vuln·us or **voln·us -ĕris** *n* wound; blow, stroke; blow, disaster
vulpēcŭl·a or **volpēcŭl·a -ae** *f* little fox, sly little fox
vulp·ēs or **volp·ēs -is** *f* fox; craftiness, cunning
vuls·us or **vols·us -a -um** *pp* of **vello**; *adj* plucked, beardless, effeminate
vulticŭl·us or **volticŭl·us -ī** *m* mere look
vult·um -ī *n* face; looks, expression, features; look, appearance
vultuōs·us or **voltuōs·us -a -um** *adj* full of airs, affected
vult·ur or **volt·ur -ŭris** *m* vulture
Vult·ur or **Volt·ur -ŭris** *m* mountain in Apulia near Venusia
vulturīn·us or **volturnīn·us -a -um** *adj* of a vulture, vulture-like
vultur·ius or **voltur·ius -iī** or **-ī** *m* vulture
Vulturn·us or **Volturn·us -ī** *m* principal river of Campania (*modern Volturno*)
vult·us or **volt·us -ūs** *m* face; looks, expression, features; look, appearance
vulv·a or **volv·a -ae** *f* wrapper, cover; womb; sow's womb (*as a delicacy*)

X

Xanthipp·ē -ēs *f* wife of Socrates
Xanth·us -ī *m* river at Troy, identified with Scamander River
xen·ium -iī or **-ī** *n* gift, present
Xenophăn·ēs -is *m* early Greek philosopher (*c.* 565-470 B.C.)
Xenŏph·ōn -ontis *m* Greek historian and pupil of Socrates (*c.* 430-*c.* 354 B.C.)
xērampelīn·ae -ārum *f pl* dark-colored clothes
Xerx·ēs -is *m* Persian king, defeated at Salamis (*c.* 519-465 B.C.)
xiphi·ās -ae *m* swordfish
xyst·us -ī *m* or **xyst·um -ī** *n* open colonnade or portico, walk, avenue

Z

Zacynth·us or **Zacynth·os -ī** *f* island off W. Greece
Zam·a -ae *f* town in Numidia where Scipio defeated Hannibal and brought the Second Punic War to an end
zāmi·a -ae *f* harm, damage, loss
Zancl·ē -ēs *f* old name of Messana in Sicily
Zēn·ō or **Zēn·ōn -ōnis** *m* founder of Stoic philosophy and a native of Citium in Cyprus (335-263 B.C.); Epicurean philosopher, the teacher of Cicero and Atticus
Zephȳr·us -ī *m* zephyr; west wind; wind
Zēth·us -ī *m* son of Jupiter and Antiope and brother of Amphion
zmaragd·us -ī *f* emerald
zōdiăc·us -ī *m* zodiac
Zōil·us -ī *m* proverbially stern Alexandrine critic of Homer
zōn·a -ae *f* belt, sash, girdle (*worn by women*); money belt; zone
zōnāri·us -a -um *adj* of a belt or girdle; *m* belt maker, girdle maker
zōnŭl·a -ae *f* little girdle
zōthēc·a -ae *f* small room
zōthēcŭl·a -ae *f* small bedroom

ENGLISH–LATIN

A

a *indefinite article, unexpressed in Latin;* **twice — year** bis in anno
aback *adv* **taken —** stupefactus, attonitus, consternatus
abandon *vt* (de)relinquĕre, destituĕre, deserĕre, abjicĕre, omittĕre
abandoned *adj* derelictus, desertus; (*fig*) nefarius, perditus, flagitiosus
abandonment *s* derelictio, destitutio *f*
abase *vt* deprimĕre, comprimĕre, frangĕre, (de)minuĕre
abash *vt* perturbare, confundĕre, pudefacĕre, percellĕre
abashed *adj* pudendus, erubescens
abate *vt* (*to lower*) imminuĕre; (*to slacken*) laxare; (*the price*) remittĕre, detrahĕre; *vi* (*to lessen*) imminuĕre, decrescĕre; (*to decline*) cadĕre, decedĕre; (*of passion*) defervescĕre
abbess *s* abbatissa *f*
abbey *s* abbatia *f*
abbot *s* abbas *m*
abbreviate *vt* abbreviare, contrahĕre, imminuĕre
abbreviation *s* abbreviatio, contractio *f*, compendium *n*
abdicate *vt* abdicare; *vi* se abdicare
abdication *s* abdicatio *f*
abdomen *s* abdomen *n*
abduct *vt* abducĕre, rapĕre
abduction *s* raptio *f*, rapt·us -ūs *m*
aberration *s* error *m*; declinatio *f*
abet *vt* adjuvare, instigare; favēre (*with dat*)
abeyance *s* **to be in —** jacēre, intermitti
abhor *vt* abhorrēre ab (*with abl*), detestari, odio habēre
abhorrence *s* detestatio *f*, odium *n*
abhorrent *adj* perosus; alienus, repugnans, abhorrens
abide *vt* tolerare, subire; *vi* (*to dwell*) habitare, manēre; **to — by** stare in (*with abl*)
abiding *adj* diuturnus, mansurus; constans, fidus
ability *s* facultas, potestas *f*; ingenium *n*; **to the best of one's —** summa ope; pro sua parte
abject *adj* abjectus, vilis; humilis; **—ly** abjecte; humiliter
abjure *vt* abjurare, ejurare
ablative *s* ablativus *m*
able *adj* potens; valens, capax, peritus; ingeniosus; **to be — to** posse, valēre, quire, sufficĕre
ablution *s* ablutio, lavatio *f*
ably *adv* experte; ingeniose
aboard *adv* in *or* super nave; **to go — a ship** navem conscendĕre
abode *s* domicilium *n*; sedes *f*; commoratio, mansio *f*
abolish *vt* abolēre; exstinguĕre, tollĕre, rescindĕre
abolition *s* abolitio, dissolutio *f*
abominable *adj* detestabilis, infandus, execrabilis; odiosus
abominably *adv* execrabiliter; odiose
abominate *vt* abominari, detestari
abomination *s* destestatio *f*
aborigines *s* aborigines, indigenae *m pl*
abortion *s* abortio *f*; abort·us -ūs *m*
abortive *adj* abortivus; (*fig*) irritus, frustratus
abound *vi* abundare, redundare, superesse; **to — in** abundare (*with abl*)
abounding *adj* abundans; copiosus, largus; creber
about *adv* circa, circiter; fere, ferme
about *prep* (*of place*) circa, circum (*with acc*); (*of number*) circa, ad (*with acc*); (*of time*) circa, sub (*with acc*); (*of respect*) de (*with abl*)
above *adv* supra; insuper; **from —** desuper, superne
above *prep* supra, super (*with acc*)
abrasion *s* attrit·us -ūs *m*
abreast *adv* pariter; ex adverso
abridge *vt* contrahĕre; abbreviare; (*fig*) privare
abridgment *s* compendium *n*, epitome *f*
abroad *adv* (*in a foreign land*) peregre; (*of motion, out of doors*) foras; (*of rest, out of doors*) foris; **from —** extrinsecus; peregre; **to be** *or* **live abroad** peregrinari; patriā carēre; **to get —** (*fig*) divulgari
abrogate *vt* rescindĕre, abrogare, dissolvĕre
abrupt *adj* praeruptus; (*fig*) subitus, repentinus; (*of style*) abruptus; **—ly** abrupte; raptim
abruptness *s* declivitas, rapiditas, festinatio *f*
abscess *s* abscess·us -ūs *m*; suppuratio *f*; vomica *f*
absence *s* absentia *f*; **in my —** me absente
absent *adj* absens; **to be —** abesse
absent *vt* **to — oneself** se removēre, non comparēre
absentee *s* qui abest *m*; peregrinator *m*
absolute *adj* absolutus, summus, perfectus; (*unlimited*) infinitus; **—ly** absolute; prorsus; penitus, omnino
absolution *s* absolutio *f*; venia, indulgentia *f*
absolve *vt* veniam dare (*with dat*); absolvĕre; dimittĕre; (*from punishment*) condonare

absorb *vt* absorbēre, combibĕre; (*fig*) distringĕre, tenēre
absorbent *adj* bibulus; absorbens
abstain *vi* abstinēre, se abstinēre
abstinence *s* abstinentia *f*; continentia *f*; jejunium *n*
abstract *vt* abstrahĕre; separare, sejungĕre, excludĕre
abstract *adj* abstractus; mente perceptus
abstract *s* compendium *n*; epitome *f*; **in the —** in abstracto
abstracted *adj* abstractus; separatus; contractus; (*in mind*) parum attentus; **—ly** separatim; in abstracto
abstraction *s* separatio *f*; (*idea*) notio *f*
abstruse *adj* abstrusus; reconditus; obscurus, occultus; **—ly** abdite, occulte
absurd *adj* absurdus, insulsus; ridiculus; **—ly** inepte, absurde
absurdity *s* ineptia, insulsitas *f*
abundance *s* abundantia, copia *f*
abundant *adj* abundans; amplus; copiosus, plenus; uber; **to be —** abundare; **—ly** abundanter, copiose; cumulate; (*fruitfully*) feliciter
abuse *s* (*wrong use*) abus·us -ūs *m*; (*insult*) injuria *f*, convicium *n*; contumelia *f*; probra *n pl*, maledicta *n pl*
abuse *vt* (*misuse*) abuti (*with abl*); (*a woman*) stuprare; (*with words*) maledicĕre (*with dat*); lacerare
abusive *adj* contumeliosus; dicax, maledicus; injuriosus; **—ly** contumeliose; maledice, injuriose
abyss *s* profundum *n*, vorago *f*, gurges *m*; (*fig*) barathrum *n*
academic *adj* scholasticus; academicus
academy *s* Academia *f*; schola *f*, collegium *n*; societas *f*
accede *vi* accedĕre, assentire *or* assentiri
accelerate *vt* accelerare, festinare, maturare
acceleration *s* acceleratio *f*
accent *s* accent·us -ūs *m*; sonus *m*; vox *f*; (*mark*) apex *m*
accent *vt* (*in speaking*) acuĕre; (*in writing*) fastigare
accentuation *s* accent·us -ūs *m*
accept *vt* accipĕre; recipĕre
acceptable *adj* acceptus, aptus, gratus; probabilis; **to be —** placēre
acceptably *adv* apte; grate
acceptance *s* acceptio *f*; approbatio *f*
access *s* adit·us -ūs, access·us -ūs *m*; **to have —** admitti
accessible *adj* (*of places*) patens; (*fig*) facilis, affabilis
accession *s* (*addition*) accessio *f*, cumulus *m*; (*to the throne*) regni principium *n*
accessory *adj* adjunctus; (*of crimes*) conscius
accessory *s* affinis, conscius *m*, particeps *m & f*
accident *s* cas·us -ūs *m*; calamitas *f*
accidental *adj* fortuitus; adventicius; **—ly** casu, forte, fortuito
acclaim *s* acclamatio *f*; clamor *m*
acclaim *vt* acclamare
acclamation *s* acclamatio *f*, clamor, consens·us -ūs, plaus·us -ūs *m*
accommodate *vt* accommodare, aptare; (*with lodgings*) hospitium parare (*with dat*)
accommodation *s* accommodatio *f*; (*convenience*) commoditas *f*; (*lodgings*) hospitium, deversorium *n*
accompaniment *s* concinentia *f*
accompany *vt* comitari; deducĕre; (*mus*) concinĕre (*with dat*)
accomplice *s* particeps, socius, conscius *m*; satelles *m*
accomplish *vt* efficĕre, perficĕre; peragĕre, implēre
accomplished *adj* completus; (*fig*) doctus, eruditus; (*eloquent*) disertus
accomplishment *s* exsecutio, peractio *f*; eruditio *f*
accord *s* consens·us, -ūs *m*, concordia *f*; **of one's own —** sua sponte; ultro; **with one —** unanimiter
accord *vt* concedĕre, dare, praebēre, praestare; *vi* convenire; inter se congruĕre; inter se consentire
accordance *s* **in — with** ex, de (*with abl*); secundum (*with acc*); pro (*with abl*)
accordingly *adv* itaque; ita; pariter; sic
according to *prep* de, ex, pro (*with abl*); secundum (*with acc*)
accost *vt* appellare; compellare; alloqui, affari
account *s* (*financial*) ratio *f*; (*statement*) memoria *f*; (*esteem*) reputatio *f*; (*story*) narratio *f*; **of little —** parvi pretii; vilis; **of no —** nullius pretii; **on — of** ob, propter (*with acc*); causā (*with genit*); **on that —** propterea; ideo; **to call to —** rationem poscĕre; **to give an —** rationem reddĕre; **to take — of** rationem habēre (*with genit*)
account *vt* numerare; (*esteem*) aestimare, habēre, pendĕre; **to — for** rationem reddĕre (*with genit*)
accountable *adj* reus
accountant *s* calculator *m*; **a rationibus** (procurator) *m*
accredited *adj* aestimatus, honoratus
accretion *s* accessio *f*
accrue *vi* accrescĕre; advenire; cedĕre; (*advantage*) redundare
accumulate *vt* accumulare, coacervare; *vi* crescĕre, augēri
accumulation *s* cumulus, acervus, congest·us -ūs *m*; collectio *f*
accuracy *s* cura *f*; subtilitas *f*
accurate *adj* exactus; subtilis; diligens; **—ly** accurate, exacte; subtiliter; diligenter
accursed *adj* exsecratus; scelestus
accusation *s* accusatio *f*; (*charge*) crimen *n*; **to bring an — against** accusare

accusative *s* accusativus *m*
accuse *vt* accusare; criminari; (*to blame*) reprehendĕre; **to — falsely** calumniari, insimulare
accuser *s* accusator, delator *m*; (*in civil suit*) petitor *m*
accustom *vt* assuefacĕre; **to — oneself** assuefieri, consuescĕre; **to be accustomed to** solēre (*with inf*)
acerbity *s* acerbitas *f*; (*fig*) severitas *f*; rigor *m*
ache *s* dolor *m*
ache *vi* dolēre; **my head —s** caput mihi dolet
achieve *vt* patrare, conficĕre, perficĕre; (*to win*) consequi
achievement *s* res gesta *f*; facinus *n*
acid *adj* acidus; vinosus
acid *s* acidum *n*
acknowledge *vt* agnoscĕre, recognoscĕre; confitēri; (*a child*) tollĕre
acknowledgment *s* recognito *f*, confessio *f*; (*receipt for money*) apocha *f*
acme *s* fastigium *n*
acorn *s* glans *f*; balanus *f*
acoustics *s* acustica *n pl*; res auditoria *f*
acquaint *vt* certiorem facĕre; **to — oneself with** noscĕre, cognoscĕre
acquaintance *s* familiaritas, notitia *f*; (*person*) familiaris *m* & *f*
acquainted *adj* notus; **— with** gnarus (*with genit*); peritus (*with genit or abl*); **to become — with** noscĕre, cognoscĕre, pernoscĕre
acquiesce *vi* acquiescĕre, assentire
acquiescence *s* assens·us -ūs *m*
acquire *vt* acquirĕre; adipisci, nancisci
acquisition *s* (*act of acquiring*) conciliatio *f*; quaest·us -ūs *m*; (*thing acquired*) quaesitum *n*
acquisitive *adj* quaestuosus
acquit *vt* absolvĕre, liberare; **to — oneself** se gerĕre
acquittal *s* absolutio *f*
acre *s* jugerum *n*; **— by —** jugeratim
acrid *adj* acer, asper
acrimonious *adj* acerbus; asper, truculentus
acrimony *s* acrimonia *f*; acerbitas, amaritudo *f*; acor *m*
acrobat *s* funambulus *m*
across *adv* transversus
across *prep* trans (*with acc*)
act *s* (*deed, action*) factum, gestum *n*; (*decree*) decretum *n*; (*in a play*) act·us -ūs *m*; **caught in the —** deprehensus; **in the very —** in flagranti
act *vt* (*role, part*) agĕre; *vi* agĕre, facĕre, gerĕre
acting *s* actio, gesticulatio *f*
action *s* actio *f*, act·us -ūs *m*; (*deed*) factum, facinus *n*; (*law*) actio *f*; (*mil*) pugna *f*, proelium *n*; (*of speaker*) gest·us -ūs *m*; **to bring an — against** actionem intendĕre (*with dat*)
active *adj* actuosus; activus; agilis; impiger, vegetus, strenuus, sedulus, navus; **—ly** impigre; strenue; (*gram*) active
activity *s* agilitas, mobilitas *f*; (*motion*) mot·us -ūs *m*; (*energy*) industria, sedulitas, gnavitas *f*
actor *s* histrio *m*; mimus *m*; (*in comedy*) comoedus *m*; (*in tragedy*) tragoedus *m*
actress *s* mima, scenica *f*
actual *adj* verus, ipse; **—ly** re vera
actuality *s* veritas *f*
acumen *s* acumen *n*; sagacitas *f*; ingenii acies *f*
acute *adj* acutus; acer; (*fig*) sagax, subtilis; **—ly** acute, acriter
acuteness *s* acies *f*; (*of the mind*) acumen *n*, subtilitas *f*
adage *s* proverbium *n*
adamant *adj* obstinatus
adamant *s* adamas *m*
adapt *vt* accommodare, aptare
adaptation *s* accommodatio *f*
adapted *adj* aptus
add *vt* addĕre, apponĕre, adjungĕre; (*in speaking*) superdicĕre; (*in writing*) subjungĕre; (*to reckon*) adscribĕre; **to — up** computare, supputare; **to be added** accedĕre
adder *s* coluber *m*, vipera *f*
addict *vt* **to be addicted** se addicĕre, se tradĕre, se dare
addition *s* additamentum *n*; adjectio, accessio *f*; appendix *f*; incrementum *n*; **in —** praeterea, insuper; **in — to** praeter (*with acc*)
additional *adj* novus, addititius, adjunctus
address *s* alloquium *n*; allocutio, compellatio *f*; (*on letter*) forma directionis, inscriptio *f*; (*speech*) contio, oratio *f*; (*adroitness*) dexteritas, comitas *f*
address *vt* (*to speak to*) alloqui, aggredi, compellare; (*letter*) inscribĕre
adduce *vt* (*witnesses*) producĕre; (*arguments*) afferre
adept *adj* peritus
adequacy *s* sufficientia *f*
adequate *adj* adaequatus, sufficiens, par; **to be —** sufficĕre; **—ly** satis, apte
adhere *vi* adhaerēre, cohaerēre; **to — to** inhaerēre (*with dat*); (*fig*) stare in (*with abl*)
adherence *s* adhaesio *f*
adherent *s* assectator, fautor, cliens *m*
adhesion *s* adhaesio *f*
adhesive *adj* tenax
adieu *interj* vale, valete; **to bid —** valedicĕre; valēre jubēre
adjacent *adj* confinis, conterminus; vicinus
adjective *s* adjectivum (nomen) *n*
adjectively *adv* adjective; ut appositum; pro apposito
adjoin *vt* adjungĕre; adjacēre (*with dat*); *vi* adjacēre
adjoining *adj* adjacens, confinis
adjourn *vt* comperendinare, differre, prorogare; *vi* deferri
adjournment *s* dilatio *f*

adjudge *vt* addicĕre, adjudicare
adjudicate *vt* addicĕre, decernĕre
adjudication *s* addictio, adjudicatio *f*; sententia *f*; arbitrium *n*
adjunct *s* adjunctum *n*, accessio, appendix *f*
adjuration *s* obtestatio *f*; obsecratio *f*
adjure *vt* adjurare; obtestari
adjust *vt* aptare, accommodare; (*put in order*) componĕre
adjustment *s* accommodatio, compositio *f*; (*of a robe*) structura *f*
adjutant *s* optio *m*
administer *vt* (*to manage*) administrare; (*medicine, etc.*) adhibēre; (*oath*) adigĕre; (*justice*) dispensare, reddĕre
administration *s* administratio, cura, procuratio *f*; jurisdictio *f*; magistrat·us -ūs *m*
administrative *adj* ad administrationem pertinens
administrator *s* administrator, procurator *m*
admirable *adj* admirabilis, mirabilis, admirandus; insignis, egregius
admiral *s* classis praefectus *m*
admiration *s* admiratio *f*
admire *vt* admirari; amare
admirer *s* admirator, mirator, laudator *m*; amator *m*
admiringly *adv* admirans
admissible *adj* accipiendus, aptus, aequus
admission *s* admissio, confessio *f*; adit·us -ūs, access·us -ūs *m*
admit *vt* admittĕre; recipĕre; (*to recognize*) asciscĕre; noscĕre; **it is admitted** constat
admittedly *adv* sane
admonish *vt* monēre, admonēre, commonēre; hortari
admonition *s* monitio, admonitio *f*; monitum *n*
adolescence *s* prima adulescentia *f*
adolescent *adj* adolescens, adulescens
adolescent *s* adulescentulus, adulescens *m*
adopt *vt* (*a minor*) adoptare; (*an adult*) arrogare; (*a custom*) asciscĕre; (*a plan*) capĕre, inire
adoption *s* adoptio, adoptatio *f*; (*of an adult*) arrogatio *f*; (*of a custom*) assumptio *f*; **by —** adoptivus
adoptive *adj* adoptivus
adorable *adj* adorandus, venerandus
adoration *s* adoratio *f*; cult·us -ūs *m*; (*of kings*) veneratio *f*
adore *vt* adorare, venerari; (*fig*) admirari, amare
adorn *vt* ornare, decorare, distinguĕre, illustrare; excolĕre, comare
adornment *s* exornatio *f*; ornat·us -ūs *m*; ornamentum *n*
Adriatic Sea *s* Hadria *m or* Adria *m*
adrift *adv* fluctuans; **to be —** fluctuare
adroit *adj* callidus, dexter, sollers, peritus; **—ly** callide, scite
adroitness *s* dexteritias, sollertia, calliditas *f*
adulation *s* adulatio, assentatio *f*
adult *adj* adultus
adult *s* adultus homo, puber *m*
adulterate *vt* adulterare, vitiare, commiscēre
adulteration *s* adulteratio, commixtio *f*
adulterer *s* adulter *m*; moechus *m*
adulteress *s* adultera *f*; moecha *f*
adulterous *adj* stuprosus, adulterinus, incestus
adultery *s* adulterium, stuprum *n*; **to commit —** moechari; adulterare
advance *vt* promovēre; admovēre; (*money*) praerogare; (*a cause*) fovēre; (*an opinion*) exhibēre, praeferre; (*to honors*) provehĕre; *vi* procedĕre, progredi, incedĕre; (*mil*) gradum *or* pedem inferre; signa proferre; (*to progress*) proficĕre
advance *s* progress·us -ūs *m*; (*step*) pass·us -ūs *m*; (*attack*) incursio *f*; impet·us -ūs *m*; (*money*) mutuae pecuniae *f pl*; **in —** maturius
advanced *adj* provectus; (*of age*) grandis
advance guard *s* primum agmen *n*
advancement *s* dignitatis accessio, promotio *f*; honos *m*
advantage *s* (*benefit*) commodum *n*, us·us -ūs *m*, bonum *n*; (*profit*) lucrum, emolumentum *n*; utilitas *f*, fruct·us -ūs *m*; **to be of —** prodesse; **to have an — over** praestare (*with dat*); superior esse (*with dat*); **to take — of** uti (*with abl*); (*to deceive*) decipĕre, fallĕre; **with —** faenerato
advantageous *adj* fructuosus, utilis; **—ly** utiliter; bene
advent *s* advent·us -ūs *m*
adventure *s* cas·us -ūs *m*; fors *f*; facinus *n*
adventurer *s* periclitator *m*; latro *m*; pirata *m*
adventurous *adj* audax
adverb *s* adverbium *n*
adverbial *adj* adverbialis; **—ly** adverbialiter
adversary *s* adversarius *m*, hostis *m*; adversatrix *f*
adverse *adj* adversus, infestus; asper; **—ly** male, contrarie, infeliciter
adversity *s* res adversae *f pl*; calamitas *f*
advertise *vt* communefacĕre; proscribĕre
advertisement *s* proscriptio *f*; libellus *m*; indicium *n*
advice *s* consilium *n*; **to ask — of** consulĕre; **to give —** suadēre (*with dat*)
advisable *adj* commodus, utilis
advise *vt* suadēre (*with dat*), censēre (*with dat*), monēre; **to — to the contrary** dissuadēre (*with dat*)
adviser *s* consultor *m*
advocate *s* (*law*) actor, causidicus *m*; (*fig*) patronus *m*; suasor *m*; auctor *m*
aedile *s* aedilis *m*

aegis *s* aegis *f*
aerial *adj* aërius, aethereus
affability *s* comitas, affabilitas, facilitas *f*
affable *adj* affabilis, comis, facilis
affably *adv* comiter
affair *s* negotium *n*; res *f*; (*love*) amores *m pl*
affect *vt* afficĕre; commovēre; jactare; ostentare; attingĕre
affectation *s* simulatio, affectatio *f*
affected *adj* simulatus, fictus; (*in style*) putidus; **—ly** putide
affection *s* amor *m*; benevolentia *f*; studium *n*
affectionate *adj* amans, benevolus; **—ly** amanter
affidavit *s* testimonium *n*
affiliate *vt* adoptare; attribuĕre
affinity *s* affinitas *f*; cognatio *f*
affirm *vt* affirmare, asseverare, testificari
affirmation *s* affirmatio *f*
affirmative *adj* affirmans; **I reply in the —** aio; **—ly** affirmative
affix *vt* affigĕre, annectĕre
afflict *vt* affligĕre, afflictare
affliction *s* afflictio, miseria *f*; res adversae *f pl*
affluence *s* abundantia, copia *f*; divitiae *f pl*
affluent *adj* affluens, abundans; dives; **—ly** abundanter
afford *vt* praebēre; (*to yield*) reddĕre, ferre; **I cannot —** res mihi non suppetit ad (*with acc*)
affront *vt* irritare; contumeliā afficĕre; offendĕre
affront *s* contumelia, injuria *f*
afield *adv* foris
afloat *adj* natans; fluctuans; **to be —** natare, fluctuare
afoot *adv* pedestris, pedibus; **to be —** geri
afraid *adj* timidus, pavidus; **to be —** timēre; **to make —** terrefacĕre
afresh *adv* de integro, iterum, de novo
after *prep* post (*with acc*); a, de, e, ex (*with abl*); (*following immediately upon*) sub (*with acc*); (*in rank or degree*) secundum (*with acc*); (*in imitation of*) ad (*with acc*); **— all** tamen; saltem; **a little —** paulo post; **the day —** postridie
after *conj* postquam
afternoon *adj* postmeridianus, pomeridianus
afternoon *s* pomeridianum *n*; **in the —** post meridiem
afterthought *s* posterior cogitatio *f*
afterwards *adv* post, postea; deinde, deinceps, dehinc
again *adv* iterum, rursus, denuo, rursum; deinde; (*hereafter*) posthac; (*likewise, in turn*) invicem, mutuo, vicissim; contra; **— and —** etiam atque etiam; identidem; **once —** denuo; **over —** de novo
against *prep* contra (*with acc*); adversus (*with acc*); (*in a hostile manner*) in (*with acc*); **— the current** adverso flumine; **to be —** adversari
age *s* (*life*) aetas *f*; (*era*) saeculum *n*, aetas *f*; **of the same —** aequaevus, aequalis; **old —** senectus *f*; **to be of —** sui juris esse; **twelve years of —** duodecim annos natus; **under —** impubis
age *vi* senescĕre; maturescĕre
aged *adj* aetate provectus; senilis; (*things*) antiquus
agency *s* actio *f*; (*medium*) opera *f*; (*office*) procuratio *f*; **through the — of** per (*with acc*)
agent *s* actor, auctor *m*; (*in crime*) minister *m*
aggravate *vt* aggravare; (*pain*) augēre; provocare; (*a wound*) ulcerare; **to become aggravated** ingravescĕre
aggravating *adj* molestus
aggravation *s* exaggeratio *f*
aggregate *adj* aggregatus, totus
aggregate *s* summa *f*
aggregation *s* collatio *f*; aggregatum *n*
aggression *s* incursio *f*
aggressive *adj* hostilis, infensus; ferox
aggressor *s* qui bellum infert *m*; qui alterum prior lacessit *m*
aggrieve *vt* dolore afficĕre
aggrieved *adj* iratus
aghast *adj* attonitus, consternatus, stupefactus; **to stand —** obstupescĕre
agile *adj* agilis; pernix
agility *s* agilitas *f*; pernicitas *f*
agitate *vt* agitare; commovēre; perturbare
agitated *adj* tumultuosus; turbulentus; (*fig*) sollicitus
agitation *s* agitatio, commotio *f*; (*of the sea*) jactatio *f*; trepidatio *f*
agitator *s* concitator, turbator *m*
ago *adv*. abhinc; **a short time —** haud ita pridem; dudum; **long —** iamdudum, iampridem, antiquitus; **some time —** pridem
agonize *vt* cruciare, excruciare; *vi* discruciari
agonizing *adj* crucians; horribilis
agony *s* dolor *m*; agonia *f*; cruciat·us -ūs *m*
agrarian *adj* agrarius
agree *vi* assentire, assentiri; convenire; (*to make a bargain*) pacisci; (*of facts*) constare, convenire; **to — with** assentiri (*with dat*), sentire cum (*with abl*)
agreeable *adj* gratus, acceptus; amabilis; congruens, conveniens; **very —** pergratus
agreeably *adv* grate, jucunde; suaviter
agreement *s* consens·us -ūs *m*; concordia *f*; (*pact*) pactio *f*, pactum *n*; (*bargain*) conditio *f*; (*proportion*) symmetria *f*; reconciliatio *f*
agricultural *adj* rusticus, agrestis
agriculture *s* agricultura *f*; res rustica *f*
agriculturist *s* agricola *m*
ah *interj* ah!, eja!, vah!, vae!

ahead *adv use verb with prefix* prae- *or* pro-
aid *s* auxilium, subsidium *n*
aid *vt* succurrĕre (*with dat*), subvenire (*with dat*), adjuvare
aide-de-camp *s* optio *m*
ail *vt* dolēre; *vi* aegrotare
ailing *adj* aegrotus, aeger
ailment *s* aegrotatio *f*; malum *n*; morbus *m*
aim *s* (*mark*) scopus *m*; (*fig*) finis *m*, propositum *n*
aim *vt* intendĕre, tendĕre; *vi* **to — at** affectare, spectare, petĕre, quaerĕre
aimless *adj* vanus, inanis; **—ly** sine ratione
air *s* aër *m*; caelum *n*; (*breeze*) aura *f*; (*attitude*) habit·us -ūs, gest·us -ūs *m*; (*tune*) modus *m*; **in the open —** sub divo *or* sub caelo; **to take the —** deambulare
air *vt* ventilare
airily *adv* hilare
airy *adj* aërius; apertus, patens; ventosus; (*fig*) hilaris
aisle *s* ala *f*
ajar *adj* semiapertus
akin *adj* cognatus, agnatus, consanguineus, propinquus
alabaster *s* alabaster *m*
alacrity *s* alacritas *f*
alarm *s* (*signal*) classicum *n*; (*sudden fright*) trepidatio *f*, pavor *m*; tumult·us -ūs *m*; **to give the —** increpare
alarm *vt* perterrefacĕre, consternĕre, perturbare
alarming *adj* formidolosus
alas *interj* eheu!, heu!
alchemist *s* alchemista *m*
alchemy *s* alchemistica *f*
alcohol *s* spirit·us -ūs vini *m*
alcoholic *adj* alcoolicus
alcove *s* zotheca *f*, cubiculum *n*
ale *s* cerevisia *f*
alert *adj* alacer, promptus, vegetus
alertness *s* alacritas *f*
alias *adv* aliter
alias *s* falsum nomen *n*
alibi *s* (law) absentia rei *f*; (*excuse*) species *f*
alien *adj* peregrinus
alien *s* peregrinus *m*; alienigena, advena *m*
alienate *vt* alienare, abalienare, avertĕre, avocare
alienation *s* abalienatio, alienatio *f*
alight *vi* descendĕre; (*from a horse*) desilire; (*of birds*) subsidĕre
alike *adj* aequus, par, similis
alike *adv* pariter, similiter, aeque
alimony *s* alimentum, alimonium *n*
alive *adj* vivus; (*fig*) alacer; **to be —** vivĕre; superesse
all *adj* omnis, cunctus, totus; integer; universus; **— over** undique, passim; **— the better** tanto melius; **— the more** eo plus
all *s* omnia *n pl*; **at —** omnino; **in —** in summa; **not at —** haudquaquam; **one's all** proprium *n*
allay *vt* sedare, lenire, mitigare; **to be allayed** defervescĕre, temperari
allegation *s* affirmatio *f*; insimulatio *f*
allege *vt* affirmare, arguĕre; citare, allegare
allegiance *s* fides, fidelitas *f*; **to swear —** sacramentum dicĕre
allegorical *adj* allegoricus; **—ly** allegorice
allegorize *vi* allegorice scribĕre; allegorice explicare
allegory *s* allegoria *f*
alleviate *vt* levare, allevare, sublevare
alleviation *s* allevamentum *n*, levatio *f*
alley *s* angiport·us -ūs *m*
alliance *s* (*by blood*) consanguinitas *f*; (*by marriage*) affinitas *f*; (*of states*) foedus *n*; societas *f*
allied *adj* foederatus, socius; junctus, propinquus
alligator *s* crocodilus *m*
alliteration *s* alliteratio *f*
allocate *vt* impertire, assignare
allot *vt* distribuĕre, assignare
allotment *s* assignatio, portio *f*; assignatum *n*
allow *vt* concedĕre (*with dat*), permittĕre (*with dat*), sinĕre, pati; **it is allowed** licet; **to — for** indulgēre (*with dat*); **to — of** admittĕre
allowable *adj* licitus
allowance *s* (*permission*) licentia, permissio *f*; (*concession*) venia, indulgentia *f*; (*portion*) portio *f*; salarium *n*; diaria *n pl*; cibaria *n pl*; demensum *n*; **to make — for** ignoscĕre (*with dat*), condonare
alloy *s* mixtura *f*
alloy *vt* miscēre, adulterare, diluĕre
allude *vi* **to — to** attingĕre, designare, denotare, spectare
allure *vt* allicĕre, allectare, pellicĕre
allurement *s* illecebra, blanditia *f*; blandimentum *n*
alluring *adj* blandus; **—ly** blande
allusion *s* parodia *f*; indicium *n*, mentio *f*
allusive *adj* obliquus; **—ly** oblique
alluvial *adj* alluvius
ally *s* socius *m*, socia *f*
ally *vt* sociare
almanac *s* fasti *m pl*
almighty *adj* omnipotens
almond *s* amygdala *f*
almond tree *s* amygdalus *f*
almost *adv* fere, paene, prope, ferme
alms *s* stips *f*
aloft *adv* sublime
alone *adj* solus, unus, solitarius, unicus; **all —** persolus; **to leave —** deserĕre; **to let —** omittĕre, mittĕre
alone *adv* solum
along *adv* porro, protinus; **all —** jamdudum; **— with** una cum (*with abl*)
along *prep* per (*with acc*), praeter (*with acc*), secundum (*with acc*)
aloof *adv* procul; **to stand —** discedĕre, abstare
aloud *adv* magna voce; clare

alphabet *s* alphabetum *n*; prima elementa *n pl*
alphabetical *adj* litterarum ordine
Alpine *adj* alpinus
already *adv* jam
also *adv* etiam, quoque, et, idem, necnon
altar *s* ara *f*; altaria *n pl*
alter *vt* mutare, commutare; variare; vertĕre
alterable *adj* mutabilis
alteration *s* mutatio, commutatio *f*
altercation *s* altercatio *f*, jurgium *n*
alternate *adj* alternus; **—ly** invicem, per vices; alternis
alternate *vt & vi* alternare, variare
alternation *s* vicissitudo *f*
alternative *adj* alter
alternative *s* discrimen *n*, optio *f*; alternata conditio *f*
although *conj* etsi, etiamsi, tametsi, quamquam, licet, cum
altitude *s* altitudo *f*
altogether *adv* omnino; prorsus, plane
altruism *s* beneficentia *f*
always *adv* semper
amalgamate *vt* miscēre, conjungĕre
amalgamation *s* mixtio *f*
amass *vt* coacervare, cumulare
amateur *s* artium amator *m*; tiro *m*
amaze *vt* obstupefacĕre
amazed *adj* attonitus, stupefactus; **to be —** stupēre; obstupescĕre
amazement *s* stupor *m*; **in —** attonitus, stupefactus
amazing *adj* mirus, mirandus, mirabilis; **—ly** mirabiliter
Amazon *s* Amazon *f*
Amazonian *adj* amazonius, amazonicus
ambassador *s* legatus *m*
amber *s* sucinum *n*; electrum *n*
ambiguity *s* ambiguitas *f*, ambages *f pl*
ambiguous *adj* ambiguus, dubius, anceps; **—ly** ambigue
ambition *s* ambitio *f*; studium *n*
ambitious *adj* laudis *or* gloriae cupidus; studiosus; ambitiosus
amble *vi* ambulare
ambrosia *s* ambrosia *f*
ambush *s* insidiae *f pl*
ambush *vt* insidiari (*with dat*)
ameliorate *vt* meliorem *or* melius facĕre, corrigĕre
amenable *adj* docilis, obediens
amend *vt* emendare, corrigĕre; *vi* proficĕre
amendment *s* emendatio, correctio *f*
amends *s* compensatio, satisfactio *f*; **to make —** expiare, satisfacĕre, compensare
amenity *s* amoenitas *f*; (*comfort*) commodum *n*
amethyst *s* amethystus *f*
amiable *adj* amabilis, suavis
amiably *adv* amabiliter, suaviter
amicable *adj* amicus; pacatus; benevolus
amicably *adv* amice; pacate; benevole
amid *prep* inter (*with acc*)
amity *s* amicitia *f*
ammonia *s* ammoniaca *f*
ammunition *s* belli apparat·us -ūs *m*; missilium copia *f*
amnesty *s* venia, abolitio *f*
among *prep* inter (*with acc*); apud (*with acc*); ad (*with acc*); **from —** e, ex (*with abl*)
amorous *adj* amatorius; libidinosus, mulierosus; **—ly** amatorie; cum amore
amount *s* summa *f*, totum *n*
amount *vi* **to — to** crescĕre, exsurgĕre; (*fig*) esse
amour *s* amores *m pl*
amphitheater *s* amphitheatrum *n*
ample *adj* amplus; copiosus; satis
amplification *s* amplificatio, auctio, dilatatio *f*
amplify *vt* amplificare, dilatare
amply *adv* ample, abunde
amputate *vt* amputare, secare
amputation *s* amputatio, sectio *f*
amuck *adv* furiose; **to run —** delirare
amulet *s* amuletum *n*
amuse *vt* oblectare, delectare; **to — oneself** ludĕre
amusement *s* delectatio, oblectatio *f*; delectamentum *n*; ludibrium *n*
amusing *adj* ridiculus; festivus; facetus
an *indefinite article, unexpressed in Latin*
anachronism *s* temporum inversio *f*
analogous *adj* analogus
analogy *s* analogia, comparatio *f*
analysis *s* analysis *f*; explicatio *f*; separatio *f*
analytical *adj* analyticus; **—ly** per analysin
analyze *vt* in principia resolvĕre; (*words*) subtiliter enodare
anapest *s* anapaestus *m*
anapestic *adj* anapaesticus
anarchist *s* civis sediotiosus *m*
anarchy *s* anarchia *f*; rei publicae perturbatio *f*; licentia *f*
anathema *s* anathema *n*; exsecratio *f*
anatomical *adj* anatomicus
anatomy *s* anatomia, dissectio *f*
ancestor *s* proavus *m*; auctor *m*; **—s** majores, priores *m pl*
ancestral *adj* avitus; proavitus; patrius
ancestry *s* genus *n*; stirps *f*; origo *f*
anchor *s* ancora *f*; **to lie at —** in ancoris stare; **to weigh —** ancoram tollĕre *or* solvĕre
anchor *vt* in ancoris tenēre; *vi* ancoram jacĕre
anchorage *s* statio *f*
ancient *adj* antiquus, vetustus; priscus; pristinus; **in — times** antiquitus; **the —s** veteres *m pl*; barbati *m pl*
and *conj* et, ac, atque, -que
anecdote *s* fabella *f*
anemic *adj* exsanguis
anew *adv* denuo; ab integro
angel *s* angelus *m*

angelic *adj* angelicus; (*fig*) egregius, excellens
anger *s* ira *f*; bilis *f*
anger *vt* irritare, exacerbare
angle *s* angulus *m*
angle *vi* hamo piscari
angler *s* piscator *m*
angrily *adv* irate, iracunde
angry *adj* iratus, iracundus, indignans; **to be —** irasci, succensēre, stomachari; **to make —** irritare, exacerbare
anguish *s* angor *m*; dolor *m*; cruciat·us -ūs *m*
anguished *adj* animo fractus
angular *adj* angularis; angulosus
animal *s* animal *n*; (*wild beast*) bestia, fera *f*; (*domestic*) pecus *n*
animal *adj* animalis
animate *vt* animare; (*fig*) excitare
animated *adj* excitatus, vegetus
animation *s* animatio *f*; vigor, ardor, spirit·us -ūs *m*
animosity *s* acerbitas *f*; invidia *f*; odium *n*; inimicitia *f*
ankle *s* talus *m*
annalist *s* annalium scriptor *m*
annals *s* annales, fasti *m pl*
annex *s* appendix *f*
annex *vt* annectĕre, adjungĕre, addĕre, supponĕre
annexation *s* adjectio *f*
annihilate *vt* delēre, exstinguĕre
annihilation *s* exstinctio *f*; internecio *f*
anniversary *adj* anniversarius; annuus
anniversary *s* festus dies anniversarius *m*
annotate *vt* annotare, commentari
annotation *s* annotatio, nota *f*
announce *vt* nuntiare; (*to report*) renuntiare; (*officially*) denuntiare, pronuntiare; (*laws, etc.*) proscribĕre
announcement *s* denuntiatio, pronuntiatio *f*; (*news*) nuntius *m*
announcer *s* nuntius *m*
annoy *vt* incommodare, vexare, male habēre; **to be annoyed** stomachari, offensus esse
annoyance *s* vexatio, molestia *f*; dolor *m*
annoying *adj* molestus, odiosus
annual *adj* anniversarius, annuus; **—ly** quotannis
annuity *s* annua pecunia *f*; annuus redit·us -ūs *m*; (*law*) annuum *n*
annul *vt* rescindĕre, tollĕre, dissolvĕre, abrogare
annulment *s* abolitio *f*; abrogatio *f*
anoint *vt* ung(u)ĕre
anointing *s* unctio *f*
anomalous *adj* anomalus; enormis
anomaly *s* anomalia *f*; enormitas *f*
anonymous *adj* sine nomine; **—ly** sine nomine
another *adj* alius; **—'s** alienus; **one after —** alius ex alio; **one —** inter se; alius alium; **to — place** alio
answer *vt* respondēre (*with dat*); (*by letter*) rescribĕre (*with dat*); (*to correspond to*) congruĕre cum (*with abl*); *vi* **to — for** rationem reddĕre (*with genit*); **to — to the name of** vocari
answer *s* responsio *f*, responsum *n*; (*solution*) explicatio *f*
answerable *adj* reus; **to be — for** praestare
ant *s* formica *f*
antagonism *s* adversitas, inimicitia *f*
antagonist *s* adversarius *m*; adversatrix *f*; hostis *m*
antarctic *adj* antarcticus
antecedent *adj* antecedens; prior
antecedent *s* antecedens *n*
antechamber *s* atriolum *n*; antithalamus *m*
antedate *vt* diem vero antiquiorem ascribĕre (*with dat*)
antelope *s* antilope *f*; dorcas *f*
antepenult *s* syllaba antepenultima *f*
anterior *adj* anterior, prior
anteroom *s* antithalamus *m*; vestibulum *n*
anthem *s* canticum sacrum *n*; hymnus elatior *m*
anthology *s* anthologia *f*; excerpta *n pl*
anticipate *vt* anticipare; (*to expect*) spectare; (*to forestall*) praevenire, praeoccupare; (*mentally*) praesumĕre
anticipation *s* anticipatio, praesumptio, anteoccupatio *f*
anticlimax *s* climax inversa *f*
antics *s* joca *n pl*; ineptiae *f pl*
antidote *s* antidotum *n*
antipathy *s* repugnantia, antipathia *f*; fastidium, odium *n*
antiquarian *adj* historicus
antiquarian *s* antiquitatis peritus *m*; antiquarius *m*
antiquated *adj* antiquatus, obsoletus
antique *adj* antiquus, vetus, priscus
antique *s* antiqui artificis opus *n*
antiquity *s* antiquitas, vetustas *f*
antithesis *s* contrarium *n*, contentio *f*
antler *s* cornu *n*
anvil *s* incus *f*
anxiety *s* anxietas, sollicitudo *f*
anxious *adj* anxius, sollicitus; trepidus; avidus; **—ly** anxie, sollicite; trepide; avide
any *adj* ullus; quivis, quilibet; aliquis; **— longer** diutius; **— more** amplius
anybody *pron* aliquis; quivis; quilibet; (*after* si, nisi, num, ne) quis; (*interrog*) ecquis, numquis; (*after negative*) quisquam
anyhow *adv* quoquomodo
anyone *see* **anybody**
anything *pron* aliquid, quicquam, quidpiam, quodvis; (*after* si, nisi, num, ne) quid; (*interrog*) ecquid, numquid; (*after negative*) quicquam; **hardly —** nihil fere
anywhere *adv* ubilibet, alicubi, ubivis
apart *adv* seorsum, separatim; **to be —** distare; **to set —** seponĕre; **to stand —** distare
apart from *prep* praeter (*with acc*)
apartment *s* conclave *n*; insula *f*

apathetic *adj* lentus, languidus
apathy *s* apathia, lentitudo *f*, languor *m*
ape *s* simius *m*, simia *f*
ape *vt* imitari
aperture *s* apertura *f*; foramen *n*
apex *s* cacumen *n*; fastigium *n*
aphorism *s* sententia *f*
apiary *s* alvearium *n*
apiece *adv* singuli
aplomb *s* confidentia *f*
apocalypse *s* apocalypsis *f*
apocryphal *adj* apocryphus, commenticius
apogee *s* apogaeum *n*
apologetic *adj* apologeticus; confitens
apologist *s* defensor *m*
apologize *vi* se excusare; veniam petĕre
apology *s* excusatio, defensio *f*; (*written treatise*) apologia *f*, liber apologeticus *m*; **to make an — for** excusare
apoplectic *adj* apoplecticus
apoplexy *s* apoplexia *f*; apoplexis *f*
apostasy *s* apostasia *f*
apostate *s* apostata *m*
apostle *s* apostolus *m*
apostolic *adj* apostolicus
apostrophe *s* apostrophe *f*; (*gram*) apostrophus *f*
apostrophize *vt* abrupte compellare
apothecary *s* (*druggist*) medicamentarius *m*; (*drugstore*) medicina taberna *f*, pharmacopolium *n*
apotheosis *s* apotheosis *f*
appall *vt* exterrēre, percellĕre
apparatus *s* apparat·us -ūs *m*
apparel *s* vestis *f*, vestit·us -ūs *m*; vestimenta *n pl*
apparel *vt* vestire; adornare
apparent *adj* manifestus, apertus, conspicuus; **to be —** apparēre; **—ly** manifeste, aperte, specie, per speciem
apparition *s* spectrum *n*; visum *n*; species *f*
appeal *vi* appellare; provocare; **to — to** (*a magistrate*) appellare; (*the people*) provocare ad (*with acc*); (*the gods*) obsecrare, invocare, testari
appeal *s* (*law*) appellatio *f*; (*entreaty*) obsecratio, testatio *f*; (*to the people*) provocatio *f*
appear *vi* apparēre, comparēre; se ostendĕre; (*to seem*) vidēri; (*to arise*) exoriri, surgĕre; **to begin to —** patescĕre
appearance *s* (*becoming visible*) aspect·us -ūs *m*; (*outward show*) species *f*; (*likelihood*) similitudo *f*; (*vision*) visum *n*; **first —** exort·us -ūs *m*; **to all —s** probabilissime; **to make an —** prodire
appease *vt* placare, sedare; mitigare; (*fig*) expiare
appeasement *s* placatio *f*; (*of an enemy*) pacificatio *f*
appellation *s* nomen *n*
appendage *s* appendix, accessio, appendicula *f*
appendix *s* appendix *f*
appetite *s* appetit·us -ūs *m*, cupiditas *f*; **to have an —** esurire
applaud *vt* applauděre; laudare
applause *s* plaus·us -ūs, applaus·us ūs *m*; laus f
apple *s* malum, pomum *n*; **— of my eye** ocellus meus *m*
apple tree *s* malus *f*
appliance *s* instrumentum *n*, apparat·us -ūs *m*
applicable *adj* commodus, conveniens
applicant *s* petitor *m*
application *s* petito *f*; adhibitio, appositio *f*; studium *n*, sedulitas, industria, diligentia *f*; (*med*) fomentum *n*
apply *vt* adhibēre, admovēre, apponěre; aptare, accommodare; (*fig*) applicare; *vi* **to — to** pertinēre ad (*with acc*); **to — for** petĕre
appoint *vt* creare; facĕre; designare; destinare; constituĕre
appointment *s* creatio *f*; (*rendezvous*) constitutum *n*; (*order*) mandatum *n*; (*office*) magistrat·us -ūs *m*
apportion *vt* dividĕre, distribuĕre
apportionment *s* divisio, distributio *f*
apposition *s* appositio *f*
appraisal *s* aestimatio *f*
appraise *vt* aestimare
appraiser *s* aestimator *m*
appreciable *adj* aestimabilis, haud exiguus
appreciate *vt* aestimare
appreciation *s* aestimatio *f*
apprehend *vt* apprehendĕre, comprehendĕre, percipĕre; (*to seize*) capĕre; (*to take by surprise*) intercipĕre; (*to fear*) timēre, metuĕre
apprehension *s* comprehensio *f*; facultas, intelligentia *f*; suspicio *f*; (*seizing*) captura *f*; (*fear*) timor, met·us -ūs *m*
apprehensive *adj* timidus, sollicitus
apprentice *s* discipulus *m*; tiro *m*
apprenticeship *s* identura *f*; tirocinium *n*
apprize *vt* docēre
approach *vt* appropinquare (*with dat*), accedĕre ad (*with acc*), adire; *vi* appropinquare, appetĕre
approach *s* access·us -ūs, adit·us -ūs *m*; appropinquatio *f*; (*by sea*) appuls·us -ūs *m*
approachable *adj* (*person*) facilis, affabilis; (*place*) patens
approbation *s* approbatio, laus *f*
appropriate *adj* proprius, aptus, idoneus; **—ly** apte, congruenter
appropriate *vt* asciscĕre, asserĕre, vindicare; assumĕre
appropriation *s* vindicatio *f*
approval *s* approbatio *f*
approve *vt* approbare, probare; (*law*) sciscĕre; *vi* **to — of** probare
approved *adj* probatus, spectatus
approximate *adj* propinquus, proximus; **—ly** prope, propemodum; (*with numbers*) ad (*with acc*)
approximate *vt* appropinquare (*with dat*); accedĕre ad (*with acc*)

approximation *s* appropinquatio *f*
apricot *s* malum armeniacum *n*
April *s* (mensis) Aprilis *m*
apron *s* praecinctorium *n*; operimentum *n*
apt *adj* aptus, idoneus; (*inclined, prone*) pronus, propensus; **—ly** apte
aptitude *s* habilitas *f*, ingenium *n*
aptness *s* convenientia, congruentia *f*; (*tendency*) proclivitas *f*
aquatic *adj* aquatilis, aquaticus
aqueduct *s* aquaeduct·us -ūs, aquarum duct·us -ūs *m*
aquiline *adj* (*of the nose*) aduncus
arable *adj* arabilis, culturae idoneus; **— land** arvum *n*
arbiter *s* arbiter *m*
arbitrament *s* arbitrat·us -ūs *m*, arbitrium *n*
arbitrarily *adv* ad arbitrium; ad libdinem; libidinoso
arbitrary *adj* libidinosus; imperiosus, superbus
arbitrate *vt & vi* disceptare
arbitration *s* arbitrium *n*, dijudicatio *f*
arbitrator *s* arbiter *m*; disceptator *m*
arbor *s* umbraculum *n*, pergula *f*
arc *s* arc·us -ūs *m*
arcade *s* portic·us -ūs *f*
arch *s* arc·us -ūs, fornix *m*
arch *adj* astutus, callidus, vafer; nimius
arch *vt* arcuare, fornicare
archaeological *adj* archaeologiae (*genit*)
archaeologist *s* antiquitatis investigator *m*
archaeology *s* rerum antiquarum scientia *f*
archaism *s* locutio obsoleta *f*
archbishop *s* archiepiscopus *m*
archer *s* sagittarius *m*; (*constellation*) Arcitenens *m*
archery *s* ars sagittandi *f*
archetype *s* archetypum *n*
archipelago *s* insulis crebrum mare *n*
architect *s* architectus *m*
architectural *adj* architectonicus
architecture *s* architectura *f*
archives *s* tabulae *f pl*; tabularium *n*
arctic *adj* arcticus
ardent *adj* ardens, fervidus; **—ly** ardenter
ardor *s* ardor, fervor *m*
arduous *adj* arduus
area *s* regio *f*; area *f*; superficies *f*
arena *s* (h)arena *f*
argonaut *s* argonauta *m*
argue *vt* arguĕre, probare; *vi* argumentari, disputare, disserĕre
argument *s* (*discussion*) disputatio *f*; controversia *f*; (*theme*) argumentum, thema *n*, ratio *f*
argumentation *s* argumentatio *f*
argumentative *adj* ratiocinativus, litigiosus
aria *s* canticum *n*
arid *adj* aridus, siccus
aright *adv* recte
arise *vi* surgĕre, exoriri, exsistĕre; **to — from** nasci ex (*with abl*)
aristocracy *s* (*class*) optimates, nobiles *m pl*; (*government*) optimatum dominat·us -ūs *m*
aristocrat *s* optimas *m*
aristocratic *adj* patricius, generosus
arithmetic *s* arithmetica *n pl*
ark *s* arca *f*
arm *s* bracchium *n*; (*of the sea*) sin·us -ūs *m*; fretum *n*; **—s** arma *n pl*; **by force of —s** vi et armis; **to be under —s** in armis esse; **to lay down —s** ab armis discedĕre; arma dedĕre; **to take up —s** armare; arma sumĕre
arm *vt* armare; *vi* armari; bellum parare
armada *s* classis magna *f*
armament *s* belli apparat·us -ūs *m*; copiae *f pl*
armchair *s* anconibus fabrefacta sella *f*
armistice *s* indutiae *f pl*
armlet *s* bracchiolum *n*; (*bracelet*) bracchiale *n*
armor *s* armatura *f*, armat·us -ūs *m*; arma *n pl*
armorbearer *s* armiger *m*
armory *s* armamentarium *n*
armpit *s* ala *f*
army *s* exercit·us -ūs *m*; (*in battle*) acies *f*; (*on the march*) agmen *n*
aroma *s* aroma *n*; (*of wine*) flos *m*
aromatic *adj* armomaticus
around *adv* circum, circa; **all —** undique, passim
around *prep* circum (*with acc*)
arouse *vt* suscitare; (*fig*) erigĕre; **to — oneself** expergisci
arraign *vt* accusare
arraignment *s* accusatio, actio *f*
arrange *vt* instruĕre, struĕre, ordinare, disponĕre, componĕre; (*to agree*) pacisci
arrangement *s* ordo *m*, collocatio *f*; dispositio *f*; pactum n
array *s* vestis f, vestit·us -ūs *m*; habit·us -ūs *m*; (*mil*) acies *f*
array *vt* vestire; adornare; instruĕre
arrears *s* reliqua *n pl*; residuum *n*, residuae pecuniae *f pl*; **to be in —** relinqui
arrest *s* prehensio *f*
arrest *vt* (*to seize*) prehendĕre, deprehendĕre, arripĕre; (*movement*) tardare, morari; (*attention*) in se convertĕre
arrival *s* advent·us -ūs *m*; (*by sea*) appuls·us -ūs *m*
arrive *vi* pervenire, advenire; (*of a ship*) advehi, appelli
arrogance *s* arrogantia, superbia *f*
arrogant *adj* arrogans, superbus; **—ly** arroganter, insolenter, superbe
arrogate *vt* arrogare, assumĕre
arrow *s* sagitta, arundo *f*
arsenal *s* armamentarium *n*; navalia *n pl*
arsenic *s* arsenicum *n*
arson *s* incendium dolo malo *n*
art *s* ars *f*; artificium *n*
artery *s* arteria *f*

artful *adj* artificialis; callidus, subtilis; **—ly** callide, eleganter
article *s* (*object*) res *f*; (*ware*) merx *f*; (*term*) condicio *f*; (*clause*) caput *n*; (*gram*) articulus *m*
articulate *adj* distinctus, dilucidus; **—ly** articulatim, distincte
articulate *vt* explanare, exprimĕre; articulatim dicĕre
articulation *s* commissura *f*; (*fig*) explanatio *f*
artifice *s* artificium *n*; ars *f*; dolum *n*
artificial *adj* artificiosus; factitius; **—ly** arte
artillery *s* tormenta *n pl*
artisan *s* faber *m*; artifex, opifex *m*
artist *s* artifex *m*
artistic *adj* artificiosus, elegans; **—ally** artificiose; affabre
as *conj & adv* ut; quam; (*of time*) dum, cum; ita ut; sicut, velut; **— far —** quoad, usque ad, quantum; **— if** quasi, perinde ac si; ita ut si; **— it were** seu, tamquam; **— long —** tamdiu, tantisper dum; **— many —** tot, totidem; quotquot, quodcumque; **— much** tantum; **— often —** toties quoties; **— soon —** cum primum, simul, simul ac, simul atque; **— well —** ut, tamquam; **— yet** adhuc; **not — yet** nondum, necdum
ascend *vt & vi* ascendĕre
ascendency *s* auctoritas *f*
ascent *s* ascensio *f*; ascens·us -ūs *m*; acclivitas *f*
ascertain *vt* confirmare, comperire
ascetic *adj* asceticus
ascetic *s* asceta *m*
asceticism *s* duritia *f*
ascribe *vt* imputare, tribuĕre, ascribĕre
ash *s* cinis *m*; (*tree*) fraxinus *f*
ashamed *adj* pudibundus; **I am — of** pudet me (*with genit*)
ashen *adj* pallidus
ashore *adv* (*motion*) in litus; (*rest*) in litore
Asiatic *adj* Asiaticus
aside *adv* seorsum, oblique; **to call —** sevocare; **to lay** *or* **set —** ponĕre, seponĕre
aside from *prep* praeter (*with acc*)
asinine *adj* asininus
ask *vt* rogare, poscĕre; interrogare; requirĕre; *vi* **to — for** petĕre
askance *adv* oblique
askew *adv* traverse
asleep *adj* dormiens; **to be —** dormire; **to fall —** obdormire, obdormiscĕre
asp *s* aspis *f*
asparagus *s* asparagus *m*
aspect *s* aspect·us -ūs, prospect·us -ūs *m*; facies *f*
aspen *s* populus tremula *f*
asperity *s* acerbitas *f*
aspersion *s* opprobrium *n*, calumniatio *f*
asphalt *s* bitumen *n*
asphyxia *s* asphyxia *f*
aspirant *s* petitor *m*
aspiration *s* affectatio, spes *f*; (*pol*) ambitio *f*
aspire *vi* **to — to** affectare, spectare, petĕre, anniti
aspiring *adj* appetens; **aspiring to** appetens (*with genit*)
ass *s* asinus *m*; asina *f*; onager *m*; (*fig*) stultus *m*
assail *vt* appetĕre; oppugnare, invehi
assailable *adj* expugnabilis
assailant *s* oppugnator *m*
assassin *s* sicarius *m*; percussor *m*
assassinate *vt* insidiis interficĕre, occidĕre
assassination *s* caedes *f*
assault *s* impet·us -ūs *m*; oppugnatio, vis *f*; **aggravated —** (*law*) vis *f*; **sexual —** stupratio *f*; **to take by —** expugnare
assault *vt* adoriri, oppugnare; manus inferre (*with dat*); aggredi; (*in speech*) invehi in (*with acc*)
assay *vt* (*metals*) spectare; tentare, conari
assay *s* (*of metals*) obrussa *f*; spectatio *f*
assemblage *s* congregatio *f*; coacervatio *f*
assemble *vt* congregare, convocare; contrahĕre; *vi* convenire
assembly *s* coet·us -ūs *m*; convent·us -ūs *m*; (*pol*) comitia *n pl*; concilium *n*; (*of troops*) contio *f*; synodus *f*
assent *s* assens·us -ūs *m*
assent *vi* assentiri, adnuĕre
assert *vt* asserĕre, affirmare, asseverare; (*to vindicate*) defendĕre
assertion *s* affirmatio, asseveratio *f*; postulatio *f*
assess *vt* (*to tax*) censēre; (*to value*) aestimare
assessment *s* cens·us -ūs *m*; aestimatio *f*; vectigal, tributum *n*
assessor *s* (*judge*) consessor *m*; (*of taxes*) censor *m*
assets *s* bona *n pl*
assiduous *adj* assiduus; **—ly** assidue
assign *vt* attribuĕre, tribuĕre; (*land*) assignare; (*place*) indicare; (*time*) praestituĕre; (*task*) delegare; (*to allege*) suggerĕre, afferre
assignment *s* assignatio, attributio *f*; delegatio *f*
assimilate *vt* assimulare; (*food*) concoquĕre; (*knowledge*) concipĕre
assimilation *s* assimulatio, appropriatio *f*
assist *vt* adesse (*with dat*), succurrĕre (*with dat*), juvare, adjuvare
assistance *s* auxilium *n*; opem (*no nominative*) *f*; **to be of — to** auxilio esse (*with dat*)
assistant *s* adjutor *m*, adjutrix *f*, administer *m*
associate *adj* socius; collegialis
associate *s* socius, sodalis, consors *m*
associate *vt* consociare, adsciscĕre, conjungĕre; *vi* **to — with** familiariter uti (*with abl*); se adjungĕre (*with dat*)

association *s* societas *f*; communitas *f*; consociatio *f*; congregatio *f*
assort *vt* digerĕre, disponĕre; *vi* congruĕre
assortment *s* digestio, dispositio *f*; variae res *f pl*
assuage *vt* allevare, placare, lenire, mitigare
assume *vt* assumĕre, arrogare; induĕre; (*office*) inire
assuming *adj* arrogans
assumption *s* assumptio *f*; arrogantio *f*; (*hypothesis*) sumptio *f*
assurance *s* fiducia *f*; (*guarantee*) fides *f*; (*boldness*) confidentia, audacia *f*
assure *vt* confirmare, affirmare; promittĕre (*with dat*); adhortari; **to be assured** confidĕre
assuredly *adv* certo, profecto
asterisk *s* asteriscus *m*
asthmatic *adj* asthmaticus; **to be —** suspirio laborare
astonish *vt* obstupefacĕre; **to be astonished at** mirari
astonishingly *adv* admirabiliter
astonishment *s* admiratio *f*; stupor *m*
astound *vt* (ob)stupefacĕre
astray *adj* vagus; **to go —** errare; **to lead —** seducĕre
astride *adj* varicus
astrologer *s* astrologus *m*; Chaldaeus *m*; mathematicus *m*
astrological *adj* astrologicus
astrology *s* astrologia *f*; Chaldaeorum divinatio *f*
astronomer *s* astrologus *m*; astronomus *m*
astronomical *adj* astronomicus
astronomy *s* astrologia, astronomia *f*
astute *adj* callidus
asunder *adv* seorsum, separatim; *use verb with prefix* dis- *or* se-
asylum *s* asylum, perfugium *n*
at *prep* (*of place*) ad (*with acc*), apud (*with acc*), in (*with abl*), *or locative case*; (*of time*) in (*with abl*), ad (*with acc*), *or abl case*
atheism *s* deos esse negare (*used as neuter noun*)
atheist *s* atheos *m*
athlete *s* athleta *m*
athletic *adj* athleticus; lacertosus
atlas *s* orbis terrarum descriptio *f*
atmosphere *s* aër *m*; caelum *n*; inane *n*
atmospheric *adj* aëris (*genit*)
atom *s* atomus *f*; corpus individuum *n*; (*fig*) mica, particula *f*
atomic *adj* atomicus; **— theory** atomorum doctrina *f*
atone *vi* **to — for** piare, expiare
atonement *s* piaculum *n*; expiatio, compensatio *f*
atrocious *adj* atrox, dirus; nefarius, nefandus; immanis; **—ly** nefarie
atrocity *s* atrocitas *f*; atrox facinus *n*
atrophy *s* tabes, atrophia *f*
atrophy *s* tabescĕre, macrescĕre
attach *vt* annectĕre, adjungĕre; applicare; affigĕre; **to be attached to** adhaerēre (*with dat*)
attachment *s* adhaesio *f*; (*emotional*) amor *m*; vinculum *n*; studium *n*
attack *s* impet·us -ūs *m*; oppugnatio *f*; (*of cavalry*) incurs·us -ūs *m*; (*of disease, etc.*) tentatio *f*
attack *vt* adoriri, aggredi, oppugnare; (*with words*) invehi in (*with acc*), insequi; (*of diseases*) corripĕre, invadĕre, tentare
attacker *s* oppugnator, provocator *m*
attain *vt* adipisci, consequi; **to — to** pervenire ad (*with acc*)
attainable *adj* impetrabilis, obtinendus
attempt *s* conat·us -ūs *m*, inceptum *n*; (*risk*) ausum, periculum *n*; **first —** tirocinium *n*
attempt *vt* conari, niti, temptare, moliri
attend *vt* (*to accompany*) comitari; (*to escort*) deducĕre; (*to be present at*) adesse (*with dat*), interesse (*with dat*); *vi* **to — on** apparēre (*with dat*); frequentare, assectari; adesse (*with dat*); **to — to** animadvertĕre, procurare; (*to comply with*) obtemperare (*with dat*); invigilare
attendance *s* frequentia *f*; expectatio, adsectatio, cura, diligentia *f*; obsequium *n*; (*retinue*) comitat·us -ūs *m*
attendant *adj* adjunctus
attendant *s* comes *m*; assecla, apparitor *m*; famulus *m*, famula *f*
attention *s* animadversio *f*; animi attentio *f*; (*to duty*) cura, diligentia *f*; **to call —** to indicare; **to pay —** to operam dare (*with dat*), studēre (*with dat*)
attentive *adj* attentus; sedulus; officiosus; **—ly** attente, intento animo; sedulo; officiose
attenuate *vt* attenuare, extenuare
attenuation *s* extenuatio *f*
attest *vt* testari, testificari
attestation *s* testificatio *f*
attic *s* cenaculum *n*
Attic *adj* Atticus; (*fig*) subtilis, elegans
attire *s* ornat·us -ūs *m*; vestis *f*; habit·us -ūs m; vestit·us -ūs *m*
attire *vt* vestire; adornare
attitude *s* habit·us -ūs, stat·us -ūs *m*; (*mental*) ratio *f*
attorney *s* cognitor, procurator, advocatus, actor *m*
attorney general *s* advocatus fisci, procurator publicus *m*
attract *vt* trahĕre, attrahĕre; (*fig*) allicĕre
attraction *s* vis attractionis *f*; (*fig*) illecebra *f*, invitamentum *n*
attractive *adj* blandus, suavis, lepidus, venustus; **—ly** blande, suaviter, venuste, lepide
attractiveness *s* lepos *m*, venustas *f*
attribute *s* proprium, attributum *n*
attribute *vt* tribuĕre, attribuĕre; assignare, delegare
attrition *s* attrit·us -ūs *m*

attune *vt* modulari
auburn *adj* fulvus; aureus
auction *s* auctio *f*; (*public*) hasta *f*; **to hold an —** auctionem facĕre; **to sell by —** sub hasta vendĕre
auctioneer *s* praeco *m*
audacious *adj* audax; **—ly** audacter
audacity *s* audacia *f*
audible *adj* quod audiri potest
audibly *adv* clara voce
audience *s* auditores *m pl*; (*bystanders*) corona *f*
audit *s* rationum inspectio *f*
audit *vt* inspicĕre
auditory *adj* auditorius
Augean *adj* Augiae (*genit*)
auger *s* terebra *f*
augment *vt* augēre, ampliare; *vi* augēri, accrescĕre
augur *s* augur *m*
augur *vi* augurari
augury *s* augurium, auspicium *n*; auguratio *f*
august *adj* augustus; magnificus
August *s* (mensis) Sextilis, (mensis) Augustus *m*
Augustan *adj* Augustalis
aunt *s* (*on father's side*) amita *f*; (*on mother's side*) matertera *f*
auspices *s* auspicium *n*; **to take —** auspicari; **without taking —** inauspicato
auspicious *adj* auspicatus; faustus, felix; **—ly** auspicato; feliciter
austere *adj* austerus, severus; **—ly** austere, severe
austerity *s* austeritas, severitas *f*
authentic *adj* certus; verus; ratus; (*law*) authenticus; fide dignus; genuinus
authenticate *vt* recognoscĕre
authentication *s* auctoritas *f*; legibus confirmatio *f*
authenticity *s* auctoritas, fides *f*
author *s* auctor, scriptor *m*; (*inventor*) conditor *m*; (*of a crime*) caput *n*
authoress *s* auctor *f*
authoritative *adj* imperiosus; fidus; **—ly** praecise
authority *s* auctoritas, potestas *f*; (*leave*) licentia *f*; jus *n*; imperium *n*; magistrat·us -ūs *m*; **to have it on good —** bono auctore habēre
authorization *s* auctoritate confirmatio *f*; licentia *f*
authorize *vt* potestatem *or* auctoritatem dare (*with dat*), mandare; (*law*) sancire
authorship *s* scriptoris munus *n*; auctoritas *f*
autobiography *s* de vita sua scriptus liber *m*
autocrat *s* dominus *m*
autograph *s* chirographum *n*
autograph *vt* manu propria scribĕre
automatic *adj* necessarius
automaton *s* automaton *n*
autumn *s* autumnus *m*
autumnal *adj* autumnalis
auxiliaries *s* (*mil*) auxilia *n pl*; auxiliarii *m pl*
auxiliary *adj* auxiliaris, auxiliarius
auxiliary *s* adjutor *m*
avail *vt* prodesse (*with dat*); **to — oneself of** uti (*with abl*); *vi* valēre
avail *s* **to be of no —** usui non esse
availability *s* utilitas *f*
available *adj* in promptu; utilis
avalanche *s* montis ruina *f*
avarice *s* avaritia *f*; sordes *f*
avaricious *adj* avarus, avidus; **—ly** avare
avenge *vt* vindicare, ulcisci
avenger *s* ultor *m*, vindex *m & f*
avenging *adj* ultrix, vindex
avenue *s* xystus *m*, xystum *n*
average *s* medium *n*; **on the —** fere
average *vi* fere esse
averse *adj* aversus; **to be — to** abhorrēre ab (*with abl*); **—ly** averse
aversion *s* odium, fastidium *n*; **to have an — for** fastidire
avert *vt* avertĕre, amovēre, abducĕre
aviary *s* aviarium *n*
avid *adj* avidus
avocation *s* officium *n*, negotia *n pl*
avoid *vt* vitare, fugĕre; (*a blow*) declinare
avoidable *adj* evitabilis
avoidance *s* vitatio *f*; declinatio *f*
avow *vt* asserĕre, profitēri
avowal *s* confessio *f*
avowedly *adv* palam, aperte, ex confesso
await *vt* exspectare
awake *adj* vigil, vigilans; **to be —** vigilare
awaken *vt* excitare, suscitare, expergefacĕre; *vi* expergisci
award *s* praemium *n*; (*decision*) arbitrium, judicium *n*
award *vt* tribuĕre; (*law*) adjudicare, addicĕre
aware *adj* gnarus, sciens; **to be — of** scire
away *adv* *use verbs with prefix* a- *or* ab-; **far —** procul, longe; **to be —** abesse; **to go —** abire
awe *s* reverentia *f*; formido f, met·us -ūs, terror *m*; **to stand in — of** verēri; venerari
awful *adj* formidulosus, dirus, terribilis; **—ly** terribiliter, formidulose
awhile *adv* paulisper, aliquamdiu, parumper
awkward *adj* ineptus; rusticus, rudis; inhabilis; (*fig*) molestus; **—ly** inepte; rustice; dure; inscite
awkwardness *s* ineptia *f*; imperitia, rusticitas *f*
awl *s* subula *f*
awning *s* velarium *n*; inductio *f*
awry *adj* obliquus; pravus
awry *adv* oblique; prave
ax *s* securis *f*
axiom *s* axioma, pronuntiatum *n*, sententia *f*
axis *s* axis *m*
axle *s* axis *m*
azure *adj* caeruleus

B

baa *s* balat·us -ūs *m*
baa *vi* balare
babble *s* garrulitas *f*
babble *vi* blaterare, garrire
babbler *s* blatero, garrulus *m*
babbling *adj* garrulus, loquax
babe *s* infans *m & f*
baboon *s* cynocephalus *m*
baby *s* infans *m & f*
babyish *adj* infantilis
bacchanal *s* bacchans *m*, baccha *f*
bacchanalian *adj* bacchanalis
Bacchic *adj* bacchicus
bachelor *s* caelebs *m*; (*degree*) baccalaureus *m*
back *s* tergum, dorsum *n*; aversum *n*; **at one's —** a tergo
back *adv* retro, retrorsum; *or use verbs with prefix* re- *or* retro-
back *vt* adjuvare; favēre (*with dat*), obsecundare (*with dat*), adesse (*with dat*); *vi* **to — away from** defugĕre; **to — up** retrogradi
backboard *s* pluteus *m*
backbone *s* spina *f*
backdoor *s* posticum *n*
backer *s* adjutor, fautor *m*
background *s* recess·us -ūs *m*
backstairs *s* scalae posticae *f pl*
backward *adv* retro; retrorsum; rursus
backward *adj* (*reversed*) supinus; (*slow*) piger, tardus; (*late*) serus; **to be —** cunctari
backwardness *s* tarditas *f*; pigritia *f*
bacon *s* lardum *n*
bad *adj* malus, parvus, nequam; improbus; aegrotus; (*of weather*) adversus; **to go —** corrumpi; **—ly** male, prave; improbe
badge *s* insigne, signum *n*
badger *s* meles *f*
badger *vt* vexare, inquietare, sollicitare
badness *s* malitia, pravitas, nequitia, improbitas *f*
baffle *vt* decipĕre, fallĕre, eludĕre
bag *s* saccus *m*; (*of leather*) uter *m*; (*of network*) reticulum *n*
baggage *s* sarcinae *f pl*; impedimenta *n pl*; scruta *n pl*
bail *s* vadimonium *n*; vas *m*; (*for debt*) praes *m*; **to accept — for** vadari; **to put up — for** spondēre pro (*with abl*), fidepromittĕre
bailiff *s* (*sergeant of court of justice*) apparitor *m*; (*manager of estate*) villicus *m*
bailiwick *s* jurisdictio *f*
bait *s* esca *f*; (*fig*) incitamentum *n*, illecebra *f*
bait *vt* inescare; (*to tease*) lacessĕre
bake *vt* torrēre, coquĕre
baker *s* pistor *m*
bakery *s* pistrina *f*, pistrinum *n*
balance *s* libra, trutina, statera *f*; (*equipoise*) aequipondium *n*; (*in bookkeeping*) reliquum *n*; (*fig*) compensatio *f*
balance *vt* librare; compensare; (*accounts*) consolidare, dispungĕre; *vi* constare; **the account balances** ratio constat
balance sheet *s* ratio accepti et expensi *f*
balcony *s* maenianum *n*; podium *n*
bald *adj* calvus, glaber; (*fig*) aridus; **—ly** (*in style*) jejune
baldness *s* calvitium *n*; (*of style*) ariditas, jejunitas *f*
bale *s* sarcina *f*, fascis *m*
bale *vt* (*e.g., hay*) involvĕre; **to — out** exhaurire
baleful *adj* funestus; perniciosus, noxius
balk *s* (*of wood*) tignum *n*; (*fig*) frustratio *f*
balk *vt* frustrari, eludĕre, decipĕre
ball *s* globulus *m*; (*for playing*) pila *f*; **to play —** pilā ludĕre
ballad *s* carmen *n*
ballast *s* saburra *f*
ballast *vt* saburrare
ballet *s* pantomimus *m*
ballet dancer *s* pantomimus *m*, pantomima *f*
ballot *s* tabella *f*; suffragium *n*
ballot box *s* cista, cistula *f*
balm *s* balsamum *n*; unguentum *n*; (*fig*) solatium *n*
balmy *adj* balsaminus; suavis, lenis
balsam *s* balsamum *n*
bamboo *s* arundo indica *f*
ban *s* edictum *n*; proscriptio *f*; interdictum *n*
ban *vt* interdicĕre (*with dat*), vetare
banana *s* ariena *f*
band *s* vinculum, ligamentum *n*; (*for the head*) redimiculum *n*, infula *f*; (*troop*) caterva *f*, chorus *m*; grex *f*; man·us -ūs *f*; **in —s** turmatim
band *vi* **to — together** conjungi, consociari
bandage *s* fascia, ligatura *f*
bandage *vt* ligare, obligare
bandit *s* latro *m*
banditry *s* latrocinium *n*
bandy *vt* jactare; **to — words** altercari
bane *s* venenum *n*; virus *n*; (*fig*) pestis, pernicies *f*
baneful *adj* pestiferus, perniciosus, exitiosus
bang *s* crepit·us -ūs, sonit·us -ūs *m*
bang *vt* verberare; *vi* sonare, crepare
banish *vt* expellĕre, pellĕre, relegare, deportare; aquā et igni interdicĕre (*with dat*)
banishment *s* (*act*) ejectio, relegatio *f*; interdictio aquae et ignis *f*; (*state*) exilium *n*
banister *s* epimedion *n*
bank *s* (*of a river*) ripa *f*; (*of earth*) agger *m*; (*com*) argentaria *f*, mensa publica *f*

banker *s* argentarius, mensarius *m*
banking *s* argentaria negotiatio *f*
bank note *s* tessera mensae publicae *f*
bankrupt *s* conturbator, decoctor *m*; **to be** *or* **become —** rationes conturbare; decoquĕre; **to go —** foro cedĕre
bankruptcy *s* rationum conturbatio *f*; (*fig*) naufragium patrimonii *n*
banner *s* vexillum *n*
banquet *s* convivium *n*, epulae *f pl*
banter *s* cavillatio *f*; jocus *m*
banter *vi* cavillari
bantering *s* cavillatio *f*
baptism *s* baptisma *n*, baptismus *m*
baptize *vt* baptizare
bar *s* vectis *f*; (*of door*) obex *m*; repagulum *n*; (*fig*) impedimentum *n*; (*ingot*) later *m*; (*in court of justice*) cancelli *m pl*, claustra *n pl*; (*legal profession*) forum *n*; (*counter*) abacus *m*; **of the —** forensis; **to practice at the —** causas agĕre
bar *vt* (*door*) obserare; (*to keep away*) obstare (*with dat*), prohibēre, intercludĕre
barb *s* hamus *m*; aculeus *m*
barbarian *adj* barbarus
barbarian *s* barbarus *m*
barbaric *adj* barbaricus
barbarism *s* barbaria, barbaries *f*; feritas *f*; (*of language*) barbarismus *m*
barbarity *s* ferocia, saevitia, immanitas *f*
barbarous *adj* barbarus; ferus, immanis; **—ly** barbare; saeve
barbed *adj* hamatus
barber *s* tonsor *m*, tonstrix *f*
bard *s* vates *m*
bare *adj* nudus; merus; (*of style*) pressus; **to lay —** nudare, detegĕre
bare *vt* nudare, denudare; detegĕre, aperire
barefaced *adj* impudens; **—ly** impudenter
barefoot *adj* nudis pedibus; discalceatus
bareheaded *adj* nudo capite
barely *adv* vix, aegre
bargain *s* pactio *f*, pactum *n*; **to strike a —** pacisci
bargain *vi* pacisci
barge *s* linter *f*
bark *s* (*of tree*) cortex *m & f*, liber *m*; (*of dog*) latrat·us -ūs *m*; (*ship*) navis, ratis *f*
bark *vi* latrare; **to — at** allatrare
barking *s* latrat·us -ūs *m*
barley *s* hordeum *n*
barley *adj* hordeacus
barmaid *s* ministra cauponae *f*
barn *s* granarium, horreum *n*
barometer *s* barometrum *n*
barometric *adj* barometricus
baron *s* baro *m*
barracks *s* castra (stativa) *n pl*
barrel *s* cadus *m*, dolium *n*, cupa *f*
barren *adj* sterilis; macer; jejunus; (*fig*) angustus
barrenness *s* sterilitas *f*
barricade *s* munimentum *n*; claustrum *n*
barricade *vt* obsaepire, obstruĕre, oppilare
barrier *s* limes *m*; cancelli *m pl*; (*fig*) claustra *n pl*
barrister *s* advocatus *m*
barter *s* permutatio *f*; merx *f*
barter *vt* mutare, commutare; *vi* merces mutare, merces pacisci
base *adj* humilis, ignobilis, obscurus; inferior; servilis; infamis, vilis, turpis; **—ly** abjecte; turpiter
base *s* basis *f*; (*mus*) sonus gravis *m*; (*fig*) fundamentum *n*; (*mil*) castra *n pl*
baseless *adj* inanis, vanus, falsus
basement *s* fundamentum *n*, basis *f*; imum tabulatum *n*
baseness *s* humilitas *f*; turpitudo *f*
bashful *adj* erubescens; pudens; modestus; verecundus; **—ly** timide, verecunde; modeste
bashfulness *s* pudor *m*; rubor *m*; verecundia *f*
basic *adj* primus, principalis
basilica *s* basilica *f*
basin *s* (*for washing*) trulleum *n*, trulla *f*; (*reservoir*) labrum *n*
basis *s* fundamentum *n*
bask *vi* apricari
basket *s* corbis *f*, canistrum *n*; (*for wool*) quasillum *n*; cophinus *m*
bas-relief *s* caelamen *n*; toreuma *n*
bass *s* sonus gravissimus *m*
bast *s* tilia *f*
bastard *adj* spurius
bastard *s* nothus, spurius *m*
baste *vt* lardo perfundĕre
bastion *s* propugnaculum, castellum *n*
bat *s* (*bird*) vespertilio *m*; (*club*) clava *f*
batch *s* massa *n*; numerus *m*
bath *s* balneum *n*; (*public*) balnea *n pl*; (*tub*) alveus *m*, labrum *n*; lavatio *f*; **cold —** frigidarium *n*; **hot —** cal(i)darium *n*
bathe *vt* lavare; *vi* balneo uti, lavari, perlui
bathing *s* lavatio *f*; natatio *f*
bathtub *s* alveus *m*
batman *s* calo *m*
baton *s* virga *f*
battalion *s* cohors *f*
batter *vt* percutĕre, obtundĕre, diruĕre, verberare, quassare
battering ram *s* aries *m*
battle *s* proelium *n*, pugna *f*; acies *f*
battle *vi* pugnare, proeliari
battle array *s* acies *f*
battle-ax *s* bipennis *f*
battlement *s* pinna *f*
bauble *s* tricae *f pl*
bawd *s* lena *f*
bawdry *s* lenocinium *n*
bawl *vi* vociferari, clamitare
bawling *s* vociferatio *f*; indecorus clamor *m*
bay *s* (*sea*) sin·us -ūs *m*; (*tree*) laurea, laurus *f*; **at —** interclusus
bay *adj* (*light-colored*) helvus; (*dark-colored*) spadix; (*of bay*) laureus

bay *vi* latrare
bayonet *s* pugio *f*
bayonet *vt* pugione foděre
bazaar *s* forum rerum venalium *n*
be *vi* esse; exsistěre; (*condition*) se habēre; **to — absent** abesse; **to — against** adversari; **to — amongst** interesse (*with dat*); **to — for** (*to side with*) favēre (*with dat*), stare cum (*with abl*); **to — present** adesse
beach *s* litus *n*, acta *f*
beach *vt* subducěre; *vi* vadis impingěre
beacon *s* ignis in specula *m*; (*lighthouse*) pharus *m*
bead *s* pilula, sphaerula *f*
beagle *s* parvus canis venaticus *m*
beak *s* rostrum *n*
beaked *adj* rostratus
beaker *s* poculum *n*, cantharus *m*
beam *s* (*of wood*) tignum *n*, trabs *f*; (*of light*) radius *m*, jubar *n*; nitor *m*
beam *vi* radiare, refulgēre; (*of a person*) arriděre
beaming *adj* nitens, lucidus
bean *s* faba *f*; phaselus *m & f*
bear *vt* (*to carry*) portare, ferre; (*to endure*) ferre, pati, tolerare; (*to produce*) ferre; (*to beget*) parěre; **to — away** auferre; **to — out** (*to confirm*) arguěre; **to — witness to** testari; *vi* **to — down on** appropinquare; **to — upon** (*to refer to*) pertiněre ad (*with acc*); **to — up under** obsistěre (*with dat*), sustiněre; **to — with** indulgēre (*with dat*)
bear *s* ursus *m*, ursa *f*
bearable *adj* tolerandus, tolerabilis
beard *s* barba *f*; (*of grain*) arista *f*
bearded *adj* barbatus; intonsus
beardless *adj* inberbis
bearer *s* (*porter*) bajulus *m*; (*of litter*) lecticarius *m*; (*of letter*) tabellarius *m*; (*of news*) nuntius *m*
bearing *s* (*posture*) gest·us -ūs, vult·us -ūs *m*; (*direction*) regio *f*; **to have a — on** pertiněre ad (*with acc*)
beast *s* belua *f*; bestia *f*; (*wild*) fera *f*; (*domestic*) pecus *f*
beast of burden *s* jumentum *n*
beastly *adj* obscenus, foedus, spurcus
beat *vt* (*to punish*) verberare; (*to knock*) pulsare; (*to conquer*) superare, vincěre; (*the body in grief*) plangěre; **to — back** repellěre; **to — down** demoliri; **to — in** perfringěre; *vi* palpitare; **to — upon** (*of rain*) impluěre; (*of waves*) illiděre
beat *s* (*blow*) plaga *f*, ict·us -ūs *m*; (*of the heart*) palpitatio *f*; (*mus*) percussio *f*; (*patrol*) vigiles nocte ambulantes *m pl*
beaten *adj* victus; (*worn*) tritus
beating *s* verberatio *f*; ict·us -ūs *m*; verbera *n pl*; (*defeat*) repulsa *f*; clades *f*; (*of the heart*) palpitatio *f*
beautiful *adj* pulcher; (*shapely*) formosus; **—ly** pulchre, belle
beautify *vt* ornare, decorare
beauty *s* pulchritudo *f*; forma *f*; (*of places*) amoenitas *f*
beaver *s* castor, fiber *m*; (*of helmet*) buccula *f*
because *conj* quod, quia, quoniam; quippe qui
because of *prep* ob (*with acc*), propter (*with acc*), gratiā (*with genit*)
beck *s* nut·us -ūs *m*; **at the — and call** ad arbitrium
beckon *vt* nutare, annuěre
become *vt* decēre; *vi* fieri
becoming *adj* decens; decorus; conveniens; **—ly** decenter; digne; honeste
bed *s* lectus *m*, cubile *n*; (*in a garden*) areola *f*; (*of a river*) alveus *m*; **to go to —** cubitum ire; **to make the —** lectum sterněre
bedding *s* stragulum *n*
bedeck *vt* decorare, ornare
bedevil *vt* (*to enchant*) fascinare
bedfellow *s* tori socius *m*, tori socia *f*
bedlam *s* tumult·us -ūs *m*
bedpost *s* fulcrum *n*
bedraggled *adj* sordidus
bedridden *adj* **to be —** lecto tenēri
bedroom *s* cubiculum *n*
bedtime *s* hora somni *f*
bee *s* apis *f*
beef *s* bubula caro *f*
beehive *s* alveus *m*; alvearium *n*
beekeeper *s* apiarius *m*
beer *s* cerevisia *f*
beet *s* beta *f*
beetle *s* scarabaeus *m*
befall *vt* acciděre (*with dat*); contingěre (*with dat*); *vi* acciděre, contingěre, evenire
befit *vt* decēre, convenire in (*with acc*)
befitting *adj* decens; conveniens, idoneus; **it is —** decet
before *prep* ante (*with acc*); prae (*with abl*); pro (*with abl*); coram (*with abl*); apud (*with acc*); **— all things** imprimis; **— long** jamdudum; **— now** antehac
before *conj* antequam, priusquam
beforehand *adv* antea
befriend *vt* favēre (*with dat*), sublevare, adjuvare
beg *vt* petěre, poscěre, orare, obsecrare; *vi* mendicare
beget *vt* gigněre, procreare, generare
beggar *s* mendicus *m*
begging *s* mendicitas *f*; **to go —** mendicare
begin *vt & vi* incipěre, incohare, exordiri; **to — with** incipěre ab (*with abl*)
beginner *s* auctor *m*; inceptor *m*; tiro *m*
beginning *s* inceptio *f*; initium *n*; exordium *n*; origo *f*; principium *n*; **at the — of winter** ineunte hieme
begone *interj* apage!
beguile *vt* fallěre, fraudare
behalf *s* **on — of** pro (*with abl*)
behave *vi* se gerěre; **to — towards**

uti (*with abl*); **well behaved** bene moratus
behavior *s* mores *m pl*
behead *vt* detruncare, obtruncare
beheading *s* decollatio *f*
behest *s* jussum *n*
behind *adv* pone, a tergo, post; **to be left —** relinqui
behind *prep* pone (*with acc*); post (*with acc*)
behold *vt* conspicĕre; obtuēri
behold *interj* ecce!, en!
being *s* ens *n*; natura *f*; essentia *f*; homo *m*
bejewelled *adj* gemmatus, gemmeus
belabor *vt* mulcare, verberare
belch *s* ruct·us -ūs *m*
belch *vi* ructare, eructare
belfry *s* campanile *n*
belie *vt* repugnare; (*to refute*) refutare, refellĕre
belief *s* fides *f*; opinio, persuasio *f*
believe *vt* (*thing*) credĕre; (*person*) credĕre (*with dat*); (*to suppose*) existimare, opinari, putare, credĕre, arbitrari; **to make —** simulare
believer *s* credens *m & f*; Christianus *m*
bell *s* (*large*) campana *f*; (*small*) tintinnabulum *n*
belle *s* formosa puella *f*
belles lettres *s* litterae *f pl*
belligerent *adj* belliger, belligerans, bellans
bellow *vi* rugire, mugire
bellowing *s* mugit·us -ūs *m*
bellows *s* follis *m*
belly *s* venter *m*; abdomen *n*
bellyache *s* tormina *n pl*
belong *vi* **to — to** esse (*with genit*); inesse (*with dat*); pertinēre ad (*with acc*)
beloved *adj* dilectus, carus; **dearly —** carissimus
below *adj* inferus
below *adv* infra; subter
below *prep* infra (*with acc*); sub (*with abl or acc*)
belt *s* cingulum *n*; (*swordbelt*) balteus *m*; zona *f*
bemoan *vt* deplorare, lamentari
bemused *adj* attonitus
bench *s* scamnum, sedile, subsellium *n*; (*for rowers*) transtrum *n*
bend *vt* flectĕre, curvare; inclinare; (*bow*) intendĕre; (*to persuade*) intendĕre; *vi* se inflectĕre; **to — back** reflectĕre; **to — down** *or* **over** se demittĕre
bend *s* plica *f*; flex·us -ūs *m*; curvamen *n*; (*fig*) inclinatio *f*
bending *s* flexura, curvatura, inclinatio *f*
bending *adj* flexus; inclinans; acclivis; declivis; (*concave*) concavus
beneath *adv* subter
beneath *prep* sub (*with acc or abl*)
benediction *s* benedictio *f*
benefaction *s* beneficium *n*
benefactor *s* largitor *m*; patronus *m*
benefactress *s* patrona *f*
beneficence *s* beneficentia *f*
beneficent *adj* beneficus, benignus, liberalis; **—ly** benefice
beneficial *adj* utilis, commodus; salutaris; **—ly** utiliter
benefit *s* beneficium *n*, gratia *f*; fruct·us -ūs *m*; **to have the — of** frui (*with abl*)
benefit *vt* juvare; prodesse (*with dat*); *vi* proficĕre; lucrari
benevolence *s* benevolentia *f*
benevolent *s* benevolus, beneficus; benignus, liberalis; **—ly** benevole
benign *adj* benignus; **—ly** benigne
bent *adj* curvus, flexus; (*of the mind*) attentus; **— backwards** recurvus; **— forwards** pronus; **— inwards** camur; sinuosus
bent *s* flex·us -ūs *m*, plica *f*; curvatura *f*; (*inclination*) ingenium *n*, inclinatio f
benumb *vt* torpore afficĕre
bequeath *vt* legare
bequest *s* legatum *n*
bereave *vt* orbare; privare; spoliare
bereavement *s* orbitas *f*; damnum *n*
bereft *adj* orbus, orbatus, privatus
berry *s* bacca *f*; acinus *m*
berth *s* statio *f*; (*cabin*) diaeta *f*; **to give wide — to** devitare
beseech *vt* obsecrare, implorare, supplicare
beset *vt* circumdare, obsidēre, circumsedēre; urgēre
beside *prep* ad (*with acc*), apud (*with acc*), juxta (*with acc*); **— the point** nihil ad rem; **to be — oneself** delirare
besides *adv* praeterea, ultro, insuper
besides *prep* praeter (*with acc*)
besiege *vt* circumsedēre, obsidēre
besieging *s* obsessio, circumsessio *f*
besmirch *vt* maculare
best *adj* optimus, praestantissimus; **the — part** major pars *f*
best *s* flos *m*; **to do one's —** pro virili parte agĕre; **to have the — of it** praevalēre, valēre; **to make the — of** aequo animo ferre; **to the — of one's ability** pro viribus
bestial *adj* bestialis; immanis
bestir *vt* **to — oneself** expergisci
bestow *vt* tribuĕre, conferre; donare, largiri
bestower *s* largitor, dator *m*
bet *s* pignus, depositum *n*
bet *vt* deponĕre; *vi* pignore contendĕre
betide *vi* evenire, accidĕre
betoken *vt* indicare, portendĕre
betray *vt* tradĕre, prodĕre; (*feelings*) arguĕre
betrayer *s* proditor, traditor *m*
betroth *vt* spondĕre, despondĕre
betrothal *s* sponsalia *n pl*; pactio nuptialis *f*
betrothed *adj* sponsus, pactus
better *adj* melior; potior, praestantior; superior; **it is —** praestat; **to get —** convalescĕre; **to get the — of** superare, vincĕre
better *adv* melius, potius; praestantius; rectius; satius

better *vt* meliorem facĕre; corrigĕre; **to — oneself** proficĕre
betters *s* superiores *m pl*
between *prep* inter (*with acc*); **— whiles** interim
betwixt *prep* inter (*with acc*)
bevel *vt* obliquare
beverage *s* potio *f*, pot·us -ūs *m*
bevy *s* grex *f*
bewail *vt* deplorare, ingemĕre, queri, lamentari
beware *vi* cavēre; **to — of** cavēre
bewilder *vt* perturbare, confundĕre
bewilderment *s* perturbatio *f*
bewitch *vt* fascinare; (*to charm*) demulcēre
beyond *adv* supra, ultra; ulterius
beyond *prep* ultra (*with acc*); (*motion*) trans (*with acc*); supra (*with acc*), extra (*with acc*); **to go —** excedĕre
bias *s* inclinatio *f*; praeponderatio *f*
bias *vt* inclinare
Bible *s* divina scriptura *f*, biblia *n pl*
Biblical *adj* biblicus
bibliography *s* bibliographia *f*
bicker *vi* jurgare, altercari
bickering *s* altercatio *f*
bid *vt* jubēre, mandare, rogare; (*to invite*) invitare; (*at auction*) licitari, licēri; **to — farewell** valedicĕre
bid *s* licitatio *f*; **to make a —** licēri
bidder *s* licitator *m*
bidding *s* jussum *n*; (*auction*) licitatio *f*
bide *vt* exspectare, manēre
biennial *adj* biennalis, bimus
bier *s* feretrum *n*, sandapila *f*
big *adj* ingens, vastus; grandis, amplus; **— with child** gravida; **— with young** praegnans; **very —** permagnus
bigamist *s* bimaritus *m*
bigamy *s* bigamia *f*
bigot *s* nimis obstinatus fautor *m*
bigoted *adj* nimis obstinatus
bigotry *s* contumacia *f*; nimia obstinatio *f*
bile *s* bilis *f*
bilge water *s* sentina *f*
bilious *adj* biliosus
bilk *vt* fraudare; frustrari
bill *s* (*of a bird*) rostrum *n*; (*proposed law*) rogatio *f*; lex *f*; plebiscitum *n*; (*com*) ratio debiti *f*; syngrapha *f*; (*notice*) libellus *m*; **to introduce a —** ferre, legem ferre; populum rogare; **to pass a —** legem perferre; **to turn down a —** antiquare
billet *s* hospitium *n*
billet *vt* per hospitia dispargĕre
billion *s* billio *m*
billow *s* fluct·us -ūs *m*
billowy *adj* fluctuosus, undabundus
bin *s* (*in wine cellar*) loculus *m*; (*for grain*) cista *f*, panarium *n*
bind *vt* ligare, nectĕre, stringĕre, vincire; (*by obligation*) obligare; (*books*) conglutinare; (*wounds*) obligare; **to — fast** devincire; **to — together** colligare; **to — up** alligare; (*med*) astringĕre

binding *adj* obligatorius; (*law*) ratus
binding *s* religatio *f*; compages *f*
biographer *s* vitae scriptor *m*
biography *s* vita *f*
biped *s* bipes *m*
birch *adj* betulinus
birch tree *s* betula *f*
bird *s* avis, volucris *f*
birdcage *s* cavea *f*
birdcall *s* fistula aucupatoria *f*
birdlime *s* viscum *n*
bird's nest *s* nidus *m*
birth *s* part·us -ūs *m*; ort·us -ūs *m*; (*race*) genus *n*
birthday *s* dies natalis *m*
birthday cake *s* libum *n*
birthplace *s* patria *f*
birthright *s* patrimonium *n*
biscuit *s* crustulum *n*
bisect *vt* dividĕre
bishop *s* episcopus *m*
bison *s* bison *m*; urus *m*
bit *s* (*for a horse*) frenum *n*; (*small amount*) pars *f*, fragmentum *n*; (*of food*) frustum *n*; **— by —** minutatim
bitch *s* canis *f*
bite *s* mors·us -ūs *m*; (*fig*) sarcasmus *m*
bite *vt* mordēre; (*as pepper, frost, etc.*) urĕre
biting *adj* mordax; (*fig*) asper; mordens
bitter *adj* amarus; (*fig*) acerbus; asper; gravis; **—ly** acerbe; aspere
bitterness *s* amaritas *f*; (*fig*) acerbitas *f*; asperitas *f*
bitters *s* absinthium *n*
bivouac *s* excubiae *f pl*
blab *s* garrulus *m*
blab *vi* garrire, deblaterare
black *adj* niger; ater; (*in looks*) trux; (*of character*) scelestus
black *s* nigrum *n*; (*negro*) Aethiops *m*; **in —** pullatus
black-and-blue *adj* lividus
blackberry *s* morum *n*
blackbird *s* merula *f*
black death *s* pestis *f*
blacken *vt* nigrare; denigrare
blackguard *s* nebulo *m*
blacklist *s* proscriptio *f*
black magic *s* magicae artes *f pl*
blackness *s* nigritia, nigrities *f*
blacksmith *s* ferrarius faber *m*
bladder *s* vesica *f*
blade *s* (*edge*) lamina *f*; (*of grass*) caulis *m*, herba *f*; (*of oar*) palma *f*
blamable *adj* culpabilis; reus
blame *vt* reprehendĕre, culpare, vituperare
blame *s* culpa *f*; reprehensio *f*
blameless *adj* integer, innoxius; irreprehensus; **—ly** integre, innocenter
blanch *vt* candefacĕre; *vi* exalbescĕre, pallescĕre
bland *adj* blandus
blandishment *s* blanditia *f*, blandimentum *n*; (*charm*) lenocinium *n*
blank *adj* vacuus, albus, purus; (*expression*) stolidus

blanket *s* lodix *f*; stragulum *n*
blare *s* strepit·us -ūs, clangor, stridor *m*
blare *vi* stridēre, canĕre
blaspheme *vi* maledicĕre, execrari; blasphemare
blasphemous *adj* maledicus, impius; blasphemus
blasphemy *s* maledicta *n pl*, impietas *f*; blasphemia, blasphematio *f*
blast *s* flat·us -ūs *m*, flamen *n*
blast *vt* discutĕre, disjicĕre; (*crops*) urĕre, robigine afficĕre
blaze *s* flamma *f*; fulgor *m*
blaze *vi* flagrare, ardēre; **to — up** exardescĕre
bleach *vt* dealbare, candefacĕre
bleak *adj* desertus; immitis
blear-eyed *adj* lippus; **to be —** lippire
bleat *vi* balare
bleating *s* balat·us -ūs *m*
bleed *vi* sanguinem fundĕre
bleeding *adj* crudus, sanguineus
bleeding *s* (*bloodletting*) sanguinis missio *f*; (*flowing of blood*) sanguinis profusio *f*
blemish *s* macula *f*, vitium *n*; labes *f*
blemish *vt* maculare, foedare
blend *vt* commiscēre, immiscēre
bless *vt* beare; (*eccl*) benedicĕre; (*consecrate*) consecrare; (*with success*) secundare
blessed *adj* beatus; pius; fortunatus; (*of emperors*) divus
blessing *s* (*thing*) bonum, commodum *n*; (*eccl*) benedictio *f*
blight *s* robigo, uredo *f*
blight *vt* urĕre; robigine afficĕre; (*fig*) nocēre (*with dat*)
blind *adj* caecus; obscurus; (*fig*) ignarus; **—ly** (*rashly*) temere
blind *vt* caecare, occaecare; (*fig*) occaecare, fallĕre
blindfold *vt* oculos obligare (*with dat*)
blindfolded *adj* obligatis oculis
blindness *s* caecitas *f*; (*fig*) temeritas *f*; stultitia *f*
blink *vi* connivēre
bliss *s* beatitudo *f*
blissful *adj* beatus; **—ly beate**
blister *s* pustula *f*
blister *vt & vi* pustulare
blithe *adj* hilaris, hilarus
bloated *adj* tumidus, turgidus
block *s* truncus, stipes *m*; (*of stone*) massa *f*; (*of houses*) insula *f*
block *vt* claudĕre; (*to impede*) obstare (*with dat*); **to — up** obstruĕre
blockade *s* obsidio *f*; **to raise a —** obsidionem solvĕre
blockade *vt* obsidēre, claudĕre
blockhead *s* caudex *m*
blood *s* sanguis *m*; (*gore*) cruor *m*, sanies *f*; (*fig*) (*slaughter*) caedes *f*; (*lineage*) genus *n*; **bad —** simultas *f*; **to staunch —** sanguinem supprimĕre
bloodless *adj* exsanguis; (*without bloodshed*) incruentus
blood-red *adj* cruentus; sanguineus, sanguinolentus
bloodshed *s* caedes *f*
bloodshot *adj* cruore suffusus
bloodstained *adj* cruentus, cruentatus, sanguinolentus
bloodsucker *s* sanguisuga *f*; hirudo *f*
bloodthirsty *adj* sanguinarius; sanguinolentus
blood vessel *s* vena *f*
bloody *adj* cruentus
bloom *s* flos *m*
bloom *vi* florēre, florescĕre; vigēre
blooming *adj* florens; floridus; nitidus
blossom *s* flos *m*
blot *s* macula, litura *f*; (*fig*) labes *f*, dedecus *n*
blot *vt* maculare; conspurcare; **to — out** delēre; (*to erase*) oblitterare
blotch *s* macula *f*; pustula *f*
blotched *adj* maculosus
blow *s* (*stroke*) plaga *f*, ict·us -ūs *m*; (*with the fist*) colaphus *m*; (*fig*) plaga *f*; calamitas *f*
blow *vt* (*instrument*) canĕre; (*breath*) anhelare; **to — out** extinguĕre; **to — the nose** emungĕre; **to — up** inflare; *vi* flare; (*of a flower*) efflorescĕre; **to — over** (*of a storm*) cadĕre; (*fig*) abire
blowing *s* sufflatio *f*; flat·us -ūs *m*; (*of the nose*) emunctio *f*
blowup *s* scandalum *n*; (*scolding*) objurgatio *f*
blubber *s* adeps balaenarum *m*
blubber *vi* lacrimas effundĕre
blue *adj* caeruleus
blueness *s* caeruleum *n*
blues *s* melancholia *f*
bluff *s* rupes *f*; promunturium *n*
bluff *adj* rusticus; declivis; ventosus
bluff *vt* fallĕre, decipĕre; *vi* ampullari, gloriari
blunder *s* (*in writing*) mendum *n*; error *m*, erratum *n*
blunder *vi* offendĕre, errare
blunderer *s* homo ineptus *m*
blunt *adj* hebes; obtusus; (*fig*) inurbanus, rusticus; **—ly** plane, liberius
blunt *vt* hebetare, obtundĕre, retundĕre
bluntness *s* hebetudo *f*; (*fig*) candor *m*
blur *s* macula *f*
blur *vt* obscurare
blurt *vt* **to — out** inconsultum projicĕre
blush *s* rubor *m*
blush *vi* erubescĕre
bluster *vi* declamitare; fremĕre, strepĕre
bluster *s* jactatio, declamatio *f*; fremit·us -ūs, strepit·us -ūs *m*
boar *s* aper *m*; verres *m*
board *s* (*plank*) tabula *f*; (*table*) mensa *f*; (*food*) vict·us -ūs *m*; (*council, etc.*) collegium *n*; consilium *n*; concilium *n*; (*judicial*) quaestio *f*; (*for games*) abacus, alveus *m*
board *vt* **to — a ship** navem conscendĕre; **to — up** contabulare; *vi* **to — with** devertĕre ad (*with acc*)
boarder *s* convictor, hospes *m*

boardinghouse *s* contubernium *n*
boast *vi* se jactare, gloriari
boast *s* jactantia, jactatio, gloriatio, vanitas *f*
boastful *adj* gloriosus; **—ly** gloriose
boasting *s* gloriatio *f*
boat *s* linter *f*; cymba *f*; scapha *f*; navicula *f*
boatman *s* nauta, lintrarius *m*
bode *vt* portendĕre, praesagire
bodiless *adj* incorporalis
bodily *adj* corporeus; corporalis; in persona
bodily *adv* corporaliter
body *s* corpus *n*; (*corpse*) cadaver *n*; truncus *m*; (*person*) homo *m*; (*of troops*) man·us -ūs, caterva *f*; (*of cavalry*) turma *f*; (*of people*) numerus *m*, multitudo *f*; (*heavenly*) astrum *n*
bodyguard *s* stipatores, satellites *m pl*; cohors praetoria *f*
bog *s* palus *f*
boil *vt* fervefacĕre, coquĕre; **to — down** decoquĕre; *vi* fervēre, effervescĕre; (*fig*) aestuare
boil *s* furunculus *m*, ulcus *n*
boiler *s* (*vessel*) ahenum, caldarium *n*; (*kettle*) lebes *m*
boisterous *adj* procellosus; violentus, turbidus; **—ly** turbide, turbulente
bold *adj* audax; impavidus; (*rash*) temerarius; (*saucy*) insolens, protervus, impudens; (*language*) liber; (*stout*) intrepidus; **—ly** audacter; temere; fortiter; insolenter
boldness *s* audacia, fidentia *f*; (*in speech*) libertas, impudentia *f*
bolster *s* pulvinar *n*; (*of a bed*) cervical *n*
bolster *vt* supportare, adjuvare; **to — up** suffulcire
bolt *s* (*of a door*) pessulus *m*; (*of thunder*) fulmen *n*; (*pin*) clavus *m*; (*missile*) sagitta *f*, telum *n*
bolt *vt* obserare, oppessulare, claudĕre, occludĕre
bomb *s* pyrobolus *m*
bombard *vt* tormentis verberare; (*fig*) lacessĕre
bombardment *s* tormentis verberatio *f*
bombast *s* ampulla *f pl*
bombastic *adj* inflatus, tumidus; **to be —** ampullari
bond *s* vinculum *n*; nodus *m*; copula, catena *f*, jugum *n*; (*document*) syngrapha *f*
bondage *s* servitus *f*, servitium *n*; captivitas *f*
bondsman *s* servus *m*; verna *m*; addictus *m*
bone *s* os *n*; (*of fish*) spina *f*
boneless *adj* exos
bonfire *s* ignes festi *m pl*
bonnet *s* redimiculum *n*
bony *adj* osseus
book *s* liber *m*; volumen *n*; codex *m*;
bookcase *s* foruli *m pl*; librarium *n*; pegma *n*
bookish *adj* libris deditus
bookkeeper *s* calculator *m*; actuarius *m*
bookshelf *s* pluteus *m*
bookstore *s* bibliopolum *n*, libraria taberna *f*
bookworm *s* tinea *f*; (*fig*) librorum helluo *m*
boom *s* (*of a ship*) longurius *m*; (*of a harbor*) obex *m* & *f*, repagulum *n*
boom *vi* resonare
boon *s* bonum, donum *n*
boor *s* rusticus *m*
boorish *adj* agrestis, rusticus; **—ly** rustice
boost *vt* efferre
boot *s* calceus *m*; caliga *f*; (*peasant's*) pero *m*; (*tragic*) cothurnus *m*; **to —** insuper
boot *vi* prodesse; **what boots it?** cui bono?
booth *s* taberna *f*, tabernaculum *n*
booty *s* praeda *f*; spolia *n pl*
border *s* (*edge*) margo *m* & *f*; (*seam*) limbus *m*, fimbria *f*; (*boundary*) finis, terminus *m*
border *vt* tangĕre, attingĕre; circumjacēre; *vi* **to — on** adjacēre (*with dat*), attingĕre; imminēre (*with dat*)
bordering *adj* affinis, finitimus
bore *vt* terebrare, perforare; excavare; (*fig*) (*to weary*) obtundĕre, fatigare
bore *s* (*tool*) terebra *f*; (*hole*) foramen *n*; (*fig*) importunus, molestus *m*
borer *s* terebra *f*
born *adj* natus; genitus; **to be —** nasci; (*fig*) oriri
borough *s* municipium *n*
borrow *vt* mutuari; (*fig*) imitari
borrowed *adj* mutuatus, mutuus; alienus
borrowing *s* mutuatio *f*
bosom *s* (*breast*) pectus *n*; sin·us -ūs *m*; (*of female*) mammillae *f pl*; (*fig*) gremium *n*
Bosphorus *s* Bosporus *m*
boss *s* bulla *f*; (*of a shield*) umbo *m*; (*of a book*) umbilicus *m*
boss *vt* (*to order about*) dominari in (*with acc*)
botanical *adj* botanicus
botanist *s* herbarius *m*
botany *s* herbaria *f*
botch *s* bubo, carbunculus *m*; (*bungling work*) scruta *n pl*
botch *vt* male sarcire; male gerĕre
both *adj* ambo; uterque
both *pron* ambo; uterque
both *conj* **— . . . and** et . . . et; cum . . . tum; vel . . . vel
bother *vt* vexare, sollicitare; molestus esse (*with dat*); *vi* **to — about** operam dare (*with dat*)
bother *s* negotium *n*; vexatio *f*; sollicitudo *f*
bottle *s* ampulla *f*; lagoena *f*
bottle *vt* in ampullas infundĕre
bottom *s* fundus *m*; (*of a ship*) carina *f*; (*dregs*) faex *f*, sedimentum *n*; (*of a mountain*) radix *f*; **the — of** imus; **the — of the sea** imum mare *n*
bottom *adj* imus, infimus

bottomless *adj* fundo carens, immensus; profundus
bough *s* ramus *m*
boulder *s* saxum *n*
bounce *vi* resilire, resultare
bound *adj* alligatus, obligatus, obstrictus; **it is — to happen** necesse est accidat; **to be — for** tendĕre ad (*with acc*)
bound *s* salt·us -us *m*; (*limit*) modus, terminus *m*; **to set —s** modum facĕre
bound *vt* finire, definire, terminare; *vi* (*to leap*) salire
boundary *s* finis, terminus *m*; (*fortified*) limes *m*
boundless *adj* infinitus, immensus; profundus
bountiful *adj* largus, benignus; **—ly** benigne, large
bounty *s* largitas, benignitas, liberalitas *f*; copia *f*
bouquet *s* corollarium *n*; (*of wine*) flos m
bow *s* arc·us -ūs *m*
bow *s* (*of a ship*) prora *f*; (*greeting*) summissio capitis *f*
bow *vt* flectĕre, inclinare; (*one's head*) demittĕre; *vi* flecti; (*fig*) **to — to** (*to accede to*) obtemperare (*with dat*), obsequi
bowels *s* intestina, viscera *n pl*
bower *s* trichlia *f*, umbraculum *n*
bowl *s* cratera, patera *f*; (*for cooking*) catina *f*
bowlegged *adj* valgus
bowman *s* sagittarius *m*
bowstring *s* nervus *m*
box *s* arca, cista *f*; scrinium *n*; (*for medicine*) pyxis *f*; (*tree*) buxus *f*
box *vt* includĕre; pugnis certare cum (*with abl*); **to — the ears of** alapam adhibēre (*with dat*)
boxer *s* pugil *m*
boxing glove *s* caest·us -ūs *m*
boxing match *s* pugilatio *f*
boy *s* puer, puerulus *m*
boyhood *s* pueritia *f*; aetas puerilis *f*
boyish *adj* puerilis; **—ly** pueriliter
brace *s* (*strap*) fascia *f*; (*couple*) par *n*; copula *f*; (*in architecture*) fibula *f*
brace *vt* ligare, alligare; (*to strengthen*) firmare
bracelet *s* armilla *f*
bracket *s* mutulus *m*; **—s** (*in writing*) unci *m pl*
brag *vi* se jactare, gloriari
braggart *s* jactator, salaco *m*
bragging *s* jactantia *f*
braid *s* limbus *m*; (*of hair*) cincinnus *m*
braid *vt* plectĕre, plicare
brain *s* cerebrum *n*; ingenium *n*
brainless *adj* stolidus, inconsultus, socors
brake *s* (*fern*) filix *f*; (*thicket*) dumetum *n*; (*on wheel*) sufflamen *n*
bramble *s* rubus *m*; (*thicket*) rubetum *n*; (*thorny bush*) sentis, vepris *m*
branch *s* (*of tree*) ramus *m*; (*of pedigree*) stemma *n*; (*division*) pars *f*
branch *vi* (*of trees*) germinare; **to — out** ramos porrigĕre; (*fig*) dividi, scindi, diffundi
brand *s* (*mark*) stigma *n*, nota *f*; (*of fire*) fax *f*, torris *m*; (*type*) genus *n*
brand *vt* inurĕre, notare
branding iron *s* cauter *m*
brandish *vt* vibrare
brandy *s* aqua vitae *f*; vini spirit·us -ūs *m*; spirit·us -ūs gallicus *m*
brass *s* orichalcum, aes *n*
brat *s* infans *m & f*
brave *adj* fortis, animosus, strenuus; **—ly** fortiter, strenue
brave *vt* sustinēre
bravery *s* fortitudo *f*; virtus *f*
bravo *interj* eu!, euge!, bene!, macte!
brawl *s* rixa *f*, jurgium *n*
brawl *vi* rixari, jurgare
brawler *s* rixator, rabula *m*
brawling *adj* contentiosus, jurgans
brawn *s* callum aprugnum *n*; (*muscle*) lacertus, torus *m*
brawny *adj* lacertosus, robustus
bray *vi* (*of asses*) rudĕre; (*of elephants*) barrire; (*to cry out*) emugire
braying *s* tritura *f*; barrit·us -ūs *m*; rugit·us -ūs *m*
brazen *adj* aënus; (*fig*) impudens
brazier *s* foculus *m*
breach *s* ruptura, ruina *f*; (*of treaty*) violatio *f*; dissidium *n*
bread *s* panis *m*; (*fig*) vict·us -ūs *m*
breadth *s* latitudo *f*
break *vt* frangĕre; rumpĕre; **to — apart** diffringĕre; **to — down** demoliri, destruĕre; **to — in** (*to tame*) domare, subigĕre; **to — in pieces** dirumpĕre; **to — off** abrumpĕre; (*friendship or action*) dirumpĕre; (*a meeting*) interrumpĕre; **to — open** effringĕre; **to — up** interrumpĕre, dissolvĕre; *vi* frangi; rumpi; (*of day*) illucescĕre; (*of strength*) deficĕre; **to — forth** erumpĕre; **to — into** irrumpĕre; invadĕre; **to — off** desinĕre; **to — out** erumpĕre; (*of trouble*) exardescĕre; (*of war*) exoriri; (*of fire*) grassari; **to — through** perrumpĕre; **to — up** dissolvi, dilabi; (*of a meeting*) dimitti; **to — with** dissidēre ab (*with abl*)
break *s* interruptio *f*, intervallum *n*; interstitium *n*
breakage *s* fractura *f*
breakdown *s* calamitas *f*; frustratio *f*; (*of health*) debilitas *f*; (*of a machine*) defect·us -ūs *m*
breaker *s* fluct·us -ūs *m*
breakfast *s* prandium *n*
breakfast *vi* prandēre
breakup *s* dissolutio *f*
breast *s* pectus *n*; (*of a woman*) mamma *f*; (*fig*) praecordia *n pl*; **to make a clean — of** confitēri
breastbone *s* sternum *n*; os pectorale *n*
breastplate *s* lorica *f*; thorax *m*
breath *s* spirit·us -ūs *m*, anima *f*; halit·us -ūs *m*; **— of air** aura *f*; **deep —** anhelit·us -ūs *m*; **to catch one's —** obstipescĕre; **to hold**

one's breath animam continēre; **to take one's — away** exanimare; **to waste one's —** operam perdĕre
breathe *vt* ducĕre; spirare; (*to whisper*) susurrare; **to — out** exspirare; *vi* spirare, respirare; **to — upon** inspirare (*with dat*)
breathing *s* respiratio *f*; halit·us -ūs *m*; (*gram*) spirit·us -ūs *m*
breathless *adj* exanimis, exanimus; exanimatus
breeches *s* bracae *f pl*
breed *s* genus *n*
breed *vt* parĕre, gignĕre; (*to cause*) producĕre; (*to engender*) procreare, educare; (*to raise*) alĕre; (*horses*) pascĕre
breeder *s* (*man*) generator *m*; (*stallion*) admissarius *m*; (*animal*) matrix; (*fig*) nutrix *f*
breeding *s* fetura *f*; educatio *f*; **good —** urbanitas, humanitas *f*
breeze *s* aura *f*
breezy *adj* ventosus
brethren *s* fratres *m pl*
brevity *s* brevitas, breviloquentia *f*
brew *vt* coquĕre; *vi* excitari, concitari
bribe *s* pretium *n*, merces *f*
bribe *vt* corrumpĕre, largiri
briber *s* corruptor, largitor *m*
bribery *s* corruptio, corruptela, largitio *f*; ambit·us -ūs *m*
brick *s* later *m*
brick *adj* latericius
bricklayer *s* laterum structor *m*
bridal *adj* nuptialis
bride *s* nupta *f*
bridegroom *s* maritus *m*
bridesmaid *s* pronuba *f*
bridge *s* pons *m*
bridge *vt* pontem imponĕre (*with dat*)
bridle *s* frenum *n*
brief *adj* brevis, concisus; **—ly** breviter, paucis verbis
brief *s* diploma *n*; sententiola *f*; summarium *n*
brigade *s* (*infantry*) legio *f*; (*cavalry*) turma *f*
brigadier *s* tribunus militum *m*
brigand *s* latro, latrunculus *m*
bright *adj* clarus; lucidus, splendidus; nitidus, candidus; (*flashing*) fulgidus; (*smart*) argutus; **—ly** lucide, clare, splendide
brighten *vt* illustrare, illuminare; *vi* lucescĕre; splendescĕre; clarescĕre; (*of a person*) in hilaritatem solvi
brightness *s* nitor, splendor, fulgor, candor *m*; (*of the sky*) serenitas *f*
brilliance *s* splendor *m*; fulgor *m*; (*of style*) nitor *m*, lumen *n*
brilliant *adj* splendidus; nitens; (*fig*) praeclarus, insignis, luculentus; **—ly** splendide, praeclare, luculenter
brim *s* ora, margo *f*, labrum *n*; **to fill to the —** explēre
brimful *adj* ad summum plenus
brimstone *s* sulfur *n*
brine *s* muria *f*, salsamentum *n*; (*sea*) salum *n*
bring *vt* ferre, afferre, inferre; (*by carriage, etc.*) advehĕre; **to — about** efficĕre, perducĕre; **to — back** referre, reducĕre; reportare; (*fig*) revocare; (*by force*) redigĕre; dejicĕre; **to — forth** prodĕre, depromĕre; parĕre; (*to yield*) ferre, efferre; **to — forward** proferre, efferre, agĕre; **to — in** inferre; invehĕre; inducĕre; (*as a farm, etc.*) reddĕre; **to — off** dissuadēre; **to — on** afferre; adducĕre; (*fig*) objicĕre; **to — out** efferre; producĕre; excire; **to — over** perducĕre, traducĕre; (*fig*) perducĕre, trahĕre; conciliare; **to — to** adducĕre; appellĕre; (*fig*) persuadēre; **to — together** conferre; (*to assemble*) contrahĕre; (*fig*) conciliare; **to — to pass** efficĕre; **to — under** subigĕre; **to — up** subducĕre; (*children*) educare; (*to vomit*) evomĕre
brink *s* margo *f*; ora *f*; (*fig*) extremitas *f*
brisk *adj* alacer, agilis, vividus; laetus; **to be —** vigēre; **—ly** alacriter, agiliter
briskness *s* alacritas *f*, vigor *m*
bristle *s* seta *f*
bristle *vi* horrēre
bristly *adj* setiger, setosus; hirsutus; horridus
Britain *s* Britannia *f*
British *adj* Britannicus
brittle *adj* fragilis
broach *vt* in medium proferre
broad *adj* latus, largus, amplus; (*fig*) manifestus, apertus; **—ly** late
broadcast *vt* divulgare, disseminare
broaden *vt* dilatare
broadsword *s* gladius *m*
brocade *s* Attalica *n pl*
broccoli *s* brassica oleracea Botrytis *f*
brochure *s* libellus *m*
broil *s* rixa, turba *f*
broil *vt* torrēre
broken *adj* fractus; intermissus; dirutus; (*fig*) confectus; (*of speech*) refractus, infractus, corrupte pronuntiatus
brokenhearted *adj* abjectus, dejectus
broker *s* transactor, institor *m*
bronze *s* aes *n*
bronze *adj* aeneus, a(h)enus, aeratus
brooch *s* fibula *f*
brood *s* proles *f*; (*chicks*) pullities *f*
brood *vi* (*as a hen*) incubare; (*fig*) **to — over** agitare, meditari
brook *vt* ferre, tolerare
broom *s* genista *f*; scopae *f pl*
broth *s* jus *n*
brothel *s* lupanar *n*, ganea *f*
brother *s* frater *m*
brotherhood *s* germanitas, fraternitas *f*; (*fig*) sodalitium *n*
brother-in-law *s* levir *m*; sororis maritus *m*
brotherly *adj* fraternus
brow *s* supercilium *n*; frons *f*; (*of a hill*) dorsum *n*
browbeat *vt* terrēre, deprimĕre, exagitare, objurgare

brown *adj* fulvus, fuscus, spadix; (*of skin*) adustus
browse *vi* depasci
bruise *vt* contunděre, sugillare; infringěre
bruise *s* contusio *f*, contusum *n*, sugillatio *f*
brunette *s* puella subfusca *f*
brunt *s* impet·us -ūs *m*; vehementia *f*
brush *s* scopula *f*; (*painter's*) penicillus *m*; (*bushy tail*) muscarium *n*; (*skirmish*) aggressio *f*
brush *vt* verrěre, purgare; **to — aside** neglegěre, sperněre; **to — away** amovēre
brutal *adj* atrox, immanis, inhumanus; **—ly** atrociter, immaniter, inhumane
brutality *s* atrocitas, ferocitas, saevitia, immanitas *f*
brute *adj* brutus; stupidus
brute *s* belua, bestia *f*
brutish *adj* ferinus; stupidus
bubble *s* bulla *f*
bubble *vi* bullire; (*to gush up*) scatēre
bubbling *s* bullit·us -ūs *m*; scatebra *f*
buccaneer *s* pirata *m*
buck *s* cervus *m*; (*he-goat*) hircus *m*; (*male rabbit*) cuniculus *m*
bucket *s* hama, situla, fidelia *f*
buckle *vt* fibulā nectěre; *vi* flectěre
buckle *s* fibula *f*, spinther *m*
buckler *s* parma *f*
bucolic *adj* bucolicus, agrestis
bud *s* gemma *f*, germen *n*; (*of a flower*) flosculus *m*
bud *vi* gemmare, germinare
budding *s* germinatio *f*; emplastratio *f*
budge *vt* ciēre, movēre; *vi* movēri, ceděre
budget *s* sáccus *m*; publicae pecuniae ratio *f*
buffalo *s* urus *m*
buffet *s* (*sideboard*) abacus *m*; (*slap*) alapa *f*; (*fig*) plaga *f*
buffet *vt* jactare
buffoon *s* scurra *m*; sannio, balatro *m*; **to play the —** scurrari
bug *s* cimex *m & f*
bugle *s* buccina *f*
build *vt* aedificare; struěre, conděre; (*road*) munire; (*hopes*) poněre; **to — up** exstruěre
builder *s* aedificator, structor *m*
building *s* (*act*) aedificatio *f*; exstructio *f*; (*structure*) aedificium *n*
bulb *s* bulbus *m*
bulge *vi* tumēre, tumescěre; prominēre
bulk *s* amplitudo, magnitudo *f*; (*mass*) moles *f*; (*greater part*) major pars *f*
bulkiness *s* magnitudo *f*
bulky *adj* crassus; ingens; corpulentus; onerosus
bull *s* taurus *m*
bulldog *s* canis Molossus *m*
bullet *s* glans *f*
bulletin *s* libellus *m*
bullfrog *s* rana ocellata *f*
bullion *s* aurum infectum *n*; argentum infectum *n*; massa *f*
bully *s* salaco, thraso *m*
bully *vt* procaciter lacessěre
bulwark *s* agger *m*; propugnaculum *n*; moenia *n pl*
bump *s* (*swelling*) tuber *n*; (*thump*) plaga *f*
bump *vt* pulsare, pellěre; *vi* **to — against** offenděre
bun *s* libum *n*, placenta *f*
bunch *s* fasciculus *m*; (*of grapes*) racemus *m*
bundle *s* fascis, fasciculus *m*; vesiculus *m*
bundle *vt* consarcinare
bungle *vt* inscite gerěre; inscite agěre; *vi* errare
bungler *s* homo rudis *m*
buoy *s* cortex *m*
buoy *vt* **to — up** attollěre, sublevare
buoyancy *s* levitas *f*; (*fig*) hilaritas *f*
buoyant *adj* levis; (*fig*) hilaris
burden *s* onus *n*; (*fig*) scrupulus *m*
burden *vt* onerare; opprimere
burdensome *adj* onerosus, gravis, molestus
bureau *s* armarium, scrinium *n*
burglar *s* fur *m*
burglary *s* (domūs) effractura *f*
burial *s* (*act*) sepultura *f*; (*ceremony*) funus *n*
burial place *s* sepulturae locus *m*; sepulcrum *n*
burlesque *s* ridicula imitatio *f*
burly *adj* corpulentus
burn *vt* urěre, cremare; (*to set on fire*) incenděre; **to — down** deurěre; **to — out** exurěre; **to — up** amburěre, comburěre; *vi* flagrare; ardēre; **to — out** extingui; **to — up** conflagrare
burn *s* adustio *f*; combustum *n*
burning *s* ustio, adustio *f*; deflagratio *f*
burning *adj* ardens; fervens
burrow *s* cuniculus *m*
burrow *vi* defoděre
bursar *s* dispensator *m*
burst *s* impet·us -ūs *m*; eruptio *f*; (*noise*) fragor *m*
burst *vt* rumpěre, dirumpěre; **to — open** effrangěre; *vi* dirumpi; **to — forth** prorumpěre; (*of tears*) prosilire; **to — in** irrumpěre; **to — out** erumpěre; **to — out laughing** cachinnum tollěre
bury *vt* sepelire; (*to hide*) abděre, conděre
bush *s* dumetum *n*, frutex *m*; (*of hair*) caesaries *f*
bushel *s* medimnus, modius *m*
bushy *adj* (*full of bushes*) dumosus; (*bush-like*) fruticosus
busily *adv* industrie, sedulo, impigre
business *s* negotium *n*; (*trade, calling*) ars *f*; (*employment*) occupatio *f*; (*matter*) res *f*; **to mind one's own —** negotium suum agěre
businessman *s* negotiator *m*
buskin *s* cothurnus *m*
bust *s* imago *f*; effigies *f*
bustle *s* festinatio *f*; trepidatio *f*

bustle *vi* festinare; trepidare; **to — about** discurrĕre
busy *adj* occupatus; negotiosus; operosus, impiger; (*meddling*) molestus
busybody *s* ardelio *m*
but *prep* praeter (*with acc*)
but *adv* modo, tantum
but *conj* sed; ast, at; atqui; ceterum; vero, verum; autem; **— if** quodsi; sin, sin autem; **— if not** sin aliter, sin minus
butcher *s* lanius *m*; (*fig*) carnifex *m*
butcher *vt* (*animals*) caedĕre; (*people*) trucidare
butcher shop *s* macellum *n*
butchery *s* caedes, trucidatio *f*
butler *s* promus *m*
butt *s* (*mark*) meta *f*; (*cask*) dolium *n*; (*mound*) agger *m*; **— of ridicule** ludibrium *n*
butt *vt* arietare; *vi* **to — in** interpellare
butter *s* butyrum *n*
butter *vt* butyro inducĕre
buttercup *s* ranunculus tuberosus *m*
butterfly *s* papilio *m*
buttermilk *s* lactis serum *n*
buttock *s* clunis *m & f*
button *s* bulla *f*
button *vt* nectĕre, confibulare
buttress *s* anterides *f pl*; fulcrum *n*
buttress *vt* suffulcire
buxom *adj* alacer, hilaris, laetus
buy *vt* emĕre, mercari; **to — back** *or* **off** redimĕre; **to — up** coemĕre
buyer *s* emptor *m*
buying *s* emptio *f*
buzz *s* bombus *m*; murmur *n*
buzz *vi* bombilare; (*in the ear*) insusurrare
buzzard *s* buteo *m*
by *prep* (*agency*) a, ab (*with abl*); (*of place*) ad (*with acc*), apud (*with acc*), juxta (*with acc*), prope (*with acc*); (*along*) secundum (*with acc*); (*past*) praeter (*with acc*); (*of time*) ante (*with acc*); (*in oaths*) per (*with acc*); **— and —** mox; **— means of** per (*with acc*); **— oneself** solus
bygone *adj* praeteritus; priscus
bylaw *s* praescriptum *n*; regula *f*
bystander *s* arbiter *m*
byway *s* trames *m*, semita *f*, deverticulum *n*
byword *s* adagium *n*

C

cabal *s* factio *f*; societas clandestina *f*
cabbage *s* brassica *f*, caulis *m*
cabin *s* (*cottage*) tugurium *n*; (*on a ship*) stega *f*
cabinet *s* armarium *n*; scrinium *n*; cistula *f*; (*in government*) principis consilium *n*
cable *s* funis, rudens *m*; (*anchor*) ancorale *n*
cackle *vi* gracillare; (*fig*) deblaterare
cackle *s* glocitatio *f*; (*fig*) gerrae *f pl*; clangor *m*
cacophony *s* dissonae voces *f pl*
cactus *s* cactus *f*
cadaver *s* cadaver *n*
cadence *s* numerus *m*
cadet *s* tiro *m*; discipulus militaris *m*
cage *s* cavea *f*, aviarium *n*; septum *n*
cage *vt* includĕre
cajole *vt* inescare, lactare, blandiri
cake *s* libum *n*, placenta *f*
calamitous *adj* calamitosus; funestus; exitiosus
calamity *s* calamitas *f*; clades *f*; malum *n*; res adversae *f pl*
calculate *vt* computare; (*fig*) aestimare, existimare
calculated *adj* aptus, accommodatus
calculation *s* computatio, ratio *f*; (*fig*) ratiocinatio *f*
calculator *s* computator *m*; ratiocinator *m*
caldron *s* ahenum *n*, lebes *m*
calendar *s* fasti *m pl*; calendarium *n*
calends *s* Kalendae *f pl*
calf *s* vitulus *m*; (*of the leg*) sura *f*
caliber *s* (*fig*) ingenium *n*, indoles *f*
call *vt* vocare; (*to name*) appellare; **to — aside** sevocare; **to — away** avocare; (*fig*) devocare; **to — back** revocare; **to — down** devocare; **to — forth** evocare, provocare; (*fig*) exciĕre, elicĕre; **to — in** advocare; (*money*) cogĕre; **to — off** avocare, revocare; **to — together** convocare; **to — to mind** recordari; **to — to witness** testari; **to — up** excitare, suscitare, elicĕre; *vi* **to — on** *or* **upon** (*for help*) implorare; (*to visit*) visĕre
call *s* vocatio *f*; clamor *m*; (*visit*) salutatio *f*; (*requisition*) postulatio *f*; (*whistle*) fistula *f*
calling *s* (*profession*) ars *f*, artificium *n*
callous *adj* callosus; (*fig*) durus; expers sensūs; **to become —** occallescĕre; obdurescĕre
calm *adj* tranquillus, placidus, sedatus, quietus; (*mentally*) aequus; **—ly** tranquille, aequo animo, placide
calm *s* tranquillitas *f*, tranquillum *n*
calm *vt* pacare, placare, sedare, mulcēre; *vi* **to — down** defervescĕre
calmness *s* tranquillitas *f*; serenitas *f*
calumny *s* maledictum *n*, obtrectatio *f*, opprobria *n pl*
camel *s* camelus *m*
cameo *s* imago ectypa *f*
camouflage *s* dissimulatio *f*
camouflage *vt* dissimulare

camp *s* castra *n pl*; **summer —** aestiva *n pl*; **to strike —** castra movēre; **winter —** hiberna *n pl*
camp *adj* castrensis
camp *vi* castra poněre
campaign *s* aestiva *n pl*; stipendium *n*; expeditio *f*
campaign *vi* stipendium merēre; expeditioni interesse
campaigner *s* veteranus *m*
camphor *s* camphora *f*
can *s* hirnea *f*
can *vi* posse; scire; **I — not** nequeo; nescio
canal *s* fossa navigabilis *f*
canary *s* fringilla Canaria *f*
cancel *vt* delēre, expungěre; abrogare, tollěre
cancellation *s* deletio, abolitio *f*
cancer *s* cancer *m*
cancerous *adj* cancerosus, canceraticus
candid *adj* candidus, apertus, liber, simplex; **—ly** candide
candidacy *s* petitio *f*
candidate *s* petitor *m*; candidatus *m*
candied *adj* saccharo conditus
candle *s* candela *f*; (*taper*) cera *f*
candlelight *s* lucerna *f*; **to study by —** lucubrare
candlestick *s* candelabrum *n*
candor *s* candor *m*, simplicitas, ingenuitas *f*
candy *s* saccharum crystallinum *n*
cane *s* baculus *m*; virga *f*; (*reed*) harundo *f*
cane *vt* baculo *or* virgā ferire; verberare
canine *adj* caninus
canister *s* canistrum *n*, pyxis *f*
canker *s* (*of plants*) rubigo, robigo *f*; (*fig*) aerugo *f*
cannibal *s* anthropophagus *m*
cannon *s* tormentum *n*
cannon shot *s* tormenti ict·us -ūs *m*
canoe *s* linter *m*
canon *s* regula, norma *f*; canon *m*
canonical *adj* canonicus
canopy *s* canopeum *n*; aulaea *n pl*
cant *s* fucus *m*
cantata *s* carmen *n*
canteen *s* caupona castrensis *f*
canter *s* lenis atque quadrupedans grad·us -ūs *m*
canter *vi* leniter quadrupedare
canticle *s* canticum *n*
canto *s* liber *m*
canton *s* pagus *m*
canvas *s* linteum crassum *n*, carbasus *f*, carbasa *n pl*
canvass *s* (*legal*) ambitio *f*; (*illegal*) ambit·us -ūs *m*
canvass *vt* circumire, prensare; *vi* ambire
cap *s* pileus *m*; calyptra *f*; (*in rituals*) galerus *m*
capability *s* facultas, habilitas *f*
capable *adj* capax; idoneus, potens, doctus
capably *adv* bene, docte
capacity *s* capacitas, mensura *f*; modus *m*; ingenium *n*
cape *s* promontorium *n*; (*garment*) humerale *n*, chlamys *f*
caper *vi* saltare, tripudire, assilire; (*of animals*) lascivire
caper *s* salt·us -ūs *m*, exsultatio *f*
capital *adj* praecipuus, princeps; (*law*) capitalis; (*of letters*) uncialis; (*outstanding*) insignis, eximius
capital *s* (*architecture*) capitulum *n*; (*chief city*) caput *n*; (*com*) sors *f*, caput *n*; faenus *n*
capitalist *s* faenerator *m*
capitol *s* capitolium *n*
capitulate *vi* ex pacto urbem traděre; se deděre
capitulation *s* deditio *f*
capon *s* capus, capo *m*
caprice *s* libido, inconstantia *f*
capricious *adj* levis, inconstans; ventosus, mobilis; **—ly** leviter, inconstanter, ex libidine
capricorn *s* capricornus *m*
capsize *vt* evertěre; *vi* everti
capsule *s* capsula *f*
captain *s* (*in infantry*) centurio *m*; (*in cavalry*) praefectus *m*; (*in navy*) navarchus *m*, (*in merchant marine*) magister *m*
caption *s* caput *n*
captious *adj* argutus; morosus; fallax; **—ly** captiose, morose
captivate *vt* captare, delenire, mulcēre
captive *adj* captivus
captive *s* captivus *m*
captivity *s* captivitas *f*
captor *s* captor *m*; expugnator *m*; victor *m*
capture *s* captura, comprehensio *f*
capture *vt* capěre, excipěre
car *s* carrus *m*
carat *s* unciae triens *m*
caravan *s* commeat·us -ūs, comitat·us -ūs *m*
carbon *s* carbonium *n*
carbuncle *s* carbunculus, furunculus *m*
carcass *s* cadaver *n*
card *s* charta *f*; (*ticket*) tessera *f*; (*for combing wool*) pecten *n*
card *vt* pectěre
cardboard *s* charta crassior *f*
cardinal *adj* principalis, praecipuus
cardinal *s* (*eccl*) cardinalis *m*
care *s* cura, sollicitudo *f*; (*diligence*) diligentia *f*; (*charge*) tutela, curatio, custodia *f*; **to take — of** curare
care *vi* curare; **to — for** (*to look after*) curare; (*to be fond of*) amare
career *s* curriculum *n*; decurs·us -ūs *m*; (*pol*) curs·us -ūs honorum *m*
carefree *adj* securus
careful *adj* (*attentive*) attentus, diligens; (*cautious*) cautus; (*of work*) accuratus; **—ly** diligenter; caute; accurate, exquisite
careless *adj* neglegens, incautus; (*loose*) dissolutus; **—ly** neglegenter; incuriose; (*loosely*) solute
carelessness *s* incuria, neglegentia *f*
caress *s* blanditiae *f pl*; complex·us -ūs *m*
caress *vt* blandiri, fovēre

cargo *s* onus *n*
caricature *s* imago in pejus detorta *f*
caricature *vt* in pejus fingĕre
carnage *s* caedes, strages *f*
carnal *adj* sensualis, carnalis
carnival *s* feriae *f pl*
carnivorous *adj* carnivorus
carol *s* cant·us -ūs *m*; carmen *n*; **Christmas —** hymnus de Christi natu *m*
carol *vi* cantare, cantillare
carouse *vi* comissari, perpotare, perbacchari
carp *s* cyprinus *m*
carp *vi* **to — at** carpĕre, mordēre, vellicare
carpenter *s* faber tignarius *m*
carpentry *s* ars fabrilis *f*
carpet *s* tapes *m*, tapeta *f*
carriage *s* (*act*) vectura *f*; (*vehicle*) vehiculum *n*; raeda *f*, petorritum *n*; (*bearing, posture*) habit·us -ūs, gest·us -ūs, incess·us -ūs *m*
carrier *s* portitor, vector, bajulus *m*; (*of letters*) tabularius *m*
carrion *s* caro morticina *f*
carrot *s* carota *f*; pastinaca *f*
carry *vt* portare, ferre; (*by vehicle*) vehĕre; gerĕre; (*law*) perferre; **to — away** auferre; evehĕre; (*fig*) rapĕre; **to — back** referre; revehĕre; **to — in** importare; invehĕre; **to — off** auferre; rapĕre; **to — on** promovēre; perducĕre; (*fig*) exercēre; gerĕre; **to — out** efferre, exportare; evehĕre; (*fig*) exsequi; **to — over** transferre; **to — round** circumferre; **to — through** perferre; *vi* (*of sound*) audiri; **to — on** pergĕre; se gerĕre
cart *s* plaustrum *n*; curr·us -ūs *m*; curriculus *m*; **to put the — before the horse** praeposteris consiliis uti
cart *vt* plaustro vehĕre; **to — away** auferre
carve *vt* sculpĕre; caelare, incidĕre; (*at table*) secare
carver *s* caelator *m*; (*at table*) carptor *m*; (*knife*) cultellus *m*
carving *s* caelatura *f*
cascade *s* praeceps aquae laps·us -ūs *m*
case *s* (*law*) causa, actio *f*; (*matter*) res *f*; (*instance*) exemplum *n*; (*container*) involucrum *n*; theca *f*; capsula *f*; (*state*) stat·us -ūs *m*; conditio *f*; (*gram*) cas·us -ūs *m*; **in —** si; **in that —** ergo; **since that is the —** quae cum ita sint
cash *s* pecunia numerata *f*; nummi *m pl*; praesens pecunia *f*
cashier *s* dispensator *m*
cash payment *s* repraesentatio *f*
cask *s* cadus *m*, dolium *n*
casket *s* arcula *f*; pyxis *f*
cast *s* (*throw*) jact·us -ūs *m*; (*mold*) typus *m*; forma *f*
cast *vt* jacĕre; (*metal*) fundĕre; **to — about** circumjacĕre; **to — away** abjicĕre; dejicĕre; **to — down** dejicĕre; (*fig*) affligĕre; **to — in** injicĕre; **to — in one's teeth** reprobrare; **to — off** (*the skin*) exuĕre; (*fig*) amovēre, ponĕre; repudiare; **to — out** ejicĕre, expellĕre; **to — over** trajicĕre; **to — upon** superinjicĕre; (*fig*) aspergĕre; conferre; *vi* **to — off** ancoram tollĕre
castaway *s* perditus *m*; ejectus *m*
caste *s* ordo *m*; **to lose —** degenerare
castigate *vt* castigare
castigation *s* castigatio *f*
castle *s* castellum *n*; arx *f*
castor oil *s* cicinum oleum *n*
castrate *vt* castrare
castration *s* castratio, castratura *f*
casual *adj* fortuitus; (*person*) neglegens; **—ly** fortuito, forte, casu
casualty *s* cas·us -ūs *m*; occisus *m*
cat *s* feles *f*
cataclysm *s* cataclysmos *m*
catacombs *s* puticuli *m pl*; catacumbae *f pl*
catalogue *s* catalogus *m*; index *m*
cataract *s* cataracta *f*, cataractes *m*; (*of the eye*) glaucoma *n*
catastrophe *s* calamitas *f*; ruina *f*; exit·us -ūs *n*
catch *vt* capĕre, captare; (*by surprise*) comprehendĕre; (*falling object*) suscipĕre; (*in a net*) illaquēre; (*with bait*) inescare; (*fire*) concipĕre; (*disease*) contrahĕre; *vi* **to — at** arripĕre; (*fig*) captare; **to — up with** consĕqui
catching *adj* contagiosus; (*fig*) gratus
categorical *adj* categoricus; **—ly** categorice, sine exceptione
category *s* categoria *f*; numerus *m*
cater *vi* obsonari; cibos suppeditare
caterer *s* obsonator *m*
caterpillar *s* eruca *f*
cathedral *s* ecclesia cathedralis *f*
catholic *adj* catholicus, generalis
cattle *s* pecus *n*
cauliflower *s* brassica oleracea botryitis *f*
cause *s* causa, res, materia *f*; (*pol*) partes *f pl*
cause *vt* facĕre, efficĕre; (*feelings*) exciēre, movēre
causeless *adj* sine causa; vanus
causeway *s* agger *m*
caustic *adj* causticus; (*fig*) mordax, acerbus
caution *s* cautio *f*; cura *f*; prudentia *f*; monitio *f*, monitum *n*
caution *vt* (ad)monēre
cautious *adj* cautus, consideratus; circumspectus; providus; **—ly** caute, prudenter; depetentim
cavalcade *s* pompa *f*
cavalier *s* eques *m*
cavalry *s* equitat·us -ūs *m*; equites *m pl*; copiae equestres *f pl*
cave *s* spec·us -ūs *m*; spelunca *f*; caverna *f*; antrum *n*
cavern *s* caverna *f*
cavernous *adj* cavernosus
caviar *s* ova acipenseris *n pl*
cavity *s* cavum *n*; caverna *f*
caw *vi* crocire, crocitare

cease *vi* desiněre, desistěre
ceaseless *adj* assiduus, perpetuus; **—ly** continenter, assidue, perpetuo
ceasing *s* cessatio, intermissio *f*
cedar *s* cedrus *f*
cedar *adj* cedreus, cedrinus
cede *vt* ceděre, conceděre
ceiling *s* laquear, lacunar *n*
celebrate *vt* celebrare; laudare, dicěre
celebrated *adj* celeber; nobilis, notus, praeclarus
celebration *s* celebratio *f*; (*of rites*) sollemne *n*
celebrity *s* celebritas *f*; fama *f*; (*person*) vir illustris *m*
celery *s* heleoselinum *n*
celestial *adj* caelestis, divinus
celibacy *s* caelibat·us -ūs *m*, caelebs vita *f*
celibate *s* caelebs *m*
cell *s* cella *f*
cellar *s* cella *f*, cellarium *n*
cement *s* ferrumen *n*; caementum *n*; (*glue*) gluten *n*
cement *vt* conglutinare; ferruminare; *vi* coalescěre
cemetery *s* sepulcretum *n*
censer *s* turibulum *n*
censor *s* censor *m*
censorship *s* censura *f*; magisterium morum *n*
censurable *adj* reprehensione dignus; culpandus
censure *s* vituperatio *f*
censure *vt* animadvertěre, vituperare
census *s* cens·us -ūs *m*; civium enumeratio *f*
centaur *s* centaurus *m*
centenary *adj* centenarius
centenary *s* centesimus annus *m*
center *s* medium *n*; **in the — of the plain** in medio campo
center *vt* in centrum poněre; *vi* **to — on** niti (*with abl*)
central *adj* medius, centralis
centralize *vt* (*authority*) ad unum deferre
centurion *s* centurio *m*
century *s* (*pol*) centuria *f*; saeculum *f*
cereal *s* frumentum *n*
ceremonial *adj* caerimonialis, sollemnis; **—ly** sollemniter, rite
ceremonial *s* rit·us -ūs *m*
ceremonious *adj* sollemnis; (*person*) officiosus; **—ly** sollemniter; officiose
ceremony *s* caerimonia *f*, rit·us -ūs *m*; (*pomp*) apparat·us -ūs *m*
certain *adj* (*sure*) certus; (*indefinite*) quidam, nonnulus; **for —** certe, pro certo; **it is —** constat; **—ly** certe; profecto
certainty *s* certum *n*; (*belief*) fides *f*
certificate *s* testimonium *n*
certify *vt* recognoscěre, confirmare
cessation *s* cessatio, intermissio *f*; **— of hostilities** indutiae *f pl*
chafe *vt* urěre; (*with the hand*) fricare; (*to excoriate*) atterěre; (*to vex*) irritare, succensēre; *vi* stomachari
chaff *s* palea *f*; (*fig*) quisquiliae *f pl*
chagrin *s* dolor *m*; stomachus *m*
chain *s* catena *f*; (*necklace*) troques *m & f*; (*fig*) series *f*
chain *vt* catenis constringěre; catenas injicěre (*with dat*)
chair *s* sella, cathedra *f*
chairman *s* praeses *m*
chalice *s* calix *m*
chalk *s* creta *f*; calx *f*
chalk *vt* cretā notare; cretā illiněre; **to — out** designare
chalky *adj* (*chalk-like*) cretaceus; (*full of chalk*) cretosus
challenge *s* provocatio *f*; (*law*) recusatio *f*
challenge *vt* provocare, lacessěre; (*law*) rejicěre; (*to reclaim*) arrogare
challenger *s* provocator *m*
chamber *s* cubiculum *n*, camera *f*, thalamus *m*; pars interior *f*
champ *vt & vi* manděre, morděre
champion *s* propugnator, defensor *m*; (*of a party*) antesignanus *m*
chance *s* (*accident*) cas·us -ūs, event·us -ūs *m*; fortuna *f*; (*fig*) alea *f*; (*probability*) spes *f*; **by —** casu, forte, fortuito
chance *vt* periclitari; *vi* acciděre, contingěre
chance *adj* fortuitus; inexpectatus
chancel *s* cancellus *m*
chancellor *s* cancellarius *m*
change *s* mutatio, commutatio, permutatio *f*; (*variety*) varietas *f*; (*pol*) res novae *f pl*; **small —** nummi *m pl*
change *vt* mutare, commutare, permutare; *vi* mutari, variare; (*of the moon*) renovari
changeable *adj* mutabilis; inconstans; (*of color*) versicolor
changeless *adj* immutabilis
changeling *s* subditus, suppositus *m*
channel *s* canalis *m*; (*of rivers*) alveus *m*; (*arm of the sea*) fretum *n*; (*in architecture*) stria *f*; (*fig*) curs·us -ūs *m*
channel *vt* sulcare, excavare; (*to guide*) ducěre
chant *s* cant·us -ūs *m*
chant *vt* cantare
chaos *s* chaos *n*; (*fig*) confusio *f*
chaotic *adj* confusus; indigestus
chap *s* fissura *f*; (*person*) homo *m*
chap *vt* scinděre, diffinděre; *vi* scindi
chapel *s* aedicula *f*, sacellum *n*
chapter *s* caput *n*
char *vt* amburěre
character *s* character *m*; mores *m pl*; (*inborn*) indoles, natura *f*; ingenium *n*; (*repute*) existimatio *f*; (*type*) genus *n*; (*letter*) littera *f*; (*in drama*) persona *f*
characteristic *adj* proprius; **—ally** proprie
characteristic *s* proprium *n*, proprietas *f*
characterize *vt* describěre, notare, designare
charade *s* aenigma syllabicum *n*
charcoal *s* carbo *m*

charge *s* (*law*) crimen *n*; accusatio *f*; (*mil*) impet·us -ūs, incurs·us -ūs *m*; (*command*) mandatum *n*; (*trust*) cura, custodia *f*; (*office*) munus *n*; (*cost*) impensa *f*, sumpt·us -ūs *m*; **to be in — of** praeesse (*with dat*); **to bring a — against** litem intenděre (*with dat*); **to put in — of** praeficěre (*with dat*)
charger *s* equus bellator *m*
chariot *s* curr·us -ūs *m*; curriculum *n*; (*mil*) essedarium *n*
charioteer *s* auriga *m*
charitable *adj* benignus, beneficus; (*fig*) mitis
charitably *adv* benigne; miti animo
charity *s* caritas *f*; liberalitas *f*
charlatan *s* pharmacopola *m*; ostentator, jactator *m*
charm *s* incantamentum *n*; (*fig*) illecebra, gratia *f*; (*amulet*) amuletum *n*
charm *vt* incantare; (*to delight*) capěre, captare, delectare; **to — away** recantare
charmer *s* fascinator *m*; (*thing*) deliciae *f pl*
charming *adj* suavis, lepidus, venustus; **—ly** lepide, suaviter, blande, venuste
chart *s* tabula *f*
charter *s* charta *f*, diploma *n*
charter *vt* conducěre
chase *s* venatio *f*, venat·us -ūs *m*
chase *vt* (*to hunt*) persequi, venari; (*to engrave*) caelare; **to — away** abigěre, pellěre
chasing *s* caelatura *f*
chasm *s* chasma *n*, hiat·us -ūs *m*
chaste *adj* castus, pudicus; (*of language*) purus; **—ly** caste, pudice; pure
chasten *vt* purificare, castigare
chastise *vt* castigare
chastisement *s* castigatio, animadversio *f*
chastiser *s* castigator *m*
chastity *s* pudicitia, castitas *f*, pudor *m*
chat *s* familiaris sermo *m*; **to have a —** fabulari, garrire
chat *vi* fabulari, garrire, colloqui
chattel *s* bona *n pl*
chatter *s* clangor *m*; (*idle talk*) garrulitas *f*, loquacitas *f*; (*of the teeth*) crepit·us -ūs *m*
chatter *vi* balbutire; (*to talk nonsense*) garrire, effutire; (*of teeth*) crepitare
cheap *adj* vilis; **— as dirt** pervilis; **—ly** bene, vili; viliter
cheapen *vt* pretium minuěre (*with genit*)
cheapness *s* vilitas *f*
cheat *vt* decipěre, fraudare
cheat *s* fraus *f*; dolus *m*; (*cheater*) fraudator *m*
check *vt* (*to restrain*) cohiběre, inhiběre; (*to stop*) retardare; (*to bridle*) refrenare; (*accounts*) dispungěre; (*to verify*) comprobare
check *s* (*hindrance*) coercitio, suppressio *f*; impedimentum *n*; (*reprimand*) reprehensio *f*; (*bridle*) frenum *n*; (*disadvantage*) detrimentum *n*; (*admission ticket*) tessera *f*
checkered *adj* varius
cheek *s* gena *f*
cheekbone *s* maxilla *f*
cheer *s* (*shout*) clamor, plaus·us -ūs *m*; hilaritas *f*
cheer *vt* hortari, hilarare, exhilarare; (*to console*) solari
cheerful *adj* hilaris, alacer, laetus; **—ly** hilare, laete; libenter
cheerfulness *s* hilaritas *f*
cheering *s* acclamatio *f*; plaus·us -ūs *m*
cheerless *adj* maestus, tristis, illaetabilis
cheese *s* caseus *m*
chemical *adj* chemicus
chemical *s* chemicum *n*
chemise *s* indusium *n*
chemist *s* chemicus, chemiae peritus *m*
chemistry *s* chemia, chymia *f*
cherish *vt* (*to nourish*) alěre; (*to treat tenderly*) fovēre; (*fig*) colěre
cherry *s* cerasum *n*
cherry tree *s* cerasus *f*
chest *s* (*of the body*) pectus *n*; (*box*) cista, arca *f*; (*for clothes*) vestiarium *n*; scrinium *n*
chestnut *s* castanea *f*
chew *vt* manděre, manducare; **to — the cud** ruminare; (*fig*) meditari
chewing *s* manducatio, ruminatio *f*
chicanery *s* calumnia, praevaricatio *f*
chick *s* pullus *m*; (*term of endearment*) pulla *f*
chicken *s* gallina *f*
chicken-hearted *adj* timidus, ignavus
chicory *s* cichoreum *n*
chide *vt* objurgare; corripěre
chief *adj* primus; praecipuus, summus; supremus; **—ly** praecipue, imprimis
chief *s* princeps, procer, dux, auctor *m*; caput *n*
chieftain *s* dux *m*
child *s* infans *m & f*; puer, filius *m*, puella, filia *f*; (*in the womb*) embryo *m*; **to bear a —** parturire; **with —** gravida
childbearing *s* part·us -ūs *m*
childbirth *s* part·us -ūs *m*; Lucinae labores *m pl*
childhood *s* infantia *f*; pueritia *f*; **from —** a puero *or* pueris; a primo tempore aetatis, a parvo
childish *adj* puerilis; **—ly** pueriliter
childless *adj* orbus
childlike *adj* puerilis
chill *s* frigusculum, frigus *n*
chill *adj* frigidulus
chill *vt* refrigerare
chilling *adj* algificus; frigidus, gelidus
chilly *adj* alsiosus; frigidulus
chime *s* sonus *m*
chime *vi* caněre, sonare; **to — in** interpellare
chimera *s* chimaera *f*; figmentum *n*
chimney *s* caminus *m*
chin *s* mentum *n*

china *s* fictilia *n pl*
chink *s* rima *f*; (*sound*) tinnit·us -ūs *m*
chink *vi* tinnire
chip *s* segmen *n*, assula *f*; (*for lighting fire*) fomes *m*
chip *vt* ascio dedolare
chirp *s* (*of birds*) pipat·us -ūs *m*; (*of crickets*) stridor *m*
chirp *vi* (*of birds*) minurire, pipilare; (*of crickets*) stridēre
chisel *s* scalprum, caelum *n*
chisel *vt* scalpro caedĕre, sculpĕre; (*fig*) decipĕre, fraudare
chivalrous *adj* magnanimus, nobilis
chivalry *s* equestris dignitas *f*; (*class*) equites *m pl*
chocolate *s* chocolatum *n*
choice *s* electio *f*, delect·us -ūs *m*; (*power of choosing*) optio *f*; (*diversity*) varietas *f*
choice *adj* electus, exquisitus
choir *s* chorus *m*
choke *vt* suffocare; strangulare; *vi* suffocari; strangulari
choking *s* suffocatio *f*; strangulatio *f*
choose *vt* eligĕre, optare; **to — to** (*to prefer to*) malle (*with inf*)
choosing *s* electio *f*
chop *s* frustum *n*; (*of meat*) ofella *f*
chop *vt* concidĕre; truncare; **to — off** detruncare; abscidĕre; **to — up** minutatim concidĕre
choral *adj* symphoniacus
chord *s* chorda *f*, nervus *m*
chorus *s* chorus *m*; symphonia *f*
Christ *s* Christus *m*
christen *vt* baptizare
Christendom *s* cuncti Christiani *m pl*
Christian *adj* Christianus
Christianity *s* Christianismus *m*
Christian name *s* praenomen in baptismo inditum *n*
Christmas *s* festum nativitatis Christi *n*
chronic *adj* diuturnus, perpetuus; inveteratus
chronicle *s* annales *m pl*; acta publica *n pl*
chronological *adj* **in — order** ordinem temporum respiciens
chronology *s* temporum ordo *m*, temporum ratio *f*
chubby *adj* crassus, pinguis
chuckle *vi* cachinnare
church *s* ecclesia *f*; templum *n*
churl *s* homo rusticus *m*
churlish *adj* agrestis, importunus; **—ly** rustice
cider *s* hydromelum *n*
cinder *s* cinis *m*, favilla *f*
cinnamon *s* cinnamomum *n*
cipher *s* (*code*) nota *f*; (*a nobody*) numerus *m*; (*zero*) nihil *n*
circle *s* circulus, orbis, gyrus *m*; (*around the moon*) halo *m*; **vicious —** circulus vitiosus *m*
circle *vt* circumdare, cingĕre; *vi* circumire
circuit *s* circuit·us -ūs, circulus *m*; **to make a —** circumire
circuitous *adj* devius
circular *adj* orbicus, rotundus
circulate *vt* spargĕre; (*news*) disseminare, divulgare; *vi* circulari
circulation *s* ambit·us -ūs *m*; (*of blood*) circulatio *f*
circumcise *vt* circumcidĕre
circumcision *s* circumcisio *f*
circumference *s* peripheria *f*, ambit·us -ūs, circulus *m*
circumflex *s* circumflex·us -ūs *m*
circumlocution *s* circumlocutio, periphrasis *f*; ambages *f pl*
circumscribe *vt* finire, terminare, circumscribĕre
circumspect *adj* prudens, cautus, providus
circumspection *s* cautio, prudentia *f*
circumstance *s* res, conditio *f*; tempus *n*; sit·us -ūs *m*; **under the —s** quae cum ita sint
circumstantial *adj* adventicius, fortuitus; enumeratus; (*of evidence*) conjecturalis; **—ly** subtiliter
circumvent *vt* circumvenire, fallĕre, circumscribĕre
circumvention *s* circumscriptio, fraus *f*
circus *s* circus *m*
cistern *s* cisterna *f*, lac·us -ūs *m*; puteus *m*
citadel *s* arx *f*
citation *s* citatio, prolatio *f*; (*law*) vocatio *f*
cite *vt* (*law*) citare, evocare; (*to quote*) proferre, memorare
citizen *s* civis *m & f*; (*of a municipality*) municeps *m*
citizen *adj* civicus
citizenship *s* civitas *f*
city *adj* urbanus; urbicus
city *s* urbs *f*
civic *adj* civilis, civicus
civil *adj* civilis; (*polite*) comis, urbanus; (*of war*) civilis, intestinus, domesticus
civilian *s* togatus *m*; privatus *m*
civility *s* urbanitas, comitas *f*
civilization *s* cult·us -ūs *m*; humanitas *f*
civilize *vt* excolĕre; expolire
clad *adj* indutus, vestitus, amictus
claim *s* postulatio, vindicatio *f*, postulatum *n*
claim *vt* postulare, poscĕre, vindicare, arrogare
claimant *s* petitor, vindicator *m*
clam *s* chama *f*
clamber *vi* scandĕre, conscendĕre
clammy *adj* umidus, viscidus, lentus
clamor *s* clamor *m*, vociferatio *f*
clamor *vi* exclamare, vociferari; **— for** flagitare
clamp *s* confibula *f*; uncus *m*
clamp *vt* constringĕre
clan *s* gens *f*
clandestine *adj* clandestinus, furtivus; **—ly** clam, furtim
clang *s* clangor *m*
clang *vi* clangĕre, strepĕre
clank *s* strepit·us -ūs *m*
clank *vi* crepare

clap *s* (*of hand*) plaus·us -ūs *m*; (*of thunder*) fragor *m*
clap *vi* plauděre, applauděre
claptrap *s* apparat·us -ūs *m*
clarification *s* explicatio *f*, explanatio *f*
clarify *vt* deliquare, explanare, explicare
clarion *s* lituus *m*
clarity *s* claritas *f*; perspicuitas *f*
clash *s* concurs·us -ūs *m*; (*sound*) crepit·us -ūs *m*; (*fig*) dissonantia *f*
clash *vi* concurrěre; increpare, increpitare; (*fig*) dissidēre, discrepare
clasp *s* fibula *f*; (*embrace*) amplex·us -ūs *m*
clasp *vt* (*to embrace*) amplecti, complecti; (*to grasp*) comprehenděre
class *s* (*pol*) classis *f*, ordo *m*; (*kind*) genus *n*
class *vt* in classes distribuěre; **to — as** in numero habēre
classical *adj* classicus
classics *s* scriptores classici *m pl*
classification *s* in classes distributio, in genera distributio *f*
classify *vt* describěre, in classes distribuěre, in genera distribuěre
clatter *s* strepit·us -ūs, crepit·us -ūs *m*
clatter *vi* crepare, crepitare, strepěre
clause *s* (*gram*) membrum, incisum *n*, articulus *m*, clausula *f*; (*law*) caput *n*
claw *s* unguis *m*
claw *vt* lacerare
clay *s* argilla, creta *f*; **made of —** fictilis
clean *adj* mundus, purus; (*fig*) purus, castus; **—ly** munde, pure
clean *vt* mundare, purgare
cleanliness *s* munditia *f*
cleanly *adj* mundus, nitidus
cleanse *vt* purgare, depurgare, abluěre, detergēre
clear *adj* clarus; (*of weather*) serenus; (*bright*) lucidus; (*of liquids*) limpidus; (*transparent*) liquidus; (*of voice*) candidus, acutus, argutus; (*manifest*) conspicuus, manifestus; (*of space*) apertus, patens; (*of language*) dilucidus; (*of conscience*) rectus; (*of the mind*) sagax; **— of** expers (*with genit*); **it is —** apparet, liquet; **to keep — of** evitare; **—ly** clare; plane, aperte, haud dubie
clear *vt* purgare; (*to acquit*) absolvěre; (*a doubt*) explanare; (*land, forests*) extricare; (*profit*) lucrari; **to — away** detergēre, amovēre, tollěre; **to — out** emundare; **to — up** enodare, explanare, explicare; *vi* **to — up** (*of weather*) disserenascěre, disserenare
clearance *s* purgatio *f*; (*space*) intervallum *n*
clearness *s* claritas *f*; (*of sky*) serenitas *f*; (*of style*) perspicuitas *f*
cleavage *s* discidium *n*
cleave *vt* finděre; *vi* **to — to** adhaerēre (*with dat*)
cleaver *s* dolabra *f*
cleft *s* rima, fissura *f*, hiat·us -ūs *m*
clemency *s* clementia *f*
clement *adj* clemens, mitis
clench *vt* compriměre
clerk *s* scriba *m*
clever *adj* sollers, ingeniosus, callidus, astutus, versutus; **—ly** sollerter, callide, ingeniose, astute
cleverness *s* dexteritas, sollertia, astutia *f*
click *s* crepit·us -ūs *m*
click *vi* crepitare
client *s* cliens *m & f*; consultor *m*
cliff *s* cautes *f*, scopulus *m*, rupes *f*
climate *s* caelum *n*
climax *s* gradatio *f*
climb *vt & vi* ascenděre, conscenděre, scanděre
climb *s* ascens·us -ūs *m*
clinch *vt* confirmare
cling *vi* adhaerēre; **to — together** cohaerēre
clink *s* tinnit·us -ūs *m*
clink *vi* tinnire
clip *s* fibula *f*
clip *vt* tondēre, praeciděre; (*words*) mutilare
clipping *s* tonsura *f*; **—s** resegmina *n pl*
cloak *s* pallium *n*; (*for travel*) paenula *f*; (*in rain*) lacerna *f*; (*mil*) sagum, paludamentum *n*
cloak *vt* dissimulare, praetenděre, tegěre
clock *s* horologium *n*; (*sundial*) solarium *n*
clod *s* glaeba *f*
clog *s* (*shoe*) sculponea *f*; (*fig*) impedimentum *n*
clog *vt* impedire
cloister *s* portic·us -ūs *f*; monasterium *n*
close *adj* (*dense*) densus, spissus; (*tight*) artus, angustus; (*shut*) occlusus, clausus; (*fast*) firmus; (*near*) propinquus; (*secret*) arcanus, obscurus; (*niggardly*) avarus, tenax, parcus; **at — quarters** comminus; **— together** confertus, refertus, densus, continuus; **to be — at hand** adesse, instare; **to keep — to** adhaerēre (*with dat*); **—ly** prope; (*attentively*) attente, exacte
close *vt* clauděre, operire; (*to end*) finire, terminare; **to — a bargain** pacisci; *vi* coire; claudi, concludi, terminari; (*in a speech*) perorare
close *s* finis, terminus *m*, terminatio, conclusio *f*; **to bring to a —** finire; **to draw to a —** terminari
close *adv* prope, promime, juxta; **— to** prope (*with acc*), juxta (*with acc*)
closet *s* conclave *n*, cella *f*; (*for clothes*) vestiarium *n*
closing *adj* ultimus
closing *s* conclusio *f*, finis *m*
clot *s* (*of blood*) cruor, concretus sanguis *m*
clot *vi* concrescěre
cloth *s* pannus *m*; (*linen*) linteum *n*
clothe *vt* vestire, induěre; velare

clothes *s* vestit·us -ūs *m*, vestimenta *n pl*, vestis *f*
clothing *s* vestit·us -ūs *m*, vestimenta *n pl*, vestis *f*
cloud *s* nubes *f*
cloud *vt* nubibus velare; (*fig*) obscurare; *vi* nubilare
cloudiness *s* nubilum *n*
cloudless *adj* serenus, purus
cloudy *adj* nubilus; **to grow —** nubilare
clout *s* ict·us -ūs *m*; alapa *f*
cloven *adj* bisulcus, bifidus
clown *s* (*boor*) rusticus *m*; (*buffoon, jester*) scurra *m*
clown *vi* scurrari
clownish *adj* rusticus; scurrilis
cloy *vt* satiare, exsaturare
cloying *adj* putidus
club *s* (*cudgel*) clava *f*, fustis *m*; (*society*) sodalitas *f*, collegium *n*
club *vt* fuste dolare
cluck *vi* glocire; singultire
clue *s* indicium *n*
clump *s* massa *f*; (*of trees*) arbustum *n*, globus *m*
clumsily *adv* rustice, inscite, ineleganter, male, inepte
clumsiness *s* rusticitas, inscitia *f*
clumsy *adj* ineptus, inscitus, rusticus, agrestis; (*of things*) inhabilis
cluster *s* (*of grapes, etc.*) racemus *m*; (*of flowers*) corymbus *m*; (*of people*) corona *f*
cluster *vi* congregari; **to — around** stipare
clutch *s* unguis *m*; comprehensio *f*; **from one's —es** e manibus; **in one's —es** in sua potestate
clutch *vt* arripěre, prehenděre
coach *s* curr·us -ūs *m*, raeda *f*; (*trainer*) magister *m*
coagulate *vt* coagulare; *vi* concrescěre
coagulation *s* coagulatio, concretio *f*
coal *s* carbo *m*
coalesce *vi* coalescěre, coire
coalition *s* conjunctio, coitio, conspiratio *f*
coal mine *s* fodina carbonaria *f*
coarse *s* (*of material*) crassus, rudis; (*of manners*) incultus, inurbanus, rusticus; **—ly** crasse; inurbane
coarseness *s* crassitudo *f*; rusticitas *f*
coast *s* ora *f*, litus *n*
coast *vi* praetervehi
coastal *adj* maritimus, litoralis
coat *s* tunica, toga *f*; (*of fur*) pellis *f*
coat *vt* illiněre, inducěre, obducěre
coating *s* corium *n*
coat of arms *s* insignia *n pl*
coat of mail *s* lorica *f*; (*skin*) pellis *f*
coax *vt* cogěre, mulcēre, blandiri
coaxing *s* blandimenta *n pl*, blanditiae *f pl*
coaxingly *adv* blande
cobbler *s* sutor *m*
cobweb *s* aranea *f*, araneum *n*
cock *s* gallus *m*
cockroach *s* blatta *f*
cocoa *s* faba Cacao *f*
cocoanut *s* nux palmae indicae *f*
cocoon *s* globulus *m*
coddle *vt* indulgēre (*with dat*)
code *s* notae *f pl*
codify *vt* digerěre
coerce *vt* coercēre, refrenare, cogěre
coercion *s* coercitio, vis *f*
coeval *adj* coaevus, aequalis
coexist *vi* simul existěre
coffee *s* coffea Arabica *f*
coffer *s* arca, cista *f*
coffin *s* arca *f*, sarcophagus *m*
cog *s* dens *m*
cogency *s* vis *f*
cogent *adj* cogens, efficax, gravis
cognate *adj* cognatus
cognizance *s* cognitio *f*
cognizant *adj* conscius, gnarus
cohabit *vi* coire, consuescěre
cohabitation *s* consuetudo *f*, convict·us -ūs *m*
coheir *s* coheres *m & f*
cohere *vi* cohaerēre; (*fig*) congruěre
coherence *s* context·us -ūs *m*, convenientia *f*
coherent *adj* cohaerens, congruens; **—ly** constanter
cohesion *s* cohaerentia *f*
cohesive *adj* tenax
cohort *s* cohors *f*
coil *s* spira *f*
coil *vt* glomerare; *vi* glomerari
coin *s* nummus *m*
coin *vt* cuděre, signare; (*fig*) fingěre
coinage *s* res nummaria, moneta *f*
coincide *vi* congruěre, convenire, concurrěre; eodem tempore fieri
coincidence *s* concursatio *f*, concurs·us -ūs *m*; (*fig*) consens·us -ūs *m*; **by —** casu
coincidental *adj* fortuitus
cold *adj* frigidus, gelidus; **to be —** algēre, frigēre; **to become —** frigescěre, algescěre; **—ly** (*fig*) frigide, gelide, lente
cold *s* frigus *n*, algor *m*, gelu *n*; (*sickness*) gravedo *f*; **to catch a —** gravedinem contraheěre; **to have a —** gravedine dolēre
coldness *s* frigus *n*, algor *m*
colic *s* tormina *n pl*
collapse *s* labes, ruina *f*
collapse *vi* collabi, conciděre, in se corruěre
collar *s* (*of garment*) collare *n*; (*for dogs*) millus *m*; jugum *n*
collar *vt* collo comprehenděre
collarbone *s* jugulum *n*
collate *vt* conferre
collateral *adj* transversus; adjunctus, consentaneus
colleague *s* collega, consors *m*
collect *vt* conferre, colligěre; (*to assemble*) convocare; (*money*) exigěre; **to — oneself** mentem colligěre, animum colligěre; *vi* colligi, aggregari
collected *adj* praesens
collection *s* collectio, conquisitio, collecta, congeries *f*; (*out of authors*) collectanea *n pl*

collective *adj* communis, collectivus; **—ly** una, simul, communiter
college *s* collegium *n*
collegiate *adj* collegialis, collegiarius
collide *vi* confligĕre, concurrĕre
collision *s* concursio, conflictio *f*, concurs·us -ūs *m*
colloquial *adj* quotidianus
collusion *s* collusio, praevaricatio *f*, dolus *m*
colon *s* colon *n*
colonel *s* legatus *m*
colonial *adj* colonicus
colonist *s* colonus *m*
colonize *vt* coloniam constituĕre in (*with abl*)
colonnade *s* portic·us -ūs *f*
colony *s* colonia *f*
color *s* color *m*, pigmentum *n*; **—s** vexillum *n*
color *vt* colorare; (*to dye*) tingĕre, inficĕre; (*fig*) obtegĕre; *vi* erubescĕre
colossal *adj* ingens, immanis
colossus *s* colossus *m*
colt *s* equulus, pullus equinus *m*
column *s* columna *f*; (*mil*) agmen *n*
comb *s* pecten *m*
comb *vt* pectĕre, comĕre
combat *s* pugna *f*, proelium, certamen *n*
combat *vt* pugnare cum (*with abl*); *vi* pugnare, proeliari
combination *s* conjunctio, junctura *f*; (*of persons*) conspiratio, conjuratio *f*
combine *vt* conjungĕre, miscēre; temperare; *vi* coire; conspirare
combustible *adj* igni obnoxius
combustion *s* concrematio, ustio *f*
come *vi* venire; (*to arrive*) pervenire; (*to happen*) fieri; **to — about** evenire; **to — after** sequi; **to — again** revenire; **to — along** procedĕre; **to — away** abscedĕre; **to — back** revenire, redire; **to — before** praevenire; **to — by** praeterire; (*to get*) acquirĕre; **to — down** descendĕre; (*to fall down*) decidĕre; **to — forth** exire; (*fig*) exoriri; **to — forward** procedĕre; **to — in** introire; **to — near** approprinquare, accedĕre; **to — off** recedĕre, discedĕre; **to — on** pergĕre; **to — out** (*to be published*) edi, emitti; **to — over** supervenire; (*the face*) obire; **to — round** (*fig*) transgredi; **to — to** advenire; (*to come to one's senses*) ad se redire; **to — to pass** evenire, fieri; **to — together** convenire, coire; **to — up** subvenire; (*to occur*) accidĕre, provenire; **to — upon** (*to find*) invenire; (*to attack*) ingruĕre
comedian *s* comoedus *m*; (*playwright*) comicus *m*
comedy *s* comoedia *f*
comely *adj* decens, venustus
comet *s* cometes *m*, stella crinita *f*
comfort *s* consolatio *f*, solatium *n*
comfort *vt* consolari, solari
comfortable *adj* commodus, amoenus
comfortably *adv* commode
comforter *s* consolator *m*
comfortless *adj* solatii expers, incommodus
comic *adj* comicus, facetus
comic *s* scurra *m*
comical *adj* comicus, ridiculus; **—ly** comice, ridicule
coming *adj* venturus
coming *s* advent·us -ūs *m*
comma *s* comma *n*
command *vt* imperare (*with dat*), jubēre; (*view*) prospectare, despectare
command *s* (*order*) jussum, mandatum, praeceptum *n*, juss·us -ūs *m*; (*mil*) imperium *n*; (*jurisdiction*) provincia *f*; **— of language** copia dicendi *f*; **to be in — of** praeesse (*with dat*); **to put someone in — of** aliquem praeficĕre (*with dat*)
commander *s* dux, praefectus *m*
commander in chief *s* imperator *m*
commandment *s* mandatum *n*
commemorate *vt* celebrare
commemoration *s* celebratio *f*
commence *vt* incipere, inchoare
commencement *s* initium, exordium, principium *n*
commend *vt* approbare, laudare; (*to recommend*) commendare; (*to entrust*) committĕre, mandare
commendable *adj* commendabilis, probabilis, laudabilis
commendation *s* commendatio *f*
commensurate *adj* adaequans, conveniens
comment *vi* commentari; **to — on** explicare, enarrare, interpretari
comment *s* sententia *f*, dictum *n*
commentary *s* commentarius *m*, commentarium *n*
commentator *s* interpres *m*
commerce *s* commercium *n*, mercat·us -ūs *m*, mercatura *f*; **to engage in —** negotiari
commercial *adj* negotialis
commiserate *vi* **to — with** miserēri
commiseration *s* misericordia *f*
commissariat *s* commeat·us -ūs *m*, res frumentaria *f*
commissary *s* procurator, curator *m*
commission *s* mandatum *n*; (*mil*) legatio *f*
commission *vt* delegare, mandare
commissioner *s* delegatus *m*
commit *vt* (*crime*) admittĕre, patrare, perpetrare; (*to entrust*) committĕre; **to — to memory** ediscĕre
commitment *s* (*obligation*) munus, officium *n*; (*to jail*) incarceratio *f*
committee *s* consilium *n*
commodity *s* res venalis, merx *f*
common *adj* communis, publicus; (*ordinary*) vulgaris, quotidianus; (*well known*) pervulgatus; (*repeated*) creber; (*inferior*) mediocris; (*gram*) promiscuus; **—ly** vulgo, fere, plerumque
commoner *s* plebeius *m*; **—s** plebs *f*
commonplace *adj* vulgaris, pervulgatus, tritus
commonwealth *s* respublica *f*

commotion *s* commotio, agitatio *f*, tumult·us -ūs *m*
commune *vi* confabulari
communicate *vt* communicare; (*information*) impertire, nuntiare; *vi* **to — with** communicare (*with dat*), agĕre cum (*with abl*)
communication *s* communicatio *f*; commercium *n*; (*information*) nuntius *m*
communicative *adj* affabilis, facilis
communion *s* communio, societas *f*
community *s* civitas *f*
commutation *s* mutatio, permutatio *f*
commute *vt* commutare
compact *adj* densus, spissus; (*of style*) pressus; **—ly** dense, spisse, confertim
compact *s* pactum, foedus *n*, pactio *f*
compact *vt* densare
companion *s* comes, socius, sodalis; (*mil*) contubernalis, commilito *m*
companionable *adj* affabilis, facilis
companionship *s* societas, sodalitas, consuetudo *f*; (*mil*) contubernium *n*
company *s* societas, consuetudo *f*; (*gathering*) convent·us -ūs *m*; (*guests*) convivium *n*; (*com*) societas *f*; (*mil*) manipulus *m*; (*theatrical*) grex *f*
comparable *adj* comparabilis
comparative *adj* comparatus, relativus; **—ly** comparate
comparative *s* grad·us -ūs comparativus *m*
compare *vt* comparare, conferre; **compared with** ad (*with acc*), adversus (*with acc*)
comparison *s* comparatio, collatio *f*; **in — with** prae (*with abl*), adversus (*with acc*)
compartment *s* loculus *m*, cella, pars *f*
compass *s* ambit·us -ūs *m*; (*limits*) fines *m pl*; (*instrument*) circinus *m*; (*magnetic*) ac·us -ūs magnetica *f*
compass *vt* circumvallare, cingĕre, circumdare; (*to attain*) consequi, patrare
compassion *s* misericordia *f*
compassionate *adj* misericors; **—ly** misericorditer
compatibility *s* congruentia, convenientia *f*
compatible *adj* congruus, conveniens
compatriot *s* civis, popularis *m*
compeer *s* par, aequalis *m*
compel *vt* cogĕre, compellĕre
compendium *s* summarium *n*
compensate *vt* compensare, renumerare; satisfacĕre (*with dat*)
compensation *s* compensatio *f*; poena *f*
compete *vi* contendĕre, petĕre, certare
competence *s* facultas *f*; (*legal capacity*) jus *n*
competent *adj* congruens, idoneus, peritus, capax; (*of authorities*) locuples; **—ly** satis, idonee
competition *s* contentio, aemulatio *f*, certamen *n*
competitor *s* petitor, rivalis, aemulus *m*
compilation *s* collectio *f*, collectanea *n pl*
compile *vt* colligĕre, componĕre
compiler *s* collector, scriptor *m*
complacency *s* amor sui *m*
complacent *adj* qui sibi placet
complain *vi* queri
complaint *s* querela, querimonia *f*; (*law*) crimen *n*; (*med*) morbus *m*
complaisance *s* comitas, accommodatio *f*, obsequium *n*
complaisant *adj* comis, officiosus; **—ly** comiter
complement *s* complementum, supplementum *n*
complete *adj* perfectus, integer, absolutus, plenus; **—ly** plane, prorsus, omnino, abolute, funditus
complete *vt* complēre; (*to accomplish*) perficĕre, conficĕre, peragĕre
completion *s* completio *f*; (*accomplishment*) perfectio *f*; (*end*) finis *m*
complex *adj* multiplex, implicatus, complicatus
complexion *s* color *m*
complexity *s* implicatio, multiplex natura *f*
compliance *s* obtemperatio *f*, obsequium *n*
compliant *adj* obsequens
complicate *vt* impedire
complicated *adj* impeditus, implicatus, complicatus, nodosus
complication *s* implicatio *f*
complicity *s* conscientia *f*
compliment *s* blandimentum *n*, verba honorifica *n pl*; **to pay one's —s** to salutare
compliment *vt* gratulari (*with dat*); laudare, blandiri
complimentary *adj* blandus, honorificus
comply *vi* **to — with** concedĕre (*with dat*), cedĕre (*with dat*), parēre (*with dat*), obsequi (*with dat*), morigerari (*with dat*)
component *s* pars *f*, elementum *n*
compose *vt* componĕre; (*verses*) condĕre, pangĕre; (*to calm*) sedare; (*quarrel*) componĕre; **to — oneself** tranquillari
composed *adj* tranquillus, quietus, placidus
composer *s* scriptor, auctor *m*
composite *adj* compositus, multiplex
composition *s* compositio, scriptura *f*; opus *n*
composure *s* tranquillitas *f*, animus aequus *m*
compound *vt* componĕre, miscēre; (*words*) jungĕre
compound *adj* compositus
compound *s* compositio *f*; (*word*) junctum verbum *n*
compound interest *s* anatocismus *m*
comprehend *vt* continēre, amplectari; (*to understand*) capĕre, percipĕre, comprehendĕre, intellegĕre
comprehensible *adj* perspicuus
comprehension *s* intellect·us -ūs *m*, intellegentia *f*

comprehensive *adj* plenus, capax; **—ly** funditus, omnino
compress *vt* comprimĕre
compression *s* compressio *f*, compress·us -ūs *m*
comprise *vt* continēre
compromise *s* (*unilateral*) accommodatio *f*; (*bilateral*) compromissum *n*
compromise *vt* compromittĕre, implicare; *vi* pacisci
compulsion *s* compulsio, vis, necessitas *f*
compulsory *adj* necessarius, debitus
compunction *s* paenitentia, compunctio *f*
computation *s* ratio, computatio *f*
compute *vt* computare
comrade *s* socius, sodalis *m*; (*mil*) contubernalis *m*
conceal *vt* celare, occultare, abdĕre, dissimulare
concealment *s* occultatio, dissimulatio *f*; (*place*) latebrae *f pl*; **to be in —** latēre
concede *vt* concedĕre
conceit *s* (*haughtiness*) arrogantia, superbia *f*; (*idea*) notio *f*
conceited *adj* arrogans, superbiā tumens
conceive *vt* concipĕre, percipĕre, intellegĕre
concentrate *vt* in unum locum contrahĕre; *vi* **to — on** animum intendĕre in (*with acc*)
concentration *s* in unum locum contractio *f*; (*fig*) animi intentio *f*
conception *s* (*in womb*) concept·us -ūs *m*; (*idea*) imago, notio *f*
concern *s* (*affair*) res *f*, negotium *n*; (*importance*) momentum *n*; (*worry*) sollicitudo, cura *f*
concern *vt* pertinēre ad (*with acc*), attinēre ad (*with acc*); (*to worry*) sollicitare; **it —s me** meā interest, meā refert
concerned *adj* sollictus, anxius
concerning *prep* de (*with abl*)
concert *s* (*music*) concent·us -ūs *m*, symphonia *f*; **in —** uno animo, ex composito
concert *vt* (*plan*) inire
concession *s* concessio *f*; (*thing*) concessum *n*; **to make —s** concedĕre
conch *s* concha *f*
conciliate *vt* conciliare
conciliation *s* conciliatio *f*
concise *adj* brevis, concisus; (*style*) densus; **—ly** breviter, concise
conciseness *s* brevitas *f*
conclave *s* conclave, consilium *n*
conclude *vt* (*to end*) conficĕre, perficĕre, terminare, finire; (*to infer*) concludĕre, colligĕre
conclusion *s* (*end*) conclusio *f*; (*decision*) determinatio, sententia *f*; (*of speech*) peroratio *f*; (*of action*) exit·us -ūs *m*; (*inference*) conjectura *f*
conclusive *adj* certus, gravis
concoct *vt* concoquĕre; (*to contrive*) excogitare, conflare
concoction *s* pot·us -ūs *m*; (*fig*) machinatio *f*
concomitant *adj* adjunctus, conjunctus
concord *s* concordia, harmonia *f*; (*mus*) concent·us -ūs *m*
concordat *s* pactum *n*
concourse *s* concurs·us -ūs *m*, concursio *f*
concrete *adj* concretus
concrete *s* concretum *n*, concret·us -ūs *m*
concubinage *s* concubinat·us -ūs *m*
concubine *s* concubina *f*
concupiscence *s* libido *f*
concur *vi* congruĕre, consentire
concurrence *s* consens·us -ūs *m*, consensio *f*
concussion *s* concussio *f*
condemn *vt* damnare, condemnare; **to — to death** capitis damnare
condemnation *s* damnatio, condemnatio *f*
condensation *s* densatio, spissatio *f*
condense *vt* (con)densare, spissare; (*words*) premĕre
condescend *vi* dignari, descendĕre, concedĕre, se submittĕre
condescending *adj* comis; **—ly** comiter
condescension *s* comitas *f*
condition *s* (*state*) stat·us -ūs *m*, condicio, res *f*; (*stipulation*) condicio, lex *f*; **on — that** ea lege ut
condition *vt* formare, informare
conditional *adj* conditionalis; **—ly** (*law*) conditionaliter; sub condicione
condole *vi* **to — with** dolēre cum (*with abl*)
condone *vt* veniam dare (*with dat*), condonare
conducive *adj* utilis, accommodatus
conduct *s* mores *m pl*, vita *f*; (*management*) administratio *f*
conduct *vt* (*to lead*) adducĕre, deducĕre, perducĕre; (*to manage*) gerĕre, administrare
conductor *s* dux, ductor *m*
conduit *s* canalis, aquaeduct·us -ūs *m*
cone *s* conus *m*
confection *s* conditura, cuppedo *f*
confectionery *s* cuppedia *n pl*, conditura *f*
confederacy *s* (*alliance*) foedus *n*, societas *f*
confederate *adj* foederatus
confederate *s* socius, conjuratus *m*
confederate *vi* foedus facĕre
confederation *s* societas *f*
confer *vt* conferre, tribuĕre; *vi* colloqui
conference *s* colloquium *n*
confess *vt* fatēri, confitēri; agnoscĕre, concedĕre
confessedly *adv* ex confesso; manifesto, aperte
confession *s* confessio *f*
confidant *s* familiaris *m & f*, conscius *m*, conscia *f*
confide *vt* committĕre, credĕre, mandare; *vi* **to — in** (con)fidĕre (*with dat*)
confidence *s* fides, confidentia, fiducia *f*; **to have — in** confidĕre (*with

dat); **to inspire — in** fidem facĕre (*with dat*)
confident *adj* confidens, fidens; **—ly** confidenter
confidential *adj* fidus; (*secret*) arcanus
configuration *s* forma, figura *f*
confine *s* finis *m*
confine *vt* includĕre; (*to restrain*) coercēre, cohibēre; (*to limit*) circumscribĕre; **to be confined to bed** lecto tenēri
confinement *s* inclusio *f*; (*imprisonment*) incarceratio, custodia *f*; (*of women*) puerperium *n*
confirm *vt* confirmare; (*to prove*) comprobare; (*to ratify*) sancire
confirmation *s* confirmatio, affirmatio *f*
confiscate *vt* proscribĕre, publicare
confiscation *s* proscriptio, publicatio *f*
conflagration *s* incendium *n*
conflict *s* conflict·us -ūs *m*, contentio, pugna *f*, certamen *n*
conflict *vi* contendĕre; (*differ*) dissentire, discrepare
conflicting *adj* contrarius, adversus
confluence *s* confluens *m*
conform *vt* accommodare; *vi* obsequi, obtemperare
conformation *s* conformatio, figura, forma *f*
conformity *s* convenientia, congruentia *f*; **in — with** secundum (*with acc*)
confound *vt* confundĕre, permiscēre, perturbare; (*to frustrate*) frustrari
confounded *adj* miser, nefandus
confront *vt* obviam ire (*with dat*), se opponĕre (*with dat*)
confrontation *s* comparatio *f*
confuse *vt* confundĕre, perturbare, permiscēre
confused *adj* confusus, perplexus; **—ly** confuse, perplexe
confusion *s* confusio, perturbatio *f*; (*shame*) pudor *m*
congeal *vt* congelare, glaciare; *vi* consistĕre, concrescĕre
congenial *adj* consentaneus, concors
congenital *adj* nativus
congested *adj* refertus, densus; frequentissimus
congestion *s* congeries, frequentia *f*
congratulate *vt* gratulari (*with dat*)
congratulation *s* gratulatio *f*
congratulatory *adj* gratulans, gratulabundus
congregate *vt* congregare, colligĕre; *vi* congregari, convenire
congregation *s* coet·us -ūs *m*, auditores *m pl*
conical *adj* conicus
conjectural *adj* conjecturalis, opinabilis; **—ly** ex conjectura
conjecture *s* conjectura *f*
conjecture *vt* conjectare, conjicĕre
conjugal *adj* conjugalis
conjugate *vt* declinare
conjugation *s* conjugatio *f*
conjunction *s* unio *f*, concurs·us -ūs *m*; (*gram*) conjunctio *f*
conjure *vt* obtestari, incantare, fascinare; *vi* praestigiis uti
conjurer *s* magus, praestigiator *m*
conjuring *s* praestigiae *f pl*
connect *vt* connectĕre, jungĕre, copulare; (*in a series*) serĕre
connected *adj* conjunctus; continuus, continens; (*by marriage*) affinis; **to be closely connected with** inhaerēre (*with dat*); **to be connected with** contingĕre
connection *s* conjunctio, colligatio *f*, nex·us -ūs, context·us -ūs *m*; (*kin*) necessitudo *f*; (*by marriage*) affinitas *f*
connivance *s* indulgentia, dissimulatio *f*
connive *vi* connivēre
connoisseur *s* doctus, peritus, intellegens *m*
conquer *vt* vincĕre, superare; domare
conqueror *s* victor *m*, victrix *f*; domitor *m*
conquest *s* victoria *f*
consanguinity *s* consanguinitas *f*
conscience *s* conscientia *f*; **guilty —** mala conscientia; **to have no —** nullam religionem habēre
conscientious *adj* integer, pius, religiosus, diligens; **—ly** diligenter
conscious *adj* conscius, gnarus; **—ly** scienter
consciousness *s* conscientia *f*
conscript *s* tiro *m*
conscript *vt* conscribĕre
conscription *s* delect·us -ūs *m*
consecrate *vt* sacrare, consecrare, dedicare, devovēre
consecration *s* consecratio, dedicatio *f*
consecutive *adj* continuus; **—ly** deinceps, continenter
consent *vi* assentire, consentire
consent *s* consens·us -ūs *m*, consensio *f*; **without my —** me invito
consequence *s* consequentia, consecutio *f*, event·us -ūs, exit·us -ūs *m*; (*logical*) conclusio *f*; (*importance*) momentum *n*
consequent *adj* consequens, consectarius; **—ly** ergo, igitur, itaque
consequential *adj* consentaneus
conservation *s* conservatio *f*
conservative *adj* reipublicae statūs conservandi studiosus; **— party** optimates *m pl*
conserve *vt* conservare, servare
consider *vt* considerare, animo agitare, revolvĕre; (*to deem*) aestimare, ducĕre, habēre; (*to respect*) respicĕre
considerable *adj* aliquantus; (*of persons*) eximius, illustris; (*of size*) amplus
considerably *adv* aliquantum; multum; (*with comp*) multo, aliquanto
considerate *adj* prudens, humanus, benignus
consideration *s* consideratio, contemplatio, deliberatio *f*; (*regard*) respect·us -ūs *m*; (*ground, motive*)

ratio *f*; (*importance*) momentum *n*; **without —** inconsulte, temere
considering *prep* pro (*with abl*)
consign *vt* committĕre, mandare, consignare, tradĕre
consignment *s* consignatio *f*
consist *vi* consistĕre; **to — of** constare ex (*with abl*)
consistency *s* congruentia, constantia *f*
consistent *adj* constans; consentaneus; **—ly** constanter, congruenter
consolable *adj* consolabilis
consolation *s* consolatio *f*; (*thing*) solacium *n*
console *vt* consolari
consolidate *vt* corroborare, firmare, consolidare, stabilire; *vi* solidescĕre
consonant *adj* consonus, consentaneus
consonant *s* consonans littera *f*
consort *s* consors *m* & *f*; (*married*) conjux *or* conjunx *m* & *f*
consort *vi* **to — with** familiariter uti (*with abl*), se associare cum (*with abl*)
conspicuous *adj* conspicuus; insignis, manifestus; **—ly** manifeste, palam
conspiracy *s* conjuratio, conspiratio *f*
conspirator *s* conjuratus *m*
conspire *vi* conjurare, conspirare
constable *s* lictor *m*
constancy *s* constantia, firmitas, perseverantia *f*
constant *adj* constans, firmus; perpetuus; fidelis; **—ly** constanter, crebro
constellation *s* sidus, astrum *n*
consternation *s* consternatio, trepidatio *f*, pavor *m*; **to throw into —** perterrēre
constituent *s* elector, suffragator *m*; (*part*) elementum *n*
constitute *vt* constituĕre, creare
constitution *s* (*of body*) habit·us -ūs *m*, constitutio *f*; (*pol*) civitatis stat·us -ūs *m*, reipublicae leges *f pl*
constitutional *adj* legitimus; (*natural*) naturā insitus; **—ly** legitime
constrain *vt* cogĕre, compellĕre, detinēre
constraint *s* vis, coercitio, necessitas *f*
construct *vt* construĕre
construction *s* constructio, aedificatio *f*; figura, forma *f*; (*meaning*) sens·us -ūs *m*, interpretatio *f*
constructor *s* structor, fabricator *m*
construe *vt* interpretari; (*gram*) construĕre
consul *s* consul *m*; **— elect** consul designatus *m*
consular *adj* consularis
consulship *s* consulat·us -ūs *m*; **to run for the —** consulatum petĕre; **during my —** me consule
consult *vt* consulĕre, consultare; *vi* deliberare
consultation *s* consultatio, deliberatio *f*
consume *vt* consumĕre, absumĕre; (*food*) edĕre
consumer *s* consumptor *m*
consummate *adj* summus, perfectus
consummate *vt* consummare
consummation *s* consummatio *f*; (*end*) finis *m*
consumption *s* consumptio *f*; (*disease*) tabes *f*
consumptive *adj* pulmonarius
contact *s* contact·us -ūs *m*, contagio *f*; **to come in — with** contingĕre
contagion *s* contagium *n*, contagio *f*
contagious *adj* contagiosus, tabificus
contain *vt* continēre; (*to restrain*) cohibēre
container *s* vas *n*
contaminate *vt* contaminare
contamination *s* contaminatio, labes *f*
contemplate *vt* contemplari, intuēri
contemplation *s* contemplatio, meditatio *f*
contemporaneous *adj* aequalis; **—ly** simul
contemporary *s* aequalis, aequaevus *m*
contempt *s* contemptio *f*, contempt·us -ūs *m*
contemptible *adj* contemnendus, abjectus, vilis
contemptibly *adv* contemptim, abjecte
contemptuous *adj* fastidiosus, superbus; **—ly** fastidiose
contend *vt* (*to aver*) affirmare, asseverare; *vi* contendĕre, certare; (*to struggle*) luctari; (*to dispute*) verbis certare; **to — against** repugnare, adversari
contending *adj* aversus, contrarius
content *adj* contentus
content *vt* satisfacĕre (*with dat*), placēre (*with dat*), mulcēre
contented *adj* contentus; **—ly** aequo animo, leniter
contention *s* contentio *f*; certamen *n*; controversia *f*
contentious *adj* litigiosus; pugnax
contentment *s* aequus animus *m*
contents *s* quod inest, quae insunt; (*of book*) argumentum *n*
contest *s* certamen *n*, contentio, certatio *f*
contest *vt* (*to dispute*) resistĕre (*with dat*), repugnare (*with dat*); (*law*) lege agĕre de (*with abl*)
contestant *s* petitor, aemulus *m*
context *s* context·us -ūs, sens·us -ūs *m*
contiguous *adj* contiguus, conterminus, adjunctus
continence *s* continentia, abstinentia *f*
continent *adj* abstinens, continens; **—ly** abstinenter, continenter
continent *s* continens *f*
continental *adj* in continenti positus; ad continentem pertinens
contingent *s* (*of troops*) numerus *m*, man·us -ūs *f*
continual *adj* continuus; perpetuus, assiduus; **—ly** assidue, semper

continuance *s* continuatio, perpetuitas, assiduitas *f*
continuation *s* continuatio *f*
continue *vt* continuare, producĕre; *vi* pergĕre; (*to last*) durare, persistĕre, perstare, (re)manēre
continuity *s* continuitas *f*; (*of speech*) perpetuitas *f*
continuous *adj* continuus, continens, perpetuus; **—ly** continenter
contortion *s* contortio, distortio *f*
contour *s* forma, figura *f*; lineamenta *n pl*
contraband *adj* interdictus, vetitus, illicitus
contract *vt* contrahĕre, astringĕre; (*to shorten*) deminuĕre; (*sickness*) contrahĕre; (*to undertake*) redimĕre; *vi* pacisci; (*to shrink*) contrahi
contract *s* pactum, conventum *n*; (*pol*) foedus *n*
contraction *s* contractio *f*; (*of word*) compendium *n*
contractor *s* redemptor, susceptor *m*
contradict *vt* contradicĕre (*with dat*), obloqui (*with dat*)
contradiction *s* contradictio *f*; (*of things*) repugnantia *f*
contradictory *adj* contrarius, repugnans
contrary *adj* (*opposite*) contrarius, diversus; (*fig*) aversus, repugnans; **— to** contra (*with acc*)
contrary *s* contrarium *n*, contraria pars *f*; **on the —** contra, e contrario
contrast *s* diversitas, dissimilitudo *f*
contrast *vt* comparare, opponĕre; *vi* discrepare
contribute *vt* contribuĕre, conferre; *vi* **to — towards** conferre ad (*with acc*)
contribution *s* contributio, collatio *f*; (*money*) stips *f*
contributory *adj* contribuens, adjunctus
contrite *adj* paenitens
contrition *s* paenitentia *f*
contrivance *s* inventio, machinatio *f*; (*thing contrived*) inventum, artificium *n*, machina *f*
contrive *vt* (*to invent*) fingĕre; excogitare, machinari, efficĕre
control *s* (*restraint*) continentia *f*; (*power*) potestas, moderatio, dictio *f*, imperium *n*; **to have — over** praeesse (*with dat*)
control *vt* moderari (*with dat*), continēre, regĕre, coercēre
controller *s* moderator *m*
controversial *adj* concertatorius
controversy *s* controversia, disceptatio, concertatio *f*
contusion *s* contusio *f*, contusum *n*
conundrum *s* aenigma *n*; (*quibble*) cavillum *n*
convalesce *vi* convalescĕre
convalescence *s* conditio convalescendi *f*
convalescent *adj* convalescens
convene *vt* convocare
convenience *s* commoditas, opportunitas, convenientia *f*; (*thing*) commodum *n*
convenient *adj* commodus, idoneus, opportunus; **—ly** commode, apte, opportune
convention *s* convent·us -ūs *m*; (*custom*) mos *m*
conventional *adj* usitatus, tralaticius, solitus
converge *vi* vergĕre, coire
conversant *adj* peritus, exercitatus; **to be — with** versari in (*with abl*)
conversation *s* colloquium *n*, sermo *m*
conversational *adj* in colloquio usitatus
converse *vi* colloqui
converse *s* contrarium *n*, convers·us -ūs *m*
conversely *adv* e contrario, e converso
conversion *s* conversio *f*
convert *vt* convertĕre, commutare; deducĕre
convert *s* neophytus, discipulus *m*
convertible *adj* commutabilis
convex *adj* convexus
convey *vt* portare, vehĕre, convehĕre; (*property*) abalienare; (*fig*) significare
conveyance *s* (*act*) advectio, vectura *f*; (*vehicle*) vehiculum *n*; (*law*) abalienatio, transcriptio *f*
convict *s* convictus, evictus, reus *m*
convict *vt* convincĕre
conviction *s* (*law*) damnatio *f*; (*certainty*) persuasio, fides *f*
convince *vt* persuadēre (*with dat*)
convivial *adj* hilaris, laetus
convocation *s* convocatio *f*
convoke *vt* convocare
convoy *s* praesidium *n*, deductor *m*
convoy *vt* deducĕre
convulse *vt* concutĕre, convellĕre
convulsion *s* convulsio *f*, spasmus *m*
convulsive *adj* spasticus
cook *s* coquus *m*, coqua *f*
cook *vt & vi* coquĕre
cool *adj* frigidulus; (*fearless*) sedatus, immotus, impavidus; (*indifferent*) lentus, frigidus; **—ly** frigide; sedate; lente
cool *vt* refrigerare; *vi* refrigerari; (*fig*) defervescĕre
coolness *s* frigus *n*; (*fig*) lentitudo, cautela *f*; animus aequus *m*
coop *s* (*for chickens*) cavea *f*
coop *vt* **to — up** includĕre
cooperate *vi* unā agĕre; **to — with** adjuvare
cooperation *s* adjumentum *n*, consociatio, opera *f*
cope *vi* **to — with** certare cum (*with abl*); **able to — with** par (*with dat*)
copious *adj* copiosus, abundans; **—ly** copiose, abundanter
copper *s* aes, cuprum *n*
copper *adj* aëneus, cuprinus
copse *s* dumetum, fruticetum *n*
copy *s* exemplar *n*, imitatio, imago *f*
copy *vt* imitari; (*writing*) transcribĕre, exscribĕre

coquette *s* lupa, lasciva *f*
coquettish *adj* lascivus
coral *adj* coralinus
coral *s* coralium *n*
cord *s* funis, restis *m*
cordial *adj* benignus, comis; **—ly** benigne, comiter, ex animo
cordiality *s* comitas *f*
cordon *s* corona *f*
core *s* (*of fruit*) volva *f*; (*fig*) nucleus *m*
Corinthian *adj* Corinthiacus, Corinthius
cork *s* cortex *m*; (*stopper*) obturamentum *n*
corn *s* (*grain*) frumentum *n*; (*on toes*) callus *m*
corner *s* angulus *m*; (*of house*) versura *f*; (*of street*) compitum *n*
cornice *s* corona *f*
corollary *s* corollarium *n*
coronation *s* coronae impositio *f*
coronet *s* diadema *n*
corporal *adj* corporeus, corporalis
corporal *s* decurio *m*
corporate *adj* corporatus
corporation *s* collegium *n*; municipium *n*
corporeal *adj* corporeus
corps *s* legio *f*
corpse *s* cadaver *n*
corpulent *adj* corpulentus
corpuscle *s* corpusculum *n*
correct *adj* correctus, rectus, accuratus; **—ly** recte, bene
correct *vt* corrigĕre, emendare; (*to punish*) animadvertĕre, castigare
correction *s* correctio, emendatio *f*; (*punishment*) animadversio, castigatio *f*
correctness *s* puritas, accuratio *f*
correlation *s* reciprocitas, mutua ratio *f*
correspond *vi* congruĕre; (*by letter*) litteras mutuas scribĕre
correspondence *s* congruentia, convenientia *f*; epistolae *f pl*
correspondent *s* epistolarum scriptor *m*
corridor *s* portic·us -ūs *f*, andron, xystus *m*
corroborate *vt* confirmare
corrode *vt* erodĕre, edĕre
corrosion *s* rosio *f*
corrosive *adj* corrosivus; (*fig*) mordax
corrupt *vt* corrumpĕre, depravare; (*a girl*) stuprare
corrupt *adj* corruptus, putridus; (*fig*) pravus, impurus; venalis; **—ly** corrupte; inceste, turpiter
corrupter *s* corruptor *m*, corruptrix *f*, perditor *m*, perditrix *f*
corruption *s* corruptio, putredo *f*; (*fig*) depravatio, pravitas *f*
corselet *s* lorica *f*
corvette *s* celox *f*
cosily *adv* commode
cosmetic *s* medicamen *n*
cost *s* pretium *n*, impensa *f*; **— of living** anona *f*
cost *vi* (con)stare, venire
costliness *s* caritas *f*
costly *adj* carus; (*extravagant*) sumptuosus, lautus
costume *s* habit·us -ūs, vestit·us -ūs *m*
cosy *adj* commodus, gratus
cot *s* lectulus *m*; (*mil*) grabatus *m*
cottage *s* casa *f*, tugurium *n*
cotton *s* xylinum *n*
cotton *adj* gossipinus
couch *s* cubile, pulvinar *n*; lectus *m*
cough *s* tussis *f*; **to have a bad —** male tussire
cough *vi* tussire
council *s* concilium *n*
councilor *s* consiliarius *m*
counsel *s* (*advice*) consilium *n*; (*person*) advocatus *m*
counsel *vt* consulĕre, monēre
counselor *s* consiliarius, consiliator *m*
count *s* computatio, ratio *f*; (*of indictment*) caput *n*
count *vt* numerare, computare; (*to regard as*) ducĕre, habēre; **to — up** enumerare; *vi* aestimari, habēri; **to — upon** confidĕre (*with dat*)
countenance *s* facies *f*, vult·us -ūs, aspect·us -ūs *m*; **to put out of —** confundĕre, perturbare
countenance *vt* favēre (*with dat*), indulgēre (*with dat*), adjuvare
counter *s* (*of shop*) abacus *m*; (*in games*) calculus *m*
counteract *vt* obsistĕre (*with dat*); (*a sickness*) medēri (*with dat*)
counteraction *s* oppositio *f*
counterfeit *vt* imitari, simulare, fingĕre, adulterare
counterfeit *adj* simulatus, spurius, ficticius, adulterinus
counterfeit *s* (*money*) nummus adulterinus *m*; simulatio, imitatio *f*
counterfeiter *s* imitator, falsarius *m*
countermand *vt* renuntiare
counterpart *s* res gemella *f*; par *m, f & n*
countersign *vt* contrascribĕre
countless *adj* innumerabilis, innumerus
country *s* terra, regio *f*; (*territory*) fines *m pl*; (*not city*) rus *n*; (*native*) patria *f*
country house *s* villa *f*
countryman *s* civis, popularis *m*
countryside *s* rus *n*, agri *m pl*
couple *s* par *n*; mariti *m pl*; **a — of** duo
couple *vt* copulare, unire; *vi* (*of animals*) coire
courage *s* virtus *f*, animus *m*, fortitudo *f*; **to lose —** animos dimittĕre; **to take —** bono animo esse
courageous *adj* fortis, animosus, acer; **—ly** fortiter, acriter
courier *s* cursor, nuntius, tabellarius *m*
course *s* (*movement*) curs·us -ūs *m*; (*of life*) ratio *f*; (*of water*) duct·us -ūs *m*; (*route*) iter *n*; (*at table*) ferculum *n*; (*order*) series *f*; (*for racing*) circus *m*, stadium *n*; **in due —** mox; **in the — of** inter (*with acc*); **of —** certe, scilicet
court *s* (*law*) forum, tribunal, judi-

cium *n*, judices *m pl*; (*open area*) area *f*; (*of house*) atrium *n*; (*palace*) aula *f*; (*retinue*) comitat·us -ūs *m*
court *vt* colĕre, ambire; (*woman*) petĕre; (*danger*) se offerre (*with dat*)
courteous *adj* comis, urbanus; **—ly** comiter, urbane
courtesan *s* meretrix *f*
courtesy *s* comitas, urbanitas *f*; (*act*) officium *n*
courtier *s* aulicus *m*
courtly *adj* aulicus; officiosus
court-martial *s* judicium castrense *n*
courtship *s* amor *m*, ambitio *f*
courtyard *s* aula *f*
cousin *s* consobrinus *m*, consobrina *f*, patruelis *m* & *f*
cove *s* sin·us -ūs *m*
covenant *s* pactum *n*, pactio *f*
covenant *vi* pacisci, stipulari
cover *s* tegmen, integumentum *n*; (*lid*) operculum *n*; (*shelter*) tectum *n*, (*mil*) praesidium *n*; (*pretense*) species *f*; **under — of** sub (*with abl*), sub specie (*with genit*)
cover *vt* tegĕre, operire; (*to hide*) celare, velare; **to — up** obtegĕre
coverlet *s* lodix *f*
covet *vt* concupiscĕre, cupĕre, appetĕre
covetous *adj* avidus, appetens, cupidus; **—ly** avide, avare, appetenter
covey *s* grex *m*
cow *vt* domare
coward *s* homo *or* miles ignavus *m*
cowardice *s* ignavia *f*
cowardly *adj* ignavus
cower *vi* sudsidĕre
cowherd *s* bubulcus *m*
cowl *s* cucullus *m*
coy *adj* verecundus, pudens; **—ly** verecunde, pudenter
coyness *s* verecundia *f*, pudor *m*
cozily *adv* commode, jucunde
cozy *adj* commodus, jucundus
crab *s* cancer *m*
crabbed *adj* morosus, difficilis
crack *s* fissura, rima *f*; (*noise*) crepit·us -ūs *m*; **at — of dawn** prima luce
cracked *adj* rimosus; (*fig*) cerritus, delirus
cracker *s* crustulum *n*
crackle *vi* crepitare
crackling *s* crepit·us -ūs *m*
cradle *s* cunae *f pl*, cunabula *n pl*
craft *s* (*cunning*) astutia *f*, artes *f pl*, dolus *m*; (*skill*) ars *f*; (*trade*) ars *f*; (*boat*) scapha, cymba *f*, navigium *n*
craftily *adv* callide, astute; dolose
crafty *adj* astutus, callidus, subdolus
craftsman *s* artifex, faber *m*
craftsmanship *s* artificium *n*, man·us -ūs *f*
cram *vt* farcire; **to — together** constipare
cramp *s* spasmus *m*
cramp *vt* comprimĕre, coartare
crane *s* (*bird*) grus *m* & *f*; (*machine*) tolleno *f*; machina *f*
crank *s* (*machine*) uncus *m*; (*person*) morosus *m*
crash *s* fragor, strepit·us -ūs *m*, ruina *f*
crash *vi* strepĕre, frangorem dare
crater *s* crater *m*
crave *vt* efflagitare, appetĕre, concupiscĕre, desiderare
craven *adj* ignavus atque abjectus
craving *s* desiderium *n*, appetitio *f*
crawl *vi* repĕre, serpĕre
crayfish *s* commarus *m*
crayon *s* creta *f*
craze *s* libido *f*
craziness *s* imbecillitas, mens alienata *f*, furor *m*
crazy *adj* imbecillus, demens, cerritus; **to drive —** mentem alienare (*with genit*)
creak *vi* stridēre, crepitare
creaking *s* stridor, crepit·us -ūs *m*
creaking *adj* stridulus
cream *s* flos lactis *m*; (*fig*) flos *m*
crease *s* plica, ruga *f*
crease *vt* corrugare, rugare
create *vt* creare; (*fig*) fingĕre
creation *s* (*act*) creatio *f*; (*world*) summa rerum *f*, mundus *m*; (*fig*) opus *n*
creative *adj* creatrix, effectrix
creator *s* creator, opifex, auctor *m*
creature *s* animal *n*; homo *m*; (*lackey*) minister *m*
credence *s* fides *f*; **to give — to** credĕre (*with dat*)
credentials *s* litterae commendaticiae *f pl*; testimonia *n pl*
credibility *s* fides, auctoritas *f*
credible *adj* credibilis; (*of persons*) locuples
credit *s* (*authority*) auctoritas *f*; (*faith*) fides *f*; (*reputation*) existimatio, fama *f*; (*com*) fides *f*; (*recognition*) laus *f*
credit *vt* credĕre (*with dat*); (*com*) acceptum referre (*with dat*)
creditable *adj* honorificus, honestus, laudabilis
creditor *s* creditor *m*
credulity *s* credulitas *f*
credulous *adj* credulus; **—ly** credens
creed *s* fides, religio *f*, dogma *n*
creek *s* aestuarium *n*; fluvius *m*
creep *vi* repĕre, serpĕre; (*of flesh*) horrēre
crescent *s* luna crescens *f*
crescent-shaped *adj* lunatus
crest *s* crista *f*
crested *adj* cristatus
crestfallen *adj* dejectus, demissus
crevice *s* rima, rimula *f*
crew *s* grex *m*; (*of ship*) remiges, nautae *m pl*
crib *s* (*manger*) praesepe *n*; (*small bed*) lectulus *m*
cricket *s* gryllus *m*, cicada *f*
crier *s* praeco *m*
crime *s* scelus, delictum, maleficium, flagitium *n*
Crimea *s* Tauris *f*
criminal *adj* criminosus, scelestus, flagitiosus; **—ly** nefarie, improbe; (*law*) criminaliter
criminal *s* reus, sceleratus *m*
crimp *vt* crispare

crimson *adj* coccineus
crimson *s* coccum *n*
cringe *vi* adulari, assentari
cringing *s* adulatio abjecta *f*
cripple *s* claudus *m*
cripple *vt* claudum facĕre, mutilare, debilitare; (*fig*) frangĕre
crippled *adj* mancus, claudus
crisis *s* discrimen *n*
crisp *adj* crispus, fragilis; (*fig*) alacer
criterion *s* norma *f*, indicium *n*, index *m*
critic *s* judex, censor, existimator *m*; (*literary*) criticus, grammaticus *m*
critical *adj* criticus, intellegens; (*careful*) accuratus; (*blaming*) fastidiosus, censorius; (*crucial*) anceps, periculosus; **—ly** accurate; periculose
criticism *s* ars critica *f*; censura, reprehensio *f*, judicium *n*
criticize *vt* judicare; carpĕre, reprehendĕre, agitare, castigare
croak *vi* coaxare; (*of raven*) crocitare, crocire; (*fig*) queritari
croaking *s* crocitatio *f*; (*fig*) querimonia *f*
croaking *adj* raucus
crock *s* olla *f*
crocodile *s* crocodilus *m*
crook *s* pedum *n*
crook *vt* curvare, flectĕre
crooked *adj* curvatus, flexus; (*fig*) pravus, dolosus; **—ly** prave
crop *s* (*of grain*) messis, seges *f*; (*of bird*) ingluvies *f*
crop *vt* abscidĕre, tondēre; (*to harvest*) metĕre; (*to browse*) carpĕre
cross *s* crux *f*; (*figure*) quincunx *m*, decussis *f*; (*fig*) molestia *f*, cruciat·us -ūs *m*
cross *adj* transversus; (*contrary*) adversus; (*peevish*) acerbus, morosus
cross *vt* transire, transgredi; (*river*) trajicĕre; (*mountain*) transcendĕre; (*to thwart*) frustrari, adversari; **to — out** expungĕre, delēre
cross-examination *s* percontatio, interrogatio *f*
cross-examine *vt* percontari, interrogare
crossing *s* transit·us -ūs, traject·us -ūs *m*; (*of roads*) bivium *n*; (*of three roads*) trivium *n*; (*of four roads*) quadrivium *n*
cross-roads *s* quadrivium *n*
crouch *vi* se submittĕre, subsidĕre
crow *s* (*bird*) cornix *f*; (*of cock*) cant·us -ūs *m*, gallicinium *n*
crow *vi* (*of cocks*) canĕre, cucurire; (*to boast*) jactare, gestire
crowbar *s* vectis *f*
crowd *s* turba, frequentia *f*, concurs·us -ūs *m*; **in —s** gregatim
crowd *vt* arctare, stipare, premĕre; *vi* frequentare; **to — around** stipare, circumfundi
crowded *adj* confertus, frequens, spissus
crowing *s* gallicinium *n*, cant·us -ūs *m*
crown *s* corona *f*, diadema *n*; (*top*) vertex *m*; (*fig*) apex *m*
crown *vt* coronare; (*with garlands, etc.*) cingĕre; (*fig*) cumulare
crucifix *s* imago Christi cruci affixi *f*
crucifixion *s* crucis supplicium *n*
crucify *vt* in cruce suffigĕre
crude *adj* crudus; rudis, incultus, informis; **—ly** imperfecte; inculte
cruel *adj* crudelis, atrox, saevus; **—ly** crudeliter, saeve, dure
cruelty *s* crudelitas, atrocitas, saevitia *f*
cruet *s* guttus *m*, acetabulum *n*
cruise *vi* circumvectari, navigare
cruise *s* navigatio *f*
crumb *s* mica *f*
crumble *vt* friare, putrefacĕre, comminuĕre, conterĕre; *vi* collabi, friari, corruĕre
crumbling *adj* puter, friabilis
crumple *vt* corrugare, duplicare
crunch *vt* dentibus frangĕre
crush *vt* contundĕre, conterĕre; (*fig*) opprimĕre, affligĕre
crush *s* contusio *f*; (*crowd*) turba, frequentia *f*
crust *s* crusta *f*, crustum *n*
crusty *adj* crustosus; (*fig*) cerebrosus, stomachosus
crutch *s* fulcrum *n*
cry *vt* clamare, clamitare; **to — out** exclamare, vociferari; *vi* (*to shout*) clamare, clamitare; (*to weep*) lacrimare, flēre; (*of infant*) vagire; **to — out** exclamare; **to — out against** objurgare
cry *s* clamor *m*; (*of infant*) vagit·us -ūs *m*; (*weeping*) plorat·us -ūs *m*
crying *s* flet·us -ūs, plorat·us -ūs *m*
crypt *s* crypta *f*
crystal *adj* crystallinus, vitreus
crystal *s* crystallum *n*
crystal-clear *adj* pellucidus
cub *s* catulus *m*
cube *s* cubus *m*
cubic *adj* cubicus
cubit *s* cubitum *n*, ulna *f*
cuckoo *s* coccyx, cuculus *m*
cucumber *s* cucumis *m*
cud *s* ruma *f*, rumen *n*; **to chew the —** ruminare
cudgel *s* fustis *m*
cue *s* (*hint*) nut·us -ūs *m*, signum, indicium *n*
cuff *s* (*blow*) colaphus *m*; (*of sleeves*) extrema manica *f*
cull *vt* carpĕre, legĕre, decerpĕre
culminate *vi* ad summum fastigium venire
culpable *adj* culpandus, nocens
culprit *s* reus *m*, rea *f*
cultivate *vt* colĕre; (*the mind*) excolĕre; (*friends*) fovēre
cultivation *s* cultura *f*, cult·us -ūs *m*
cultivator *s* cultor, colonus *m*
culture *s* cultura *f*, cult·us -ūs *m*
cumbersome *adj* onerosus, impediens
cunning *adj* sollers, callidus, doctus, peritus; (*in bad sense*) astutus
cunning *s* calliditas, peritia; astutia *f*
cup *s* poculum *n*, calix *m*; (*of flower*) calyx *m*

cupbearer *s* pocillator *m*
cupboard *s* armarium *n*
Cupid *s* Cupido, Amor *m*
cupidity *s* cupiditas *f*
cupola *s* tholus *m*; turricula rotunda *f*
cur *s* canis *m*; (*fig*) scelestus *m*
curable *adj* medicabilis, sanabilis
curative *adj* medicabilis
curator *s* curator *m*
curb *s* frenum *n*; (*fig*) coercitio *f*, frenum *n*
curb *vt* frenare, infrenare; (*fig*) coercēre, cohibēre
curdle *vt* coagulare; *vi* coagulare, concrescĕre
cure *s* (*remedy*) remedium *n*; (*process*) sanatio *f*
cure *vt* medēri (*with dat*), sanare; (*to pickle*) salire
curiosity *s* curiositas *f*; (*thing*) miraculum *n*
curious *adj* curiosus; (*strange*) mirus, novus, insolitus; **—ly** curiose; mirabiliter, mirum in modum
curl *vt* (*hair*) crispare; torquēre; *vi* crispari; (*of smoke*) volvi
curl *s* (*natural*) cirrus *m*; (*artificial*) cincinnus *m*
curly *adj* crispus
currency *s* (*money*) moneta *f*; (*use*) us·us -ūs *m*
current *adj* vulgaris, usitatus; **—ly** vulgo
current *s* flumen *n*; (*of air*) afflat·us -ūs *m*, aura *f*; **against the —** adverso flumine; **with the —** secundo flumine
curse *s* exsecratio, maledictio *f*, maledictum *n*; (*fig*) pestis *f*
curse *vt* maledicĕre (*with dat*), exsecrari; *vi* exsecratione uti
cursed *adj* exsecrabilis
cursorily *adv* breviter, summatim
cursory *adj* levis, brevis
curt *adj* abruptus; **—ly** breviter
curtail *vt* minuĕre, coartare; decurtare
curtain *s* velum, aulaeum *n*
curvature *s* curvatura *f*
curve *s* curvamen *n*, flex·us -ūs *m*, curvatura *f*
curve *vt* incurvare, flectĕre, inflectĕre, arcuare
curved *adj* curvatus, curvus; (*as a sickle*) falcatus
cushion *s* pulvinar *n*; (*on a seat*) sedularia *n pl*
custard *s* artolaganus *m*
custody *s* custodia, tutela *f*; (*imprisonment*) carcer *m*; **to keep in —** custodire
custom *s* mos, us·us -ūs *m*, consuetudo *f*, institutum, praescriptum *n*; (*duty*) portorium, vectigal *n*
customary *adj* usitatus, consuetus, tralaticius
customer *s* emptor *m*
customs officer *s* portitor *m*
cut *vt* secare; (*to fell*) caedĕre; (*to mow*) succidĕre; **to — apart** intercidĕre, dissecare; **to — away** recidĕre, abscindĕre; (*to amputate*) amputare; **to — down** caedĕre; (*to kill*) occidĕre; **to — in pieces** concidĕre; **to — off** praecidĕre, abscindĕre; (*the head*) detruncare; (*to intercept*) intercludĕre, prohibēre; (*to destroy*) exstinguĕre; **to — open** incidĕre; **to — out** exsecare; (*out of rock, etc.*) excidĕre; **to — short** intercidĕre; (*to abridge*) praecidĕre; (*fig*) (*to interrupt*) interpellare; **to — up** minutatim concidĕre; (*enemy*) trucidare
cutlass *s* ensis, gladius *m*
cutlery *s* cultri *m pl*
cutlet *s* offa *f*, frustum *n*
cutthroat *s* sicarius *m*
cutting *adj* (*sharp*) acutus; (*fig*) mordax
cutting *s* (*act*) sectio, consectio, exsectio *f*; (*thing*) segmen *n*
cuttlefish *s* loligo, sepia *f*
cycle *s* orbis *m*
cylinder *s* cylindrus *m*
cylindrical *adj* cylindratus
cymbal *s* cymbalum *n*
cynic *adj* cynicus
cynic *s* cynicus *m*
cynical *adj* mordax, difficilis; **—ly** mordaciter
cynicism *s* acerbitas *f*
cypress *s* cupressus *f*

D

dab *vt* illidĕre
dab *s* massula *f*
dabble *vi* **to — in** gustare
dactyl *s* dactylus *m*
dactylic *adj* dactylicus
daffodil *s* asphodelus, narcissus *m*
dagger *s* pugio *m*, sica *f*
daily *adj* diurnus, quotidianus *or* cottidianus
daily *adv* quotidie *or* cottidie, in dies
dainty *adj* (*of persons*) fastidiosus, mollis, elegans; (*of things*) delicatus, exquisitus
dairy *s* cella lactaria *f*
daisy *s* bellis *f*
dale *s* vallis *f*
dalliance *s* lus·us -ūs *m*, lascivia *f*
dally *vi* morari; (*to trifle*) nugari, ludificari
dam *s* moles *f*, agger *m*; (*of animals*) mater *f*
damage *s* damnum, incommodum, detrimentum *n*; (*injury*) injuria, noxa *f*
damage *vt* nocēre (*with dat*), laedĕre; (*reputation*) violare

dame *s* domina, hera, matrona *f*
damn *vt* damnare, exsecrari
damnable *adj* damnabilis, detestabilis
damnably *adv* damnabiliter, improbe
damnation *s* damnatio *f*
damp *adj* (h)umidus
dampen *vt* humectare; (*fig*) infringĕre, restinguĕre
dampness *s* uligo *f*
damsel *s* puella, virgo *f*
dance *s* saltat·us -ūs *m*, saltatio *f*
dance *vi* saltare
dancer *s* saltator *m*
dancing *s* saltatio *f*, saltat·us -ūs *m*
dandelion *s* taraxacum *n*
dandruff *s* porrigo *f*
dandy *s* homo bellus et lepidus *m*
danger *s* periculum *n*
dangerous *adj* periculosus; **—ly** periculose, graviter
dangle *vi* pendēre, dependēre
dangling *adj* pendulus
dank *adj* (h)umidus, uvidus, udus
dappled *adj* variatus, variegatus
dare *vt* provocare; *vi* audēre
daring *adj* audax; **—ly** audacter
daring *s* audacia, audentia *f*
dark *adj* obscurus, opacus; (*in color*) ater, fuscus; (*fig*) obscurus, ambiguus; atrox; **—ly** obscure
dark *s* tenebrae *f pl*; obscurum *n*; **to keep in the —** celare
darken *vt* obscurare, occaecare; (*of colors*) infuscare
darkness *s* obscuritas, opacitas *f*, tenebrae *f pl*
darling *adj* suavis, mellitus, carus, dilectus
darling *s* deliciae *f pl*, corculum *n*
darn *vt* resarcire
dart *s* jaculum, spiculum *n*
dart *vt* jaculari, jacĕre; *vi* provolare, emicare, se conjicĕre
dash *vt* (*to splash*) aspergĕre; (*hopes*) frustrari, frangĕre; **to — against** illidĕre, incutĕre, offendĕre; **to — off** (*to write hurriedly*) scriptitare; **to — to pieces** discutĕre; **to — to the ground** prosternĕre; *vi* (*to rush*) ruĕre, ferri
dash *s* impet·us -ūs *m*; curs·us -ūs *m*; (*animation*) alacritas *f*; (*small amount*) admixtio *f*
dashing *adj* acer, alacer, fulgidus, splendidus
data *s* facta *n pl*
date *s* (*time*) dies *m & f*, tempus *n*; (*fruit*) palmula *f*; **to become out of —** exolescĕre; **to —** adhuc; **out of —** obsoletus
date *vt* diem ascribĕre (*with dat*); *vi* **to — from** oriri ab (*with abl*), originem trahĕre ab (*with abl*)
date palm *s* phoenix, palma *f*
dative *s* dativus *m*
daub *vt* oblinĕre, illinĕre
daughter *s* filia *f*
daughter-in-law *s* nurus *f*
daunt *vt* pavefacĕre, perterrēre
dauntless *adj* impavidus, intrepidus; **—ly** impavide, intrepide
dawdle *vi* morari, cessare, cunctari
dawn *s* aurora, prima lux *f*, diluculum *n*; **at —** prima luce
dawn *vi* illucescĕre, dilucescĕre; (*fig*) **to — on** occurrĕre (*with dat*)
day *s* dies *m & f*; lux *f*, sol *m*; **by —** interdiu; **— by —** in dies; **every —** quotidie, cottidie; **from — to —** in dies; **next —** postridie; **some —** olim; **the — after tomorrow** perendie; **the — before** pridie
day *adj* diurnus, dialis
daybreak *s* lux prima *f*; **before —** antelucio
daylight *s* lux *f*, dies *m & f*
daystar *s* Lucifer, Phosphorus *m*
daytime *s* dies *m*, tempus diurnum *n*; **in the —** interdiu
daze *s* stupor *m*
daze *vt* obstupefacĕre
dazzle *vt* obcaecare, praestringĕre
dazzling *adj* fulgidus, splendidus
deacon *s* diaconus *m*
dead *adj* mortuus; defunctus; (*fig*) torpidus, segnis, iners
dead *s* manes *m pl*; **— of night** media nox *f*; **— of winter** summa hiems *f*
dead *adv* omnino, totaliter, prorsus
deaden *vt* hebetare, obtundĕre; *vi* hebetari, obtundi
deadly *adj* mortifer, letalis; (*fig*) capitalis, implacabilis
deaf *adj* surdus; **to be — to** non audire
deafen *vt* exsurdare, obtundĕre
deaf-mute *adj* surdus idemque mutus
deafness *s* surditas *f*
deal *s* (*quantity*) numerus *m*, copia *f*; (*com*) negotium *n*; **a good — longer** multo diutius; **a good — of** aliquantus
deal *vt* partiri, dividĕre, distribuĕre; *vi* (*com*) mercari, negotiari; **to — with** (*to treat of*) agĕre de (*with abl*), tractare
dealer *s* mercator, negotiator, distributor *m*
dealing *s* negotiatio, mercatura *f*; (*doing*) facta *n pl*
dean *s* decanus *m*
dear *adj* carus, dulcis, gratus; (*costly*) carus, preciosus; **—ly** valde, ardenter; (*at high cost*) magni, magno
dear *interj* (*dismay*) hei!; (*surprise*) ahem!
dearness *s* caritas *f*
dearth *s* inopia, penuria, fames *f*
death *s* mors *f*, obit·us -ūs, interit·us -ūs *m*; (*in violent form*) nex *f*
deathbed *s* **on the —** moriens, moribundus
deathless *adj* immortalis
deathlike *adj* cadaverosus, luridus
deathly *adj* pallidus
debase *vt* depravare, corrumpĕre; (*coinage*) adulterare; **to — oneself** se demittĕre, se prosternĕre
debasement *s* adulteratio *f*; ignominia *f*, dedecus *n*
debatable *adj* disputabilis, controversiosus, ambiguus

debate *vt* disputare, disceptare; *vi* argumentari, disserĕre
debate *s* disceptatio, controversia, altercatio *f*; (*law*) actio *f*
debater *s* disputator *m*
debauch *vt* stuprare, corrumpĕre, vitiare; *vi* (*to revel*) debacchari
debauchery *s* ganea *f*, stuprum *n*
debilitate *vt* debilitare
debit *s* expensum *n*
debit *vt* in expensum referre
debt *s* aes alienum *n*; (*fig*) debitum *n*; **to pay off a —** aes alienum persolvĕre; **to run up a —** aes alienum contrahĕre
debtor *s* debitor *m*
decade *s* decem anni *m pl*
decadence *s* occas·us -ūs *m*
decadent *adj* degener
decalogue *s* decalogus *m*
decamp *vi* (*mil*) castra movēre; (*fig*) aufugĕre, discedĕre
decant *vt* diffundĕre
decanter *s* lagoena *f*
decapitate *vt* detruncare
decay *s* tabes, ruina *f*, laps·us -ūs *m*; (*fig*) defectio *f*
decay *vi* putrescĕre, tabescĕre, senescĕre
decease *s* mors *f*, obit·us -ūs *m*, decess·us -ūs *m*
deceased *adj* mortuus, defunctus
deceit *s* fraus *f*, dolus *m*
deceitful *adj* fallax, dolosus, fraudulentus; **—ly** fallaciter, dolose
deceive *vt* decipĕre, fallĕre, fraudare
December *s* (mensis) December *m*
decency *s* decorum *n*, honestas *f*
decent *adj* honestus, pudicus; **—ly** honeste, pudenter
deception *s* deceptio, fallacia, fraus *f*
deceptive *adj* fallax, fraudulentus, vanus, falsus
decide *vt & vi* (*dispute*) disceptare, dijudicare, decernĕre; **to — to** constituĕre (*with inf*), statuĕre (*with inf*); **the senate decided** placuit senatui; visum est senatui
decided *adj* firmus, constans; (*of things*) certus; **—ly** certe, plane
deciduous *adj* caducus
decimate *vt* decimare; (*fig*) depopulari
decipher *vt* explicare, expedire, enodare
decision *s* sententia *f*; judicium, arbitrium, decretum *n*; (*of senate*) auctoritas *f*
decisive *adj* certus, firmus; **—ly** praecise
deck *vt* exornare, ornare; (*table*) sternĕre
deck *s* pons *m*
declamatory *adj* declamatorius; (*fig*) inflatus
declaration *s* declaratio, professio, affirmatio *f*; (*of war*) denuntiatio *f*
declare *vt* declarare, affirmare, aperire, profitēri; (*war*) denuntiare, indicĕre; (*proclamation*) edicĕre; *vi* **to — for** favēre (*with dat*)
declension *s* declinatio *f*
declinable *adj* declinabilis, casualis
declination *s* declinatio *f*; (*decay*) defectio *f*
decline *s* (*slope*) declive *n*; (*of strength*) defectio, diminutio *f*
decline *vt* (*to refuse*) recusare, renuĕre, abnuĕre; (*gram*) declinare, flectĕre; (*battle*) detrectare; *vi* vergĕre, inclinare; (*to decay, fail*) deficĕre, minui, decrescĕre; (*of prices*) laxare
decode *vt* enodare
decompose *vt* dissolvĕre, resolvĕre; *vi* tabescĕre, putescĕre, dissolvi
decomposition *s* dissolutio *f*
decorate *vt* ornare, decorare
decoration *s* ornatio *f*; (*ornament*) ornamentum *n*; (*distinction*) decus *n*
decorator *s* exornator *m*
decorous *adj* decorus, modestus, pudens; **—ly** decore, modeste, pudenter
decorum *s* decorum, honestum *n*, pudor *m*
decoy *s* illecebra *f*, illicium *n*
decoy *vt* allicĕre, inescare; (*fig*) illicĕre
decrease *s* deminutio, imminutio *f*
decrease *vt* (de)minuĕre, imminuĕre, extenuare; *vi* decrescĕre, (de)minui
decree *s* decretum, edictum *n*; (*of senate*) consultum *n*, auctoritas *f*; (*of assembly*) scitum *n*
decree *vt* decernĕre, edicĕre; (*of assembly*) jubēre, sciscĕre; **the senate —s** senatui placet, senatui videtur
decrepit *adj* decrepitus, debilis
decry *vt* detrectare, obtrectare, vituperare
dedicate *vt* dedicare, consecrare, devovēre
dedication *s* dedicatio, devotio *f*; (*of a book*) nuncupatio *f*
deduce *vt* deducĕre, concludĕre
deducible *adj* consectarius
deduct *vt* detrahĕre, subtrahĕre, demĕre
deduction *s* deductio, deminutio *f*; (*inference*) conclusio *f*, consequens *n*
deed *s* factum, facinus *n*; (*law*) syngrapha *f*, instrumentum *n*
deem *vt* judicare, existimare, ducĕre, habēre
deep *adj* altus, profundus; (*of sounds*) gravis; (*of color*) satur; (*fig*) abstrusus, gravis; **—ly** alte, profunde; (*inwardly*) penitus; (*fig*) valde, graviter, vehementer
deep *s* profundum, altum *n*
deepen *vt* defodĕre; (*fig*) augēre; *vi* altior fieri; (*fig*) crescĕre, densare
deer *s* cervus *m*, cerva *f*; (*fallow deer*) dama *f*
deface *vt* deformare, turpare, foedare
defaced *adj* deformis
defacement *s* deformitas *f*
defamation *s* calumnia *f*, opprobrium *n*
defamatory *adj* probrosus, contumeliosus
defame *vt* diffamare, infamare, calumniari

default *s* culpa *f*, delictum *n*, defect·us -ūs *m*
defeat *s* clades *f*; (*at polls*) repulsa *f*
defeat *vt* vincĕre, superare; (*to baffle*) frustrari
defect *s* vitium, mendum *n*; (*lack*) defect·us -ūs *m*
defect *vi* (*to desert*) deficĕre
defection *s* defectio *f*
defective *adj* vitiosus, imperfectus, mancus; (*gram*) defectivus
defend *vt* defendĕre, custodire, tuēri; (*in court*) patrocinari
defendant *s* reus *m*, rea *f*
defender *s* defensor, propugnator *m*; (*law*) patronus *m*
defense *s* (*act*) defensio *f*; praesidium, munimentum *n*, tutela *f*; (*law*) patrocinium *n*; (*speech*) defensio *f*
defenseless *adj* inermis, infensus; defensoribus nudatus
defensible *adj* excusabilis, justus; inexpugnabilis
defensive *adj* defendens; **— weapons** arma *n pl*
defer *vt* differre; *vi* obsequi
deference *s* observantia, reverentia *f*, obsequium *n*; **out of —** reverenter
defiance *s* provocatio, ferocia *f*
defiant *adj* minax, insolens; **—ly** insolenter
deficiency *s* defectio, inopia, penuria *f*, defect·us -ūs *m*
deficient *adj* inops, mancus; **to be —** deficĕre, deesse
deficit *s* lacuna *f*
defile *s* fauces *f pl*
defile *vt* contaminare, inquinare; (*fig*) foedare
define *vt* (*meaning*) explicare; (*limits*) (de)finire, circumscribĕre, terminare
definite *adj* definitus, certus; **—ly** certe, certo, prorsus; definite
definition *s* definitio *f*
definitive *adj* definitivus; **—ly** definite, distincte
deflect *vt* deflectĕre, declinare; *vi* deflectĕre, errare
deflection *s* deflexio, declinatio *f*, flex·us -ūs *m*
deflower *vt* stuprare
deform *vt* deformare
deformed *adj* deformatus, deformis, distortus, pravus
deformity *s* deformitas, pravitas *f*
defraud *vt* fraudare, defraudare
defray *vt* praebēre, suppeditare
defunct *adj* defunctus, mortuus
defy *vt* provocare, contemnĕre, spernĕre
degeneracy *s* mores corrupti *m pl*
degenerate *adj* degener
degenerate *vi* degenerare
degradation *s* dedecus *n*, ignominia, infamia *f*
degrade *vt* dejicĕre, abdicare; ex loco movēre
degrading *adj* indignus
degree *s* grad·us -ūs, ordo *m*
deification *s* apotheosis *f*
deify *vt* divum habēre, inter deos referre, consecrare
deign *vt* dignari, curare
deism *s* deismus *m*
deity *s* numen *n*; deus *m*, dea *f*
dejected *adj* afflictus, demissus; **—ly** maeste
dejection *s* animi abjectio, maestitia *f*
delay *s* mora, cunctatio *f*
delay *vt* detinēre, tardare, remorari; *vi* morari, cunctari
delectable *adj* amoenus, jucundus
delegate *s* legatus *m*
delegate *vt* delegare, mandare, committĕre
delegation *s* delegatio, legatio *f*
delete *vt* delēre
deletion *s* litura *f*
deliberate *adj* deliberatus, consideratus, cautus, prudens; (*speech*) lentus; **—ly** deliberate, de industria; lente
deliberate *vi* deliberare, considerare, consulĕre
deliberation *s* deliberatio, consultatio *f*
delicacy *s* subtilitas, tenuitas *f*; elegantia *f*; (*manner*) lux·us -ūs *m*; (*health*) suavitas *f*; (*food*) cuppedia *f*
delicate *adj* (*tender*) delicatus, tener, mollis, exquisitus; (*of texture*) subtilis; (*in taste*) elegans, fastidiosus; (*in health*) infirmus; **—ly** delicate; eleganter; subtiliter
delicious *adj* suavis, dulcis
delight *s* delectatio *f*, gaudium *n*, voluptas *f*
delight *vt* delectare, oblectare; *vi* **to — in** delectari (*with abl*)
delightful *adj* suavis, jucundus; **—ly** suaviter, jucunde
delineate *vt* delineare, describĕre, adumbrare
delineation *s* designatio, descriptio *f*
delinquency *s* delictum *n*
delinquent *s* nocens *m & f*, noxius *m*
delirious *adj* delirus, phreneticus
delirium *s* delirium *n*, phrenesis *f*
deliver *vt* (*to hand over*) tradĕre, dare; (*to free*) liberare, eripĕre; (*to surrender*) prodĕre; (*speech*) habēre; (*sentence*) dicĕre; (*message*) referre; (*blow*) intendĕre; (*child*) obstetricari
deliverance *s* liberatio *f*
deliverer *s* liberator *m*; nuntius *m*
delivery *s* liberatio *f*; (*of goods*) traditio *f*; (*of speech*) actio, pronuntiatio *f*; (*of child*) part·us -ūs *m*
delude *vt* decipĕre, deludĕre
deluge *s* diluvium *n*, inundatio *f*
deluge *vt* inundare, obruĕre
delusion *s* delusio *f*, error *m*
demagogue *s* plebicola *m*
demand *s* postulatio, petitio *f*, postulatum *n*
demand *vt* postulare, flagitare, poscĕre; exigĕre
demarcation *s* confinium *n*
demean *vt* **to — oneself** se demittĕre
demeanor *s* gest·us -ūs *m*, mores *m pl*

demerit *s* culpa *f*, delictum *n*
demigod *s* heros *m*
demise *s* decess·us -ūs, obit·us -ūs *m*
democracy *s* civitas popularis *f*, liber populus *m*
democrat *s* homo popularis *m*
democratic *adj* popularis; **—ally** populi voluntate
demolish *vt* demoliri, disjicĕre, diruĕre, destruĕre
demolition *s* demolitio, destructio *f*
demon *s* daemon *m*
demonstrable *adj* demonstrabilis
demonstrably *adv* clare, manifeste
demonstrate *vt* (*to show*) monstrare, ostendĕre; (*to prove*) demonstrare
demonstration *s* demonstratio *f*
demonstrative *adj* demonstrativus; **—ly** demonstrative
demoralization *s* depravatio *f*
demoralize *vt* depravare, labefactare
demote *vt* loco movēre
demure *adj* taciturnus, modestus; **—ly** modeste, pudice
den *s* latibulum *n*
deniable *adj* infitiandus
denial *s* negatio, repudiatio *f*
denomination *s* nominatio *f*, nomen *n*; secta *f*
denote *vt* significare
denounce *vt* denuntiare, deferre
dense *adj* densus, spissus, confertus; **—ly** dense, crebro
density *s* densitas, crassitudo *f*; (*crowd*) frequentia *f*
dent *s* nota *f*
dentist *s* dentium medicus *m*
denude *vt* nudare, denudare
denunciation *s* denuntiatio, accusatio *f*
deny *vt* negare, abnegare; (*to renounce*) renuntiare
depart *vi* abire, discedĕre, proficisci; (*to die*) obire
departed *adj* mortuus, defunctus
department *s* pars, provincia *f*
departure *s* abit·us -ūs, discess·us -ūs, digress·us -ūs *m*; (*deviation*) digressio *f*; (*death*) obit·us -ūs *m*
depend *vi* **to — on** pendēre ex (*with abl*), niti (*with abl*); (*to rely on*) fidĕre (*with dat or abl*)
dependable *adj* fidus
dependence *s* clientela *f*; (*reliance*) fiducia *f*
dependency *s* provincia *f*
dependent *adj* subjectus, obediens, obnoxius
depict *vt* (de)pingĕre; describĕre, exprimĕre
deplete *vt* deminuĕre
depletion *s* deminutio *f*
deplorable *adj* miserabilis, flebilis, plorabilis
deplorably *adv* misere, pessime
deplore *vt* deplorare, deflēre
deploy *vt* (*mil*) explicare, expedire
deponent *adj* (*gram*) deponens
deportment *s* gest·us -ūs, habit·us -ūs *m*
depose *vt* (de)movēre
deposit *vt* deponĕre
deposit *s* depositum *n*, fiducia *f*
deposition *s* depositio *f*, testimonium *n*
depositor *s* depositor *m*
depot *s* (*com*) emporium *n*; (*for military supplies*) armamentarium *n*
deprave *vt* depravare
depravity *s* depravatio, turpitudo, pravitas *f*
deprecate *vt* deprecari
deprecation *s* deprecatio *f*
depreciate *vt* detrectare, obtrectare
depreciation *s* detrectatio, obrectatio *f*; (*of price*) vilitas *f*
depredation *s* spoliatio, direptio *f*
depress *vt* deprimĕre; (*fig*) infringĕre, affligĕre
depressed *adj* depressus, afflictus; (*flat*) planus; (*hollow*) cavus
depression *s* depressio, imminutio *f*; (*fig*) tristitia *f*
depressive *adj* tristis, affligens
deprivation *s* privatio, orbatio *f*; (*state*) inopia *f*
deprive *vt* privare, spoliare
depth *s* altitudo, profunditas *f*, profundum *n*; (*bottom*) fundus *m*
deputation *s* legatio *f*, legati *m pl*
deputy *s* legatus, vicarius *m*
derange *vt* (per)turbare, conturbare
deranged *adj* mente captus
derangement *s* perturbatio, confusio *f*; (*of mind*) mentis alienatio *f*
dereliction *s* derelictio, destitutio *f*
deride *vt* deridēre, irridēre
derision *s* ris·us -ūs *m*, irrisio *f*
derisive *adj* irridens
derivation *s* derivatio, origo *f*
derivative *adj* derivativus, derivatus
derive *vt* derivare, deducĕre; *vi* procedĕre, oriri
derogatory *adj* inhonestus, indignus
descend *vi* descendĕre, delabi; **to — upon** (*to attack*) irrumpĕre in (*with acc*)
descendant *s* progenies *f*; **—s** posteri *m pl*
descent *s* descens·us -ūs *m*; (*slope*) declivitas *f*, clivus *m*; (*lineage*) genus *n*
describe *vt* describĕre, perscribĕre; depingĕre; narrare
description *s* descriptio *f*; narratio *f*
desecrate *vt* profanare, polluĕre
desecration *s* profanatio, violatio *f*
desert *s* (*wilderness*) loca deserta *n pl*, solitudo *f*
desert *s* (*merit*) meritum *n*, dignitas *f*
desert *vt* deserĕre, relinquĕre; *vi* transfugĕre, deficĕre
deserter *s* desertor *m*; (*mil*) transfuga *m*
desertion *s* desertio, defectio *f*; transfugium *n*
deserve *vt* merēre, merēri
deserving *adj* meritus, dignus
design *s* (*drawing*) adumbratio *f*; (*plan*) consilium, propositum *n*
design *vt* designare; (*to sketch*) adumbrare; (*fig*) machinari

designate *vt* designare, nominare, appellare
designation *s* designatio *f*; vocabulum, nomen *n*, titulus *m*
designer *s* inventor, auctor, fabricator, machinator *m*
designing *adj* callidus
desirable *adj* optabilis, desiderabilis
desire *s* appetitio, cupiditas, cupido *f*; (*request*) rogat·us -ūs *m*
desire *vt* cupĕre, optare, expetĕre; (*to request*) orare, petĕre
desirous *adj* cupidus, appetens
desist *vi* desistĕre; (*to cease*) desinĕre
desk *s* scrinium, pulpitum *n*, mensa scriptoria *f*
desolate *adj* desolatus, solitarius; (*of persons*) afflictus
desolate *vt* devastare
desolation *s* vastatio *f*; (*state*) solitudo, vastitas *f*
despair *s* desperatio *f*
despair *vi* desperare
desperado *s* sicarius *m*
desperate *adj* desperatus; (*dangerous*) periculosus; **—ly** desperanter; **to be —ly in love** perdite amare
desperation *s* desperatio *f*
despicable *adj* abjectus, vilis, turpis
despise *vt* despicĕre, spernĕre, contemnĕre
despite *prep* contra (*with acc*)
despite *s* malevolentia *f*, odium *n*
despoil *vt* nudare, spoliare
despondency *s* animi abjectio *f*
despondent *adj* abjectus, demissus; **—ly** animo demisso
despot *s* dominus, tyrannus *m*
despotic *adj* tyrannicus; **—ally** tyrannice
despotism *s* dominatio *f*
dessert *s* secunda mensa *f*, bellaria *n pl*
destination *s* destinatio *f*, propositum *n*
destine *vt* destinare, designare
destiny *s* fatum *n*, sors *f*
destitute *adj* egens, inops, destitutus; **— of** expers (*with genit*)
destitution *s* inopia, mendicitas *f*
destroy *vt* destruĕre, subvertĕre, abolēre, delēre, vastare; **to be destroyed** interire
destroyer *s* deletor, vastator *m*
destruction *s* eversio, clades *f*, exitium *n*
destructive *adj* exitialis, perniciosus; **—ly** perniciose
desultory *adj* inconstans
detach *vt* sejungĕre, separare, amovēre
detached *adj* sejunctus; (*of houses*) solus
detachment *s* separatio *f*; (*mil*) man·us -ūs *f*; (*aloofness*) secess·us -ūs *m*
detail *s* singula *n pl*, singulae res *f pl*
detail *vt* enumerare
detain *vt* detinēre, retinēre, retardare
detect *vt* detegĕre, comperire, patefacĕre
detection *s* patefacio *f*, indicium *n*
detective *s* inquisitor *m*
detention *s* retentio *f*; (*law*) mora *f*
deter *vt* deterrēre, avertĕre
detergent *s* smegma *n*
deterioration *s* depravatio, corruptio *f*
determination *s* constantia, obstinatio *f*; (*intention*) propositum *n*
determine *vt* (*to decide*) statuĕre, constituĕre, discernĕre; (*to fix*) determinare, definire
determined *adj* certus; (*resolute*) firmus, obstinatus
detest *vt* abominari, detestari
detestable *adj* detestabilis, foedus
dethrone *vt* regno depellĕre
detonate *vi* crepare
detonation *s* fragor *m*
detour *s* circuit·us -ūs *m*
detour *vi* iter flectĕre, circumagi
detract *vt* detrahĕre; *vi* **to — from** detrectare, obtrectare
detraction *s* obtrectatio *f*
detractor *s* obtrectator *m*
detriment *s* detrimentum, damnum *n*
detrimental *adj* injuriosus, damnosus; **to be — to** detrimento esse (*with dat*)
devastate *vt* vastare, depopulari
devastation *s* (*act*) vastatio, populatio *f*; (*state*) vastitas *f*
develop *vt* evolvĕre, explicare; (*person*) alĕre; *vi* crescĕre; **to — into** evadĕre in (*with acc*)
development *s* explicatio *f*, progress·us -ūs *m*
deviate *vi* aberrare, degredi, decedĕre
deviation *s* aberratio, declinatio, digressio *f*
device *s* (*contrivance*) artificium *n*, machina *f*; (*plan*) consilium *n*; (*emblem*) insigne *n*
devil *s* diabolus, daemon *m*; **go to the —!** abi in malam crucem!
devilish *adj* diabolicus, daemonicus; (*fig*) nefandus
devious *adj* devius; vagus, erraticus
devise *vt* fingĕre, excogitare, concoquĕre
devoid *adj* inanis, vacuus, expers; **to be — of** carēre (*with abl*)
devolve *vi* **to — upon** obtingĕre, pervenire ad (*with acc*)
devote *vt* devovēre, consecrare; **to — oneself to** studĕre (*with dat*), se dedĕre (*with dat*)
devoted *adj* deditus, studiosus; **— to** studiosus (*with genit*)
devotee *s* cultor *m*
devotion *s* devotio, addictio *f*, studium *n*
devour *vt* devorare; (*fig*) haurire
devout *adj* pius, religiosus; **—ly** pie, religiose
dew *s* ros *m*
dewdrop *s* gutta roscida *f*
dewy *adj* roscidus, roridus
dexterity *s* sollertia, calliditas *f*
dexterous *adj* sollers, callidus, habilis; **—ly** sollerter, callide, habiliter
diabolical *adj* nefarius, nefandus
diagnose *vt* dijudicare, discernĕre

diagnosis *s* judicium *n*
diagonal *adj* diagonalis; **—ly** in transversum
diagram *s* forma, descriptio *f*
dial *s* solarium *n*
dialect *s* dialectus *f*, sermo *m*
dialectic *adj* dialecticus
dialogue *s* sermo *m*, colloquium *n*; (*written discussion*) dialogus *m*
diameter *s* diametros *f*
diamond *s* adamas *m*
diaper *s* striatura *f*
diaphragm *s* praecordia *n pl*
diarrhea *s* alvi profluvium *n*
diary *s* diarium *n*, commentarii diurni *m pl*
diatribe *s* convicium *n*
dice *s* tali *m pl*; (*game*) alea *f*
dictate *vt* dictare, praescribĕre
dictate *s* praescriptum, praeceptum, jussum *n*
dictation *s* dictatio *f*; dictatum *n*
dictator *s* dictator *m*
dictatorial *adj* imperiosus, dictatorius
dictatorship *s* dictatura *f*
diction *s* dictio, elocutio *f*
dictionary *s* lexicon *n*, thesaurus linguae *m*
didactic *adj* didascalicus
die *s* alea *f*
die *vi* mori, obire, perire; **to — off** demori; **to — out** emori
diet *s* (*food*) vict·us -ūs *m*; (*med*) diaeta *f*
diet *vi* secundum diaetam vivĕre
dietary *adj* diaeteticus
differ *vi* differre, discrepare, distare; (*in opinion*) dissentire
difference *s* differentia, diversitas, dissimilitudo *f*; (*of opinion*) discrepantia, dissensio *f*
different *adj* diversus, dissimilis, dispar; alius; **—ly** diverse, aliter
difficult *adj* difficilis, arduus
difficulty *s* difficultas *f*, labor *m*, negotium *n*; **with —** aegre
diffidence *s* diffidentia, verecundia *f*
diffident *adj* diffidens, verecundus, modestus; **—ly** diffidenter
diffuse *adj* diffusus; (*fig*) verbosus; **—ly** effuse, latius
diffuse *vt* diffundĕre
diffusion *s* diffusio *f*
dig *vt* fodĕre
digest *s* summarium *n*
digest *vt* (*to arrange*) digerĕre; (*food*) concoquĕre
digestion *s* concoctio *f*
digestive *adj* pepticus
digging *s* fossio, fossura *f*
digit *s* numerus *m*
dignified *adj* gravis, augustus
dignify *vt* honestare, honorare
dignitary *s* vir amplissimus *m*
dignity *s* dignitas *f*, honor *m*
digress *vi* digredi, aberrare, abire
digression *s* digressio *f*, digress·us -ūs *m*
dike *s* agger *m*
dilapidated *adj* ruinosus, obsoletus
dilate *vt* dilatare; *vi* dilatari
dilatory *adj* cunctabundus, lentus, segnis
dilemma *s* dilemma *n*; nodus *m*, angustiae *f pl*
diligence *s* diligentia *f*
diligent *adj* diligens, sedulus; **—ly** diligenter, sedulo
dilute *vt* diluĕre, miscēre
dilution *s* temperatio, mixtura *f*
dim *adj* hebes, obscurus; **to become —** hebescĕre; **—ly** obscure, obtuse
dim *vt* hebetare, obscurare; *vi* hebescĕre
dimension *s* dimensio, mensura *f*
diminish *vt* minuĕre, deminuĕre, extenuare; *vi* decrescĕre, minui
diminutive *adj* exiguus, parvulus; (*gram*) deminutivus
diminutive *s* (nomen) deminutivum *n*
dimness *s* hebetudo, obscuritas, caligo *f*
dimple *s* lacuna *f*, gelasinus *m*
din *s* strepit·us -ūs, sonit·us -ūs, fragor *m*; **to make a —** strepare
dine *vi* cenare
diner *s* conviva *m*
dingy *adj* fuscus, squalidus
dining room *s* cenatio *f*, triclinium *n*
dinner *s* cena *f*
dinner party *s* convivium *n*
dint *s* ict·us -ūs *m*; **by — of** per (*with acc*)
dip *vt* immergĕre, ting(u)ĕre; *vi* mergi, tingi; (*to sink*) premi, declinare
dip *s* devexitas, declinatio *f*
diploma *s* diploma *n*
diplomacy *s* (*function*) officium legationis *m*; (*tact*) dexteritas *f*
diplomat *s* legatus *m*
diplomatic *adj* sagax, callidus, astutus
dire *adj* dirus
direct *adj* rectus, directus; **—ly** directe, rectā; (*immediately*) statim
direct *vt* dirigĕre; (*to administer*) administrare; (*to rule*) gubernare; (*to order*) jubēre; imperare (*with dat*); (*weapon*) intendĕre; (*letter*) inscribĕre; (*attention*) admovēre
direction *s* (*act*) directio *f*; (*quarter*) pars, regio *f*; (*management*) administratio *f*; (*instruction*) mandatum *n*; (*order*) praeceptum *n*
director *s* rector, magister, gubernator, curator *m*
directory *s* (*office of director*) curatio *f*, magisterium *n*; (*body of directors*) magistri, curatores *m pl*
dirge *s* nenia *f*
dirt *s* sordes *f*; (*mud*) lutum *n*, limus *m*
dirtiness *s* spurcitia *f*; (*fig*) obscenitas *f*
dirty *adj* spurcus, sordidus; (*fig*) obscenus
dirty *vt* foedare, spurcare
disability *s* impotentia *f*
disable *vt* debilitare, enervare
disabled *adj* inhabilis, debilis, mancus

disabuse *vt* errorem eripĕre (*with dat*)
disadvantage *s* incommodum, detrimentum *n*
disadvantageous *adj* incommodus, iniquus
disagree *vi* discrepare, dissidēre, dissentire
disagreeable *adj* injucundus, molestus, insuavis, gravis; (*of smells*) graveolens; (*of persons*) difficilis, morosus
disagreeably *adv* moleste, graviter, ingrate
disagreement *s* dissensio, discordia *f*, dissidium *n*
disappear *vi* vanescĕre, fugĕre, diffugĕre, abire, perire
disappearance *s* fuga *f*, exit·us -ūs *m*
disappoint *vt* fallĕre, frustrari
disappointment *s* frustratio *f*; incommodum, malum *n*
disapproval *s* reprehensio, improbatio *f*
disapprove *vt* reprehendĕre, improbare
disarm *vt* exarmare
disarrange *vt* (per)turbare, confundĕre
disarray *s* perturbatio *f*
disaster *s* calamitas *f*, incommodum *n*
disastrous *adj* calamitosus, funestus, exitiosus; **—ly** calamitose
disavow *vt* diffitēri, infitiari
disavowal *s* infitiatio *f*
disband *vt* dimittĕre; *vi* dimitti
disbelief *s* diffidentia, incredulitas *f*
disbeliever *s* incredulus *m*
disburse *vt* erogare, expendĕre
disbursement *s* erogatio, solutio *f*
disc *s* orbis *m*
discard *vt* ponĕre, mittĕre; repudiare
discern *vt* discernĕre, distinguĕre
discernible *adj* dignoscendus
discerning *adj* perspicax, sagax, prudens
discernment *s* (*act*) perspicientia *f*; (*faculty*) discrimen, judicium *n*
discharge *vt* (*to unload*) exonerare; (*to dismiss*) dimittĕre; (*to perform*) perfungi (*with abl*); (*debt*) exsolvĕre; (*weapon*) immittĕre, jacĕre, jaculari; (*defendant*) absolvĕre
discharge *s* (*unloading*) exoneratio *f*; (*shooting*) emissio, conjectio *f*; (*dismissal*) missio *f*; (*payment*) solutio *f*; (*bodily*) defluxio *f*
disciple *s* discipulus *m*; (*fig*) sectator *m*
discipline *s* disciplina *f*
discipline *vt* assuefacĕre, coercēre
disclaim *vt* infitiari, diffitēri, negare
disclaimer *s* infitiatio *f*
disclose *vt* aperire, detegĕre, enuntiare
disclosure *s* patefactio *f*
discomfit *vt* fundĕre
discomfort *s* incommoda *n pl*, molestiae *f pl*
disconcerting *adj* molestus
disconnect *vt* sejungĕre, disjungĕre
disconsolate *adj* tristis, afflictus; **—ly** insolabiliter, triste
discontent *s* taedium *n*, molestia, offensio *f*
discontented *adj* parum contentus; **—ly** animo iniquo
discontinue *vt* intermittĕre; *vi* desinĕre, desistĕre
discord *s* discordia, dissensio *f*; (*mus*) dissonantia *f*
discordant *adj* discors, discrepans; (*mus*) dissonus
discount *vt* deducĕre; (*to disregard*) praetermittĕre
discount *s* (*com*) decessio *f*
discourage *vt* deterrēre, examinare; **to be discouraged** animum demittĕre
discouragement *s* animi abjectio *or* infractio *f*
discouraging *adj* adversus, incommodus
discourse *s* sermo *m*, colloquium *n*; (*written*) libellus *m*
discourse *vi* disserĕre, colloqui, verba facĕre
discourteous *adj* inurbanus; **—ly** inurbane
discourtesy *s* inurbanitas *f*
discover *vt* invenire, reperire; (*to find out*) explorare; (*to disclose*) patefacĕre
discoverable *adj* indagabilis, visibilis
discoverer *s* inventor, repertor *m*
discovery *s* inventio *f*; (*things discovered*) inventum *n*
discredit *s* dedecus *n*, ignominia *f*
discredit *vt* notare, infamare
discreet *adj* cautus, prudens; **—ly** consulto, prudenter
discrepancy *s* discrepantia *f*
discretion *s* pudentia, circumspectio *f*; (*tact*) judicium *n*
discretionary *adj* interminatus, liber
discriminate *vt* distinguĕre, dijudicare, discernĕre
discriminating *adj* sagax, discernens
discrimination *s* distinctio *f*; judicium, discrimen *n*
discuss *vt* agĕre, disputare, disserĕre
discussion *s* disputatio, disceptatio *f*
disdain *vt* fastidire, despicĕre, aspernari
disdain *s* fastidium *n*, despect·us -ūs, contempt·us -ūs *m*
disdainful *adj* fastidiosus, superciliosus; **—ly** fastidiose, contemptim
disease *s* morbus *m*, malum *n*
diseased *adj* aegrotus
disembark *vt* e navi exponĕre; *vi* e navi conscendĕre
disenchant *vt* errorem demĕre (*with dat*)
disengage *vt* expedire, eximĕre, avocare
disentangle *vt* expedire, extricare, explicare
disfavor *s* invidia *f*

disfigure *vt* deformare, turpare, mutilare
disfranchise *vt* civitatem adiměre (*with dat*)
disgorge *vt* revoměre, evoměre
disgrace *s* dedecus *n*, infamia *f*; (*thing*) flagitium *n*
disgrace *vt* dedecorare
disgraceful *adj* dedecorus, turpis, flagitiosus; **—ly** turpiter, flagitiose
disguise *s* (*mask*) persona *f*; simulatio *f*; (*pretense*) praetext·us -ūs *m*
disguise *vt* obtegěre; (*fig*) celare, dissimulare
disgust *s* (*loathing*) fastidium, taedium *n*, nausea *f*
disgust *vt* fastidium movēre (*with dat*); **I am disgusted with** me taedet (*with genit*), me piget (*with genit*)
disgusting *adj* taeter, foedus; **—ly** foede
dish *s* (*flat*) patina *f*; (*large*) lanx *f*; (*course*) ferculum *n*, dapes *f pl*
dishearten *vt* exanimare, percellěre; **to be disheartened** animum demittěre
disheveled *adj* passus, effusus
dishonest *adj* improbus, perfidus; **—ly** improbe, dolo malo
dishonesty *s* improbitas *f*, dolus malus *m*, fraus, perfidia *f*
dishonor *s* dedecus *n*, infamia, ignominia *f*
dishonor *vt* dedecorare
dishonorable *adj* inhonestus, turpis
disillusion *vt* errorem adiměre (*with dat*)
disinfect *vt* purgare
disinherit *vt* exheredare
disintegrate *vi* dilabi
disinter *vt* effoděre
disinterested *adj* integer; (*of judge*) severus; **—ly** integre, gratuito
disjoin *vt* segregare, disjungěre
disjointed *adj* incompositus; **—ly** incomposite
disk *s* orbis *m*
dislike *s* odium, fastidium *n*, aversatio *f*
dislike *vt* aversari, odisse, fastidire
dislocate *vt* extorquēre, luxare
dislocation *s* luxatura *f*
dislodge *vt* movēre, depellěre
disloyal *adj* perfidus; **—ly** perfide
disloyalty *s* infidelitas, perfidia *f*
dismal *adj* maestus, funestus, miser; **—ly** maeste, misere
dismantle *vt* diruěre, spoliare, nudare
dismay *s* pavor *m*, consternatio *f*
dismay *vt* terrēre, perterrefacěre, territare
dismember *vt* membratim dividěre, lacerare, discerpěre
dismemberment *s* mutilatio *f*
dismiss *vt* dimittěre; (*fear*) mittěre; (*to discharge, to cashier*) exauctorare
dismissal *s* missio, dimissio *f*
dismount *vi* ex equo desilire
disobedience *s* inobedientia, contumacia *f*
disobedient *adj* contumax
disobey *vt* non obedire (*with dat*), non parēre (*with dat*)
disorder *s* confusio *f*; (*med*) aegrotatio *f*; (*of mind*) perturbatio *f*; (*pol*) tumult·us -ūs *m*
disordered *adj* turbatus; (*fig*) dissolutus
disorderly *adj* inordinatus, incompositus, (per)turbatus; (*insubordinate*) turbulentus
disorganization *s* dissolutio *f*
disorganize *vt* conturbare, confunděre; **to be disorganized** dilabi
disown *vt* (*statement*) diffiteri, infitiari; (*heir*) abdicare; (*thing*) repudiare
disparage *vt* obtrectare, detrectare
disparagement *s* obtrectatio *f*
disparaging *adj* obtrectans
disparate *adj* dispar
disparity *s* inaequalitas, discrepantia *f*
dispassionate *adj* sedatus, tranquillus, frigidus; **—ly** sedate, frigide
dispatch *vt* mittěre, dimittěre, legare; (*to finish*) absolvěre, perficěre; (*to kill*) interficěre
dispel *vt* dispellěre; (*worries*) poněre
dispensary *s* medicamentaria taberna *f*
dispensation *s* distributio, partitio *f*; (*exemption*) immunitas, exemptio *f*
dispense *vt* distribuěre, dispertiri; (*to release*) solvěre; *vi* **to — with** indulgēre (*with dat*), omittěre, praetermittěre
dispenser *s* dispensator *m*
disperse *vt* spargěre, dispergěre, dissipare; *vi* dilabi, diffugěre
dispersion *s* dispersio, dissipatio *f*
dispirited *adj* abjectus, demissus, animo fractus
displace *vt* summovēre; exauctorare
displacement *s* amotio *f*
display *s* (*exhibit*) ostent·us -ūs *m*; (*ostentation*) ostentatio, jactatio *f*
display *vt* ostenděre, ostentare, exhibēre
displease *vt* displicēre (*with dat*)
displeased *adj* offensus; **to be — at** aegre ferre
displeasing *adj* odiosus, ingratus
displeasure *s* offensa, offensio *f*
disposable *adj* in promptu
disposal *s* dispositio *f*; arbitrium *n*; **at the — of** penes (*with acc*)
dispose *vt* disponěre, ordinare; (*to incline*) parare, praeparare; *vi* **to — of** abalienare, venděre; (*to get rid of*) tollěre
disposed *adj* inclinatus; (*in bad sense*) pronus
disposition *s* (*arrangement*) dispositio *f*; (*character*) natura, mens *f*, ingenium *n*, animus *m*
dispossess *vt* ejicěre, detruděre, pellěre
disproportion *s* inaequalitas, inconcinnitas *f*
disproportionate *adj* inaequalis, im-

par, inconcinnus; **—ly** impariter, inaequaliter
disprove *vt* refutare, confutare, redarguěre
disputable *adj* disputabilis, ambiguus
dispute *s* (*debate*) disputatio *f*; (*quarreling*) altercatio, controversia *f*; **beyond —** indisputabilis
dispute *vt & vi* disputare, contenděre
disqualification *s* impedimentum *n*
disqualify *vt* inhabilem redděre, impedire
disquiet *vt* inquietare, vexare
disregard *s* incuria, negligentia *f*
disregard *vt* negligěre, omittěre
disreputable *adj* infamis
disrepute *s* infamia *f*
disrespect *s* negligentia, insolentia *f*
disrespectful *adj* irreverens, insolens; **—ly** insolenter, irreverenter
disrupt *vt* dirumpěre
disruption *s* diruptio *f*; (*fig*) discidium *n*
dissatisfaction *s* molestia, offensio *f*
dissatisfied *adj* parum contentus
dissatisfy *vt* parum satisfacěre
dissect *vt* dissecare
dissection *s* incisio *f*
dissemble *vt & vi* dissimulare
disseminate *vt* disseminare, divulgare
dissension *s* dissensio *f*, dissidium *n*
dissent *vi* dissentire, dissidēre
dissent *s* dissensio *f*
dissertation *s* disputatio, dissertatio *f*
dissimilar *adj* dissimilis, dispar
dissimilarity *s* dissimilitudo *f*
dissipate *vt* dissipare, diffunděre; *vi* dissipari, diffundi
dissipation *s* dissipatio *f*
dissolute *adj* dissolutus, corruptus, perditus; **—ly** immoderate, prodige
dissolution *s* dissolutio *f*
dissolve *vt* dissolvěre; (*to melt*) liquefacěre; (*meeting*) dimittěre; *vi* liquescěre; (*to break up*) dissolvi
dissonance *s* dissonantia *f*
dissonant *adj* dissonus
dissuade *vt* dissuadēre (*with dat*), dehortari
dissuasion *s* dissuasio *f*
distaff *s* colus *f*
distance *s* distantia *f*, intervallum *n*; (*fig*) frigus *n*; (*long way*) longinquitas *f*; **at a —** procul, longe
distant *adj* distans, disjunctus, longinquus; (*fig*) parum familiaris; **to be —** abesse
distaste *s* fastidium *n*
distasteful *adj* (*of taste*) teter; (*fig*) molestus, odiosus
distemper *s* morbus *m*
distend *vt* distenděre
distil *vt & vi* stillare, destillare
distillation *s* destillatio *f*
distinct *adj* (*different*) diversus, alius; (*clear*) distinctus; **—ly** clare, distincte, certe
distinction *s* distinctio, discrepantia *f*, discrimen *n*; (*status*) amplitudo *f*; (*honor*) honos *m*; **there is no —** nil interest
distinctive *adj* proprius; **—ly** proprie
distinguish *vt* distinguěre, discerněre; **to — oneself** enitēre
distinguished *adj* insignis, clarus, notus, eximius
distort *vt* distorquēre; (*fig*) depravare
distortion *s* distortio *f*; (*fig*) depravatio *f*
distract *vt* distrahěre, avocare; (*to madden*) furiare
distracted *adj* amens, insanus; **—ly** amens, mente alienatus
distraction *s* (*cause*) invitamentum *n*; (state) negligentia *f*; **to —** efflictim
distress *s* afflictio, aegrimonia, aerumna *f*, dolor, labor *m*
distress *vt* afflictare, angěre
distressed *adj* anxius, afflictus, sollicitus
distressing *adj* tristis, gravis, acerbus
distribute *vt* distribuěre
distributer *s* distributor *m*
distribution *s* distributio *f*
district *s* regio *f*
distrust *s* diffidentia *f*
distrust *vt* diffiděre (*with dat*)
distrustful *adj* diffidens; **—ly** diffidenter
disturb *vt* perturbare; sollicitare, inquietare
disturbance *s* perturbatio *f*; confusio *f*; (*pol*) mot·us -ūs, tumult·us -ūs *m*
disturber *s* turbator, concitator *m*
disuse *s* desuetudo *f*
ditch *s* fossa *f*
ditty *s* cantilena *f*, canticum *n*
divan *s* lectulus *m*
dive *vi* mergi
diver *s* urinator *m*
diverge *vi* deflectěre, declinare, devertěre; (*of views*) discrepare
diverse *adj* alius, varius, diversus
diversification *s* variatio *f*
diversify *vt* variare
diversion *s* (*recreation*) oblectamentum *n*; (*of thought*) avocatio *f*; (*of river, etc.*) derivatio *f*
diversity *s* diversitas, varietas *f*
divert *vt* avertěre, divertěre; (*attention*) avocare; (*to amuse*) oblectare
divest *vt* exuěre, nudare, privare; **to — oneself of** exuěre, poněre
divide *vt* dividěre, partiri, distribuěre; *vi* disceděre, se scinděre
divination *s* divinatio, vaticinatio *f*
divine *adj* divinus; **—ly** divine
divine *s* theologus *m*
divine *vt* divinare, augurari, vaticinari; (*to guess*) conjicěre
diviner *s* augur, haruspex *m*
divinity *s* divinitas *f*; (*god*) numen *n*; divus *m*, diva *f*
divisible *adj* dividuus, divisibilis
division *s* divisio, partitio *f*; (*part*) pars *f*; (*mil*) legio *f*; **— of opinion** dissensio *f*

divorce *s* divortium *n*
divorce *vt* repudiare, dimittĕre
divulge *vt* vulgare, palam facĕre, aperire, patefacĕre
dizziness *s* vertigo *f*
dizzy *adj* vertiginosus
do *vt* agĕre, facĕre, efficĕre; *vi* agĕre; **how do you —?** quid agis?; **to — away with** tollĕre, perdĕre
docile *adj* docilis, tractabilis
dock *s* navale *n*; (*law*) cancelli *m pl*
dock *vt* subducĕre
docket *s* lemniscus *m*
dockyard *s* navalia *n pl*
doctor *s* medicus *m*; (*teacher*) doctor *m*
doctor *vt* medicari, curare
doctorate *s* doctoris grad·us -ūs *m*
doctrine *s* doctrina *f*, dogma *n*
document *s* documentum, instrumentum *n*
dodge *s* dolus *m*
dodge *vt* eludĕre; *vi* tergiversari
doe *s* cerva *f*
dog *s* canis *m* & *f*
dogged *adj* pervicax, pertinax; **—ly** pertinaciter
doggedness *s* pervicacia *f*
doggerel *s* versus inepti *m pl*
dog kennel *s* canis cubile *n*
dogma *s* dogma, placitum, praeceptum *n*
dogmatic *adj* dogmaticus; arrogans; **—ally** arroganter
dogmatism *s* arrogantia doctrinae *f*
dog star *s* canicula *f*, Sirius *m*
doing *s* factum, facinus *n*
dole *s* sportula *f*; donatio *f*
dole *vt* **to — out** parce dare
doleful *adj* lugubris, maestus, flebilis; **—ly** maeste, flebiliter
doll *s* pupa *f*
dollar *s* thalerus *m*
dolphin *s* delphinus, delphin *m*
dolt *s* caudex, stipes *m*
domain *s* (*estate*) possessio *f*; (*kingdom*) regnum *n*
dome *s* tholus *m*
domestic *adj* domesticus, familiaris; intestinus
domestic *s* famulus, servus, verna *m*, famula, serva *f*
domesticate *vt* domare, assuefacĕre
domicile *s* domicilium *n*, dom·us -ūs *f*
dominant *adj* praevalens
domination *s* dominium *n*
domineer *vi* dominari
domineering *adj* imperiosus
dominion *s* imperium, regnum *n*
don *vt* induĕre
donation *s* donum *n*, stips *f*
donkey *s* asinus, asellus *m*
donor *s* donator *m*, donatrix *f*
doom *s* fatum, exitium *n*
doom *vt* damnare, condemnare
door *s* janua *f*, ostium *n*, fores *f pl*
doorkeeper *s* janitor *m*, janitrix *f*
doorpost *s* postis *f*
doorway *s* ostium *n*
Doric *adj* Doricus
dormant *adj* sopitus; (*hidden*) latens; **to lie —** jacĕre
dormitory *s* cubiculum, dormitorium *n*
dorsal *adj* dorsualis
dose *s* potio *f*
dot *s* punctum *n*
dot *vt* punctum imponĕre (*with dat*)
dotage *s* senium *n*
dotard *s* senex delirus *m*
dote *vi* **to — upon** deamare, deperire
doting *adj* deamans, desipiens; **—ly** perdite amans
double *adj* duplex; (*of pairs*) geminus; (*as much again*) duplus; (*meaning*) ambiguus
double *s* duplum *n*; **to march on the —** currĕre
double *vt* duplicare; (*cape*) praetervehi; *vi* duplicari; (*to run*) currĕre
doubly *adv* bis, dupliciter
doubt *s* dubitatio *f*, dubium *n*; (*distrust*) suspicio *f*
doubt *vt* dubitare; suspicari
doubtful *adj* (*of persons*) dubius; (*of things*) incertus, ambiguus, anceps; **—ly** dubie; (*hesitatingly*) dubitanter
doubtless *adv* scilicet, haud dubie, sine dubio
dough *s* farina *f*
doughty *adj* strenuus, fortis
douse *vt* (*to put out*) exstinguĕre; (*to drench*) madefacĕre
dove *s* columba *f*
dowdy *adj* inconcinnus
down *s* pluma *f*; (*of hair*) lanugo *f*; (*of plants*) pappus *m*
down *adv* deorsum; **— from** de (*with abl*); **— to** usque ad (*with acc*)
down *prep* de (*with abl*)
down *adj* declivis; tristis; ad inopiam redactus
downcast *adj* (*of eyes or head*) dejectus, demissus; (*fig*) afflictus, maestus
downfall *s* occas·us -ūs *m*, ruina *f*
downhill *adj* declivis
downright *adj* directus, sincerus
downright *adv* prorsus, plane
downstream *adv* secundo flumine
downward *adj* declivis; pronus
downwards *adv* deorsum
downy *adj* plumeus; lanuginosus
dowry *s* dos *f*
doze *vi* dormitare
dozen *s* duodecim
drab *adj* cinereus
draft *s* (*act of drawing*) lineatio *f*; (*drink*) haust·us -ūs *m*; (*of ship*) immersio *f*; (*first copy*) exemplar *n*; (*of air*) aura *f*; (*mil*) dilect·us -ūs *m*; (*money*) syngrapha *f*; (*of net*) jact·us -ūs *m*
draft *vt* conscribĕre
draft horse *s* equus rhedarius *m*
drag *vt* trahĕre, rapĕre; *vi* trahi
drag *s* (*fig*) impedimentum *n*
dragnet *s* tragula *f*
dragon *s* draco, anguis *m*
drain *s* cloaca *f*
drain *vt* siccare; derivare; (*to drink*)

exhaurire, ebibĕre; (*strength*) exhaurire
drainage *s* derivatio, exsiccatio *f*; colluvies cloacarum *f*
draining *s* exsiccatio *f*
drake *s* anas *m*
drama *s* drama *n*, fabula *f*
dramatic *adj* dramaticus, scaenicus
dramatist *s* poeta scaenicus, scriptor fabularum *m*
dramatize *vt* ad scaenam componĕre
drape *vt* induĕre, amicire, velare
drapery *s* aulaeum *n*
drastic *adj* vehemens
draw *vt* (*to pull*) trahĕre, ducĕre; (*picture*) scribĕre, delineare; (*sword*) destringĕre; (*bow*) adducĕre; (*inference*) colligĕre; **to — aside** abducĕre, seducĕre; **to — away** avertĕre, distrahĕre; **to — back** retrahĕre; **to — off** detrahĕre, abducĕre; (*wine*) depromĕre; **to — out** extrahĕre; (*sword, etc.*) educĕre; (*fig*) elicĕre; **to — together** contrahĕre; **to — up** subducĕre; scribĕre; (*troops*) instruĕre, constituĕre; *vi* **to — back** pedem referre, cedĕre; (*fig*) recedĕre; **to — near** appropinquare; **to — off** cedĕre; **to — up to** (*of ships*) appetĕre
drawback *s* impedimentum, incommodum *n*, retardatio *f*
drawbridge *s* pons *m*
drawer *s* (*sliding compartment*) loculus *m*; (*chest*) armarium *n*
drawing *s* descriptio *f*; (*art*) graphice *f*
drawing room *s* exedra *f*
drawl *vi* lentius loqui
dray *s* plaustrum *n*
dread *s* terror, pavor *m*, formido *f*
dread *adj* terribilis, dirus
dread *vt* expavescĕre, formidare
dreadful *adj* terribilis, horribilis, atrox; **—ly** horrendum in modum, atrociter
dream *s* somnium *n*; **in a —** in somno
dream *vt & vi* somniare; (*fig*) dormitare
dreamer *s* (*fig*) nugator *m*
dreamy *adj* somniculosus
drearily *adv* triste, misere
dreariness *s* (*place*) solitudo, vastitas *f*; (*mind*) tristitia *f*
dreary *adj* (*place*) vastus, solus, incultus; (*person*) tristis, miser
dredge *s* everriculum *n*
dregs *s* faex *f*; (*fig*) sentina *f*
drench *vt* madefacĕre, perfundĕre
dress *s* habit·us -ūs, vestit·us -ūs *m*, vestis *f*, vestimenta *n pl*
dress *vt* vestire, induĕre; (*to deck out*) (ex)ornare; (*wounds*) curare; (*to bind up*) obligare; *vi* se induĕre
dressing *s* ornatio *f*; (*of foods*) coctio, coctura *f*; (*med*) fomentum *n*
dressing room *s* procoeton *m*
dribble *vi* stillare
drift *s* propositum *n*; (*purpose*) scopus *m*; (*of sand*) cumulus *m*; (*of snow*) vis *f*
drift *vi* ferri, fluitare
drill *s* (*tool*) terebra *f*; (*mil*) exercitatio *f*
drill *vt* (*to bore*) terebrare; (*mil*) exercēre; (*pupil*) instituĕre
drink *vt* bibĕre, potare; **to — in** absorbēre, haurire; **to — up** epotare; *vi* bibĕre, potare; **to — to** propinare (*with dat*)
drink *s* pot·us -ūs *m*, potio *f*
drinkable *adj* potabilis
drinker *s* potor, potator *m*; (*drunkard*) bibax *m*
drinking *adj* (*given to drink*) bibosus
drinking cup *s* poculum *n*
drip *s* stillicidium *n*
drip *vi* stillare
drive *vt* agĕre, pellĕre, impellĕre; (*to force*) compellĕre, cogĕre; (*a nail, etc.*) infigĕre; **to — away** abigĕre; (*fig*) depellĕre; (*to dislodge*) dejicĕre; **to — back** repellĕre; **to — in** (*sheep, etc.*) cogĕre; (*fig*) compellĕre; **to — off** abigĕre; **to — on** impellĕre; **to — out** expellĕre; **to — out of one's senses** infuriare; **to — up** subigĕre; *vi* (*in carriage*) vehi; **to — off** avehi; **to — on** praetervehi; **to — past** praetervehi
drive *s* (*in carriage*) vectio *f*; (*energy*) impigritas *f*
drivel *s* saliva *f*, sputum *n*; (*nonsense*) ineptiae, nugae *f pl*
drivel *vi* (*fig*) delirare
driver *s* agitator *m*; (*of carriage*) auriga *m*
drizzle *vi* leniter pluĕre
drizzle *s* lenis pluvia *f*
dromedary *s* dromas *m*
drone *s* (*bee*) fucus *m*; (*person*) nebulo *m*; (*buzz*) bombus *m*
drone *vi* fremĕre
droop *vt* demittĕre; *vi* languēre; (*of flowers*) languescĕre, tabescĕre
drooping *adj* languidus
drop *s* gutta, stilla *f*; (*a little bit*) paululum *n*; **— by —** guttatim
drop *vt* stillare; (*to let slip*) omittĕre; (*to lay low*) sternĕre; (*hint*) emittĕre; (*anchor*) jacĕre; (*work*) desistĕre ab (*with abl*); *vi* destillare; (*to fall*) cadĕre; **to — behind** cessare; **to — off to sleep** obdormire; **to — out** excidĕre
drought *s* siccitas, ariditas *f*
drove *s* grex *m*
drown *vt* immergĕre, demergĕre; (*fig*) opprimĕre; **to — out** obscurare; *vi* in aqua perire
drowsily *adv* somniculose
drowsy *adj* somniculosus, somnolentus; (*fig*) ignavus
drudge *s* (*slave*) mediastinus *m*; (*fig*) plagiger *m*
drudgery *s* opera servilis *f*
drug *s* medicamentum *n*
drug *vt* medicare
druggist *s* medicamentarius *m*
drugstore *s* taberna medicina, apotheca *f*

Druids *s* Druidae *m pl*
drum *s* typanum *n*
drum *vi* tympanum pulsare
drummer *s* tympanista *m*
drunk *adj* ebrius
drunkard *s* ebriosus, temulentus *m*
drunken *adj* ebrius, ebriosus
drunkenness *s* ebrietas, temulentia *f*
dry *adj* aridus, siccus; (*thirsty*) siticulosus; (*fig*) jejunus; insulsus
dry *vt* siccare, desiccare, arefacĕre; (*in the sun*) insolare; *vi* arescĕre
dryad *s* dryas *f*
dryly *adv* (*fig*) insulse; (*of jokes*) facete
dryness *s* ariditas, siccitas *f*; (*fig*) aridum sermonis genus *n*
dual *adj* duplex
dub *vt* supernominare
dubious *adj* dubius; **—ly** dubie
duck *s* anas *f*
duck *vt* submergĕre, demergĕre; (*an issue*) evitare; *vi* (*under water*) urinari
duckling *s* anaticula *f*
due *adj* debitus, justus, meritus; **to be — to** fieri (*with abl*)
due *adv* rectā; **due east** rectā ad orientem
due *s* debitum *n*
duel *s* certamen *n*
duet *s* bicinium *n*
duke *s* dux *m*
dull *adj* hebes; (*of mind*) tardus, segnes, insulsus; (*of style*) frigidus
dull *vt* hebetare, obtundĕre; stupefacĕre
dullness *s* stupiditas, tarditas *f*
duly *adv* rite; recte
dumb *adj* mutus; **to be —** obmutescĕre
dumbfound *vt* obstupefacĕre
dumb show *s* mimus *m*
dumpling *s* farinae subactae globulus *m*
dumpy *adj* brevis atque obesus
dun *adj* fuscus, furvus
dun *vt* flagitare, exposcĕre
dunce *s* homo stupidus *m*
dung *s* stercus *n*, fimus *m*; (*of birds*) merda *f*
dungeon *s* carcer *m*, ergastulum *n*
dupe *s* homo credulus, homo stolidus *m*
dupe *vt* decipĕre
duplicate *adj* duplex
duplicate *s* duplicitas, fallacia *f*
duplicate *vt* duplicare
duplicity *s* duplicitas *f*
durability *s* firmitudo, stabilitas *f*
durable *adj* firmus, durabilis, stabilis
duration *s* spatium temporis *n*, diuturnitas, perpetuitas *f*
during *prep* per (*with acc*), inter (*with acc*)
dusk *s* crepusculum, obscurum *n*
dusky *adj* obscurus, tenebrosus; fuscus
dust *s* pulvis *m*
dust *vt* detergēre
dusty *adj* pulverulentus, pulvereus
dutiful *adj* pius, officiosus; **—ly** pie, officiose
duty *s* (*social or moral*) officium *n*; (*task*) munus *n*; (*tax*) vectigal *n*; **to be on —** (*mil*) stationem agĕre
dwarf *s* nanus, pumilio *m*
dwarfish *adj* pumilus
dwell *vi* habitare, inhabitare; **to — upon** commorari in (*with abl*)
dweller *s* incola *m & f*, habitator *m*
dwelling place *s* domicilium *n*, sedes, habitatio *f*
dwindle *vi* decrescĕre, imminui
dye *vt* ting(u)ĕre, colorare, inficĕre, fucare
dye *s* tinctura *f*, color *m*
dying *adj* moriens, moribundus; (*last*) ultimus, extremus
dynamics *s* dynamica *f*
dynasty *s* dynastia, dom·us -ūs *f*
dysentery *s* dysenteria *f*

E

each *adj & pron* quisque; (*of two*) uterque; **— other** inter se, invicem
eager *adj* cupidus, avidus, acer, vehemens; **—ly** cupide, avide, acriter, vehementer
eagerness *s* aviditas, cupiditas, alacritas *f*, studium *n*
eagle *s* aquila *f*
ear *s* auris *f*; (*of corn*) spica *f*; **to give —** aurem praebēre
earache *s* aurium dolor *m*
earl *s* comes *m*
early *adj* (*in morning*) matutinus; (*in season*) maturus; (*of early date*) antiquus; (*beginning*) primus, novus
early *adv* (*in morning*) mane; (*too soon*) praemature; (*quickly, soon*) cito
earn *vt* lucrari, merēre *or* merēri, consequi
earnest *adj* intentus, serius, impensus, vehemens; **in —** serio, sedulo, bona fide; **—ly** intente, impense, acriter, graviter
earnestness *s* assiduitas, gravitas *f*, ardor *m*
earnings *s* quaest·us -ūs *m*, lucrum *n*
earring *s* elenchus *m*
earth *s* terra, tellus *f*; (*soil*) solum *n*; (*globe*) orbis (terrarum) *m*
earthen *adj* terrenus; fictilis
earthenware *s* fictilia *n pl*
earthly *adj* terrenus; terrestris; humanus
earthquake *s* terrae mot·us -ūs *m*
earthwork *s* opus terrenum *n*, agger *m*
earthy *adj* terrenus

ease *s* (*leisure*) otium *n*, quies *f*; (*grace*) lepor *m*, facilitas *f*; (*pleasure*) voluptas *f*; **at —** otiosus, vacuus; securus
ease *vt* levare, exonerare, expedire; (*fig*) lenire, mitigare
east *adj* orientalis
east *s* oriens *m*
Easter *s* pascha *f*, sollemnia paschalia *n pl*
eastern *adj* orientalis
eastward *adv* ad orientem
east wind *s* Eurus *m*
easy *adj* facilis; expeditus; (*manner*) facilis, affabilis; (*graceful*) lepidus
eat *vi* vesci (*with abl*), esse; (*fig*) roděre; **to — away** pereděre; (*fig*) corroděre; **to — up** comesse, devorare, exesse
eating *s* es·us -ūs *m*
eaves *s* suggrundia *n pl*
eavesdropper *s* auceps, auricularius *m*
ebb *s* recess·us -ūs *m*; **to be at a low —** jacēre
ebb *vi* receděre; (*fig*) decrescěre
eccentric *adj* insolens, inusitatus, abnormis
ecclesiastic *adj* ecclesiasticus
echo *s* echo, imago *f*
echo *vt* repercutěre, resonare; (*fig*) subsequi; *vi* resonare, resultare
eclipse *s* (*of sun or moon*) obscuratio solis *or* lunae *f*, defect·us -ūs *m*
eclipse *vt* obscurare, obumbrare
eclogue *s* ecloga *f*
economic *adj* economicus
economical *adj* frugi (*indecl*), parcus; **—ly** parce
economics *s* publicarum opum scientia *f*
economize *vi* parcěre
economy *s* parsimonia, frugalitas *f*; rei familiaris administratio *f*
ecstasy *s* ecstasis, insania *f*, furor *m*
eddy *s* vortex *m*
eddy *vi* volutari
edge *s* (*brink*) margo *m & f*; (*of knife, etc.*) acies *f*; (*of forest*) ora *f*
edge *vt* (*garment*) praetexěre; (*to sharpen*) acuěre; *vi* **to — closer** appropinquare
edged *adj* acutus
edging *s* limbus *m*
edible *adj* esculentus, edulis
edict *s* edictum, decretum *n*
edification *s* eruditio *f*
edify *vt* docēre
edit *vt* eděre, recensēre
edition *s* editio *f*
editor *s* editor *m*
educate *vt* educare, erudire
education *s* educatio, eruditio *f*
educator *s* praeceptor, magister *m*
eel *s* anguilla *f*
efface *vt* delēre, oblitterare, tollěre
effect *s* effectum *n*, effect·us -ūs; (*show*) jactatio *f*; **—s** bona *n pl*; **in —** re vera; **without —** irritus
effect *vt* efficěre, exsequi, facěre
effective *adj* efficiens, efficax, valens; **—ly** valide, graviter
effectual *adj* efficax, valens, potens, **—ly** efficaciter, potenter
effeminacy *s* mollities *f*
effeminate *adj* effeminatus, mollis, muliebris; **—ly** effeminate, muliebriter
effete *adj* effetus
efficacious *adj* efficax; **—ly** efficaciter
efficacy *s* efficacia, vis *f*
efficiency *s* virtus, peritia *f*
efficient *adj* efficiens, aptus, idoneus; efficax; **—ly** perite, bene
effigy *s* effigies *f*
effort *s* labor, conat·us -ūs, nis·us -ūs *m*, opera *f*; **to make an —** eniti
effrontery *s* audacia, impudentia *f*
effusion *s* effusio *f*
effusive *adj* officiosus
egg *s* ovum *n*; **to lay —s** ova parěre
egotism *s* amor sui *m*
egotist *s* sui amator *m*
egotistical *adj* sibi soli consulens
egress *s* egress·us -ūs, exit·us -ūs *m*
eight *adj* octo; **— times** octies
eighteen *adj* duodeviginti, decem et octo
eighteenth *adj* decimus octavus, duodevicesimus
eighth *adj* octavus
eighth *s* octava pars *f*
eightieth *adj* octogesimus
eighty *adj* octoginta
either *pron* alteruter; uter; alter
either *conj* **— . . . or** aut . . . aut; vel . . . vel
ejaculate *vt* emittěre
ejaculation *s* clamor *m*
eject *vt* ejicěre
ejection *s* dejectio *f*
eke *vt* **to eke out a livelihood** victum aegre parare
elaborate *adj* elaboratus; **—ly** elaborate
elaborate *vt* elaborare
elaboration *s* nimia diligentia *f*
elapse *vi* praeterire, abire, labi
elastic *adj* resiliens; (*fig*) mobilis
elate *vt* inflare, superbum redděre; **to be elated** efferri
elation *s* gaudium *n*, laetitia *f*, animus elatus *m*
elbow *s* ulna *f*, cubitus *m*
elbow *vt* cubitis depulsare, cubitis truděre
elder *adj* major natu
elderly *adj* aetate provectior
eldest *adj* maximus natu
elect *vt* eligěre, deligěre, creare
elect *adj* designatus; (*elite*) lectus
election *s* electio *f*, delect·us -ūs *m*; (*pol*) comitia *n pl*
electioneering *s* ambitio *f*
elective *adj* suffragatorius
elector *s* suffragator *m*
electrical *adj* electricus
electricity *s* vis electrica *f*
electrify *vt* electricā *vi* afficěre; (*fig*) percellěre
elegance *s* elegantia *f*
elegant *adj* elegans, concinnus; **—ly** eleganter, cum elegantia

elegiac *adj* elegiacus; **— verse** elegi *m pl*
elegy *s* elegia *f*
element *s* elementum *n*; **—s** principia, initia *n pl*; (*fig*) rudimenta *n pl*
elementary *adj* elementarius
elephant *s* elephantus, elephas *m*
elevate *vt* levare, attollĕre; (*fig*) efferre, inflare
elevated *adj* editus
elevation *s* elatio *f*; (*height*) altitudo *f*; (*hill*) locus superior *m*
eleven *adj* undecim; **— times** undecies
eleventh *adj* undecimus
elf *s* larva *f*, numen pumilum *n*
elicit *vt* elicĕre
eligible *adj* eligibilis, idoneus
eliminate *vt* amovēre, tollĕre
elision *s* elisio *f*
elite *adj* lectus
elite *s* flos *m*, lecti *m pl*
elk *s* alces *f*
ellipsis *s* ellipsis *f*
elliptical *adj* ellipticus; **—ly** per defectionem
elm *s* ulmus *f*
elocution *s* pronuntiatio *f*
elongate *vt* producĕre
elope *vi* clam fugĕre, aufugĕre
elopement *s* fuga clandestina *f*
eloquence *s* eloquentia *f*; (*natural*) facundia *f*
eloquent *adj* eloquens, disertus; **—ly** diserte, eloquenter, graviter
else *adj* alius; **no one —** nemo alius; **who —** quis alius
else *adv* (*besides*) praeterea; (*otherwise*) aliter
elsewhere *adv* alibi; (*motion*) alio
elucidate *vt* illustrare, explicare
elucidation *s* explicatio *f*
elude *vt* eludĕre, frustrari, evitare
Elysian *adj* Elysius
Elysian fields *s* Elysii campi *m pl*
emaciate *vt* emaciare, macerare
emaciated *adj* macer, macilentus
emaciation *s* macies, tabes *f*
emanate *vi* emanare, oriri
emanation *s* emanatio, exhalatio *f*
emancipate *vt* emancipare, manumittĕre; (*fig*) liberare
emancipation *s* (*of slave*) manumissio *f*; (*of son*) emancipatio *f*; (*fig*) liberatio *f*
emasculate *vt* castrare, emasculare; (*fig*) enervare
embalm *vt* condire, pollingĕre
embalming *s* pollinctura *f*
embankment *s* agger *m*, moles *f*
embargo *s* retentio navium *f*, interdictum *n*; **to lay an — upon a ship** navem retinēre
embark *vt* imponĕre; *vi* conscendĕre; **to — upon** (*fig*) ingredi
embarkation *s* conscensio *f*
embarrass *vt* perturbare, confundĕre, impedire
embarrassing *adj* incommodus, difficilis
embarrassment *s* conturbatio, implicatio *f*; (*financial*) angustiae *f pl*
embassy *s* legatio *f*, legati *m pl*
embellish *vt* ornare, exornare
embellishment *s* ornamentum, decus *n*, exornatio *f*
embers *s* cinis *m*, favilla *f*
embezzle *vt* peculari
embezzlement *s* peculat·us -ūs *m*
embezzler *s* peculator *m*
embitter *vt* exacerbare
emblazon *vt* insignire
emblem *s* emblema, insigne, signum *n*
emblematic *adj* symbolicus
embody *vt* includĕre, repraesentare
emboss *vt* caelare
embrace *s* amplex·us -ūs, complex·us -ūs *m*
embrace *vt* amplecti, complecti; comprehendĕre
embroider *vt* acu pingĕre
embroidery *s* vestis picta *f*
embroil *vt* permiscēre, implicare
embroilment *s* implicatio *f*
embryo *s* immaturus part·us -ūs *m*
emend *vt* emendare, corrigĕre
emendation *s* correctio, emendatio *f*
emerald *s* smaragdus *m*
emerge *vi* emergĕre; (*to arise*) exsistĕre
emergency *s* tempus, discrimen *n*, cas·us -ūs *m*
emigrant *s* emigrans *m*
emigrate *vi* emigrare
emigration *s* migratio *f*
eminence *s* praestantia, amplitudo *f*; (*rise of ground*) locus editus *m*
eminent *adj* eminens, egregius, praestans; **—ly** eximie, insigniter
emissary *s* emissarius, legatus *m*
emit *vt* emittĕre; exhalare
emotion *s* animi mot·us -ūs *m*, commotio *f*
emotional *adj* mobilis
emperor *s* imperator, princeps *m*
emphasis *s* energia, vis *f*, pondus *n*; impressio *f*
emphasize *vt* exprimĕre
emphatic *adj* emphaticus, gravis; **—ally** emphatice, graviter
empire *s* imperium, regnum *n*
empirical *adj* empiricus; **—ly** ex experimentis
empiricism *s* empirice *f*
employ *vt* uti (*with abl*), adhibēre, exercēre, occupare
employer *s* conductor, dominus *m*
employment *s* (*act*) us·us -ūs *m*; (*occupation*) quaest·us -ūs *m*; (*business*) negotium *n*
empower *vt* potestatem facĕre (*with dat*)
empress *s* imperatrix *f*
emptiness *s* inanitas *f*; (*fig*) vanitas *f*
empty *adj* vacuus, inanis; (*of street*) desertus; (*fig*) vanus
empty *vt* evacuare; exhaurire; *vi* (*of river*) influĕre
empyrean *s* aether *m*
emulate *vt* aemulari, imitari
emulation *s* aemulatio *f*
enable *vt* facultatem facĕre (*with dat*)
enact *vt* decernĕre, sancire

enactment *s* lex, sanctio *f*, decretum *n*
enamel *s* smaltum, vitrum metallicum *n*
enamel *adj* smaltinus
enamoured *adj* amans; **to be — of** amare, deamare
encamp *vi* castra poněre
encampment *s* castra *n pl*
encase *vt* includěre
enchant *vt* fascinare; (*fig*) capěre, captare, delectare
enchanter *s* incantator *m*
enchanting *adj* (*fig*) venustus, suavissimus
enchantment *s* incantamentum *n*; (*fig*) illecebrae *f pl*
enchantress *s* maga, cantatrix *f*; venefica *f*
encircle *vt* cingěre, circumdare, circumplecti
enclose *vt* includěre, saepire
enclosure *s* saeptum *n*
encompass *vt* complecti
encounter *s* (*meeting*) congress·us -ūs *m*; (*fight*) certamen *n*, pugna *f*
encounter *vt* congredi cum (*with abl*), obviam ire (*with dat*), occurrěre (*with dat*); (*in battle*) concurrěre cum (*with abl*)
encourage *vt* cohortari, confirmare; favēre (*with dat*)
encouragement *s* hortat·us -ūs *m*, confirmatio *f*, favor *m*
encroach *vi* invaděre; **to — upon** usurpare, occupare, invaděre
encroachment *s* usurpatio *f*
encumber *vt* impedire, onerare, praegravare
encumbrance *s* impedimentum, onus *n*
encyclopedia *s* encyclopaedia *f*
end *s* finis, terminus, exit·us -ūs *m*; (*aim*) propositum *n*; (*of a speech*) peroratio *f*; **in the —** denique; **to put an — to** finem imponěre (*with dat*); **to what —?** quo?, quorsum?
end *vt* finire, terminare, conficěre; *vi* desiněre; (*of time*) exire; (*of events*) evaděre
endanger *vt* periclitari
endear *vt* carum redděre, devincire
endearing *adj* carus, blandus
endearment *s* blanditiae *f pl*, blandimenta *n pl*
endeavor *s* conat·us -ūs, nis·us -ūs *m*
endeavor *vi* conari, eniti, laborare, contenděre
ending *s* finis, exit·us -ūs *m*
endless *adj* infinitus; perpetuus; **—ly** sine fine, perpetuo
endorse *vt* ratum facěre
endow *vt* dotare, donare, instruěre
endowed *adj* praeditus
endowment *s* dotatio, dos *f*, donum *n*
endurable *adj* tolerabilis
endurance *s* tolerantia, patientia *f*; (*duration*) duratio *f*
endure *vt* tolerare, pati; *vi* durare; permaněre
enduring *adj* tolerans; durabilis
enemy *s* (*public*) hostis *m*; (*private*) inimicus, adversarius *m*
energetic *adj* impiger, acer, strenuus, navus; **—ally** acriter, impigre, strenuo
energy *s* vis, vehementia, efficacia *f*, impet·us -ūs *m*
enervate *vt* enervare, debilitare
enforce *vt* exsequi, cogěre; (*arguments*) confirmare
enforcement *s* coactio, sanctio *f*
enfranchise *vt* (*slave*) manumittěre; civitate donare
enfranchisement *s* (*of slave*) manumissio *f*; civitatis donatio *f*
engage *vt* (*to employ*) adhibēre; (*to reserve*) conducěre; (*attention*) occupare; (*to involve*) implicare; (*enemy*) proelium facěre cum (*with abl*); *vi* **to — in** suscipěre, ingredi; **to engage in battle** proeliari, manum *or* manus conserěre
engaged *adj* (*to marry*) sponsus; **to be — in** versari in (*with abl*)
engagement *s* (*to marry*) pactio nuptialis *f*; (*business*) negotium *n*, occupatio *f*; (*mil*) proelium *n*, pugna *f*; (*promise*) pactum *n*, pactio *f*, promissum *n*
engaging *adj* suavis, blandus, amabilis
engender *vt* ingenerare, gigněre
engine *s* machina, machinatio *f*
engineer *s* machinator, faber *m*
engineering *s* machinalis scientia *f*; **civil —** architectura *f*
England *s* Anglia, Britannia *f*
English *adj* Anglicus, Britannicus
Englishman *s* Anglus, Britannus, Britannicus *m*
engrave *vt* inciděre, caelare, insculpěre, scalpěre
engraver *s* sculptor, caelator *m*
engraving *s* sculptura, caelatura *f*
engross *vt* occupare; **to be engrossed in** totus esse in (*with abl*)
enhance *vt* augēre, amplificare, ornare
enigma *s* aenigma *n*, ambages *f pl*
enigmatic *adj* ambiguus, obscurus; **—ally** ambigue
enjoin *vt* jubēre, injungěre
enjoy *vt* frui (*with abl*); uti (*with abl*)
enjoyment *s* fruct·us -ūs *m*, voluptas *f*, gaudium *n*; possessio *f*
enlarge *vt* amplificare, augēre, dilatare; *vi* **to — upon** amplificare, prosequi
enlargement *s* amplificatio, dilatio *f*, auct·us -ūs *m*
enlighten *vt* illustrare, illuminare; erudire
enlightenment *s* eruditio, humanitas *f*
enlist *vt* (*support*) conciliare; (*mil*) conscriběre; *vi* sacramentum dicěre
enlistment *s* conscriptio *f*
enliven *vt* animare, incitare; exhilarare
enmity *s* inimicitia *f*, odium *n*
ennoble *vt* honestare
ennui *s* taedium *n*
enormity *s* immanitas *f*; atrocitas *f*

enormous *adj* ingens, enormis, immanis; **—ly** immensum, praeter modum
enough *adj* satis; **— trouble** satis laboris
enough *adv* satis; **more than —** satis superque
enrage *vt* infuriare, exasperare, incenděre
enrapture *vt* rapěre, captare
enrich *vt* locupletare, ditare
enroll *vt* adscriběre, inscriběre; *vi* nomen dare
enshrine *vt* consecrare, dedicare
enshroud *vt* involvěre, amicire
ensign *s* (*flag*) vexillum *n*; (*officer*) signifer *m*
enslave *vt* in servitutem redigěre
enslavement *s* servitus *f*
ensnare *vt* illaquēre, irretire; (*fig*) illicěre
ensue *vi* sequi, insequi
ensuing *adj* insequens, posterus, proximus
entail *vt* afferre, inferre
entangle *vt* illaquēre, irretire, impedire, implicare
entanglement *s* implicatio *f*
enter *vt* intrare, inire, ingredi; introire in *or* ad (*with acc*); **to — politics** ad rem publicam acceděre; *vi* intrare, inire, ingredi, introire; **to — upon** (*to undertake*) suscipěre, ingredi
enterprise *s* (*undertaking*) inceptum, ausum *n*; (*in bad sense*) facinus *n*; (*quality*) animus alacer, animus promptus *m*
enterprising *adj* acer, promptus
entertain *vt* (*guest*) excipěre, invitare, adhibēre; (*idea*) admittěre, habēre; (*to amuse*) oblectare, delectare
entertainer *s* hospes *m*
entertainment *s* (*amusement*) oblectatio *f*, oblectamentum *n*; (*cultural*) acroama *n*; (*by guest*) hospitium *n*
enthrall *vt* captare
enthusiasm *s* studium *n*, fervor, furor, ardor *m*
enthusiastic *adj* fanaticus, ardens, fervidus; **—ally** fanatice, ardenter
entice *vt* allicěre, elicěre
enticement *s* illecebra *f*
enticing *adj* blandus
entire *adj* totus, integer, solidus; **—ly** omnino, plane, penitus
entirety *s* integritas, universitas *f*
entitle *vt* (*to name*) appellare, nominare; inscriběre; (*to give title to*) potestatem dare (*with dat*)
entity *s* ens *n*, res *f*
entomologist *s* entomologicus *m*
entomology *s* entomologia *f*
entrails *s* viscera, exta, intestina *n pl*
entrance *s* adit·us -ūs, introit·us -ūs *m*; ostium *n*; (*act*) introit·us -ūs *m*, ingressio *f*
entrance *vt* rapěre, consopire, capěre
entrance hall *s* vestibulum *n*
entrap *vt* illaquēre, inescare; capěre
entreat *vt* obsecrare, orare, deprecari
entreaty *s* rogatio, obsecratio *f*, preces *f pl*
entrust *vt* creděre, mandare, committěre
entry *s* (*act*) introit·us -ūs *m*, ingressio *f*; (*of house*) vestibulum *n*; adit·us -ūs *m*; (*in accounts*) nomen *n*
entwine *vt* implicare, nectěre
enumerate *vt* enumerare
enumeration *s* enumeratio, recensio *f*
enunciate *vt* enuntiare, pronuntiare, expriměre
enunciation *s* enuntiatio *f*
envelop *vt* involvěre, amicire, implicare
envelope *s* involucrum *n*
enviable *adj* invidiosus
envious *adj* invidus, lividus
envoy *s* nuntius, legatus, orator *m*
envy *s* invidia *f*
envy *vt* invidēre (*with dat*)
ephemeral *adj* brevis; caducus
epic *adj* epicus, heroicus
epic *s* epos *n*
epicure *s* helluo, homo voluptarius *m*
Epicurean *adj* Epicureus
Epicurean *s* Epicureus *m*; (*hedonist*) voluptarius *m*
epidemic *adj* epidemus, contagiosus
epidemic *s* pestilentia *f*
epidermis *s* summa cutis, epidermis *f*
epigram *s* epigramma *n*
epilepsy *s* morbus comitialis *m*, epilepsia *f*
epilogue *s* epilogus *m*
epiphany *s* epiphania *f*
episode *s* embolium, eventum *n*, excurs·us -ūs *m*
epistle *s* epistola *f*
epistolary *adj* epistolaris
epitaph *s* epitaphium *n*, titulus *m*
epithet *s* epitheton *n*
epitome *s* epitome, epitoma *f*
epoch *s* epocha *f*, saeculum *n*
equal *adj* aequalis, aequus, par; **—ly** aeque, aequaliter, pariter
equal *s* par *m, f & n*
equal *vt* aequare, adaequare
equality *s* aequalitas *f*, aequum *n*
equalization *s* (act) aequatio, exaequatio *f*; (*state*) aequalitas *f*
equalize *vt* adaequare, exaequare
equanimity *s* aequus animus *m*
equation *s* aequatio *f*
equator *s* aequinoctialis circulus *m*
equatorial *adj* aequinoctialis
equestrian *adj* equestris
equestrian *s* eques *m*
equidistant *adj* **to be —** aequo intervallo inter se distare
equilibrium *s* aequilibrium *n*
equinox *s* aequinoctium *n*
equip *vt* armare, ornare, instruěre
equipment *s* arma, instrumenta, armamenta *n pl*, armatura *f*, apparat·us -ūs *m*
equitable *adj* aequus, justus
equitably *adv* aeque, juste
equity *s* aequitas *f*, aequum *n*

equivalent *adj* aequus, par
equivocal *adj* ambiguus, anceps; **—ly** ambigue
equivocate *vi* tergiversari
era *s* tempus, saeculum *n*
eradicate *vt* eruĕre, exstirpare, eradicare
eradication *s* exstirpatio *f*
erase *vt* delēre, eradĕre
erasure *s* litura *f*
ere *conj* priusquam
ere *prep* ante (*with acc*); **— long** brevi, mox; **— now** ante hoc tempus
erect *adj* erectus, arrectus
erect *vt* (*to raise*) erigĕre; (*to build*) exstruĕre; (*statue*) ponĕre
erection *s* erectio, aedificatio, exstructio *f*
erotic *adj* amatorius, eroticus
err *vi* (ab)errare, peccare
errand *s* mandatum *n*
erratic *adj* inconstans
erroneous *adj* falsus, errore implicitus; **—ly** falso, perperam
error *s* error *m*; vitium *n*; delictum, peccatum *n*; (*in writing*) mendum *n*
erudite *adj* eruditus, doctus
erudition *s* eruditio *f*
erupt *vi* erumpĕre
eruption *s* eruptio *f*
escape *s* fuga *f*, effugium *n*
escape *vt* fugĕre, evitare; **to — the notice of** fallĕre; *vi* effugĕre, evadĕre, elabi; (*secretly*) subterfugĕre
escort *s* comitat·us -ūs *m*; (*protection*) praesidium *n*
escort *vt* comitari, deducĕre
especially *adv* praecipue, praesertim, maxime, in primis
essay *s* experimentum *n*, conat·us -ūs *m*; (*treatise*) libellus *m*
essay *vt* conari, tentare
essence *s* essentia, natura *f*
essential *adj* necessarius, propius; **—ly** naturā, necessario
establish *vt* constituĕre, statuĕre; (*firmly*) stabilire, confirmare; (*to prove*) probare, arguĕre
establishment *s* (*act*) constitutio *f*; (*com*) negotium *n*
estate *s* (*state*) stat·us -ūs *m*, conditio *f*; (*property*) fundus *m*, praedium *n*; (*pol*) ordo *m*, dignitas *f*
esteem *s* aestimatio *f*, honor *m*
esteem *vt* aestimare, putare; (*to respect*) magni facĕre
estimable *adj* aestimandus
estimate *vt* aestimare, censēre
estimate *s* aestimatio *f*, judicium *n*
estimation *s* aestimatio, opinio, sententia *f*, judicium *n*
estimator *s* aestimator, calculator *m*
estrange *vt* abalienare
estrangement *s* alienatio *f*, discidium *n*
estuary *s* aestuarium *n*
eternal *adj* aeternus, sempiternus; **—ly** in aeternum, semper
eternity *s* aeternitas *f*
ether *s* aether *m*
ethereal *adj* aethereus
ethical *adj* moralis
ethics *s* mores *m pl*, ethice *f*; philosophia moralis *f*
etymology *s* etymologia, verborum notatio *f*
eulogize *vt* collaudare
eulogy *s* laudatio *f*, panegyricus *m*
eunuch *s* eunuchus *m*; (*in contempt*) spado *m*
euphony *s* euphonia *f*, sonus dulcis *m*
European *adj* Europaeus
Euxine *s* Euxinus pontus *m*
evacuate *vt* vacuare, vacuefacĕre; (*people*) deducĕre
evacuation *s* discessio *f*; (*of bowels*) egestio *f*
evade *vt* subterfugĕre, eludĕre, devitare
evaporate *vt* exhalare, evaporare; *vi* exhalari
evaporation *s* exhalatio *f*
evasion *s* effugium *n*, tergiversatio *f*
evasive *adj* ambiguus; **—ly** ambigue
eve *s* vesper *m*; (*of feast*) vigiliae *f pl*; **on the — of** sub (*with acc*)
even *adj* aequalis, aequus; (*level*) planus; (*of numbers*) par; **—ly** aequaliter
even *adv* et, etiam, vel; **— if** etsi, etiamsi; **not —** ne . . . quidem
evening *s* vesper *m*; **in the —** vespere, vesperi
evening *adj* vespertinus
evening star *s* Hesperus, Vesper *m*
evenness *s* aequalitas, aequabilitas *f*
event *s* cas·us -ūs *m*, factum *n*; (*outcome*) event·us -ūs, exit·us -ūs *m*; **in any —** saltem
eventful *adj* memorabilis
eventual *adj* ultimus; **—ly** aliquando, olim, denique
ever *adv* (*always*) semper; (*at any time*) umquam; (*after* si, nisi, num, ne) quando; **for —** in aeternum
evergreen *adj* sempervivus
everlasting *adj* sempiternus; **—ly** in aeternum
evermore *adv* semper, in aeternum
every *adj* quisque, omnis; **— now and then** interdum; **— other day** alternis diebus
everybody *pron* quisque, nemo non; omnes *m pl*
everyday *adj* quotidianus *or* cottidianus; usitatus
everything *pron* omnia *n pl*
everywhere *adv* ubique, ubivis
evict *vt* expellĕre, dejicĕre, detrudĕre
evidence *s* testimonium, indicium, argumentum *n*; (*witness*) testis *m & f*
evidence *vt* testari
evident *adj* apertus, manifestus; **it is —** apparet; **—ly** aperte, manifesto
evil *adj* malus, pravus, improbus
evil *s* malum *n*, improbitas *f*
evildoer *s* maleficus, malefactor *m*
evil-minded *adj* malevolus, malignus
evoke *vt* evocare, excitare, elicĕre
evolution *s* progress·us -ūs *m*, progressio *f*
evolve *vt* evolvĕre, explicare
exact *adj* exactus, subtilis, diligens;

—ly accurate, subtiliter, diligenter; **—ly as** sic ut
exact *vt* exigĕre
exaction *s* exactio *f*
exactitude *s* diligentia *f*
exaggerate *vt* exaggerare, augēre, in majus extollĕre
exaggeration *s* trajectio, superlatio *f*
exalt *vt* extollĕre, amplificare, evehĕre
exaltation *s* elatio *f*
examination *s* investigatio *f*; (*in school*) probatio *f*; (*of witnesses*) interrogatio *f*
examine *vt* investigare, inquirĕre, scrutari; (*witnesses*) interrogare
examiner *s* scrutator, investigator *m*
example *s* exemplum, exemplar, documentum *n*; **for —** exempli gratiā, verbi gratiā
exasperate *vt* exasperare, exacerbare, irritare
exasperation *s* ira *f*
excavate *vt* excavare, effodĕre
excavation *s* fossio, excavatio *f*, cavum *n*
exceed *vt* superare, excedĕre
exceedingly *adv* valde, magnopere
excel *vt* superare, praestare (*with dat*); *vi* excellĕre
excellence *s* excellentia, praestantia *f*
Excellency *s* illustrissimus *m*
excellent *adj* praestans, egregius, optimus; **—ly** egregie, optime
except *vt* excipĕre
except *prep* praeter (*with acc*); nisi (*followed by appropriate case*); **— that** nisi quod
exception *s* exceptio *f*; **with the — of** praeter (*with acc*)
exceptional *adj* egregius, praestans, singularis; **—ly** praeter modum
excess *s* excess·us -ūs *m*, intemperantia *f*
excessive *adj* immodicus, nimius; **—ly** immodice, nimis
exchange *s* (*barter*) commutatio *f*; (*of money*) collybus *m*
exchange *vt* mutare, permutare
excise *vt* excidĕre
excision *s* excisio *f*
excitable *adj* irritabilis, fervidus
excite *vt* excitare, stimulare; (*to inflame*) incendĕre
excitement *s* commotio *f*; perturbatio *f*; incitamentum *n*
exclaim *vt* exclamare; (*as a group*) conclamare; *vi* **to — against** acclamare (*with dat*); declamitare in (*with acc*)
exclamation *s* exclamatio *f*, clamor *m*
exclude *vt* excludĕre, prohibēre
exclusion *s* exclusio *f*
exclusive *adj* proprius; **— of** praeter (*with acc*); **—ly** solum
excommunicate *vt* excommunicare
excommunication *s* excommunicatio *f*
excrement *s* excrementum, stercus *n*
excretion *s* excrementum *n*, excretio *f*
excruciating *adj* acerbissimus
exculpate *vt* (ex)purgare, excusare, absolvĕre
excursion *s* excursio *f*, iter *n*
excusable *adj* excusabilis
excuse *vt* excusare; ignoscĕre (*with dat*), veniam dare (*with dat*)
excuse *s* excusatio *f*; (*pretense*) pretext·us -ūs *m*, species *f*
execute *vt* (*to perform*) exsequi, efficĕre; (*to punish*) necare, securi ferire
execution *s* effect·us -ūs *m*, effectio *f*; (*capital punishment*) supplicium *n*
executioner *s* carnifex *m*
executive *adj* ad administrationem pertinens
executive *s* administrator *m*
executor *s* curator testamenti *m*
exemplary *adj* egregius, eximius
exemplification *s* expositio *f*
exemplify *vt* explicare
exempt *vt* eximĕre, liberare
exempt *adj* exemptus, immunis, liber
exemption *s* exemptio, immunitas, liberatio *f*
exercise *s* exercitatio *f*, us·us -ūs *m*; (*mil*) exercitium *n*; (*literary*) thema *n*
exercise *vt* exercēre; uti (*with abl*)
exert *vt* adhibēre; **to — oneself** viribus eniti
exertion *s* contentio *f*, nis·us -ūs *m*
exhalation *s* exhalatio *f*, vapor *m*
exhale *vt* exhalare, spargĕre; *vi* exspirare
exhaust *vt* exhaurire; (*to tire*) defatigare, conficĕre, debilitare
exhaustion *s* defatigatio, defectio virium *f*
exhibit *vt* exhibēre, exponĕre, ostendĕre
exhibition *s* exhibitio, propositio *f*; spectaculum *n*
exhilarate *vt* exhilarare
exhilaration *s* hilaritas *f*
exhort *vt* hortari
exhortation *s* hortatio *f*, hortamen *n*
exhume *vt* exhumare, eruĕre
exigency *s* necessitas *f*, angustiae *f pl*
exile *s* (*banishment*) ex(s)ilium *n*; (*person*) exsul, profugus *m*
exile *vt* relegare, in exilium pellĕre, deportare
exist *vi* esse, exsistĕre; vivĕre
existence *s* existentia *f*; vita *f*
exit *s* exit·us -ūs *m*; ostium *n*
exonerate *vt* absolvĕre
exorbitant *adj* nimius, immodicus
exotic *adj* externus, peregrinus
expand *vt* expandĕre, extendĕre, dilatare; *vi* expandi, extendi, dilatari
expanse *s* spatium, expansum *n*
expansion *s* expansio *f*, spatium *n*
expatriate *vt* expellĕre
expect *vt* exspectare, sperare
expectancy *s* spes *f*
expectation *s* exspectatio, spes *f*
expectorate *vt* exspuĕre, exscreare
expediency *s* utilitas *f*
expedient *adj* utilis, commodus; **—ly** apte, commode

expedient *s* modus *m*, ratio *f*
expedite *vt* expedire, maturare
expedition *s* (*mil*) expeditio *f*; (*speed*) celeritas *f*
expeditious *adj* celer, promptus; **—ly** celeriter, mature
expel *vt* expellĕre, ejicĕre
expend *vt* expendĕre, impendĕre
expenditure *s* sumpt·us -ūs *m*, impensa *f*
expense *s* impensa *f*, sumpt·us -ūs *m*
expensive *adj* carus, pretiosus; sumptuosus, lautus; **—ly** sumptuose
experience *s* experientia, peritia *f*, us·us -ūs *m*
experience *vt* experiri, cognoscĕre, pati
experienced *adj* peritus, expertus
experiment *s* experimentum *n*
experiment *vi* **to — with** experiri
experimental *adj* usu comparatus
expert *adj* sciens, peritus, callidus; **—ly** callide, scienter
expertness *s* calliditas, sollertia *f*
expiate *vt* expiare, luĕre
expiation *s* expiatio *f*; piaculum *n*
expiration *s* exspiratio *f*, finis, exit·us -ūs *m*
expire *vi* exspirare; (*of time*) exire
explain *vt* explanare, explicare, exponĕre
explanation *s* explanatio, explicatio, enodatio, interpretatio *f*
explicit *adj* apertus, expressus; **—ly** aperte, plane
explode *vt* displodĕre, discutĕre; *vi* displodi, dirumpi
exploit *s* res gesta *f*, factum, facinus *n*
exploit *vt* uti (*with abl*), abuti (*with abl*)
exploration *s* indagatio, investigatio *f*
explore *vt* explorare, scrutari, perscrutari
explorer *s* explorator *m*
explosion *s* fragor *m*
exponent *s* interpres *m*
export *vt* exportare, evehĕre
exporter *s* exportator *m*
exports *s* merces quae exportantur *f pl*
expose *vt* exponĕre; nudare, detegĕre, patefacĕre; (*to danger*) objicĕre, offerre
exposition *s* explicatio, expositio, interpretatio *f*; (*show*) spectaculum *n*
expostulation *s* expostulatio, querela *f*
exposure *s* (*of guilt*) deprehensio *f*; (*to cold*) expositio *f*
expound *vt* exponĕre, interpretari
express *adj* clarus, expressus; **—ly** plane
express *vt* exprimĕre, eloqui, dicĕre; significare
expression *s* vox *f*, verbum *n*; (*of face*) vult·us -ūs *m*
expressive *adj* significans; (*fig*) loquax; **— of** index (*with genit*)
expulsion *s* exactio, ejectio, expulsio *f*
expunge *vt* delēre, oblitterare
expurgate *vt* expurgare
exquisite *adj* exquisitus, elegans; **—ly** eleganter, exquisite
extant *adj* superstes, exsistens; **to be —** exstare
extempore *adv* ex tempore, subito
extemporize *vi* subito dicĕre, subita dicĕre
extend *vt* extendĕre, producĕre, propagare; *vi* extendĕre, porrigi
extension *s* extensio *f*; (*space*) spatium *n*; (*of boundaries*) prolatio *f*
extensive *adj* amplus, latus; **—ly** late
extent *s* spatium *n*; (*of a country*) tract·us -ūs *m*, fines *m pl*; **to a great —** magna ex parte; **to some —** aliqua ex parte; **to this —** hactenus
extenuate *vt* mitigare, minuĕre
extenuation *s* imminutio *f*
exterior *adj* externus, exterior
exterior *s* species *f*
exterminate *vt* exstirpare, exterminare, eradicare
extermination *s* exstirpatio *f*; internecio, occidio *f*
external *adj* externus, extraneus; **—ly** extrinsecus
extinct *adj* exstinctus, obsoletus; **to become —** obsolescĕre
extinction *s* exstinctio *f*, interit·us -ūs *m*
extinguish *vt* exstinguĕre, restinguĕre
extol *vt* laudibus efferre
extort *vt* extorquēre, diripĕre, exprimĕre
extortion *s* res repetundae *f pl*
extortioner *s* exactor, extortor *m*
extra *adj* additus
extra *adv* insuper, praeterea
extract *vt* extrahĕre, excerpĕre; (*teeth, etc.*) evellĕre
extract *s* (*chemical*) expressio *f*; (*literary*) excerptum *n*; (*synopsis*) compendium *n*
extraction *s* (*act*) evulsio *f*; (*birth, origin*) stirps, origo *f*, genus *n*
extraneous *adj* extraneus, alienus, adventicius
extraordinarily *adv* mire, praeter solitum, extra modum
extraordinary *adj* extraordinarius, insolitus; (*outstanding*) eximius, mirus
extravagance *s* intemperantia *f*; sumpt·us -ūs *m*
extravagant *adj* immodicus, nimius; profusus, luxuriosus; (*spending*) prodigus; **—ly** immodice, absurde; prodige
extreme *adj* extremus, ultimus; **—ly** valde, summe
extreme *s* extremum, summum *n*
extremity *s* extremitas *f*, extremum *n*, finis *m*; (*distress*) miseria *f*
extricate *vt* expedire, extrahĕre, liberare

exuberance *s* ubertas, luxuria, redundantia *f*
exuberant *adj* uber, luxuriosus; **—ly** ubertim
exude *vt* exudare; *vi* emanare
exult *vi* exsultare, gestire
exultant *adj* laetabundus, laetus; **—ly** laete
exultation *s* laetitia *f*
eye *s* oculus *m*; (*of needle*) foramen *n*; (*of plant*) gemma *f*; **to keep one's —s on** oculos defigĕre in (*with abl*)
eye *vt* aspicĕre, intuēri
eyebrow *s* supercilium *n*
eyelash *s* palebrarum pilus *m*
eyelid *s* palpebra *f*
eyesight *s* acies, acies oculi *f*
eyewitness *s* arbiter *m*

F

fable *s* fabula, narratio commenticia *f*
fabric *s* fabrica *f*; (*piece of cloth*) textile *n*
fabricate *vt* fabricare, struĕre; (*fig*) fingĕre
fabrication *s* fabricatio *f*; (*fig*) mendacium *n*
fabulous *adj* fictus, commenticius; **—ly** ficte
face *s* facies *f*, os *n*, vult·us -ūs *m*; **— to —** coram
face *vt* aspicĕre, intuēre; se opponĕre (*with dat*), obviam ire (*with dat*); obire; *vi* spectare, vergĕre; **to — about** (*mil*) signa convertĕre
facet *s* pars *f*
facetious *adj* facetus; **—ly** facete
facilitate *vt* facilius reddĕre
facility *s* facilitas *f*; opportunitas *f*
facing *adj* adversus, spectans
facsimile *s* imago *f*, exemplar *n*
fact *s* factum, verum *n*, res *f*; **as a matter of —** enimvero; **in —** vero, re ipsa; enim, etenim; **the — that** quod
faction *s* factio *f*
factory *s* officina, fabrica *f*
faculty *s* facultas, vis *f*; (*of university*) ordo *m*
fade *vi* marcescĕre, deflorescĕre, pallescĕre
fail *vt* (*to disappoint*) relinquĕre, deserĕre, deficĕre; *vi* succumbĕre, concidĕre, cadĕre; (*com*) decoquĕre, foro cedĕre
fail *s* **without —** certo, plane, omnino
failing *s* (*deficiency*) defect·us ūs *m*; (*fault*) culpa *f*, delictum, vitium *n*; (*disappointment*) frustratio *f*; (*ceasing*) remissio *f*
failure *s* defectio *f*, defect·us -ūs *m*; (*fault*) culpa *f*, delictum *n*
faint *adj* (*weary*) defessus; (*drooping*) languidus; (*of sight, smell, etc.*) hebes; (*of sound*) surdus; (*of color*) pallidus; (*of courage*) timidus; **—ly** languide; timide
faint *vi* collabi, intermori, (animo) linqui
fainthearted *adj* timidus, imbellis, ignavus
faintness *s* (*of impression*) levitas *f*; (*of body*) languor *m*
fair *adj* (*in appearance*) formosus, pulcher; (*of complexion*) candidus; (*of hair*) flavus; (*of weather*) serenus; (*of wind*) secundus; (*impartial*) aequus; (*of ability*) mediocris; **— and square** sine fuco ac fallaciis; **—ly** aeque, juste; (*moderately*) mediocriter
fair *s* nundinae *f pl*
fairness *s* (*of complexion*) candor *m*; (*justice*) aequitas *f*
fairy *s* nympha *f*
faith *s* (*trust*) fides *f*; religio *f*; **to have — in** credĕre (*with dat*), confidĕre (*with dat*)
faithful *adj* fidelis, fidus; **—ly** fideliter
faithfulness *s* fidelitas, integritas *f*
faithless *adj* infidus, infidelis, perfidus; **—ly** perfide
falcon *s* falco *m*
fall *s* cas·us -ūs, laps·us -ūs *m*; (*season*) autumnus *m*
fall *vi* cadĕre, concidĕre, labi; (*to die*) occidĕre; (*to abate*) decrescĕre; (*violently*) corruĕre; **to — apart** dilabi; **to — at** accidĕre ad (*with acc*); **to — back** recidĕre; (*to retreat*) pedem referre; **to — down** decidĕre; concidĕre; **to — forwards** procidĕre, prolabi; **to — foul of** incurrĕre; **to — in(to)** incidĕre; **to — in with** (*to meet*) incidĕre; (*to agree*) congruĕre; **to — in love with** amare, adamare; **to — off** (*fig*) in deterius mutari; **to — out with** (*to have a disagreement with*) dissedēre; dissentire ab (*with abl*); **to — short of** non contingĕre; **to — sick** in morbum incidĕre; **to — to** (*of inheritances, etc.*) obvenire (*with dat*); **to — under** succumbĕre; (*to be reckoned*) pertinēre; (*to become subjected to*) pati; **to — upon** incidĕre ad (*with acc*); (*to assail*) incidĕre in (*with acc*), ingruĕre in (*with acc*)
fallacious *adj* fallax, captiosus; **—ly** fallaciter
fallacy *s* captio *f*
fallible *adj* errori obnoxius
fallow *adj* (*of land*) novalis; **to lie —** cessare
false *adj* falsus, fictus; **—ly** falso
falsehood *s* mendacium *n*
falsify *vt* supponĕre, corrumpĕre; (*documents*) vitiare, interlinĕre

falter vi (to stammer) haesitare; (to totter) titubare

fame s fama f, nomen n

famed adj clarus, illustris

familiar adj familiaris, notus; intimus; —ly familiariter

familiarity s familiaritas, consuetudo f, us·us -ūs m

familiarize vt assuefacĕre

family s familia, dom·us -ūs, gens f, genus n

family adj familiaris; (of home) domesticus; (relating to race) gentilicus

famine s fames f

famished adj famelicus; fame confectus

famous adj clarus, celeber, inclitus; —ly praeclare, insigniter

fan s flabellum n; (admirer) fautor m; (winnowing) vannus f

fan vt ventilare; (fire) accendĕre; (fig) excitare, inflammare

fanatic adj fanaticus; —ly fanatice

fanaticism s furor religiosus m

fancied adj opinatus

fanciful adj (capricious) inconstans, levis; (imagined) commenticius

fancy s opinio, imaginatio f; (caprice) libido f; (liking) prolubium n; (faculty) phantasia f

fancy vt imaginari

fang s dens m

fantastic adj vanus; monstruosus

far adj longinquus, remotus

far adv procul, longe; **as — as** quantum, quatenus; tenus (with abl); by **— longe, multo; — and near** longe lateque; — **be it from me to say** equidem dicĕre nolim; — **off** procul; **so — hactenus; thus —** hactenus

farce s mimus m

farcical adj mimicus; —ly mimice

fare s (food) cibus, vict·us -ūs m; (money) vectura f, portorium n

fare vi agĕre, se habēre

farewell interj vale!; salve!

farm s fundus m, praedium n

farm vt (to till) arare, colĕre; (taxes) redimĕre; **to — out** locare

farmer s agricola, colonus m; (of revenues) publicanus m

farming s agricultura f; res rustica f

farsighted adj providus

farther adj ulterior

farther adv longius, ulterius, ultra

farthermost adj remotissimus, ultimus

farthest adj ultimus, extremus

fasces n fasces m pl

fascinate vt fascinare

fascination s fascinatio f, fascinum n

fashion s (form) forma, figura f; (manner) mos, modus, rit·us -ūs m; (custom) consuetudo f, us·us -ūs m

fashion vt formare, fabricare, effingĕre

fashionable adj elegans, concinnus; **it is — in usu est

fashionably adv ad morem; eleganter

fast adj (swift) celer; (firm) firmus, stabilis; (tight) astrictus; (shut) occlusus

fast adv celeriter; firmiter

fast s jejunium n

fast vi jejunare, cibo abstinēre

fasten vt affigĕre, astringĕre; **to — down** defigĕre; **to — to** annectĕre, impingĕre; **to — together** configĕre, colligare; vi **to — upon** arripĕre

fastening s colligatio f, vinculum n

fastidious adj fastidiosus, delicatus, elegans, morosus; —ly fastidiose, morose

fasting s jejunium n, abstinentia f

fat adj pinguis, obsesus; (productive) fertilis

fat s adeps m & f, lardum n

fatal adj fatalis; exitialis, funebris; —ly fataliter; funeste

fatality s fatum n; (misfortune) infortunium n

fate s fatum n, sors f

fated adj fatalis

Fates s Parcae f pl

father s pater m; **— of the family** paterfamilias m

fatherhood s paternitas f

father-in-law s socer m

fatherless adj orbus

fatherly adj paternus, patrius

fathom s ulna f

fathom vt exputare

fathomless adj profundissimus

fatigue s (de)fatigatio, lassitudo f

fatigue vt (de)fatigare, delassare

fatigued adj (de)fatigatus, (de)fessus

fatten vt saginare, farcire; vi pinguescĕre

fattening s saginatio f

fatty adj pinguis

fatuous adj fatuus, insulsus

fault s culpa f, delictum, vitium n, error m; (in writing) mendum n; **to find — with** vituperare, carpĕre, incusare

faultless adj integer, perfectus; (corrected) emendatus

faulty adj vitiosus; mendosus

faun s faunus m

favor s favor m, gratia f; (goodwill) benevolentia f; (good turn) beneficium n; (present) munus n

favor vt favēre (with dat), secundare

favorable adj prosperus, secundus; commodus, idoneus; benignus, propitius

favorably adv fauste, felicter, benigne; opportune

favorite adj dilectus, gratus

favorite s deliciae f pl

favoritism s indulgentia f; iniquitas f

fawn s hinnuleus m

fawn vi **to — on** or **upon** adulari

fawning adj blandus, adulatorius; —ly blande, adulatorie

fawning s adulatio f

fear s timor, met·us -ūs m, formido f

fear vt & vi timēre, metuĕre, verēri

fearful *adj* timidus, pavidus; (*terrible*) dirus, terribilis; **—ly** timide
fearless *adj* impavidus, intrepidus; **—ly** impavide, intrepide
feasibility *s* possibilitas *f*
feasible *adj* efficiendus, possibilis
feast *s* (*banquet*) convivium *n*, epulae *f pl*; (*holy day*) dies festus *m*
feast *vt* pascĕre; *vi* epulari, convivari
feat *s* facinus, factum *n*
feather *s* penna *f*; (*downy*) pluma *f*
feather *vt* **to — one's nest** opes accumulare
feathered *adj* pennatus; plumosus
feathery *adj* plumeus, plumosus
feature *s* lineamentum *n*; (*fig*) proprietas *f*, proprium *n*
February *s* (mensis) Februarius *m*
federal *adj* foederatus; rei publicae (*genit*)
federalize *vt* confoederare
federation *s* confoederatio *f*
fee *s* merces *f*
feeble *adj* infirmus, debilis; **to grow —** languescĕre
feebly *adv* infirme, languide
feed *vt* (*animals*) pascĕre; (*to nourish*) alĕre; (*fig*) (*of streams, etc.*) servire (*with dat*); *vi* pasci; **to — on** vesci (*with abl*)
feed *s* pabulum *n*
feel *vt* sentire; (*with hand*) tangĕre, tractare; **to — pain** dolore affici; **to — pity for** misereri (*with genit*); *vi* **to — happy** gaudēre; **to — sad** maestus esse
feel *s* tact·us -ūs *m*
feeling *s* (*touch*) tact·us -ūs *m*; (*sensibility*) sens·us -ūs *m*; (*emotion*) affect·us -ūs *m*; (*taste*) judicium *n*; (*pity*) miseratio *f*
feign *vt* fingĕre, dissimulare, mentiri
feint *s* simulatio *f*
felicitation *s* congratulatio *f*
felicitous *adj* felix; **—ly** feliciter
felicity *s* felicitas *f*
feline *adj* felin(e)us
fell *adj* atrox, saevus, crudelis
fell *vt* (*trees*) caedĕre; (*person*) sternĕre
fellow *s* socius, aequalis *m*
felon *s* scelestus, sceleratus *m*
felonious *adj* scelestus, sceleratus
felony *s* scelus *n*
felt *s* coacta *n pl*
female *adj* muliebris
female *s* femina *f*
feminine *adj* muliebris, femineus; (*gram*) femininus
fence *s* saepes *f*, saepimentum *n*
fence *vt* saepire; **to — off** intersaepire; *vi* batuĕre
fencing *s* ludus gladiatorius *m*
fend *vt* **to — off** arcēre; *vi* **to — for oneself** sibi providēre, sibi consulĕre
ferment *s* fermentum *n*; (*fig*) aest·us -ūs *m*
ferment *vt* fermentare; excitare; *vi* fermentari; (*fig*) fervēre
fermentation *s* fermentatio *f*
fern *s* filix *f*
ferocious *adj* ferox, truculentus, saevus, atrox; **—ly** truculente
ferocity *s* ferocitas, saevitia *f*
ferret *vt* **to — out** eruĕre
ferry *s* traject·us -ūs *m*
ferry *vt* trajicĕre, transvehĕre
ferryboat *s* scapha, cymba *f*
ferryman *s* portitor *m*
fertile *adj* fertilis, fecundus
fertility *s* fertilitas, ubertas *f*
fertilize *vt* fecundare
fervent *adj* fervidus, ardens; **—ly** ardenter, vehementer
fervid *adj* fervidus; **—ly** fervide
fervor *s* fervor, ardor *m*
fester *vi* suppurare, ulcerari
festival *s* dies festus *m*, sollemne *n*
festive *adj* festus
festivity *s* sollemnia *n pl*; (*gaiety*) festivitas *f*
fetch *vt* adducĕre, afferre, arcessĕre
fetid *adj* foetidus, graveolens
feud *s* simultas, inimicitia, lis *f*
fever *s* febris *f*; **to have a —** febrire
feverish *adj* febriculosus
few *adj* pauci; **a —** aliquot; **in a — words** paucis, breviter
fiasco *s* calamitas *f*
fiber *s* fibra *f*
fibrous *adj* fibratus
fickle *adj* inconstans, mobilis, instabilis
fiction *s* fictio *f*, commentum *n*; fabula *f*
fictitious *adj* fictus, commenticius; **—ly** ficte
fiddle *s* fides *f*
fiddle *vi* fide ludĕre
fiddler *s* fidicen *m*
fidelity *s* fidelitas, constantia *f*
fidget *vi* trepidare
fidgety *adj* inquietus
field *s* ager *m*; (*plowed*) arvum *n*; (*mil*) acies *f*, campus *m*; (*grassy*) pratum *n*; (*of grain*) seges *f*; (*sphere*) area *f*, locus, campus *m*
fieldpiece *s* tormentum *n*
fiend *s* inimicus *m*; diabolus *m*
fiendish *adj* diabolicus
fierce *adj* atrox, saevus, vehemens; **—ly** atrociter, saeve, vehementer
fierceness *s* atrocitas, saevitia, ferocitas *f*
fiery *adj* igneus; (*fig*) ardens, fervidus
fife *s* tibia *f*
fifteen *adj* quindecim; **— times** quindecies
fifteenth *adj* quintus decimus
fifth *adj* quintus; **for the — time** quintum, quinto
fifth *s* quinta pars *f*
fiftieth *adj* quinquagesimus
fifty *adj* quinquaginta
fig *s* ficus *f*
fight *s* pugna *f*, proelium *n*; (*struggle*) contentio, luctatio *f*
fight *vt* pugnare cum (*with abl*); **to — it out** decernĕre, depugnare; *vi* pugnare, dimicare; (*in battle*) proeliari; (*with sword*) digladiari; **to — hand to hand** cominus pugnare

figment *s* commentum *n*
figurative *adj* translatus, assumptus; **—ly** per translationem, tropice
figure *s* figura, forma, imago *f*; (*of speech*) tropus *m*, translatio *f*; (*in art*) signum *n*
figure *vt* figurare, formare; putare, opinari
figured *adj* sigillatus
filament *s* filum *n*, fibra *f*
filbert *s* nux avellana *f*
file *s* (*tool*) lima *f*; (*for papers*) scapus *m*; (*row*) ordo *m*, agmen *n*
file *vt* limare; (*papers*) in scapo conděre; *vi* **to — off** (*mil*) decurrěre
filial *adj* pius
filigree *s* diatreta *n pl*
filings *s* scobis *f*
fill *vt* complēre, implēre; (*office*) fungi (*with abl*); **to — out** implēre; **to — up** explēre, complēre, supplēre
fill *s* satietas *f*
fillip *s* talitrum *n*
filly *s* equula *f*
film *s* membranula *f*
filmy *adj* membranaceus; (*fig*) caliginosus
filter *s* colum *n*
filter *vt* percolare; *vi* percolari
filtering *s* percolatio *f*
filth *s* sordes, colluvies *f*, squalor *m*
filthiness *s* foeditas *f*, squalor *m*; (*fig*) obscenitas *f*
filthy *adj* sordidus, spurcus; (*fig*) obscenus
filtration *s* percolatio *f*
fin *s* pinna *f*
final *adj* ultimus, postremus, extremus; **—ly** denique, tandem; postremo
finance *s* (*private*) res familiaris *f*; (*public*) aerarium *n*, ratio aeraria *f*, vectigalia *n pl*
financial *adj* aerarius
find *vt* invenire, reperire; (*to hit upon*) offenděre; **to — out** comperire, cognoscěre
fine *adj* (*thin*) subtilis, tenuis; (*of gold*) purus; (*handsome*) bellus, elegans; (*of weather*) serenus; **—ly** subtiliter
fine *s* mul(c)ta *f*, damnum *n*
fine *vt* mul(c)tare
finery *s* ornat·us -ūs *m*
finesse *s* astutia *f*, argutiae *f pl*
finger *s* digitus *m*; (*of glove*) digitale *n*
finger *vt* tractare
finish *vt* conficěre, perficěre; (*to put an end to*) terminare; **to — off** conficěre; peragěre; *vi* desiněre
finish *s* finis *m*; (*in art*) perfectio *f*
finite *adj* finitus, circumscriptus
fire *s* ignis *m*; (*conflagration*) incendium *n*; (*of artillery*) conject·us -ūs *m*; (*fig*) fervor, ardor, impet·us -ūs *m*; **by — and sword** ferro igníque; **to be on —** flagrare; **to catch —** flammam concipěre; **to set on —** incenděre
fire *vt* accenděre, incenděre; (*fig*) inflammare; (*missile*) jaculari; (*to dismiss*) dimittěre
firefly *s* elater noctilucus *m*
fireplace *s* focus, caminus *m*
fireproof *adj* ignibus impervius
fireside *s* focus *m*
firewood *s* lignum *n*
firm *adj* firmus, solidus; constans; **to be —** perseverare; **to stand —** perstare; **—ly** firme, firmiter; solide; constanter
firm *s* societas *f*
firmament *s* firmamentum *n*
firmness *s* firmitas, constantia *f*
first *adj* primus; (*of two*) prior
first *adv* primum; **at —** primo; **— of all** imprimis
firstborn *adj* primogenitus
firstfruits *s* primitiae *f pl*
fiscal *adj* aerarius, fiscalis
fish *s* piscis *m*
fish *vi* piscari; (*fig*) expiscari
fisherman *s* piscator *m*
fishing *s* piscat·us -ūs *m*, piscatio *f*
fish market *s* forum piscarium *n*
fish pond *s* piscina *f*
fishy *adj* piscosus
fissure *s* fissura, rima *f*
fist *s* pugnus *m*
fit *s* (*of anger, etc.*) impet·us -ūs *m*; (*med*) access·us -ūs *m*; convulsio *f*; (*whim*) libido *f*; **by —s and starts** carptim
fit *adj* aptus, idoneus; habilis; (*becoming*) decens; (*ready*) paratus
fit *vt* accommodare; (*to apply*) applicare; (*to furnish*) instruěre; *vi* (*fig*) convenire
fitful *adj* mutabilis, inconstans
fitness *s* convenientia *f*; (*of persons*) habilitas *f*
fitting *adj* decens, idoneus; **it is —** convenit, decet
five *adj* quinque; **— times** quinquies
fix *vt* (*to repair*) reficěre; resarcire; (*to fasten*) figěre, firmare; (*the eyes*) intenděre; (*time*) dicěre; *vi* **to — upon** inhaerēre (*with dat*)
fixed *adj* firmus, fixus; certus; **— on** (*intent upon*) intentus (*with dat*)
fixture *s* affixum *n*
fizz *vi* sibilare
flabbiness *s* mollitia *f*
flabby *adj* flaccidus, flaccus; (*drooping*) marcidus
flaccid *adj* flaccidus
flag *s* vexillum *n*
flagrant *adj* impudens, apparens, nefarius
flail *s* pertica, tribula *f*
flake *s* squama *f*; (*of snow*) nix *f*
flaky *adj* squameus
flame *s* flamma *f*
flame *vi* flammare, flagrare; **to — up** scintillare; (*fig*) exardescěre
flank *s* (*of animal*) ilia *n pl*; (*mil*) latus *n*; **on the —** a latere
flank *vt* tegěre latus (*with genit*)
flap *s* (*of dress*) lacinia *f*
flap *vt* plauděre (*with abl*); *vi* (*to hang loosely*) fluitare
flare *s* flamma *f*, fulgor *m*
flare *vi* flagrare, exardescěre

flash *s* fulgor *m*; (*of fire*) coruscatio *f*; (*of lightning*) fulmen *n*; **— of wit** sales *m pl*
flash *vi* fulgēre, coruscare, micare
flask *s* ampulla, laguncula *f*
flat *adj* (*level*) planus, aequus; (*not mountainous*) campester; (*on back*) supinus; (*on face*) pronus; (*insipid*) vapidus; (*fig*) frigidus, insulsus; **to fall —** (*fig*) frigēre
flatness *s* planities *f*
flatten *vt* complanare, planum reddĕre
flatter *vt* adulari (*with dat*), blandiri (*with dat*), assentari (*with dat*)
flatterer *s* adulator, assentator *m*
flattering *adj* adulans, blandus, adulatorius
flattery *s* adulatio *f*, blanditiae *f pl*
flaunt *vt* jactare; *vi* tumēre, gloriari
flaunting *adj* lautus, gloriosus
flaunting *s* jactatio *f*
flavor *s* sapor, gustat·us -ūs *m*
flavor *vt* imbuĕre, condire
flaw *s* (*defect*) vitium *n*; (*chink*) rimula *f*
flawless *adj* emendatus
flax *s* linum *n*
flaxen *adj* lineus
flay *vt* deglubare
flea *s* pulex *m*
fleck *s* macula *f*
fledged *adj* plumatus
flee *vi* fugĕre; **to — away** aufugĕre; **to — back** refugĕre; **to — to** confugĕre ad *or* in (*with acc*)
fleece *s* vellus *n*
fleece *vt* tondēre; (*fig*) spoliare
fleecy *adj* laniger
fleet *s* classis *f*
fleet *adj* celer; (*winged*) volucer; (*fig*) fugax
fleeting *adj* fugax; (*flowing*) fluxus
flesh *s* caro *f*; **in the —** vivus
fleshy *adj* carnosus
flexibility *s* flexibilitas *f*; (*fig*) mollitia *f*
flexible *adj* flexibilis, lentus; (*fig*) exorabilis
flicker *vi* coruscare
flickering *adj* tremulus
flight *s* (*flying*) volat·us -ūs *m*; (*escape*) fuga *f*, effugium *n*; (*covey*) grex *m*; (*of stairs*) scala *f*; **to put to —** fugare; **to take to —** aufugĕre, terga vertĕre
flighty *adj* levis
flimsy *adj* nimis subtilis, praetenuis; (*fig*) frivolus
flinch *vi* retrocedĕre, tergiversari; (*to start*) absilire
fling *vt* jacĕre, conjicĕre; **to — away** abjicĕre; **to — down** dejicĕre; **to — off** rejicĕre; **to — open** vehementer aperire
fling *s* jact·us -ūs *m*
flint *s* silex *m & f*
flinty *adj* siliceus
flippancy *s* petulantia *f*
flippant *adj* petulans; temere loquens; **—ly** temere ac leviter
flirt *s* lupus *m*, lupa *f*
flirt *vi* ludĕre, lascivire
flirtation *s* amores *m pl*
flit *vi* volitare
float *s* (*raft*) rates *f*; (*on fishing line*) cortex *m*
float *vt* (*to launch*) demittĕre; *vi* fluitare, (in)natare; (*in air*) volitare
flock *s* grex *m*; **in —s** gregatim
flock *vi* concurrĕre, convenire, coire
floe *s* fragmentum glaciei *n*
flog *vt* verberare
flogging *s* verberatio *f*, verbera *n pl*
flood *s* (*deluge*) diluvies *f*; (*of river*) torrens *m*; (*tide*) access·us -ūs *m*; (*fig*) flumen *n*
floor *s* (*story of building*) tabulatum *n*; (*on the ground*) solum; (*paved*) pavimentum *n*
floor *vt* (*to throw down*) sternĕre
flooring *s* contabulatio *f*
floral *adj* floreus
florid *adj* floridus
flotilla *s* classicula *f*
flounce *s* fimbria *f*
flounder *vi* volutari; (*in speech*) haesitare
flour *s* farina *f*; (*finest*) pollen *m*
flourish *vt* vibrare; (*to sound*) canĕre; *vi* florēre, virēre; (*mus*) praeludĕre
flourish *s* ornamentum *n*; (*of style*) calamistri *m pl*; (*mus*) praelusio *f*; (*of trumpet*) cant·us -ūs *m*
flout *vt* deridēre, contumeliis afficĕre, aspernari
flow *vi* fluĕre; (*of tide*) affluĕre, accedĕre
flow *s* fluxio *f*, laps·us -ūs *m*; (*of tide*) access·us -ūs *m*
flower *s* flos *m*; (*fig*) (*the best*) flos *m*; (*of army*) robur *n*; (*of age*) adulescentia *f*
flower *vi* florescĕre
flowery *adj* floreus; floridus
fluctuate *vi* fluctuari; (*fig*) jactare
fluctuation *s* fluctuatio *f*; (*fig*) mutatio *f*
flue *s* cuniculus fornacis *m*
fluency *s* copia verborum, volubilitas linguae *f*
fluent *adj* volubilis; (*eloquent*) disertus; **—ly** volubiliter
fluid *adj* fluidus, liquidus
fluid *s* fluidum *n*, fluor *m*
fluke *s* (*of anchor*) dens *m*; (*luck*) fortuitum *n*
flurry *s* commotio *f*, tumult·us -ūs *m*
flurry *vt* perturbare, inquietare
flush *s* rubor *m*
flush *vi* erubescĕre
fluster *vt* turbare, inquietare
flute *s* tibia *f*; (*in architecture*) stria *f*
flutist *s* tibicen *m*
flutter *s* volitatio *f*, tremor *m*; (*fig*) trepidatio *f*
flutter *vi* (*of the heart*) palpitare; (*of bird*) volitare; (*with alarm*) trepidare
flux *s* flux·us -ūs *m*; **to be in a state of —** fluĕre
fly *s* musca *f*
fly *vi* volare; (*to flee*) fugĕre; **to — apart** dissilire; **to — off** avolare;

to — open dissilire; to — out provolare; to — up subvolare
flying *adj* volatilis, volucer
foal *s* pullus *m*; (*of asses*) asellus *m*; (*of horses*) equulus *m*
foal *vi* parěre
foam *s* spuma *f*
foam *vi* spumare; (*to boil*) exaestuare
foamy *adj* spumans; spumeus, spumosus
focus *vt* (*the mind*) intenděre
fodder *s* pabulum *n*
fodder *vt* pabulum praebēre (*with dat*)
foe *s* (*public*) hostis *m*; (*private*) inimicus *m*
fog *s* caligo, nebula *f*
foggy *adj* caliginosus, nebulosus
foible *s* vitium *n*, error *m*
foil *s* (*for fencing*) rudis *f*; (*leaf of metal*) lamina *f*; (*very thin*) bractea *f*; (*contrast*) repulsa *f*
foil *vt* eluděre; repellěre
fold *s* sin·us -ūs *m*, plica *f*; (*wrinkle*) ruga *f*; (*for sheep*) ovile *n*; (*for cattle*) stabulum *n*
fold *vt* plicare, complicare
foliage *s* frons *f*, folia *n pl*
folio *s* liber maximae formae *m*
folk *s* homines *m pl*
follow *vt* sequi; (*close*) instare (*with dat*), assectari; (*a calling*) facěre; (*instructions*) parēre (*with dat*); (*road*) pergěre; (*to understand*) intellegěre; **to — out** exsequi, prosequi; **to — up** subsequi
follower *s* sectator *m*; (*of teacher*) auditor *m*
following *adj* sequens; posterus, proximus
folly *s* stultitia, insipientia *f*
foment *vt* fovēre
fond *adj* amans, studiosus; ineptus; **to be — of** amare; **—ly** amanter; (*foolishly*) inepte
fondle *vt* mulcēre, fovēre
fondness *s* caritas *f*, studium *n*
food *s* cibus *m*
fool *s* stultus, fatuus *m*; **to make a — of** ludificare; **to play the —** ineptire
fool *vt* ludificari
foolhardy *adj* temerarius
foolish *adj* stultus, fatuus, ineptus, stolidus; **—ly** stulte, inepte
foot *s* pes *m*; (*of mountain*) radix *f*; (*of pillar*) basis *f*; **on —** pedester
football *s* pila pedalis *f*
footing *s* locus *m*; (*condition*) stat·us -ūs *m*
footprint *s* vestigium *n*
foot soldier *s* pedes *m*
footstool *s* scabellum, scamnum *n*
fop *s* bellus homo *m*
foppish *adj* nitidus, delicatus
for *prep* (*extent of time or space*) *render by acc*; (*price*) *render by genit or abl*; (*on behalf of*) pro (*with abl*); (*cause*) causā (*with genit*), ob (*with acc*), propter (*with acc*); (*after negatives*) prae (*with abl*); (*toward*) erga (*with acc*)
for *conj* nam; enim
forage *s* pabulum *n*
forage *vi* pabulari, frumentari
foray *s* incursio *f*
forbear *vi* parcěre (*with dat*), desistěre
forbearance *s* patientia, indulgentia *f*
forbid *vt* vetare, prohibēre, interdicěre
forbidding *adj* insuavis, odiosus
force *s* vis *f*; (*law*) man·us -ūs *f*; (*mil*) copiae *f pl*, impet·us -ūs *m*; **in —** validus
force *vt* cogěre, impellěre; (*door, etc.*) rumpěre; **to — down** detruděre; **to — out** extruděre, extorquēre
forced *adj* (*unnatural*) arcessitus, quaesitus
forced march *s* magnum *or* maximum iter *n*
forceps *s* forceps *m & f*
forcible *adj* per vim factus; (*of force*) validus; (*violent*) vehemens; (*weighty*) gravis
forcibly *adv* per vim, vi; violenter; graviter
ford *s* vadum *n*
ford *vt* vado transire
fore *adj* anterior, prior
forearm *s* bracchium *n*
forearm *vt* praemunire; **to be forearmed** praecavēre
forebode *vt* (*to foretell*) portenděre; (*to be prescient of*) praesagire
foreboding *s* portentum, praesagium *n*; (*feeling*) praesensio *f*
foreboding *adj* praesagus
forecast *vt* providēre, prospicěre; praedicěre
forecast *s* praedictio *f*
forecastle *s* prora *f*
foredoom *vt* praedestinare
forefather *s* atavus *m*; **—s** majores *m pl*
forefinger *s* digitus index *m*
forego *vt* abdicare, dimittěre
foregoing *adj* prior, proximus
forehead *s* frons *f*
foreign *adj* externus, alienus, peregrinus
foreigner *s* peregrinus, advena *m*
foreknowledge *s* providentia *f*
foreman *s* procurator, villicus *m*
foremost *adj* primus, princeps
forenoon *s* antemeridianum tempus *n*; **in the —** ante meridiem
forensic *adj* forensis
fore part *s* prior pars *f*
forerunner *s* praenuntius, antecursor *m*
foresee *vt* providēre, praevidēre, prospicěre
foreseeing *adj* providus
foresight *s* providentia, prudentia *f*; (*precaution*) provisio *f*
forest *adj* silvestris
forest *s* silva *f*
forestall *vt* occupare, anticipare
foretell *vt* praedicěre, vaticinari
forethought *s* providentia *f*
forewarn *vt* praemonēre
forewarning *s* praemonit·us -ūs *m*
forfeit *s* multa, poena *f*, damnum *n*

forfeit *vt* mul(c)tari (*with abl*), amittĕre, perdĕre
forfeiture *s* damnum *n*, amissio *f*
forge *vt* fabricari, excudĕre; (*document*) subjicĕre; (*signature*) imitari; **to — money** adulterinos nummos cudĕre
forge *s* furnus fabrilis *m*
forged *adj* falsus, adulterinus
forger *s* fabricator *m*; (*of writings*) falsarius *m*; (*of money*) qui adulterinos nummos cudit
forgery *s* falsum *n*
forget *vt* oblivisci (*with genit*)
forgetful *adj* immemor, obliviosus
forgetfulness *s* oblivio *f*
forgive *vt* ignoscĕre (*with dat*), veniam dare (*with dat*); condonare
forgiveness *s* venia *f*
forgiving *adj* clemens
fork *s* furca *f*; (*of roads*) bivium *n*
forked *adj* bifurcus, bicornis
forlorn *adj* destitutus, derelictus
form *s* forma, figura *f*; **in due —** rite
form *vt* formare, fingĕre; (*to produce*) efficĕre
formal *adj* justus; nimis accuratus; **—ly** frigide ac nimis accurate
formality *s* rit·us -ūs *m*; **with due —** rite
formation *s* conformatio, forma, figura *f*; **in —** (*mil*) instructus
former *adj* prior; (*immediately preceding*) superior; antiquus, priscus; **the —** ille; **—ly** antehac, olim, quondam
formidable *adj* formidabilis
formidably *adv* formidolose
formless *adj* informis, rudis
formula *s* formula *f*, exemplar *n*
forsake *vt* deserĕre, derelinquĕre
forswear *vt* abjurare, repudiare
fort *s* castellum *n*
forth *adv* foras; (*of time*) inde; **and so —** et cetera
forthwith *adv* protinus, statim, extemplo
fortieth *adj* quadragesimus
fortification *s* munitio *f*, munimentum *n*
fortify *vt* munire
fortitude *s* fortitudo *f*
fortress *s* arx *f*, castellum *n*
fortuitous *adj* fortuitus; **—ly** fortuito
fortunate *adj* fortunatus, felix, prosperus; **—ly** feliciter
fortune *s* fortuna, felicitas *f*; (*estate*) opes *f pl*, res *f*, divitiae *f pl*; **to tell —s** hariolari
fortune-teller *s* fatidicus, sortilegus, astrologus *m*
forty *adj* quadraginta
forum *s* forum *n*
forward *adv* porro, prorsus, prorsum
forward *adj* (*person*) audax, protervus; anterior
forward *vt* (*letter*) perferre; (*cause*) adjuvare, promovēre
foster *vt* alĕre, fovēre, nutrire
foster brother *s* collacteus *m*
foster child *s* alumnus *m*, alumna *f*
foster father *s* altor, nutritor, educator *m*
foster mother *s* altrix, nutrix, educatrix *f*
foul *adj* (*dirty*) foedus, lutulentus, squalidus; (*ugly*) deformis; (*of language*) obscenus; (*of weather*) turbidus; **to fall — of** incurrĕre in (*with acc*), inruĕre in (*with acc*); **—ly** foede
foul *vt* foedare, inquinare
found *vt* condĕre, fundare, constituĕre, instituĕre
foundation *s* fundamentum *n*, substructio *f*
founder *s* conditor, fundator, auctor *m*
founder *vi* titubare, submergi
foundling *s* expostititius *m*, expositia *f*
fountain *s* fons *m*
fountainhead *s* caput fontis *n*
four *adj* quattuor; **— each** quaterni; **— times** quater; **— years** quadriennium *n*; **on all —s** repens
fourfold *adj* quadruplex, quadruplus
fourscore *adj* octoginta
fourteen *adj* quattuordecim
fourteenth *adj* quartus decimus
fourth *adj* quartus; **—ly** quarto
fourth *s* quadrans *n*, quarta pars *f*; **three —s** tres partes *f pl*
fowl *s* avis, volucris *f*; (*domestic*) gallina *f*
fox *s* vulpes *f*; **an old —** (*fig*) veterator *m*
fraction *s* pars exigua *f*
fracture *s* fractura *f*
fracture *vt* frangĕre
fragile *adj* fragilis; (*fig*) caducus
fragility *s* fragilitas *f*
fragment *s* fragmentum *n*
fragrance *s* odor *m*
fragrant *adj* suaveolens, odorus; **—ly** suavi odore
frail *adj* fragilis; caducus, infirmus
frailty *s* fragilitas, debilitas *f*; (*moral*) error *m*
frame *s* (*of buildings, etc.*) compages *f*; (*of body*) figura *f*; (*of bed*) sponda *f*; (*of mind*) habit·us -ūs *m*
frame *vt* fabricari; (*to contrive*) moliri; (*a picture*) in forma includĕre; (*a document*) componĕre
France *s* Gallia *f*
franchise *s* civitas *f*, suffragium *n*
frank *adj* candidus, sincerus, simplex; **—ly** candide, aperte
frankness *s* libertas, simplicitas, ingenuitas *f*
frantic *adj* amens, furiosus, furens; **—ally** furenter
fraternal *adj* fraternus; **—ly** fraterne
fraternity *s* fraternitas *f*; (*association*) sodalitas *f*
fratricide *s* (*doer*) fratricida *m*; (*deed*) fratris parricidium *n*
fraud *s* fraus *f*, dolus *m*; (*person*) dolus malus *m*
fraudulence *s* fraus *f*

fraudulent *adj* fraudulentus, dolosus; **—ly** fraudulenter, dolo malo
fraught *adj* plenus
fray *s* pugna *f*; (*brawl*) rixa *f*
freak *s* (*whim*) libido *f*; monstrum *n*
freckle *s* lentigo *f*
freckled *adj* lentiginosus
free *adj* liber; (*disengaged*) vacuus, otiosus; (*generous*) liberalis; (*from duty*) immunis; (*unencumbered*) expeditus; (*in speech*) liber, candidus; **—ly** libere; (*of one's own accord*) sponte, ultro; (*frankly*) aperte; (*generously*) large, copiose
free *vt* liberare; (*slave*) manumittĕre; (*son*) emancipare
freeborn *adj* ingenuus
freedman *s* libertus *m*
freedom *s* libertas *f*; (*from duty*) immunitas *f*
freehold *s* praedium liberum *n*
freeholder *s* dominus *m*
freeman *s* liber *m*
free will *s* voluntas *f*, liberum arbitrium *n*; **of one's own —** suā sponte, ultro, arbitrio suo
freeze *vt* congelare, glaciare; *vi* consistĕre, rigescĕre; **it is freezing** gelat
freezing *adj* gelidus
freight *s* onus *n*, vectura *f*
freight *vt* onerare
French *adj* Gallicus; **in —** Gallice; **the —** Galli *m pl*
Frenchman *s* Gallus *m*
frenzied *adj* furens, lymphatus
frenzy *s* furor *m*, insania *f*
frequency *s* crebritas, assiduitas *f*
frequent *adj* creber, frequens; **—ly** crebro, frequenter, saepe
frequent *vt* frequentare
frequenter *s* frequentator *m*
fresco *s* opus tectorium *n*
fresh *adj* (*new*) recens, novus; (*cool*) frigidulus; (*not tired*) integer; (*forward*) protervus; (*green*) viridis; **—ly** recenter
freshen *vt* recreare, renovare; *vi* (*of wind*) increbrescĕre
freshman *s* tiro *m*
freshman *adj* novicius
freshness *s* novitas, viriditas *f*
fret *vi* dolēre, angi
fretful *adj* morosus, stomachosus; **—ly** morose, stomachose
fretted *adj* laqueatus
friction *s* frictio *f*, attrit·us -ūs *m*
friend *s* amicus *m*, amica *f*, familiaris *m & f*; (*of a thing*) amator *m*
friendless *adj* amicorum inops, desertus
friendliness *s* benevolentia, comitas, affabilitas *f*
friendly *adj* amicus, benevolus, comis; **in a — manner** amice
friendship *s* amicitia *f*
frieze *s* zoophorus *m*
fright *s* pavor, terror *m*
frighten *vt* (per)terrēre; **to — away** absterrēre
frightful *adj* terribilis, terrificus; **—ly** foede
frigid *adj* frigidus; **—ly** frigide
frigidity *s* frigiditas *f*
frills *s* segmenta *n pl*; (*rhet*) calamistri *m pl*
fringe *s* fimbria *f*, cirrus *m*; (*fig*) limbus *m*
frisk *vt* scrutari; *vi* lascivire, exsilire
fritter *vt* **to — away** conterĕre, comminuĕre, dissipare
frivolity *s* levitas *f*, nugae *f pl*
frivolous *adj* levis, frivolus, inanis; **—ly** inaniter
fro *adv* **to and —** huc illuc, ultro citroque
frock *s* palla, stola *f*
frog *s* rana *f*
frolic *s* lascivia *f*, ludus *m*
frolic *vi* exsultare, hilarescĕre
from *prep* a *or* ab (*with abl*); de (*with abl*); e *or* ex (*with abl*); (*cause*) ob (*with acc*); **— above** desuper; **— abroad** peregre; **— day to day** de die in diem; **— time to time** interdum, passim; **— within** intus; **— without** extrinsecus
front *s* frons *f*; (*mil*) acies *f*, primum agmen *n*; (*fig*) impudentia *f*; **in —** a fronte, adversus; **in — of** pro (*with abl*)
front *adj* prior
frontier *s* limes *m*, confinia *n pl*
frost *s* gelu *n*, pruina *f*
frostbitten *adj* praeustus, adustus
frosty *adj* gelidus, glacialis
froth *s* spuma *f*
froth *vi* spumare, spumas agĕre
frothy *adj* spumeus, spumosus
frown *s* contractio frontis *f*
frown *vi* frontem contrahĕre *or* aducĕre
frozen *adj* conglaciatus, gelatus, gelu rigens
frugal *adj* parcus, frugi (*indecl*); **—ly** frugaliter, parce
frugality *s* parsimonia, frugalitas *f*
fruit *s* fruct·us -ūs *m*, frux *f*; (*of tree*) mala *n pl*; **—s of the earth** fruges *f pl*
fruitful *adj* fructuosus, fecundus, fertilis; **—ly** fecunde, feraciter
fruitfulness *s* fecunditas, fertilitas, ubertas *f*
fruitless *adj* sterilis; (*fig*) irritus; **—ly** frustra
fruit tree *s* pomus *f*
frustrate *vt* frustrari; (*to baffle*) decipĕre
frustration *s* frustratio *f*
fry *s* (*dish of things fried*) frixa *f*
fry *vt* frigĕre
frying pan *s* sartago *f*
fuel *s* fomes *m*, materia *f*
fugitive *adj* fugitivus
fugitive *s* profugus, transfuga, fugitivus *m*; (*from abroad*) extorris *m*
fulcrum *s* (*of a lever*) pressio *f*
fulfil *vt* explēre, exsequi, perficĕre
fulfilment *s* exsecutio, peractio, perfectio *f*
full *adj* plenus; (*filled up*) expletus; (*entire*) integer, solidus; (*satiated*) satur; (*of dress*) fusus; **—ly** plene, funditus, penitus
full moon *s* plenilunium *n*

fumble *vi* haesitare
fume *s* fumus, vapor, halit·us -ūs *m*
fume *vi* irasci
fumigate *vt* fumigare, suffire
fumigation *s* suffit·us -ūs *m*
fun *s* jocus *m*, ludibrium *n*
function *s* munus, officium *n*
function *vi* munus implēre
functionary *s* magistrat·us -ūs *m*
fund *s* copia *f*, pecuniae *f pl*
fundamental *adj* fundamentalis, primus; **—ly** penitus, funditus
funeral *s* funus *n*, exsequiae *f pl*
funeral *adj* funebris
funereal *adj* funereus, lugubris
fungus *s* fungus *m*
funnel *s* infundibulum *n*
funny *adj* ridiculus, jocularis
fur *s* villi *m pl*, pellis *m*
furious *adj* furiosus, furens; **—ly** furiose, furenter
furl *vt* complicare; (*sail*) legĕre
furlough *s* commeat·us -ūs *m*; **on —** in commeatu
furnace *s* fornax *f*
furnish *vt* suppeditare, ministrare; ornare, exornare, instruĕre
furniture *s* supellex *f*
furrow *s* sulcus *m*
furry *adj* pelle insutus
further *adj* ulterior
further *adv* ultra, longius, ulterius
further *vt* promovēre, provehĕre; (*to aid*) adjuvare
furtherance *s* progress·us -ūs *m*
furthermore *adv* insuper, porro, praeterea
furthest *adj* ultimus, extremus
furthest *adv* longissime
furtive *adj* furtivus; **—ly** furtim, furtive
fury *s* furor *m*
fuse *vt* fundĕre; *vi* coalescĕre
fusion *s* fusura *f*
fuss *s* strepit·us -ūs, tumult·us -ūs *m*
fuss *vi* sollicitari
fussy *adj* fastidiosus, importunus
futile *adj* futilis, inanis
futility *s* futilitas *f*
future *adj* futurus, posterus
future *s* futura *n pl*, posterum tempus *n*; **in the —** posthac
futurity *s* posteritas *f*

G

gab *s* garrulitas *f*
gab *vi* garrire
gable *s* fastigium *n*
gadfly *s* tabanus, oestrus *m*
gag *s* jocus *m*
gag *vt* os obstruĕre (*with dat*)
gaiety *s* hilaritas *f*; nitor, splendor *m*
gaily *adv* hilare, festive
gain *s* quaest·us -ūs *m*, lucrum *n*
gain *vt* consequi, acquirĕre, capĕre; (*profit*) lucrari; (*victory*) reportare; (*case*) vincĕre; **to — possession of** potiri (*with abl*)
gainful *adj* quaestuosus, lucrosus
gainsay *vt* contradicĕre (*with dat*)
gait *s* incess·us -ūs *m*
gala *s* dies festus *m*
galaxy *s* orbis lacteus *m*
gale *s* ventus *m*
gall *s* fel *n*, bilis *f*
gall *vt* urĕre
gallant *adj* fortis, animosus; (*to ladies*) officiosus; **—ly** fortiter
gallant *s* amator *m*
gallantry *s* virtus, fortitudo *f*; (*to ladies*) urbanitas *f*
galleon *s* navis oneraria *f*
gallery *s* portic·us -ūs *f*; (*open*) peristylium *n*; (*for pictures*) pinacotheca *f*
galley *s* navis longa, triremis *f*; (*kitchen*) culina *f*
Gallic *adj* Gallicus, Gallicanus
galling *adj* mordax
gallon *s* congius *m*
gallop *s* citatissimus curs·us -ūs *m*; **at a —** citato equo, admisso equo
gallop *vi* quadrupedare
gallows *s* patibulum *n*
gamble *vt* **to — away** ludĕre, amittĕre; *vi* aleā ludĕre
gambler *s* aleator, lusor *m*
gambling *s* alea *f*
gambol *s* salt·us -ūs *m*
gambol *vi* lascivire, ludĕre
game *s* ludus *m*; (*with dice*) alea *f*; (*quarry*) praeda *f*, ferae *f pl*; **to make — of** ludificari
gander *s* anser *m*
gang *s* grex *m*, caterva *f*
gangster *s* grassator *m*
gangway *s* forus *m*
gap *s* apertura, fissura, lacuna *f*, hiat·us -ūs *m*
gape *vi* hiare, dehiscĕre
gaping *adj* hians, hiulcus, oscitans; (*fig*) stupidus
garb *s* vestit·us -ūs, habit·us -ūs *m*
garbage *s* quisquiliae *f pl*
garble *vt* vitiare, corrumpĕre
garden *s* hortus *m*
gardener *s* hortulanus, olitor *m*
gardening *s* hortorum cult·us -ūs *m*
gargle *vi* gargarizare
gargling *s* gargarizatio *f*
garland *s* sertum *n*, corona *f*
garlic *s* alium *n*
garment *s* vestimentum *n*, vestit·us -ūs *m*
garner *s* horreum *n*
garnish *vt* decorare, ornare
garret *s* cenaculum *n*
garrison *s* praesidium *n*
garrison *vt* praesidio munire, praesidium collocare in (*with abl*), praesidium imponĕre (*with dat*)

garrulity *s* garrulitas *f*
garrulous *adj* garrulus, loquax
garter *s* periscelis *f*
gas *s* spiritūs naturales *m pl*
gash *s* patens plaga *f*
gash *vt* caesim ferire
gasp *s* anhelit·us -ūs, singult·us -ūs *m*
gasp *vi* anhelare, singultare
gastric *adj* ad stomachum pertinens
gastronomy *s* gula *f*
gate *s* janua *f*, ostium *n*; (*of town*) porta *f*
gatekeeper *s* janitor *m*
gateway *s* porta *f*, postis *m*
gather *vt* (*to assemble*) congregare, colligĕre; (*fruit, etc.*) legĕre; (*to pluck*) decerpĕre, carpĕre; (*in logic*) concludĕre; (*to suspect*) suspicare; *vi* convenire, concurrĕre
gathering *s* convent·us -ūs *m*, congregatio *f*; collectio *f*
gaudily *adv* laute
gaudiness *s* lautitia *f*, ornat·us -ūs, nitor *m*
gaudy *adj* lautus, speciosus, splendidus
gauge *s* modulus *m*
gauge *vt* metiri
gaunt *adj* macer
gauntlet *s* manica *f*
gauze *s* coa *n pl*
gawky *adj* ineptus, stolidus
gay *adj* laetus, hilaris, festivus
gaze *s* conspect·us -ūs *m*; (*fixed look*) obtut·us -ūs *m*
gaze *vi* intuēri; **to — at** intuēri, adspectare, contemplari
gazelle *s* dorcas *f*
gazette *s* acta diurna *n pl*
gazetteer *s* itinerarium *n*
gear *s* instrumenta *n pl*, apparat·us -ūs *m*
gelatin *s* glutinum *n*
gelding *s* (*horse*) canterius *m*
gem *s* gemma *f*
gender *s* genus *n*
genealogical *adj* genealogicus
genealogy *s* genealogia *f*
general *adj* generalis; vulgaris, publicus, universus; **in —** omnino; **—ly** plerumque, fere; generatim
general *s* dux, imperator *m*
generalize *vi* in summam loqui
generalship *s* duct·us -ūs *m*; (*skill*) consilium *n*
generate *vt* generare, gignĕre
generation *s* generatio *f*; (*age*) aetas *f*, saeculum *n*
generic *adj* generalis
generosity *s* liberalitas, largitas *f*
generous *adj* liberalis, largus; **—ly** large, liberaliter
genesis *s* origo *f*
genial *adj* comis, benignus; **—ly** comiter, benigne
geniality *s* comitas, benignitas *f*
genitals *s* genitalia *n pl*, veretrum *n*
genitive *s* genitivus *m*
genius *s* ingenium *n*, indoles *f*; vir ingeniosus *m*; **of —** ingeniosus
genteel *adj* elegans, urbanus; **—ly** eleganter
gentile *adj* gentilicus, gentilis
gentile *s* gentilis *m*
gentility *s* nobilitas, elegantia *f*
gentle *adj* lenis, mitis, clemens; (*gradual*) mollis; (*thing*) lenis
gentleman *s* vir honestus, homo liberalis *m*
gentleness *s* lenitas, clementia *f*; (*tameness*) mansuetudo *f*
gently *adv* leniter, clementer, placide; (*gradually*) sensim
gentry *s* optimates *m pl*
genuine *adj* sincerus, purus, verus; **—ly** sincere, vere
genus *s* genus *n*
geographer *s* geographus *m*
geographical *adj* geographicus
geography *s* geographia *f*
geological *adj* geologicus
geologist *s* geologus *m*
geology *s* geologia *f*
geometrical *adj* geometricus
geometry *s* geometria *f*
germ *s* germen *n*
German *adj* Germanus
germane *adj* affinis
Germanic *adj* Germanicus
Germany *s* Germania *f*
germinate *vi* germinare
germination *s* germinat·us -ūs *m*
gesticulate *vi* gestus agĕre, gestu uti
gesture *s* gest·us -ūs, mot·us -ūs *m*
get *vt* nancisci, adipisci, consequi, acquirĕre; (*by entreaty*) impetrare; **to — back** recuperare; **to — down** depromĕre; **to — hold of** prehendĕre, occupare; **to — out** delēre, oblitterare; **to — rid of** amovēre, tollĕre; **to — the better of** superare; **to — together** colligĕre, cogĕre; congregare; *vi* (*to become*) fieri; (*to arrive at*) pervenire; **to — abroad** (*to spread*) palam fieri, emanare; **to — along** procedĕre; **to — away** aufugĕre; **to — back** revertĕre *or* reverti; **to — down** descendĕre; **to — in** pervenire; **to — off** aufugĕre, dimitti; **to — on** procedĕre, proficisci; (*to succeed*) bene succedĕre; **to — out** exire; (e curru) descendĕre; **to — over** transgredi; **to — together** congregari; **to — up** surgĕre; (*from sleep*) expergisci
ghastly *adj* luridus; (*shocking*) foedus
ghost *s* larva *f*, phantasma *n*; umbra *f*
ghostly *adj* spiritualis
giant *s* gigas *m*
gibberish *s* barbaricus sermo *m*
gibbet *s* furca *f*, patibulum *n*
gibe *s* sanna *f*
gibe *vt* illudĕre, subsannare
giblets *s* gigeria *n pl*, anseris trunculi *m pl*
giddiness *s* vertigo *f*
giddy *adj* vertiginosus; (*fig*) levis, inconsultus
gift *s* donum *n*; (*talent*) ingenium *n*
gifted *adj* (*endowed*) praeditus; ingeniosus
gig *s* (*carriage*) cisium *n*

gigantic *adj* ingens, immanis, praegrandis
giggle *vi* summissim cachinnare
gild *vt* inaurare
gilding *s* (*art*) auratura *f*; (*gilded work*) aurum inductum *n*
gill *s* branchia *f*
gilt *adj* auratus
gin *s* junipero infectus spirit·us -ūs *m*
ginger *s* zinziberi *n* (*indecl*)
gingerly *adv* pedetemptim
giraffe *s* camelopardalis *f*
gird *vt* cingĕre; **to — oneself** cingi
girder *s* tignum *n*
girdle *s* cingulum *n*, zona *f*
girdle *vt* cingĕre
girl *s* puella, virgo *f*
girlhood *s* puellaris aetas *f*
girlish *adj* puellaris, virginalis
girth *s* (*of horse*) cingula *f*; amplitudo *f*, ambit·us -ūs *m*
gist *s* cardo *m*
give *vt* dare, donare; (*to deliver*) tradĕre; **to — away** donare; **to — back** reddĕre; **to — forth** emittĕre; **to — oneself up to** se addicĕre (*with dat*); **to — out** edĕre, emittĕre; nuntiare, proclamare; distribuĕre; **to — over** transferre; relinquere; **to — up** tradĕre; (*to betray*) prodĕre; (*to abandon*) dimittĕre; *vi* **to — in** (*to yield*) cedĕre; **to — way** (*mil*) pedem referre; (*to yield*) cedĕre; (*to comply*) obsequi
giver *s* donator *m*
giving *s* datio, largitio *f*
glacial *adj* glacialis
glacier *s* moles conglaciata *f*
glad *adj* laetus, contentus; **to be —** gaudĕre; **—ly** libenter
gladden *vt* laetificare
glade *s* salt·us -ūs *m*
gladiator *s* gladiator *m*
gladness *s* gaudium *n*, laetitia *f*
glamorous *adj* venustus, nitidus; **to be —** nitēre
glamour *s* venustas *f*, nitor *m*
glance *s* aspect·us -ūs *m*
glance *vi* aspicĕre; **to — at** aspicĕre; **to — off** stringĕre
gland *s* glandula *f*
glare *s* fulgor *m*
glare *vi* fulgēre; torvis oculis aspicĕre; **to — at** torvis oculis aspicĕre *or* intuēri
glaring *adj* fulgens; manifestus
glass *s* vitrum *n*; (*for drinking*) calix vitreus *m*
glass *adj* vitreus
glassmaker *s* vitrarius *m*
glassware *s* vitrea *n pl*
glaze *vt* vitrum illinĕre (*with dat*), polire
gleam *s* fulgor *m*, jubar *n*; (*fig*) aura *f*
gleam *vi* coruscare, micare, fulgēre
gleaming *adj* coruscus, renidens
glean *vt* colligĕre, legĕre
gleaning *s* spicilegium *n*
glee *s* laetitia, hilaritas *f*
gleeful *adj* laetus, hilaris; **—ly** laete, hilare
glen *s* vallis *f*
glib *adj* lubricus, volubilis; **—ly** volubiliter
glide *vi* labi
glimmer *s* lux dubia *f*; **— of hope** specula *f*
glimmer *vi* sublucēre
glimpse *s* aspect·us -ūs *m*; **to have a — of** despicĕre
glisten *vi* nitēre
glitter *s* fulgor *m*
glitter *vi* fulgēre, micare, coruscare
gloat *vi* oculos pascĕre; **to — over** inhiare (*with abl*), oculos pascĕre (*with abl*)
globe *s* globus *m*; orbis terrarum *m*
globular *adj* globosus
globule *s* globulus *m*, pilula *f*
gloom *s* tenebrae *f pl*; (*fig*) tristitia *f*
gloomily *adv* maeste
gloomy *adj* tenebrosus, furvus; (*fig*) maestus, tristis
glorification *s* laudatio, glorificatio *f*
glorify *vt* celebrare, glorificare, extollĕre
glorious *adj* gloriosus, illustris; **—ly** gloriose
glory *s* gloria, laus *f*
glory *vi* gloriari, se jactare
gloss *s* interpretatio *f*; (*sheen*) nitor *m*
gloss *vt* annotare; **to — over** extenuare, dissimulare
glossary *s* glossarium *n*
glossy *adj* nitidus, expolitus
glove *s* chirotheca *f*
glow *s* ardor, fervor, calor *m*
glow *vi* candēre, ardēre, calēre
glowing *adj* candens, fervens; (*fig*) fervidus
glue *s* gluten, glutinum *n*
glue *vt* glutinare
glum *adj* maestus, tristis
glut *s* satietas *f*
glut *vt* satiare, saturare
glutton *s* helluo, homo gulosus, ganeo *m*
gluttonous *adj* gulosus, edax; **—ly** gulose
gnarled *adj* nodosus
gnash *vt* **to — one's teeth** dentibus frendĕre
gnat *s* culex *m*
gnaw *vt & vi* rodĕre
gnawing *adj* mordax
go *vi* ire, incedĕre, proficisci; **to — about** circumire, perambulari; (*fig*) aggredi; **to — abroad** peregrinari; **to — after** sequi, petĕre; **to — aside** discedĕre; **to — astray** aberrare, vagari; **to — away** abire; **to — back** reverti; **to — before** praeire, antecedĕre; **to — between** intervenire; **to — beyond** egredi; (*fig*) excedĕre; **to — by** praeterire; (*fig*) (*to follow*) sequi; **to — down** descendĕre; (*of sun*) occidĕre; **to — for** petĕre; **to — forth** exire; **to — in** introire; **to — into** inire; **to — off** abire; (*as gun*) displodi; **to — on** (*to continue*) pergĕre; (*to happen*)

fieri; (*to succeed, thrive*) succedĕre; **to — out** exire; (*of fire*) extingui; **to — over** transgredi; (*fig*) (*a subject*) percurrĕre; **to — round** circumire; **to — through** obire, pertendĕre; **to — to** adire, accedĕre; **to — towards** petĕre; **to — under** subire; submergi; **to — up** ascendĕre; **to let —** dimittĕre; (*to let fall*) omittĕre

goad *s* pertica *f*, stimulus *m*

goad *vt* instigare; (*fig*) stimulare; (*to exasperate*) exasperare

goal *s* finis *m*; (*at racetrack*) calx *f*

goat *s* caper *m*, capra *f*

gobble *vt* devorare, deglutire

gobbler *s* helluo *m*

goblet *s* poculum *n*, scyphus *m*

goblin *s* larva *f*

god *s* deus, divus *m*

God *s* Deus *m*

goddess *s* dea, diva *f*

godhead *s* deitas *f*, numen *n*

godless *adj* atheus; improbus

godlike *adj* divinus

godliness *s* pietas *f*

gold *adj* aureus

gold *s* aurum *n*

golden *adj* aureus

goldfish *s* hippurus *m*

gold leaf *s* auri breactea *f*

gold mine *s* aurifodina *f*

goldsmith *s* aurifex *m*

good *adj* bonus, probus; (*beneficial*) salutaris; (*kindhearted*) benevolus; (*fit*) aptus, idoneus; **— for nothing** nequam (*indecl*); **to do —** prodesse; **to make —** compensare, restituĕre; **to seem —** vidēri

good *s* bonum *n*; (*profit*) commodum, lucrum *n*, utilitas *f*; **to be — for** prodesse (*with dat*); **—s** bona *n pl*, res *f*; (*for sale*) merx *f*

good *interj* bene!; euge!

good-by *interj* vale!; (*to more than one*) valete!; **to say —** valēre jubēre

goodly *adj* pulcher; (*quantity*) amplus; **a — number of** nonnulli

good-natured *adj* comis, benignus, facilis

goodness *s* bonitas *f*; (*moral*) probitas, virtus *f*; (*generosity*) benignitas *f*

goose *s* anser *m*

gooseberry *s* acinus grossulae *m*

gore *s* cruor *m*

gore *vt* cornu perforare, cornu ferire

gorge *s* fauces *f pl*; (*defile*) angustiae *f pl*

gorge *vt* **to — oneself** se ingurgitare

gorgeous *adj* splendidus, lautus; **—ly** splendide, laute

gory *adj* cruentus, cruentatus

gospel *s* evangelium *n*

gossamer *s* aranea *f*

gossip *s* (*talk*) nugae, gerrae *f pl*; (*person*) garrulus *m*, garrula *f*, loquax *m & f*, lingulaca *f*

gossip *vi* garrire

gouge *vt* evellĕre, eruĕre

gourd *s* cucurbita *f*

gourmand *s* helluo, popino *m*

gout *s* morbus articularis *m*, arthritis *f*; (*in the legs*) podagra *f*; (*in hands*) chiragra *f*

govern *vt* imperare (*with dat*), regĕre, administrare, gubernare

governable *adj* tractabilis

governess *s* magistra, educatrix *f*

government *s* gubernatio, administratio, res publica *f*

governor *s* gubernator, moderator, praefectus *m*; (*of province*) proconsul, legatus *m*; procurator *m*

governorship *s* praefectura *f*

gown *s* (*of Roman citizen*) toga *f*; (*of women*) stola *f*

grace *s* gratia *f*; (*elegance, etc.*) venustas *f*, lepos *m*; (*pardon*) venia *f*; **to say —** gratias agĕre

grace *vt* exornare; honestare

graceful *adj* gratiosus, venustus, lepidus; **—ly** venuste, lepide

gracefulness *s* venustas *f*

graceless *adj* deformis, illepidus

Graces *s* Gratiae *f pl*

gracious *adj* benignus, misericors; **—ly** benigne, humane

gradation *s* grad·us -ūs *m*; (*in speech*) gradatio *f*

grade *s* grad·us -ūs *m*

gradient *s* proclivitas *f*

gradual *adj* lenis, mollis; per gradus; **—ly** gradatim, pedetentim

graduate *vt* gradibus distinguĕre; *vi* gradum suscipĕre

graduate *s* qui gradum academicum adeptus est

graft *s* surculus *m*; (*pol*) ambit·us -ūs *m*

graft *vt* inserĕre

grain *s* granum *n*; (*fig*) particula *f*; **against the —** (*fig*) Minervā invitā

grammar *s* grammatica *f*

grammarian *s* grammaticus *m*

grammatical *adj* grammaticus

granary *s* horreum *n*, granaria *n pl*

grand *adj* grandis

grandchild *s* nepos *m*, neptis *m & f*

granddaughter *s* neptis *f*

grandeur *s* magnificentia, majestas *f*

grandfather *s* avus *m*

grandiloquent *adj* magniloquus

grandmother *s* avia *f*

grandson *s* nepos *m*

granite *s* granites lapis *m*

grant *vt* concedĕre, permittĕre; (*to acknowledge*) fatēri; dare, praebēre

grant *s* concessio *f*

grape *s* uva *f*, acinus *m*

grapevine *s* vitis *f*

graphic *adj* expressus, significans, manifestus; **—ally** expresse

grapple *vt* compleci; *vi* luctari

grasp *s* complex·us -ūs *m*, comprehensio *f*; pugillum *n*; (*power*) potestas *f*; (*of the hand*) man·us -ūs *f*

grasp *vt* prehendĕre, tenēre, arripĕre; (*fig*) appetĕre, percipĕre, intellegĕre; *vi* **to — at** captare, appetĕre

grasping *adj* avidus, cupidus

grass *s* gramen *n*, herba *f*

grasshopper *s* grillus *m*
grassy *adj* graminosus, herbosus, herbidus
grate *s* clathri *m pl*; (*hearth*) caminus *m*
grate *vt* raděre, conterěre; *vi* striděre; **to — upon** offenděre
grateful *adj* gratus, juncundus; **—ly** grate
gratification *s* gratificatio *f*; (*pleasure, delight*) voluptas, oblectatio *f*
gratify *vt* gratificari (*with dat*), morigerari (*with dat*)
gratifying *adj* gratus
grating *s* clathri, cancelli *m pl*; (*sound*) stridor *m*
gratis *adv* gratuito, gratis
gratitude *s* gratitudo *f*, gratus animus *m*
gratuitous *adj* gratuitus; **—ly** gratuito
gratuity *s* stips *f*, munus, praemium *n*
grave *adj* gravis, serius; (*stern*) severus; **—ly** graviter; severe
grave *s* sepulcrum *n*, tumulus *m*
gravedigger *s* tumulorum fossor *m*
gravel *s* glarea *f*
gravelly *adj* glareosus
gravestone *s* monumentum *n*
gravitate *vi* vergěre
gravitation *s* ponderatio *f*
gravity *s* gravitas *f*, pondus *n*; (*personal*) severitas, dignitas *f*; momentum *n*
gravy *s* (*broth*) jus *n*; (*juice*) sucus *m*
gray *adj* canus; **to become —** canescěre
gray-eyed *adj* caesius
gray-headed *adj* canus
grayish *adj* canescens
grayness *s* canities *f*
graze *vt* (*cattle*) pascěre; (*to touch lightly*) perstringěre, raděre; *vi* pasci
grease *s* adeps *m*, pinguitudo, arvina *f*
grease *vt* ung(u)ěre
greasy *adj* pinguis; unctus; (*dirty*) squalidus
great *adj* magnus; ingens, amplus, grandis; **as — as** tantus quantus; **—ly** magnopere, valde
great-grandfather *s* proavus *m*
greatness *s* magnitudo *f*
greaves *s* ocreae *f pl*
Grecian *adj* Graecus
greed *s* aviditas, avaritia *f*; voracitas *f*
greedily *adv* avide, cupide
greedy *adj* avarus, cupidus; vorax
Greek *adj* Graecus
Greek *s* Graecus *m*
green *adj* viridis; (*fig*) recens; (*unripe*) crudus, immaturus; **to become —** virescěre
green *s* color viridis *m*; (*lawn*) locus herbidus *m*; **—s** olera *n pl*
greenhouse *s* viridarium hibernum *n*
greenish *adj* subviridis
greenness *s* viriditas *f*; (*fig*) cruditas, immaturitas *f*
greet *vt* salutem dicěre (*with dat*), salutare
greeting *s* salutatio *f*
gregarious *adj* gregalis
grenade *s* pyrobolus *m*
greyhound *s* vertagus *m*
gridiron *s* craticula *f*
grief *s* maeror, dolor, luct·us -ūs *m*; **to come to —** perire
grievance *s* injuria, querimonia, querela *f*
grieve *vt* dolore afficěre; *vi* maerēre, dolēre, lugēre
grievous *adj* gravis, durus, atrox; **—ly** graviter, aegre
griffin *s* gryps *m*
grill *vt* torrēre
grim *adj* torvus, atrox, truculentus; **—ly** torve, truculente, atrociter
grimace *s* distortus vult·us -ūs *m*, oris depravatio *f*
grimace *vi* os ducěre
grimy *adj* niger, squalidus
grin *vi* distorto vultu ridēre
grin *s* ris·us -ūs *m*
grind *vt* (*grain*) molěre; (*in mortar*) contunděre; (*on whetstone*) exacuěre; **to — the teeth** dentibus freděre
grindstone *s* cos *f*
grip *s* pugillum *n*, comprehensio *f*
grip *vt* arripěre, comprehenděre
grisly *adj* horrendus, horridus
grist *s* farina *f*
gristle *s* cartilago *f*
gristly *adj* cartilagineus, cartilaginosus
grit *s* harena *f*
gritty *adj* harenosus, sabulosus
grizzly *adj* canus
groan *s* gemit·us -ūs *m*
groan *vi* geměre
groin *s* inguen *n*
groom *s* agaso, equiso *m*
groom *vt* curare
groove *s* canalis *m*, stria *f*
groove *vt* striare
grope *vi* praetentare
gropingly *adv* pedetentim
gross *adj* crassus, pinguis; turpis, foedus; nimius; **—ly** nimium, valde
grotesque *adj* distortus
grotto *s* antrum *n*
ground *s* solum *n*, terra, humus *f*; (*reason*) causa, ratio *f*; (*place*) locus *m*; **on the —** humi; **to give —** ceděre
ground *vt* fundare; (*to teach*) instruěre; (*a ship*) subducěre
groundless *adj* vanus, falsus, fictus; **—ly** temere, de nihilo
group *s* corona, turba *f*, globus *m*
group *vt* disponěre; *vi* **to — around** circulari, stipari
grouse *s* (*bird*) tetrao *m*
grove *s* lucus *m*, nemus *n*
grovel *vi* serpěre, se prosterněre
grow *vt* colěre, serěre; *vi* crescěre, augēri; (*to become*) fieri; **to — out of** (*fig*) oriri ex (*with abl*); **to — up** adolescěre, pubescěre
grower *s* cultor *m*
growl *s* fremit·us -ūs *m*
growl *vi* freměre

grown-up *adj* adultus; puber
growth *s* incrementum *n*, auct·us -ūs *m*
grub *s* vermiculus, lombricus *m*
grub *vi* effodĕre
grudge *s* odium *n*, invidia *f*; **to hold a — against** succensēre (*with dat*)
grudgingly *adv* invitus, aegre
gruesome *adj* taeter
gruff *adj* torvus, asper; **—ly** torve, aspere
gruffness *s* asperitas *f*
grumble *vi* murmurare, mussitare
grunt *s* grunnit·us -ūs *m*
grunt *vi* grunnire; (*fig*) fremĕre
guarantee *s* fides *f*; (*money*) sponsio *f*; (*person*) praes, vas, sponsor *m*; (*bail money*) vadimonium *n*
guarantee *vt* praestare, spondēre
guarantor *s* sponsor *m*
guard *s* custodia, tutela *f*; (*mil*) praesidium *n*; (*person*) custos *m & f*; **to be on one's —** cavēre
guard *vt* custodire, defendĕre; *vi* **to — against** cavēre
guarded *adj* cautus, circumspectus; **—ly** caute
guardian *s* custos, praeses *m & f*, defensor *m*; (*of minor or orphan*) tutor *m*
guardianship *s* custodia, tutela, curatio *f*
guerdon *s* merces *f*
guess *s* conjectura *f*
guess *vt & vi* conjicĕre, divinare, opinari
guest *s* hospes *m*; advena *m*; (*at dinner*) conviva *m*
guidance *s* duct·us -ūs *m*, curatio, moderatio *f*
guide *s* dux, ductor *m*
guide *vt* ducĕre, regĕre; (*to control*) moderari
guidebook *s* itinerarium *n*
guild *s* collegium, corpus *n*, sodalitas *f*
guile *s* dolus *m*
guileful *adj* dolosus
guileless *adj* simplex, sincerus
guilt *s* culpa *f*, crimen, vitium *n*
guiltless *adj* innocens, insons
guilty *adj* sons, noxius, nocens, sceleratus
guinea hen *s* meleagris *f*
guise *s* species *f*
guitar *s* cithara Hispanica *f*; fides *f pl*; **to play the —** fidibus canĕre
gulf *s* sin·us -ūs *m*; (*abyss*) abyssus *f*, gurges *m*
gull *s* larus marinus, mergus *m*
gullet *s* gula *f*, guttur *n*
gullible *adj* credulus
gulp *vt* absorbēre, glutire, haurire; *vi* singultare
gulp *s* haust·us -ūs, singult·us -ūs *m*
gum *s* (*of mouth*) gingiva *f*; gummi *n* (*indecl*)
gumption *s* alacritas *f*
gun *s* sclopetum *n*; tormentum *n*
gunner *s* tormentarius *m*
gurgle *vi* singultare; (*of stream*) murmurare
gurgling *s* singult·us -ūs *m*; (*of stream*) murmur *n*, murmuratio *f*
gush *vi* micare, scaturire
gush *s* scaturigines *f pl*
gust *s* impet·us -ūs *m*, flamen *n*
gusty *adj* ventosus, procellosus
gut *s* intestinum *n*
gut *vt* exenterare; (*fig*) diripĕre, amburĕre
gutted *adj* (*by fire*) ambustus
gutter *s* canalis *m*; (*rain gutter*) compluvium *n*; (*in fields or upon roofs*) colliciae *f pl*
guttural *adj* gutturalis
guzzle *vi* potare
guzzler *s* potor *m*
gymnasium *s* gymnasium *n*, palaestra *f*
gymnastic *adj* gymnicus
gymnastics *s* palaestra, palaestrica *f*

H

haberdasher *s* linteo *m*
habit *s* consuetudo *f*, mos *m*; (*dress*) habit·us -ūs, vestit·us -ūs *m*
habitation *s* habitatio, dom·us -ūs *f*
habitual *adj* usitatus, inveteratus; **—ly** de more, ex more
habituate *vt* insuescĕre, assuefacĕre
hack *vt* caedĕre; **to — to pieces** concidĕre
hack *s* (*horse*) caballus *m*
hackneyed *adj* tritus, pervulgatus
haddock *s* gadus morhua *m*
hag *f* an·us -ūs *f*
haggard *adj* macer; ferus
haggle *vi* cavillari, licitare
haggler *s* licitator *m*
hail *s* grando *f*
hail *vt* salutare, appellare
hail *vi* **it is hailing** grandinat
hail *interj* salve!; (*to several*) salvete!
hailstone *s* saxea grando *f*
hair *s* capillus, crinis *m*; (*single*) pilus *m*; (*of animals*) saeta *f*, villus *m*
haircloth *s* cilicium *n*
hairdresser *s* concinnator, tonsor *m*
hairless *adj* (*of head*) calvus; (*of body*) glaber, depilis
hairpin *s* crinale *n*
hairy *adj* pilosus, crinitus; (*shaggy*) hirsutus
halberd *s* bipennis *f*
halcyon *s* alcedo, alcyon *f*
halcyon days *s* alcedonia *n pl*
hale *adj* robustus, validus
hale *vt* rapĕre, trahĕre
half *s* dimidia pars *f*, dimidium *n*

half *adj* dimidius, dimidiatus
half-hour *s* semihora *f*
half-moon *s* luna dimidiata *f*; (*shape*) lunula *f*
half-open *adj* semiapertus
half year *s* semestrium *n*
hall *s* atrium *n*; (*entrance*) vestibulum *n*
hallo *interj* heus!, ohe!
hallow *vt* consecrare
hallucination *s* error *m*, somnium *n*, alucinatio *f*
halo *s* corona *f*
halt *vt* sistĕre; *vi* consistĕre; (*fig*) haesitare; (*to limp*) claudicare
halt *s* pausa, mora *f*; **to come to a —** consistĕre
halter *s* capistrum *n*
halting *adj* claudus
halve *vt* ex aequo dividĕre
ham *s* poples *m*; (*smoked, etc.*) perna *f*
hamlet *s* vicus, viculus *m*
hammer *s* malleus *m*
hammer *vt* tundĕre, cudĕre
hamper *s* corbis *f*
hamper *vt* impedire, implicare
hamstring *s* poplitis nervus *m*
hamstring *vt* poplitem succidĕre (*with dat*)
hand *s* man·us -ūs *f*; (*handwriting*) chirographum *n*; (*of dial*) gnomon *m*; **at —** ad manum, praesto, prae manibus, prope; **by —** manu; **— in —** junctis manibus; **— to —** cominus; **on the other —** altera parte; **on the right —** a dextra; **to have a — in** interesse (*with dat*); **to take in —** suscipĕre
hand *vt* tradĕre, porrigĕre; **to — down** tradĕre; **to — over** referre; (*to betray*) prodĕre; **to — round** circumferre
handbill *s* libellus *m*
handbook *s* enchiridion *n*
handcuffs *s* manicae *f pl*
handful *s* manipulus *m*
handicraft *s* artificium *n*
handiwork *s* opus, opificium *n*
handkerchief *s* sudarium *n*
handle *s* manubrium *n*; (*of cup*) ansa, ansula *f*
handle *vt* tractare
handling *s* tractatio *f*
handsome *adj* pulcher, formosus; **—ly** pulchre; (*liberally*) liberaliter
handsomeness *s* pulchritudo, forma, venustas *f*
handwriting *s* man·us -ūs *f*, chirographum *n*
handy *adj* (*of things*) habilis; (*of person*) sollers; (*at hand*) praesto
hang *vt* suspendĕre; (*by a line*) appendĕre; (*head*) demittĕre; *vi* pendēre; **hanging down** demissus; **hanging loose** fluens; **to — down** dependēre; **to — on to** haerēre (*with dat*); **to — over** imminēre (*with dat*)
hanging *adj* pensilis
hanging *s* (*execution*) suspendium, *n*; **—s** aulaea *n pl*
hangman *s* carnifex *m*
haphazard *adj* fortuitus
happen *vi* accidĕre, fieri, evenire, contingĕre; **to — upon** incidĕre in (*with acc*)
happily *adv* beate, feliciter
happiness *s* felicitas *f*
happy *adj* beatus, felix, fortunatus, faustus
harangue *s* contio *f*
harangue *vt & vi* contionari
harass *vt* vexare, inquietare, exagitare, fatigare
harassing *adj* molestus
harassment *s* vexatio *f*
harbinger *s* praenuntius, antecursor *m*
harbor *s* port·us -ūs *m*
harbor *vt* excipĕre
hard *adj* durus; (*difficult*) difficilis, arduus; (*severe*) acer, rigidus, asper; **to become —** durescĕre
hard *adv* valde, sedulo, summa vi
harden *vt* durare; (*fig*) indurare; *vi* durescĕre; (*fig*) obdurescĕre
hardhearted *adj* durus, crudelis, inhumanus
hardihood *s* audacia *f*
hardiness *s* robur *n*
hardly *adv* vix, aegre; **— any** nullus fere
hardness *s* duritia *f*; (*fig*) iniquitas, acerbitas *f*; (*difficulty*) difficultas *f*
hardship *s* labor *m*, difficultas, aerumna *f*
hardware *s* ferramenta *n pl*
hardy *adj* robustus, durus
hare *s* lepus *m*
harem *s* gynaeceum *n*
hark *interj* heus!
harken *vi* audire; **to — to** auscultare (*with dat*)
harlot *s* meretrix *f*
harm *s* injuria *f*, damnum *n*; **to come to —** detrimentum accipĕre
harm *vt* nocēre (*with dat*), laedĕre
harmful *adj* noxius, nocivus, damnosus
harmless *adj* (*person*) innocens; (*thing*) innocuus; **—ly** innocenter, incolumis
harmonious *adj* canorus, consonus; (*fig*) concors, consentiens; **—ly** consonanter; (*fig*) concorditer, convenienter
harmonize *vt* componĕre; *vi* concinĕre; (*fig*) consentire
harmony *s* harmonia *f*, concent·us -ūs *m*; (*fig*) concordia *f*
harness *s* equi ornamenta *n pl*
harness *vt* ornare, insternĕre
harp *s* lyra *f*
harpist *s* psaltes *m*
harpoon *s* jaculum hamatum *n*
harpoon *vt* jaculo hamato transfigĕre
harpy *s* harpyia *f*
harrow *s* rastrum *n*, irpex *m*
harrow *vt* occare
harsh *adj* asper, raucus, discors, stridulus; (*in taste*) acer; (*fig*) durus, severus, inclemens; **—ly** aspere, acerbe, severe
harshness *s* asperitas, acerbitas, severitas *f*

harvest *s* messis, seges *f*
harvest *vt* metĕre
hash *vt* comminuĕre
hash *s* minutal *n*
haste *s* festinatio, celeritas *f*; **in —** propere; **to make —** properare
hasten *vt* accelerare, properare, praecipitare; *vi* properare, festinare
hastily *adv* propere, raptim; (*without reflection*) temere, inconsulte
hastiness *s* celeritas, temeritas *f*
hasty *adj* properus, praeceps, temerarius, inconsultus
hat *s* pileus, galerus, petasus *m*
hatch *vt* (*fig*) coquĕre, machinari; (*of chickens*) ex ovis excludĕre
hatchet *s* ascia, securis, dolabra *f*
hate *s* odium *n*, invidia *f*
hate *vt* odisse
hateful *adj* odiosus, invisus; **to be — to** odio esse (*with dat*); **—ly** odiose
hatred *s* odium *n*, invidia *f*
haughtily *adv* superbe, arroganter, insolenter
haughtiness *s* superbia, arrogantia *f*, fastidium *n*
haughty *adj* superbus, arrogans, insolens
haul *s* bolus *m*
haul *vt* trahĕre; **to — up** subducĕre
haunch *s* clunis, coxa *f*
haunt *vt* frequentare; (*fig*) agitare, inquietare
haunt *s* locus *m*; (*of animals*) lustra *n pl*, latebrae *f pl*
have *vt* habēre, possidēre, tenēre
haven *s* port·us -ūs *m*
havoc *s* strages *f*
hawk *s* accipiter *m & f*
hawk *vt* venditare
hawser *s* retinaculum *n*
hawthorn *s* crataegus oxyacantha *f*
hay *s* faenum *n*
hayloft *s* faenilia *n pl*
haystack *s* faeni meta *f*
hazard *s* periculum *n*
hazard *vt* periclitari
hazardous *adj* periculosus, anceps; **—ly** periculose
haze *s* nebula *f*
hazy *adj* caliginosus, nebulosus
he *pron* hic, is, ille; (*male*) mas *m*
head *s* caput *s*; (*mental faculty*) ingenium *n*; (*fig*) princeps; **— first** praeceps
head *adj* primus, principalis, capitalis
head *vt* praeesse (*with dat*), ducĕre; *vi* **to — for** petĕre
headache *s* capitis dolor *m*
heading *s* caput *n*, titulus *m*
headland *s* promuntorium *n*
headless *adj* truncus
headlong *adv* praeceps
headquarters *s* praetorium *n*
headstrong *adj* pervicax, contumax
headway *s* profect·us -ūs *m*; **to make —** proficĕre
headwind *s* ventus adversus *m*
heady *adj* (*of drinks*) fervidus, vehemens
heal *vt* medēri (*with dat*), sanare; *vi* sanescĕre; (*of wounds*) coalescĕre
healer *s* medicus *m*
healing *adj* salubris, salutaris
health *s* valetudo, salus *f*; **to be in good —** valēre; **to drink to the — of** propinare (*with dat*)
healthful *adj* salutaris, salubris
healthily *adv* salubriter
healthy *adj* sanus, integer; (*places*) salubris
heap *s* acervus, cumulus *m*, congeries *f*
heap *vt* acervare; **to — up** accumulare, exstruĕre
hear *vt* audire, exaudire; (*to learn*) certior fieri, accipĕre, cognoscĕre
hearing *s* (*act*) auditio *f*; (*sense*) audit·us -ūs *m*; (*law*) cognitio *f*; **hard of —** surdaster
hearken *vi* auscultare
hearsay *s* fama *f*, rumor *m*
heart *s* cor *n*; (*fig*) pectus *n*; (*courage*) animus *m*; **to learn by —** ediscĕre
heartache *s* cura *f*, angor *m*
heartbreak *s* angor *m*
heartbroken *adj* aeger
hearth *s* focus *m*
heartily *adv* sincere, vehementer, valde
heartiness *s* studium *n*, alacritas *f*
heartless *adj* crudelis, inhumanus; **—ly** crudeliter, inhumane
heartlessness *s* inhumanitas *f*
hearty *adj* sincerus, vehemens, alacer
heat *s* calor, ardor *m*; (*fig*) fervor *m*
heat *vt* calefacĕre; *vi* calescĕre
heath *s* (*plant*) erice *f*; (*place*) loca inculta *n pl*
heathen *adj* paganus
heathen *s* paganus *m*
heather *s* erice *f*
heating *s* calefactio *f*
heave *vt* attollĕre, levare; **to — a sigh** gemitum ducĕre; *vi* tumēre, aestuare, fluctuare
heaven *s* caelum *n*; (*fig*) dii, superi *m pl*
heavenly *adj* caelestis, divinus
heavily *adv* graviter; (*slowly*) tarde
heaviness *s* gravitas *f*; (*slowness*) tarditas *f*
heavy *adj* gravis, ponderosus; (*fig*) tardus, segnis, iners; (*sad*) maestus
Hebraic *adj* Hebraicus
Hebrew *s* Hebraeus *m*; (*language*) Hebraea lingua *f*
hecatomb *s* hecatombe *f*
hectic *adj* fervidus, febriculosus
hedge *s* saepes *f*
hedge *vt* **to — in** saepire; **to — off** intersaepire; *vi* tergiversari
hedgehog *s* ericius *m*
heed *s* cura, opera *f*; **to take —** cavēre, curare
heed *vt* curare, observare, respicĕre; (*to obey*) parēre (*with dat*)
heedless *adj* incautus, temerarius; **— of** immemor (*with genit*)
heedlessness *s* neglegentia *f*
heel *s* calx *m & f*
heifer *s* bucula, juvenca *f*
height *s* altitudo *f*; (*of person*) pro-

ceritas *f*; (*top*) culmen *n*; (*fig*) fastigium *n*
heighten *vt* amplificare, exaggerare, augēre
heinous *adj* atrox, nefarius, foedus; **—ly** atrociter
heir *s* heres *m*; **sole** *or* **universal —** heres ex asse
heiress *s* heres *f*
heirloom *s* res hereditaria *f*
hell *s* Tartarus *m*, inferi *m pl*
Hellenic *adj* Hellenicus, Graecus
Hellenism *s* Hellenismus *m*
hellish *adj* infernus, diabolicus, nefarius
helm *s* gubernaculum *n*
helmet *s* cassis, galea *f*
helmsman *s* gubernator, rector *m*
help *s* auxilium, subsidium *n*
help *vt* adjuvare (*with acc*), auxiliari (*with dat*), succurrĕre (*with dat*), opem ferre (*with dat*)
helper *s* adjutor *m*, adjutrix *f*
helpful *adj* utilis
helpless *adj* inops
helplessness *s* inopia *f*
hem *s* ora *f*, limbus *m*
hem *vt* (*to sew*) suĕre; **to — in** circumsidēre, obsidēre
hem *interj* hem!, ehem!
hemisphere *s* hemisphaerium *n*
hemlock *s* cicuta *f*
hemp *s* cannabis *f*
hempen *adj* cannabinus
hen *s* gallina *f*
hence *adv* hinc; (*consequently*) igitur, ideo
henceforth *adv* posthac, dehinc
henpecked *adj* uxorius
her *pron* eam, illam, hanc
her *adj* ejus, illius, hujus; **— own** suus, proprius
herald *s* fetialis *m*; (*crier*) praeco *m*
herald *vt* nuntiare, praenuntiare
herb *s* herba *f*; **—s** herbae *f pl*, olus *n*
herd *s* grex *m*; armentum *n*; (*in contempt*) vulgus *n*
herd *vt* **to — together** congregare, cogĕre; *vi* congregari
herdsman *s* pastor, armentarius *m*
here *adv* hic; **— and there** passim
hereafter *adv* posthac, in reliquum tempus
hereby *adv* ex hoc, ex hac re, hinc
hereditary *adj* hereditarius, patrius
heredity *s* genus *n*; **by —** jure hereditario, per successiones
herein *adv* in hoc, in hac re, hic
heresy *s* haeresis *f*
heretical *adj* haereticus; falsus, pravus
hereupon *adv* hic
herewith *adv* una cum hac re
heritage *s* hereditas *f*
hermaphrodite *s* androgynus, Hermaphroditus *m*
hermit *s* eremita *m*
hermitage *s* eremitae cella *f*
hernia *s* hernia *f*
hero *s* vir *m*; (*demigod*) heros *m*
heroic *adj* fortissimus, magnanimus, heroicus; **—ally** fortissime
heroine *s* virago *f*
heroism *s* virtus, fortitudo *f*
heron *s* ardea *f*
herring *s* harenga *f*
hers *pron* ejus, illius
herself *pron* (*refl*) se; (*intensive*) ipsa; **to —** sibi; **with —** secum
hesitant *adj* dubius, incertus; **—ly** cunctanter, dubitanter
hesitate *vi* dubitare, haesitare
hesitation *s* dubitatio, haesitatio, cunctatio *f*
Hesperian *adj* Hesperius
heterogeneous *adj* diversus
hew *vt* dolare, caedĕre
hey *interj* ohe!
hiatus *s* hiat·us -ūs *m*
hiccup *s* singult·us -ūs *m*
hiccup *vi* singultare
hide *s* pellis *f*, corium *n*
hide *vt* abdĕre, abscondĕre, celare, occultare; (*to flog*) verberare; *vi* latēre, se abdĕre
hideous *adj* foedus, perhorridus, turpis; **—ly** foede, turpiter
hideousness *s* foeditas *f*, horror *m*
hiding *s* occultatio *f*; (*whipping*) verberatio *f*
hiding place *s* latebra *f*
hierarchy *s* hierarchia *f*
high *adj* altus, excelsus, sublimis; (*tall*) procerus; (*of price*) pretiosus, carus; (*of ground*) editus; (*of rank*) amplus; **—ly** (*value*) magni; (*intensity*) vehementer, valde
high *adv* alte, sublimiter; **to aim —** magnas res appetĕre
highborn *adj* generosus, ingenuus, nobilis
high-flown *adj* inflatus, tumidus
highhanded *adj* insolens, superbus; **—ly** insolenter, superbe
highland *s* regio montuosa *f*
highlander *s* montanus *m*
high-minded *adj* (*noble*) magnanimus; (*arrogant*) arrogans, insolens
high priest *s* pontifex maximus *m*
highway *s* via *f*
highwayman *s* latro, grassator *m*
hilarity *s* hilaritas *f*
hill *s* collis, tumulus *m*; (*slope*) clivus *m*
hillock *s* tumulus *m*
hilly *adj* montuosus, clivosus
hilt *s* capulus *m*
him *pron* eum, hunc, illum; **of —** ejus, hujus, illius; de eo, de hoc, de illo
himself *pron* (*refl*) se; (*intensive*) ipse; **to —** sibi; **with —** secum
hind *s* cerva *f*
hind *adj* posterior
hinder *vt* obstare (*with dat*); impedire, morari
hindmost *adj* postremus, ultimus, novissimus
hindrance *s* impedimentum *n*
hinge *s* cardo *m*
hinge *vi* **to — on** (*fig*) niti (*with abl*)
hint *s* indicium *n*, significatio *f*
hint *vt & vi* significare, innuĕre, suggerĕre
hip *s* coxendix *f*

hippodrome *s* hippodromos *m*
hire *s* conductio, locatio *f*; (*wages*) merces *f*
hire *vt* conducĕre; **to — out** locare; *vi* **to — out** operam suam locare
hired *adj* conductus, conducticius, mercenarius
hireling *s* mercenarius *m*
his *adj* ejus, illius, hujus; **— own** suus, proprius
his *pron* ejus, illius, hujus
hiss *vt & vi* sibilare
hissing *s* sibilus *m*
historian *s* historicus, rerum gestarum scriptor *m*
historical *adj* historicus
history *s* historia, memoria rerum gestarum *f*; **ancient —** antiquitas *f*; **modern —** memoria recentioris aetatis *f*
histrionic *adj* histrionalis
hit *s* ict·us -ūs *m*, plaga *f*; **to be a —** bene succedĕre
hit *vt* icĕre, ferire, percutĕre; *vi* **to — upon** invenire
hitch *s* impedimentum *n*, mora *f*
hitch *vt* (ad)jungĕre
hither *adv* huc
hither *adj* citerior
hitherto *adv* (*of time*) adhuc; (*of place*) huc usque
hive *s* alvus *m*, alvearium *n*
hoard *s* acervus *m*
hoard *vt* coacervare, recondĕre
hoarder *s* accumulator *m*
hoarse *adj* raucus; **to get —** irraucescĕre; **—ly** raucā voce
hoary *adj* canus
hoax *s* fraus, ludificatio *f*
hoax *vt* fallĕre, decipĕre, ludificari
hobble *vi* claudicare
hobby *s* avocamentum *n*
hock *s* poples *m*
hoe *s* sarculum *n*
hoe *vt* sarculare; (*weeds*) pectĕre
hog *s* porcus, sus *m*
hoist *vt* sublevare, tollĕre
hold *vt* tenēre, possidēre, habēre; (*to* (*contain*) capĕre; (*to think*) habēre, existimare, censēre; **to — back** retinēre; **to — forth** porrigĕre, extendĕre; (*to offer*) praebēre; **to — in** inhibēre, cohibēre; **to — off** abstinēre, arcēre; **to — up** (*to lift up*) attollĕre, sustinēre; *vi* **to — back** cunctari; **to — out** (*to last*) durare, permanēre
holder *s* possessor *m*; (*handle*) manubrium *n*
holding *s* possessio *f*
hole *s* foramen *n*; (*fig*) latebra *f*; (*of mice*) cavum *n*
holiday *s* dies festus *m*; **—s** feriae *f pl*
holiness *s* sanctitas *f*
hollow *adj* cavus; (*fig*) vanus, inanis
hollow *s* caverna *f*, cavum *n*; (*depression*) lacuna *f*
hollow *vt* **to — out** cavare, excavare
holly *s* ilex aquifolium *n*
holocaust *s* holocaustum *n*
holy *adj* sanctus
homage *s* obsequium *n*, cult·us -ūs *m*; **to pay — to** colere
home *s* domicilium *n*, dom·us -ūs *f*; **at —** domi; **from —** domo
home *adv* (*motion*) domum; (*place where*) domi
home *adj* domesticus
homeless *adj* tecto carens, profugus
homeliness *s* rusticitas *f*
homely *adj* rusticus, simplex
homemade *adj* domesticus, vernaculus, domi factus
homesickness *s* tecti sui desiderium *n*, nostalgia *f*
homestead *s* sedes *f*, fundus *m*
homeward *adv* domum
homicidal *adj* cruentus, sanguinolentus
homicide *s* (*person*) homicida *m*; (*deed*) homicidium *n*
homily *s* sermo, tractat·us -ūs *m*
homogeneous *adj* pari naturā praeditus
hone *vt* acuĕre
honest *adj* probus, sincerus; **—ly** probe, sincere
honesty *s* probitas, sinceritas *f*
honey *s* mel *n*
honeybee *s* apis mellifera *or* mellifica *f*
honeycomb *s* favus *m*
honeysuckle *s* clymenus *m*
honor *s* honos *m*; (*repute*) fama *f*; (*trust*) fides *f*; (*award*) decus *n*; (*official distinction*) dignitas *f*; **sense of —** pudor *m*
honor *vt* honorare; (*to respect*) colĕre
honorable *adj* honestus
honorably *adv* honeste
honorary *adj* honorarius
hood *s* cucullus *m*
hoof *s* ungula *f*
hook *s* hamus, uncus *m*; **by — or by crook** quocumque modo
hook *vt* inuncare; confibulare; (*fig*) capĕre
hooked *adj* hamatus; (*crooked*) curvatus, aduncus
hoop *s* circulus *m*; (*toy*) trochus *m*; (*shout*) clamor *m*
hoop *vi* exclamare
hoot *vt* explodĕre; *vi* obstrepĕre; (*of owls*) canĕre
hop *s* salt·us -ūs *m*
hop *vi* salire, subsultare
hope *s* spes *f*
hope *vt* sperare; **to — for** exspectare
hopeful *adj* bonae spei; **—ly** magna cum spe
hopeless *adj* exspes, desperatus; **—ly** desperanter
hopelessness *s* desperatio *f*
horde *s* turba, caterva *f*, grex *m*
horizon *s* orbis finiens *m*
horizontal *adj* libratus; **—ly** ad libram
horn *s* cornu *n*; (*as trumpet*) buccina *f*
horned *adj* cornutus, corniger
hornet *s* crabo *m*
horoscope *s* horoscopus *m*

horrible *adj* horribilis, foedus; (*excessive*) immoderatus
horribly *adv* horribili modo, foede
horrid *adj* horridus, horrens; **—ly** horride
horrify *vt* horrificare, perterrēre
horror *s* horror *m*; (*deep hatred*) odium *n*
horse *s* equus *m*, equa *f*
horseback *s* **on —** in equo; ex equo; **to fight on —** ex equo pugnare; **to ride on —** in equo vehi
horsehair *s* pilus equinus *m*
horseman *s* eques *m*
horse race *s* curriculum equorum *n*, certatio equestris *f*
horseradish *s* armoracia *f*
horseshoe *s* solea *f*
horsewhip *s* flagellum *n*, scutica *f*
horsewhip *vt* verberare
horticultural *adj* ad hortorum cultum pertinens
horticulture *s* hortorum cult·us -ūs *m*
hose *s* (*stocking*) tibiale *n*; (*tube*) tubulus *m*
hosiery *s* feminalia *n pl*
hospitable *adj* hospitalis
hospitably *adv* hospitaliter
hospital *s* valetudinarium *n*
hospitality *s* hospitalitas *f*
host *s* (*entertainer*) hospes *m*; (*army*) copiae *f pl*, exercit·us -ūs *m*; (*crowd*) multitudo *f*; (*wafer*) hostia *f*
hostage *s* obses *m & f*
hostess *s* hospita *f*; (*at inn*) caupona *f*
hostile *adj* hostilis, infensus, inimicus; **in a — manner** hostiliter, infense
hot *adj* calidus *or* caldus; fervidus; (*boiling*) fervens; (*seething*) aestuosus; (*of spices*) acer; (*fig*) ardens; **to be —** calēre; **to become —** calescĕre; **—ly** acriter, ardenter
hotel *s* hospitium *n*, caupona *f*
hound *s* catulus *m*
hound *vt* instare (*with dat*)
hour *s* hora *f*
hourglass *s* horarium *n*
hourly *adv* in horas
house *s* dom·us -ūs *f*, aedes *f pl*, tectum *n*; (*family*) dom·us -ūs, gens *f*; (*in country*) villa *f*; **at the — of** apud (*with acc*)
house *vt* domo excipĕre; (*things*) condĕre
housebreaker *s* fur, effractarius *m*
housebreaking *s* domūs effractura *f*
household *adj* familiaris, domesticus
household *s* familia, dom·us -ūs *f*
householder *s* paterfamilias *m*
household gods *s* Lares *m pl*; Penates *m pl*
housekeeper *s* promus *m*
housekeeping *s* rei familiaris cura *f*
housemaid *s* ancilla, vernacula *f*
housewife *s* materfamilias *f*
hovel *s* tugurium, gurgustium *n*
hover *vi* pendēre, volitare; **to — over** impendēre (*with dat*)
how *adv* quomodo, quo pacto, qui; (*to what degree*) quam; **— many** quot; **— much** quantum; **— often** quotiens
however *adv* tamen, nihilominus, autem; quamvis, quamlibet; **— great** quantuscunque; **— many** quotquot; **— often** quotiescunque
howl *s* ululat·us -ūs *m*
howl *vi* ululare, fremĕre
hub *s* axis *m*
huckster *s* propola, institor *m*
huddle *vi* congregari
huddle *s* corona *f*
huddled *adj* confertus
hue *s* color *m*
hue and cry *s* conclamatio *f*
huff *s* offensio *f*; **in a —** offensus
huff *vi* stomachari
hug *s* complex·us -ūs *m*
hug *vt* complecti, amplecti
huge *adj* ingens, immensus, vastus, immanis
hulk *s* alveus *m*; navis oneraria *f*
hull *s* alveus *m*
hum *s* murmur *n*, murmuratio *f*; (*of bees*) bombus *m*
hum *vi* murmurare; (*of bees*) bombilare
human *adj* humanus; **— feelings** humanitas *f*; **—ly** humane, humaniter, humanitus
human being *s* homo *m & f*
humane *adj* humanus, misericors; **—ly** humaniter, misericorditer, humanitus
humanity *s* humanitas *f*; homines *m pl*
humanize *vt* excolĕre
humble *adj* (*obscure*) humilis, obscurus; (*modest*) summissus, modestus; **—ly** summisse
humble *vt* deprimĕre, infringĕre; **to — oneself** se summittĕre
humid *adj* humidus
humidity *s* humor *m*
humiliate *vt* humiliare, deprimĕre
humiliation *s* humiliatio *f*, dedecus *n*
humility *s* animus summissus *m*, modestia, humilitas *f*
humor *s* (*disposition*) ingenium *n*, natura *f*; (*whim*) libido *f*; **sense of —** facetiae *f pl*, festivitas *f*
humor *vt* obsequi (*with dat*), morigerari (*with dat*), indulgēre (*with dat*)
humorous *adj* facetus, ridiculus, jocularis; **—ly** facete
hump *s* gibber, gibbus *m*
humpbacked *adj* gibber
hunch *s* opinio *f*; **to have a —** opinari
hundred *adj* centum; **— times** centie(n)s
hundredfold *adj* centuplex
hundredfold *s* centuplum *n*
hundredth *adj* centesimus
hunger *s* fames *f*
hunger *vi* esurire
hungrily *adv* avide, voraciter, rabide; jejune
hungry *s* esuriens, jejunus; (*fig*) avide; **to be —** esurire
hunt *s* venatio *f*, venat·us -ūs *m*

hunt *vt* venari, indagare; *vi* **to — for** quaerĕre, exquirĕre
hunter *s* venator *m*; (*horse*) equus venaticus *m*
hunting *s* venatio *f*, venat·us -ūs *m*
hunting *adj* venaticus
huntress *s* venatrix *f*
huntsman *s* venator *m*
hurdle *s* crates *f*; (*obstacle*) obex *m & f*
hurl *vt* jacĕre, conjicĕre, jaculari
hurray *interj* io!, evax!
hurricane *s* procella *f*
hurriedly *adv* raptim, festinanter; (*carelessly*) negligenter
hurry *vt* rapĕre, accelerare, maturare; *vi* festinare, properare, maturare
hurry *s* festinatio *f*; **in a —** festinanter
hurt *vt* nocēre (*with dat*), laedĕre; (*fig*) offendĕre; *vi* dolēre
hurt *s* vulnus *n*; damnum *n*, injuria *f*
hurt *adj* saucius; (*emotionally*) saucius, offensus
husband *s* maritus, vir *m*
husbandry *s* agricultura, res rustica *f*
hush *s* silentium *n*
hush *vt* comprimĕre, pacare; (*a secret*) celare; *vi* tacēre
hush *interj* st!, tace!; (*to several*) tacete!
husk *s* folliculus *m*; (*of beans, etc.*) siliqua *f*; (*of grain*) gluma *f*
husky *adj* robustus; (*of voice*) raucus
hustle *vt* trudĕre, pulsare; *vi* festinare
hut *s* tugurium *n*, casa *f*
hyacinth *s* hyacinthus *m*
hydra *s* hydra *f*
hyena *s* hyaena *f*
hymen *s* Hymenaeus *m*
hymn *s* carmen *n*, hymnus *m*
hyperbole *s* superlatio *f*
hypercritical *adj* nimis severus
hyphen *s* hyphen *n* (*indecl*)
hypochondriac *s* melancholicus *m*
hypocrisy *s* simulatio, dissimulatio *f*
hypocrite *s* simulator, dissimulator *m*
hypocritical *adj* simulatus, fictus
hypothesis *s* hypothesis, sumptio, conjectura *f*
hypothetical *adj* hypotheticus, sumptus
hysteria *s* deliratio *f*
hysterical *adj* hystericus

I

I *pron* ego; **— myself** egomet, ego ipse
iambic *adj* iambeus
ice *s* glacies *f*
icicle *s* stiria *f*
icy *adj* glacialis
idea *s* notio, notitia, imago, conceptio *f*
ideal *adj* perfectus, summus, optimus; (*as mere mental image*) mente conceptus, idealis
ideal *s* exemplar *n*
identical *adj* idem
identify *vt* agnoscĕre
idiocy *s* fatuitas, animi imbecillitas *f*
idiom *s* proprietas linguae, consuetudo *f*
idiomatic *adj* proprius linguae
idiosyncrasy *s* proprium *n*
idiot *s* fatuus, excors *m*
idiotic *adj* fatuus, stultus, ineptus
idle *adj* otiosus, vacuus; (*pointless*) vanus, inanis; (*lazy*) ignavus, iners, deses; **to be —** cessare
idle *vt* **to — away** terĕre; *vi* cessare
idleness *s* otium *n*; ignavia, inertia, desidia *f*
idler *s* cessator, homo ignavus *m*
idle talk *s* nugae *f pl*
idly *adv* otiose; ignave, segniter; (*in vain*) vane, frustra
idol *s* simulacrum *n*; (*eccl*) idolum *n*; (*person*) deliciae *f pl*
idolater *s* simulacrorum cultor *m*
idolatrous *adj* idololatricus
idolatry *s* simulacrorum cult·us -ūs *m*
idolize *vt* venerari
idyl *s* idyllium *n*
if *conj* si; **as —** quasi, tamquam; **and —** quodsi; **but —** sin; quodsi; **even —** etiamsi; **— not** ni, nisi, si non; **— only** si modo, dummodo
igneous *adj* igneus
ignite *vt* accendĕre, incendĕre; *vi* exardescĕre, flammam concipĕre
ignoble *adj* ignobilis, obscurus; (*base*) turpis
ignobly *adv* turpiter
ignominious *adj* ignominiosus, turpis; **—ly** ignominiose, turpiter
ignominy *s* ignominia *f*
ignoramus *s* idiota *m*
ignorance *s* ignoratio, ignorantia *f*
ignorant *adj* ignarus, nescius; (*unlearned*) indoctus; **to be — of** ignorare, nescire; **—ly** inscienter, inscite, indocte
ignore *vt* praetermittĕre, neglegĕre
Iliad *s* Ilias *f*
ill *adj* aegrotus, aeger; (*evil*) malus; **to be —** aegrotare; **to fall — in** morbum incidĕre
ill *adv* male, prave
ill *s* malum *n*
ill-bred *adj* inurbanus, agrestis
illegal *adj* vetitus, illicitus; **—ly** contra leges, illicite
illegitimate *adj* haud legitimus; (*of birth*) spurius, nothus
illiberal *adj* illiberalis; **—ly** illiberaliter
illicit *adj* illicitus; **—ly** illicite

illiterate *adj* illitteratus, indoctus, ineruditus
illness *s* morbus *m*, aegritudo, aegrotatio, valetudo *f*
illogical *adj* absurdus; **—ly** absurde
ill-starred *adj* infelix
ill-tempered *adj* iracundus, stomachosus, difficilis
illuminate *vt* illustrare, illuminare
illumination *s* illuminatio *f*, lumina *n pl*
illusion *s* error *m*
illusive *adj* falsus, vanus
illusory *adj* fallax
illustrate *vt* illustrare; (*fig*) explanare
illustration *s* illustratio *f*; (*fig*) exemplum *n*
illustrative *adj* exemplaris
illustrious *adj* illustris, insignis, praeclarus; **—ly** praeclare
image *s* signum, simulacrum *n*; (*likeness*) effigies, imago *f*
imagery *s* figurae *f pl*
imaginary *adj* fictus, commenticius
imagination *s* cogitatio *f*
imaginative *adj* ingeniosus
imagine *vt* imaginari, fingĕre; (*to suppose*) opinari
imbecile *adj* (*weak*) imbecillus; (*of mind*) animo imbecillus, fatuus
imbecile *s* fatuus *m*
imbibe *vt* imbibĕre
imbue *vt* imbuĕre, tingĕre
imitate *vt* imitari
imitation *s* imitatio *f*; (*copy*) imago *f*
imitative *adj* ad imitandum aptus
imitator *s* imitator *m*, imitatrix *f*, aemulator *m*
immaculate *adj* integer, castus
immaterial *adj* incorporalis; (*unimportant*) nullius momenti
immeasurable *adj* immensus, infinitus
immeasurably *adv* infinito
immediate *adj* praesens, proximus; **—ly** statim, confestim, extemplo; **—ly after** sub (*with acc*)
immemorial *adj* antiquissimus; **from time —** ex omni memoria aetatum
immense *adj* immensus; **—ly** vehementer
immensity *s* immensitas *f*
immerge *vt* mergĕre, immergĕre
immersion *s* immersio *f*
imminent *adj* imminens, impendens
immobility *s* immobilitas *f*
immoderate *adj* immodicus; **—ly** immoderate, nimie
immodest *adj* immodestus, impudicus; **—ly** immodeste, inverecunde
immodesty *s* immodestia *f*
immolate *vt* immolare
immolation *s* immolatio *f*
immoral *adj* pravus, improbus, corruptus; **—ly** prave
immorality *s* mores mali *m pl*, turpitudo, improbitas *f*
immortal *adj* immortalis
immortality *s* immortalitas *f*
immortalize *vt* aeternare, ad deos evehĕre
immovable *adj* immobilis, immotus
immunity *s* immunitas, vacatio *f*
immure *vt* includĕre
immutability *s* immutabilitas *f*
immutable *adj* immutabilis
imp *s* larva *f*; (*child*) puer lascivus *m*
impair *vt* imminuĕre, atterĕre, debilitare
impale *vt* infigĕre
impart *vt* impertire, communicare
impartial *adj* aequus, aequabilis, severus; **—ly** severe
impartiality *s* aequitas, aequabilitas *f*
impassable *adj* insuperabilis, impervius
impassive *adj* impassibilis, frigidus, lentus
impatient *adj* impatiens, trepidus; **—ly** impatienter, aegre
impeach *vt* accusare
impeachment *s* accusatio *f*
impede *vt* obstare (*with dat*), impedire, retardare
impediment *s* impedimentum *n*; (*in speech*) haesitatio *f*
impel *vt* impellĕre
impenetrable *adj* impenetrabilis; (*fig*) occultus
impenitence *s* impaenitentia *f*
imperative *adj* necessarius; (*gram*) imperativus
imperceptible *adj* tenuissimus, obscurus
imperceptibly *adv* sensim
imperfect *adj* imperfectus, mancus, vitiosus; **—ly** imperfecte, vitiose
imperfection *s* vitium *n*, defect·us -ūs *m*
imperial *adj* imperatorius, regius; **—ly** regie
imperil *vt* in periculum adducĕre
imperishable *adj* perennis, aeternus, immortalis
impermeable *adj* impervius
impersonal *adj* impersonalis; **—ly** impersonaliter
impersonate *vt* sustinēre partes (*with genit*), imitari
impertinence *s* insolentia, protervitas *f*
impertinent *adj* (*rude*) insolens, protervus; (*not to the point*) ineptus, nihil ad rem; **—ly** insolenter, proterve; inepte
impervious *adj* impervius, impenetrabilis
impetuosity *s* impet·us -ūs *m*, vehementia, violentia *f*
impetuous *adj* vehemens, fervidus, violentus; **—ly** vehementer, fervide, violenter
impetus *s* impet·us -ūs *m*, vis *f*
impiety *s* impietas *f*
impinge *vi* incidĕre
impious *adj* impius, nefarius; **—ly** impie, nefarie
implacable *adj* implacabilis, inexorabilis, durus
implacably *adv* implacabiliter, dure
implant *vt* ingignĕre, inserĕre, ingenerare
implement *s* instrumentum *n*

implement *vt* exsequi
implicate *vt* implicare, impedire
implication *s* indicium *n*; **by —** tacite
implicit *adj* tacitus, totus; **—ly** tacite, omnino
implore *vt* implorare, obsecrare
imply *vt* significare; **to be implied in** inesse in (*with abl*)
impolite *adj* inurbanus; **—ly** inurbane
impoliteness *s* inurbanitas *f*
impolitic *adj* inconsultus
imponderable *adj* ponderis expers
import *vt* importare, invehĕre; (*to mean*) significare, velle
import *s* significatio *f*; **—s** importaticia *n pl*
importance *s* momentum *n*, gravitas *f*
important *adj* magnus, magni momenti, gravis
importunate *adj* importunus; **—ly** importune
importune *vt* fatigare, efflagitare, sollicitare
impose *vt* imponĕre; (*to enjoin*) injungĕre; **to — upon** abuti (*with abl*)
imposition *s* (*tax*) vectigal, tributum *n*; (*excessive burden*) importunitas *f*
impossibility *s* impossibilitas *f*
impossible *adj* impossibilis
imposter *s* fraudator *m*
imposture *s* fraus *f*
impotence *s* imbecillitas, infirmitas *f*
impotent *adj* imbecillus, infirmus
impound *vt* publicare; (*animals*) includĕre
impoverish *vt* in egéstatem redigĕre
impractical *adj* inutilis
imprecate *vt* imprecari, exsecrari
imprecation *s* exsecratio *f*, dirae *f pl*
impregnable *adj* inexpugnabilis
impregnate *vt* imbuĕre, gravidam facĕre
impregnation *s* fecundatio *f*
impress *vt* imprimĕre; (*person*) movēre; **to — something on** inculcare aliquid (*with dat*); (*e.g., someone's mind*) infigĕre aliquid (*with dat*)
impression *s* impressio *f*; (*copy*) exemplar *n*; (*mark*) vestigium *n*; (*idea*) opinio, opinatio *f*; **to make an — on** commovēre
impressive *adj* gravis; **—ly** graviter
imprint *s* impressio *f*
imprint *vt* imprimĕre, infigĕre
imprison *vt* in vincula conjicĕre
imprisonment *s* custodia *f*
improbable *adj* haud credibilis, parum verisimilis
impromptu *adv* ex tempore
improper *adj* indecorus; **—ly** indecore, perperam
impropriety *s* indecorum *n*
improve *vt* emendare, corrigĕre, excolĕre; *vi* melior fieri, proficĕre
improvement *s* emendatio, correctio *f*, profect·us -ūs *m*
improvident *adj* improvidus, imprudens; **—ly** improvide
improvise *vt* ex tempore dicĕre *or* componĕre
imprudence *s* imprudentia *f*
imprudent *adj* imprudens, inconsultus, temerarius; **—ly** imprudenter, inconsulte, temere
impugn *vt* impugnare, in dubium vocare
impulse *s* impuls·us -ūs *m*
impulsive *adj* vehemens, violentus; **—ly** impulsu
impunity *s* impunitas *f*; **with —** impune
impure *adj* impurus, obscenus, incestus; contaminatus; **—ly** impure, obscene, inceste
impurity *s* impuritas, obscenitas, impudicitia *f*
in *prep* in (*with abl*); (*in the writings of*) apud (*with acc*); (*of time*) *render by abl*
in *adv* (*motion*) intro; (*rest*) intra, intus
inability *s* impotentia *f*
inaccessible *adj* inaccessus
inaccuracy *s* neglegentia *f*
inaccurate *adj* neglegens, parum accuratus, minime exactus; **—ly** parum accurate
inactive *adj* iners, quietus, ignavus
inactivity *s* inertia, socordia, cessatio *f*
inadequate *adj* impar; **—ly** parum
inadmissible *adj* illicitus
inadvertence *s* imprudentia *f*
inadvertent *adj* imprudens; **—ly** imprudenter
inalienable *adj* proprius
inane *adj* inanis
inanimate *adj* inanimus, inanimatus
inapplicable *adj* **to be —** non valēre
inappropriate *adj* haud idoneus, parum aptus; **—ly** parum apte
inarticulate *adj* indistinctus
inartistic *adj* durus
inasmuch as *conj* quandoquidem
inattentive *adj* haud attentus, neglegens; **—ly** neglegenter
inaudible *adj* **to be —** audiri non posse
inaugurate *vt* inaugurare, consecrare
inauguration *s* inauguratio, consecratio *f*
inauspicious *adj* infaustus; **—ly** malo omine
inborn *adj* ingenitus, innatus
incalculable *adj* inaestimabilis; (*fig*) immensus, incredibilis
incantation *s* carmen, incantamentum *n*
incapable *adj* incapax, inhabilis; **to be — of** non posse (*with inf*)
incapacitate *vt* debilitare
incarcerate *vt* in vincula conjicĕre
incarnate *adj* incarnatus
incarnation *s* incarnatio *f*
incautious *adj* incautus; **—ly** incaute
incendiary *adj* incendiarius

incense *s* tus *n*
incense *vt* ture fumigare; (*to anger*) irritare, exasperare
incentive *s* incitamentum *n*
incessant *adj* continuus, assiduus; **—ly** assidue
incest *s* incest·us -ūs *m*
incestuous *adj* incestus
inch *s* uncia *f*; **— by —** unciatim
incident *s* cas·us -ūs, event·us -ūs *m*
incidental *adj* fortuitus; **—ly** fortuito, casu, forte
incipient *adj* nascens, primus
incision *s* incis·us -ūs *m*, incisura *f*
incisive *adj* acer
incite *vt* incitare, stimulare
incitement *s* incitamentum *n*, incitatio *f*
incivility *s* rusticitas *f*
inclemency *s* inclementia *f*; (*of weather*) asperitas *f*
inclination *s* (*act*) inclinatio *f*; (*slope*) proclivitas *f*; (*propensity*) libido, inclinatio *f*
incline *vt* inclinare; *vi* propendēre
incline *s* acclivitas *f*
inclined *adj* inclinatus, propensus, pronus
include *vt* includěre, comprehenděre
inclusive *adj* comprehendens
incognito *adv* clam
incoherent *adj* interruptus; **—ly** interrupte
income *s* redit·us -ūs, fruct·us -ūs *m*, merces *f*
incomparable *adj* incomparabilis, singularis, unicus, eximius
incomparably *adv* eximie, unice
incompatibility *s* repugnantia, diversitas *f*
incompatible *adj* repugnans, discors
incompetence *s* jurisdictionis defect·us -ūs *m*; inscitia *f*
incompetent *adj* inscitus, inhabilis
incomplete *adj* imperfectus
incomprehensible *adj* haud comprehensibilis
inconceivable *adj* incredibilis
inconclusive *adj* anceps
incongruous *adj* inconveniens, male congruens; **—ly** parum apte
inconsiderable *adj* levis, exiguus
inconsiderate *adj* inconsultus
inconsistency *s* inconstantia, discrepantia *f*
inconsistent *adj* inconstans, absonus, contrarius; **to be — with** abhorrēre ab (*with abl*); **—ly** inconstanter
inconsolable *adj* inconsolabilis
inconstancy *s* inconstantia, levitas *f*
inconstant *adj* inconstans, levis
incontestable *adj* non contentendus
incontinence *s* incontinentia, impudicitia *f*
incontinent *adj* incontinens, intemperans, impudicus; **—ly** incontinenter
incontrovertible *adj* quod refutari non potest
inconvenience *s* incommodum *n*
inconvenience *vt* incommodare
inconvenient *adj* incommodus; **—ly** incommode
incorporate *vt* concorporare, inserěre
incorporation *s* coagmentatio, cooptatio *f*
incorporeal *adj* incorporalis
incorrect *adj* mendosus, vitiosus, falsus; **—ly** mendose, falso, perperam
incorrigible *adj* incorrigibilis; (*fig*) perditus
incorrupt *adj* incorruptus, integer
incorruptibility *s* incorruptibilitas *f*, incorrupti mores *m pl*
incorruptible *adj* incorruptibilis, integer
increase *s* (*act*) accretio *f*; incrementum, additamentum *n*
increase *vt* augēre, ampliare; *vi* augēri, crescěre
incredible *adj* incredibilis
incredibly *adv* incredibiliter, ultra fidem
incredulity *s* incredulitas *f*
incredulous *adj* incredulus
increment *s* incrementum *n*
incriminate *vt* criminari
incubation *s* incubatio *f*
inculcate *vt* inculcare
inculcation *s* inculcatio *f*
incumbent *adj* **it is — on** oportet (*with acc*)
incur *vt* contrahěre, subire; (*guilt*) admittěre
incurable *adj* insanabilis
incursion *s* incursio *f*
indebted *adj* obaeratus; (*obliged*) obligatus, devinctus, obnoxius
indecency *s* indecorum *n*, obscenitas *f*
indecent *adj* indecorus, obscenus; **—ly** indecore, obscene
indecision *s* haesitatio, dubitatio *f*
indecisive *adj* anceps, dubius, incertus
indeclinable *adj* indeclinabilis
indeed *adv* vere, profecto, sane; (*concessive*) quidem; (*reply*) certe, vero; (*interr*) itane?, verone?
indefatigable *adj* indefatigabilis, indefessus
indefensible *adj* non excusandus; **to be —** defendi non posse; (*mil*) tenēri non posse
indefinite *adj* infinitus, incertus, anceps, obscurus; **—ly** indefinite
indelible *adj* indelebilis
indelicacy *s* indecorum *n*
indelicate *adj* putidus, indecorus
indemnify *vt* compensare; damnum restitutěre (*with dat*)
indemnity *s* indemnitas *f*
independence *s* libertas *f*
independent *adj* sui potens, sui juris, liber; **—ly** libere, suo arbitrio
indescribable *adj* inenarrabilis; **—ly** inenarrabiliter
indestructible *adj* perennis, perpetuus
indeterminate *adj* indefinitus
index *s* index, elenchus *m*; (*of dial*) gnomon *m*
Indian *adj* Indicus
Indian *s* Indus *m*

indicate *vt* indicare, significare
indication *s* indicatio *f*, signum, indicium *n*
indicative *adj* indicativus
indict *vt* accusare; diem dicĕre (*with dat*)
indictment *s* libellus *m*, accusatio *f*
indifference *s* neglegentia, incuria, lentitudo *f*
indifferent *adj* (*apathetic*) remissus, neglegens, lentus; (*mediocre*) mediocris; **—ly** neglegenter, lente; (*without discrimination*) promiscue
indigenous *adj* indigena
indigent *adj* egens, inops
indigestible *adj* crudus
indigestion *s* cruditas *f*
indignant *adj* indignans, indignabundus, iratus; **to be —** indignari; **—ly** indignanter
indignation *s* indignatio *f*, dolor *m*
indignity *s* indignitas, contumelia *f*
indirect *adj* indirectus, obliquus; **—ly** indirecte, oblique
indiscreet *adj* inconsultus; **—ly** inconsulte, temere
indiscretion *s* immodestia *f*; (*act*) culpa *f*
indiscriminate *adj* promiscuus; **—ly** promiscue, sine discrimine
indispensable *adj* omnino necessarius
indisposed *adj* aversus; (*in health*) aegrotus; **to be —** aegrotare
indisputable *adj* manifestus, certus
indissoluble *adj* indissolubilis
indistinct *adj* indistinctus, parum clarus, obscurus; **—ly** indistincte
individual *adj* proprius, singularis, singuli; **—ly** singulatim
individual *s* homo *m & f*; **—s** singuli *m pl*
individuality *s* proprium ingenium *n*
indivisible *adj* indivisibilis, individuus
indolence *s* inertia, desidia *f*
indolent *adj* iners, ignavus; **—ly** ignave, segniter
indomitable *adj* indomitus
indorse *vt* ratum facĕre
indubitable *adj* indubitabilis
indubitably *adv* sine dubio
induce *vt* persuadēre (*with dat*), inducĕre
inducement *s* incitamentum *n*, illecebra *f*
indulge *vt* indulgēre (*with dat*), servire (*with dat*)
indulgence *s* indulgentia, venia *f*
indulgent *adj* indulgens, benignus; **—ly** indulgenter, benigne
industrious *adj* industrius, sedulus, strenuus; **—ly** industrie
industry *s* industria, assiduitas *f*
inebriated *adj* ebrius, madidus
ineffable *adj* ineffabilis
ineffective *adj* irritus, inutilis; **to be —** effectu carēre
ineffectual *adj* inefficax; **—ly** frustra, nequiquam
inefficiency *s* inutilitas *f*
inefficient *adj* inscitus, inhabilis
ineligible *adj* non eligibilis
inept *adj* ineptus
inequality *s* inaequalitas *f*
inert *adj* iners, segnis, socors
inertia *s* inertia *f*
inevitable *adj* necessarius
inexact *adj* haud accuratus; (*of persons*) indiligens
inexcusable *adj* inexcusabilis
inexhaustible *adj* inexhaustus
inexorable *adj* inexorabilis, durus
inexperience *s* imperitia, inscitia *f*
inexperienced *adj* imperitus, inexpertus
inexplicable *adj* inexplicabilis, inenodabilis
inexpressible *adj* inenarrabilis
inextricable *adj* inexplicabilis, inextricabilis
infallible *adj* certus, erroris expers
infamous *adj* infamis, turpis, flagitiosus; **—ly** flagitiose
infamy *s* infamia *f*, probrum *n*
infancy *s* infantia *f*
infant *adj* infans; puerilis
infant *s* infans *m & f*
infanticide *s* (*person*) infanticida *m*; (*deed*) infanticidium *n*
infantile *adj* infantilis
infantry *s* peditat·us -ūs *m*, pedites *m pl*
infatuate *vt* infatuare
infatuation *s* amentia, dementia *f*
infect *vt* inficĕre; (*fig*) contaminare
infection *s* contagium *n*, contagio *f*
infectious *adj* contagiosus
infer *vt* inferre, conjicĕre
inference *s* conjectura, conclusio *f*
inferior *adj* inferior, deterior, minor
infernal *adj* infernus
infertility *s* sterilitas *f*
infest *vt* infestare, frequentare
infidel *s* infidelis *m & f*
infidelity *s* infidelitas, perfidia *f*
infiltrate *vi* se insinuare
infinite *adj* infinitus, immensus; **—ly** infinite; (*very greatly*) infinito
infinitive *s* infinitivus modus *m*
infinity *s* infinitas, infinitio *f*
infirm *adj* infirmus, debilis
infirmary *s* valetudinarium *n*
infirmity *s* infirmitas, imbecillitas *f*
inflame *vt* inflammare, incendĕre, accendĕre
inflammable *adj* ad exardescendum facilis
inflammation *s* inflammatio *f*
inflammatory *adj* turbulentus, ardens
inflate *vt* inflare; **to be inflated** tumēre
inflation *s* inflatio *f*
inflect *vt* inflectĕre, curvare
inflection *s* flex·us -ūs *m*, declinatio *f*
inflexible *adj* rigidus; (*fig*) obstinatus, pertinax
inflexibly *adv* obstinate
inflict *vt* infligĕre, imponĕre
infliction *s* malum *n*, poena *f*
influence *s* gratia, auctoritas *f*, momentum *n*; **to have — on** valēre apud (*with acc*)
influence *vt* movēre, impellĕre
influential *adj* gravis, potens

influenza *s* catarrh·us -ūs *m*, gravedo *f*
influx *s* influxio *f*
inform *vt* (*to teach*) instruĕre; certiorem facĕre; *vi* **to — against** deferre de (*with abl*)
informant *s* index, delator *m*
information *s* informatio *f*, indicium *n*, nuntius *m*
informer *s* delator *m*
infraction *s* infractio *f*
infrequency *s* raritas *f*
infrequent *adj* rarus
infringe *vt* infringĕre, violare; *vi* **to — upon** occupare, usurpare
infringement *s* violatio, usurpatio *f*
infuriate *vt* efferare
infuse *vt* infundere; (*fig*) injicĕre
infusion *s* infusio *f*
ingenious *adj* sollers, callidus, ingeniosus; (*of thing*) artificiosus; **—ly** callide, artificiose
ingenuity *s* ars, sollertia *f*
ingenuous *adj* simplex
inglorious *adj* inglorius, inhonestus; **—ly** sine gloria, in honeste
ingrained *adj* insitus, inveteratus
ingratiate *vt* **to — oneself with** gratiam inire ab (*with abl*)
ingratitude *s* ingratus animus *m*
ingredient *s* pars *f*
inhabit *vt* incolĕre, habitare
inhabitable *adj* habitabilis
inhabitant *s* incola *m & f*
inhale *vt* haurire; *vi* spiritum ducĕre
inharmonious *adj* dissonus, absonus
inherent *adj* inhaerens, insitus; **to be — in** inesse (*with dat*)
inherit *vt* excipĕre
inheritance *s* hereditas, successio *f*, patrimonium *n*; **to come into an —** hereditatem adire
inheritor *s* heres *m & f*
inhospitable *adj* inhospitalis
inhospitably *adv* minime hospitaliter
inhospitality *s* inhospitalitas *f*
inhuman *adj* inhumanus; **—ly** inhumane
inhumanity *s* inhumanitas *f*
inimical *adj* inimicus
inimitable *adj* inimitabilis
iniquitous *adj* iniquus, improbus
iniquity *s* iniquitas, injustitia *f*
initial *adj* primus
initiate *vt* initiare, instituĕre
initiation *s* initiatio *f*
initiative *s* initium *n*
inject *vt* injicĕre, infundĕre, immittĕre
injection *s* injectio *f*
injudicious *adj* inconsultus; **—ly** inconsulte, temere
injunction *s* mandatum, imperatum *n*
injure *vt* nocēre (*with dat*), laedĕre
injurious *adj* noxius, damnosus, gravis; **—ly** male
injury *s* injuria f, damnum, detrimentum, malum *n*
injustice *s* injustitia *f*; (*act*) injuria *f*
ink *s* atramentum *n*
inkling *s* (*hint*) rumusculus *m*, obscura significatio *f*
inland *adj* mediterraneus
inlay *vt* inserĕre; (*with mosaic*) tessellare
inlet *s* sin·us -ūs *m*, aestuarium *n*
inmate *s* incola, inquilinus *m*
inmost *adj* intimus, imus
inn *s* caupona *f*, deversorium *n*
innate *adj* innatus, insitus
inner *adj* interior
innermost *adj* intimus, imus
innkeeper *s* caupo *m*
innocence *s* innocentia *f*; castitas *f*
innocent *adj* insons, innocens, integer, castus; **—ly** innocenter, integre, caste
innocuous *adj* innocuus; **—ly** innocue
innovation *s* novum *n*, res nova *f*
innovator *s* rerum novarum auctor *m*
innumerable *adj* innumerabilis
inoffensive *adj* innocens, innoxius
inopportune *adj* inopportunus; **—ly** parum in tempore
inordinate *adj* immoderatus; **—ly** immoderate
inquest *s* inquisitio *f*; (*law*) quaestio *f*; **to hold an —** quaerĕre
inquire *vi* inquirĕre, rogare; **to — into** investigare
inquiry *s* quaestio, investigatio *f*
inquisition *s* inquisitio *f*
inquisitive *adj* curiosus; **—ly** curiose
inquisitor *s* quaesitor *m*
inroad *s* incursio, irruptio *f*
insane *adj* insanus, vecors; **—ly** insane
insanity *s* insania, dementia *f*
insatiable *adj* insatiabilis, inexplebilis
inscribe *vt* inscribĕre, insculpĕre, incidĕre
inscription *s* inscriptio *f*, titulus *m*
inscrutable *adj* occultus, obscurus
insect *s* insectum *n*, bestiola *f*
insecure *adj* incertus, intutus, instabilis
insecurity *s* periculum *n*
insensible *adj* insensilis; (*fig*) durus
inseparable *adj* inseparabilis
insert *vt* inserĕre; (*in writing*) ascribĕre
insertion *s* insertio, interpositio *f*
inside *adj* interior
inside *adv* intrinsecus
inside *s* interior pars *f*, interiora *n pl*
inside *prep* intro (*with acc*)
insidious *adj* insidiosus, subdolus; **—ly** insidiose, subdole
insight *s* (*knowledge*) cognitio, intellegentia *f*; (*intelligence*) consilium, judicium *n*
insignia *s* insignia *n pl*
insignificance *s* exiguitas, levitas *f*
insignificant *adj* exiguus, levis, nullius momenti; (*rank*) humilis
insincere *adj* insincerus, simulatus, fucosus; **—ly** haud sincere, simulate
insincerity *s* simulatio, fallacia *f*

insinuate *vt* insinuare; (*to hint*) significare
insinuation *s* significatio *f*
insipid *adj* insulsus, hebes, frigidus; **—ly** insulse
insist *vt* flagitare, exposcĕre; *vi* instare; **to — on** urgĕre, postulare
insistence *s* pertinacia *f*
insolence *s* insolentia, arrogantia *f*
insolent *adj* insolens, arrogans; **—ly** insolenter
insoluble *adj* insolubilis; (*fig*) inexplicabilis
insolvent *adj* **to be —** solvendo non esse
inspect *vt* inspicĕre, introspicĕre, intuēri; (*mil*) recensēre
inspection *s* inspectio, cura *f*; (*mil*) recensio *f*
inspector *s* curator *m*
inspiration *s* (*divine*) afflat·us -ūs *m*; instinct·us -ūs *m*; (*prophetic*) furor *m*
inspire *vt* inspirare, incendĕre, injicĕre
instability *s* instabilitas *f*
install *vt* inaugurare, constituĕre
installation *s* inauguratio *f*
instalment *s* pensio, portio *f*
instance *s* exemplum *n*; **at my —** me auctore; **for —** exampli gratiā
instance *vt* memorare
instant *adj* instans, praesens; **—ly** extemplo, statim
instant *s* momentum *n*; **this —** statim, actutum
instantaneous *adj* praesens; **—ly** continuo
instead *adv* potius, magis
instead of *prep* pro (*with abl*), loco (*with genit*)
instigate *vt* instigare
instigation *s* incitatio *f*, stimulus *m*
instigator *s* instigator *m*, instigatrix *f*
instill *vt* instillare, imbuĕre, injicĕre
instinct *s* instinct·us -ūs *m*, natura *f*
instinctive *adj* naturalis; **—ly** instinctu
institute *vt* instituĕre, constituĕre, condĕre
institute *s* institutum *n*
institution *s* (*act*) institutio *f*; (*thing instituted*) institutum *n*
instruct *vt* (*to teach*) docēre, instituĕre; (*to order*) praecipĕre (*with dat*), mandare
instruction *s* institutio, eruditio, doctrina *f*; **—s** mandata *n pl*
instructive *adj* ad docendum aptus
instructor *s* praeceptor, magister, doctor *m*, magistra *f*
instrument *s* instrumentum *n*; (*mus*) organum *n*; (*law*) tabula, syngrapha *f*
instrumental *adj* aptus, utilis
insubordinate *adj* seditiosus, male parens
insubordination *s* inobedientia, intemperantia *f*
insufferable *adj* intolerandus, intolerabilis
insufficiency *s* defect·us -ūs *m*, inopia *f*
insufficient *adj* impar, parum sufficiens; **—ly** haud satis
insular *adj* insulanus
insulate *vt* segregare
insult *s* probrum *n*, injuria, contumelia *f*
insult *vt* insultare; contumeliam imponĕre (*with dat*), contumeliā afficĕre
insultingly *adv* contumeliose
insure *vt* tutum praestare
insurgent *adj* rebellis
insurgent *s* rebellis *m*
insurmountable *adj* inexsuperabilis
insurrection *s* rebellio, seditio *f*
intact *adj* integer, intactus, incolumis
intangible *adj* intactilis
integral *adj* necessarius
integrity *s* integritas, innocentia, fides *f*
intellect *s* intellect·us -ūs, animus *m*, mens *f*, ingenium *n*
intellectual *adj* ingeniosus
intelligence *s* ingenium *n*, intellegentia *f*; (*information*) nuntius *m*
intelligent *adj* sapiens, argutus, prudens; **—ly** intellegenter, sapienter, prudenter
intelligible *adj* intellegibilis, perspicuus
intelligibly *adv* intellegibiliter, perspicue
intemperance *s* intemperantia *f*
intemperate *adj* immodicus, intemperatus; **—ly** intemperanter
intend *vt* (*with inf*) intendĕre, in animo habēre; (*with object*) destinare
intended *adj* destinatus; (*of future spouse*) sponsus
intense *adj* acer, fervidus; (*of heat*) rapidus; (*excessive*) nimius; **—ly** vehementer, valde, nimium
intensify *vt* augēre
intensity *s* vehmentia, vis *f*; (*of winter, etc.*) rigor *m*
intent *adj* intentus, attentus; **to be — on** animum intendĕre in (*with acc*); **—ly** intente
intention *s* propositum, consilium *n*; (*meaning*) significatio *f*
intentionally *adv* de industria
inter *vt* inhumare, sepelire
intercede *vi* intercedĕre, deprecari, se interponĕre
intercept *vt* excipĕre, intercipĕre, intercludĕre
intercession *s* deprecatio *f*; (*of tribune*) intercessio *f*
intercessor *s* deprecator *m*
interchange *vt* permutare, commutare
interchange *s* permutatio, vicissitudo *f*
intercourse *s* commercium *n*; (*social*) consuetudo *f*; (*sexual*) congress·us -ūs, coit·us -ūs *m*
interdict *vt* interdicĕre, prohibēre
interdiction *s* interdictio *f*, interdictum *n*
interest *s* (*attention*) studium *n*; (*advantage*) utilitas *f*, us·us -ūs *m*,

commodum *n*; (*money*) faenus *n*, usura *f*; **it is of — to me** meā interest, meā refert
interested *adj* **— in** studiosus (*with genit*), attentus (*with dat*)
interfere *vi* intercedĕre, intervenire, interpellare
interference *s* intercessio *f*, dissidium *n*, intervent·us -ūs *m*
interim *s* intervallum *n*; **in the —** interim, interea
interior *adj* interior
interior *s* interior pars *f*
interjection *s* interjectio *f*
interlinear *adj* interscriptus
interlude *s* embolium *n*
intermarriage *s* connubium *n*
intermarry *vi* matrimonio inter se conjungi
intermediary *s* internuntius *m*
intermediate *adj* medius
interment *s* sepultura, humatio *f*
interminable *adj* infinitus
intermission *s* intermissio, intercapedo *f*
intermittent *adj* intermittens, interruptus; **—ly** interdum, aliquando
internal *adj* intestinus, domesticus; **—ly** intus, interne; domi
international *adj* inter gentes
interpolate *vt* interpolare
interpolation *s* interpolatio *f*
interpret *vt* interpretari
interpretation *s* interpretatio *f*
interpreter *s* interpres *m*
interrogate *vt* interrogare, percontari
interrogation *s* interrogatio, percontatio *f*
interrogative *adj* interrogativus
interrupt *vt* interrumpĕre, interpellare
interruption *s* interruptio, interpellatio *f*
intersect *vt* intersecare
intersection *s* quadrivium *n*
intersperse *vt* inmiscēre
intertwine *vt* intertexĕre
interval *s* intervallum, spatium *n*
intervene *vi* (*to be between*) interjacēre; (*to come between*) intercedĕre, intervenire
intervening *adj* medius
intervention *s* intercessio *f*, intervent·us -ūs *m*
interview *s* colloquium *n*, congress·us -ūs *m*
interview *vt* percontari
interweave *vt* intertexĕre, intexĕre
intestinal *adj* ad intestina pertinens
intestine *adj* intestinus; (*pol*) domesticus, civicus
intestines *s* intestina *n pl*; (*of victim*) exta *n pl*
intimacy *s* familiaritas, consuetudo *f*
intimate *adj* familiaris; intimus; **—ly** familiariter; intime
intimate *vt* indicare, innuĕre, denuntiare
intimation *s* indicium *n*, denuntiatio *f*
intimidate *vt* minari (*with dat*), metum injicĕre (*with dat*), terrēre
intimidation *s* minae *f pl*
into *prep* in (*with acc*)
intolerable *adj* intolerabilis, intolerandus
intolerably *adv* intoleranter
intolerance *s* intolerantia *f*; superbia *f*
intolerant *adj* intolerans, impatiens
intonation *s* accent·us -ūs *m*
intone *vt* cantare
intoxicate *vt* ebrium reddĕre
intoxicated *adj* ebrius
intoxication *s* ebrietas *f*
intractable *adj* intractabilis, indocilis
intrepid *adj* intrepidus, impavidus; **—ly** intrepide
intricacy *s* perplexitas, implicatio *f*
intricate *adj* contortus, implicatus, perplexus; **—ly** contorte, perplexe
intrigue *s* conspiratio *f*, dolus *m*, artificia *n pl*
intrigue *vt* fascinare; *vi* machinari, dolis contendĕre
intrinsic *adj* innatus, verus; **—ally** vere, per se
introduce *vt* introducĕre, inducĕre
introduction *s* (*preface*) praefatio *f*, exordium, prooemium *n*; (*to person*) introductio *f*, adit·us -ūs *m*
intrude *vi* se interponĕre, se inculcare, intervenire
intruder *s* interpellator, advena *m*; homo molestus *m*
intrusion *s* interpellatio, usurpatio *f*
intuition *s* intuit·us -ūs *m*, cognitio *f*, acumen *n*
intuitive *adj* intuitivus; **—ly** mentis propriā vi ac naturā
inundate *vt* inundare
inundation *s* inundatio *f*, diluvium *n*
invade *vt* incurrĕre in (*with acc*), invadĕre
invader *s* invasor *m*
invalid *adj* infirmus, vitiosus; (*sick*) aeger, aegrotus
invalid *s* aegrotus *m*
invalidate *vt* irritum facĕre, rescindĕre
invaluable *adj* inaestimabilis
invariable *adj* constans, immutabilis
invariably *adv* semper
invasion *s* incursio, irruptio *f*
invective *s* convicium, probrum *n*
inveigh *vi* **to — against** invehi in (*with acc*), insectari
invent *vt* invenire, reperire; (*to contrive*) excogitare, fingĕre
invention *s* (*act*) inventio *f*; (*thing invented*) inventum *n*
inventive *adj* sollers, ingeniosus
inventor *s* inventor, auctor *m*
inventory *s* bonorum index *m*
inverse *adj* inversus, conversus; **—ly** inverso ordine
inversion *s* inversio, conversio *f*
invert *vt* invertĕre
invest *vt* (*money*) collocare, ponĕre; (*to besiege*) obsidēre
investigate *vt* investigare, indagare; (*law*) quaerĕre, cognoscĕre
investigation *s* investigatio *f*; (*law*) cognitio *f*

investigator *s* investigator, indagator *m*; (*law*) quaesitor *m*
investment *s* (*of money*) collocatio *f*; (*money invested*) locata pecunia *f*; (*mil*) obsessio *f*
inveterate *adj* inveteratus
invigorate *vt* corroborare, recreare
invincible *adj* invictus, insuperabilis
inviolable *adj* inviolatus, sacrosanctus
inviolate *adj* inviolatus, intactus
invisible *adj* invisibilis, caecus
invitation *s* invitatio *f*
invite *vt* invitare, adhibēre
inviting *adj* suavis, gratus, blandus; **—ly** blande
invocation *s* invocatio, testatio *f*
invoice *s* libellus *m*
invoke *vt* vocare, invocare, obtestari
involuntarily *adv* invite, coacte
involuntary *adj* non voluntarius, coactus
involve *vt* implicare, involvĕre; (*to comprise*) continēre
involved *adj* **to be —** illigari; **to be — in debt** aere alieno laborare
invulnerable *adj* invulnerabilis
inward *adj* interior; **—ly** intus, intrinsecus
inwards *adv* introrsus
Ionian *adj* Ionicus
irascible *adj* iracundus
ire *s* ira *f*
Ireland *s* Hibernia *f*
iris *s* iris *f*
Irish *adj* Hibernicus
irk *vt* incommodare; **I am irked** taedet me, piget me
irksome *adj* molestus, odiosus
iron *s* ferrum *n*
iron *adj* ferreus
ironical *adj* ironicus, deridens; **—ly** per ironiam
irony *s* ironia, dissimulatio *f*
irradiate *vt* illustrare; *vi* effulgēre
irrational *adj* rationis expers, irrationalis, absurdus; **—ly** absurde
irreconcilable *adj* implacabilis; (*incompatible*) repugnans, insociabilis
irrecoverable *adj* irreparabilis
irrefutable *adj* certus, invictus
irregular *adj* irregularis, abnormis; (*disorderly*) tumultuarius; (*gram*) anomalus; **—ly** irregulariter
irregularity *s* irregularitas *f*; (*of conduct*) luxuries, pravitas *f*; (*gram*) anomalia *f*
irrelevant *adj* non pertinens, alienus; **it is —** nil ad rem pertinet
irreligious *adj* impius
irremediable *adj* insanabilis
irreparable *adj* irreparabilis, irrevocabilis
irreproachable *adj* irreprehensus, integer
irresistible *adj* inexsuperabilis, invictus
irresolute *adj* dubius, incertus animi; (*permanent characteristic*) parum firmus; **—ly** dubitanter
irresolution *s* dubitatio *f*; animus parum firmus *m*
irresponsibility *s* incuria *f*
irresponsible *adj* incuriosus
irretrievable *adj* irreparabilis, irrevocabilis
irreverence *s* impietas *f*
irreverent *adj* impius, inverecundus; **—ly** impie
irrevocable *adj* irrevocabilis
irrigate *vt* irrigare
irrigation *s* irrigatio, inductio aquae *f*
irritability *s* iracundia *f*
irritable *adj* irritabilis, iracundus, difficilis
irritate *vt* irritare; (*wound*) inflammare
irritation *s* irritatio, iracundia *f*, stomachus *m*
island *s* insula *f*
islander *s* insulanus *m*
islet *s* parva insula *f*
isolate *vt* sejungĕre, secernĕre
issue *s* (*result*) event·us -ūs, exit·us -ūs *m*; (*question*) res *f*; (*offspring*) proles *f*; (*of book*) editio *f*; (*of money*) emissio *f*
issue *vt* (*to distribute*) distribuĕre; (*orders, etc.*) edĕre, proponĕre, promulgare; (*money*) erogare; (*book*) edĕre; *vi* emanare, egredi; (*to turn out, result*) evenire, evadĕre
isthmus *s* isthmus *m*
it *pron* id, hoc
itch *s* prurigo *f*, prurit·us -ūs *m*; (*disease*) scabies *f*
itch *vi* prurire; (*fig*) gestire
item *s* res *f*
itinerant *adj* circumforaneus, vagus
itinerary *s* itinerarium *n*
its *pron* ejus; **— own** suus
itself *pron* (*refl*) se, sese; (*intensive*) ipsum
ivory *s* ebur *n*
ivory *adj* eburneus
ivy *s* hedera *f*

J

jabber *vi* blaterare
jackass *s* asinus *m*; (*fig*) stultus *m*
jacket *s* tunica *f*
jaded *adj* defessus
jagged *adj* serratus; (*of rocks*) praeruptus
jail *s* carcer *m*
jailer *s* carcerarius *m*
jam *s* baccarum conditura *f*
jam *vt* frequentare, stipare; (*to obstruct*) impedire, obstruĕre
jamb *s* postis *m*
jangle *vi* crepitare
January *s* (mensis) Januarius *m*

jar *s* olla, amphora *f*, urceus, cadus *m*
jar *vt* vibrare; offendĕre; *vi* discrepare
jargon *s* confusae voces *f pl*
jarring *adj* dissonus, discors
jaundice *s* morbus regius *m*
jaundiced *adj* ictericus, felle suffusus; (*fig*) lividus, morosus
jaunt *s* excursio *f*; **to take a —** excurrĕre
javelin *s* pilum, jaculum *n*; **to hurl a —** jaculari
jaw *s* mala, maxilla *f*; **—s** (*fig*) fauces *f pl*
jawbone *s* maxilla *f*
jay *s* graculus *m*
jealous *adj* invidus, lividus; **to be — of** invidēre (*with dat*)
jealousy *s* invidia, aemulatio *f*
jeer *s* irrisio *f*, irris·us -ūs *m*
jeer *vt* deridēre, explodĕre; *vi* **to — at** irridēre, alludĕre
jelly *s* cylon, quilon *n*
jellyfish *s* pulmo, halipleumon *m*
jeopardize *vt* periclitari, in periculum adducĕre
jeopardy *s* periculum *n*
jerk *s* verber, ict·us -ūs, impet·us -ūs *m*
jerk *vt* calcitrare, icĕre
jerky *adj* (*of style*) salebrosus
jest *s* jocus *m*; **in —** joco, jocose
jest *vi* jocari, ludĕre
jester *s* joculator *m*; (*buffoon*) scurra *m*
jestingly *adv* per jocum
Jesus *s* Jesus *m*
jet *s* scatebra *f*
jetty *s* moles *f*
Jew *s* Judaeus *m*
jewel *s* gemma *f*
jeweled *adj* gemmeus, gemmifer
jeweler *s* gemmarius *m*
jewelry *s* gemmae *f pl*
Jewish *adj* Judaicus
jig *s* tripudium *n*
jilt *vt* repudiare
jingle *vi* tinnire
jingle *s* tinnit·us -ūs *m*
job *s* negotiolum, opus *n*
jockey *s* agaso *m*
jocose *adj* jocosus; **—ly** jocose
jocular *adj* jocularis, facetus
jog *vi* **to — along** lente progredi
join *vt* (*to connect*) jungĕre, conjungĕre; (*to come into the company of*) se jungĕre (*with dat*), se jungĕre cum (*with abl*); *vi* conjungi, adjungi, cohaerēre; **to — in** particeps esse (*with genit*), interesse (*with dat*); **to — together** inter se conjungi
joint *adj* communis; **—ly** una, conjunctim, communiter
joint *s* (*of body*) articulus *m*, commissura *f*; (*of plant*) geniculum *n*; (*of any structure*) compages *f*
jointed *adj* geniculatus
joist *s* tignum *n*
joke *s* jocus *m*
joke *vi* jocari, ludĕre
joker *s* joculator *m*
joking *s* jocus *m*; **all — aside** joco remoto; **—ly** per jocum
jolly *adj* hilaris, festivus
jolt *vt* jactare, concutĕre; (*fig*) percellĕre; *vi* jactari
jolting *s* jactatio *f*
jostle *vt* pulsare, agitare, fodicare
jot *s* hilum *n*; **not a —** minime; **to care not a —** non flocci facĕre
jot *vt* **to — down** notare, subscribĕre
journal *s* ephemeris *f*, acta diurna *n pl*
journey *s* iter *n*
journey *vi* iter facĕre; **to — abroad** peregrinari
journeyman *s* opifex *m*
Jove *s* Jupiter *m*
jovial *adj* hilaris
jowl *s* bucca *f*
joy *s* gaudium *n*, laetitia *f*
joyful *adj* laetus; **—ly** laete, libenter
joyless *adj* illaetabilis
joyous *adj* hilaris, festivus
jubilant *adj* laetus, gaudio exsultans, gaudio triumphans
jubilation *s* exsultatio *f*
jubilee *s* dies anniversarius *m*, solemne *n*
Judaic *adj* Judaicus
Judaism *s* Judaismus *m*
judge *s* judex, quaesitor, arbiter *m*
judge *vt* judicare; (*to think*) existimare, censēre; (*to value*) aestimare; (*to decide between*) dijudicare
judgment *s* judicium, arbitrium *n*; (*opinion*) sententia *f*, judicium *n*; **to pass — on** statuĕre de (*with abl*); **to pronounce —** jus dicĕre
judgment seat *s* tribunal *n*
judicial *adj* judicialis, judicarius; **—ly** jure, lege
judicious *adj* sapiens, sagax, prudens; **—ly** sapienter, sagaciter, prudenter
jug *s* urceus *m*
juggle *vi* praestigias agĕre
juggler *s* praestigiator *m*
juice *s* sucus, liquor *m*
juicy *adj* sucidus
July *s* (mensis) Quintilis *or* Julius *m*
jumble *s* congeries, confusio *f*
jumble *vt* confundĕre, permiscēre
jump *s* salt·us -ūs *m*
jump *vt* transilire; *vi* salire; **to — at** (*opportunity*) captare; **to — for joy** exsultare
junction *s* conjunctio *f*
juncture *s* tempus *n*; **at this —** hic
June *s* (mensis) Junius *m*
jungle *s* salt·us -ūs *m*
junior *adj* junior, minor natu
juniper *s* juniperus *m*
jurisdiction *s* jurisdictio *f*
jurisprudence *s* jurisprudentia *f*
jurist *s* jurisconsultus *m*
juror *s* judex *m*
jury *s* judices *m pl*
just *adj* justus, aequus; (*deserved*) meritus; **—ly** juste; jure, merito
just *adv* (*only*) modo; (*exactly*) prorsus; (*with adv*) demum, denique; **— after** sub (*with acc*); **— as** aeque ac, perinde ac, sic ut, haud secus

ac; — **before** sub (*with acc*); — **now** modo; — **so** ita prorsus
justice *s* justitia, aequitas *f*; (*just treatment*) jus *n*; (*person*) praetor *m*
justifiable *adj* justus, legitimus, excusatus
justifiably *adv* jure
justification *s* purgatio, excusatio *f*
justify *vt* purgare, excusare, approbare
jut *vi* prominēre; **to — out** prominēre, eminēre, procurrĕre
juvenile *adj* juvenilis, puerilis

K

kale *s* crambe *f*
keel *s* carina *f*
keen *adj* acer, sagax; **—ly** acute, acriter; sagaciter
keenness *s* (*of scent*) sagacitas *f*; (*of sight*) acies *f*; (*of pain*) acerbitas *f*; (*enthusiasm*) studium *n*
keep *vt* tenēre, habēre; (*to preserve*) servare; (*to celebrate*) agĕre, celebrare; (*to guard*) custodire; (*to obey*) observare; (*to support*) alĕre; (*animals*) pascĕre; (*to store*) condĕre; **to — apart** distinēre; **to — away** arcēre; **to — back** retinēre, cohibēre; (*to conceal*) celare; **to — company** comitari; **to — from** prohibēre; **to — in** cohibēre, claudĕre; **to — off** arcēre, defendĕre; **to — secret** celare; **to — together** continēre; **to — under** compescĕre, supprimĕre; **to — up** sustinēre; *vi* remanēre, durare; **to — away** abstinēre; **to — up with** subsequi
keep *s* custodia, cura *f*
keeper *s* custos *m*
keeping *s* tutela, custodia, cura *f*; **in — with** pro (*with abl*)
keepsake *s* monumentum, pignus *n*
keg *s* cadus *m*, testa *f*
ken *s* conspect·us -ūs *m*
kennel *s* stabulum *n*
kernel *s* nucleus *m*; (*fig*) medulla *f*
kettle *s* lebes *f*
kettledrum *s* tympanum aeneum *n*
key *s* clavis *f*; (*of a position*) claustra *n pl*
keyhole *s* foramen *n*
kick *vt* calce ferire; *vi* calcitrare
kid *s* haedus *m*
kidnap *vt* surripĕre
kidnapper *s* plagiarius *m*
kidney *s* ren *m*
kill *vt* interficĕre, caedĕre, occidĕre, necare; (*time*) perdĕre
killer *s* interfector, necator *m*
kiln *s* fornax *f*
kin *s* cognati, consanguinei, necessarii *m pl*
kind *adj* amicus, benignus, benevolus; **—ly** benigne, clementer
kind *s* genus *n*; **what — of** qualis
kindhearted *adj* benignus
kindle *vt* incendĕre, accendĕre, inflammare
kindly *adj* benignus
kindness *s* benignitas, benevolentia *f*; (*deed*) beneficium, officium *n*
kindred *adj* consanguineus, cognatus
kindred *s* consanguinitas, cognatio *f*; cognati, propinqui *m pl*
king *s* rex *m*
kingdom *s* regnum *n*
kingfisher *s* alcedo *f*
kingly *adj* regius, regalis
kinsman *s* necessarius, cognatus, propinquus *m*
kinswoman *s* necessaria, cognata, propinqua *f*
kiss *s* osculum, basium *n*
kiss *vt* osculari
kissing *s* osculatio *f*
kitchen *s* culina *f*
kite *s* (*bird*) milvus *m*
kitten *s* catulus felinus *m*
knack *s* sollertia, calliditas *f*
knapsack *s* sarcina *f*
knave *s* nebulo, veterator *m*
knavish *adj* nefarius, improbus; (*mischievous*) malitiosus
knead *vt* subigĕre
knee *s* genu *n*
kneel *vi* genibus niti
knell *s* campana funebris *f*
knife *s* culter *m*; (*for surgery*) scalprum *n*
knight *s* eques *m*
knighthood *s* equestris dignitas *f*
knightly *adj* equester
knit *vt* texĕre; **to — the brow** frontem contrahĕre
knob *s* tuber *n*, nodus *m*; (*of door*) bulla *f*
knock *vt* **to — down** dejicĕre, sternĕre; (*fig*) (*at auction*) addicĕre; **to — in** impellĕre, infigĕre; **to — off** excutĕre, decidĕre; **to — out** excutĕre; *vi* **to — about** (*to ramble*) vagari; **to — at** pulsare
knock *s* pulsatio *f*, puls·us -ūs *m*
knoll *s* tumulus *m*
knot *s* nodus *m*, geniculum *n*; (*of people*) corona *f*
knot *vt* nodare, nectĕre
knotty *adj* nodosus; (*fig*) spinosus
know *vt* scire; (*person*) novisse; **not to —** ignorare, nescire; **to — how to** scire (*with inf*)
knowing *adj* callidus, prudens; **—ly** sciens, de industria, consulto
knowledge *s* scientia, doctrina *f*; (*of something*) cognitio *f*; (*skill*) peritia *f*; (*learning*) eruditio *f*
known *adj* notus; (*common*) tritus; **to become —** enotescĕre; **to make —** divulgare, declarare
knuckle *s* articulus, condylus *m*
kowtow *vi* adulari

L

label *s* titulus *m*
labor *s* labor *m*; (*manual*) opera *f*; (*work done*) opus *n*; **to be in —** laborare utero; **woman in —** puerpera *f*
labor *vi* laborare, eniti; **to — under** laborare (*with abl*)
laboratory *s* officina *f*
labored *adj* affectatus
laborer *s* operarius *m*
labyrinth *s* labyrinthus *m*
labyrinthine *adj* labyrinthicus; (*fig*) inextricabilis
lace *s* opus reticulatum *n*
lace *vt* (*to tie*) nectĕre, astringĕre; (*to beat*) verberare
lacerate *vt* lacerare, laniare
laceration *s* laceratio *f*
lack *s* inopia *f*, defect·us -ūs *m*, defectio *f*
lack *vt* carēre (*with abl*), egēre (*with abl*)
lackey *s* pedisequus, servus a pedibus *m*
laconic *adj* brevis, astrictus; **—ally** breviter, paucis
lad *s* puer, adulescens *m*
ladder *s* scala *f*
ladle *s* ligula, spatha *f*, cochlear *n*
lady *s* domina, matrona *f*
lag *vi* cessare, morari, cunctari
lagoon *s* lacuna *f*, stagnum *n*
lair *s* cubile, latibulum *n*
laity *s* laici *m pl*
lake *s* lac·us -ūs *m*
lamb *s* agnus *m*, agna *f*; (*meat*) agnina *f*
lame *adj* claudus; **to walk —** claudicare; **—ly** (*fig*) inconcinne
lameness *s* clauditas *f*
lament *s* lamentum *n*, lamentatio *f*
lament *vt* lamentari, deplorare; *vi* flēre
lamentable *adj* lamentabilis, miserabilis
lamentably *adv* miserabiliter
lamentation *s* lamentatio *f*
lamp *s* lucerna *f*, lychnus *m*
lampoon *s* satira *f*, libellus *m*
lampoon *vt* famosis carminibus lacessĕre
lance *s* lancea, hasta *f*
lance *vt* incidĕre
land *s* (*soil*) terra, tellus *f*; (*country*) regio *f*; (*estate*) fundus *m*, praedium *n*
land *vt* in terram exponĕre; *vi* egredi, appellĕre
landing place *s* egress·us -ūs *m*
landlord *s* (*of inn*) caupo *m*; (*of land*) dominus *m*
landmark *s* lapis, terminus *m*
landscape *s* regionis sit·us -ūs *m*
landslide *s* terrae laps·us -ūs *m*
land tax *s* vectigal *n*
lane *s* semita *f*
language *s* lingua *f*; (*style or manner of verbal expression*) oratio *f*, sermo *m*, verba *n pl*
languid *adj* languidus; **—ly** languide
languish *vi* languēre, languescĕre
languishing *adj* languidus, tabescens
languor *s* languor *m*
lanky *adj* prolixus, exilis
lantern *s* la(n)terna *f*
lap *s* sin·us -ūs *m*; (*fig*) gremium *n*; (*in racing*) spatium *n*
lap *vt* lambĕre
lapse *s* laps·us -ūs *m*; (*error*) erratum, peccatum *n*, error *m*
lapse *vi* labi; (*of agreement*) irritus fieri; (*to err*) peccare
larceny *s* furtum *n*
lard *s* laridum, lardum *n*, adeps *m & f*
large *adj* magnus, amplus, grandis; **to a — extent** magna ex parte; **—ly** plerumque
largess *s* donativum *n*, largitio *f*; **to give a —** largiri
lark *s* alauda *f*
larynx *s* guttur *n*
lascivious *adj* lascivus, salax, libidinosus; **—ly** lascive, libidinose
lash *s* verber, flagellum *n*, scutica *f*; (*mark*) vibex *m*
lash *vt* (*to whip*) flagellare; (*to fasten*) alligare; (*fig*) castigare
lashing *s* verberatio *f*
lass *s* puella, virgo *f*
lassitude *s* lassitudo *f*
last *adj* postremus, ultimus; (*in line*) novissimus; (*preceding*) proximus; **at —** demum, tandem; **for the — time** postremo
last *vi* durare, perdurare
lasting *adj* diuturnus, perennis
lastly *adv* denique, postremo
latch *s* obex *m & f*
latch *vt* oppessulare
late *adj* serus, tardus; (*new*) recens; (*deceased*) demortuus; (*said of deceased emperor*) divus
late *adv* sero; **too —** sero, serius
lately *adv* modo, recens, nuper
latent *adj* latens, latitans, occultus
lateral *adj* lateralis
lather *s* spuma *f*
Latin *adj* Latinus; **to speak —** Latine loqui; **to translate into —** Latine reddĕre; **to understand —** Latine scire
Latinity *s* Latinitas *f*
latitude *s* latitudo *f*; (*liberty*) licentia *f*
latter *adj* posterior; **the —** hic
lattice *s* cancelli *m pl*
laudable *adj* laudabilis
laudably *adv* laudabiliter
laudatory *adj* laudativus, honorificus
laugh *s* ris·us -ūs *m*
laugh *vi* ridēre; **to — at** deridēre; **to — with** arridēre (*with dat*)
laughingstock *s* ludibrium *n*

laughter *s* ris·us -ūs *m*; (*loud*) cachinnus *m*, cachinnatio *f*
launch *vt* deducĕre; (*to hurl*) jaculari, contorquēre; *vi* **to — forth** *or* **out** proficisci
laundress *s* lotrix *f*
laundry *s* lavatorium *n*
laureate *adj* laureatus
laurel *adj* laureus
laurel tree *s* laurus *f*
lava *s* liquefacta massa *f*
lavish *adj* prodigus; **—ly** prodige
lavish *vt* prodigĕre, profundĕre
lavishness *s* prodigalitas, profusio *f*
law *s* lex *f*; (*right*) jus *n*; (*rule*) norma *f*; (*divine*) fas *n*; **to break the —** leges violare; **to pass a —** legem perferre
law-abiding *adj* bene moratus
law court *s* judicium *n*; (*building*) basilica *f*
lawful *adj* legitimus, licitus, fas; **—ly** legitime, lege
lawless *adj* exlex, illegitimus; **—ly** illegitime, licenter
lawlessness *s* licentia *f*
lawn *s* pratulum *n*
lawsuit *s* lis, causa *f*
lawyer *s* jurisconsultus, causidicus *m*
lax *adj* remissus; (*fig*) neglegens; **—ly** remisse; neglegens
laxity *s* remissio *f*
lay *vt* ponĕre; (*eggs*) parĕre; (*foundations*) jacĕre; (*hands*) injicĕre; (*plans*) capĕre, inire; **to — an ambush** insidiari; **to — aside** ponĕre, amovēre; **to — before** proponĕre; **to — claim to** arrogare, vindicare; **to — down** (*office*) resignare; (*rules*) statuĕre; **to — down arms** ab armis discedĕre; **to — hold of** prehendĕre, arripĕre; **to — open** patefacĕre; **to — out** (*money*) expendĕre; (*plans*) designare; **to — up** condĕre, reponĕre; **to — waste** vastare
lay *s* cantilena *f*
layer *s* (*stratum*) corium *n*; (*of a plant*) propago *f*
lazily *adv* ignave, pigre
laziness *s* segnities, pigritia *f*
lazy *adv* ignavus, piger, iners
lead *s* plumbum *n*
lead *vt* ducĕre; (*life*) agĕre; **to — about** circumducĕre; **to — away** abducĕre; **to — off** divertĕre; **to — on** conducĕre; *vi* **to — up to** tendĕre ad (*with acc*)
leaden *adj* plumbeus
leader *s* dux, ductor *m*; (*fig*) auctor *m*
leadership *s* duct·us -ūs *m*
leading *adj* princeps, primus, praecipuus
leaf *s* folium *n*; (*of vine*) pampinus *m*; (*of paper*) pagina, scheda *f*; (*of metal*) bractea *f*
leafless *adj* fronde nudatus
leafy *adj* frondosus, frondeus
league *s* foedus *n*, societas *f*
leak *s* rima *f*, hiat·us -ūs *m*
leak *vi* perfluĕre, rimas agĕre
leaky *adj* rimosus
lean *adj* macer, macilentus
lean *vt* inclinare; *vi* inclinare, niti; **to — back** se reclinare; **to — on** inniti in (*with abl*), incumbĕre (*with dat*)
leap *s* salt·us -ūs *m*
leap *vi* salire; **to — for joy** exsultare
leap year *s* bisextilis annus *m*
learn *vt* discĕre, cognoscĕre; (*news*) accipĕre, audire; **to — by heart** ediscĕre
learned *adj* eruditus, doctus; **—ly** docte
learning *s* (*act*) discĕre; (*knowledge*) eruditio *f*
lease *s* conductio, locatio *f*
lease *vt* conducĕre; **to — out** locare
leash *s* lorum *n*
least *adj* minimus
least *adv* minime; **at —** saltem; **not in the —** ne minimum quidem
leather *s* corium *n*; (*tanned*) aluta *f*
leather *adj* scorteus
leathery *adj* lentus
leave *vt* relinquĕre, deserĕre, destituĕre; (*to entrust*) mandare, tradĕre; (*legacy*) legare; **to — behind** relinquĕre; **to — out** omittĕre, praetermittĕre; *vi* (*to depart*) discedĕre, proficisci, abire; **to — off** desinĕre, desistĕre
leave *s* permissio *f*; **— of absence** commeat·us -ūs *m*; **to ask —** veniam petĕre; **to obtain —** impetrare; **to take — of** valēre jubēre; **with your —** pace tua
leaven *s* fermentum *n*
leaven *vt* fermentare
lecherous *adj* libidinosus, salax
lecture *s* lectio, praelectio, acroasis *f*
lecture *vi* (*to reprove*) objurgare; *vi* praelegĕre
lecturer *s* lector, praelector *m*
ledge *s* projectura *f*, limen, dorsum *n*
ledger *s* codex (accepti et expensi) *m*
leech *s* sanguisuga, hirudo *f*
leer *vi* limis oculis spectare
leering *adj* limus, lascivus
left *adj* laevus, sinister; **on the —** a sinistra; **to the —** ad sinistram, sinistrorsum
leftover *adj* reliquus
leftovers *s* reliquiae *f pl*
leg *s* crus *n*; (*of table, etc.*) pes *m*
legacy *s* legatum *n*
legal *adj* legalis, legitimus; judicialis; **—ly** legitime, lege
legalize *vt* sancire
legate *s* legatus *m*
legation *s* legatio *f*
legend *s* fabula *f*; (*inscription*) titulus *m*
legendary *adj* commenticius, fabulosus
legging *s* ocrea *f*
legible *adj* clarus
legion *s* legio *f*
legislate *vi* leges facĕre

legislation *s* leges *f pl*
legislator *s* legum lator *m*
legitimate *adj* legitimus; **—ly** legitime
leisure *s* otium *n*; **at —** otiosus, vacuus
leisure *adj* otiosus, vacuus; **—ly** otiose
leisurely *adj* lentus
lemon *s* pomum citreum *n*
lemonade *s* aqua limonata *f*
lend *vt* commodare; **to — money** pecuniam mutuam dare; (*at interest*) pecuniam faenerare *or* faenerari; **to — one's ear** aures praebēre
length *s* longitudo *f*; (*of time*) longinquitas, diuturnitas *f*; **at —** tandem
lengthen *vt* extendĕre, protrahĕre, producĕre
lengthwise *adv* in longitudinem
lengthy *adj* longus, prolixus
leniency *s* lenitas, clementia, mansuetudo *f*
lenient *adj* lenis, mitis, clemens; **—ly** leniter, clementer
lentil *s* lens *f*
leopard *s* leopardus, pardus *m*
leper *s* leprosus *m*
leprosy *s* leprae *f pl*
less *adj* minor
less *adv* minus
lessee *s* conductor *m*
lessen *vt* minuĕre; *vi* decrescĕre, minui
lesson *s* documentum *n*; **to give —s in** docēre
lessor *s* locator *m*
lest *conj* ne
let *vt* (*to allow*) sinĕre, pati, permittĕre; (*to lease*) locare; **to — alone** omittĕre; **to — down** (*to disappoint*) deesse (*with dat*), destituĕre; **to — fall** a manibus mittĕre; **to — fly** emittĕre, contorquēre; **to — go** (di)mittĕre; **to — in** admittĕre; **to — off** absolvĕre; **to — out** emittĕre; **to — pass** omittĕre; **to — slip** omittĕre
lethargic *adj* lethargicus
lethargy *s* lethargus *m*; (*fig*) veternus *m*
letter *s* (*of alphabet*) littera *f*; (*epistle*) litterae *f pl*, epistula *f*; **by —** per litteras; **to the —** ad verbum
letter carrier *s* tabellarius *m*
lettered *adj* litteratus
lettering *s* titulus *m*
lettuce *s* lactuca *f*
level *adj* planus, aequus
level *s* planities *f*; (*tool*) libra, libella *f*
level *vt* aequare, adaequare; (*to the ground*) solo aequare, sternĕre
lever *s* vectis *m*
levity *s* levitas *f*
levy *s* delect·us -ūs *m*
levy *vt* (*troops*) conscribĕre; (*tax*) exigĕre
lewd *adj* impudicus, incestus
lewdness *s* impudicitia *f*
liable *adj* obnoxius
liar *s* mendax *m & f*
libation *s* libatio *f*; **to pour a —** libare
libel *s* calumnia *f*
libel *vt* calumniari
libelous *adj* famosus, probrosus
liberal *adj* liberalis, munificus; (*fig*) ingenuus; **—ly** liberaliter
liberality *s* liberalitas, munificentia *f*
liberate *vt* liberare; (*slave*) manumittĕre
liberation *s* liberatio *f*
liberator *s* liberator *m*
libertine *s* homo dissolutus *m*
liberty *s* libertas *f*; licentia *f*; **at —** liber
librarian *s* librarius *m*
library *s* bibliotheca *f*
license *s* (*permission*) copia, potestas *f*; (*freedom*) licentia *f*
license *vt* potestatem dare (*with dat*)
licentious *adj* dissolutus, impudicus; **—ly** dissolute, impudice
lick *vt* lambĕre; (*daintily*) liqurrire
lictor *s* lictor *m*
lid *s* operculum, operimentum *n*
lie *s* mendacium *n*; **to give the — to** redarguĕre; **to tell a —** mentiri
lie *vi* (*to tell a lie or lies*) mentiri; (*to be lying down*) jacēre, cubare; (*to be situated*) situs esse; **to — down** jacēre; **to — in wait** insidiari; **to — on** *or* **upon** incubare (*with dat*), incumbĕre (*with dat*)
lieu *s* **in — of** loco (*with genit*), pro (*with abl*)
lieutenant *s* legatus, praefectus *m*
life *s* vita, anima *f*; (*fig*) vigor *m*, alacritas *f*
lifeblood *s* sanguis *m*
life history *s* vita *f*
lifeless *adj* inanimus, exanimis; (*fig*) exsanguis, frigidus; **—ly** (*fig*) frigide
lifetime *s* aetas *f*
lift *vt* tollĕre, attollĕre, sublevare; **to — up** attollĕre, efferre
ligament *s* ligamentum, ligamen *n*
ligature *s* ligatura *f*
light *s* lux *f*, lumen *n*; (*lamp*) lucerna *f*; **to bring to —** in lucem proferre; **to throw — on** lumen adhibēre (*with dat*)
light *adj* (*bright*) lucidus, fulgens; (*in weight*) levis; (*of colors*) candidus, dilutus; (*easy*) facilis; (*nimble*) agilis; **—ly** leviter
light *vt* accendĕre, incendĕre; (*to illuminate*) illuminare; *vi* flammam concipĕre; **to — on** *or* **upon** incidĕre (*with dat*), offendĕre; **to — up** (*fig*) hilaris fieri
lighten *vt* (*to illumine*) illustrare; (*weight*) allevare, exonerare; *vi* (*in sky*) fulgurare
lighthouse *s* pharus *f*
lightness *s* levitas, agilitas *f*
lightning *s* fulmen, fulgur *n*; **struck by —** fulmine ictus, de caelo tactus

like *adj* similis (*with dat*); (*equal*) par (*with dat*), aequus (*with dat*)
like *prep* instar (*with genit*); tamquam, ut, velut
like *vt* amare, diligĕre; **I — this** hoc mihi placet; **I — to do this** me juvat hoc facĕre
likelihood *s* verisimilitudo *f*
likely *adj* verisimilis, probabilis
likely *adv* probabiliter
liken *vt* comparare
likeness *s* similitudo *f*; (*portrait*) imago, effigies *f*
likewise *adv* pariter, similiter, item
liking *s* amor *m*; (*fancy*) libido *f*
lilac *s* syringa vulgaris *f*
lily *s* lilium *n*
lily of the valley *s* convallaria majalis *f*
limb *s* art·us -ūs *m*, membrum *n*
limber *adj* flexilis
lime *s* calx *f*
limestone *s* calx *f*
lime tree *s* tilia *f*
limit *s* finis, terminus, modus *m*
limit *vt* terminare, finire, definire; (*to restrict*) circumscribĕre
limitation *s* determinatio *f*; (*exception*) exceptio *f*
limp *s* claudicatio *f*
limp *vi* claudicare
limp *adj* flaccidus, languidus
limpid *adj* limpidus
linden tree *s* tilia *f*
line *s* (*drawn*) linea *f*; (*row*) series *f*, ordo *m*; (*lineage*) stirps *f*, genus *n*; (*mil*) acies *f*; (*of poetry*) vers·us -ūs *m*; (*cord*) funis *m*
line *vt* (*streets*) saepire
lineage *s* stirps *f*, genus *n*
lineal *adj* linearis; **—ly** rectā lineā
lineament *s* lineamentum *n*
linear *adj* linearis
linen *adj* linteus, lineus
linen *s* linteum, linum *n*
linger *vi* morari, cunctari, cessare
lingering *adj* cunctabundus, tardus; **—ly** cunctanter
lingering *s* cunctatio *f*
linguist *s* linguarum peritus *m*
liniment *s* unguentum *n*, linit·us -ūs *m*
link *s* (*of chain*) anulus *m*; (*bond*) vinculum *n*, nex·us -ūs *m*
link *vt* connectĕre, conjungĕre
linseed *s* lini semen *n*
lint *s* linamentum *n*
lintel *s* limen superum *n*
lion *s* leo *m*
lioness *s* lea, leaena *f*
lip *s* labrum *n*; (*edge*) ora *f*
liquefy *vt* liquefacĕre
liquid *adj* liquidus
liquid *s* liquidum *n*, liquor *m*; **to become —** liquescĕre
liquidate *vt* solvĕre, persolvĕre
liquor *s* liquor *m*
lisp *vi* balbutire
lisping *adj* blaesus
list *s* index *m*, tabula *f*; (*of ship*) inclinatio *f*
list *vt* enumerare; *vi* inclinare
listen *vi* auscultare, audire; **to — to** auscultare, audire
listless *adj* remissus, languidus; **—ly** languide
litany *s* litania *f*
literal *adj* litteralis; **—ly** ad litteram, ad verbum
literary *adj* (*person*) litteratus; **— style** scribendi genus *n*
literature *s* litterae *f pl*
litigant *s* litigator *m*
litigate *vi* litigare
litigation *s* lis *f*
litter *s* (*vehicle*) lectica *f*; (*of straw, etc.*) stramentum *n*; (*brood*) fet·us -ūs, part·us -ūs *m*
litter *vt* sternĕre
little *adj* parvus, exiguus
little *adv* parum, paulum; **a —** paulum, aliquantulum; **— by —** paulatim
little *s* paulum, aliquantulum *n*
live *vi* vivĕre, vitam agĕre; (*to reside*) habitare; **to — on** vesci (*with abl*)
live *adj* vivus; (*of colors*) vegetus
livelihood *s* vict·us -ūs *m*
lively *adj* vivus, vīvidus, alacer; (*of colors*) vegetus
liver *s* jecur *n*
livid *adj* lividus; **to be —** livēre
living *adj* vivus, vivens
living *s* (*livelihood, food*) vict·us -ūs *m*
lizard *s* lacerta *f*
load *s* onus *n*
load *vt* onerare
loaf *s* panis *m*
loaf *vi* grassari
loafer *s* grassator *m*
loam *s* lutum *n*
loan *s* mutuum *n*, pecunia mutua *f*
loathe *vt* fastidire
loathing *s* fastidium *n*
loathsome *adj* foedus, taeter
lobby *s* vestibulum *n*
lobe *s* lobus *m*
lobster *s* astacus *m*
local *adj* indigena; loci (*genit*), regionis (*genit*)
locality *s* locus *m*, natura loci *f*
lock *s* (*of hair*) cinnus, floccus *m*; (*of door*) sera *f*
lock *vt* obserare, oppessulare; **to — in** includĕre; **to — out** exludĕre; **to — up** concludĕre
locker *s* loculamentum, armarium *n*
lockjaw *s* tetanus *m*
locust *s* locusta *f*
lodge *s* casa *f*
lodge *vt* (*complaint*) deferre; *vi* (*to stay*) deversari; (*to stick*) inhaerēre
lodger *s* inquilinus *m*
lodging *s* hospitium, deversorium *n*
loft *s* tabulatum, cenaculum *n*
lofty *adj* (ex)celsus, sublimis; (*fig*) sublimis, superbus
log *s* tignum *n*, stipes *m*
logic *s* dialectica *n pl*
logical *adj* logicus, dialecticus; **—ly** dialectice, ex ratione
loin *s* lumbus *m*
loiter *vi* cessare, cunctari, grassari
loiterer *s* cessator, grassator *m*

loll *vi* recumbĕre
lone *adj* solus
loneliness *s* solitudo *f*
lonely *adj* solitarius; desolatus
long *adj* longus; (*of time*) diuturnus; (*lengthened*) productus
long *adv* diu; — **after** multo post; — **ago** jamdudum, jampridem; — **before** multo ante
long *vi* avēre; **to — for** desiderare
longevity *s* longaevitas *f*
longing *s* desiderium *n*
longing *adj* avidus; **—ly** avide
longitude *s* longitudo *f*
long-lived *adj* vivax
long-suffering *adj* patiens
long-winded *adj* longus
look *s* aspect·us -ūs, vult·us -ūs *m*; (*appearance*) facies, species *f*
look *vi* vidēre; (*to seem*) vidēri; **to — about** circumspicĕre; **to — after** curare; **to — around** circumspicĕre, respicĕre; **to — at** intuēri, aspicĕre; **to — back** respicĕre; **to — for** quaerĕre; **to — forward to** exspectare; **to — into** inspicĕre, introspicĕre; (*to examine*) perscrutari; **to — on** intuēri; **to — out** prospicĕre; **to — out for** quaerĕre; **to — towards** spectare; **to — up** suspicĕre; **to — upon** habēre, aestimare
loom *s* tela *f*
loom *vi* in conspectum prodire
loop *s* sin·us -ūs *m*
loophole *s* fenestra *f*; (*fig*) effugium *n*
loose *adj* laxus, solutus, remissus; (*morally*) dissolutus; **—ly** laxe; dissolute
loosen *vt* solvĕre, laxare; *vi* solvi
loquacious *adj* loquax, garrulus
lord *s* dominus *m*
Lord *s* Dominus *m*
lord *vi* **to — it over** dominari in (*with acc*)
lordly *adj* imperiosus
lordship *s* dominatio *f*, imperium *n*
lore *s* doctrina *f*
lose *vt* amittĕre, perdĕre; **to — one's way** aberrare
loss *s* (*act*) amissio *f*; damnum, detrimentum *n*; (*mil*) repulsa *f*
lost *adj* perditus; **to be —** perire
lot *s* pars, portio, sors *f*; **casting of —s** sortitio *f*, sortit·us -ūs *m*; **to draw —s for** sortiri
lotion *s* lotio *f*
lottery *s* sortitio *f*
loud *adj* magnus; **—ly** magnā voce
lounge *vi* cessare, otiari
lounge *s* lectulus *m*
louse *s* pediculus *m*
lousy *adj* pediculosus; (*fig*) vilis
lout *s* rusticus *m*
loutish *adj* agrestis, rusticus
love *s* amor *m*; **to fall in —** amare, adamare
love *vt* amare, diligĕre
love affair *s* amores *m pl*
lovely *adj* venustus, amabilis
love potion *s* philtrum *n*
lover *s* amator, amans *m*
lovesick *adj* amore aeger
loving *adj* amans; **—ly** amanter
low *adj* humilis; (*of price*) vilis; (*of birth*) obscurus; (*of voice*) summissus; (*vile*) turpis; (*downcast*) abjectus
low *adv* humiliter; summissā voce
low *vi* mugire
lowborn *adj* obscurus, degener
lower *vt* demittĕre, deprimĕre; (*price*) imminuĕre; *vi* (*of sky*) obscurari
lower *adj* inferior; **of the — world** infernus; **the — world** inferi *m pl*
lowermost *adj* infimus
lowing *s* mugit·us -ūs *m*
lowlands *s* loca plana, campestria *n pl*, campi *m pl*
lowly *adj* humilis, obscurus
loyal *adj* fidelis, fidus; **—ly** fideliter
loyalty *s* fidelitas, fides *f*
lubricate *vt* unguĕre
lucid *adj* lucidus, clarus, perspicuus; (*transparent*) pellucidus
Lucifer *s* Lucifer *m*
luck *s* fortuna *f*; **bad —** fortuna *f*, infortunium *n*; **good —** fortuna *f*, felicitas *f*
luckily *adv* feliciter, fauste
luckless *adj* infelix
lucky *adj* felix, faustus
lucrative *adj* quaestuosus
lucre *s* lucrum *n*, quaest·us -ūs *m*
ludicrous *adj* ridiculus; **—ly** ridicule
luggage *s* sarcinae *f pl*, impedimenta *n pl*
lukewarm *adj* tepidus; (*fig*) segnis, frigidus; **—ly** (*fig*) segniter
lull *s* quies, intermissio *f*
lull *vt* sopire; (*to calm, as a storm*) sedare; (*fig*) demulcēre
lumber *s* scruta *n pl*
luminary *s* lumen *n*
luminous *adj* lucidus, illustris; (*fig*) dilucidus
lump *s* glaeba, massa, congeries *f*; (*on body*) tuber *n*
lump *vt* **to — together** coacervare
lumpy *adj* glaebosus, crassus
lunacy *s* alienatio mentis *f*
lunar *adj* lunaris
lunatic *s* insanus *m*
lunch *s* merenda *f*, prandium *n*
lunch *vi* prandēre
luncheon *s* prandium *n*
lung *s* pulmo *m*
lunge *s* ict·us -ūs *m*, plaga *f*
lunge *vi* prosilire
lurch *s* impedimentum *n*; **to leave in the —** deserĕre, destituĕre
lurch *vi* titubare
lure *s* illecebra, esca *f*
lure *vt* illicĕre, inescare
lurk *vi* latēre, latitare
luscious *adj* suavis, praedulcis
lush *adj* luxuriosus
lust *s* libido *f*
lust *vi* concupiscĕre
luster *s* splendor, nitor *m*
lustful *adj* libidinosus, salax; **—ly** libidinose, lascive

lustily *adv* valide, strenue
lusty *adj* validus, robustus
lute *s* cithara *f*, fides *f pl*
luxuriance *s* luxuries, ubertas *f*
luxuriant *adj* luxuriosus; (*fig*) luxurians
luxuriate *vi* luxuriare, luxuriari
luxurious *adj* sumptuosus, lautus; **—ly** sumptuose, laute
luxury *s* luxuria *f*, lux·us -ūs *m*
lye *s* lixivia *f*
lying *adj* mendax, fallax
lying *s* mendacium *n*
lymph *s* lympha *f*
lynx *s* lynx *m* & *f*
lyre *s* lyra *f*, fides *f pl*, barbitos *m*
lyric *adj* lyricus
lyric *s* carmen *n*

M

macaroni *s* collyra *f*
mace *s* fasces *m pl*
mace bearer *s* lictor *m*
macerate *vt* macerare
machination *s* dolus *m*
machine *s* machina *f*
machinery *s* machinamentum *n*, machinatio *f*
mackerel *s* scomber *m*
mad *adj* insanus, vesanus, demens, furiosus; **to be —** furĕre, insanire; **—ly** insane, dementer
madam *s* domina *f*
madden *vt* mentem alienare (*with dat*); (*fig*) furiare
maddening *adj* furiosus
madman *s* homo furiosus *m*, demens *m*
madness *s* insania, dementia *f*, furor *m*
magazine *s* (*journal*) ephemeris *f*; (*storehouse*) horreum, armamentarium *n*
maggot *s* vermis, vermiculus *m*
magic *adj* magicus
magic *s* ars magica *f*
magically *adv* velut magica quadam arte
magician *s* magus *m*
magisterial *adj* ad magistratum pertinens
magistracy *s* magistrat·us -ūs *m*
magistrate *s* magistrat·us -ūs *m*
magnanimity *s* magnanimitas *f*
magnanimous *adj* magnanimus
magnet *s* magnes *m*
magnetic *adj* magneticus
magnetism *s* vis magnetica *f*
magnetize *vt* magnetica vi afficĕre
magnificence *s* magnificentia *f*, splendor *m*
magnificent *adj* magnificus, splendidus; **—ly** magnifice, splendide
magnify *vt* amplificare, exaggerare
magnitude *s* magnitudo *f*
maid *s* ancilla *f*
maiden *s* virgo, puella *f*
maidenhood *s* virginitas *f*
maidenly *adj* puellaris, virginalis
mail *s* (*letters*) epistulae *f pl*; (*armor*) lorica *f*
maim *vt* mutilare
maimed *adj* mancus
main *adj* primus, praecipuus, princeps; **— point** caput *n*; **—ly** praecipue, maxime
main *s* (*sea*) altum *n*, pelagus *m*
mainland *s* continens *f*
maintain *vt* (*to keep*) tenēre; (*to keep alive*) nutrire, alĕre, sustentare; (*to defend*) tuēri, sustinēre; (*to argue*) affirmare
maintenance *s* (*support*) defensio, sustentatio *f*; (*means of living*) vict·us -ūs *m*, alimentum *n*
majestic *adj* augustus, imperatorius; **—ally** auguste
majesty *s* majestas, dignitas *f*
major *adj* major
major *s* (*mil*) tribunus militum *m*; (*in logic*) major praemissa *f*
majority *s* major pars *f*
make *vt* facĕre; (*to form*) fingĕre; (*to render*) reddĕre, facĕre; (*to appoint*) creare, facĕre, instituĕre; **to — amends** corrigĕre; **to — good** resarcire, reparare; **to — haste** accelerare, festinare; **to — much of** magni facĕre; **to — over** transferre; **to — ready** praeparare; **to — up** (*story*) fingĕre; (*to compensate*) resarcire; (*one's mind*) decernĕre; **to — way** cedĕre; *vi* **to — away with** tollĕre, amovēre; **to — for** petĕre
make *s* forma, figura, formatio *f*
maker *s* fabricator *m*; auctor *m*
maladministration *s* administratio mala *f*
malady *s* morbus *m*
male *adj* mas, masculinus
male *s* mas, masculus *m*
malediction *s* dirae *f pl*, exsecratio *f*
malefactor *s* homo maleficus, reus *m*
malevolence *s* malevolentia *f*
malevolent *adj* malevolus
malice *s* malevolentia, invidia *f*
malicious *adj* malevolus, invidiosus, malignus; **—ly** malevolo animo
malign *vt* obtrectare, vexare
malign *adj* malignus, invidiosus
malignant *adj* malevolus
malleable *adj* ductilis
mallet *s* malleus *m*
malpractice *s* delicta *n pl*
maltreat *vt* vexare, mulcare
man *s* (*human being*) homo *m*; (*male human being*) vir *m*
man *vt* (*ship*) complēre; (*walls*) praesidio firmare
manacle *s* manica *f*, compes *m*
manacle *vt* manicas injicĕre (*with dat*)
manage *vt* administrare, curare

manageable *adj* tractabilis
management *s* administratio, cura *f*
manager *s* curator *m*; (*steward*) procurator *m*; (*of estate*) villicus *m*
mandate *s* mandatum *n*
mandrake *s* mandragora *f*
mane *s* juba *f*
maneuver *s* (*mil*) decurs·us -ūs *m*, decursio *f*; (*trick*) dolus *m*, artificium *n*
maneuver *vi* (*mil*) decurrĕre; (*fig*) machinari
mange *s* scabies *f*
manger *s* praesepe *n*
mangle *vt* lacerare, laniare
mangy *adj* scaber
manhood *s* pubertas *f*; virilitas, fortitudo *f*
mania *s* insania *f*
maniac *s* furiosus *m*
manifest *adj* manifestus, apertus; **—ly** manifeste, aperte
manifest *vt* declarare, ostendĕre, aperire
manifestation *s* patefactio *f*
manifesto *s* edictum *n*
manifold *adj* multiplex, varius
manipulate *vt* tractare
manipulation *s* tractatio *f*
mankind *s* genus humanum *n*
manliness *s* virtus, fortitudo *f*
manly *adj* virilis
manner *s* modus *m*, ratio *f*; (*custom*) consuetudo *f*, mos *m*; **after the — of** ritu (*with genit*), more (*with genit*); **bad —s** rusticitas *f*; **good —s** urbanitas *f*
mannerism *s* affectatio *f*
mannerly *adj* urbanus
mannikin *s* homunculus, homuncio *m*
man-of-war *s* navis longa *f*
manor *s* praedium *n*, fundus *m*
man servant *s* servus, famulus *m*
mansion *s* dom·us -ūs, sedes *f*
manslaughter *s* homicidium *n*
mantle *s* penula, palla *f*
mantle *vt* celare, tegĕre, dissimulare
manual *adj* manualis
manual *s* enchiridion *n*
manufacture *s* fabrica *f*
manufacture *vt* fabricari, fabrefacĕre
manufacturer *s* fabricator, opifex *m*
manure *s* stercus *n*, fimus *m*
manure *vt* stercorare
manuscript *s* codex, liber *m*
many *adj* multi, plerique, complures; **a good —** nonnulli; **as — . . . as** quot . . . tot; **how —** quot; **— ways** multifariam; **so —** tot
many-colored *adj* multicolor
map *s* tabula geographica *f*
map *vt* **to — out** designare, describĕre
maple *adj* acernus
maple tree *s* acer *n*
mar *vt* foedare, vitiare, corrumpĕre
marauder *s* praedator, latro *m*
marauding *s* praedatio *f*, latrocinium *n*
marble *adj* marmoreus
marble *s* marmor *n*
March *s* (mensis) Martius *m*
march *s* iter *n*
march *vt* ducĕre; *vi* iter facĕre, incedĕre, gradi; **to — on** signa proferre; **to — on a town** oppidum aggredi
mare *s* equa *f*
margin *s* margo *m & f*
marginal *adj* margini ascriptus
marigold *s* caltha *f*
marine *adj* marinus
marine *s* miles classicus, miles classiarius *m*
mariner *s* nauta *m*
maritime *adj* maritimus
mark *s* nota *f*, signum *n*; (*brand*) stigma *n*; (*impression*) vestigium *n*; (*target*) scopus *m*; (*of wound*) cicatrix *f*; (*fig*) indicium *n*
mark *vt* notare, signare; (*to observe*) animadvertĕre; (*with pencil, etc.*) designare; **to — out** metari
marker *s* index *m*
market *s* macellum *n*, mercat·us -ūs *m*
marketable *adj* venalis
market day *s* nundinae *f pl*
marketing *s* emptio *f*
market place *s* forum *n*
market town *s* emporium *n*
marksman *s* jaculandi peritus *m*
marmalade *s* quilon ex aurantiis confectum *n*
marquee *s* tabernaculum *n*
marriage *s* matrimonium *n*, nuptiae *f pl*
marriageable *adj* nubilis
marriage contract *s* pactio nuptialis *f*
married *adj* (*of woman*) nupta; (*of man*) maritus
marrow *s* medulla *f*
marry *vt* (*said of man*) in matrimonium ducĕre, uxorem ducĕre (*with acc*); (*said of woman*) nubĕre (*with dat*); **to get married** matrimonio *or* nuptiis conjungi
marsh *s* palus *f*
marshal *s* dux, imperator *m*
marshal *vt* disponĕre
marshy *adj* paluster
mart *s* forum, emporium *n*
martial *adj* bellicosus, ferox, militaris
martyr *s* martyr *m & f*
martyrdom *s* martyrium *n*
marvel *s* res mira *f*, mirum *n*
marvel *vi* **to — at** mirari, admirari
marvelous *adj* mirus, mirabilis; **—ly** mire
masculine *adj* masculus, virilis; (*gram*) masculinus
mash *s* mixtura *f*; (*for cattle*) farrago *f*
mash *vt* commiscĕre; (*to bruise*) contundĕre
mask *s* persona, larva *f*; (*fig*) praetext·us -ūs *m*
mask *vt* (*fig*) dissimulare
mason *s* lapicida, caementarius *m*
masonry *s* opus caementicium *n*

mass *s* moles *f*; (*of people*) turba *f*; (*eccl*) missa *f*; **the —es** vulgus *n*
mass *vt* congerĕre, coacervare
massacre *s* caedes, trucidatio *f*
massacre *vt* trucidare
massive *adj* solidus, ingens
mast *s* (*of ship*) malus *m*; (*for cattle*) glans *f*, balanus *m*
master *s* dominus, herus *m*; (*teacher*) magister, praeceptor *m*; (*controller*) arbiter *m*; **to be — of** potens esse (*with genit*), compos esse (*with genit*); **not to be — of** impotens esse (*with genit*)
master *vt* superare, vincĕre; (*to learn*) perdiscĕre; (*passion*) continēre
masterly *adj* (*artist*) artificiosus; imperiosus
masterpiece *s* magnum opus *n*
mastery *s* dominatio *f*, imperium, arbitrium *n*
masticate *vt* mandĕre
mastiff *s* Molossus *m*
mat *s* teges, storea, matta *f*
match *s* (*marriage*) nuptiae *f pl*; (*contest*) certamen *n*; (*an equal*) par, compar *m & f*; **a — for** par (*with dat*); **not a — for** impar (*with dat*)
match *vt* adaequare, exaequare; *vi* quadrare
matchless *adj* incomparabilis
mate *s* socius, collega *m*; conju(n)x *m & f*
mate *vi* conjungi
material *adj* corporeus; (*significant*) haud levis, magni momenti; **—ly** magnopere
material *s* materia, materies *f*
maternal *adj* maternus
maternity *s* conditio matris *f*
mathematical *adj* mathematicus
mathematician *s* mathematicus *m*
mathematics *s* mathematica *f*, numeri *m pl*
matricide *s* (*murder*) matricidium *n*; (*murderer*) matricida *m & f*
matrimony *s* matrimonium *n*
matrix *s* forma *f*
matron *s* matrona *f*
matronly *adj* matronalis
matter *s* (*substance*) materia *f*; (*affair*) res *f*, negotium *n*; pus *n*; **no —** nihil interest
matter *v impers* **it does not —** nihil interest, nihil refert
matting *s* tegetes *f pl*
mattress *s* culcita *f*
mature *adj* maturus, adultus; **—ly** mature
mature *vi* maturescĕre
maturity *s* maturitas, aetas matura *f*
maudlin *adj* flebilis
maul *vt* mulcare, delaniare
mausoleum *s* mausoleum *n*
maw *s* ingluvies *f*
mawkish *adj* putidus; **—ly** putide
maxim *s* axioma, praeceptum *n*, sententia *f*
maximum *adj* quam maximus, quam plurimus
May *s* (mensis) Maius *m*
may *vi* posse; **I —** licet mihi
maybe *adv* forsitan
mayor *s* praefectus urbi *m*
maze *s* labyrinthus *m*
me *pron* me; **by —** a me; **to —** mihi; **with —** mecum
mead *s* (*drink*) mulsum *n*
meadow *s* pratum *n*
meager *adj* macer, exilis, jejunus; **—ly** exiliter, jejune
meagerness *s* macies *f*; (*of soil*) exilitas *f*; exigua copia *f*
meal *s* farina *f*; (*food*) cibus *m*; (*dinner*) epulae *f pl*
mean *adj* (*middle*) medius; (*low*) humilis; (*cruel*) crudelis, vilis
mean *s* medium *n*, mediocritas *f*
mean *vt* dicĕre, significare; (*to intend*) velle, cogitare, in animo habēre; (*to refer to*) significare, intellegĕre
meander *vi* sinuoso cursu labi
meaning *s* significatio, vis *f*, sens·us -ūs *m*
meanness *s* humilitas *f*; (*cruelty*) crudelitas *f*
means *s* (*way, method*) ratio, via *f*, consilium *n*; (*wealth*) opes *f pl*; **by all —** maxime, omnino; **by — of** *render by abl or* per (*with acc*); **by no —** nullo modo, haudquaquam
meanwhile *adv* interea, interim
measles *s* morbilli *m pl*
measurable *adj* mensurabilis
measure *s* mensura *f*, modus *m*; (*course of action*) ratio *f*, consilium *n*; (*law*) rogatio, lex *f*; **in some —** aliqua ex parte
measure *vt* metiri; (*land*) metari; **to — out** admetiri, dimetiri
measurement *s* mensura *f*
meat *s* caro *f*; (*food*) cibus *m*
mechanic *s* opifex, faber *m*
mechanical *adj* mechanicus, machinalis; **—ly** mechanica quadam arte
mechanics *s* mechanica ars, machinalis scientia *f*
mechanism *s* machinatio *f*
medal *s* insigne *n*
medallion *s* numisma sollemne *n*
meddle *vi* se interponĕre
meddler *s* ardelio *m*
mediate *vi* intercedĕre
mediation *s* intercessio *f*
mediator *s* intercessor, conciliator *m*
medical *adj* medicus, medicinalis
medicate *vt* medicare
medicinal *adj* medicus, salutaris
medicine *s* (*science*) medicina *f*; (*remedy*) medicamentum *n*
medieval *adj* medii aevi (*genit, used as adj*)
mediocre *adj* mediocris
mediocrity *s* mediocritas *f*
meditate *vi* meditari, cogitare
meditation *s* meditatio, cogitatio *f*
meditative *adj* cogitabundus
Mediterranean *s* mare internum *or* medium, mare nostrum *n*
medium *s* (*middle*) medium *n*; (*expedient*) modus *m*, ratio *f*; (*agency*) conciliator *m*

medium *adj* mediocris
medley *s* farrago *f*
meek *adj* mitis, demissus; **—ly** summisse
meekness *s* animus demissus *m*
meet *adj* aptus, idoneus; **it is —** convenit
meet *vt* obviam ire (*with dat*), occurrĕre (*with dat*); (*fig*) obire; *vi* convenire; **to — with** offendĕre, excipĕre
meeting *s* congressio *f*; (*assembly*) convent·us -ūs *m*
melancholy *s* tristitia, maestitia *f*
melancholy *adj* tristis, maestus
mellow *adj* maturus, mitis; (*from drinking*) temulentus
mellow *vt* maturare, coquĕre; *vi* maturescĕre
melodious *adj* canorus; **—ly** canore, modulate
melody *s* melos *n*, modus *m*
melt *vt* liquefacĕre, dissolvĕre; *vi* liquescĕre, tabescĕre
member *s* membrum *n*; (*fig*) sodalis *m*
membrane *s* membrana *f*
memento *s* monumentum *n*
memoirs *s* commentarii *m pl*
memorable *adj* memorabilis, memoriā dignus
memorandum *s* nota *f*
memorial *s* monumentum *n*
memory *s* memoria *f*; **from —** ex memoria, memoriter; **in the — of man** post hominum memoriam; **to commit to —** ediscĕre, memoriae mandare
menace *s* minae *f pl*
menace *vt* minari, minitari; (*of things*) imminēre (*with dat*)
menacing *adj* minax; (*only of persons*) minitabundus
mend *vt* emendare, corrigĕre, restaurare, reparare; (*clothes*) sarcire; *vi* melior fieri
mendicant *s* mendicus *m*, mendica *f*
menial *adj* servilis, sordidus
menial *s* servus, famulus *m*
mental *adj* mente conceptus; **—ly** mente
mention *s* mentio, commemoratio *f*; **to make — of** mentionem facĕre (*with genit*)
mention *vt* commemorare, nominare; **to not —** silentio praeterire
mercantile *adj* mercatorius
mercenary *adj* mercenarius, venalis
mercenary *s* miles mercenarius *m*
merchandise *s* merces *f pl*
merchant *s* mercator, negotiator *m*
merciful *adj* misericors, clemens; **—ly** misericorditer, clementer
merciless *adj* immisericors, inclemens; **—ly** duriter, inhumane
mercurial *adj* vividus, acer, levis
Mercury *s* Mercurius *m*
mercury *s* argentum vivum *n*
mercy *s* misericordia *f*
mere *adj* merus; **—ly** tantummodo, solum, modo
meretricious *adj* meretricius, fucatus
merge *vt* confundĕre; *vi* confundi
meridian *s* meridianus circulus *m*; meridies *m*
merit *s* meritum *n*
merit *vt* merēre, merēri
meritorious *adj* laudabilis
mermaid *s* nympha *f*
merrily *adv* hilare, festive
merry *adj* hilaris, festivus
mesh *s* (*of net*) macula *f*
mess *s* (*dirt*) squalor *m*; (*confusion*) turba, rerum perturbatio *f*
messenger *s* nuntius *m*
metal *adj* metallicus, ferreus, aereus
metal *s* metallum *n*
metallurgy *s* metallurgia, scientia metallorum *f*
metamorphosis *s* transfiguratio *f*
metaphor *s* translatio *f*
metaphorical *adj* translatus; **—ly** per translationem
mete *vt* metiri
meteor *s* fax caelestis *f*
meteorology *s* prognostica *n pl*
meter *s* metrum *n*, numerus *m*
method *s* ratio *f*, modus *m*
methodical *adj* dispositus; (*person*) diligens; **—ly** ratione et viā
meticulous *adj* accuratus; **—ly** accurate
metonymy *s* immutatio *f*
metrical *adj* metricus, numerosus
metropolis *s* caput *n*
mettle *s* animus *m*, virtus, magnanimitas *f*
miasma *s* halit·us -ūs *m*
microscope *s* microscopium *n*
mid *adj* medius
midday *adj* meridianus
midday *s* meridies *m*, meridianum tempus *n*
middle *adj* medius
middle *s* medium *n*; **in the — of the road** in media via
midget *s* pumilio *m & f*
midnight *s* media nox *f*
midriff *s* diaphragma *n*, praecordia *n pl*
midst *s* medium *n*; **in the — of** inter (*with acc*)
midsummer *s* summa aestas *f*
midway *adv* medius; **he stood — between the lines** stabat medius inter acies
midwife *s* obstetrix *f*
midwinter *s* bruma *f*
midwinter *adj* brumalis
mien *s* vult·us -ūs *m*
might *s* vis, potestas, potentia *f*; **with all one's —** summa ope
might *vi render by imperfect subjunctive*
mightily *adv* valde, magnopere
mighty *adj* potens, validus
migrate *vi* migrare, abire
migration *s* peregrinatio *f*
migratory *adj* advena, migrans
mild *adj* mitis, lenis; (*person*) placidus, clemens; **—ly** leniter, clementer
mildew *s* robigo *f*, mucor, sit·us -ūs *m*
mildness *s* clementia, lenitas, mansuetudo *f*

mile *s* mille passuum, milliare *n*
milestone *s* milliarium *n*
militant *adj* ferox
military *adj* militaris
militia *s* milites *m pl*
milk *s* lac *n*
milk *vt* mulgēre
milky *adj* lacteus
Milky Way *s* orbis lacteus *m*, via lactea *f*
mill *s* mola *f*, pistrinum *n*
millennium *s* mille anni *m pl*
miller *s* molitor, pistor *m*
million *adj* decies centena milia (*with genit*)
millionaire *s* homo praedives *m*
millionth *s* pars una ex decies centenis milibus partium *f*
millstone *s* mola *f*
mime *s* mimus *m*
mimic *s* mimus *m*
mimic *vt* imitari
mimicry *s* imitatio *f*
mince *vt* concidĕre; **not to — words** plane aperteque loqui
mind *s* mens *f*, animus *m*, ingenium *n*; (*opinion*) sens·us -ūs *m*, sententia *f*; **to call to —** recordari; **to make up one's —** animum inducĕre, statuĕre, constituĕre; **to show presence of —** praesenti animo uti
mind *vt* (*to look after*) curare; (*to regard*) respicĕre; (*to object to*) aegre ferre; **to — one's own business** suum negotium agĕre
mindful *adj* attentus, diligens; memor
mine *s* fodina *f*, metallum *n*; (*mil*) cuniculus *m*; (*fig*) thesaurus *m*
mine *vt* effodĕre
mine *pron* meus
miner *s* (*of metals*) metallicus *m*; fossor *m*
mineral *s* metallum *n*
mineral *adj* metallicus, fossilis
mineralogist *s* metallorum peritus *m*
mineralogy *s* metallorum scientia *f*
mingle *vt* commiscēre, confundĕre; *vi* commiscēri, se immiscēre
miniature *s* pictura minuta *f*
minimum *adj* quam minimus
minimum *s* minimum *n*
minion *s* cliens *m & f*
minister *s* minister, administer *m*
minister *vi* ministrare, servire
ministry *s* ministratio *f*, munus, officium *n*
minor *s* pupillus *m*, pupilla *f*
minor *adj* minor
minority *s* minor pars *f*
minstrel *s* fidicen *m*
mint *s* (*plant*) mentha *f*; (*for making money*) moneta *f*
mint *vt* cudĕre
minute *s* temporis momentum *n*
minute *adj* (*small*) minutus, exiguus, pusillus; (*exact*) accuratus, subtilis; **—ly** accurate, subtiliter
minx *s* puella procax *f*
miracle *s* miraculum, monstrum *n*
miraculous *adj* miraculosus; **—ly** divinitus
mirage *s* falsa species *f*
mire *s* lutum *n*
mirror *s* speculum *n*
mirth *s* hilaritas, laetitia *f*
mirthful *adj* hilaris
misadventure *s* infortunium *n*
misalliance *s* matrimonium impar *n*
misapply *vt* abuti (*with abl*)
misapprehend *vt* male intellegĕre
misapprehension *s* falsa conceptio *f*
misbehave *vi* indecore se gerĕre
misbehavior *s* morum pravitas *f*
misbelief *s* fides prava *f*
miscalculate *vi* errare
miscalculation *s* error *m*
miscarriage *s* abort·us -ūs *m*; (*fig*) malus success·us -ūs *m*
miscarry *vi* abortum facĕre; (*fig*) male succedĕre
miscellaneous *adj* promiscuus
miscellany *s* conjectanea, miscellanea *n pl*
mischance *s* infortunium *n*
mischief *s* incommodum, maleficium *n*; (*of children*) lascivia *f*
mischievous *adj* maleficus, noxius; (*playful*) lascivus
misconceive *vt* male intellegĕre
misconception *s* falsa conceptio, falsa opinio *f*
misconduct *s* delictum, peccatum *n*
misconstruction *s* sinistra interpretatio *f*
misconstrue *vt* male interpretari; perverse interpretari
misdeed *s* delictum, peccatum *n*
misdemeanor *s* levius delictum *n*
misdirect *vt* fallĕre
miser *s* avarus, sordidus *m*
miserable *adj* miser, infelix, aerumnosus
miserably *adv* misere
miserly *adj* avarus, sordidus
misery *s* miseria, aerumna *f*
misfortune *s* infortunium, incommodum *n*
misgiving *s* sollicitudo *f*
misgovern *vt* male regĕre
misguide *vt* seducĕre, fallĕre
misguided *adj* (*fig*) demens
mishap *s* incommodum *n*
misinform *vt* falsa docēre (*with acc*)
misinterpret *vt* male interpretari
misinterpretation *s* prava interpretatio *f*
misjudge *vt* male judicare
mislay *vt* amittĕre
mislead *vt* seducĕre, decipĕre
mismanage *vt* male gerĕre
mismanagement *s* mala administratio *f*
misnomer *s* falsum nomen *n*
misplace *vt* alieno loco ponĕre
misprint *s* erratum typographicum, mendum *n*
misquote *vt* falso citare, falso proferre
misquotation *s* falsa prolatio *f*
misrepresent *vt* calumniari
misrepresentation *s* calumnia *f*; falsa descriptio *f*

misrule *s* prava administratio *f*
miss *s* adulescentula, virgo *f*; error *m*
miss *vt* (*to overlook*) omittĕre, praetermittĕre; (*one's aim*) non ferire, non attingĕre; (*to feel the want of*) desiderare; (*to fail to find*) requirĕre; *vi* (*to fall short*) errare
misshapen *adj* pravus, deformis
missile *s* telum, missile, tormentum *n*
missing *adj* absens; **to be —** deesse
mission *s* legatio, missio *f*
misspell *vt* perperam scribĕre
misspend *vt* prodigĕre, perdĕre, dissipare
misstate *vt* parum accurate memorare
misstatement *s* falsum, mendacium *n*
mist *s* nebula, caligo *f*
mistake *s* error *m*, erratum *n*; (*written*) mendum *n*; **to make a —** errare, peccare
mistake *vt* habēre pro (*with abl*)
mistaken *adj* falsus; **to be —** falli; **unless I am —** ni fallor
mistletoe *s* viscum *n*
mistress *s* domina, hera *f*; (*sweetheart*) amica *f*; (*paramour*) concubina *f*; (*teacher*) magistra *f*
mistrust *s* diffidentia, suspicio *f*
mistrust *vt* diffidĕre (*with dat*)
mistrustful *adj* diffidens; **—ly** diffidenter
misty *adj* nebulosus, caliginosus; (*fig*) obscurus
misunderstand *vt* perperam intellegĕre
misunderstanding *s* error *m*; (*disagreement*) offensio *f*, dissidium *n*
misuse *vt* abuti (*with abl*); (*to revile*) conviciari
misuse *s* abus·us -ūs *m*; (*ill treatment*) injuria *f*
mite *s* (*bit*) parvulus *m*; (*coin*) sextans *m*
miter *s* mitra *f*
mitigate *vt* mitigare, lenire
mitigation *s* mitigatio *f*
mix *vt* miscēre; **to — in** admiscēre; **to — up** commiscēre; (*fig*) confundĕre
mixed *adj* promiscuus, confusus
mixture *s* mixtura, farrago *f*
moan *vi* gemĕre, ingemiscĕre
moan *s* gemit·us -ūs *m*
moat *s* fossa *f*
mob *s* turba *f*, vulgus *n*
mob *vt* conviciis insectari, stipare
mobile *adj* mobilis
mobility *s* mobilitas *f*
mock *s* irrisio, derisio *f*
mock *vt* ludĕre, ludificari, irridēre
mock *adj* fictus, fucatus
mockery *s* irrisio *f*, irris·us -ūs *m*
mode *s* modus *m*, ratio *f*; (*fashion*) us·us -ūs *m*
model *s* exemplar, exemplum *n*
model *vt* formare, delineare, fingĕre
moderate *adj* moderatus, mediocris, modicus; **—ly** moderate, mediocriter, modice
moderate *vt* moderari, temperare, coercēre
moderation *s* moderatio, temperantia *f*, modus *m*
moderator *s* praeses *m*
modern *adj* recens, hodiernus, novus
modest *adj* (*restrained*) modestus, pudens, verecundus; (*sight*) modicus, mediocris; **—ly** pudenter, verecunde
modesty *s* modestia, pudicitia, verecundia *f*
modification *s* modificatio, mutatio *f*
modify *vt* (im)mutare
modulate *vt* (*voice*) flectĕre; modulari
modulation *s* flexio *f*, flex·us -ūs *m*
moist *adj* humidus, uvidus, madidus
moisten *vt* (h)umectare, rigare
moisture *s* humor *m*
molar *s* dens genuinus *m*
molasses *s* sacchari faex *f*
mold *s* (*form*) forma, matrix *f*; (*mustiness*) mucor *m*
mold *vt* formare, fingĕre; (*to knead*) subigĕre; *vi* mucescĕre
molder *vi* putrescĕre, dilabi
moldiness *s* mucor, sit·us -ūs *m*
moldy *adj* mucidus, situ corruptus
mole *s* (*animal*) talpa *f*; (*sea wall*) moles *f*, agger *m*; (*on skin*)naevus *m*
molecule *s* particula *f*
molehill *s* **to make a mountain out of a —** e rivo flumina magna facĕre
molest *vt* vexare, sollicitare
molt *vi* plumas ponĕre
molten *adj* liquefactus
moment *s* (*of time*) punctum temporis *n*; (*importance*) momentum *n*; **in a —** statim; **of great —** magni ponderis; **this —** ad tempus
momentarily *adv* statim, confestim
momentary *adj* brevis
momentous *adj* gravis, magni momenti (*genit, used adjectively*)
monarch *s* rex, princeps, dominus *m*
monarchical *adj* regius
monarchy *s* regnum *n*
monastery *s* monasterium *n*
monetary *adj* pecuniarius, argentarius, nummarius
money *s* pecunia *f*, nummi *m pl*; **for —** mercede
moneychanger *s* nummularius *m*
moneylender *s* faenerator *m*
mongrel *s* hybrida *m*
monitor *s* admonitor *m*
monk *s* monachus *m*
monkey *s* simia *f*
monogram *s* monogramma *n*
monologue *s* oratio *f*
monopolize *vt* monopolium exercēre in (*with acc*)
monopoly *s* monopolium *n*
monosyllabic *adj* monosyllabus
monosyllable *s* monosyllabum *n*
monotonous *adj* semper idem; (*singsong*) canorus
monotony *s* taedium *n*
monster *s* monstrum, portentum *n*, belua *f*
monstrosity *s* monstrum *n*
monstrous *adj* monstrosus, portentosus, prodigiosus; **—ly** monstrose

month *s* mensis *m*
monthly *adj* menstruus
monthly *adv* singulis mensibus
monument *s* monumentum *n*
monumental *adj* (*important*) gravis, magnus; (*huge*) ingens
mood *s* animi affect·us -ūs, habit·us -ūs *m*; (*gram*) modus *m*
moodiness *s* morositas *f*
moody *adj* morosus, maestus
moon *s* luna *f*
moonlight *s* lunae lumen *n*; **by —** per lunam
moonstruck *adj* lunaticus
Moor *s* Maurus *m*
moor *vt* religare, anchoris retinēre
moor *s* tesca *n pl*
mop *s* peniculus *m*
mop *vt* detergēre
mope *vi* maerēre
moral *adj* (*relating to morals*) moralis, ethicus; (*morally proper*) honestus; **—ly** moraliter; honeste
moral *s* (*of story*) documentum *n*
morale *s* animus *m*, animi *m pl*; **— is low** animus jacet, animi deficiunt
morality *s* boni mores *m pl*
moralize *vi* de moribus disserĕre
morals *s* mores *m pl*
morass *s* palus *f*
morbid *adj* morbidus, morbosus
more *adj* plus (*with genit*); plures
more *adv* plus, magis, amplius; ultra; **— and —** magis magisque; **— than** plus quam; **— than enough** plus satis; **no —** non diutius
moreover *adv* praeterea, ultro, etenim vero
morning *s* mane *n* (*indecl*); tempus matutinum *n*; **early in the —** multo mane, bene mane, prima luce; **in the —** mane, matutino tempore; **this —** hodie mane
morning *adj* matutinus
morning star *s* Lucifer, phosphorus *m*
morose *adj* morosus; **—ly** morose
moroseness *s* morositas *f*
morsel *s* offa *f*, frustulum *n*
mortal *adj* mortalis; (*deadly*) mortifer, letalis; **—ly** letaliter
mortal *s* mortalis *m & f*, homo *m & f*
mortality *s* mortalitas *f*
mortar *s* mortarium *n*
mortgage *s* hypotheca *f*, pignus *n*
mortgage *vt* obligare
mortification *s* dolor *m*
mortify *vt* mortificare, coercēre; (*to vex*) offendĕre
mosaic *s* tessellatum opus *n*
mosaic *adj* tesselatus
mosquito *s* culex *m*
moss *s* muscus *m*
mossy *adj* muscosus
most *adj* plurimus, maximus, plerusque; **for the — part** maximam partem
most *adv* maxime, plurimum
mostly *adv* plerumque, fere
mote *s* corpusculum *n*
moth *s* blatta *f*
mother *s* mater *f*
motherhood *s* matris conditio *f*
mother-in-law *s* socr·us -ūs *f*
motherless *adj* matre orbus
motherly *adj* maternus
motion *s* motio *f*, mot·us -ūs *m*; (*proposal of bill*) rogatio *f*; **to make a —** ferre; **to set in —** ciēre
motion *vi* significare, innuĕre
motionless *adj* immotus, immobilis
motive *s* causa, ratio *f*, incitamentum *n*
motive *adj* movens, agens
motley *adj* varius, versicolor
mottled *adj* maculosus
motto *s* sententia *f*, praeceptum *n*
mound *s* tumulus, agger *m*, moles *f*
mount *s* mons *m*; (*horse*) equus *m*
mount *vt* scandĕre, ascendĕre, conscendĕre; *vi* ascendĕre, conscendĕre, sublime ferri; subvolare
mountain *s* mons *m*
mountaineer *s* montanus *m*
mountainous *adj* montuosus, montanus
mounted *adj* (*on horseback*) inscensus
mourn *vt* lugēre, deflēre; *vi* lugēre, maerēre
mourner *s* plorator *m*
mournful *adj* lugubris, luctuosus, tristis, flebilis, maestus; **—ly** maeste, flebiliter
mourning *s* luct·us -ūs, maeror *m*; (*dress*) vestis lugubris *f*; **in —** pullatus, sorditatus; **to go into —** vestitum mutare
mouse *s* mus *m*
mousetrap *s* muscipulum *n*
mouth *s* os *n*; (*of beast*) faux *f*; (*of river*) ostium *n*; (*of bottle*) lura *f*
mouthful *s* buccella *f*
mouth piece *s* interpres *m*
movable *adj* mobilis
movables *s* res *f pl*, supellex *f*
move *vt* movēre; (*emotionally*) commovēre; (*to propose*) ferre; *vi* movēri, se movēre; (*to change residence*) migrare; **to — on** progredi
movement *s* mot·us -ūs *m*
moving *adj* flebilis, miserabilis
mow *vt* demetĕre, secare
mower *s* faenisex *m & f*
mowing *s* faenisicium *n*
much *adj* multus; **as — . . . as** tantus . . . quantus; **how —** quantus; **so —** tantus; **too —** nimius; **very —** plurimus
much *adv* multum, valde; (*with comparatives*) multo; **too —** nimium; nimis; **very —** plurimum
muck *s* stercus *n*
mucous *adj* mucosus
mud *s* lutum *n*, limus *m*
muddle *vt* turbare; (*fig*) perturbare
muddle *s* confusio, turba *f*
muddy *adj* lutosus, lutulentus; (*troubled*) turbidus
muffle *vt* involvĕre; **to — up** obvolvĕre
muffled *adj* surdus
mug *s* poculum *n*
muggy *adj* humidus
mulberry *s* morum *n*

mulberry tree *s* morus *f*
mule *s* mulus *m*
muleteer *s* mulio *m*
mulish *adj* obstinatus
multifarious *adj* varius, multiplex
multiplication *s* multiplicatio *f*
multiply *vt* multiplicare; *vi* augēri, crescĕre
multitude *s* multitudo, turba *f*
multitudinous *adj* creberrimus
mumble *vt* opprimĕre; *vi* murmurare
munch *vt* manducare, mandĕre
mundane *adj* mundanus
municipal *adj* municipalis
municipality *s* municipium *n*
munificence *s* munificentia, largitas *f*
munificent *adj* munificus, liberalis; **—ly** munifice
munitions *s* belli apparat·us -ūs *m*
mural *adj* muralis
murder *s* caedes, nex *f*, homicidium *n*
murder *vt* necare, trucidare, obtruncare
murderer *s* homicida *m & f*, sicarius *m*
murderous *adj* (*fig*) sanguinarius, cruentus
murky *adj* caliginosus, tenebrosus
murmur *s* murmur *n*, fremit·us -ūs *m*
murmuring *s* admurmuratio *f*
muscle *s* musculus, lacertus, torus *m*
muscular *adj* lacertosus, robustus
Muse *s* Musa *f*
muse *vi* meditari, secum agitare
mushroom *s* fungus, boletus *m*
music *s* musica *f*; (*of instruments and voices*) cant·us -ūs, concent·us -ūs *m*
musical *adj* (*of person*) musicus; (*of sound*) canorus
musician *s* musicus *m*; (*of stringed instrument*) fidicen *m*; (*of wind instrument*) tibicen *m*
muslin *s* sidon *f*
must *s* mustum *n*
must *vi* **I — go** mihi eundum est, me oportet ire, debeo ire, necesse est (ut) eam
mustard *s* sinapi *n*
muster *vt* lustrare; (*fig*) cogĕre, convocare; **to — up courage** animum sumĕre; *vi* convenire, coire
muster *s* copiarum lustratio *f*, recens·us -ūs *m*
musty *adj* mucidus
mutable *adj* mutabilis
mute *adj* mutus
mutilate *vt* mutilare, truncare
mutilated *adj* mutilus, truncus
mutilation *s* mutilatio, laceratio *f*
mutineer *s* seditiosus *m*
mutinous *adj* seditiosus
mutiny *s* seditio *f*, mot·us -ūs *m*
mutiny *vi* tumultuari, seditionem facĕre
mutter *vi* murmurare, mussitare
mutter *s* murmuratio *f*
mutton *s* ovilla *f*
mutual *adj* mutuus; **—ly** mutuo, inter se
muzzle *s* capistrum *n*
muzzle *vt* capistrare
my *adj* meus; **— own** proprius
myriad *adj* decem milia (*with genit*); (*innumerable*) sescenti
myrrh *s* myrrha, murrha *f*
myrtle *s* myrtus *f*
myself *pron* (*reflexive*) me; **to —** mihi; (*intensive*) ipse, egomet
mysterious *adj* arcanus, occultus; **—ly** arcane, occulte
mystery *s* mysterium, arcanum *n*; (*fig*) res occultissima *f*
mystical *adj* mysticus; **—ly** mystice
mystification *s* ambages *f pl*
mystify *vt* confundĕre, fallĕre
myth *s* mythos *m*, fabula *f*
mythical *adj* fabulosus
mythology *s* fabulae *f pl*, mythologia *f*

N

nab *vt* prehendĕre
nadir *s* fundus *m*
nag *s* caballus *m*
nag *vt* objurgitare
naiad *s* naias *f*
nail *s* clavus *m*; (*of finger*) unguis *m*
nail *vt* defigĕre
naive *adj* simplex; **—ly** simpliciter
naked *adj* nudus, apertus; **—ly** aperte
name *s* nomen *n*, appellatio *f*; (*reputation*) fama, celebritas *f*; (*term*) vocabulum *n*; **by —** nominatim
name *vt* nominare, appellare; (*to appoint*) dicĕre
nameless *adj* nominis expers
namely *adv* scilicet, videlicet
nap *s* brevis somnus *m*; (*of cloth*) villus *m*; **to take a —** meridiari, jacēre
nape *s* **— of the neck** cervix *f*
napkin *s* mappa *f*, mantele *n*
narcotic *adj* somnificus
narcotic *s* medicamentum somnificum *n*
nard *s* nardus *f*, nardum *n*
narrate *vt* narrare
narration *s* narratio, expositio *f*
narrative *s* fabula *f*
narrator *s* narrator *m*
narrow *adj* angustus; (*fig*) arctus; **—ly** vix, aegre
narrow *vt* coarctare; *vi* coarctari
narrow-minded *adj* animi angusti *or* parvi (*genit, used adjectively*)
narrowness *s* angustiae *f pl*
nasty *adj* (*foul*) foedus; (*mean*) amarus

natal *adj* natalis
nation *s* gens, natio *f*; (*as political body*) populus *m*; (*state*) res publica *f*
national *adj* publicus, civilis; rei publicae (*genit, used adjectively*)
nationality *s* civitas *f*
native *adj* indigena
native *s* indigena *m & f*
native land *s* patria *f*
native tongue *s* patrius sermo *m*
nativity *s* ort·us -ūs *m*
natural *adj* naturalis; (*innate*) nativus, innatus, insitus; (*fig*) sincerus, simplex; **—ly** naturā; (*unaffectedly*) simpliciter; (*of its own accord*) sponte
naturalization *s* civitatis donatio *f*
naturalize *vt* civitate donare
nature *s* natura, rerum natura *f*; (*character*) ingenium *n*, indoles *f*
naught *pron* nihil; **to set at —** parvi facĕre
naughty *adj* improbus, malus
nausea *s* nausea *f*; (*fig*) fastidium *n*
nauseate *vt* fastidium movēre (*with dat*); **to be nauseated** nauseare, fastidire
nautical *adj* nauticus
naval *adj* navalis, maritimus
nave *s* (*of church*) navis *f*
navel *s* umbilicus *m*
navigable *adj* navigabilis, navium patiens
navigate *vt* gubernare; *vi* navigare
navigation *s* navigatio *f*, res nauticae *f pl*
navigator *s* nauta, gubernator *m*
navy *s* classis *f*, copiae navales *f pl*
nay *adv* non ita
near *prep* prope (*with acc*), ad (*with acc*)
near *adj* propinquus, vicinus; (*of relation*) proximus; **— at hand** propinquus, in promptu
near *adv* prope, juxta
near *vt* appropinquare (*with dat*)
nearly *adv* prope, paene, fere, ferme
nearness *s* propinquitas *f*
nearsighted *adj* myops
neat *adj* mundus, nitidus, concinnus; **—ly** munde, concinne
neatness *s* munditia, concinnitas *f*
nebulous *adj* nebulosus
necessarily *adv* necessario
necessary *adj* necessarius; **it is —** opus est
necessitate *vt* cogĕre
necessity *s* necessitas *f*; (*want*) egestas, necessitudo *f*; (*thing*) res necessaria *f*
neck *s* collum *n*, cervis *f*
necklace *s* monile *n*, torques *m*
necktie *s* collare *n*
nectar *s* nectar *n*
need *s* (*necessity*) opus *n*, necessitas *f*; (*want*) inopia, egestas, penuria *f*; **there is — of** opus est (*with abl*)
need *vt* egēre (*with abl*), indigēre (*with abl*); (*to require*) requirĕre
needle *s* ac·us -ūs *f*
needless inutilis, minime necessarius, vanus; **—ly** sine causa
needy *adj* egens, indigens, inops
nefarious *adj* nefarius
negation *s* negatio *f*
negative *adj* negans, negativus; **—ly** negando
negative *s* negatio *f*; **to answer in the —** negare
neglect *vt* neglegĕre, omittĕre; deserĕre
neglect *s* neglegentia, incuria *f*, neglect·us -ūs *m*
neglectful *adj* neglegens
negligence *s* neglegentia, incuria *f*
negligent *adj* neglegens; **—ly** neglegenter
negligible *adj* levis, tenuis
negotiable *adj* mercabilis
negotiate *vt* (*a deal*) agĕre; agĕre de (*with abl*); *vi* negotiari
negotiation *s* transactio, actio *f*, pactum *n*
negotiator *s* conciliator, orator *m*
Negro *s* Aethiops *m*
neigh *vi* hinnire
neigh *s* hinnit·us -ūs *m*
neighbor *s* vicinus, finitimus *m*
neighborhood *s* vicinia, vicinitas *f*; proximitas *f*
neighboring *adj* vicinus, finitimus
neighborly *adj* familiaris, comis, benignus
neither *pron* neuter
neither *conj* nec, neque, neve, neu; **neither . . . nor** neque . . . neque
neophyte *s* tiro *m*
nephew *s* fratris filius, sororis filius *m*
Nereid *s* Nereis *f*
nerve *s* nervus *m*; (*fig*) temeritas, audacia *f*
nervous *adj* trepidus; **—ly** trepide
nervousness *s* diffidentia, sollicitudo *f*
nest *s* nidus *m*
nest *vi* nidificare
nestle *vi* recubare
net *s* rete *n*
net *vt* irretire
netting *s* reticulum *n*
nettle *s* urtica *f*
nettle *vt* (*fig*) vexare
network *s* reticulum, opus reticulatum *n*
neuter *adj* neuter, neutralis
neutral *adj* medius, neuter
neutrality *s* nullam in partem propensio *f*
neutralize *vt* aequare
never *adv* nunquam
nevermore *adv* nunquam posthac
nevertheless *adv* nihilominus, attamen
new *s* novus, recens, integer; **—ly** nuper, modo
newcomer *s* advena *m & f*
news *s* fama *f*, rumor, nuntius *m*
newspaper *s* acta diurna *n pl*
next *adj* proximus; (*of time*) insequens; **— day** postridie
next *adv* dein, deinde, deinceps
nibble *vt* arrodĕre; (*fig*) carpĕre; *vi* rodĕre
nice *adj* (*dainty*) delicatus; (*choice*)

exquisitus; (*exact*) accuratus; (*fine*) bellus; (*effeminate*) mollis; (*amiable*) suavis; (*of weather*) serenus; **—ly** delicate, exquisite, belle; accurate
nicety *s* accuratio, subtilitas, elegantia *f*
niche *s* aedicula *f*
nick *s* incisura *f*; **in the very — of time** in ipso articulo temporis
nick *vt* incidĕre
nickname *s* agnomen *n*
niece *s* fratris filia, sororis filia *f*
niggardly *adj* parcus, avarus
nigh *adj* propinquus
night *s* nox *f*; **by —** nocte, noctu; **to spend the —** pernoctare
nightfall *s* primae tenebrae *f pl*; **at —** sub noctem
nightingale *s* luscinia *f*
nightly *adj* nocturnus
nightly *adv* noctu, de nocte
nightmare *s* incubus *m*
night watch *s* vigilia *f*; (*guard*) vigil *m*
nimble *adj* pernix, agilis
nine *adj* novem; **— times** noviens
nineteen *adj* undeviginti, decem et novem
nineteenth *adj* undevicesimus
ninetieth *adj* nonagesimus
ninety *adj* nonaginta
ninth *adj* nonus
nip *vt* vellicare; (*of frost*) urĕre; **to — off** desecare
nippers *s* forceps *m*
nipple *s* papilla *f*
no *adj* nullus; **— one** nemo *m*
no *adv* non, minime; **to say —** negare
nobility *s* nobilitas *f*; nobiles, optimates *m pl*; (*moral excellence*) honestas *f*
noble *adj* nobilis, generosus; (*morally*) ingenuus, honestus, liberalis
noble *s* optimas *m*
nobleman *s* vir nobilis *m*
nobly *adv* nobiliter, praeclare, generose
nobody *pron* nemo *m*
nocturnal *adj* nocturnus
nod *s* nut·us -ūs *m*
nod *vi* nutare; (*to doze*) dormitare; (*in assent*) annuĕre
noise *s* strepit·us -ūs *m*; (*high-pitched*) stridor *m*; (*loud*) fragor *m*; **to make —** strepĕre, strepitare, increpare
noise *vt* **to — abroad** promulgare, divulgare
noiseless *adj* tacitus; **—ly** tacite
noisily *adv* cum strepitu
noisome *adj* noxius, foedus, taeter
noisy *adj* clamosus
nomad *s* nomas *m & f*
nomadic *adj* vagus, vagabundus
nominal *adj* nominalis; **—ly** nomine, verbo
nominate *vt* nominare, designare
nomination *s* nominatio, designatio *f*; (*of heir*) nuncupatio *f*
nominative *adj* nominativus
nominee *s* nominatus, designatus *m*
none *pron* nemo *m*
nonentity *s* nihilum *n*
nones *s* Nonae *f pl*
nonplus *vt* (*to puzzle*) ad incitas redigĕre
nonsense *s* ineptiae, nugae *f pl*; **to talk —** absurde loqui, garrire
nonsense *interj* gerrae!
nonsensical *adj* ineptus, absurdus
nook *s* angulus *m*
noon *s* meridies *m*; **before —** ante meridiem
noonday *adj* meridianus
no one *pron* nemo *m*
noose *s* laqueus *m*
nor *conj* nec, neque, neve, neu
norm *s* norma *f*
normal *adj* solitus; **—ly** plerumque
north *s* septentriones *m pl*
north *adj* septentrionalis
northern *adj* septentrionalis
northern lights *s* aurora Borealis *f*
north pole *s* arctos *f*
northwards *adv* septentriones versus
north wind *s* aquilo *m*
nose *s* nas·us -ūs *m*, nares *f pl*; **to blow the —** emungĕre
nostril *s* naris *f*
not *adv* non, haud; **— at all** nullo modo, haudquaquam; **— even** ne . . . quidem
notable *adj* notabilis, insignis, insignitus
notably *adv* insignite
notary *s* scriba *m*
notation *s* notatio *f*, signum *n*
notch *s* incisura *f*
notch *vt* incidĕre
note *s* (*mark*) nota *f*; (*comment*) adnotatio *f*; (*mus*) sonus *m*, vox *f*; (*com*) chirographum *n*; (*letter*) litterulae *f pl*
note *vt* notare; (*to notice*) animadvertĕre
notebook *s* commentarius *m*, tabulae *f pl*, pugillares *m pl*
noted *adj* insignis, insignitus, notus, praeclarus
noteworthy *adj* notabilis, memorabilis
nothing *pron* nihil, nil, nihilum; **for —** (*free*) gratis, gratuito; (*in vain*) frustra; **good for —** nequam; **— but** nihil nisi; **to think — of** nihili facĕre
notice *s* (*act of noticing*) notatio, animadversio *f*; (*announcement*) denuntiatio *f*; (*sign*) proscriptio *f*, titulus, libellus *m*; **to escape —** latēre; **to escape the — of** fallĕre; **to give — of** denuntiare
notice *vt* animadvertĕre, observare
noticeable *adj* insignis, conspicuus
noticeably *adv* insigniter
notification *s* denuntiatio, declaratio *f*
notify *vt* certiorem facĕre
notion *s* notio, suspicio *f*
notoriety *s* infamia *f*
notorious *adj* famosus, infamis, notus, manifestus; **—ly** manifeste
notwithstanding *adv* nihilominus

nought *pron* nihil; **to set at —** parvi facĕre
noun *s* nomen *n*
nourish *vt* alĕre, nutrire
nourishment *s* (*act*) alimentum *n*, cibus *m*
novel *adj* novus, inauditus
novel *s* fabula *f*
novelty *s* res nova *f*; novitas *f*
November *s* (mensis) November *m*
novice *s* tiro *m*
now *adv* nunc; (*past*) jam; **— and then** interdum, nonnunquam; **— . . . —** modo . . . modo
nowhere *adv* nusquam
noxious *adj* noxius
nozzle *s* ansa *f*
nude *adj* nudus
nudge *vt* fodicare
nudity *s* nudatio *f*
nugget *s* massa *f*
nuisance *s* incommodum *n*, molestia *f*
null *adj* irritus
nullify *vt* irritum facĕre
numb *adj* torpidus, torpens; **to become —** torpescĕre; **to be —** torpēre
numb *vt* torpefacĕre; (*fig*) obstupefacĕre
number *s* numerus *m*; **a — of** aliquot; **without —** innumerabilis
number *vt* numerare, enumerare, dinumerare
numberless *adj* innumerus, innumerabilis
numbness *s* torpor *m*; (*fig*) stupor *m*
numerical *adj* numeralis; **—ly** numero, ad numerum
numerous *adj* frequens, creber, multus
numismatics *s* doctrina nummorum *f*
nuptial *adj* nuptialis, conjugalis
nuptials *s* nuptiae *f pl*
nurse *s* nutrix *f*
nurse *vt* (*a baby*) nutrire; (*fig*) fovēre; (*the sick*) ancillari (*with dat*), curare
nursery *s* (*for children*) infantium cubiculum *n*; (*for plants*) plantarium, seminarium *n*
nurture *vt* nutrire, educare
nut *s* nux *f*; **a hard — to crack** (*fig*) quaestio nodosa *f*
nutriment *s* nutrimentum, alimentum *n*
nutrition *s* nutritio *f*, nutrimentum *n*
nutritious *adj* alibilis, salubris
nutshell *s* putamen *n*; **in a —** (*fig*) paucis verbis
nymph *s* nympha *f*

O

oaf *s* stultus, hebes *m*
oak *adj* querceus, quernus
oak *s* querc·us -ūs *f*; (*evergreen*) ilex *f*; (*timber*) robur *n*
oakum *s* stuppa *f*
oar *s* remus *m*; **to pull the —s** remos ducĕre
oarsman *s* remex *m*
oath *s* jusjurandum *n*; (*mil*) sacramentum *n*; **false —** perjurium *n*; **to take an —** jurare; (*mil*) sacramentum dicĕre
oats *s* avena *f*
obdurate *adj* obstinatus, pertinax; **—ly** obstinate, pertinaciter
obedience *s* obedientia *f*, obsequium *n*
obedient *adj* obediens, obsequens; **—ly** obedienter
obeisance *s* obsequium *n*, capitis summissio *f*; **to make —** to flectĕre ante (*with acc*); (*fig*) obsequi (*with dat*)
obelisk *s* obeliscus *m*
obese *adj* obesus
obesity *s* obesitas *f*
obey *vt* parēre (*with dat*), obedire (*with dat*), obtemperare (*with dat*), obsequi (*with dat*)
obituary *s* Libitinae index *m*
object *s* objectum *n*, res *f*; (*aim*) finis *m*, propositum *n*
object *vi* (*to feel annoyance*) gravari; (*to make objections*) recusare; **to —** to aegre ferre
objection *s* objectio *f*; impedimentum *n*, mora *f*
objectionable *adj* injucundus, improbabilis
objective *s* finis *m*, propositum *n*
objective *adj* externus, objectivus, verus
oblation *s* donum *n*
obligation *s* debitum, officium *n*; **under —** noxius
obligatory *adj* necessarius, debitus
oblige *vt* (*to force*) cogĕre, impellĕre; (*to put under obligation*) obligare, obstringĕre; (*to do a favor for*) morigerari (*with dat*); **to be obliged to** debēre (*with inf*); (*to feel gratitude toward*) gratiam habēre (*with dat*)
obliging *adj* officiosus, comis, blandus; **—ly** officiose, comiter
oblique *adj* obliquus; **—ly** oblique
obliterate *vt* delēre, oblitterare
oblivion *s* oblivio *f*
oblivious *adj* obliviosus, immemor
oblong *adj* oblongus
obloquy *s* vituperatio *f*, maledictum *n*
obnoxious *adj* invisus, noxius
obscene *adj* obscenus; **—ly** obscene
obscenity *s* obscenitas *f*
obscure *adj* obscurus; **—ly** obscure

obscure *vt* obscurare
obscurity *s* obscuritas *f*, tenebrae *f pl*; (*of birth*) humilitas *f*
obsequies *s* exsequiae *f pl*
obsequious *adj* officiosus, morigerus, nimis obsequens
obsequiousness *s* obsequium *n*, assentatio *f*
observable *adj* notabilis
observance *s* observantia *f*; (*rite*) rit·us -ūs *m*
observant *adj* attentus; **— of** diligens (*with genit*)
observation *s* observatio, animadversio *f*; (*remark*) notatio *f*, dictum *n*
observe *vt* (*to watch*) observare, contemplari, animadvertĕre; (*to keep*) conservare, observare; (*to remark*) dicĕre
observer *s* spectator *m*
obsess *vt* occupare
obsession *s* studium *n*
obsolescent *adj* **to be —** obsolescĕre
obsolete *adj* obsoletus, antiquatus; **to become —** exolescĕre
obstacle *s* impedimentum *n*; (*barrier*) obex *m*
obstinacy *s* obstinatio *f*, animus obstinatus *m*
obstinate *adj* obstinatus, pertinax; **—ly** obstinate
obstreperous *adj* tumultuosus, clamosus
obstruct *vt* obstare (*with dat*), obstruĕre, impedire
obstruction *s* obstructio *f*, impedimentum *n*; (*pol*) intercessio *f*
obtain *vt* nancisci, adipisci, consequi; (*by entreaty*) impetrare; *vi* valēre
obtainable *adj* impetrabilis
obtrusive *adj* molestus, importunus
obtuse *adj* obtusus, hebes, stolidus
obviate *vt* praevertĕre
obvious *adj* apertus, manifestus, perspicuus; **—ly** aperte, manifesto
occasion *s* occasio *f*, locus *m*; (*reason*) causa *f*; (*time*) tempus *n*
occasion *vt* locum dare (*with dat*), movēre
occasionally *adv* interdum
occidental *adj* occidentalis
occult *adj* occultus, arcanus
occupant *s* possessor *m*
occupation *s* possessio *f*; (*engagement*) occupatio *f*; (*employment*) negotium *n*, quaest·us -ūs *m*
occupy *vt* occupare, tenēre; (*to possess*) possidēre; (*space*) complēre
occur *vi* accidĕre, evenire; (*to the mind*) occurrĕre, in mentem venire
occurrence *s* cas·us -ūs, event·us -ūs *m*
ocean *s* oceanus *m*, mare oceanum *n*
oceanic *adj* oceanus, oceanensis
October *s* (mensis) October *m*
ocular *adj* ocularis
oculist *s* ocularius medicus *m*
odd *adj* (*of number*) impar; (*quaint*) insolitus, novus; **—ly** mirum in modum
oddity *s* raritas *f*, ridiculum *n*
odds *s* **the — are against us** impares summus; **to be at — with** dissidēre ab (*with abl*)
odious *adj* odiosus, invisus
odium *s* invidia *f*
odor *s* odor *m*
odorous *adj* odoratus
Odyssey *s* Odyssea *f*
of *prep* (*possession*) *rendered by genit*; (*origin*) de (*with abl*), ex (*with abl*)
off *adv* procul; **far —** longe, procul; **well —** bene nummatus
off *prep* de (*with abl*)
offend *vt* offendĕre, laedĕre; *vi* **to — against** violare
offender *s* peccator, reus *m*
offense *s* (*fault*) offensa, culpa *f*; (*insult*) injuria *f*; (*displeasure*) offensio *f*
offensive *adj* injuriosus; (*odors, etc.*) odiosus, foedus, gravis; (*language*) malignus, contumeliosus; (*aggressive*) bellum inferens; **—ly** injuriose; odiose
offer *vt* offerre, donare, praebēre; (*violence*) adferre; (*help*) ferre
offer *s* conditio *f*
offhand *adj* incuriosus
offhand *adv* confestim, illico
office *s* (*place of work*) officina *f*; (*pol*) honos, magistrat·us -ūs *m*; (*duty*) munus, officium *n*
officer *s* magistrat·us -ūs *m*; (*mil*) praefectus *m*
official *adj* publicus
official *s* minister, magistrat·us -ūs *m*
officiate *vi* officio *or* munere fungi, interesse; (*of clergyman*) rem divinam facĕre
officious *adj* officiosus, molestus; **—ly** officiose, moleste
offing *s* **in the —** procul
offset *vt* compensare
offspring *s* proles, progenies *f*
often *adv* saepe; **very —** persaepe
ogre *s* larva *f*, monstrum *n*
oh *interj* oh!, ohe!
oil *s* oleum *n*
oil *vt* ung(u)ĕre
oily *adj* oleosus; (*like oil*) oleaceus
ointment *s* unguentum *n*
old *adj* (*aged*) senex; (*out of use*) obsoletus; (*worn*) exesus, tritus; (*ancient*) antiquus, priscus; **of —** olim, quondam; **to grow —** senescĕre
old age *s* senectus *f*
old-fashioned *adj* priscus, antiquus
old man *s* senex *m*
old woman *s* an·us -ūs *f*
oligarchy *s* optimates *m pl*
olive *s* olea *f*
olive grove *s* olivetum *n*
Olympiad *s* Olympias *f*
Olympic *adj* Olympicus
omelet *s* laganum de ovis confectum *n*
omen *s* omen, auspicium *n*
ominous *adj* infaustus; **—ly** malis ominibus
omission *s* praetermissio, neglegentia *f*

omit *vt* omittěre, mittěre, praetermittěre
omnipotence *s* omnipotentia, infinita potentia *f*
omnipotent *adj* omnipotens
omnivorous *adj* omnivorus
on *prep* (*place*) in (*with abl*); (*time*) *render by abl*; (*about, concerning*) de (*with abl*); (*ranged with*) a(b) (*with abl*); (*depending, hanging on*) de (*with abl*); (*near*) ad (*with acc*)
on *adv* porro; (*continually*) usque; **and so —** et cetera, ac deinceps; **to go —** pergěre
once *adv* (*one time*) semel; (*formerly*) olim, quondam; **at —** statim, illico, ex templo; **for —** aliquando; **— and for all** semel in perpetuum; **— more** iterum; **— upon a time** olim
one *adj* unus
one *pron* unus; unicus; (*a certain person or thing*) quidam; **it is all —** perinde est; **— after another** alternus; **— another** inter se, alius alium; **— by —** singulatim; **— or the other** alteruter; **— or two** unus et alter
one-eyed *adj* luscus
onerous *adj* onerosus, gravis
oneself *pron* (*refl*) se; **to —** sibi; **with —** secum; (*intensive*) ipse
one-sided *adj* inaequalis, iniquus, impar
onion *s* caepa *f*
only *adj* unicus, unus, solus
only *adv* solum, tantum, modo; **not — . . . but also** non solum . . . sed etiam
only-begotten *adj* unigenitus
onset *s* impet·us -ūs *m*
onslaught *s* incurs·us -ūs *m*
onward *adv* porro
ooze *vi* manare, (de)stillare
opaque *adj* densus, opacus
open *adj* (*not shut*) apertus, patens; (*evident*) manifestus; (*sincere*) candidus, ingenuus; (*public*) publicus, communis; (*of space*) apertus; (*of question, undecided*) integer; **in the — air** sub divo; **to lie —** patēre; **—ly** aperte, palam
open *vt* aperire, patefacěre; (*to uncover*) retegěre; (*letter*) resignare; (*book*) evolvěre; (*to begin*) exordiri; (*with ceremony*) inaugurare; *vi* patescěre, se panděre; (*to gape*) dehiscěre; (*of wound*) recrudescěre
open-handed *adj* liberalis, largus
open-hearted *adj* simplex, ingenuus
opening *s* (*act*) apertio *f*; (*aperture*) foramen *n*, hiat·us -ūs *m*; (*opportunity*) locus *m*, occasio *f*
open-minded *adj* docilis
operate *vt* agěre, gerěre; *vi* operari
operation *s* effectio *f*; (*business*) negotium *n*; (*med*) sectio *f*
operative *adj* efficax, activus
operator *s* opifex *m*
opiate *s* mendicamentum somnificum *n*
opinion *s* opinio, sententia, mens *f*; (*esteem*) existimatio *f*; **public —** fama *f*
opium *s* opion *n*
opponent *s* adversarius *m*
opportune *adj* opportunus, idoneus, commodus; **—ly** opportune, in tempore
opportunity *s* copia, occasio, opportunitas *f*
oppose *vt* opponěre, objicěre; *vi* repugnare, resistěre, adversari
opposite *adj* adversus, contrarius, diversus
opposite *prep* contra (*with acc*)
opposite *adv* contra, ex adverso
opposition *s* oppositio, repugnantia, discrepantia *f*; (*obstacle*) impedimentum *n*; (*party*) adversa factio *f*
oppress *vt* oppriměre, vexare, gravare, onerare
oppression *s* gravatio, injuria *f*
oppressive *adj* praegravis, acerbus, molestus; **to become —** ingravescěre
oppressor *s* tyrannus *m*
opprobrious *adj* turpis, probrosus
opprobrium *s* dedecus, probrum *n*
optical *adj* opticus
option *s* optio *f*
opulence *s* opulentia *f*
opulent *adj* opulens, opulentus
or *conj* vel, aut, —ve; (*in questions*) an; **— else** aut, alioquin; **— not** annon; (*in indirect questions*) necne
oracle *s* oraculum *n*
oracular *adj* fatidicus
oral *adj* verbalis, verbo traditus; **—ly** voce, verbis
orange *s* malum aurantium *n*
oration *s* oratio *f*
orator *s* orator *m*
oratorical *adj* oratorius
oratory *s* ars oratoria, eloquentia, rhetorice *f*
orb *s* orbis, gyrus *m*
orbit *s* orbis *m*; (*in astronomy*) ambit·us -ūs *m*
orchard *s* pomarium *n*
orchestra *s* symphoniaci *m pl*
ordain *vt* (*to appoint*) edicěre
ordeal *s* discrimen *n*, labor *m*
order *s* (*class, arrangement*) ordo *m*; (*command*) mandatum, jussum, imperatum *n*; (*fraternity*) collegium *n*; **by — of** jussu (*with genit*); **in —** dispositus; **in — that** ut; **in — that not** ne; **out of —** incompositus; **to put in —** ordinare, disponěre
order *vt* (*to command*) imperare (*with dat*), jubēre; (*to demand*) imperare (*with acc*); (*to put in order*) ordinare, disponěre, digerěre
orderly *adj* compositus, ordinatus; (*well-behaved*) modestus
orderly *s* accensus *m*; (*mil*) tesserarius *m*
ordinal *adj* ordinalis
ordinance *s* edictum, rescriptum *n*
ordinarily *adv* fere, plerumque
ordinary *adj* usitatus, vulgaris, solitus, quottidianus
ordnance *s* tormenta *n pl*
ore *s* aes *n*

organ *s* (*of body*) membrum *n*; (*musical*) organum *n*
organic *adj* organicus
organism *s* compages *f*
organization *s* ordinatio *f*, structura *f*
organize *vt* ordinare, instituĕre
orgy *s* comissatio *f*
Orient *s* oriens *m*
oriental *adj* Asiaticus
orifice *s* foramen, os *n*
origin *s* origo *f*, principium *n*; (*birth*) genus *n*; (*source*) fons *m*
original *adj* pristinus, primitivus, primus; (*one's own*) proprius; (*new*) novus, inauditus; **—ly** primum, principio, initio
original *s* archetypum, exemplar *n*; (*writing*) autographum *n*
originality *s* proprietas ingenii *f*
originate *vt* instituĕre; *vi* oriri
originator *s* auctor *m*
ornament *s* ornamentum *n*, ornat·us -ūs *m*
ornament *vt* ornare, decorare
ornamental *adj* decorus
ornate *adj* ornatus; **—ly** ornate
orphan *s* orbus *m*, orba *f*
orphaned *adj* orbatus
orphanage *s* orphanotrophium *n*
oscillate *vi* agitari; (*fig*) dubitare
oscillation *s* agitatio *f*; (*fig*) dubitatio *f*
ostensible *adj* simulatus, fictus
ostensibly *adv* specie, per speciem
ostentation *s* ostentatio, jactatio *f*
ostentatious *adj* ambitiosus, gloriosus, jactans; **—ly** ambitiose, jactanter
ostracism *s* ostracismus *m*
ostrich *s* struthiocamelus *m*
other *adj* (*different*) alius, diversus; (*remaining*) ceterus; **every — day** tertio quoque die; **on the — hand** contra, autem; **the —** alter
otherwise *adv* aliter
otter *s* lutra *f*
ought *vi* **I —** debeo, oportet me
ounce *s* uncia *f*
our *adj* noster
ours *pron* noster
ourselves *pron* (*reflex*) nos, nosmet; **to —** nobis; (*intensive*) nosmet ipsi
oust *vt* ejicĕre
out *adv* (*outside*) foris; (*motion*) foras; **— of** de (*with abl*), e(x) (*with abl*); (*on account of*) propter (*with acc*); **— of the way** devius
outbreak *s* eruptio *f*; (*fig*) seditio *f*
outburst *s* eruptio *f*
outcast *s* exsul, extorris, profugus *m*
outcome *s* event·us -ūs *m*
outcry *s* clamor *m*, acclamatio *f*, convicium *n*
outdo *vt* superare
outdoors *adv* foris, sub divo
outer *adj* exterior
outermost *adj* extremus
outfit *s* apparat·us -ūs *m*; (*costume*) vestimenta *n pl*
outflank *vt* circumire, circumvenire
outgrow *vt* excedĕre ex (*with abl*), staturā superare
outing *s* excursio *f*
outlandish *adj* externus, barbarus
outlast *vt* diutius durare (*with abl*)
outlaw *s* proscriptus *m*
outlaw *vt* aquā et igni interdicĕre (*with dat*), proscribĕre
outlay *s* sumpt·us -ūs *m*, impensa *f*
outlet *s* exit·us -ūs *m*
outline *vt* describĕre, adumbrare
outline *s* adumbratio *f*
outlive *vt* supervivĕre (*with dat*), superesse (*with dat*)
outlook *s* prospect·us -ūs *m*
outlying *adj* externus; (*distant*) remotus
outnumber *vt* multitudine superare
outpost *s* statio *f*
outpouring *s* effusio *f*
output *s* fruct·us -ūs *m*
outrage *s* injuria *f*, flagitium *n*
outrage *vt* flagitio afficĕre, violare
outrageous *adj* flagitiosus, atrox; (*excessive*) immodicus; **—ly** flagitiose; immodice
outright *adv* (*at once*) statim; (*completely*) prorsus, penitus
outrun *vt* praevertĕre, linquĕre
outset *s* initium, inceptum *n*
outshine *vt* praelucĕre (*with dat*)
outside *s* pars exterior, superficies *f*; (*appearance*) species *f*; **on the —** extrinsecus
outside *adj* externus
outside *adv* foris, extra; (*motion*) foras; **from —** extrinsecus
outside *prep* extra (*with acc*)
outskirts *s* suburbium *n*, ager suburbanus *m*
outspoken *adj* candidus, liber
outspread *adj* patulus
outstanding *adj* praestans; (*of debts*) residuus
outstretched *adj* extentus, porrectus, passus
outstrip *vt* praevertĕre, cursu superare
outward *adj* externus
outward *adv* extra, extrinsecus
outweigh *vt* praevertĕre (*with dat*), praeponderare
outwit *vt* deludĕre, decipĕre
oval *adj* ovatus
ovation *s* plaus·us -ūs *m*; (*triumph*) ovatio *f*
oven *s* furnus *m*, fornax *f*
over *prep* (*across*) super (*with acc*), trans (*with acc*), per (*with acc*); (*above*) super (*with abl*), supra (*with acc*); (*with numbers*) plus quam
over *adv* supra; (*excess*) nimis; **all —** ubique, passim; **— and above** insuper; **— and — again** iterum ac saepius, identidem
overall *adj* totus
overawe *vt* (de)terrēre
overbalance *vt* praeponderare
overbearing *adj* superbus, insolens
overboard *adv* ex nave; **to jump —** ex nave desilire
overburden *vt* nimis onerare
overcast *adj* obnubilus

overcharge *vt* plus aequo exigĕre ab (*with abl*)
overcoat *s* paenula, lacerna *f*
overdo *vt* exaggerare, in majus extollĕre
overdue *adj* (*money*) residuus
overestimate *vt* majoris aestimare
overflow *s* inundatio *f*
overflow *vt* inundare; *vi* abundare, redundare
overgrown *adj* obductus, obsitus; (*too big*) praegrandis
overhang *vt* impendēre
overhaul *vt* reficĕre
overhead *adv* desuper, insuper
overhear *vt* excipĕre, auscultare
overjoyed *adj* **to be —** nimio gaudio exsultare
overladen *adj* praegravatus
overland *adj* per terram
overlay *vt* inducĕre, illinĕre
overload *vt* nimis onerare
overlook *vt* (*not to notice*) praetermittĕre; (*to pardon*) ignoscĕre (*with dat*); (*a view*) despectare
overlord *s* dominus *m*
overpower *vt* exsuperare, opprimĕre
overrate *vt* nimis aestimare
overreach *vt* circumvenire
overriding *adj* praecipuus
overripe *adj* praematurus
overrun *vt* (per)vagari; (*fig*) obsidēre
overseas *adj* transmarinus
oversee *vt* praeesse (*with dat*)
overseer *s* curator, praeses, custos *m*
overshadow *vt* obumbrare; (*fig*) obscurare
overshoot *vt* excedĕre, transgredi
oversight *s* incuria, neglegentia *f*, error *m*
oversleep *vi* diutius dormire
overspread *vt* obducĕre
overstate *vt* in majus extollĕre
overstep *vt* excedĕre, transgredi
overt *adj* apertus; **—ly** palam
overtake *vt* consequi
overtax *vt* (*fig*) abuti (*with abl*)
overthrow *s* eversio, ruina *f*, excidium *n*
overthrow *vt* subvertĕre, evertĕre, dejicĕre
overture *s* (*mus*) exordium *n*; (*proposal*) conditio *f*; **to make —s to** agĕre cum (*with abl*)
overturn *vt* evertĕre, subvertĕre
overweening *adj* superbus, insolens, arrogans
overwhelm *vt* obruĕre, opprimĕre
overwork *vt* **to — oneself** plus aequo laborare
owe *vt* debēre
owing to *prep* propter (*with acc*)
owl *s* bubo *m*, strix *f*
own *adj* proprius; **one's —** suus, proprius
own *vt* possidēre, tenēre; (*to acknowledge*) fatēri, confitēri
owner *s* dominus, possessor *m*
ownership *s* possessio *f*, mancipium, dominium *n*
ox *s* bos *m*
oyster *s* ostrea *f*
oyster shell *s* ostreae testa *f*

P

pace *s* (*step*) pass·us -ūs, grad·us -ūs *m*; (*measure*) pass·us -ūs *m*; (*speed*) velocitas *f*, grad·us -ūs *m*
pace *vi* incedĕre, gradi; **to — up and down** spatiari
pacific *adj* pacificus, tranquillus
pacification *s* pacificatio *f*
pacify *vt* pacare, placare, sedare
pack *s* (*bundle*) sarcina *f*, fasciculus *m*; (*of animals*) grex *m*; (*of people*) turba *f*, grex *m*
pack *vt* (*items of luggage*) colligĕre, componĕre; (*to fill completely*) frequentare, complēre; (*to compress*) stipare; *vi* vasa colligĕre
package *s* sarcina *f*, fasciculus *m*
packet *s* fasciculus *m*
pack horse *s* equus clitellarius *m*
packsaddle *s* clitellae *f pl*
pact *s* pactum *n*, pactio *f*; **to make a —** pacisci
pad *s* pulvinus, pulvillus *m*
pad *vt* suffarcinare
padding *s* fartura *f*
paddle *s* remus *m*
paddle *vi* remigare
paddock *s* saeptum *n*
pagan *s* paganus *m*
page *s* (*of book*) pagina, scheda *f*; puer *m*
pageant *s* pompa *f*, spectaculum *n*
pail *s* hama, situla *f*
pain *s* dolor *m*; (*fig*) angor *m*; **to be in —** dolēre; **to take —s** operam dare
pain *vt* dolore afficĕre, excruciare; *vi* dolēre
painful *adj* gravis, acerbus, molestus; **—ly** graviter, magno cum dolore
painless *adj* doloris expers
painstaking *adj* operosus
paint *s* pigmentum *n*; (*for face*) fucus *m*
paint *vt* pingĕre, depingĕre
paintbrush *s* penicillus *m*
painter *s* pictor *m*
painting *s* pictura *f*
pair *s* par *n*; (*of oxen*) jugum *n*
pair *vt* conjungĕre, componĕre
palace *s* regia *f*, palatium *n*
palatable *adj* jucundus, suavis, sapidus
palate *s* palatum *n*
palatial *adj* regius

pale *adj* pallidus; **to be —** pallēre; **to grow —** pallescĕre
pale *s* palus *m*
paling *s* saepes *f*
palisade *s* vallum *n*
pall *s* pallium *n*
pall *vt* satiare; *vi* vapescĕre
pallet *s* grabat·us -ūs *m*
palliative *s* lenimentum *n*
pallid *adj* pallidus
pallor *s* pallor *m*
palm *s* (*of hand*) palma *f*; (*tree*) palma *f*
palpable *adj* tractabilis; (*fig*) apertus, manifestus
palpitate *vi* palpitare
palsied *adj* paralyticus
palsy *s* paralysis *f*
paltry *adj* vilis, minutus
pamper *vt* indulgēre (*with dat*)
pamphlet *s* libellus *m*
pan *s* patina, patella *f*; (*for frying*) sartago *f*
pancake *s* laganum *n*
pander *s* leno *m*
pander *vi* lenocinari
panegyric *s* laudatio *f*
panel *s* (*of wall*) abacus *m*; (*of ceiling*) lacunar *n*; (*of jury*) decurio *m*; (*of door*) tympanum *n*
paneled *adj* laqueatus
pang *s* dolor *m*
panic *s* pavor *m*
panic-stricken *adj* pavidus
panoply *s* arma *n pl*
panorama *s* conspect·us -ūs *m*
pant *vi* palpitare, anhelare; **to — after** (*fig*) gestire
pantheism *s* pantheismus *m*
pantheist *s* pantheista *m*
pantheon *s* Pantheon *n*
panther *s* pantera *f*
panting *adj* anhelus
panting *s* anhelit·us -ūs *m*
pantomime *s* (*play and actor*) mimus *m*
pantry *s* cella penaria *f*
pap *s* papilla, mamilla *f*
paper *s* (*stationery*) charta *f*; (*newspaper*) acta diurna *n pl*; **—s** scripta *n pl*
paper *adj* chartaceus, charteus
papyrus *s* papyrus *f*
par *s* **to be on a — with** par esse (*with dat*)
parable *s* parabole *f*
parade *s* (*mil*) decurs·us -ūs *m*; pompa *f*; (*display*) apparat·us -ūs *m*, pompa *f*
parade *vt* (*fig*) ostentare, jactare; *vi* (*mil*) decurrĕre
paradise *s* paradisus *m*
paradox *s* oxymora verba *n pl*
paragon *s* specimen, exemplar *n*
paragraph *s* caput *n*
parallel *adj* parallelus; (*fig*) consimilis
parallel *vt* exaequare
paralysis *s* paralysis *f*; (*fig*) torpedo *f*
paralytic *adj* paralyticus
paralyze *vt* debilitare, enervare, percellĕre
paramount *adj* supremus
paramour *s* (*man*) moechus, adulter *m*; (*woman*) meretrix, pellex *f*
parapet *s* pluteus *m*
paraphernalia *s* apparat·us -ūs *m*
paraphrase *s* paraphrasis *f*
paraphrase *vt* vertĕre, interpretari
parasite *s* parasitus *m*
parasol *s* umbella *f*, umbraculum *n*
parcel *s* fasciculus *m*; (*plot of land*) agellus *m*
parcel *vt* **to — out** partire, dispertire
parch *vt* torrēre
parched *adj* torridus, aridus; **to be —** arēre
parchment *s* membrana *f*
pardon *s* venia *f*
pardon *vt* ignoscĕre (*with dat*); (*an offense*) condonare
pardonable *adj* ignoscendus, condonandus
pare *vt* (*vegetables*) deglubĕre; (*the nails*) resecare
parent *s* parens *m & f*
parentage *s* genus *n*, stirps *f*
parental *adj* patrius
parenthesis *s* interpositio, interclusio *f*
parity *s* paritas, aequalitas *f*
park *s* horti *m pl*
parlance *s* sermo *m*
parley *s* colloquium *n*
parley *vi* colloqui
parliament *s* senat·us -ūs *m*
parliamentary *adj* senatorius
parlor *s* exedrium *n*
parody *s* ridicula imitatio *f*
parole *s* fides *f*
paroxysm *s* access·us -ūs *m*
parricide *s* (*murder*) parricidium *n*; (*murderer*) parricida *m & f*
parrot *s* psittacus *m*
parry *vt* avertĕre, defendĕre
parse *vt* flectĕre
parsimonious *adj* parcus; **—ly** parce
parsing *s* partium orationis flexio *f*
parsley *s* apium *n*
part *s* pars *f*; (*in play*) partes *f pl*; (*duty*) officium *n*; **for the most —** maximam partem; **in —** partim; **on the — of** ab (*with abl*); **to act the — of** sustinēre partes (*with genit*); **to take — in** interesse (*with dat*), particeps esse (*with genit*)
part *vt* separare, dividĕre; **to — company** discedĕre; *vi* discedĕre, abire; (*to go open*) dehiscĕre; **to — with** dimittĕre
partial *adj* iniquus; (*incomplete*) mancus; **to be —** favēre (*with dat*); **—ly** aliqua ex parte
partiality *s* iniquitas *f*
participant *s* particeps *m & f*
participate *vi* interesse; **to — in** interesse (*with dat*), particeps esse (*with genit*)
participation *s* participatio, societas *f*
participle *s* participium *n*
particle *s* particula *f*

particular *adj* (*own*) proprius; (*special*) peculiaris, singularis, praecipuus; (*fussy*) fastidiosus; **—ly** praecipue, praesertim
particularize *vt* exsequi
particulars *s* singula *n pl*
parting *s* discess·us -ūs, digress·us -ūs *m*
partisan *s* fautor *m*
partition *s* partitio *f*; (*between rooms*) paries *m*; (*enclosure*) saeptum *n*
partly *adv* partim, ex parte
partner *s* socius *m*, socia *f*, particeps *m & f*; (*in office*) collega *m*; (*in marriage*) conju(n)x, consors *m & f*
partnership *s* consociatio, societas, consortio *f*
partridge *s* perdix *m & f*
party *s* (*entertainment*) convivium *n*; (*pol*) factio *f*, partes *f pl*; (*detachment*) man·us -ūs *f*; **to join a —** partes sequi
pass *s* angustiae *f pl*
pass *vt* (*to go by*) praeterire, transire, transgredi; (*to exceed*) excedĕre; (*to approve*) probare; (*time*) agĕre, degĕre; (*a law*) perferre; **to — around** circumferre, tradĕre; **to — down** tradĕre; **to — sentence** jus dicĕre; **to — the test** approbari; *vi* (*of time*) transire, abire, praeterire; **to come to —** evenire, fieri; **to let —** praetermittĕre, dimittĕre; **to — away** (*to die*) perire, abire; **to — for** habēri, vidēri; **to — on** (*to go forward*) pergĕre; (*to die*) perire; **to — out** collabi, intermori; **to — over** transire
passable *adj* (*of road*) pervius; (*fig*) mediocris, tolerabilis
passably *adv* mediocriter, tolerabiliter
passage *s* (*act*) transit·us -ūs *m*; (*by water*) transmissio, trajectio *f*; (*of book*) locus *m*
passenger *s* viator *m*; (*on ship*) vector *m*
passer-by *s* praeteriens *m*
passing *s* obit·us -ūs *m*
passion *s* cupiditas, permotio *f*, fervor *m*; (*anger*) ira *f*; (*lust*) libido *f*
passionate *adj* fervidus, ardens; iracundus; **—ly** ardenter; iracunde
passive *adj* passivus; **—ly** passive
passport *s* diploma *n*
password *s* tessera *f*
past *adj* praeteritus; (*immediately preceding*) proximus, superior
past *s* tempus praeteritum *n*
past *prep* praeter (*with acc*), post (*with acc*)
paste *s* gluten *n*
paste *vt* agglutinare, conglutinare
pasteboard *s* charta crassa *f*
pastime *s* oblectamentum *n*, ludus *m*
pastoral *adj* pastoralis, bucolicus
pastoral *s* poema bucolicum *n*
pastry *s* crustum *n*
pasture *s* past·us -ūs *m*, pascuum *n*, pastio *f*
pasture *vt* pascĕre; *vi* (*to graze*) pasci
pat *adj* idoneus
pat *vt* permulcēre, demulcēre
patch *s* assumentum *n*, pannus *m*
patch *vt* resarcire, assuĕre
patchwork *s* cento *m*
patent *adj* apertus, manifestus; **—ly** manifesto
patent *s* privilegium *n*
paternal *adj* paternus
paternity *s* paternitas *f*
path *s* semita *f*, trames, callis *m*; (*fig*) via *f*
pathetic *adj* maestus; **—ally** maeste
pathless *adj* invius
pathos *s* pathos *n*, dolor *m*
pathway *s* semita *f*, callis, trames *m*
patience *s* patientia *f*
patient *adj* patiens, tolerans; **—ly** patienter, aequo animo
patient *s* aegrotus *m*, aegrota *f*
patriarch *s* patriarcha *m*
patriarchal *adj* patriarchicus
patrician *adj* patricius
patrician *s* patricius *m*
patrimony *s* patrimonium *n*
patriot *s* amans patriae *m*
patriotic *adj* amans patriae
patriotism *s* amor patriae, amor in patriam *m*
patrol *s* excubiae *f pl*
patrol *vt* circumire; *vi* excubias agĕre
patron *s* patronus *m*
patronage *s* patrocinium, praesidium *n*
patroness *s* patrona *f*
patronize *vt* favēre (*with dat*), fovēre
patronymic *s* patronymicum nomen *n*
pattern *s* exemplar, exemplum, specimen *n*
paucity *s* paucitas *f*
paunch *s* ingluvies *f*
pauper *s* pauper *m*
pause *s* pausa, mora *f*; (*mus*) intermissio *f*, intervallum *n*
pause *vi* insistĕre, intermittĕre
pave *vt* sternĕre
pavement *s* pavimentum *n*, stratura *f*
pavilion *s* tentorium *n*
paving stone *s* saxum quadratum *n*
paw *s* ungula *f*, pes *m*
paw *vt* pedibus pulsare
pawn *s* pignus *n*
pawn *vt* pignerare
pawnbroker *s* pignerator *m*
pay *s* merces *f*; (*mil*) stipendium *n*
pay *vt* solvĕre; (*in full*) persolvĕre, pendĕre; (*mil*) stipendium numerare (*with dat*); **to — a compliment to** laudare; **to — for** solvĕre (*with acc of thing and dat of person*); **to — respects to** salutare; **to — the penalty** poenam dare, poenam luĕre; *vi* **it pays** operae pretium est, prodest, lucro est
payable *adj* solvendus
paymaster *s* dispensator *m*; (*mil*) tribunus aerarius *m*
payment *s* (*act*) solutio *f*; (*sum of money*) pensio *f*

pea *s* pisum, cicer *n*
peace *s* pax *f*; quies *f*, otium *n*
peaceful *adj* tranquillus, placidus, pacatus; **—ly** tranquille, placide, cum bona pace
peacemaker *s* pacificator *m*
peace offering *s* placamen, placamentum, piaculum *n*
peacetime *s* otium *n*
peach *s* malum Persicum *n*
peacock *s* pavo *m*
peak *s* (*of mountain*) cacumen *n*; vertex, apex *m*
peal *s* (*of thunder*) fragor *m*; (*of bells*) concent·us -ūs *m*
peal *vi* resonare
pear *s* pirum *n*
pearl *s* margarita *f*
pearly *adj* gemmeus
peasant *s* agricola, colonus *m*
peasantry *s* agricolae, agrestes *m pl*
pebble *s* lapillus, calculus *m*
peck *s* modius *m*
peck *vt* rostro impetĕre, vellicare
peculation *s* peculat·us -ūs *m*
peculiar *adj* proprius, peculiaris, praecipuus, singularis; **—ly** praecipue
peculiarity *s* proprietas *f*
pecuniary *adj* pecuniarius
pedagogue *s* paedagogus *m*; (*schoolmaster*) magister *m*
pedant *s* scholasticus *m*
pedantic *adj* putidus, nimis diligens; **—ally** nimis diligenter
pedantry *s* eruditio insulsa *f*
peddle *vt* venditare, circumferre
peddler *s* venditor, institor *m*
pedestal *s* basis *f*
pedestrian *adj* pedester
pedestrian *s* pedes *m*
pedigree *s* stemma *n*, stirps *f*
pediment *s* fastigium *n*
peel *s* cortex *m*
peel *vt* decorticare, glubĕre
peep *s* aspect·us -ūs, tuit·us -ūs *m*
peep *vi* inspicĕre
peephole *s* conspicillum *n*
peer *s* par *m*; (*of peerage*) patricius *m*
peer *vi* **to — at** intuēri
peerless *adj* unicus, incomparabilis
peevish *adj* stomachosus, morosus, difficilis; **—ly** stomachose, morose
peg *s* clavus, paxillus *m*
pelican *s* pelicanus, onocrotalus *m*
pellet *s* globulus *m*
pelt *s* pellis *f*
pelt *vt* (*to hurl*) jacĕre; (*to beat*) verberare, petĕre
pen *s* (*to write with*) calamus, stylus *m*; (*enclosure*) saeptum *n*; (*for sheep*) ovile *n*; (*for pigs*) suile *n*
pen *vt* scribĕre, componĕre; **to — in** includĕre
penal *adj* poenalis
penalize *vt* poenā afficĕre, mul(c)tare
penalty *s* poena, mul(c)ta *f*
penance *s* satisfactio *f*
pencil *s* stilus *m*, graphis *f*
pending *adj* suspensus; (*law*) sub judice
pending *prep* inter (*with acc*)
pendulum *s* libramentum *n*
penetrate *vt* penetrare
penetrating *adj* acer, perspicax
penetration *s* acies mentis *f*, acumen *n*
peninsula *s* paeninsula *f*
penitence *s* paenitentia *f*
penitent *adj* paenitens; **—ly** paenitenter
penitentiary *s* carcer *m*
penknife *s* scalpellum *n*
penmanship *s* man·us -ūs *f*
pennant *s* vexillum *n*
penniless *adj* inops
penny *s* quadrans *m*
pension *s* annua *n pl*
pensive *adj* meditabundus
penultimate *s* paenultima syllaba *f*
penurious *adj* parcus, sordidus
penury *s* egestas, inopia *f*
people *s* (*nation*) populus *m*; homines *m pl*; (*common people*) plebs *f*; **— say** dicunt
people *vt* frequentare
pepper *s* piper *n*
pepper *vt* pipere condire; (*fig*) (*with blows*) verberare
peppermint *s* mentha *f*
perceive *vt* percipĕre, sentire, vidēre, intellegĕre
percentage *s* portio *f*
perceptible *adj* percipiendus, manifestus
perceptibly *adv* sensim
perception *s* perceptio *f*, sens·us -ūs *m*
perch *s* (*for birds*) pertica *f*; (*type of fish*) perca *f*
perch *vi* insidēre
perchance *adv* forte
percolate *vt* percolare; *vi* permanare
percussion *s* ict·us -ūs, concuss·us -ūs *m*
perdition *s* interit·us -ūs *m*; exitium *n*
peremptory *adj* arrogans
perennial *adj* perennis
perfect *adj* perfectus, absolutus; (*gram*) praeteritus; **—ly** perfecte, absolute; (*entirely*) plane
perfect *vt* perficĕre, absolvĕre
perfection *s* perfectio, absolutio *f*
perfidious *adj* perfidus, perfidiosus; **—ly** perfidiose
perfidy *s* perfidia *f*
perforate *vt* perforare, terebrare
perforation *s* foramen *n*
perform *vt* perficĕre, peragĕre; (*duty*) fungi (*with abl*); (*to play*) agĕre
performance *s* perfunctio, executio *f*; (*work*) opus *n*; (*of a play*) actio *f*; (*play, drama*) fabula *f*
performer *s* actor *m*; (*in play*) histrio *m*
perfume *s* odor *m*, unguentum *n*
perfume *vt* odoribus imbuĕre
perhaps *adv* forte, forsitan, fortasse
peril *s* periculum *n*
perilous *adj* periculosus; **—ly** periculose
period *s* (*gram*) periodus *f*; tempus, spatium *n*, aetas *f*; (*rhet*) circuit·us -ūs *m*

periodic *adj* certus; (*style*) periodicus; **—ally** certis temporibus
periphery *s* peripheria *f*, ambit·us -ūs *m*
periphrastic *adj* per periphrasin dictus
perish *vi* perire, interire
perishable *adj* fragilis, caducus, mortalis
peristyle *s* peristyl(i)um *n*
perjure *vt* **to — oneself** pejerare, perjurare
perjured *adj* perjurus
perjury *s* perjurium *n*; **to commit —** pejerare, perjurare
permanence *s* stabilitas, constantia *f*
permanent *adj* diuturnus, perpetuus, mansurus; **—ly** perpetuo
permeable *adj* pervius
permeate *vt* penetrare; *vi* permanare
permission *s* permissio, venia, potestas *f*
permit *vt* permittěre (*with dat*), siněre
permutation *s* permutatio *f*
pernicious *adj* perniciosus; **—ly** perniciose
peroration *s* peroratio *f*
perpendicular *adj* perpendicularis, directus
perpendicular *s* linea perpendicularis *f*
perpetrate *vt* facěre, perficěre
perpetrator *s* auctor, reus *m*
perpetual *adj* perpetuus, perennis, sempiternus; **—ly** perpetuo
perpetuate *vt* perpetuare, continuare
perpetuity *s* perpetuitas *f*
perplex *vt* turbare, confunděre
perplexing *adj* perplexus, ambiguus
perplexity *s* perturbatio, dubitatio *f*
persecute *vt* persequi, insequi, vexare
persecution *s* insectatio *f*
persecutor *s* insectator *m*
perseverance *s* perseverantia, constantia *f*
persevere *vi* perseverare, perstare, constare
persevering *adj* perseverans, constans, tenax; **—ly** perseverante, constanter
persist *vi* perstare, perseverare
persistence *s* permansio, pertinacia, perseverantia *f*
persistent *adj* pertinax; **—ly** pertinaciter
person *s* homo *m & f*, quidam *m*; (*body*) corpus *n*; **in —** ipse
personage *s* persona *f*
personal *adj* privatus, suus; (*gram*) personalis; **—ly** ipse, per se, coram
personality *s* persona, natura *f*, ingenium *n*
personification *s* prosopopoeia *f*
personify *vt* personā induěre
personnel *s* membra *n pl*, socii *m pl*
perspective *s* scaenographia *f*
perspicacious *adj* perspicax
perspicacity *s* perspicacitas *f*
perspiration *s* sudatio *f*, sudor *m*
perspire *vi* sudare
persuade *vt* persuadēre (*with dat*)
persuasion *s* persuasio *f*
persuasive *adj* suasorius; **—ly** persuasibiliter
pert *adj* procax; **—ly** procaciter
pertain *vi* pertinēre, attinēre
pertinent *adj* appositus; **to be —** ad rem pertinēre; **—ly** apposite
perturb *vt* turbare, perturbare
perturbation *s* perturbatio *f*
perusal *s* perlectio *f*
peruse *vt* perlegěre, evolvěre
pervade *vt* invaděre, permanare, perfunděre
perverse *adj* perversus, pravus; **—ly** perverse
perversion *s* depravatio *f*
perversity *s* perversitas, pravitas *f*
pervert *vt* (*words*) detorquēre; depravare, corrumpěre
pest *s* pestis *f*
pester *vt* vexare, infestare, sollicitare
pestilence *s* pestilentia *f*
pestle *s* pilum *n*
pet *s* corculum *n*, deliciae *f pl*
pet *vt* fovēre, in deliciis habēre
petal *s* floris folium *n*
petition *s* petitio *f*, preces *f pl*; (*pol*) libellus *m*
petition *vt* supplicare, orare
petitioner *s* supplex *m*
petrify *vt* in lapidem convertěre; *vi* lapidescěre
petticoat *s* subucula *f*
pettiness *s* animus angustus *m*
petty *adj* minutus, angustus, levis
petulance *s* petulantia, protervitas *f*
petulant *adj* protervus
phalanx *s* phalanx *f*
phantom *s* simulacrum, phantasma *n*, species *f*
pharmacy *s* ars medicamentaria *f*; (*drugstore*) taberna medicina, apotheca *f*
phase *s* (*of moon*) lunae facies *f*; (*fig*) vices *f pl*
pheasant *s* phasianus *m*, phasiana *f*
phenomenal *adj* singularis
phenomenon *s* res *f*; (*remarkable event*) portentum, prodigium *n*
philanthropic *adj* humanus
philanthropy *s* humanitas *f*
philologist *s* philologus, grammaticus *m*
philology *s* philologia *f*
philosopher *s* philosophus, sapiens *m*
philosophical *adj* philosophicus; **—ly** philosophice, sapienter; (*calmly*) aequo animo
philosophize *vi* philosophari
philosophy *s* philosophia, sapientia *f*; (*theory*) ratio *f*
philter *s* philtrum *n*
phlegm *s* pituita *f*, phelgma *n*
phlegmatic *adj* (*fig*) lentus
phosphorus *s* phosphorus *m*
phrase *s* locutio *f*; (*gram*) incisum *n*
phraseology *s* locutio, loquendi ratio *f*
physical *adj* physicus; (*natural*) corporis (*genit, used adjectively*); **—ly** naturā

physician *s* medicus *m*
physicist *s* physicus *m*
physics *s* physica *n pl*
physiognomy *s* oris habit·us -ūs *m*
physique *s* vires *f pl*
pick *vt* (*to choose*) eligĕre; (*to pluck*) carpĕre; (*to gather*) decerpĕre; **to — off** avellĕre; **to — out** eligĕre; **to — up** tollĕre
pick *s* (*tool*) dolabra *f*; (*best part*) flos *m*, lecti *m pl*
pickax *s* dolabra *f*
picked *adj* electus, delectus
picket *s* (*mil*) statio *f*
pickle *s* muria *f*
pickle *vt* in aceto condire, in muriā condire
pickled *adj* muriā conditus
picture *s* tabula picta, pictura *f*; (*fig*) descriptio *f*
picture *vt* (*to imagine*) fingĕre, ante oculos ponĕre
picture gallery *s* pinacotheca *f*
picturesque *adj* venustus, amoenus
pie *s* crustum *n*
piece *s* pars, portio *f*; (*of food*) frustum *n*; (*of cloth*) pannus *m*; (*broken off*) fragmentum *n*; (*coin*) nummus *m*; (*drama*) fabula *f*; **to fall to —s** dilabi; **to tear to —s** dilaniare, lacerare
piece *vt* resarcire; **to — together** fabricari, consuĕre
piecemeal *adv* frustatim, membratim
pier *s* moles *f*, agger *m*
pierce *vt* perforare; (*with sword, etc.*) transfigĕre, perfodĕre; (*fig*) pungĕre
piercing *adj* acutus, stridulus
piety *s* pietas, religio *f*
pig *s* porcus *m*, sus *m & f*
pigeon *s* columba *f*
pigment *s* pigmentum *n*
pigsty *s* hara *f*, suile *n*
pike *s* (*weapon*) hasta *f*; (*fish*) lupus *m*
pilaster *s* parasta, columella *f*
pile *s* (*heap*) acervus, cumulus *m*; (*for cremation*) rogus *m*; (*for building*) moles *f*; (*nap of cloth*) villus *m*
pile *vt* coacervare, congerĕre; **to — up** exstruĕre
pilgrim *s* peregrinator *m*
pilgrimage *s* peregrinatio *f*
pill *s* pilula *f*
pillage *s* vastatio, direptio, expilatio, rapina *f*
pillage *vt* vastare, diripĕre, depopulari, expilare, praedari
pillar *s* columna, pila *f*, columen *n*
pillow *s* pulvinus *m*, culcita *f*, cervical *n*
pillowcase *s* cervicalis integumentum *n*
pilot *s* gubernator *m*
pilot *vt* gubernare
pimp *s* leno *m*
pimple *s* pustula *f*
pimply *adj* pustulosus
pin *s* ac·us -ūs, acicula *f*; (*peg*) clavus *m*
pin *vt* acu figĕre; affigĕre
pincers *s* forceps *m & f*
pinch *vt* vellicare; (*as cold*) (ad)urĕre; (*to squeeze*) coartare; (*of shoe*) urĕre
pine *s* pinus *f*
pine *vi* **to — away** tabescĕre, languēre; **to — for** desiderare
pineapple *s* (nux) pinea *f*
pink *adj* rosaceus, rubicundus
pinnacle *s* fastigium *n*, summus grad·us -ūs *m*
pint *s* sextarius *m*
pioneer *s* praecursor *m*
pious *adj* pius; (*scrupulous*) religiosus; (*saintly*) sanctus; **—ly** pie, religiose, sancte
pipe *s* (*tube*) tubus *m*; (*mus*) fistula *f*
pipe *vt* fistulā canĕre
piper *s* tibicen *m*
piquant *s* salsus, facetus; **—ly** salse
pique *s* offensio *f*
pique *vt* offendĕre
piracy *s* latrocinium *n*
pirate *s* pirata, praedo *m*
piratical *adj* praedatorius
pit *s* fossa, fovea *f*, puteus *m*; (*in theater*) cavea *f*; (*quarry*) fodina *f*
pitch *s* pix *f*; (*sound*) sonus *m*; (*degree*) grad·us -ūs *m*, fastigium *n*; (*slope*) fastigium *n*; **to such a — of** eo (*with genit*)
pitch *vt* (*to fling*) conjicĕre; (*camp*) ponĕre; (*tent*) tendĕre
pitcher *s* urceus *m*
pitchfork *s* furca *f*
piteous *adj* miserabilis; **—ly** miserabiliter, misere
pitfall *s* fovea *f*
pith *s* medulla *f*
pithy *adj* (*fig*) sententiosus
pitiable *adj* miserandus
pitiful *adj* misericors; (*pitiable*) miserabilis, miserandus; **—ly** misere
pitiless *adj* immisericors, durus; **—ly** immisericorditer
pittance *s* (*allowance for food*) demensum *n*; (*trifling sum*) mercedula *f*
pity *s* misericordia, miseratio *f*
pity *vt* miserēri (*with genit*); **I — him** miseret me ejus
pivot *s* axis, paxillus *m*; (*fig*) cardo *m*
placard *s* titulus, libellus *m*
place *s* locus *m*; **in — of** pro (*with abl*), loco (*with genit*); **in the first —** primum, primo; **out of —** intempestivus; **to take —** fieri, accidĕre
place *vt* ponĕre, locare, collocare
placid *adj* placidus, tranquillus; **—ly** placide, tranquille
plagiarism *s* furtum litterarium *n*
plagiarist *s* fur litterarius *m*
plagiarize *vt* furari
plague *s* pestilentia *f*; (*fig*) pestis *f*
plague *vt* vexare, exagitare
plain *s* campus *m*, planities *f*; **of the —** campester
plain *adj* (*clear*) apertus, manifestus, perspicuus; (*unadorned*) inornatus, simplex; (*of one color*) unicolor; (*frank*) sincerus; (*homely*)

invenustus; **—ly** aperte, manifeste; simpliciter; sincere
plaintiff *s* petitor *m*
plaintive *adj* querulus, flebilis; **—ly** flebiliter
plan *s* consilium, propositum *n*; (*drawing*) descriptio *f*; (*layout*) forma *f*
plan *vt* (*to scheme*) excogitare, meditari; (*to intend to*) in animo habēre (*with inf*); (*to draw*) designare, describĕre
plane *s* (*tool*) runcina *f*; (*level surface*) planities *f*
plane *vt* runcinare
planet *s* planeta, stella errans *or* vaga *f*
plank *s* assis *m*, tabula *f*
plant *s* planta, herba *f*
plant *vt* serĕre, conserĕre; (*feet*) ponĕre
plantation *s* plantarium *n*
planter *s* sator *m*
planting *s* sat·us -ūs *m*, consitura *f*
plaster *s* tectorium, gypsum *n*; (*med*) emplastrum *n*
plaster *vt* gypsare, dealbare
plastic *adj* plasticus, ductilis
plate *s* (*dish*) patella *f*, catillus *m*; (*coating*) lamina *f*; (*silver*) argentum *n*
plated *adj* bracteatus
platform *s* suggest·us -ūs *m*, suggestum *n*
platitude *s* trita sententia *f*
Platonic *adj* Platonis (*genit, used adjectively*)
platter *s* patella, lanx *f*
plausible *adj* verisimilis
play *s* ludus *m*; (*drama*) fabula *f*
play *vt* ludĕre; (*instrument*) canĕre (*with abl*); (*game*) ludĕre (*with abl*) (*role*) agĕre; **to — a trick on** ludificari
player *s* (*in game*) lusor *m*; (*on stage*) histrio, actor *m*; (*on wind instrument*) tibicen *m*; (*on string instrument*) fidicen *m*
playful *adj* lascivus, jocosus, ludibundus; (*words*) facetus; **—ly** per ludum, per jocum
playmate *s* collusor *m*
plaything *s* ludibrium *n*
playwright *s* fabularum scriptor *m*
plea *s* (*law*) petitio, exceptio, defensio *f*; (*excuse*) excusatio *f*
plead *vi* (*in court*) causam agĕre; (*to beg*) obsecrare, implorare, orare; **to — against** causam dicĕre contra (*with acc*); **to — for** defendĕre
pleasant *adj* amoenus, gratus, jucundus, suavis; **—ly** jucunde, suaviter
pleasantry *s* jocosa dicacitas *f*, facetiae *f pl*
please *vt* placēre (*with dat*), delectare; **if you —** si placet; **please!** obsecro!; sis!, amabo! (*colloquial*)
pleasing *adj* gratus, jucundus
pleasurable *adj* jucundus
pleasure *s* voluptas *f*; **it is my —** libet; **to derive —** voluptatem capĕre
plebeian *adj* plebeius
plebeians *s* plebs *f*
pledge *s* pignus *n*; (*proof*) testimonium *n*
pledge *vt* (op)pignerare, obligare; **to — one's word** fidem obligare
Pleiads *s* Pleiades *f pl*
plenary *adj* plenus, perfectus
plenipotentiary *s* legatus *m*
plentiful *adj* largus, affluens, uber; **—ly** large, ubertim
plenty *s* copia, abundantia *f*
plethora *s* pletura *f*
pleurisy *s* pleuritis *f*
pliable *adj* flexibilis, tractabilis, mansuetus
pliant *adj* lentus
plight *s* conditio *f*, stat·us -ūs *m*, discrimen *n*
plod *vi* assidue laborare
plodder *s* sedulus homo *m*
plodding *adj* laboriosus, assiduus, sedulus
plot *s* (*conspiracy*) conjuratio *f*, insidiae *f pl*; (*of drama*) argumentum *n*; (*of ground*) agellus *m*
plot *vi* conjurare, moliri
plow *s* aratrum *n*
plow *vt* arare; **to — up** exarare
plowing *s* aratio *f*
plowman *s* bubulcus, arator *m*
plowshare *s* vomer *m*
pluck *s* animus *m*
pluck *vt* carpĕre; **to — off** avellĕre, decerpĕre; **to — out** evellĕre, eripĕre; **to — up** eruĕre; **to — up courage** animo esse
plug *s* obturamentum *n*
plug *vt* obturare
plum *s* prunum *n*
plumage *s* plumae, pennae *f pl*
plumber *s* plumbarius *m*
plume *s* crista *f*
plummet *s* perpendiculum *n*
plump *adj* pinguis, obesus
plum tree *s* prunus *f*
plunder *s* (*act*) rapina *f*; (*booty*) praeda *f*
plunder *vt* praedari
plunderer *s* praedator *m*
plundering *s* rapina, praedatio *f*
plundering *adj* praedatorius, praedabundus
plunge *vt* mergĕre, submergĕre; (*sword, etc.*) condĕre; *vi* immergi, se mergĕre
pluperfect *s* plus quam perfectum tempus *n*
plural *adj* pluralis
plurality *s* multitudo *f*, numerus major *m*
plush *adj* lautus
ply *vt* exercēre, urgēre
poach *vt* (*eggs*) frigĕre; *vi* illicita venatione uti
poacher *s* fur *m*
pocket *s* sin·us -ūs, sacculus *m*
pocket *vt* in sacculis condĕre
pocket book *s* pugillaria *n pl*
pockmark *s* cicatrix *f*
pod *s* siliqua *f*
poem *s* poema, carmen *n*
poet *s* poeta, vates *m*

poetess *s* poetria, poetris *f*
poetic *adj* poeticus; **—ly** poetice
poetics *s* ars poetica *f*
poetry *s* (*art*) poetice *f*; (*poems*) poemata, carmina *n pl*, poesis *f*
poignancy *s* acerbitas *f*
poignant *adj* acerbus, pungens
point *s* punctum *n*; (*pointed end*) acumen *n*, acies *f*; (*of swords, etc.*) mucro *m*; (*fig*) quaestio, res *f*, stat·us -ūs *m*, argumentum *n*; **beside the —** ab re; **from this — on** posthac, hinc; **— of view** sententia *f*; **to the —** ad rem; **up to this —** adhuc, hactenus
point *vt* (*to sharpen*) acuĕre; **to — out** monstrare, indicare
pointed *adj* acutus; (*fig*) salsus; (*stinging*) aculeatus; **—ly** acute, aperte
pointer *s* index *m & f*
pointless *adj* (*fig*) insulsus, frigidus; **—ly** insulse
poise *s* (*fig*) urbanitas *f*
poise *vt* ponderare, pendĕre, librare
poison *s* venenum, virus *n*
poison *vt* venenare, veneno necare; (*fig*) vitiare
poisoning *s* veneficium *n*
poisonous *adj* venenatus, venenosus
poke *vt* (*to jab*) cubito pulsare, fodicare; (*fire*) fodĕre
polar *adj* arcticus
polarity *s* polaritas *f*
pole *s* asser, contus *m*, pertica *f*; (*of earth*) polus *m*
polemic *s* controversiae *f pl*
pole star *s* stella polaris *f*
police *s* vigiles, custodes *m pl*
policeman *s* vigil *m*
policy *s* ratio *f*, consilium *n*
polish *vt* polire; **to — up** expolire
polish *s* nitor, levor *m*; (*refined manners*) urbanitas *f*; (*literary*) lima *f*
polite *adj* comis, urbanus; **—ly** comiter, urbane
politeness *s* urbanitas, comitas *f*
politic *adj* prudens, astutus
political *adj* civilis, publicus
politician *s* magistrat·us -ūs *m*
politics *s* res publica *f*; **to enter —** ad rem publicam accedĕre
poll *s* caput *n*; **—s** comitia *n pl*
poll *vt* suffragiis petĕre
polling booth *s* saeptum *n*
poll tax *s* capitum exactio *f*
pollute *vt* polluĕre, inquinare, contaminare
pollution *s* (*act*) contaminatio *f*; (*filth*) colluvio, impuritas *f*
polygamy *s* polygamia *f*
polysyllabic *adj* polysyllabus
polytheism *s* multorum deorum cult·us -ūs *m*
pomegranate *s* malum Punicum *n*
pommel *vt* pulsare, verberare
pomp *s* pompa *f*, apparat·us -ūs *m*
pomposity *s* magnificentia *f*
pompous *adj* magnificus, gloriosus; **—ly** magnifice, gloriose
pond *s* stagnum *n*
ponder *vt* in mente agitare, considerare, ponderare
ponderous *adj* ponderosus, praegravis
pontiff *s* pontifex *m*
pontifical *adj* pontificalis
pontificate *s* pontificat·us -ūs *m*
pontoon *s* ponto *m*
pony *s* mannulus, equulus *m*
pool *s* lacuna *f*, stagnum *n*
pool *vt* conferre
poor *adj* (*needy*) pauper, inops, egens; (*inferior*) tenuis, mediocris; (*of soil*) macer; (*pitiable*) miser; (*meager*) exilis; **—ly** parum, mediocriter, misere, tenuiter
pop *s* crepit·us -ūs *m*
pop *vi* crepare; **to — out** exsilire
poplar *s* populus *f*
poppy *s* papaver *n*
populace *s* vulgus *n*, plebs *f*
popular *adj* popularis; **—ly** populariter
popularity *s* populi favor *m*, populi studium *n*
populate *vt* frequentare
population *s* civium numerus, incolarum numerus *m*
populous *adj* frequens
porcelain *s* fictilia *n pl*
porch *s* vestibulum *n*, portic·us -ūs *f*
porcupine *s* hystrix *f*
pore *s* foramen *n*
pore *vi* **to — over** assidue considerare, scrutari
pork *s* porcina *f*
porous *adj* rarus
porpoise *s* porculus marinus *m*
porridge *s* puls *f*
port *s* port·us -ūs *m*
portal *s* porta *f*
portend *vt* praesagire, portendĕre, significare
portent *s* monstrum, portentum, prodigium *n*
portentous *adj* monstruosus, prodigiosus
porter *s* janitor, ostiarius *m*; (*carrier*) bajulus *m*
portfolio *s* scrinium *n*
portico *s* portic·us -ūs *f*
portion *s* portio, pars *f*
portion *vt* partire
portly *adj* amplus, opimus
portrait *s* imago, effigies *f*
portray *vt* depingĕre, exprimĕre
pose *s* stat·us -ūs, habit·us -ūs *m*
pose *vi* habitum *or* statum sumĕre
position *s* positio *f*, sit·us -ūs *m*; (*of body*) gest·us -ūs *m*; (*office*) honos *m*; (*state*) conditio *f*, stat·us -ūs *m*; (*rank*) amplitudo, dignitas *f*
positive *adj* certus; (*gram*) positivus; (*fig*) confidens; **—ly** praecise, certo
possess *vt* possidēre, tenēre
possession *s* possessio *f*; (*estate*) bona *n pl*; **in the — of** penes (*with acc*); **to gain — of** potiri (*with abl*), occupare
possessive *adj* quaestuosus, avarus; (*gram*) possessivus
possessor *s* possessor, dominus *m*
possibility *s* facultas *f*
possible *adj* **as quickly as —** quam celerrime; **it is —** fieri po-

test; **it is — for me to** possum (*with inf*)
possibly *adv* fortasse
post *s* (*stake*) postis, cippus *m*; (*station*) statio, sedes stativa *f*; (*position*) munus *n*
post *vt* collocare, poněre, constituěre; **to — a letter** tabellario litteras dare
postage *s* vectura (epistulae) *f*
postdate *vt* diem seriorem scriběre (*with dat*)
poster *s* libellus *m*
posterior *adj* posterior
posterity *s* posteri, minores *m pl*, posteritas *f*
posthaste *adv* quam celerrime
posthumous *adj* postumus
postman *s* tabellarius *m*
postpone *vt* differre, prorogare
postscript *s* ascriptio *f*
posture *s* stat·us -ūs, habit·us -ūs, gest·us -ūs *m*
pot *s* olla *f*, ahenum *n*
potato *s* solanum tuberosum *n*
potentate *s* tyrannus *m*
potential *adj* futurus
potion *s* potio *f*
potter *s* figulus *m*
pottery *s* fictilia *n pl*
pouch *s* sacculus *m*, pera *f*
poultry *s* aves cohortales *f pl*
pounce *vi* **to — on** insilire (*with dat or* **in** + *acc*)
pound *s* libra *f*
pound *vt* contunděre, conterěre
pour *vt* funděre; **to — in** infunděre; **to — out** effunděre; *vi* fundi, fluěre; **to — down** (*of rain*) ruěre
pouring *adj* (*of rain*) effusus
pout *vi* stomachari
poverty *s* paupertas, pauperies *f*
powder *s* pulvis *m*
powder *vt* pulvere conspergěre
power *s* vis, potestas *f*; (*pol*) imperium *n*; (*mil*) copiae *f pl*; (*excessive*) potentia *f*; (*divine*) numen *n*; **to have great —** multum posse, multum valēre
powerful *adj* validus, potens; (*effectual*) efficax; **—ly** valde
powerless *adj* invalidus, impotens; (*vain*) irritus; **to be —** nil valēre
practical *adj* utilis, habilis; **—ly** fere, paene
practice *s* us·us -ūs *m*, experientia, exercitatio *f*; (*custom*) mos *m*, consuetudo *f*
practice *vt* (*to engage in*) exercēre, tractare; (*to rehearse*) meditari
practitioner *s* exercitator *m*; (*medical*) medicus *m*
pragmatic *adj* pragmaticus
prairie *s* campus *m*
praise *s* laus *f*
praise *vt* laudare
praiseworthy *adj* laudabilis, laudandus
prance *vi* exsultare, subsultare; (*of persons*) jactare
prank *s* ludus *m*; (*trick*) jocus, dolus *m*
pray *vt* precari, orare; *vi* precari, orare; **to — for** petěre, precari; **to — to** adorare, supplicare
prayer *s* preces *f pl*
preach *vt & vi* praedicare
preamble *s* prooemium, exordium *n*
precarious *adj* precarius, periculosus, incertus; **—ly** precario
precaution *s* cautio, provisio *f*; **to take —** cavēre, praecavēre
precede *vt* praeire (*with dat*), anteceděre
precedence *s* prior locus *m*; **to take — over** anteceděre
precedent *s* exemplum *n*
preceding *adj* prior, superior
precept *s* praeceptum *n*
preceptor *s* praeceptor, magister *m*
precinct *s* termini, limites *m pl*, templum *n*; (*ward*) regio *f*
precious *adj* pretiosus, carus; **— stone** gemma *f*
precipice *s* praeceps *n*; **down a —** in praeceps
precipitate *vt* praecipitare
precipitous *adj* praeceps, praeruptus, declivis
precise *adj* certus, definitus; (*exact*) accuratus, exactus; **—ly** subtiliter, accurate
precision *s* accuratio, cura *f*
preclude *vt* praecluděre, excluděre
precocious *adj* praecox
preconceive *vt* praeciperě, praesentire; **preconceived idea** praejudicium *n*
preconception *s* praeceptio, praejudicata opinio *f*
precursor *s* praenuntius *m*
predatory *adj* praedatorius, praedabundus
predecessor *s* antecessor, decessor *m*
predestine *vt* praedestinare
predicament *s* discrimen *n*, angustiae *f pl*
predicate *vt* praedicare
predicate *s* praedicatum *n*
predict *vt* praedicěre, augurari
prediction *s* praedictio *f*, praedictum, vaticinium *n*
predilection *s* studium *n*
predispose *vt* inclinare
predisposition *s* inclinatio *f*
predominant *adj* praevalens
predominate *vi* praevalēre
preeminence *s* praestantia, excellentia *f*
preeminent *adj* praecipuus, praestans, excellens; **—ly** praecipue, excellenter
preexist *vi* antea exstare *or* esse
preface *s* praefatio *f*
prefatory *adj* **to make a few — remarks** pauca praefari
prefect *s* praefectus *m*
prefecture *s* praefectura *f*
prefer *vt* praeponěre, anteponěre; (*charges*) deferre; **to — to** (*would rather*) malle (*with inf*)
preferable *adj* potior, praestantior
preference *s* favor *m*; **in — to** potius quam; **to give — to** anteponěre
preferment *s* honos *m*
prefix *s* syllaba praeposita *f*

prefix *vt* praefigĕre, praeponĕre
pregnancy *s* graviditas *f*
pregnant *adj* gravida; (*of language*) pressus
prejudge *vt* praejudicare
prejudice *s* praejudicata opinio *f*, praejudicium *n*
prejudice *vt* **to be prejudiced against** praejudicatam opinionem habēre in (*with acc*), invidēre (*with dat*); **to — the people against** studia hominum inclinare in (*with acc*)
prejudicial *adj* noxius
preliminary *adj* praevius; **to make a few — remarks** pauca praefari
prelude *s* (*mus*) prooemium *n*, praelusio *f*
prelude *vt* praeludĕre
premature *adj* praematurus, immaturus, praeproperus; **—ly** ante tempus
premeditate *vt* praemeditari
premier *s* princeps *m*
premise *s* (*major*) propositio *f*; (*minor*) assumptio *f*; **—s** fundus *m*, praedium *n*
premium *s* praemium *n*; **at a —** carus
premonition *s* monit·us -ūs *m*, monitum *n*
preoccupation *s* praeoccupatio *f*
preoccupy *vt* praeoccupare
preparation *s* comparatio, praeparatio *f*, apparat·us -ūs *m*; (*rehearsal*) meditatio *f*
prepare *vt* parare, comparare, apparare; (*to rehearse*) meditari; **to — to** parare (*with inf*)
preponderance *s* praestantia *f*
preposition *s* praepositio *f*
preposterous *adj* praeposterus; **—ly** praepostere, absurde
prerogative *s* jus *n*
presage *s* praesagium *n*
presage *vt* praesagire, portendĕre, significare
prescience *s* providentia *f*
prescient *adj* providus, sagax
prescribe *vt* praescribĕre, proponĕre
prescription *s* praescriptum *n*; (*of physician*) medicamenti formula *f*
presence *s* praesentia *f*; (*look*) aspect·us -ūs *m*; **in my —** me praesente; **in the — of** coram (*with abl*)
present *adj* praesens, hic; **for the — in** praesens tempus; **to be —** adesse; **—ly** mox, illico, statim
present *s* donum, munus *n*
present *vt* donare, offerre; introducĕre; (*in court*) sistĕre; (*to bring forward*) praebēre, offerre; **to — itself** *or* **oneself** occurrĕre, obvenire
presentation *s* donatio *f*; (*on stage*) fabula *f*
presentiment *s* praesagitio *f*, praesagium *n*
preservation *s* conservatio *f*
preserve *vt* conservare; (*fruits*) condire
preserver *s* conservator *m*
preside *vi* praesidēre, praeesse; **to — over** praesidēre (*with dat*), praeesse (*with dat*)
presidency *s* praefectura *f*
president *s* praeses, praefectus *m*
press *s* (*for wine*) prelum *n*; (*of people*) turba *f*
press *vt* premĕre, comprimĕre; (*fig*) urgēre; **to — down** deprimĕre; *vi* **to — forward** anniti; **to — on** pergĕre, contendĕre
pressing *adj* gravis, urgens
pressure *s* pressio, pressura *f*, press·us -ūs *m*
pressure *vt* urgēre
prestige *s* auctoritas *f*
presumably *adv* sane
presume *vt* sumĕre, credĕre, conjicĕre; (*to take liberties*) sibi arrogare
presumption *s* (*conjecture*) conjectura *f*; (*arrogance*) arrogantia *f*
presumptuous *adj* arrogans, insolens, audax; **—ly** insolenter, arroganter
presuppose *vt* praesumĕre
pretend *vt* simulare, dissimulare, fingĕre
pretender *s* simulator, captator *m*
pretense *s* simulatio, species *f*; **under — of** per speciem (*with genit*); **without —** sine fuco
pretension *s* (*claim*) postulatio *f*; (*display*) ostentatio *f*; **to make —s to** affectare
preterite *s* tempus praeteritum *n*
preternatural *adj* praeter naturam
pretext *s* species *f*, praetextum *n*; **under the — of** specie (*with genit*), sub specie (*with genit*), sub praetextu (*with genit*)
pretor *s* praetor *m*
pretorian *adj* praetorianus
pretorship *s* praetura *f*
prettily *adv* belle, concinne
pretty *adj* bellus, venustus, lepidus
pretty *adv* satis, admodum; **— well** mediocriter
prevail *vi* (*to be prevalent*) esse, obtinēre; (*to win*) vincĕre; **to — upon** persuadēre (*with dat*)
prevalent *adj* (per)vulgatus; **to become —** increbrescĕre
prevaricate *vi* tergiversari
prevarication *s* praevaricatio, tergiversatio *f*
prevaricator *s* praevaricator, mendax *m*
prevent *vt* impedire, prohibēre
prevention *s* anticipatio, impeditio *f*
preventive *adj* prohibens, anticipans
previous *adj* prior, superior; **—ly** antea, antehac
prey *s* praeda *f*
prey *vi* **to — on** praedari, rapĕre; (*fig*) vexare, consumĕre
price *s* pretium *n*; **at a high —** magni; **at a low —** parvi
priceless *adj* inaestimabilis
prick *vt* pungĕre; (*fig*) stimulare; **to — up the ears** aures arrigĕre
prickle *s* aculeus *m*
prickly *adj* spinosus

pride *s* superbia *f*; (*source of pride*) decus *n*
pride *vt* **to — oneself on** jactare
priest *s* sacerdos *m*; (*of particular god*) flamen *m*
priestess *s* sacerdos *f*
priesthood *s* (*office*) sacerdotium *n*; (*collectively*) sacerdotes *m pl*
priestly *adj* sacerdotalis
prig *s* homo fastidiosus *m*
prim *adj* (nimis) diligens
primarily *adv* praecipue
primary *adj* primus, principalis; (*chief*) praecipuus
prime *s* flos *m*; **to be in one's —** florēre, vigēre
prime *adj* primus, egregius, optimus, exquisitus
primeval *adj* pristinus, priscus
primitive *adj* priscus, antiquus, incultus
primordial *adj* priscus
primrose *s* primula vulgaris *f*
prince *s* regulus, regis filius *m*; (*king*) rex, princeps *m*
princely *adj* regius, regalis
princess *s* regia puella, regis filia *f*
principal *adj* principalis, praecipuus; **—ly** praecipue, maxime
principal *s* caput *n*, praeses, praefectus, princeps *m*; (*money*) caput *n*, sors *f*
principality *s* principat·us -ūs *m*
principle *s* principium *n*; (*in philosophy*) axioma *n*; (*maxim*) institutum *n*
print *s* nota impressa *f*; (*of foot*) vestigium *n*
print *vt* imprimĕre
prior *adj* prior, potior
priority *s* primat·us -ūs *m*
prism *s* prisma *n*
prison *s* carcer *m*, vincula *n pl*
prisoner *s* reus *m*, rea *f*; (*for debt*) nex·us -ūs *m*
prisoner of war *s* captivus *m*
pristine *adj* pristinus
privacy *s* solitudo *f*, secretum *n*
private *adj* (*secluded*) secretus; (*person*) privatus; (*home*) domesticus; (*one's own*) proprius; (*mil*) gregarius; **—ly** clam, secreto; (*in a private capacity*) privatim
private *s* miles, miles gregarius *m*
privation *s* egestas, inopia *f*
privilege *s* privilegium *n*, immunitas *f*
privy *adj* privatus, secretus; **— to** conscius (*with genit*)
privy *s* forica, latrina *f*
prize *s* (*reward*) praemium *n*, palma *f*; (*prey*) praeda *f*
prize *vt* magni aestimare, magni facĕre
prize fighter *s* pugil *m*
probability *s* veri similitudo, probabilitas *f*
probable *adj* verisimilis, probabilis
probably *adv* probabiliter
probation *s* probatio *f*
probe *vt* scrutari, inspicĕre
probity *s* probitas, honestas *f*
problem *s* quaestio *f*; **to have —s** laborare
problematical *adj* anceps, incertus
procedure *s* progress·us -ūs, modus *m*, ratio *f*
proceed *vi* (*to go on*) pergĕre, procedĕre, incedĕre; **to — against** persequi; **to — from** oriri ex (*with abl*)
proceedings *s* acta *n pl*; (*law*) lis, actio *f*
proceeds *s* redit·us -ūs *m*
process *s* ratio *f*; (*law*) lis, actio *f*
proclaim *vt* promulgare, edicĕre, pronuntiare, declarare
proclamation *s* pronuntiatio *f*, edictum *n*
proconsul *s* proconsul *m*
proconsular *adj* proconsularis
proconsulship *s* proconsulat·us -ūs *m*
procrastinate *vi* cunctari, procrastinare
procrastination *s* procrastinatio *f*
procreate *vt* procreare, generare
procreation *s* procreatio *f*
proctor *s* procurator *m*
procurable *adj* procurandus
procurator *s* procurator *m*
procure *vt* parare, acquirĕre, nancisci, adipisci
procurement *s* comparatio *f*
procurer *s* leno *m*
prodigal *adj* prodigus
prodigal *s* ganeo *m*
prodigality *s* dissipatio, effusio *f*
prodigious *adj* prodigiosus, immanis, ingens
prodigy *s* prodigium, monstrum, portentum *n*; (*fig*) miraculum *n*
produce *s* fruct·us -ūs *m*; (*of earth*) fruges *f pl*; (*in money*) redit·us -ūs *m*
produce *vt* (*to bring forward*) proferre, producĕre; (*to bring into existence*) parĕre, procreare, gignĕre; (*to cause*) efficĕre, facĕre; (*to put on, as a play*) docēre; (*crops*) ferre
product *s* (*of earth*) fruges *f pl*; opus *n*
production *s* productio *f*
productive *adj* ferax, fecundus, uber
productivity *s* feracitas, ubertas *f*
profanation *s* violatio *f*
profane *adj* profanus, impius; **—ly** impie
profane *vt* vilare, profanare, polluĕre
profanity *s* impietas *f*, nefas *n*
profess *vt* profitēri
professed *adj* apertus, manifestus
profession *s* professio *f*
professional *adj* ad professionem pertinens; (*expert*) peritus
professor *s* doctor *m*
professorship *s* doctoris munus *n*
proffer *vt* offerre, promittĕre, proponĕre
proficiency *s* progress·us -ūs *m*, peritia *f*
proficient *adj* habilis, peritus
profile *s* facies obliqua *f*; (*portrait*) imago obliqua *f*

profit *s* quaest·us -ūs, redit·us -ūs *m*, lucrum *n*
profit *vt* prodesse (*with dat*); *vi* proficĕre; **to — by** uti (*with abl*), frui (*with abl*)
profitable *adj* fructuosus, quaestuosus, utilis; **to be —** prodesse
profitably *adv* utiliter
profitless *adj* inutilis, vanus
profligacy *s* nequitia *f*, perditi mores *m pl*
profligate *adj* perditus, flagitiosus, nequam (*indecl*)
profligate *s* nepos, ganeo *m*
profound *adj* altus, subtilis, abstrusus; **—ly** penitus
profundity *s* altitudo *f*
profuse *adj* profusus, effusus; **—ly** effuse
profusion *s* effusio, profusio, abundantia *f*
progeny *s* progenies, proles *f*
prognosticate *vt* praedicĕre
prognostication *s* praedictio *f*, praedictum *n*
program *s* libellus *m*
progress *s* progress·us -ūs *m*; **to make —** proficĕre
progress *vi* progredi
progression *s* progress·us -ūs *m*
progressive *adj* proficiens; **—ly** gradatim
prohibit *vt* interdicĕre (*with dat*), vetare
prohibition *s* interdictum *n*
project *s* propositum, consilium *n*
project *vt* projicĕre; *vi* prominēre, exstare; (*of land*) excurrĕre
projectile *s* missile *n*
projecting *adj* eminens, prominens
projection *s* projectura, eminentia *f*
proletarian *adj* proletarius
proletariat *s* plebs *f*
prolific *adj* fecundus
prolix *adj* longus, verbosus
prolixity *s* verbositas *f*
prologue *s* prologus *m*
prolong *vt* producĕre, prorogare, extendĕre
prolongation *s* proragatio, dilatio *f*
promenade *s* (*walk*) ambulatio *f*; (*place*) xystus *m*
promenade *vi* spatiari, ambulare
prominence *s* eminentia *f*
prominent *adj* prominens, insignis
promiscuous *adj* promiscuus; **—ly** promiscue, sine ullo discrimine
promise *s* promissio *f*, promissum *n*; **to break a —** fidem fallĕre; **to make a —** fidem dare
promise *vt* promittĕre, pollicēri; (*in marriage*) despondēre
promising *adj* bonā spe (*abl used adjectively*)
promissory note *s* chirographum *n*
promontory *s* promontorium *n*
promote *vt* (*in rank*) producĕre, provehĕre; (*a cause, etc.*) favēre (*with dat*), adjuvare
promoter *s* adjutor, fautor *m*
promotion *s* amplior grad·us -ūs *m*, dignitas *f*
prompt *adj* promptus, paratus; **—ly** statim, extemplo
prompt *vt* subjicĕre, suggerĕre; (*to incite*) impellĕre, commovēre
promulgate *vt* promulgare
promulgation *s* promulgatio *f*
prone *adj* pronus, propensus
prong *s* dens *m*
pronominal *adj* pronominalis
pronoun *s* pronomen *n*
pronounce *vt* (*to declare*) pronuntiare; (*to articulate*) enuntiare, eloqui; (*sentence*) dicĕre, pronuntiare
pronunciation *s* appellatio, elocutio, locutio *f*
proof *s* documentum, argumentum, indicium, signum *n*
proof *adj* tutus, securus; **— against** invictus ab (*with abl*), adversus (*with acc*)
prop *s* tibicen *m*, fulcrum *n*; (*for vines*) adminiculum *n*
prop *vt* fulcire, sustinēre
propaganda *s* divulgatio *f*
propagate *vt* propagare, vulgare, disseminare
propagation *s* propagatio *f*
propel *vt* impellĕre, propellĕre
propeller *s* impulsor *m*
propensity *s* propensio, inclinatio *f*
proper *adj* (*becoming*) decorus, decens; (*suitable*) aptus, idoneus; **it is —** decet; **—ly** decore; apte
property *s* (*characteristic*) proprium *n*, proprietas *f*; (*things owned*) res *f*, bona *n pl*, fortuna *f*; **private —** res familiaris *f*
prophecy *s* praedictum *n*, praedictio, vaticinatio *f*
prophesy *vt* vaticinari, praedicĕre
prophet *s* vates *m & f*, fatidicus *m*; (*Biblical*) propheta *f*
prophetess *s* vates, fatiloqua *f*
prophetic *adj* fatidicus, divinus, vaticinus; **—ally** divinitus
propitiate *vt* propitiare, placare
propitiation *s* propitiatio *f*, placamentum *n*
propitious *adj* felix, faustus; **—ly** fauste
proportion *s* ratio, proportio *f*; **in —** pro rata parte; **in — to** pro (*with abl*)
proportionately *adv* pro portione
proposal *s* propositio, conditio *f*; (*of senate*) rogatio *f*
propose *vt* ferre, rogare; **to — a toast to** propinare (*with dat*)
proposition *s* (*offer*) condicio *f*; (*logic*) propositio *f*, pronuntiatum *n*
propound *vt* proponĕre, exponĕre
proprietor *s* possessor, dominus *m*
propriety *s* decorum *n*, convenientia *f*
propulsion *s* propulsio *f*
prosaic *adj* aridus, jejunus
proscribe *vt* proscribĕre
proscription *s* proscriptio *f*
prose *s* prosa *f*
prosecute *vt* (*to carry out*) exsequi; (*law*) litem intendĕre (*with dat*), accusare
prosecution *s* executio *f*; (*law*) accusatio *f*
prosecutor *s* accusator, actor *m*

prospect *s* prospect·us -ūs *m*; (*hope*) spes *f*
prospective *adj* futurus
prosper *vt* prosperare, secundare; *vi* prosperā fortunā uti, florēre, vigēre
prosperity *s* res secundae *f pl*
prosperous *adj* prosperus, secundus; **—ly** prospere, bene
prostitute *s* scortum *n*, meretrix *f*
prostitute *vt* prostituĕre
prostrate *vt* sternĕre, projicĕre; (*fig*) affligĕre
prostrate *adj* prostratus, projectus; (*fig*) afflictus, fractus; **to fall —** se projicĕre
prostration *s* (*act*) prostratio *f*; (*state*) animus fractus *m*
protect *vt* tuēri, protegĕre, defendĕre, custodire
protection *s* praesidium *n*, tutela *f*
protector *s* defensor, patronus *m*
protest *s* obtestatio, denuntiatio *f*
protest *vt* affirmare; *vi* obtestari, reclamare; (*pol*) intercedĕre
protestation *s* affirmatio *f*
prototype *s* exemplar *n*
protract *vt* protrahĕre, differre
protrude *vt* protrudĕre; *vi* prominēre
protuberance *s* tuber *n*, tumor, gibbus *m*
proud *adj* superbus, arrogans; **to be —** superbire; **—ly** superbe, arroganter
prove *vt* probare, confirmare, evincĕre, arguĕre; *vi* (*of person*) se praebēre, se praestare; (*of thing, event, etc.*) evadĕre, fieri, exire
proverb *s* proverbium *n*
proverbial *adj* proverbialis, tritus, notus
provide *vt* (*to furnish*) suppeditare, (com)parare, praebēre; *vi* **to — for** providēre (*with dat*), consulĕre (*with dat*); (*of laws*) jubēre
provided that *conj* dum, modo, dummodo, eā condicione ut
providence *s* providentia *f*
provident *adj* providus, cautus; **—ly** caute
providential *adj* divinus; **—ly** divinitus
province *s* provincia *f*
provincial *adj* provincialis; (*countrified*) inurbanus, rusticus; (*narrow*) angusti animi (*genit, used adjectively*)
provincialism *s* dialectos *f*
provision *s* (*stipulation*) condicio *f*; **—s** cibus, vict·us -ūs *m*, alimentum *n*; (*mil*) commeat·us -ūs *m*, res frumentaria *f*
provisional *adj* temporarius; **—ly** ad tempus
proviso *s* condicio *f*; **with the — that** eā lege ut
provocation *s* provocatio, offensio *f*
provoke *vt* provocare, irritare, stimulare
provoking *adj* molestus, odiosus
prow *s* prora *f*
prowess *s* virtus *f*
prowl *vi* vagari, grassari
prowler *s* praedator *m*
proximity *s* propinquitas *f*
proxy *s* vicarius *m*
prude *s* fastidiosa *f*
prudence *s* prudentia *f*
prudent *adj* prudens; **—ly** prudenter
prudish *adj* tetricus
prune *s* prunum conditum *n*
prune *vt* (am)putare, resecare, recidĕre
pruning *s* putatio *f*
pry *vi* perscrutor; **to — into** investigare, explorare
prying *adj* curiosus
pseudonym *s* falsum nomen *n*
puberty *s* pubertas *f*
public *adj* publicus, communis; (*known*) vulgatus; **—ly** palam, aperte
public *s* homines *m pl*, vulgus *n*
publican *s* publicanus *m*
publication *s* publicatio, promulgatio *f*; (*of book*) editio *f*; (*book*) liber *m*
publicity *s* celebritas, lux *f*
publish *vt* publicare, divulgare, patefacĕre; (*book*) edĕre
publisher *s* editor *m*
pucker *vt* corrugare
pudding *s* placenta *f*
puddle *s* lacuna *f*, stagnum *n*
puerile *adj* puerilis
puerility *s* puerilitas *f*
puff *s* aura *f*, flamen *n*
puff *vt* inflare, sufflare; *vi* anhelare
puffy *adj* sufflatus, tumens
pugilist *s* pugil *m*
pugnacious *adj* pugnax
pull *vt* (*to drag*) trahĕre, tractare; **to — apart** distrahĕre; **to — away** avellĕre; **to — down** detrahĕre; (*buildings*) demoliri, destruĕre, evertĕre; **to — off** avellĕre; **to — out** extrahĕre; (*hair, etc.*) evellĕre; *vi* **to — at** vellicare; **to — through** pervincĕre; (*illness*) convalescĕre
pull *s* (*act*) tract·us -ūs *m*; (*effort*) nis·us -ūs *m*; (*influence*) gratia *f*
pulley *s* trochlea *f*
pulmonary *adj* pulmoneus, pulmonaceus, pulmonarius
pulp *s* pulpa, caro *f*
pulpit *s* suggest·us -ūs *m*, rostra *n pl*
pulsate *vi* palpitare
pulse *s* puls·us -ūs *m*; (*plant*) legumen *n*; **to feel the —** venas temptare
pulverization *s* pulveratio *f*
pulverize *vt* pulverare, contundĕre
pumice *s* pumex *m*
pump *s* antlia *f*
pump *vt* haurire, exantlare; **to — with questions** percontari
pumpkin *s* pepo, melopepo *m*
pun *s* verborum lus·us -ūs *m*, agnominatio *f*
punch *s* (*tool*) veruculum *n*; (*blow*) pugnus, ict·us -ūs *m*
punch *vt* pugnum ducĕre (*with dat*)
punctilious *adj* scrupulosus, religiosus
punctual *adj* promptus, accuratus, diligens; **—ly** ad tempus, ad horam

punctuality *s* diligentia *f*
punctuate *vt* interpungĕre
punctuation *s* interpunctio *f*
punctuation mark *s* interpunctum *n*
puncture *s* punctio *f*, punctum *n*
pungent *adj* pungens, acutus; (*caustic, as speech*) mordax, aculeatus
Punic *adj* Punicus
punish *vt* punire
punishable *adj* puniendus, poenā dignus
punishment *s* (*act*) punitio, castigatio *f*; (*penalty*) poena *f*, supplicium *n*; **without —** impune
punster *s* argutator *m*
puny *adj* pusillus
pup *s* catulus *m*
pupil *s* pupillus, discipulus *m*, pupilla, discipula *f*; (*of eye*) pupilla, pupula *f*
puppet *s* pupa *f*
puppy *s* catulus *m*
purchase *s* (*act*) emptio *f*; (*merchandise*) merx *f*
purchase *vt* emĕre
purchase price *s* pretium *n*; (*of grain*) annona *f*
purchaser *s* emptor *m*
pure *adj* mundus, purus; (*unmixed*) merus; (*morally*) castus, integer; **—ly** pure, integre; (*quite*) omnino; (*solely*) solum
purgation *s* purgatio *f*
purge *vt* purgare, mundare
purge *s* purgatio *f*; (*pol*) proscriptio *f*
purification *s* purificatio, purgatio *f*
purify *vt* purgare; (*fig*) expiare
purity *s* puritas, munditia *f*; (*moral*) castitas, integritas *f*
purple *s* purpura *f*; **dressed in —** purpuratus
purple *adj* purpureus
purport *s* significatio, sententia, vis *f*
purport *vt* significare, spectare ad (*with acc*)
purpose *s* propositum, consilium *n*, animus *m*; (*end, aim*) finis *m*; (*wish*) mens *f*; **on —** consulto; **to good —** ad rem; **to no —** frustra, nequaquam; **to what —** quo, quorsum
purpose *vt* in animo habēre, velle
purposely *adv* consulto, de industria
purr *s* murmur *n*
purr *vi* mumurare
purring *s* murmuratio *f*
purse *s* crumena *f*, marsupium *n*
purse *vt* corrugare, contrahĕre
pursuance *s* continutatio *f*; **in — of** ex (*with abl*), secundum (*with acc*)
pursuant *adj* **— to** ex (*with abl*), secundum (*with acc*)
pursue *vt* (per)sequi, insequi, insectari; (*plan, course*) insistĕre
pursuit *s* persecutio, insectatio *f*; (*occupation*) studium, artificium *n*, occupatio *f*
pus *s* pus *n*, sanies *f*
push *vt* trudĕre, urgēre, impellĕre; *vi* **to — on** contendĕre, iter facĕre
push *s* ict·us -ūs, puls·us -ūs, impuls·us -ūs *f*; (*fig*) conat·us -ūs *m*
pushing *adj* audax, confidens; (*energetic*) strenuus
pusillanimous *adj* timidus
put *vt* ponĕre, collocare; **to — an end to** finem facĕre (*with dat*); **to — aside** ponĕre; **to — away** seponĕre, abdĕre, amovēre; (*in safety*) recondĕre; **to — back** reponĕre; **to — down** deponĕre; (*to suppress*) supponĕre, sedare; (*in writing*) scribĕre; **to — in** inserĕre; **to — in order** ordinare; **to — off** (*to postpone*) differre; **to — on** imponĕre; (*clothes*) se induĕre (*with abl*); (*to add*) addĕre; **to — out** ejicĕre, extrudĕre; (*fire*) extinguĕre; (*money*) ponĕre; **to — out of the way** demovēre; **to — together** componĕre, conferre; **to — up** erigĕre, statuĕre; **to — up for sale** proponĕre, venum dare; *vi* **to — in** (*of ships*) portum petĕre, appellĕre; **to — out to sea** solvĕre; **to — up with** tolerare
putrefaction *s* putredo *f*
putrefy *vi* putrescĕre, putrefieri
putrid *adj* puter *or* putris, putridus
puzzle *s* quaestio abstrusa *f*, nodus *m*, aenigma *n*
puzzle *vt* confundĕre, perturbare; **to be puzzled** haerēre, dubitare
puzzling *adj* perplexus, ambiguus
pygmy *s* nanus, pumilio, pumilus *m*
pyramid *s* pyramis *f*
pyre *s* rogus *m*
Pythagorean *adj* Pythagoraeus
Pythian *adj* Pythius

Q

quack *s* (*charlatan*) circulator, pharmacopola *m*
quack *vi* tetrinnire
quadrangle *s* area *f*
quadruped *s* quadrupes *m & f*
quadruple *adj* quadruplex, quadrūplus
quadruple *vt* quadruplicare
quaestor *s* quaestor *m*
quaestorship *s* quaestura *f*
quaff *vt* ducĕre, haurire
quagmire *s* palus *f*
quail *s* coturnix *f*
quail *vi* pavēre
quaint *adj* rarus, insolitus, novus
quake *vi* tremĕre
qualification *s* (*endowment*) indoles *f*; (*limitation*) exceptio, condicio *f*
qualified *adj* (*suited*) aptus, idoneus, dignus; (*competent*) peritus, doctus

qualify *vt* aptum *or* idoneum redděre, instruěre; (*to limit*) temperare, mitigare, extenuare
quality *s* proprietas, qualitas *f*; **—s** ingenium *n*, indoles *f*
qualm *s* fastidium *n*; **— of conscience** religio *f*, scrupulus *m*
quandry *s* confusio *f*, angustiae *f pl*
quantity *s* numerus *m*, multitudo, vis, copia *f*; (*in scansion*) quantitas, mensura *f*
quarrel *s* jurgium *n*; (*dispute*) altercatio, controversia *f*; (*violent*) rixa *f*
quarrel *vi* altercari, jurgare, rixari
quarrelsome *adj* jurgiosus, rixosus, pugnax
quarry *s* lapicidinae, lautumiae *f pl*; (*prey*) praeda *f*
quart *s* duo sextarii *m pl*
quarter *s* quarta pars *f*, quadrans *m*; (*side, direction*) pars, regio *f*; (*district*) regio *f*; **at close —s** comminus; **—s** (*dwelling*) tectum *n*, habitatio *f*; (*temporary abode*) hospitium *n*; (*mil*) castra, contubernia stativa *n pl*; (*of moon*) lunae phases *f pl*; **to give — to** parcěre (*with dat*)
quarter *vt* in quattuor partes dividěre; (*to receive in one's house*) hospitium praebēre (*with dat*)
quarterly *adj* trimestris
quarterly *adv* quadrifariam, tertio quoque mense
quartermaster *s* castrorum praefectus *m*
quash *vt* (*to subdue*) opprimĕre; (*law*) rescindĕre, abolēre
quatrain *s* tetrastichon *n*
queasy *adj* fastidiosus; **to feel —** nauseare
queen *s* regina *f*
queen bee *s* rex *m*
queer *adj* novus, insolitus, rarus, ineptus
quell *vt* opprimĕre, sedare, domare
quench *vt* exstinguĕre; **to — the thirst** sitim sedare
querulous *adj* querulus, queribundus
query *s* quaestio, interrogatio *f*
query *vt* dubitare; *vi* quaerĕre, quaeritare
quest *s* inquisitio *f*; **to be in — of** quarĕre, requirĕre; **to go in — of** investigare
question *s* interrogatio *f*; (*doubt*) dubitatio *f*, dubium *n*; (*matter*) res, causa *f*; **there is no — that** non dubium est quin; **to ask a —** quaerĕre, rogare; **to call in —** dubitare; **without —** sine dubio, haud dubie
question *vt* interrogare, percontari; (*to doubt*) dubitare, in dubium vocare; (*to examine*) scrutari
questionable *adj* dubius, incertus
questioning *s* interrogatio, inquisitio *f*
questor *s* quaestor *m*
questorship *s* quaestura *f*
quibble *s* captio, argutiola *f*
quibble *vi* cavillari
quibbler *s* cavillator, sophista *m*
quibbling *s* cavillatio, captio *f*
quick *adj* (*swift*) celer, velox; (*nimble*) agilis; (*mentally*) sagax, astutus, acutus; (*with hands*) facilis; (*of wit*) argutus; **—ly** cito, velociter; (*with haste*) propere, festinanter
quicken *vt* accelerare; (*to enliven*) vivificare, animare; (*to rouse*) excitare
quicksand *s* syrtis *f*
quicksilver *s* argentum vivum *n*
quiet *adj* quietus, tranquillus, placidus; (*silent*) tacitus, taciturnus; **to keep —** quiescěre; (*to refrain from talking*) silēre, tacēre; **—ly** quiete, tranquille; tacite, per silentium
quiet *s* quies, tranquillitas *f*; (*leisure*) otium *n*; (*silence*) silentium *n*
quiet *vt* tranquillare, pacare, sedare
quill *s* penna *f*, calamus *m*
quilt *s* culcita *f*
quince *s* cydonium *n*
quince tree *s* cydonia *f*
quintessence *s* vis, medulla *f*, flos *m*
quip *s* dictum *n*, facetiae *f pl*
quirk *s* cavillatio, proprium *n*
quit *vt* relinquěre, deserěre
quite *adv* omnino, penitus, prorsus, magnopere; **not —** minus, parum; (*not yet*) nondum
quiver *s* pharetra *f*; **wearing a —** pharetratus
quiver *vi* treměre, contremiscěre, trepidare
quivering *s* tremor *m*, trepidatio *f*
Quixotic *adj* ridiculus
quoit *s* discus *m*
quota *s* portio, pars, rata pars *f*
quotation *s* (*act*) prolatio *f*; (*passage*) locus *m*
quote *vt* adducěre, proferre, commemorare

R

rabbit *s* cuniculus *m*
rabble *s* plebecula, faex populi *f*; (*crowd*) turba *f*
rabid *adj* rabidus; **—ly** rabide
race *s* (*lineage*) genus *n*, stirps *f*; (*nation*) gens *f*; (*contest*) certamen *n*; curs·us -ūs *m*, curriculum *n*
race *vi* certare, cursu contenděre
race horse *s* equus cursor *m*
racer *s* (*person*) cursor *m*; (*horse*) equus cursor *m*
racetrack *s* circus *m*, curriculum *n*
rack *s* (*shelf*) pluteus *m*; (*for punishment*) equuleus *m*, tormentum *n*
racket *s* (*noise*) strepit·us -ūs *m*

radiance *s* fulgor, splendor *m*
radiant *adj* radians, fulgidus, spendidus
radiate *vt* emittěre; *vi* radiare, fulgēre, nitēre
radiation *s* radiatio *f*
radical *adj* insitus, innatus; (*thorough*) totus; **—ly** penitus, omnino
radical *s* rerum novarum cupidus *m*
radish *s* raphanus *m*
radius *s* radius *m*
raffle *s* alea *f*
raffle *vt* **to — off** aleā venděre
raft *s* ratis *f*
rafter *s* trabs *f*
rag *s* panniculus, pannus *m*
rage *s* furor *m*, rabies *f*
rage *vi* furěre, saevire
ragged *adj* pannosus
raid *s* incursio, invasio *f*, latrocinium *n*
raider *s* praedator, latro *m*
raid *vt* praedari
rail *s* palus, asser transversus, longurius *m*
rail *vt* **to — off** consaepire; *vi* **to — at** insectari, conviciari
railing *s* (*fence*) saepimentum *n*; (*abuse*) convicium, maledictum *n*
raiment *s* vestis *f*, vestit·us -ūs *m*
rain *s* pluvia *f*, imber *m*
rain *vi* pluěre; **it is raining** pluit
rainbow *s* pluvius arc·us -ūs *m*
rain cloud *s* imber *m*
rainy *adj* pluvius, pluvialis; pluviosus
raise *vt* tollěre, elevare; (*to erect*) erigěre; (*to build*) exstruěre; (*money*) cogěre; (*army*) conscriběre; (*siege*) solvěre; (*to stir up*) excitare; (*children*) educare; (*to promote*) provehěre, producěre; (*price*) augēre; (*crops*) colěre; (*beard*) demittěre; **to — up** sublevare
raisin *s* astaphis *f*
rake *s* rastellus, irpex *m*; (*person*) nebulo, nepos *m*
rake *vt* raděre; **to — together** corraděre
rally *s* convent·us -ūs *m*, contio *f*
rally *vt* in aciem revocare; *vi* ex fuga convenire; (*from sickness*) convalescěre
ram *s* aries *m*
ram *vt* fistucare, paviare; (*to cram*) infercire
ramble *s* vagatio *f*
ramble *vi* vagari, errare; **to — on** (*in speech*) garrire
rambling *adj* errans; (*fig*) vagus
ramification *s* ramus *m*
rampage *vi* saevire
rampant *adj* ferox
rampart *s* vallum, propugnaculum *n*
rancid *adj* rancidus
rancor *s* simultas *f*, dolor *m*
random *adj* fortuitus; **at —** temere
range *s* series *f*, ordo *m*; (*of mountains*) jugum *n*; (*reach*) jact·us -ūs *m*
range *vt* ordinare, disponěre; *vi* pervagari
rank *s* series *f*, ordo, grad·us -ūs *m*, dignitas *f*
rank *vt* in numero habēre; *vi* in numero habēri
rank *adj* luxuriosus; (*extreme*) summus, maximus; (*of smell*) foetidus, gravis, graveolens
rankle *vi* suppurare, exulcerare
ransack *vt* diripěre, spoliare; (*to search thoroughly*) exquirěre
ransom *s* (*act*) redemptio *f*; pretium *n*
ransom *vt* rediměre
rant *vi* ampullari; **to — and rave** debacchari
rap *s* (*slap*) alapa *f*; (*blow*) ict·us -ūs *m*; (*at door*) pulsatio *f*; (*with knuckles*) talitrum *n*
rap *vt* (*to criticize*) exagitare; *vi* **to — at** pulsare, ferire
rapacious *adj* rapax, avidus
rapacity *s* rapacitas, aviditas *f*
rape *s* stuprum *n*; (*act of carrying away*) rapt·us -ūs *m*
rape *vt* violare, per vim stuprare
rapid *adj* rapidus, celer, velox; **—ly** rapide, cito, velociter
rapidity *s* rapiditas, velocitas *f*
rapier *s* verutum *n*
rapine *s* rapina *f*
rapture *s* exsultatio *f*, animus exsultans *m*
rapturous *adj* mirificus
rare *adj* rarus, inusitatus; (*fig*) eximius, singularis; (*thin*) tenuis; **—ly** raro
rarefy *vt* extenuare, rarefacěre
rarity *s* raritas, paucitas *f*; (*thing*) res rara, res singularis *f*
rascal *s* homo nequam, scelestus *m*
rascally *adj* scelestus, flagitiosus; nequam (*indecl*)
rash *adj* praeceps, temerarius; **—ly** temere, inconsulte
rash *s* eruptio pustulae *f*
rashness *s* temeritas *f*
raspberry *s* morum idaeum *n*
raspberry bush *s* rubus idaeus *m*
rat *s* sorex, mus *m*; (*person*) transfuga *m*
rate *s* proportio *f*; (*price*) pretium *n*; (*scale*) norma *f*; (*tax*) vectigal *n*; **— of interest** faenus *n*, usura *f*
rate *vt* aestimare
rather *adv* potius, prius, libentius; (*somewhat*) aliquantum, paulo, *or render by comparative of adjective*
ratification *s* sanctio *f*
ratify *vt* ratum facěre, sancire
rating *s* aestimatio *f*
ratio *s* proportio *f*
ration *s* (*portion*) demensum *n*; (*mil*) cibaria *n pl*
ration *vt* demetiri
rational *adj* ratione praeditus, intellegens; **—ly** ratione, sapienter
rationalize *vi* ratiocinari
rattle *s* crepit·us -ūs, strepit·us -ūs *m*; (*toy*) crepitaculum *n*
rattle *vt* crepitare (*with abl*); *vi* increpare, crepitare; **to — on** inepte garrire
raucous *adj* raucus
ravage *vt* vastare, spoliare, populari
ravages *s* vastatio, direptio *f*
rave *vi* furěre, saevire, bacchari

ravel *vt* involvĕre, implicare
raven *s* corvus *m*, cornix *f*
ravenous *adj* rapax, vorax; **—ly** voraciter
ravine *s* fauces *f pl*
raving *adj* furiosus, furens, insanus
ravish *vt* constuprare
raw *adj* crudus, incoctus; (*of person*) rudis, imperitus; (*of weather*) asper
rawboned *adj* strigosus
ray *s* radius *m*
raze *vt* solo aequare, excidĕre
razor *s* novacula *f*
reach *s* (*grasp, capacity*) capt·us -ūs *m*; (*of weapon*) ict·us -ūs, jact·us -ūs *m*; **out of my —** extra ictum meum
reach *vt* attingĕre; (*of space*) pertinēre ad (*with acc*), extendi ad (*with acc*); (*to come up to*) assequi; (*to arrive at*) pervenire ad (*with acc*); (*to hand*) tradĕre
react *vi* affici; **to — to** ferre
read *vt & vi* legĕre; **to — aloud** recitare
readable *adj* lectu facilis
reader *s* lector *m*; (*lecturer*) praelector *m*
readily *adv* (*willingly*) libenter; (*easily*) facile
readiness *s* facilitas *f*; **in —** in promptu
ready *adj* paratus, promptus, expeditus; (*easy*) facilis; **— money** praesens pecunia *f*; **to be —** praesto esse
real *adj* verus, sincerus; **—ly** re vera; (*surely*) sane, certe
real estate *s* fundus *m*
realistic *adj* verisimilis
reality *s* veritas, res ipsa *f*, verum *n*
realization *s* effectio *f*; (*of ideas*) cognitio, comprehensio *f*
realize *vt* (*to understand*) intellegĕre, vidēre, comprehendĕre; (*to effect*) efficĕre, ad exitum perducĕre; (*to convert into money*) redigĕre
realm *s* regnum *n*
ream *s* (*of paper*) scapus *m*
reap *vt* metĕre, desecare; (*fig*) percipĕre, capĕre
reaper *s* messor *m*
reappear *vi* redire, revenire, resurgĕre
rear *vt* educare, alĕre; *vi* (*of horses*) arrectum se tollĕre
rear *s* tergum *n*; (*mil*) novissimum agmen *n*, novissima acies *f*; **on the —** a tergo; **to bring up the —** agmen cogĕre
rearing *s* educatio *f*
reascend *vt & vi* denuo ascendĕre
reason *s* (*faculty*) mens, ratio, intellegentia *f*; (*cause*) causa *f*; (*moderation*) modus *m*; **by — of** ob (*with acc*), propter (*with acc*), a(b) (*with abl*); **there is no — why** non est cur
reason *vi* ratiocinari; **to — with** disceptare cum (*with abl*)
reasonable *adj* (*fair*) aequus, justus; (*moderate*) modicus; (*judicious*) prudens
reasonably *adv* ratione, juste; modice
reasoning *s* ratiocinatio, ratio *f*; (*discussing*) disceptatio *f*
reassemble *vt* recolligĕre, cogĕre
reassert *vt* iterare
reassume *vt* resumĕre
reassure *vt* confirmare, redintegrare
rebel *s* rebellis *m*
rebel *vi* rebellare, desciscĕre, seditionem commovēre
rebellion *s* rebellio, seditio *f*, rebellium *n*
rebellious *adj* rebellis, seditiosus; (*disobedient*) contumax
rebound *s* result·us -ūs *m*
rebound *vi* resilire, resultare
rebuff *s* repulsa *f*
rebuff *vt* repellĕre, rejicĕre
rebuild *vt* reparare, reficĕre
rebuke *s* reprehensio *f*
rebuke *vt* reprehendĕre, vituperare
rebuttal *s* refutatio *f*
recall *s* revocatio *f*
recall *vt* revocare; **to — to mind** in memoriam redigĕre
recant *vt* retractare, revocare
recantation *s* recept·us -ūs *m*
recapitulate *vt* repetĕre, summatim colligĕre
recapitulation *s* repetitio, enumeratio *f*
recapture *s* recuperatio *f*
recapture *vt* recipĕre, recuperare
recede *vi* recedĕre, refugĕre
receipt *s* (*act*) acceptio *f*; (*note of acceptance*) apocha *f*; (*money*) acceptum *n*
receive *vt* accipĕre, capĕre, excipĕre
receiver *s* receptor *m*
recent *adj* recens; **—ly** nuper
receptacle *s* receptaculum *n*
reception *s* adit·us -ūs *m*, admissio *f*; (*of guest*) hospitium *n*
recess *s* (*place*) recess·us -ūs *m*; (*in wall*) adytum *n*, angulus *m*; (*intermission*) intermissio *f*; (*vacation*) feriae *f pl*
recipe *s* praescriptum, compositio *f*
recipient *s* acceptor *m*
reciprocal *adj* mutuus; **—ly** mutuo, vicissim, inter se
reciprocate *vt* reddĕre
reciprocity *s* reciprocatio *f*
recital *s* narratio, enumeratio, recitatio *f*
recitation *s* recitatio, lectio *f*
reckless *adj* temerarius; **—ly** temere
reckon *vt* numerare, computare, aestimare; *vi* **to — on** confidĕre (*with dat*)
reckoning *s* numeratio *f*; (*account to be given*) ratio *f*
reclaim *vt* reposcĕre, repetĕre
recline *vi* recubare, recumbĕre; (*at table*) accumbĕre
recluse *s* homo solitarius *m*
recognition *s* cognitio, agnitio *f*
recognize *vt* agnoscĕre, recognoscĕre; (*to acknowledge*) noscĕre; (*to admit*) fatēri
recoil *vi* resilire; **to — from** rece-

dĕre ab (*with abl*), refugĕre ab (*with abl*)
recoil *s* recessio *f*
recollect *vt* recordari
recollection *s* memoria, recordatio *f*
recommence *vt* redintegrare, renovare
recommend *vt* commendare
recommendation *s* commendatio, laudatio *f*; **letter of —** litterae commendaticiae *f pl*
recompense *s* remuneratio *f*
recompense *vt* remunerare; (*to indemnify*) compensare
reconcilable *adj* placabilis; (*of things*) conveniens
reconcile *vt* reconciliare, componĕre; **to be reconciled** in gratiam restitui
reconciliation *s* reconciliatio *f*, in gratiam redit·us -ūs *m*
reconnoiter *vt* explorare
reconquer *vt* revincĕre, recuperare
reconsider *vt* revolvĕre, retractare
reconstruct *vt* restituĕre, renovare
reconstruction *s* renovatio *f*
record *s* monumentum *n*, historia *f*; **—s** annales *m pl*, tabulae *f pl*
recorder *s* procurator ab actis *m*
recount *vt* referre, enarrare, commemorare
recoup *vt* recuperare
recourse *s* refugium *n*; **to have — to** (*for safety*) fugĕre ad (*with acc*); (*to resort to*) descendĕre ad (*with acc*)
recover *vt* recuperare, recipĕre; *vi* (*from illness*) convalescĕre; (*to come to one's senses*) ad se redire
recoverable *adj* reparabilis, recuperandus; (*of persons*) sanabilis
recovery *s* recuperatio, reparatio *f*; (*from illness*) recreatio *f*
recreate *vt* recreare
recreation *s* oblectatio, remissio *f*, lus·us -ūs *m*
recriminate *vi* invicem accusare
recrimination *s* mutua accusatio *f*
recruit *vt* (*mil*) conscribĕre; (*strength*) reficĕre
recruit *s* tiro *m*
recruiting *s* delect·us -ūs *m*
recruiting officer *s* conquisitor *m*
rectification *s* correctio *f*
rectify *vt* corrigĕre, emendare
rectitude *s* probitas *f*
recumbant *adj* resupinus
recur *vi* recurrĕre, redire
recurrence *s* redit·us -ūs *m*
recurrent *adj* assiduus
red *adj* ruber; (*ruddy*) rubicundus; **to be —** rubēre; **to grow —** rubescĕre
redden *vt* rubefacĕre, rutilare; *vi* rubescĕre; (*to blush*) erubescĕre
reddish *adj* subrufus, subruber, rubicundulus
redeem *vt* redimĕre, liberare
redeemer *s* liberator *m*
Redeemer *s* Redemptor *m*
redemption *s* redemptio *f*
redhead *s* rufus *m*
red-hot *adj* candens
redness *s* rubor *m*
redolence *s* fragrantia *f*
redolent *adj* fragrans, redolens; **to be —** redolēre
redouble *vt* ingeminare
redoubt *s* propugnaculum *n*
redoubtable *adj* formidolosus
redound *vi* redundare
redress *vt* restituĕre
redress *s* satisfactio *f*; **to demand —** res repetĕre
reduce *vt* minuĕre, deminuĕre; (*to a condition*) redigĕre; (*mil*) vincĕre, expugnare
reduction *s* deminutio *f*; (*mil*) expugnatio *f*
redundancy *s* redundantia *f*
redundant *adj* redundans, superfluus
reed *s* harundo *f*, calamus *m*
reef *s* scopulus *m*, saxa *n pl*
reek *s* fumus, vapor *m*
reek *vi* fumare; **to — of** olēre
reel *s* fusus *m*
reel *vi* (*to stagger*) titubare
reestablish *vt* restituĕre
reestablishment *s* restitutio *f*
refer *vt* referre, remittĕre; *vi* **to — to** perstringĕre, attingĕre
referee *s* arbiter *m*
reference *s* ratio *f*; (*in book*) locus *m*
refine *vt* purgare, excolĕre, expolire; (*metals*) excoquĕre
refined *adj* politus; (*fig*) elegans, urbanus, humanus
refinement *s* (*of liquids*) purgatio *f*; (*fig*) urbanitas, humanitas, elegantia *f*
reflect *vt* repercutĕre, reverberare; (*fig*) afferre; *vi* **to — on** considerare, revolvĕre
reflection *s* repercussio *f*, repercuss·us -ūs *m*; (*thing reflected*) imago *f*; (*fig*) consideratio, meditatio, cogitatio *f*; **without —** inconsulte
reflective *adj* cogitabundus
reflexive *adj* reciprocus
reform *vt* reficĕre, refingĕre; (*to amend*) corrigĕre, emendare; *vi* se corrigĕre
reform *s* correctio, emendatio *f*
reformation *s* correctio *f*
reformer *s* corrector, emendator *m*
refract *vt* refringĕre
refraction *s* refractio *f*
refractory *adj* contumax, indocilis
refrain *s* vers·us -ūs intercalaris *m*
refrain *vi* **to — from** abstinēre ab (*with abl*), parcĕre (*with dat*); **I — from speaking** abstineo quin dicam
refresh *vt* recreare, reficĕre; (*the memory*) redintegrare
refreshing *adj* jucundus, dulcis
refreshment *s* (*food*) cibus *m*; (*drink*) pot·us -ūs *m*
refuge *s* refugium, perfugium, asylum *n*; **to take — with** confugĕre in (*with acc*)
refugee *s* profugus *m*, ex(s)ul *m & f*
refulgence *s* fulgor *m*
refulgent *adj* fulgidus
refund *vt* refundĕre, rependĕre

refusal *s* recusatio, repulsa *f*
refuse *vt* recusare, negare; (*scornfully*) repudire, renuĕre
refutation *s* refutatio, confutatio *f*
refute *vt* refutare, refellĕre, redarguĕre
regain *vt* recipĕre, recuperare
regal *adj* regalis, regius; **—ly** regaliter
regale *vt* excipĕre
regalia *s* insignia regia *n pl*
regard *s* respect·us -ūs *m*, ratio *f*; (*care*) cura *f*; (*esteem*) gratia *f*
regard *vt* (*to look at*) respicĕre, intuēri; (*to concern*) spectare ad (*with acc*); (*to esteem*) aestimare; (*to consider*) habēre
regarding *prep* de (*with abl*)
regardless *adj* neglegens, incuriosus
regency *s* procuratio regni *f*, interregnum *n*
regenerate *vt* regenerare
regeneration *s* regeneratio *f*
regent *s* interrex *m*
regicide *s* (*murderer*) regis occisor *m*; (*murder*) caedes regis *f*
regime *s* administratio *f*
regimen *f* vict·us -ūs *m*
regiment *s* cohors, caterva *f*
region *s* regio, plaga *f*, tract·us -ūs *m*
register *s* tabulae *f pl*, catalogus *m*, album *n*
register *vt* in tabulas referre; (*emotion*) ostendĕre; *vi* profitēri, nomen dare
registrar *s* tabularius, actuarius *m*
registration *s* perscriptio, in tabulas relatio *f*
registry *s* tabularium *n*
regret *s* indignatio, paenitentia *f*, dolor *m*
regret *vt* dolēre; **I —** paenitet me (*with genit*), piget me (*with genit*)
regretful *adj* paenitens
regular *adj* (*common*) usitatus; (*proper*) justus, rectus; (*consistent*) constans, certus; **—ly** ordine, constanter; juste, recte
regularity *s* symmetria *f*; (*consistency*) constantia *f*
regulate *vt* ordinare, disponĕre, dirigĕre; (*to control*) moderari
regulation *s* ordinatio, temperatio, moderatio *f*; (*rule*) lex *f*, jussum *n*
rehabilitate *vt* restituĕre
rehearsal *s* meditatio *f*
rehearse *vt* meditari
reign *s* regnum *n*
reign *vi* regnare, dominari
reimburse *vt* rependĕre
reimbursement *s* pecuniae restitutio *f*
rein *s* habena *f*; **to give full —** habenas immittĕre (*with dat*); **to loosen the —s** frenos dare; **to tighten the —s** habenas adducĕre
reindeer *s* reno *m*
reinforce *vt* firmare, supplēre
reinforcement *s* supplementum, subsidium *n*; **—s** (*mil*) novae copiae *f pl*
reinstate *vt* restituĕre
reinstatement *s* restitutio *f*
reinvest *vt* iterum locare
reiterate *vt* iterare
reiteration *s* iteratio *f*
reject *vt* rejicĕre, repudiare, repellĕre, respuĕre
rejection *s* rejectio, repulsa *f*
rejoice *vi* gaudēre, exsultare
rejoin *vt* redire ad (*with acc*); *vi* respondēre
rejoinder *s* responsum *n*
rekindle *vt* resuscitare
relapse *s* novus laps·us -ūs *m*
relate *vt* referre, memorare, narrare; (*to compare*) conferre; *vi* **to — to** pertinēre ad (*with acc*)
related *adj* propinquus, conjunctus; (*by blood*) consanguineus, cognatus; (*by marriage*) affinis
relation *s* narratio *f*; (*reference*) ratio *f*; (*relationship*) cognatio *f*; (*relative*) cognatus *m*, cognata *f*
relationship *s* (*by blood*) consanguinitas, cognatio *f*; (*by marriage*) affinitas *f*; (*connection*) necessitudo, vicinitas, conjunctio *f*
relative *adj* attinens; cum ceteris comparatus; **—ly** pro ratione, ex comparatione
relative *s* cognatus, propinquus *m*, cognata, propinqua *f*
relax *vt* remittĕre, laxare; *vi* languescĕre
relaxation *s* remissio, relaxatio, requies *f*
relaxing *adj* remissivus
release *s* liberatio, absolutio, missio *f*
release *vt* (*prisoner*) liberare; solvĕre, resolvĕre
relegate *vt* relegare
relent *vi* mitescĕre, mollescĕre, flecti
relentless *adj* immisericors, inexorabilis, atrox; **—ly** atrociter
relevant *adj* **to be —** ad rem attinēre
reliance *s* fiducia, fides *f*
reliant *adj* fretus
relic *s* reliquiae *f pl*
relief *s* (*alleviation*) levatio *f*, levamentum *n*; (*comfort*) solatium, lenimen *n*; (*help*) auxilium *n*; (*in sculpture*) toreuma *n*; (*of sentries*) mutatio *f*
relieve *vt* levare, allevare, mitigare; (*to aid*) succurrĕre (*with dat*); (*a guard*) succedĕre (*with dat*), excipĕre
religion *s* religio *f*, deorum cult·us -ūs *m*
religious *adj* religiosus, pius; **—ly** religiose
relinquish *vt* relinquĕre; (*office*) se abdicare ab (*with abl*)
relish *s* (*flavor*) sapor *m*; (*enthusiasm*) studium *n*; (*seasoning*) condimentum *n*
relish *vt* gustare
reluctance *s* aversatio *f*; **with —** invite
reluctant *adj* invitus; **—ly** invite
rely *vi* **to — on** confidĕre (*with dat*), niti (*with abl*)
remain *vi* manēre, permanēre; (*of things*) restare

remainder *s* reliquum *n*
remains *s* reliquiae *f pl*
remark *vt* dicĕre
remark *s* dictum *n*
remarkable *adj* insignis, memorabilis, mirus, egregius
remarkably *adv* insignite, mire, egregie
remediable *adj* sanabilis
remedial *adj* medicabilis; emendatorius
remedy *s* remedium *n*; (*law*) regress·us -ūs *m*
remedy *vt* mederī (*with dat*), sanare, corrigĕre
remember *vt* meminisse (*with genit*); reminisci (*with genit*); recordari
remembrance *s* memoria, commemoratio *f*
remind *vt* admonēre, commonefacĕre
reminder *s* admonitio *f*, admonitum *n*
reminisce *vi* meditari; **to — about** recordari
reminiscence *s* recordatio *f*
remiss *adj* neglegens
remission *s* venia, remissio *f*
remit *vt* remittĕre, condonare
remittance *s* remissio *f*
remnant *s* reliquum, residuum *n*; **—s** reliquiae *f pl*
remodel *vt* reformare, transfigurare
remonstrance *s* objurgatio *f*
remonstrate *vi* reclamare, reclamitare; **to — with** objurgare
remorse *s* paenitentia *f*
remorseless *adj* immisericors
remote *adj* remotus, longinquus, reconditus; **—ly** procul
remoteness *s* longinquitas, distantia *f*
removable *adj* mobilis
removal *s* amotio *f*; (*banishment*) amandatio *f*; (*change of residence*) migratio *f*
remove *vt* amovēre, tollĕre, auferre; *vi* migrare
remunerate *vt* remunerari
remuneration *s* remuneratio *f*
rend *vt* lacerare, scindĕre; (*to split*) findĕre
render *vt* reddĕre, tradĕre; (*to translate*) vertĕre; (*thanks*) referre
rendering *s* (*translation*) conversio *f*; (*interpretation*) interpretatio *f*
rendezvous *s* constitutum *n*
renegade *s* desertor, transfuga *m*
renew *vt* renovare, instaurare, redintegrare
renewal *s* renovatio, instauratio, repetitio *f*
renounce *vt* renuntiare, repudiare, abdicare; (*an office*) se abdicare (*with abl*)
renovate *vt* renovare, reficĕre
renovation *s* renovatio, reparatio *f*
renown *s* fama, gloria *f*
renowned *adj* praeclarus, insignis, celebris
rent *s* (*of lands*) vectigal *n*; (*of houses*) merces, pensio *f*; (*tear; fissure*) scissura *f*
rent *vt* (*to let out*) locare; (*to hire*) conducĕre
renunciation *s* repudiatio, cessio, abdicatio *f*
reopen *vt* iterum aperire
repair *vt* reparare, reficĕre, restituĕre; (*clothes*) resarcire
repair *s* refectio *f*; **in bad —** ruinosus
reparation *s* satisfactio *f*
repartee *s* sales *m pl*
repast *s* cena *f*
repay *vt* remunerari; (*money*) reponĕre, retribuĕre
repayment *s* solutio, remuneratio *f*
repeal *vt* abrogare, rescindĕre, tollĕre
repeal *s* abrogatio *f*
repeat *vt* iterare, repetĕre; (*ceremony*) instaurare
repeatedly *adv* iterum atque iterum, identidem
repel *vt* repellĕre; (*fig*) aspernari
repent *vi* **I —** paenitet me
repentance *s* paenitentia *f*
repentant *adj* paenitens
repercussion *s* repercuss·us -ūs *m*
repetition *s* iteratio, repetitio *f*
repine *vi* conquĕri
replace *vt* reponĕre, restituĕre
replant *vt* reserĕre
replenish *vt* replēre
replete *adj* repletus, plenus
repletion *s* satietas *f*
reply *vi* respondēre
reply *s* responsum *n*
report *vt* referre, narrare, nuntiare; (*officially*) renuntiare
report *s* (*rumor*) fama *f*, rumor *m*; (*official*) renuntiatio *f*; (*noise*) fragor *m*
repose *vt* ponĕre, reponĕre; *vi* quiescĕre
repose *s* quies, requies *f*
repository *s* receptaculum *n*
reprehend *vt* reprehendĕre, vituperare
reprehensible *adj* culpā dignus, improbus
represent *vt* repraesentare, exprimĕre, describĕre, proponĕre; (*a character*) partes agĕre (*with genit*)
representation *s* (*act*) repraesentatio *f*; (*likeness*) imago *f*
representative *s* legatus, vicarius *m*
repress *vt* reprimĕre, coercēre, cohibēre
repression *s* coercitio, cohibitio *f*
reprieve *s* supplicii dilatio, mora, venia *f*; **to grant a —** supplicium differre, veniam dare
reprieve *vt* veniam dare (*with dat*)
reprimand *s* reprehensio *f*
reprimand *vt* reprehendĕre
reprint *vt* denuo imprimĕre
reprisal *s* ultio *f*; **to make —s on** ulcisci
reproach *s* exprobratio, vituperatio *f*, probrum *n*; (*cause for reproach*) opprobrium *n*
reproach *vt* opprobrare, vituperare, increpitare
reproachful *adj* objurgatorius, contumeliosus; **—ly** contumeliose
reprobate *s* perditus *m*

reproduce *vt* regenerare, propagare; (*likeness*) referre
reproduction *s* regeneratio, propagatio *f*; (*likeness*) effigies *f*
reproof *s* reprehensio, vituperatio, objuratio *f*
reprove *vt* reprehenděre, objurgare
reptile *s* serpens, bestia serpens *f*
republic *s* civitas popularis, libera civitas *f*
republican *adj* popularis
repudiate *vt* repudiare
repudiation *s* repudiatio *f*
repugnance *s* fastidium *n*, aversatio *f*
repugnant *adj* aversus, repugnans, alienus
repulse *s* depulsio *f*; (*political defeat*) repulsa *f*
repulse *vt* repellěre
repulsion *s* repulsio *f*
repulsive *adj* odiosus, foedus
reputable *adj* honestus
reputation *s* fama *f*, nomen *n*
repute *s* fama, opinio *f*, nomen *n*
request *s* petitio, rogatio *f*; **to obtain a —** impetrare
request *vt* rogare, petěre
require *vt* postulare, poscěre; (*to need*) egēre (*with abl*); (*to call for*) requirěre
requirement *s* necessarium *n*
requisite *adj* necessarius
requisition *s* postulatio *f*, postulatum *n*
requital *s* retributio, merces *f*; (*return for a service*) gratia *f*
requite *vt* compensare, retribuěre; (*for a favor*) remunerari
rescind *vt* rescinděre, tollěre
rescue *s* liberatio, salus *f*; **to come to the — of** subvenire (*with dat*)
rescue *vt* liberare, servare, eripěre
research *s* investigatio *f*
resemblance *s* similitudo, imago *f*, instar *n* (*indecl*)
resemble *vt* similis esse (*with genit, esp. of persons, or with dat*)
resembling *adj* similis (*with genit, esp. of persons, or with dat*)
resent *vt* aegre ferre
resentful *adj* iracundus, indignans
resentment *s* indignatio *f*, dolor *m*
reservation *s* retentio *f*; (*mental*) exceptio *f*; (*proviso*) condicio *f*
reserve *s* (*restraint*) pudor *m*, taciturnitas *f*; (*stock*) copia *f*; (*mil*) subsidium *n*; **in —** subsidiarius; **without —** aperte
reserve *vt* servare, reservare, reponěre
reserved *adj* (*of seat*) assignatus; (*of disposition*) taciturnus
reservoir *s* cisterna *f*, lac·us -ūs *m*
reset *vt* reponěre
reside *vi* habitare, commorari; **to — in** inhabitare
residence *s* habitatio, sedes *f*, domicilium *n*
resident *s* incola *m & f*
residue *s* residuum *n*
resign *vt* ceděre, remittěre; se abdicare a(b) (*with abl*); **to — oneself** animum summittěre (*with dat*); *vi* se abdicare
resignation *s* (*act*) abdicatio *f*; (*fig*) aequus animus *m*
resigned *adj* summissus; **to be —** aequo animo esse; **to be — to** aequo animo ferre
resilience *s* mollitia *f*
resilient *adj* resultans, mollis
resin *s* resina *f*
resist *vt* resistěre (*with dat*), obstare (*with dat*), repugnare (*with dat*)
resistance *s* repugnantia *f*; **to offer to —** obsistěre (*with dat*), repugnare (*with dat*)
resolute *adj* firmus, constans, fortis; **—ly** constanter, fortiter
resolution *s* (*determination*) constantia *f*; (*decision, decree*) decretum *n*; (*of senate*) consultum *n*
resolve *s* constantia *f*
resolve *vt* decerněre, statuěre, constituěre; (*to reduce, convert*) resolvěre, dissolvěre
resonance *s* resonantia *f*
resonant *adj* resonus
resort *s* locus celeber *m*; (*refuge*) refugium *n*
resort *vi* **to — to** (*to frequent*) frequentare, celebrare; (*to have recourse to*) confugěre ad (*with acc*)
resource *s* subsidium *n*; **—s** facultates, opes, copiae *f pl*
respect *s* (*regard*) respect·us -ūs *m*; (*reference*) ratio *f*; **in every —** ex omni parte
respect *vt* (re)verēri, observare
respectability *s* honestas *f*
respectable *adj* honestus, bonus
respectably *adv* honeste
respectful *adj* observans, reverens; **—ly** reverenter
respecting *prep* de (*with abl*)
respective *adj* proprius, suus; **—ly** mutuo
respiration *s* spirit·us -ūs *m*
respite *s* intermissio, cessatio, requies *f*
resplendence *s* nitor, splendor *m*
resplendent *adj* resplendens, splendidus; **—ly** splendide
respond *vi* responděre
respondent *s* (*law*) reus *m*
response *s* responsum *n*
responsibility *s* cura *f*; **it is my —** est mihi curae
responsible *adj* obnoxius, reus
rest *s* quies, requies *f*; (*support*) fulcrum, statumen *n*; (*remainder*) reliqua pars *f*, reliquum *n*; **the — of the men** ceteri *m pl*
rest *vt* (*to lean*) reclinare; *vi* (re)quiescěre; (*to pause*) cessare; **to — on** inniti in (*with abl*), niti (*with abl*)
restitution *s* restitutio *f*; (*restoration*) refectio *f*
restive *adj* (*balky, unruly*) contumax; (*impatient*) impatiens
restless *adj* inquietus, turbidus, tumultuosus; (*agitated*) sollicitus; **—ly** inquiete, turbulenter
restoration *s* restauratio, refectio, renovatio *f*
restore *vt* restituěre, redděre; (*to re-*

build) restaurare, reficĕre; (*to health*) recurare, recreare; **to — to order** in integrum reducĕre
restrain *vt* cohibēre, coercēre, continēre; (*to prevent*) impedire
restraint *s* temperantia, moderatio *f*
restrict *vt* cohibēre, restringĕre, circumscribĕre, (de)finire
restriction *s* modus, finis *m*, limitatio *f*
result *s* exit·us -ūs, event·us -ūs *m*; eventum *n*; **without —** nequiquam
result *vi* evenire, fieri, evadĕre
resume *vt* resumĕre, repetĕre
resumption *s* resumptio, continuatio *f*
resurrection *s* resurrectio *f*
resuscitate *vt* resuscitare
retail *vt* divendĕre
retailer *s* caupo, propola *m*
retain *vt* retinēre, obtinēre, conservare
retainer *s* (*adherent*) cliens, asectator, satelles *m*; (*fee*) arrabo *m*
retake *vt* recipĕre, recuperare
retaliate *vi* ulcisci
retaliation *s* ultio *f*
retard *vt* retardare
retch *vi* nauseare
retention *s* retentio, conservatio *f*
retentive *adj* tenax
reticence *s* taciturnitas *f*
reticent *adj* taciturnus
retinue *s* comitat·us -ūs *m*
retire *vi* recedĕre, regredi; (*from office*) abire; (*for the night*) dormitum ire
retired *adj* (*of place*) remotus, solitarius; (*from work*) emeritus
retirement *s* (*act*) recess·us -ūs *m*, abdicatio *f*; (*state*) otium *n*, solitudo *f*
retiring *adj* modestus
retort *s* responsum *n*
retort *vt* respondēre
retrace *vt* repetĕre, iterare
retract *vt* revocare, recantare, renuntiare
retraction *s* retractatio *f*
retreat *vi* recedĕre, refugĕre, se recipĕre, pedem referre
retreat *s* (*act*) recess·us -ūs *m*, fuga *f*; (*place*) recess·us -ūs *m*, refugium *n*; (mil) recept·us -ūs *m*
retrench *vt* recidĕre
retrenchment *s* recisio *f*
retribution *s* compensatio, poena *f*
retrieve *vt* recuperare, recipĕre
retrogression *s* regress·us -ūs, retrogress·us -ūs *m*
retrospect *s* retrospect·us -ūs *m*; **in —** respicienti
retrospective *adj* respiciens; **—ly** retro
return *s* (*coming back*) redit·us -ūs *m*; (*repayment*) remuneratio *f*; (*income, profit*) fruct·us -ūs *m*
return *vt* (*to give back*) reddĕre, restituĕre, referre; *vi* (*to go back*) redire; (*to come back*) revenire, reverti
reunion *s* readunatio *f*, convivium *n*
reunite *vt* iterum conjungĕre; reconciliare; *vi* reconciliari
reveal *vt* retegĕre, recludĕre, aperire; (*to unveil*) revelare
revel *s* comissatio, bacchatio *f*; **—s** orgia *n pl*
revel *vi* comissari, debacchari, luxuriare *or* luxuriari
revelation *s* patefactio, revelatio *f*
reveler *s* comissator *m*
revelry *s* comissatio *f*, orgia *n pl*
revenge *vt* ulcisci
revenge *s* ultio, vindicta *f*; **to take — on** se vindicare in (*with acc*)
revengeful *adj* ulciscendi cupidus
revenue *s* redit·us -ūs, fruct·us -ūs *m*, vectigal *n*
reverberate *vi* resonare
reverberation *s* repercuss·us -ūs *m*, resonantia *f*
revere *vt* reverēri, venerari
reverence *s* reverentia, veneratio, religio, pietas *f*
reverend *adj* reverendus
reverent *adj* reverens, pius, religiosus; **—ly** reverenter, religiose
reverential *adj* venerabundus
reverie *s* cogitatio, meditatio *f*
reversal *s* infirmatio *f*
reverse *s* contrarium *m*; (*change*) conversio, commutatio *f*; (*defeat*) clades *f*
reverse *vt* invertĕre, (com)mutare; (*decision*) rescindĕre, abrogare
revert *vi* redire, reverti
review *s* recognitio *f*; (*critique*) censura *f*; (*mil*) recensio, lustratio *f*
review *vt* recensēre, inspicĕre; (*mil*) recensēre, lustrare
reviewer *s* censor, editor *m*
revile *vt* maledicĕre (*with dat*), insectari
revise *vt* corrigĕre, recognoscĕre
revision *s* emendatio *f*; (*of literary work*) recensio, lima *f*
revisit *vt* revisĕre, revisitare
revival *s* redanimatio *f*; (*fig*) renovatio *f*
revive *vt* resuscitare; (*to renew*) renovare; (*to encourage*) animare, instigare, excitare; *vi* reviviscĕre
revocation *s* revocatio *f*
revoke *vt* revocare, renuntiare; (*a law*) rescindĕre
revolt *vt* offendĕre; *vi* rebellare, desciscĕre, deficĕre
revolt *s* rebellio, seditio, defectio *f*
revolting *adj* taeter, foedus
revolution *s* conversio *f*; (*change*) commutatio *f*; (*of planets*) ambit·us -ūs *m*; (*pol*) res novae *f pl*, mot·us -ūs *m*
revolutionary *adj* seditiosus, novarum rerum cupidus
revolutionize *vt* novare
revolve *vt* (*in mind*) meditari, volutare; *vi* revolvi, se (re)volvĕre
revulsion *s* taedium, fastidium *n*; **to cause —** fastidium movĕre
reward *s* praemium *n*
reward *vt* remunerare, compensare
rewrite *vt* rescribĕre
rhapsody *s* rhapsodia *f*
rhetoric *s* rhetorica *n pl* **or** *f*

rhetorical *adj* rhetoricus, oratorius; **to practice —** declamare
rhetorician *s* rhetor *m*
rheumatism *s* dolor artuum *m*
rhinoceros *s* rhinoceros *m*
rhubarb *s* radix Pontica *f*
rhyme *s* homoeteleuton *n*
rhythm *s* numerus, rhythmus *m*
rhythmical *adj* numerosus
rib *s* costa *f*
ribald *adj* obscenus, spurcus
ribaldry *s* obscenitas *f*
ribbed *adj* costatus, striatus
ribbon *s* infula *f*
rice *s* oryza *f*
rich *adj* dives, locuples; (*of soil*) fertilis, uber, opimus; (*food*) pinguis; (*costly*) pretiosus, lautus; **—ly** copiose, pretiose, laute
riches *s* divitiae, opes *f pl*
rickety *adj* instabilis
rid *vt* liberare; **to get — of** dimittěre, deponěre, exuěre
riddle *s* aenigma *n*
ride *vt* **to — a horse** equo vehi; *vi* equitare; vehi; **to — away** *or* **off** avehi
ride *s* (*on horseback*) equitatio *f*; (*in carriage*) vectio *f*
rider *s* eques *m*; (*in carriage*) vector *m*; (*attached to documents*) adjectio *f*
ridge *s* jugum, dorsum *n*
ridicule *s* ridiculum, ludibrium *n*, irris·us -ūs *m*
ridicule *vt* irriděre
ridiculous *adj* ridiculus; **—ly** ridicule
riding *s* equitatio *f*
rife *adj* frequens
riffraff *s* plebecula, faex populi *f*
rifle *vt* despoliare, diripěre
rig *vt* adornare; (*ship*) armare, ornare
rigging *s* armamenta *n pl*, rudentes *m pl*
right *adj* rectus; (*just*) aequus, justus; (*opposed to left*) dexter; (*suitable*) idoneus, aptus; (*true*) verus, rectus; **—ly** recte, rite, juste, vere
right *s* (*hand*) dextra *f*; (*law*) jus, fas, aequum *n*; **on the —** a dextra
right *vt* emendare, corrigěre; (*to replace*) restituěre; (*to avenge*) vindicare, ulcisci
righteous *adj* justus, pius; **—ly** juste, pie
righteousness *s* justitia, pietas, probitas *f*
rightful *adj* legitimus, justus; **—ly** juste
rigid *adj* rigidus; **—ly** rigide
rigidity *s* rigiditas *f*
rigor *s* severitas, duritia *f*
rigorous *adj* severus, asper; (*hardy*) durus
rill *s* rivulus *m*
rim *s* ora, margo *f*, labrum *n*
rind *s* crusta *f*
ring *s* anulus *m*; (*of people*) corona *f*; (*for fighting*) arena *f*; (*sound*) sonit·us -ūs *m*; (*of bells*) tinnit·us -ūs *m*
ring *vt* **to — a bell** tintinnabulum tractare; *vi* tinnire, resonare
ringing *s* tinnit·us -ūs *m*
ringleader *s* auctor, dux *m*
rinse *vt* colluěre, eluěre
rinsing *s* colluvies *f*
riot *s* tumult·us -ūs, mot·us -ūs *m*; **to run —** luxuriari
riot *vi* seditionem movēre, tumultuari
rioter *s* seditiosus *m*
riotous *adj* seditiosus, tumultuosus; **— living** luxuria *f*
rip *vt* scinděre; **to — apart** discinděre, diffinděre; (*fig*) discerpěre
ripe *adj* mitis, maturus, tempestivus
ripen *vt* maturare; *vi* maturescěre
ripple *s* fluctuculus *m*
ripple *vi* trepidare
rise *vi* oriri, surgěre; (*from sleep*) expergisci; (*to mount*) ascenděre; (*to increase*) crescěre; (*of rioters*) consurgěre; (*of passion*) tumescěre; **to — again** resurgěre, reviviscěre; **to — up** exsurgěre
rise *s* (*ascent*) ascens·us -ūs *m*; (*origin*) origo *f*, ort·us -ūs *m*; (*increase*) incrementum *n*; (*slope*) clivus *m*; **to give — to** parěre
rising *s* (*of sun*) ort·us -ūs *m*; (*insurrection*) mot·us -ūs, tumult·us -ūs *m*
risk *s* periculum *n*; **to run a —** periculum subire, periclitari
risk *vt* in periculum vocare, periclitari
rite *s* rit·us -ūs *m*
ritual *s* rit·us -ūs *m*, caeremonia *f*
rival *s* rivalis, aemulus, competitor *m*
rival *vt* aemulari
rivalry *s* aemulatio *f*, certamen *n*; (*in love*) rivalitas *f*
river *s* flumen *n*, amnis *m*
rivet *s* clavus *m*
rivet *vt* (*eyes, attention*) defigěre
rivulet *s* rivus, rivulus *m*
road *s* via *f*, iter *n*; **on the —** in itinere; **to build a —** viam munire
roam *vi* errare, vagari
roar *s* fremit·us -ūs, rugit·us -ūs, strepit·us -ūs *m*
roar *vi* freměre, ruděre, rugire
roast *vt* torrēre; (*in a pan*) frigěre, assare, coquěre
roast *adj* assus
roast *s* assum *n*
rob *vt* spoliare, compilare, latrocinari
robber *s* latro, fur *m*
robbery *s* latrocinium *n*, spoliatio *f*
robe *s* vestis, palla *f*
robe *vt* vestire
robin *s* sylvia rubecula, rubisca *f*
robust *adj* robustus, validus, lacertosus
rock *s* saxum *n*; (*cliff*) scopulus *m*, rupes *f*
rock *vt* jactare; **to — a cradle** cunas agitare; *vi* vibrare, vacillare
rocket *s* missile *n*
rocky *adj* saxosus, scopulosus
rod *s* virga, ferula *f*
roe *s* caprea *f*; (*of fish*) ova *n pl*
roebuck *s* capreolus *m*
rogue *s* nequam (homo), furcifer *m*
roguish *adj* malus, improbus

roll *vt* volvĕre, versare; *vi* volvi; (*of tears*) labi
roll *s* (*book*) volumen *n*; (*of names*) catalogus *m*, album *n*; (*of bread*) collyra *f*
roller *s* cylindrus *m*
Roman *adj* Romanus
Roman *s* Romanus, Quiris *m*
romance *s* fabula, narratio ficta *f*; (*affair*) amores *m pl*
romantic *adj* fabulosus, commenticius, amatorius
roof *s* tectum, fastigium *n*; (*of mouth*) palatum *n*
roof *vt* contegĕre, integĕre
room *s* (*space*) spatium *n*, locus *m*; (*of house*) conclave *n*
roomy *adj* laxus, spatiosus
roost *s* pertica *f*
roost *vi* cubitare, insidēre
root *s* radix *f*; (*fig*) fons *m*, origo *f*; **to take —** coalescĕre
root *vt* **to become rooted** (*fig*) inveterascĕre; **to be rooted** inhaerēre; **to — out** eradicare, exstirpare; *vi* radices agĕre; (*fig*) inveterascĕre
rope *s* funis *m*, restis *f*
rose *s* rosa *f*
roseate *adj* roseus
rosy *adj* roseus, rosaceus
rot *vi* putrescĕre, tabescĕre
rot *s* putredo, tabes, caries *f*
rotate *vi* volvi, se convertĕre
rotation *s* ambit·us -ūs *m*, conversio *f*; (*succession*) vicissitudo *f*; **in —** ordine
rote *s* **by —** memoriter
rotten *adj* putridus, tabidus, cariosus
rotunda *s* tholus *m*
rouge *s* fucus *m*
rough *adj* asper; (*of character*) agrestis, durus; (*of weather*) inclemens; (*shaggy*) hirsutus; **—ly** aspere, duriter
roughen *vt* asperare
roughness *s* asperitas *f*; (*brutality*) feritas *f*
round *adj* rotundus, globosus; **—ly** aperte, plane, praecise
round *s* orbis, circulus *m*; (*series*) ambit·us -ūs *m*
round *vt* (*a corner*) circumire, flectĕre; (*a cape*) superare; **to — off** concludĕre, complēre
rouse *vt* excitare, animare
rout *s* fuga *f*; (*defeat*) clades *f*; (*crowd*) turba *f*
rout *vt* fugare, fundĕre
route *s* via *f*, iter *n*
routine *s* consuetudo *f*, ordo, us·us -ūs *m*
rove *vi* vagari, errare
rover *s* ambulator *m*
row *s* series *f*, ordo *m*; (*quarrel*) rixa *f*
row *vt* remis propellĕre; *vi* remigare
rower *s* remex *m*
rowing *s* remigatio *f*, remigium *n*
royal *adj* regalis, regius; **—ly** regaliter, regie
royalty *s* regia potestas *f*, regnum *n*
rub *vt* fricare; **to — away** *or* **off** detergēre
rub *s* fricatio *f*; (*fig*) difficultas *f*
rubbing *s* attrit·us -ūs, affrict·us -ūs *m*, fricatio, frictio *f*
rubbish *s* rudus *n*; (*fig*) quisquiliae *f pl*
rubble *s* rudus *n*
rubric *s* rubrica *f*
ruby *s* rubinus, carbunculus *m*
rudder *s* gubernaculum *n*
ruddy *adj* rubicundus, rubens, rutilus
rude *adj* rudis, rusticus, inurbanus; (*impertinent*) impudicus; **—ly** rustice, incondite
rudeness *s* rusticitas, inhumanitas, insolentia *f*
rudiment *s* elementum, initium, rudimentum, principium *n*
rudimentary *adj* inchoatus, elementarius
rue *vt* **I —** me paenitet (*with genit*)
rueful *adj* maestus, luctuosus
ruffian *s* sicarius, grassator *m*
ruffle *vt* agitare, turbare; (*to irritate*) commovēre
ruffle *s* limbus *m*
rug *s* stragulum *n*
rugged *adj* asper, praeruptus
ruin *s* pernicies *f*, exitium *n*; ruina *f*; **—s** ruinae *f pl*
ruin *vt* perdĕre, corrumpĕre; (*morally*) depravare
ruination *s* vastatio *f*
ruinous *adj* damnosus, exitiosus
rule *s* (*regulation*) praeceptum *n*, lex *f*; (*government*) regimen, imperium *n*, dominatio *f*; (*instrument*) regula, norma *f*
rule *vt* regĕre, moderari; *vi* regĕre, dominari
ruler *s* (*person*) rector, dominus, rex *m*; (*instrument*) regula *f*
ruling *s* edictum *n*
rum *s* sicera *f*
rumble *s* murmur *n*
rumble *vi* murmurare, crepitare, mugire
rumbling *s* murmur *n*, mugit·us -ūs *m*
ruminate *vi* ruminare
rumination *s* ruminatio *f*
rummage *vi* **to — through** rimari
rumor *s* rumor *m*, fama *f*
rump *s* clunis *f*
rumple *s* (*in garment*) plica, ruga *f*
rumple *vt* corrugare
run *vt* (*to manage*) gerĕre, administrare; **to — aground** impingĕre; **to — up** (*an account*) augēre; *vi* currĕre; (*to flow*) fluĕre; **to — about** discurrĕre, cursare; **to — after** sequi, petĕre, sectari; **to — aground** offendĕre; **to — away** aufugĕre; **to — away from** defugĕre; **to — down** decurrĕre; (*as water*) defluĕre; **to — for** conquirĕre; **to — foul of** collidi; **to — into** (*to meet*) incidĕre in (*with acc*); **to — off** aufugĕre; (*as water*) defluĕre; **to — on** percurrĕre, continuare; **to — out** excurrĕre; (*of time*) exire; (*of supplies*) deficĕre; **to — over** (*details*) percurrĕre; (*of fluids*) superfluĕre; **to — short** deficĕre; **to — through** (*to dissipate*)

dissipare; to — together concurrĕre; to — up accurrĕre; to — up against incurrĕre in (*with acc*)
runaway *s* transfuga *m*
runner *s* cursor *m*
running *s* curs·us -ūs *m*; (*flowing*) flux·us -ūs *m*
rupture *s* hernia *f*; seditio, dissensio *f*
rupture *vt* rumpĕre, abrumpĕre; *vi* rumpi
rural *adj* agrestis, rusticus
ruse *s* dolus *m*, fraus *f*
rush *s* (*plant*) juncus *m*; (*charge*) impet·us -ūs *m*
rush *vt* rapĕre; *vi* ruĕre, ferri; **to — forward** prorumpĕre, se proripĕre; **to — in** inruĕre, incurrĕre; **to — out** erumpĕre, evolare
russet *adj* russus, rufus, ravus
rust *s* rubigo, aerugo *f*; (*of iron*) ferrugo *f*
rust *vi* rubiginem contrahĕre
rustic *adj* rusticus, agrestis
rustic *s* rusticus *m*, ruricola *m & f*
rustle *vi* crepitare, increpare
rustle *s* crepit·us -ūs *m*
rusty *adj* rubiginosus, aeruginosus; **to become —** rubigine obduci; (*fig*) desuescĕre
rut *s* (*of wheel*) orbita *f*
ruthless *adj* immisericors, inexorabilis, crudelis; **—ly** incrudeliter
rye *s* secale *n*

S

Sabbath *s* sabbata *n pl*
saber *s* acinaces *m*
sable *adj* pullus, ater, niger
sable *s* (*fur*) pellis zibellina *f*
sack *s* saccus *m*; (*mil*) direptio *f*
sack *vt* (*mil*) vastare, diripĕre
sackcloth *s* cilicium *n*
sacred *adj* sacer, sanctus, sacrosanctus
sacrifice *s* (*act*) sacrificium *n*, immolatio *f*; (*victim*) hostia, victima *f*; (*fig*) jactura *f*
sacrifice *vt* immolare, mactare, sacrificare; (*fig*) devovēre
sacrilege *s* sacrilegium *n*
sacrilegious *adj* sacrilegus
sad *adj* tristis, maestus, miserabilis; **—ly** maeste
sadden *vt* contristare, dolore afficĕre
saddle *s* ephippium *n*
saddle *vt* imponĕre (*with acc of thing and dat of person*); **to — a horse** equum sternĕre
saddlebags *s* clitellae *f pl*
sadness *s* tristitia, maestitia *f*
safe *adj* tutus; (*without hurt*) incolumis; **— and sound** salvus; **—ly** tute
safe-conduct *s* tutela *f*, commeat·us -ūs *m*
safeguard *s* praesidium *n*, tutela *f*
safety *s* salus, incolumitas *f*; **in —** tuto
saffron *adj* croceus
sagacious *adj* sagax; **—ly** sagaciter
sagacity *s* sagacitas *f*
sage *s* (*wise man*) sapiens *m*
sage *adj* sapiens, prudens; **—ly** sapienter
sail *s* velum *n*; **to set —** vela dare
sail *vi* nave vehi, vela facĕre, navigare
sailing *s* navigatio *f*
sailor *s* nauta *m*
saint *s* vir sanctus *m*, femina sancta *f*
saintly *adj* sanctus, pius
sake *s* **for the — of** gratiā (*with genit*), causā (*with genit*), pro (*with abl*)
salad *s* acetaria *n pl*, moretum *n*
salamander *s* salamandra *f*
salary *s* salarium *n*, merces *f*
sale *s* venditio *f*; **for —** venalis; **to put up for —** venum dare
salesman *s* venditor *m*
salient *adj* prominens, saliens
saline *adj* salsus
saliva *s* saliva *f*, sputum *n*
sallow *adj* pallidus, luridus
sally *s* eruptio *f*, impet·us -ūs *m*
sally *vi* eruptionem facĕre, erumpĕre
salmon *s* salmo *m*
saloon *s* caupona *f*
salt *s* sal *m*
salt *vt* salire, sale condire
salting *s* salsura *f*
saltless *adj* insulsus
salt mine *s* salifodina *f*
salt shaker *s* salinum *n*
salt water *s* aqua marina *f*
salubrious *adj* salubris
salutary *adj* salutaris, utilis
salutation *s* salutatio, salus *f*
salute *s* salus, salutatio *f*
salute *vt* salutare
salvage *vt* servare, eripĕre
salvation *s* salus *f*
salve *s* unguentum *n*
same *adj* idem; **at the — time** eodem tempore, simul; **the very —** ipsissimus
sameness *s* identitas *f*
sample *s* exemplum, specimen *n*
sample *vt* libare
sanctify *vt* sanctificare, consecrare
sanctimonious *adj* sanctitatem affectans
sanction *s* comprobatio, auctoritas, confirmatio *f*
sanction *vt* ratum facĕre, sancire
sanctity *s* sanctitas, sanctimonia *f*
sanctuary *s* sanctuarium *n*; (*refuge*) asylum *n*
sand *s* (h)arena *f*
sandal *s* solea, crepida *f*
sandstone *s* tofus, tophus *m*
sandy *adj* (h)arenosus, sabulosus, (h)arenaceus; (*in color*) rufus

sane *adj* sanus
sanguinary *adj* sanguinarius, cruentus
sanguine *adj* sanguineus, alacer
sanitary *adj* salubris
sanity *s* sanitas, mens sana *f*
sap *s* sucus *m*
sap *vt* subruĕre, haurire
sapling *s* surculus *m*
Sapphic *adj* Sapphicus
sapphire *s* sapphirus *f*
sarcasm *s* dicacitas *f*
sarcastic *adj* acerbus, mordax; **—ally** acerbe, amare
sarcophagus *s* sarcophagus *m*
sardine *s* sarda *f*
sardonic *adj* amarus
sash *s* cingillum *n*, zona *f*
Satan *s* Satanas, Satan *m*
satchel *s* sacculus *m*, pera *f*
satellite *s* satelles *m & f*
satiate *vt* satiare, saturare
satire *s* satura *f*
satirical *adj* acerbus, satiricus
satirist *s* derisor, saturarum scriptor *m*
satirize *vt* notare, perstringĕre
satisfaction *s* compensatio *f*; (*feeling*) voluptas *f*
satisfactorily *adv* ex sententia (meā, tuā, *etc.*)
satisfactory *adj* idoneus, jucundus, gratus
satisfied *adj* contentus
satisfy *vt* satisfacĕre (*with dat*); (*to indemnify*) compensare; (*desires*) explēre
satrap *s* satrapes *m*
saturate *vt* saturare, imbuĕre
satyr *s* satyrus *m*
sauce *s* condimentum *n*; (*of meat*) eliquamen *n*
saucer *s* patella, scutella *f*
saucily *adv* petulanter
saucy *adj* petulans, procax, protervus
saunter *vi* vagari, ambulari
sausage *s* farcimen *n*
savage *adj* ferus, efferatus; (*cruel*) saevus, atrox, immanis; **—ly** crudeliter, immaniter
save *vt* servare, conservare; (*from danger*) liberare, eripĕre; **to — up** reservare
save *prep* praeter (*with acc*)
saving *s* conservatio *f*; **—s** peculium *n*
savior *s* servator, liberator *m*
Saviour *s* Salvator (mundi) *m*
savor *s* sapor, gust·us -ūs *m*
savor *vi* sapĕre
savory *adj* sapidus
saw *s* (*tool*) serra *f*; (*saying*) proverbium *n*
saw *vt* serrā secare; *vi* serram ducĕre
sawdust *s* scobis *f*
say *vt* dicĕre; **that is to —** scilicet; **to — that . . . not** negare
saying *s* dictum, proverbium *n*
scab *s* crusta *f*
scabbard *s* vagina *f*
scaffold *s* tabulatum *n*, fala *f*
scald *vt* urĕre
scale *s* (*of fish*) squama *f*; (*for weighing*) libra, trutina *f*; (*mus*) diagramma *n*; (*gradation*) grad·us -ūs *m*
scale *vt* (*fish*) desquamare; **to — a wall** murum per scalas ascendĕre
scallop *s* pecten *m*
scalp *s* pericranium *n*
scaly *adj* squamosus, squameus
scamp *s* furcifer *m*
scamper *vi* cursare; **to — about** discurrĕre, cursitare; **to — away** aufugĕre
scan *vt* examinare, explorare; (*verses*) scandĕre
scandal *s* ignominia *f*, opprobrium *n*
scandalize *vt* offendĕre
scandalous *adj* probrosus, flagitiosus
scantily *adv* exigue, anguste
scanty *adj* tenuis, exiguus, exilis
scapegoat *s* piaculum *n*
scar *s* cicatrix *f*
scarce *adj* rarus; **—ly** vix, aegre
scarcity *s* paucitas, inopia *f*
scare *vt* terrēre, territare
scarecrow *s* terriculum *n*
scarf *s* fascia *f*, focale *n*
scarlet *s* coccum *n*
scarlet *adj* coccinus, coccineus
scathing *adj* acerbus, aculeatus
scatter *vt* spargĕre, dispergĕre, dissipare; *vi* dilabi, diffugĕre
scavenger *s* cloacarius *m*
scene *s* prospect·us -ūs *m*, spectaculum *n*; (*on stage*) scaena *f*; (*place*) locus *m*
scenery *s* (*in theater*) scaenae apparat·us -ūs *m*; (*of nature*) species regionis *f*
scent *s* (*sense*) odorat·us -ūs *m*; (*of dogs*) sagacitas *f*; (*fragrance*) odor *m*
scent *vt* odorari
scented *adj* odoratus
scepter *s* sceptrum *n*
sceptic *s* scepticus *m*
sceptical *adj* dubitans, incredulus
schedule *s* ratio *f*
scheme *s* consilium *n*
scheme *vt & vi* moliri, machinari
schism *s* schisma, discidium *n*
scholar *s* litteratus *m*
scholarly *adj* litteratus, doctus
scholarship *s* litterae *f pl*, eruditio *f*
scholastic *adj* scholasticus
scholiast *s* scholiastes, interpres *m*
school *s* ludus *m*, schola *f*; (*group holding like opinions*) secta *f*
schoolboy *s* discipulus *m*
schoolmaster *s* magister *m*
schoolroom *s* schola *f*
science *s* scientia, doctrina, disciplina, ars *f*
scientific *adj* physicus; **—ally** physice; (*systematically*) ratione
scientist *s* physicus *m*
scimitar *s* acinaces *m*
scion *s* edit·us -ūs *m*, progenies *f*
scissors *s* forfex *f*
scoff *s* irrisio, derisio, cavillatio *f*
scoff *vi* cavillari; **to — at** irridēre, deridēre
scoffer *s* derisor, irrisor *m*

scold *vt* objurgare, increpare; *vi* desaevire
scolding *s* objurgatio *f*
scoop *s* trulla *f*
scoop *vt* **to — out** excavare
scope *s* campus *m*, spatium *n*
scorch *vt* adurĕre, torrēre
score *s* nota *f*; (*total*) summa *f*; (*twenty*) viginti; (*reckoning*) ratio *f*
score *vt* notare
scorn *s* contemptio *f*
scorn *vt* contemnĕre, spernĕre, aspernari
scornful *adj* fastidiosus; **—ly** fastidiose, contemptim
scorpion *s* scorpio, scorpius *m*
Scot *adj* Scoticus
Scotchman *s* Scotus *m*
Scotland *s* Scotia *f*
Scottish *adj* Scoticus
scoundrel *s* nebulo, furcifer *m*
scour *vt* (*to rub clean*) (de)tergēre; (*to range over*) pervagari, percurrĕre
scourge *s* flagellum *n*; (*fig*) pestis *f*
scourge *vt* verberare
scourging *s* verberatio *f*, verbera *n pl*
scout *s* explorator, speculator *m*
scout *vt* speculari, explorare
scowl *vi* frontem contrahĕre
scowlingly *adv* fronte contractā
scramble *vi* **to — up** scandĕre, escendĕre
scrap *s* fragmentum, frustum *n*
scrape *vt* radĕre, scabĕre; **to — together** corradĕre
scrape *s* difficultas *f*; (*quarrel*) rixa *f*
scraper *s* radula *f*
scraping *s* rasura *f*; **—s** ramenta *n pl*
scratch *s* levis incisura *f*
scratch *vt* radĕre, scalpĕre
scrawl *s* scriptio mala *f*
scrawl *vt & vi* male scribĕre
scream *s* ululat·us -ūs, clamor *m*; (*of an infant*) vagit·us -ūs *m*
scream *vi* ululare, clamitare
screech *s* stridor *m*
screech *vi* stridēre
screen *s* umbraculum *n*, obex *m*
screen *vt* protegĕre
screw *s* cochlea *f*
screw *vt* torquēre
scribble *vt & vi* scriptitare
scribe *s* scriba *m*
script *s* scriptum *n*; (*hand*) man·us -ūs *f*
scrofulous *adj* strumosus
scroll *s* volumen *n*, schedula *f*
scrub *vt* defricare, detergēre
scruple *s* scrupulus *m*, religio, dubitatio *f*
scrupulous *adj* religiosus, anxius; **—ly** religiose
scrutinize *vt* scrutari, perscrutari
scrutiny *s* scrutatio, perscrutatio *f*
scud *vi* celeriter aufugĕre
scuffle *s* rixa *f*
scuffle *vi* rixari
sculptor *s* sculptor, scalptor *m*
sculpture *s* (*art*) sculptura *f*; (*work*) opus, signum *n*
sculpture *vt* sculpĕre
scum *s* spuma *f*; (*fig*) sentina *f*
scurrilous *adj* scurrilis
scurvy *s* scorbutus *m*
scutcheon *s* scutum *n*
scythe *s* falx *f*
sea *s* mare, aequor *n*, pontus *m*
sea captain *s* navarchus *m*
seacoast *s* ora maritima *f*
seafaring *adj* maritimus, nauticus
sea gull *s* larus *m*
seal *s* sigillum, signum *n*; (*animal*) phoca *f*
seal *vt* signare; (*fig*) sancire; **to — up** obsignare
seam *s* sutura *f*
seaman *s* nauta *m*
seamanship *s* nauticarum rerum us·us -ūs *m*, ars navigandi *f*
sear *vt* adurĕre
search *s* investigatio, scrutatio *f*
search *vt* investigare, explorare; (*a person*) excutĕre; *vi* **to — for** quaerĕre, exquirĕre; **to — out** explorare
seasick *adj* nauseabundus; **to be —** nauseare
season *s* tempestas *f*, anni tempus *n*; (*proper time*) opportunitas *f*, tempus *n*; **in —** tempestive
season *vt* condire; (*fig*) assuefacĕre, durare
seasonable *adj* tempestivus, opportunus
seasoning *s* condimentum *n*
seat *s* sedes, sella *f*; (*dwelling*) sedes *f*, domicilium *n*
seat *vt* sede locare; **to — oneself** considĕre
seaweed *s* alga *f*
secede *vi* secedĕre
secession *s* secessio *f*
seclude *vt* secludĕre, removēre, abdĕre
secluded *adj* remotus, solitarius
seclusion *s* solitudo *f*, locus remotus *m*
second *adj* secundus, alter; **a — time** iterum; **—ly** deinde, tum
second *s* (*person*) adjutor *m*; (*of time*) punctum temporis *n*
second *vt* adesse (*with dat*), favēre (*with dat*), adjuvare
secondary *adj* secundarius, inferior
secondhand *adj* alienus, tritus
second-rate *adj* inferior
secrecy *s* secretum *n*; (*keeping secret*) silentium *n*
secret *adj* secretus, occultus, arcanus; **to keep —** celare; **—ly** clam
secret *s* secretum *n*, res arcana *f*; **in —** clam
secretary *s* scriba, amanuensis *m*
secrete *vt* celare, occultare, abdĕre
secretion *s* secretio *f*
sect *s* secta *f*
section *s* pars, sectio *f*
sector *s* sector *m*, regio *f*
secular *adj* profanus
secure *adj* tutus; **—ly** tuto
secure *vt* confirmare, munire; (*to obtain*) parare, nancisci; (*to fasten*) religare

security *s* salus, incolumitas *f*; (*pledge*) satisdatio *f*, pignus *n*
sedan *s* lectica *f*
sedate *adj* gravis, sedatus; **—ly** graviter, sedate
sedentary *adj* sedentarius
sedge *s* ulva, carex *f*
sediment *s* sedimentum *n*, faex *f*
sedition *s* seditio, rebellio *f*
seditious *adj* seditiosus, turbulentus; **—ly** seditiose
seduce *vt* seducĕre, corrumpĕre, depravare
seducer *s* corruptor *m*
seduction *s* corruptela *f*
seductive *adj* blandus; **—ly** blande
see *vt & vi* vidēre, cernĕre, conspicĕre; (*to understand*) vidēre, intellegĕre, sentire; **to go to —** visĕre; **to — to** curare
seed *s* semen *n*; (*offspring*) progenies *f*; (*of fruit*) acinum *n*
seedling *s* surculus *m*
seek *vt* quaerĕre, petĕre; **to — to** conari (*with inf*), laborare (*with inf*)
seem *vi* vidēri
seeming *adj* speciosus; **—ly** in speciem, ut videtur
seemly *adj* decens, decorus
seep *vi* manare
seer *s* vates *m*
seethe *vi* fervēre, aestuare
segment *s* segmentum *n*
segregate *vt* segregare, secernĕre
segregation *s* separatio *f*
seize *vt* prehendĕre, arripĕre, rapĕre; (*mil*) occupare; (*fig*) afficĕre
seizure *s* comprehensio, occupatio *f*
seldom *adv* raro
select *vt* seligĕre, eligĕre, deligĕre
select *adj* electus, lectus, exquisitus
selection *s* (*act*) selectio *f*; (*things chosen*) electa *n pl*
self-confident *adj* sibi fidens, confidens
self-conscious *adj* pudibundus
self-control *s* continentia, temperantia *f*
self-denial *s* abstinentia *f*
self-evident *adj* manifestus
self-indulgent *adj* intemperans
selfish *adj* avarus
selfishness *s* avaritia *f*
self-respect *s* pudor *m*
sell *vt* vendĕre; *vi* venire
seller *s* venditor *m*
semblance *s* species, similitudo *f*
semicircle *s* hemicyclium *n*
semicircular *adj* semicirculus
senate *s* senat·us -ūs *m*; (*building*) curia *f*
senator *s* senator *m*
senatorial *adj* senatorius
send *vt* mittĕre; (*on public business*) legare; **to — away** dimittĕre; **to — for** arcessĕre; **to — forward** praemittĕre
senile *adj* senilis, aetate provectus
senior *adj* natu major
seniority *s* aetatis praerogativa *f*
sensation *s* sens·us -ūs *m*; (*fig*) mirum *n*
sense *s* (*faculty; meaning*) sens·us -ūs *m*; (*understanding*) prudentia *f*; (*meaning*) vis, significatio *f*
sense *vt* sentire
senseless *adj* absurdus, ineptus; (*unconscious*) omni sensu carens
sensible *adj* sapiens, prudens
sensibly *adv* prudenter, sapienter
sensitive *adj* sensilis, patibilis; (*touchy*) mollis
sensual *adj* voluptarius, libidinosus; **—ly** libidinose
sensualist *s* homo voluptarius *m*
sensuality *s* libido *f*
sentence *s* (*gram*) sententia *f*; (*law*) judicium *n*; **to pass —** judicare
sentence *vt* damnare, condemnare
sententious *adj* sententiosus; **—ly** sententiose
sentiment *s* (*opinion*) sententia, opinio *f*; (*feeling*) sens·us -ūs *m*
sentimental *adj* mollis, effeminatus
sentimentality *s* mollities animi *f*
sentinel *s* custos, vigil *m*
sentry *s* custos, vigil *m*; **sentries** excubiae, stationes, vigiliae *f pl*
separable *adj* separabilis
separate *adj* separatus, disjunctus; **—ly** separatim
separate *vt* separare, disjungĕre, dividĕre; *vi* separari, disjungi
separation *s* separatio, disjunctio *f*
September *s* (mensis) September *m*
sepulcher *s* sepulcrum *n*
sepulchral *adj* sepulcralis
sequel *s* exit·us -ūs *m*
sequence *s* ordo *m*, series *f*
seraph *s* seraphus *m*
serenade *vt* occentare
serene *adj* serenus, tranquillus; **—ly** serene
serenity *s* serenitas, tranquillitas *f*
serf *s* servus *m*
serfdom *s* servitium *n*, servitus *f*
sergeant *s* optio *m*
series *s* series *f*, ordo *m*
serious *adj* serius, gravis; **—ly** serio
seriousness *s* gravitas *f*, serium *n*
sermon *s* oratio sacra *f*
serpent *s* serpens *f*, anguis *m & f*
servant *s* famulus *m*, famula *f*, servus *m*, serva *f*; (*public servant*) minister *m*
serve *vt* servire (*with dat*); (*food*) apponĕre; (*to be useful to*) prodesse (*with dat*); **to — a sentence** poenam subire; *vi* (*mil*) merēre, militare; (*to suffice*) sufficĕre
service *s* (*favor*) officium *n*; (*mil*) militia *f*, stipendia *n pl*; (*work*) ministerium *n*; **to be of — to** prodesse (*with dat*), bene merēri de (*with abl*)
serviceable *adj* utilis
servile *adj* servilis, humilis
servility *s* humilitas *f*, animus abjectus *m*
servitude *s* servitus *f*
session *s* sessio *f*, convent·us -ūs *m*
set *vt* ponĕre, sistĕre, collocare; (*course*) dirigĕre; (*example*) dare; (*limit*) imponĕre; (*sail*) dare; (*table*) instruĕre; **to — apart** secernĕre, seponĕre; **to — aside** ponĕre; (*fig*)

rescindĕre; **to — down** deponĕre; (*in writing*) perscribĕre; **to — forth** exponĕre; **to — free** liberare; **to — in motion** ciēre; **to — in order** componĕre; **to — off** (*to adorn*) adornare; **to — on fire** incendĕre, accendĕre; **to — someone over** aliquem praeficĕre (*with dat*); **to — up** statuĕre; *vi* (*of stars, etc.*) occidĕre; **to — in** (*to begin*) incipĕre; **to — out** proficisci
set *adj* (*fixed*) certus, praescriptus
set *s* congeries *f*
setting *s* occas·us -ūs *m*
settle *vt* statuĕre; (*business*) transigĕre; (*colony*) deducĕre; (*argument*) componĕre; (*debts*) solvĕre, expedire; *vi* (*to take up residence*) considĕre; (*to sink*) subsidĕre
settlement *s* constitutio *f*; (*agreement*) pactum *n*; (*colony*) colonia *f*; (*of liquids*) sedimentum *n*
settler *s* colonus *m*
seven *adj* septem; **— times** septies
sevenfold *adj* septemplex
seventeen *adj* septemdecim, decem et septem
seventeenth *adj* septimus decimus
seventh *adj* septimus; **the — time** septimum
seventieth *adj* septuagesimus
seventy *adj* septuaginta
sever *vt* separare; *vi* disjungi
several *adj* aliquot, complures; **—ly** singulatim
severe *adj* severus, gravis, durus; (*of weather*) asper; **—ly** severe, graviter
severity *s* severitas, gravitas *f*
sew *vt* suĕre; **to — up** consuĕre
sewer *s* cloaca *f*
sewing *s* sutura *f*
sex *s* sex·us -ūs *m*
sextant *s* sextans *m*
sexton *s* aedituus *m*
sexual *adj* sexualis
shabbily *adv* sordide, obsolete
shabbiness *s* sordes *f pl*
shabby *adj* sordidus, obsoletus
shackle *vt* compedibus constringĕre
shackles *s* vincula *n pl*, compedes *f pl*
shade *s* umbra *f*; **—s** (*of the dead*) manes *m pl*
shade *vt* opacare, adumbrare
shadow *s* umbra *f*
shadowy *adj* umbrosus, opacus; (*fig*) inanis, vanus
shady *adj* umbrosus, opacus
shaft *s* (*arrow*) sagitta *f*; (*of spear*) hastile *n*; (*of mine*) puteus *m*
shaggy *adj* hirsutus, villosus
shake *vt* quatĕre, concutĕre; (*head*) nutare; *vi* tremĕre; (*to totter*) vacillare
shaking *s* quassatio *f*; (*with cold, fear, etc.*) tremor, horror *m*
shaky *adj* instabilis
shallow *adj* brevis, vadosus; (*fig*) insulsus, levis
sham *s* dolus *m*, simulatio, species *f*
sham *adj* fictus, simulatus
shambles *s* laniena *f*, laniarium *n*
shame *s* pudor *m*; (*disgrace*) dedecus *n*, infamia, ignominia *f*
shame *vt* ruborem incutĕre (*with dat*)
shamefaced *adj* pudens, verecundus
shameful *adj* probrosus, turpis; **—ly** probrose, turpiter
shameless *adj* impudens; **—ly** impudenter
shamrock *s* trifolium *n*
shank *s* crus *n*
shanty *s* tugurium *n*
shape *s* forma, figura, facies *f*
shape *vt* formare, fingĕre
shapeless *adj* informis, deformis
shapely *adj* formosus
share *s* pars, portio *f*; (*of plow*) vomer *m*
share *vt* partire, impertire; particeps esse (*with genit*)
shark *s* p(r)istix *m*
sharp acutus; (*bitter*) acer, acerbus; (*keen*) acutus, acer, sagax; **—ly** acriter, acute; (*bitterly*) acerbe
sharpen *vt* acuĕre
shatter *vt* quassare, confringĕre; (*fig*) frangĕre
shave *vt* radĕre
shavings *s* ramenta *n pl*
shawl *s* amiculum *n*
she *pron* ea, illa, haec
sheaf *s* manipulus, fascis *m*
shear *vt* tondēre
shearing *s* tonsura *f*
shears *s* forfices *f pl*
sheath *s* vagina *f*
sheathe *vt* in vaginam recondĕre
shed *vt* fundĕre, effundĕre
shed *s* tugurium *n*; (*mil*) vinea *f*
sheep *s* ovis *f*
sheepfold *s* ovile *n*
sheephook *s* pedum, baculum pastorale *n*
sheepish *adj* pudibundus; **—ly** pudenter
sheepskin *s* pellis ovilla *f*
sheer *adj* merus
sheet *s* linteum *n*; (*of paper*) plagula, scheda *f*; (*of metal*) lamina *f*
shelf *s* pluteus *m*, tabula *f*, pegma *n*
shell *s* concha, crusta *f*; (*husk*) folliculus *m*; (*of nuts, etc.*) putamen *n*
shell *vt* decorticare
shellfish *s* concha *f*
shelter *s* tegmen *n*; (*refuge*) refugium *n*; (*lodgings*) hospitium *n*
shelter *vt* tegĕre, defendĕre; (*refugee*) excipĕre
shepherd *s* pastor, opilio, pecorum custos *m*
shield *s* scutum *n*, parma *f*
shield *vt* tegĕre, protegĕre
shield bearer *s* scutigerulus, armiger *m*
shift *vt* mutare, amovēre; *vi* (*as the wind*) vertĕre; (*to change position*) se movēre, mutari
shift *s* (*change*) mutatio *f*
shifty *adj* varius, mobilis
shin *s* tibia *f*, crus *n*
shine *s* nitor *m*
shine *vi* lucēre, fulgēre, nitēre; **to — forth** elucēre, enitēre, exsplen-

descĕre; **to — on** *or* **upon** affulgēre (*with dat*)
shiny *adj* lucidus, fulgidus, nitidus
ship *s* navis *f*, navigium *n*
ship *vt* navi invehĕre
shipbuilder *s* naupegus *m*
shipbuilding *s* architectura navalis *f*
shipmaster *s* navicularius *m*
shipwreck *s* naufragium *n*; **to suffer —** naufragium facĕre
shipwrecked *adj* naufragus
shirk *vt* defugĕre, detrectare
shirt *s* subulca, camisia *f*
shiver *vi* contremiscĕre, horrēre
shoal *s* caterva *f*, grex *m*; (*shallow*) brevia *n pl*
shock *vt* percutĕre, percellĕre; (*fig*) offendĕre
shock *s* concussio *f*, impet·us -ūs *m*; (*fig*) offensio *f*
shocking *adj* flagitiosus, atrox
shoe *s* calceus *m*
shoemaker *s* sutor *m*
shoot *vt* (*missile*) conjicĕre, jaculari; (*person*) transfigĕre; *vi* volare
shoot *s* surculus *m*
shooting star *s* fax caelestis *f*
shop *s* taberna, officina *f*
shopkeeper *s* tabernarius *m*
shore *s* litus *n*, ora *f*
short *adj* brevis; **to run —** deficĕre; **—ly** brevi, mox
shortage *s* inopia *f*
shortcoming *s* defect·us -ūs *m*, delictum *n*
shorten *vt* coarctare, contrahĕre; *vi* contrahi, minui
shorthand *s* notae breviores *f pl*
shortness *s* brevitas, exiguitas *f*; **— of breath** asthma *n*
short-sighted *adj* myops; (*fig*) improvidus, imprudens
short-winded *adj* anhelus
shot *s* ict·us -ūs *m*; (*reach, range*) jact·us -ūs *m*
should *vi* debēre; **I — go** mihi eundum est
shoulder *s* (h)umerus *m*; (*of animal*) armus *m*
shoulder *vt* suscipĕre
shout *s* clamor *m*, acclamatio *f*
shout *vt & vi* clamare, acclamare, vociferari
shove *vt* trudĕre, pulsare
shovel *s* pala *f*, rutrum *n*
shovel *vt* palā tollĕre
show *vt* monstrare; (*to display*) exhibēre; (*to teach*) docēre; **to — off** ostendĕre; *vi* **to — off** se jactare
show *s* (*appearance*) species *f*; (*display*) ostentatio *f*; (*pretense*) simulatio *f*; (*entertainment*) spectaculum *n*
shower *s* imber *m*
shower *vt* fundĕre, effundĕre
showy *adj* speciosus
shred *s* segmentum panni *n*; (*scrap*) frustum *n*
shrew *s* mulier jurgiosa *f*
shrewd *adj* acutus, astutus, callidus, sagax; **—ly** acute, callide, sagaciter
shrewdness *s* calliditas, astutia, sagacitas *f*
shriek *s* ululat·us -ūs *m*, ejulatio *f*
shriek *vi* ululare, ejulare
shrill *adj* peracutus, stridulus
shrimp *s* cancer pagurus *m*; (*person*) pumilio, homulus *m*
shrine *s* fanum, delubrum *n*
shrink *vt* contrahĕre; *vi* contrahi; (*to withdraw*) refugĕre; **to — from** abhorrēre ab (*with abl*), refugĕre ab (*with abl*)
shrivel *vt* corrugare, torrefacĕre; *vi* corrugari, torrescĕre
shroud *s* integumentum *n*; (*of ship*) rudentes *m pl*
shroud *vt* involvĕre, obducĕre
shrub *s* frutex *m*
shrubbery *s* fruticetum *n*
shrug *s* (h)umerorum allevatio *f*
shrug *vt* **to — the shoulders** (h)umeros contrahĕre *or* allevare
shudder *vi* horrēre; **to — at** horrēre
shuffle *vt* miscēre; *vi* claudicare
shun *vt* vitare, devitare, fugĕre
shut *vt* claudĕre, occludĕre; **to — out** excludĕre; **to — up** concludĕre; *vi* **to — up** conticescĕre
shutter *s* claustrum *n*, foricula *f*
shy *adj* timidus, pudibundus; **—ly** timide
shyness *s* timiditas, verecundia *f*
sibyl *s* sibylla *f*
sick *adj* (*mentally or physically*) aeger; (*physically*) aegrotus; **I am — of** me taedet (*with genit*), fastidio; **to be —** aegrotare
sicken *vt* fastidium movēre (*with dat*); *vi* in morbum incidĕre, nauseare
sickle *s* falx *f*
sickly *adj* infirmus
sickness *s* morbus *m*, aegrotatio *f*
side *s* latus *n*; (*direction*) pars *f*; (*district*) regio *f*; (*faction*) partes *f pl*; (*kinship*) genus *n*; **at the — of a** latere (*with genit*); **on all —s** undique; **on both —s** utrimque; **on one —** unā ex parte; **on that —** illinc; **on the mother's —** materno genere; **on this —** hinc; **on this — of** cis (*with acc*), citra (*with acc*); **to be on the — of** stare ab (*with abl*), sentire cum (*with abl*)
side *adj* lateralis, obliquus
side *vi* **to — with** partes sequi (*with genit*), stare ab (*with abl*), sentire cum (*with abl*)
sideboard *s* abacus *m*
sidelong *adj* obliquus, transversus
sideways *adv* in obliquum, oblique
siege *s* obsessio, oppugnatio, obsidio *f*; **to lay — to** obsidēre
siesta *s* meridiatio *f*; **to take a —** meridiare
sieve *s* cribrum *n*; (*little sieve*) cribellum *n*
sift *vt* cribrare; (*fig*) scrutari
sigh *s* suspirium *n*
sigh *vi* suspirare; **to — for** desiderare
sight *s* (*sense*) vis·us -ūs *m*; (*act of seeing*) aspect·us -ūs *m*; (*range*) conspect·us -ūs *m*; (*appearance*) species *f*; (*show*) spectaculum *n*; **at**

first — primo aspectu; **to catch — of** conspicĕre; **to lose — of** e conspectu amittĕre
sight *vt* conspicari
sightless *adj* caecus
sightly *adj* decorus, decens
sign *s* signum, indicium *n*; (*mark*) nota *f*; (*distinction*) insigne *n*; omen, portentum *n*
sign *vt* (*e.g., a document*) subscribĕre, signare, consignare
signal *vi* signum dare; (*by a nod*) annuĕre
signal *s* signum *n*; (*mil*) classicum *n*
signal *adj* insignis, egregius
signature *s* signatura *f*, nomen *n*
signer *s* signator *m*
signet *s* sigillum *n*
significance *s* (*meaning*) significatio, vis *f*, sens·us -ūs *m*; (*importance*) momentum *n*
significant *adj* gravis, magnus, magni momenti (*genit*)
signify *vt* significare, portendĕre
silence *s* silentium *n*
silence *interj* tace!; (*to more than one person*) tacete!
silence *vt* comprimĕre; (*by argument*) refutare
silent *adj* tacitus, taciturnus; **to become —** conticescĕre; **to be —** tacēre; **—ly** tacite
silk *s* sericum *n*, bombyx *m & f*
silk *adj* sericus, bombycinus
silkworm *s* bombyx *m & f*
sill *s* limen inferum *n*
silly *adj* stultus, ineptus
silver *s* argentum *n*
silver *adj* argenteus
silversmith *s* faber argentarius *m*
silvery *adj* argenteus; (*of hair*) canus
similar *adj* similis; **—ly** similiter, pariter
similarity *s* similitudo *f*
simile *s* translatio, similitudo *f*
simmer *vi* lente fervēre
simper *vi* inepte ridēre
simple *adj* simplex; (*easy*) facilis; (*frank*) sincerus; (*silly*) stultus
simpleton *s* stultus, ineptus *m*
simplicity *s* simplicitas *f*
simplify *vt* faciliorem reddĕre
simply *adv* simpliciter; solum, tantummodo
simulate *vt* simulare
simulation *s* simulatio *f*
simultaneous *adj* eodem tempore; **—ly** simul, unā, eodem tempore
sin *s* peccatum, delictum *n*
sin *vi* peccare
since *prep* ex (*with abl*), ab (*with abl*), post (*with acc*); **ever —** usque ab (*with abl*)
since *adv* abhinc; **long —** jamdudum, jampridem
since *conj* (*temporal*) ex quo tempore, postquam, cum; (*causal*) quod, quia, quoniam, cum
sincere *adj* sincerus, candidus; **—ly** sincere, vere
sinew *s* nervus, lacertus *m*
sinewy *adj* nervosus, lacertosus
sinful *adj* impius, pravus; **—ly** impie, improbe
sing *vt & vi* canĕre, cantare
singe *vt* adurĕre, amburĕre
singer *s* cantator *m*, cantatrix *f*
singing *s* cant·us -ūs *m*
single *adj* solus, unicus, unus, singularis; (*unmarried*) caelebs; **not a — one** ne unus quidem
single *vt* **to — out** eligĕre
singly *adv* singulatim, viritim
singsong *s* canticum *n*
singsong *adj* canorus
singular *adj* unicus, singularis; (*outstanding*) egregius, eximius; **—ly** singulariter, unice, egregie
sinister *adj* infaustus, malevolus, iniquus
sink *vt* submergĕre, demergĕre, deprimĕre; (*money*) collocare; *vi* considĕre, subsidĕre; (*in water*) mergi; (*of morale, etc.*) cadĕre
sink *s* sentina *f*
sinless *adj* peccati expers
sinner *s* peccator *m*, peccatrix *f*
sinuous *adj* sinuosus
sip *vt* libare, sorbillare, degustare
siphon *s* sipho *m*
sir *s* (*title*) eques *m*
sir *interj* (*to a master*) ere!; (*to an equal*) bone vir!, vir clarissime!
sire *s* genitor *m*
siren *s* siren *f*
sister *s* soror *f*
sister-in-law *s* glos *f*
sisterly *adj* sororius
sit *vi* sedēre; **to — beside** assidēre (*with dat*); **to — down** considēre; **to — on** insidēre (*with dat*); **to — up** (*to be awake at night*) vigilare
site *s* sit·us -ūs *m*
situated *adj* situs, positus
situation *s* sit·us -ūs *m*; (*circumstances*) res, conditio *f*
six *adj* sex; **— times** sexies
sixfold *adj* sextuplus
sixteen *adj* sedecim
sixteenth *adj* sextus decimus
sixth *s* sexta pars *f*
sixtieth *adj* sexagesimus
sixty *adj* sexaginta
size *s* magnitudo, mensura *f*
skein *s* glomus *m*
skeleton *s* sceletos *m*, ossa *n pl*
sketch *s* adumbratio, lineatio *f*
sketch *vt* adumbrare, delineare; (*fig*) describĕre
skiff *s* scapha *f*
skilful *adj* dexter, peritus, scitus; (*with hands*) habilis; **—ly** perite, scite
skill *s* sollertia, calliditas, peritia *f*
skilled *adj* peritus, doctus
skillet *s* cucumella *f*
skim *vt* despumare; (*fig*) percurrĕre, stringĕre
skin *s* (*of men*) cutis *f*; (*of animals*) pellis *f*; (*prepared*) corium *n*
skin *vt* pellem exuĕre (*with abl*)
skinny *adj* macilentus
skip *vt* praeterire; *vi* subsultare; **to — over** transilire
skirmish *s* concursatio, velitatio *f*
skirmish *vi* velitari

skirmisher *s* veles *m*
skirt *s* instita *f*; (*border*) fimbria *f*
skirt *vt* tangĕre, legĕre
skull *s* cranium, caput *n*
sky *s* caelum *n*, aether *m*; **under the open —** sub divo
slab *s* tabula, tessera *f*
slack *adj* remissus, laxus; (*fig*) piger, neglegens
slacken *vt* remittĕre, laxare, minuĕre; *vi* minui, remitti
slag *s* scoria *f*
slain *adj* occisus
slake *vt* exstinguĕre, sedare
slander *s* calumnia, obtrectatio *f*
slander *vt* obtrectare (*with dat*), calumniari
slanderer *s* obtrectator *m*
slanderous *adj* calumniosus, maledicus
slang *s* vulgaria verba *n pl*
slant *vt* acclinare; (*fig*) detorquēre
slanting *adj* obliquus
slap *s* alapa *f*
slap *vt* alapam dare (*with dat*), palmā ferire
slash *s* (*cut*) caesura *f*; (*blow*) ict·us -ūs *m*; (*wound*) vulnus *n*
slash *vt* caedĕre, incidĕre
slaughter *s* caedes, trucidatio *f*
slaughter *vt* mactare, trucidare
slaughterhouse *s* laniena *f*
slave *s* servus *m*, serva *f*
slave dealer *s* venalicius, manciporum negotiator *m*
slavery *s* servitus *f*, servitium *n*
slave trade *s* venalicium *n*
slavish *adj* servilis; **—ly** serviliter
slay *vt* interficĕre, occidĕre, necare
slayer *s* necator, homicida *m*
sledge *s* traha, trahea *f*
sleek *adj* levis, politus, nitidus, pinguis
sleep *s* somnus *m*
sleep *vi* dormire
sleepless *adj* insomnis, pervigil
sleepy *adj* somniculosus, semisomnis; (*fig*) iners
sleet *s* nivosa grando *f*
sleeve *s* manica *f*
slender *adj* gracilis, tenuis
slice *s* segmentum, frustum *n*, offula *f*
slice *vt* secare
slide *vi* labi
slight *adj* levis, exiguus, tenuis; **—ly** leviter, paululum
slight *s* neglegentia, contemptio *f*
slight *vt* neglegĕre, contemnĕre
slily *adv* astute, callide, vafre
slim *adj* gracilis
slime *s* limus *m*
slimy *adj* limosus, mucosus, viscosus
sling *s* funda *f*; (*for arm*) fascia *f*
sling *vt* iaculari
slink *vi* **to — away** furtim se subducĕre
slip *s* laps·us -ūs *m*; (*of paper*) scheda *f*; (*in grafting*) surculus *m*; (*error*) peccatum *n*, culpa *f*
slip *vt* (*to give furtively*) furtim dare; *vi* labi; **to let —** omittĕre; **to — away** elabi
slipper *s* solea, crepida *f*
slippery *adj* lubricus; (*deceitful*) subdolus
slit *s* incisura *f*
slit *vt* incidĕre, discidĕre
slop *s* vilis pot·us -ūs *m*
slope *s* declivitas *f*, clivus *m*
slope *vi* proclinari, vergĕre
sloping *adj* declivis, pronus; (*upward*) acclivis
sloppy *adj* lutulentus, sordidus
slot *s* rima *f*
sloth *s* ignavia, pigritia, inertia *f*
slothful *adj* piger, segnis, iners; **—ly** pigre, segniter, ignave
slouch *vi* languide incedĕre
slough *s* (*of snake*) exuviae *f pl*; (*mire*) caenum *n*
slovenly *adj* sordidus, ignavus
slow *adj* tardus, lentus; (*gentle*) lenis; **—ly** tarde, lente, sensim
sluggard *s* homo piger *m*
sluggish *adj* piger, ignavus, segnis; **—ly** pigre, segniter
sluice *s* cataracta *f*
slumber *s* somnus, sopor *m*
slumber *vi* obdormiscĕre, dormitare
slur *s* macula *f*
slur *vt* inquinare; *vi* **to — over** extenuare, leviter attingĕre
slut *s* meretrix *f*
sly *adj* astutus, vafer, callidus; **on the —** clam; **—ly** astute, callide, vafre
smack *s* (*flavor*) sapor *m*; (*blow*) alapa *f*
smack *vt* (*to strike*) ferire; *vi* **to — of** sapĕre
small *adj* parvus, exiguus, tenuis
smart *adj* (*clever*) sollers, callidus; (*elegant*) lautus, nitidus; (*of pace*) velox; **—ly** callide; nitide
smart *s* dolor *m*
smart *vi* dolēre
smash *s* concussio, fractura *f*
smash *vt* confringĕre
smattering *s* cognitio manca, levis scientia *f*
smear *vt* illinĕre, oblinĕre
smell *s* (*sense*) odorat·us -ūs *m*; (*odor*) odor *m*
smell *vt* olfacĕre, odorari; *vi* olēre; **to — of** olēre, redolēre
smelly *adj* olidus, graveolens
smelt *vt* (ex)coquĕre, fundĕre
smile *s* ris·us -ūs *m*; **with a —** subridens
smile *vi* subridēre; **to — at** arridēre (*with dat*)
smirk *vi* subridēre
smite *vt* ferire, percutĕre
smith *s* faber *m*
smithy *s* ferramentorum fabrica *f*
smock *s* tunica *f*
smoke *s* fumus *m*
smoke *vt* (*to cure by smoking*) infumare; *vi* fumare
smoky *adj* fumeus, fumidus, fumosus
smooth *adj* levis; (*of skin*) glaber; (*polished*) teres; (*calm*) placidus; (*of talk*) blandus; **—ly** leviter; blande
smooth *vt* polire, limare
smother *vt* suffocare, opprimĕre
smudge *s* sordes *f*

smudge *vt* inquinare, conspurcare
smug *adj* lautus, nitidus, sui contentus
smuggle *vt* furtim importare, sine portorio importare
smut *s* fuligo *f*
smutty *adj* obscenus; (*blackened*) fumosus
snack *s* portio, morsiuncula *f*
snail *s* cochlea *f*, limax *m & f*
snake *s* anguis *m & f*, serpens *f*
snap *vt* (*to break*) frangĕre; **to — the fingers** digitis concrepare; **to — up** corripĕre; *vi* disilire, frangi; **to — at** mordēre
snap *s* crepit·us -ūs *m*
snare *s* laqueus *m*, pedica *f*; (*fig*) insidiae *f pl*
snare *vt* illaquēre, irretire
snarl *vi* (*as a dog*) ringĕre, hirrire
snatch *vt* rapĕre, corripĕre; **to — away** eripĕre; **to — up** surripĕre
sneak *s* perfidus *m*
sneak *vi* repĕre, serpĕre, latitare
sneer *s* rhonchus *m*, irrisio *f*
sneer *vi* irridēre, deridēre
sneeringly *adv* cum irrisione
sneeze *s* sternutamentum *n*
sneeze *vi* sternuĕre
sniff *vt* odorari, naribus captare
snip *vi* amputare; **to — off** decerpĕre, praecidĕre
snivel *s* mucus *m*
snivel *vi* mucum resorbēre
snob *s* homo arrogans *m*, homo fastidiosus *m*
snobbish *adj* fastidiosus
snore *s* rhonchus *m*
snore *vi* stertĕre
snort *s* fermit·us -ūs *m*
snort *vi* fremĕre
snout *s* rostrum *n*
snow *s* nix *f*
snow *vi* ningĕre; **it is snowing** ningit
snowball *s* glebula nivis *f*
snowdrift *s* niveus agger *m*
snowstorm *s* ningor *m*
snowy *adj* niveus, nivalis; (*full of snow*) nivosus
snub *vt* reprehendĕre, neglegĕre
snub *s* repulsa *f*
snuff *vt* **to — out** exstinguĕre
snug *adj* commodus; **—ly** commode
so *adv* sic, ita, (*before adjectives*) tam; **— far** eatenus, adhuc; **— much** tantum; **— so** mediocriter; **— that** ita ut; **— that not** ne; **— then** quare, quapropter
soak *vt* madefacĕre, macerare; *vi* madēre
soap *s* sapo *m*
soar *vi* in sublime ferri; (*of birds*) subvolare
sob *s* singult·us -ūs *m*
sob *vi* singultare
sober *adj* sobrius; (*fig*) moderatus, modestus; **—ly** sobrie; moderate
sobriety *s* sobrietas *f*; (*fig*) continentia *f*
sociable *adj* sociabilis, facilis, affabilis
social *adj* socialis, civilis, communis
society *s* societas *f*; **high — optimates** *m pl*; **secret —** sodalitas *f*
sock *s* pedale *n*, udo *m*
socket *s* (*in anatomy*) cavum *n*
sod *s* caespes *m*, glaeba *f*
soda *s* (*in natural state*) nitrum *n*; (*prepared*) soda *f*
sofa *s* lectulus, grabatus *m*
soft *adj* mollis, tener; (*fig*) delicatus, effeminatus; **—ly** molliter, leniter
soften *vt* mollire, mitigare; (*fig*) lenire, placare; *vi* mollescĕre; (*of fruits*) mitescĕre; (*fig*) mansuescĕre, mitescĕre
softness *s* mollitia, teneritas, lenitas *f*; (*effeminacy*) mollities *f*
soil *s* solum *n*, terra *f*
soil *vt* inquinare, contaminare
sojourn *s* commoratio, mansio *f*
sojourn *vi* commorari
solace *s* solatium *n*
solace *vt* consolari
solar *adj* solaris; solis (*genit*)
soldier *s* miles *m*
soldierly *adj* militaris
soldiery *s* miles *m*
sole *adj* solitarius; **—ly** solum, modo, tantum
sole *s* (*of foot*) planta *f*; (*of shoe*) solea *f*; (*fish*) solea *f*
solemn *adj* sollemnis; gravis; **—ly** sollemniter; graviter
solemnity *s* sollemne *n*, sollemnitas *f*; gravitas *f*
solemnization *s* celebratio *f*
solemnize *vt* celebrare
solicit *vt* rogare, flagitare
solicitation *s* flagitatio *f*
solicitor *s* flagitator *m*; (*law*) advocatus *m*
solicitous *adj* anxius, trepidus; **—ly** anxie, trepide
solicitude *s* sollicitudo, anxietas *f*
solid *adj* solidus; purus; (*fig*) verus, firmus; **—ly** solide
soliloquize *vi* secum loqui
soliloquy *s* soliloquium *n*
solitary *adj* solitarius; (*of places*) desertus
solitude *s* solitudo *f*
solstice *s* solstitium *n*
soluble *adj* dissolubilis
solution *s* dilutum *n*; (*fig*) solutio, explicatio *f*
solve *vt* solvĕre, explicare
solvency *s* facultas solvendi *f*
some *adj* aliqui; (*a certain*) quidam; nonnulli, aliquot
some *pron* aliqui; nonnulli; (*certain people*) quidam
somebody *pron* aliquis; **— or other** nescio quis
someday *adv* olim
somehow *adv* quodammodo, nescio quomodo, aliquā (viā)
someone *pron* aliquis; **— else** alius
something *pron* aliquid; **— else** aliud; **— or other** nescio quid
sometime *adv* aliquando
sometimes *adv* interdum, nonnumquam; **sometimes . . . sometimes** modo . . . modo

somewhat *adv* aliquantum; (*with comparatives*) aliquanto, paulo
somewhere *adv* alicubi; (*with motion*) aliquo; — **else** alibi; (*with motion*) alio
somnolence *s* somni cupiditas *f*
somnolent *adj* semisomnus
son *s* filius *m*
song *s* cant·us -ūs *m*; (*tune*) melos *n*
son-in-law *s* gener *m*
sonorous *adj* sonorus, canorus; **—ly** sonore, canore
soon *adv* brevi tempore, mox; **as — as** simul, simulac, simulatque; **as — as possible** quamprimum; **— after** paulo post
sooner *adv* prius; (*preference*) potius; **— or later** serius ocius
soot *s* fuligo *f*
soothe *vt* permulcēre, mitigare, delenire
soothsayer *s* hariolus, sortilegus *m*
soothsaying *s* vaticinatio *f*
sooty *adj* fumosus
sop *s* offa, offula *f*
sophism *s* sophisma *n* cavillatio *f*
sophist *s* sophistes *m*
sophisticated *adj* urbanus, lepidus
sophistry *s* cavillatio captiosa *f*
soporific *adj* soporifer
sorcerer *s* magus *m*
sorceress *s* maga, saga *f*
sorcery *s* veneficium *n*
sordid *adj* sordidus, foedus; **—ly** sordide
sore *adj* (*aching*) tener; (*grievous*) atrox, durus; **—ly** graviter, vehementer
sore *s* ulcus *n*
sorrow *s* dolor, maeror, luct·us -ūs *m*
sorrow *vi* dolēre, lugēre
sorrowful *adj* luctuosus, tristis, maestus; **—ly** maeste
sorry *adj* (*pitiable*) miser; **I am — about** me paenitet (*with genit*); **I feel — for** me miseret (*with genit*), misereo (*with genit*)
sort *s* genus *n*, species *f*; **of that —** ejusmodi
sort *vt* digerěre, ordinare
sot *s* fatuus *m*; (*drunkard*) ebrius, potator *m*
sottish *adj* ebriosus
soul *s* (*principle of life*) anima *f*; (*principle of intellection and sensation*) animus *m*; (*person*) caput *n*
sound *adj* (*healthy*) validus, sanus; (*strong*) robustus; (*entire*) integer; (*in mind*) mentis compos; (*true, genuine*) verus; (*of sleep*) artus; (*valid*) ratus; **—ly** (*of beating*) vehementer, egregie; (*of sleeping*) arte
sound *s* sonus *m*; (*noise*) strepit·us -ūs, sonit·us -ūs *m*; (*of trumpet*) clangor *m*; (*strait*) fretum *n*
sound *vt* (*trumpet*) caněre; *vi* caněre, sonare; (*to seem*) vidēri
soundness *s* sanitas, integritas *f*
soup *s* jus *n*
sour *adj* acidus, acerbus; (*fig*) amarus, morosus; **to turn —** acescěre; (*fig*) coacescěre
source *s* fons *m*; (*of stream*) caput *n*; (*fig*) origo *f*, fons *m*
South *s* meridies, auster *m*
southern *adj* australis, meridionalis
southward *adv* in meridiem, meridiem versus
south wind *s* auster, notus *m*
souvenir *s* monumentum *n*
sovereign *adj* supremus
sovereign *s* princeps, rex, regnator *m*
sovereignty *s* dominatio *f*, principat·us -ūs *m*
sow *s* sus *m & f*
sow *vt* serěre, seminare; (*a field*) conserěre
space *s* spatium *n*; (*of time*) intervallum *n*
spacious *adj* spatiosus, amplus
spade *s* ligo *m*, pala *f*
span *s* (*extent*) spatium *n*; (*measure*) palmus *m*
spangle *s* bractea *f*
spangle *vt* bracteis ornare
Spaniard *s* Hispanus *m*
Spanish *adj* Hispanicus, Hispaniensis
spar *s* tignum *n*
spar *vi* dimicare; (*fig*) digladiari
spare *vt* parcěre (*with dat*), parce uti (*with abl*)
spare *adj* parcus, frugalis, exilis
sparing *adj* parcus; **—ly** parce
spark *s* scintilla *f*; (*fig*) igniculus *m*
sparkle *vi* scintillare; (*as wine*) subsilire
sparkling *adj* coruscans
sparrow *s* passer *m*
Spartan *adj* Laconicus, Spartanus
spasm *s* spasmus *m*, convulsio *f*
spasmodically *adv* interdum
spatter *vt* aspergěre, inquinare
spatula *s* spatha *f*
spawn *s* ova *f pl*
spawn *vi* ova gigněre
speak *vt & vi* loqui, fari, dicěre; **to — of** dicěre de (*with abl*); **to — to** alloqui (*with acc*); **to — with** colloqui cum (*with abl*)
speaker *s* orator *m*
spear *s* hasta *f*
spear *vt* hastā transfigěre
special *adj* specialis, praecipuus; **—ly** specialiter, praecipue
specialty *s* proprietas *f*
species *s* species *f*, genus *n*
specific *adj* certus
specify *vt* enumerare, designare
specimen *s* specimen, exemplum *n*
specious *adj* speciosus
speck *s* macula *f*
speckle *vt* maculis variare
spectacle *s* spectaculum *n*
spectator *s* spectator *m*
specter *s* larva *f*, phantasma *n*
spectral *adj* larvalis
spectrum *s* spectrum *n*
speculate *vi* cogitare, conjecturam facěre; (*com*) foro uti
speculation *s* cogitatio, conjectura *f*; (*com*) alea *f*
speculative *adj* conjecturalis
speculator *s* contemplator *m*; (*com*) aleator *m*

speech *s* oratio *f*, sermo *m*; (*faculty*) lingua *f*
speechless *adj* mutus, elinguis; (*fig*) obstupefactus
speed *s* celeritas, velocitas *f*
speed *vt* accelerare, maturare; *vi* properare, festinare
speedily *adv* cito, celeriter
speedy *adj* citus, velox, celer
spell *s* incantamentum, carmen *n*
spelling *s* orthographia *f*
spelt *s* far *n*
spend *vt* impenděre, consuměre; (*to exhaust*) effunděre; (*time*) agěre
spendthrift *s* nepos, prodigus *m*
spew *vt* voměre
sphere *s* sphaera *f*, globus *m*; (*fig*) provincia *f*
spherical *adj* sphaericus, sphaeralis, globosus
sphinx *s* sphinx *f*
spice *s* condimentum *n*
spice *vt* condire
spicy *adj* conditus, aromaticus
spider *s* aranea *f*
spider web *s* araneum *n*
spigot *s* epistomium *n*
spike *s* clavus *m*
spill *vt* effunděre, profunděre
spin *vt* (*thread*) nēre; **to — round** versare, circumagěre; *vi* versari
spinach *s* spinacea oleracea *f*
spinal *adj* dorsalis
spine *s* spina *f*
spinster *s* innupta *f*
spiral *adj* intortus
spiral *s* spira, involutio *f*
spirit *s* spirit·us -ūs *m*, anima *f*; (*character*) ingenium *n*; (*ghost*) anima *f*; **—s** (*of the dead*) manes *m pl*
spirited *adj* animosus, alacer
spiritless *adj* piger, ignavus
spiritual *adj* animi (*genit*)
spit *s* veru *n*; (*spittle*) sputum *n*
spit *vt & vi* sputare, spuěre
spite *s* livor *m*, malevolentia *f*, odium *n*
spite *vt* offenděre
spiteful *adj* lividus, malevolus; **—ly** malevole
spittle *s* sputum *n*
splash *vt* asperġěre
splash *s* fragor *s*
splendid *adj* splendidus; **—ly** splendide
splendor *s* splendor *m*
splint *s* ferula *f*
splinter *s* assula *f*
splinter *vt* assulatim finděre
split *s* fissura *f*
split *vt* finděre; *vi* findi
spoil *vt* spoliare; (*to mar*) corrumpěre; (*to ruin*) perděre, depravare, vitiare
spoils *s* spolia *n pl*, praeda *f*
spoke *s* radius *m*
spokesman *s* orator *m*
spondee *s* spondeus *m*
sponge *s* spongia *f*
spongy *adj* spongiosus
sponsor *s* sponsor *m*
spontaneity *s* impuls·us -ūs *m*
spontaneous *adj* voluntarius; **—ly** sponte, ultro
spool *s* fusus *m*
spoon *s* cochleare *n*
spoonful *s* cochleare *n*
sport *s* ludus, lus·us -ūs *m*; (*mockery*) ludibrium *n*, irrisio *f*
sport *vi* luděre, lascivire
sportive *adj* jocosus; **—ly** jocose
sportsman *s* venator *m*
spot *s* macula *f*; (*stain*) macula, labes *f*; (*place*) locus *m*
spot *vt* (*to speckle*) maculis notare; (*to stain*) inquinare, maculare
spotless *adj* integer, purus, castus
spotted *adj* maculosus, maculis distinctus
spouse *s* conju(n)x *m & f*
spout *s* (*pipe*) canalis *m*; (*of jug*) os *n*; (*of water*) torrens *m*
spout *vt* ejaculare; (*speeches*) declamare; *vi* emicare
sprain *vt* intorquēre, convellěre
sprawl *vi* se funděre, prostratus jacēre
spray *s* aspergo *f*
spray *vt* asperġěre
spread *vt* panděre, distenděre, extenděre; diffunděre; (*to make known*) divulgare; *vi* patēre; (*of news*) manare, divulgari; (*of disease*) evagari
sprig *s* ramusculus *m*, virgula *f*
sprightly *adj* alacer, vegetus
spring *s* (*season*) ver *n*; (*leap*) salt·us -ūs *m*; (*of water*) fons *m*, scaturgo *f*
spring *adj* vernus
spring *vi* (*to come from*) oriri, enasci; (*as rivers, etc.*) scatēre, effluěre; (*to leap*) salire, exsilire
springtime *s* vernum tempus *n*
sprinkle *vt* sparġěre, asperġěre; *vi* rorare
sprite *s* spectrum *n*
sprout *s* pullus, surculus *m*
sprout *vi* pullulare
spruce *adj* lautus, nitidus, comptus; **—ly** nitide
spur *s* calcar *n*; (*fig*) incitamentum *n*
spur *vt* calcaribus concitare; (*fig*) urgēre
spurious *adj* fictus, fucosus, spurius
spurn *vt* sperněre, aspernari
spurt *vi* emicare
sputter *vi* balbutire
spy *s* explorator, speculator *m*
spy *vt* conspicěre; *vi* speculari
squabble *s* jurgium *n*, rixa *f*
squabble *vi* rixari
squad *s* manipulus *m*, decuria *f*
squadron *s* (*of cavalry*) ala, turma *f*; (*of ships*) classis *f*
squalid *adj* squalidus, sordidus
squall *s* procella *f*
squalor *s* squalor *m*, sordes *f*
squander *vt* dissipare, effunděre
squanderer *s* prodigus *m*
square *adj* quadratus; (*fig*) honestus, probus
square *s* quadratum *n*, quadra *f*; (*tool*) norma *f*
square *vt* quadrare; *vi* convenire, congruěre
squash *vt* conterěre, contunděre

squat *vi* succumbĕre, recumbĕre, subsidĕre
squat *adj* parvus atque obesus
squeak *vi* stridēre; (*as a mouse*) dintrire
squeak *s* stridor *m*
squeamish *adj* fastidiosus; **to feel —** fastidire
squeeze *vt* comprimĕre, premĕre; **to — out** exprimĕre
squint *vi* strabo esse
squint-eyed *adj* paetus
squire *s* armiger *m*; (*landowner*) dominus *m*
squirrel *s* sciurus *m*
squirt *vt* projicĕre; *vi* emicare
stab *s* ict·us -ūs *m*, puncta *f*
stab *vt* fodĕre, perforare
stability *s* stabilitas *f*
stabilize *vt* stabilire, firmare
stable *adj* stabilis, solidus
stable *s* stabulum *n*; (*for horses*) equile *n*; (*for cows, oxen*) bubile *n*
stack *s* acervus *m*, strues *f*
stack *vt* coacervare, cumulare
staff *s* baculum *n*, scipio *m*, virga *f*; (*of a magistrate*) consilium *n*; (*mil*) contubernales *m pl*
staff officer *s* contubernalis *m*
stag *s* cervus *m*
stage *s* (*in theater*) scaena *f*; (*degree*) grad·us -ūs *m*; (*on journey*) iter *n*
stagger *vt* obstupefacĕre; *vi* titubare
stagnant *adj* stagnans, torpens; (*fig*) iners
stagnate *vi* stagnare; (*fig*) refrigescĕre
stagnation *s* cessatio *f*, torpor *m*
staid *adj* gravis
stain *s* macula, labes *f*
stain *vt* maculare, contaminare; (*to dye*) tingĕre
stainless *adj* immaculatus, purus, integer
stair *s* scala *f*, grad·us -ūs *m*
staircase *s* scalae *f pl*
stake *s* palus *m*; (*wager*) depositum *n*; **to be at —** agi
stake *vt* deponĕre, appignerare
stale *adj* vetus, obsoletus; (*of bread*) secundus; (*of wine*) vapidus
stalk *s* (*of plant*) caulis, stipes *m*; (*of grain*) calamus *m*
stalk *vt* venari; *vi* incedĕre
stall *s* stabulum *n*
stall *vt* sistĕre; *vi* consistĕre
stallion *s* admissarius *m*
stamina *s* patientia *f*
stammer *vi* balbutire, linguā haesitare
stammering *adj* balbus
stammering *s* balbuties *f*
stamp *s* (*mark*) nota *f*; (*with the foot*) vestigium *n*; (*impression made*) impressio *f*
stamp *vt* imprimĕre, notare; (*money*) cudĕre; (*feet*) supplodĕre
stand *s* locus *m*, statio *f*; (*halt*) mora *f*; (*platform*) suggest·us -ūs *m*
stand *vt* (*to set upright*) statuĕre, constituĕre; (*to tolerate*) tolerare, perferre, sustinēre; *vi* stare; **to — aloof** abstare; **to — by** adesse (*with dat*); **to — fast** consistĕre; **to — for office** petĕre; **to — in awe of** in metu habēre; **to — in need of** indigēre (*with abl*); **to — on end** horrēre; **to — out** exstare, eminēre, prominēre; **to — still** consistĕre, subsistĕre
standard *adj* solitus
standard *s* (*mil*) vexillum, signum *n*; (*measure*) norma, mensura *f*
standard-bearer *s* vexillarius, signifer *m*
standing *s* stat·us -ūs, ordo *m*, conditio *f*; **of long —** vetus
standing *adj* perpetuus
standstill *s* **to be at a —** haerēre
stanza *s* tetrastichon *n*
staple *adj* praecipuus
star *s* stella *f*, sidus *n*; (*fig*) lumen *n*
starch *s* amylum *n*
starch *vt* amylare
stare *s* obtut·us -ūs *m*, oculorum intentio *f*
stare *vi* stupēre; **to — at** intuēri
stark *adj* rigidus
stark *adv* omnino, penitus
starlight *s* siderum lumen *n*
starling *s* sturnus *m*
starry *adj* sidereus, stellatus
start *s* initium *n*; (*sudden movement*) salt·us -ūs *m*; (*of journey*) profectio *f*
start *vt* incipĕre, instituĕre; (*game*) excitare; *vi* (*to begin*) incipĕre, (ex)ordiri; (*to take fright*) resilire
starting gate *s* carceres *m pl*
startle *vt* terrēre, territare
starvation *s* fames *f*
starve *vt* fame interficĕre; *vi* fame confici
state *s* stat·us -ūs, locus *m*; (*pol*) civitas, respublica *f*; (*pomp*) magnificentia *f*
state *vt* declarare, dicĕre, affirmare
state *adj* publicus
stately *adj* grandis, lautus, splendidus
statement *s* affirmatio *f*, dictum *n*; testimonium *n*
statesman *s* vir reipublicae regendae peritus *m*
statesmanship *s* reipublicae regendae ars *f*
station *s* statio *f*, locus *m*
station *vt* locare, disponĕre
stationary *adj* stabilis, statarius, immotus
stationery *s* res scriptoriae *f pl*
statistics *s* cens·us -ūs *m*
statue *s* statua *f*, signum *n*
stature *s* statura *f*
statute *s* statutum, decretum *n*, lex *f*
staunch *adj* certus, firmus, fidus
staunch *vt* (*blood*) sistĕre
stave *vt* perrumpĕre; **to — off** arcēre
stay *vt* detinēre, sistĕre; (*to curb*) coercēre; *vi* manēre, commorari
stay *s* (*sojourn*) commoratio, mansio *f*; (*delay*) mora *f*; (*prop*) fulcrum *n*
steadfast *adj* constans, firmus, stabilis; **—ly** constanter

steadily *adv* constanter, firme, magis magisque
steadiness *s* stabilitas, constantia *f*
steady *adj* stabilis, firmus; (*fig*) constans, gravis
steak *s* offa, offula *f*
steal *vt* furari; *vi* furari; **to — away** se subducĕre
stealing *s* furtum *n*
stealthily *adv* furtim
steam *s* vapor *m*
steam *vi* fumare
steed *s* equus bellator *m*
steel *s* chalybs *m*
steep *adj* arduus, praeceps, praeruptus
steep *vt* imbuĕre, madefacĕre
steeple *s* turris *f*
steepness *s* acclivitas, declivitas *f*
steer *s* juvencus *m*
steer *vt* gubernare, dirigĕre
steering *s* gubernatio *f*
stem *s* stipes *m*; (*of ship*) prora *f*
stem *vt* obsistĕre (*with dat*), cohibēre, reprimĕre
stench *s* foetor *m*
step *s* pass·us -ūs, grad·us -ūs *m*; (*plan, measure*) ratio *f*; **flight of —s** scalae *f pl*; **— by —** gradatim, pedetentim
step *vi* gradi
stepbrother *s* (*on father's side*) vitrici filius *m*; (*on mother's side*) novercae filius *m*
stepdaughter *s* privigna *f*
stepfather *s* vitricus *m*
stepmother *s* noverca *f*
stepson *s* privignus *m*
sterile *adj* sterilis
sterility *s* sterilitas *f*
sterling *adj* verus, bonus
stern *adj* durus, severus, torvus; **—ly** dure, severe, torve
stern *s* puppis *f*
sternness *s* severitas *f*
stew *s* carnes cum condimentis elixae *f pl*
stew *vt* lento igne coquĕre
steward *s* procurator *m*; (*of estate*) vilicus *m*
stewardship *s* procuratio *f*
stick *s* fustis *m*; (*cane*) baculum *n*
stick *vt* affigĕre; *vi* haerēre, haesitare
sticky *adj* viscosus, viscidus
stiff *adj* rigidus; (*fig*) severus, frigidus; **—ly** rigide
stiffen *vt* rigidum facĕre; (*with starch*) amylare; *vi* obdurescĕre
stifle *vt* suffocare; (*fig*) restinguĕre
stigma *n* stigma *n*, nota *f*
stigmatize *vt* notare
still *adj* quietus, immotus, tranquillus
still *adv* (*adversative*) tamen, nihilominus; (*yet*) adhuc, etiamnum; (*with comparatives*) etiam
still *vt* pacare, sedare
stillborn *adj* abortivus
stillness *s* silentium *n*, taciturnitas *f*
stilts *s* grallae *f pl*
stimulant *s* irritamentum *n*, stimulus *m*
stimulate *vt* stimulare, excitare
stimulus *s* stimulus *m*
sting *s* aculeus *m*; (*fig*) (*of conscience*) angor *m*
sting *vt* pungĕre, mordēre
stinginess *s* avaritia *f*, sordes *f pl*
stingy *adj* avarus, sordidus
stink *s* foetor *m*
stink *vi* foetēre; **to — of** olēre (*with acc*)
stint *s* modus *m*
stint *vt* coercēre
stipend *s* salarium *n*, merces *f*
stipulate *vt* stipulari
stipulation *s* stipulatio, conditio, lex *f*
stir *vt* excitare; *vi* se movēre
stir *s* tumult·us -ūs *m*
stirring *adj* (*of a speech*) ardens
stitch *vt* suĕre
stock *s* (*supply*) copia *f*; (*race*) stirps *f*, genus *n*; (*handle*) lignum *n*
stock *vt* instruĕre; suppeditare
stockade *s* vallum *n*
stockbroker *s* argentarius *m*
stocking *s* tibiale *n*
Stoic *s* Stoicus *m*
stoical *adj* patiens, durus; **—ly** patienter
Stoicism *s* Stoica disciplina *f*
stole *s* stola *f*
stolen *adj* furtivus
stomach *s* stomachus *m*
stomach *vt* tolerare, perferre, pati
stone *s* lapis *m*, saxum *n*
stone *vt* lapidare
stonecutter *s* lapicida, lapidarius *m*
stone quarry *s* lapidicina *f*
stony *adj* (*full of stones*) lapidosus; (*of stone*) saxeus; (*fig*) durus
stool *s* scabellum *n*
stoop *vi* proclinare; (*fig*) se summittĕre
stop *vt* sistĕre, obturare, prohibēre; *vi* subsistĕre; (*to cease*) desistĕre
stop *s* mora, pausa *f*
stopgap *s* tibicen *m*
stoppage *s* obstructio *f*, impedimentum *n*
stopper *s* obturamentum *n*
store *s* (*supply*) copia *f*; (*shop*) taberna *f*
store *vt* condĕre, reponĕre
storehouse *s* promptuarium *n*; (*for grain*) horreum *n*; (*fig*) thesaurus *m*
stork *s* ciconia *f*
storm *s* tempestas, procella *f*
storm *vt* (*mil*) expugnare; *vi* desaevire
stormy *adj* turbidus, procellosus; (*fig*) tumultuosus
story *s* narratio, fabula *f*; (*lie*) mendacium *n*; (*of house*) tabulatum *n*
storyteller *s* narrator *m*; (*liar*) mendax *m*
stout *adj* corpulentus; (*brave*) fortis; (*strong*) firmus, validus; **—ly** fortiter
stove *s* focus, caminus *m*
stow *vt* condĕre, recondĕre; *vi* **to — away** in navi delitescĕre
straddle *vi* varicare
straggle *vi* palari
straggler *s* palans *m*
straight *adj* rectus, directus
straight *adv* directo, rectā

straighten *vt* rectum facĕre; **to — out** corrigĕre
straightforward *adj* apertus, simplex, directus
straightway *adv* statim
strain *vt* contendĕre; (*muscle*) luxare; (*to filter*) percolare; *vi* eniti
strain *s* contentio *f*; (*effort*) labor *m*; (*mus*) modus *m*
strained *adj* (*style*) arcessitus
strainer *s* colum *n*
strait *adj* angustus, artus
strait *s* fretum *n*; **—s** (*fig*) angustiae *f pl*
straiten *vt* contrahĕre, artare
strand *s* litus *n*; (*of hair*) floccus *m*
strand *vt* vadis illidĕre; *vi* impingi
strange *adj* insolitus, novus; mirus; (*foreign*) peregrinus; **— to say** mirabile dictu; **—ly** mirum in modum
strangeness *s* novitas *f*
stranger *s* advena, peregrinus *m*
strangle *vt* strangulare
strap *s* lorum *n*, strupus *m*
strapping *adj* robustus
stratagem *s* stratagema *n*; (*trickery*) dolus *m*
strategic *adj* idoneus
strategy *s* consilium *n*
straw *adj* stramineus
straw *s* stramentum *n*; (*for thatch*) stipula *f*
strawberry *s* fragum *n*
stray *vi* errare, aberrare
streak *s* linea *f*; (*of character*) vena *f*
streak *vt* lineis distinguĕre
stream *s* flumen *n*, amnis *m*
stream *vi* fluĕre, currĕre
streamer *s* vexillum *n*
street *s* via *f*; (*narrow*) vicus *m*
strength *s* robur *n*, vires *f pl*, nervi *m pl*
strengthen *vt* roborare, confirmare; munire
strenuous *adj* strenuus, sedulus; **—ly** strenue
stress *s* (*accent*) ict·us -ūs *m*; (*meaning*) vis *f*, pondus *n*; (*effort*) labor *m*
stress *vt* exprimĕre
stretch *vt* tendĕre, extendĕre, distendĕre; **to — oneself** pandiculari; **to — out** (*hands*) porrigĕre; (*to lengthen*) producĕre; *vi* extendi, distendi; produci; patescĕre
stretch *s* spatium *n*
stretcher *s* lecticula *f*
strew *vt* spargĕre, sternĕre
stricken *adj* saucius, vulneratus
strict *adj* (*severe*) severus, rigidus; (*accurate*) accuratus, exactus, diligens; **—ly** severe, diligenter; **—ly speaking** immo
stricture *s* vituperatio *f*
stride *s* grad·us -ūs, pass·us -ūs *m*
stride *vi* varicare
strife *s* jurgium *n*, lis, pugna, discordia *f*
strike *vt* ferire, pulsare, percutĕre; **to — fear into** incutĕre in (*with acc*)
strike *s* cessatio operis *f*; (*blow*) ict·us -ūs *m*
strikingly *adv* mirum in modum
string *s* filum *n*; (*for bow*) nervus *m*; (*for musical instrument*) chorda *f*; (*fig*) series *f*
string *vt* (*bow*) intendĕre
stringent *adj* severus
stringy *adj* fibratus
strip *vt* spoliare; denudare; (*clothes*) exuĕre
strip *s* (*of cloth*) lacinia *f*; (*of paper*) scheda *f*; (*of land*) spatium *n*
stripe *s* linea *f*; (*blow*) ict·us -ūs *m*; (*mark of blow*) vibex *f*; (*on toga*) clavus *m*
strive *vi* (e)niti, moliri, conari, laborare; **to — for** anniti, sectari
striving *s* contentio *f*, nis·us -ūs *m*
stroke *s* ict·us -ūs *m*, plaga *f*; (*with pen*) pennae duct·us -ūs *f*; (*of oar*) puls·us -ūs *m*
stroke *vt* (per)mulcēre
stroll *s* ambulatio *f*
stroll *vi* perambulare, spatiari
strong *adj* robustus, firmus, validus; (*smell*) gravis; (*powerful*) potens; (*feeling*) acer; (*language*) vehemens; **—ly** valide, graviter, vehementer, acriter
stronghold *s* arx *f*, castellum *n*
structure *s* structura *f*; (*building*) aedificium *n*
struggle *s* certamen *n*, pugna *f*; (*fig*) luctatio *f*
struggle *vi* contendĕre, (ob)niti, luctari
strumpet *s* scortum *n*, meretrix *f*
strut *s* incess·us -ūs *m*
strut *vi* turgēre, tumēre
stubble *s* stipula *f*
stubborn *adj* obstinatus, contumax, pervicax; **—ly** obstinate, pervicaciter
stubbornness *s* obstinatus animus *m*, obstinatio, pertinacia *f*
stud *s* clavus *m*; equus admissarius *m*
student *s* discipulus *m*
studied *adj* meditatus; (*style*) exquisitus
studious *adj* studiosus discendi; (*careful*) attentus
study *s* studium *n*; (*room*) bibliotheca *f*
study *vt* studēre (*with dat*); (*to scrutinize*) perscrutari
stuff *s* materia, materies *f*
stuff *vt* farcire; (*with food*) saginare
stuffing *s* (*in cooking*) fartum *n*; (*in upholstery*) tomentum *n*
stultify *vt* ad irritum redigĕre
stumble *vi* offendĕre; **to — upon** incidĕre in (*with acc*)
stumbling block *s* offensio *f*
stump *s* truncus, caudex *m*
stun *vt* stupefacĕre; (*fig*) confundĕre, obstupefacĕre
stunted *adj* curtus
stupefy *vt* obstupefacĕre, perturbare
stupendous *adj* mirus, admirabilis
stupid *adj* stupidus, fatuus; **—ly** stupide
stupidity *s* stupiditas, fatuitas *f*
stupor *s* stupor, torpor *m*
sturdiness *s* robur *n*, firmitas *f*
sturdy *adj* robustus, validus, firmus

sturgeon *s* acipenser *m*
stutter *vi* balbutire
sty *s* suile *n*, hara *f*
style *s* (*literary*) scribendi genus *n*; (*rhetorical*) dicendi genus *n*; (*architectural*) rit·us -ūs *m*; (*of dress*) habit·us -ūs *m*
style *vt* appellare, nominare
stylish *adj* speciosus, affectatus, elegans
suave *adj* suavis, urbanus
subdivide *vt* iterum dividĕre
subdivision *s* pars *f*
subdue *vt* subjicĕre, domare, vincĕre
subject *adj* **— to** obnoxius (*with dat*), subjectus (*with dat*)
subject *s* homo subditus *m*; civis *m*; (*topic*) materia *f*, argumentum *n*; (*matter*) res *f*; (*gram*) subjectum *n*
subject *vt* subjicĕre, subigĕre
subjection *s* servitus *f*; patientia *f*
subjective *adj* proprius
subjugate *vt* subigĕre, domare
subjunctive *s* subjunctivus modus *m*
sublime *adj* sublimis, excelsus; **—ly** excelse
sublimity *s* elatio, sublimitas *f*
submerge *vt* demergĕre, inundare; *vi* se demergĕre
submission *s* obsequium, servitium *n*, reverentia *f*
submissive *adj* summissus, obsequiosus; **—ly** summisse
submit *vt* (*e.g., a proposal*) referre; *vi* se dedĕre; **to — to** obtemperare (*with dat*)
subordinate *vt* subjicĕre, supponĕre
subordinate *adj* secundus, subjectus, inferior
suborn *vt* subornare
subscribe *vt* (*to contribute*) conferre; *vi* **to — to** assentiri (*with dat*)
subscriber *s* subscriptor *m*
subscription *s* collatio *f*
subsequent *adj* sequens, posterior, serior; **—ly** postea, deinde
subserve *vt* subvenire (*with dat*)
subservient *adj* obsequiosus
subside *vi* desidĕre; (*of wind*) cadĕre; (*of passion*) defervescĕre
subsidiary *adj* secundus
subsidy *s* subsidium *n*, collatio *f*, vectigal *n*
subsist *vi* subsistĕre
subsistence *s* vict·us -ūs *m*
substance *s* substantia *f*; res *f*; (*gist*) summa *f*; (*wealth*) opes *f pl*
substantial *adj* solidus, firmus; (*real*) verus; (*rich*) opulentus; (*important*) magnus; **—ly** magnā ex parte, re
substantiate *vt* confirmare
substantive *s* nomen, substantivum *n*
substitute *s* vicarius *m*
substitute *vt* supponĕre
substitution *s* substitutio *f*
subterfuge *s* effugium *n*, praetext·us -ūs *m*
subterranean *adj* subterraneus
subtle *adj* subtilis, tenuis; (*shrewd*) acutus, vafer
subtlety *s* subtilitas, tenuitas *f*; (*cleverness*) astutia *f*
subtract *vt* subtrahĕre, detrahĕre, deducĕre
subtraction *s* detractio, deductio *f*
suburb *s* suburbium *n*
suburban *adj* suburbanus
subversion *s* eversio *f*
subversive *adj* seditiosus
subvert *vt* evertĕre
succeed *vt* succedĕre (*with dat*), insequi, excipĕre; *vi* (*of persons*) rem bene gerĕre; (*of activities*) prospere evenire, succedĕre
success *s* success·us -ūs, bonus event·us -ūs *m*, res secundae *f pl*
successful *adj* fortunatus, prosper; **—ly** fortunate, prospere
succession *s* successio *f*; (*series*) series *f*
successive *adj* continuus; **—ly** in ordine, continenter
successor *s* successor *m*
succinct *adj* succinctus, brevis, pressus; **—ly** presse
succor *s* subsidium, auxilium *n*
succor *vt* succurrĕre (*with dat*), subvenire (*with dat*)
succulence *s* sucus *m*
succulent *adj* sucosus, suculentus
succumb *vi* succumbĕre
such *adj* talis; **— . . . as** talis . . . qualis
suck *vt* sugĕre; **to — in** sorbēre; **to — up** exsorbēre, ebibĕre; *vi* ubera ducĕre
suckle *vt* nutricari
suction *s* suct·us -ūs *m*
sudden *adj* subitus, repentinus, inexpectatus; **—ly** subito, repente
sue *vt* litem intendĕre (*with dat*); *vi* **to — for** orare, rogare, petĕre
suffer *vt* pati, tolerare, sustinĕre; *vi* dolēre, affici
sufferable *adj* tolerabilis, tolerandus
suffering *s* dolor *m*
suffice *vi* sufficĕre, satis esse
sufficient *adj* satis (*with genit*); **—ly** satis
suffocate *vt* suffocare
suffocation *s* suffocatio *f*
suffrage *s* suffragium *n*
suffuse *vt* suffundĕre
suffusion *s* suffusio *f*
sugar *s* saccharum *n*
sugar *vt* saccharo condire
sugar cane *s* arundo sacchari *f*
suggest *vt* suggerĕre, subjicĕre, admonēre
suggestion *s* suggestio, admonitio *f*
suicide *s* suicidium *n*; **to commit —** sibi mortem consciscĕre
suit *s* lis, causa *f*; (*clothes*) vestit·us -ūs *m*
suit *vt* accommodare; convenire (*with dat*), congruĕre (*with dat*)
suitable *adj* aptus, idoneus, congruus
suite *s* comitat·us -ūs *m*; (*apartment*) conclave *n*
suitor *s* procus *m*
sulfur *s* sulfur *n*
sulk *vi* aegre ferre
sulky *adj* morosus

sullen *adj* torvus, tetricus, morosus; **—ly** morose
sully *vt* inquinare, contaminare
sultry *adj* aestuosus, torridus
sum *s* summa *f*
sum *vt* **to — up** computare; (*to summarize*) summatim describĕre, breviter repetĕre
summarily *adj* breviter, summatim
summarize *vt* summatim describĕre
summary *adj* subitus, brevis
summary *s* epitome *f*, summarium *n*
summer *adj* aestivus
summer *s* aestas *f*
summit *s* culmen *n*; (*fig*) fastigium *n*
summon *vt* arcessĕre; (*a meeting*) convocare; **to — up courage** animum erigĕre, animum colligĕre
summons *s* vocatio *f*
sumptuary *adj* sumptuarius
sumptuous *adj* sumptuosus, lautus; **—ly** sumptuose
sun *s* sol *m*
sunbeam *s* radius *m*
sunburnt *adj* adustus
Sunday *s* Dominica *f*
sunder *vt* separare, sejungĕre
sundial *s* solarium *n*
sundry *adj* diversi, varii
sunlight *s* sol *m*
sunny *adj* apricus
sunrise *s* solis ort·us -ūs *m*
sunset *s* solis occas·us -ūs *m*
sunshine *s* sol *m*
sup *vi* cenare
superabundant *adj* nimius; **—ly** satis superque
superannuated *adj* emeritus
superb *adj* magnificus; **—ly** magnifice
supercilious *adj* superbus, arrogans
superficial *adj* levis; **—ly** leviter
superfluity *s* redundantia *f*
superfluous *adj* superfluus, supervacaneus
superhuman *adj* divinus, major quam humanus
superintend *vt* praeesse (*with dat*), administrare
superintendence *s* cura, curatio *f*
superintendent *s* praefectus, curator *m*
superior *adj* superior, melior; **to be — to** praestare (*with dat*)
superior *s* praepositus *m*
superiority *s* praestantia *f*
superlative *adj* eximius; (*gram*) superlativus
supernatural *adj* divinus
supernumerary *adj* ascripticius, accensus
supersede *vt* succedĕre (*with dat*)
superstition *s* superstitio *f*
superstitious *adj* superstitiosus
supervise *vt* procurare
supervision *s* cura, curatio *f*
supine *adj* supinus; **—ly** supine
supper *s* cena *f*; **after —** cenatus
supple *adj* flexibilis, flexilis
supplement *s* supplementum *n*, appendix *f*
supplement *vt* amplificare
suppliant *s* supplex *m & f*
supplicate *vt* supplicare
supplication *s* supplicatio, obsecratio *f*
supply *s* copia *f*; **supplies** (*mil*) commeat·us -ūs *m*
supply *vt* praebēre, suppeditare
support *s* (*prop*) fulcrum *n*; (*help*) subsidium *n*; (*maintenance*) alimentum *n*
support *vt* (*to hold up*) fulcire, sustinēre; (*to help*) adjuvare; (*to maintain*) alĕre
supportable *adj* tolerabilis
supporter *s* adjutor, fautor *m*
suppose *vt* opinari, putare, credĕre
supposition *s* opinio *f*
supremacy *s* dominat·us -ūs, principat·us -ūs *m*, imperium *n*
supreme *adj* supremus, summus; **—ly** unice, maxime
sure *adj* certus; (*faithful*) fidus; (*safe*) tutus; **—ly** certe, scilicet, profecto
surety *s* vas *n*; (*person*) sponsor *m*
surf *s* aest·us -ūs *m*
surface *s* superficies *f*; **the — of the sea** summum mare *n*
surfeit *s* satietas *f*; (*fig*) taedium *n*
surfeit *vt* saturare; (*fig*) satiare
surge *s* fluct·us -ūs, aest·us -ūs *m*
surge *vi* tumescĕre, surgĕre; **to — forward** proruĕre
surgeon *s* chirurgus *m*
surgery *s* chirurgia *f*
surgical *adj* chirurgicus
surly *adj* morosus, difficilis
surmise *s* conjectura *f*
surmise *vt* conjicĕre, suspicari
surmount *vt* superare, vincĕre
surmountable *adj* superabilis
surname *s* cognomen *n*
surpass *vt* superare, excedĕre, antecedĕre
surplus *s* reliquum, residuum *n*
surprise *s* (ad)miratio *f*; **to take by —** deprehendĕre
surprise *vt* admirationem movēre (*with dat*); (*mil*) opprimĕre; **to be surprised at** mirari, admirari
surprising *adj* mirus, mirabilis; inexpectatus; **—ly** mire, mirabiliter
surrender *s* (*mil*) deditio *f*; (*law*) cessio *f*
surrender *vt* dedĕre, tradĕre, cedĕre; *vi* se tradĕre, se dedĕre
surreptitious *adj* furtivus, clandestinus; **—ly** furtim, clam
surround *vt* circumdare, circumvenire, cingĕre
surroundings *s* vicinia *f*
survey *s* inspectio, contemplatio *f*; (*of land*) mensura *f*
survey *vt* inspicĕre, contemplari; (*land*) permetiri
surveyor *s* agrimensor, metator *m*
survival *s* salus *f*
survive *vt* supervivĕre (*with dat*); *vi* superstes esse
survivor *s* superstes *m & f*
susceptible *adj* mollis
suspect *vt* suspicari, suspicĕre; **to be suspected of** in suspicionem

venire quasi (*with verb in subjunctive*)
suspend *vt* suspendĕre, intermittĕre, differre
suspense *s* dubitatio *f*; **in —** suspensus
suspension *s* suspensio, dilatio *f*
suspicion *s* suspicio *f*; **to throw — on** suspicionem adjungĕre ad (*with acc*)
suspicious *adj* suspicax; (*suspected*) suspectus; **—ly** suspiciose
sustain *vt* sustinēre, sustentare; (*hardships, etc.*) ferre
sustenance *s* vict·us -ūs *m*
swab *s* peniculus *m*
swab *vt* detergēre
swaddling clothes *s* fasciae *f pl*, incunabula *n pl*
swagger *vi* se jactare
swaggerer *s* homo gloriosus *m*
swallow *s* (*bird*) hirundo *f*
swallow *vt* vorare, sorbēre; **to — up** devorare, absorbēre
swamp *s* palus *f*
swamp *vt* demergĕre
swampy *adj* paludosus
swan *s* cygnus *m*
swank *adj* lautus
swarm *s* examen *n*
swarm *vi* congregari
swarthy *adj* fuscus
swathe *s* fascia *f*
sway *s* dicio, dominatio *f*, imperium *n*
sway *vt* regĕre, movēre; *vi* vacillare
swear *vt* jurare; **to — in** sacramento adigĕre, sacramento rogare; *vi* jurare
sweat *s* sudor *m*
sweat *vi* sudare
sweep *vt* verrĕre; **to — out** everrĕre; *vi* **to — by** (*to dash by*) praetervolare; **to — over** (*to move quickly over*) percurrĕre
sweet *adj* dulcis, suavis; (*fig*) blandus, jucundus; **—ly** suaviter
sweeten *vt* dulcem facĕre; (*fig*) lenire, mulcēre
sweetheart *s* deliciae *f pl*, amica *f*
sweetness *s* dulcedo, suavitas *f*
sweets *s* cuppedia *n pl*
swell *s* aest·us -ūs *m*, unda *f*
swell *vt* inflare, tumefacĕre; *vi* tumēre
swelling *s* tumor *m*
swelter *vi* aestu laborare
swerve *vi* aberrare, vagari
swift *adj* celer, velox; **—ly** celeriter, velociter
swiftness *s* celeritas, velocitas *f*
swim *vi* natare, nare
swimmer *s* natator *m*
swimming *s* natatio *f*; (*of head*) vertigo *f*
swimming pool *s* piscina *f*
swindle *vt* fraudare, circumvenire
swindle *s* fraus *f*
swindler *s* fraudator *m*
swine *s* sus *m & f*
swineherd *s* suarius *m*
swing *s* oscillatio *f*
swing *vt* librare; *vi* oscillare
switch *s* (*stick*) virga, virgula *f*; (*change*) commutatio *f*
switch *vt* (*to flog*) flagellare; (*to change* (com)mutare
swoon *vi* intermori, collabi
swoop *s* impet·us -ūs *m*
swoop *vi* incurrĕre; **to — down on** involare in (*with acc*)
sword *s* gladius, ensis *m*, ferrum *n*; **with fire and —** ferro ignique
sycamore *s* sycomorus *f*
sycophant *s* sycophanta, assentator *m*
syllable *s* syllaba *f*
syllogism *s* syllogismus *m*, ratiocinatio *f*
symbol *s* signum, symbolum *n*
symbolical *adj* symbolicus; **—ly** symbolice
symmetrical *adj* congruens, concinnus
symmetry *s* symmetria, concinnitas *f*
sympathetic *adj* concors, misericors
sympathize *vi* consentire; **to — with** miserēri (*with genit*)
sympathy *s* consens·us -ūs *m*, misericordia, concordia *f*
symphony *s* symphonia *f*, concent·us -ūs *m*
symptom *s* indicium, signum *n*
synagogue *s* synagoga *f*
syndicate *s* societas *f*
synonym *s* verbum idem declarans *n*
synonymous *adj* idem declarans, idem valens
synopsis *s* breviarium *n*, epitome *f*
syntax *s* syntaxis *f*
system *s* ratio, disciplina *f*
systematic *adj* ordinatus; **—ally** ratione, ordine

T

tab *vt* designare, notare
tabernacle *s* tabernaculum *n*
table *s* mensa *f*; (*list*) index *m*, tabula *f*
tablecloth *s* mantele *n*
table napkin *s* mappa *f*
tablet *s* tabula, tabella *f*, album *n*
tacit *adj* tacitus; **—ly** tacite
taciturn *adj* taciturnus
tack *s* clavulus *m*
tack *vt* **to — on** assuĕre, affigĕre; *vi* (*of ships*) reciprocari
tact *s* judicium *n*, dexteritas *f*
tactful *adj* prudens, dexter; **—ly** prudenter, dextere
tactician *s* rei militaris peritus *m*
tactics *s* res militaris, belli ratio *f*
tadpole *s* ranunculus *m*

tag *s* appendicula *f*
tail *s* cauda *f*
tailor *s* vestitor, textor *m*
taint *s* contagio *f*, vitium *n*
taint *vt* inficĕre, contaminare; (*fig*) corrumpĕre
take *vt* capĕre, sumĕre, accipĕre; **to — away** demĕre, auferre, adimĕre; **to — down** (*in writing*) exscribĕre; **to — for** habēre pro (*with abl*); **to — hold of** prehendĕre; **to — in** (*e.g., a guest*) recipĕre; (*through deception*) decipĕre; **to — in hand** suscipĕre; **to — off** exuĕre; **to — out** eximĕre; (*from storage*) promĕre; **to — up** suscipĕre; **to — upon oneself** sibi sumĕre; *vi* **to — after** similis esse (*with genit or dat*); **to — off** (*to depart*) abire; **to — to** amare, diligĕre
tale *s* fabula, narratio *f*
talent *s* talentum *n*; (*fig*) ingenium *n*
talented *adj* ingeniosus
talk *s* sermo *m*, colloquium *n*; **idle —** nugae *f pl*
talk *vi* loqui; **to — with** colloqui cum (*with abl*)
talkative *adj* loquax, garrulus
talker *s* (*idle*) gerro *m*
tall *adj* altus, celsus, procerus
tallow *s* sebum *n*
tally *s* tessera *f*
tally *vi* convenire
talon *s* unguis *m*
tambourine *s* tympanum *n*
tame *adj* cicur, mansuetus, domitus; **—ly** mansuete, leniter
tame *vt* domare, mansuefacĕre
tamer *s* domitor *m*
tamper *vi* **to — with** (*persons*) sollicitare; (*writings*) depravare
tan *vt* (*by sun*) adurĕre; (*hides*) perficĕre
tangible *adj* tractabilis
tangle *s* implicatio *f*, nodus *m*
tangle *vt* implicare
tank *s* lac·us -ūs *m*
tankard *s* cantharus *m*
tantalize *vt* vexare
tantamount *adj* par
tap *s* levis ict·us -ūs *m*
tap *vt* leviter ferire; (*wine, etc.*) relinĕre
tape *s* taenia *f*
taper *s* cereus *m*
taper *vt* fastigare; *vi* fastigari
tapestry *s* aulaeum, tapete *n*
taproom *s* taberna *f*
tar *s* pix *f*
tardily *adv* tarde, lente
tardiness *s* tarditas, segnitia *f*
tardy *adj* tardus, lentus
target *s* scopus *m*
tariff *s* portorium *n*
tarnish *vt* infuscare; *vi* infuscari
tarry *vi* commorari, cunctari
tart *adj* acerbus, amarus
tart *s* scriblita *f*, crustulum *n*
task *s* pensum, opus *n*; **to take to —** objurgare
taste *s* (*sense*) gustat·us -ūs *m*; (*flavor*) sapor *m*; (*fig*) judicium *n*
taste *vt* (de)gustare; *vi* sapĕre
tasteful *adj* elegans; **—ly** eleganter
tasteless *adj* insipidus; (*fig*) insulsus, inelegans; **—ly** insulse
tasty *adj* sapidus, dulcis
tattered *adj* pannosus
tatters *s* panni *m pl*
taunt *s* convicium *n*
taunt *vt* exprobrare
taut *adj* intentus
tavern *s* taberna, caupona *f*
tavern keeper *s* caupo *m*
tawdry *adj* fucatus, vilis
tawny *adj* fulvus
tax *s* vectigal, tributum *n*
tax *vt* vectigal imponĕre (*with dat*)
taxable *adj* vectigalis, stipendiarius
taxation *s* vectigalia *n pl*
tax collector *s* exactor *m*
teach *vt* docēre, instituĕre, erudire
teachable *adj* docilis
teacher *s* magister, praeceptor *m*; (*of primary school*) litterator *m*; (*of secondary school*) grammaticus *m*; (*of rhetoric*) rhetor *m*
teaching *s* institutio, eruditio *f*
team *s* jugales *m pl*; (*of animals*) jugum *n*
tear *s* lacrima *f*, flet·us -ūs *m*; (*a rent*) scissura *f*
tear *vt* scindĕre; **to — apart** discindĕre; **to — in pieces** dilacerare, dilaniare; **to — off** abscindĕre; **to — open** rescindĕre; **to — out** evellĕre; **to — up** convellĕre
tease *vt* vexare, ludĕre
teat *s* mamma *f*
technical *adj* (*term*) proprius; technicus, artificialis
technique *s* ars *f*
technology *s* officinarum artes *f pl*
tedious *adj* molestus; **—ly** moleste
tedium *s* taedium *n*
teem *vi* scatēre, redundare
teethe *vi* dentire
teething *s* dentitio *f*
tell *vt* narrare, memorare, referre; (*to order*) imperare (*with dat*), jubēre; **— me the truth** dic mihi verum
teller *s* numerator *m*
temerity *s* temeritas *f*
temper *s* temperatio *f*, animus *m*, ingenium *n*; (*bad*) iracundia *f*
temper *vt* temperare; (*fig*) lenire
temperament *s* animus *m*
temperance *s* temperantia *f*
temperate *adj* temperatus, moderatus, sobrius; **—ly** temperanter, sobrie
temperature *s* calor *m*, caloris grad·us -ūs *m*
tempest *s* tempestas *f*
tempestuous *adj* turbulentus, procellosus
temple *s* templum *n*, aedes *f*; (*of forehead*) tempus *n*
temporal *adj* humanus; profanus
temporarily *adv* ad tempus
temporary *adj* brevis
temporize *vi* tergiversari
tempt *vt* temptare, illicĕre
temptation *s* illecebra *f*
ten *adj* decem; **— times** decies

tenable *adj* defensibilis, stabilis
tenacious *adj* tenax, pertinax; **—ly** tenaciter, pertinaciter
tenacity *s* tenacitas, pertinacia *f*
tenancy *s* conductio *f*
tenant *s* conductor, colonus, incola *m*
tend *vt* curare; *vi* tendĕre, spectare
tendency *s* inclinatio *f*
tender *adj* tener, mollis; **—ly** tenere, indulgenter
tender *vt* offerre
tenderness *s* mollitia *f*; (*affection*) indulgentia *f*
tendon *s* nervus *m*
tendril *s* (*of vine*) pampinus *m*; (*of plants*) claviculus *m*
tenement *s* conductum *n*
tenement house *s* insula *f*
tenet *s* dogma *n*
tenfold *adj* decemplex, decuplus
tennis *s* **to play —** pilā ludĕre
tennis court *s* sphaeristerium *n*
tenor *s* tenor, sens·us -ūs *m*
tense *adj* intentus, attentus
tense *s* tempus *n*
tension *s* intentio *f*
tent *s* tentorium, tabernaculum *n*
tentative *adj* tentans
tenth *adj* decimus
tenth *s* decima pars *f*
tenuous *adj* tenuis, rarus
tenure *s* possessio *f*
tepid *adj* tepidus
term *s* (*word*) verbum *n*; (*limit*) terminus *m*; (*condition*) condicio, lex *f*
terminate *vt* terminare, finire; *vi* terminari, desinĕre; (*of words*) cadĕre
termination *s* terminatio *f*, finis, exit·us -ūs *m*
terrace *s* ambulatio *f*
terrestrial *adj* terrestris, terrenus
terrible *adj* terribilis
terribly *adv* horrendum in modum
terrific *adj* terrificus, terrens, formidabilis
terrify *vt* terrēre, perterrēre
territory *s* regio *f*, ager *m*, fines *m pl*
terror *s* terror *m*, formido *f*
terse *adj* brevis, pressus; **—ly** presse
test *s* probatio *f*, experimentum *n*
test *vt* probare, experiri
testament *s* testamentum *n*
testamentary *adj* testamentarius
testator *s* testator *m*
testify *vt* testificari, testari
testimonial *s* laudatio *f*
testimony *s* testimonium *n*
testy *adj* stomachosus, obstinatus, morosus
tether *s* retinaculum *n*
tether *vt* religare
text *s* verba *n pl*
textbook *s* enchiridion *n*
textile *adj* textilis
texture *s* textura *f*
than *adv* quam; atque, ac
thank *vt* gratias agĕre (*with dat*)
thankful *adj* gratus; **—ly** grate
thankless *adj* ingratus; **—ly** ingrate
thanks *s* gratiae, grates *f pl*
thanks *interj* gratias!
thanksgiving *s* grates *f pl*, gratulatio *f*; (*public act*) supplicatio *f*
that *adj* ille, is, iste
that *pron demonstrative* ille, is, iste; *pron rel* qui
that *conj* (*purpose, result, command*) ut; (*after verbs of fearing*) ne
thatch *s* stramentum *n*
thatch *vt* stramento tegĕre
thaw *vt* (dis)solvĕre; *vi* tabescĕre
the *article, not expressed in Latin*
the *adv* (*with comparatives*) **the . . . the** quo . . . eo
theater *s* theatrum *n*
theatrical *adj* scenicus, theatralis
thee *pron* te; **of —** de te; **to —** tibi; **with —** tecum
theft *s* furtum *n*
their *adj* illorum, eorum, istorum; **— own** suus
them *pron* eos, illos, istos; **to —** eis, illis, istis
theme *s* thema, argumentum *n*
themselves *pron reflex* se; **to —** sibi; **with —** secum; *pron intensive* ipsi
then *adv* (*at that time*) tum, tunc; (*after that*) deinde, inde; (*therefore*) igitur, ergo; **now and —** interdum, nonnumquam
thence *adv* inde, illinc; (*therefore*) ex eo, exinde
thenceforth *adv* ex eo tempore, dehinc
theologian *s* theologus *m*
theological *adj* theologicus
theology *s* theologia *f*
theoretical *adj* contemplativus
theory *s* ratio *f*
there *adv* ibi, illic; (*thither*) illuc; **— are** sunt; **— is** est
thereabouts *adv* circa, circiter, fere
thereafter *adv* deinde, postea
thereby *adv* eā re, eo
therefore *adv* itaque, igitur, idcirco, ergo
therefrom *adv* exinde, ex eo
therein *adv* in eo, in ea re
thereupon *adv* exinde, subinde
thesis *s* thesis *f*, propositum *n*
they *pron* ii, illi, isti
thick *adj* densus, spissus; **—ly** dense
thicken *vt* densare, spissare; *vi* concrescĕre
thicket *s* dumetum, fruticetum *n*
thickness *s* crassitudo *f*
thief *s* fur *m*
thievery *s* furtum *n*
thigh *s* femur *n*
thin *adj* tenuis, exilis, rarus; (*lean*) macer; **—ly** tenuiter, rare
thin *vt* attenuare; **to — out** rarefacĕre
thine *adj* tuus
thine *pron* tuus
thing *s* res *f*; **—s** (*possessions*) bona *n pl*; (*clothes*) vestimenta *n pl*
think *vt* cogitare; (*to believe, imagine, etc.*) putare, credĕre, opinari; **to — over** in mente agitare; *vi* **to — highly of** magni habēre
thinker *s* philosophus *m*
thinking *s* cogitatio *f*
thinness *s* tenuitas, raritudo *f*; (*of person*) macies *f*

third *adj* tertius; **—ly** tertio
third *s* tertia pars *f*
thirst *s* sitis *f*
thirst *vi* sitire; **to — for** sitire
thirstily *adv* sitienter
thirsty *adj* sitiens
thirteen *adj* tredecim, decem et tres
thirteenth *adj* tertius decimus
thirtieth *adj* tricesimus
thirty *adj* triginta
this *adj* hic
thistle *s* carduus *m*
thither *adv* illuc, istuc, eo
thong *s* lorum *n*
thorn *s* spina *f*, aculeus *m*
thorny *adj* spinosus; (*fig*) nodosus
thorough *adj* germanus, perfectus; **—ly** penitus, funditus
thoroughbred *adj* generosus, genuinus
thoroughfare *s* pervium *n*, via pervia *f*
though *conj* quamquam, quamvis
thought *s* (*act and faculty*) cogitatio *f*; (*product of thinking*) cogitatum *n*
thoughtful *adj* cogitabundus; providus; **—ly** anxie, provide
thoughtless *adj* inconsultus, improvidus; **—ly** temere, inconsulte
thousand *adj* mille; **a — times** millies
thousandth *adj* millesimus
thraldom *s* servitus *f*
thrall *s* servus *m*
thrash *vt* terĕre; (*fig*) verberare
thrashing *s* verbera *n pl*
thread *s* filum *n*
thread *vt* inserĕre
threadbare *adj* tritus, obsoletus
threat *s* minae *f pl*, minatio *f*
threaten *vt* minari (*with dat of person*); *vi* impendēre, imminēre
three *adj* tres; **— times** ter
threefold *adj* triplex, triplus
three-legged *adj* tripes
thresh *vt* terĕre
threshing floor *s* area *f*
threshold *s* limen *n*
thrice *adv* ter
thrift *s* frugalitas, parsimonia *f*
thriftily *adv* frugaliter
thrifty *adj* parcus, frugalis
thrill *s* gaudium *n*, voluptas *f*; (*of fear*) horror *m*
thrill *vt* commovēre, percellĕre
thrilling *adj* mirus, mirabilis
thrive *vi* virēre, vigēre, valēre
thriving *adj* vegetus, prosperus
throat *s* jugulum, guttur *n*, fauces *f pl*
throb *s* palpitatio *f*, puls·us -ūs *m*
throb *vi* palpitare
throes *s* dolor *m*
throne *s* solium *n*; (*fig*) regia dignitas *f*
throng *s* multitudo, turba, frequentia *f*
throng *vi* **to — around** stipare
throttle *vt* strangulare
through *prep* per (*with acc*); (*on account of*) ob (*with acc*), propter (*with acc*)
through *adv render by compound verb with* trans- *or* per-, e.g., **to read —** perlegĕre; **— and —** penitus, omnino
throughout *adv* prorsus, penitus
throughout *prep* per (*with acc*)
throw *vt* jacĕre, conjicĕre; (*esp. weapons*) mittĕre, jaculari; **to — away** abjicĕre; **to — back** rejicĕre; **to — down** dejicĕre; **to — open** patefacĕre; **to — out** ejicĕre; **to — together** conjicĕre in unum; *vi* **to — up** vomĕre
throw *s* jact·us -ūs *m*
thrush *s* turdus *m*
thrust *s* impet·us -ūs, ict·us -ūs *m*
thrust *vt* trudĕre, impellĕre; (*with sword*) perfodĕre
thumb *s* pollex *m*
thump *s* percussio *f*
thump *vt* tundĕre
thunder *s* tonitr·us -ūs *m*
thunder *vi* tonare
thunderbolt *s* fulmen *n*
thunderstruck *adj* attonitus, obstupefactus
thus *adv* ita, sic; **and —** itaque
thwart *vt* obstare (*with dat*), frustrari
thy *adj* tuus
tiara *s* diadema *n*
tick *s* (*insect*) ricinus *m*; (*clicking*) levis ict·us -ūs *m*
ticket *s* tessera *f*
tickle *vt & vi* titillare
tickling *s* titillatio *f*
ticklish *adj* periculosus
tide *s* aest·us -ūs *m*
tidings *s* nuntius *m*
tie *s* vinculum *n*; (*relationship*) necessitudo *f*
tie *vt* (al)ligare; (*in a knot*) nodare, nectĕre
tier *s* ordo *m*
tiger *s* tigris *m*
tight *adj* strictus, astrictus, artus; **—ly** arte
tighten *vt* astringĕre, adducĕre, contendĕre
tile *s* tegula, imbrex *f*
till *conj* dum, donec
till *prep* usque ad (*with acc*)
till *vt* colĕre
tillage *s* agricultura *f*
tiller *s* (*person*) agricola *m*; (*helm*) gubernaculum *n*
tilt *vt* proclinare
timber *s* materia *f*, lignum *n*
time *s* tempus *n*, dies *f*; (*age, period*) aetas *f*; (*leisure*) otium *n*; (*opportunity*) occasio *f*; (*interval*) intervallum, spatium *n*; (*of day*) hora *f*; **another —** alias; **at the same —** simul; **for a —** parumper; **for a long —** diu; **for some —** aliquamdiu; **from — to —** interdum; **in a short —** brevi; **in —** ad tempus; **on —** tempestive; **what — is it?** quota hora est?
timely *adj* tempestivus, opportunus
timepiece *s* horarium, horologium *n*
timid *adj* timidus
timidity *s* timiditas *f*
timorous *adj* pavidus
tin *s* stannum, plumbum album *n*
tin *adj* stanneus

tincture *s* color *m*
tinder *s* fomes *m*
tinge *vt* tingĕre, imbuĕre
tingle *vi* formicare, verminare
tinkle *vi* tinnire
tinsel *s* bractea, bracteola *f*
tip *s* cacumen, acumen *n*, apex *m*
tip *vt* praefigĕre; (*to incline*) invertĕre
tipple *vi* potare
tippler *s* potor *m*
tipsy *adj* ebriolus, temulentus
tiptoe *adv* in digitos erectus
tire *vt* fatigare, lassare; *vi* defatigari
tired *adj* fessus, lassus; **I am — of me** taedet (*with genit*); **— out** defessus
tiresome *adj* laboriosus; molestus
tissue *s* text·us -ūs *m*
titanic *adj* ingens
tithe *s* decuma *f*
title *s* titulus *m*; (*of book*) inscriptio *f*; (*of person*) appellatio, dignitas *f*; (*claim*) jus *n*
title page *s* index *m*
titter *s* ris·us -ūs *m*
to *prep commonly rendered by the dative;* (*motion, except with names of towns, small islands and* rus) ad (*with acc*), in (*with acc*); **— and fro** huc illuc
toad *s* bufo *m*
toast *s* (*bread*) panis tosti offula *f*; (*health*) propinatio *f*; **to drink a — to** propinare (*with dat*)
toast *vt* torrēre; (*in drinking*) propinare (*with dat*)
today *adv* hodie
today *s* hodiernus dies *m*
toe *s* digitus *m*
together *adv* simul, unā
toil *s* labor *m*, opera *f*
toil *vi* laborare
toilsome *adj* laboriosus, operosus
token *s* signum, pignus, indicium *n*
tolerable *adj* tolerabilis; mediocris
tolerably *adv* tolerabiliter; mediocriter
tolerance *s* patientia *f*
tolerant *adj* tolerans, indulgens, patiens; **—ly** indulgenter
tolerate *vt* tolerare, ferre
toleration *s* toleratio, indulgentia, patientia *f*
toll *s* vectigal *n*; (*at ports*) portorium *n*
toll collector *s* exactor, portitor *m*
tomb *s* sepulcrum *n*
tombstone *s* lapis, cippus *m*
tomorrow *adv* cras
tomorrow *s* crastinus dies *m*; **the day after —** perendie
tone *s* sonus *m*, vox *f*; (*in painting*) color *m*
tongs *s* forceps *m & f*
tongue *s* lingua *f*; (*of shoe*) ligula *f*; (*pole of carriage*) temo *m*
tonsils *s* tonsillae *f pl*
too *adv* nimis, nimium; (*also*) quoque, insuper
tool *s* instrumentum *n*; (*dupe*) minister *m*
tooth *s* dens *m*; **— and nail** totis viribus
toothache *s* dentium dolor *m*
toothless *adj* edentulus
toothpick *s* dentiscalpium *n*
tooth powder *s* dentifricium *n*
top *adj* summus
top *s* vertex, apex *m*; (*of tree*) cacumen *n*; (*of house*) fastigium *n*; (*toy*) turbo *m*; **the — of the mountain** summus mons *m*
top *vt* superare
topic *s* res *f*, argumentum *n*
topmost *adj* summus
topography *s* regionum descriptio *f*
topple *vt* evertĕre; *vi* titubare
torch *s* fax *f*
torment *s* tormentum *n*, cruciat·us -ūs *m*
torment *vt* (ex)cruciare, torquēre
tormenter *s* tortor *m*
torpid *adj* torpens; **to be —** torpēre
torpor *s* torpor *m*
torrent *s* torrens *m*
torrid *adj* torridus
tortoise *s* testudo *f*
tortoise shell *s* testudo *f*
torture *s* tormentum *n*, cruciat·us -ūs *m*
torture *vt* torquēre, (ex)cruciare
torturer *s* cruciator, tortor *m*
toss *s* jact·us -ūs *m*
toss *vt* jactare; *vi* jactari
total *adj* totus, universus; **—ly** omnino, prorsus
totality *s* summa, universitas *f*
totter *vi* vacillare, titubare
touch *vt* tangĕre, attingĕre; (*to stir emotionally*) movēre, commovēre, afficĕre; *vi* inter se contingĕre; **to — on** attingĕre
touch *s* (con)tact·us -ūs *m*, tactio *f*
touching *adj* mollis, flexanimus
touchstone *s* (*fig*) obrussa *f*
touchy *adj* stomachosus
tough *adj* durus, lentus; (*fig*) strenuus; difficilis
tour *s* (*rounds*) circuit·us -ūs *m*; (*abroad*) peregrinatio *f*
tourist *s* peregrinator *m*
tournament *s* certamen *n*
tow *s* stuppa *f*
tow *vt* remulco trahĕre
toward *prep* versus (*with acc*), ad (*with acc*); (*of feelings*) erga (*with acc*), in (*with acc*); (*of time*) sub (*with acc*)
towel *s* mantele *n*; sudarium *n*
tower *s* turris *f*
tower *vi* **to — over** imminēre (*with dat*)
towering *adj* excelsus, arduus
towline *s* remulcum *n*
town *s* urbs *f*; (*fortified*) oppidum *n*
town hall *s* curia *f*
townsman *s* oppidanus *m*
toy *s* crepundia *n pl*, oblectamentum *n*
trace *s* vestigium *n*; (*for horse*) helcium *n*
trace *vt* delinēre, describĕre; indagare, investigare; **to — back** repetĕre
track *s* vestigium *n*; (*path*) semita *f*, calles *m*
track *vt* investigare
trackless *adj* avius, invius

tract *s* (*of land*) tract·us -ūs *m*, regio *f*; (*treatise*) tract·us -ūs *m*
tractable *adj* tractabilis, docilis, obsequiosus
trade *s* mercatura *f*, commercium *n*; (*calling*) ars *f*, quaest·us -ūs *m*
trade *vt* commutare; *vi* negotiari, mercaturas facĕre
trader *s* mercator *m*
tradesman *s* opifex *m*
tradition *s* traditio, fama, memoria *f*, mos majorum *m*
traditional *adj* patrius, a majoribus traditus
traduce *vt* calumniari, infamare
traffic *s* commercium *n*; (*on street*) vehicula *n pl*
tragedian *s* (*playwright*) tragoedus, tragicus poeta *m*; (*actor*) tragicus actor *m*
tragedy *s* tragoedia *f*
tragic *adj* tragicus; (*fig*) tristis, miserabilis; **—ally** tragice; miserabiliter
trail *vt* investigare; (*to drag*) trahĕre; *vi* trahi, verrĕre
trail *s* vestigium *n*; (*path*) calles *m*
train *s* (*line*) series *f*, ordo *m*; (*of robe*) instita *f*; (*retinue*) comitat·us -ūs *m*; (*of army*) impedimenta *n pl*
train *vt* educare, instruĕre, assuefacĕre
trainer *s* lanista, aliptes *m*
training *s* disciplina, institutio *f*; (*practice*) exercitatio *f*
trait *s* mos *m*
traitor *s* proditor *m*
traitorous *adj* perfidus; **—ly** perfide
trammel *vt* impedire, vincire, irretire
tramp *s* vagabundus, homo vagus *m*; (*of feet*) puls·us -ūs *m*
tramp *vi* gradi
trample *vt* calcare, conculcare; *vi* **to — on** obterĕre, proterĕre, opprimĕre
trance *s* stupor *m*, ecstasis *f*
tranquil *adj* tranquillus; **—ly** tranquille
tranquillity *s* tranquillitas *f*, tranquillus animus *m*
tranquilize *vt* tranquillare
transact *vt* transigĕre, gerĕre
transaction *s* negotium *n*, res *f*
transcend *vt* superare, vincĕre
transcendental *adj* sublimis, divinus
transcribe *vt* transcribĕre
transcription *s* transcriptio *f*
transfer *s* translatio *f*; (*of property*) alienatio *f*
transfer *vt* transferre; (*property*) abalienare
transference *s* translatio *f*
transfigure *vt* tranfigurare
transform *vt* vertĕre, commutare
transformation *s* commutatio *f*
transgress *vt* violare, perfringĕre; *vi* peccare, delinquĕre
transgression *s* violatio *f*, delictum *n*
transgressor *s* violator, maleficus *m*
transient *adj* transitorius, brevis, fluxus
transition *s* transitio *f*, transit·us -ūs *m*
transitive *adj* transitivus; **—ly** transitive
transitory *adj* transitorius, brevis, fluxus
translate *vt* vertĕre, transferre
translation *s* translata *n pl*
translator *s* interpres *m*
transmission *s* transmissio *f*
transmit *vt* transmittĕre
transmutation *s* transmutatio *f*
transparent *adj* pellucidus; (*fig*) perspicuus
transpire *vi* perspirare, emanare; (*to happen*) evenire
transplant *vt* transferre
transport *vt* transportare, transvehĕre
transport *s* vectura *f*; (*ship*) navigium vectorium *n*, navis oneraria *f*; (*rapture*) sublimitas *f*
transportation *s* vectura *f*
transpose *vt* transponĕre
transposition *s* transpositio, trajectio *f*
trap *s* laqueus *m*, pedica *f*; (*fig*) insidiae *f pl*; **to lay a —** insidiari
trap *vt* (*to snare*) irretire; (*fig*) inlaqueare
trappings *s* ornamenta *n pl*, apparat·us -ūs *m*; (*of horse*) phalerae *f pl*
trash *s* scruta *n pl*; (*fig*) nugae *f pl*
trashy *adj* vilis; obscenus
travel *vi* iter facĕre; **to — abroad** peregrinari
traveler *s* viator, peregrinator *m*
traverse *vt* transire, peragrare, lustrare
travesty *s* perversa imitatio *f*
tray *s* ferculum *n*, trulla *f*
treacherous *adj* perfidus, dolosus; **—ly** perfidiose
treachery *s* perfidia *f*
tread *vt* calcare; *vi* incedĕre
tread *s* grad·us -ūs, incess·us -ūs *m*, vestigium *n*
treason *s* perduellio, proditio *f*
treasonable *adj* perfidus, proditorius
treasure *s* thesaurus *m*
treasure *vt* fovēre, magni aestimare
treasurer *s* aerarii praefectus *m*
treasury *s* aerarium *n*, fiscus *m*
treat *vt* uti (*with abl*), tractare; (*patient*) curare; (*topic*) tractare; (*to entertain*) invitare
treatise *s* libellus *m*, dissertatio *f*
treatment *s* tractatio *f*; (*by doctor*) curatio *f*
treaty *s* foedus, pactum *n*; **to make a —** foedus icĕre
treble *adj* triplex, triplus; (*of sound*) acutus
treble *vt* triplicare
tree *s* arbor *f*
trellis *s* clathrus *m*
tremble *vi* tremĕre, tremiscĕre
trembling *adj* tremulus
trembling *s* trepidatio *f*
tremendous *adj* immanis, ingens, vastus; **—ly** valde, maxime
tremulous *adj* tremulus, vacillans
trench *s* fossa *f*

trespass *vt* violare, offenděre; *vi* delinquěre
trespass *s* violatio, culpa *f*
tress *s* crinis, cirrus *m*
trestle *s* fulcimentum *n*
trial *s* tentatio, experientia *f*; (*test*) probatio *f*; (*trouble*) labor *m*; (*law*) judicium *n*, quaestio *f*
triangle *s* triangulum *n*
triangular *adj* triangulus, triquetrus
tribe *s* trib·us -ūs *f*
tribulation *s* tribulatio, afflictio *f*
tribunal *s* (*raised platform*) tribunal *n*; (*court*) judicium *n*
tribune *s* tribunus *m*
tribuneship *s* tribunat·us -ūs *m*
tributary *adj* vectigalis, stipendiarius
tributary *s* amnis in alium influens *m*
tribute *s* tributum, vectigal *n*
trick *s* dolus *m*, artificium *n*, fraus, ars *f*
trick *vt* fallěre, deciperě
trickle *s* guttae *f pl*
trickle *vi* stillare, manare
trickster *s* veterator, fraudator *m*
trident *s* tridens *m*
triennial *adj* triennis
trifle *s* res parvi momenti *f*, nugae *f pl*
trifle *vi* nugari
trifling *adj* levis, exiguus, frivolus
trill *s* sonus modulatus *m*
trill *vt* vibrare
trim *adj* nitidus, comptus, bellus
trim *vt* adornare; (*to prune*) putare, tonděre
trinket *s* tricae *f pl*
trip *s* iter *n*
trip *vt* supplantare; *vi* titubare; (*fig*) errare
tripartite *adj* tripartitus
tripe *s* omasum *n*
triple *adj* triplex
triple *vt* triplicare
tripod *s* tripus *m*
trireme *s* triremis *f*
trite *adj* tritus
triumph *s* (*entry of victorious Roman general*) triumphus *m*; (*victory*) victoria *f*
triumph *vi* triumphare; vincěre; **to — over** devincěre
triumphal *adj* triumphalis
triumphant *adj* victor; elatus, laetus
trivial *adj* levis, tenuis
triviality *s* nugae *f pl*
troop *s* turma, caterva *f*, grex, globus *m*; **—s** (*mil*) copiae *f pl*
trooper *s* eques *m*
trope *s* tropus *m*
trophy *s* tropaeum *n*
tropical *adj* tropicus
tropics *s* loca fervida *n pl*
trot *vi* tolutim ire
trouble *s* labor, dolor *m*, incommodum *n*, aerumna, molestia *f*
trouble *vt* turbare, vexare, angěre
troublesome *adj* molestus, operosus
trough *s* alveus *m*
trounce *vt* (*to punish*) castigare; (*to defeat decisively*) devincěre
troupe *s* grex *m*
trousers *s* bracae *f pl*
trout *s* tru(c)ta *f*
trowel *s* trulla *f*
truant *s* cessator *m*
truce *s* indutiae *f pl*
truck *s* carrus *m*
truculent *adj* truculentus
trudge *vi* repěre
true *adj* verus; (*genuine*) germanus; (*faithful*) fidus; (*exact*) rectus, justus
truism *s* verbum tritum *n*
truly *adv* vere, profecto
trump *vt* **to — up** effingěre, ementiri
trumpet *s* tuba, bucina *f*
trumpeter *s* tubicen, bucinator *m*
truncheon *s* fustis *m*
trundle *vt* volvěre
trunk *s* truncus *m*; (*for luggage*) cista *f*; (*of elephant*) proboscis *f*
trust *s* fiducia, fides *f*
trust *vt* fiděre (*with dat*), creděre (*with dat*); (*to entrust*) committěre
trustee *s* fiduciarius, tutor *m*
trusteeship *s* tutela *f*
trustful *adj* credulus
trusting *adj* fidens; **—ly** fidenter
trustworthiness *s* integritas, fides *f*
trustworthy *adj* fidus; (*of witness*) locuples; (*of an authority*) bonus
trusty *adj* fidus
truth *s* veritas *f*, verum *n*; **in —** vero
truthful *adj* verax; **—ly** veraciter, vere
try *vt* tentare, probare, experiri; (*law*) cognoscěre; (*to endeavor*) laborare; **to — one's patience** patientiā abuti
trying *adj* molestus, incommodus, gravis
tub *s* labrum, dolium *n*
tube *s* fistula *f*
tuck *vt* **to — up** succingěre
tuft *s* floccus, cirrus *m*, crista *f*
tug *s* conat·us -ūs, nis·us -ūs *m*; (*ship*) navis tractoria *f*
tug *vt* trahěre
tuition *s* tutela *f*
tumble *vi* corruěre, collabi, volvi
tumbler *s* poculum vitreum *n*
tumor *s* tumor, tuber *m*
tumult *s* tumult·us -ūs *m*
tumultuous *adj* tumultuosus, turbulentus; **—ly** tumultuose
tune *s* tonus *m*, moduli *m pl*
tuneful *adj* canorus
tunic *s* tunica *f*
tunnel *s* canalis, cuniculus *m*
turban *s* mitra, tiara *f*
turbid *adj* turbidus, turbulentus
turbulence *s* tumult·us -ūs *m*
turbulent *adj* turbulentus; **—ly** turbulente
turf *s* caespes *m*
turgid *adj* turgidus
turkey *s* meleagris gallopavo *f*
turmoil *s* turba, perturbatio *f*, tumult·us -ūs *m*
turn *s* (*circuit*) circuit·us -ūs *m*; (*revolution*) conversio *f*, circumact·us -ūs *m*; (*change, course*) vicissitudo *f*; (*inclination of mind*) inclinatio

f, ingenium *n*; **a good —** officium, beneficium *n*; **in —** invicem
turn *vt* vertĕre, convertĕre; (*to twist*) torquēre; (*to bend*) flectĕre; **to — aside** deflectĕre; **to — away** avertĕre; **to — down** (*refuse*) recusare, denegare, respuĕre; **to — into** mutare in (*with acc*), vertĕre in (*with acc*); **to — over** (*to hand over*) tradĕre, transferre; (*property*) alienare; (*in mind*) agitare; **to — one's attention to** animadvertĕre; **to — out** ejicĕre, expellĕre; **to — round** volvĕre, circumagĕre, rotare; **to — up** (*with hoe*) invertĕre; **to — up the nose** nares corrugare; *vi* verti, converti, versari; **to — against** disciscĕre ab (*with abl*), alienari ab (*with abl*); **to — aside** devertĕre, se declinare; **to — away** discedĕre, aversari; **to — back** reverti; **to — into** (*to be changed into*) vertĕre in (*with acc*), mutari in (*with acc*); **to — out** cadĕre, evadĕre, contingĕre, evenire; **to — round** converti; **to — up** intervenire, adesse
turnip *s* rapum *n*
turpitude *s* turpitudo *f*
turret *s* turricula *f*
turtle *s* testudo *f*
turtledove *s* turtur *m*
tusk *s* dens *m*
tutelage *s* tutela *f*
tutor *s* praeceptor, magister *m*
tutor *vt* edocēre
tweezers *s* volsella *f*
twelfth *adj* duodecimus
twelve *adj* duodecim; **— times** duodecies
twentieth *adj* vicesimus
twenty *adj* viginti; **— times** vicies
twice *adv* bis
twig *s* surculus, ramulus *m*, virga, virgula *f*
twilight *s* crepusculum *n*; (*dawn*) diluculum *n*
twin *adj* geminus
twin *s* geminus, gemellus *m*
twine *s* filum *n*, resticula *f*
twine *vt* circumplicare, contorquēre; *vi* circumplecti
twinge *s* dolor *m*
twinkle *vi* micare, coruscare
twinkling *s* (*of eye*) nict·us -ūs *m*
twirl *vt* versare, circumagĕre; *vi* versari
twist *vt* torquēre; *vi* flecti
twit *vt* exprobrare, objurgare
twitch *s* vellicatio *f*
twitch *vt* vellicare; *vi* micare
twitter *vi* minurire
two *adj* duo; **— at a time** bini; **— times** bis
twofold *adj* duplex, duplus
type *s* (*model*) exemplum, exemplar *n*; (*class*) genus *n*, forma, figura *f*
typhoon *s* turbo *m*
typical *adj* solitus, proprius
tyrannical *adj* tyrannicus, superbus; **—ly** tyrannice, superbe
tyrannicide *s* (*act*) tyrannicidium *n*; (*person*) tyranni interfector, tyrannicida *m*
tyrannize *vi* dominari
tyranny *s* tyrannis, dominatio *f*
tyrant *s* tyrannus, dominus superbus *m*
tyro *s* tiro *m*

U

udder *s* uber *n*
ugliness *s* deformitas, foeditas *f*
ugly *adj* deformis, turpis, foedus
ulcer *s* ulcus *n*
ulcerous *adj* ulcerosus
ultimate *adj* ultimus, extremus; **—ly** tandem
umbrage *s* offensio *f*; **to take — at** aegre ferre
umbrella *s* umbella *f*
umpire *s* arbiter, disceptator *m*
unabashed *adj* intrepidus
unabated *adj* integer
unable *adj* impotens, invalidus; **to be — to** non posse, nequire
unaccented *adj* accentu carens
unacceptable *adj* ingratus, odiosus
unaccompanied *adj* incomitatus, solus
unaccomplished *adj* infectus, imperfectus
unaccountable *adj* inexplicabilis, inenodabilis
unaccountably *adv* praeter opinionem, sine causa
unaccustomed *adj* insolitus, insuetus, inexpertus
unacquainted *adj* **— with** ignarus (*with genit*), expers (*with genit*)
unadorned *adj* inornatus, incomptus, simplex
unadulterated *adj* merus, integer
unaffected *adj* simplex, candidus
unafraid *adj* impavidus
unaided *adj* non adjutus, sine ope
unalterable *adj* immutabilis
unaltered *adj* immutatus
unanimous *adj* unanimus, concors; **—ly** concorditer, consensu omnium
unanswerable *adj* irrefragabilis
unappeased *adj* implacatus
unapproachable *adj* inaccessus
unarmed *adj* inermis
unasked *adj* injussus, non vocatus
unassailable *adj* inexpugnabilis
unassuming *adj* modestus, moderatus, demissus
unattached *adj* liber, vacuus
unattainable *adj* arduus
unattempted *adj* inexpertus, inausus, intentatus
unattended *adj* incomitatus, sine comitibus

unattractive *adj* invenustus
unauthorized *adj* illicitus
unavailing *adj* inutilis, irritus
unavenged *adj* inultus
unavoidable *adj* inevitabilis
unaware *adj* inscius, nescius, ignarus
unbearable *adj* intolerabilis
unbeaten *adj* invictus
unbecoming *adj* indecorus, indecens; **it is —** dedecet
unbefitting *adj* indecorus
unbend *vi* animum remittĕre
unbending *adj* inflexibilis, inexorabilis
unbiased *adj* incorruptus, integer
unbidden *adj* injussus, ultro
unbleached *adj* crudus
unblemished *adj* integer, intactus
unblest *adj* infortunatus
unborn *adj* nondum natus
unbroken *adj* irruptus; integer; (*of horses*) indomitus
unbuckle *vt* refibulare
unburden *vt* exonerare
unbutton *vt* refibulare
unceasing *adj* constans, assiduus; **—ly** assidue
uncertain *adj* incertus, dubius; **—ly** incerte, dubie
uncertainty *s* dubium *n*, dubitatio *f*
unchangeable *adj* immutabilis
unchanged *adj* immutatus
unchanging *adj* integer, idem
uncharitable *adj* immisericors
unchaste *adj* impudicus, obscenus; **—ly** impudice, impure
uncivil *adj* inurbanus
uncivilized *adj* incultus
unclasp *vt* defibulare
uncle *s* (*father's brother*) patruus *m*; (*mother's brother*) avunculus *m*
unclean *adj* immundus
uncomfortable *adj* incommodus, molestus
uncommon *adj* rarus, insolitus, inusitatus; **—ly** raro, praeter solitum
unconcerned *adj* securus, incuriosus
unconditional *adj* absolutus, sine exceptione; **—ly** nullā condicione
unconnected *adj* disjunctus
unconquerable *adj* invictus
unconscionable *adj* iniquus, injustus, absurdus
unconscious *adj* omni sensu carens; **— of** ignarus (*with genit*), inscius (*with genit*)
unconstitutional *adj* illicitus; **—ly** contra leges
uncontrollable *adj* impotens
unconventional *adj* insolitus
unconvinced *adj* non persuasus
unconvincing *adj* non verisimilis
uncooked *adj* rudus
uncorrupted *adj* incorruptus
uncouth *adj* inurbanus, agrestis
uncover *vt* detegĕre, recludĕre, nudare
uncritical *adj* credulus
uncultivated *adj* incultus; indoctus
uncut *adj* intonsus
undamaged *adj* integer, inviolatus
undaunted *adj* impavidus, intrepidus
undecided *adj* incertus, dubius, anceps
undefended *adj* indefensus, nudus
undefiled *adj* purus, incontaminatus
undefined *adj* infinitus
undeniable *adj* haud dubius
under *adv* subter, infra
under *prep* (*position*) sub (*with abl*); (*motion*) sub (*with acc*); (*less than*) intra (*with acc*), infra (*with acc*)
underage *adj* impubes
underestimate *vt* minoris aestimare
undergarment *s* subucula *f*
undergo *vt* subire, pati
underground *adj* subterraneus
undergrowth *s* virgulta *n pl*
underhanded *adj* clandestinus, furtivus; **—ly** clam, furtive
underline *vt* subnotare
underling *s* minister, assecla *m*
undermine *vt* subruĕre, suffodĕre; (*fig*) labefacĕre, labefactare
underneath *adv* infra, subter
underneath *prep* (*position*) infra (*with acc*), sub (*with abl*); (*motion*) sub (*with acc*)
underrate *vt* minoris aestimare
understand *vt* intellegĕre, comprehendĕre
understanding *adj* prudens, sapiens
understanding *s* mens *f*, intellectus -ūs *m*; (*agreement*) consens·us -ūs *m*; (*condition*) condicio *f*
undertake *vt* adire ad (*with acc*), suscipĕre; (*to begin*) incipĕre
undertaker *s* vespillo, libitinarius *m*
undertaking *s* inceptum, coeptum *n*
undervalue *vt* minoris aestimare
underworld *s* inferi *m pl*
undeserved *adj* immeritus, injustus; **—ly** immerito
undeserving *adj* indignus
undiminished *adj* imminutus
undiscernible *adj* imperceptus, invisus
undisciplined *adj* immoderatus; (*mil*) inexercitatus
undisguised *adj* apertus
undismayed *adj* impavidus, intrepidus
undisputed *adj* certus
undistinguished *adj* ignobilis, inglorius
undisturbed *adj* imperturbatus, immotus
undivided *adj* indivisus
undo *vt* (*knot*) expedire; (*fig*) infectum reddĕre; (*to ruin*) perdĕre
undone (*adj*) (*not completed*) infectus, imperfectus; (*ruined*) perditus
undoubted *adj* certus, haud dubius; **—ly** haud dubie
undress *vt* exuĕre; *vi* vestes exuĕre
undressed *adj* nudus; (*fig*) rudis
undue *adj* nimius, iniquus
undulate *vi* undare, fluctuare
undulation *s* undarum agitatio *f*
unduly *adv* nimis, plus aequo
undying *adj* aeternus, sempiternus
unearth *vt* detegĕre, effodĕre
unearthly *adj* humano major, divinus
uneasiness *s* sollicitudo, anxietas *f*

uneasy *adj* sollicitus, anxius
uneducated *adj* indoctus, illiteratus
unemployed *adj* vacuus, otiosus
unemployment *s* otium *n*, cessatio *f*
unencumbered *adj* expeditus
unending *adj* infinitus, perpetuus
unendurable *adj* intolerandus
unenjoyable *adj* injucundus
unenlightened *adj* ineruditus
unenviable *adj* non invidendus, miser
unequal *adj* inaequalis, dispar, impar; **—ly** inaequaliter, impariter, inique
unequaled *adj* singularis, eximius
unerring *adj* certus; **—ly** certe
uneven *adj* inaequalis, iniquus; (*rough*) asper
unexpected *adj* inopinatus, insperatus, improvisus; **—ly** de improviso
unexplored *adj* inexploratus
unfading *adj* semper recens
unfailing *adj* certus, perpetuus; **—ly** semper
unfair *adj* iniquus; **—ly** inique
unfaithful *adj* infidus, perfidus, infidelis; **—ly** perfide
unfamiliar *adj* ignotus, alienus
unfashionable *adj* obsoletus
unfasten *vt* laxare, resolvěre
unfavorable *adj* adversus, iniquus, inopportunus
unfavorably *adv* male, inique
unfed *adj* impastus
unfeeling *adj* durus, crudelis; **—ly** dure, crudeliter
unfetter *vt* vincula deměre (*with dat*)
unfinished *adj* imperfectus; (*crude*) rudis, impolitus
unfit *adj* inhabilis, ineptus, inutilis
unfold *vt* explicare, evolvěre; (*story*) enarrare; *vi* dehiscěre, patescěre
unforeseeing *adj* imprudens, improvidus
unforeseen *adj* improvisus, insperatus
unforgiving *adj* inexorabilis
unfortified *adj* immunitus, nudus
unfortunate *adj* infelix, infortunatus, nefastus; **—ly** infeliciter
unfounded *adj* vanus, fictus
unfriendly *adj* parum amicus, inimicus, alienus
unfruitful *adj* infructuosus, sterilis, infecundus
unfulfilled *adj* infectus
unfurl *vt* panděre, solvěre
unfurnished *adj* imparatus
ungainly *adj* ineptus, inhabilis
ungenerous *adj* illiberalis
ungentlemanly *adj* inurbanus, illepidus
ungird *vt* discingěre
ungodly *adj* impius
ungovernable *adj* indomabilis, intractabilis
ungracious *adj* iniquus, asper
ungrateful *adj* ingratus; **—ly** ingrate
ungrudging *adj* non invitus; **—ly** sine invidia
unguarded *adj* incustoditus, indefensus; (*of words*) inconsultus
unhandy *adj* inhabilis
unhappily *adv* infeliciter, misere
unhappiness *s* tristitia, miseria, maestitia f
unhappy *adj* infelix, infortunatus, miser
unharness *vt* disjungěre
unhealthiness *s* valetudo, gravitas *f*
unhealthy *adj* infirmus, morbosus; (*unwholesome*) gravis, insalubris
unheard-of *adj* inauditus
unheeded *adj* neglectus
unhelpful *adj* invitus, difficilis
unhesitating *adj* promptus, confidens; **—ly** confidenter
unhinge *vt* de cardine detrahěre; (*fig*) perturbare
unholy *adj* impius, profanus
unhoped-for *adj* insperatus
unhurt *adj* incolumis, salvus
unicorn *s* monoceros *m*
uniform *adj* constans, aequabilis; **—ly** constanter, aequabiliter
uniform *s* vestit·us -ūs *m*; (*mil*) sagum *n*
uniformity *s* constantia, aequabilitas *f*
unify *vt* conjungěre
unilateral *adj* unilaterus
unimaginative *adj* hebes
unimpaired *adj* integer, intactus
unimpeachable *adj* probatissimus
unimportant *adj* nullius momenti (*genit*), levis
uninformed *adj* indoctus
uninhabitable *adj* non habitabilis, inhabitabilis
uninhabited *adj* desertus
uninjured *adj* incolumis
uninspired *adj* hebes
unintelligible *adj* obscurus
uninteresting *adj* frigidus, jejunus
uninterrupted *adj* continuus, perpetuus
uninviting *adj* injucundus, non alliciens
union *s* (*act*) conjunctio *f*; (*social*) consociatio, societas *f*; (*agreement*) consens·us -ūs *m*; (*marriage*) conjugium *n*
unique *adj* unicus, singularis
unison *s* concent·us -ūs *m*
unit *s* monas *f*, unio *m*
unite *vt* conjungěre, consociare; *vi* coalescěre, coire; conjurare
unity *s* concordia *f*
universal *adj* universus, universalis; **—ly** universe, ubique
universe *s* mundus *m*, summa rerum *f*
university *s* academia, universitas *f*
unjust *adj* injustus, iniquus; **—ly** injuste, inique
unjustifiable *adj* indignus
unkempt *adj* incomptus, neglectus
unkind *adj* inhumanus; **—ly** inhumane
unknowingly *adv* insciens
unknown *adj* ignotus, incognitus
unlawful *adj* illegitimus, illicitus; **—ly** contra legem *or* leges
unless *conj* nisi
unlike *adj* dissimilis, dispar, diversus
unlikely *adj* parum verisimilis
unlimited *adj* infinitus, immensus
unload *vt* exonerare

unluckily *adv* infeliciter
unlucky *adj* infelix, infaustus
unmanageable *adj* intractabilis, contumax
unmanly *adj* mollis
unmannerly *adj* male moratus, inurbanus
unmarried *adj* (*man*) caelebs; (*woman*) innupta
unmask *vt* detegĕre
unmatched *adj* unicus, singularis
unmerciful *adj* immisericors; **—ly** immisericorditer
unmindful *adj* immemor
unmistakable *adj* certissimus
unmistakably *adv* sine dubio
unmoved *adj* immotus
unnatural *adj* (*event*) monstruosus; (*deed*) immanis, crudelis; **—ly** contra naturam
unnecessarily *adv* ex supervacuo, nimis
unnecessary *adj* haud necessarius, supervacaneus
unnerve *vt* debilitare
unnoticed *adj* praetermissus; **to go —** latēre
unobjectionable *adj* culpae expers, honestus
unoccupied *adj* vacuus; otiosus; (*of land*) apertus
unofficial *adj* privatus
unpack *vt* e cistis eximĕre
unpaid *adj* (*of money*) debitus; (*of a service*) gratuitus
unpalatable *adj* amarus, insuavis
unparalleled *adj* unicus, singularis
unpardonable *adj* inexcusabilis
unpatriotic *adj* immemor patriae
unpitying *adj* immisericors, inexorabilis
unpleasant *adj* injucundus, incommodus; **—ly** injucunde, incommode
unpolluted *adj* impollutus; (*fig*) integer, intactus
unpopular *adj* invisus, invidiosus
unpracticed *adj* inexpertus, imperitus
unprecedented *adj* novus, inauditus
unprejudiced *adj* aequus
unpremeditated *adj* subitus, ex tempore
unprepared *adj* imparatus
unprincipled *adj* improbus
unproductive *adj* infecundus, infructuosus, sterilis
unprofitable *adj* vanus, inutilis
unprofitably *adv* inutiliter, frustra
unprotected *adj* indefensus
unprovoked *adj* non lacessitus, ultro
unpunished *adj* inpunitus, inultus
unqualified *adj* haud idoneus, inhabilis
unquenchable *adj* inexstinctus
unquestionable *adj* haud dubius, certissimus
unquestionably *adv* certe
unquestioning *adj* credulus
unravel *vt* retexĕre; (*fig*) enodare, explicare
unreasonable *adj* rationis expers, absurdus; iniquus
unreasonably *adv* absurde, inique
unrefined *adj* rudis, crudus, incultus
unrelenting *adj* implacabilis, inexorabilis
unremitting *adj* assiduus, continuus
unrepentant *adj* impaenitens
unrestrained *adj* effrenatus, indomitus, effusus
unrighteous *adj* injustus, iniquus; **—ly** injuste
unripe *adj* immaturus, crudus
unroll *vt* evolvĕre, explicare
unruliness *s* petulantia *f*
unruly *adj* effrenatus, turbulentus
unsafe *adj* intutus, periculosus
unsatisfactory *adj* non idoneus, malus
unsavory *adj* insipidus, insulsus, insuavis
unseasonable *adj* intempestivus, immaturis; incommodus, importunus
unseemly *adj* indecorus, indecens
unseen *adj* invisus
unselfish *adj* suae utilitatis immemor, liberalis; **—ly** liberaliter
unsettle *vt* turbare, sollicitare
unsettled *adj* incertus, inconstans; (*of mind*) sollicitus
unshaken *adj* immotus
unshaved *adj* intonsus
unsheathe *vt* destringĕre, e vagina educĕre
unsightly *adj* turpis, foedus
unskilful *adj* imperitus, inscitus; **—ly** imperite, inscite
unskilled *adj* imperitus, indoctus
unsophisticated *adj* simplex
unsound *adj* infirmus; (*mentally*) insanus; (*ill-founded*) vanus
unsparing *adj* inclemens; (*lavish*) prodigus, largus; **—ly** inclementer; prodige, large
unspeakable *adj* ineffabilis, inenarrabilis
unstable *adj* instabilis; (*fig*) levis, inconstans
unstained *adj* incontaminatus, purus
unsteadily *adv* inconstanter, instabiliter
unsteady *adj* inconstans, instabilis
unsuccessful *adj* infelix, infaustus; **—ly** infeliciter
unsuitable *adj* inhabilis, incommodus, alienus
unsuited *adj* haud idoneus
unsullied *adj* incorruptus
unsuspected *adj* non suspectus
untamed *adj* indomitus, ferus
untasted *adj* ingustatus
untaught *adj* indoctus, rudis
unteachable *adj* indocilis
untenable *adj* infirmus, inanis
unthankful *adj* ingratus
untie *vt* solvĕre
until *conj* dum, donec, quoad
until *prep* usque ad (*with acc*), in (*with acc*); **— now** adhuc
untimely *adj* intempestivus, importunus, immaturus
untiring *adj* assiduus, indefessus
untold *adj* innumerus
untouched *adj* intactus, integer; (*fig*) immotus
untrained *adj* inexercitatus

untried *adj* inexpertus, intemptatus
untrodden *adj* non tritus, avius
untroubled *adj* placidus, tranquillus; (*of sleep*) levis
untrue *adj* falsus, mendax; (*disloyal*) infidus
untrustworthy *adj* infidus
unusual *adj* inusitatus, insolitus, insuetus; **—ly** praeter solitum, raro
unutterable *adj* infandus, inenarrabilis
unvarnished *adj* (*fig*) nudus, simplex
unveil *vt* detegĕre, patefacĕre
unversed *adj* imperitus
unwarranted *adj* injustus, iniquus
unwary *adj* imprudens, incautus
unwearied *adj* indefessus, impiger
unwelcome *adj* ingratus, injucundus
unwholesome *adj* insalubris
unwieldy *adj* inhabilis
unwilling *adj* invitus; **—ly** invite
unwind *vt* revolvĕre, retexĕre
unwise *adj* imprudens, insipiens; **—ly** imprudenter, insipienter
unworthy *adj* indignus
unwrap *vt* explicare, evolvĕre
unwritten *adj* non scriptus
unyielding *adj* inflexibilis, obstinatus
unyoke *vt* disjungĕre
up *adv* sursum; **— and down** sursum deorsum
upbringing *s* educatio *f*
upheaval *s* eversio *f*
uphold *vt* servare, sustinēre, sustentare
upkeep *s* impensa *f*
uplift *vt* sublevare
upon *prep* (*position*) super (*with abl*), in (*with abl*); (*motion*) super (*with acc*), in (*with acc*); (*directly after*) e(x) (*with abl*); (*dependence*) e(x) (*with abl*)
upper *adj* superus, superior
uppermost *adj* summus, supremus
upright *adj* erectus; (*of character*) honestus, integer; **—ly** recte; integre
uproar *s* tumult·us -ūs *m*, turba *f*
uproot *vt* eradicare, eruĕre
upset *vt* evertĕre, subvertĕre, percellĕre
upset *adj* perculsus
upstream *adv* adverso flumine
up to *prep* usque ad (*with acc*), ad (*with acc*), tenus (*postpositive, with abl or genit*)
upwards *adv* sursum, sublime; **— of** (*of number*) plus quam
urban *adj* urbanus, oppidanus
urge *vt* urgēre, impellĕre, hortari; **to — on** stimulare
urge *s* impuls·us -ūs *m*
urgency *s* gravitas, necessitas *f*
urgent *adj* gravis, instans, vehemens; **to be —** instare; **—ly** vehementer, magnopere, graviter
urn *s* urna *f*
us *pron* nos; **to —** nobis; **with —** nobiscum
usage *s* mos *m*, consuetudo *f*
use *s* us·us -ūs, mos *m*, consuetudo, usura *f*; **no —!** frustra!; **to be of —** usui esse, prodesse; **to make — of** uti (*with abl*)
use *vt* uti (*with abl*); (*to take advantage of*) abuti (*with abl*); **to — something for** aliquid adhibēre (*with dat*); **to — up** consumĕre, exhaurire; *vi* **I used to** solebam (*with inf*)
used *adj* usitatus; **— to** (*accustomed to*) assuetus (*with dat*)
useful *adj* utilis, commodus, aptus; **—ly** utiliter, commode, apte
useless *adj* inutilis, inhabilis; (*of things*) inanis; **—ly** inutiliter, frustra
usual *adj* usitatus, solitus, consuetus; **—ly** plerumque, fere, ferme; **I — go** soleo ire
usurp *vt* usurpare, occupare
usurper *s* usurpator *m*
usury *s* usura *f*; **to practice —** faenerari
utensils *s* utensilia, vasa *n pl*, supellex *f*
utility *s* utilitas *f*
utilize *vt* uti (*with abl*), adhibēre
utmost *adj* extremus, ultimus, summus; **to do one's —** omnibus viribus contendĕre
utter *adj* totus, extremus, summus; **—ly** omnino, funditus
utter *vt* eloqui, proferre, pronuntiare, edĕre
utterance *s* elocutio, pronuntiatio *f*, dictum *n*
uttermost *adj* extremus, ultimus

V

vacant *adj* vacuus, inanis; **to be —** vacare
vacation *s* vacatio *f*, feriae *f pl*
vacillate *vi* vacillare
vacuum *s* inane *n*
vagabond *s* vagabundus, grassator *m*
vagrant *adj* vagabundus, vagus
vague *adj* vagus, dubius, ambiguus; **—ly** incerte, ambigue
vain *adj* vanus, futilis; superbus, arrogans; **in —** frustra; **—ly** frustra
valet *s* cubicularius *m*
valiant *adj* fortis; **—ly** fortiter
valid *adj* validus, legitimus, ratus; (*argument*) gravis
valley *s* vallis *f*
valor *s* fortitudo *f*
valuable *adj* pretiosus
valuation *s* aestimatio *f*
value *s* pretium *n*, aestimatio *f*
value *vt* aestimare, ducĕre; **to — highly** magni aestimare, magni habēre
valueless *adj* vilis, inutilis
vanguard *s* (*mil*) primum agmen *n*

vanish *vi* vanescĕre, diffugĕre
vanity *s* gloria, ostentatio *f*
vanquish *vt* vincĕre, superare
vapor *s* vapor *m*, exhalatio *f*
variable *adj* commutabilis, varius
variation *s* varietas, commutatio, vicissitudo *f*
variety *s* varietas, diversitas, multitudo *f*
various *adj* varii, diversi; **—ly** varie, diverse
vary *vt* variare, mutare; *vi* mutari
vase *s* amphora *f*, vas *n*
vast *adj* vastus, ingens, immensus; **—ly** valde
vastness *s* immensitas *f*
vault *s* fornix, camera *f*; (*leap*) salt·us -ūs *m*
vault *vi* salire
vaunt *vt* jactare; *vi* se jactare
veal *s* caro vitulina *f*
vegetable *s* holus *n*
vegetable *adj* holitarius
vehemence *s* vehementia, vis *f*, impet·us -ūs *m*
vehement *adj* vehemens, violentus, fervidus; **—ly** vehementer, valde
vehicle *s* vehiculum *n*
veil *s* velamen *n*, rica *f*; (*bridal*) flammeum *n*; (*fig*) integumentum *n*
veil *vt* velare, tegĕre
vein *s* vena *f*
velocity *s* velocitas, celeritas *f*
velvet *s* velvetum *n*
vend *vt* vendĕre
veneer *s* ligni bractea *f*; (*fig*) species *f*
venerable *adj* venerabilis
venerate *vt* venerari, colĕre
veneration *s* adoratio *f*, cult·us -ūs *m*
vengeance *s* ultio, poena *f*; **to take — on** vindicare in (*with acc*), ulcisci
venom *s* venenum, virus *n*
vent *s* spiramentum, foramen *n*
vent *vt* aperire; **to — one's wrath on** iram erumpere in (*with acc*)
ventilate *vt* ventilare
venture *s* ausum *n*
venture *vt* periclitari; audēre
veracious *adj* verax
veracity *s* veracitas *f*
verb *s* verbum *n*
verbal *adj* verbalis; **—ly** verbo tenus
verbatim *adv* ad verbum
verbose *adj* verbosus; **—ly** verbose
verdict *s* sententia *f*; **to deliver a —** sententiam pronuntiare
verge *s* margo, ora *f*; **to be on the — of** non procul abesse ut
verge *vi* vergĕre
verification *s* affirmatio *f*
verify *vt* ratum facĕre, confirmare
vermin *s* bestiolae *f pl*
versatile *adj* varius, agilis, versatilis
verse *s* vers·us -ūs *m*
versed *adj* peritus, exercitatus
version *s* forma, translatio *f*
vertex *s* vertex, vortex *m*
vertical *adj* rectus, directus; **—ly** ad lineam, ad perpendiculum
very *adj* ipse
very *adv* valde, admodum
vessel *s* vas *n*; (*ship*) navigium *n*
vest *s* subucula *f*
vestal *s* virgo vestalis *f*
vestige *s* vestigium, indicium *n*
vestment *s* vestimentum *n*
veteran *s* (*mil*) veteranus, vexillarius, emeritus *m*; (*fig*) veterator *m*
veterinarian *s* veterinarius *m*
veto *s* intercessio *f*, interdictum *n*
veto *vt* interdicĕre (*with dat*); (*as tribune*) intercedĕre (*with dat*)
vex *vt* vexare, sollicitare
vexation *s* vexatio, offensio *f*, stomachus *m*
via *prep* per (*with acc*)
vial *s* phiala *f*
vibrate *vi* tremĕre, vibrare
vibration *s* tremor *m*
vicar *s* vicarius *m*
vice *s* vitium *n*, turpitudo *f*
vicinity *s* vicinitas, vicinia *f*
vicious *adj* vitiosus, perditus; (*of temper*) ferox; **—ly** ferociter
vicissitude *s* vicissitudo *f*
victim *s* victima, hostia *f*; (*exploited*) praeda *f*
victimize *vt* circumvenire
victor *s* victor *m*, victrix *f*
victorious *adj* victor; (*of woman*) victrix; **to be —** vincĕre
victory *s* victoria *f*; **to win a —** victoriam reportare
vie *vi* certare, contendĕre; **to — with** aemulari (*with dat*)
view *s* aspect·us -ūs, conspect·us -ūs *m*; (*from above*) despect·us -ūs *m*; (*opinion*) opinio, sententia *f*, judicium *n*; **in my —** me judice; **to have in —** praevidēre
view *vt* visĕre, conspicĕre, intuēri, inspicĕre
vigil *s* pervigilatio *f*, pervigilium *n*
vigilance *s* vigilantia, diligentia *f*
vigilant *adj* vigilans, diligens, intentus; **—ly** vigilanter, diligenter
vigor *s* vigor, impet·us -ūs *m*, robur *n*
vigorous *adj* strenuus, acer, vegetus; **—ly** strenue, acriter
vile *adj* vilis, abjectus, perditus, flagitiosus
vilify *vt* infamare, calumniari
villa *s* villa *f*
village *s* vicus, pagus *m*
villager *s* vicanus, paganus *m*
villain *s* scelestus, nequam (*indecl*) *m*
villany *s* scelus *n*, improbitas, nequitia *f*
vindicate *vt* vindicare; (*to justify*) purgare; (*person*) defendĕre
vindictive *adj* ultionis cupidus
vine *s* vitis *f*
vinegar *s* acetum *n*
vineyard *s* vinea *f*, vinetum *n*
violate *vt* violare
violation *s* violatio *f*
violator *s* violator *m*
violence *s* violentia, vis *f*, impet·us -ūs *m*; (*cruelty*) saevitia *f*
violent *adj* violentus, vehemens; **—ly** violenter, vehementer
virgin *adj* virginalis
virgin *s* virgo *f*
virile *adj* virilis
virility *s* virilitas *f*
virtually *adv* fere

virtue *s* virtus, probitas *f*; (*power*) vis *f*; **by — of** per (*with acc*), ex (*with abl*)
virtuous *adj* probus, honestus; (*chaste*) castus, pudicus; **—ly** honeste, caste
virulence *s* vis *f*, virus *n*; (*fig*) acerbitas *f*
visage *s* facies *f*, os *n*
viscous *adj* viscosus, lentus
visible *adj* aspectabilis, conspicuus, manifestus; **to be —** apparēre
visibly *adv* manifesto
vision *s* (*sense*) vis·us -ūs *m*; (*apparition*) visum *n*, visio *f*
visionary *adj* vanus, fictus, inanis
visit *s* salutatio *f*
visit *vt* visĕre, visitare
visitor *s* salutator *m*, salutatrix *f*; advena, hospes *m*
visor *s* buccula *f*
vista *s* prospect·us -ūs *m*
visual *adj* oculorum (*genit*)
vital *adj* vitalis; (*essential*) necessarius; **—ly** praecipue
vitality *s* vis *f*, animus *m*
vitiate *vt* vitiare, corrumpĕre
vituperate *vt* vituperare, reprehendĕre
vituperative *adj* maledicus
vivacious *adj* vividus, alacer, hilaris; **—ly** acriter
vivacity *s* alacritas *f*
vivid *adj* vividus, acer; **—ly** acriter
vivify *vt* animare, vivificare
vocabulary *s* verborum copia *f*
vocal *adj* vocalis, canorus
vocation *s* officium, munus *n*
vociferous *adj* clamosus
vogue *s* mos *m*; **to be in — in** honore esse
voice *s* vox *f*, sonus *m*; (*vote*) suffragium *n*
void *s* inane, vacuum *n*
volatile *adj* levis, volaticus
volcanic *adj* flammas eructans
volcano *s* mons ignivomus *m*
volition *s* voluntas *f*
volley *s* conject·us -ūs *m*
voluble *adj* volubilis
volume *s* (*book*) volumen *n*; (*quantity*) copia, multitudo *f*; (*size*) amplitudo *f*
voluminous *adj* copiosus, amplus, magnus
voluntary *adj* voluntarius; (*unpaid*) gratuitus
volunteer *s* voluntarius *m*; (*mil*) miles voluntarius, evocatus *m*
volunteer *vi* sponte nomen dare
voluptuous *adj* voluptarius, voluptuosus, delicatus
vomit *vt* vomĕre, evomĕre
voracious *adj* vorax; **—ly** voraciter
voracity *s* voracitas *f*
vortex *s* vortex *m*
vote *s* suffragium *n*; (*fig*) (*judgment*) sententia *f*
vote *vi* suffragium ferre, suffragium inire; (*of judge*) sententiam ferre; (*of senator*) censēre; **to — against** antiquare; **to — for** suffragari (*with dat*)
votive *adj* votivus
vouch *vi* spondēre; **to — for** testificari, asseverare
voucher *s* (*person*) auctor *m*; (*document*) testimonium *n*
vow *s* votum *n*
vow *vt* (*to promise*) (de)vovēre, spondēre, promittĕre
vowel *s* vocalis littera *f*
voyage *s* navigatio *f*
voyage *vi* navigare
voyager *s* navigator *m*
vulgar *s* vulgaris, communis; (*low*) plebeius, vilis
vulgarity *s* insulsitas *f*
vulnerable *adj* obnoxius
vulture *s* vultur *m*

W

wade *vi* per vada ire; **to — across** vado transire
wag *vt* vibrare, agitare
wage *vt* **to — war** bellum gerĕre
wager *vt* deponĕre; *vi* sponsionem facĕre
wages *s* merces *f*, stipendium *n*
wagon *s* carrus *m*, plaustrum *n*
wail *vi* plorare, plangĕre, ululare
wailing *s* plorat·us -ūs, planct·us -ūs *m*
waist *s* medium corpus *n*
wait *vi* manēre; **to — for** exspectare; **to — on** servire (*with dat*)
wait *s* mora *f*; **to lie in — for** insidiari (*with dat*)
waive *vt* decedĕre de (*with abl*), remittĕre
wake *vt* exsuscitare, excitare; *vi* expergisci
wake *s* vestigia *n pl*; **in the — of** post (*with acc*)
wakeful *adj* insomnis, vigil
waken *vt* exsuscitare, excitare; *vi* expergisci
walk *s* (*act*) ambulatio *f*; (*place*) ambulacrum *n*, xystus *m*; (*covered*) portic·us -ūs *m*; (*gait*) incess·us -ūs *m*
walk *vi* incedĕre, ambulare, gradi
wall *s* (*of house*) paries *f*; (*of town*) moenia *n pl*, murus *m*
wall *vt* muro cingĕre, moenibus munire
wallow *vi* volutari
walnut *s* juglans *f*
wan *adj* pallidus, exsanguis
wander *vi* vagari, errare; **to — about** pervagari; **to — over** pererrare
wanderer *s* erro, vagus *m*
wandering *s* erratio *f*
wane *vi* decrescĕre, minui, tabescĕre

want *s* egestas, inopia, indigentia, defectio *f*
want *vt* (*to wish*) velle; (*to lack*) egēre (*with abl*), indigēre (*with abl*), carēre (*with abl*); (*to miss*) desiderare
wanting *adj* (*defective*) vitiosus; (*missing*) absens; **to be —** deficĕre, deesse
wanton *adj* protervus, lascivus, petulans; **—ly** lascive, petulanter
war *s* bellum *n*; **to declare —** bellum indicĕre; **to declare — on** bellum indicĕre (*with dat*); **to enter —** bellum suscipĕre; **to wage —** bellum gerĕre
war *vi* bellare
war cry *s* ululat·us -ūs *m*
ward *s* (*of town*) regio *f*; (*guard*) custodia *f*; (*minor*) pupillus *m*, pupilla *f*
ward *vt* **to — off** arcēre, avertĕre, defendĕre
warden *s* custos *m*; (*of prison*) carcerarius *m*
warehouse *s* apotheca *f*
wares *s* merx *f*
warfare *s* bellum *n*, res bellica *f*
war horse *s* equus bellator *m*
warlike *adj* militaris, bellicosus
warm *adj* calidus; (*fig*) acer; **to be —** calēre; **—ly** ardenter, acriter
warm *vt* calefacĕre, tepefacĕre
warmth *s* calor, fervor *m*
warn *vt* monēre, praemonēre
warning *s* monitio *f*, monit·us -ūs *m*; (*object lesson*) exemplum *n*
warrant *s* auctoritas *f*, mandatum *n*
warrant *vt* praestare, promittĕre
warranty *s* satisdatio *f*
warrior *s* bellator, miles *m*, bellatrix *f*
wart *s* verruca *f*
wary *adj* cautus, providus, circumspectus
wash *vt* lavare; **to — away** abluĕre, diluĕre; **to — out** eluĕre; *vi* lavari
wash *s* (*clothes*) lintea lavanda *n pl*
washing *s* lavatio, lotura *f*
wasp *s* vespa *f*
waste *s* detrimentum *n*, effusio, dissipatio *f*; (*of time*) jactura *f*
waste *adj* vastus, desertus; **to lay —** vastare, (de)populari
waste *vt* consumĕre, perdĕre, dissipare; (*time*) absumĕre, terĕre; *vi* **to — away** tabescĕre, intabescĕre
wasteful *adj* profusus, prodigus; **—ly** prodige
wasteland *s* solitudo, vastitas *f*
watch *s* (*guard*) vigilia *f*; (*sentry*) excubiae *f pl*; **to keep —** excubare; **to keep — over** invigilare (*with dat*), custodire
watch *vt* (*to observe*) observare, spectare, intuēri; (*to guard*) custodire; *vi* **to — out for** exspectare
watchful *adj* vigilans; **—ly** vigilanter
watchman *s* vigil, excubitor *m*
watchtower *s* specula *f*
watchword *s* tessera *f*, signum *n*
water *s* aqua *f*
water *vt* irrigare; (*animals*) adaquare
waterfall *s* cataracta *f*
watering place *s* aquarium *n*
watery *adj* aquaticus, aquosus
wave *s* unda *f*, fluct·us -ūs *m*
wave *vt* agitare, vibrare, jactare; *vi* undare, fluctuare
waver *vi* fluctuare, labare, dubitare
wavering *adj* dubius, incertus
wavy *adj* undans, undosus; (*of hair*) crispus
wax *s* cera *f*
wax *vt* incerare; *vi* crescĕre, augēri
waxen *adj* cereus
way *s* via *f*, iter *n*; (*manner*) ratio *f*, modus *m*; (*habit*) mos *m*; **all the — from** usque ab (*with abl*); **all the — to** usque ad (*with acc*); **to get in the — of** intervenire (*with dat*); **to give —** (*of a structure*) labare; (*mil*) pedem referre; **to give — to** indulgēre (*with dat*); **to stand in the — of** obstare (*with dat*)
wayfarer *s* viator *m*
waylay *vt* insidiari (*with dat*)
wayward *adj* inconstans, levis, mutabilis
we *pron* nos; **— ourselves** nosmet ipsi
weak *adj* infirmus, debilis, imbecillus; (*argument*) tenuis; (*senses*) hebes; **—ly** infirme
weaken *vt* infirmare, debilitare, enervare; *vi* labare, hebescĕre, infirmus fieri
weakness *s* infirmitas, debilitas *f*; (*of mind*) imbecillitas *f*; (*flaw*) vitium *n*; (*of arguments*) levitas *f*
wealth *s* divitiae, opes *f pl*; copia, abundantia *f*
wealthy *adj* dives, opulentus; abundans
wean *vt* ab ubere depellĕre; (*fig*) desuefacĕre
weapon *s* telum *n*
wear *vt* (*clothes*) gerĕre; **to — out** terĕre, exedere; *vi* durare
weariness *s* lassitudo *f*
wearisome *adj* molestus
weary *adj* lassus, fessus, fatigatus
weather *s* caelum *n*, tempestas *f*
weather *vt* **to — a storm** procellam superare
weave *vt* texĕre
web *s* (*on loom*) tela, textura *f*; (*spider's*) araneum *n*
wed *vt* (*a woman*) ducĕre; (*a man*) nubĕre (*with dat*); *vi* (*of husband*) uxorem ducĕre; (*of bride*) nubĕre
wedge *s* cuneus *m*
wedlock *s* matrimonium *n*
weed *s* herba inutilis *f*
weed *vt* eruncare
week *s* hebdomas *f*
weekly *adj* hebdomadalis
weep *vi* flēre, lacrimare; **to — for** deplorare
weeping *s* plorat·us -ūs *m*, lacrimae *f pl*
weigh *vt* pendĕre, ponderare, trutinari; (*fig*) meditari; **to — down** degravare; (*fig*) opprimĕre; *vi* **to — much** magni ponderis esse

weight *s* pondus *n*, gravitas *f*; (*influence*) (*fig*) auctoritas *f*; (*importance*) momentum *n*
weighty *adj* ponderosus, gravis
welcome *s* gratulatio, salutatio *f*
welcome *vt* salvēre jubēre, excipĕre
welcome *interj* salve!; (*to several*) salvēte!
weld *vt* (con)ferruminare
welfare *s* salus *f*
well *s* puteus, fons *m*
well *adj* sanus, validus, salvus
well *adv* bene, recte, probe; **very —** optime
well *interj* heia!
well-bred *adj* generosus, liberalis
well-known *adj* pervulgatus; notus, nobilis
welter *s* congeries, turba *f*
west *s* occidens, occas·us -ūs *m*
western *adj* occidentalis
westward *adv* in occasum, occasum versus
west wind *s* Zephyrus, Favonius *m*
wet *adj* humidus, uvidus, madidus
wet *vt* madefacĕre, rigare
whale *s* balaena *f*, cetus *m*
wharf *s* navale *n*, crepido *f*
what *pron interrog* quid, quidnam, ecquid
what *adj interrog* qui; **— sort of** qualis
whatever *pron* quisquis
whatever *adj* quicumque
wheat *s* triticum *n*
wheedle *vt* blandiri, delenire
wheedling *adj* blandus
wheel *s* rota *f*
wheelbarrow *s* pabo *m*
whelp *s* catulus *m*
when *adv* quando
when *conj* cum, ubi, ut
whence *adv* unde
whenever *conj* quandocumque, utcumque, quotiens
where *adv* ubi
where *conj* quā, ubi
whereas *conj* quandoquidem
whereby *adv* re, quā viā, quo, per quod
wherefore *adv* quare, quamobrem, quapropter
wherein *adv* in quo, in quibus, ubi
whereof *adv* cujus, quorum; de quo, de quibus
whereto *adv* quo, quorsum
whereupon *adv* quo facto, post quae
wherever *conj* quacumque, ubicumque
whet *vt* acuĕre; (*fig*) exacuĕre
whether *conj* (*in single indirect question*) num, -ne, an; **whether . . . or** (*in multiple indirect questions*) utrum . . . an, -ne . . . an, . . . an; (*in disjunctive conditions*) sive . . . sive, seu . . . seu; **whether . . . or not** utrum . . . necne
whetstone *s* cos *f*
which *pron interrog* quis; (*of two*) uter; *pron rel* qui
which *adj interrog* qui; (*of two*) uter; *adj rel* qui
whichever *pron* quisquis, quicumque; (*of two*) utercumque
while *s* tempus, spatium *n*; **a little —** paulisper; **a long —** diu; **it is worth —** operae pretium est; **once in a —** interdum
while *conj* dum, quoad, donec
whim *s* libido *f*
whimper *vi* vagire
whimper *s* vagit·us -ūs *m*
whimsical *adj* levis, mobilis
whine *vi* miserabiliter vagire
whip *s* flagellum *n*, scutica *f*
whip *vt* flagellare, verberare
whirl *vt* torquēre, rotare; *vi* torquēri, rotari
whirlpool *s* vertex, gurges *m*
whirlwind *s* turbo, typhon *m*
whisper *s* susurrus *m*
whisper *vt & vi* susurrare
whistle *s* (*pipe*) fistula *f*; (*sound*) sibilus *m*; (*of wind*) stridor *m*
whistle *vi* sibilare
white *adj* albus; (*brilliant*) candidus; (*of hair*) canus
whiten *vt* dealbare, candefacĕre; *vi* albescĕre, canescĕre
who *pron interrog* quis; *pron rel* qui
whoever *pron* quicumque, quisquis
whole *adj* totus, cunctus; integer
whole *s* totum *n*, summa *f*; **on the —** plerumque
wholesome *adj* saluber, salutaris
wholly *adv* omnino, prorsus
whose *pron* cujus; quorum
why *adv* cur, quare, quamobrem
wicked *adj* improbus, nefarius, impius; **—ly** improbe, nefarie
wickedness *s* nequitia, improbitas, impietas *f*, scelus *n*
wicker *adj* vimineus
wide *adj* latus, amplus; **—ly** late
widen *vt* dilatare, laxare, extendĕre; *vi* patescĕre, dilatari, laxari
widow *s* vidua *f*
widower *s* viduus *m*
widowhood *s* viduitas *f*
width *s* latitudo, amplitudo *f*
wield *vt* tractare, vibrare
wife *s* uxor, conju(n)x *f*
wifely *adj* uxorius
wig *s* capillamentum *n*
wild *adj* ferus; (*of trees, plants, etc.*) silvestris; (*of land*) vastus, incultus; (*of disposition*) saevus, amens, ferox; **—ly** saeve, ferociter
wilderness *s* vastitas, solitudo *f*, loca deserta *n pl*
wile *s* fraus *f*, dolus *m*
wilful *adj* pervicax, consultus; **—ly** de industria
will *s* voluntas *f*, animus *m*; (*intent*) propositum, consilium *n*; (*document*) testimonium *n*; (*of gods*) nut·us -ūs *m*; **at —** ad libidinem
will *vt* velle; (*legacy*) legare, relinquĕre
willing *adj* libens, promptus; **to be —** velle; **—ly** libenter
willow *s* salix *f*
wily *adj* vafer, astutus
win *vt* adipisci, nancisci, consequi, (*victory*) reportare; (*friends*) sibi

conciliare; **to — over** conciliare; *vi* vincĕre, superare
wind *s* ventus *m*
wind *vt* circumvolvĕre, circumvertĕre, glomerare, torquēre; **to — up** (*to bring to an end*) concludĕre; *vi* sinuare
windfall *s* (*fig*) lucrum insperatum *n*
winding *adj* sinuosus, flexuosus
windmill *s* venti mola *f*
window *s* fenestra *f*
windpipe *s* aspera arteria *f*
windy *adj* ventosus
wine *s* vinum *n*; (*undiluted*) merum *n*; (*sour or cheap*) vappa *f*; (*new*) mustum *n*
wing *s* ala *f*; (*mil*) cornu *n*
winged *adj* alatus, volucer
wink *vi* nictare, connivēre
winner *s* victor *m*
winning *adj* (*fig*) blandus, amoenus
winnings *s* lucrum *n*
winnow *vt* ventilare
winter *s* hiems *f*; **in the dead of —** media hieme; **to spend the —** hiemare
winter *vi* hiemare, hibernare
winter *adj* hibernus
winter quarters *s* hiberna *n pl*
wintry *adj* hiemalis, hibernus
wipe *vt* detergēre; **to — away** abstergēre; **to — out** delēre, abolēre, expungĕre
wire *s* filum aeneum *n*
wisdom *s* sapientia, prudentia *f*
wise *adj* sapiens, prudens; **—ly** sapienter, prudenter
wise *s* modus *m*; **in no —** nequaquam
wish *s* optatum, votum *n*; **best —es** salus *f*
wish *vt* optare, velle, cupĕre; *vi* **to — for** exoptare, expetĕre
wisp *s* manipulus *m*
wistful *adj* desiderii plenus; **—ly** oculis intentis
wit *s* (*intellect*) ingenium *n*, argutiae *f pl*; (*humor*) sales *m pl*, facetiae *f pl*; (*person*) homo facetus *m*; **to be at one's —s' end** delirare; **to —** scilicet
witch *s* venefica, saga *f*
witchcraft *s* ars magica *f*, veneficium *n*
with *prep* cum (*with abl*); apud (*with acc*)
withdraw *vt* seducĕre, avocare; (*words*) revocare; *vi* recedĕre, discedĕre
wither *vt* torrēre, corrumpĕre; *vi* marcēre, arescĕre
withered *adj* marcidus
withhold *vt* retinēre, abstinēre, cohibēre
within *adv* intus, intra; (*motion*) intro
within *prep* intro (*with acc*), in (*with abl*); **— a few days** paucis diebus
without *adv* extra, foris; **from —** extrinsecus
without *prep* sine (*with abl*), absque (*with abl*), expers (*with genit*); **to be —** carēre (*with abl*)
withstand *vt* obsistĕre (*with dat*), resistĕre (*with dat*)
witness *s* testis *m & f*; (*to a signature*) obsignator *m*; **to bear —** testificari; **to call to —** testari, antestari
witness *vt* testificari; (*to see*) intuēri, vidēre
witticism *s* sales *m pl*
witty *adj* facetus, salsus, acutus
wizard *s* magus, veneficus *m*
woe *s* dolor, luct·us -ūs *m*; **—s** mala *n pl*
woeful *adj* tristis, luctuosus, miser; **—ly** triste, misere
wolf *s* lupus *m*, lupa *f*
woman *s* mulier, femina *f*
womanhood *s* muliebris stat·us -ūs *m*
womanly *adj* muliebris
womb *s* uterus *m*
wonder *s* admiratio *f*; (*astonishing object*) miraculum, mirum *n*
wonder *vi* (ad)mirari; **to — at** admirari
wonderful *adj* mirabilis, admirandus; **—ly** mirabiliter, mirifice
wont *adj* **to be — to** solēre (*with inf*)
woo *vt* petĕre
wood *s* lignum *n*; (*forest*) silva *f*, nemus *n*
wooded *adj* lignosus, silvestris
wooden *adj* ligneus
woodland *s* silvae *f pl*
woodman *s* lignator *m*
wood nymph *s* Dryas *f*
wooer *s* procus, amator *m*
wool *s* lana *f*
woolen *adj* laneus
word *s* verbum, vocabulum *n*; (*spoken*) vox *f*; (*promise*) fides *f*; (*news*) nuntius *m*; **in a —** denique; **to break one's —** fidem fallĕre; **to give one's —** fidem dare; **to keep one's —** fidem praestare; **— for —** ad verbum
wordy *adj* verbosus
work *s* opera *f*, opus *n*; (*trouble*) labor *m*; (*task*) pensum *n*
work *vt* (*to exercise*) exercēre; (*to till*) colĕre; *vi* laborare, operari
workman *s* (*unskilled*) operarius *m*; (*skilled*) faber, opifex *m*
workmanship *s* opus *n*, ars *f*
workshop *s* officina *f*
world *s* (*universe*) mundus *m*, summa rerum *f*; (*earth*) orbis terrarum *m*; (*nature*) rerum natura *f*; (*mankind*) homines *m pl*
worldly *adj* profanus
worm *s* vermis, vermiculus *m*, tinea *f*
worm-eaten *adj* vermiculosus
worry *s* sollicitudo, cura *f*
worry *vt* vexare, sollicitare; *vi* sollicitari
worse *adj* pejor, deterior; **to grow —** ingravescĕre
worsen *vi* ingravescĕre
worship *s* veneratio *f*, cult·us -ūs *m*
worship *vt* venerari, adorare, colĕre
worshiper *s* cultor, venerator *m*
worst *adj* pessimus, deterrimus
worst *vt* vincĕre

worth *s* (*value*) pretium *n*; (*merit*) dignitas, virtus *f*; **to be —** valēre
worthless *adj* vilis, inutilis; (*of person*) nequam (*indecl*)
worthy *adj* dignus
wound *s* vulnus *n*
wound *vt* vulnerare; (*fig*) offendĕre, laedĕre
wounded *adj* saucius
wrap *vt* involvĕre; **to — up** complicare
wrath *s* ira, iracundia *f*
wrathful *adj* iratus, iracundus; **—ly** iracunde
wreak *vt* **to — vengeance on** ulcisci, vindicare
wreath *s* sertum *n*, corona *f*
wreathe *vt* (*to twist*) torquēre; (*to adorn with wreaths*) coronare, nectĕre
wreck *s* naufragium *n*
wreck *vt* frangĕre; (*fig*) perdĕre
wren *s* regulus *m*
wrench *vt* detorquēre, luxare
wrest *vt* extorquēre, eripĕre
wrestle *vi* luctari
wrestler *s* luctator, athleta *m*
wretch *s* miser, perditus, nequam (*indecl*) *m*
wretched *adj* miser, infelix, abjectus; **—ly** misere, abjecte
wretchedness *s* miseria, aerumna *f*
wring *vt* contorquēre, stringĕre; **to — the neck** gulam frangĕre
wrinkle *s* ruga *f*
wrinkle *vt* corrugare; **to — the forehead** frontem contrahĕre
wrinkled *adj* rugosus
writ *s* (*law*) mandatum *n*
write *vt* scribĕre, perscribĕre; (*poetry*) componĕre; (*history*) perscribĕre
writer *s* scriptor, auctor *m*
writhe *vi* torquēri
writing *s* (*act*) scriptio *f*; (*result*) scriptum *n*, scriptura *f*; (*hand*) man·us -ūs *f*
wrong *adj* pravus, perversus, falsus; (*unjust*) injustus, iniquus; **—ly** falso, male, perperam; **to be —** errare, falli
wrong *s* nefas *n*, injuria *f*, malum *n*; **to do —** peccare
wrong *vt* nocēre (*with dat*), injuriam inferre (*with dat*), laedĕre
wrought *adj* factus, confectus, fabricatus
wry *adj* distortus, obliquus

Y

yard *s* (*court*) area *f*; (*measure*) tres pedes *m pl*; **a — long** tripedalis
yawn *vi* oscitare, hiare; (*to gape open*) dehiscĕre
year *s* annus *m*; **every —** quotannis; **five —s** quinquennium *n*; **four —s** quadriennium *n*; **three —s** triennium *n*; **two —** biennium *n*
yearly *adj* annuus, anniversarius
yearly *adv* quotannis
yearn *vi* **to — for** desiderare
yeast *s* fermentum *n*
yell *s* ululat·us -ūs *m*, ejulatio *f*
yell *vi* ululare, ejulare
yellow *adj* flavus, luteus, gilvus, croceus
yelp *vt* gannire
yes *adv* ita, immo, sane
yesterday *adv* heri
yet *adv* (*contrast, after adversative clause*) tamen, nihilominus; (*time*) adhuc; (*with comparatives*) etiam; **as —** adhuc; **not —** nondum
yield *vt* (*to produce*) ferre, parĕre, praebēre; (*to surrender*) dedĕre, concedĕre; *vi* cedĕre
yoke *s* jugum *n*; (*fig*) servitus *f*
yoke *vt* jugum imponĕre (*with dat*), conjungĕre
yonder *adv* illic
you *pron* (*thou*) tu; (*ye*) vos; **— yourself** tu ipse
young *adj* juvenis, adulescens; (*of child*) parvus; (*fig*) novus
younger *adj* junior, minor natu
youngster *s* adulescentulus *m*
your *adj* tuus; vester
yours *pron* tuus; vester
yourself *pron reflex* te; **to —** tibi; **with —** tecum; *intensive* tu ipse
yourselves *pron reflex* vos; **to —** vobis; **with —** vobiscum; *intensive* vos ipsi, vosmet ipsi
youth *s* (*age*) adulescentia *f*; (*collectively*) juventus *f*; (*young man*) juvenis, adulescens *m*
youthful *adj* juvenalis, puerilis; **—ly** juveniliter, pueriliter

Z

zeal *s* studium *n*, ardor, fervor *m*
zealous *adj* studiosus, ardens; **—ly** studiose, ardenter *m*
zenith *s* vertex *m*
zephyr *s* Zephyrus, Favonius *m*
zero *s* nihil, nihilum *n*
zest *s* (*taste*) sapor, gust·us -ūs *m*; (*fig*) gustat·us -ūs, impet·us -ūs *m*
zigzag *adj* tortuosus
zodiac *s* signifer orbis *m*
zone *s* zona, regio *f*
zoology *s* zoologia, animantium descriptio *f*